INVESTMENTS

Haim Levy

Hebrew University of Jerusalem

and

Thierry Post

Erasmus University Rotterdam

Assisted by

Deborah L. Murphy, University of Tennessee

Philippe Versijp, Erasmus University Rotterdam

 **Prentice Hall**
FINANCIAL TIMES

An imprint of **Pearson Education**
Harlow, England • London • New York • Boston • San Francisco • Toronto • Sydney • Singapore • Hong Kong
Tokyo • Seoul • Taipei • New Delhi • Cape Town • Madrid • Mexico City • Amsterdam • Munich • Paris • Milan

Pearson Education Limited
Edinburgh Gate
Harlow
Essex CM20 2JE
England

and Associated Companies throughout the world

Visit us on the World Wide Web at:
www.pearsoned.co.uk

_____

First published by South-Western College Publishing
This edition first published 2005

© Pearson Education Limited 2005

ISBN: 978-0-273-65164-2

British Library Cataloguing-in-Publication Data
A catalogue record for this book is available from the British Library

Library of Congress Cataloging-in-Publication Data
Levy, Haim.
    Investments / Haim Levy and Thierry Post.
       p. cm.
    Includes bibliographical references and index.
      ISBN 0-273-65164-1 (pbk.)
      1. Investments. 2. Securities. 3. Capital market. 4. Portfolio management. I. Post,
Thierry. II. Title.

  HG4521.L632 2005
  332.6—dc22

                                                                                    2004043194

ARP impression 98

Typeset in 10/12pt Minion by 35
Printed and bound in Great Britain by Ashford Colour Press Ltd

The publisher's policy is to use paper manufactured from sustainable forests.

Brief contents

Visit the *Investments* Companion Website at www.booksites.net/levy to access a rich, free resource of valuable teaching and learning material, including the following content:

<u>For the lecturer</u>

- A secure, **password-protected** site offering downloadable teaching support
- Customisable **PowerPoint slides**, including key figures and tables from the main text
- Extensive **Instructor's Problem Set**, including review and practice problems with solutions

<u>For the student</u>

- **Multiple Choice Questions** for every chapter, with instant feedback
- Interactive **Spreadsheets**, that accompany the Appendices in the book
- A searchable, online **Glossary** of key investments terminology
- Interactive **Flashcards** that allow you to check definitions against the key terms during revision
- **Learning Objectives** from every chapter

<u>Also</u>

This site has a syllabus manager, search functions and email results functions.

Contents in detail

Part 3 CAPITAL MARKETS IN EQUILIBRIUM

Preface

This book offers a general introduction to investment in security markets. To some people, security markets are like casinos and investing is about predicting security prices and speculating that those predictions will come true. This book will be of little use to those people. Reading this book won't enable you to make predictions about security prices that are any better than simply flipping a coin or reading a horoscope. That is not to say that this book won't help you to become a better investor. Indeed, one of the basic insights that you will obtain from reading this book is that good investments generally do not require forecasting skills. Rather, in many cases, good investments require the matching of the investments with the objectives and constraints of the investor. Frequently, this can be achieved by means of spreading the investments over many, preferably unrelated, securities (diversification), selecting securities whose risks offset the risks of the investors' liabilities (immunisation) and/or using derivative securities to protect against downside risk (hedging). These strategies do not require any forecasting ability whatsoever. However, they do require a thorough understanding of securities, securities markets and investment strategies. This is exactly what this book aims to achieve.

Intended audience

This book is geared to both undergraduate and graduate students. The subject matter can be covered in a two-semester course, but the text can also be used for a one-semester course by selecting the chapters considered most important. Generally, this course is taken after principles of finance have been studied. However, all concepts needed for this book are discussed here, in order to achieve a self-contained text. With regard to mathematics, no more than high-school-level algebra is assumed.

Special features and ancillary material

This text and its special features were carefully developed by the authors and evaluated by a dedicated panel of reviewers. The goal throughout has been to spark the interest of students and enhance their motivation to learn about the field of investments. Some of the material is placed on the accompanying Levy–Post investment website to allow for regular updates. The URL of the website is: www.booksites.net/levy

The following special features are included in this book:

Up-to-date coverage of investment practice and academic research

Throughout the book, we have attempted to give an up-to-date coverage of current investment practice and academic research. For example, the table below gives a small sample of ten key words that are found in this book but would not have appeared in a typical investment book ten years ago – most of them not even five years ago. Indeed, the financial markets have changed beyond recognition during the past decade.

Key word	Chapter
Behavioural finance	12
Electronic communication network (ECN)	3
Exchange-traded fund (ETF)	2
Hedge funds	4
Microsoft Excel spreadsheet application	Appendix B
Socially responsible investment (SRI)	5
Style analysis	22
Three-factor model	11
Treasury inflation-protected security (TIPS)	13
Value-at-risk (VaR)	21

Pedagogical structure of the text

The book was designed to facilitate easy absorption of the material. Each chapter begins with Learning objectives and ends with a Summary section. Key terms are presented in bold type the first time they are introduced. These terms also appear in the end-of-chapter Key terms section and in the end-of-book Glossary. Throughout the chapters, Practice boxes are used to illustrate the key concepts. Every chapter also includes a Selected references section, which guides the student to further literature on the subject covered in that chapter.

Real-life material: recent newspaper articles and case studies

Included are a wealth of articles and discussions from the *Financial Times* and other sources, as well as the financial statements of corporations, in order to introduce students to real-life scenarios that will give them the opportunity to apply investment theory and techniques. Each chapter opens with Investments in the News, a newspaper article highlighting the main topic discussed in the chapter. Additional material from the financial media is used throughout each chapter in the Connecting Theory to Practice sections.

Extensive sets of review and practice questions and answers (online)

We have spent much time and effort in developing a wealth of questions and answers for purposes of review, practice and examination. This material is divided into three parts:

■ Review and practice problems apply the concepts discussed in every chapter. We include samples of both multiple-choice questions and essay questions. Many problems are taken from the financial media and use real cases to show the relevance of the concepts studied. This material is split into two parts: one part that is available to both students and academic staff and another part that is available exclusively to academic staff. This allows academic staff to use exclusive questions as classroom enrichment problems, homework assignments and examination questions.
■ Multiple-choice self-evaluation tests for every chapter. Students can take these tests and will receive online a grade and feedback on the topics and sections that require further study.
■ Special CFA examination questions are practice problems that prepare students for the series of Chartered Financial Analyst (CFA) examinations administered by the Association

for Investment Management and Research (AIMR). For more information regarding the CFA Candidate Program, address enquiries to the Association for Investment Management and Research, Department of Candidate Programs, 5 Boar's Head Lane, PO Box 3668, Charlottesville, VA 22903-0668, USA, or visit www.aimr.org/cfaprogram/

All material is posted on the accompanying Levy–Post investment website. This allows us to regularly add new material and correct possible flaws in the existing material.

Appendices with regression and Excel tools for empirical research and practical application

An introduction to the field of investments is not complete without an introduction to the basic tools for empirical research and quantitative problem-solving. For this purpose, we have developed two appendices that help students to independently conduct research and solve decision-support problems. Appendix A, developed by Thierry Post, gives a step-by-step introduction to regression analysis. Appendix B introduces the student to the use of Microsoft Excel spreadsheets. The latter appendix was produced by Michael J. Seiler.

Ready Microsoft PowerPoint slides (online)

We have developed a collection of visually stimulating Microsoft PowerPoint slides for use during classroom lectures. The slides are designed to allow the instructor to modify and adapt each slide to meet individual classroom needs. The slides are posted on the accompanying Levy–Post investment website.

Software and Internet links (online)

Microsoft Excel spreadsheet software is provided free to adopters of the text in order to give students the opportunity to implement techniques presented in the text. Another feature includes Internet references that lead academics and students to pertinent investment-related websites. The software and Internet links will be updated regularly and are posted on the accompanying Levy–Post investment website.

Acknowledgements

This project could never have been completed without the help of many colleagues and friends. We would like to thank the following for providing valuable feedback and contributions:

Michael J. Alderson, St Louis University; Yakov Amihud, New York University; Hames J. Angel, Georgetown University; Sung C. Bae, Bowling Green State University; Guido Baltussen, Erasmus University Rotterdam; Kegian Bi, University of San Francisco; Avi Bick, Simon Fraser University; Gilbert Bickum, Eastern Kentucky University; Richard H. Borgman, University of Maine; Denis O. Boudreaux, University of Southern Louisiana; Stephen Caples, McNeese State University; John Clark, University of Alabama; John Clinebell, University of

Northern Colorado; Charles J. Corrado, University of Missouri-Columbia; Arthur T. Cox, University of Northern Iowa; Richard F. DeMong, University of Virginia; Giorgio De Santis, University of Southern California; Elroy Dimson, London School of Business; John W. Ellis, Colorado State University; Thomas H. Eyssell, University of Missouri at St Louis; Daniel Falkowski, Canisius College; James Feller, Middle Tennessee State University; J. Howard Finch, University of Tennessee at Chattanooga; Adam K. Gehr, Jr, DePaul University; Deborah W. Gregory, University of Otago; Frank M. Hatheway, Pennsylvania State University; David Heskel, Bloomsburg College; Stan Jacobs, Central Washington University; Vahan Janjigian, Boston College; Hazel J. Johnson, University of Louisville; Edward M. Kaitz, Marymount University; Andrew Karolyi, Ohio State University; Mike Keenan, New York University; Yoram Kroll, Hebrew University; Ladd Kochman, Kennesaw State College; Thomas Krueger, University of Wisconsin LaCrosse; Yoram Landskroner, Hebrew University; Graham K. Lemke, Pennsylvania State University; Azriel Levy, Hebrew University; K. C. Lim, City Polytechnic, Hong Kong; K. C. Ma, Investment Research Company; Steven V. Mann, University of South Carolina; Ralph D. May, Southwestern Oklahoma State University; William M. Mayfield, Northwestern Oklahoma State University; Michael L. McBain, Marquette University; Robert McConkie, Sam Houston State University; Robert McElreath, Clemson University; Bruce McManis, Nicholls State University; Edward Miller, University of New Orleans; Lalatendu Misra, University of Texas at San Antonio; Santhosh B. Mohan, Ohio Northern University; Deborah L. Murphy, University of Tennessee; Eli Ofek, New York University; Joseph P. Ogden, State University of New York at Buffalo; Rajeev N. Parikh, St Bonaventure University; Rose Prasad, Michigan State University; Hugh M. Pratt, University of Manitoba; Jerry Prock, University of Texas; Shafiqur Rahman, Portland State University; Venkateshward K. Reddy, University of Colorado, Colorado Springs; William Reichenstein, Baylor University; Stan Reyburn, Commercial Investment Counsellor, Professional Realty Associates; Meir Schneller, Virginia Polytechnic Institute; Michael J. Seiler, Hawaii Pacific University; Latha Shanker, Concordia University; Neil Sicherman, University of South Carolina; Raymond W. So, Louisiana State University; Meir Statman, Santa Clara University; Stacey L. Suydam, Montana State University, Billings; Antoinette Tessmer, University of Illinois; David E. Upton, Virginia Commonwealth University; Martijn J. van den Assem, Erasmus University Rotterdam; Jan van der Meulen, Erasmus University Rotterdam; Pim van Vliet, Erasmus University Rotterdam; Gopala K. Vasudevan, Suffolk University; Joseph D.Vu, DePaul University; William Wells, Merrimack University; Darin While, Union University; James A. Yoder, University of South Alabama.

We would also like to thank Hyla Berkowitz and Maya Landau for their editorial help, as well as Yael Ben-David, Daniel Berkowitz, Natali Eisof, Allon Cohen, Eitan Goldman, Doron Lavee, Tijmen Beetz and Bart de Klerk for their assistance in preparing the manuscript. Special thanks also go to Colette Holden for her excellent and thorough copy-editing, Lesley Thomas for obtaining copyright permissions, Georgina Clark-Mazo for attentively consolidating all editorial changes on to a master copy for the typesetter, and Amanda Thomas for overseeing production of the book.

Finally, we would like to thank the hardworking team at Pearson: Colin Reed, Senior Text Designer; Kevin Ancient, Design Manager, who designed the cover; and Jo Barber, Marketing Manager. In particular, we thank Justinia Seaman, Acquisitions Editor, and David Cox, Development Editor, for coordinating and driving this entire project.

Haim Levy, Jerusalem, Israel
Thierry Post, Rotterdam, the Netherlands

Acknowledgements

We are grateful to the following for permission to reproduce copyright material:

Exhibits 1.2, 1.3, 2.1, 2.2, 3.8, 5.1, 6.1, 6.2, 6.3, 6.4, 6.7, 6.8, 6.9, 6.10, 8.3, 8.7, 8.8, 8.9, 8.10, 8.11, 8.13, 8.14, 10.1a, 10.1b, 10.2, 10.3, 10.4, 10.6, 10.7, 11.1, 11.2, 11.4, 11.5, 11.6, 11.7, 12.1, 12.2, 12.3, 12.4, 12.7, 12.8, 13.2, 13.3, 13.4, 13.8, 13.9, 13.B1, 14.1, 14.2, 14.3, 14.4, 14.5, 14.7, 14.8, 14.9, 15.1, 15.2, 15.5, 15.6, 15.7, 17.5, 18.2, 18.3, 18.7, 18.8, 18.9, 18.10, 19.2, 19.5, 19.7, 20.1, 20.2, 20.3, 20.4, 20.5, 20.6, 20.7, 20.8, 20.9, 20.10, 20.13, 22.1, 22.2, 22.4, 22.7 and two figures in Practice Box 18 from *Introduction to Investments*, 2nd edn, by Levy, © 1999, reprinted with permission of South-Western, a division of Thomson Learning: www.thomsonrights.com, fax 800 730 2215; Exhibits 3.1, 3.2 and 3.5 from *World Online Preliminary Prospectus*, 1 March 2000, Utrecht, World Online International NV; Exhibit 3.4 reproduced with permission from Van den Assem; Exhibit 3.7 from *Financial Market Trends*, Vol. 65, 1996, pp. 16–17, © OECD *Financial Market Trends*, 1996; Exhibit 3.9 from www.archipelago.com, 5 January 2003, reproduced with permission of Archipelago Exchange® (ArcEx®); Exhibit 3.10 image of the NYSE Trading Floor® a federally registered service mark of the New York Stock Exchange, Inc., from www.nyse.com/pdfs/2001.factbook.06.pdf, photograph used with permission of NYSE; Exhibits 4.1, 4.3 and 4.4 from *Low of Funds*, www.federalreserve.gov, public domain, Washington, DC, Federal Reserve Board; Exhibit 4.2 from *Insurance City Business Series 2001*, www.ifsl.org.uk, London, International Financial Services London (IFSL, 2001); Exhibit 5.3 from *Progress on the Financial Services Action Plan*, www.europa.eu.int/comm/internalmarket/enfinances/actionplan/index.htm, 31 July 2003, Brussels, European Communities; Exhibit 6.5 from *MSCI Net Indices for UK and South African Equity*, www.msci.com, London, Morgan Stanley Capital International, Inc.; Exhibit 6.6 from *The Dow Jones Averages 1885–1995*, © Dow Jones & Company, Inc., 2003 (Pierce, P. S.); Exhibits 6.11 and 16.6, copyright 1992, 1987, respectively, CFA Institute, reproduced and republished from *Financial Analysts Journal* with permission from the CFA, all rights reserved (Reilly, F. and Kao, G. W. 1992; Gibson, C. 1987); Exhibit 6.12 reprinted from Robertson, Malcolm J., *Directory of World Futures and Options Markets*, 1st edn, © 1991; Exhibit 12.6 reprinted from *Journal of Financial Economics*, Vol. 3, Rendleman, R. *et al.*, 'Empirical anomalies based on unexpected earnings and the importance of risk adjustment', pp. 285–6, copyright 1982, with permission from Elsevier; Exhibit 12.9 from 'The cross section of expected returns', *Journal of Finance*, Vol. 47, pp. 427–65, Oxford, Blackwell Publishing Ltd (Fama, E. F. and French, K. R., 1992); Exhibit 13.5 from *Moody's 17th Annual Survey of Global Corporate Defaults and Rating Performance* and Exhibit 13.7 based on data from *Moody's Corporate Baa Series*, www.moodys.com, © Moody's Investors Service, Inc., and/or its affiliates, reprinted with permission, all rights reserved; Exhibit 13.6 from *Corporate Defaults in 2003 Recede from Recent Highs*, copyright 2004 by Standard & Poor's, material reproduced with permission of Standard & Poor's, a division of The McGraw-Hill Companies, Inc. (Brady, B., 2004); Exhibit 13C.1 adapted from Livingston, Miles, *Money and Capital Markets: Financial Instruments and Their Uses*, 1st edn, © 1990, by permission of Pearson Education, Inc., Upper Saddle River, NJ; Exhibit 15.10 from 'Break the barrier between you and your analyst', *Financial Executive*, September, p. 19, Florham Park, NJ, Financial Executives Institute (Chugh, L. C. and Meador, J. W., 1984); Exhibit 16.1 adapted from *Financial Statement Analysis: Theory, Application and Interpretation*, 4th edition, Homewood, IL, Irwin (Bernstein, L. A., 1989); Exhibit 16.2 from Pfizer 1996 Annual Report: Quarterly Consolidate Balance Sheet; Exhibit 16.3 from Consolidated Statement of Income for Pfizer, Inc.; and Subsidiary Companies; Exhibit 16.4 from Statement of Cash Flows for Pfizer, Inc.; Exhibit 16.5 from Pfizer 1996 Annual Report: Shareholder's Equity; Exhibit 16.8 from Percentage Balance Sheet for Pfizer, Inc.; and Exhibit 16.9 from Percentage Income Statement for Pfizer, Inc., http://www.pfizer.com/are/mn_investors.cfm, 1996, reproduced with permission of Pfizer, Inc.; Exhibit 16.7 © 2004, CCH INCORPORATED. All rights reserved. Reprinted with permission from *Almanac of Business and Industrial Financial Ratios* (Troy, L.); Exhibit 17.1 'The procedure for reporting the GDP', Exhibit 17.3 'Measuring inflation and components of the GDP when they are reported' and Exhibit 17.6 'The actions of the Federal Reserve Bank and its influence on the economy', from *The Atlas of Economic Indicators* by W. Stansbury Carnes and Stephen D. Slifer, copyright © 1991 by HarperCollins Publishers Inc., reprinted by permission of HarperCollins Publishers, Inc.; Exhibit 17.2 from www.bea.gov/bea/dn/nipaweb/index.asp, public domain, US Bureau of Economic Analysis; Exhibit 17.4 from Abel/Bernanke, *Macroeconomics*, Fig. 9.1 (p. 291), © 1995 by Addison-Wesley Publishing Company, Inc., and Exhibit 17.10 from Solnik, *International Investments*, Exhibit 1.1 (p. 9), © 1991, both reprinted by permission of Pearson Education, Inc., publishing as Pearson Addison Wesley; Exhibit 18.1 from *Technical Analysis Explained*, New York, McGraw-Hill, p. 14 (Pring, M. J., 1991); Exhibits 18.4, 18.5, 18.6 and 18.12 from *The Technical Analysis Course*, Chicago, IL, Probus Publishing, pp. 102–3, 109–10, 120–1, 137 (Meyers, T., 1989), reproduced with permission of The McGraw-Hill Companies; Exhibit 18.11 from Standard & Poor's (1997), *Daily Stock Record*, material reproduced with permission of Standard & Poor's. Copyright © 1997 Standard & Poor's, a division of The McGraw-Hill Companies, Inc. Standard & Poor's, including its subsidiary corporations ('S&P'), is a division of The McGraw-Hill Companies, Inc. Reproduction of this S&P Data in any form is prohibited without S&P's prior written permission. Because of the possibility of human or mechanical error by S&P's sources, S&P or others, S&P does not guarentee the accuracy, adequacy, completeness or availability of any information or any errors or omissions or for the results obtained from the use of such information. S&P GIVES NO EXPRESS OR IMPLIED WARRANTIES, INCLUDING, BUT NOT LIMITED TO, ANY WARRANTIES OF MERCHANTIBILITY OR FITNESS FOR A PARTICULAR PURPOSE OR USE. In no event shall S&P be liable for any indirect, special or consequential damages in connection with any use of the S&P Data; Exhibits 19.9 and 19.10 from *Futures Magazine Source Book 2003 and 2004*, Chicago, IL, Futures Magazine, Inc. (Robertson, R., 1990); Exhibit 19.11 from www.amex.com, 24 February 2004, copyright American Stock Exchange LLC 2004, reprinted with permission of American Stock Exchange LLC; Exhibit 21.5 from *The Report of the Board of Banking Supervision Inquiry into the Circumstances of the Collapse of Bearings, Ordered by the House of Common*, Crown copyright material is reproduced with the permission for the Controller of HMSO and the Queen's Printer for Scotland (HMSO, 1995); Exhibit 22.6 from Asset allocation: management style and performance measurement. *The Journal of Portfolio Management*, Vol. 18, pp. 7–19, published by Institutional Investor, Inc., W. F. Sharpe (1992); Screenshots A.1, A.2, A.3, A.4, A.5, A.6 from *EViews Regression*, reprinted by permission from Quantitative Micro Systems; Screenshots B.1, B.2, B.3, B.4, B.5, B.6, B.7, B.8, B.9, B.10, B.11, B.12, B.13, B.14, B.15, B.16, B.17, B.18, B.19, B.20, B.21, B.22, B.23 of *Microsoft Excel*® reprinted by permission from Microsoft Corporation, © 2003 Microsoft Corporation, One Microsoft Way, Redmond, Washington 98052-6399, USA, all rights reserved.

Bulls back as indicators point to growth, © *Financial Times*, 17 September 2003; Riskier assets do well thanks to US recovery, in 2003: the year in global markets, FT.com, © *Financial Times*, 31 December 2003; Exhibit 2.3 UK (Gilts) Treasury Bills, © *Financial Times*, 26 September 2003; Exhibit 2.4 Money market interest rates (%), © *Financial Times*, 10 October 2003; Exhibit 2.5 UK Notes and bonds, © *Financial Times*, 24 November 2003; Exhibit 2.6 UK index-linked bonds, © *Financial Times*, 24 November 2003; Exhibit 2.7 New corporate bond issues, © *Financial Times*, 9 October 2003; Exhibit 2.8 London Stock Exchange benchmark government bonds, © *Financial Times*, 7 October 2003; Exhibit 2.9 Extract from the Financial Times Stock Market tables, © *Financial Times*, 28 October 2003; Exhibit 2.10 Some Stock Market indices, © *Financial Times*, 11/12 October 2003; Big Board must end its costly drama, FT.com, © *Financial Times*, 11 November 2003; Equity loans: how to sell what you do not own, © *Financial Times*, 28 May 2001; Over-the-counter status presents an image problem, © *Financial Times*, 7 May 2001; Record inflow to mutual funds, © *Financial Times*, 28 February 2001; Share rises fail to ease pension deficits, © *Financial Times*, 17 January 2004; Mutual funds join the world of shorting, FT.com, © *Financial Times*, 7 November 2002; Why risk management is not rocket science, © *Financial Times*, 27 June 2000; Wall Street banks draw up new code for analysts, FT.com, © *Financial Times*, 21 May 2001; Corporate America in crisis: proposed reform, FT.com, © *Financial Times*, 2 July 2002; Out of sight, not out of mind: over-the-counter derivatives, © *Financial Times*, 20 September 1999; Putnam assets fall 11 per cent in November, FT.com, © *Financial Times*, 6 December 2003; Positive about 'best' stocks, © *Financial Times*, 2 March 2002; Dubious practices are outlawed, © *Financial Times*, 12 May 2000; 'Correlation' a key to smart investment, © *Financial Times*, 31 May 2003; Fund managers cautious over equities, © *Financial Times*, 19 February 2003; Equity investments by pension funds projected to surge, © *Financial Times*, 5 March 2002; A puzzle at the heart of equities, FT.com, © *Financial Times*, 19 March 2003; The enlightening struggle against uncertainty, © *Financial Times*, 25 April 2000; Pension plans under scrutiny, © *Financial Times*, 7 December 2001; Investors seek escape from ties that bind, © *Financial Times*, 22 November 2002; Why enough is never enough: a new study shows that you may need more shares in your portfolio than you think, © *Financial Times*, 24 June 2000; Investors get a lesson in home economics, © *Financial Times*, 25 February 2002; A model weighting game in estimating expected returns, © *Financial Times*, 21 May 2001; In search of money for nothing, © *Financial Times*, 11 June 2001; Dow inches forward into the black, © *Financial Times*, 24 September 2003; The curious case of Palm and 3Com, © *Financial Times*, 18 June 2001; Markets behaving badly, FT.com, © *Financial Times*, 7 April 2001; Few countries enforcing insider trading laws, © *Financial Times*, 12 April 2001; I'm a tracker punter and proud of it, © *Financial Times*, 17 August 2002; Hewitt Bacon recommends 'blindfolded monkey' way, FT.com, © *Financial Times*, 16 June 2003; Funds get caught in a bond bubble bind, © *Financial Times*, 8 July 2003; Euro-zone yield curve on inversion course, © *Financial Times*, 19 May 2000; Bond and rating agencies: scores are often junk, say critics, © *Financial Times*, 8 March 2003; A fad for junk bonds, © *Financial Times*, 28 June 2003; Lex column: telephone exchanges, © *Financial Times*, 9 January 2001; Balancing risk and return in volatile market conditions, © *Financial Times*, 21 August 2001; Low rates prompt bond buybacks, FT.com, © *Financial Times*, 20 June 2003; Markets/yields, FT.com, © *Financial Times*, 26 July 2002; DaimlerChrysler board poised to make its first dividend cut, © *Financial Times*, 4 February 2002; Equities in wonderland, FT.com, © *Financial Times*, 2 July 2001; Conceptual, © *Financial Times*, 28 August 2000; True diligence, © *Financial Times*, 15 April 2002; Ahold scandal stokes EU–US row over accounts regulation, © *Financial Times*, 26 February 2003; Job losses mean no end in sight for US recession, © *Financial Times*, 5 April 2003; The art and craft of reading the market, © *Financial Times*, 9 July 2001; FTSE rally gathers technical steam,

FT.com, © *Financial Times*, 18 March 2003; Technically, these methods don't work, © *Financial Times*, 7 June 2003; The secret formula that saved Salomon North: Wall Street steps in to rescue the fund that thought it was too smart to fail, © *Financial Times*, 25 September 1998; Exhibit 19.1 Spot and forward exchange rates against the dollar, © *Financial Times*, 2 December 2003; Euro markets: corporate sector embraces credit swaps, © *Financial Times*, 9 March 2000; Exhibit 19.8 Futures prices for December 2, 2003, © *Financial Times*, 3 December 2003; Eurex makes inroads into US, FT.com, © *Financial Times*, 28 May 2003; Overview: essential controversial, popular and profitable, FT.com, © *Financial Times*, 5 November 2003; Banks wake up to risk management challenge, FT.com, © *Financial Times*, 7 May 2003; Long march into markets' hell for a heavenly cause, © *Financial Times*, 22 February 2003; Weighing up the risks, © *Financial Times*, 2 December 1998; Sharpe's the word for risk and return, © *Financial Times*, 12 April 2003.

Diversification: Your excuses don't add up, from *The Financial Times Limited*, 15 March 2003, © Alpesh Patel, email: alpesh.patel@tradermind.com; The great technology bubble has been purged, from FT.com, *The Financial Times Limited*, 28 October 2002, © Jeremy Siegel; Getting the measure of Wall Street, from *The Financial Times Limited*, 19 February 2000, © Edward Chancellor; Undue pessimism is driving the Eurozone's recession, from *The Financial Times Limited*, 8 August 2003, © Paul de Grauwe; The costs of sterling, from FT.com, *The Financial Times Limited*, 4 July 2002, © David Cobham.

In some instances we have been unable to trace the owners of the copyright material, and we would appreciate any information that would enable us to do so.

Guided tour to the book

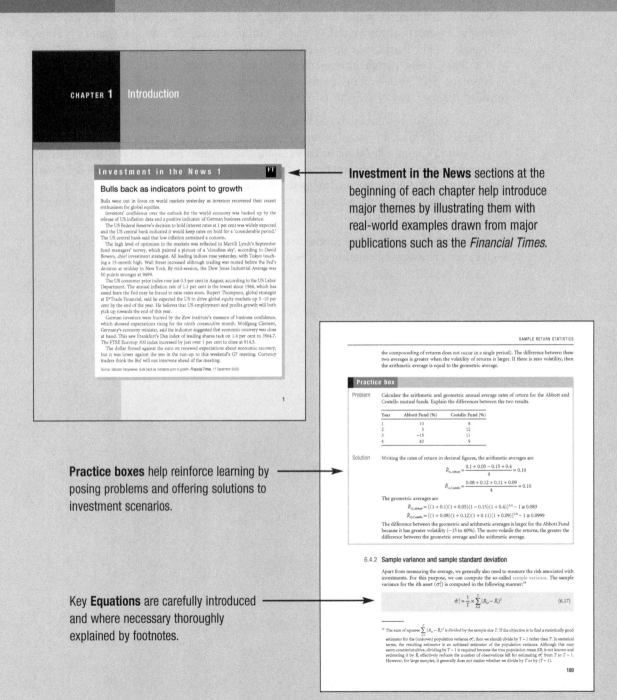

CHAPTER 1 Introduction

Investment in the News sections at the beginning of each chapter help introduce major themes by illustrating them with real-world examples drawn from major publications such as the *Financial Times*.

SAMPLE RETURN STATISTICS

the compounding of returns does not occur in a single period). The difference between these two averages is greater when the volatility of returns is larger. If there is zero volatility, then the arithmetic average is equal to the geometric average.

Practice box

Problem Calculate the arithmetic and geometric annual average rates of return for the Abbott and Costello mutual funds. Explain the differences between the two results.

Year	Abbott Fund (%)	Costello Fund (%)
1	10	8
2	5	12
3	−15	11
4	40	9

Solution Writing the rates of return in decimal figures, the arithmetic averages are

$$\bar{R}_{A,Abbott} = \frac{0.1 + 0.05 - 0.15 + 0.4}{4} = 0.10$$

$$\bar{R}_{A,Costello} = \frac{0.08 + 0.12 + 0.11 + 0.09}{4} = 0.10$$

The geometric averages are

$$\bar{R}_{G,Abbott} = [(1 + 0.1)(1 + 0.05)(1 - 0.15)(1 + 0.4)]^{1/4} - 1 \cong 0.083$$

$$\bar{R}_{G,Costello} = [(1 + 0.08)(1 + 0.12)(1 + 0.11)(1 + 0.09)]^{1/4} - 1 \cong 0.0999$$

The difference between the geometric and arithmetic averages is larger for the Abbott Fund because it has greater volatility (−15 to 40%). The more volatile the returns, the greater the difference between the geometric average and the arithmetic average.

Practice boxes help reinforce learning by posing problems and offering solutions to investment scenarios.

6.4.2 Sample variance and sample standard deviation

Apart from measuring the average, we generally also need to measure the risk associated with investments. For this purpose, we can compute the so-called sample variance. The sample variance for the ith asset ($\hat{\sigma}_i^2$) is computed in the following manner:[19]

$$\hat{\sigma}_i^2 = \frac{1}{T} \times \sum_{t=1}^{T} (R_{it} - \bar{R}_i)^2 \qquad (6.17)$$

Key **Equations** are carefully introduced and where necessary thoroughly explained by footnotes.

_____

[19] The sum of squares $\sum_{t=1}^{T} (R_{it} - \bar{R}_i)^2$ is divided by the sample size T. If the objective is to find a statistically good estimator for the (unkown) population variance σ_i^2, then we should divide by $T - 1$ rather than T. In statistical terms, the resulting estimator is an unbiased estimator of the population variance. Although this may seem counterintuitive, dividing by $T - 1$ is required because the true population mean ER_i is not known and estimating it by $\bar{R}_i$ effectively reduces the number of observations left for estimating σ_i^2 from T to $T - 1$. However, for large samples, it generally does not matter whether we divide by T or by $(T - 1)$.

189

→ Connecting Theory to Practice 4.3   FT

Where did LTCM come from?

In the 1980s and early 1990s, Salomon Brothers made billions of dollars through its proprietary trading. Most of those profits came from its bond arbitrage group led by John Meriwether. This group was created to take advantage of misvaluations of securities with correlated risks by taking a short position in the overpriced security and a long position in the underpriced one, hedging those risks that could be hedged.

To understand this approach, suppose the group decided that the yield on a particular US agency bond was too high compared with US Treasury bonds (yields in fixed income markets are inversely related to the price of a security). Certain agency bonds benefit from various guarantees from the US government. Yet such bonds trade at a higher yield than comparable government bonds. The group would purchase the agency bond and sell short government bonds with the view that eventually the yields would converge – hence the term 'convergence trade' to denote such a position.

Because of government guarantees, the main risk of the bonds is interest rate risk, but the position would have little interest rate risk because of the offsetting bond positions. The position would generate cash because of the difference between the coupon received and the coupon to be paid on the short position. Further, any narrowing of the spread between the yields of the agency bonds and the Treasury bonds would create a capital gain.

Eventually, Salomon Brothers was embroiled in a scandal when an employee was charged with manipulating auctions for Treasury bonds. Several senior managers at Salomon left the institution in 1991, including Meriwether. Two years later, Meriwether founded Long-Term Capital Management (LTCM) to manage a hedge fund, the Long-Term Capital Portfolio. Hedge funds are unregulated, managed pools of money. LTCM was organised to pursue the strategies that the arbitrage group at Salomon Brothers had implemented and very quickly several members of this group joined LTCM, along with future Nobel Laureates Robert Merton and Myron Scholes.

Source: Rene Stulz, Why risk management is not rocket science, Financial Times, 27 June 2000.

→ Making the connection

This newspaper article explains that LTCM was a continuation of the successful arbitrage group at Salomon Brothers. Note that the term 'arbitrage' does not properly describe the actual trading activities, as arbitrage is supposed to be risk-free. Also, the term 'hedge fund' is somewhat misleading. In general, hedging means to offset the risk of a set of securities with another set of securities, usually derivatives. For example, an investor may hedge the risk of Microsoft stock by selling futures or buying put options on Microsoft stock. However, hedge funds typically are not (fully) hedged; they hedge against adverse movements of the general market but at the same time speculate on price differences between individual assets or asset classes. Hence, hedge funds can be very risky. Further details on LTCM can be found in Connecting Theory to Practice 21.2 and 21.2 and Investment in the News 19.

116

Connecting Theory to Practice boxes contain a wide range of recent international examples that help underline the major themes and theories of the chapter.

Making the connection describes and explains exactly why the example is important, and provides guidance for the reader to related topics elsewhere in the book.

Key terms

Advance-funded pension plan 000	Institutional investors 000	Mutual fund 000
Asset-liability management (ALM) 000	Insurance company 000	NASDAQ 100 Shares 000
Conduit theory 000	Investment company 000	Net asset value (NAV) 000
Closed-end fund 000	Investment trust 000	No-load mutual fund 000
Discount 000	Open-end fund 000	Regulated investment
Defined-benefit pension plan 000	Life insurance company 000	company 000
Defined-contribution pension plan 000	Load 000	Standard & Poor's Depository
Dow Diamonds 000	Load mutual funds 000	Receipts 000
Family of funds 000	Pay-as-you-go (PAYG) pension plan 000	State pension fund 000
Hedge fund 000	Pension plan 000	Trust company 000
	Pension fund 000	Turnover 000
	Premium 000	Unit trust 000
	Private pension plan 000	World Equity Benchmark Shares (WEBS) 000

Review questions

1 Why can a defined-contribution pension plan never be underfunded?

2 What's the difference in investment behaviour between life insurers and property-casualty insurers; and what's the reason for this difference?

3 Why must open-end funds keep more cash on hand than closed-end funds?

4 The ABC Fund, a closed-end fund, consists of three securities – 1000 shares of Security A, which is currently trading at $35; 2000 shares of Security B, which is trading at $45; and 3000 shares of Security C, which is trading at $55. What is ABC Fund's NAV if it has $87 000 in net liabilities and 10 000 shares outstanding?

5 Suppose the return on the S&P 500 index is 12%. A mutual fund has a group of experts who can earn 15%. The load is 2%, and the management fee is 1.5%. Supposing that you can buy the S&P 500 index, which of these two investments would you prefer?

 For an extensive set of review and practice questions and answers, visit the Levy-Post investment website at www.booksites.net/levy-post

Selected references

Anderson, S. C. and J. A. Born, 1989, 'The Selling and Seasoning of Closed-End Investment Company's IPOs', *Journal of Financial Services Research*, 2, 131–150.

Anderson, S. C. and J. A. Born, 1992, *Closed-End Investment Companies: Issues and Answers*, Boston, MA: Kluwer Academic Publishers.

118

Key terms provide a convenient reference point for the concepts discussed within the chapter, with full definitions to be found in the Glossary at the back of the book.

Each chapter ends with **Review questions**, which test understanding with problems and practical exercises. Sample answers can be found at the back of the book.

Selected references provide sources for additional study on key topics and themes.

About the authors

Professor Haim Levy is the Miles Robinson Professor of Finance at Hebrew University of Jerusalem, Israel. He has also taught at the universities of California (Berkeley), Pennsylvania (Wharton), Illinois and Florida. In addition to his teaching responsibilities, he is an active consultant to firms and governments worldwide. Professor Levy is among the most published and most frequently cited researchers in modern finance. In addition to almost 200 journal articles, many of them in leading journals such as *Journal of Finance*, *Review of Financial Studies*, *Journal of Business*, *American Economic Review*, *Review of Economics and Statistics*, *Journal of Economic Theory* and *Econometrica*, he has published numerous books, including *Principles of Corporate Finance* (South-Western College Publishing, 1998). He has also found time to serve on the editorial boards of the *Journal of Finance*, *Management Science*, *Journal of Banking and Finance*, *Journal of Portfolio Management* and the *Financial Analysts Journal*.

Professor Thierry Post is Professor of Finance at the Rotterdam School of Economics of the Erasmus University Rotterdam, the Netherlands. His main research interests are understanding the economic forces behind the prices of financial assets (stocks, bonds and derivatives) and developing economically and statistically sound methods to support financial decision-making problems such as portfolio selection, performance evaluation and risk management. He has published in a wide variety of international journals, including *Journal of Finance*, *Review of Financial Studies*, *Review of Economics and Statistics* and *Operations Research*.

Introduction

Investment in the News 1

FT

Bulls back as indicators point to growth

Bulls were out in force on world markets yesterday as investors recovered their recent enthusiasm for global equities.

Investors' confidence over the outlook for the world economy was backed up by the release of US inflation data and a positive indicator of German business confidence.

The US Federal Reserve's decision to hold interest rates at 1 per cent was widely expected and the US central bank indicated it would keep rates on hold for a 'considerable period.' The US central bank said that low inflation remained a concern.

The high level of optimism in the markets was reflected in Merrill Lynch's September fund managers' survey, which painted a picture of a 'cloudless sky', according to David Bowers, chief investment strategist. All leading indices rose yesterday, with Tokyo touching a 15-month high. Wall Street increased although trading was muted before the Fed's decision at midday in New York. By mid-session, the Dow Jones Industrial Average was 50 points stronger at 9499.

The US consumer price index rose just 0.3 per cent in August, according to the US Labor Department. The annual inflation rate of 1.3 per cent is the lowest since 1966, which has eased fears the Fed may be forced to raise rates soon. Rupert Thompson, global strategist at E*Trade Financial, said he expected the US to drive global equity markets up 5–10 per cent by the end of the year. He believes that US employment and profits growth will both pick up towards the end of this year.

German investors were buoyed by the Zew institute's measure of business confidence, which showed expectations rising for the ninth consecutive month. Wolfgang Clement, Germany's economy minister, said the indicator suggested that economic recovery was close at hand. This saw Frankfurt's Dax index of leading shares tack on 1.4 per cent to 3564.7. The FTSE Eurotop 300 index increased by just over 1 per cent to close at 914.5.

The dollar firmed against the euro on renewed expectations about economic recovery, but it was lower against the yen in the run-up to this weekend's G7 meeting. Currency traders think the BoJ will not intervene ahead of the meeting.

Source: Deborah Hargreaves, 'Bulls Back As Indicators Point to Growth', *Financial Times*, 17 September 2003.

After studying this chapter, you should be able to:

1 Differentiate between corporate finance and investments.

2 State some good reasons to study investments.

3 Summarise the overall investment process.

4 Discuss several recent developments in the field of investments.

Happy days are here again! Forty-two months after the dot.com bubble burst in March 2000, stock prices are moving upwards strongly once again.[1] The Dow's peak, which came in January 2000, was 11 723, but the index dropped below 8000 afterwards. As this article was written, the Dow Jones Industrial Average stock index was again close to the psychologically important level of 10 000. The Dow was above this level when this book was written half a year later. Investors are becoming increasingly confident that the bull market has returned.

Bulls, or those who believe that the market will rise, may point at the recovery of the US economy. Economic growth in the third quarter of 2003 was 8.2% on an annual basis. World trade is booming thanks in part to the remarkable strength of the Chinese economy. Corporate profits are growing, business confidence has rebounded and analysts are upgrading their earnings forecasts.

However, not all is well that looks well. Bears, or those who think the market will fall, may point at uncertain prospects for US unemployment and high levels of consumer debt. Further, the rebound in profits is not primarily the result of faster revenue growth. A good deal is the result of the falling dollar, which increases the value of the revenues of the US corporate sector's overseas subsidiaries. Also, it has required remarkable fiscal and monetary stimulus to achieve the profit rebound: the lowest short-term interest rates for a generation and a federal budget deficit running at about 5% of gross domestic product (GDP). Eventually, some of this stimulus will be withdrawn; the Federal Reserve Bank (Fed) will eventually be raising interest rates and the federal government will probably have to apply the fiscal brakes once the 2004 presidential election is out of the way.

So where do we go from here? Should we follow the bulls or the bears? Will the Dow Jones soon advance beyond its old levels or will it fall back again? We, the authors of this book, would not bet our money on this. Conventional wisdom says that the stock market always goes up in the long run. Exhibit 1.1 confirms this; the long-term trend of the Dow

---

[1] The dot.com bubble was a speculative frenzy of investment in 'dot.coms' or companies selling products or services related to the Internet in the late 1990s. On 10 March 2000, the technology-heavy Nasdaq stock market index reached its peak of 5048.62, more than double its value just a year before. Arguably, the bubble burst as investors finally understood that the dot.com model was inherently flawed. A typical dot.com's business model relied on network effects to justify losing money in the short run to build market share through giving their product away in the hope that they could monopolise their sector and charge for their product in the long run. However, there could only be at most one network-effects winner in each sector and therefore most companies with the same business plan would fail. A majority of the dot.coms have now ceased trading, after having burnt through their capital, often without ever making a gross profit. A few established dot.com companies, including Amazon.com and eBay, have survived and appear to have a good chance of long-term survival.

Exhibit 1.1	Bull and bear periods of the Dow Jones

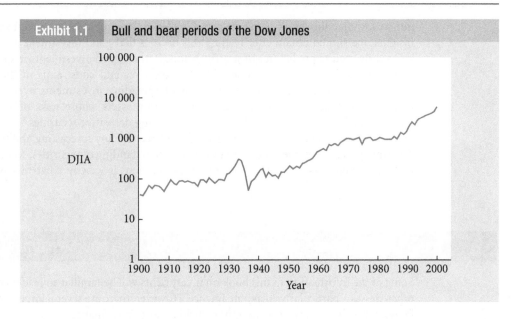

is up. However, sometimes the long run takes quite a while – there is no way of knowing whether the trend will persist the coming year. During the past century, there have been long periods when the stock market made little, if any, progress. For example, the index took off during the 'Roaring Twenties', peaking in 1929, followed by the the Great Crash and the Great Depression. The Dow Jones did not regain its 1929 level for 25 years. The real annual return for investors who bought at the peak was just 0.4% in the subsequent 20 years. Another peak occurred in 1966, the high-water mark of the optimistic Kennedy/Johnson New Economics era. In that year, the Dow almost breached the 1000 level, hitting 995.15. It did break 1000 in 1973, just before a calamitous bear market associated with the oil crisis and stagflation. It was not until 1982 that the market broke decisively past the 1000 mark. Over the 15-year period from 1966, the real return to equity investors averaged minus 0.5% a year.

In brief, forecasting stock prices is extremely difficult, even for periods of 15–20 years. If the authors of this book could predict stock prices, then probably we would not work in academia but rather use our time to make a fortune. However, the truth is that we cannot predict stock prices. And research shows that it is unlikely that other people can do so unless they have access to insider information – and using such information is illegal.

Generally, academics and practitioners agree on the effects on security prices of changes in the most important factors. For example, almost all agree that when the Federal Reserve cuts interest rates more than expected, or when it announces no increase in the interest rate when such an increase is expected, then the overall stock market will go up. Similarly, investors routinely observe that when a firm announces greater-than-expected quarterly earnings and dividends, the stock price of the firm goes up. Note that the factor must change by *more than expected* to influence prices. What if the Federal Reserve does not cut the interest rate, or the cut is less than what investors expected? In either case, the market will be disappointed, and prices will fall as a result. Thus, an investor who correctly predicted a rate cut may still end up losing money. In general, the average investor cannot make predictions that are better than average (unless he or she uses insider information).

In brief, reading this book won't enable the reader to make 'short-run' predictions about stock prices that are any better than simply flipping a coin or reading a horoscope. That is not to say that this book won't help the reader to become a better investor. One of the insights one should obtain after reading this book is that good investment decisions do not necessarily require predictions of security prices. Rather, good investments frequently require matching the investment portfolio with the objectives and constraints of the investor. In many cases, this can be achieved by means of spreading investments over many, preferably unrelated, securities (diversification), selecting assets whose risks offset the risks of the investors' liabilities (immunisation) and/or using derivative securities to protect against downside risk (hedging). These strategies do not require any forecasting ability whatsoever. The strategies do, however, require a thorough understanding of securities, securities markets and investment strategies. Gaining this understanding is exactly what this book aims to achieve.

1.1 The difference between corporate finance and investments

Some of the information in this book on investments will be familiar to readers from work in other classes – particularly corporate finance. However, there are several important differences between the field of investments and the field of corporate finance.

Corporate finance typically covers issues such as project analysis, capital structure, capital budgeting and working capital management. Project analysis is concerned with determining whether a project should be undertaken, for example whether a new warehouse should be built. Capital structure addresses the question of what type of long-term financing is best. Capital budgeting addresses the question of what long-term investments to undertake. Working capital management addresses how to manage a firm's day-to-day cash flow. Corporate finance is also concerned with how to allocate profits. Profits are divided among shareholders (through dividends), the government (through taxes) and the firm itself (through retained earnings).

Firms raise money by issuing stocks and bonds in the primary security markets. These securities are subsequently traded in the secondary security markets, where they are bought and sold by investors. Thus, both investors and the firm have an interest in the workings of financial markets. Corporate finance involves the interaction between firms and financial markets, whereas the field of investments addresses the interaction between investors and financial markets.

Apart from this different orientation, investments also differ from corporate finance in the use of relevant research methods. Specifically, investment problems in many cases allow for a quantitative modelling approach, while qualitative research methods, such as surveys and case studies, are used more frequently in corporate finance. Further, due to the large data sets available, for example on high-frequency stock returns, the field of investments often uses sophisticated statistical time-series estimation techniques.

Due to these differences, investments and corporate finance are typically covered in separate courses, although both build upon a common set of financial principles, such as the present value and the opportunity cost of capital. Of course, investments and corporate finance cannot possibly be treated as entirely separate fields. The similarities are most striking between capital budgeting and security analysis. Specifically, in capital budgeting, we need an asset-pricing theory that stipulates how investor preferences affect the relevant discount rate for risky projects. Similarly, in security analysis, we need an assessment of the investment projects and the financial policy of the firm.

1.2 The benefits of studying investments

Why study investments? There are several reasons why it is worthwhile. First, in this day and age, you can hardly go through life totally oblivious to terms such as 'swaps', 'options', 'bonds', 'stocks' and 'yields'. The media will not let you. To understand the financial news, you need some understanding of such terms.

Second, a thorough knowledge of the investment process can greatly enhance a person's welfare. By understanding how to make wise investments and manage finances prudently, people can greatly reduce the contributions required for retirement or obtain more income to support a better lifestyle.

Many people spend most of their lives trying to generate additional income rather than focusing on properly managing the income that they currently generate. For example, consider a group of physicians who focus on running an office practice and providing for their patients but neglect their day-to-day cash-flow management. As a result, the group has over $32 000 in a cheque account that does not earn interest. By taking a little time, they could immediately generate an additional $1120 per year. That is, they could open a money-market account from which they could write cheques (usually in excess of some minimum amount, say $250). Suppose the money-market account is earning about 4% per year. Then, by moving $28 000 to the money-market account (leaving $4000 for daily, small cash outflows), the physicians could earn $1120 ($28 000 × 0.04) a year. Just as the physicians' office could make $1120 a year, all individuals can save money by managing their personal finances wisely. The proper management of personal finances can result in a significantly higher future income. From the efficient management of day-to-day cash flow to retirement planning, a thorough knowledge of investments will provide lifelong benefits. Thus, even non-professional investors can benefit from understanding investments.

Third, studying investments is very challenging. It is a practical field in which highly sophisticated models are applied. For example, the theoretical underpinnings of investments received recognition by the Nobel Committee in 1990, when it awarded the Nobel Prize in Economics to financial economists Harry Markowitz, Merton Miller and William Sharpe. A large part of this book relies on the work of Markowitz and Sharpe, which laid the foundation for portfolio decision-making models and equilibrium risk–return relationships. (Miller's main contribution is in the area of corporate finance.) The work of Markowitz and Sharpe is used widely for various practical financial management applications, such as portfolio selection performance, capital budgeting, risk management and performance evaluation. In 1997, Robert Merton and Myron Scholes won the Nobel Prize in Economics for their contribution to research in derivatives, with an emphasis on options valuation models. The Black–Scholes option-pricing model (discussed in Chapter 20 of this book) is employed regularly by practitioners and traders in the financial markets. Thus, the topics covered in this book are not only intellectually challenging but also are important in day-to-day decision-making.

Fourth, this knowledge can lead to a rewarding career. As the financial markets become increasingly complex, job opportunities for professional investors increase. Even though job opportunities declined after the October 1987 stock market crash and recently after the 2000–02 bear market, the overall trend has been expansion. Increasingly, firms and institutions are looking for people with specialised skills. Exhibit 1.2 provides a sampling of job opportunities in the investments field. These jobs can be highly rewarding in terms of salary and bonuses, intellectual challenge and prestige.

Exhibit 1.2	Job opportunities in investments	
Job title	**Typical firms**	**Description**
Broker, registered representative, account executive	Brokerage firms, financial institutions	Provide sales and financial planning services
Analyst	Brokerage firms, financial institutions	Conduct research and security analysis
Financial planner	Private firms, certified public accountant (CPA) firms	Advise individual investors
Portfolio manager	Mutual fund groups, pension funds, money managers	Perform asset allocation and security selection
Asset/liability manager	Insurance companies, financial institutions	Perform research, actuarial work and asset allocation
Auditor	All firms	Monitor and devise internal controls
Regulator	Government agencies, exchanges	Oversee and police market activity
Surveillance	Exchanges	Oversee and monitor trading behaviour

Source: From *Introduction to Investments*, 2nd edn, by Levy. © 1999. Reprinted with permission of South-Western, a division of Thomson Learning: www.thomsonrights.com. Fax 800 730-2215.

1.3 The investment process

The process of managing investments is never completed; it is a dynamic and ongoing process. Generally speaking, the investment process includes five basic components: investor characteristics, investment vehicles, strategy development, strategy implementation and strategy monitoring. Exhibit 1.3 shows the relationship between these components.

1.3.1 Investor characteristics

The first element in the investment process is the investor and his or her characteristics. The investor may be an individual or an institutional investor, such as a manager of a pension fund or a mutual fund. The investor should first establish an investment policy; in the case of a large or institutional investor, this will be a written document detailing the objectives and constraints (characteristics) of the investor.

The investment policy should have specific objectives regarding the return requirement and risk tolerance. For example, the investment policy may state that the portfolio's target average return should exceed 8% and the portfolio should avoid exposure to more than 10% in losses. Typically, identifying the tolerance for risk is the most important objective, because every investor would like to earn the greatest return possible.

The investment policy should also state any constraints that will affect the day-to-day management of the funds. Constraints can include any liquidity needs, projected time horizons (when should the resources become available again for consumption?), tax considerations, and legal and regulatory requirements, as well as unique needs, circumstances and preferences. For example, the policy may call for 5% of the portfolio to remain liquid. The projected time horizon may be short, long or indefinite. The policy will usually state the tax status of the account.

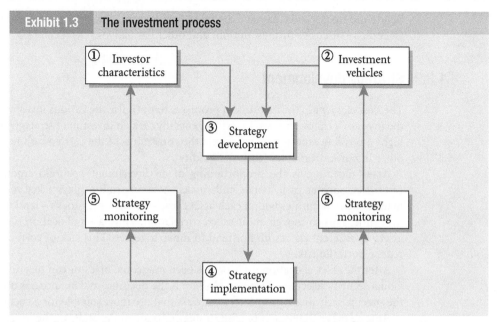

Exhibit 1.3   The investment process

Source: From *Introduction to Investments*, 2nd edn, by Levy. © 1999. Reprinted with permission of South-Western, a division of Thomson Learning: www.thomsonrights.com. Fax 800 730-2215.

Here are some typical questions that the individual investor must address before reaching an investment decision: What is the investor's current financial situation? What are the available investable resources? What is the investable income over the foreseeable future? What cash flows are needed at different dates in the future? How much risk can be tolerated by the investor? What type of investments would cause the investor to lose sleep? What is the tax status of the investment funds?

These types of questions must be addressed at the beginning of the investment-management process. For example, parents who want to invest for the college education of their newborn child have different answers, and therefore different investment policies, than an investor who is planning to get married and who wants to buy a house in one year.

1.3.2 Investment vehicles: the trade-off between risk and return

After an assessment of the investor's characteristics has been made, the available investment opportunities can be explored. Financial assets are classified broadly as money market securities, bonds, stocks and derivative securities. Money-market securities are securities with a short maturity (less than one year), such as Treasury bills, commercial paper and negotiable certificates of deposit. Bonds are financial assets that represent a creditor relationship with an entity. They are debt instruments of a firm. Stocks represent an ownership position in a corporation. Derivative securities (also called contingent claims), such as options and futures, are tied to the performance of another security (hence, the term 'derivative'). Of the four categories, money-market instruments are generally the least risky and also offer the lowest return. Bonds offer a higher return on average; however, they are exposed to interest-rate risk and, for corporate bonds, credit risk. Stocks offer even higher average returns; these are a reward for higher risks. Derivative securities have the highest potential risk level as well as the highest potential return. Chapter 2 elaborates further on money-market instruments, bonds and stocks, and Chapter 6 discusses the historical risk–return profile of these securities. Chapter 19 discusses futures, options and other derivatives.

1.3.3 Strategy development

The next element in the investment process is to optimise the various investment vehicles and the investor's characteristics. Investors generally seek an investment strategy that provides the highest possible expected return within the constraints of the desired cash flow, risk level and other important variables (such as liquidity).

Asset allocation is the proportioning of an investment portfolio among various asset categories, such as cash, bonds and stocks. Asset allocation plays a key role in investment management. Securities within each asset class – for example, stocks – tend to move together over time. This co-movement is called correlation. Thus, asset allocation is essential because assets in different classes do not tend to move together. This lack of co-movement helps to reduce portfolio risk.

After the asset-allocation decision has been made, the investor can turn to the task of individual security selection. Security selection is the decision-making process used to determine the specific securities within each asset class that are most suitable for a client's needs.

Among other things, the precise strategy developed depends on the investor's perception of how good capital markets are at processing information. If the capital markets process information quickly and accurately, then we say that the markets are efficient. An efficient market is one in which stock prices reflect all relevant information about the stock.

If an investor believes that the market is efficient, then the investment focus will be on designing well-diversified portfolios, immunised portfolios or hedging investment risks. (The investor sees no benefit in trying to uncover mispriced securities.) However, the investor who does not believe that the markets are efficient may wish to acquire all of the latest information and attempt to strategically alter his or her asset allocation or to buy underpriced securities and sell overpriced securities. In this book, we discuss various approaches to collecting relevant information: financial-statement analysis (see Chapter 16), macroeconomic analysis (see Chapter 17) and technical analysis (see Chapter 18).

1.3.4 Strategy implementation

After a strategy has been developed, the asset-allocation decisions are implemented and the specific securities are selected. Successful implementation of the strategy can be difficult in practice, especially if it involves frequent changes to the portfolio composition. One problem is transaction costs: changing the composition is costly because buying and selling securities generally carry a brokerage commission and a bid–ask spread (the difference between the price for buying and selling securities). Another problem is liquidity: buying or selling large blocks of securities may require significant price concessions, especially for inactively traded securities.

1.3.5 Strategy monitoring

Once the investment process has begun, it is important to re-evaluate the approach periodically. This monitoring is necessary because financial markets change, tax laws and security regulations change, and other events alter stated investment goals.

Economies and markets are in constant flux, which changes the optimal investment strategy. These changes result in assets either being allocated in a suboptimal fashion or incurring transaction costs. For example, in the late 1980s, interest rates were high and inflation was expected to fall. This situation induced some investors to allocate a large portion of their assets to bonds. Also, as interest rates fell in the early 1990s, bond prices rose. This condition further increased the allocation to bonds, since their expected returns were revised upwards. In contrast, when interest rates are relatively low and there is an expectation that firms will earn a lot of money, as occurred in the prosperity of the late 1990s, investors want to invest mainly in stocks. These constantly changing circumstances result in the need of investors to constantly change their asset allocations.

Another problem is changing investor objectives and constraints. Over time, the needs of an individual or institution change, requiring rebalancing of the portfolio. In this respect, investor objectives and constraints typically evolve during the different stages of the investor's lifecycle. For example, the situation of a young DINK (double income, no kids) couple is very different from that of a middle-aged man who is married with children or that of a retired widower. Similarly, an immature pension fund having few pensions in payment has different investment objectives and constraints than a mature fund where sizeable retirement payments are required, or a fund that is closing down (or 'winding up'). Investors must regularly examine and question their strategy to make sure it is the best one. Primarily, they need to monitor goals and objectives and review the available financial assets.

1.4 Recent developments in investments

Recent years have witnessed various developments that have revolutionised the capital market. The most important tends are discussed briefly below and will be elaborated in greater detail in the following chapters of this book.

1.4.1 Institutionalisation

The capital market has shifted from dominance by households to specialised institutional investors that manage saving collectively on behalf of individuals and sometimes non-financial companies. In part, this process is driven by the economies of scale in managing and diversifying financial assets and liabilities, and the demographic pressure of an ageing population on social security systems. Nowadays, institutional investors account for the largest part of the security holdings and security trading activity. At the end of 2002, US institutional investors, who owned only 7.2% of total outstanding equities in 1950, held a total of roughly $6.5 trillion or about half of all US equities. The manner in which these institutions invest their funds and exercise shareholder control over firm management has a pronounced effect on capital markets.

1.4.2 Advances in telecommunication and computer technology

Trading financial instruments has historically required face-to-face communication at physical locations. However, progress in telecommunication and computer technology changed this situation. The National Association of Securities Dealers Automated Quotations (NASDAQ) over-the-counter (OTC) market for stocks was one of the first markets where technology replaced physical interaction. Subsequently, most of the world's stock exchanges, including the Tokyo Stock Exchange (TSE) and the London Stock Exchange (LSE), moved to electronic trading. The New York Stock Exchange (NYSE) still uses physical trading but has introduced systems to let investors engage in electronic trading. Also, in the USA, new electronic markets have emerged, which are known as electronic communication networks (ECNs; see below). In brief, the world security markets are changing rapidly into virtual marketplaces. The technological progress also fuels an ongoing process of fragmentation to cater to individual needs of different investors and consolidation to create a compatible information and order-routing system that effectively connects the various marketplaces. This process explains many of the recent alliances, mergers and acquisitions between different exchanges. Currently, the landscape of tomorrow's security markets is uncertain. However, one thing is clear. The names and faces of stock exchanges may change radically in the next few years, but the real winners in these markets will be the investors. Due to competition and technological progress, investors will have access to more information and liquidity and at a higher speed and lower cost.

1.4.3 New investment vehicles and investment strategies

The capital market has been bombarded with new investment vehicles and investment strategies. Derivatives securities such as futures and options have hit the headlines, and financial engineering is popular. The role of futures and options as speculative investment tools, as well as risk management tools, has expanded rapidly. Exchange-traded funds (ETFs), also called index shares, track a specific basket of securities and trade continuously on the major exchanges like an ordinary stock. ETFs bring investors instant exposure to a diversified portfolio of stocks at lower costs than traditional mutual funds. Even though they have been around only since 1999, ETFs such as Nasdaq 100 Shares (QQQs) are so popular that their daily trading volume rivals the companies on the NYSE. An electronic communication network (ECN) is a trading system that allows investors to clear trades through a electronic open-limit order book. Due to their low costs and fast executions, ECNs are a competitive threat to the established NYSE and NASDAQ markets. In fact, in 2003, the ECNs dominated trading in NASDAQ stocks: some 55% of trades were carried out wholly on ECNs, most notably Instinet, Island and Archipelago, while the traditional NASDAQ dealers accounted for only 16.5%.

1.4.4 Market globalisation

The financial markets have become truly global. Because of fast-flowing communication systems and relaxation of capital flow restrictions worldwide, transactions between all parts of the world can be executed with a few computer keystrokes. Globalisation offers investors improved possibilities to diversify their portfolio across various countries and regions. However, at the same time, globalisation also reduces the risk-reduction benefits of diversification, as correlations have increased significantly. This can be seen in particular when short-term panic occurs in the market, as in the October 1987 crisis, the October 1997 crash and the aftermath of the terrorist attacks of 11 September 2001. In these three events, almost all major stock markets worldwide fell sharply.

1.4.5 Advances of academic knowledge

The field of financial economics has shown remarkable advances in the knowledge of how to price and analyse risky assets and how to manage investment portfolios. As discussed above, the theoretical underpinnings of investments received recognition with the Nobel Prize for Markowitz, Miller and Sharpe and the Nobel Prize for Merton and Scholes. Apart from the theoretical work, a wealth of decision-support tools has been developed for portfolio selction, risk management and performance evaluation, in many cases building on the Nobel Prize-winning work.

1.4.6 Increased focus on security regulation and investment ethics

Security markets cannot function properly without rules, institutions enforcing the rules and market participants (issuers, investment banks, retail and institutional investors, brokers, dealers, auditors, etc.) obeying the rules. Following the 1990s bull market, the financial world was shaken by a series of scandals. Among the many scandals were investment banks issuing overoptimistic investment advice and steering allocations of shares in much-sought-after initial public offerings to executives, prominent companies (including Enron and Worldcom) misstating their financial reports to give an overoptimistic impression of their financial health, and mutual funds favouring select investors in exchange for payments and other inducements at the expense of ordinary investors. These scandals have had a profoundly negative effect on the public confidence in the functioning of financial markets. For this reason, there appears to be a need to overhaul the regulatory system so as to convince investors that the financial markets can be transparent and trustworthy. Also, market participants are facing growing pressure, both public and internal, to ensure ethical practices in the financial marketplace.

All these rapid changes can make the field of investments more difficult for students to understand and for academics to teach. At the same time, however, the changes also make the field more challenging and interesting.

1.5 Where do we go from here? A brief overview of the book

This book has six parts. The contents of each of these parts will be discussed briefly below.

1.5.1 The investment environment

Part 1 discusses the investment environment. This part introduces many practical and institutional issues about security markets, the securities that are traded and the individuals and organisations that operate in the financial markets. These practical and institutional issues are useful in order to place the remaining parts of the book in the proper perspective. While the other parts can be read independently of each other, the reader is advised to first master the practical and institutional knowledge before proceeding with any of the other parts. Chapter 2 discusses the basic types of securities and the opportunities and risks these securities offer to investors. Chapter 3 explains how these securities are issued by corporations and governments in the primary market and subsequently traded among investors in the secondary market. Chapter 4 analyses the important roles of mutual funds, insurance companies and pension funds in securities markets today. Finally, Chapter 5 explains that security markets cannot function properly without rules and institutions enforcing those rules so that market participants obey them.

1.5.2 Risk and return

Part 2 introduces the reader to the most fundamental principle of investments: the trade-off between risk and return. For this purpose, Chapter 6 first explains how return is measured and the impact of taxes, inflation and exchange rates on rate-of-return calculations. Next, Chapter 7 explains how economists try to model the risk–return trade-off using the so-called expected utility theory (EUT). This chapter introduces several fundamental economic concepts, including the portfolio possibilities set, the probability distribution of returns and the utility function. EUT is a very useful conceptual framework for structuring investment decision-making, but it is by itself of little practical use. Therefore, Chapter 8 introduces the mean–variance analysis, which currently is the most popular practical framework for structuring investment decision-making. Mean–variance analysis is used widely for applications of portfolio selection, performance evaluation and risk management. Not surprisingly, many of the remaining chapters of the book will build on mean–variance analysis. Chapter 9 concludes Part 2. Building on the mean–variance framework introduced in the previous chapter, this chapter discusses the potential gains from spreading an investment portfolio over many assets and the potential problems investors encounter in constructing well-diversified portfolios.

1.5.3 Capital markets in equilibrium

Part 3 deals with economic theories about the pricing of securities. This section introduces the capital asset-pricing model (see Chapter 10), the arbitrage pricing theory (see Chapter 11) and the efficient market theory (see Chapter 12). The theories are explained and illustrated with simple examples. We also discuss the results of empirical research directed to validate these theories. Apart from the theoretical models and empirical studies, we also discuss how the theories can be used in practice. Indeed, the equilibrium models are the foundation for many popular decision-support tools for portfolio selection, capital budgeting, risk management and performance evaluation – many of which are covered in the remaining chapters. We deliberately choose to treat the efficient market theory *after* the capital asset pricing model and the arbitrage pricing theory because empirical tests of market efficiency cannot be understood without a prior understanding of asset-pricing theories; such tests invariantly are joint tests of market efficiency and an asset-pricing model.

1.5.4 Security analysis

Part 4 turns to security analysis. The first three chapters deal with the framework for security analysis, with an emphasis on computing the intrinsic value of securities or the present value of expected future cash flow to investors discounted at an appropriate risk-adjusted discount rate. Chapters 13 and 14 focus on the risk and return associated with investing in bonds and on managing an investment in bonds in a climate of volatile interest rates. Chapter 15 deals with the valuation and selection of stocks. It pays special attention to valuation multiples and their relationship with the conceptual dividend discount model to clarify their strengths and weaknesses. These three chapters assume that information about the future cash flows of bonds and stocks and relevant discount rates is readily available and say little about the source of these model inputs. The next three chapters discuss various approaches to collecting such information; they give an introduction to financial statement analysis (see Chapter 16), macroeconomic analysis (see Chapter 17) and technical analysis (see Chapter 18).

1.5.5 Derivative securities

Part 5 deals with derivatives, the asset class with the highest risks and the largest returns. These instruments (options, futures, forwards and swaps) are distinctly different from bonds and stocks in a number of ways, such as their payoffs and the fact that derivatives are located entirely in the secondary market. The characteristics of derivatives and their markets are discussed in Chapter 19. One of the most interesting (and complex) parts of investments is the valuation of derivatives, in particular options. Chapter 20 introduces option valuation based on the no-arbitrage argument, enabling the reader to value standard derivatives – an essential feature of modern risk and portfolio management.

1.5.6 Portfolio management

Part 6 turns to the issue of portfolio management. At this stage, many practical tools have already been discussed in the earlier chapters, most notably Part 4 on security analysis. However, we have not yet covered the extensive set of tools currently available for managing risk and measuring performance. These include, for instance, models for quantifying market risk and credit risk and models for measuring and decomposing investment performance. Chapter 21 deals with risk management and Chapter 22 deals with performance evaluation.

1.5.7 Appendices

Investments is a relatively quantitative discipline that often uses statistical estimation and mathematical optimisation models. An introduction to the field of investments is not complete without an introduction to the basic tools for empirical research and quantitive modelling. For this purpose, we have developed two appendices that help students to independently conduct empirical research and solve decision-support problems. Appendix A gives a step-by-step introduction to regression analysis. Appendix B introduces the student to the use of Microsoft Excel spreadsheets. The former appendix is developed by Thierry Post, while the latter is produced by Michael J. Seiler. We believe that the student will benefit greatly from mastering these multipurpose tools, which can be applied to a wide variety of problems in investments, as well as other fields.

Summary

Differentiate between corporate finance and investments.

Corporate finance addresses the relationship between the financial markets and firms, whereas the field of investments addresses the relationship between investors and the financial markets. In addition, investment problems in many cases allow for a quantitative modelling approach, while qualitative research methods, such as surveys and case studies, are used more frequently in corporate finance. Further, due to the large data sets available, for example on high-frequency stock returns, investments often uses sophisticated statistical time-series estimation techniques.

State some good reasons for the study of investments.

The benefits of understanding investments include helping you to become a better manager of your own personal wealth, the intellectual challenge of mastering Nobel Prize-winning insights, and learning about the possibilities of a dynamic and exciting career.

Summarise the overall investment process.

The investment process consists of five components: investor characteristics, investment vehicles, strategy development, strategy implementation and strategy monitoring.

Discuss several recent development in the field of investments.

Broad trends in the capital markets include (1) the growing importance of institutional investors, (2) the advances in telecommunication and computer technology, (3) the introduction of new investment vehicles and strategies, (4) the globalisation of the marketplace, (5) the advances in academic knowledge and (6) the increased focus on security regulation and investor ethics.

Key terms

Asset allocation 8
Bears 2
Bonds 7
Bulls 2
Consolidation 10
Derivatives securities 7
Diversification 4

Efficient market 8
Electronic communication
  network (ECN) 10
Exchange-traded funds
  (ETFs) 10
Fragmentation 10
Hedging 4

Immunisation 4
Institutional investor 9
Investment policy 6
Money-market securities 7
Security selection 8
Stocks 7

Review questions

1   Discuss briefly the difference between the field of Corporate Finance and the field of Investments.

2   List the five basic components of the investment process.

3   Explain why different investors adopt different investment strategies. Use the concept of the investment process to explain your answer.

4   Explain why a given investor may adopt different investment strategies at different points in time. Use the concept of the investment process to explain your answer.

5   Identify six important developments in the capital market in recent years, and elaborate briefly on each of them.

 For review and practice questions and answers, visit the Levy–Post investment website at
www.booksites.net/levy

Selected references

Bernstein, P. L., 1993, *Capital Ideas: The Improbable Origins of Modern Wall Street*, New York: Free Press.

Lee, Helen, 2001, *The Harvard Business School Guide to Careers in Finance 2001*, Boston, MA: Harvard Business School Publishing.

Levy, Moshe and Haim Levy, 2003, 'Investment Talent and the Pareto Wealth Distribution: Theoretical and Experimental Analysis', *Review of Economics and Statistics*, **85**, 709–725.

Maginn, John L. and Donald L. Tuttle (eds), 1990, *Managing Investment Portfolios: A Dynamic Process*, 2nd edn, New York: Warren, Gorham & Lamont.

Malkiel, B., 2000, *A Random Walk Down Wall Street*, 7th edn, New York: W.W. Norton & Company.

Schiller, R., 2001, *Irrational Exuberance*, Princeton, NJ: Broadway Books.

Schiller, R., 2003, *The New Financial Order: Risk in the 21st Century*, Princeton, NJ: University Press.

Siegel, J. J., 2002, *Stocks for the Long Run: The Definitive Guide to Financial Market Returns and Long-Term Investment Strategies*, 3rd edn, New York: McGraw-Hill.

Part 1

THE INVESTMENT ENVIRONMENT

CHAPTER 2

Bonds, stocks and other securities

FT

Riskier assets do well thanks to US recovery

It paid to take risks in 2003. Government bonds, the 'safe haven' assets of 2001 and 2002, significantly underperformed. Instead, investors who prospered bought technology stocks, emerging market equities, commodities and junk bonds.

Choosing such assets in 2002 would probably have got a fund manager fired. But in 2003, riskier assets performed well thanks to growing confidence in US economic recovery on the back of interest rate cuts and increased government spending.

Asset classes 2003		Equity markets 2003		Equity sectors 2003	
	Return		Performance		Performance
Equities	to Dec 29* (%)	**Best**	to Dec 29 (%)	**Best**	to Dec 29* (%)
FTSE All World	32.8	Argentina	121.2	Steel & other metals	87.2
S&P 500	28.4	Thailand	118.2	IT hardware	64.8
FTSE Eurotop 300	36.5	China	117.3	Mining	55.8
		India	101.6	Construction & building materials	52.2
Bonds**		Brazil	89.6	Engineering & machinery	52.2
US Treasuries	2.4				
Emerging markets	29.9	**Worst**	% change	**Worst**	% change
Corporate investment grade	14.0	Venezuela	20.0	Food producers & processors	14.2
Corporate high yield	32.2	Finland	21.1	Personal care & household	14.3
		Malaysia	21.3	Beverages	16.8
Commodities		Netherlands	23.8	Pharmaceuticals & biotech	17.7
GSCI Commodity Index	20.2	Poland	24.3	Food & drug retailers	24.2
Gold ($ price)	20.3				

* $ terms
** Lehman Brothers' global indices

Sources: Thomson Datastream; Lehman Brothers

Nigel Richardson, chief strategist at AXA Investment Managers in London, said: 'The big picture is one of confidence in US recovery. The world realised the US was able to respond to monetary and fiscal stimulus. Back in June, people were talking about the threat of outright deflation. That threat has, to a great extent, receded.'

Investment in the News 2 continued

The S&P 500 index has risen by about 40 per cent from its low in mid-March – before the war in Iraq began – while the MSCI World index is up about 30 per cent this year. Reflecting a brighter industrial outlook, metal prices have risen about 30 per cent.

Improving US data in the second half of the year, added to the removal of uncertainty leading up to the Iraq war, help explain the change in market psychology. Although US forces are still bogged down in Iraq, some of the worst post-Iraq scenarios, such as a wider Middle East war, did not occur.

In the US the Dow Industrial average rose about 25 per cent this year while the technology-heavy Nasdaq is up 50 per cent. Some of the best share price performers of the year were some of the worst casualties of the bear market, such as Alcatel and Nortel Networks.

In the fixed-income market, investors took on more risk in a desperate search for yield after 13 US interest rate cuts since the start of 2001 brought rates to their lowest since 1958. That drove a boom in junk bonds, which have returned about 32 per cent globally, their highest total return since 1991, according to Lehman Brothers.

Junk bonds also benefited from increasing investor confidence about corporate credit-worthiness as profits recovered strongly and companies took action to improve balance sheets. But government bond markets delivered barely positive returns, as investors worried about rising issuance and potential inflationary pressures.

Emerging markets tend to outperform in a rising cyclical environment. And in both equities and bonds, emerging markets stood out in 2003, with the FTSE emerging markets index up about 65 per cent and the Lehman Brothers emerging markets bond index up about 30 per cent on a total return basis. The rise of industrial commodities has played a part in the performance of resource-rich countries.

For ordinary investors, the main way of gaining exposure to commodities is through the equity markets, for example buying mining shares.

While a US-led recovery played a part in rising industrial commodity prices, so did the emergence of China as a leading trading nation, with an explosion of demand for industrial metals in particular.

Source: Adrienne Roberts, 'Riskier Assets Do Well Thanks to US Recovery', In: 2003: The Year in the Global Markets, FT.com site; 31 December 2003.

Learning objectives

After studying this chapter, you should be able to:

1 Differentiate between investments in physical assets and investments in financial assets (securities).

2 Describe basic characteristics and types of bonds, stocks and derivatives.

3 Describe investment opportunities in international markets and investment companies.

4 Compare different types of derivative securities.

5 Explain the risks involved in investing in securities.

In this Investment in the News article, we see that there exist many different types of traded financial assets and securities. The history of security markets is long and varied. Babylonian merchants financed their activities with the savings of the rich around 2000 BC. By 400 BC the Greeks had their equivalent of a modern joint-stock company and markets for handling currencies and interest-bearing securities. Although there has always been a demand for some sort of securities, the security markets have become much more sophisticated during the past centuries.

Today's world security markets include bond, stock and derivative securities, and in a larger diversity then ever before. This chapter describes the basic characteristics of these securities and the different types of risks (for example, interest rate risk and exchange rate risk) associated with these securities. We also illustrate how to read the quotes for these securities as they appear in the financial media.

Different securities generally have a different expected rate of return or yield. We stress that the yield is the expected return and not necessarily the actual return that the investor will realise during his or her holding period, which is not known in advance (except for risk-free securities such as US Treasury bills). For example, the table in Investment in the News displays the realised returns on various types of securities during 2003. The returns over 2004 may be very different. In general, the higher the yield, the higher the uncertainty about the actual return. This pattern arises because investors generally dislike risk and, hence, demand a higher yield for risky securities.

2.1 The nature of securities

An asset is something that is owned by a business, institution, partnership, or individual and that has monetary value. There are two categories of assets: physical assets, which are tangible, such as precious metals or real estate, and financial assets, which are intangible, such as corporate stocks and bonds. Although financial assets are typically represented by tangible certificates of ownership, the financial asset itself is intangible. Financial assets are also called securities. A key distinction between financial and physical assets is that the latter are income-generating assets used to produce goods or services. Financial assets, in contrast, represent claims against the income generated by real assets.

Investment in financial assets differs from investment in physical assets in several ways:

2.1.1 Divisibility

One unique characteristic of investments in financial assets (as opposed to investments in real assets) is that financial assets are easily divisible. For example, you can buy a small fraction of General Electric (GE) through common stock, i.e. you do not have to buy the entire company. Thus, you can buy or sell a portion of a corporation with common stock. It is much harder, however, to buy or sell a portion of a manufacturing plant or other physical asset. An asset is said to be divisible if you can buy and sell small portions of it. Financial assets are divisible, whereas most physical assets are not.

2.1.2 Marketability

Financial assets (or securities) can be classified by how easily they can be bought and sold. Marketable securities, such as 100 shares of AT&T stock, can easily be bought and sold by a phone call to a broker or via the Internet and are therefore very liquid. Non-marketable securities, such as stamps or Chinese ceramics, cannot be sold readily. Marketability reflects not necessarily the market value but simply the ease and speed with which an asset can be traded without having to incur a substantial price concession. Clearly, if you wanted to sell a house in one day, then you would have to offer a substantial discount to attract someone to buy it immediately.

Marketability is a characteristic of financial assets that is not shared by real assets. Marketability, or liquidity, reflects the feasibility of converting an asset into cash quickly and without affecting its price significantly. Stocks with a large number of shares outstanding that are actively traded are very liquid. These securities are preferred by investors who trade large quantities of securities, because their trading activity will have no (or minimal) impact on the security's price. Many financial assets are very easy to buy and sell. However, most real assets are not very liquid and hence are described as illiquid. An investor who owns textile machines and who wants to sell them, for example, will generally have difficulty doing so.

2.1.3 The holding period

When investors acquire a real asset, they normally plan to hold it for a relatively long period. Buying new steel-producing machines, for example, requires large installation costs. Therefore, no one would plan to hold these machines for a month or even just a year. However, the transaction costs of buying securities are relatively low, and investing for a month or a year may be reasonable. Thus, the planned holding period of securities can be much shorter than the corresponding holding period of most real assets.

2.1.4 Information availability

Information about financial assets is abundant. Although in principle all investors can obtain information on real assets, it is typically hard to acquire and may be costly. For example, suppose you enquire about buying an oil-drilling machine. Where would you get information on the value of the machine? What are the transportation and installation costs of the machine? Probably only a few people in the oil industry have the information to determine these costs. The situation is different with stocks and bonds. Anyone can open the *Wall Street Journal* or the *Financial Times*, look on the Internet or call a broker to find out how much a share of AT&T stock costs. Similarly, a person who wants to buy shares of AT&T stock can obtain information (at almost no cost) on earnings, dividends and so forth. Since this information is available publicly, the impact of many published factors on the value of the financial asset can be analysed. This type of analysis cannot be done easily with real assets, at least not by all investors.

These four factors – divisibility, marketability (also called liquidity), holding period and information availability – make investments in financial assets different from investments in physical assets.

2.2 Fixed-income securities

A fixed-income security is a financial contract with predetermined payoffs; you know in advance the amount you'll receive, hence the name. A major part of fixed-income securities are bonds, which we'll use to illustrate the characteristics of fixed-income securities.

2.2.1 Basic characteristics of fixed-income securities

Bonds have three major identifying characteristics. First, they are typically securities issued by a corporation or governmental body for a specified term. The Federal Government, states, cities, corporations, and many other types of institutions sell bonds. Bonds are issued with the purpose of raising capital by borrowing money. When a bond becomes due for payment, at maturity, the nominal dollar amount assigned to a security by the issuer, par value, face value or principal value, is returned to the investors.

Second, bonds usually pay fixed periodic interest instalments, called coupon payments. Most bonds are fixed-rate bonds, because the stated payments are contractual and constant over time and normally defined as a percentage of the par value. However, some bonds pay variable income and are referred to as floating-rate bonds. For example, in July 1999, Ford Unit (Ford Motor Credit Co.) launched the largest corporate bond issue in US history ($8.6 billion) at a floating rate that holds for 32 years at 140 basis points (i.e. 1.4%) over the Treasury rates.[1] Shorter maturity bonds were issued by Ford at 26 basis points (0.26%) over the three-month London interbank offer rate (LIBOR) (see Section 2.2.2) rate. With a floating-rate or fixed-rate bond, the issuer is obligated to pay the bondholder at specified dates and has no discretion as to the amount that will be paid. As long as the maturity of the bond is not too long, and there is little risk of bankruptcy (for example, US government bonds), the risks of bonds are generally low, with correspondingly low returns. Bonds are usually less liquid than stocks and generate relatively high periodic cash flows (the interest payments).

Third, when an investor buys a bond, he or she becomes a creditor of the issuer. However, the buyer does not gain any kind of ownership rights to the issuer, unlike in the case of equities. On the other hand, a bondholder has a greater claim than a shareholder on an issuer's assets in the case of financial distress (this is true for all creditors). Bonds are traded in the bond market and have a market price that may change over time.

Bonds are typically classified into two groups based on their length of time to maturity. Money market securities are short-term (less than one year) obligations (for example, Treasury bills). In contrast, capital market securities are long-term securities (more than one year), such as Treasury bonds (usually having initial maturities in excess of ten years). The term 'capital market securities' also applies to stocks.

Exhibit 2.1(a) shows the cash-flow characteristics of a bond in general. Exhibit 2.1(b) shows an example of cash flows from a particular bond. The downward-pointing arrows in Exhibit 2.1 depict the cash payments from the investor, and the upward-pointing arrows depict cash receipts to the investor. By investing the current market price of the bond today ($Price), there is a promised stream of cash receipts in the future, called coupon payments ($C), and principal payment (or par value, $Par).

As we will see in Chapter 13, the bond price today is the present value of its future coupons and par value, discounted with the appropriate discount rate. If interest rates rise, then the present value of the future cash flows ($C and $Par) will decrease, thereby decreasing the price of the bond. The opposite holds when the interest rate decreases. For example, on 27 October 2003, the bonds of DaimlerChrysler with an 8.50% coupon interest and maturity in 2031 were traded at $112.15, while the par value is only $100. Due to a decrease in the interest rates, the discount rate decreased and the present value of future cash flows on DaimlerChrysler's bonds increased, which explains the gap between the market value and par value of these

---

[1] A basis point is 1/100 of a per cent, or 0.0001.

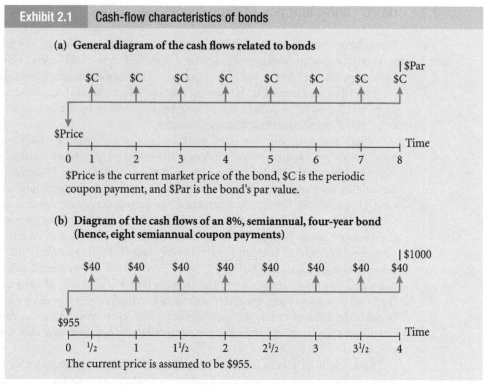

Exhibit 2.1   Cash-flow characteristics of bonds

(a) General diagram of the cash flows related to bonds

$Price is the current market price of the bond, $C is the periodic coupon payment, and $Par is the bond's par value.

(b) Diagram of the cash flows of an 8%, semiannual, four-year bond (hence, eight semiannual coupon payments)

The current price is assumed to be $955.

Source: From *Introduction to Investments*, 2nd edn, by Levy. © 1999. Reprinted with permission of South-Western, a division of Thomson Learning: www.thomsonrights.com. Fax 800 730-2215.

bonds. Thus, bond prices are sensitive to interest rate changes. The larger the change in the interest rate, the larger the potential loss or gain.

The advantages of bonds to an investor relative to stocks are that they are good sources of current income and their investment is relatively safe from large losses (unless, of course, the bonds have a large risk of default by the issuer). Another advantage is that in case of default, bondholders receive their payments before shareholders can be compensated. A major disadvantage of bonds relative to stocks is that the potential profit is limited.

Several types of fixed-income securities are available to investors, including short-term and long-term, high-risk and low-risk, and taxable and non-taxable. Exhibit 2.2 lists the different

Exhibit 2.2   Types of bonds

Money-market securities	Capital-market securities
Treasury bills	Treasury notes
Commercial paper	Treasury bonds
Bankers' acceptances	Federal agency bonds
Negotiable certificates of deposit	Municipal bonds
Repurchase agreements	Corporate bonds
Federal funds	Mortgages and mortgage-backed securities
Eurodollars	

Source: From *Introduction to Investments*, 2nd edn, by Levy. © 1999. Reprinted with permission of South-Western, a division of Thomson Learning: www.thomsonrights.com. Fax 800 730-2215.

types of bonds, classified by whether they are money-market securities or capital-market securities. The following section provides a brief description of various types of bonds.

2.2.2 Money-market securities

The money market (maturity less than a year) includes a wide range of securities, including Treasury bills, commercial paper, bankers' acceptances, negotiable certificates of deposit, repurchase agreements, Federal funds and eurodollars. Investors in the money market include speculators, hedge funds and also insitutional investors, such as pension funds. Let us elaborate briefly on each type of security.

Treasury bills (also called T-bills) are securities representing financial obligations of the US government. Treasury bills have maturities of less than one year. They have the unique feature of being issued at a discount from their stated value at maturity. In other words, a sum of money is paid today for a greater fixed dollar amount in the future at maturity; usually the payment at maturity is $100 000 (no coupon payments are made). For example, Treasury bills may sell for $98 000 when issued and have a maturity value of $100 000 in six months. Thus, the dollar return to the investor is $2000. During this six-month period, the investor earns interest, although the interest is not paid in cash but is merely accrued.

Another unique feature of T-bills is that they are virtually risk-free. Ignoring inflation and default of a government (which is rare in developed countries), the T-bill will pay the stated yield with certainty. Also, because it is a short-term asset, changes in interest rates do not affect the price significantly. Therefore, it is common to refer to the yield on T-bills as the 'risk-free interest rate'. It is true that, over time, the yield on T-bills changes. However, when you purchase a given T-bill, the rate of return you earn is fixed if you hold it to maturity.

Gilts are Treasury securities (bills and bonds) issued by the British government and equivalent to Treasury securities in the USA, in that they are perceived to have no risk of default. This is also the case for the major euro countries in Europe who issue their own government bonds (Germany, France, Spain and the Netherlands).

Exhibit 2.3 shows recent quotes for UK Treasury bills. The first column gives the name of the UK T-Bill. In the name, we can deduce the coupon percentage and the maturity. The second column gives the closing mid-prices, while the third column summarises the weekly price change. The fourth column gives the amount issued in sterling. The fifth column shows

Exhibit 2.3	UK (Gilts) Treasury bills							FT
Sep 26	Notes	Price £	W'k % chng	Amnt £m	Interest due		Last xd	Red Yield
Shorts' (Lives up to Five Years)								
Tr 12$\frac{1}{2}$ pc '03–5.............*		101.27	–.1	152	My21	Nv21	5'2	3.50
Tr 6$\frac{1}{2}$ pc '03		100.54	...	8095	Je7	De7	29.5	3.56
Tr 13$\frac{1}{2}$ pc '04–8 ....*		104.75xd	–.1	96	Se26	Mr26	17.9	3.66
Tr 10pc '04......................*		103.93	...	20	Nv18	My18	8.5	3.68
Tr 5pc '04		100.92	...	7504	Je7	De7	29.5	3.63
Cn 9$\frac{1}{2}$ pc '04 ....*		105.92	...	307	Ap25	Oc25	16.4	3.80
Tr 6$\frac{3}{4}$ pc '04		103.33xd	0.1	6597	My26	Nv26	17.9	3.78
Cn 9$\frac{1}{2}$ pc '05		108.33	0.1	4469	Oc18	Ap18	16.4	3.91
Ex 10$\frac{1}{2}$ pc '05.................*		112.18	0.2	24	Mr20	Se20	11.9	4.02

Source: *Financial Times*, 26 September 2003.

the interest date (note that all Gilts have semiannual coupon payments). The sixth column shows the ex-dividend data followed by the gross redemtion yield (Red Yield), which is the expected rate of return for an investor who holds the bills to maturity or yield to maturity. For example, the bid price of the 7 December 2003 UK Gilt (Tr61/2pc'03) is quoted as 100.54 (recall that par value is the lump sum paid at maturity). The amount issued is £8095 million. The gross redemption yield (or yield to maturity) is 3.56 per annum.

T-bills and their counterparts are issued on an auction basis. The issuer accepts competitive bids and allocates bills to those offering the highest prices. Non-competitive bids are also accepted. A non-competitive bid is an offer to purchase the bills at a price that equals the average of the competitive bids.

For example, on 10 October 2003, the total UK Treasury Bills on offer was £1500 million. There was a total of £7637 million applications. There cannot be allocated more than what is offered in an auction, and therefore the allocated amount is £1500 million. The highest accepted yield was 3.6150% and the lowest accepted yield was 3.5400%.[2]

The yields on T-bills are watched closely in the money market for signs of interest rate trends. Many floating-rate loans have interest rates tied to the yield on T-bills.

Another type of money market security is a commercial paper, which is a means of short-term borrowing by large corporations. Large, well-established corporations have found that borrowing directly from investors through commercial paper is cheaper than relying solely on bank loans. Commercial paper is unsecured, which means that these loans are not backed by specific assets (no collateral). Commercial paper is issued either directly from the firm to the investor or through an intermediary. Like T-bills, commmercial paper is usually issued at a discount. Issuers of commercial paper are typically corporations that have a high credit rating. However, other firms can use the commercial paper market if they 'enhance' the credit quality of the commercial paper by purchasing a guarantee from another, more well-established firm or by pledging collateral of quality assets with the issue.

Commercial paper is riskier than Treasury bills, because there is a larger risk that a corporation will default. Also, commercial paper is not easily bought and sold after it is issued, because the issues are relatively small compared with T-bills and hence the market is not liquid. The lenders are generally investors with temporarily idle cash. The majority of investors in this market are institutions such as money-market mutual funds and pension funds. By the end of October 2003, the commercial paper market in the USA exceeded $1312 billion.[3]

Bankers' acceptances are short-term fixed-income securities that are created by a non-financial firm whose payment is guaranteed by a bank. Bankers' acceptances arise from the financial needs of corporations engaged mainly in international commerce. To demonstrate how a firm and its customer use bankers' acceptances, suppose a US firm ships a 3-ton engine to a UK firm and delivery takes two months. The US firm would like payment from the sale today, and the UK firm wants to wait until the engine is delivered. The UK firm's bank provides the UK firm with a short-term loan. The UK firm pays the US firm a discounted amount now. The UK bank (which will be paid by the UK firm in two months) could then sell this short-term loan contract to an outside party, recouping its initial outlay. This short-term loan contract, called a banker's acceptance, will typically have a higher interest rate than similar money-market securities, so as to compensate for the credit (default) risk. Since bankers' acceptances are not standardised, there is no active trading of these securities.

---

[2] Source: Bureau of Public Debt, www.publicdebt.treas.gov
[3] Source: Board of governors of the Federal Reserve System, www.federalreserve.gov

Certificates of deposit (CDs) are debt instruments issued by banks and usually pay interest. Most CDs cannot be traded, and they incur penalties for early withdrawal. To accommodate large money-market investors, financial institutions allow their large-denomination CD deposits to be traded as negotiable CDs. Negotiable CDs can be as small as $100 000, but they tend to trade in increments of $5 million. The maturity ranges from a few weeks to several years. The largest investors in this market are money-market mutual funds and investment companies.

The repurchase agreements (repos) market affords additional liquidity to the money market. Firms are able to raise additional capital by selling securities held in inventory to another institution with an agreement to buy them back at a specified higher price at a specified time. The securities are usually government securities. In effect, a repurchase agreement is a short-term loan. Because of concerns about default risk, the length of maturity of a repurchase agreement is usually very short. Typically, repos are used for overnight borrowing needs.

As an example of how repos work, suppose that, for cash-management purposes, Ford Motor Corporation holds $4 million in three-month US Treasury bills yielding 5%. Now Ford has an immediate need for $4 million so it can purchase a specialised piece of equipment being offered at a bankruptcy liquidation. Ford's cash manager also knows that in a week, Ford will receive a $4 million payment for auto sales in Canada. What can Ford do?

One solution would be to take a bank loan at, say, 8%. Ford could also sell the T-bills and buy them back in one week. Ford would incur transaction costs twice (the bills have to be repurchased). In addition, there would be a price risk in this transaction: the price of the T-bills could rise in a week. Alternatively, Ford could enter into a repurchase agreement using its T-bills. Ford could sell the T-bills to an outside firm with a guarantee to buy them back in two weeks at a specified price. From the difference between the sale price and the purchase price, an implied interest rate, known as the repo rate, can be computed. Obviously, Ford should employ the transaction that is the cheapest after all transaction costs have been considered.

A term repo has a longer holding period. A reverse repo is the opposite of a repo. In this transaction, a corporation buys the securities with an agreement to sell them at a specified price and time.

The federal funds market helps banks place reserves on deposit at the Federal Reserve Bank. Banks that do not have sufficient funds on reserve can borrow from other banks that have excess reserves. Most of this borrowing is for one day, although some agreements are for as long as six months. Central banks use this market to implement monetary policy.

Finally, eurodollars are US dollar deposits held outside the USA. These deposits are not subject to the same regulations as bank deposits held within the USA. Hence, the interest rate offered on eurodollar deposits is typically different from the rate offered in the USA. The interest rate quoted for these deposits between major banks is referred to as the London interbank offer rate (LIBOR). This is the rate that one bank asks from another bank for borrowing. London is the main trading centre for eurodollars. The London interbank bid rate (LIBID) is the rate at which major banks will offer eurodollars as deposits to other banks. The interest on loans is sometimes linked to the LIBOR. Quotes such as 'LIBOR + 1%' or 'LIBOR + 2%' are very common, where the riskier the borrower, the higher the increase in the interest rate above the LIBOR.

Exhibit 2.4 shows the various short-term interest rates in the USA and the UK as of 10 October 2003. The differences between the rates reflect the exchange rate and other macroeconomic expectations, as for example inflation.

The discount rate is the interest rate that the Federal Reserve (or, in general, the central bank) charges member banks for loans (with collateral usually in the form of government securities). This is the lowest interest rate on the floor, and banks set their loan rate to their

Exhibit 2.4	Money-market interest rates		**FT**
		USA	UK
Discount rate (%)		2.00	3.52
Prime rate (%)		4.00	3.75
T-bills rate (3 months) (%)		0.90	3.59
CDs rate (6 months) (%)		1.09	3.75
Commercial paper rate (3 months) (%)		1.05	3.65
LIBOR (6 months) (%)		1.18	2.15

Source: *Financial Times*, 10 October 2003.

most creditworthy customers a notch above the discount rate. When the Federal Reserve changes the discount rate, the other money-market rates adjust in the same direction. The European Central Bank (ECB) calls this rate the refinancing rate.

The prime rate is the interest rate that banks charge their most creditworthy customers. Thus, for less creditworthy customers, the interest rate is high, e.g. prime + 2%, prime + 3%, etc. When the banks borrow from customers by selling CDs, they pay the investors in the CDs only (for example) 1.87%, and the difference between the prime rate and the CDs rate accounts for the banks' costs and profits.

Individuals who buy stocks on margin borrow part of their investment from their brokers. The broker loan call rate is the rate at which the brokers borrow from banks to finance these loans to the customers. Because these loans are callable by the banks on a 24-hour notice, they are called call rates.

2.2.3 Capital-market securities

Like T-bills, Treasury notes and Treasury bonds are US government securities used to finance the government debt. In contrast to T-bills, which have maturities of less than one year, Treasury notes and bonds have maturities greater than one year at the time they are issued. They pay stated coupon amounts semiannually and are exempt from state and local taxes. When first issued, notes have maturities of two to ten years and bonds have maturities of more than ten years. The minimum denomination is $1000 for US government securities. Other countries issue similar instruments.

Apart from the par, the investor also receives coupon payments every (semiannual) period up to the maturity date. Note, however, that the price of bonds as quoted in the financial media is not equal to the amount the investor has to pay for the bond. The investor also has to pay the accrued interest because bond prices are quoted without the accrued interest. Accrued interest is found by multiplying the fraction of the semiannual coupon period that has elapsed by the coupon payment. For example, if 142 days have elapsed since the last coupon has been paid and the semiannual coupon is £45, then one has to add (142/183) × £45 = £34.91 to the quoted price of a bond, where 183 days is the number of calender days in half a year. Investors sometimes neglect the fact that the bond is worth more than the quoted price. Thus, when you buy or sell bonds, always remember that the accrued interest should be added.

Exhibit 2.5 lists UK Treasury notes and bonds. The first column gives the name of the security, which also contains information about the coupon percentage and the maturity date.

| Exhibit 2.5 | UK notes and bonds | | | | | | FT |

		Yield				52-week	
	Notes	Int	Red	Price (£)	Change	High	Low
5–10 years							
Tr 5$\frac{1}{2}$pc '08–12		5.39	5.01	102.05	−.32	109.02	101.71
Tr 9pc '08..........................+		7.68	4.98	117.24	−.30	126.17	116.83
Tr 4pc '09..........................		4.18	4.95	95.63	−.28	101.96	95.12
Tr 8pc '09..........................+		6.95	4.98	115.12	−.37	124.08	114.75
Tr 5$\frac{3}{4}$pc '09		5.53	4.97	104.03	−.35	111.94	103.57
Tr 6$\frac{1}{4}$pc '10		5.83	5.01	107.24xd	−.42	116.12	106.79
Cn 9pc Ln '11		7.21	5.04	124.82	−.51	135.92	124.45
10–15 years							
Tr 7$\frac{3}{4}$pc '12–15....................		6.66	5.25	116.45	−.52	126.67	116.04
Tr 5pc '12..........................		5.02	5.06	99.62	−.48	108.42	99.18
Tr 9pc '12..........................+		7.09	5.12	126.99	−.58	138.62	126.66
Tr 8pc '13..........................		6.52	5.05	122.68	−.63	134.66	122.28
Tr 5pc '14..........................		5.03	5.08	99.31	−.58	109.00	98.97
Tr 8pc '15..........................		6.35	5.08	126.02	−.73	138.76	125.75
Tr 8$\frac{3}{4}$pc '14		6.44	5.09	135.84xd	−.86	149.74	134.54
>15 years							
Ex 12pc '13–17 ....+		7.79	5.08	153.97	−.75	169.09	153.60
Tr 8pc '21..........................		5.96	5.04	134.22	−.97	147.98	133.96
Tr 5pc '25..........................		4.99	4.99	100.18	−.89	110.90	99.99
Tr 6pc '28..........................		5.22	4.95	115.05	−1.03	127.33	114.86
Tr 4$\frac{1}{4}$pc '32		4.72	4.90	90.01	−.94	100.09	89.80
Tr 4$\frac{1}{4}$pc '36		4.72	4.86	90.05	−1.00	100.19	89.80

+, indicative price; Tr, Treasury; Cn, conversion; Ex, Exchequer (convertible).

Source: *Financial Times*, 24 November 2003.

The second column gives the annualised coupon yield and the red yield (gross redemption yield).[4] The third column gives the price in pounds, while the fourth column gives the daily percentage price change. Finally, in the sixth column, the highest and lowest prices of the past 52 weeks are given.

The USA, the UK and other nations also issue also inflation-indexed Treasury securities. The coupons and the principal (the par value) are linked to the cost of living index. Exhibit 2.6 lists UK index-linked notes. The first column gives the name of the note from which the coupon rate and the maturity date can be derived. The second column gives the base for indexing, with 1987 as 100. The third colum gives the yield with an expected inflation of (1) 5% annually and (2) 3%. The third column gives the price in sterling, while the fourth column gives the daily percentage price change. Finally, in the fifth and sixth columns, the 52-week high and low prices, respectively, are given.

Agency securities differ from Treasury securities. Agency securities are issued by federal government-sponsored corporations, such as the Federal Home Loan Banks, and not directly from the US government. Agency securities are perceived to be slightly more risky than Treasuries from a default risk viewpoint. The US government may not be as likely to come

---

[4] The annualised coupon yield is defined as the annual coupon divided by the price. For the first bond in Exhibit 2.5, the coupon yield is 5.5/102.05 = 0.0539 or 5.39%.

| Exhibit 2.6 | UK index-linked bonds | | | | | FT |

		Yield				52-week	
	Notes	(1)	(2)	Price (£)	Change	High	Low
Index-linked ....(b)							
4³₈pc '04 ....(135.6)		–	1.11	136.27	–.06	138.53	132.12
2pc '06 ....(69.5)		1.27	1.69	260.51	–.42	268.20	239.60
2¹₂pc '09 ....(78.8)		1.79	2.00	233.83xd	–.72	244.75	215.12
2¹₂pc '11 ....(74.6)		1.96	2.12	247.22	–1.09	260.98	227.44
2¹₂pc '13 ....(89.2)		2.04	2.17	207.17	–1.12	220.17	191.28
2¹₂pc '16 ....(81.6)		2.12	2.23	226.34	–1.45	241.51	210.93
2¹₂pc '20 ....(83.0)		2.14	2.22	224.71	–1.74	238.61	210.65
2¹₂pc '24 ....(97.7)		2.13	2.20	192.98	–1.86	204.32	182.60
4¹₈pc '30 ....(135.1)		2.11	2.17	185.18	–2.04	196.40	177.11
2pc '35 ....(173.6)		2.09	2.14	100.10	–1.43	106.94	94.71

–, non-available; xd, for ex divided.

Source: *Financial Times*, 24 November 2003.

to the rescue of an agency as it would be for securities issued by the US goverment. In the USA, the Federal National Mortgage Association (FNMA; pronounced 'Fannie Mae') and the Federal Home Loan Mortgage Corporation ('Freddie Mac') issue federal agency bonds. Both are publicly owned and sponsored by the government to purchase mortgages from lenders and resell them to investors. They are usually in $100 000 denominations. Recently, FNMA and Freddie Mac were associated with management and accounting scandals. The basic problem at Freddie Mac and FNMA is their aggressive investment strategy, which attempts to leverage their implicit guarantee to accumulate vastly increasing amounts of mortgage investments with a huge amount of debt. State and local governments issue municipal bonds to finance highways, water systems, cover deficits, schools and other capital projects. There are two basic types of municipal bonds: general obligation bonds and revenue bonds. General obligation bonds are backed by the full faith and power of the municipality. Revenue bonds are backed by the income generated from a specific project, such as a toll bridge. The income from these bonds is exempt from federal, state and local taxes if the investor lives in that locality, but the income is subject to state and local taxes if the investor does not live in the jurisdiction issuing the bonds. Because investors are interested in after-tax returns, we would not anticipate the yields to be as high as those from their fully taxable counterparts.

Corporate bonds are issued to finance corporate investment, for example in new plant equipment, and to finance take-overs. Corporate bonds are an attractive means of raising capital, because the interest expense is tax-deductible (whereas dividend payments are not). However, recall that corporate bonds also increase the likelihood that the firm will go bankrupt in hard economic times. Corporate bonds are traded on most major securities exchanges, such as the NYSE and the American Stock Exchange (AMEX), as well as on the OTC market (see Chapter 3). These bonds usually have a par or face value of $1000. Corporate bonds vary in their risk and their returns to investors. Exhibit 2.7 lists new corporate bonds issues worldwide. The first column gives the name of the issuing entity and the second column the amount that is issued. The third column gives information about the coupon that will be paid. Price and maturity information is given in the fourth and fifth columns, respectively. The last two columns give information about the fees that are paid by the issuing entity for the issue and information regarding the yield spread over the relevant government bond.

Exhibit 2.7	New corporate bond issues					

Borrower	Amount (m.)	Coupon (%)	Price	Maturity	Fees (%)	Spread (bp)
US Dollars						
Wells Fargo & Co(S)	1 bn	4.95#	99.688	Oct 2013	undiscl	+75(4^1/$_4$Aug13)
BNG(a)	750	2.375	95.02R	Sep 2008	0.10R	+32(3^1/$_8$Oct08)
Eastman Kodak Co(b)§	500	3.375#	100.00	Oct 2033	2.50	–
Fannie Mae(c)	500	2.75#	99.856	Aug 2006	undiscl	+11^1/$_8$(OASF)
Anheuser-Busch Companies(d)	400	5.05#(l)	99.435	Oct 2016	undiscl	+90(4^1/$_4$Aug13)
Mobile Telesystems Fin SA	400	8.375#	100.00	Oct 2010	0.75	+527(3^1/$_8$Oct08)
VF Corp(g)	300	6.00#(l)	97.37	Oct 2033	undiscl	+105(5^3/$_8$Feb31)
Magnitogorsk Iron & Steel	300	8.00#	98.992	Oct 2008	0.70	+511(3^1/$_8$Oct08)
NBP Capital Trust III(h)	200	7.375(q)	100.00	undated	2.00	–
Banco de Oro Universal Bk(r)	150	6.50#	99.331	Oct 2008	0.75	+465(2^2/$_8$Aug06)
Euros						
UniCredito Italiano SpA‡	500	(j)	99.88R	Oct 2008	0.10R	–
Credito Valtellinese Scarl‡	250	(k)	99.817	Oct 2008	0.15	–
Land Meckenburg-Vorpommern‡	125	(m,s)	100.0193	Oct 2007	undiscl	–
CRH France(n)	85	5.00	104.864	Oct 2013	0.325	–
Sterling						
Severn Trent Wtr Utilities(o)	50	5.25(s)	98.025	Dec 2014	0.375	+58(5%Feb14)

Source: *Financial Times*, 9 October 2003.

Explaining the new international bond issues in the Financial Times

Bond issue details are online at www.ft.com/bondissues. Final terms, non-callable unless stated. Yield spread (over relevant government bond) at launch supplied by lead manager. J Convertible. Floating-rate note. #Semi-annual coupon. R: fixed re-offer price; fees shown at re-offer level. a) Fungible with $1.25 bn. Plus 31 days accrued. b) Conversion price: $31.02. Puttable on 15/10/10, 13, 18, 23 & 28 at par. Callable from 15/10/10 at par. c) Fungible with $2 bn. Plus 59 days accrued. Callable on 11/8/04 at par. d) Makewhole call at T +20 bp. g) Makewhole call at T +15 bp. h) Preferred securities for Natexis Banques Populaires SA. Callable from 27/10/09 at par. j) 3-mth Euribor +7 abp. k) 3-mth Euribor +25 bp. l) Long 1st coupon. m) 6-mth Euribor flat. n) Fungible with $2.8 bn. Plus 4 days accrued. o) Fungible with £150 m. Plus 24 days accrued. q) Quarterly. r) Puttable on 16/10/06 at par. s) Short 1st coupon. S) Subordinated.

Source: *Financial Times*, 9 October 2003.

Some highly rated bonds are very safe but pay low yield. Junk bonds, in contrast, are very risky and thus pay much higher yield. For such bonds, there is a higher risk that the firm will go bankrupt and the investor will lose the entire investment – hence the name junk bonds.

Some bonds do not pay any coupons and are called zero-coupon bonds, in contrast with coupon-bearing bonds.

Mortgages are bonds in which the borrower (the mortgagor) provides the lender (the mortgagee) collateral, which is usually real estate that cannot be traded.[5] In the USA, default risk related to mortgages can be insured either privately or through government insurance

---

[5] Other mortgage bonds are collateralised by corporate assets, such as property and equipment.

agencies such as the Federal Housing Authority or the Veterans Administration. Mortgages are typically pooled (packaged together in portfolios) and sold so thay can be traded. These pools of securities are called mortgage-backed securities. The originator of the mortgage will sell the mortgage through another firm (called a conduit), such as the FNMA. Mortgage-backed securities may or may not be backed by a federal agency. The most difficult aspect of managing a mortgage portfolio is assessing the risk that the mortgages will be prepaid; if the mortgager pays his or her debt early, then a new investment has to found for this amount. Mortgage holders generally prepay when interest rates are down, so this tends to be unfavourable for the mortgagee.

A callable bond contains a call provision that allows the issuing firm to repurchase its bonds at a stated price after a stated date. The purchase price is usually the face value plus one year of coupon payments. This call provision can adversely affect the value of the bonds if interest rates decrease dramatically and the bond's value rises above the stated price. A bond that is not able to be redeemed before maturity is referred to as a bullet bond.

For example, an 8% coupon bond with a face value of $1000 that matures in 15 years may be callable after eight years. According to the call provision, the firm could repurchase the bonds any time after the eighth year if it is willing to pay the face value ($1000) plus one year of interest ($80), i.e. $1080.

If interest rates fall to 5%, then a non-callable bond gains from having an 8% coupon. However, for callable bonds, the firm could call the bonds and issue new ones at 5%, saving 3% per year. Thus, in the case of a sharp decrease in interest rate, the callable bonds will not provide the capital gain as will the non-callable bonds, because they can be called back at $1080.

On the one hand, a callable bond, like all other bonds, also suffers losses when interest rates go up (because the price falls). On the other hand, as shown above, a callable bond's price will not go up in the same way as a non-callable bond's price. Thus, why would anyone want to buy such bonds, which seem to be an inferior investment? The reason is simple. The firm issuing the bonds must issue them at a higher interest rate than the rate for non-callable bonds; otherwise, a rational investor will not buy the callable bonds. Thus, in the event that the interest rate does not go down and the bonds are not called, the bondholder enjoys a relatively high interest rate.

A convertible bond is a corporate bond with an option to convert the bond into a fixed number of stocks. The bondholder receives coupon payments that are lower than those on non-convertible bonds with the same risk. Since the bond is convertible, it provides the possibility to participate in a rise in the stock price. In essence, a convertible bond is an ordinary bond with a call option added.

Suppose Bozdemir Inc. 8%, 2011 convertible bonds issued in 2003 were trading at £105.40 in October 2003. That is, the bonds offer a 8% coupon and will mature in 2011. To understand the price of the Bozdemir Inc. bond, we need more information. We need the conversion ratio, the number of common shares a bondholder will receive for one bond if the bond is tendered for conversion. Suppose for Bozdemir Inc. convertible bonds that the conversion ratio is 11. That is, each bond with £1000 par is convertible into 11 shares of stock. The conversion price is the par value of a bond divided by the conversion ratio, which for Bozdemir Inc. is about £91 (i.e. £1000/11). Bozdemir Inc. stock is currently trading at £32 per share. The conversion value is the current value of a bond if it is converted. If we converted the Bozdemir bonds, our equity would be worth £352 (i.e. £32 × 11), which is far less than the bonds' current trading price of £1054. The conversion premium is the value of the option to convert the bond into stocks, which is the difference between the current market value of the bonds and the comparable market price of a non-convertible bond. In this case, the option to convert the bond to stocks at a price of £91, when the stock is presently trading at £32, is not worth very much.

2.2.4 World bond markets

US and UK Treasury securities constitute one of the largest and most liquid fixed-income markets in the world. Other major governments, however, also have substantial treasury issues. Exhibit 2.8 summarises the government bond series. The first column gives the country name, the second column the coupon date, the third column the coupon percentage, and the fourth column the bid price. The yield at which investors can buy securities, the bid yield, is shown in the fifth column. The daily, weekly, monthly and yearly changes in the yield are shown, respectively, in the sixth, seventh, eighth and ninth columns.

The international arena has a special type of bond, called a crossborder bond. Crossborder bonds are bonds issued in a different country from that of the issuer. For example, a bond that a US firm issues that is denominated in Swiss francs, paying interest and principal in Swiss francs, would be classified as a crossborder bond. The crossborder bond has been one of the fastest-growing segments of the bond market.

2.3   Stocks

This section covers the basic characteristics of common and preferred stock. It compares and contrasts these different types of stock issues and concludes with a description of published stock quotations.

2.3.1 Basic characteristics of common stock

A common stock represents part ownership in a firm. Common stocks are also referred to as 'common shares' and 'equity'. Typically, each common stock owned entitles an investor to one vote in corporate shareholders' meetings. Shareholders vote on issues such as who will be in senior management positions, who will be the outside auditor, and what to do with merger offers.

Historically, common stocks on the whole have provided a higher return than bonds, but they also have higher risk. For example, in the stock market crash of 19 October 1987, the overall value of the market declined more than 20% in one day. More recently, the stock markets have fallen after the 11 September terrorist attacks and have declined for an extended period after the 'tech-boom' of the late 1990s came to an end. The Japanese Nikkei index once traded around 40 000 points, but it had fallen to around 10 000 points 15 years later.

With common stocks, the ownership of the firm is residual; that is, common shareholders receive what is left over after all other claims on the firm have been satisfied. Because they are residual claims, common stocks have no stated maturity. In other words, unlike corporate bonds, common stocks do not have a date on which the corporation must buy them back. The shareholder receives these residual benefits in the form of dividends, capital gains or both.

Dividends are paid to shareholders only after other liabilities such as interest payments have been settled. Cash dividends are cash payments made to shareholders by the firm that issued the stock. Typically, the firm does not pay all its earnings in cash dividends. Usually, the firm will retain some of its earnings to reinvest in other projects in an effort to enhance the firm's value. For example, a pharmaceutical company will take some or all of its earnings and invest them in research and development in an effort to discover new and better drugs, thereby aiming for future profits. A special form of dividend is the stock dividend, in which the corporation pays in stocks rather than cash.

| Exhibit 2.8 | London Stock Exchange benchmark government bonds | | | | | | | FT |

Country	Red date	Coupon	Bid price	Bid yield	Day's change in yield	Week's change in yield	Month's change in yield	Year's change in yield
Australia	7 May	7.5	104.01	5.09	−0.02	0.13	−0.01	0.2
	1 May	6.5	106.83	5.57	−0.02	0.17	−0.05	0.12
Austria	10 May	3.9	102.67	2.53	0	0.21	−0.14	−0.53
	1 Oct	3.8	96.44	4.24	0.03	0.18	−0.11	−0.24
Belgium	9 May	4.75	104.14	2.56	0.01	0.22	−0.13	−0.46
	1 Sep	4.25	99.78	4.28	0.04	0.2	−0.1	−0.23
Canada	6 May	3.5	101.01	2.87	0	0	−0.23	−0.41
	1 Jun	5.25	104.12	4.71	0	0.07	−0.15	−0.2
Denmark	11 May	4	102.48	2.77	−0.01	0.22	−0.18	−0.45
	1 Nov	5	104.82	4.4	0.03	0.21	−0.11	−0.16
Finland	7 Jun	2.75	99.84	2.81	0.01	0.22	−0.13	−0.16
	1 Jul	5.375	109.20	4.2	0.03	0.19	−0.12	−0.15
France	1 May	3.5	101.55	2.23	−0.01	0.14	−0.12	−0.73
	7 Aug	3	98.17	3.42	0.02	0.27	−0.17	−0.17
	1 Apr	4	98.48	4.19	0.03	0.18	−0.12	−0.2
Germany	6 May	2	99.35	2.42	0	0.19	−0.14	−0.55
	4 Aug	3	98.55	3.35	0.02	0.26	−0.17	−0.22
	1 Jul	3.75	96.49	4.19	0.03	0.19	−0.12	−0.11
	1 Jul	4.75	97.09	4.93	0.04	0.12	−0.04	0.02
Greece	6 May	4.65	103.55	2.48	0	0.19	−0.25	−0.51
	1 May	4.6	102.17	4.31	0.03	0.19	−0.13	−0.33
Ireland	10 May	3.5	101.71	2.62	0.01	0.29	−0.08	−0.72
	1 Apr	5	106.24	4.19	0.03	0.19	−0.15	−0.36
Italy	9 May	3.5	101.73	2.58	0.01	0.23	−0.11	−0.39
	1 Aug	3.5	100.55	3.36	0.02	0.26	−0.15	−0.32
	1 Aug	4.25	99.63	4.3	0.03	0.21	−0.08	−0.18
	1 Feb	5.75	110.15	5.08	0.04	0.11	−0.05	−0.02
Japan	9 May	3.3	106.11	0.13	−0.02	−0.08	−0.07	0.11
	9 Oct	1.7	104.92	0.97	−0.02	−0.07	−0.2	0.72
	1 Sep	5.5	138.69	1.33	−0.03	−0.04	−0.09	0.27
	1 Jun	0.8	82.80	1.85	0	0.01	0.04	0.01
Netherlands	7 May	4	102.60	2.47	0.01	0.19	−0.13	−0.49
	1 Jul	4.25	100.21	4.21	0.03	0.19	−0.11	−0.21
New Zealand	2 May	6.5	101.52	5.31	−0.03	0.06	−0.12	−0.31
	1 Apr	6.5	103.77	5.97	−0.01	0.14	−0.14	−0.2
Norway	11 Apr	5.75	102.94	3.08	0.05	0.13	−0.07	−3.16
	1 May	6.5	111.90	4.91	0.01	0.18	−0.12	−1.12
Portugal	10 May	5.25	105.17	2.58	0.01	0.23	−0.09	−0.53
	1 Sep	5.45	108.94	4.33	0.04	0.2	−0.08	−0.32
Spain	7 May	4.95	104.36	2.44	−0.03	0.17	−0.1	−0.63
	1 Jul	4.2	99.96	4.2	0.03	0.19	−0.11	−0.23
	1 Oct	5.75	112.17	4.95	0.04	0.13	−0.04	0
Sweden	4 Jun	3.5	99.97	3.51	−0.02	0.24	−0.07	−0.63
	1 May	6.75	116.20	4.76	0.01	0.24	−0.02	−0.11
Switzerland	1 May	5.5	106.30	0.39	−0.03	0.07	−0.23	−0.51
	1 Feb	4	110.94	2.66	−0.02	0.12	−0.15	0.06
UK	6 Apr	5	100.78	3.79	−0.01	0.14	0.13	0.15
	3 Aug	5	101.86	4.53	0	0.23	0.07	0.36
	1 Sep	5	101.67	4.8	0.05	0.19	0.05	0.35
	1 Jun	4.25	91.63	4.79	0.04	0.13	0.02	0.43
USA	7 May	1.5	100.04	1.48	0	0.11	−0.16	−0.11
	8 Aug	3.25	101.11	3	0	0.21	−0.26	0.53
	1 Aug	4.25	100.80	4.15	0	0.21	−0.46	0.54
	1 Feb	5.375	104.69	5.06	0	0.17	−0.3	0.35

Source: *Financial Times*, 7 October 2003. www.ft.com/markets&data

Corporations try to maintain a constant dividend payment, because this situation tends to enhance share prices (or at least it is perceived by some investors to do so). An investor earns capital gains (the difference between the asset's purchase price and selling price) when he or she sells stocks at a price higher than the purchase price. If the stock is sold at a price below the purchase price, then a capital loss is incurred.

Several dates are important when investing in dividend-paying common stock. Dividends are typically paid semiannually, although there are many other payment schemes. The declaration date is the day on which the board of directors actually announces that shareholders on the date of record will receive a dividend. The date of record is the day on which the shareholder must actually own the shares to be able to receive the dividend. The date of record is usually several weeks after the declaration date. The ex-dividend date is the first day on which, if the stock is purchased, shareholders are no longer entitled to receive the dividend. Stocks on the NYSE go ex-dividend four trading days before the date of record. This allows for the official records to be adjusted. Typically, there is a price effect around the ex-dividend period of stock. A stock's price moves up by the amount of the dividend as the ex-dividend day approaches, then falls by the amount of the dividend after that date. The payment date is the day that the company actually mails the dividend cheques to its shareholders. The payment date is about three weeks after the ex-dividend date. Finally, some corporations pay cash to their shareholders by purchasing their own shares. These are known as share buybacks.

2.3.2 Classifications of common stocks

Stocks are usually classified using the following categories: (1) growth, (2) income, (3) blue-chip, (4) speculative, (5) cyclical and (6) defensive. A stock may be classified in more than one category. For example, Wal-Mart stock is rated as both growth and blue-chip. Some stocks may fall into only one or two categories, and other stocks may avoid classification because of their unique features. In brief, the classification is neither exhaustive nor exclusive.

Growth stocks are usually common stocks of firms having expected sales and earnings growth in excess of the industry average. The company pays very low or no dividends and reinvests its earnings for expansion. For example, many dot.com firms have never paid any dividend (or made any accounting profit).

Income stocks or value stocks are common stocks of older, more mature firms that pay high dividends and are not growing rapidly. Stocks of utility companies are examples of income stocks. Income stocks are usually in low-risk industries, and their price increases little. For example, IBM is an example of a value stock that returns a steady dividend return without large downside risk for investors.

Blue-chip stocks are common stocks of large, generally financially sound corporations with a good history of dividend payments and consistent earnings growth. These stocks tend to have very a low risk of default. For years, IBM has been well-known as a blue-chip stock.

Speculative stocks are the opposite of blue-chip stocks. These are stocks with a higher-than-average possibility of gain or loss, due to the fact that they are very risky and have considerable short-term volatility (the prices move by relatively large amounts). Generally, stocks with a big difference between the high and the low price corresponding to the past 52 weeks are considered speculative stocks.

Cyclical stocks are common stocks that tend to move with the business cycle. When the economy is doing well, these stocks do well. When the country is in recession, these stocks do poorly. Automobile sales are typically a leading indicator of economic activity because cars are durable consumer goods and people can often postpone the purchase of a new car for months or years. Hence, as the economy slips into a recession, so do the earnings of automobile companies.

Defensive stocks are, in a sense, the opposite of cyclical stocks. Defensive stocks tend to do relatively well in recessionary periods but do not do very well when the economy is booming. These stocks are more difficult to find than cyclical stocks. Stocks of automobile-parts makers may be defensive. When the economy is in a recession, consumers are much more likely to attempt to maintain their motor vehicles rather than purchase new ones. Hence, sales by auto-parts makers tend to increase in recessions and decrease in expansions.

2.3.3 Preferred stocks

Preferred stocks typically pay a fixed dividend and have preference over the payments to common shareholders. Thus, preferred stock is a 'hybrid security' that has some of the properties of bonds and some properties of stocks. Investors are attracted to this type of investment as an alternative to bonds, but they sometimes overlook the additional risk. It is true that preferred stocks may provide a relatively high yield, but this high yield is not guaranteed: interest on bonds and loans is paid before dividends on preferred stock. Also, if the firm goes bankrupt, the preferred shareholder stands in the credit line behind bondholders. A company's failure to pay preferred stock dividends, however, does not result in bankruptcy. Sometimes, the firm can even call back the preferred stock, thus avoiding the high dividend. Finally, owners of preferred stock do not enjoy the same benefits as owners of common stock when the firm is doing well. That is, the common stock price could increase sharply, offering shareholders high capital gains, in anticipation of higher future dividends. However, the preferred stock price gains are limited, much like the earning potential of bonds, because the dividends are fixed.

Cumulative preferred stocks are preferred stocks whose dividends accumulate if they are not paid. That is, before common shareholders can receive a dividend, the preferred shareholders receive all prior dividends that are due. Participating preferred stocks are preferred stocks whose dividends are tied to the success of the firm according to some stated formula based on the earnings of the firm. Preference shares are preferred stocks with a higher claim to any dividend payments than other preferred stock issues. That is, in hard times, these shares' dividends are paid before any other dividends are paid (see BMW stock in Exhibit 2.9(a)). Notice that behind the names of the stocks in price lists, 'pr' stands for 'preference shares' and 'pf' stands for 'preferred stock'.

2.3.4 Reading the stock pages

Exhibit 2.9 shows an extract of interesting markets in the world from a stock page from the financial pages of a newspaper. The first column gives the stock's abbreviated name. The second column gives the daily closing price. The third column gives the daily price change. The s by AEP stock means the firm has recently had a stock split. A stock split occurs when a company issues more new shares in return for existing shares. For example, a two-for-one split means that a company issues two new shares for every one share currently outstanding. Stock splits are a method that firms use to control the per-share price of their stock, for example to signal their growth potential. After a two-for-one split, a firm's stock will trade at about half of its previous price, because the value of the firm will not change but the number of shares outstanding will double.

| Exhibit 2.9 | Extract from the *Financial Times* stock market tables | FT |

Stock	Price	Change	52-week high	52-week low	Yield (%)	P/E	Volume (000s)
AMERICA							
NYSE (US$)							
3M	75.74	+.06	76.18	59.73	1.7	25.8	1 881
ACM Inc	8.28	+.03	9.56	7.70	10.5	9.1	205
AEPs	28.78	−.47	31.51	19.03	4.9	12.3	1 256
AESCrp	7.99	−.15	8.49	1.15			758
AFLAC	35.89	+.49	35.96	28.00	0.9	20.2	1 523
AMBPrp	30.80	+.60	31.68	25.90	5.4	19.1	204
AMR	12.90	+.04	15.45	1.28			3 401
At&TWr	7.15	−.10	9.18	5.17		51.1	21 443
AT&T	19.79	−.11	28.88	13.49	4.8	18.2	3 853
Abbttl	41.43	−.33	46.94	33.75	2.4	20.4	1 826
ADRs (US$)							
ABN Am	20.25	+.27	20.75	12.98	3.7	15.1	128
AstZen	49.13	+.49	49.32	29.41	1.9	26.1	938
Aventis	53.64	−.06	61.82	41.85	1.1	19.4	218
Axa	18.44	+.25	19.41	9.96	1.8		162
AMEX (US$)							
Bio-Rad A	51.55	+.54	62.85	33.20		16.3	55
DevEgy	46.90	−.11	56.65	41.14	0.4	9.0	542
EqInFd	76.32	+.63	91.75	62.52	3.3	36.0	4
Iivax	18.00	+.05	20.74	10.50		9.9	476
NASDAQ (US$)							
3Com	6.71	+.03	7.01	3.88			2 814
Dell	36.08	+.08	37.18	22.59			12 634
eBay	55.87	+.93	61.60	30.13			6 683
Intel	31.42	+.34	32.78	14.88	0.3	45.5	36 737
EUROPE (Eurozone)							
France (euro)							
BNPpprb	44.16	+.82	49.49	32.65	2.7	11.7	32.96
Casino	78	+1.25	81.40	47.80	2.3	19.0	322
Total	133.10	+1.60	144.20	110.50	3.1	14.2	1390
Wanadoo	6.32	+.04	6.42	3.40			3295
Germany (euro)							
Adidas	79.85	+.46	86.90	68.80	1.3	15.8	229
BMW*pf*	23.48	+.36	26.20	14.44	2.3	14.4	112
Cmmzbk	16.06	+.45	16.83	5.22	0.6		2329
SAP	122.61	+3.48	130.19	66.13	0.5	75.2	1130
Cmmzbk	16.06	+.45	16.83	5.22	0.6		2329
SAP	122.61	+3.48	130.19	66.13	0.5	75.2	1130
EUROPE (non-Eurozone)							
Russia (US$)							
YukosOil	12.40	−2.02	16.02	8.86		0.9	940
Turkey (Turkish lira)							
Akbank	6150	−50	6800	2730	0.6	10.8	948 271

Exhibit 2.9 continued

Stock	Price	Change	52-week high	52-week low	Yield (%)	P/E	Volume (000s)
UK (pence)							
3i	633	+12.50	673.50	403.50	2.1	27.6	2 215
Aviva	487.50	+7	576.50	332	4.8		6 873
Reuters	249	+14.50	272	95.25	4.0		44 197
Unilever	495.50	+1.50	640	473	3.2	23.5	66 780
Vodafone	119.75	−50	134.75	97.50	1.4	16.7	268 206
ASIA-PACIFIC							
Australia (Aust$)							
AMP	6.63	+.10	13.35	4.26	4.1		12 246
China (renminibi)							
Oriental P	12.26	−.53	21.60	12.10	0.6		2 131
India (rupee)							
ITC	863	+6	912.90	602	1.7	15.6	63
Singapore (S$)							
City Dvlpt	5.90	−.15	6.70	3.10	1.3	31.3	2 261

Source: *Financial Times*, 28 October 2003.

The fourth and fifth columns give the 52-week high and low stock prices. The sixth column gives the dividend yield. The dividend yield is found by dividing the annual (52-week) dollar dividend, D, by the closing price per share (denoted by P). The dividend yield is stated as a percentage. For example, the dividend yield for 3M is 1.7%. The seventh column gives the price/earnings (P/E) ratio, which is the closing price divided by the past year's earnings per share. When the earnings are negative or very close to zero, the P/E ratio is meaningless and hence not reported. The dividend yield and the P/E ratio are widely used ratios in evaluating common stocks. Chapter 15 discusses the interpretation of these ratios. The eighth column gives the previous day's volume of shares trading in thousands.

When you want to know the sentiment in the general stock market or some segment of the market, generally you should not look at prices of one stock but should rely on an index of stocks or some average price of many stocks. There are many indices that measure the changes in the price of various groups of stocks. Probably the most well-known indices are the Dow Jones index, the Standard & Poor's index, the FTSE 100 and the NASDAQ index. Exhibit 2.10(a) shows that on 10 October 2003, the closing price of the FTSE 100 was 4311.0. Furthermore, we see some European indices. The first column gives the name of the index, while the closing level for the past three days is shown in the next columns. The next two columns give information about the year-to-date (YTD) high and low, and the last column shows the YTD yield. Exhibit 2.10(b) lists other FTSE and European indices. This exhibit also gives information about European indices that track industry sectors. The first column gives the name of the index. The closing level and the day's percentage and absolute change are given next. The fifth column gives the YTD yield and the sixth column gives the dividend-adjusted YTD yield (xd adj ytd). The last column gives the total euro return index. Exhibit 2.10(c) shows the major US indices such as the Dow Jones index (DJI), the S&P and the NASDAQ. Chapter 6 elaborates further on the subject of indices.

Exhibit 2.10 Some stock market indices

(a) FTSE 100 and other major European indices

	2003					
	Oct 8	Oct 9	Oct 10	High (dd/mm)	Low (dd/mm)	Yield
FTSE 100-UK	4268.6	4313.9	4311.0	4314.7 (18/9)	3287 (12/3)	3.53
FTSE All-Share-UK	2113.6	2135.2	2135	2135.8 (10/10)	1593.3 (12/3)	3.30
CAC 40-France	3248.6	3324.9	3306.1	3422.8 (13/9)	2403.0 (12/3)	3.27
XETRA DAX-Germany	3395.3	3481.9	(u)	3668.6 (4/9)	2202.9 (12/3)	2.11
AEX-The Netherlands	317.1	324.6	323.1	342.2 (8/9)	218.4 (12/3)	3.68

(b) Major US share indices

		Oct 10	Oct 9	Oct 8	2003 high	2003 low	Yield	P/E
DJ Industrials	(u)		9 680.90	9 630.90	9 680.01	7 524.06	1.62	23
DJ Composite	(u)		2 809.00	2 783.12	2 809.00	2 108.95		
DJ Transport	(u)		2 850.73	2 791.62	2 850.73	1 942.19		
DJ Utilities	(u)		253.56	252.46	255.00	190.22		
S&P 500	(u)		1 038.73	1 033.78	1 039.58	800.73		
NASDAQ cmp	(u)		1 911.90	1 893.78	1 911.90	1 271.47		
NASDAQ 100	(u)		1 396.90	1 382.40	1 400.13	951.90		
Russell 2000	(u)		521.34	515.68	521.34	345.94		
NYSE Comp	(u)		5 886.89	5 855.34	5 886.89	4 486.70		
Wilshire 5000	(u)		10 092.92	10 038.58	10 092.92	7 610.47		

(c) Major Asian stock markets

	2003					
	Oct 8	Oct 9	Oct 10	High (dd/mm)	Low (dd/mm)	Yield
Hang Seng-Hong Kong	11 720	11 800	11 935	11 935 (10/10)	8 409 (25/4)	3.1
Nikkei 225-Japan	10 542	10 531	10 786	11 033 (18/09)	7 607 (28/4)	0.89
Strait Times-Singapore	1 733	1 738	1 746	1 746 (10/10)	1 213 (10/03)	2.44
KOSPI-South Korea	722	736	757	767 (9/9)	515 (17/3)	1.61

(u), unavailable.

Source: *Financial Times*, 11/12 October 2003.

2.4   Investment companies

Many investors choose to invest their money in investment companies, which receive money from investors with the common objective of pooling the funds and then investing them in securities. There are many different types of investment companies, as well as a range of ways to classify them. For example, there are open-end funds or mutual funds, which can issue additional shares upon demand and eliminate shares when they are redeemed. The price is determined not by demand and supply but rather by the net asset value (NAV) per share, which is the current market value of the assets per share (based on the market value of the underlying securities in the mutual fund). Conversely, closed-end funds or investment trusts cannot increase or decrease the number of shares easily.[6] Closed-end funds have their shares traded on a stock exchange, such as the NYSE or the AMEX. Investors can buy or sell shares of closed-end funds like any other stock in the market. In closed-end funds, market supply and demand drive the trading prices. Closed-end funds trade at a premium above or a discount below net asset value, depending on a range of factors (including how well the fund is run, the expenses charged, and the particular focus of the fund).

Some open-end funds are no-load and some are load. The load is a sales charge paid by an investor who buys a share in a load mutual fund. A fund that does not charge this fee is called a no-load fund. On a closed-end fund, the investor pays transaction costs exactly as paid on stocks bought in the stock market.

New investment vehicles are competing with the traditional investment companies. Exchange-traded funds (ETFs), also called index shares, track a specific basket of securities and trade continuously on the major exchanges like an ordinary stock. The first index shares created by the AMEX were Standard & Poor's depository receipts (SPDRs; pronounced 'spiders'). Separate SPDRs were created for the S&P 500 and the S&P Mid-Cap 400. Trading in S&P 500 SPDRs was introduced in 1993, and S&P Mid-Cap 400 trading began in 1995.

Seventeen World Equity Benchmark Shares (WEBS) began trading the Morgan Stanley Capital International (MSCI) stock market indices of a single foreign country in 1996. Dow Diamonds, an index product based on the Dow Jones Industrial Average, began trading in early 1998. Each of these unit trusts represents a stake in the 30 stocks that make up the Dow Jones index. Each Diamond is sold for the equivalent of 1% of the value of the index. Thus, if the index is traded for, say, 8000, then the Diamond price is determined as $80. The Diamonds were followed by the NASDAQ 100 Shares, also known as QQQs or Qubes, which track the NASDAQ 100 stock index. Even though they have been around only since March 1999, Qubes are so popular that their daily trading volume rivals the companies on the NYSE.

As is true for traditional investment companies, an important benefit of ETFs is that they bring investors instant exposure to a diversified portfolio of stocks. In addition, the annual expenses on EFTs are lower than those on most traditional funds, since there is no need to hire professionals to determine which securities to invest in.

Chapter 4 elaborates further on investment companies.

---

[6] A closed-end fund, with shareholder approval, can undertake a new issue or change the nature of the fund (for example, change it to an open-end fund).

2.5 International investment

For all investors, even US investors, the bulk of the investment opportunities are outside their home countries. The benefits of international diversification have been well-documented since the 1960s (see Chapter 9). An investor who wishes to invest internationally can use several instruments. A straightforward method is to purchase foreign securities directly in foreign capital markets. This approach, however, is not simple, due to complications such as foreign currency transactions and associated exchange rate risk, foreign taxes and foreign regulations. In practice, this approach is available primarily to larger institutional investors. However, even small individual investors can take advantage of international diversification by means of investing in (1) multinational corporations, (2) foreign ordinaries, (3) American depository receipts (ADRs) and (4) crossborder investment funds and WEBS.

2.5.1 Multinational

ating directly in foreign markets by buying market. Many of the world's largest com- d acquisitions in recent years. The share the end of 2002 – and the earnings com- any of the big UK-listed companies such nd Shell, the Anglo-Dutch oil operator, corporations offer exposure to economic an easy way to diversify internationally.

ly in their home capital markets but also rs can escape many of the drawbacks of oreign securities in their home country.

ssued by a US depository bank, repres- anch or correspondent in the country n a non-US exchange, while the ADRs straightforward for a US investor to en the corporation provides financial y subsidise the administration of the e.

ADR on a US exchange: an investment bank and a bank purchases the foreign shares on a foreign market and offers them for in the USA. The depository bank handles the issuance and cancellation of ADRs certificates backed by ordinary shares based on investor orders, as well as other services provided to an issuer of ADRs, but is not involved in selling the ADRs.

```
        ALDI  STORES
          2 Burnett Close
            WINCHESTER
                                  GBP
                                  0.89 A
54150 GARLIC                      0.99 A
1249  CHICKEN READY MEALS         0.23 A
1031  RED KIDNEY BEANS            0.23 A
1031  RED KIDNEY BEANS            0.55 A
61886 LEMONGRASS/GINGER           0.79 A
61924 POTATOES - BAKING 4 PK      0.69 A
51176 BUTTERNUT SQUASH            0.89 A
60969 LARGE RED ONIONS            0.79 B
45453 POPCORN                     0.59 A
51227 TOMATOES 6 PK               0.20 A
49754 SPAGHETTI - 500G            0.85 A
64489 ALL BUTTER MADEIRA/ANG
                      Subtotal    7.69

Card Number: ************0934
VISA DEBIT
Merchant ID: *********22028
Terminal ID: ****4642
EFT No.: 20014118150

SALE

Your account will be debited
with the total amount shown:

Goods: 7.69

Total: GBP7.69
```

41

One ADR may represent a portion of a foreign share, one share or a bundle of shares of a foreign corporation. The depositary bank sets the ratio of US ADRs per home country share. This ratio can be less than or greater than one. Basically, the ratio is set to get the ADR within a price that Americans are comfortable with, say a range between $15 and $75 per share. If, in the home country, the shares are worth considerably less, then each ADR would represent several real shares. If, in the home country, shares were trading for the equivalent of several hundred dollars, then each ADR would be only a fraction of a normal share.

For example, ADRs trade on the NYSE for ABN AMRO, a Dutch bank (see Exhibit 2.9). These ADRs trade in dollars on the NYSE with ticker symbol ABN, and ABN AMRO also trades in euros on Euronext Amsterdam. Each ADR allows the holder the rights to one common share. For example, on Tuesday 28 October 2003, ABN was trading at $20.25 on the NYSE, and ABN AMRO was trading at 17.70 euro at Euronext Amsterdam. Since one ADR equals one common share, the exchange rate for the euro must have been about $20.25/E17.70 = 1.144.

American depository shares (ADS) are a similar form of certification; they represent foreign stock issued in the USA and registered in the ADR system.

2.5.4 Crossborder mutual funds, index funds and World Equity Benchmark Shares

There is a wide range of investment companies with an international focus. Country funds invest in the securities of one country. An international fund invests in several foreign countries. Regional funds specialise in one region, such as Europe or Latin America. While international funds include the entire world, excluding your home country, a global fund includes the entire world. There are also emerging markets funds, which invest in countries with younger, less developed economies. Like their counterparts at home, international index funds offer key advantages over actively managed funds: broad diversification and low costs. A number of funds try to match international indices such as the MSCI EAFE index, which tracks blue-chip stocks in Europe, Australia and the Far East. WEBS are ETFs that passively track an MSCI country index in the same way that, for example, SPDRs track the S&P 500 index for the US stock market (see Section 2.4). Active funds such as hedge funds also offer a wide range of international investment strategies.

2.6 Derivative securities

A derivative security is one whose value depends directly on, or is derived from, the value of another asset. The cash flow at the end of the lifetime of a derivative is determined solely by the value of that underlying asset and the terms of the contract. The two main types of derivative securities are forwards and options; however, these basic contracts come in various forms: for example, swaps and futures are varieties of forwards (however, futures have greater importance in practice than forwards themselves). There also exists many types of 'exotic' options. Derivatives will be discussed in greater detail in Chapters 19 and 20.

2.6.1 Forwards, futures and swaps

A forward contract is a security that *obligates* one to buy or sell a specified amount of an asset at a stated price on a particular date, regardless of the market price at that moment.

If the forward is traded on an exchange (implying standardised terms), it is called a futures contract. For example, the buyer of a 100 Troy oz (about 31.1 g) gold futures contract that matures in three months agrees to buy 100 Troy oz gold of a specified quality at a specific location at a specific price (the futures price). Like many other commodities, a very small percentage of all gold contract futures result in delivery. In general, traders offset their futures position before the contracts mature.

For example, on 31 October 2003, the price of gold futures that expire in December 2003 was $384.60 per Troy oz. This means that if you buy a 100 Troy oz/lb (which is the minimum in the case of gold) contract, you are obligated to pay on the delivery date 100 × $384.60 = $38 460, regardless of the gold price that will prevail on that date. An investor can make a profit out of this contract (by subsequently selling the gold) if the price of gold on the expiration day is above $384.60 per Troy oz. If the price is below $384.60, then the investor makes a loss.

Futures contracts exist on metals, energy products, interest rates, currencies and various (mainly stock) indices. Futures are used mainly to hedge financial price risk and to speculate on the direction of future prices, although one can also use them for arbitrage and portfolio diversification. For example, a multinational corporation that has large accounts receivable in Japanese yen may sell yen futures contracts to hedge against a weakening yen relative to the dollar. A speculator who believes the dollar will weaken against the yen may buy yen futures in the hope of profiting. Thus, futures can transfer financial price risk from the hedger to the speculator (or from one hedger to another hedger, or from one speculator to another speculator).

A swap is an agreement to exchange a specific series of cash flows at future points in time. For example, a currency swap is an agreement to exchange currencies – say, US dollars for euros – at specific dates and for specific amounts in the future. In fact, a swap is a series of forward contracts. The seminal example is the first modern swap between IBM and the World Bank. IBM held fixed-rate debt in German marks (DM) and Swiss francs (SF). IBM wanted to convert its DM and SF liabilities to US dollar liabilities. In August 1981, the World Bank issued fixed-rate bonds in dollars with the exact maturities of the IBM debt. The World Bank and IBM then agreed to 'swap' the interest payments. The interest payments were calculated based on the par value of the bonds. This par value is referred to as the notional principal. The net result of these transactions was that the World Bank would, in effect, make IBM's debt payments in DM and SF, and IBM would make the World Bank's debt payments in US dollars. Thus, IBM eliminated its currency risk. Why did the World Bank take this currency risk? Probably, it had assets in Germany and Switzerland that generated cash flows in DM and SF. These assets could then be used to pay the World Bank's debts without having to be concerned about changes in exchange rates. Thus, both sides of this transaction benefited. This transfer of risk is a basic characteristic of forwards, futures and swaps.

2.6.2 Options

A call option gives the holder of the option (the buyer) the right to buy a specified security (for example, a stock or a bond or an index of stocks and bonds) at a specified price on or before a specified date. A put option gives the holder the right to sell a security at a predetermined price on or before a specified date. Investors buy call options in the hope that the security's price will rise so they may buy the security at a discount. Investors buy put options hoping that the security's price will fall so they may sell the security at a premium, or to protect them from losses in case they also own the stock itself.

For example, a call option on the FTSE 100 Index with a strike price of 4625 and a maturity until next October entitles the investor to buy, up to the end of October, the underlying index for £46 250 (£10 per full index point; in other words, the contract is for ten times the index). The FTSE index on this date was 4311.0. Thus, if the index increases until October, say to 4630, the investor can buy the underlying index for only 4625 (that is, exercise the call option) and earn £50 (£46 300 – £46 250) minus the price he or she paid for the call option. Similarly, a put option on the FTSE 100 Index with a strike price of 4625 and a maturity until next October entitles the investor to sell, up to the end of October, the underlying index value for £46 250. If the FTSE 100 Index drops to, say, 4200, the investor earns £250 (£42 250 – £42 000) minus the price paid for the put option.

The advantage of options is that owning them can provide a much higher return than simply owning the underlying asset (or short-selling the underlier). However, there is a risk that a call option will expire worthless if the stock price falls, and a put option may expire worthless if the stock price rises. In these cases you lose your entire investment; that is, you make a −100% rate of return.

2.7 Investment risks

Investing in securities involves three major sources of risk: market risk, credit risk, and operational risk. (The order of coverage here does not suggest the relative importance of the risks, as risks vary among different securities.)

2.7.1 Market risk

Market risk results from unexpected movements of general market prices. Much of the research conducted on securities markets has documented that the prices of all securities in a particular market tend to move together. This correlation arises because different securities are exposed to the same set of general risk factors. There are several different types of market risk. Interest-rate risk, equity risk, foreign-exchange risk and commodity risk all deal with market risk spurred by their respective risk factors: fluctuations in interest rates, stock indices, exchange rates and commodity prices (gold, oil and so on). Market risk also includes market-liquidity risk, or the risk that securities cannot be sold quickly and/or only with price concessions due to an unexpected liquidity dry-up.

Interest-rate risk is the exposure to adverse changes in interest rates. This type of market risk is especially important for bonds and interest-rate derivatives. Would you want to buy a bond offering an annual 8% coupon rate when the market is paying 10% on newly issued bonds? Since investors will prefer a 10% bond to the 8% bond, the price of the 8% bonds falls if interest rates increase to 10%. The falling price will result in rising yields. For example, if an 8% coupon bond is selling for 90% of the price of the new 10% bond, then for the same investment you can buy more of the old bond and earn more interest and receive more principal. The price adjustment will continue until both the old and the new bonds yield approximately 10%. Of course, changes in interest rates may also be a source of gain. If you hold a bond with a fixed coupon of 8% and the interest rate goes down in the market to 6%, then you are locked into a good agreement. Everyone will buy the 8% bond, and its market price will go up (which gives you a capital gain as a bondholder) until both the old and the new bonds yield the same return of 6%. In general, the risk of a change in the bond price because of an increase in the interest rate is called the price risk.

Price risk is only one part of interest-rate risk. Specifically, if interest rates increase, then one can reinvest coupon and principal payments at a higher yield. By contrast, if the interest rate goes down, then the coupon reinvestment rate will be smaller and, hence, the terminal value of the investment will be smaller. This possible decrease in the reinvestment rate is called the reinvestment rate risk.

For example, suppose a government bond with 8% coupon and maturity date of August 2020 is trading for 131.50. The long-term interest rate has fallen to about 4.06% since the bond was issued in 1998, hence the large coupons (plus the par value) discounted at 4.06% yield more than 31% capital gain. However, reinvestment risk shows its ugly face: when the large coupons are reinvested, the profit on them is 4.06% rather than 8%, which was the reinvestment rate when the bond was issued.

Shareholders also can lose or win when interest rates change. However, the effect of interest rates on stock prices is complex. For example, an interest-rate rise means that the interest expenses of corporations that are financed partly with bank loans or corporate bonds will increase (immediately or in the future). However, the interest rate rise itself may be caused by an increased demand for consumer loans to fund consumption, and hence the higher interest rates may reflect improved prospects for future corporate sales, earnings and dividends to shareholders.

Equity risk is the exposure to the stock market as a whole. Even if you hold a well-diversified stock portfolio, you cannot avoid the fluctuations of the whole stock market. For example, on 19 October 1987, the whole US stock market went down by more than 20%. Exhibit 2.11 shows the ten biggest one-day declines of the Dow Jones Industrial Average (DJIA) in terms of the percentage change. No matter how well diversified your stock portfolio was on 19 October 1987, or any of the other days shown in Exhibit 2.11, you could not have avoided this loss. In Chapter 10, we will see that the equity risk of a security is typically measured by means of its market beta, or the coefficient of regression between its returns and the returns on a broad stock market index.

Exchange-rate risk is the exposure to adverse changes in exchange rates. Why would an American investor buy long-term US bonds yielding only 4.50% when you could earn 5.01% in the UK? The answer is simple: when you invest in the UK, you have to convert your US dollars to sterling. However, when you want your money back – say, at the end of the year – you must

Exhibit 2.11	Biggest one-day percentage declines in DJIA			
Rank change	Date	Close	Net change	%
1	10/19/87	1738.74	−508.00	−22.61
2	10/28/29	260.64	−38.33	−12.82
3	10/29/29	230.07	−30.57	−11.73
4	11/06/29	232.13	−25.55	−9.92
5	12/18/29	58.27	−5.57	−8.72
6	08/12/32	63.11	−5.79	−8.40
7	03/14/07	76.23	−6.89	−8.29
8	10/26/87	1793.93	−156.83	−8.04
9	07/21/33	88.71	−7.55	−7.84
10	10/18/37	125.73	−10.57	−7.75

sell the UK bonds for sterling and then convert the proceeds to US dollars. Of course, there is a risk that for each pound you receive, you may get fewer dollars because of changes in the exchange rate. In dollars, you may end up with a yield much lower than 5.01%; indeed, the yield may be even less than the 4.50% that you can get on the US bonds. Thus, the high yield of 5.01% may not apply to foreign investors. Bonds are bought and sold in local currencies. This exchange-rate risk adds one more layer of risk for the international investor.

Commodity risk is the risk that arises from holding securities with an underlying exposure to commodities such as oil and precious metals. Consider an investor who has bought a six-month crude oil futures contract (1000 barrels) on the New York Mercantile Exchange with a strike price of $32.79 per barrel. Thus, the underlying value of the contract is $32 790. The current price of a barrel of oil is $36.16. Had the contract been terminated today, the investor would have made $3.37 profit per barrel. However, the contract has not yet expired, and until it is terminated the profits and losses on the contract depend on changes in the oil price. The risk the investor faces due to these price changes is called commodity risk.

Market-liquidity risk is the risk that it could be very costly for the investor to sell the securities. There may be no one who wishes to buy the securities at that time. To get a buyer quickly, the investor may have to sell the security at an unreasonably low price relative to its true value and thus incur a substantial price concession.

Investors typically do not have a liquidity-risk problem with government bonds and actively traded bonds and stocks of larger corporations, such as those issued by AT&T and GM. However, investors must anticipate a liquidity risk with the bonds or stocks of small firms, because they are not actively traded. To compensate for the lack of liquidity, small firms must offer investors a higher yield on bonds and a higher expected return on stocks.

A well-known example of liquidity risk is the downfall of the hedge fund Long-Term Capital Management (LTCM).[8] When the Russian government defaulted on its debts in 1998, liquidity suddenly evaporated from international financial markets. LTCM suffered massive losses because it could not liquidate its assets before the value of its portfolio dropped.

2.7.2 Credit risk

One risk that affects bond investors is default risk. The issuer may fail to pay either the coupon payments or the face value in a timely manner. Of course, federal government bonds do not have default risk, because the Treasury Department can print money. By contrast, corporate bonds, municipal bonds and stocks are exposed to default risk. A recent example of a default is the Enron case. This case is the biggest corporate bankruptcy case in US history. Enron was a Houston, Texas-based company, formed in 1985, which grew into the USA's seventh-biggest company in revenue by buying electricity from generators and selling it to consumers. In 2001, Enron unexpectedly went bankrupt after it became clear that the company had deceived its investors by inflating its financial statements for years. The company used complex partnerships to keep some $500 million in debt off its books and mask its financial problems so it could continue to get cash and credit to run its trading business.

Apart from the risk of default, credit risk also includes credit-migration risk, or the risk that the probability of default on future obligations increases. For example, in 2003, the Dutch retail group Royal Ahold disclosed that its earnings had been inflated by hundreds of millions

---

[8] The LTCM case is discussed further in Investment in the News 19 and Connecting Theory to Practice 4.3, 21.1 and 21.2.

of dollars (see Chapter 16). In reaction, credit-rating agencies reduced the rating of Ahold's bonds to junk, and the prices of Ahold's bonds fell to reflect the unexpected possibility of default. Hence, bondholders suffered large losses, even though Ahold did not actually default on its obligations to bondholders. Thus, credit risk is the risk that a counterparty will default on its obligations or the risk that the creditworthiness will change.

Generally, we can make a distinction between issuer-specific credit risk and systematic credit risk. Issuer-specific risk results from default of a single counterparty. Hence, the issuer-specific credit risk can be reduced by holding a diversified portfolio. In contrast, systematic risk cannot be reduced by diversifying investments because it depends on factors that change the default risk of individual corporations simultaneously. For example, a recession or a catastrophic event like the terrorist attacks of 11 September 2001 can increase the average default risk of the corporations in the economy, which leads to greater systematic credit risk. Besides the risk resulting from default of a single company or the entire economy, credit risk also includes sovereign risk. Rather than being firm-specific or economy-wide, sovereign risk is country-specific. This risk occurs when debtors are unable to honour their obligations as a result of actions taken by foreign governments. A company might not be able to pay the interest or principal on a loan even if it would want to. The government of the country in which the debtor is located may prohibit debt payments for political reasons as well as economic reasons, such as foreign-currency shortages. Rating companies and other institutions provide investors with ratings and information on the political and economic risks of investing in a foreign country.

2.7.3 Operational risk

Operational risk is the least well-defined of all the types of risk. In fact, the term 'operational risk' is usually used as an umbrella term for various investment risks other than market risk and credit risk. This risk category includes a wide variety of risks resulting from, for instance, malfunction of systems, flawed organisational structure, management failure, faulty control, fraud, human error and incorrect models. Additionally, it includes the risk that comes from the external environment, such as legal and regulatory uncertainty. Contrary to market risk and credit risk, these risks generally are difficult to quantify and control.

There is no generally accepted classification scheme for operational risk. However, Exhibit 2.12 attempts to classify some of the risks that are typically seen as operational. Some of these risks are especially important for institutional investors (insurance companies, pension funds and investment companies), which tend to be large, complex organisations. The management and control of such organisations entail risks not faced by individual retail investors.

The above discussion gives a general overview of the different types of risk an investor is faced with (market risk, credit risk and operational risk). However, one should note that this list is not exhaustive and the individual types of risk usually do not stand alone. A typical investor is exposed to several risks at the same time, and there can be a degree of interdependence among these risks. For example, during a financial crisis, stock and bond prices may fall sharply, causing the value of investment portfolios to fall. At the same time, bond issuers may default on their obligations and market liquidity may dry up, causing potential funding problems. Clearly, an investor should keep this dependency in mind when managing risk. Several financial debacles, including the LTCM and Barings Bank cases discussed in Chapter 21, have shown that the failure to identify and manage different risks can have enormous financial repercussions. Although today most investors take risk management very seriously, there are still numerous examples of financial debacles that came as a result of insufficient identification of the different risk exposures.

| Exhibit 2.12 | Subtypes of operational risk |

Type of risk	Description
Organisational risk	This type of risk can result from a flawed organisational structure, for example in terms of internal controls and supervision. Hence, this includes failure of management to actively monitor behaviour of individuals in the organisation or the absence of a clear separation of responsibilities. Such a failure of management supervision or separation of functions increases the chance of inefficiencies, mistakes and fraud.
Funding liquidity risk	Derivative instruments such as futures and swaps are largely marked to market, meaning paper gains and losses can have cash consequences well before the maturity dates. Insufficient cash reserves can lead to problems in fulfilling the obligation and may result in the need for early liquidation, sometimes at below-market values. The insufficiency of cash may be caused by two factors. First, a sharp unexpected movement in the market may lead to cash drains. Second, the company itself may not have enough cash reserves.
Reputational risk	This is the risk that a company suffers from events that might mitigate their brands. For financial firms, their reputation is paramount to how much business they attract. In effect, reputational risk may arise from losses due to any of the other risks (including market and credit risks) that the firm potentially could have avoided by prudent measures.
Legal risk	This risk arises through uncertainty in laws and legal actions. Sources of legal risk include capacity and enforceability issues, as well as the legality of financial instruments The most important legal risk is legal capacity, or *ultra vires* risk, which arises when a counterparty does not have the legal authority to engage in a transaction.
Regulatory risk	This risk results from the exposure to unanticipated changes in regulations.
Strategic risk	The risk of adverse changes in industry environment such as entry of new competitors and product innovation or price cuts by existing rivals.
External risk or force majeure risk	Natural disasters, geopolitical turmoil, terrorism, strikes.
Security risk	Technical security of company is breached when, for example, employees and/or outside parties gain unauthorised access to systems.
Systems risk	Technology failure (telecommunications, energy, system crashes).
Transactions risk	Human error in carrying out transactions (booking, execution, etc.). It typically occurs when front-office and back-office operations are not connected in an efficient manner, for example when the back office fails to recognise a discrepancy between a reported trade by a broker and the counterparty confirmation.
Fraud	Purposeful wrongdoings by employees for personal gain. In the finance industry, the most prominent case is that of the fall of Barings Bank in 1995 due to unauthorised trading activities by rogue trader Nick Leeson.
Model risk	The investor may be unable to capture investment risks effectively due to the incorrect specification, poor data feeding or erroneous use of models. Such mistakes can lead to faulty risk estimates and flawed valuations of assets and liabilities.

Summary

Differentiate between investments in physical assets and investments in financial assets (securities).

The differences include the divisibility of investment in securities (you can buy a small fraction of a firm), marketability (you can sell a $100 000 investment in stock with one phone call to a broker or a few with a few computer keystrokes), the investment holding period (which can be shorter for financial assets), and the more abundant information available on financial assets as compared with real assets.

Describe the basic characteristics and types of bonds and stocks.

Fixed-income securities are instruments that are useful primarily when investors have specific income requirements, whereas stocks are purchased primarily for growth potential. Money-market securities are short-term obligations, including Treasury bills, commercial paper, bankers' acceptances, negotiable certificates of deposit, repurchase agreements, federal funds and eurodollars. Capital market securities are long-term obligations, including Treasury notes and bonds, federal agency bonds, municipal bonds, corporate bonds, mortgages and mortgage-backed securities. A convertible bond is just like a regular bond, but with an added feature: if you own a convertible bond, you can convert the bond into a specified number of stocks. The term 'capital-market securities' also applies to stocks. A common stock represents part ownership in a firm.

Describe investment opportunities in international securities and investment companies.

International securities increase the investor's opportunities. Mutual funds receive money from investors with common objectives, pool the funds together, and then invest them in securities. Shares of open-end funds are purchased and sold exclusively with the fund, whereas shares of closed-end funds are traded on stock exchanges. International securities can be purchased directly from an international stock exchange or indirectly through an American depository receipt (ADR) or a mutual fund.

Compare the different types of derivative securities.

A derivative security is a security whose value is derived from the value of another asset. Examples of derivative securities include options, futures and swaps. A call option gives the holder the right to buy, whereas a put option gives the holder the right to sell, a specified stock at a specified price on or before a specified date (for an American option). A futures contract is a security that obligates the investor to buy or sell a specified amount of an asset at a stated price on a particular date. A swap is an agreement to exchange specific assets at future points in time.

Explain the risks involved in bond and stock investment.

There are three categories of risks related to investing in securities: market risk (the exposure to general risk factors such as interest rates, exchange rates, stock indices, commodity prices and market liquidity), credit risk (the risk that a counterparty will default on its obligations and the risk that the creditworthiness will change) and operational risk (the risk resulting from inadequate or failed internal processes, people and systems, or from external events). Understanding the risks related to investments is an important first step in successful money management.

Key terms

American depository
    receipts 41
Asset 21
Bankers' acceptances 26
Bid yield 33
Blue-chip stocks 35
Broker loan call rate 28
Bullet bond 32
Callable bond 32
Call option 43
Capital gains 35
Capital loss 35
Capital market securities 23
Certificates of deposit 26
Closed-end funds 40
Commercial paper 26
Commodity risk 46
Common stock 33
Conduit 32
Conversion premium 32
Conversion price 32
Conversion ratio 32
Conversion value 32
Convertible bond 32
Corporate bonds 30
Coupon-bearing bonds 31
Coupon payments 23
Credit-migration risk 46
Crossborder bond 33
Cumulative preferred
    stocks 36
Cyclical stocks 35
Date of record 35
Declaration date 35
Default risk 46
Defensive stocks 36
Discount rate 27
Dividends 33
Dow Diamonds 40

Equity risk 45
Eurodollars 27
Exchange-rate risk 45
Exchange-traded funds
    (ETFs) 40
Ex-dividend date 35
Face value 23
Federal funds 27
Financial assets 21
Fixed-rate bonds 23
Floating-rate bonds 23
Forward contract 42
Futures contract 43
General obligation bonds 30
Gilts 25
Growth stocks 35
Illiquid 22
Income stocks (value stocks) 35
Inflation-indexed Treasury
    securities 29
Interest-rate risk 44
Investment companies 40
Investment trusts 40
Issuer-specific risk 47
Junk bonds 31
Liquidity 22
Market beta 45
Market-liquidity risk 46
Market risk 44
Maturity 23
Money market securities 23
Mortgage-backed
    securities 32
Mortgages 31
Municipal bonds 30
Mutual funds 40
NASDAQ 100 shares 40
Net asset value 40
Notional principal 43

Open-end funds 40
Operational risk 47
Participating preferred
    stocks 36
Par value 23
Payment date 35
Physical assets 21
Preference shares 36
Price risk 45
Prime rate 28
Principal value 23
Put option 43
Refinancing rate 28
Repo rate 27
Repurchase agreements 27
Reinvestment rate risk 45
Revenue bonds 30
Reverse repo 27
Securities 21
Share buybacks 35
Sovereign risk 47
Speculative stocks 35
Standard & Poor's depository
    receipts 40
Stock dividend 33
Stock split 36
Swap 43
Systematic risk 47
T-bills 25
Term repo 27
Treasury bills 25
Treasury bonds 28
Treasury notes 28
Unsecured 26
World Equity Benchmark
    Shares (WEBS) 40
Yield 21
Yield to maturity 25
Zero-coupon bonds 31

Review questions

1 Describe the difference between financial assets and physical assets for each of the following characteristics:

   a. Divisibility
   b. Marketability
   c. Holding period
   d. Information availability

2 Classify each of the following types of assets as either money market securities or capital market securities:

Treasury notes	Commercial paper
Municipal bonds	Mortgages
Federal funds	Treasury bills
Eurodollars	Corporate bonds
Repurchase agreements	Negotiable CDs

3 Explain what is meant by the following statement: 'The ownership of the firm is residual in nature.

4 Suppose a bond has a par value of $1000 and a market value of $1100. It is convertible into 40 shares of stock, and the current stock price is $26:

   a. What is the conversion ratio?
   b. What is the conversion price?
   c. What is the conversion value?

5 Briefly explain the origin of the following sources of risk:

   a. Interest-rate risk
   b. Equity risk
   c. Commodity risk
   d. Default risk
   e. Credit-migration risk

 For an extensive set of review and practice questions and answers, visit the Levy–Post investment website at www.booksites.net/levy

Selected references

Baumol, W., S. Goldfeld, L. Gordon and M. Koehn, 1989, *The Economics of Mutual Funds Markets*, Boston, MA: Kluwer.

Caglayan, M. O. and R. E. Franklin, 2001, 'Hedge Fund and Commodity Fund Investments in Bull and Bear Markets', *Journal of Portfolio Management*, **27** (4), 97–108.

Cook, T. Q. and T. D. Rowe (eds), 1986, *Instruments of the Money Market*, Richmond, VA: Federal Reserve Bank of Richmond.

Fabozzi, F. J. and D. Fabozzi, 1989, *Bond Market Analysis and Strategies*, Englewood Cliffs, NJ: Prentice-Hall.

Fabozzi, F. J. and I. M. Pollack (eds), 1987, *Handbook of Fixed Income Securities*, Homewood, IL: Dow Jones–Irwin.

Investment Company Institute, *Mutual Fund Fact Book*, Washington, DC: The Investment Company Institute.

Kihn, J., 1996, 'To Load or not to Load? A Study of the Marketing and Distribution Changes of Mutual Funds', *Financial Analysts Journal*, **52** (3), 28–37.

Lederman, J. and K. Park (eds), 1991, *Global Bond Markets*, Chicago: Probus Publishing.

Schwartz, R. and D. G. Weaver, 2001, 'What We Think about the Quality of our Equity Markets', *Journal of Portfolio Management*, **27** (4), 63–70.

Solnik, B., 1991, *International Investments*, 2nd edn, Reading, MA: Addison-Wesley.

Stigum, M., 1989, *The Money Market*, 3rd edn, Homewood, IL: Dow Jones–Irwin.

CHAPTER 3   Security markets

Investment in the News 3

Big Board must end its costly drama

It seems like only yesterday. As each initial public offering came to the New York Stock Exchange, the company's directors would gather around ... [the NYSE chair] to ring the opening bell, and cheers would swell up from the packed trading floor below.

The Big Board [the NYSE] is a visual godsend in the technological world of modern finance: Amsterdam's *hoekmen*, Liffe's brightly jacketed brokers and the London Stock Exchange's jobbers have given way to machines. The NYSE's specialists and floor brokers are the only surviving human interest at the world's big stock exchanges.

Source: John Gapper, 'Big Board Must End Its Costly Drama', FT.com site; 10 November 2003.

Images of invited guests, who have included Arnold Schwarzenegger and Nelson Mandela, ringing the opening bell at the NYSE reach millions of television viewers around the world every trading day. Apart from the opening bell, the exchange's grand Wall Street façade and the crowded trading floor are well-known pictures. Ironically, these images give an antiquated impression of current security markets. Trading financial instruments has historically required face-to-face communication at physical locations. However, progress in telecommunications and computer technology changed this situation. The NASDAQ over-the-counter (OTC) market for stocks was one of the first markets in which technology replaced physical interaction. Subsequently, most stock exchanges in the world, including the Tokyo Stock Exchange (TSE) and the London Stock Exchange (LSE), moved to electronic trading. The NYSE still uses physical trading but has introduced systems to let investors engage in electronic trading. Also, in the USA, new electronic markets have emerged, which are known as electronic communication networks (ECNs). In brief, the world security markets are changing rapidly into virtual marketplaces. Bricks-and-mortar exchanges with a physical trading floor are becoming institutions from a bygone age.

This chapter studies security markets – the markets where corporations and governments issue new securities and where investors subsequently trade the securities. This is not a simple task, because security markets are evolving constantly due to competition and technological innovation. For example, in recent history, there have been several alliances, entries, exits, mergers and acquisitions that substantially changed the landscape of global security markets. Also, technology has recently made various electronic trading methods available, including online brokers, electronic exchanges and ECNs. For this reason, describing security markets is like aiming at a moving target.

Despite the continuous change, the security markets are designed to allow corporations and governments to raise new funds and to allow investors to execute their buying and selling orders. Thus, a security market that functions effectively provides society with two benefits. First, it allocates investors' funds to those corporations and governments that will make the best economic use of them. Second, a well-functioning security market will reduce the cost of moving in and out of securities. This chapter focuses especially on these two tasks of security markets.

Our investigation of security markets begins with a description of the primary market, where corporate and government entities can raise additional capital by selling stocks, bonds and other securities. The issuing entity receives the proceeds from the sale of securities after they have been issued in the primary market. All securities are first traded in the primary market, and the proceeds from the sale of securities go to the issuing firm. Next, Section 3.2 describes the secondary market, where previously issued securities are traded among investors. Note that the issuing entity does not receive any funds when its securities are traded in the secondary market.

However, the secondary market provides liquidity for the securities after they have been issued in the primary market. Investors are more willing to buy securities in the primary market when they know that there will be a market in which to trade them in the future. The existence of a well-functioning secondary market thus makes buying securities in the primary market more appealing.

3.1   The primary security market[1]

The primary market is the mechanism through which firms raise additional capital by selling stocks, bonds and other securities, and through which current suppliers of capital can sell their privately held stake in the company to the public. The remainder of this section will focus on offerings of common shares. Recall that the primary market encompasses also all other securities.

3.1.1 Going public

If a company's share is traded in the primary market for the very first time, then it is referred to as an initial public offering (IPO). By performing an IPO, the company changes from being a privately held firm into being a publicly held firm. If a company has sold stock previously and its shares are already listed, then the sale of shares through the primary market is called a seasoned equity offering (SEO). IPOs are sometimes referred to as unseasoned equity offerings. IPOs and SEOs can consist of solely existing shares (secondary shares, for example shares of founders, venture capitalists or a parent company), solely new shares (primary shares) or a combination of both.[2] For example, in the case of the IPO of World Online (a Dutch Internet provider that went public around the peak of US and European stock markets in March 2000), the number of primary and secondary shares amounted to, respectively, 46 906 454 and 20 656 365 shares (see Exhibit 3.1). The proceeds from the sale of primary shares, net of issue costs, flow into the company's accounts. By contrast, the proceeds from the sale of secondary shares go into the pockets of existing shareholders. Usually, existing shareholders do not sell all the shares they hold. Their retained number of shares as a fraction of the number of post-IPO outstanding shares is called the retained ownership percentage.

The whole process of preparing and executing an IPO is often referred to as going public. In addition to allowing existing shareholders to exit and allowing the company to raise new capital (for example, to fund investment opportunities or to repay debt), IPOs are also undertaken for other reasons. For instance, an IPO is a useful leg-up to a future SEO (which might be of a much larger magnitude), it often yields a lot of free publicity, it enhances company status due to visibility and media coverage, and it also provides the opportunity to implement bonus and options schemes that are linked to the share price in the secondary market as an external performance measure. Very importantly, the public valuation of the shares ensures

---

[1] This section is a contribution by Martijn J. van den Assem, Assistant Professor at the Department of Finance and Investments of the Erasmus University of Rotterdam, the Netherlands. Homepage: www.few.eur.nl/few/people/vandenassem. Email: vandenassem@few.eur.nl. He would like to express his appreciation to Coen Mensink, Thierry Post and Nico van der Sar for providing valuable comments, and to Olivier Beck and Cederic Cremers for composing Exhibit 3.4.
[2] One should not confuse the difference between primary and secondary shares with the difference between the primary and the secondary market. The first distinction refers to the origin of shares traded (newly issued or existing), the second to the stage where trading takes place.

| Exhibit 3.1 | Cover of the preliminary prospectus or red herring of World Online for its March 2000 initial public offering |

The information contained in this Preliminary Offering Circular is subject to completion and may be changed.

Subject to completion. Dated March 1, 2000.

World Online International N.V.

(a company incorporated under the laws of the Netherlands with its corporate seat in Rotterdam)

67 562 819 Ordinary Shares

(nominal value €0.40 per share)

This Offering Circular relates to an international offering, including a retail offering in the Netherlands, of 50 672 114 shares outside the United States in reliance on Regulation S under the United States Securities Act of 1933. In addition, 16 890 705 shares are being offered in a concurrent offering of shares in the United States only to qualified institutional buyers in reliance on Rule 144A under the Securities Act.

As part of the international offering, there will be a preferential allotment to subscribers of World Online resident in the Netherlands and, to the extent permitted by law, to employees and 'friends and family' of World Online, whose applications are received by march 13, 2000, 16.30 (CET). The maximum number of shares reserved for preferential allotment is 4 285 714 for such subscribers and 3 428 571 for employees, friends and family, respectively.

Of the total shares being offered, we are offering 46 906 454 newly issued shares and the selling shareholders identified herein are offering 20 656 365 shares. We will not receive any proceeds from the sale of the shares by the selling shareholders.

The international underwriters may, under certain circumstances, purchase up to an additional 7 600 817 shares from us at the initial public offering price less the underwriting discount. The U.S. underwriters may similarly purchase up to an aggregate of 2 533 606 additional shares.

It is currently estimated that the initial public offering price will be between €35 and €43 per share. Prior to the offering, there has been no public market for the shares. An application has been made to list the shares on the Official Segment of the stock market of Amsterdam Exchanges N.V. under the symbol 'WOL'.

See 'Risk Factors' beginning on page 13 for a discussion of certain factors to be considered in connection with an investment in the shares.

Offering Price: €   per share.

The shares are offered severally by the underwriters specified herein, subject to receipt and acceptance by them and subject to their right to reject any order in whole or in part.

The underwriters expect to deliver the shares through the book-entry facilities of NECIGEF, Euroclear and Clearstream Banking against payment on or about March   , 2000.

Joint Global Coordinators

Goldman Sachs International   **ABN AMRO Rothschild**

Joint Lead Managers and Joint Bookrunners

ABN AMRO Rothschild   **Goldman Sachs International**

Co-Lead Managers

Morgan Stanley Dean Witter   **Rabo Securities**

Co-Managers

Kempen & Co N.V.   **Robertson Stephens International**

The date of this Offering Circular is   , 2000.

Source: Preliminary prospectus, World Online, 1 March 2000.

Exhibit 3.2	Table of contents from the World Online preliminary prospectus dated 1 March 2000

TABLE OF CONTENTS

Source: Preliminary prospectus, World Online, 1 March 2000.

that shares can be used easily as acquisition currency. Disadvantages of going public include the substantial costs (not to trivialise management time consumed) and the tight disclosure requirements imposed by security market regulation.

An important element of going public is the writing and subsequent distribution of the prospectus. The prospectus is a legal document containing the business plan, financial statements, details on the offering and other information that will help investors make well-informed investment decisions. It simultaneously serves as a marketing instrument. Information contained in the prospectus should give an unbiased picture of the firm. In a so-called comfort letter, lawyers state that the prospectus provides a complete, clear and verified picture of the firm. Accountants do the same with regard to the financial statements. Exhibit 3.2 shows the table of contents from the IPO prospectus of World Online.

Issues in the primary market are usually handled by investment banks. These provide advice and arrange and execute most of the tasks involved, including promoting the issue and collecting investors' applications. Investment banks also act as underwriters of a new issue. As intermediaries between the issuer and potential investors, underwriters guarantee the proceeds from the transaction to the issuer and/or the selling shareholders. Multiple types of underwriting exist, but most common are firm-commitment and best-efforts contracts. In the case of a firm commitment, the underwriter agrees to purchase the entire issue and absorb all unsold shares for its own account at a predetermined price. Under a best-efforts contract, the underwriter markets the new issue as well as it can but takes no price risk; the underwriter does not take ownership of the securities. Strictly, the appellation 'underwriter' is not appropriate in best-effort cases.

Investment banks generally cooperate on IPOs and form syndicates to share the underwriting and legal risks and to reach a sufficient number of potential investors. Many functional names for syndicate members are in use. Because professional credibility and reputation are very important goods among investment bankers, all these namings suggest great importance. However, among insiders, it is well known that the higher an investment bank is mentioned on the cover of the prospectus, the more prestige is awarded. In international (often large) offers, the leading investment bank is named global coordinator. The joint global coordinators of the World Online IPO were Goldman Sachs and ABN AMRO. Smaller offers (often oriented towards local investors) are usually managed solely by a single lead manager. At least one syndicate member has to execute the important and prestigious role of bookrunner. The bookrunner maintains the order book during the subscription period and plays a decisive role with regard to final pricing and allocation. Examples of well-known US investment banks are Goldman Sachs, Merrill Lynch, Morgan Stanley, Citigroup, JP Morgan Chase and Lehman Brothers. Credit Suisse First Boston, UBS and Deutsche Bank are dominant players of European origin. In the case of large IPOs, there is often an additional selling group linked to the syndicate. In the most stringent form of the definition, banks in the selling group typically do not bear any risk, their sole focus being to distribute shares.

As a formal compensation for risk and efforts, syndicate members receive an underwriting commission, or gross spread.[3] Generally, this is composed of three components: a management fee (for managing the issue), an underwriting fee (for bearing the risks inherent to underwriting) and a selling concession (compensation for distribution). Total commission can add up to about 7%, depending on the country, the underwriting risk and the transaction size.

In most countries, an underwriter may support share prices after the IPO (in the secondary market) for a limited period of time (usually 30–45 days).[4] Both issuer and underwriter generally want to prevent prices in the aftermarket declining below the introduction price, because they want to avoid reputational damage. To facilitate underwriter price support, the selling shareholder or the issuer usually grants a so-called Green Shoe option or overallotment option (often with a duration of 30 days) to the underwriters.[5] Under an overallotment option agreement, the underwriter is allowed to buy additional shares at the offering price. Mostly, the option concerns 15% of the regular total transaction size. For example, in the case of World Online, the underwriters were allowed to purchase an additional 10 134 423 primary shares (7 600 817 + 2 533 606, equal to 15% of the regular transaction size of 67 562 819 shares; see Exhibit 3.1). Price support is facilitated as follows. In the case of sufficient public demand for the IPO shares, the underwriter initially allocates all shares, including those from the overallotment option. If aftermarket prices remain well above the introduction price, the underwriter does not interrupt trading and simply exercises his or her right to buy additional shares through the overallotment option. If the share price declines to or below the introduction price and support is deemed necessary, shares are bought back by the underwriter up to the extent of the overallotment option, thereby supporting the stock price. Depending on the number of shares bought back, the underwriter does not exercise – or exercises only partially – the overallotment option. An underwriter preferably abstains from price support beyond the extent of the overallotment option, since any additional share bought ends up on the underwriter's own shelves and thus exposes the underwriter to full price risk.

---

[3] The preliminary prospectus of World Online mentions the gross spread as 'the underwriting discount' (see Exhibit 3.1).

[4] In the case of World Online, one of the joint global coordinators was fined for manipulating the opening price on the first trading day. Once trading started, ABN AMRO immediately bought more than four million shares in the market, which contributed to an opening price of €50.20, €7.20 above the offering price. This could have caused misrepresentation of true market demand. According to the Dutch supervising authority Autoriteit Financiële Markten (AFM), ABN AMRO exceeded the limits of what is permitted in stabilisation transactions.

[5] The Green Shoe option is named after the Green Shoe Manufacturing Company, which first granted this option to an underwriter in 1963.

| Exhibit 3.3 | Summary of initial listing requirements for the AMEX, the NASDAQ[1] and the NYSE |

Minimum requirement	AMEX	NASDAQ	NYSE
Post-issue publicly held shares[2]	1.0 million[3]	1.1 million	–
Number of public shareholders	400[3]	400	2000
Offering price	$3	$5	–
Pre-tax income	$750 000[4]	$1 million[5]	$2.5 million[6]
Book value of shareholders' equity	$4 million[7]	$15 million	–
Expected market value of publicly held shares[2]	$3 million	$8 million	$60 million

Note that summarised and IPO-tapered figures for US companies are presented; consult official listing manuals for a detailed overview. Historically, listing requirements have been subject to amendments; the above requirements went into effect around February 2004.

[1] The exhibited NASDAQ requirements relate to the NASDAQ National Market. Requirements for the NASDAQ SmallCap Market are less stringent.

[2] Shares held by directors, officers or their immediate families and other concentrated holdings of 10% or more are excluded in calculating the number of publicly held shares.

[3] AMEX requires 800 post-issue public shareholders and 500 000 shares publicly held, or 400 public shareholders and 1 000 000 shares publicly held.

[4] $750 000 in past fiscal year or in two of the three past fiscal years. This requirement does not apply if the expected market value of publicly held shares is $15 million or more, together with a two-year history of operations or together with an expected market capitalisation (= issue price × post-issue number of shares outstanding) of $50 million.

[5] $1 million in latest fiscal year or in two of three past fiscal years. This requirement does not apply if both stockholders' equity equals $30 million or more, expected market value of publicly held shares is at least $18 million and operating history entails at least two years. It is also waived if the expected market value of listed securities is $75 million or more or if both total assets and total revenues are at least $75 million.

[6] $2.5 million in the latest fiscal year together with $2 million in each of the preceding two years; or $6.5 million in the aggregate for the past three fiscal years together with a minimum of $4.5 million in the most recent fiscal year, and positive amounts for each of the preceding years. If expected market capitalisation is $500 million or more and revenues exceed $100 million, an aggregate cash flow of $25 million for the past three years suffices. Companies with at least $1 billion in expected market capitalisation and not less than $100 million in revenues are exempt from income requirements.

[7] This requirement does not apply if both expected market capitalisation is $75 million or more and expected market value of publicly held shares is at least $20 million.

Not every company is allowed to perform an IPO. All regulated exchanges impose listing requirements. These are roughly aimed at attracting viable companies, securing sufficient liquidity in the secondary market, promoting transparency and reducing insiders' opportunities to exploit information backlogs of investors. Requirements concern mainly financial track record (for example, three years), market capitalisation, post-issue free float (for example, 25% of total shares outstanding), transaction composition (the ratio of primary to secondary shares), transaction size (number or value of shares), number of post-issue public shareholders, lock-up provisions for existing shareholders (for example, six months for retained shares) and accounting principles applied. Exhibit 3.3 displays a summary of the initial listing requirements for AMEX, NASDAQ and NYSE.

Between the mid- and late 1990s, many European stock exchanges set up new markets for young firms with extraordinary potential for autonomous growth. Examples are the French Nouveau Marché and the German Neuer Markt. Although the listing requirements with respect to track record and profitability are less stringent, disclosure requirements and lock-up provisions are often tighter for these markets. In the late 1990s, numerous biotech, Internet and media firms obtained a listing on one of these new markets. Ultimately, due to the collapse of Internet-related stocks in the early 2000s, many new markets became insignificant or even dissolved (the Neuer Markt was closed mid-2003).

3.1.2 Selling mechanisms and the pricing process

Most exchanges permit the following three methods by which IPOs can be publicly priced and sold:[6]

- In the case of bookbuilding, investors submit orders based on a price range published in a preliminary prospectus. This preliminary prospectus is often referred to as the red herring because the cover contains a disclaimer printed in red ink. Exhibit 3.1 shows the red herring cover of World Online. Note both the price range mentioned as €35–€43 and the blank space reserved for the temporarily unknown final offering price. Investors indicate their demand at different price levels within the given range. Compared to large (institutional) investors, smaller (retail) investors can usually only submit market orders (that is, orders that only indicate quantity demanded, regardless of price). As a result, bookbuilding provides the underwriter with a sound grasp of the interest in the offered shares at different price levels. Once subscription is closed, the underwriter and the issuer/selling shareholders jointly determine or negotiate the final offer price. Trading starts almost immediately thereafter, often within 24 hours. Logically, demand for almost any executable IPO exceeds the number of shares offered,[7] which means that demand can be met only partially. In the case of bookbuilding, allocation of oversubscribed issues typically occurs at the underwriter's discretion. This can leave some investors with empty hands, while others are favoured generously.
- In a fixed-price offering, subscription commences with a complete prospectus, including both offer size and price. Investors submit quantity orders based on this known and fixed price. Allocation rules and practices on oversubscribed fixed-price issues differ per country, but the allocation of oversubscribed issues is usually much more even-handed than in bookbuilding issues.
- In the case of IPOs by means of the uniform price auction or tender mechanism, a minimum price is stated in the prospectus. Investors indicate the highest price they are willing to pay for the number of shares they demand. Orders below the minimum price are rejected. The final offering price is generally the highest price accommodating the sale of all shares. This price applies to all successful bidders. Logically, rationing is absent or minimal in IPOs sold by auction. To prevent irrational bidding, a maximum price is sometimes applied after the closing of subscription.[8]

---

[6] In addition, sometimes a flotation occurs by means of 'introduction'. This fourth method isn't essentially an IPO method because there's no preceding 'offering' or public subscription period. In fact, shares are sold and traded directly in the secondary market against current prices.

[7] Recall that many IPOs are underwritten. At first sight, undersubscribed issues might thus be about as common as oversubscribed issues. However, the definitive version of the underwriting agreement is signed by the underwriter usually only after expected demand has turned out to be sufficient. Disappointing demand generally necessitates postponement or a substantial reduction of the offering price or price range.

[8] Uninformed participants tend to overbid in order to secure a stake in the offering. Each individual expects insignificant influence of his or her own bidding on the final offering price because he or she relies on rational bids by others. In order to prevent irrational bidding, investors are warned in advance that extreme bids will be rejected. The precise limit for order-acceptance is determined only after the close of subscription.

Bookbuilding is the most popular method used in the USA. In Europe, bookbuilding became more common and eventually dominant around the mid-1990s.[9] The lack of regulation and the opacity surrounding the allocation process made the bookbuilding mechanism vulnerable to abuse. The box below discusses the abusive practices known as spinning and laddering. In the late 1990s, many issues were priced suspiciously far below their feasible levels and shares were subsequently allotted to parties affiliated to the underwriter or even to the company's management. Recent developments indicate a change in regulation and supervision in order to enhance transparency. For example, in November 2003, the US financial regulator, the National Association of Security Dealers (NASD), proposed various amendments to rules governing allocations and disclosure of demand.

→ **Connecting Theory to Practice 3.1**

Spinning and laddering

Spinning

Spinning refers to the allocation of attractive IPO shares to the personal brokerage accounts of individuals with investment banking business to offer. A special examining committee of the US congress chaired by Michael G. Oxley found that spinning occurred on a large scale in the late 1990s. Numerous officers and directors whose companies were investment banking clients of Goldman Sachs or Credit Suisse First Boston (CSFB) received substantial amounts of IPO shares, generating huge cumulative profits. There is no doubt that the trading of their companies' investment banking business for their own personal gain can be considered highly immoral. Documents obtained by Oxley also showed the use of research reports to hype companies that were investment banking clients, the possibly illegal (excess) underpricing of IPOs, potentially improper due diligence* in bringing companies to the market, and questionable use of analytics by analysts to justify unrealistic price targets.

Laddering

Laddering exceeds the stage of allocation. In the case of laddering, the underwriter requires investors to purchase additional shares in the aftermarket in return for being assigned substantial quantities of IPO shares. A cooperative customer could count on a favourable allocation in the next IPO. It cannot be excluded that laddering contributed to the high stock prices in the late 1990s. Favoured investors were mainly institutional money managers generating high commissions by active trading styles and high commission brackets.

In December 2002, a settlement by many large US investment banks amounting to $1.4 billion was announced. This settlement related to the consequences of investment banks' conflicts of interest on various fields and to their misleading behaviour towards (retail) investors. Earlier that year, the Securities and Exchange Commission (SEC) and NASD dropped charges against CSFB for abusive IPO allocation practices, but only after settlement for a payment of $100 million. The SEC accused CSFB of allocating IPOs for a large part to investors that had to transfer a considerable part of their subsequent gains to CSFB by paying excessively high brokerage commissions on other trades.

* A due diligence analysis includes reviewing all financial records plus anything else deemed important. The accompanying investment bank is required to judge the condition of the firm going public and to ascertain the correctness and completeness of the information to be contained in the prospectus.

---

[9] See, for instance, Sherman (2003) or Ljungqvist *et al.* (2003).

Before setting the price in fixed-price introductions or the range in IPOs by bookbuilding, most underwriters perform so-called premarketing activities. Premarketing serves as an important check on preceding theoretical valuation exercises and as a means to inform major investors about the forthcoming IPO. Premarketing embraces both investor education and an activity called sounding out investors. Both terms are typically investment bankers' jargon.

Investor education is carried out by an independently acting equity research analyst affiliated to the underwriter or another syndicate member. The analyst (personally and on his or her personal account) visits his or her institutional clients, informs them about the forthcoming IPO and provides them with his or her personal judgement about the price his or her fellow investment bankers have in mind. At the end of the meeting, the analyst gauges the interest from the client. Afterwards, the analyst presents the findings to his or her banking colleagues. The latter draw up a so-called feedback book, which is discussed with the issuer or selling shareholders. Investor education activities can exceed the commencement of the subscription period.

Sounding out investors refers to investment bankers directly (without an intervening analyst) gauging interest from institutional investors, generally by telephone.

In the USA, premarketing is not allowed, together with any written material, except for an official (preliminary) prospectus. Because the 'red herring' is not available in this phase (recall that this document by definition contains the price range, the appropriateness of which is gauged by premarketing), US underwriters use a preliminary red herring without a price range, called the 'pink herring'.[10]

Once a reasonable fixed price or price range is determined, the formal subscription period commences. At the same time a 'road show' starts, during which (executive) directors of the company present themselves and their company to the community of institutional investors and try to win them over. One-on-ones are discrete meetings between management/bankers and representatives of institutional investors.

3.1.3 IPO underpricing

Except for IPOs sold by auction, new issues on average have been significantly underpriced compared with their aftermarket value. Usually, underpricing (or initial return, IR) is measured as the relative difference between the first-day closing price (P_1) and the introduction price (P_0):[11]

$$IR = (P_1 - P_0)/P_0$$

Since this return is not corrected for the share-price performance of comparable firms between the pricing date and the introduction date, it is called the raw or unadjusted initial return. Although dependent on period and country considered, it can be stated that average initial returns per country vary roughly between 10% and 20%. Exhibit 3.4 shows average

---

[10] In Europe, premarketing can also be accompanied by less formal documents, such as a predeal research report from a research analyst associated with one of the syndicate's investment banks. The investment bank and the issuing firm and/or selling shareholder are obliged to provide equal information to all approached investors.

[11] It is sometimes argued that the offering price should be compared with the stock price after several trading days, in order to exclude eventual influences of initial market inefficiencies. Although this argument might hold for some illiquid or restricted markets, persistent patterns of abnormal return in the immediate aftermarket are rarely if ever observed.

| Exhibit 3.4 | Initial public offering (IPO) underpricing in Europe, 1994–2001 |

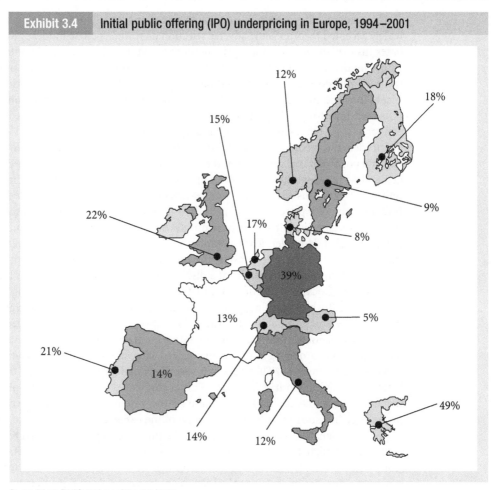

Source: Private EU IPO database of Van den Assem.

initial returns for several European countries between 1994 and 2001. This period includes the notorious Internet-bubble period, which manifested itself not only in high valuations but also in high initial returns. Note the relatively high level of average underpricing in Germany (39%), which can be attributed to the enormous flow of small young growth firms towards the Neuer Markt.[12] Because of high uncertainty about future earnings and due to other causes, particularly IPOs of small young growth firms were coupled with high and sometimes incredible levels of underpricing. For comparison, for the AMEX, NASDAQ and NYSE, Bradley, Jordan and Ritter (2003) report an average level of underpricing over a roughly similar period (1996–2000) of 37.3%. The difference from the European average can be attributed (at least partially) to the exclusion of the years 1994, 1995 and 2001, which gives the results of the US study a larger weight of the Internet-bubble period (roughly concerning 1999 and early 2000).

[12] A possible explanation for the high level of underpricing in Greece (49%) is the large number of IPOs issued on the Greek Parallel Market. This market is relatively easily accessible for issuers and it accordingly attracts relatively risky companies.

The academic literature offers several explanations for IPO underpricing. Among the most widely accepted theories is the adverse selection or winner's curse model of Rock (1986). Rock bases his explanation for underpricing on the supposition of unequally informed investors. In his model, he distinguishes only two types of investors: the perfectly informed and the relatively uninformed. Note that although the latter lack complete information, they still have access to some information and they act rationally given this information. Since perfectly informed investors will apply only for underpriced issues, the uninformed investor faces a winner's curse. On the one hand, in underpriced issues they are confronted with competition due to demand from informed investors, so they end up with rationed allocations of shares yielding positive initial returns. On the other hand, in overpriced issues there is no competing demand, so uninformed investors end up with full allocations of shares yielding negative initial returns. Overall, this adverse selection results in negative allocation-weighted initial returns if IPOs are averagely priced according to their (fair) market value. The harmful consequence of the winner's curse is that all relatively uninformed investors will abstain from participating in the IPO market. However, Rock assumes that both types of investors are needed to take up all shares in IPOs; in order to prevent the uninformed investors from disappearing from the scene, all offerings need to be sold at a discount to compensate them for this bias in allocation. According to Rock, it is this discount that we observe and call underpricing.

Following Rock's reasoning, positive initial returns are also regarded as a compensation for informed investors. The ability to distinguish between hot IPOs (underpriced) and cold IPOs (overpriced) is not for free. Informed investors incur so-called information-acquisition costs. Since the costs of acquiring information are fixed, large investors will have relatively low research costs per dollar invested. Therefore, it is very likely that large investors will, on average, be the better-informed individual investors. This is confirmed indirectly by the practice of underwriters. During the premarketing phase of the pricing process, underwriters particularly probe large investors in order to get a sense of the expected market value of the shares.

Rock's explanation simultaneously puts the intuitively appealing initial returns in another perspective: it might be very difficult to obtain shares in an underpriced IPO, due to high demand from other investors and thus severe rationing. The winner's curse also teaches that overstating the number of shares applied for might be very risky if fair (aftermarket) value turns out to be overestimated.

In addition to the information asymmetry-based theory of Rock, the following theories for IPO underpricing should be mentioned. Notice that information asymmetry underlies many explanations.

- In Logue's (1973) view, underwriters operate in an environment that lacks competition. This provides the underwriter with some bargaining power over the firm that goes public. By neglecting the will of the firm and its selling shareholders to a certain extent by pricing the IPO shares at a discount, the underwriter minimises his or her marketing efforts (cheap shares are easier to sell) and reduces his or her risks (price support, reputation damage and legal liability are less likely). Furthermore, the investment bank gains popularity among investors by regularly selling IPOs at significant discounts. Of course, the underwriter will weigh these advantages against lower commission proceeds and the deterrence of potential future issuers.

- Baron (1982) also considers the relationship between the issuer/selling shareholder and the investment bank. In contrast to Logue, Baron focuses not on bargaining power but rather on information asymmetry: the underwriter is assumed to have more information about demand for the shares than the firm going public. By allowing underpricing, the underwriter is rewarded for valuing and selling the company's shares. The underwriter gains by the strengthening of its reputation among investors. The more ex-ante uncertainty surrounding the company's value, the more importance is assigned to the underwriter's expertise and, therefore, the larger the underpricing discount will be.

- Welch (1992) regards underpricing as a trigger to initiate massive demand. According to Welch, investors do not rely only on their own assessment of the IPO; above all, they keep an eye on the behaviour of others. To prevent investors from keeping aloof from the IPO, the issuer and/or selling shareholders need to apply a discount – underpricing – to win over the first investors. Their buying behaviour initiates demand from other investors and a cascade is originated.

- Signalling models by Allen and Faulhaber (1989) and others regard underpricing as a means for firms and existing shareholders to establish a good reputation, enhancing the opportunities (increasing the proceeds) for a following large seasoned equity offering. A high initial return on the IPO is costly but leaves a good taste in the investor's mouth. By showing favourable profits or dividend payments up to the SEO, a superior company proves itself to be a high-quality firm, inducing a high stock price. Inferior companies do not benefit from underpricing, because they cannot imitate high-quality firms: they risk revelation of their inferiority and a declined stock price before the SEO is executed. Inferior companies act optimally when pursuing a hit-and-run strategy at the time of the IPO. Because of this distinction, the level of underpricing is considered a credible signal about the true nature of a firm.

- Benveniste and Spindt (1989) take underpricing to be a compensation for the revelation of costly private information by well-informed (large) investors. Ideally, underwriters wish to collect information about market demand in advance, so they can price the issue accordingly. Premarketing can be a fruitful way to gauge this demand, but without compensation, the consulted investors have no incentive to reveal positive information. By repeatedly consulting the same investors, by allocating them favourably and by adjusting the offering price only partially for the new information obtained, investors do have an incentive to cooperate. In line with Benveniste and Spindt's reasoning, empirical analyses indeed show that issues with positive revisions of the final offering price compared with the initial price range in the preliminary prospectus are still severely underpriced – despite these revisions. This finding is referred to as the partial adjustment phenomenon.[13]

- The underpricing theory of Tiniç (1988) is frequently referred to as the implicit insurance model or lawsuit-avoidance hypothesis. By substantially underpricing the issue, underwriters reduce the chance of lawsuits from investors whose new investment has declined below its offering price. Accompanying and underwriting an IPO entails legal responsibilities (depending on national legislation). Apart from legal liabilities, lawsuits might cause uninvited damage to an investment bank's reputation. The IPO of World Online serves as an example of an IPO that activated many lawyers. Among the accusations was the proposition that World Online and the underwriters left out important notifications and provided misleading information in the prospectus. A noteworthy detail is that the World Online IPO coincided with the peak of Internet stocks. World Online happened to be among the last to go public during the Internet hype before the hype collapsed. It is hard to determine which part of the stock's dramatic decline can be contributed to the charges (if justified) and which part is merely a consequence of broad market developments. Exhibit 3.5 shows World Online's post-IPO stock-price development.

---

[13] Examples of studies demonstrating the partial adjustment phenomenon are Hanley (1993) and Loughran and Ritter (2002).

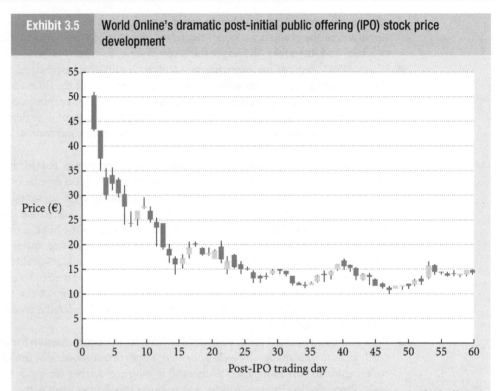

Exhibit 3.5 World Online's dramatic post-initial public offering (IPO) stock price development

World Online's initial price range was set at €35–€43. After the close of subscription, the final offering price was fixed at €42. The opening price was €50.20. After peaking at €51, the stock ended its first trading day on 17 March 2000 at €43.20. World Online's closing price after 60 trading days (14 June 2000) was €14.35 (−67%). For comparison, from 17 March to 14 June, the NASDAQ Composite went down from 4798 to 3797 points (−21%) and the Dow Jones Internet Composite fell from 467 to 280 (−40%).

3.2 The secondary security market

In the secondary market, previously issued securities are traded between investors. The proceeds from selling the securities go to the current owners of the securities, not to the original issuers. Generally, not every individual investor has direct access to security markets. Rather, retail investors generally need to employ security brokers. Brokers act as intermediaries between buyers and sellers, a service for which they charge brokerage commission. Exhibit 3.6 illustrates the basics of trading in the secondary market. If an investor wants to execute a particular trade, then the brokerage function delivers an order with the specified terms to a marketplace. There, buy and sell orders are executed. Finally, clearing and settlement ensure that both sides of the transaction honour their commitments.

While these basics are simple, there is a wide variety in orders, including market orders and limit orders. Also, there is a variety of brokers, ranging from full-service brokers to deep-discount brokers, and a variety of marketplaces, including securities exchanges, OTC markets and alternative trading systems (ATSs). By contrast, the settlement of the trades is usually centralised. In the USA, the Depository Trust & Clearing Corporation (DTCC) is the focal point for this transferring of ownership from one entity to another. In addition to the mechanics,

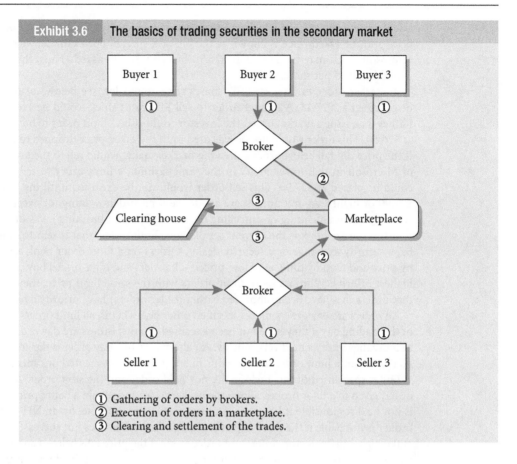

Exhibit 3.6 The basics of trading securities in the secondary market

① Gathering of orders by brokers.
② Execution of orders in a marketplace.
③ Clearing and settlement of the trades.

the DTCC guarantees counterparty risk, the risk that the counterparty will default, leaving the dealer with an unmatched position.

This section discusses various issues related to the secondary market. We first focus on the different types of order an investor can place (Section 3.2.1), the different types of security broker (Section 3.2.2), and various special trading methods, such as margin trading and short-selling (Section 3.2.3). Next, we discuss features of the security market that are of interest to investors, such as liquidity, execution quality and anonymity (Section 3.2.4), different types of trading system, including the dealer system, the auction system and the specialist system (Section 3.2.5), and different marketplaces, such as exchanges, OTC markets and ATSs (Section 3.2.6). Finally, we discuss the process of fragmentation and consolidation of marketplaces.

3.2.1 Types of order

Investors can use different types of order to buy and sell securities. The most common is a market order, which is an order to buy or sell a certain quantity of a security *at the best price currently available*. In contrast, a limit order is an order to buy or sell a specified quantity of a security *at a specified price or better*. The trade will occur only when the specified price is available.

Normally, there is a difference between the price for buying securities and the price for selling securities. The bid price is the price at which investors can buy a security and the asked price is the price at which investors can sell a security. The difference between the bid price and the asked price is known as the bid–ask spread. For example, we can assume that Microsoft stock may be quoted at $26.90 bid and $27.25 asked. Thus, the bid–ask spread would be $0.35 per share.

A market order to buy, say, 100 shares (one round lot, see below) of Microsoft would be executed at $27.25. A market order to sell Microsoft stock would be executed at $26.90. Rather than issue a market order, the investor could issue a limit order to buy Microsoft stock at $26.50. This order would not be executed until the asked price dropped to $26.50 or lower. If the price did fall below $26.50, then the market maker would sell to the investor 100 shares of Microsoft in that lower price. In the same fashion, a limit order to sell Microsoft stock could be placed at $27.90. This sell order would not be executed until the bid price rose to $27.90 or higher. At any time, there are active limit orders waiting for execution or further action (such as amending or cancelling the order) by the submitting investor.

A limit order book is the current set of active limit orders that is sent to, and maintained by, a security exchange or a security dealer. Orders on a limit order book are arranged first by price and then by time, with low-priced sell orders and high-priced buy orders having the highest priority. Within a set of limit orders with the same limit price, they are arranged so that orders that have been submitted earlier (older orders) have priority over later orders.

All orders are day orders unless specified otherwise. That is, all limit orders expire at the end of the trading day if they have not been executed. Market orders are day orders by definition, because they are executed very quickly. An alternative to a day order is the good-till-cancelled (GTC) order, a limit order that remains in effect until it is executed or cancelled.

Other specialised orders include the not-held order and the stop order. A not-held (NH) order, given to a floor broker, allows the broker to try and obtain a better price, but the broker is not held responsible if he or she is unsuccessful. For example, on an NH order to sell, the broker is not liable if the price falls sharply and the broker does not successfully sell an order at the higher price. A stop order is an order to sell if the price falls below a specified minimum, whereas it becomes an order to buy if the price rises above a specified maximum. Stop orders are used to limit losses or protect accumulated gains. If an investor purchased Microsoft when it was trading at $20, and it rose to $30, the investor could limit his or her risk of losing this gain with a stop order to sell if the price falls below $25. Thus, you protect your accumulated gain by a sell stop order. Similarly, you can give a buy order to stockholders. Such an order is usually given by investors who are in short position (see below), hence they lose money when the stock price rises. By buying the stock if it goes above $25, they put a limit on the losses in the short position. Exhibit 3.7 lists other unusual types of orders that currently exist.

Finally, although most orders are for round lots (increments of 100 shares), trading can be in odd lots, which is any number of shares not in increments of 100. For example, a 50-share trade would be an odd-lot trade. Odd-lot trades, however, incur substantially higher fees; thus, it is more economical to trade round lots.

3.2.2 Types of broker

Unlike a discount banker, who executes only trades, a full-service broker provides a wide range of additional services to clients, for example, advice on which securities to buy or sell. A full-service broker may also offer an asset-management account, advice on financial planning, tax shelters, income-limited partnerships and new securities issues. A full-service broker's commission will be higher than that of a discount broker. Importantly, many of the special trading methods discussed below require a full-service broker. Examples of full-service brokers

Exhibit 3.7	Specialised orders for securities
Type of order	**Definition**
All-or-nothing order	Partial execution of an order is prohibited. For example, assume you have a seller wishing to sell 1000 shares of IBM stock at $80 per share, and the buy limit order is for 2000 shares at $80. Because the order would be filled only partially, it would not be executed.
Minimum-fill order	Execution of the order will take place at a prespecified minimum volume of trading.
Market opening/closing order	Order is executed only at the opening or closing of the market.
Last-sale-price order	Order must be executed at a price equal to or better than the last sale price.
Mid-market order	Execution of this order must be at the middle of the most recent bid–offer spread only.
Basket trade	Purchase (or sale) of a given security may be executed only in conjunction with the sale (or purchase) of another security.
Index-related trade	The execution price is related to the value of a specified market index (could be considered a type of limit order).
Spot/future trade	Execution of a cash position is permitted only if a prespecified and simultaneous execution occurs in a futures market.

Source: © OECD *Financial Market Trends*, 1996.

include Merrill Lynch and Morgan Stanley Dean Witter. There are two levels of discount brokers: standard discounters, whose commissions are at least 50% less than those of full-service brokers; and deep discounters, whose commissions are 60% to 90% less than those of full-service brokers. Discount brokers are able to offer competitive commission rates by unbundling traditional brokerage services; unlike full-service brokers, they generally do not have research departments and do not offer investment advice.

Discount brokers frequently operate as online brokers. An online broker is a brokerage firm that allows investors to execute trades electronically using the Internet. Online brokerages vary somewhat in the types of investment they offer to customers. They all offer common stock, but some issues (such as OTC stocks and foreign stocks) remain unavailable at certain brokerages. Mutual fund offerings are becoming increasingly popular. Stock and index options are also offered online widely but not universally. Bonds are sometimes offered, but futures are offered rarely (although this is increasing). Several major online brokers are Ameritrade, Datek, E-trade, Fidelity, Schwab and TD Waterhouse.

3.2.3 Special trading methods

Investors may engage in margin trading. That is, they may borrow a portion of the funds needed to buy securities from their brokers. By borrowing, the investor can take a larger position than would be possible otherwise; hence, the investor is able to 'leverage' the investment. If the security price appreciates, the investor's return is enhanced. If the security price declines, however, the investor's losses are magnified.

The interest rate charged by the broker on the borrowed funds is known as the call loan rate or the broker loan rate. In the USA, the maximum amount that can be borrowed is established by the Federal Reserve Board's Regulation and is currently 50% of the purchase price. However, brokers may require investors to put up more than half of the purchase price.

As security prices fall, the percentage of borrowed money in relation to the security value will rise. If this percentage rises above the allowed limit, the investor must supply more funds to reduce the amount borrowed. When a broker calls for more money, it makes a margin call. One factor to consider before buying on margin is at what price level a margin call will go out.

The initial margin (IM) is the percentage of the dollar amount originally required by the lender to be put up by the borrower:

$$IM = \frac{\text{total amount invested} - \text{borrowing}}{\text{total amount invested}} = \frac{N \times P - B}{N \times P} \tag{3.1}$$

where N is the number of securities, P is the price and B is the borrowing. For example, if you purchased 200 shares of ABC stock at $60 per share, then the total cost is $12 000. An initial margin of 50% would require that you borrow no more than 50% of $12 000, namely, $6000:

$$IM = \frac{(\$60 \times 200) - \$6000}{\$200 \times \$60} = 0.5, \text{ or } 50\%$$

The percentage of the total current market value that an investor originally put up is known as the actual margin. Under regulation of the Federal Reserve Board, the initial margin is currently 50% of the purchase price when buying eligible stock or convertible bonds or 50% of the proceeds of a short sale. As prices fall, the actual margin will also fall. For example, if the ABC stock price falls to $55, then the investor's actual margin (AM) is:

$$AM = \frac{\text{value of stock} - \text{borrowing}}{\text{value of stock}} = \frac{(200 \times \$55) - \$6000}{200 \times \$55} = 0.45, \text{ or } 45\%$$

To minimise the risk of default by the investor, the broker has a minimum margin requirement, known as the maintenance margin, which is the percentage of the dollar amount of the securities market value that must always be set aside as a margin. If the actual margin falls below the maintenance margin, then the investor pays the broker cash to reduce the amount of borrowing. When the account is not brought up to the required levels, some of the client's securities may be sold to remedy the deficiency. The maintenance margin is always less than the initial margin. The maintenance margin (MM) can be written as:

$$MM = \frac{(N \times P') - B}{N \times P'} \tag{3.2}$$

where P' is the price at which a margin call will be issued. Solving for P', we find:

$$P' = \frac{B}{N(1 - MM)} \tag{3.2a}$$

Suppose you purchased 100 shares ($N = 100$) of ABC common stock for $90 by borrowing $4500 and providing $4500 of your own funds (because of the initial margin of 50%). Suppose the maintenance margin is 40% (MM = 0.4). You will receive a margin call when the price is below:

$$P' = \frac{4500}{100(1 - 0.4)} = \frac{4500}{60} = \$75$$

Hence, you will not receive a margin call as long as the price remains above $75. If the price suddenly falls to $60, how much will you have to add in cash to hold your position? To reduce the amount of money borrowed, you will have to add the amount of cash that will bring the maintenance margin back to 40%, or from Equation 3.2:

$$MM = 0.40 = \frac{(100 \times 60) - \$4500 + cash}{100 \times \$60}$$

or

$$cash = (0.40 \times 100 \times \$60) - (100 \times \$60) + \$4500 = \$900$$

where $4500 is the borrowing and $60 is the new market price of the stock.

Indeed, the amount borrowed decreases to $4500 − $900 = $3600, and the maintenance margin (MM) is:

$$\frac{(100 \times 60) - \$3600}{(100 \times 60)} = \frac{6000 - 3600}{6000} = \frac{2400}{6000} = 0.40, \text{ or } 40\%$$

as required.

Most investors buy securities with the expectation that they will appreciate in value. Margin trading is one method to enhance the return when a security's price rises.

Short-selling is a method that allows you to profit when a security's price falls by selling securities that you borrow. Actually, your broker borrows these securities from the inventory of other clients. If the price falls, the short-seller can buy the securities back at a lower price. By selling high and buying low, the short-seller can make a profit. Thus, the short-seller is hoping prices will fall.

To demonstrate how a short-sale works, assume you borrow from your broker 1000 shares of Microsoft stock, and you sell them for $25. Assume that the price falls to $22. Now you buy back the stock and return it to the broker. From this transaction, you make a profit of $3 per share. However, if the price goes up to $27, you have to pay $27 to buy it in order to reimburse your broker, and you lose $2 per share.

The short-seller must pay any dividends due to the original owner of the shorted securities. Also, the proceeds from the short-sale are held by the broker as collateral for the borrowed securities, and the short-seller receives interest on the held proceeds. The short-seller must provide additional money to insure against default. If 1000 shares of Microsoft are sold short at $25, and Microsoft's stock price rises to $27, then the brokerage firm will lose $2000, or 1000($27 − $25), if the short-seller defaults.

Short-selling is a high-risk activity. When investors buy stock (a long position), the most they can lose is the investment itself (when or if the stock price falls to zero). However, when investors sell short (a short position), their loss is unlimited because there is no upper limit to the stock price. The higher the price, the larger the loss. For example, if an investor had sold short 1000 shares of Microsoft when it was trading at $25 per share, then the investor would be required to cover this short position by buying Microsoft. If Microsoft common stock is currently trading for about $27, then the investor is facing a $2 loss per share, a total loss of 1000 × $2 = $2000. The investor could wait, but then the price might increase even more.

Connecting Theory to Practice 3.2 gives further details on the working of short-selling.

Equity loans: how to sell what you do not own

It is tempting to view a short trade as simply the opposite of a long one, but the logistics are different and sometimes difficult or even impossible. The reason is that the short-seller must deliver like any other seller – but does not have what is sold.

Loan pricing

The problem of delivering shares one does not have is solved by equity lending. An equity loan is best thought of as a temporary swap of legal ownership. The lender transfers ownership of some shares to the borrower, who is then free to pass the ownership on to someone else. At the same time as the shares are transferred, the borrower transfers ownership of collateral, usually cash. In the US, the standard collateral is cash amounting to 102 per cent of the value of the shares, to be adjusted daily as their value fluctuates.

So, to borrow 20 000 shares of a company trading at Dollars 50 a share, the borrower would remit Dollars 1.02 m to the lender and would pay in or get back collateral as the shares rise or fall respectively. The loan is closed out when the borrower transfers the 20 000 shares back to the lender, who simultaneously returns the collateral.

But who gets the interest on the collateral? This is the key to pricing the loan. The lender invests the collateral and collects the interest, and the standard investment is a minimal-risk overnight instrument earning close to the Federal Funds rate (this being the inter-bank lending market where repayment is almost certain). If the lender simply kept all interest, the loan's cost and the lender's gross revenue would be as follows. Assuming the loan lasts n days, the lender would receive n days of interest on the collateral at the Fed Funds rate, that is: $1.02 \times$ security value $\times$ Fed Funds rate $\times (n/360)$.

For the example earlier, this would be Dollars 992 for 7 days (assuming the Fed Funds rate is 5 per cent and the price stays at Dollars 50 a share). But the lending market is not so kind to lenders; they have to give back most of this interest.

Rebates

The loan contract will specify a rebate rate, which is the interest the lender must repay to the borrower. This rebate is usually almost everything. Securities that are not scarce in the lending market – which includes most stocks on a given day and almost always the large ones – have the same rebate rate, known as the general rate.

The general rate is around 20 basis points below the going overnight rate (one basis point being 0.01 per cent), so the rebate in the loan described above would not be [5] per cent, but more like 4.8 per cent. This implies a cost to the borrower and gross revenue to the lender of just Dollars 40. It is important to note that these are wholesale terms for large loans; retail brokerage customers get a much smaller rebate because of the proportionately larger fixed costs they incur on each loan and the intermediary layers they encounter. But even the big wholesale customers see their rebates shrink as the security gets scarce.

When supply of a stock is small enough relative to its borrowing demand, lenders negotiate lower rebates. A stock in this situation is said to be "on special" and the shortfall in its rebate is called its specialness. Why would a stock go on special? For one thing, it probably started there.

Stocks are notoriously hard to borrow in the first days after their initial public offerings. In our research we find IPOs to be invariably on special at first, with an average specialness of more than 300 basis points. Specialness gradually settles down to mature-stock levels, in particular after the insider-selling restrictions end at 180 days. Once a stock emerges from the initial shortage it is usually not scarce unless a new event associated with widespread shorting occurs.

The major event associated with borrowing scarcity is merger arbitrage. When one company proposes to absorb another, arbitrageurs such as hedge funds often wish to buy the target and short-sell the acquirer. This generally pays off if the merger goes through and loses if it does not. An example is At Home's acquisition of Excite, which made At Home very expensive to borrow. Specialness in these situations can sometimes reach 90 per cent. This means the arbitrageur's profit net of borrowing costs can be much lower than it first appears.

Source: Chris Geczy, David Musto and Adam Reed, 'Equity Loans: How To Sell What You Do Not Own', *Financial Times*, 28 May 2001.

There are day-trading brokers that allow investors to trade using the firm's computers. The day trader usually buys a security and sells it several times a day and closes the position before he or she leaves the trading room. Such clients believe they discover some pattern in the security's price – for instance, the price fluctuates within the day between $98 and $99, so they adopt a policy to buy at $98 and sell at $99. Sitting all day in front of the computer and using some technical indicators telling you when to buy or sell a security is very similar to gambling in the casino. The clients frequently do not know what the company's profit is or even to which industry it belongs. On average, the stock market goes up (unlike gambling in a casino, where, on average, you lose money), so one would believe that, on average, day traders would gain, even if they had no superior investment information or skills. However, because they conduct many transactions within a day, they pay the day-trading company transaction costs; hence, on average, they lose money.

Day trading should not be confused with active trading. Unlike day traders, active traders trade once or twice a day and don't close out all their positions at the end of the day. While a day trader might hold a given position for only a few minutes, active traders often hold on to their stocks for days, weeks or even months. Also, while a day trader generally pays a large fee to their firm to use special trading software as well as a commission, an active trader usually sticks with a deep-discount online broker. Active trading typically requires the following:

- All the information you need to make decisions fast, including real-time quotes, ideally the bid–ask spread and the supply/demand depth for each security.
- Fast order execution.
- Real-time execution reports.
- A broker who offers low commissions or rebates for active traders.
- A broker who allows all the types of trades that the investor wants to perform, such as buying on margin, short-selling, trading in derivatives, etc.

Programme trading is the simultaneous purchase or sale of an entire basket of securities in a coordinated programme. A computer program constantly monitors the stock, bond, futures and option markets. It gives a buy or sell signal when opportunities for arbitrage profits (sure profits with no risk) occur, or when market conditions warrant portfolio accumulation or liquidation. Programme trading was blamed for the large decline in the stock market that occurred on Black Monday (19 October 1987), because when the market was down, the computer programs triggered a sale order that enhanced the price fall.

Programme trading does not necessarily have to be transacted via computer. The idea of trading baskets of securities has been around for a long time; however, it was not until the advent of computerised trading that it became very efficient.

3.2.4 Market microstructure

The actual mechanisms in a security market that facilitate trading are known as market microstructure. Many different trading systems make up the landscape of today's global capital markets. The basic features are: (1) level of transaction costs, (2) liquidity, (3) degree of anonymity, (4) degree of continuity, (5) execution quality, (6) price discovery and (7) transparency.

Transaction costs

Transaction costs are the costs of buying or selling a security, which consists mainly of the brokerage commission, the bid–ask spread and direct taxes, such as the SEC fee, any imposed transfer taxes and other direct taxes.[14] The brokerage commission covers order delivery and clearing (clearing fees are paid indirectly through the broker). An investor who submits a market order also pays for immediacy via the bid–ask spread. In return for a quick transaction, a buy order pays the higher asked or offer price, while a sell order receives the lower bid price.

In recent years, trading costs around the world have fallen dramatically. The USA is a case in point. The average quoted bid–ask spreads (as a percentage of price) on the 30 stocks in the Dow Jones Industrial averaged 0.175% of the share price in 1998, less than a third of the 1980 figure. Commissions follow an even steeper downward curve. For example, one-way commission rates for NYSE stocks were about 0.55% in 1980 and have since plunged to about 0.10%.[15]

Competition between brokerages, increases in trading volume and technological progress probably explain the decline in transaction costs. But the way in which trading is conducted matters as well. A good example is the minimum price increment or minimum tick size. Before 1997, the minimum tick in the USA was, for the most part, an eighth of a dollar, or $0.125. In the spring of 1997, US exchanges adopted sixteenths, halving the minimum tick, and currently the exchanges use decimal prices, so a tick can be as low as a cent. In the future, competition and technological progress could bring further reductions in transaction costs.

Liquidity

The liquidity of a security market is the ease with which securities can be purchased or sold without a delay and without an impact on the prices. When markets are liquid, transactions are completed quickly and without a substantial price impact. For example, the market for US Treasury bills is more liquid than the market for real estate, because $10 million in US Treasury bills can be traded in seconds at their fair market price, whereas trading real estate may take months. The market for stocks and bonds of big companies is more liquid than the market for securities of smaller firms. For example, shares in large blue-chip organisations like IBM and Microsoft are liquid because they are actively traded and therefore the stock price will not be moved dramatically by a few buy or sell orders. However, shares in small

---

[14] The SEC fee is a small fee to recover the costs incurred by the government, including the SEC, for supervising and regulating the securities markets and securities professionals. Self-regulatory organisations (SROs) – such as the NASD and all of the national securities exchanges, including the NYSE and AMEX – must pay transaction fees to the SEC based on the volume of securities that are sold on their markets. The SROs have adopted rules that require their broker-dealer members to pay their fair share of these fees. Broker-dealers, in turn, pass the responsibility of paying the fees to their customers.

[15] Glosten and Jones (2001).

Exhibit 3.8	Hypothetical stock orders			

Price ($)	Alternative hypothetical orders			
	A	B	C	D
100.00	0	100	0	1300
99.90	0	100	1200	2000
99.80	200	200	0	1200
99.70	100	100	0	1400
99.60	100	200	2100	1500
99.50	0	100	0	1200
99.40	0	200	0	1100
Market condition	Thin and shallow	Thin and deep	Broad and shallow	Broad and deep

Source: From *Introduction to Investments*, 2nd edn, by Levy. © 1999. Reprinted with permission of South-Western, a division of Thomson Learning: www.thomsonrights.com. Fax 800 730-2215.

companies with few shares outstanding are not considered liquid, because one or two big orders can move the price up or down sharply. When markets are liquid, market participants execute trades at existing prices or at prices that are very close to the existing prices.

We can measure the liquidity of different security markets by looking at the depth, breadth and resilience of transactions that occur in each market. If a sufficient number of (limit) orders exists at prices above and below the price at which shares are currently trading, then the market has depth.[16] Otherwise the market is shallow. If a large volume of orders exists at prices above and below the current price, then the market has breadth. Otherwise, it is called a thin market.

Exhibit 3.8 illustrates these concepts when the current price is assumed to be $99.70. The exhibit shows hypothetical stock orders at various prices. Column A demonstrates a thin and shallow market; Column B, a thin and deep market; Column C, a broad and shallow market; and Column D, a broad and deep market. If the market for a given stock is broad and deep, as well as resilient, it is considered to be a relatively liquid market. A transaction can be made in such a market quickly, with no significant price change.

If new orders come into the market rapidly when prices change due to an imbalance of orders, then the market is said to have resilience.

Liquidity requires a critical mass of trading. Since the incumbent marketplaces already have that mass, it is difficult, although not impossible, for another marketplace to establish itself. Investors will not move to a new and illiquid market unless the new market offers, for example, higher execution quality or higher transparency.

Anonymity

For some investors, it is important to trade anonymously (the counterparty does not know the identity of the investor); for others, non-anonymity is important. As an example of an investor who prefers anonymity, consider a pension fund that is trying to buy a large block of shares of IBM. In an anonymous market, no broker knows the identity of the pension fund and is able to buy IBM in advance and drive up the price before the pension fund's order is executed. Avoiding such 'front-running' has obvious appeal for the pension fund.

---

[16] These orders are known as 'limit orders' and are covered on p. 67.

Other investors may actually prefer non-anonymity. To understand this, we must first distinguish between two types of investors. First, there are uninformed investors who need to trade for reasons of liquidity, for example a mutual fund such as Vanguard, which routinely trades stocks in response to additions and redemptions. Second, there exists a group of informed investors who possess unrevealed information about the true price of the security. Investors do not know whether an anomymous counterparty is uninformed or informed and face the risk of trading with an informed investor. For this reason, buyers will post lower asked prices and sellers will post higher bid prices. In economics jargon, the bid–ask spread will include an adverse selection component to protect investors against the possibility of trading with informed parties. If an investor can convince the counterparty that he or she is uninformed, then he or she may be able to get a more favourable quote.

Continuity

Trading systems can be classified as call market or continuous market. In a call market, trading and prices are determined at a specified time in such a way that supply and demand are equal. For example, suppose that by 2.00 p.m. the total accumulated buy orders by all investors in ABC stock is as follows:

Buy 600 shares at $12.86 per share or less.
Buy 700 shares at $12.84 per share or less.
Buy 800 shares at $12.83 per share or less.
Buy 1000 shares at $12.82 per share or less.
Buy 1200 shares at $12.81 per share or less.
Buy 1500 shares at $12.80 per share or less.

Note that the higher price is associated with a smaller number of shares demanded. Similarly, the following might be the aggregate supply of orders:

Sell 100 shares at $12.79 per share or more.
Sell 400 shares at $12.81 per share or more.
Sell 600 shares at $12.82 per share or more.
Sell 800 shares at $12.83 per share or more.
Sell 1300 shares at $12.84 per share or more.
Sell 1400 shares at $12.88 per share or more.

Note that the higher the price, the more shares that are made available for sale. From the aggregate supply and demand information, we see that the equilibrium price is $12.83 per share and 800 shares traded. Those investors wanting to sell securities at a higher price than $12.83 will be unable to find a buyer, and those wishing to buy securities at a price less than $12.83 will be unable to find a seller. When trade in one security is finished, trade in the second security takes place, and so on until all securities are traded. All unfulfilled orders can be resubmitted the following day or the next time the security is traded. Call-market trading usually occurs once a day, but in some countries it can occur two to three times a day.

In a continuous-market system, trades in each security occur at any time the stock exchange is open. If there is a seller and a buyer of Microsoft shares at an agreed price, for example at 10.15 a.m., then the transaction can be conducted in a few seconds (or a fraction of a second with some electronic trading systems). Five minutes later, another transaction in the same stock may be executed at a different price. For example, on some of the business television news networks in the USA, you can view the NYSE and NASDAQ transactions occurring throughout the day by watching the information scrolling across the television screen. This information includes, for example, the ticker symbol of the stock, volume traded, last price, and change in price from the previous price.

In some markets, a mixed-market system exists. For example, a group of securities is traded continuously for, say, half an hour, and then another group of securities is traded continuously for half an hour, and so forth throughout the day. In a way, all markets currently have a mixed system, as no market is open 24 hours a day. Still, ECNs have recently expanded the trading hours, and some believe it is inevitable that some markets will soon begin to run around the clock.

Execution quality

An investor who issues a buy or sell order is not guaranteed that his or her order will be executed quickly (for market orders) or even that the order will be executed at all (for limit orders). The fill rate is the percentage of limit orders that is executed. The execution speed is the time required to execute a market order. A recent survey conducted by Sanford C. Bernstein & Co., Inc., found that 58% of online traders rate immediacy of execution as more important than a favourable price in evaluating the quality of a trade execution.[17]

Price discovery

Another important feature of a well-functioning securities market is efficient price discovery. Market prices should reflect all the available information; that is, the market price should not misrepresent known information. Inaccurate price discovery refers to securities trading at prices that do not reflect true value. Clearly, buying a stock that is 10% overpriced will be costly. In a well-functioning security market, prices adjust quickly to new information and securities are priced correctly. If there is a lag between the time when information is available and a price change, then price discovery is inaccurate during this period.

Transparency

Transparency is defined as the amount of price and trading information that is disseminated to investors. In a transparent security market, investors have access to all relevant information regarding traded prices and volumes, quoted prices and depths and execution quality (execution speed and fill rate).

Markets differ widely in what information is be made available and at what time intervals. For example, the US stock exchanges are relatively transparent with last trade and quote information available to the public. Due to the emergence of electronic trading systems and the Internet, today's investors can have real-time access to this information. Some major television stations routinely provide a sampling of last trade prices and volume of stocks listed on both the NYSE and NASDAQ. The Web pages of many trading portals provide real-time quotes and last trade prices to investors. Recently, the SEC enacted regulation requiring exchanges to publish regularly statistics on execution quality. The goal is to inform market participants about the quality of the liquidity provision service, so they may make informed choices about where and how to trade. However, the limit order books of the exchanges currently are not available to the public.

---

[17] Sanford C. Bernstein & Co, Inc., 'Weekly notes', *Bernstein Research*, 12 May 2000.

In contrast to the US stock exchanges, the US corporate bond market is relatively opaque, with virtually no trading information available to the public or dissemination of information to the public occurring with delays.

3.2.5 Trading systems

There are two different basic trading systems: a quote-driven dealer system and an order-driven auction system. Different marketplaces use one of these two systems or a mixture (a hybrid system). There is an ongoing debate about what constitutes the best trading system. It is not likely that this debate will end soon, because different investors have different needs in terms of transaction costs, execution quality, anonymity, etc. Also, technological progress continuously changes the way in which the trading systems can be operated.

Dealer system

In a dealer system, dealers (or market makers) are the only providers of liquidity; they are the counterparties to every transaction. The dealers maintain their own inventory of securities and buy and sell securities from this inventory. In this capacity, they do not serve as intermediaries but rather take the risk of holding the securities in their own account. The dealers quote prices at which they are willing to buy and sell, the bid prices and the asked prices. Clearly, for the dealer to make a living, the bid price must be less than the asked price. The bid–ask spread set by the dealer is determined by several factors:

- Fixed operating costs (such as leasing an office and computer terminals).
- Non-financing variable cost per transaction (labour and supplies).
- Cost of financing the inventory of securities.
- Risk of price depreciation if inventory is held, and risk of price appreciation if sales have exceeded inventory (a short position).
- Likelihood of trading with investors with ready access to late-breaking news and possibly inside information.

Since the first three factors are relatively stable, many investors monitor the size of the bid–ask spread for clues regarding how the dealer views the volatility of a stock. Larger bid–ask spreads signal greater uncertainty and a greater likelihood of price changes. Important examples of the dealer system include NASDAQ, the SEAQ system for trading small and mid-cap stocks at the London Stock Exchange (LSE), and the Nouveau Marché in Paris, a market for new and smaller publicly traded companies.

Auction market

In contrast to the dealer system, the auction system has no designated dealers or market makers. Investors trade directly with each other or with the intervention of a broker acting only as an intermediary. The quotes come from limit orders submitted to a centralised limit order book. Investors who wish to buy or sell, but are patient, submit limit orders specifying buy or sell, number of shares and a price. The highest-limit buy orders become the market bid price and the lowest-limit sell orders form the market asked price. Investors who wish to trade immediately submit market orders that trade with the limit orders at the prevailing market bid and asked prices. Regulation of auction markets typically requires that orders in the book

Exhibit 3.9	Electronic open limit order book for Microsoft stock						
ECN	Bid	Size	Time	ECN	Ask	Size	Time
ARCHIP*	27.96	26 326	11.04	ISLAND	27.97	8 200	11.04
ISLAND	27.96	13 114	11.04	ARCHIP	27.97	19 585	11.04
ISLAND	27.95	3 200	11.04	ISLAND	27.98	2 600	11.04
ARCHIP	27.95	22 500	11.04	ARCHIP	27.98	17 200	11.04
ISLAND	27.94	2 600	11.04	ISLAND	27.99	3 100	11.04
ARCHIP	27.96	6 400	11.05	ISLAND	27.97	13 700	11.05
ISLAND	27.96	3 190	11.05	ARCHIP	27.97	23 051	11.05
ARCHIP	27.95	26 200	11.05	ARCHIP	27.98	18 400	11.05
ISLAND	27.95	8 800	11.04	ISLAND	27.98	7 314	11.05
ISLAND	27.94	2 800	11.05	ARCHIP	27.99	18 000	11.05

Source: www.archipelago.com, 5 January 2004.
* ARCHIP: Archipelago remains a fully electronic market place, but is now a US-registered stock exchange – the Archipelago Exchange: Archipelago Exchange® (ArcEx®) – rather than an ECN.

are executed according to price–time priority. Price priority requires that no market execute a trade at a worse price than available on another market. Thus, if one investor posts an offer to sell or buy at $10 for some stock, then no investor should pay more or less than $10. Time priority requires that in the presence of two of more offers to sell/buy at the same price, the offers be executed in the time order in which they are submitted.

The auction system offers investors several advantages relative to the dealer system. First, if their orders execute, then they avoid paying the bid–ask spread. Second, the anonymity is appealing to investors who do not want to reveal their identity. The limitations of an auction market are that it provides little liquidity for securities that have low trading volume and that large investors have no possibility of negotiating deals for large blocks of securities. By contrast, in a dealer market, the dealers act as liquidity providers.

Due to advances in communication and computer technology, electronic limit order book (ELOB) systems have emerged in many stock markets. Examples of ELOBs include the Tokyo Stock Exchange (TSE), the Toronto Stock Exchange (TSX), the Stock Exchange Electronic Trading System (SETS) of the London Stock Exchange (LSE) for trading the LSE's most liquid securities, the Nouveau Système de Cotation (NSC) system of Euronext, and the Xetra system of the Deutsche Börse in Frankfurt, Germany.[18] This type of system has also sprung up in the USA in the form of electronic communication networks (ECNs), like Instinet and Archipelago (see p. 86), now a fully electronic US stock exchange, ArcEx®, and NASDAQ's SuperMontage electronic order book, built to compete with them.

Exhibit 3.9 shows two snapshots of the ELOB of electronic markets for Microsoft stock at 5 January 2004. The two snapshots are taken at 11.04 a.m. and 11.05 a.m. As you can see, the market is very liquid, with many buy and sell orders at the various prices. Also, many trades are executed, even in a one-minute time interval. In a liquid market such as the market for Microsoft stock, there is no need for dealers who provide liquidity and post bid–ask quotes, and the ELOB seems the optimal trading system. Indeed, ECNs and alternative electronic markets are rapidly replacing the traditional NASDAQ dealers for trading in NASDAQ stocks.

---

[18] In 2001, the Amsterdam, Brussels, Lisbon, LIFFE and Paris stock exchanges merged to form the pan-European exchange Euronext, using a single order-driven trading platform based on the French NSC electronic order book system.

Hybrid market

Some markets have a hybrid system that combines elements of the dealer system and the auction system. The specialist system used on the NYSE and the AMEX is the canonical example. The specialist is an exchange member who is charged with the responsibility of maintaining a fair and orderly market for one or more securities. Specialists buy and sell (or even short-sell) securities for their own accounts to counteract any temporary imbalance in supply and demand for the stock. In this way, they prevent large fluctuations in the price of the stock in which they trade. Specialists also run the limit order book. Specialists are prohibited from buying or selling securities for their own accounts if there are any outstanding orders that have not been executed for the same security at the same price in the specialist's limit order book.[19] Only one specialist who has a post on the floor of the exchange trades each security. If you want IBM shares, you must go to the IBM specialist. However, one specialist can handle the trade of several securities. The specialist who maintains an inventory of securities publishes quotes of bid and ask prices and is obliged to execute (even from his or her portfolio) at least a limited number of market orders at these quotes. Then, the specialist may decide to have another bid–ask quote against which he or she is once again obliged to trade the minimum amount.

The specialist has an important role in making the market a continuous one. To illustrate, suppose that the highest limit order to buy IBM stock is $85, whereas the lowest limit order to sell is $95. As market buy and sell orders come to the floor, the market price of IBM stock fluctuates from $85 to $95. The specialist is expected, and has agreed, to reduce this relatively large fluctuation by stepping in and buying and selling IBM stock for his or her own account at bid and ask prices between these two prices, such that the range would be only between 0.25 and 0.5. In this way, the specialist provides continuity.

3.2.6 Marketplaces

There exist several marketplaces for executing orders to trade securities. Below, we distinguish between the (1) organised security exchanges, (2) the OTC markets, (3) alternative trading systems (ATSs) and (4) the upstairs market.

Organised security exchanges

A security exchange provides a facility for its members to trade securities, and only exchange members may trade there. For this reason, memberships, or seats, are valuable assets. For example, the price of a seat on the NYSE was as high as $1.85 million in 2003. The members include brokerage firms, which offer their services to individual investors, charging commissions for executing trades on their behalf. Other exchange members buy or sell for their own account, functioning as dealers or market makers who set prices at which they are willing to buy and sell for their own account.

---

[19] Related to the dual role of maintaining the limit order book and acting as a monopoly dealer, specialists earn income in two ways. First, as brokers, they receive commission fees for executing orders. Second, as dealers, they receive income by selling securities held in their own inventory at prices greater than the original purchase price.

| Exhibit 3.10 | Part of the New York Stock Exchange (NYSE) trading floor |

Image of the NYSE Trading Floor® a federally registered service mark of the New York Stock Exchange, Inc., from www.nyse.com/pdfs/2001.factbook.06.pdf, used with permission of NYSE.

In the USA, exchanges are regulated by the SEC. Although the exchanges operate under rules mandated by the SEC, they are self-regulatory organisations that are required to perform a significant degree of internal regulation of their members. In Chapter 5, we elaborate further on the regulation of security markets.

The most well-known and active stock exchanges in the world are the NYSE, the AMEX, the TSE, the LSE and Euronext. The Chicago Board of Trade (CBOT) and the Chicago Mercantile Exchange (CME) are examples of exchanges where commodity and derivative securities such as stock options are traded (see Chapter 19).

As discussed in the previous section, the NYSE and the AMEX have a specialist system that combines elements of the dealer system and the auction system; in brief, the specialist is a monopolist dealer who also maintains a centralised limit order book. Exhibit 3.10 shows the post of a specialist (left corner) as well as the various people involved with the trade and the various screens with current information on the traded stocks. The floor houses 20 such specialist posts.

NYSE member firms may either send orders via a floor broker or send orders electronically from the floor directly to the specialist through the super designated order turnaround (superDOT) system. SuperDOT is an electronic order-routing system that transmits member firms' market and limit orders to the proper trading-floor workstation. Specialists receiving orders through SuperDOT execute them in the trading crowd at their posts, as quickly as market interest and activity permit, and return reports to the originating firm's offices via the same electronic circuit that brought them to the floor.

In Europe, the exchanges have adopted electronic trading systems. By contrast, the US exchanges have been much slower in adopting the new technology, and they adhere to a physical trading floor. Indeed, some commentators claim that trading floors are dinosaurs; see, for instance, Connecting Theory to Practice 3.3. However, defenders claim that hybrid markets can be all things to all investors by providing cheap execution for small orders and providing liquidity in case of large orders and securities with a small market capitalisation.

Big Board must end its costly drama

Even at a theoretical level, the specialist system makes little sense for the top 500 listed US companies. Why have a middle man to ease trading in the most liquid stocks in the world? In practical terms, it is a recipe for abuse: specialists can 'trade ahead' of large customer orders, using privileged knowledge to make proprietary profits, or favour other investors.

It is small wonder that institutions fume. But there has been little they can do up to now: in most cases, their orders for listed stocks are routed to the Big Board under the so-called 'trade-through' rule, enacted 20 years ago as part of SEC efforts to preserve an integrated national market. It says a trade must be executed where the best price is quoted.

As a result, 82 per cent are done on the NYSE rather than through banks, or on Electronic Communication Networks, such as Island, that match orders automatically. The NYSE tends to have the best immediate quotes because it is a central marketplace, but they are 'maybe prices' – they can move after big orders are placed – while ECN quotes are fixed.

This has led to growing pressure to end the trade-through rule. Specialist firms are resisting doggedly, since they do not have to look far to see what could happen.

Specialists claim that abolishing the trade-through rule would fragment the trading of listed stocks, reducing transparency and widening spreads. But even retail investors can now find price information on dispersed networks via the internet. Furthermore, spreads on large-cap stocks are likely to be tight wherever they are traded: for the Big Board to take credit for that is, as Benn Steil of the Council of Foreign Relations puts it, 'like Yankee Stadium claiming credit for the Yankees'.

In any case, competition does not necessarily lead to fragmentation, as demonstrated by the European experience of reforms to trading on national stock exchanges in the late 1990s. London's experience mirrors that of Paris, Frankfurt and Amsterdam, which eliminated its *hoekmen* in 2001. While specialists have a place for illiquid small-cap stocks, an electronic auction book is sufficient for large listed companies.

The way ahead for the SEC and the Big Board is clear. If the SEC wants an efficient stock exchange, it will abolish the trade-through rule. It will then be up to the NYSE whether fragmentation follows. If it tries to preserve specialists for large-cap stocks, it will have little hope of resisting the ECNs; if it has the courage to change, the Big Board can stay big.

Source: John Gapper, 'Big Board Must End Its Costly Drama', FT.com site, 10 November 2003.

→ **Making the connection**

In this newspaper article, the author suggests that the NYSE specialist system is an inefficient system that survives only because of the trade-through rule of the SEC. This rule requires all orders submitted in a US marketplace (on or off the NYSE) to be routed to the NYSE if the NYSE gives the best quote (National Best Bid and Offer; NBBO). According to the author, if the rule were abolished, then competitions by ECNs would force the NYSE to adopt a more efficient electronic limit order book system. Nevertheless, others believe that the trading floor is the NYSE's most valuable asset; the exchange handles large trades effectively and the floor is the reason. Also, the NYSE is working hard to automate some of the specialists' simpler tasks, freeing them to focus on larger trades and the bigger picture of maintaining and allocating liquidity across market participants.

Over-the-counter markets

Securities not traded on any exchange can be traded in the OTC market. The OTC market is not a formal exchange. Rather, it is a loosely organised network of brokers and dealers who negotiate sales of securities. Security dealers quote prices at which they are willing to buy or sell securities. Buyers use a broker to locate the dealer with the lowest offer price and sellers locate the dealer with the highest bid price. A broker can execute a trade by contacting the dealer issuing an attractive quote.

The OTC market has several distinguishing features compared with exchanges. First, there are no membership requirements, and thousands of brokers register as dealers on the OTC market. For example, the requirements for a firm to become a NASDAQ dealer are relatively small, including certain capital requirements, electronic interfaces, and a willingness to make a two-sided market. Second, there are no listing requirements, and thousands of securities are traded in the OTC market.[20] Third, while most exchanges have an auction market (or a specialist system) with a concentrated order flow, OTC markets generally operate as a dealer market with multiple dealers per security. As of June 2000, there was an average of 14.9 market makers per stock listed, while for the top 1% of issues by dollar volume, there was an average of 72.6 market makers on the NASDAQ.[21]

Stocks traded on the OTC market are generally less active issues that are usually traded in regional brokerage offices. For example, a small Alabama firm's stock may trade only within the south-eastern USA. This firm could opt for a regional stock exchange. The OTC market also trades less active issues that have national trading activity. Sometimes, companies prefer to be listed on an OTC market instead of listing on a stock exchange. For example if they are unable or unwilling to abide by the information-disclosure rules of an exchange (the disclosure standards for the OTC market are not as stringent as those imposed by a stock exchange).

OTC stocks are usually considered very risky since they are the stocks that are not considered large or stable enough to trade on a major exchange. They also tend to trade infrequently, making the bid–ask spread larger. Also, research about these stocks is more difficult to obtain.

However, the negative image of the OTC market is not entirely justified. First, the OTC market also has an important role to play in the primary stock market; many new stock issues are sold over the counter initially, and for these issues the OTC market forms a springboard to the exchanges in a later stage.

Second, large blocks of outstanding shares offered for a sale by a single investor, whether listed on an exchange or not, are sometimes sold in the OTC stock market. An example would be an AT&T trade that is conducted through an OTC market (AT&T is listed on the NYSE). Institutional investors such as pension funds and mutual funds (see Chapter 4) frequently trade blocks of several thousands of securities. Security dealers who do not wish

---

[20] However, particular segments of the OTC market, such as NASDAQ stocks, do have to meet stringent listing requirements.

[21] Although these numbers seem large, there is a high degree of concentration of order flow in any stock in a limited number of market makers. Further, all of these market makers are linked together electronically. Some of these links are bilateral, while others, such as the small order execution system (SOES), are provided by NASDAQ. SOES was implemented following the market crash of 1987. During this crash, investors panicked and attempted to sell their shares. The market makers, in turn, simply refused to pick up their phones and fulfil these orders. The SEC reacted by mandating the creation of the SOES, which is a direct-access system that matches bids and asks and executes orders. This system forces liquidity and automatically ensures that at least part of an investor's order is fulfilled.

to hold such a large amount of securities in their inventory often cannot handle such large blocks comfortably.[22]

Third, the OTC market also includes stocks listed on the NASDAQ (see below). These stocks do have to meet high listing requirements. Examples include technology giants such as Intel and Microsoft.

Finally, although most common stocks are traded on exchanges, most bonds and money-market instruments are not. Corporate bonds are traded both on exchanges and on the OTC markets, but all federal and municipal government bonds are traded only over the counter. Also, forwards and swaps are traded in the OTC market.

In the USA, there are rules for OTC trading, written and enforced largely by the NASD, which is a self-regulatory group overseen by the SEC. NASD members include virtually all investment houses and firms dealing with the OTC market. The NASD establishes and enforces fair and equitable rules for security trading on the OTC.

The NASD owns the NASDAQ, which is a computerised trading system that provides investors, brokers and dealers with price quotations for securities traded on OTC markets. NASDAQ lists more companies and trades more shares per day than any other US market.[23] In 2003, NASDAQ listed approximately 3600 companies across all areas of business. However, technology and Internet companies constitute the majority of the market value.

The NASDAQ system consists of two areas: the National Market System (NMS) and the OTC market. The NMS comprises the so-called Tier 1 OTC stocks, a selected part of the OTC market whose issues meet higher volume and price requirements than the remainder of the NASDAQ market.

→ **Connecting Theory to Practice 3.4**   **FT**

Over-the-counter status presents an image problem

Over-the-counter trading is the bottom of the barrel in the eyes of most US investors, calling to mind failed dotcoms, penny stocks and boiler-room investment scams.

But the OTC market is also full of household names, from Nestle to Nintendo to Volkswagen – large foreign companies that have not listed their American depositary receipts on a US exchange.

The 970 ADRs that trade on the OTC 'pink sheets' – a name derived from the coloured paper on which the listings were once printed – are not nearly as liquid as the 540 ADRs on the New York Stock Exchange or the NASDAQ. The few that do trade regularly have attracted only 10 per cent of ADR investors, according to Robert Colle, who heads JP Morgan Chase's ADR group, mainly because companies with OTC ADRs do not have to meet US accounting standards.

But new technology – combined with already prominent brand names – could boost volumes, said Cromwell Coulson, chairman of Pink Sheets, formerly called the National Quotation Board. In 1999, the pink sheets moved online and into real time.

▶

---

[22] Trades in exchange-listed issues that take place in the OTC market are sometimes referred to as the 'third market'. The 'first market' refers to trades in exchange-listed issues that take place on the exchanges, and the 'second market' refers to trades in OTC-listed issues that take place in the OTC market. Before (1972), members of the NYSE were required to execute their trades of exchange-listed securities on the exchange and to charge commissions according to a predetermined schedule. This requirement prevented brokers from offering discounts on large orders. This led brokerage firms that were not members of the NYSE to establish trading of NYSE firms in the OTC market, hence creating the third market.

[23] However, when size is measured by volume in dollars, its proportion declines, because relatively small stocks are traded on the NASDAQ. No matter how it is measured, the NASDAQ is one of the most important trading systems, and its role continues to grow.

'Before, you would look up the security and call all the market makers to get prices. It was very inefficient. No one knew who was giving what,' Mr Coulson said. 'Now market makers can publish their bids and offers. Spreads tighten but liquidity goes up. The dealers are willing to trade at a lower spread because there's less risk.'

Lukoil, the Russian oil company, has seen its ADR trading volume jump to Dollars 6.7 m this year, while both Nestle, the Swiss food and drinks company, and Roche Holdings, the Swiss healthcare group, have topped Dollars 5m. Invensys, a UK software and electronics business, is the OTC share volume leader this year, and the spread between the bid and asked prices has narrowed to 10 cents.

ADRs account for only about 5 per cent of the companies on the pink sheets but they represent about half the dollar volume, Mr Coulson added. But investors are still reluctant to bet on OTC ADRs, said Nina Pawlak, account director at Brunswick Group, the communications and investor relations company. Several of her corporate clients have OTC ADRs sponsored by US depositary banks.

'The ownership is still in the home market,' she said. At the same time, 'it demonstrates that you are interested in making a commitment to be here. It is nice (for investors) to have a ticker symbol to look up.'

Larger companies may not be ready to shift to US accounting but they have operations in the US and employees they would like to reward with US-traded stock. And an OTC ADR programme costs less than a formal listing.

'You have exchange fees on the NYSE and the NASDAQ, lawyers, accountants, even promoting the listing,' Ms Pawlak said. 'It all adds up.'

The pink sheets can be a springboard to the NYSE, the NASDAQ or the American Stock Exchange, however. Companies such as Switzerland's Novartis and Brazil's Petrobras have recently shifted from OTC to listed ADRs, and other big names, including Bayer, the German pharmaceutical company, are expected to make the jump later this year.

Source: Alison Beard, 'Over-the-Counter Status Presents An Image Problem', *Financial Times*, 7 May 2001.

→ **Making the connection**

As discussed in the main text, OTC securities are usually considered very risky because they do not trade on a major exchange, they trade infrequently, and research information is difficult to obtain. As discussed in this newspaper article, this image is not correct for OTC ADRs of large foreign companies such as Nestlé, Nintendo and Volkswagen, which have various reasons not to list their ADRs on a US exchange and to opt for the OTC market instead.

Alternative trading systems

Technological progress enables the erection of new marketplaces, called alternative trading systems (ATSs). An ATS is an electronic trading mechanism developed independently from the established marketplaces and designed to match buyers and sellers on an agency basis, i.e. brokers who use ATSs are acting on behalf of their clients and do not trade on their own account.[24] Within the ATS, we can distinguish between ECNs and crossing networks.

---

[24] Not every electronic trading system is an ATS. For example, TradeWeb has garnered an important amount of US Treasury securities trading volumes. TradeWeb allows investors to solicit quotes electronically from a number of dealers and execute a trade with the dealer of their choice, which in essence replaces the need for investors to sequentially call dealers for a quote on a bond and then trade with their preferred dealer. TradeWeb is not an ATS, because it does not work on an agency basis; rather, TradeWeb is an electronic custromer-to-dealer system for the OTC bond market.

An electronic communication network (ECN) is a trading system that allows investors to clear trades through an electronic open limit order book. Rather than place orders with a specialist or dealer, investors on ECNs may anonymously submit buy or sell orders and trade with each other directly (with the help of a broker). An ECN is essentially a virtual exchange that works as a massive bulletin board where investors can post the price at which they are willing to buy or sell a security. When there is a match, a trade executes. ECNs internally match buy and sell orders or represent the highest bid prices and lowest asked prices on the open market.

An ECN has distinct advantages over traditional markets:

- Cost savings: the ECN does not incur the high overhead costs required to maintain both hosts of human conduits and expensive locales. They also avoid market makers (and their spreads).[25]
- The execution typically takes only a split second for liquid securities and less than a minute for less actively traded securities.
- The extended hours of trading of an ECN allow investors to enter the marketplace at their own convenience.[26]
- Anonymity (which is often important for large trades).[27]
- Since their systems operate electronically and automatically, it is much more difficult to use an ECN to collude or 'move the market', resulting in a level playing field.

ECNs evolved quickly in the late 1990s. They are competing with NASDAQ and NYSE for volume. In fact, in 2003, the ECNs dominated trading in NASDAQ stocks: some 55% of trades were carried out wholly on ECNs, most notably Instinet, Island and Archipelago, while the traditional NASDAQ dealers accounted for only 16.5%, despite the recent introduction of SuperMontage, NASDAQ's electronic execution platform designed to meet the challenge of its rivals. One of the driving forces behind ECNs in the USA is the regulatory change by the SEC, who opened up the stock markets for competition.[28] Also, the auction system of the ECNs seems more suitable for large, liquid NASDAQ stocks than the OTC dealer system. By contrast, the NYSE is already an auction market (with a specialist) and enjoys an incumbency advantage due to the liquidity of the market. Nevertheless, ECNs have also successfully increased trading hours of NYSE stocks.

Although ECNs have come to play a very important role in equity trading, the bond markets suggest that electronic trading might not be preferable to all investors, types of securities and market environments. Secondary government, municipal and corporate bond markets remain predominantly traditional OTC dealer markets that operate over the telephone. The reason for this is that these markets are dominated by large institutional investors. While a retail investor may value the high speed and low transaction costs of an ECN, an institutional trader who wishes to trade a large block of securities may value the liquidity and the possibility to negotiate price improvements offered by a dealer market.

---

[25] However, anonymous trading can increase the 'adverse selection' component of the spread.

[26] However, volume of after-hours trading can be extremely low, leading to high volatility and large bid–ask spreads.

[27] Of course, this is a drawback for investors who seek non-anonymous markets in which they can negotiate and/or avoid 'adverse selection' premiums.

[28] In 1975, Congress directed the SEC to develop a national market system in which all orders to buy or sell equities would interact. In recent years, the SEC has been extremely active in encouraging competition across market centres. There are three main initiatives: the Manning rules, the order display rules, and ATS (alternative trading system) rules (see Chapter 5). These opened the market for ECNs.

A second category of ATS is external crossing networks such as POSIT and E-Crossnet. Crossing networks are electronic systems that cross multiple orders at a single price at pre-specified times and that do not allow orders to be crossed or executed outside of the specified times. Traders enter unpriced buy or sell orders, which are then crossed at prespecified times, at prices prevailing in the security's primary market. Crossing systems thus are call markets that trade at scheduled times, as opposed to the continuous trading of exchanges or ECNs. Also, since traders enter unpriced buy or sell orders, crossing systems do not contribute to price discovery, while ECNs actively contribute to the price-discovery process.

Execution risk remains at crossing networks since the trade is not necessarily executed. The advantage of a crossing network is that it minimises market impact. Trades are typically executed at the midpoint of the bid–ask spread in the primary market. Crossing networks cater to institutional investors placing larger-sized orders in less liquid securities. While ECNs have been especially successful for NASDAQ stocks, crossing networks have been especially successful for NYSE stocks. Crossing systems compete with the NYSE in terms of their ability to more cheaply (measured in terms of lower price-impact costs) match larger uninformed buy and sell orders at the prevailing NYSE price.

ATSs are evolving quickly and their future remains quite uncertain. One possible business model for ATS is to become an exchange (for instance, Island and Archipelago have already filed with the SEC to become an exchange). This implies that the ATS becomes an organised market allowing them to become a destination for listed shares. Another business model is to become a regular broker at several exchanges. However, independent ATSs may also disappear as some of the specific aspects of ATS have already been incorporated into the traditional exchanges (NYSE Direct+ offers a crossing network and NASDAQ offers SuperMontage, a fully integrated order-display and execution-trading platform).

Currently, trading volume on ATSs in Europe is rather low compared with the established marketplaces. In Europe, European traditional marketplaces were automated earlier than their American counterparts. In the USA, the traditional US marketplaces (most notably the NYSE and NASDAQ) have been slow to adopt the new technology. Entrepreneurial financial service providers quickly took advantage of this new opportunity. Moreover, continental European exchanges are typically organised as auction systems, and the importance of having a large liquidity pool for such systems makes it more difficult for ECNs to develop a successful business model in Europe. Nevertheless, there may still be a role for crossing networks in Europe.

Upstairs market

When it comes to large transactions, many institutions try to completely avoid exchanges by using the upstairs market for institutions trading with one another. This trading of large blocks typically occurs without formally posting limit orders, which is the heart of most electronic trading systems. Instead, institutions do not reveal orders until a party willing to take the opposite side of the transaction is available for a large trade.

3.2.7 Competition, fragmentation and consolidation

A security market is constantly trying to attract issuers that will allow it to trade their securities and investors who are willing to trade those securities. Providing a secondary market is a competitive business, with the market shares going to those markets that best serve the investors at the lowest cost. For example, JASDAQ, the Japanese OTC market, recently lost the jewel in its crown, Yahoo Japan, to the TSE. Also, as discussed above, the ECNs have captured the majority of the NASDAQ market at the cost of traditional dealers. The NYSE competes with the NASDAQ for listing the top US technology companies. Indeed, it is so certain that Microsoft and Intel will one day migrate to its famed trading floor that the NYSE has reserved the ticker symbols 'M' and 'I' for the eventuality.

The variety of security markets can be explained in part by the varying needs of different investors (or the varying needs of the same investor at different times or for different assets). Again, a small retail investor may value the high speed and low transaction costs of an ECN, while an institutional trader may value the liquidity and the possibility to negotiate price improvements offered by a dealer market. It should be expected, as has occurred in the past, that different ways of trading will evolve to satisfy the varying needs of investors.

However, the emergence of competing marketplaces also has a downside. Market fragmentation refers to the splintering of order flow and liquidity provision that occurs when several marketplaces are available to execute an order. It is especially pronounced for NASDAQ stocks. Twenty years ago, almost every trade in a NASDAQ stock was done over the phone with a dealer. NASDAQ dealers still make markets, but now there is a range of alternatives, most notably the ECNs. The main argument against fragmentation is that there are important economies of scale in providing trading facilities. Specifically, centralised reporting of transactions, quotes and the limit order book gives investors, brokers and dealers access to the widest possible information set. Also, there needs to be an efficient means of transferring excess supply in one marketplace to excess demand in another, so as to create a deep liquidity pool. These economies of scale explain much of the recent alliances, mergers and acquisitions between different marketplaces.[29] In many cases, the objective is an information and order-routing system that effectively connects the various marketplaces. This process is called consolidation.

The end result of consolidation could be a consolidated limit order book (CLOB). In a CLOB, all limit orders for a given security are submitted anonymously to a centralised book. The orders in this book are executed according to price–time priority. To provide strict price–time priority, all trades must take place through this CLOB; no orders can be executed outside the CLOB. This is in contrast to the existing fragmented system, whereby limit orders are maintained by individual marketplaces.[30]

Proponents of a CLOB argue that this system is eminently fair. Any investor who submitted a limit order would be assured that his or her order would be executed according to price–time priority. Any investor who submitted a market order would receive the best price available at the time. No one would have an unfair advantage. Also, the integration of all limit books for a given security would ensure the largest possible liquidity pool for that security.

However, CLOB opponents argue against the one-shoe-fits-all approach, because different investors have different needs. Price–time priority assures the best price, but investors may rationally choose to bypass the market with the best price and, for example, choose the market with the lowest transaction costs or the fastest execution, or a non-anonymous market.

---

[29] For example, NASDAQ and the AMEX merged in 1999, resulting in the NASDAQ–Amex Market Group. Also, the French, Dutch and Belgian bourses have merged into Euronext, now the second largest European exchange.

[30] The US markets are currently linked by the Intermarket Trading System (ITS). However, this does not mean that there is a CLOB. Since the ITS reports only the best prices and corresponding depths at each marketplace rather than the entire limit order book, it does not maintain price–time priority across marketplaces, even though the limit order books adhere to price–time priority within each marketplace. Also, the existence of trading floors that are not completely electronic (such as the NYSE, the AMEX and regional exchanges) implies that not all available liquidity is necessarily displayed within a venue's quotes.

Another potential concern is that a CLOB may make prices more volatile. After all, there are no dealers to provide liquidity for large orders and for small funds.

An important issue in the process of fragmentation and consolidation is the ownership structure of marketplaces. Traditionally, exchanges were organised as mutuals that served the interest of the exchange members. However, stock exchanges began moving with time, gradually edging away from the sway of their members to become proper companies with proper shareholders. Exchanges in Europe and Asia sought stock-market listings to raise capital to invest in new technology and to acquire smaller rivals with shares. US exchanges have been slower to go down the listing route. By contrast, the rival ECNs are commercial private companies and the NASDAQ stock market has become a publicly traded company. Demutualisation would also enable the NYSE to respond more quickly and nimbly to competitive threats from other exchanges and quasi-exchanges. This might take the form of an alliance with a European exchange to provide a transatlantic equity-trading platform. It would also allow the NYSE to buy an ECN outright.[31]

Currently, the landscape of tomorrow's security markets is uncertain. However, one thing is clear. The names and faces of securities marketplaces may change radically in the next few years, but the real winners in these markets will be the investors. Due to competition and technological progress, investors will have access to more information and liquidity and at a higher speed and lower cost.

Summary

Contrast the primary and secondary markets.

In the primary security market, corporate and government entities can raise additional capital by selling stocks, bonds and other securities with the help of investment banks. The issuing entity receives the proceeds from the sale of securities after they have been issued in the primary market. All securities are first traded in the primary market. In the secondary security market, previously issued securities are traded among investors with the help of brokers. The issuing entity does not receive any funds when its securities are traded in the secondary market. However, the secondary market provides liquidity for the securities after they have been issued in the primary market. Investors are more willing to buy securities in the primary market when they know there will be a liquid market in which to trade them in the future. The existence of a well-functioning secondary market thus makes buying securities in the primary market more appealing.

Summarise the operation of the primary security market.

An initial public offering (IPO) refers to a company's share being offered in the primary market for the very first time. IPOs can consist of secondary shares and primary shares. Not all firms qualify for an IPO: all regulated exchanges impose listing requirements. The process of preparing and executing an IPO is often referred to as 'going public'. An important element of going public is the realisation of a prospectus. Firms going public are often guided by investment banks, who provide advice and arrange and execute most of the tasks involved. Often, they also act as underwriters, guaranteeing the proceeds from the transaction. The most

---

[31] Nevertheless, a flotation of the NYSE is not inevitable, given the steep capital gains tax liability that might be incurred by exchange members. Furthermore, a flotation may raise questions about whether the NYSE should be allowed to continue regulating itself.

common selling mechanisms are bookbuilding, fixed-price and tender methods. On average, IPOs are significantly underpriced compared with their aftermarket value. Several theoretical explanations for underpricing exist. Among the most widely accepted explanations is Rock's winner's curse model, which focuses on the relatively unfavourable allocation of IPO shares to the relatively uninformed investors.

Summarise the operation of the secondary security market.

If an investor wants to execute a particular trade, a security broker delivers an order with the specified terms to a marketplace. There, buy and sell orders are executed. Finally, clearing and settlement ensures that both sides of the transaction honour their commitments. While these basics are simple, there is a wide variety of orders (including market orders and limit orders), brokers (full-service brokers, discount brokers and online brokers) and marketplaces (securites exchanges, OTC markets, alternative trading systems and the upstairs market). By contrast, the settlement of the trades is usually centralised, with the DTCC playing a central role in the USA. Currently, the secondary markets are in an ongoing process of fragmentation and consolidation that is fuelled by competition and recent advances in telecommunication and computer technology. However, one thing seems clear: competition and technology will lead to better-functioning markets in terms of transparency, transaction costs, liquidity and execution quality.

Key terms

Active trading 73
Actual margin 70
Adverse selection component 76
Alternative trading system (ATS) 85
Asked price 68
Auction system 78
Best efforts 57
Bid–ask spread 68
Bid price 67
Bookbuilding 60
Bookrunner 58
Breadth 75
Broker loan rate 70
Call loan rate 70
Call market 76
Clearing 66
Cold IPOs 62
Consolidated limit order book (CLOB) 88
Consolidation 88
Continuous market 76
Continuous-market system 76
Crossing networks 87

Day orders 68
Day trader 73
Dealer system 78
Deep discounters 69
Depth 75
Discount banker 68
Discount broker 68
Electronic communication network (ECN) 86
Electronic limit order book (ELOB) 79
Firm commitment 57
Fixed price 60
Full-service broker 68
Global coordinator 58
Going public 55
Good-till-cancelled (GTC) order 68
Green Shoe option 58
Hot IPOs 64
Hybrid system 78
Information acquisition costs 64
Initial margin (IM) 70
Initial public offering (IPO) 55
Initial return 62

Investment bank 57
Investor education 62
Laddering 61
Lead manager 58
Limit order 67
Limit order book 68
Liquidity 74
Maintenance margin 70
Margin call 70
Margin trading 69
Market fragmentation 88
Market makers 78
Market microstructure 74
Market order 67
Marketplace 66
Mixed-market system 77
Not-held (NH) order 68
Odd lots 68
One-on-ones 62
Online broker 69
Overallotment option 58
Pink herring 62
Premarketing 62
Price discovery 77
Price–time priority 79

Primary market 55	Secondary market 66	Standard discounters 69
Primary shares 55	Secondary shares 55	Stop order 68
Programme trading 73	Security brokers 66	Syndicates 57
Prospectus 57	Security exchange 80	Tender 60
Red herring 60	Selling group 58	Thin market 75
Resiliency 75	Settlement 66	Transparency 77
Retained ownership percentage 55	Shallow market 75	Underpricing 62
	Short-selling 71	Underwriters 57
Road show 62	Sounding out investors 62	Underwriting commission 58
Round lots 68	Specialist 80	Uniform price auction 60
Seasoned equity offering 55	Specialist system 80	Unseasoned equity offerings 55
Seats 80	Spinning 61	Winner's curse 64

Review questions

1 What is the most widely accepted model explaining IPO underpricing, and what is this model's main assumption?

2 The price (P'), below which a maintenance margin call will be issued, can be expressed without the amount borrowed (B). Develop and explain this formula (Hint: see Equations 3.1 and 3.2.)

3 On 1 May, Heloise opened a margin account, buying 400 shares of ABC Company stock for $33 per share. Her initial margin requirement was 55%, and the maintenance margin is 25%:

   a. At what stock price will Heloise receive a margin call (assuming that Heloise borrowed as much as possible to open the account)?

   b. On 1 June, ABC's stock price fell to $15, and Heloise received a margin call. She decided to fulfil the margin requirements by depositing cash in her account. How much cash must Heloise deposit if she is required to restore the margin of 55%?

4 The table below shows four different examples of stock orders at various bid prices as they could appear in a market-maker's limit order book. For each example, determine whether the market is (a) deep or shallow, or (b) broad or thin.

	Number of shares ordered at each bid price			
Bid price	Example 1	Example 2	Example 3	Example 4
$80	1200	1200	100	100
$79.95	1300	1300	50	150
$79.90	0	1400	0	200
$79.85	0	1500	0	225

5 Describe the role of the specialist on the NYSE.

For an extensive set of review and practice questions and answers, visit the Levy–Post investment website at www.booksites.net/levy

Selected references

Allen, F. and G. R. Faulhaber, 1989, 'Signaling by Underpricing in the IPO Market', *Journal of Financial Economics*, **23**, 303–324.

Bae, S. C. and H. Levy, 1990, 'The Valuation of Firm Commitment Underwriting Contracts for Seasoned New Equity Issues: Theory and Evidence', *Financial Management*, **19**, 48–59.

Barclay, M., 1997, 'Bid–Ask Spreads and the Avoidance of Odd-Eighth Quotes on NASDAQ: An Examination of Exchange Listings', *Journal of Financial Economics*, **45**, 35–58.

Barclay, M. J., W. G. Christie, J. H. Harris, E. Kandel and P. Schultz, 1999, 'The Effects of Market Reform on the Trading Costs and Depths on Nasdaq Stocks', *Journal of Finance*, **54**, 1–35.

Baron, David P., 1982, 'A Model of the Demand for Investment Banking Advising and Distribution Services for New Issues', *Journal of Finance*, **37**, 955–976.

Benveniste, Lawrence M. and Paul A. Spindt, 1989, 'How Investment Bankers Determine the Offer Price and Allocation of New Issues', *Journal of Financial Economics*, **24**, 343–361.

Bessembinder, H., 1999, 'Trade Execution Costs on NASDAQ and the NYSE: A Post-Reform Comparison', *Journal of Financial and Quantitative Analysis*, **34**, 387–407.

Bloomfield, R. and M. O'Hara, 2000, 'Can Transparent Markets Survive?', *Journal of Financial Economics*, **55** (3), 425–459.

Bloomfield, R. and M. O'Hara, 1999, 'Market Transparency: Who Wins and Who Loses?', *Review of Financial Studies*, **12** (1), 5–35.

Bradley, Daniel J., Bradford D. Jordan and Jay R. Ritter, 2003, 'The Quiet Period Goes Out With a Bang', *Journal of Finance*, **58**, 1–36.

Brown, David P. and Zhi Ming Zhang, 1997, 'Market Orders and Market Efficiency', *Journal of Finance*, **52**, 277–308.

Christie, W. and P. Schultz, 1994, 'Why do NASDAQ Market Makers Avoid Odd-Eighth Quotes?', *Journal of Finance*, **49**, 1813–1840.

Chung, K. H., B. F. Van Ness and R. A. Van Ness, 1999, 'Limit Orders and the Bidask Spread – A Paired Comparison of Execution Costs on Nasdaq and the NYSE', *Journal of Financial Economics*, **53**, 255–287.

Demsetz, Harold, 1997, 'Limit Orders and the Alleged Nasdaq Collusion', *Journal of Financial Economics*, **45**, 91–96.

Dutta, Prajit and Ananth Madhavan, 1997, 'Competition and Collusion in Dealer Markets', *Journal of Finance*, **52**, 245–276.

Flood, M. D., R. Huisman, K. G. Koedijk and R. J. Mahieu, 1999, 'Quote Disclosure and Price Discovery in Multiple-Dealer Financial Markets', *Review of Financial Studies*, **12**, 37–59.

Glosten, L. R., 1994, 'Is the Electronic Open Limit Order Book Inevitable?', *Journal of Finance*, **49**, 1127–1161.

Glosten, L. and C. Jones, 2001, 'The Past, Present and Future of Trading Stocks', *Financial Times*, 14 May 2001.

Goldstein, M. A. and Kavajecz, K. A., 2000, 'Eighths, Sixteenths and Market Depth: Changes in Tick Size and Liquidity Provision on the NYSE', *Journal of Financial Economics*, **56**, 125–149.

Grossman, Sanford J., 1992, 'The Informational Role of Upstairs and Downstairs Trading', *Journal of Business*, **65**, 509–528.

Hanley, Kathleen W., 1993, 'The Underpricing of Initial Public Offerings and the Partial Adjustment Phenomenon', *Journal of Financial Economics*, **34**, 231–250.

Harris, L., 2002, *Trading and Exchanges: Market Microstructure for Practitioners*, Oxford: Oxford University Press.

Huang, R. D. and H. R. Stoll, 1996, 'Dealer Versus Auction Markets: A Paired Comparison of Execution Costs on Nasdaq and the Nyse', *Journal of Financial Economics*, **41**, 313–357.

Jones, C. M. and Lipson, M. L., 2001, 'Sixteenths: Direct Evidence on Institutional Execution Costs', *Journal of Financial Economics*, **59**, 253–278.

Kandel, E. and Marx, L. M., 1997, 'Nasdaq Market Structure and Spread Patterns', *Journal of Financial Economics*, **45**, 61–89.

Kavajecz, K. A., 1999, 'The Specialist's Quoted Depth and the Limit Order Book', *Journal of Finance*, **54**, 747–771.

Ljungqvist, Alexander P., Tim Jenkinson and William J. Wilhelm, 2003, 'Global Integration in Primary Equity Markets: the Role of US banks and US Investors', *Review of Financial Studies*, **16**, 63–99.

Logue, Dennis E., 1973, 'Of the Pricing of Unseasoned Equity Issues: 1965–1969', *Journal of Financial and Quantitative Analysis*, **8**, 91–103.

Loughran, Tim and Jay R. Ritter, 2002, 'Why Don't Issuers Get Upset About Leaving Money on the Table in IPOs?', *Review of Financial Studies*, **15**, 413–443.

Madhavan, A., 2000, 'Market Microstructure: A Survey', *Journal of Financial Markets*, **3**, 205–258.

O'Hara, M., 1995, *Market Microstructure Theory*, Oxford: Blackwell.

Pagano, M. and R. Ailsa, 1996, 'Transparency and Liquidity: A Comparison of Auction and Dealer Markets with Informed Trading', *Journal of Finance*, **51**, 579–611.

Rock, Kevin, 1986, 'Why are New Issues Underpriced?', *Journal of Financial Economics*, **15**, 187–212.

Sherman, Ann E., 2003, 'Global Trends in IPO Methods: Book Building vs. Auctions with Endogenous Entry', working paper, University of Notre Dame, Indiana.

Smith, C. W., 1986, 'Investment Banking and the Capital Acquisition Process', *Journal of Financial Economics*, **15**, 3–29.

Snell, Andy and Ian Tonks, 2003, 'A Theoretical Analysis of Institutional Investors' Trading Costs in Auction and Dealer Markets', *Economic Journal*, **113**, 576–597.

Tiniç, M. Seha, 1988, 'Anatomy of Initial Public Offerings of Common Stock', *Journal of Finance*, **43**, 789–822.

Viswanathan, S. and Wang, J. J. D., 2002, 'Market Architecture: Limit-Order Books Versus Dealership Markets', *Journal of Financial Markets*, **5**, 127–167.

Welch, Ivo, 1992, 'Sequential Sales, Learning, and Cascades', *Journal of Finance*, **47**, 695–732.

Weston, J., 2000, 'Competition on the NASDAQ and the Impact of Recent Market Reforms', *Journal of Finance*, **55**, 2565–2598.

CHAPTER 4

Institutional investors

Investment in the News 4

Record inflow to mutual funds

US mutual funds took in a record amount of new money from investors in January, accord-ing to the Investment Company Institute, an industry trade group, but the bulk of it went to money market funds, seen by many investors as a safe haven.

Of the Dollars 102.78 bn that rolled into money market funds last month, Dollars 82.47 bn went to funds used primarily by institutional investors, according to the ICI.

In all of 2000 money market funds gathered Dollars 159.55 bn, while in December institutional and retail investors combined sent the funds Dollars 16.63 bn.

Retail investors were less conservative than institutions, sending money market funds Dollars 20.31 bn in January, a total that the ICI said was in line with recent monthly averages.

In addition, retail investors were more enthusiastic this year about stocks than in the fourth quarter of 2000, sending equity funds Dollars 24.58 bn – double December's Dollars 11.64 bn.

However, bond funds showed their first net inflow in six months, at Dollars 8.6 bn.

Source: Elizabeth Wine, 'Record Inflow To Mutual Funds', *Financial Times*, 28 February 2001.

Nowadays, large institutions rather than individuals account for the largest part of security holdings and security trading activity. Institutional investors are specialised financial intermediaries that manage savings collectively on behalf of individuals and sometimes non-financial companies. Investment in the News 4 mentions two types of institutional investors: pension funds and mutual funds. Other types of institutional investors include insurance companies, closed-end funds and hedge funds. Many individuals use these institutions as their primary investment vehicle. This makes institutional investors a potentially powerful force if they choose to exercise shareholder control over firm management. Clearly, when a pension fund manager who manages a large block of shares calls a corporate officer, the officer is going to listen carefully.

This chapter discusses the role of institutional investors in today's financial markets. We will explain the growth of institutional investors, distinguish between the different types of institution (insurance companies, pension funds and investment companies) and discuss their investment behaviour. We note at the outset that the sharp distinctions made in this section are not always appropriate, given the blurring of differences between financial institutions. In particular, both life insurance and pension business is often conducted via products employing mutual funds as an investment vehicle. Examples of products concerned are unit-linked life policies and many types of personal pension products, such as the US 401(k) plans.

4.1   Institutionalisation

Institutional investors, particularly insurance companies, pension funds and investment companies (mutual funds, closed-end funds and hedge funds), are major collectors of savings and suppliers of funds to financial markets. As shown in Exhibit 4.1, institutional investors hold an increasing portion of the value of US equities. At the end of 2002, US institutional investors, who owned only 7.2% of total outstanding equities in 1950, held a total of roughly $6.5 trillion or about half of all equities.

This phenomenon is not restricted to the USA. The Organisation for Economic Co-operation and Development (OECD) estimates the average annual growth in OECD countries during the period from 1990 to 1999 at 13% for insurance companies, 11% for pension funds and 20% for investment companies.[1]

---

[1] Source: OECD Institutional Investors database, www.oecd.org

Exhibit 4.1	Institutional holdings of corporate equities in the USA (end of year, in billions of dollars)						
	1950	1970	1990	1995	1999	2000	3Q 2001
Private pension funds	1.1	67.1	595.0	1 289.2	2 156.9	2 001.1	1 591.3
State and local pension funds	0.0	10.1	270.7	678.9	1 343.2	1 335.1	1 100.3
Life insurance companies	2.1	14.6	81.9	315.4	964.5	940.8	820.8
Other insurance companies	2.6	13.2	79.9	134.2	207.9	194.3	169.6
Mutual funds	2.9	39.7	2 33.2	1 024.9	3 400.0	3 250.8	2 442.0
Closed-end funds	1.6	4.3	16.2	38.2	39.9	35.7	28.4
Bank personal trusts	0.0	87.9	190.1	224.9	338.3	280.0	206.2
Foreign sector	2.9	27.2	243.8	527.6	1 537.8	1 748.3	1 524.4
Households and non-profit organisations	128.7	572.5	1 806.5	4 182.9	9 342.8	7 487.1	5 471.8
Other	0.8	4.8	25.3	79.5	249.9	293.2	270.4
Total equities outstanding	142.7	841.4	3 542.6	8 495.7	19 518.2	17 566.4	13 625.2
% held by US institutions	*7.2*	*28.2*	*41.4*	*43.6*	*43.2*	*45.8*	*46.7*

Source: Federal Reserve Board Flow of Funds, www.federalreserve.gov

The shifting of the capital market from dominance by retail investors to financial institutions is often referred to as the institutionalisation of capital markets. Several economic, demographic and regulatory factors have been crucial in driving this phenomenon:

4.1.1 Efficient management and diversification of assets and liabilities

Institutional investors can achieve economies of scale in the management and diversification of assets and liabilities. An important risk in investing in a single company is the possibility that the company goes bankrupt and the securities held in that company become worthless. This risk can be reduced through diversification, i.e. by investing in many companies, industries and markets. Unfortunately, for a small investor, maintaining a diversified portfolio can be difficult and costly. Collecting and analysing information can be a full-time job, and diversification can also involve significant transaction costs. To add to the problem, to remain optimally diversified, a portfolio needs to be rebalanced periodically, which further increases the transaction and information costs. Institutional investors offer investors an easy way to diversify. The costs of buying and selling securities in large quantities are considerably less than those for buying and selling in small quantities. Also, the institutions' funds are managed by professional portfolio managers, assisted by a team of professional analysts who research the companies, industries and markets in which they invest. Similarly, institutions enjoy economies of scale in the pooling of liabilities. For example, an insurance company is based on the fact that the individual risks of adverse events such as traffic accidents are highly uncorrelated. Managing a pool of pension or insurance liabilities is much simpler than managing the financial implications of the individual risks.

4.1.2 Demographic pressure on social security

The ageing and growing wealth of the populations in the OECD area has produced a growing demand for retirement and life and health insurance products. Simultaneously, the baby-boom cohort of the 1940s and 1950s is causing looming fiscal problems in countries (notably in Continental Europe) relying predominantly on pension and healthcare systems financed from tax revenues. The percentage of the US population over 60 years old, which stood at 16.3% in 2000, is expected to rise to 27.7% by 2030. This trend is typical for high-income OECD countries in general. For example, in the UK, Germany and France, the percentages for 2000 are 20.7%, 20.6% and 20.2%, respectively, and the expected percentages for 2030 are 30.1%, 36.35% and 30.0%, respectively.[2] Consequently, public pension and healthcare expenditure as a share of GDP is projected to increase sharply if the policy is unchanged. This has stimulated the introduction of advance-funded public pension schemes and private pensions and life and health insurance as a supplement to social security.

4.1.3 The changing role of banks

Since the 1970s, there has been a shift from bank deposits and traditional savings vehicles to more performance-oriented instruments such as money-market funds and mutual funds investing in equity. A key determinant is Regulation Q, which imposes a ceiling on the deposit rates that banks and thrifts could pay to their clients in order to promote stability in the banking sector by preventing destructive competition among depository institutions to get funds by offering higher deposit rates. One of the effects of these restrictions was the evolution of money-market mutual funds (MMMFs), in which small investors pool their funds to buy a portfolio of money-market instruments (Treasury bills, commercial paper, negotiable certificates of deposit, and so on) that offered money-market interest rates in excess of that permitted by regulation Q. Also, the deregulation of the banking and securities industries since the beginning of the 1980s has heightened competition between and among banks and other financial institutions. Together with the introduction of international capital standards for banks, this caused a massive move by banks into the fee and commission business associated with capital-market transactions, thereby further blurring demarcation lines between banks and insurance and fund-management organisations.

4.2 Insurance companies

Individuals and corporations protect themselves by buying insurance against many possible adverse events, such as fire, floods and accidents. Insurance companies are in the business of assuming the risks of these adverse events in exchange for a flow of insurance premiums. Most people hold one or more types of insurance policies (life, health, homeowner, disability, automobile, and so on). Indeed, the insurance industry is an important industry, measured by annual revenues (over $600 bn in the USA in 2000) and the number of people employed in the industry (over two million in the USA in the 2000).

4.2.1 The function of insurance companies

The economic idea behind the insurance business is to reduce risk by pooling many individual risks. The risk-reduction effect makes it possible that insurance companies can offer insurance products for a relative low premium in combination with a high level of security. Furthermore, most insurance companies reinsure the risk they cannot bear or diversify.

---

[2] Source: R. Palacios and M. Pallarès-Miralles (2000), *International Patterns of Pension Provision*, Washington, DC: World Bank.

The major operations of an insurance company are underwriting, the determination of which risks the insurer can take on, rate-making, the decisions regarding necessary premiums for such risks, and asset–liability management (ALM), the matching of investment assets with insurance liabilities. The underwriter is responsible for guarding against adverse selection, wherein there is excessive coverage of high-risk candidates in proportion to the coverage of low-risk candidates. Besides preventing adverse selection, the underwriter must also consider physical and moral hazards in relation to applicants. Physical hazards include those dangers that surround the individual or property, jeopardising the wellbeing of the insured. Moral hazards include the danger that coverage against a loss might actually increase the risk-taking behaviour of the insured.

Insurance companies charge premiums that are sufficient to cover the expected insurance claims plus a profit. The difficult part is to estimate the claims: rate-making involves quantifying the probability of the insured event and the loss in case the event occurs. Although such computations are very difficult for individual applicants, predictions can be made on an aggregate level. Since insurance companies insure millions of people, the law of large numbers makes the company's predictions quite reliable, which allows companies to price the policies so that they can expect to make a profit. For example, a life insurance company can predict with a high degree of accuracy the amount of death benefits that must be made by using actuarial tables that predict life expectancies.

While the premiums are generally received at the beginning of the insurance period, the payments resulting from adverse events happen after or during that period, and many insurance policies have far less than one adverse event per period, so most premiums have to be invested for a long time. Therefore, the insurance companies invest the premiums in financial assets. In this sense, the insurance company is holding two portfolios: a portfolio of insurance liabilities and a portfolio of financial assets. Both portfolios are exposed to uncertainty regarding their future value. The uncertainty of the portfolio of insurance contracts results from the uncertainty of the timing and volume of the aforementioned adverse events. The uncertainty of the portfolio of assets results from fluctuations of security prices. The task of insurance companies is to match the risks of the insurance liabilities with offsetting risks of the financial assets. However, the risks of the liabilities are often estimated more accurately than those of the assets, where the law of large numbers does not apply (all securities are exposed to systematic risk factors).

4.2.2 Types of insurance

Life insurance, originally conceived to protect a man's family members when his death left them without income, has developed into a variety of policy plans, some of which are also important savings vehicles. Term-life insurance, also called temporary insurance, covers a person against death for a limited time, the term. For example, the term might be until children are grown-up, or until college is paid for, or until retirement. You pay for the policy period, and at the end of the term, the contract or policy expires. If no claims are made against the policy during the term, you don't receive any benefits after the policy expires, just like auto or homeowner insurance. In a whole-life policy, also called permanent insurance, fixed premiums are paid throughout the insured's lifetime. This accumulated amount, augmented by compound interest, is paid to a beneficiary in a lump sum upon the insured's death; the benefit is paid even if the insured had terminated the policy beforehand. Under a universal life policy, the insured can vary the amount and timing of the premiums; the funds compound to create the death benefit. With variable life policies, the fixed premiums are invested in a portfolio (with earning reinvested), and the death benefit is based on the performance of the investment. Annuity policies, which pay the insured a yearly income after a certain age as long as he or she lives, have also been developed. While the aforementioned policies protect against an early death, annuities protect against the risk of running out of retirement assets when one lives longer than expected. In the 1990s, life insurance companies began to allow early payouts to terminally ill patients.

Non-life insurance, also known as property-casualty insurance, provides cover for a wide variety of incidents, for example fire, car accidents, destruction of property and theft. A major type of non-life insurance is private health insurance, which covers mainly two kinds of losses: disability income losses and medical care expenses. Fire insurance usually includes damage from arson and lightning; other elements that may be insured against are include hail, tornado, flood and drought. Complete automobile insurance includes not only insurance against fire and theft but also compensation for damage to the car and for personal injury to the victim of an accident (liability insurance); many car owners, however, carry only partial insurance. In many countries, liability insurance is compulsory, and a number of countries (including most European countries) have instituted so-called no-fault insurance laws, whereby automobile accident victims receive compensation without having to initiate a liability lawsuit, except in special cases. Fidelity insurance is designed to protect an employer against dishonesty or default on the part of an employee. Credit insurance safeguards businesses against loss from the failure of customers to meet their obligations. Marine insurance protects shipping companies against the loss of a ship or its cargo, as well as many other items; inland marine insurance covers a vast miscellany of items, including tourist baggage, express and parcel-post packages, truck cargoes, goods in transit, and even bridges and tunnels – not to mention beaches that get polluted by oil spills. In recent years, the insurance industry has broadened to guard against almost any conceivable risk; companies such as Lloyd's will insure a dancer's legs, a pianist's fingers, or an outdoor event against loss from rain on a specified day.

Reinsurance is a financial agreement between a reinsurance company and an insurance company, whereby the reinsurer agrees to compensate part of the uncertain payments for losses that the ceding insurer is called upon to pay the original policyholders, of course against payment of a reinsurance premium. In other words, reinsurers take over the risks covered by non-life insurers and, to a lesser extent, life insurers. Reinsurance commonly knows two types: treaty reinsurance and facultative reinsurance. Under a treaty reinsurance contract, an insurer commits to ceding and a reinsurer to accept a share of risks on a new business over an agreed period. Under facultative reinsurance, insurers and reinsurers agree to cover for particular exposures.

Exhibit 4.2 shows the largest life insurance companies, non-life insurance companies and reinsurance companies in 2000.

Exhibit 4.2	Largest global insurers by revenue (June 2004)				
Largest life insurance groups	Revenue (US$ bn)	Largest property/ casualty insurance companies	Revenue (US$ bn)	Largest reinsurance groups	Gross premiums written (US$ bn)
ING group	88.1	Allianz	101.9	Munich Re – Segment Reins	24.9
AXA	62.1	AIG	67.5	Swiss Re Group	21.6
Nippon Life	61.2	Munich Re Group	52.0	Berkshire Hathaway	13.1
Assicurazioni Generali	53.6	State Farm	49.7	Hannover Re	8.5
Aviva	49.5	Berkshire Hathaway	42.4	Employers Re Group	7.9

Source: *Insurance*, City Business Series 2004. London: International Financial Services, London (2004).

4.2.3 Investment policy of insurance companies

To repeat, insurers match their insurance liabilities with financial assets, a process called asset–liability management. Life insurers are especially important investors. Many life insurance products also serve as savings vehicles, for instance through annuities. These products entail a high probability of paying out large sums of money or payments during long periods of time. For example, assuming a 5% discount rate, the obligation to pay $50 000 annually (at the end of the year, so with the first payment in 12 months' time) to an individual beneficiary during 20 years is a liability with a present value of:[3]

$$\$50\ 000/0.05 - (\$50\ 000/0.05) \times 1.05^{-20} \cong \$623\ 111$$

Related to this, life insurers typically hold very large portfolios of long-term financial assets. Property-casualty insurance usually has a much shorter term than most life insurance. Also, the risks of the property-casualty sector are 'insurance risks' that arise from highly uncertain flows of claims depending on major disasters and court cases offsetting the benefits of the 'law of large numbers'. A property-casualty insurer can face a large payout on short notice. Because of these considerations, property-casualty insurers hold fewer long-term financial assets than life-insurers; their portfolios tend to include a high proportion of short-term assets that can be liquidated easily with little loss of value. For these reasons, we focus throughout this section on life insurers and abstract from property-casualty insurers.

Life insurance company liabilities tended historically to be defined in nominal terms. These nominal liabilities would include those arising from term, whole-life and universal policies and annuities. Guaranteed investment contracts (GICs) – a form of zero coupon bond typically sold to pension funds – are a modern variant. Insurers may also offer nominal, insured defined-benefit pension plans. These nominal liabilities can be matched or immunised using long-term bonds, private placements and mortgages (see Chapter 14 for more details on immunisation strategies).[4] Life insurers' portfolios also need some short-term liquidity to cover liabilities arising from early surrender of policies and policy loans.[5]

However, life insurers also invest a significant part of their fund in equities, real estate and international investments. Undoubtedly, the following insights about risks and return help explain these investments:

■ With the rise of modern portfolio theory came the insight that much of the risk of individual investments can be diversified away in the context of well-diversified portfolio. For example, junk bonds are very sensitive to the overall health of the issuing firm and hence their price moves more with information related to the firm than with changes in overall interest rates. It turns out that a diversified portfolio of junk bonds with a relatively low correlation is less volatile than a diversified portfolio of US Treasury securities.

---

[3] This figure is the difference between the value of an annuity paying $50 000 per annum that starts next year and the value of an annuity paying $50 000 per annum that starts after 21 years. The present value of the former annuity is $50 000/0.05 = $1 000 000. The present value of the latter annuity is ($50 000/0.05) $\times (1.05)^{-20} \cong \$376\ 889$.

[4] A private placement is the sale of bonds directly to an investor such as an insurance company. Because private placements are not registered with the SEC, the original purchasers cannot easily resell them to other investors.

[5] Many life insurance contracts include mandatory or customary early surrender guarantees or rights to take policy loans (a loan made by a life insurance company to a policy owner on the security of a policy's cash surrender value).

■ Long-run investors are not affected by day-to-day fluctuations of asset prices and the long-run risk of stocks is lower than their short-term risk. For example, even during the Depression of 1929–39, a well-diversified investor who continued to reinvest his or her dividends in the stock market would have seen their stock portfolio fall by only 18%.

■ Risky investments generally yield a higher return and hence allow for higher retirement benefits or lower retirement contributions. For example, the average annual real return (i.e. the inflation-adjusted return) on the US stock market over the past 110 years has been about 7.9%. Over the same period, the return on T-bills was a paltry 1%. The difference is known as the equity premium.

The investments in high-risk, high-return assets is especially relevant for variable policies. Life companies are increasingly offering variable policies such as variable life policies, variable annuities, with-profits endowment and unit (mutual fund)-linked policies. Also, policies may have option features, with, for instance, variable returns but a guaranteed floor. Unlike traditional policies, variable policies allow for risk-taking, because the beneficiary rather than the insurer bears the risk. The related assets may often be held in the form of mutual funds. Pension liabilities, to be discussed below, are another factor increasing equity and foreign investment. Insurance companies are involved heavily in investing pension monies. This may occur directly on the balance sheet, generally on a 'defined-contribution' basis (i.e. the contribution is fixed and the pension benefits are variable; see later in this chapter) or externally as asset managers on behalf of pension funds.

Exhibit 4.3 shows the distribution of the financial assets of US life insurance companies for the years 1990–2002. Clearly, the amounts invested are enormous. With more than $3.3 trillion of financial assets in 2002, life insurers are among the largest institutional investors in security markets today. Roughly 75% of the financial assets are held in money-market and credit-market instruments to provide liquidity and to match the nominal liabilities. About 21% is placed in corporate equities. Note that these figures represent aggregates over all life insurance companies in the USA. The investment portfolio of individual companies may

Exhibit 4.3	Financial assets of US life insurance companies (end of year, dollars in billions)						
	1990	1992	1994	1996	1998	2000	2002
Chequeable deposits and currency	4.9	4.8	5.6	4.3	5.4	5	35.3
Money-market fund shares	18.1	25	16.2	61.9	110.4	142.3	163.8
Credit-market instruments	1134.5	1304.4	1487.5	1657	1828	1943.9	2307.8
Open-market paper	45.7	43.2	52.8	48.4	73.4	71.2	74
US government securities	180.2	281.8	341.2	337.4	288.4	293.5	409.4
Treasury	59.2	88.8	107.1	93.2	71.3	58.1	78.5
Agency	121	193	234.1	244.1	217	235.4	330.9
Municipal securities	12.3	11.4	12.8	13.4	18.4	19.1	19.9
Corporate and foreign bonds	566.9	653.9	779.4	949.3	1130.4	1222.2	1449.3
Policy loans	61.6	72.1	85.5	100.5	103.8	101.9	105.1
Mortgages	267.9	242	215.8	208.2	213.6	235.9	250
Corporate equities	81.9	151.6	231.4	404.6	679.5	887	705
Mutual fund shares	30.7	18.2	24.4	44.7	77	101.9	80.5
Miscellaneous assets	81.3	83	97.9	73.7	69.2	55.6	42.8
Total financial assets	*1351.4*	*1587*	*862.9*	*2246.3*	*2769.5*	*3135.7*	*3335*

Source: Federal Reserve Board Flow of Funds, www.federalreserve.gov

differ substantially, for example depending on the chosen balance between fixed and variable policies. Another issue is the extent by which the insurance companies' assets exceeds the value of liabilities or the 'surplus'. The surplus is intended to protect the firms against insolvency over time and to finance future growth. Not held explicitly to back liabilities, the surplus is likely to be invested aggressively for return to shareholders and development of reserves.

4.3 Pension funds

A pension fund is an asset pool that accumulates over an employee's working years and pays retirement benefits during the employee's non-working years. Pension funds collect, pool and invest funds contributed by sponsors and employees to provide for the future benefits of employees. The sponsors often are employers, although personal pensions (generally contracts between individuals and life insurance companies) are also common.

4.3.1 Public versus private pension plans

Many different pension systems exist. Most industrialised countries either have or are evolving toward pension systems that contain three basic elements:

- A state pension to ensure a minimum income for elderly people. In this system, the pensioners are paid from the yearly proceeds of taxes that are paid by the actively working people in the system. Therefore, the system is called a pay-as-you-go (PAYG) system. Social security in the USA is a prime example.
- Mandatory programmes for employees that provide retirement benefits scaled to salary and service years. These programmes can be either publicly managed or managed by private pension companies. Also, the programmes can be financed either using a PAYG system (from current tax revenues) or an advance-funded system. In an advance-funded system, funds are set aside and invested in the capital market in advance of the date of retirement.
- Programmes that encourage voluntary supplementation by individual workers and their employers. These programmes are almost always operated by the private sector and are usually financed on an advanced-funded basis (an exception is unfunded defined-benefit plans, which is the private sector variant of a PAYG system).

In most industrialised countries, the public pension schemes are now faced with the difficulty that the number of contributors is in rapid decline compared with the number of those in receipt of a pension. The problems are most severe in countries that face the dangerous combination of (1) an ageing population, (2) a generous public pension system and (3) a PAYG system. Countries such as Germany, France and Italy have large unfunded pension liabilities. The problems are less severe in countries where the ageing is less pronounced (for example, due to immigration) and the public pensions are less generous and/or use advance-funded systems for their mandatory earnings-related programmes.

Due to the enormity of pension-payment obligations, falling relative levels of public pension payments, as well as increased levels of contributions, are to be expected in many countries. More and more people are becoming aware of the increasing financial difficulties of public pension schemes and are turning to private pension products to close the resulting gaps. Also, many governments are actively stimulating private retirement savings by means of tax incentives. Thus, there currently is a shift from a publicly managed, defined-benefit programme financed on a PAYG basis to privately managed, individual defined-contribution accounts, financed on an advance-funding basis.[6,7]

4.3.2 Defined-benefit versus defined-contribution pension plans

Pension funds may operate under different types of pension plans or agreements about the amounts and timing of the contributions to the fund and distributions from the fund. Pension plans can be categorised as defined-benefit or defined-contribution.

Under a defined-benefit pension plan, the plan sponsor promises the employee a specific benefit when they retire. The benefits are usually determined according to a formula that accounts for the years of service and the salary history of the employee. For example, the plan sponsor may agree to pay the employee for life, starting at the age of 65, an annual pension that is computed according to the following formula:

Benefit = 2% × average salary of final 5 years of service × years of service

If an employee had worked for 28 years and the average salary during the last five years of service was $80 000, then the annual benefit would be:

Benefit = 2% × $80 000 × 28 = $44 800

The defined-benefit plan puts the burden on the plan sponsor to provide sufficient funds to ensure that the benefits can be paid out. Hence, the sponsor absorbs the investment risk associated with investing the contributions made to cover the benefits. The obligation to pay the promised benefits functions as a fixed long-run liability for the sponsor.

In defined-benefit pension plans, there is a distinction between the liabilities and the funds invested to cover the liabilities. If no funds are reserved, then the plan is said to be unfunded. When the reserves are worth less than the promised payments, then the plan is underfunded. If the plan's assets have a market value that exceeds the value of the liabilities, it is overfunded.

In contrast to a defined-benefit plan, a defined-contribution pension plan specifies only what will be contributed into the fund. The retirement benefits are dependent entirely on the investment performance of the contributed funds. Hence, the employee bears all the investment risk. Sponsors of defined-contribution plans, and in most cases also the employees, pay a predetermined fraction of the employee's salary into the pension account each pay period, although that fraction need not be constant over the course of the employee's career. An insurance company or fund manager acts as a trustee and invests the fund's assets. Frequently, the employee has some choice in asset allocation. For example, a conservative employee may choose to invest in government bonds, while a more aggressive employee may choose to invest in corporate bonds or stocks. By contrast, the participant in a defined-benefit

---

[6] Although we use the term 'defined benefit', state pensions usually have the caveat that the government can adjust the benefits, whereas a defined benefit programme in the private sector is often contractually bound to a predefined level of benefits.

[7] Alternative means of addressing the pension problem, such as raising the general taxation level and/or the mandatory social charges on employees and employers, show themselves to be politically difficult or impossible to implement.

plan is not required (or able) to make investment decisions. At retirement, the balance in the pension account can be transferred into an annuity or some other form of distribution. A defined-contribution plan can never be unfunded or underfunded, because the value of the retirement benefit by definition equals the value of the assets in the pension account.

In a 401(k) plan, the most common type of defined-contribution plan in the USA, income that would have been paid to the employee is deposited pretax in an account and invested; it may be matched to some degree by a contribution from the employer. Such plans also differ from traditional defined-benefit plans in that the contributions are voluntary, and as a result employees are covered only if they choose to contribute to an account. Under a 401(k) plan, employees also may be allowed some degree of control over how the contributions are invested.

During the 1980s, there was a shift in the type of pension plan that employees were covered by. The number of people covered by defined-benefit pension plans levelled off as companies attempted to reduce costs by forcing employees to contribute to their own plans, such as 401(k) plans (defined-contribution plans), or by terminating the plans. One reason for the increased popularity of defined-contribution plans is that the burden is put on the employee rather than the sponsor to look out for the investment performance. This reduces the liability of the sponsor and increases the flexibility for the employee to control the asset allocation of their investment and to transfer funds when changing employer. Still, the two types of pension plans are not mutually exclusive. Many sponsors adopt a defined-benefit plan as their primary plan, in which participation is mandatory, and supplement it with a defined-contribution plan in which participation is voluntary.

4.3.3 Investment policy of pension funds

Like life insurance companies, pension funds have very large liabilities; they have to pay out large sums of retirement money during the entire retirement period of a pensioner. Pension funds that are operated under an advance-payment scheme rather than a PAYG scheme accumulate large pools of money to cover these liabilities and invest this money in the capital market. Hence, like life insurers, pension funds are among the largest investors in the world. For example, the California Public Employees' (Calpers) and Teachers' Pension Funds (Calstrs) and the New York State Pension Fund are the three largest public pension funds in the USA and had a combined portfolio of more than $340 billion in 2003. Europe's largest pension fund, ABP Investments, the Dutch public employees' pension fund, had roughly 140 billion euros in assets in 2003.

At the heart of every pension company is matching the risks of the pension liabilities with offsetting risks of the financial assets. The liabilities of a pension fund are complex and depend on many factors, such as the workforce characteristics (for example, the ratio of active members to retirees), the type of pension scheme (for example, the share of defined-benefit plans) and actuarial assumptions (for example, life expectancy, promotion chances and disability chances). Asset–liability management aims to match the expected future cash flow of the pensioners with the assets, i.e. invest in such a manner that future flows can be financed with a high degree of confidence.

Despite the similarities, the typical investment policy of pension funds differs from that of life insurers. Most notably, while life insurers invest predominantly in money-market and credit-market investments, pension funds typically invest more in equity and real estate. Partly, the use of these instruments can be explained by the aforementioned insights about risk and return; risky assets are useful in order to increase the replacement ratio (ratio of pension benefits to final salary) in defined-contribution plans and reduce the sponsor's contributions in defined-benefit schemes. However, there are also several key differences between life insurance and pension funds:

- Defined-benefit plans are typically linked to the wage level, and hence the liabilities are denominated in real terms rather than fixed in nominal terms. Also, the pensions in payment to pensioners are typically indexed to correct for inflation. However, the coupon and principal payments of fixed-income instruments are stated in nominal terms. By contrast, the prices of commercial and residential property generally increase during periods of inflation and increasing wages. Similarly, corporations frequently can pass on inflation and rising labour costs (in part or in whole) to their customers by increasing the prices of their products and services, hence mitigating the effects of inflation on corporate earnings and dividends.[8] By contrast, life insurers' liabilities are typically fixed in nominal terms.

- Unlike insurance companies, occupational pension funds have a link to a non-financial firm, whose own capital is effectively the backup for a defined-benefit fund. Where the firm is solvent, this is often a more extensive source of capital than a life insurer's capital base – in principle, the entire equity of a firm could be used. Furthermore, a company's equity is subject to shocks that are relatively independent of those affecting pension assets. Arguably, this more extensive backup could justify riskier strategies in pension funds than for life insurers.[9]

- The adoption of defined-contribution plans that do not fix the pension fund's liabilities and allow employees to take risks. In a defined-contribution pension fund, the sponsors are responsible only for making contributions to the plan. There is no guarantee regarding assets at retirement, which allows for active investment in high-risk, high-return assets to maximise the growth of the assets of the plan.

- Life insurance companies are subject to risks not present for pension funds to the same degree, such as liquidity risk for policy loans and guaranteed early surrender values. As noted, these have traditionally been seen as requiring heavy investment in low-yielding, capital-certain assets.

Some pension funds carry out their investment functions in house. More commonly, a share of the funds under management is placed with professional fund managers, who develop asset-allocation strategies and make investment decisions on behalf of their institutional investor clients. Fund management is typically carried out by investment banks, insurance companies or independent fund-management companies. Fund managers actively compete for mandates to manage funds from pension plans, life insurance companies, and others.

Some funds use active investment strategies, while others use passive investment strategies based on indexing to broad market benchmarks or immunisation, a passive bond-management strategy that aims to match the risk profile of assets and liabilities. There is a large body of evidence that shows that, for most fund managers, it is difficult to outperform or beat their benchmark performance indexes consistently (see Chapter 22). Nevertheless, many institutional

---

[8] Inflation protection also provides the rationale for inflation-indexed bonds (see Chapter 13).

[9] On the other hand, pension funds have no explicit capital base of a pension fund, unlike an insurer. There may be surplus assets, but these are typically limited by tax regulations and may be run down by the sponsor (via 'contribution holidays') in order to boost its profitability. In contrast, life companies have their capital as a cushion against errors and also non-guaranteed bonuses on variable policies. A corollary is that any excess returns on defined-benefit pension funds accrue to the sponsor gradually over time (via 'contribution holidays'), while excess returns on investments profit the insurance company directly.

Exhibit 4.4	Financial assets of US private pension funds (end of year, dollars in billions)						
	1990	1992	1994	1996	1998	2000	2002
Chequeable deposits and currency	3.3	3	4	5.4	5.7	7.1	6.5
Time and savings deposits	110.4	98.8	102.1	111.9	147.7	147.6	152.6
Money-market fund shares	17.8	19.8	31.6	48.4	63.4	79.6	71.8
Security repurchase agreements	23.5	27.4	22.2	26.7	28.8	29.6	32.3
Credit-market instruments	464.2	515.6	591.4	601.4	621.1	666.5	700.5
Open-market paper	26.3	29.4	23.9	30.1	34.3	35.8	44.4
US government securities	255.5	265.2	332.6	319.5	279.9	301.4	309.4
Treasury	122.4	108.7	121.1	115.8	85.1	76.1	66.9
Agency	133.1	156.5	211.5	203.7	194.8	225.2	242.5
Corporate and foreign bonds	157.1	206.5	227.1	242.9	297.5	317.9	332.2
Mortgages	24.9	14.5	7.8	9	9.3	11.5	14.5
Corporate equities	605.9	873.7	1013.7	1445.2	1947.9	2137.8	1417.6
Mutual fund shares	40.5	96.2	205.9	412.3	668.2	733.6	533.5
Miscellaneous assets	361.1	401.5	462.9	555.5	622.2	621.3	617.8
Total financial assets	1626.7	2036	2433.8	3206.8	4104.8	4423.1	3532.6

Source: Federal Reserve Board Flow of Funds, www.federalreserve.gov

investors are still willing to pay for active management – and the more an institution believes that the skills of a portfolio manager are worth paying for, the more the manager will be allowed to deviate from the benchmark index. In fact, many pension funds follow a hybrid strategy, where the fund maintains a passive core, which is an indexed or immunised position, and augments that position with actively managed portfolios.

Exhibit 4.4 shows the distribution of the financial assets of US private pension funds. Clearly, the amounts invested are enormous. With more than $3.5 trillion of financial assets, private pension funds are the largest institutional investor. In this exhibit, we see that a large portion of pension fund assets is held in corporate equities. Another sizeable portion is placed in mutual funds. The growing role of defined-contribution plans has led to strong linkages between pension funds and mutual funds; numerous mutual funds (most notably in the equities sector) are strongly influenced by 401(k) and other pension inflows. The reliance on corporate equity also explains why the total asset portfolio of private pension grew quickly in the late 1990s and fell sharply in the early 2000s. By contrast, the portfolio value of life insurance assets increased more gradually (see Exhibit 4.4).

Again, this exhibit represents the aggregate over all private pension funds in the USA. The investment portfolio of individual funds may be very different, depending on, for example, the balance between defined-benefit and defined-contribution plans. An additional factor that will influence the portfolio distributions of an individual pension fund is maturity – the ratio of active to retired members. The duration of liabilities (i.e. the average time to discounted pension payment requirements) is much longer for an immature fund having few pensions in payment than for a mature fund where sizeable repayments are required. A fund that is closing down (or 'winding up') will have even shorter duration liabilities. It is often suggested that given the varying duration of liabilities, it is rational for immature funds having 'real' liabilities as defined above to invest mainly in equities (whose cash flows have a long duration), for mature funds to invest in a mix of equities and bonds, and funds that are winding-up to invest mainly in bonds (whose cash flows have a short duration).

Share rises fail to ease pension deficits

Members of UK pension schemes are no better off today than they were a year ago, despite the best stock market performance seen since the heyday of the late 1990s.

The drop in interest rates over the past year has all but wiped out the impact of strong equity returns, according to Watson Wyatt, the actuarial consultant. The firm says it would take three more such years of surging equities to wipe out the pension deficit of UK companies. It calculates that the underfunding in UK employers' schemes is now roughly equal to that at the start of 2003. Among FTSE 100 companies, the aggregate deficit on company balance sheets is about £60 bn. Across the UK as a whole, company deficits are probably twice that, Watson Wyatt says.

Robert Hailes, a partner in the benefits consultancy practice at the firm, said: 'In order for [. . .] deficits to be removed through stock market rises alone, we would need to see the very strong recovery in equity markets experienced in 2003 be repeated for at least another three years. This is substantially above the level expected by many commentators, and so it could well take substantially longer than this.'

The new calculation underscores why the UK's pensions deficit is a much more intractable problem than many had believed – the deficits are created as much by low interest rates as they are by falling stock markets. In other words, although rising share prices may give people in company pension schemes a bigger pot, the retirement income available from those savings falls when interest rates are low.

Even people who are not relying on a pension from their employer but are saving for their own pension are affected. This is because they must buy an annuity – a contract that exchanges a lump sum for a regular income until your death – when they retire. And these are more expensive when interest rates are low.

'While a rising stock market has been positive, the liabilities of pension schemes have increased because of higher inflation expectations and lower corporate bond yields,' said Mr Hailes. 'The stock market recovery was clearly welcome but rising liabilities mean it has done little to eat into these accounting deficits,' he said.

Source: Norma Cohen, Share rises fail to ease pension deficits, *Financial Times*, 17 January 2004.

→ Making the connection

As discussed in Section 4.2.1, public pension schemes that are operated on a PAYG basis are facing increasing difficulties due to the ageing of the population. Meanwhile, advance-funded private pension funds in many countries are facing their own problems. There currently is not enough money in pension funds to guarantee a comfortable retirement for today's working population. There are several factors that explain why pension funds are underfunded. Medical advances over the past few decades have greatly prolonged our lifespan, forcing the pensions industry to support a greater number of pensioners for longer periods. However, many funds were slow to respond to longer life expectancy. In fact, several of the funds admitted to having taken 'pension holidays' in recent years when they were overfunded due to the sustained equity bull market. The bear stock market severely reduced the funds reserves and caused many funds to be underfunded. According to the article above, the pension deficit is £120 bn in the UK alone. In 2003, stock markets rebounded. For example, UK equities delivered total returns exceeding 21%. Surprisingly, these stock returns did not reduce the pension deficits. The problem is that the increased value of the assets is offset by the increased value of the retirement liabilities, leaving the pension deficit unaffected.

To see the problem pension funds face, suppose you currently have $100 000 invested in equity mutual fund shares for your retirement income in 30 years' time. Based on your calculations, you will need a final value of about $400 000 to lead a pleasant life as a pensioner. If the expected return on this investment currently is 5% per annum, then the expected value of the portfolio after 30 years is $100 000 × 1.05^{30} = $432 194, which exceeds the desired amount.

Now suppose the value of the investments increases by 20% to $120 000 due to a stock-market rally. Surely this is positive news if you immediately liquidate the portfolio and use the proceeds to fund current consumption? However, your objective is to fund your future retirement income rather than your current consumption. Of course, if the expected return on investment remains 5% per year, then the expected value of the portfolio after 30 years increases to $120 000 × 1.05^{30} = $518 633. However, if the expected return falls to 3% per year, then the expected future value of the portfolio decreases to $120 000 × 1.03^{30} = $291 272, which is far less than the desired amount.

Thus, we see that rising stock prices do not necessarily make long-run investors better off. Pension funds face exactly the same problem. To reduce the current deficits of pension schemes, both rising stock prices and rising interest rates are needed, so that the value of the assets increases relative to the value of the liabilities.

Later on in this book, we will see that the price of stocks is equal to the discounted value of the expected future dividend payments to the stockholder, where dividends are discounted at the current risk-free interest rate plus a risk premium. Rising stock prices may reflect (1) improved prospects about the corporate sales, earnings and dividends, (2) an increased willingness to invest and take investment risk at a lower rate of return, or (3) a combination of these two explanations. For a long-run investor, rising stock prices are not good news if they reflect lower rates of return rather than improved corporate prospects.

4.4 Investment companies

An investment company or trust company is an organisation that takes a pool of investors' money and invests it in securities according to a stated set of investment objectives. Like other publicly held companies, investment companies start by selling shares to a group of investors. These investment companies invest in securities rather than plant and equipment. Thus, investment companies manage a portfolio of securities on behalf of their shareholders. In contrast to pension funds and insurance companies, mutual funds do not have fixed pension or insurance liabilities and their investment strategies are determined by client demand rather than by their financial liabilities.

Investment companies run three basic types of funds: open-end funds, closed-end funds and hedge funds. Open-end funds (also known as mutual funds) are able to issue new shares on a daily basis. Specifically, supply and demand for mutual fund shares govern how many shares are outstanding at any point in time. When an investor buys shares of a mutual fund, the purchase is made directly from the mutual fund that issues new shares. When an investor sells shares of a mutual fund, the sale is made directly with the mutual fund, which redeems the old shares. Closed-end funds (also known as investment trusts) are not able to issue new shares daily.[10] The investor who wishes to purchase shares of a closed-end fund must find a willing seller, whereas an investor can purchase shares of an open-end fund directly from the investment company. Most closed-end company shares trade on an exchange such as the NYSE or the AMEX. Therefore, the behaviour of closed-end funds is much like that of common stock. As a particular fund becomes popular, demand rises, as does the market value of the closed-end fund shares. Investors do not trade the closed-end fund shares directly with the investment company; they trade in the secondary market. From time to time, closed-end investment companies do issue new shares in the same manner as other corporations.

Hedge funds are different from open-end and closed-end funds. A hedge fund is an unregistered, privately offered, managed pool of capital for wealthy, financially sophisticated investors. Hedge funds are usually structured as private partnerships, with the general partner being the portfolio manager and making the investment decisions and the investors being the limited partners.

4.4.1 Open-end funds

Unlike closed-end funds, open-end funds (or mutual funds) can issue additional shares and buy shares when investors wish to sell. Thus, a mutual fund trades directly with investors. The price is not determined by demand and supply but rather by an estimate of the current market value of the fund's net assets per share and a commission (see below). This estimate of current value is called the net asset value (NAV). Specifically, NAV is the current market value of all securities held by the fund less any net liabilities divided by the total number of shares outstanding. NAV is adjusted for liabilities to better represent the true value of a share in a closed-end fund, just as the book value of equity for a normal corporation is assets minus liabilities. One liability is securities purchased but not yet paid. (On most security exchanges, there is a two-day or three-day settlement period between the time securities are purchased and their payment date.) Other liabilities include accrued fees, options that have been written, dividends payable and other accrued expenses.

Mutual funds can be classified broadly as either no-load or load. Load mutual funds are sold in the OTC market by dealers who do not receive an up-front sales commission. Instead, a load (or sales commission) is added to the NAV at the time of the purchase. A load is a fee paid to the seller of mutual funds. For example, a 3% load means that for every dollar invested in the OTC fund, three cents go to the dealer and only 97 cents are actually invested in the fund. If an investor bought a mutual fund for only one year and it earned 10%, the load would take about 30% of the earnings, resulting in a gain of only 7%. However, over a long period of time, this cost would decline on a percentage basis.[11] For many years, the typical load was 8.5%, but currently one often finds funds with loads of 4–5%. Many load funds do not have an up-front load but rather impose a back-end load, which customers pay if they sell the fund

---

[10] This terminology of investment companies is not always well-defined, and it can be confusing. For example, in the UK, mutual funds are called unit trusts. Also, it is common practice to refer loosely to both closed-end and open-end companies as mutual funds. This chapter adheres to the strict definition and uses the term 'mutual fund' to refer only to open-end companies.

[11] However, a load is still costly over time in absolute dollar terms. For example, for 25 years, a $10 000 investment in the load fund would be worth $(\$10\,000 \times 0.97)(1 + 0.1)^{25} = \$105\,096.65$, which is a 9.866% annual rate of return. The no-load fund, with the same 10% annual rate of return, would be worth $\$10\,000(1 + 0.1)^{25} = \$108\,347.06$, or $3250.41 more. Thus, this load would result in the investor losing $3250.41, but only 0.134% on an annual percentage basis.

shares within a stated period of time (for example, five years). Note that loaded funds may also charge fees on an annual basis (for instance, custodian fees). No-load mutual funds are bought directly from the funds, and no sales commission is added to the NAV. Of course, no-load funds also incur selling and advertising expenses. However, rather than charging a load, these expenses are treated as part of the ongoing expenses of the fund and are included in the annual management fees (also called the expense ratio when expressed as a percentage of assets) of the fund.[12]

Each mutual fund is required by law to provide a prospectus to investors. The prospectus contains information regarding the fund's objectives, fund expenses, historical performance, risks, who should invest and who is managing the fund. The Investment Company Act of 1940 requires every mutual fund to state its specific investment objectives in the prospectus. By reading a mutual fund's prospectus, an investor can easily determine its objective – in other words, what type of fund it is.

There exist many different types of mutual funds. Bonds and income funds and equity funds are are long-term oriented. Money-market mutual funds (MMMFs) invest in debt securities of very short maturities. Most money-market funds allow investors to write cheques on the balance invested in the fund. Hence, these funds have to be highly liquid. Moreover, they are a legal way to circumvent the unpopular Regulation Q, which prohibits banks from paying interest on current accounts; MMMFs can be almost as liquid, making them a popular alternative. Money-market funds typically invest in US government debt, commercial paper, bank certificates of deposit, repurchase agreements, banker's acceptances and other short-term securities. Money-market funds have very little risk and have many restrictions on how they can invest shareholders' money. For example, the SEC requires money-market funds to invest solely in commercial paper in the top two grades as evaluated by the rating agencies Moody's and Standard & Poor's.

Most mutual funds are members of a group of mutual funds known as a family of funds, such as American Funds, Fidelity Investments and Vanguard. One benefit of a family of funds is the ease with which investors can reallocate their investment money among funds in a family.

Exhibit 4.5 shows data on the largest ten mutual funds operating in the USA.[13] Fidelity Magellan is the biggest, with an average $60.3 billion of assets, followed by the Fidelity Growth & Income Fund, with $56.8 billion of assets. For the five-year period, American Funds Growth Fund shows the highest rate of return, while for 2003 (up to 11 December 2003), American Funds New Perspective Fund has the highest year-to-date (YTD) rate of return.

Index funds are mutual funds that simply replicate a given index. For example, S&P index funds simply invest in the stocks and weights that compare with the S&P 500 index. Due to this simple investment strategy, index funds generally have relatively low management fees; for example, the Vanguard 500 index, which tracks the S&P 500 index, charges only 0.2% annually as a management fee. However, index funds hold no cash (because they replicate the

---

[12] In the USA, fees for selling and advertisement expenses are known as 12b-1 fees. On 28 October 1980, the SEC adopted Rule 12b-1, allowing mutual funds to pay selling expenses directly rather than charging investors a load. At issue is whether selling expenses are part of the ongoing expenses of the fund or whether they are a one-time expense that is charged at the purchase date. By law, fund managers have to decide whether to invest in securities or to pay a sales force. From the time of the passage of Rule 12b-1, many funds have opted to use 12b-1 fees to pay selling and advertising costs.

[13] These data are taken from Morningstar. Morningstar, Inc., located in Chicago, is one of the most prominent providers of information about returns and characteristics of mutual funds. The homepage can be found at www/morningstar.com/

Exhibit 4.5	The ten largest mutual funds in the USA (end 2003)					

Fund	NAV ($bn)	Investment objective[1]	YTD return	Three-year return	Five-year return
Fidelity Magellan	60.3	Large blend stocks	18.95	−8.49	−0.39
Fidelity Growth & Income	56.8	Large blend stocks	14.01	−6.17	−0.56
Vanguard 500	42.5	Large blend stocks	22.29	−6.87	−0.52
American Funds Invmt Co of America	34.3	Large value stocks	20.41	−0.27	4.49
American Funds Washington Mutual A	30.7	Large value stocks	19.61	2.54	3.4
American Funds New Perspective A	28.6	Large growth stocks	28.94	−0.42	6.07
American Funds Growth Fund of America A	22.9	Large growth stocks	26.48	−5.94	7.79
American Funds EuroPacific Gr	15.8	Large blend stocks	26.12	−1.92	4.78
Fidelity Contrafund	11.5	Large growth stocks	21.89	−1.62	4.1
Pimco Total Return		High intermediary bonds	4.91	8.66	7.15

[1] The investment objective is characterised by the Morningstar style category. For stocks, Morningstar distinguishes between large, medium and small cap stocks and value, blend and growth stocks. For bonds, Morningstar distinguishes between short, intermediate and long maturity bonds and between high, medium and low credit quality.

NAV, net asset value; YTD, year to date.

Source: www.morningstar.com, 11 December 2003.

S&P 500 index); hence, stocks held by the fund must be sold whenever investors redeem shares. This characteristic can cause difficulties for the fund's management and place some annoying obstacles in the way of investors seeking quick redemptions. For example, index funds may not allow investors to sell shares by a telephone call, and they may charge a redemption fee for shares held for less than a given period, say six months. For instance, Dreyfus Corporation, a $1.2 billion S&P 500 index fund, charges a 1% redemption fee for shares held for less than six months.

→ **Connecting Theory to Practice 4.2**   **FT**

Mutual funds join the world of shorting

One way to beat this bear market has been to bet against it. A host of mutual funds is offering investors the means to short stocks and entire indices, a strategy that had been the exclusive domain of hedge funds serving institutions and high net worth investors.

Fund companies such as Rydex, ProFunds, Comstock and Prudent Bear are allowing individual investors to short the market with remarkable success. While the S&P 500 has been off by 22 per cent in the year to the end of October, the bear funds surveyed here are all up by more than 20 per cent, with several significantly leveraged versions soaring close to 70 per cent. And, at least in the near term, they may still have further to rise.

Richard Bernstein, Merrill Lynch's chief market strategist, believes the equity prospects remain muddled, with earnings growth being the least predictable in more than 60 years. Throw in the possibility of war with Iraq, continued fear of terrorism, and doubts that consumer spending will continue to buoy the economy, and shorting the market does not appear an unreasonable proposition.

Bear funds offer individual investors two basic strategies: passive and active shorting. The argument for the former: if index investing was the most efficient way to play the bulls, then shorting indices may indeed be one of the most effective ways to dance with the bear.

Rydex and ProFunds offer investors funds that perform in direct opposition to the S&P 500 and the Nasdaq 100 indices. If the indices drop 10 per cent, the funds rise 10 per cent.

Charles Tennes, director of portfolios at Rydex, says these funds were established because of the familiarity of these two big indices. 'Unlike actively managed short funds that could bet against an unknown mix of companies,' says Mr Tennes, 'our strategy is transparent and more cost-efficient, given the liquidity of futures contracts that track these indices.' Instead of buying puts on every one of their constituent holdings, Rydex shorts the widely traded, three-month futures contracts of the S&P 500 and Nasdaq 100. Because these are leveraged investments, requiring only about 5 per cent of assets to gain inverse exposure to the indices, the bulk of the funds' assets are kept in short-term fixed-income instruments. This enables Rydex to maintain call protection against its contracts so that the maximum loss can never exceed the amount of the investment. 'When investors short a stock or an index,' explains Mr Tennes, 'they are taking on limitless liability. We have capped this risk.'

Because Rydex and ProFunds do not charge to get into or out of their funds, investors can constantly adjust their bearishness, an essential appeal of these investments. 'We view the funds as short-term plays,' explains Michael Sapir, chief executive of ProFunds, 'because over the long term, we expect the markets to increase in value.' Accordingly, investors should look at these funds as tactical weapons to control losses when they think the market has clear reason to sag. These funds can also be useful in hedging one's technology exposure without having to unwind extensive positions and incur undesirable tax consequences.

However, George Nichols, a Morningstar analyst, warns that 'it is notoriously tough to time the markets and downside risk of these funds is huge since equity markets have tended to go up over time'. For those undeterred by such advice and who remain extraordinarily bearish, Rydex and ProFunds also offer funds designed to move 200 per cent in opposition with the S&P 500 and Nasdaq 100.

Some investors may be attracted by these higher leveraged funds as means to defend long positions with half the investment required by the 100 per cent versions, albeit with substantially greater volatility. For others, these plays transform the role of the short fund from a hedge to an aggressive growth strategy in a depressed market.

Instead of betting broadly against the market's big indices, Comstock Capital Value Fund and the Prudent Bear Funds offer investors an active management approach. Both have racked up stunning three-year annualised returns, with Comstock having realised annualised gains of nearly 19 per cent and Prudent Bear appreciating by more than 26 per cent. And their year-to-date returns are double these averages.

Source: 'Mutual Funds Join the World of Shorting', FT.com, 7 November 2002.

→ Making the connection

For small investors, holding shares of a mutual fund is an efficient means to diversify. If the market declines unexpectedly, the investor's losses will be limited. Unfortunately, until recently, there was no way by which a small investor could profit if he or she *expected* that the market would decline – the best the investor could do was to redeem his or her shares and thereby avoid a loss. However, as this newspaper article shows, nowadays the investor can invest also in a short position with a mutual fund when he or she expects that the market will decline.

4.4.2 Closed-end funds

A closed-end fund (investment trust) is a publicly traded investment company. Closed-end funds (or investment trusts) issue a specified number of shares, after which no additional shares are issued, unless a new public issue is conducted.

While open-end fund shares are purchased directly from the fund, most closed-end company shares trade on an exchange such as the NYSE or the AMEX. A mutual fund investor, depending on whether the fund is no-load or load, may pay a commission to buy and sell shares of the mutual fund. By contrast, a closed-end-fund investor pays a commission to a broker to buy or sell shares. Thus, trading closed-end fund shares is similar to trading individual stocks.

Closed-end funds are easier to manage than open-end funds. After the initial issue, the portfolio manager does not have to be concerned with day-to-day liquidity needs of the shareholders. Unlike open-end funds, which allow investors to redeem their shares at any time and which consequently must have funds available to provide for possible redemption, closed-end funds do not need to have a large amount of liquid funds available.

The pricing of closed-end funds differs from the pricing of open-end funds in that there are quotes for both the market price and the net asset value (NAV). The premium is the percentage difference between the current market price (P) and the NAV (dividing by the NAV) if the difference is positive. If the difference is negative, it is called the discount. For example, the Adams Express Fund was trading on Friday 27 July 2001 for $17.25 and the NAV was $19.34. Hence, the discount was:

$$\text{Discount} = \frac{P - \text{NAV}}{\text{NAV}} = \frac{\$17.25 - \$19.34}{\$19.34} = -0.108$$

or a 10.8% discount.

Although some funds trade at a premium, the majority of closed-end funds trade at a discount, often as much as 15–20%. The premium or discount is not constant but usually fluctuates with market conditions. The following are some of the factors that affect the premium or discount are as follows:

- The premium or discount may reflect inferior or superior investment performance of the fund. A fund that consistently underperforms the market or other relevant benchmarks (for example, due to excessive transaction costs or management costs) will eventually trade at a discount as investors leave the fund and fewer investors buy into the fund. Similarly, a fund that consistently outperforms (for example, due to superior skills of market timing or stock-pickings) will trade at a premium.

- Many of the older closed-end funds may have substantial capital gains since the securities they bought years ago may be worth a lot more now. New investors who buy such funds may find themselves with a large capital gains tax liability if the funds unwind some of their older profitable positions. For example, if an investor buys shares worth $1000, and the next day the fund returns $200 as a capital gains distribution, the investor pays taxes on the $200 returned to him or her (assuming it is a taxable investment), even though he or she did not own the fund during the time it racked up the substantial gains. Such funds tend to trade at a discount.

- Some funds tend to trade at premiums because they offer the only vehicle for unique investment opportunities that are not directly accessible to individual investors. For example, many countries do not allow individual investors to participate in their securities markets or restrict the foreign ownership of their securities. Funds that invest in such markets often trade at a premium, since investors who seek to participate in these markets are forced to buy these funds.

■ Many closed-end funds invest in private placements, provide venture capital, or invest in companies under bankruptcy reorganisation. The valuation of such investments is difficult since no direct measure of the marketability of the shares of these companies is available. Funds with such hard-to-evaluate investments often trade at a discount.

■ Closed-end funds operate in relative obscurity, and hence the price may drift away from the NAV due to investor ignorance. Mutual funds advertise extensively to attract new capital, because the management is paid a percentage of the assets managed. By contrast, closed-end funds generally operate with a fixed capital base. Advertising will not increase the assets managed; instead, the cost of advertising erodes the assets of the fund.

Real-estate investment trusts (REITs) are a special type of closed-end fund. REITs invest in real-estate property in a wide array of sectors, such as apartments, shopping malls and offices. The Real Estate Investment Trust Act of 1960 granted tax-exempt status to REITs. If certain conditions are met, a REIT may deduct all dividends paid to its shareholders and avoid federal taxation at the corporate level on the amount distributed. A REIT normally begins as a simple business trust or corporation. If a number of requirements are met on a year-by-year basis, the business trust or corporation may choose to be considered a REIT for federal tax purposes. REITs offer investors an efficient way to invest in real estate and diversify their portfolio whithout commiting large amounts of money. In the USA, the total market capitalisation of REITs stood at $162 billion at the end of 2002. The idea of REITs has also spurred to Europe, Japan and many other countries.

A unit investment trust (UIT) is an investment company that buys and holds a fixed portfolio of stocks, bonds, or other securities. 'Units' in the trust are sold to investors, who receive a proportionate share of dividends or interest received by the UIT. Unlike other investment companies, a UIT has a stated date for termination that varies according to the investments held in its portfolio. At termination, investors receive their proportionate share of the UIT net assets. At the end of 2002, UITs held $36.0 billion in assets. Of that total, more than half of the assets were held in bond trusts. Assets in bond trusts were $21.37 billion; assets in equity trusts were $14.65 billion.

An exchange-traded fund (ETF) is another type of closed-end fund. ETF shares are created by an institutional investor depositing a specified block of securities with the ETF. In return for this deposit, the institutional investor receives a fixed amount of ETF shares, some or all of which may then be sold on a stock exchange.

The first index shares created by AMEX were Standard & Poor's Depository Receipts (SPDRs). Separate SPDRs were created for the S&P 500 and the S&P Mid-Cap 400. Trading in S&P 500 SPDRs was introduced in 1993, and trading in the S&P Mid-Cap 400 began in 1995.

Seventeen World Equity Benchmark Shares (WEBS) began trading the Morgan Stanley Capital International (MSCI) stock market indices of a single foreign country in 1996. Dow Diamonds, an index product based on the Dow Jones Industrial Average, began trading in early 1998. Each of these unit trusts represents a stake in the 30 stocks that make up the Dow Jones index. Each Diamond is sold for the equivalent of 1% of the value of the index. Thus, if the index is traded for, say, 8000, then the Diamond price is determined as $80. The Diamonds were followed by the NASDAQ 100 Shares, also known as QQQs or Qubes, which track the NASDAQ 100 stock index. Even though they have only been around since March 1999, Qubes are so popular that their daily trading volume rivals that of companies on the NYSE.

Although we classify ETFs as closed-end funds, they actually function as open-end funds to large investors. Specifically, ETF shares can be redeemed in large quantities. For instance, the

S&P 500 SDPR can be redeemed in lots of 50 000 SPDRs, for which the investor then receives 5000 packets of the stocks in the S&P index (one SPDR represents one-tenth of the S&P index). Of course, small investors do not hold such large blocks of ETF shares and, hence, ETFs function like closed-end funds for them. However, large investors can redeem large blocks of ETF shares. This also means that the discount remains relatively low, since a large discount would make redemption profitable.

4.4.3 Hedge funds

A hedge fund is a private unadvertised investment partnership that is limited to institutions and high-net-worth individuals. Most hedge funds use strategies with high (short-term) risk, often specialising in a particular type of securities such as high-yield bonds or currency exposures. The minimum investment ranges from $250 000 to $10 million. There were an estimated 6000–7000 hedge funds in the USA with an estimated $650 billion in managed assets in 2003.

Hedge funds may engage in unlimited short-term trading, take short positions, use derivatives and borrow to a greater extent than other investment companies. Because of their ability to leverage and willingness to take risks, hedge funds may create sharp day-to-day security price movements and thereby provoke other institutions to similar action (for example, in exerting pressure on currency pegs).

Since hedge funds may take concentrated speculative positions, they can be very risky. For example, suppose that a fund takes a short position in government bonds and a long position in junk bonds, hoping that the price of junk bonds will increase relative to the price of government bonds. Put differently, the fund takes a bet that the credit spread or the default premium will fall.[14] If the spread increases, the hedge fund will incur losses. Having such a speculative position combined with a high degree of financial leverage may cause bankruptcy. Indeed, this is what almost happened to Long-Term Capital Management (LTCM), a large hedge fund that nearly collapsed in 1998.

Founded in 1993, LTCM initially was very successful. The early successes included the purchase of $2 billion 29.5-year US Treasury Bonds and short sale of $2 billion 30-year Treasury Bonds to exploit what it concluded was an unwarranted spread between the prices of these two securities. LTCM did not care whether interest rates went up, forcing all bond prices down, or interest rates went down, forcing all bond prices up. It was 'market-neutral', or 'hedged' against such uniform price moves in the bond market. It sought merely to take advantage of the historically wide spread between the prices of these two securities. Indeed, the fund made a $25 million profit on this transaction in a very short period of time.

In 1998, LTCM took a large position in Russian bonds and a large short position in US Treasuries when the spread between these two bonds was considered by LTCM to be very wide. It assumed that the spread could only narrow. The opposite occurred; the spread widened still further, inducing a massive loss to LTCM on 21 August 1998. By late 1998, LTCM's investors had lost over 90% of their capital. Thus, we see that despite its name, 'hedge fund', LTCM was a very speculative fund that took very risky positions.

---

[14] If the price of junk bonds falls, then the yield or internal rate of return of junk bonds will fall relative to the yield on Treasuries, narrowing the credit spread or the difference between the two yields. See Chapter 13 for more details on bond prices and bond yields.

Where did LTCM come from?

In the 1980s and early 1990s, Salomon Brothers made billions of dollars through its proprietary trading. Most of those profits came from its bond arbitrage group led by John Meriwether. This group was created to take advantage of misvaluations of securities with correlated risks by taking a short position in the overpriced security and a long position in the underpriced one, hedging those risks that could be hedged.

To understand this approach, suppose the group decided that the yield on a particular US agency bond was too high compared with US Treasury bonds (yields in fixed income markets are inversely related to the price of a security). Certain agency bonds benefit from various guarantees from the US government. Yet such bonds trade at a higher yield than comparable government bonds. The group would purchase the agency bond and sell short government bonds with the view that eventually the yields would converge – hence the term 'convergence trade' to denote such a position.

Because of government guarantees, the main risk of the bonds is interest rate risk, but the position would have little interest rate risk because of the offsetting bond positions. The position would generate cash because of the difference between the coupon received and the coupon to be paid on the short position. Further, any narrowing of the spread between the yields of the agency bonds and the Treasury bonds would create a capital gain.

Eventually, Salomon Brothers was embroiled in a scandal when an employee was charged with manipulating auctions for Treasury bonds. Several senior managers at Salomon left the institution in 1991, including Meriwether. Two years later, Meriwether founded Long-Term Capital Management (LTCM) to manage a hedge fund, the Long-Term Capital Portfolio. Hedge funds are unregulated, managed pools of money. LTCM was organised to pursue the strategies that the arbitrage group at Salomon Brothers had implemented and very quickly several members of this group joined LTCM, along with future Nobel Laureates Robert Merton and Myron Scholes.

Source: Rene Stultz, 'Why Risk Management Is Not Rocket Science', *Financial Times*, 27 June 2000.

→ Making the connection

This newspaper article explains that LTCM was a continuation of the successful arbitrage group at Salomon Brothers. Note that the term 'arbitrage' does not properly describe the actual trading activities, as arbitrage is supposed to be risk-free. Also, the term 'hedge fund' is somewhat misleading. In general, hedging means to offset the risk of a set of securities with another set of securities, usually derivatives. For example, an investor may hedge the risk of Microsoft stock by selling futures or buying put options on Microsoft stock. However, hedge funds typically are not (fully) hedged; they hedge against adverse movements of the general market but at the same time speculate on price differences between individual assets or asset classes. Hence, hedge funds can be very risky. Further details on LTCM can be found in Connecting Theory to Practice 21.2 and 21.2 and Investment in the News 19.

Summary

Define and explain the term 'institutionalisation'.

Institutionalisation refers to the rise of financial intermediaries such as pension funds, insurance companies and investment companies, which collect savings of individuals and non-financial companies and invest those savings in the financial markets. Institutionalisation can be explained by economies of scale in managing and diversifying financial assets and liabilities, demographic pressure on social security systems and the changing role of banks.

Discuss various types of insurance company and the investment behaviour of insurance companies.

We may distinguish between life insurers and property-casualty insurers. To cover their liabilities, life insurers build up large pools of funds that are invested in long-run financial assets. They invest heavily in credit-market and money-market investments in order to match their traditional nominal liabilities (term, whole life, universal policies and annuities) and to provide short-term liquidity to cover liabilities arising from early surrender of policies and policy loans. However, they may also invest a significant part of their fund in high-risk, high-return assets such as equities, real estate and international investments, depending on the share of variable life policies and the size of the surplus of the firm. Property-casualty insurance usually has a much shorter term than most life insurance and their risks are insurance risks that benefit less from the law of large numbers. Hence, property-casualty insurers hold less long-term financial assets than life-insurers.

Discuss various types of pension funds and the investment behaviour of pension funds.

Recently, there has been a shift from publicly managed pension schemes that are financed on a pay-as-you-go (PAYG) basis to private pension fund and advanced-funded systems. There are two primary types of pension plan: defined-benefit and defined-contribution. Defined-benefit plans pay benefits according to a predetermined formula that depends on salary and service. Defined-contribution plans specify only how much is to be saved; benefits depend on the returns generated by the plans. The employees in such plans bear all the risk of the plan's assets and often have some choice in asset allocation. Recently, there has been a shift towards defined-contribution plans, to reduce the liability of the sponsor and increase the flexibility for the employee to control the asset allocation of their investment and to transfer funds when changing employers. On average, pension funds invest heavily in corporate equities and property, so as to hedge against their natural exposure to wage level and price level increases.

Compare and contrast hedge funds with closed-end and open-end funds.

A closed-end fund rarely issues more shares after the original issue; open-end (mutual) funds continue to issue more shares as well as redeem outstanding shares at the request of investors. Closed-end funds can trade at either a premium or a discount from the net asset value (NAV). One benefit of buying closed-end funds is the ability to purchase them at a discount from the funds' intrinsic net asset value. Mutual funds can be purchased at NAV plus a load, if there is one. Mutual funds are sold at NAV and can expand or contract according to investors' demands. Hedge funds are partnerships, which are less regulated than mutual funds and may take very risky, speculative positions using derivatives, short-selling and borrowing.

Key terms

401(k) plan 104
Actuarial tables 98
Advance-funded
    pension 102
Adverse selection 98
Annuity policy 99
Asset-liability management
    (ALM) 98
Automobile insurance 99
Closed-end fund 95
Credit insurance 99
Defined-benefit pension
    plan 103
Defined-contribution
    pension plan 103
Discount 113
Dow Diamonds 114
Exchange-traded fund 114
Facultative reinsurance 99
Family of funds 110
Fidelity insurance 99
Fire insurance 99
Guaranteed investment
    contracts 100
Hard-to-evaluate
    investments 114
Hedge fund 95
Index funds 110
Inland marine insurance 99

Institutional investors 95
Institutionalisation 96
Insurance company 95
Insurance premiums 97
Investment company 95
Investment performance 113
Investment trust 108
Investor ignorance 114
Law of large numbers 98
Life insurance company 98
Load 99
Marine insurance 99
Maturity 106
Money-market mutual
    funds 110
Mutual fund 95
NASDAQ 100 Shares 114
Net asset value (NAV) 109
No-load mutual fund 110
Non-life insurance 99
Open-end fund 108
Overfunded 103
Pay-as-you-go (PAYG)
    pension plan 102
Pension fund 95
Pension plan 103
Premium 113
Private health insurance 99
Private pension plan 102

Professional fund managers
    105
Property-casualty insurance
    99
Rate-making 98
Real-estate investment trusts
    114
Reinsurance 99
Standard & Poor's
    Depository Receipts
    (SPDRs) 114
State pension fund 102
Tax liability 113
Term-life insurance
    (temporary insurance) 98
Treaty reinsurance 99
Trust company 108
Underfunded 103
Underwriting 98
Unfunded 103
Unique investment
    opportunities 113
Unit investment trust 114
Universal life policy 98
Variable life policy 98
Whole-life policy
    (permanent insurance) 98
World Equity Benchmark
    Shares (WEBS) 114

Review questions

1 Why can a defined-contribution pension plan never be underfunded?

2 What's the difference in investment behaviour between life insurers and property-casualty insurers; and what's the reason for this difference?

3 Why must open-end funds keep more cash on hand than closed-end funds?

4 The ABC Fund, a closed-end fund, consists of three securities – 1000 shares of Security A, which is currently trading at $35; 2000 shares of Security B, which is trading at $45; and 3000 shares of Security C, which is trading at $55. What is ABC Fund's NAV if it has $87 000 in net liabilities and 10 000 shares outstanding?

5 Suppose the return on the S&P 500 index is 12%. A mutual fund has a group of experts who can earn 15%. The load is 2%, and the management fee is 1.5%. Supposing that you can buy the S&P 500 index, which of these two investments would you prefer?

 For an extensive set of review and practice questions and answers, visit the Levy–Post investment website at www.booksites.net/levy

Selected references

Anderson, S. C. and J. A. Born, 1989, 'The Selling and Seasoning of Closed-End Investment Company's IPOs', *Journal of Financial Services Research*, **2**, 131–150.

Anderson, S. C. and J. A. Born, 1992, *Closed-End Investment Companies: Issues and Answers*, Boston, MA: Kluwer Academic Publishers.

Anderson, S. C., J. A. Born and T. R. Beard, 1991, 'An Analysis of Bond Investment Company IPOs: Past and Present', *Financial Review*, **26**, 211–222.

Bodie Z., 1990, 'Pensions as Retirement Income Insurance', *Journal of Economic Literature*, **28**, 28–49.

Brauer, G. A., 1984, 'Open Ending Closed-End Funds', *Journal of Financial Economics*, **13** (4), 491–507.

Brown, K. C., W. V. Harlow and L. T. Starks, 1996, 'Of Tournaments and Temptations, an Analysis of Managerial Incentives in the Mutual Fund Industry', *Journal of Finance*, **51**, 85–110.

Cappiello, F., W. D. Dent and P. W. Madlem, 1990, *The Complete Guide to Closed-End Funds*, Chicago: International Publishing.

Corsetti, G. and K. Schmidt-Hebbel, 1997, 'Pension Reform and Growth', in Valdes-Prieto, S. (ed.), *The Economics of Pensions*, Cambridge: Cambridge University Press.

Crawford, P. J. and C. P. Harper, 1985, 'An Analysis of the Discounts on Closed-End Mutual Funds', *Financial Review*, **20**, 30–38.

Davis, E. P., 1995, *Pension Funds, Retirement-Income Security and Capital Markets – An International Perspective*, Oxford: Oxford University Press.

Davis, E. P. and Steil, B., 2001, *Institutional Investors*, Cambridge, MA: MIT Press.

Feldstein, M., 1978, 'Do Private Pensions Increase National Savings?', *Journal of Public Economics*, **10**, 277–293.

Ferris, S. P. and D. Chance, 1987, 'The Effect of 12b-1 Plans on Mutual Fund Expense Ratios: A Note', *Journal of Finance*, **42**, 1077–1082.

Financial Times (1999), 'Financial Times Survey: Pension Fund Investment', *Financial Times*, 21 May 1999.

Fredman, A. J. and G. C. Scott, 1991, *Investing in Closed-End Funds: Finding Value and Building Wealth*, New York: New York Institute of Finance.

Hendricks, D., J. Patel and R. Zeckhauser, 1993, 'Hot Hands in Mutual Funds: Short-Run Persistence of Relative Performance, 1974–1988', *Journal of Finance*, **48** (1), 93–130.

Hubbard R. G., 1986, 'Pension Wealth and Individual Saving, Some New Evidence', *Journal of Money, Credit and Banking*, **18**, 167–178.

Internet Closed-End Fund Investor (ICEFI), www.icefi.com

Investment Company Institute, *Mutual Fund Fact Book*, Washington, DC: Investment Company Institute.

Lee, C. C., A. Shleifer and R. H. Thaler, 1990, 'Closed-End Mutual Funds', *Journal of Economic Perspectives*, **4** (4), 153–164.

Lee, C. C., A. Shleifer and R. H. Thaler, 1991, 'Investor Sentiment and the Closed-End Fund Puzzle', *Journal of Finance*, **46**, 75–109.

Malkiel, B. G. and A. Radisich, 2001, 'The Growth of Index Funds and the Pricing of Equity Securities', *Journal of Portfolio Management*, **27** (2), 9–21.

Morningstar, *Mutual Fund Sourcebook*, Chicago: Mutual Fund Sourcebook.

Munnell, A. H., 1986, 'Private Pensions and Saving: New Evidence', *Journal of Political Economy*, **84**, 1013–1031.

O'Neal, E. S., 1997, 'How Many Mutual Funds Constitute a Diversified Mutual Fund Portfolio?', *Financial Analysts Journal*, **53** (2), 37–46.

Peavy, J. M., 1990, 'Returns on Initial Public Offerings of Closed-End Funds', *Review of Financial Studies*, **3**, 695–708.

Standard & Poor's/Lipper, *Mutual Fund Profiles*, New York: Standard & Poor's.

Trzcinka, C. and R. Zweig, 1990, *An Economic Analysis of the Cost and Benefits of S.E.C. Rule 12b-1*, Monograph 1990–1, New York: Salomon Brothers Center for the Study of Financial Institutions, Leonard N. Stern School of Business, New York University.

Wahal, S., 1996, 'Public Pension Fund Activism and Firm Performance', *Journal of Financial and Quantitative Analysis*, **31**, 1–23.

Weiss, K., 1989, 'The Post-Offering Price Performance of Closed-End Funds', *Financial Management*, **18**, 57–67.

CHAPTER 5

Security regulation and investment ethics

Investment in the News 5

FT

Wall Street banks draw up new code for analysts

Wall Street investment banks are planning concerted action to counter public concerns that their research analysts lack independence. Heads of research from the world's leading investment banks are in the final stages of negotiating an industry-wide code of best practice.

Investors, regulators and the media have criticised Wall Street banks for compromising the integrity of their research by using star analysts to attract corporate finance business and market stock issues.

Richard Baker, chairman of the House of Representatives' subcommittee on capital markets, has scheduled a hearing next month to explore potential conflicts of interest. In the meantime, trade bodies are working on remedies including disclosure of potential conflicts.

One person involved in one of the plans says it consists of 'a solid dozen' principles, to which Wall Street, asset managers and companies that issue securities would subscribe.

They include guidelines aimed at ending 'do a deal, get a dollar' compensation. This links the pay of analysts who work on initial public offerings or mergers to the amount the firm earns for advising on the deal. Bank chiefs will be expected to sign up to the idea that bonuses should be paid from a pool drawn from all fee income.

Another principle lays down that research departments should report to the chief executive rather than to business units. Although many banks recognise the problem, they tend to suggest it is worse at competitors, making it hard to agree on 'zero tolerance' of conflicts.

'If we don't clear up this public perception then the whole industry is going to be tarred with the same brush,' said Frank Fernandez, chief economist of the Securities Industry Association.

In a separate initiative, the Association for Investment Management and Research is due to unveil its planned code of conduct during its annual meeting today. Rich Wyler, AIMR spokesman, said it would include ways to measure compliance with the existing AIMR code of ethics.

Source: Andrew Hill and Gary Silverman, 'Wall Street Banks Draw Up New Code For Analysts', FT.com site, 21 May 2001.

After studying this chapter, you should be able to:

1 Explain why regulation is critical to the security markets.

2 Summarise the history and evolution of US securities regulation.

3 Discuss recent regulatory developments in the European Union.

4 Discuss the need for regulation at an international level.

5 Distinguish between regulation and ethics and describe key ethical issues of investment.

Football would not be enjoyable for players and spectators if there were no rules, no referee to enforce the rules and no players obeying the rules. Similarly, security markets cannot function properly without rules, institutions enforcing the rules and market participants (issuers, investment banks, retail and institutional investors, brokers, dealers, auditors, etc.) obeying the rules. In this respect, we must distinguish between regulations and ethics. Regulations are rules established by governments and imposed externally on market participants. Ethics embodies market participants' internal rules or their virtues and vices. A behaviour that is unacceptable based on ethical standards may be found acceptable by existing regulations. For example, paying an analyst to promote a certain stock in the hope that the promotional campaign will drive up demand will, in many cases, be considered unethical. However, it is not illegal, and it is a frequent practice in the market for penny-stocks. Indeed, it is hard to legislate some ethical issues.

Following the 1990s' bull market, the financial world was shaken by a series of scandals that have had a devastating effect on the public confidence in the functioning of financial markets. Investment in the News 5 discusses one of these scandals: the behavior of Wall Street analysts. It became painfully clear that investment analysts of many of the large Wall Street investment banks did not provide unbiased advice. Rather, the analysts issued overoptimistic recommendations to investors in return for securing investment bank business.

Analysts such as Jack Grubman (telecommunications analyst of Citigroup's Salomon Smith Barney investment bank) and Henry Blodget (Internet analyst of Merrill Lynch) each earned more than $20 million a year as they endorsed stocks that they privately disparaged. Blodget once described as 'a piece of shit' a stock that he was publicly touting, according to an email message released by regulators.

Apart from issuing favourable analyst research, regulators also accused investment banks of steering allocations of shares in much sought-after initial public offerings to executives in order to win investment banking work from companies.

Due to these and other scandals (including the accounting scandals discussed in Chapter 16), many investors now question the appropriateness of the existing regulations, the effectiveness of regulators to enforce regulations, and the discipline of key market participants to obey regulations and ethical standards. For this reason, there appears to be a need to overhaul the regulatory system so as to convince investors that the financial markets can be transparent and trustworthy.

This chapter discusses the regulation of security markets and investment ethics. Section 5.1 explains the need for regulation of financial markets. Next, Section 5.2 discusses US and international securities regulation. Section 5.3 reviews some of the major ethical problems confronting security market participants.

5.1 The need for security regulation

Basically, there exist three main rationales for regulation of security markets: systemic risk, information asymmetry and market entry and competition.

5.1.1 Systemic risk

Through securities markets, companies and governments can raise new capital and individuals can fund future expenses (for example, retirement income or the education of their children). The economy as a whole benefits from financial stability or the unimpaired functioning of financial markets; financial stability is a collective good.

To maintain a stable system, it is essential that market participants are confident that the financial system functions properly. In order for an individual to invest his or her money in a company's stock, he or she must feel confident that the company strives to create value for its shareholders and that the stock market functions properly by providing investors with timely and accurate information and the possibility to liquidate the stocks quickly and with low costs.

Systemic risk is the risk that the unscrupulous actions of a few market participants could undermine public confidence in the financial system. The security markets could stop functioning properly if market participants no longer believe that other participants will obey the rules. If public confidence is damaged, the cost of capital for security issuers will increase and the liquidity for investors will fall, causing enormous loss for the whole economy.[1]

Few people would want to deliberately diminish the public trust in the financial system, because everybody loses if the functioning of the system is impaired. Nevertheless, some unscrupulous people might place their short-term gain above the damage they might inflict on the financial system. Also, grave mistakes may shake the system even without malice playing a part. Either way, such cases often damage the confidence in the market as a whole. A few analysts issuing overly optimistic advice, a few auditors approving overly optimistic financial statements or a few mutual funds failing to fulfil their fiduciary duties may suffice for investor confidence to be damaged for a long time. In other words, regulation aims to raise the costs of pursuing personal gains at the risk of damaging public confidence in the financial system.

5.1.2 Information asymmetry

The economist's assumptions about market efficiency cease to be valid in the face of information asymmetry or differences in information available to buyers and sellers. A seminal article by Nobel Laureate George Akerlof described the market for lemons – that is, low-quality second-hand cars. Suppose 10% of all second-hand cars were lemons. You might expect the price of a second-hand car to reflect the frequency of lemons in the overall car population. But if it did, then selling at that price would be attractive to the owners of lemons

---

[1] Systemic risk is also an important reason for prudential regulation of banks. Banks are particularly subject to systemic risk because their liabilities are at call, meaning that a loss of confidence can lead to a 'run' on a bank. Banks are also a major source for transferring systemic risk to the wider economy because of their central role in the payments system. The payments system is the process by which obligations are settled between financial institutions. If a bank is unable to meet its settlement obligations, then problems in one institution can be transferred to others within the system and into the economy as a whole.

and unattractive to the owners of normal cars. Hence, there would be a disproportionate number of lemons in used-car showrooms. Realising this, buyers would reduce the price they were willing to pay. The result would be that only those with really dreadful cars, or who were desperate for money, would put their cars on the market. Hence, the new price would not be low enough to reflect the quality of the offered cars, the price would fall further, and so on. In the end, there may be very little trade at very low prices. It is even possible for the market to decay to the point of non-existence.

A lemon market can occur in all markets where the seller knows more than the buyer about a product (or cannot convince the buyer of the quality) and the seller doesn't bear fully the consequences of selling a lemon (that is, the seller is not required to provide a full warranty). The decay of the market is the logical implication of buyers rationally discounting the probability of a rip-off (which lowers the price), and the owners of high-quality products rationally withdrawing their products from the market (which lowers the quality).

The security market is also a possible lemon market because small individual investors have access to less information than security issuers and intermediaries. For example, in IPOs, investors will not know as much about the issuing firms as the firms' managers and investment banks. To compensate for the risk of adverse selection, the uninformed investor will bid a lower price for securities than the average value of the IPOs. Hence, underpriced IPOs will be withdrawn and only overpriced IPOs would remain for sale. With only these IPOs offered, the average price would fall to reflect the overpricing. Now, any IPO that is worth more than the new price would be withdrawn, and so on, and eventually the market would fail because only the lowest-quality IPOs were being marketed.

The authorities can mitigate the effect of information asymmetry by regulating disclosure and certification of information so that investors can make better-informed decisions. In most developed securities markets, regulation requires issuers to register new security offerings and to disclose all relevant information to potential investors. Also, publicly held companies are typically required to file reports periodically and when events of significant interest occur. These reports sometimes contain information not only about the company itself but also about its shareholders. For example, in the European Union, regulations require disclosure of stock ownership for investors who hold more than a certain percentage of the company's total stock.[2]

5.1.3 Market access and competition

Regulation of securities markets is also needed to enhance competition. Effective competition can promote efficiency and innovation and, eventually, lower prices and higher service quality for investors. For example, when the NYSE and NASDAQ failed to take full advantage of advances in communication and computer technology, the alternative trading systems (ATSs) entered the market to offer electronic trading, and the NYSE and the NASDAQ had to respond by also adopting the new technology (see Chapter 3).

Regulation is needed to eliminate unnecessary barriers to entry. For example, the ATSs could not have started to challenge the established markets without the SEC being extremely active in encouraging competition across market centres. Nevertheless, regulators face a difficult trade-off. On the one hand, market entry restriction is required to protect customers as well as to encourage incumbent market parties to make long-term investments in technology

---

[2] The concentration of shareholdership is relevant for issues such as the market liquidity of the shares, the effectiveness of corporate govenance and the possibilities for a hostile take-over.

and security. On the other hand, the imposition of unnecessarily high regulation and overly intrusive monitoring of institutions and markets can seriously inhibit competition, innovation and flexibility in the marketplace.

→ **Connecting Theory to Practice 5.1**

The SEC: who we are, what we do

The primary mission of the U.S. Securities and Exchange Commission (SEC) is to protect investors and maintain the integrity of the securities markets. As more and more first-time investors turn to the markets to help secure their futures, pay for homes, and send children to college, these goals are more compelling than ever.

The world of investing is fascinating, complex, and can be very fruitful. But unlike the banking world, where deposits are guaranteed by the federal government, stocks, bonds and other securities can lose value. There are no guarantees. That's why investing should not be a spectator sport; indeed, the principal way for investors to protect the money they put into the securities markets is to do research and ask questions.

The laws and rules that govern the securities industry in the United States derive from a simple and straightforward concept: all investors, whether large institutions or private individuals, should have access to certain basic facts about an investment prior to buying it. To achieve this, the SEC requires public companies to disclose meaningful financial and other information to the public, which provides a common pool of knowledge for all investors to use to judge for themselves if a company's securities are a good investment. Only through the steady flow of timely, comprehensive and accurate information can people make sound investment decisions.

The SEC also oversees other key participants in the securities world, including stock exchanges, broker-dealers, investment advisors, mutual funds, and public utility holding companies. Here again, the SEC is concerned primarily with promoting disclosure of important information, enforcing the securities laws, and protecting investors who interact with these various organizations and individuals.

Crucial to the SEC's effectiveness is its enforcement authority. Each year the SEC brings between 400–500 civil enforcement actions against individuals and companies that break the securities laws. Typical infractions include insider trading, accounting fraud, and providing false or misleading information about securities and the companies that issue them.

Fighting securities fraud, however, requires teamwork. At the heart of effective investor protection is an educated and careful investor. The SEC offers the public a wealth of educational information on its Internet website at www.sec.gov. The website also includes the EDGAR database of disclosure documents that public companies are required to file with the Commission.

Though it is the primary overseer and regulator of the U.S. securities markets, the SEC works closely with many other institutions, including Congress, other federal departments and agencies, the self-regulatory organizations (e.g. the stock exchanges), state securities regulators, and various private sector organizations.

Source: www.sec.gov

→ **Making the connection**

In the USA, the SEC is the central regulatory agency responsible for enforcing securities legislation. In the past, the SEC has repeatedly intervened in order to promote the integrity of the securities markets, the disclosure of information by issuers and intermediaries and competition between marketplaces and intermediaries.

5.2 Securities regulation[3]

In the previous section, we discussed reasons for regulation in general; these issues are relevant for any developed market. Despite these similar problems, the actual implementation of a regulatory framework differs significantly from market to market and from country to country. This section illustrates regulation in practice with Europe and the USA as its major examples.

5.2.1 History of US security regulation

In the USA, a national securities regulator was created only after the Wall Street panic of 1929. The crash and the following Great Depression provided arguments for those who desired to regulate the securities industry. During the decade following the crash, the US Congress passed several major securities acts designed to protect investors.

Often referred to as the 'truth in securities law', the Securities Act of 1933 has two basic objectives: (1) to require that investors receive financial and other significant information concerning securities being offered for public sale in the primary market and (2) to prohibit deceit, misrepresentations and other fraud in the sale of securities.

A primary means of accomplishing these goals is the disclosure of important financial information through the registration of securities. In general, securities sold in the USA must be registered. The registration forms that companies file provide essential facts while minimising the burden and expense of complying with the law. In general, registration forms call for (1) a description of the company's properties and business, (2) a description of the security to be offered for sale, (3) information about the management of the company, and (4) financial statements certified by independent accountants. This information enables investors to make informed judgements about whether to purchase a company's securities. While the SEC requires that the information provided be accurate, it does not guarantee it. Investors who purchase securities and suffer losses have important recovery rights if they can prove that there was incomplete or inaccurate disclosure of important information.

Registration statements and prospectuses become public shortly after filing with the SEC. If filed by US domestic companies, the statements are available on the Electronic Data Gathering, Analysis and Retrieval System (EDGAR) database accessible at www.sec.gov. Registration statements are subject to examination for compliance with disclosure requirements.

Not all offerings of securities must be registered with the SEC. Some exemptions from the registration requirement include: (1) private offerings to a limited number of people or institutions, (2) offerings of limited size, (3) intrastate offerings and (4) securities of municipal, state and federal governments. By exempting many small offerings from the registration process, the SEC seeks to foster capital formation by lowering the cost of offering securities to the public.

The US Banking Act of 1933, four sections of which are commonly referred to as the Glass–Steagall Act, required the separation of commercial and investment banking. This separation was motivated by the investment bankers' practice of using their commercial banking resources to manipulate stock prices. Recently, the Gramm–Leach–Bliley Act (GLBA) ended this separation (see below).

---

[3] This section is based in part on information from the SEC homepage, www.sec.gov

The Securities Exchange Act of 1934 regulates the secondary market (the security exchanges and the OTC market). The act also created the SEC to enforce securities legislation. Before 1934, there was no central regulatory agency responsible for enforcing securities legislation (although there was not much legislation to enforce). The SEC has the power to regulate commission rates established by the exchanges, to prohibit manipulative trading practices, and to monitor traders' practices.

The SEC is an independent, quasi-judiciary regulatory agency. The SEC is broken up into four basic divisions. The Division of Corporate Finance is in charge of making sure all publicly traded companies disclose the required financial information to investors. The Division of Market Regulation oversees all legislation involving brokers and brokerage firms. The Division of Investment Management regulates the mutual fund and investment advisor industries. Finally, the Division of Enforcement enforces the securities legislation and investigates possible violations.

Further, the 1934 act provides for the registration of exchanges, which are to be self-regulatory organisations (SROs). As self-regulatory organisations, US exchanges are required to perform a significant degree of internal regulation of their members; although they operate under rules mandated by the SEC, they are responsible for their own day-to-day regulation.[4]

Finally, Regulation T of the Securities Exchange Act gave the Federal Reserve Board (FRB) the authority to establish margin requirements for securities. The current margin requirement under Regulation T is 50%, which means that customers of brokerage firms who purchase securities deposit 50% of the total market value. The brokerage firm may lend the customer the remaining 50%. Marginable securities include all stocks listed on an exchange or on NASDAQ and those OTC stocks approved for margin by the FRB. Under Regulation T, the FRB can set payment dates for customers. Customers purchasing securities in a cash or margin account must pay for their purchase within seven days.

The Securities Acts Amendments of 1975 provided major changes to the Securities Exchange Act of 1934. Specifically, these amendments eliminated fixed commissions charged by brokers in order to make the exchanges more competitive and called for the establishment of a national market system.

The Public Utility Holding Company Act of 1935 (PUHCA) forces public-utility-holding companies to register with the SEC. This law requires utilities to file financial statements and other documents. The registration process puts more information about a company into the public domain. This legislation gave the SEC broad powers related to the management of public utilities.

The Maloney Act of 1938 amended the Securities Exchange Act of 1934 to bring the OTC market under SEC jurisdiction and encourages the development of associations such as the NYSE. The Maloney Act resulted in the development of the National Association of Securities Dealers (NASD), which was registered with the SEC in 1939.

The NASD is a self-regulatory non-governmental agency that regulates the sales of securities and oversees licences for brokers and brokerage firms. It investigates complaints against member firms and tries to ensure that all of its members adhere to both its own standards and

---

[4] The SEC has recently started discussion on the overhaul of the current regulatory system based on self-regulation. Increased competition for trading volume has diminished the effectiveness of market regulation. It is difficult to monitor trading in a stock if the stock trades in multiple markets with different SROs, such that each SRO has access to only a part of the audit trail. Moreover, it is possible for some market centres to dilute their regulatory structure to enhance their competitive advantage, wreaking havoc in the marketplace as a whole. Possible solutions include establishing a single regulatory body for all stocks and inviting multiple parties to compete on price and regulation quality for the business of regulating the markets.

those laid out by the SEC. The NASD has the power to expel its members from an exchange in the case of wrongdoing (it cannot, however, take legal action against a member other than by reporting it to the SEC). The association is run by a board that takes half of its representatives from the securities industry and half of its representatives from the public. In total, the NASD oversees more than 5000 securities firms.

The Trust Indenture Act of 1939 applies to debt securities such as bonds, debentures and notes that are offered for public sale. It requires that debt issues have both a disinterested trustee and provisions to protect the rights of the bondholders. For example, the board of directors cannot pay a large cash dividend to common stockholders and then immediately default on the bond payment. Also, bondholders are required to receive from the firm a semiannual report documenting the firm's adherence to terms of the bond indenture.

The Investment Company Act of 1940 regulates the organisation of companies, including mutual funds, that engage primarily in investing, reinvesting and trading in securities and whose own securities are offered to the investing public. The regulation is designed to minimise conflicts of interest that arise in these complex operations. The act requires these companies to disclose their financial condition and investment policies to investors when stock is initially sold and, subsequently, on a regular basis. The focus of this act is on disclosure to the investing public of information about the fund and its investment objectives, as well as on investment company structure and operations. It is important to remember that the act does not permit the SEC to directly supervise the investment decisions or activities of these companies or judge the merits of their investments.

The Investment Advisor Act of 1940 regulates investment advisers. With certain exceptions, this act requires that firms or sole practitioners compensated for advising others about securities investments must register with the SEC and conform to regulations designed to protect investors. Since the act was amended in 1996, generally only advisers who have at least $25 million of assets under management or advise a registered investment company must register with the Commission.

The Williams Act of 1968 provided legislation on attempts to take over a publicly held firm. An attempt to buy large portions of a publicly held firm is known as making a tender offer. The Williams Act was enacted in response to a series of unannounced take-overs, during which stockholders had to make decisions under duress. This act requires parties attempting to buy a company to file an information document with the SEC as well as with the company under consideration. This document must contain information on the terms of the offer, the source of financing, the competence of the bidder, and a company plan after the take-over.

The US government acquired an interest in the management of brokerage firms when it passed the Securities Investor Protection Act of 1970. In the event of default by a brokerage firm, this act provides insurance to customers' accounts of up to $500 000 each by the Securities Investor Protection Corporation (SIPC).

The Employee Retirement Income Security Act of 1974 (ERISA) regulates the management of pension funds and retirement accounts. Managers of these types of accounts have a fiduciary relationship. A fiduciary is a person who acts in the best interest of his or her clients on issues related to their relationship. In other words, money managers must act in the best interest of their clients. A money manager is a fiduciary under ERISA when at least one of the following criteria is true: (1) the money manager exercises any authority related to portfolio management decisions, (2) the money manager is paid a fee for investment advice, and/or (3) the money manager has any control over the administration of a portfolio.[5]

---

[5] See Section 404(a)(1) of ERISA of 1974.

Based on ERISA, an investment manager must be loyal. This requires that any expenses charged to an ERISA account must be reasonable, and the fund must be managed with the client's best interests in mind. Specifically, an investment manager must act prudently. That is, the manager should always act with care and work diligently when conducting business for clients. One recently added requirement is that a customer account should be diversified to minimise losses. (See Chapter 9 for a complete discussion of the benefits of diversification.)

The Foreign Corrupt Practices Act of 1977 (FCPA) places restrictions on the behaviour of domestic firms operating in international markets. Specifically, firms are not allowed to bribe foreign officials, even if bribery is legal in that country. The FCPA also requires issuers of securities to meet its accounting standards. These accounting standards, which were designed to operate in tandem with the antibribery provisions of the FCPA, require corporations covered by the provisions to maintain books and records that accurately and fairly reflect the transactions of the corporation and to design an adequate system of internal accounting controls.

In 1983, firms were given the ability to sell new securities over a period of time rather than all at once. This ability helps firms that have to sell securities at depressed prices; it is called shelf registration.

In 1984 and 1988, two acts were passed that gave the SEC greater enforcement powers. The 1984 Insider Trading Sanctions Act made it illegal to trade a security while in possession of material non-public information. Although the act is vague as to what kind of information is material and when information is non-public, it has been used to restrict insider trading. The 1988 Insider Trading and Securities Fraud Enforcement Act increased the fines and punishment for insider trading and other fraudulent activities.

In 1990, several new regulations were enacted, ranging from expanding the SEC's enforcement powers to facilitating the resale of a private placement. In 1995, under the Securities Exchange Act of 1934, two new rules were enacted that became effective in January 1997. The Display Rule (Rule 11Ac1-4) requires that limit orders placed by customers and priced better than a specialist's or market maker's quote must be displayed. Similarly, the Quote Rule (Rule 11Ac1-1) requires market makers to publish quotations for any listed security when a quote represents more than 1% of the aggregate trading volume for that security. The intent of these two rules is to enhance competition and pricing efficiency by openly disclosing the trading activity on each security.

In 1999, after ten years of discussion in the US Congress, President Clinton signed the Financial Services Modernization Act or Gramm–Leach–Bliley Act (GLBA) into law. The GLBA primarily ended regulation that prevented banks, stock-brokerage companies and insurance companies from affiliating and entering each other's markets. The removal of these regulations, however, raised significant risks that these new financial institutions would have access to an incredible amount of personal information, with no restrictions upon its use. Prior to GLBA, the insurance company that maintained a customer's health records was distinct from the bank that mortgaged his or her house and the stockbroker that traded his or her stocks. Once these companies merged, however, they would have the ability to consolidate, analyse and sell the personal details of their customers' lives. Because of these risks, the GLBA included three simple requirements to protect the personal data of individuals: (1) financial institutions must store personal financial information securely, (2) they must advise customers of their policies on sharing of personal financial information, and (3) they must give consumers the option to opt out of some sharing of personal financial information.

More recently, President Bush signed into law the Sarbanes–Oxley Act of 2002, which he characterised as 'the most far reaching reforms of American business practices since the time of Franklin Delano Roosevelt'. This was the answer of the administration on the ongoing scandals that shake corporate America. The act mandated a number of reforms to enhance corporate responsibility, enhance financial disclosures and combat corporate and accounting fraud, and created the Public Company Accounting Oversight Board (PCAOB) to oversee the activities of the auditing profession.

The major US legislation related to investment management up to 2003 is summarised in Exhibit 5.1.

Exhibit 5.1	Summary of US securities laws	

Year	Legislation	Purpose
1933	Securities Act	Requires initial public offering (IPO) disclosure, registration with Federal Trade Commission (FTC), and certification; addresses fraud
1933	Banking Act	Created Federal Deposit Insurance Corporation (FDIC), separates commercial banking from investment banking
1934	Securities Exchange Act	Regulates secondary market, established Securities and Exchange Commission (SEC), provides for exchange self-rule, gives federal authority to establish margin, forbids insider trading
1935	Public Utility Holding Company Act	Requires utilities to register with SEC
1938	Maloney Act	Places over-the-counter (OTC) market under SEC supervision, results in development of National Association of Securities Dealers (NASD)
1939	Trust Indenture Act	Requires a bond trustee and protective provisions in bond indentures
1940	Investment Company Act	Regulates investment companies
1940	Investment Advisors Act	Requires registration of investment advisors and regulates activities
1968	Williams Act	Regulates tender offers
1970	Securities Investor Protection Act	Provides governmental insurance through the Securities Investor Protection Corporation (SIPC) for defaults by brokers
1974	Employee Retirement Income Security Act	Regulates the management of pension funds
1975	Securities Acts Amendments	Eliminates fixed commissions, requires the development of a national market system
1977	Foreign Corrupt Practices Act	Makes it illegal to bribe foreign officials, regulates internal controls of multinational corporations
1983	Shelf Registration	Allows for the sale of securities over a period of time rather than a specific day
1984	Insider Trading Sanctions Act	Makes it illegal to trade while in possession of 'material non-public' information
1988	Insider Trading and Securities Fraud Enforcement Act	Increases potential liabilities for insider trading or other fraudulent activities
1990	Shareholder Communications Improvement Act	Requires banks and brokers holding shares for beneficial owners of securities in nominee name to forward to the beneficial owners the proxy and information statements of investment companies
1990	Securities Law Enforcement Remedies Act	Provides the SEC with significant additional enforcement powers; civil penalties can now go up to $500 000; officers or directors whose conduct demonstrates 'substantial unfitness' can be barred

▶

Exhibit 5.1 continued

Year	Legislation	Purpose
1990	Market Reform Act	A response to the October 1987 and October 1989 market breaks; permits the SEC, during 'periods of extraordinary volatility', to 'prohibit or constrain' trading practices such as programme trading
1990	Rule 144A	Designed to facilitate the resale of privately placed securities without SEC registration: the SEC wanted to develop 'a more liquid and efficient institutional resale market for unregistered securities'
1995	Rule 11Ac1-4	'Display Rule' requires that limit orders placed by customers and priced better than a specialist's or market maker's quote must be displayed
1995	Rule 11Ac1-1	'Quote Rule' requires market makers to publish quotations for any listed security when a quote represents more than 1% of the aggregate trading volume for that security
1999	Gramm–Leach–Bliley Act	Allows US financial services providers, including banks, securities firms and insurance companies, to affiliate with each other and enter each other's markets. Also includes provisions to protect consumers' personal financial information held by financial institutions
2002	Sarbanes–Oxley Act	Mandated a number of reforms to enhance corporate responsibility, enhance financial disclosures and combat corporate and accounting fraud, and created the Public Company Accounting Oversight Board (PCAOB) to oversee the activities of the auditing profession

Sources: C. Steven Bradford (1992), 'Rule 144A and integration' *Securities Regulation Law Journal*, **20** (37); http://www.sec.gov/rules/final/34-38110.txt

As discussed in the introductory section, several scandals have recently undermined investor confidence. Many investors now question the appropriateness of the existing regulations, the effectiveness of regulators to enforce regulations, and the discipline of key market participants to obey regulations and ethical standards. To regain investor confidence, a mass of legislation overhauling the current regulatory framework has been proposed and implemented, and it is likely that more will follow. Connecting Theory to Practice 5.2 list various recent proposed and adopted rule changes intended achieve stricter oversight of auditors, more shareholder-oriented corporate governance, and rules to improve objectivity and disclosure.

→ **Connecting Theory to Practice 5.2**   FT

Corporate America in crisis: proposed reform

Corporate America is under fire for undermining investor confidence. Calls for accountability and transparency are getting louder. Investors are scrutinising everything from executive compensation to disclosure practices. The legislative mood in Washington is now shifting toward tighter controls on companies. And regulators like the Securities and Exchange Commission, the New York Stock Exchange and the National Association of Securities Dealers are proposing new rules on corporate governance.

Below is a table that shows how agencies are aiming to change the way America does business.

▶

Agency	Proposal	Purpose	Summary	Status
Senate Banking Committee	Ban performing non-audit services for clients	Improve oversight; restrict ability of firms to offer consultancy services to their audit clients	Toughen regulation of accountancy profession; create an independent five-member board to oversee work of auditors	Passed by the Senate's banking committee, still to face Senate vote
House Financial Committee	Create a five-member board to oversee work of auditors	Conduct investigations and bring disciplinary action against accounting industry	Looser version of legislation debated in the Senate; Board will hold power to bar individuals and firms from carrying out audit work	Passed by the House in early 2002
SEC	New disclosure requirements and acceleration of filing date of Form 8-K, which describes officers' transactions in company equity securities	Provide investors with faster disclosure of company's important events; enable investors to make voting decisions on a better-informed basis	Require companies to file Form 8-K and shorten filing deadline to two business days after important event; create a safe harbour for certain violations of Form 8-K filing requirements	Proposed rule
SEC	Certification of disclosure in companies' quarterly and annual reports	Improve quality of disclosure and encourage investor confidence in company officials	Require a company's officers to certify that information in the financial report is correct	Proposed rule
SEC	Amendments to mutual fund advertising rules	Ensure advertisements convey balanced information to prospective customers, do not overhype hot performance	Require enhanced disclosure in mutual fund advertisements; reinforce antifraud protections	Proposed rule
SEC	Disclosure and explanation of the application of critical accounting policies	Improve transparency of companies' financial disclosure	Require that companies enhance investors' understanding of policies; force companies to identify estimates reflected in its financial statements	Proposed rule
NYSE	Tighten the definition of 'independent' director; independent directors must comprise majority of a company's corporate board	Ensure that independent directors have no 'material' relationship with the company; increase authority of independent directors to eliminate conflict	Allow each company to determine what constitutes 'material', Mandate a 'cooling off' period where directors cannot be considered for the board if they have worked for the company in the past five years	Proposed rule

▶

Agency	Proposal	Purpose	Summary	Status
NYSE	Adopt corporate governance guidelines and a code of business conduct	Encourage a focus on good corporate governance	Require companies to adopt and disclose guidelines; require chief executive to attest to accuracy of information provided to investors	Proposed rule
NYSE	Shareholder vote on all compensation plans	Give shareholders more opportunity to monitor and participate in the governance of companies	Require that shareholders vote on equity based compensation plans, including stock options	Proposed rule
NASD	Changes to rule concerning reporting criminal offences by members	Provide investors with ample disclosure of criminal offences by securities dealers	Require companies to report any felony regarding sale of a security, forgery, extortion, larceny, embezzlement, fraud	Proposed rule; adopted by the SEC
NASD	Changes to rule concerning research analysts and research reports	Improve objectivity of research and provide investors with more useful, reliable information	Require that analysts' compensation not be tied to investment banking; prohibit firms from offering positive research to induce business	Proposed rule; adopted by the SEC

Source: 'Corporate America in Crisis: Proposed Reform', FT.com site; 2 July 2002

5.2.2 Securities regulation in the European Union

In the USA, the SEC is the central regulatory agency responsible for enforcing securities legislation. By contrast, in the European Union (EU), security regulation is very fragmented. There is neither a (supranational) regulatory body for the EU nor a common regulatory framework; different national securities regulators operate without much coordination. Currently, with the exception of a number of institutional markets and the Eurobond market, Europe continues to operate as a collection of national financial markets. This situation is seen as undesirable because it hinders a further integration of the European financial markets. In a single market, financial institutions authorised to provide financial services in one member state would be able to provide the same services throughout the EU, competing on a level playing field within a consistent regulatory environment. Such a single market could promote economic growth across all sectors of the economy, boost productivity and provide lower-cost and better-quality financial products for consumers and enterprises. The current fragmentation of financial markets is caused in large part by differences in regulations and lack of coordination and cooperation between regulators. However, this situation is changing due to the several recent trends in security regulation in EU member states:

- Consolidation of supervisory structures within EU member states.
- Harmonisation of member state regulations through the Financial Services Action Plan (FSAP).
- Intensified crossborder coordination and cooperation of national regulators through the Lamfalussy process.

These trends are discussed in greater detail below.

Consolidation of supervisory structures in Europe

Regulation and supervision within EU member states is organised along one of three basic models: (1) agencies responsible for sectors (securities, banking and insurance), (2) agencies responsible for different kinds of supervision (for example, licensing, disclosure and disciplinary issues), and (3) a single supervisory agency that performs all tasks.[6] The most recent developments seem to indicate a broad tendency towards the latter model. For example, fully integrated financial supervisors have been established in Norway, Denmark, Sweden, the UK, Germany, Austria and Belgium.[7] The logic is impeccable: these industries sell similar products to the same customers using similar distribution channels – which is why the first model (supervision based on industry) is becoming outdated. In many cases, the supervisor works in close collaboration with the national central bank, which traditionally has authority over banks in order to minimise systemic risk. Exhibit 5.2 lists the securities supervisors and central banks of several European countries, together with Internet links to the home pages of the supervisors and central banks.

The Financial Services Action Plan

EU countries have recognised the need to create a more integrated market. The Financial Services Action Plan (FSAP) agreed between heads of governments and the European Commission aims to complete the single market for financial services by the end of 2005.[8] The FSAP consists of a set of measures to fill gaps and remove remaining barriers so as to provide a legal and regulatory environment that supports the integration of EU financial markets. The main instrument for the FSAP is the EU directive. An EU directive is a legal instrument instructing national governments to take action to reach certain results. Directives set baseline requirements and minimum standards, and national governments are obliged to translate a directive into national legislation and make decisions for implementation consistent with those requirements and standards.[9] In other words, harmonisation takes place not by creating one set of rules for the entire EU but by rewriting existing rules in all the member states such that they are (or at least, should be) essentially the same. Exhibit 5.3 summarises the main FSAP and related measures. The measures can be divided into four categories: (1) measures that have not yet been proposed, (2) measures that have been proposed but not yet adopted, (3) measures that have been adopted but not yet implemented, and (4) measures that have been implemented. The exhibit shows the status as of 31 July 2003. The final date for adoption of EU directives is mid-2004, allowing 18 months for transposition by the deadline of the end of 2005.[10]

---

[6] For example, until recently, securities market oversight in France was shared by the Commission des Opérations de Bourse (COB), the Conseil des Marchés Financiers (CMF) and the Conseil de Discipline de la Gestion Financière (CDGF). The COB's responsibilities were focused on approving prospectuses and licensing and overseeing asset-management companies, supported by the CDGF for any disciplinary issues. The CMF focused on the conduct of brokers, dealers and clearing houses as well as on market rules applicable to them. The CMF also provided an opinion in licensing of investment service providers. However, in 2003, the COB, CMF and CDGF merged into Autorité des Marchés Financiers (AMF).

[7] For example, in 2002, the German supervisors for securities (Bundesaufsichtsamt für den Wertpapierhandel; BAWe), banking (Bundesaufsichtsamt für das Kreditwesen; BAKred) and insurance (Bundesaufsichtsamt für das Versicherungswesen; BAV) merged into Bundesanstalt für Finanzdienstleistungsaufsicht (BaFin), an integrated financial sector supervisor.

[8] Not all financial markets in Europe are in EU member states; the Swiss market is one example of considerable importance. However, there is coordination and cooperation between European countries inside and outside the EU.

[9] The EU directive is different from a EU regulation, which does bind citizens directly.

[10] Member States are given a period (usually of 18 months) to implement EU directives, by transposing the provisions into their national law.

Exhibit 5.2	European securities supervisors and central banks	
Member state	**Securities supervisor/central bank**	**URL**
Austria	Finanzmarktaufsicht	www.fma.gv.at
	Österreichische Nationalbank	www.oenb.co.at
Denmark	Finanstilsynet	www.ftnet.dk
	Danmarks Nationalbank	www.nationalbanken.dk
Belgium	Commission Bancaire, Financière et des Assurances/	www.cbfa.be
	Commissie voor het Bank-, Financie- en Assurantiewezen	
	Bank Nationale de Belgique/Nationale Bank van België	www.bnb.be
Finland	Rahoitustarkastus	www.rata.bof.fi
	Suomen Pankki	www.bofi.fi
France	Autorité des Marchés Financiers	www.amf-france.org
	Banque de France	www.banque-france.fr
Germany	Bundesanstalt für Finanzdienstleistungsaufsicht	www.bafin.de
	Deutsche Bundesbank	www.bundesbank.de
Greece	Capital Market Commission	www.hcmc.gr
	Bank of Greece	www.bankofgreece.gr
Iceland	Fjármálaeftirlitid	www.fme.is
	Central Bank of Iceland	www.sedlabanki.is
Ireland	Irish Financial Services Regulatory Authority	www.ifsra.ie
	Central Bank of Ireland	www.centralbank.ie
Italy	Commissione Nazionale per le Società e la Borsa	www.consob.it
	Banca d'Italia	www.bancaditalia.it
Luxembourg	Commission de Surveillance du Secteur Financier	www.cssf.lu
	Banque Centrale du Luxembourg	www.bcl.lu
Netherlands	Autoriteit Financiële Markten	www.afm.nl
	De Nederlandsche Bank	www.dnb.nl
Norway	Kredittilsynet	www.kredittilsynet.no
	Norges Bank	www.norges-bank.no
Portugal	Comissão do Mercado de Valores Mobiliários	www.cmvm.pt
	Banco de Portugal	www.bportugal.pt
Spain	Comisión Nacional del Mercado de Valores	www.cnmv.es
	Banco de España	www.bde.es
Sweden	Finansinspektionen	www.fi.se
	Sveriges Riksbank	www.riksbank.se
UK	Financial Services Authority	www.fsa.gov.uk
	Bank of England	www.bankofengland.co.uk

Harmonisation in the EU: the Lamfalussy process

In 2001, a Committee of Wise Men, headed by the former Belgian central banker Alexandre Lamfalussy, analysed the obstacles to deliver the FSAP by the target deadline. Lamfalussy found that the existing legislative and regulatory system was not working: it was too slow and too rigid, produced too much ambiguity and failed to make a distinction between core principles

Exhibit 5.3	EU Financial Services Action Plan (FSAP)

A. Securities issuance and trading

- The *Market Abuse Directive* harmonises rules on the prevention of insider dealing and market manipulation in both regulated and unregulated markets.[1]
- The *Prospectus Directive* is designed to provide a 'single passport' for issuers of equity and debt securities so that, once an issue of securities meets prospectus requirements in one country, the securities can be sold across the EU.[1]
- A revision to the *Investment Services Directive* is due to replace the 1993 Directive, which regulates the authorisation, behaviour and conduct of business of securities firms and markets, including exchanges.[2]
- The *Transparency Directive* is set to impose an obligation on issuers to meet continuing disclosure requirements after issue.[2]

B. Securities settlement

- The *Settlement Finality Directive* aims to reduce systemic risk in payment and securities settlement systems, in particular the risk of the insolvency of a participant.[3]
- The *Collateral Directive* provides greater legal certainty about the validity and enforceability of collateral backing transactions across borders.[1]

C. Accounting

- The *Fair Value Accounting Directive* brings up to date existing EU accounting directives for companies, banks and other financial institutions, on the valuation of assets at methods other than purchase price and cost.[1]
- A regulation applying *International Accounting Standards* (IAS) to all listed companies across the EU.[1]
- The *Accounting Modernisation Directive* amends the Fourth and Seventh Company Directives.[1]

D. Corporate restructuring

- The *European Company Statute* (ECS) consists of a regulation enabling companies in the EU to set up under a European charter, so that they do not need to register in a number of different countries, together with a directive on employee involvement.[1]
- The *Takeover Bids Directive* proposes a minimum framework for the national approval of takeovers, including applicable law, protection of shareholders and disclosure.[2]
- New Commission proposals for 10th and 14th *Company Law Directives*.[4]

E. Insurance

- Amendment to the *Insurance Directives* and the *Investment Services Directive* to permit information exchange with third countries.[3]
- Two directives updating solvency standards for life and non-life insurers, and a scheme for the protection of policyholders.[1]
- The *Insurance Mediation Directive* introduces a EU framework for the authorisation, capitalisation and regulation of intermediaries and brokers who sell insurance products.[1]
- A Commission proposal to harmonise the framework for reinsurance supervision in the EU.[4]

F. Long-term savings

- Two *UCITS Directives* amend earlier (1985) directives by liberalising the types of asset in which undertakings for collective investment in transferable securities (i.e. mutual funds) can invest, and regulating management companies and the production of simplified prospectuses.[1]
- The *Distance Marketing Directive* governs conditions on the sale of retail financial services products, if they are not sold face to face.[1]
- The *Pension Funds Directive* regulates the operation of employment-related pension schemes across borders in the EU. This is based on mutual recognition of home state regulation, and establishes a 'prudent person' approach in Community law, so that a prudent investment policy can be followed for scheme members in each member state.[1]

▶

Exhibit 5.3 continued

G. Retail payments

- A communication on the EU *Legal Framework for Payments in the Internal Market*, which aims to rationalise existing EU legislation on retail payments.[4]
- A framework directive *Insurance Solvency II* and *Insurance Guarantee Schemes*.[4]

H. Electronic money

- The *E-Money Directive* defines electronic money and governs the capital and authorisation requirements for a new category of electronic money institution.[3]
- The *Electronic Commerce Directive* aims to create a legal framework for the free movement across the EU of electronic commerce, including financial services.[3]

I. Money laundering

- The *Second Money Laundering Directive* (2001) extends the scope of predicate offences for which reporting of suspicious activity is mandatory, and broadens the regulated sector to include new professions, such as solicitors and accountants, and activities, such as casinos.[1]
- A proposal from the Commission for a *Third Money Laundering Directive*.[4]

J. Financial supervision

- The *Financial Conglomerates Directive* determines how the lead supervisor of a financial conglomerate should be decided and ensures that gaps in supervisory arrangements are filled.[1]
- A proposal from the Commission for a *Risk-based Capital Directive* to implement in the EU the capital framework for banks and investment firms planned in the revised Basel Capital Accord. While the Basel Capital Accord will apply only to internationally active banks, the Risk-based Capital Directive is expected to apply to all banks and investment firms.[4]

K. Corporate insolvency

- The *Insurance Winding-up Directive* (2001) ensures that the principle of mutual recognition is applied to the winding-up and reorganisation of insurance undertakings in the EU.[3]
- The *Bank Winding-up Directive* (2001) ensures that banks can be wound up and reorganised in the EU as a single entity.[1]

L. Taxation of savings income

- The *Taxation of Savings Income Directive* is designed to prevent cross-border tax evasion by individuals within the EU. It provides for Member States to exchange information on interest income paid to non-residents, or (in Austria, Belgium and Luxembourg) to tax that income at source, with equivalent treatment in Switzerland and the dependent territories.[1]

[1] Adopted but not yet implemented in 31 July 2003.
[2] Proposed but not yet adopted in 31 July 2003.
[3] Implemented in 31 July 2003.
[4] Planned but not yet proposed in 31 July 2003.

Source: EU Financial Services Action Plan (FSAP), from *Progress on the Financial Services Action Plan*,
http://www.europa.eu.int/comm/internalmarket/en/finances/actionplan/index.htm, 31 July 2003, reprinted with permission of the European Communities.

and detail. Insufficient consultation and transparency plus uneven transposition and erratic implementation by member states of agreed rules were other handicaps. To circumvent this remarkable cocktail of Kafkaesque inefficiency that served no one, Lamfalussy proposed to install two powerful pan-European committees of national finance ministry officials/ regulators to assist the Commission in drafting laws and supervise their implementation: the

European Securities Committee (ESC) and the European Securities Regulators Committee (ESRC). This speeds up EU legislative processes by:

- allowing the Commission, the European Parliament and the Council to concentrate their efforts on developing key policy principles for securities regulation by means of framework directives or regulations (so-called level 1 regulation);
- leaving the technical details needed to implement those key principles efficiently to the ESC and to the advice of the ESRC (so-called level 2 regulation).

Further, Lamfalussy opened the process of framing securities market legislation to the widest possible consultation with market professionals.

5.2.3 International regulation

The securities markets are becoming increasingly global, and national regulators need to adopt an international orientation. Certainly within ten years and probably within a much shorter period of time, the trading of the larger and more active stocks will be worldwide. Today, foreign investors can buy a US stock on a US market in US dollars during US trading hours. In the future, investors all over the globe will be able to buy US stocks during their normal business hours in their local currency.

Today, the cost and awkwardness of the clearing and settlement processes across nations restrain global trading of equities. For example, Germany has a two-day settlement period while the USA has a three-day settlement period. Further, there is a difference in time zones. Even if the settlement period becomes the same across countries, at one day, as currently envisioned, the settlement times of each side of a trade between an US investor and a German investor will still be different. To bridge this gap, funds or stocks need to be borrowed, increasing the cost of settlement and adding to counterparty risk. Another hindrance is the difference in regulatory rules between different countries. Once it becomes cheap and easy to settle trades across borders, the location of the market centre, the currency and the time of trade become a matter of choice and crossborder trading will increase.

Of great significance to US and EU regulators is that an investor will be able to trade domestic stocks in foreign markets. By doing so, US and EU investors may be able to circumvent some US and EU regulations legally. They might also hide some questionable, and possibly illegal, activities from US and EU surveillance.

Further, technology will allow a marketplace or order-gathering function to be located anywhere in the world. Just as US banks locate their credit-card activities in states with favourable laws, marketplaces and order-gathering firms will be able to locate their activities in any country of choice. The marketplace could be located in Japan, the USA, the EU or the Cayman Islands. This threat of relocation will place constraints on regulators, and global trading will make it more difficult for authorities to regulate investment practices and to protect domestic investors.

Regulatory authorities worldwide will have to coordinate their activities. A non-exhaustive list of challenges in regulating worldwide trading includes the oversight of a global clearing and settlement system, the prevention of fraud, the maintenance of transparency, the enforcement of stockholder rights, the collection of taxes, and the integration of disparate and perhaps contradictory laws.

Out of sight, not out of mind: over-the-counter derivatives

While the volume of derivatives dealing continues to expand very rapidly, a number of disquieting features have become apparent, both from a supervisory point of view and from a broader economic perspective.

Derivatives are used increasingly for regulatory arbitrage. Indeed, such instruments offer a whole array of possibilities for those who want to avoid or evade regulatory controls or taxes. This is because swaps and options can be used to provide investors with synthetic exposure to foreign assets and liabilities. That is, they make it possible to swap domestic returns for international returns without any leakage of capital beyond national frontiers. Many economic liberals argue that arbitrage of this kind enhances economic efficiency and welfare. But that cannot detract from the fact that a decisive power shift has taken place. The increasing efficacy of derivative-based tax and regulatory arbitrage has significantly diminished the armoury of the nation state.

The big economic, as opposed to political, concern about derivatives relates to systemic risk in global finance. The crucial point, from a supervisory perspective, is that the growth in derivatives is largely in the opaque and relatively illiquid OTC market rather than on more visible organised exchanges. In the five years to the end of 1998 the notional amount of exchange-traded derivatives outstanding rose from Dollars 7771 bn to Dollars 13 549 bn. Over the same period the comparable growth in OTC derivatives was from Dollars 8474 to Dollars 50 997.

The speed of growth in the less regulated OTC sector is worrying. As Alfred Steinherr [Steinherr, 1998] rightly remarks in the most thought-provoking of recent books on derivatives, much more systemic risk is generated by OTC contracts than exchange-traded contracts. Exchanges require their members to put up margin in the form of cash and securities. These margins are adjusted daily according to price movements. Users of the exchange and the related clearing house are thus charged with the full cost of the risks they undertake. In the OTC market, in contrast, book losses can be accumulated over the life of the contract. Risk is not covered on a day-to-day basis. The result is that systemic risk – an externality – is not fully priced in OTC contracts. As a result, says Mr Steinherr, OTC contracts are inevitably more attractive from a private viewpoint and less attractive from a social viewpoint than exchange-traded products.

For banking supervisors, then, the OTC market poses a special challenge, not least because 41 per cent of the total notional sums in this market involve non-bank counterparties including hedge funds that act, in effect, as market makers. The dangers became apparent last year when Long-Term Capital Management, the hedge fund run by John Meriwether, ran into trouble. Only when this low-profile but hyper-leveraged fund admitted to its problems did it emerge that it was probably the world's most active user of interest rate swaps. In August 1998 around Dollars 750 bn of its total Dollars 1000 bn notional derivatives exposure was in such swaps with about 50 counterparties around the world. None of them was aware of LTCM's total exposure. The BIS notes that while this exposure was fully collateralised, the banks had taken no protection against the potential increases in exposures resulting from changes in market values. Only when the full extent of LTCM's problems became clear did the banks seek additional collateral.

Nothing better illustrates Steinherr's point about systemic risk. For when the hedge fund was forced to raise cash by selling its most liquid securities, the shock was felt in markets all around the world. The contagion quickly spread from low-rated and illiquid securities to benchmark government bonds. The US Federal Reserve felt obliged to broker a rescue.

Source: John Plender, 'Out of Sight, Not Out Of Mind: Over-the-Counter Derivatives', *Financial Times*, 20 September 1999.

→ **Making the connection**

The growth in the OTC derivatives market is making regulators reconsider the probability and danger of systemic risk. It also demonstrates that the need for international cooperation among regulators is not a hypothetical problem to be solved when we finally have global clearing: contagion is already a very real threat. The problem is that the informal and wholly unsupervised OTC market in contrast to regulated derivatives exchanges does not have clearing houses and margin requirements to reduce default risk. As a consequence, parties that trade in the OTC derivatives market are exposed to large default risks that could have dire consequences for world financial markets. After the near-collapse of the hedge fund LTCM in 1998, many called for tighter regulation of the OTC derivatives market and its market participants.* Proposed measures include requiring banks to set aside more capital to cover the risks of derivatives exposures and dealings with highly leveraged counterparties such as hedge funds.

* Further details on the LTCM case are given in Investment in the News 19 and Connecting Theory to Practice 4.3, 21.1 and 21.2.

5.3 Ethics

Frequently, the words 'unethical' and 'fraudulent' are used in the same breath. However, there is a clear distinction between the two. Fraud involves breaking the law or the existing regulations. Ethics embodies the ideals we should strive for and how we should behave.

Unlawful acts are considered by most people to be unethical. That is, most ethical frameworks hold as essential the responsibility to obey the law. However, not all unethical actions are regulated. As an example of an issue that is unethical but not unlawful, say a CEO nominates people who are dependent on him or her to the board of directors, which determines his or her compensation. This action is clearly unethical. It is not unlawful, however. In the future, we may see a law regulating the nomination of the board of directors; if such a law is passed, this CEO's action will move from the unethical category to the unlawful category. Still, the point is that regulators cannot possibly impose laws and regulations on every possible unethical action that investors can take. Such far-reaching regulation is also seen as undesirable because each regulation involves costs and adds to an already substantial administrative burden. Furthermore, enforcement of such regulations can be very difficult and requires resources. An additional problem is that while the law is the same for everyone (at least within a single jurisdiction), ethics is a set of ideals and norms, and opinion on what is (un)ethical behaviour differs substantially from person to person. Hence, there will always be an area that is legal but is considered unethical.

If unethical behaviour is not illegal, then why would people behave in an ethical manner? First, moral and religious beliefs are important deterrents to unethical behaviour. Many people want to make a positive contribution to society and they account for the interests of other people simply because this is the right thing to do. Still, the case is probably easier to make in the negative. By behaving in an unethical manner, you risk self-regulatory sanctions by your employer or industry organisation or, possibly worse, your customers (for example, by means of a customer boycott). Consequences can range from a simple reprimand to bankruptcy. In this respect, many professions have codes of ethics to establish which activities and behaviours are considered acceptable. For example, the US Association for Investment Management and Research (AIMR), a leading professional organisation in the financial sector, has adopted its Code of Ethics and Standards of Professional Conduct to be adhered to by over 68 000 members. This code is included in Appendix 5 at the end of this chapter. In addition, by behaving in an unethical manner, you might find yourself on the front page or the evening news, which could be worse than landing in court or self-regulatory sanctions. In the past few years, most media have given much more coverage to business. Newspapers and magazines now employ investigative reporters with MBAs and business experience to dig into the affairs of companies. The old advice is still the best: don't do anything on the job you wouldn't want your mother to read about with her morning coffee.

Below, we discuss some important ethical issues for various market participants.

5.3.1 Independent investment advice

Many investors rely on investment advice from financial analysts. Exercising independent judgement is a cornerstone of the AIMR's Code of Ethics. It is critical that financial analysts issue their own assessment of the value of individual securities. The financial analyst is not to succumb to outside pressure; rather, the analyst should 'exercise diligence and thoroughness in making an investment recommendation to others'. Analysts should do their own home-work and clearly present their own opinions about a given security. They should not rely (exclusively) on other analysts' opinions but rather should have a credible basis for their own recommendations.

As discussed in Investment in the News 5, it recently became painfully clear that investment analysts of many of the large Wall Street investment banks did not provide independent advice. Rather, the analysts issued overoptimistic recommendations to investors in return for securing investment bank business.

Early 2003, ten US securities firms agreed to pay $1.4 billion, the biggest-ever settlement for violating securities laws.[11] This figure included a $400 million penalty for Citigroup and $200 million penalties for Credit Suisse and Merrill Lynch. Pending civil suits by investors against the firms will bring further scrutiny to Wall Street misconduct. For this reason, financial firms have set aside billions of dollars to pay for the costs of litigating and settling claims.[12]

Further, in an effort to restore integrity to US financial services, the SEC and the NYSE proposed several rule changes intended to separate analyst research and investment banking. Measures to minimise contacts between people working for the same company to avoid conflicts of interest are known as 'Chinese walls'.[13] As discussed in Investment in the News 5, industry organisations are also developing an industry-wide code of best practice.

---

[11] $1.4 billion is a large number. However, it pales by comparison with the harm caused to investors or the earnings of the ten companies in the settlement, which exceeded $10 billion in the first quarter of 2003 alone.

[12] Former analysts Grubman and Blodget agreed with regulators to pay multimillion-dollar fines and be barred from the securities industry for life. They also face civil suits for their actions.

[13] In the UK, the *Financial Services Act* (1986) has even incorporated this principle into regulations.

5.3.2 Corporate governance

Corporate governance is the method or system of controlling the corporation. Corporate control usually rests with a board of directors. This group of individuals is usually elected by the common shareholders and given specific powers as allowed in the corporate charter and by-laws. The most important power of the board of directors is the appointment of senior managers, who carry out the day-to-day affairs of the corporation and delegate authority to employees.

The board also determines the compensation of the CEO. The CEO's compensation generally is indexed to the firm's performance. However, recently the compensation of many CEOs has increased even though their firms were losing money. The financial media are full of criticism of this phenomenon. Clearly, excessive compensation of executives will result in shareholders losing return on their investments. The corporate governance of the firm is supposed to prevent executive interest from replacing that of shareholders' interest.

Corporate governance is important because it is the framework through which shareholders can be assured of legal compliance, and it establishes the appropriate ethical conduct of the corporation. Through judicious use of corporate governance, shareholders can implement ethical standards throughout the corporation.

With the increasing concentration of shares held by large institutional investors, the role of active corporate governance on the part of shareholders will certainly increase. When shares of a company are held widely by individual investors, it is difficult for any one shareholder to exercise much control. However, when a few large institutional investors get together, they can easily exercise control of a corporation. Moreover, a few investors are more likely to agree upon the ethical standards that they consider to be proper than a group of perhaps tens of thousands of indiviuals.

One major concern is what happens if institutional money managers fail to keep as their priority the interests of their clients? For example, if institutional money managers use their authority to vote themselves on to the board of directors so they can personally benefit, then they are no longer acting in their clients' best interest. Furthermore, pension funds in the USA may invest in the parent company.[14] The management of company pension funds may not be totally independent from the company itself, raising questions regarding whether some pension funds are used to limit the influence of outside shareholders. Obviously, this problem has consequences beyond corporate governance: a high percentage of a single stock implies a poor diversification of the investment portfolio as well.

A second issue is that enforcement of ethical practices may harm the return of the company (for example, by forgoing certain investment opportunities), and hence the return of the institutional investors' clients. In that case, it isn't immediately clear as to what the ethical course of action is: harming clients – especially without their consent – is clearly unethical, but the plans proposed by the company may be unethical as well.

5.3.3 Insider information

Investors are allowed to use any information that is acquired lawfully for making their investment decisions. Examples of such information include the financial statements issued by Pfizer, the labour market statistics reported by the US Labor Department and financial news

---

[14] Part of the ERISA (see Section 5.2.1) limits this to 10% of the total assets for most plans, but this legislation contains many exception clauses; see US code title 19 section 1107.

from the *Wall Street Journal* and the *Financial Times*. However, investors are not allowed to base investment decisions on information that is not publicly available or on insider information. For example, a person cannot buy stock in a company based on inappropriately acquired information of a pending take-over. However, if the pending take-over was announced, say, in the *Wall Street Journal* or the *Financial Times*, both public sources, then the investor can buy shares legally.

Insiders are usually the officers of a company, but they can also include officers relatives or employees of the firm. In fact, in the USA, anyone who comes across inside information through any means and then trades upon it can be found guilty of insider trading. However, the definition of 'inside information' is not as clear-cut as it seems: a rumour printed in a local newspaper few people read might be considered insider information. A conversation overheard on a train is another matter – but did the investor know that the conversation was between insiders? All these questions might be answered differently – or not at all – in different countries, making insider trading a legal minefield that one should avoid completely.

In 1984, the US Congress passed the Insider Trading Sanctions Act of 1984 to 'amend the Securities Exchange Act of 1934 to increase the sanctions against trading in securities while in possession of material nonpublic information'.[15] Specifically, the 1984 act states that the SEC can bring court action against anyone who has purchased or who sells 'a security while in possession of material nonpublic information. The amount of such penalty shall be determined by the court in light of the facts and circumstances, but shall not exceed three times the profit gained or loss avoided as a result of such unlawful purchase or sale, and shall be payable into the Treasury of the United States.' And it didn't stop there: the Insider Trading and Securities Fraud Enforcement Act of 1988 dramatically increased maximum jail terms and fines for inside trades, provides for cash bounties to informers, allows for lawsuits by those claiming to have been harmed, and attempts to induce firms to institute better internal controls. This act was passed in response to insider trading litigation and was intended to dampen the amount of insider trading done.[16]

One illegal practice of using private information is front running. Suppose that a money manager intends to have a large buy order of a given stock, which might affect the stock price. If the manager delays the transaction because he or she wishes to buy stock for him- or herself and thus then enjoy the stock price's appreciation when the big buy order is translated, it is called front running and is illegal.

5.3.4 Commission brokers and mutual funds

Full-service brokers face some difficult ethical decisions. The broker is paid by commission. The fees earned are determined by the amount of trading that the broker convinces the clients to undertake. However, an active investment strategy may not be the best for many clients. For example, transactions involve transaction costs (commission fees and bid–ask spreads). Also, the turnover may affect the client's tax bill. In the USA, a holding period of less than

---

[15] Public Law 98–376, 98th Congress, 10 August 1984 (98 Stat. 1264), H.R. 559. Exactly defining 'material nonpublic information', however, may be difficult. For example, is there a difference between rumour and substantive facts?

[16] The impact of this regulation is an open question. Arshadi and Eyssell (1991) found that the more stringent regulations reduced both the amount and profitability of insider trading before tender offers. However, Nejat (1992) claims there is no evidence that the more stringent legislation had any effect on the profitability or volume of overall insider trading.

one year implies a possible 39.6% marginal tax on all profits, including capital gains. Holding the financial asset for a longer period may result in only a 20% tax on capital gains.

The buying and selling of excessive amounts for a client by a stockbroker is called churning. Specifically, churning exists when a stockbroker has control over an account and causes it to be traded excessively for the primary purpose of generating commissions.[17] Churning is illegal under SEC rules (specifically, Rule 10b-(5)) as well as under the rules of all major exchanges. However, in most cases it is difficult to prove whether churning has occurred or whether the broker was pursuing some sort of investment management strategy. The courts have used three tests to determine whether excessive trading existed:

- Annualised turnover ratio (how frequently securities are traded).
- Ratio of commissions to invested equity.
- The proportion of commissions derived by the broker from the account in question compared with all other accounts handled by that broker.[18]

In spite of these criteria, the issue of churning is left mainly in the ethical arena.

Mutual funds face a similar ethical problem of putting personal gains above client interests. Connecting Theory to Practice 5.4 reports on a recent scandal in which fund managers favoured select investors, in exchange for payments and other inducements, at the expense of ordinary investors.

→ **Connecting Theory to Practice 5.4**

Putnam assets fall 11 per cent in November

Putnam, the mutual fund company which is under investigation for improper trading practices, has had an outflow of $32 bn in assets in November, or more than 11 per cent of its total, as retail and institutional investors pulled their money out after hearing of the group's involvement.

Calstrs, the Californian Teachers' Retirement System, also said on Friday it had just pulled its $312 m allocation to Putnam, indicating that the outflow is set to continue as pension fund trustees meet to consider their allocations.

Morningstar, the influential mutual fund rating agency, has advised investors to steer clear of Putnam, along with four other funds named or charged by regulators. It is expected shortly to also advise investors to avoid the products of Invesco Funds (IFG), a US arm of Amvescap.

The move will come as a further blow to Invesco, which was hit this week with civil charges by both the Securities and Exchange Commission and Eliot Spitzer, the New York attorney general. Raymond Cunningham, IFG's chief executive, is also facing civil charges from the SEC and Mr Spitzer.

The eight US fund managers charged or named by Mr Spitzer over market timing, including Putnam, Alliance Capital and Janus, have seen big outflows.

[Mr Spitzer] has claimed that Denver-based Invesco had engaged in massive mutual fund timing – allowing excessive trading or investors to take advantage of stale prices. 'The evidence in this case speaks for itself,' Mr Spitzer said. 'Top managers knew market timing was harming buy-and-hold investors but they condoned and facilitated it because it was a lucrative source of management fee revenues.'

▶

---

[17] See Richard A. Booth, 'Damages in Churning Cases', *Securities Regulation Law Journal*, **20**, (3), 3.
[18] *Ibid.*, p. 5.

Documents filed by Mr Spitzer's office to support his charges show parts of memos and emails from senior executives detailing the damage caused by market timers and the reasons why the timing deals should stop.

In one memo cited in the complaint, Mr Spitzer said a compliance officer said that a fund that Invesco marketed to children as part of a special promotional programme to encourage young investors was being 'whipsawed by large dollar amounts of timing activity'.

Source: Deborah Brewster and Tony Tassell, 'Putnam Assets Fall 11 Per Cent in November', FT.com site, 5 December 2003.

→ **Making the connection**

Mutual funds have long been advocated as one of the best investment choices for small investors for their diversification and management expertise. But in late 2003, investors got a fresh lesson from Wall Street: several US mutual fund companies, including Invesco and Putnam, were hit by civil charges by both the US SEC and Eliot Spitzer, the New York Attorney-General. The companies were charged with improper trading that took place in their funds. In exchange for payments and other inducements, they allowed select customers to practise certain trading strategies, which resulted in the 'dilution' of the value of these funds to the detriment of long-term mutual fund shareholders.

The two primary issues central to the fund scandal described in Connecting Theory to Practice 5.4 are late trading and market timing.

Late trading is the illegal practice of allowing certain investors to purchase fund shares at that day's closing price, even several hours after the market's close – when they should technically be buying the fund at the following day's opening price. As described by Attorney-General Spitzer, late trading is 'like allowing betting on a horse race after the horses have crossed the finish line'.

Market timing is an investment technique involving short-term, 'in-and-out' trading of mutual fund shares. The technique of timing is designed to exploit market inefficiencies when the NAV price of the mutual fund shares does not reflect the current market value of the stocks held by the mutual fund. When a 'market timer' buys mutual fund shares at the stale NAV, it realises a profit when it sells those shares the next trading day or thereafter.

The victims of the fraud were the regular, long-term investors in the mutual funds. Each of these illegal trading practices diluted the value of shares held by long-term investors because the favoured investors who were allowed to use these illegal trading practices reaped extraordinary profits that were skimmed out of long-term shareholders' accounts.

The full extent of the alleged fraud within the mutual fund industry is not presently known. However, the trading practices of leading mutual fund families are under investigation, and lawsuits have been filed against certain of these companies. Mutual fund companies could end up paying more than $1 billion in civil and regulatory penalties as a result of the scandals.

5.3.5 Initial public offerings

Another ethical problem that commission brokers face is that their firms are also major underwriters of new securities. Thus, these brokers have to sell a set number of these securities, regardless of whether the client needs them. These brokers are working for two competing parties. The firm issuing the securities wants the highest price for the securities. The client wants the lowest price. The broker must exercise considerable fortitude to make sure the clients are well served.

5.3.6 Independent regulators

As discussed in Section 5.1, stock exchanges in the USA historically have been self-regulating organisations (SROs). Hence, the exchanges are two things: they are a business and they are the regulator of a business that happens to be itself. This dual role creates a possible conflict of interest, as the interests of the members of an exchange do not always coincide with the interests of the investors.

Recently, this conflict of interests was illustrated by the controversy that surrounded the compensation package granted to Richard Grasso, the former chairman of the NYSE. Among other outrages, Mr Grasso got a bonus of $10.6 million in 2002, a year when the exchange's own net income hit a recent low of $28 million – down 61% from two years earlier. His salary and bonus were set by a compensation committee whose members were selected by Mr Grasso himself!

Mr Grasso's flamboyant compensation has played a role in a series of scandals and embarrassments that have recently plagued the NYSE, including alleged abuses by the specialist firms that match buyers and sellers on the trading floor. According to some people, the specialist process itself is a costly anachronism, but specialists are important owners of the NYSE and many of them sit on the exchange's board, so it is unlikely they would put themselves out of a job.

Presumably, the only solution is to separate the regulator and the regulated by creating an independent regulator. Such a separation is especially important if exchanges pursue a for-profit business model. For example, exchanges in Europe have already moved towards a public offering of their own shares, and a recent SEC rule change allows US exchanges to pursue a for-profit business model as well.

5.3.7 Socially responsible investment

The issuers of securities and the intermediaries in securities markets need to behave in an ethical manner in order for investors to maintain confidence in security markets. However, there also is an ethical dimension to selection of securities by the investors, as the investment process determines the allocation of scarce resources to industries and firms.

Socially responsible investing (SRI) accounts for the societal and environmental impact of investment decisions. A fast-growing number of mutual funds use screens to select or omit firms on the basis of them undertaking particular activities with social or environmental effects. Examples are funds that exclude firms involved in the production and/or distribution of tobacco, alcohol and weapons. Gambling, animal testing, labour relations, human rights, environmental issues and community relations also are used as negative or positive screens. As of November 1999, the Social Investment Forum reports that one in eight dollars of assets under management in the USA, a total of $2.16 trillion, is in investments that integrate social and environmental concerns. Connecting Theory to Practice 5.5 discusses the SRI trend.

An important issue in this respect is whether the socially responsible investor forgoes returns or diversification from using (positive or negative) social and environmental screens. However, there is some empirical evidence that the actual financial cost of SRI in terms of opportunity costs is not substantial (see Chapter 22). Also, as discussed in Connecting Theory to Practice 5.5, even conventional fund managers now analyse social and environmental factors, simply because these factors affect the earnings prospects of firms and sectors.

Positive about 'best' stocks

Managers selling individual savings accounts are finding there is nothing like the image of war, children, endangered animals or the Amazonian rainforest to make people cough up. More and more fund managers are offering Isa-eligible ethical or socially responsible investment (SRI) funds to private investors.

However, the sceptics believe that ethical investment is a subjective quagmire of ill-defined good intentions and that investors do not look hard enough at what they are buying or what they may have to sacrifice in returns. The sceptics have a point. Socially responsible investing can cover anything from religious prohibitions to environmental issues, community investing, shareholder activism and corporate governance. 'Ethical or socially responsible investing means so many different things to different people,' admits Charles Henderson, who manages Aegon's SRI funds. 'It doesn't make customers' job easy with about 60 funds that are not comparable in the sector.'

In the UK, the starting point for most funds sold to private investors is screens applied to stock selection. Funds only invest in specific industries and are forbidden from investing in others – for example, animal testing, oils, arms or tobacco.

But analysts have long been concerned that excluding companies hampers returns. The Florida Board of Administration, which runs the US state's pension fund, instituted a ban on tobacco four years ago, but lifted it last June, because the sector has outperformed others and the board reckoned it was too costly to miss out on such good returns. Analysts worry that strict SRI screening restricts investment choice and limits flexibility and diversification.

The WM Company, which reviews fund performance, calculated in 2001 that average relative returns from ethical funds sold to private investors underperformed mainstream trusts over five years. The trouble is that most environmental funds have strong biases to certain sectors – for example, resources, technology and financials. A more optimistic report from UBS Warburg last year found that while screened portfolios undoubtedly take industry bets, returns are no more affected than any actively managed fund driven by an investment style. Nonetheless, 'the history of mutual fund performance tells us that most will underperform their passive benchmarks. We do not expect socially responsible funds to be any different', the report adds. Importantly, says the WM Company, whatever the returns, ethical screens increase volatility.

Perhaps as a consequence of such findings, managers are broadening the scope of SRI research and freeing funds to invest in more stocks. 'There has to be a certain pragmatism about SRI,' says Simon Baker, Jupiter's SRI fund manager. In addition to negative screens, fund managers are imposing positive screens, picking companies that are involved in specified 'industries of the future', say, renewable energy. These companies may have a good safety record or a policy on equal opportunities, pollution controls and recycling.

SRI fund managers are also embracing the idea of 'active engagement', whereby managers can exert their power as shareholders to change management practices for the better. The theory is that managers can pick companies seen as leaders in environmental and social issues. 'This is a more subjective method of finding reasons to invest in companies,' says Aegon's Charles Henderson. Out of active engagement has evolved the notion of 'best in class'. Managers pick out companies that are doing the best they can to be socially responsible. These may be oil companies that have pioneered renewable energy technologies or embraced social accounting policies.

Increasingly, conventional fund managers are looking at SRI and the wider impact of corporate social responsibility, which encompasses corporate governance, transparency, employee and shareholder welfare and social accounting, on profits. Investment houses, including Henderson, Morley and Friends Provident Ivory & Sime, employ SRI analysts to add to conventional stock

▶

market research. The idea is that these analysts study information others ignore and can quantify risks the market is unaware of. 'We can discount the risks early and identify the opportunities in key sectors, such as chemicals and motoring, which will undergo profound change,' says Mark Campanale, who heads up Henderson Global Investment's SRI team. He cites the health and safety risks at Railtrack, and the risks to insurance companies linked to asbestosis claims. This inclusive approach is developing into a mainstream investment style, says Campanale, which in time will be offered alongside trackers and growth funds.

Source: 'Positive About "Best" Stocks', *Financial Times*, 2 March 2002.

→ Making the connection

This article discusses a number of important issues about SRI: (1) despite concerns that negative screens (excluding certain industries and companies) hamper returns, there is little evidence that the opportunity cost is in fact substantial, (2) SRI managers are increasingly using positive screens (selecting the 'industries of the future') and active engagement, and (3) even conventional fund managers cannot afford to ignore social and environmental factors nowadays.

Summary

Explain why regulation is critical to the security markets.

Regulation of security markets is needed since the market mechanism may fail because (1) the actions of a few unscrupulous market participants can damage public confidence (systemic risk), (2) 'markets for lemons' may arise due to information asymmetry between issuers of securities, financial intermediaries and investors, and (3) barriers to market entry may block competition.

Summarise the history and evolution of US securities regulation.

Since the depression in the early 1930s, many laws have been enacted that were designed to make financial markets fair and orderly. For example, the Securities Act of 1933 requires disclosure of information about an initial public offering and has general anti-fraud provisions. The Glass–Steagall Banking Act of 1933 required the separation of commercial and investment banking but was repealed in 1999. The Securities Exchange Act of 1934 provides regulation for the secondary market and created the Securities and Exchange Commission (SEC). The 1990 Market Reform Act permits the SEC to 'prohibit or constrain' programme trading during periods when the market is showing 'extraordinary' movements. The 1995 rules provide regulation related to limit orders and quotations that are published by the market makers. After the devastating accounting and investment frauds that shook corporate America in the late 1990s and the early 2000s, president Bush signed the Sarbanes–Oxley Act in order to regain confidence in the financial system.

Discuss recent regulatory developments in the European Union.

The regulatory framework in the EU is changing rapidly. In recent years, we have seen the consolidation of national supervisors, in some cases leading to fully integrated financial supervisors for securities, banking and insurance. Further, regulations in the various member states are being harmonised through the FSAP. Finally, securities markets are now overseen by two powerful pan-European committees of national regulators, which assist the Commission in drafting laws and supervise their implementation: the ESC and the ESRC.

Discuss the need for regulation at an international level.

Once it becomes cheap and easy to settle trades across borders, US and EU investors may be able to circumvent some US and EU regulations legally and to hide some questionable, and possibly illegal, activities from US and EU surveillance. Further, technology will allow a marketplace or order-gathering function to be located anywhere in the world. This threat of relocation will place constraints on regulators, and global trading will make it more difficult for authorities to regulate investment practices and to protect domestic investors. For these reasons, domestic regulators need to adopt an international orientation and cooperate and coordinate their activities with foreign regulators.

Distinguish between regulation and ethics and describe key ethical issues of investment.

Regulations are 'external' rules that governments impose on market participants. Ethics embodies 'internal rules' of market participants or what are considered to be – under the prevailing set of ideals – 'vices' and 'virtues'. Although not all ethical issues are regulated and one may not land in court for unethical behaviour, most investors obey ethical standards because this is the right thing to do, the threat of self-regulatory sanctions by employers and industry organisations, or the risk of ending up on the front page of the evening newspaper. Common ethical issues in investments include independent advice, corporate governance, insider trading, churning, independent regulators and socially responsible investment. Since ethical boundaries (as well as actual regulations) are often vague, the investor is well-advised to act with caution.

Key terms

Churning 144

Collective good 123

Corporate governance 142

Display rule 129

Employment Retirement Income Security Act of 1974 128

Ethics 140

EU directive 134

Financial Services Action Plan (FSAP) 134

Financial Services Modernization Act of 1999 (Gramm–Leach–Bliley Act) 129

Financial stability 123

Foreign Corrupt Practices Act of 1977 129

Fraud 140

Front running 143

Independent investment advice 141

Information asymmetry 123

Insider information 142

Insider Trading Sanctions Act of 1984 129

Insider Trading and Securities Fraud Enforcement Act of 1988 129

Investment Advisor Act of 1940 128

Investment Company Act of 1940 128

Late trading 145

Maloney Act of 1938 127

Market timing 145

National Association of Securities Dealers (NASD) 127

National market system 127

Public Utility Holding Company Act of 1935 127

Quote rule 129

Regulation 122

Sarbanes–Oxley Act of 2002 129

Securities Act of 1933 126

Securities Acts Amendments of 1975 127

Securities and Exchange Commission (SEC) 125

Securities Exchange Act of 1934 127

Securities Investor Protection Act of 1970 128

Self-regulatory organisations (SROs) 127

Shelf registration 129

Socially Responsible Investment (SRI) 146

Systemic risk 123

Trust Indenture Act of 1939 128

US Banking Act of 1933 (Glass–Steagall Act) 126

Williams Act of 1968 128

Review questions

1 Explain the role of regulation in enhancing competition in the marketplace.

2 Which five major securities acts designed to protect investors were passed by Congress between 1933 and 1938?

3 You are sitting on the board of directors of ABC Company that plans to repurchase its stock at $80 per share. The current price is $72 per share. You tell your brother-in-law to buy 5000 shares before the information becomes public. Is the purchase illegal?

4 What are the differences between regulations and ethics?

5 Mutual funds sometimes face the ethical problem of putting personal gains above client interests. Explain the two primary issues central to the fund scandal described in Connecting Theory to Practice 5.4.

 For an extensive set of review and practice questions and answers, visit the Levy–Post investment website at www.booksites.net/levy

Selected references

Arshadi, Nasser and Thomas H. Eyssell, 1991, 'Regulatory Deterrence and Registered Insider Trading: The Case of Tender Offers', *Financial Management*, **Summer**, 30–39.

Association for Investment Management and Research, 1990, *Standards of Practice Handbook*, 5th edn, Charlottesville, VA: AIMR.

Baker, H. Kent, 1994, *Good Ethics: The Essential Element of a Firm's Success*, Charlottesville, VA: Association for Investment Management and Research.

Berenbeim, Ronald E., 1987, *Corporate Ethics*, New York: The Conference Board.

Casey, John L., 1990, *Ethics in the Financial Marketplace*, New York: Scudder, Stevens & Clark.

Cavanagh, Gerald F., 1990, *American Business Values*, 3rd edn, Englewood Cliffs, NJ: Prentice-Hall.

Hammer, Richard M., Gilbert Simonetti, Jr and Charles T. Crawford, 1983, *Investment Regulation around the World*, Somerset, NJ: Ronald Press.

Hawkins, David, 1986, *Corporate Financial Reporting and Analysis*, 2nd edn, Homewood, IL: Dow Jones–Irwin.

Hu, Henry T. C., 1992, 'New Financial Products, The Modern Process of Financial Innovation and the Puzzle of Shareholder Welfare', *Financial Management Collection*, **7** (1), 1–13.

Lowenstein, Louis, 1988, *What's Wrong with Wall Street*, Reading, MA: Addison-Wesley.

Meulbroek, Lisa K., 1992, 'An Empirical Analysis of Illegal Insider Trading', *Journal of Finance*, **47**, 1661–1699.

Nejat, Seyhun H., 1992, 'The Effectiveness of Insider-Trading Sanctions', *Journal of Law and Economics*, **April**, 149–182.

Schwartz, Robert A., 1988, *Equity Markets Structure, Trading and Performance*, New York: Harper & Row.

Shefrin, Hersh and Meir Statman, 1992, *Ethics, Fairness, Efficiency and Financial Markets*, Charlottesville, VA: Research Foundation of the Institute of Chartered Financial Analysts.

Steinherr, Alfred, 1998, *Derivatives: The Wild Beast of Finance*, Hoboken, NJ: John Wiley & Sons.

Tewles, Richard J. and Edward S. Bradley, 1987, *The Stock Market*, 5th edn, New York: John Wiley & Sons.

Viet, E. Theodore and Michael R. Murphy, 1992, *Ethics in the Investment Profession: A Survey*, Charlottesville, VA: Research Foundation of the Institute of Chartered Financial Analysts.

Williams, Gerald J., 1992, *Ethics in Modern Management*, New York: Quorum Books.

More data on ethics are available in the following journals: *Ethics*, *Journal of Business Ethics* and *Professional Ethics*.

The following websites offer updated (1998) data about ethics:

www.condor.depaul.edu/ethics

www.babson.edu/

www.ethics.ubc.ca/

AIMR Code of Ethics and Standards of Professional Conduct[19]

The code of ethics

Members of the Association for Investment Management and Research shall:

- Act with integrity, competence, dignity, and in an ethical manner when dealing with the public, clients, prospects, employers, employees, and fellow members.
- Practice and encourage others to practice in a professional and ethical manner that will reflect credit on members and their profession.
- Strive to maintain and improve their competence and the competence of others in the profession.
- Use reasonable care and exercise independent professional judgment.

Standards of professional conduct

Standard I: Fundamental responsibilities

Members shall:

A. Maintain knowledge of and comply with all applicable laws, rules, and regulations (including AIMR's Code of Ethics and Standards of Professional Conduct) of any government, governmental agency, regulatory organization, licensing agency, or professional association governing the members' professional activities.

B. Not knowingly participate or assist in any violation of such laws, rules, or regulations.

Standard II: Relationships with and responsibilities to the profession

A. **Use of professional designation.**
   1. Membership in AIMR, the Financial Analyst Federation (FAF), or the Institute of Chartered Financial Analysts (ICFA) may be referenced by members of these organizations only in a dignified and judicious manner. The use of the reference may be accompanied by an accurate explanation of the requirements that have been met to obtain membership in these organizations.
   2. Holders of the Chartered Financial Analyst designation may use the professional designation 'Chartered Financial Analyst,' or the mark 'CFA,' and are encouraged to do so, but only in a dignified and judicious manner. The use of the designation may be accompanied by an accurate explanation of the requirements that have been met to obtain the designation.
   3. Candidates may reference their participation in the CFA Program, but the reference must clearly state that an individual is a candidate for the CFA designation and may not imply that the candidate has achieved any type of partial designation.

---

[19] Source: excerpted with permission from Association for Investment Management Research, *Standards of Practice Handbook*, 7th edn, Charlottesville, VA: Association for Investment Management and Research, Copyright 1996, All Rights Reserved.

B. **Professional misconduct.** Members shall not engage in any professional conduct involving dishonesty, fraud, deceit, or misrepresentation or commit any act that reflects adversely on their honesty, trustworthiness, or professional competence.

C. **Prohibition against plagiarism.** Members shall not copy or use, in substantially the same form as the original, material prepared by another without acknowledging and identifying the name of the author, publisher, or source of such material. Members may use without acknowledgment factual information published by recognized financial and statistical reporting services or similar sources.

Standard III: Relationships with and responsibilities to the employer

A. **Obligation to inform employer of code and standards.** Members shall:
   1. Inform their employer, through their direct supervisor, that they are obligated to comply with the Code and Standards and are subject to disciplinary sanctions for violations thereof.
   2. Deliver a copy of the Code and Standards to their employer if the employer does not have a copy.

B. **Duty to employer.** Members shall not undertake any independent practice that could result in compensation or other benefit in competition with their employer unless they obtain written consent from both their employer and the persons or entities for whom they undertake independent practice.

C. **Disclosure of conflicts to employer.** Members shall:
   1. Disclose to their employer all matters, including beneficial ownership of securities or other investments, that reasonably could be expected to interfere with their duty to their employer or ability to make unbiased and objective recommendations.
   2. Comply with any prohibitions on activities imposed by their employer if a conflict of interest exists.

D. **Disclosure of additional compensation arrangements.** Members shall disclose to their employer in writing all monetary compensation or other benefits that they receive for their services that are in addition to compensation or benefits conferred by a member's employer.

E. **Responsibilities of supervisors.** Members with supervisory responsibility, authority, or the ability to influence the conduct of others shall exercise reasonable supervision over those subject to their supervision or authority to prevent any violation of applicable statutes, regulations, or provisions of the Code and Standards. In so doing, members are entitled to rely on reasonable procedures designed to detect and prevent such violations.

Standard IV: Relationships with and responsibilities to clients and prospects

A. **Investment process.**

A.1. **Reasonable basis and representations.** Members shall:
   a. Exercise diligence and thoroughness in making investment recommendations or in taking investment actions.
   b. Have a reasonable and adequate basis, supported by appropriate research and investigation, for such recommendations or actions.
   c. Make reasonable and diligent efforts to avoid any material misrepresentation in any research report or investment recommendation.
   d. Maintain appropriate records to support the reasonableness of such recommendations or actions.

A.2. Research reports. Members shall:

    a. Use reasonable judgment regarding the inclusion or exclusion of relevant factors in research reports.

    b. Distinguish between facts and opinions in research reports.

    c. Indicate the basic characteristics of the investment involved when preparing for public distribution a research report that is not directly related to a specific portfolio or client.

A.3. Independence and objectivity. Members shall use reasonable care and judgment to achieve and maintain independence and objectivity in making investment recommendations or taking investment action.

B. Interactions with clients and prospects.

B.1. Fiduciary duties. In relationships with clients, members shall use particular care in determining applicable fiduciary duty and shall comply with such duty as to those persons and interests to whom the duty is owed. Members must act for the benefit of their clients and place their clients' interests before their own.

B.2. Portfolio investment recommendations and actions. Members shall:

    a. Make a reasonable inquiry into a client's financial situation, investment experience, and investment objectives prior to making any investment recommendations and shall update this information as necessary, but no less frequently than annually, to allow the members to adjust their investment recommendations to reflect changed circumstances.

    b. Consider the appropriateness and suitability of investment recommendations or actions for each portfolio or client. In determining appropriateness and suitability, members shall consider applicable relevant factors, including the needs and circumstances of the portfolio or client, the basic characteristics of the investment involved, and the basic characteristics of the total portfolio. Members shall not make a recommendation unless they reasonably determine that the recommendation is suitable to the client's financial situation, investment experience, and investment objectives.

    c. Distinguish between facts and opinions in the presentation of investment recommendations.

    d. Disclose to clients and prospects the basic format and general principles of the investment process by which securities are selected and portfolios are constructed and shall promptly disclose to clients and prospects any changes that might significantly affect those processes.

B.3. Fair dealing. Members shall deal fairly and objectively with all clients and prospects when disseminating investment recommendations, disseminating material changes in prior investment recommendations, and taking investment action.

B.4. Priority of transactions. Transactions for clients and employers shall have priority over transactions in securities or other investments of which a member is the beneficial owner so that such personal transactions do not operate adversely to their clients' or employer's interests. If members make a recommendation regarding the purchase or sale of a security or other investment, they shall give their clients and employer adequate opportunity to act on the recommendation before acting on their own behalf. For purposes of the Code and Standards, a member is a 'beneficial owner' if the member has

    a. a direct or indirect pecuniary interest in the securities;

    b. the power to vote or direct the voting of the shares of the securities or investments;

    c. the power to dispose or direct the disposition of the security or investment.

B.5. **Preservation of confidentiality.** Members shall preserve the confidentiality of information communicated by clients, prospects, or employers concerning matters within the scope of the client-member, prospect-member, or employer-member relationship unless the member receives information concerning illegal activities on the part of the client, prospect, or employer.

B.6. **Prohibition against misrepresentation.** Members shall not make any statements, orally or in writing, that misrepresent
   a. the services that they or their firms are capable of performing;
   b. their qualifications or the qualifications of their firm;
   c. the member's academic or professional credentials.
   Members shall not make or imply, orally or in writing, any assurances or guarantees regarding any investment except to communicate accurate information regarding the terms of the investment instrument and the issuer's obligations under the instrument.

B.7. **Disclosure of conflicts to clients and prospects.** Members shall disclose to their clients and prospects all matters, including beneficial ownership of securities or other investments, that reasonably could be expected to impair the member's ability to make unbiased and objective recommendations.

B.8. **Disclosure of referral fees.** Members shall disclose to clients and prospects any consideration or benefit received by the member or delivered to others for the recommendation of any services to the client or prospect.

Standard V: Relationships with and responsibilities to the investing public

A. **Prohibition against use of material nonpublic information.** Members who possess material nonpublic information related to the value of a security shall not trade or cause others to trade in that security if such trading would breach a duty or if the information was misappropriated or relates to a tender offer. If members receive material nonpublic information in confidence, they shall not breach that confidence by trading or causing others to trade in securities to which such information relates. Members shall make reasonable efforts to achieve public dissemination of material nonpublic information disclosed in breach of a duty.

B. **Performance presentation.**
   1. Members shall not make any statements, orally or in writing, that misrepresent the investment performance that they or their firms have accomplished or can reasonably be expected to achieve.
   2. If members communicate individual or firm performance information directly or indirectly to clients or prospective clients, or in a manner intended to be received by clients or prospective clients, members shall make every reasonable effort to assure that such performance information is a fair, accurate, and complete presentation of such performance.

Part 2

RETURN AND RISK

CHAPTER 6

Rates of return

Investment in the News 6

FT

Dubious practices are outlawed

With surprising speed, global investment performance standards (Gips) are being adopted by countries around the world. Based on the well-established US performance presentation standards developed by the Association for Investment Management and Research, they are intended to make it possible for fund managers to compete efficiently and fairly for business across borders.

Traditionally the calculation and presentation of performance numbers has been a dirty process. Marketing executives are under enormous pressure to make their firms' investment results appear as good as possible. Among the common pre-Gips distortions have been the manipulative selection of favourable measurement periods; the cherry-picking of the best portfolios and their presentation as broadly representative; and the corresponding exclusion of small, weak and failed accounts – a statistical phenomenon known as 'survivorship bias' which is especially prevalent in the mutual funds industry. Sometimes fund managers try to present the figures of performance by a purely notional or 'modelled' portfolio as representing how a real fund would perform. Occasionally the performance of different funds is strung together over time, usually to indicate the success of an individual manager (or team) across different employments; these have been dubbed Frankenstein figures.

Gips will outlaw most, if not all, of these dubious practices. But is the fuss worthwhile? There is a substantial amount of academic evidence that past investment performance has little or no bearing on the future. Bacon & Woodrow (B&W), the UK arm of the international consultants Woodrow Milliman, last year carried out research for the UK regulatory body, the Financial Services Authority, on the value of performance league tables. 'In fact,' says Andrew Warwick-Thompson, the B&W partner, in the firm's current Investment News Quarterly, 'as a means of predicting the future, past performance is about as useful as the dregs in your teacup or an end-of-the-pier fortune-teller'. Although the report to the FSA mainly concerned retail funds, the conclusion, says Mr Warwick-Thompson, is just as true for pension fund trustees as for private investors. But academic theory counts for little in the cut-throat business of fund marketing. In practice, good historical data is a vital element for success in any beauty contest for pension fund or endowment mandates. The statistics must be genuine and comparable, however.

▶

Investment in the News 6 continued

Various countries, including the UK and Switzerland, as well as the US, have developed their own performance codes over the years. The growth of international marketing, though, now requires the acceptance of a common standard. Late last year the UK's version – called the UK Investment Performance Standard, or Ukips – was launched through a consultative paper, and given official status at the National Association of Pension Funds' investment conference in March this year. Firms can now become compliant with the Ukips, and thus with Gips. The standard will remain voluntary until 2005, however, allowing scope for an orderly transition from the existing UK code. The expectation is that most British fund managers will make the switch quite quickly. 'In time non-compliance will cease to be an option for most investment firms,' says David MacKendrick, the former UK pensions chief of IBM who is now chairman of the European Investment Performance Committee.

The Gips formula sets out how investment returns are to be calculated, and lays down rules about how portfolios are to be grouped in 'composites' or groups of funds which have similar investment objectives. For practical reasons a minimum five-year performance history is accepted, compared with the 10 years for AIMR-PPS.

Source: Barry Riley, 'Dubious Practices Are Outlawed', *Financial Times*, 12 May 2000.

Learning objectives

After studying this chapter, you should be able to:

1 Understand the different methods for computing rates of return.

2 Analyse the impact of taxes, inflation and exchange rates on rate-of-return calculations.

3 Contrast the different types of stock and bond indices.

4 Discuss the basic sample statistics for summarising historical return data.

5 Compare the historical risk–return trade-off for stocks and bonds.

Rates of return can be calculated and presented in more than one way. Different methods can yield different results, and investment managers, who are rated on their performance, have an incentive to use those methods that make them look best. With this problem in mind, in 1992 the Committee for Performance Presentation Standards (CPPS) of the Association of Investment Management and Research (AIMR) established strict guidelines for its members to follow in calculating and presenting historical performance measures.[1] These guidelines

---

[1] The AIMR is an international, non-profit organisation of more than 68 000 investment practitioners and educators in over 117 countries. Its members are employed as securities analysts, portfolio managers, strategists, consultants, educators and other investment specialists. These professionals practise in a variety of fields, including investment counselling and management, banking, insurance and investment banking and brokerage firms.

are intended to ensure fair representation and full disclosure of an investment manager's performance. As discussed in Investment in the News 6, similar investment performance standards have been developed by countries around the world, and a common standard called global investment performance standards (GIPS) is evolving. Global standardisation of investment performance reporting will allow investors to compare investment managers and will allow managers to compete for new business in foreign markets. The AIMR–PPS and GIPS standards have received widespread acceptance in various markets throughout the global investment industry.

Rates of return are used for various different purposes. One important use for rates of return is evaluating historical performance. For example, mutual funds are commonly evaluated based on their previous one- and five-year performances compared with a broad market index such as the S&P 500. The historical rates of return or ex-post rates of return are rates of return that have already been earned. These ex-post returns are also useful for estimating the rates of return that are expected to occur in the future, or ex-ante rates of return. Such expected rates of return are a key input to the investment process, for example for security selection and risk management. Another important use of rates of return is to estimate a firm's cost of equity (as part of the total cost of capital) for capital budgeting decisions (as studied in corporate finance), such as evaluating future investment projects. One method for estimating the appropriate discount rate to use in net-present-value calculations utilises historical rates of return on equity.

Note that generally we are not interested in the rate of return over a single time period, especially if that period is short, for example a day, a week or a month. Of course, an investor will be excited if he or she achieves a high rate of return over a certain period. However, the returns over short time periods generally are very volatile, which makes it difficult for the purpose of performance evaluation to distinguish between investment skill and chance. Also, rates of return over a single short period are an unreliable guide for estimating future expected rates of returns. For this reason, we generally need to collect a sample of historical rates of return over a longer period of time. From such a sample, we may then compute summary statistics, such as the average rate of return. Averages generally are affected by chance less than individual returns, and hence they are better guides for performance evaluation and for estimating future expected returns. Apart from the average rate of return, we generally also wish to measure the dispersion of the returns around the average. The dispersion indicates the risk that investors were exposed to in the past, and it may also help to estimate the risk that investors will face in the future. Finally, for selecting investment portfolios, we generally need to assess the degree of dependence between the various assets. One way of estimating the dependence between the rates of return of two assets is by looking at the historical co-movements of the rates of return. If the two assets tended to move in sync, then the estimate of future dependency should be high. By contrast, if one asset zigs when the other zags, then the estimate should be low.

The remainder of this chapter is structured as follows. Section 6.1 reviews various methods for computing rates of return. Specifically, we review the techniques used in complying with the AIMR standards. Section 6.2 discusses the effects that taxes, inflation and exchange rates have on rates of return. Next, Section 6.3 discusses stock and bond indices, which are useful benchmarks for performance evaluation. Section 6.4 discusses several summary statistics that can be computed from a sample of historical returns or sample statistics. Finally, Section 6.5 analyses the historical record; it shows the sample statistics for several asset classes over the past century.

6.1 Calculating rates of return

Rates of return measure the profitability of financial assets in percentage figures rather than in dollar amounts. This enables investors to compare the profitability on various assets, independent of the number of assets held and the price level of the assets. For example, you can determine which of two investments has been more profitable by comparing the rate of return on AT&T with that of Microsoft. Suppose you earned $200 on AT&T stock and $100 on Microsoft stock. Was the investment in AT&T more profitable than the investment in Microsoft? If you had invested $1000 in AT&T but only $200 in Microsoft, then the investment in Microsoft surely was more profitable. Comparing the profit in percentage form gives you the information you need. AT&T's rate of return is $200/$1000 = 0.20, or 20%. Microsoft's rate of return is $100/$200 = 0.50, or 50%. Recall that unlike an investment in physical assets (such as an oil field), you can increase (or decrease) the size of an investment in the stock market. That is, financial assets are divisible, whereas most physical assets are not. You could have invested $1000 (instead of $200) in Microsoft and you would have received $500 (= $100 × 5). Since the investment scale can be changed, for comparing the profitability of financial assets, the absolute dollar profit is meaningless and percentage figures are more appropriate.

As discussed in the introductory section, rates of return can be calculated and presented in more than one way, and investment managers have an incentive to use those methods that make them look best. This section reviews the techniques used in complying with the AIMR standards.

6.1.1 Simple rates of return

The simple rate of return of an investment measures the dollar capital gain or loss and the dollar income from the investment during a period as a percentage of the dollar amount invested. Specifically, the simple rate of return (R) is computed as

$$R = \frac{EMV - BMV + I}{BMV} \tag{6.1}$$

where EMV is the ending market value, BMV is the beginning market value, and I is income received from the investment during the evaluation period. The income may include cash dividend payments on stocks and coupon payments on bonds. Equation 6.1 gives rates of return in decimal form. To get percentages, simply multiply by 100. We can decompose the rate of return into two components:

$$R = \underbrace{\frac{EMV - BMV}{BMV}}_{\substack{\text{Capital gain} \\ \text{or loss}}} + \underbrace{\frac{I}{BMV}}_{\substack{\text{Cash flow} \\ \text{yield}}} \tag{6.1a}$$

There are two components to the simple rate of return: (1) capital gains or losses and (2) the cash flow yield. The first term on the right of the equals sign is the capital gain or loss as a percentage of the initial investment in the security. The second term is the cash flow yield, such as the dividend yield on a stock or the current yield on a bond.

To demonstrate the simple-rate-of-return calculation, assume you purchased 200 shares of stock at the beginning of the year for $100 per share. At the end of the year, you receive an $8 cash dividend per share. The stock is trading at the end of the year at $110 per share. The rate of return in this case is

$$R = \frac{(200 \times \$110) - (200 \times \$100) + (200 \times \$8)}{(200 \times \$100)}$$

$$= \frac{200}{200}\left(\frac{\$110 - \$100 + \$8}{\$100}\right) = \frac{\$18}{\$100} = 0.18, \text{ or } 18\%$$

which consists of a 10% capital gain and an 8% dividend yield. Note that the rate of return does not depend on whether you buy 200, 100 or even one share of stock, because the number of shares (200, in this example) is common to every term in the equation and hence cancels.

Note that Equation 6.1 can also be written as

$$R = \frac{EMV + I}{BMV} - \frac{BMV}{BMV} = \frac{EMV + I}{BMV} - 1$$

and hence,

$$1 + R = \frac{EMV + I}{BMV} \tag{6.1b}$$

which, in this example, would be

$$1 + R = \frac{(200 \times \$110) + (200 \times \$8)}{(200 \times \$100)} = \$1.18$$

This tells us that an investment of $1 at the beginning of the period is worth $1.18 at the end of the period.

The simple rate of return is useful because it measures profitability of financial assets in percentage figures rather than in dollar amounts, and hence it can be used to compare the profitability on various assets, independent of the number of assets held and the price level of the assets. Still, the simple rate of return has an important limitation. Specifically, it does not account accurately for the timing of the cash flows (dividends and coupons) that are received during the evaluation period. The simple rate of return simply aggregates all cash flows, irrespective of whether they are received at the beginning, in the middle or at the end of the evaluation period. However, an investor would rather have the cash flows at the beginning of the year than at the end; cash flows received at the beginning of the year can be reinvested to yield extra wealth by the end of the period. Thus, the simple-rate-of-return method is correct only if all cash flows are received at the end of the investment period; reinvestment is not possible in that case.

6.1.2 Adjusted rate of return

The adjusted rate of return is used to calculate rates of return by taking into account the timing of cash flows. Therefore, it is also referred to as the time-weighted rate of return. This rate of return is used throughout the rest of the book, so it will be called the rate of return to distinguish it from the simple rate of return. The rate of return assumes that all interim cash flows are reinvested in the security under consideration. For example, if an investor wants to measure the rate of return for 2003 on Xerox stock, and $10 dividends are paid in January, then the $10 is used to purchase more Xerox stock immediately after the dividends are received. The AIMR (1991, p. 28) explains the philosophy of this adjustment as follows:

> If cash flows occur during the period, they must theoretically be used, in effect, 'to buy additional units' of the portfolio at the market price on the day that they are received. Thus, the most accurate approach is to calculate the market value of the portfolio on the date of each flow, calculate an interim rate of return for the subperiod [according to Equation 6.1], and then link the subperiod returns to get the return for the month or quarter.[2]

There are two approaches to computing the time-weighted rate of return:

■ The linking method calculates the simple rate of return to each subperiod, where the timing of the cash flows determines the end of the subperiods and then calculates the rate of return from these simple rates of return.
■ The index method focuses on the notion that cash flows are used to purchase additional units of the portfolio.

Both approaches yield the same adjusted rate-of-return values.[3] The index method is useful in understanding time-weighted computations, whereas the linking method is simpler to calculate in practice.

The following numerical example illustrates these two approaches to computing rates of return. For simplicity, we ignore taxes and inflation for the moment (these topics are discussed in Section 6.2). Assume you are investing in shares of ABC, Inc. Exhibit 6.1a shows the necessary data for your calculations. Notice that ABC, Inc., paid quarterly cash dividends and that its stock price fluctuated considerably during this year.[4] Specifically, notice that the price fell early in the year, rose during the latter part of the year and fell again to its original level by year's end.

By the linking method, the simple rate of return (r_t) is calculated for each subperiod (t). Then the rate of return (R) for the entire period is obtained by the following formula:[5]

$$R = \prod_{t=1}^{n}(1 + r_t) - 1 = [(1 + r_1)(1 + r_2) \ldots (1 + r_n)] - 1 \qquad (6.2)$$

where n is the number of subperiods (in the case of ABC, $n = 5$).

---

[2] Adapted with permission from Association for Investment Management and Research, 1991, *Report of the Performance Presentation Standards Implementation Committee*, Charlottesville, VA: Association for Investment Management and Research. Copyright © 1991, All rights reserved.

[3] The equality between the two methods holds only if the interim periods are of equal length. If large differences occur, then we should use the following general expression for the linking method $R = \prod_{t=1}^{n}(1 + r_t)^{l_t} - 1$, where l_t denotes the length of the t-th interim period. In this way, the longer an interim period, the higher its weight. In the examples in Exhibits 6.1–3, the length of the interim periods is approximately equal and the general expression is not needed.

[4] Dividends are typically declared about a month after the end of a fiscal quarter and paid two weeks later. Hence, most firms pay dividends in February, May, August and November.

[5] The symbol $\prod$ means 'take the product of'. For example, $y = \prod_{i=1}^{3} x_i$ means $y = x_1 \times x_2 \times x_3$. Thus, if $x_1 = 1$, $x_2 = 2$ and $x_3 = 3$, then $y = 1 \times 2 \times 3 = 6$.

Exhibit 6.1	Calculating a time-weighted rate of return for ABC, Inc.

(a) Table of input information

Date	Dollar dividend per share ($)	Market price when dividend is received ($)
1 January		100
15 February	2	80
15 May	2	95
15 August	2	105
15 November	2	120
31 December		100

(b) Calculating a time-weighted rate of return by the linking method

Date	Interim period	Interim rate of return	Time-weighted rate of return
1 January			
15 February	1	−0.18	−0.18
15 May	2	0.2125	−0.0057
15 August	3	0.1263	0.1198
15 November	4	0.1619	0.3011
31 December	5	−0.1667	0.0842

Source: From *Introduction to Investments*, 2nd edn, by Levy. © 1999. Reprinted with permission of South-Western, a division of Thomson Learning: www.thomsonrights.com. Fax 800 730-2215.

Exhibit 6.1b illustrates the linking method of computing returns. The simple rate of return over period 1 (1 January–15 February) is −0.18 (i.e. ($80 − $100 + $2)/$100), and over period 2 (15 February–15 May) it is 0.2125 (i.e. ($95 − $80 + $2)/$80). Thus, the time-weighted rate of return over the period 1 January–15 May is given by −0.0057 (i.e. ([1 + (−0.18)][1 + 0.2125] − 1)). Continuing this procedure, the time-weighted rate of return for the whole year is found to be 0.0842, or 8.42% (see the last entry in the last column of Exhibit 6.1b).

Note that an 8% return is obtained (i.e. ($100 − $100 + $2 × 4)/$100) if the timing of dividends is ignored and the simple rate of return given by Equation 6.1 is used. How can the 42-basis-point difference in the rates of return (8.42% − 8.00%) be explained?[6] This question can be answered by working through the index method for the same investment (see Exhibit 6.2).

By looking at the index method calculations, we notice that the 42-basis-point difference results from the additional shares received by reinvesting the dividends. For example, on 15 February each shareholder received $2 per share in dividends, which could have been invested in the stock at a cost of $80 per share. Thus, Exhibit 6.2 shows that on 15 February, the owner of 100 shares of ABC, Inc., would receive $200 (or $2 × 100), with which the shareholder could purchase 2.5 additional shares ($200/$80). Therefore, on 15 May this shareholder would receive $2 dividends on the original 100 shares, as well as $2 dividends on the additional 2.5 shares. Exhibit 6.2 illustrates how this reinvestment process would work throughout the entire year.

The additional shares purchased in period t (AS_t) are calculated by the following formula:

$$AS_t = \frac{N_{t-1} D_t}{P_t}$$

---

[6] Recall that a basis point is 1% of 1%, or 0.01%.

Exhibit 6.2	Calculating a time-weighted rate of return for ABC, Inc., by the index method

Date	Dollar dividend per share ($)	Market price when dividend is received ($)	Additional shares purchased	Number of shares owned
1 January		100		100
15 February	2	80	2.5	102.5
15 May	2	95	2.1579	104.6579
15 August	2	105	1.9935	106.6514
15 November	2	120	1.7775	108.4289
31 December		100		108.4289

Source: From *Introduction to Investments*, 2nd edn, by Levy. © 1999. Reprinted with permission of South-Western, a division of Thomson Learning: www.thomsonrights.com. Fax 800 730-2215.

where N_{t-1} is the number of shares owned at the end of period $t-1$ (for example, the number of shares owned on the ex-dividend date), D_t is the cash dividend paid in period t, and P_t is the price per share in period t after the dividends are paid. For example, 2.1579 additional shares are purchased on 15 May, where

$$AS_t = (102.5 \text{ shares} \times \$2)/\$95 = 2.1579$$

The number of shares owned is simply the number from the previous period plus any additional shares purchased during the period. Specifically,

$$N_t = N_{t-1} + AS_t$$

Notice in Exhibit 6.2 that when share prices are low, the dividends' receipts will buy more shares than when share prices are high. Since share prices are low early in the year, this investor is able to buy more shares early and hence receive more dividends during the rest of the year. By year's end, the investor has approximately 108.43 shares worth $100 per share. The rate of return over this year can be found by dividing the value of the investment at the end by the amount invested at the beginning and subtracting 1. That is,

$$R = \frac{P_n N_n}{P_0 N_0} - 1 = \frac{100 \times 108.4289}{100 \times 100} - 1 = 0.084289, \text{ or } 8.4289\% \qquad (6.3)$$

where P_n is the stock price at the end of the year, N_n is the number of shares owned at the end of the year, P_0 is the stock price at the beginning of the year, and N_0 is the number of shares owned at the beginning of the year. Equation 6.3 is similar to the equation for the simple rate of return given in Equation 6.1. Equation 6.3 assumes income to be zero, but the ending market value contains the cash flows, as well as earnings on the cash flows, that were reinvested during the year.

Note that the index method given in Equation 6.3 yields exactly the same rate of return as the linking method (ignoring rounding errors and the effect of small differences in the length of the interim periods). Based on this, we conclude that the linking method appropriately handles interim cash flows such as dividend payments on common stocks and coupon payments on bonds.

To sum up, the time-weighted rate of return is the superior calculation because it addresses the timing of cash flows appropriately. Investors prefer to receive money now rather than later, a fact that is ignored by the simple method. For example, suppose that firms A and B have the same data as those given in Exhibit 6.1, with only one difference: firm A pays an $8 cash dividend at the beginning of the period, whereas Firm B pays an $8 cash dividend at the end of the period. Are investors indifferent regarding the dividend payment date, as Equation 6.1 implies? They are not, because of the time value of money. However, the simple-rate-of-return calculation can mislead investors into believing that the rate of return for both firms is the same. The time-weighted rate-of-return method accounts for the timing of cash flows by assuming that interim cash flows from a security are reinvested in the security itself.

Nonetheless, in many cases, the return from reinvesting the interim cash flows are relatively small; hence, the simple and adjusted rates of return are often not that different. This explains why the simple (and quick) method is sometimes employed despite its lack of precision.

Notice that the different calculation methods attempt not to identify the best strategy for the investor but rather to measure the correct rate of return. For example, sometimes reinvesting the dividends is bad (for example, when the stock price falls). However, only the time-weighted rate-of-return method accounts adequately for interim cash flows.

6.1.3 Some further adjustments

Thus far, we have demonstrated how to adjust the rate of return for cash dividends on stocks and coupon payments on bonds. However, we also have to account for other distributions to stockholders apart from cash dividends, such as stock dividends and rights. Similarly, rates of return on bonds need to account for accrued interest. Finally, another complication in computing average returns over multiple periods is that the dollar amount invested may change over time, for example if the investor sells part of his or her portfolio or invests new funds.

Stock splits

Stock splits increase the number of shares with no additional investment. Thus, no cash flows are involved. How does such a split affect the rate-of-return calculation? The practice box below demonstrates how to incorporate stock splits and cash dividends into the rate of return calculations.

Practice box

Problem   Suppose you purchase 100 shares of ABC on 1 January at $50 per share. ABC pays $2.30 annual dividend per share on 15 March, when the stock is trading at $55. On 23 February 2001, ABC Company splits its stock in a three-for-two ratio effective on 30 May, when the stock is trading at $60. (A three-for-two stock split implies three new shares are substituted for two old shares held if ABC closes on 31 December at $35 per share.) What would your rate of return be using the linking method?

Solution   The following table summarises the basic data regarding ABC that are relevant for the rate of return calculation:

Date	Dividend ($)	Split	Market price of stock ($)
1 January			50
15 March	2.30		55
30 May		3-for-2 shares	40
31 December			35

▶

The simple rate of return for the period 1 January–15 March is:

$$\frac{\$55 + \$2.30 - \$50}{\$50} = \frac{\$7.3}{\$50} = 0.1466, \text{ or } 14.6\%$$

The simple rate of return for the period 15 March–30 May is:

$$\frac{(1.5 \times \$40) - \$55}{\$55} = \frac{\$60 - \$55}{\$55} = \frac{\$5}{\$55} \cong 0.0909, \text{ or } 9.09\%$$

Note that we multiply the end of the period price of $40 by 1.5 because a three-for-two split implies a 50% increase in the number of shares we are holding. As we assume in the calculation that one share was bought at the beginning of the period, 1.5 shares are held at the end of the period due to the split. Finally, the rate of return for the last period is:

$$\frac{\$35 - \$40}{\$40} = \frac{-\$5}{\$40} \cong -0.125, \text{ or } -12.5\%$$

Using the linking method (from Equation 6.2), the rate of return for the year is given by

$$R = [(1 + 0.1466)(1 + 0.0909)(1 - 0.125)] - 1 = 0.09447, \text{ or about } 9.447\%$$

Stock dividends

Stock dividends are incorporated into the calculation exactly as is the split. This is because the stock dividend increases the number of shares held with no cash flow involved. To illustrate, suppose that 10% stock dividends are paid, the stock price being $38 at the beginning of the period and $40 at the end. Then, for each share bought at the beginning of the period, the investor would hold 1.1 shares after the dividend payment (due to the 10% stock dividends); hence, we should multiply $40 by 1.1 to obtain the value of the investor's holding at the end of the period. The rate of return for our example at the end of the period would be

$$\frac{1.1 \times \$40 - \$38}{\$38} = \frac{\$44 - \$38}{\$38} = \frac{\$6}{\$38} \cong 0.1579, \text{ or } 15.79\%$$

Rights

Firms may raise equity by rights offerings, whereby existing stockholders have the right to buy new shares at a price lower than the market price, called the subscription price. Rights offerings are incorporated into the simple rate of return, like cash dividends. To illustrate, suppose that for every two shares held the investor earns the right to buy one share at the subscription price. One right is linked to each old stock, which means that in our specific example the investor has a right to buy half a new share for every single stock that he or she owns. These rights are traded separately from the stock and have market value. Since existing stockholders receive a right to buy new shares at a price lower than the market price of the stock, the stock price generally drops when the rights are issued. Suppose that the stock price at the beginning of the period on 1 January was $100 and on 10 March the rights were traded for $5 a right (thus, the value of the right attached to each share was $5). On 10 March, when the right started trading separately from the stock for the first time, the stock price was $107. Assuming no other distributions, the rate of return for this period is then given by

$$\frac{\$107 + \$5 - \$100}{\$100} = \frac{\$12}{\$100} = 0.12, \text{ or } 12\%$$

It is assumed that investors will sell the stock and the right at the end of the subperiod and receive $107 plus $5. Therefore, the $5 right is treated the same as a cash dividend.

We would like to emphasise that the price of rights as published in the media reflects the value attached to each old stock, regardless of the allocation ratio. So if, for example, the right allocation ratio is one right for each two old stocks and an investor wishes to exercise his or her rights (i.e. buy more shares at the relatively low price), then he or she needs two rights (or a value of $10) to buy one new share.

Indeed, investors who do not hold firm stocks can buy two rights for $10 and add the subscription price, say $97, to purchase one share of the firm. What is important for the rate-of-return calculation is that the value of the right is added to the end-of-period value exactly as cash dividends are added, regardless of whether the investor exercises the rights or simply sells them in the market.

Accrued interest on bonds

Calculating the rate of return on bonds raises one more issue regarding the timing of cash flows. Whereas the cash dividends on stocks are paid on a periodic (most often quarterly) basis, bond coupon interest accrues daily. The bond prices quoted by the financial media and market makers do not include accrued interest in most cases. However, the actual price paid for the bonds does include accrued interest. That is, the buyer in the secondary market must pay to the seller any interest accrued up to the selling date. Therefore, when calculating the interim return on bonds, the investor must incorporate accrued interest. The CPPS of the AIMR describes the underlying philosophy of rate-of-return calculations for bonds:

> The Standards clearly state that an accrual basis, rather than a cash basis, should be used for calculating interest income. The guiding premise, again, should be to include that income to which the portfolio was truly entitled if the security were sold at the end of the performance interval. Stock dividends do not become payable unless the stock is owned on the ex-dividend date. Dividends should therefore be accrued as income as of their ex-date. Interest on most fixed-income securities becomes payable pro rate as long as the security is held. Interest should therefore be accrued according to whatever method is appropriate for the specific issue.[7]

To account for accrued interest, simply add the values for accrued interest at the beginning and end of the period to the respective beginning and ending prices in Equation 6.1. Formally, the simple rate of return (R_t) can be expressed as

$$R_t = \frac{[(P_t + AI_t) - (P_{t-1} + AI_{t-1}) + C_t]}{(P_{t-1} + AI_{t-1})} \tag{6.4}$$

where P_t is the price of the bond at the end of period t, P_{t-1} is the price of the bond at the end of period $t - 1$, AI_t is the accrued interest as of the end of period t (investors get it if they sell the bonds), AI_{t-1} is the accrued interest as of the end of period $t - 1$ (investors have to pay it

---

[7] Adapted with permission from AIMR (1991, pp. 31–32). All rights reserved.

when they buy the bonds), and C_t is the coupon paid at the end of subperiod t (the coupon dates determine the end of the interim subperiods). As discussed later, if the coupon is paid at the end of the period, the accrued interest will be zero, and the formula will be

$$R_t = \frac{[P_t - P_{t-1} + C_t]}{P_{t-1}} \tag{6.4a}$$

Hence, we need to account only for the accrued interest at the beginning of the first interim period, or AI_0, and the accrued interest at the end of the last interim period, or AI_n (unless these dates also happen to be coupon dates).

Let us illustrate how to calculate rates of return for bonds on an accrual basis. Consider a coupon bond that pays 8% on a semiannual basis. Assume that $40 in interest is paid on 15 May and 15 November. Exhibit 6.3a illustrates how to calculate the time-weighted rate of return using the linking method. The exhibit lists the coupon payments, market prices and accrued interest for each date. Recall from Equation 6.1 that the simple rate of return requires calculating the beginning and ending market values. The accrual basis incorporates accrued interest in these values. For example, consider the simple return during the period

---

Exhibit 6.3   Calculating the rate of return for an 8% semiannual coupon-bearing bond

(a) Computing a time-weighted rate of return by the linking method

Date (t)	Interim period	Coupon ($)	Market price ($)	Accrued interest ($)	Accrued rate of return	Rate of return to t
1 January			990	10[a]		
15 May	1	40	1030	0	0.07[b]	0.07
15 November	2	40	1020	0	0.0291	0.1011[c]
31 December	3		1000	10[a]	−0.0098	0.0903[d]

[a] $(1000)(0.08)(1.5/12) = \$10$ (interest is paid on 15 May and 15 November).

[b] $\dfrac{[\$1030 - (\$990 + \$10) + \$40]}{\$990 + \$10} = 0.07$

[c] $(1 + 0.07) \times (1 + 0.0291) - 1 = 0.1011$.

[d] $(1 + 0.1011) \times (1 - 0.0098) - 1 = 0.0903$, or $(1 + 0.07) \times (1 + 0.0291) \times (1 - 0.0098) - 1$.

(b) Computing a time-weighted rate of return by the index method

Date (t)	Interim period	Coupon ($)	Market price ($)	Accrued interest ($)	Additional bonds purchased	Number of bonds owned
1 January			990	10[a]		100
15 May	1	40	1030	0	3.8835[b]	103.8835
15 November	2	40	1020	0	4.0738[c]	107.9573
31 December	3		1000	10		107.9573

[a] $(1000)(0.08)(1.5/12) = \$10$ (interest is paid on 15 May and 15 November).

[b] $(\$40 \times 100$ bonds$)/\$1030 = 3.8835$ bonds.

[c] $(\$40 \times 103.8835$ bonds$)/\$1020 = 4.0738$ bonds.

Source: From *Introduction to Investments*, 2nd edn, by Levy. © 1999. Reprinted with permission of South-Western, a division of Thomson Learning: www.thomsonrights.com. Fax 800 730-2215.

1 January–15 May, where the beginning market value is $1000 ($990 + $10, where $10 is accrued interest). The calculation of accrued interest will be handled in detail in Chapter 13. Until then, accrued interest can be estimated as the fraction of the period since the last payment multiplied by the payment amount. In this case, it is (1.5 months/6 months) × $40 = $10. The 1.5 months represent the period from 15 November to 1 January. The ending market value is $1030. The income paid in this period is the coupon payment of $40. Thus, the simple rate of return for the first interim period is

$$R_1 = \frac{[\$1030 - (\$990 + \$10) + \$40]}{\$990 + \$10} = \frac{\$70}{\$1000} = 0.07, \text{ or } 7\%$$

Note that the accrued interest at the end of period i will be zero if there is a coupon payment. That is, all interest that has been accrued was paid via the coupon payment. From Exhibit 6.3 we find that the rate of return over this year was 9.03%.

Exhibit 6.3b illustrates how to calculate the rate of return with the index method. Assuming the investor buys 100 bonds, then the rate of return, using the index method, is

$$R = \frac{(\$1000 + \$10)(107.9573)}{(\$990 + \$10)(100)} - 1 \cong 0.09037$$

or approximately 9.037%. Once again, the results of the index method are approximately equal to the results obtained by the linking method, and the slight difference is due to rounding and small differences in the length of the interim periods.

Changes to the amount invested

The simple rate of return and the adjusted rate of return are not affected by the dollar amount invested. However, in some cases the dollar amount invested changes across time. The dollar-weighted average rate of return takes this factor into account.

To illustrate, consider the following example. Suppose a stock's price at the beginning of the first year is $100, and at the end of the first year it is $110. At the end of the second year, the share price is $132. For simplicity, assume that no dividend is paid and that an investor buys one share at the beginning of the first year and buys one more share at the beginning of the second year. Then, at the end of the second year, the two shares are sold. The rate of return for the first year is 10%, or [($110/$100) − 1], and for the second year it is 20%, or [($132/$110) − 1]. In this case, the time-weighted rate of return is

$$R = [(1 + 0.1)(1 + 0.2)]^{1/2} - 1 \cong 0.1489, \text{ or } 14.89\%$$

This rate of return is not affected by the dollar amount invested in each year. It will be the same, regardless of whether the investor buys, say, five shares rather than one share at the beginning of the first year.

The dollar-weighted average rate of return is the internal rate of return (IRR), which solves the following equation:

$$100 = -\frac{1 \times \$110}{1 + \text{IRR}} + \frac{2 \times \$132}{(1 + \text{IRR})^2}$$

where $110 is the dollar amount invested in purchasing one more share. We find, then, that IRR is 16.54%.

Note that the IRR is the rate of return on the investment, taking into account that $100 is invested at the beginning of the first year and that an additional $110 is invested in the second year. If the investor buys, say, an additional five shares rather than one share at the end of the first year, then the IRR is the value that solves the following equation:

$$100 = -\frac{5 \times \$110}{(1 + \text{IRR})} + \frac{6 \times \$132}{(1 + \text{IRR})^2}$$

Hence, IRR is 18.48%.

Thus, the IRR is affected by the amount invested in each period of time – hence the term 'dollar-weighted average rate of return'. In our example, investing more monies in the second year increases the rate of return. This result is not surprising because, in this case, the rate of return in the second year exceeds the rate of return in the first year.

6.2 Adjustments for tax, inflation and exchange rates

In practice, the computation of rates of return is complicated by taxes and inflation and also, for foreign investments, exchange rates. The ultimate objective of investment is to fund the investor's consumption of goods and services in the future. Hence, investors typically are interested in the rate of return after tax and inflation and expressed in their domestic currency. After all, the investor cannot buy additional goods and services with the parts of his or her investment revenue that are (a) paid as taxes, (b) required to compensate for increased prices of goods and services, or (c) lost in currency transactions. For this reason, unless stated differently, we will use after-tax rates of return that are corrected for inflation and exchange rates throughout the remainder of this book.

6.2.1 After-tax rates of return

Taxes generally change the return an investor receives. Unfortunately, we cannot possibly give a detailed analysis of the fiscal treatment of investments here. This subject warrants a book in its own right, since taxes amount to numerous complications. One complication is that tax rules change often, and typically the tax rates are determined more by political negotiation than by economic reasoning. Also, the fiscal treatment of investments differs strongly across different investors, different securities and different countries. The differences include the tax rate that applies and also the timing of the taxation; taxes may be levied when the gains or losses are realised or upon accrual of the gains or losses. For example, in the USA, many pension funds and other institutional investors are tax-exempt so as to avoid double taxation, while the security holdings of individual investors are taxable. Also, the tax rate faced by different individual investors differs, depending, for example, on their income level. Further, different securities are treated in a different way. For instance, in the USA, the income from municipal bonds is exempt from taxes.[8] For these reasons, we cannot possibly give an exhaustive treatment of taxation. However, we can provide the general procedure for adjusting the rates of return if the tax rates for a given investor are known. The procedure is conceptually similar to the simple-rate-of-return calculations in the previous section. The only difference is the reduction of capital gain (or loss) and income resulting from taxes (at the time the tax is levied).

---

[8] Municipal bonds are bonds issued in the USA by municipal organisations, such as city, county and state governments and school districts.

To illustrate this, assume that the income from assets (cash dividends or coupon payments) is subject to the income tax rate (T_i) and that capital gain is subject to the capital gain tax rate (T_g) when realised, i.e. when the assets are sold at time n.[9] To include the impact of taxes in an interim period before time n, adjust the simple-rate-of-return calculation as follows:

$$R_t = \frac{\text{EMV}_t - \text{BMV}_t + I_t(1 - T_i)}{\text{BMV}_t} \tag{6.5}$$

where R_t is the interim after-tax rate of return, EMV_t is the market value at the end of interim period t, BMV_t is the market value at the beginning of interim period t, I_t is the income (cash dividends or coupon payments) paid at the end of interim period t, and T_i is the income tax rate.

Capital gains taxes are incorporated only when the gains or losses are realised at time n. The after-tax, simple rate of return for the last interim period (R_n) is

$$R_n = \frac{(\text{EMV}_n - \text{BMV}_n) - (\text{EMV}_n - \text{BMV}_1)T_g + I_n(1 - T_i)}{\text{BMV}_n} \tag{6.6}$$

The term $(\text{EMV}_n - \text{BMV}_1)T_g$ accounts for the loss due to payment of capital gains taxes (or gains due to tax reduction with capital losses). This is actually only an approximation because of the reinvestment-of-dividends assumption. Technically, one should also consider the capital gains and losses on reinvested dividends. However, this would increase the computational difficulties greatly without significantly altering the results.

Assuming a 25% tax rate on dividends, Exhibit 6.4 uses the information from Exhibit 6.1 on ABC, Inc., stock and illustrates the after-tax computations for five periods. It is assumed that shares are bought on 1 January and sold on 31 December. The simple rate of return for the first period is −0.1850 (i.e. [$80 − $100 + $2(1 − 0.25)]/$100 = −18.50/100). This is lower than the interim rate of return of −0.18 calculated with no taxes in Exhibit 6.1b. Notice that taxes reduced the time-weighted rate of return from 8.42% before taxes (see Exhibit 6.1b) to 6.27% after taxes (see Exhibit 6.4). Also notice that in this example, there are no capital gains, because the beginning price is equal to the ending price.

Exhibit 6.4	Calculating a time-weighted rate of return for ABC, Inc., on an after-tax basis assuming a 25% income and capital gains tax				
Date (t)	Interim period	Dollar dividend ($)	Market price ($)	Simple rate of return	Rate of return to t
1 January			100	N/A	N/A
15 February	1	2	80	−0.1850	−0.1850
15 May	2	2	95	0.2063	−0.0169
15 August	3	2	105	0.1211	0.1022
15 November	4	2	120	0.1571	0.2753
31 December	5		100	−0.1667	0.0627

Source: From *Introduction to Investments*, 2nd edn, by Levy. © 1999. Reprinted with permission of South-Western, a division of Thomson Learning: www.thomsonrights.com. Fax 800 730-2215.

---

[9] The tax system in most countries distinguishes between income and capital gains; usually they are taxed at different rates.

6.2.2 Inflation-adjusted rates of return

Thus far, we have calculated rates of return in nominal dollars, ignoring the effect of inflation.[10] Inflation causes investors to lose purchasing power when they sell their assets in the future and wish to buy goods and services with the proceeds.

The consumer price index (CPI) measures the cost of living and is used for determining the inflation rate. The change in the CPI over a given time period represents the percentage change in the price of a specified basket of consumer goods during this time period. The index was normalised to 100 in 1982. That is, the value of the basket of goods in 1982 was divided by itself and multiplied by 100. In order to get the index value for the following years, the value of the basket of goods for each year is divided by the basket's value in 1982 and multiplied by 100. From these index values, we can then calculate the inflation rate during a given period. For example, in September 2002 the CPI was 181.0, and in September 2003 the CPI was 185.2. Hence, the inflation rate (h) for the year September 2002–September 2003 was

$$h = \frac{CPI_{2003} - CPI_{2002}}{CPI_{2002}} = \frac{185.2 - 181.0}{181.0} \cong 0.0232, \text{ or } 2.32\% \qquad (6.7)$$

Inflation reduces the purchasing power of an investment. That is, a person may invest $1000 with the expectation of getting $1100 back in a year and of using this sum to purchase goods and services. If the overall cost of these goods and services rises more than 10% over the year, however, the purchasing power of the investor's wealth has dropped. To include inflation in our calculations, we must first determine the real rate of return.

The real rate of return is the nominal rate of return adjusted for inflation. The real rate of return (R_{real}) is calculated as

$$R_{real} = \frac{1 + R_{nom}}{1 + h} - 1 \qquad (6.8)$$

where R_{nom} is the nominal rate of return and h is the inflation rate.[11]

Note two properties of real rates of return:

- If there is no inflation ($h = 0$), then the real rate of return is equal to the nominal rate of return.
- If the nominal rate of return is equal to the inflation rate ($R_{nom} = h$), then in real terms the rate of return is zero.

Let us turn to our previous example, where the before-tax rate of return was 8.42% and the after-tax rate of return was 6.27%. Assuming a 5% annual inflation, the after-tax real rate of return would be:

$$R_{real} = \frac{1.0627}{1.05} - 1 = 0.0121, \text{ or } 1.21\%$$

Thus, in our example, both inflation and taxes reduce the nominal rate of return of 8.42% to 1.21%.

---

[10] Inflation is the increase over time in the cost of goods and services. Deflation refers to the decrease over time in the cost of goods and services.

[11] Equation 6.8 can be approximated by $R_{real} = R_{nom} - h$, where R_{real} is the real rate of return, R_{nom} is the nominal rate of return and h is the inflation rate. This is known as the Fisher relationship and was originally proposed by Fisher (1930).

6.2.3 Exchange-rate-adjusted rates of return

Today, many investors invest abroad either directly or indirectly (through mutual funds). Exchange rates can alter the rate of return realised on an international investment. Although a falling dollar may be good for US investors in a foreign country, it is bad for foreign investors in the USA. Chapter 9 gives a detailed treatment of foreign investment and exchange-rate risk. This section illustrates how foreign exchange influences rates of return.

Suppose a US investor is interested in buying a UK stock that currently trades at £70. Suppose the foreign exchange rate today is $fx_0(£/\$) = 1.43$. That is, 100 pounds (£) will buy about 143 dollars ($). Alternatively, $fx_0(\$/£) = 1/fx_0(£/\$) = 1/1.43 = 0.7$, and $100 is worth £70. The process of international investment involves three steps. Step 1 is to convert the $100 to £70. Step 2 is to invest in the UK stock. In this example, the rate of return on the stock is 15% in the UK during the year. The US investor ends up with £80.5, or £70 × (1 + 0.15). Finally, step 3 is to convert the £80.5 back to US dollars at the new exchange rate, which has fallen to £0.6/$ (or $1.67/£). The investor is left with $134.17, or £80.5 × $1.67/£. That is, the US dollar became less valuable relative to the UK pound. At the beginning of the year, $100 would buy £70. At the end of the year, $100 would buy £60. Thus, we say that the dollar depreciated. Alternatively, the pound appreciated from $1.43 at the beginning of the year to $1.67 at the end.

In this case, the actual return to the US investor was a gain of 34.17%, or $[(\$134.17/\$100) - 1]$. Although the investor earned 15% in the local currency of UK pounds, the exchange-rate decline from 0.7 to 0.6 boosted the rate of return in domestic currency of US dollars. Thus, foreign investments contain two components: the return in local currency and the return on foreign exchange.

Formally, the rate of return adjusted for foreign exchange risk (R_D) is as follows:

$$R_D = \frac{fx_n(DC/FC)}{fx_0(DC/FC)}(1 + R_L) - 1 \tag{6.9}$$

where $fx_n(DC/FC)$ is the foreign exchange rate at time n in domestic currency (DC) per foreign currency (FC), $fx_0(DC/FC)$ is the rate at time 0, and R_L is the rate of return on the foreign investment in local currency.

Note that the rate of return on foreign exchange alone (R_{fx}) can be calculated as

$$R_{fx} = \frac{fx_n(DC/FC)}{fx_0(DC/FC)} - 1 \tag{6.10}$$

For example, in the case of the pound,

$$R_{fx} = \frac{1.67}{1.43} - 1 \cong 0.167, \text{ or } 16.7\%$$

Thus, this investor gained 16.7% simply from changes in the exchange rate. Substituting Equation 6.10 into Equation 6.9, we obtain an alternative method to compute returns in domestic currency:

$$R_D = (1 + R_{fx})(1 + R_L) - 1 \tag{6.9a}$$

In our illustration with the pound, we have

$$R_D = (1 + 0.167)(1 + 0.15) - 1 \cong 0.342$$

Exhibit 6.5 illustrates the effect of foreign exchange rates. Exhibit 6.5(a) shows the monthly rate of return to a US investor from investing in a UK stock index during the period from January 2000 to August 2003. There is a noticeable exchange rate effect, as the exchange rate fluctuated between about 1.4 and 1.6 dollars for one pound. Exhibit 6.5(b) shows the results for investing

Exhibit 6.5	Exchange-rate-adjusted rates of return of investing in overseas equity indices (January 2000–August 2003)

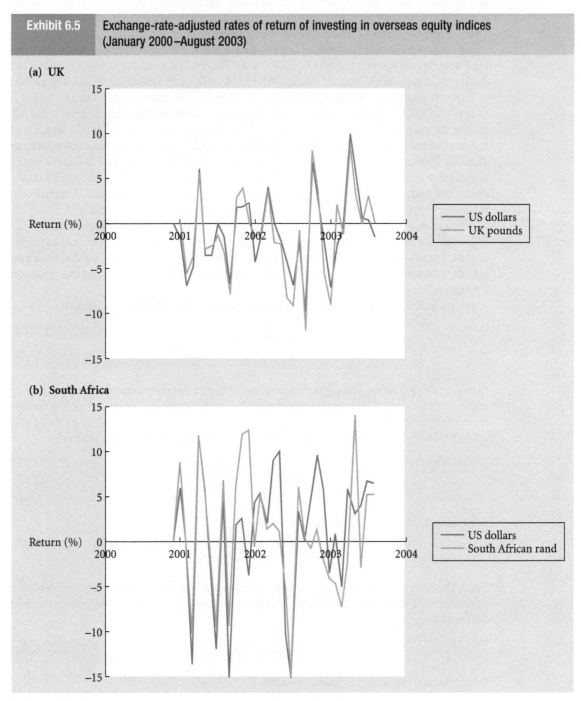

(a) UK

(b) South Africa

Source: www.msci.com

in South African equity during the same period. In this case, the effect of exchange-rate adjustments is enormous. Specifically, the exchange rate first depreciated from below eight rand for one dollar in early 2001 to about 12 rand for one dollar in late 2001; then it fell back to about eight rand for one dollar in late 2002. Related to this, the South African index realised gains of about 25% in November–December 2001, but the rate of return in US dollars was about zero. This difference is not surprising, because the weakness of the rand was an important driver of the advance of the resource-heavy Johannesburg Stock Exchange (JSE); many South-African companies have a large exposure to the exchange rate as they have a rand costs base but big dollar revenues. By contrast, in April–May 2002, the return in dollars was about 20% while the return in rands was only about 3%. This example shows clearly that the returns to a US investor in overseas markets can be much different after adjusting for exchange rates.

6.3 Indices

Indices are used widely to measure historical rates of return across several securities. Almost all evening newscasts and newspapers report the changes in the Dow Jones index. What is the Dow Jones index, what do these changes mean, and why is the index important? A securities index measures the performance of a certain basket of securities in the same way that the CPI measures consumer prices. For example, the Dow Jones Industrial Average (DJIA) is a stock index that consists of 30 blue-chip stocks.[12] Exhibit 6.6 lists the 30 stocks that made up the DJIA as of 1 January 2003 as well as the original 12 stocks that were included in the index. It is interesting to note that of the original stocks, only General Electric (GE) is still in the index. However, GE has been removed and reinstated twice since the inception of the index. The most recent change to the index occurred on 1 November 1999, when Microsoft Corporation, Intel Corporation, SBC Communications and Home Depot Incorporated replaced Chevron Corporation, Goodyear Tire & Rubber Company, Union Carbide Corporation and Sears, Roebuck. Many other indices are used in the securities markets, and new ones are being introduced constantly.

Indices are important for several reasons. First, stock indices measure the general performance of an economy. It is unusual to have a stock market that is rising sharply if the economy is falling sharply.[13] Interestingly, stock indices measure investors' expectations about the future performance of the economy, while statistics like the GDP measure the past performance. Second, indices are useful as a benchmark for gauging the performance of investment managers. For example, bond fund managers could be evaluated against a bond index, such as the Lehman Brothers Aggregate Bond Index, to determine how well they are doing. Also, stock mutual fund managers are typically evaluated against some index, such as the S&P 500. Third, indices serve as a guide for passively managed mutual funds. That is, an investor who wanted to match the performance of the DJIA could invest in a mutual fund that mimics the DJIA. Nowadays, an investor can buy SPDRs, which mimic the Standard and Poor's 500 index, QQQs which mimic the NASDAQ, and Diamonds, which mimic the Dow Jones index. Fourth, indices are used by investment analysts to assess the overall direction of the market.

---

[12] Blue-chip stocks are common stocks of large, financially sound corporations with a good history of dividend payments and consistent earnings growth.

[13] There are exceptions, such as the US bull market in the early 1990s.

Exhibit 6.6	The Dow Jones Industrial Average then and now

(a) Thirty stocks included in the DJIA, as of 1 January 2003

3M Company	Home Depot Incorporated
Alcoa Incorporated	Honeywell International Inc.
Altria Group, Incorporated	Intel Corporation
American Express Company	International Business Machines
AT&T Corporation	International Paper Company
Boeing Company	J.P. Morgan Chase & Company
Caterpillar Incorporated	Johnson & Johnson
Citigroup Incorporated	McDonald's Corporation
Coca-Cola Company	Merck & Company, Incorporated
DuPont	Microsoft Corporation
Eastman Kodak Company	Procter & Gamble Company
Exxon Mobil Corporation	SBC Communications Incorporated
General Electric Company	United Technologies Corporation
General Motors Corporation	Wal-Mart Stores Incorporated
Hewlett-Packard Company	Walt Disney Company

(b) Twelve stocks originally included in the DJIA, as of 26 May 1896

American Cotton Oil	LaClede Gas
American Sugar	National Lead
American Tobacco	North American
Chicago Gas	Tennessee Coal & Iron
Distilling & Cattle Feeding	U.S. Leather Preferred
General Electric	U.S. Rubber

Source: Phyllis S. Pierce, *The Dow Jones Averages 1885–1995*, HG 4915.D6434 1996, www.djindexes.com, © Dow Jones & Company, Inc., 2003.

Fifth, indices are used to estimate statistical parameters such as market beta, a measure of risk that is developed further in Chapter 10. Finally, indices are used as underlying securities in various derivative securities like futures and options.

The various indices differ in three major aspects: (1) which securities are included in the index, and how many, (2) how the index is adjusted over time for changes in securities (such as take-overs and mergers), and (3) which method is used to calculate the index. The following sections focus on these three factors as they examine some of the more popular indices.

6.3.1 Stock indices

Indices are designed to monitor the performance of some segment of the financial markets. For example, the Gold/Silver Stock Index tracks mining stocks, whereas the Wilshire Small Cap Index tracks small-company stocks. The number of securities within an index varies widely. For example, the Gold/Silver Stock Index contains 12 stocks whereas the Wilshire 5000 Index consists of 5000 stocks.

Indices can generally be categorised as price-weighted, value-weighted or equally weighted indices. The difference depends on how much significance, or weight, is given to each security. The price-weighted index weights its component securities according to their market price, whereas the value-weighted index weights its component securities by their equity market value. The equally weighted indices weight each security equally. For example, the DJIA is based on the stock price of each security, whereas the S&P 500 is based on the market value of each firm's equity.

Price-weighted index

The value of a price-weighted index is found by adding the prices of each security and dividing by a divisor. Namely, the index (I_t) at date t is given by

$$I_t = \frac{1}{divisor} \times \sum_{i=1}^{n} P_{i,t} \tag{6.10}$$

where n is the number of assets in the index and $P_{i,t}$ is the price of asset i in period t. The divisor is a number that is adjusted periodically for stock dividends, stock splits and other changes. For example, when a stock splits two-for-one, the stock price typically falls by about 50% but the economic value of the stock holding has not changed. Changing the divisor is a means to adjust an index for these artificial changes so that the index continues to reflect the actual value of the securities.

Exhibit 6.7 provides a simple illustration of how a price-weighted index is calculated for three securities. For simplicity, the divisor is set equal to 3. Exhibit 6.7 shows five periods for each security price, index value and percentage change. Notice that from period 1 to period 2, all three securities rise by 10%. As expected, this results in a 10% increase in the index. However, in the next three periods, only one security rises by 10%; the rest remain the same. Notice that a 10% increase in the highest-priced security has a greater influence on the index than a 10% increase in the lowest-priced security. When only security 1 rises by 10%, to $181.50, the index rises by 5%. However, when only security 3 rises by 10%, to $60.50, the index rises only by 1.54%. This pattern is generally true for price-weighted indices. High-priced securities

Exhibit 6.7	Calculating a price-weighted index					
Security		Period (t)				
	Price	1	2	3	4	5
1	P_1 ($)	150	165	181.50	181.50	181.50
	% change (%)		10	10	0	0
2	P_2 ($)	100	110	110	121	121
	% change (%)		10	0	10	0
3	P_3 ($)	50	55	55	55	60.50
	% change (%)		10	0	0	10
	Index (I_t)[a]	100	110	115.50	119.17	121
	% change		10	5[b]	3.18	1.54

[a] $I_t = \sum_{i=1}^{n} Q_t P_{i,t}$, where $Q_t = 1/divisor = 1/3$.

[b] Let us illustrate one of the calculations. The 5% rate of return in period 3 is obtained in the following way: the index is $I_3 = 1/3(\$181.50) + 1/3(\$110) + 1/3(\$55) = 115.50$, and the index percentage change is $(115.50/110) - 1 = 0.05$, or a 5% increase.

influence the index more than lower-priced securities. We know that a firm's stock price is a function of the number of shares outstanding and is easily changed by stock splits. Therefore, there is no intuitive justification for higher-priced stocks having more influence.

The popular DJIA is a price-weighted average of 30 US industrial stocks. Hence, this index can be expressed as

$$I_{DJIA,t} = \frac{1}{divisor} \sum_{i=1}^{30} P_{i,t}$$

To avoid adverse effects of artificial changes, such as stock splits, on this price-weighted index, a procedure has been developed to adjust the divisor to get the index back to its original level before the artificial change. The divisor of the DJIA was initially set at 30 in 1928. With time, stock dividends and stock splits, however, the divisor continued to decrease, and it is now only a small fraction.

As mentioned earlier, a price-weighted index has to be adjusted when a security in the index has a stock split. Recall that when a stock splits, its price falls, which would result in an artificial decline in a price-weighted index if no adjustments were made. For example, on 15 May 1992, Disney's stock split four-for-one. The stock price before the split was $152.875. As soon as the stock had split, one share was worth only $38.21875 ($152.875/4). On the day of the split, the DJIA was reported at 3353.09. Had the DJIA not been adjusted for the Disney stock split, it would have fallen to 3143.27, a 6.26% decline (i.e. (3143.27 − 3353.09)/3353.09). Before Disney had the stock split, the divisor was 0.54643593 and the sum of the other 29 stocks totalled 1679.375. Thus, the DJIA, if unadjusted for the stock split of Disney, would have been

$$I_{DJIA,unadjusted} = \frac{1}{0.54643593}(1679.375 + 38.21875) = 3143.27$$

In the case of Disney, the adjusted divisor is 0.51225107, and thus

$$I_{DJIA,adjusted} = \frac{1}{0.51225107}(1679.375 + 38.21875) = 3353.03$$

which is equal to the original level of the DJIA, except for slight rounding errors. Although the adjustment in the divisor makes sure that the index is unaffected by stock dividends and stock splits, the influence of Disney stock on the DJIA also becomes much smaller after the split, because the stock's price is lower (see Exhibit 6.8).

One advantage of price-weighted indices is that it is relatively easy to mimic the rate of return of the index simply by buying the same number of shares of each stock in the index. Many mutual funds, for example, are in essence 'index funds' that strive only to mimic a particular index, such as the DJIA. However, the bias of price-weighted indices toward high-priced stocks lacks any economic justification, because a stock's price is easily manipulated with stock splits. For example, why should Disney's stock become less influential within the index after its split?[14] The value-weighted indices were developed to address this shortcoming of price-weighted indices.

---

[14] In particular, after the four-for-one split, a portfolio seeking to mimic the DJIA would have to sell three-quarters of its Disney stocks, because price-weighted indices assume that the same number of shares are held. The proceeds must be reinvested equally in all the stocks within the index.

Exhibit 6.8	Calculating a value-weighted index				

	Period (t)				
	1	2	3	4	5
$P_{1,t}$ (\$)	150	165	181.50	181.50	181.50
$N_{1,t} \times P_{1,t}$ (\$)	45 000	49 500	54 450	54 450	54 450
% change (%)		10	10	0	0
$P_{2,t}$ (\$)	100	110	110	121	121
$N_{2,t} \times P_{2,t}$ (\$)	15 000	16 500	16 500	18 150	18 150
% change (%)		10	0	10	0
$P_{3,t}$ (\$)	50	55	55	55	60.5
$N_{3,t} \times P_{3,t}$ (\$)	5 000	5 500	5 500	5 500	6 050
% change (%)		10	0	0	10
Index (I_t)[a]	100	110	117.6[b]	120.2	121
% change (%)		10	6.9	2.2	0.67

[a] $Q_{i,t} = 100 \times \left(\dfrac{N_{i,t}}{\sum\limits_{i=1}^{n} N_{i,1} \times P_{i,1}} \right)$ and $I_t = \sum\limits_{i=1}^{n} Q_{i,t} \times P_{i,t}$, where $N_{1,t} = 300$, $N_{2,t} = 150$ and $N_{3,t} = 100$.

[b] For example, the index value (based on the information in Equation 6.12) is $I_3 = (100/65\,000) \times [(300 \times \$181.50) + (150 \times \$110) + (100 \times \$55)] = 0.001538(54\,450 + 16\,500 + 5500) = 117.6$, and the percentage change in the index is $(117.6/110) - 1 = 0.069$, or 6.9%.

Value-weighted index

A value-weighted index is based on the total market value of each security or a firm's equity value rather than just the price of each share. If we let $N_{i,t}$ represent the number of shares of stock outstanding of firm i at time t, then the firm's equity value, or its market capitalisation, is $N_{i,t} \times P_{i,t}$. Shares of stock are called outstanding if they are not held by the company that issued them. The value-weighted index is given by

$$I_t = \left(\frac{100}{\sum\limits_{i=1}^{n} N_{i,1} P_{i,1}} \right) \sum\limits_{i=1}^{n} N_{i,t} P_{i,t} \qquad (6.11)$$

where 100 represents the beginning value of the index. Note that the term within the parentheses is constant across time. Also, when $t = 1$, the two summation equations are identical and the value of the index is 100.

For the securities given in Exhibit 6.8, assume that $N_{1,1} = 300$, $N_{2,1} = 150$ and $N_{3,1} = 100$. Therefore, each stock has different market capitalisations: \$45 000 (i.e. $300 \times \$150$) for security 1, \$15 000 (i.e. $150 \times \$100$) for security 2 and \$5000 (i.e. $100 \times \$50$) for security 3. Given the prices of the three securities in Exhibit 6.8 and the values of $N_{i,1}$, the denominator of Equation 6.11 is

$$\sum\limits_{i=1}^{n} N_{i,1} P_{i,1} = (300 \times \$150) + (150 \times \$100) + (100 \times \$50) = \$65\,000$$

Substituting this result in Equation 6.11 yields

$$I_t = \frac{100}{65\ 000} \times \sum_{i=1}^{3} N_{i,t} P_{i,t} \tag{6.12}$$

Exhibit 6.8 carries out the calculations for the five periods. For simplicity, it is assumed that the number of shares outstanding remains the same during these five periods. Notice that for value-weighted indices, a 10% change in all securities has the same influence on the percentage change in the index. However, when all prices are not changed by the same percentage, the value-weighted index depends directly on each security's relative market capitalisation. The greater the market capitalisation of a security, the larger its influence (see the percentage change of the index in columns 3, 4 and 5 of Exhibit 6.8).

The main advantage of the value-weighted index is that it is not affected by stock splits and stock dividends. For example, if the firm with security 1 in Exhibit 6.8 declared a two-for-one split in period 4, then $N_{1,4} = 300 \times 2$, but also $P_{1,4} = 181.50/2$ and the total market capitalisation remains \$54 450. From Equation 6.12, we see that the index is not affected by this change, because the 2 in $N_{1,4}$ cancels with the 2 in the denominator of $P_{1,4}$ (or $(300 \times 2) \times (181.5/2) = (300 \times 181.5)$).

Equally weighted index

An equally weighted index is calculated by giving each security the same weight, regardless of its price or market capitalisation. If we think of the index as a portfolio, we can imagine that investors purchase an equal dollar amount of each security.

Two methods are used to construct an equally weighted index: the arithmetic method and the multiplicative method. (The multiplicative method is also known as the geometric method.) Both methods employ the rate of return on the securities in the index corresponding to some interim period. This interim period is typically one day. The value of an index by the arithmetic method is found using the following formula:

$$I_t = I_{t-1} \times \left(1 + \frac{1}{n} \times \sum_{i=1}^{n} R_{i,t} \right) \tag{6.13}$$

The term $\frac{1}{n} \times \sum_{i=1}^{n} R_{i,t}$ is an arithmetic average of the rates of return of all the securities in the index.

Exhibit 6.9 provides the index calculations for this method. From $t = 1$ to $t = 2$, the rates of return on all three securities are 10%. Thus, the index value at $t = 2$ is

$$I_2 = 100[1 + (1/3)(0.1 + 0.1 + 0.1)] = 100(1.1) = 110$$

From $t = 2$ to $t = 3$, only security 1 changes, and the new index level is

$$I_3 = 110[1 + (1/3)(0.1 + 0.0 + 0.0)] = 110(1.033) = 113.63$$

Thus, we see that the percentage change in the index is 3.3% (see the last row in Exhibit 6.9), regardless of the stock's price level or market capitalisation.

The arithmetic method is used in the equally weighted index series provided by the Center for Research in Securities Prices (CRSP) and is available in two versions. One version includes dividends in the return corresponding to each interim period calculation, and one version

| Exhibit 6.9 | Calculating an equally weighted index with the arithmetic method |

Security	Price	Period (t)				
		1	2	3	4	5
1	P_1 ($)	150	165	181.50	181.50	181.50
	% change (%)		10	10	0	0
2	P_2 ($)	100	110	110	121	121
	% change (%)		10	0	10	0
3	P_3 ($)	50	55	55	55	60.5
	% change (%)		10	0	0	10
	Index $(I_t)^a$	100	110	113.63	117.38	121.25
	% change (%)		10	3.3	3.3	3.3

$$^a\, I_t = I_{t-1} \times \left(1 + \frac{1}{n} \times \sum_{i=1}^{n} R_{i,t} \right)$$

Source: From *Introduction to Investments*, 2nd edn, by Levy. © 1999. Reprinted with permission of South-Western, a division of Thomson Learning: www.thomsonrights.com. Fax 800 730-2215.

does not. The index is also calculated with either daily prices or monthly prices. In addition, the CRSP provides a value-weighted series.[15]

The multiplicative or geometric method differs from the arithmetic method solely on how returns are averaged across securities. Specifically, the value of an index by the multiplicative method is found with the following formula:

$$I_t = I_{t-1} \times \left(\prod_{t=1}^{n} (1 + R_{i,t}) \right)^{1/n} \tag{6.14}$$

The term $\left(\prod_{t=1}^{n} (1 + R_{i,t}) \right)^{1/n}$ is a geometric average of the rates of return of all the securities in the index.

Exhibit 6.10 shows the index calculations for the multiplicative method. A comparison of Exhibits 6.9 and 6.10 reveals that the arithmetic method of averaging results in higher values than the multiplicative method.

The difference between the arithmetic method and the geometric method is illustrated by two well-known equal-weighted stock indices provided by Value Line, a securities analysis firm that offers opinions on the investment potential of various securities. On 30 June 1961, Value Line introduced the Value Line Composite Index. This index presupposed that an equal dollar amount is invested in each and every stock covered in the Value Line Investment Survey. The returns from doing so are averaged geometrically every day across all the stocks in the survey; consequently, this index is frequently referred to as the Value Line Geometric Index (VLG). The VLG was intended to provide a rough approximation of how the median stock in the Value Line universe performed. However, the performance of the VLG over time proved to underestimate the portfolio performance by too large a factor. Specifically, it can be

---

[15] The CRSP is the University of Chicago's Center for Research in Security Prices, which supplies security data and is used widely by academic investment researchers.

Exhibit 6.10	Calculating an equally weighted index with the multiplicative or geometric method					

Security	Price	Period (t)				
		1	2	3	4	5
1	P_1 ($)	150	165	181.50	181.50	181.50
	% change (%)		10	10	0	0
2	P_2 ($)	100	110	110	121	121
	% change (%)		10	0	10	0
3	P_3 ($)	50	55	55	55	60.5
	% change (%)		10	0	0	10
	Index (I_t)[a]	100	110	113.55[b]	117b.2	121
	% change (%)		10	3.2	3.2	3.2

[a] $I_t = I_{t-1} \times \left(\prod_{i=1}^{n} (1 + R_{it}) \right)^{1/n}$

[b] For example, the index value is $I_3 = 110[(1 + 0.1)(1 + 0.0)(1 + 0.0)]^{1/3} = 110(1.1)^{1/3} = 110 \times 1.03228 \cong 113.55$, and the percentage change in the index is $(113.55/110) - 1 \cong 0.032$, or 3.2%.

proven mathematically that the daily return of a geometric index will always be smaller than the return of an arithmetic index. The difference becomes larger if the differences in return between the individual stocks become larger, for example in volatile markets. Accordingly, it was easy for astute investors to 'game' the early Value Line futures with a representative basket of the underlying securities, since the basket would always outperform the VLG. On 1 February 1988, Value Line began publishing the Value Line Arithmetic Index (VLA), which is calculated using the arithmetic method rather than the multiplicative method. The VLA provides an estimate of how an equal-dollar weighted portfolio of stocks performed. Or, put another way, it tracks the performance of the mean, rather than the median, stock in the index. The two indices can yield very different results, especially in volatile markets. For example, in the three-year period from 1 January 2000 to 31 December 2002, the VLG had an annualised return of −15.1% in comparison with 0.3% for the VLA.

6.3.2 Bond indices

Bond indices are designed to track different segments of the bond market. Bond indices that incorporate total returns (coupon and price changes) were developed in the 1970s. Before this, indices ignored coupon payments, which make up a large portion of a bond's return.

Bond indices have several problems that stock indices do not have. First, because bonds have a finite maturity, the set of bonds within an index is always changing. A change in a bond's maturity affects the risk of the basket of bonds. Also, because of the call features within bonds, the overall set of bonds is changing constantly. When interest rates fall sharply, most firms call their bonds and reissue new bonds with lower coupon rates. For example, after eight years, a ten-year bond in the index will be a two-year bond, and two-year bonds have different risk characteristics than ten-year bonds. Second, many bonds are not actively traded, which leads to pricing problems. How do you compute the value of a bond index at the end of the day

Exhibit 6.11	Characteristics of four bond indices			
Characteristic	Lehman Brothers	Merrill Lynch	Ryan	Salomon Brothers
Number of issues within index	Over 6500	Over 5000	7 Treasury issues	Over 5000
Maturity	>1 year	>1 year	>2 years	>1 year
Weighting	Value	Value	Equal	Value
Reinvestment of intramonth cash flows	No	Yes, in specific bond	Yes, in specific bond	Yes, at 1-month T-bill rate

Source: Adapted with permission from Frank K. Reilly *et al.*, 1992, 'Alternative Bond Market Indexes', *Financial Analysts Journal*, **May–June**, 47. Copyright © 1992, Association for Investment Management and Research, Charlottesville, VA. All Rights Reserved.

when a particular bond within the index did not trade? Do you use the price from the last time the bond traded, which could be days earlier, when market conditions were much different? Do you estimate the current market price by some other method? Clearly, an investor should be cautious when using bond indices that contain inactive bonds.

Exhibit 6.11 lists the characteristics of four major bond indices. Notice that the approaches vary. The Ryan Index uses equal weighting, whereas the others use value weighting. Lehman Brothers ignores the reinvestment of intramonth cash flows, and Salomon Brothers assumes the monies are invested at the one-month Treasury bill rate. Over the long run, the movements of these indices are very similar; however, in the short run they may not move in tandem. Notice that three of the four indices are broad-based. Thus, we know that they will contain prices that are not based on literal trades and that the component bonds will be changing constantly. For example, in 1996, several firms issued long-maturity bonds: International Business Machines (IBM) issued 100-year bonds and Time–Warner issued 40-year bonds. As more companies start issuing long-term bonds, indices will also represent, on average, longer-maturity bonds. Thus, the maturity structure of an index itself can change over time.[16]

6.3.3 Major stock indices around the world

Indices for stocks are easier to develop and maintain than bond indices. Exhibit 6.12 presents a partial listing of stock indices. Notice that most indices are value-weighted; price weighting is the next most popular method. Recall that a value-weighted index has the advantage of automatically adjusting for stock splits and is weighted based on market capitalisation.

Most major exchanges have indices that track how the stocks on their particular exchange are performing. For example, the NYSE Composite Index is a value-weighted index of all the stocks on the NYSE. Similarly, the TOPIX Index covers almost 1500 stocks on the Tokyo Stock Exchange. Another widely watched index is the S&P 500, which is value-weighted. Many professional investment managers are evaluated based on how well they perform relative to the S&P 500. Many vendors of indices now maintain a whole range of indices. For example, Dow Jones has indices that cover the entire globe as well as indices covering each major industry. Similarly, Wilshire maintains a whole set of different indices.

---

[16] For more details, see Reilly *et al.* (1992).

Exhibit 6.12   Partial listing of stock indices

Stock index name	Weighting method	Purpose of index
US stock indices		
AMEX Composite Index	Value	American Stock Exchange Index
AMEX Oil Stock Index	Price	Index of 13 oil companies traded on the AMEX
Dow Jones indices	Price and value	US blue-chip stocks and broad-based global indices
AMEX Major Market Index	Price	Index of 20 blue-chip stocks; mimics the DJIA
NASDAQ Composite Index	Value	All 5000+ stocks listed on the NASDAQ
National OTC stock indices	Value	US OTC stocks
NYSE Composite stock index	Value	All NYSE stocks
Russell indices	Value	Russell 3000: 3000 largest US stocks; Russell 1000: 1000 of the highest of the 3000 stocks in Russell 3000, ranked by size; Russell 2000: consists of the other 2000 stocks
S&P indices	Value	Large US stocks
Value Line	Geometric	Over 1700 smaller US stocks
Wilshire indices	Value	Small US stocks
European market indices		
Amsterdam AEX	Value	Index of 25 most traded stocks in the Netherlands
CAC 40 Stock Index	Value	French stock market index of the 40 largest companies based on market capitalisation
FTSE 100 Index	Value	Index of top 100 UK companies ranked by market capitalisation
Swiss Market Index (SMI)	Value	Swiss blue-chip stock index with the 30 most significant stocks traded on the Swiss Stock Exchange
Xetra Dax Index	Value	Index of 30 blue-chip stocks traded on the Frankfurt Stock Exchange
Asian market indices		
Hang Seng Index (Hong Kong)	Value	Index that tracks the performance of the Hong Kong Stock Exchange
Nikkei 225 Stock Average	Price	Index that tracks the performance of the Tokyo Stock Exchange
Straits Time IDX (Singapore)	Value	Index that tracks the performance of the Stock Exchange of Singapore
Tokyo Stock Price (TOPIX)	Value	Almost 1500 stocks on the Tokyo Stock Exchange Index
Other market indices		
All Ordinaries Index	Value	Index of the 500 largest companies listed on the Australian Stock Exchange
TA-100	Value	Index of the 100 largest shares in terms of market capitalisation on the Tel Aviv Stock Exchange
S&P TSX Composite	Value	Index that tracks the performance of the Toronto Stock Exchange
Other stock indices		
Center for Research in Security Prices (CRSP)	Arithmetic	NYSE/AMEX and OTC, with and without dividends and value
Computer Technology Stock Index	Value	Index of 30 widely held computer technology stocks
Gold/Silver Stock Index (XAU)	Value	Index of 12 large mining stocks
Institutional Stock Index	Value	Index of 75 stocks largely held by institutions
International (ADR) Market Stock Index	Value	Index of 50 foreign stocks traded on the NYSE as American depository receipts
Morgan Stanley Capital International World Index (MSCI)	Value	Global index consisting of 23 developed market country indices

6.4 Sample return statistics

In this section, we will discuss several statistics for describing or summarising a sample of past rates of return or sample statistics. Specifically, we will consider the sample mean, the sample variance, the sample standard deviation, the sample covariance and the sample correlation coefficient. All these measures are after-the-fact or ex-post measures, i.e. they look at the past. Chapter 7 will discuss the corresponding statistics for summarising the statistical distribution of before-the-fact, or ex-ante, returns. These statistics are known as population statistics.

6.4.1 Sample mean

To measure the return on a portfolio of multiple assets in a given year or to measure the return on a specific security (or a portfolio) across multiple periods, some averages must be calculated. There are two main methods for calculating averages of financial assets. These methods use the arithmetic average and the geometric average. Because the two methods yield different results, it is important to study them and be able to understand the interpretation of these two averages.

The arithmetic method of determining the average rate of return adds the realised rate of return over different periods[17] identified by subscript t ($R_{i,t}$) and divided by the number of periods (T). That is,

$$\bar{R}_{A,i} = \frac{\displaystyle\sum_{t=1}^{T} R_{i,t}}{T} \tag{6.15}$$

where $\bar{R}_{A,i}$ is the average (or mean) arithmetic rate of return.

For example, if AT&T stock had returned −10%, 0%, 25% and 9% over the past four years, then the average rate of return using the arithmetic method is

$$\bar{R}_A = \frac{-0.10 + 0.0 + 0.25 + 0.09}{4} = 0.06, \text{ or } 6\%$$

The geometric method is an averaging method that compounds rates of return. That is, if \$1 is invested in period 1, then it will be worth \$$(1 + R_1)$ at the end of period 1. The geometric method assumes that \$$(1 + R_1)$ is invested in period 2. At the end of period 2, the investment will be worth the amount invested at the beginning of period 2 multiplied by the value of a dollar invested in period 2. That is, the investment at the end of period 2 is worth \$$(1 + R_1)(1 + R_2)$. Continuing this procedure over all ex-post periods would give us the value at the end of T periods of a \$1 investment at the beginning of the period. This total return is averaged by taking the Tth root. Therefore, the geometric average can be expressed as

$$\bar{R}_{G,i} = \left[\prod_{t=1}^{T} (1 + R_{i,t}) \right]^{1/T} - 1 \tag{6.16}$$

---

[17] At this point, the length of the period (t) does not matter. It can be a year, a quarter, or even a day.

where $\bar{R}_{G,i}$ is the mean geometric rate of return. Using the example of AT&T stock, we have

$$\bar{R}_{G,AT\&T} = [(1 - 0.1)(1 + 0)(1 + 0.25)(1 + 0.09)]^{1/4} - 1 \cong 0.0523, \text{ or } 5.23\%$$

Notice that the geometric average of 5.23% is different from the arithmetic average of 6%.

Let us look at a more dramatic case to illustrate the different results obtained from these two methods. Suppose a mutual fund paid no dividends and began with a market value of $100 per share. At the end of the first year the fund was worth $50 per share, and at the end of the second year the fund was once again worth $100 per share. The rate of return in the first year was $[(\$50 - \$100)/\$100] = -0.50$, or a loss of 50%. The rate of return in the second year was $[(\$100 - \$50)/\$50] = 1.0$, or an increase of 100%. The arithmetic average is $(-0.5 + 1.0)/2 = 0.25$, or 25%. The geometric average, however, is $[(1 - 0.5)(1 + 1)]^{1/2} - 1 = 0\%$.

Suppose you invest for two years in the fund. Which averaging method is correct – the 0% geometric average rate of return or the 25% arithmetic average rate of return? In this case, you originally invested $100, and after two years ended up with $100. Clearly, from an investor's viewpoint, there was no profit, or a 0% rate of return. The geometric average, therefore, is the correct calculation, because it shows a zero rate of return that reflects the change in the value to the investor. Indeed, the geometric average can be interpreted as being the actual growth of the assets, and the arithmetic average is meaningless in this case. Thus, the geometric average is appropriate to compute the average rate of return over multiple periods. Indeed, the linking method for computing rates of return (see Section 6.1.2) computes the geometric average of the simple rates of return over the subperiods.

In two situations, however, the arithmetic average is accurate and should be used:

■ The arithmetic method is correct when estimating the average performance across different securities for one period of time. For example, you would use the arithmetic average when calculating the average return for securities within a specific industry. If you wanted to assess the performance of the automobile industry over the previous year, you would take the arithmetic average of the rates of return of automobile stocks. Hence, you would not be measuring growth over time but rather performance during one period of time.

■ The arithmetic average is an unbiased estimate of future expected rates of return.[18] Suppose we want to invest in Microsoft for just one year. By taking the arithmetic average of the past ten years, we get the best estimate of next year's rate of return. To see this, recall the mutual fund example. Looking at the past performance, we know that in the first year the rate of return was −50% and in the second year it was +100%. Suppose further that these are the only two possible outcomes for the future. Because we do not know which outcome will occur next year, our best estimate is that, on average, we will make 25%, a case where the arithmetic average is relevant. Note that we are addressing not the long-run performance of the fund but only what we expect to earn over the next year. Hence, to estimate the expected rate of return on an asset or a portfolio of assets, we use the arithmetic average rather than the geometric average.

These are precisely the two situations that we will consider in this book. Hence, when we refer to the sample mean $\bar{R}_i$, we mean the arithmetic average $\bar{R}_{A,i}$.

The arithmetic average will exceed the geometric average as long as rates of returns are not constant. Hence, the arithmetic average is sometimes said to be upwardly biased (because

---

[18] This assumes, of course, that the probability distribution is stable. That is, the distribution from which historical observations were made is the same as the distribution from which future observations will be made. The mathematical proof of this assertion can be found in most basic statistics books.

the compounding of returns does not occur in a single period). The difference between these two averages is greater when the volatility of returns is larger. If there is zero volatility, then the arithmetic average is equal to the geometric average.

Practice box

Problem

Calculate the arithmetic and geometric annual average rates of return for the Abbott and Costello mutual funds. Explain the differences between the two results.

Year	Abbott Fund (%)	Costello Fund (%)
1	10	8
2	5	12
3	−15	11
4	40	9

Solution

Writing the rates of return in decimal figures, the arithmetic averages are

$$\bar{R}_{A,Abbott} = \frac{0.1 + 0.05 - 0.15 + 0.4}{4} = 0.10$$

$$\bar{R}_{A,Costello} = \frac{0.08 + 0.12 + 0.11 + 0.09}{4} = 0.10$$

The geometric averages are

$$\bar{R}_{G,Abbott} = [(1 + 0.1)(1 + 0.05)(1 - 0.15)(1 + 0.4)]^{1/4} - 1 \cong 0.083$$

$$\bar{R}_{G,Costello} = [(1 + 0.08)(1 + 0.12)(1 + 0.11)(1 + 0.09)]^{1/4} - 1 \cong 0.0999$$

The difference between the geometric and arithmetic averages is larger for the Abbott Fund because it has greater volatility (−15 to 40%). The more volatile the returns, the greater the difference between the geometric average and the arithmetic average.

6.4.2 Sample variance and sample standard deviation

Apart from measuring the average, we generally also need to measure the risk associated with investments. For this purpose, we can compute the so-called sample variance. The sample variance for the ith asset (σ_i^2) is computed in the following manner:[19]

$$\hat{\sigma}_i^2 = \frac{1}{T} \times \sum_{t=1}^{T} (R_{i,t} - \bar{R}_i)^2 \tag{6.17}$$

---

[19] The sum of squares $\sum_{t=1}^{T} (R_{i,t} - \bar{R}_i)^2$ is divided by the sample size T. If the objective is to find a statistically good estimator for the (unkown) population variance σ_i^2, then we should divide by $T - 1$ rather than T. In statistical terms, the resulting estimator is an unbiased estimator of the population variance. Although this may seem counterintuitive, dividing by $T - 1$ is required because the true population mean ER_i is not known and estimating it by $\bar{R}_i$ effectively reduces the number of observations left for estimating σ_i^2 from T to $T - 1$. However, for large samples, it generally does not matter whether we divide by T or by $(T - 1)$.

where σ is the Greek letter sigma and the circumflex indicates that the variance is computed from a sample of past observations rather than from the future return distribution. Thus, the variance is the average squared deviation from the mean. The higher the dispersion as measured by deviations from the mean, the higher the variance. Sometimes the following equivalent expression is more convenient:[20]

$$\hat{\sigma}_i^2 = \frac{1}{T} \times \sum_{t=1}^{T} R_{i,t}^2 - \bar{R}_i^2 \qquad (6.17a)$$

If the rates of return are expressed in percentage figures, then the unit of variance is per cent squared. If the rates of return are in dollar figures, then the unit of variance is dollars squared. These terms can be difficult to interpret. Therefore, it is common to take the square root of the sample variance or $\hat{\sigma}_i$, which is called the sample standard deviation; this measure is stated in percentages or dollars.

For the AT&T example, the variance is

$$\hat{\sigma}_{AT\&T}^2 = \frac{1}{4} \times [(-0.10 - 0.06)^2 + (0 - 0.06)^2 + (0.25 - 0.06)^2 + (0.09 - 0.06)^2]$$

$$= \frac{1}{4} \times (0.0256 + 0.0036 + 0.0361 + 0.0009) = 0.0166$$

The standard deviation is found by taking the square root of the variance:

$$\hat{\sigma}_{AT\&T} = 0.0166^{1/2} = 0.1286, \text{ or } 12.86\%$$

6.4.3 Sample covariance and sample correlation

The mean and variance give information about the risk and return of individual assets, but they are silent on dependency between various assets or how various assets move together. An investor who considers holding a portfolio that combines various assets needs information on the dependence between the assets. If both go up or down together, we say they have positive dependency. If one asset goes up when the other goes down, or vice versa, we say that they have negative dependency. In general, the lower the dependency between assets in a portfolio, the lower the risk of the portfolio and, hence, the more effective the asset becomes as a means for risk reduction (see Chapter 8).

It is easiest to see positive co-movement in a graph. Exhibit 6.13 shows the monthly rates of return (in excess of the riskless one-month T-bill rate) for Microsoft stocks and a value-weighted index of NYSE, AMEX and NASDAQ stocks for the period from January 1991 to December 2000, a total of 120 monthly observations. Clearly, there is a positive dependency between Microsoft and the market index. When the market index is doing relatively well, Microsoft is also doing relatively well, and vice versa. Conversely, when the market index is down, so is Microsoft. Notice that the pattern moves upward as you look from left to right. This upward pattern characterises a positive dependency.

---

[20] The following chain of equalities shows that these expressions are equivalent:

$$\hat{\sigma}_i^2 = \frac{1}{T} \times \sum_{t=1}^{T} (R_{i,t} - \bar{R}_i)^2 = \frac{1}{T} \times \sum_{t=1}^{T} (R_{i,t}^2 - 2 \times R_{i,t} \times \bar{R}_i + \bar{R}_i^2) = \frac{1}{T} \times \sum_{t=1}^{T} R_{i,t}^2 - 2 \times \bar{R}_i^2 + \bar{R}_i^2 = \frac{1}{T} \times \sum_{t=1}^{T} R_{i,t}^2 - \bar{R}_i^2.$$

| Exhibit 6.13 | Monthly returns on Microsoft stocks and a US stock market index (1991–2000) |

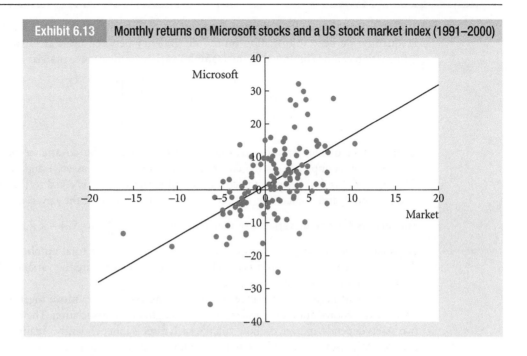

A common statistic for measuring the degree of dependence between two historical return series is the sample covariance. Formally, the sample covariance between the ith asset and the sth asset ($\sigma_{i,s}$) is defined as:

$$\hat{\sigma}_{i,s} = \frac{1}{T} \times \sum_{t=1}^{T} (R_{i,t} - \bar{R}_i)(R_{s,t} - \bar{R}_s) \tag{6.18}$$

Thus, covariance measures the average of the product of the deviation of the ith asset from its mean ($R_{i,t} - \bar{R}_i$) and the deviation of the sth asset from its mean ($R_{s,t} - \bar{R}_s$). If the two assets yield above-average returns at the same time, then the covariance will be positive. Sometimes the following equivalent expression is more convenient:[21]

$$\hat{\sigma}_{i,s} = \frac{1}{T} \times \sum_{t=1}^{T} (R_{i,t}R_{s,t}) - \bar{R}_i\bar{R}_s \tag{6.18a}$$

In our example, the covariance between the return on Microsoft stock and the market index is 23.743, which indicates a positive dependency. By contrast, a negative covariance implies a negative dependency.

---

[21] The following chain of equalities shows that these expressions are equivalent:

$$\hat{\sigma}_{i,s} = \frac{1}{T} \times \sum_{t=1}^{T} (R_{i,t} - \bar{R}_i) \times (R_{s,t} - \bar{R}_s) = \frac{1}{T} \times \sum_{t=1}^{T} (R_{i,t} \times R_{s,t} - R_{i,t} \times \bar{R}_s - \bar{R}_i \times R_{s,t} + \bar{R}_i \times \bar{R}_s)$$

$$= \frac{1}{T} \times \sum_{t=1}^{T} (R_{i,t} \times R_{s,t}) - \bar{R}_i \times \bar{R}_s - \bar{R}_i \times \bar{R}_s + \bar{R}_i \times \bar{R}_s = \frac{1}{T} \times \sum_{t=1}^{T} (R_{i,t} \times R_{s,t}) - \bar{R}_i \times \bar{R}_s.$$

This example includes only two investments (Microsoft stock and the market index). Frequently, we need information on the dependency between more than two assets. Such information can be combined in the (sample) variance–covariance matrix:

$$\begin{bmatrix} \hat{\sigma}_1^2 & \hat{\sigma}_{1,2} & \cdots & \hat{\sigma}_{n,1} \\ \hat{\sigma}_{1,2} & \hat{\sigma}_2^2 & \cdots & \hat{\sigma}_{n,2} \\ \vdots & \vdots & \ddots & \vdots \\ \hat{\sigma}_{1,n} & \hat{\sigma}_{2,n} & \cdots & \hat{\sigma}_n^2 \end{bmatrix}$$

Each element of the variance–covariance matrix contains the covariance between a pair of assets. For example, $\hat{\sigma}_{1,2}$ is the covariance corresponding to assets 1 and 2, and so forth. Obviously, $\hat{\sigma}_{1,2} = \hat{\sigma}_{2,1}$, because the covariance of assets 1 and 2 is equal to the covariance of assets 2 and 1 and, hence, the matrix is symmetric. Note that the covariance between an asset and itself gives the variance of that assets as $\hat{\sigma}_{i,i} = \dfrac{1}{T} \times \sum_{t=1}^{T} (R_{i,t} R_{i,t}) - \bar{R}_i \bar{R}_i = \hat{\sigma}_i^2$. Hence, the diagonal in the matrix gives the variances $\hat{\sigma}_1^2, \hat{\sigma}_2^2, \ldots, \hat{\sigma}_n^2$. The total number of elements in the variance–covariance matrix is n^2. The n diagonal elements are the variance terms, which leaves $n^2 - n$ or $n(n-1)$ covariance terms.

Positive and negative covariances imply that the assets either move together or move in opposite directions, but they are silent on the strength of this association. The co-movement of two assets depends, in part, on how volatile each asset is independently. Again, the covariance between Microsoft stock and the market index in our example is 23.743. Is this covariance very large? Is it modestly large? Is it twice as strong as a covariance of 11.872? If the two assets are not very volatile, then 23.743 may indicate a strong dependency. However, if the two assets are highly volatile, then a covariance of 23.743 may indicate a weak dependency.

By dividing the sample covariance by the product of the sample standard deviations of each asset, we can determine the strength of their dependency, or their sample correlation. The number we obtain is called the sample correlation coefficient

$$\hat{\rho}_{i,s} = \frac{\hat{\sigma}_{i,s}}{\hat{\sigma}_i \hat{\sigma}_s} \tag{6.19}$$

Both covariance and correlation measure the association between the rates of return on two assets. When the covariance is positive, the correlation also will be positive, and vice versa. The advantage of correlation, though, is that it is a number ranging between -1 and $+1$, and it is not in units, such as dollars or percentages. Thus, correlations are directly comparable. For example, if the correlation of rates of return between stocks A and B is 0.8 and the correlation between rates of return between stocks C and D is 0.6, then we can state that stocks A and B have a stronger positive dependency. If there is a perfect positive association between rates of return, then the correlation is $+1$. If there is a perfect negative association, then the correlation is -1. Finally, if the rates of return are unrelated (i.e. uncorrelated), then the correlation is zero.

Let us calculate the sample correlation coefficient between Microsoft stock and the market index in our example. The sample covariance is 23.743. In addition, the sample standard deviation for Microsoft is 11.080, while the standard deviation for the index is 3.949. Hence, the sample correlation coefficient is:

$$\hat{\rho}_{i,s} = \frac{23.743}{11.080 \times 3.949} = 0.542$$

A correlation of about 50% is not very strong. In Exhibit 6.13, this is reflected in a relatively high dispersion of the points around the straight line.

Again, this example includes only two investments (Microsoft stock and the market index). The sample correlation coefficients between all pairs of assets can be combined in a (sample) correlation matrix:

$$\begin{bmatrix} 1 & \hat{\rho}_{1,2} & \cdots & \hat{\rho}_{n,1} \\ \hat{\rho}_{1,2} & 1 & \cdots & \hat{\rho}_{n,2} \\ \vdots & \vdots & \ddots & \vdots \\ \hat{\rho}_{1,n} & \hat{\rho}_{2,n} & \cdots & 1 \end{bmatrix}$$

The diagonal in the matrix gives the correlation of an asset with itself, which is always 1, as $\hat{\rho}_{i,i} = \dfrac{\hat{\sigma}_{i,i}}{\hat{\sigma}_i \hat{\sigma}_i} = \dfrac{\hat{\sigma}_i^2}{\hat{\sigma}_i^2} = 1$. The off-diagonal terms in the exhibit give all the correlations between different assets; for example, $\hat{\rho}_{1,2}$ is the covariance corresponding to assets 1 and 2, and so forth. Like the variance–covariance matrix, the correlation matrix is symmetric, because the correlation of assets 1 and 2 is equal to the correlation of assets 2 and 1, or $\hat{\rho}_{1,2} = \hat{\rho}_{2,1}$.

→ **Connecting Theory to Practice 6.1**   **FT**

'Correlation': a key to smart investing

Stock market investing is becoming increasingly global and it is fashionable to assume that most of the larger markets will move together and by similar amounts.

So if, for instance, the Dow Jones moves up by 10 per cent we might get roughly the same movement in the FTSE100. Like many aspects of investing, there is a grain of common sense in this assumption. But the truth is more complicated.

The shorthand term for the way market movements are connected is correlation. Correlation is a statistical concept. It measures the strength and direction of a series of values from each of two different variables. To translate, the series of values could be the movements in an index or a share, and the different variables two stock markets or two different shares. The result of calculating this statistic, called the correlation coefficient, varies between −1 and 1.

If the correlation coefficient is positive it means that, in the case of two stock markets, an upward or downward movement in one tends to be accompanied by an upward or downward movement in the other. A negative correlation coefficient means that the two markets tend to move in opposite directions.

Investors can reduce the degree to which their portfolio's value swings by trying to invest in the markets that only have a loose, or non-existent, relationship with each other. Some emerging markets are a popular choice for professional investors, because they are only loosely linked to movements in larger ones.

As well as working for different country stock markets, correlation can also measure the relationship between different shares and different sectors, and between different types of assets, shares, bonds, property, venture capital, commodities, hedge funds, and so on. This is one reason for the attraction to some investors of hedge funds and private equity investments. Their returns do not correlate highly with more conventional stock market investments.

Correlation coefficients can be deceptive. First, their reliability depends on the amount of the data being analysed. Looking at the correlation between two stock markets using data covering 20 years might tell you more about their long-term relationship than one that looked at it over just two years. Correlation can also vary over the different stages of a market cycle.

It is also drummed into tyro statisticians that correlation does not imply causality. In other words, if the FTSE100 and Dow Jones tend to move in a similar fashion that does not necessarily

▶

mean that the Dow Jones movement 'causes' the movement in the FTSE100, even though it might sometimes seem that way. One reason is that both markets could be responding to an external stimulus – global interest rates, for example – that causes each of them to move the same way at the same time.

The way the number-crunchers tend to measure the strength of the relationship is by looking at 'r-squared'. R-squared is the square of the correlation coefficient, normally given as a percentage.

Two markets with a correlation coefficient of 0.9 would have an r-squared of 0.81, or 81 per cent. The statisticians would claim that, in this example, this means that 81 per cent of the movement in one index is 'explained' by the movement in the other, and only 19 per cent by other factors. Two markets with a correlation coefficient of 0.8, however, would only have an r-squared of 64 per cent. With a correlation coefficient of 0.7 (r-squared of 0.49, or 49 per cent), the movement in one market would explain less than half the movement in the other.

So how does it work in practice? The web site Graphic Investor (www.graphicinvestor.com) studied the relative movements of a large number of markets between May 2000 and April 2003. The results are on a matrix that shows the correlation coefficients of different pairs of markets.

As you might expect, the FTSE100 correlation coefficient with the FTSE350 is high, at 0.95, not surprising since 100 of the 350 stocks are the same as the FTSE100's. The Mid 250 has a correlation of 0.85. The Dutch and German markets also correlate highly with the UK benchmark.

The correlation of S&P500 with the 'footsie' is 0.89, suggesting that around 89 per cent of the FTSE100's movement can be explained by the movement in the S&P, with the Dow slightly more loosely related.

What about big overseas markets? Surprising perhaps, but the Nikkei 225 correlates most highly with the NASDAQ, while the S&P's closest relationships are with the Dow Jones and the Swedish stock market.

The site has done the same calculation looking at the relationship of UK sectors with each other, and the relationships between different unit trust categories and different insurance company funds. If your portfolio has tracker funds or exchange traded funds, or for that matter a selection of different unit trust styles, you can avoid some potentially unpleasant surprises by checking out how closely their performance might be linked.

Using knowledge like this can give your investing extra insight, which is the best way to improve your results.

Source: Peter Temple, ' "Correlation" A Key To Smart Investing', *Financial Times*, 31 May 2003.

6.5 The historical record

An investor can choose to invest in various types of assets, with different risk and return characteristics. In this section, we will look at the historical performance of several asset classes: large company stocks, small company stocks, (corporate and government) bonds with long maturity (20 years), (government) bonds with intermediate maturity (five years) and US Treasury bills with 30 days maturity. Generally, stocks of small firms are considered to be very risky, and they yield a relatively high average rate of return. Also, long-term bonds are considered to be riskier than short-term bonds, and corporate bonds are riskier than government bonds. Finally, US Treasury bills are the assets with the smallest risk and the smallest average rate of return.

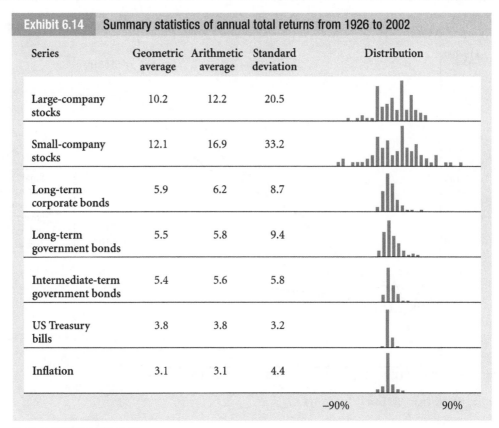

Series	Geometric average	Arithmetic average	Standard deviation	Distribution
Large-company stocks	10.2	12.2	20.5	
Small-company stocks	12.1	16.9	33.2	
Long-term corporate bonds	5.9	6.2	8.7	
Long-term government bonds	5.5	5.8	9.4	
Intermediate-term government bonds	5.4	5.6	5.8	
US Treasury bills	3.8	3.8	3.2	
Inflation	3.1	3.1	4.4	

Exhibit 6.14 Summary statistics of annual total returns from 1926 to 2002

Source: www.ibbotson.com/dataupdate

Exhibit 6.14 and Appendix 6 (which includes the raw data used to construct the exhibit) reveal the historical record regarding these assets. Notice that the historical rates of return on these assets appear to be consistent with their degree of risk. For example, small-company stocks yielded the highest (arithmetic) average rate of return during the period 1926–2002, i.e. 12.1% per year. However, if an investor invested in one year selected at random from these years, he or she would also be exposed to the highest risk. This can be seen from the standard deviation corresponding to small-company stocks (33.2%), as well as from the histogram given on the right-hand side of Exhibit 6.14. Small-company stocks were characterised by very large negative and positive rates of return over the years, while much less dispersion was observed with the other assets.

In a similar manner, the graph in Exhibit 6.15 shows what happened to an investment of $1 in 1926 in each of these assets: for example, a $1 investment in small-company stocks in 1926 would have yielded about $6816 in 2002. However, the same investment in US Treasury bills would have been worth only a fraction of this amount at the end of 2002 (i.e. $17).

The main conclusion from Exhibits 6.14 and 6.15 is that, historically, the higher the volatility or risk as measured by standard deviation, the higher the average rate of return. As we shall see, this is consistent with the concept of risk aversion – investors dislike volatility or risk, and the larger the volatility, the larger the required risk premium. Based on this past observation, in the next chapter we will analyse risk aversion and volatility when probabilities and future possible rates of return rather than past annual rates of return are employed. However, keep in mind that history teaches us that investors dislike volatility and require compensation for

| Exhibit 6.15 | Wealth indices of investments in the US capital markets, 1926–2002 (year-end 1925 = $1.00) |

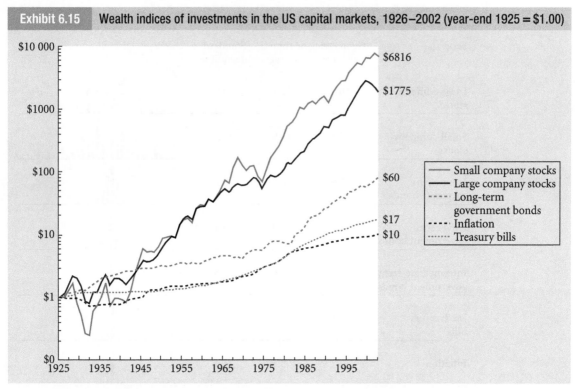

Source: www.ibbotson.com/dataupdate

the risk of fluctuation in the rates of return. So far, we have examined the individual risk and return characteristics of different types of assets. But investors are also interested in the (historical) correlations between asset classes. Exhibit 6.16 shows the historical variance–covariance matrix and the historical correlation matrix for the different assets. Among other things, this exhibit demonstrates that the correlation between the two stock classes (big caps and small caps) is relatively high (78%). Also, the three bond classes are highly correlated, with correlation coefficients ranging from 91 to 93%. However, the correlation between the stock classes on the one hand and the bond classes on the other is much lower (between −6 and 19%). Indeed, as discussed in Chapter 9, much of the gains from portfolio diversification can be achieved through diversification across asset classes.

Summary

Understand the different methods for computing rates of return.

Rates of return can be calculated using different methods. The simple rate of return is the dollar capital gain or loss plus the dollar income (dividends or coupons) divided by the dollar amount invested. It ignores the timing of the cash flows during the evaluation period. The method that uses the adjusted rate of return, or the time-weighted rate of return (which we call *rate of return* to distinguish it from the simple rate of return), has the endorsement of the Association of Investment Management and Research (AIMR). Rates of return are found by first calculating simple rates of return for the subperiods and then linking these returns

Exhibit 6.16	Dependence between asset classes

(a) Variance–covariance matrix

	Large	Small	Long-term corporate	Long-term government	Intermediate-term government	T-bill	Inflation
Large	414.4[a]	–	–	–	–	–	–
Small	526.8[b]	1087.3	–	–	–	–	–
Long-term corporate	33.9	22.2	74.2	–	–	–	–
Long-term government	24.2	−3.5	75.2	87.2	–	–	–
Intermediate-term government	5.6	−12.0	44.8	48.6	32.8	–	–
T-bill	−1.0	−9.3	5.5	6.7	8.5	9.8	–
Inflation	−1.8	6.6	−5.7	−5.8	0.2	5.5	18.8

(b) Correlation matrix

	Large	Small	Long-term corporate	Long-term government	Intermediate-term government	T-bill	Inflation
Large	1.00	–	–	–	–	–	–
Small	0.78[b]	1.00	–	–	–	–	–
Long-term corporate	0.19	0.08	1.00	–	–	–	–
Long-term government	0.13	−0.01	0.93	1.00	–	–	–
Intermediate-term government	0.05	−0.06	0.91	0.91	1.00	–	–
T-bill	−0.02	−0.09	0.20	0.23	0.47	1.00	–
Inflation	−0.02	0.05	−0.15	−0.14	0.01	0.41	1.00

[a] The standard deviation of the large cap stocks is found as $\sqrt{414.4} = 20.5$; see Exhibit 6.14.

[b] The standard deviation is 20.5 for large-cap stocks and 33.2 for small-cap stocks. Given the correlation of 0.78 between these asset classes, the covariance is computed as $0.78 \times 20.5 \times 33.2 = 526.8$. Similarly, given the covariance of 526.8, the correlation is found as $526.8/(20.5 \times 33.2) = 0.78$.

together. The idea of time-weighted rates of return is that any interim cash flow is reinvested in the asset under consideration. An alternative way to calculate time-weighted rates of return is known as the index method. It yields the same results as the linking method; in addition, it provides the intuition behind that method.

Analyse the impact of taxes, inflation and exchange rates on rate-of-return calculations.

Taxes and inflation influence the rate-of-return calculation and reduce the overall rate of return. In the case of taxes, there is a reduction of income (tax payment), which reduces the after-tax rate of return. In the inflation case, there is a reduction in the investor's purchasing power, which reduces the real rate of return to the investor. For foreign investments, exchange rates also affect the rate of return in the domestic currency. Investors generally are interested in after-tax, exchange-rate-adjusted, real rates of return because they cannot buy additional goods and services with the parts of their investment revenue that are paid as taxes, required to compensate for inflation or lost in currency transactions.

Contrast the different types of stock and bond indices.

The price-weighted index is found by adding the prices of each security and dividing by a divisor. The value-weighted index is based on the total market capitalisation (the market price multiplied by the number of securities outstanding) of each security rather than merely on the market price of each security. Equally weighted indices are calculated by giving each security the same weight, regardless of its market price or market capitalisation.

Discuss the basic sample statistics for summarising historical return data.

The basic sample statistics include the sample mean, the sample variance, the sample standard deviation, the sample covariance and the sample correlation coefficient. The sample mean and sample variance (or its square root, the sample standard deviation) measure the risk and return of individual assets or portfolios. To measure the dependency between two investments, one may use the sample covariance or the sample correlation coefficient (which is a standardised version of the sample covariance). All these measures are after-the-fact or ex-post measures, i.e. they look at the past. By contrast, population statistics look at future returns.

Compare the historical risk–return trade-off for stocks and bonds.

Historically, common stocks have been more volatile than bonds. Also, common stocks have offered a higher average return than bonds, whereas bonds offered a higher average return than T-bills, which are practically riskless. Hence, there appears to be a positive relationship between volatility and return. Presumably, this relationship reflects that the majority of the investors are risk averse.

Key terms

Adjusted rate of return 163	Ex-post rate of return 161	Sample correlation
After-tax rate of return 172	Geometric average 187	coefficient 192
Arithmetic average 187	Geometric method 187	Sample covariance 191
Arithmetic method 187	Index method 164	Sample mean 188
Bond index 184	Linking method 164	Sample standard deviation 190
Correlation matrix 193	Market capitalisation 181	Sample statistics 187
Divisor 179	Negative dependency 190	Sample variance 189
Dollar-weighted average rate of	Nominal rate of return 174	Stock index 177
return 171	Population statistics 187	Time-weighted rate of return
Equally weighted index 179	Positive dependency 190	163
Exchange-rate-adjusted rate of	Price-weighted index 178	Value-weighted index 178
return 175	Real rate of return 174	Variance–covariance
Ex-ante rate of return 161	Sample correlation 192	matrix 192

Review questions

1 Stock A generates a capital gain of 8% every 6 months. Dividends are paid semiannually and the stock's 6-month dividend yield is 4%. Use the linking method and the index method to calculate the 1-year rate of return to an investor who pays $100 to buy the stock and holds it for 1 year. Assume that the first dividend will be paid exactly 6 months from the purchase date.

2 Preferred stock pays a perpetual annual $4-per-share dividend. Corporations that invest in preferred stock pay taxes on only 30% of dividends received. The risk of ABC's preferred stock

is such that investors require a 6% after-tax return. Assume the corporate tax rate is 34% and the tax rate for individuals is 28%. Also assume that the price of the preferred stock is expected to remain constant indefinitely.

a. How much would a corporate investor be willing to pay for one share of ABC's preferred stock?

b. How much would an individual investor be willing to pay for one share of ABC's preferred stock?

c. Suppose the actual market price of the preferred stock is equal to the price you computed in part a. What after-tax return would individual investors realise if they bought the preferred stock at this price?

3 Joaquin invested $10 747 when he was 25 years old. He earned 12% per year on his investment until he was 65 years old. During the 40 years that Joaquin's money was invested, inflation was 3% per year. Calculate Joaquin's nominal ending wealth, real annual return, and real ending wealth.

4 Use the following data to calculate the value of an equally weighted index on Tuesday and Wednesday. Use the arithmetic method and assume that the value of the index on Monday is 100.

	Market prices		
Stock	Monday	Tuesday	Wednesday
A	$50	$55	$59.40
B	$60	$60	$61.20

5 The following table shows the NYSE composite index over a recent 15-year period:

End of year	NYSE composite
1988	156.26
1989	195.01
1990	180.49
1991	229.44
1992	240.21
1993	259.08
1994	250.94
1995	329.51
1996	392.30
1997	511.19
1998	595.81
1999	650.30
2000	656.87
2001	589.80
2002	472.87
2003	646.40

a. Ignoring dividends, calculate the simple annual rates of return.

b. Calculate the arithmetic average of the annual rates of return.

c. Calculate the geometric average of the annual rates of return.

d. Compare your answers in parts b and c. How do you account for the difference between these averages?

For an extensive set of review and practice questions and answers, visit the Levy–Post investment website at www.booksites.net/levy

Selected references

Association for Investment Management and Research, 1991, *Report of the Performance Presentation Standards Implementation Committee*, Charlottesville, VA: AIMR.

Eiteman, D. K., A. I. Stonehill and M. H. Moffett, 1992, *Multinational Business Finance*, 6th edn, Reading, MA: Addison-Wesley.

Fisher, I., 1930, *The Theory of Interest*, New York: Macmillan.

Jakobsen, J. and O. Sorensen, 2001, 'Decomposing and Testing Long-Term Returns: An Application of Danish IPO', *European Financial Management*, **7** (2), 393–415.

Larsen, G. A., Jr and B. G. Resnick, 2001, 'Parameter Estimation Techniques, Optimization Frequency and Portfolio Return Enhancement', *Journal of Portfolio Management*, **27** (4), 27–34.

Levy, H. and M. Sarnat, 1984, *Portfolio and Investment Selection: Theory and Practice*, Englewood Cliffs, NJ: Prentice-Hall.

Reilly, F. K., G. W. Kao and D. J. Wright, 1992, 'Alternative Bond Market Indexes', *Financial Analysts Journal*, **48** (3), 44–58.

Siegel, J. J., 1992, 'The Equity Premium: Stock and Bond Returns since 1802', *Financial Analysts Journal*, **48** (1), 28–46.

Annual US rates of return, 1926–2002

Year	Large company stocks	Small company stocks	Long-term corporate bonds	Long-term government bonds	Intermediate-term government bonds	US Treasury bills	Inflation
1926	11.62	0.28	7.37	7.77	5.38	3.27	−1.49
1927	37.49	22.10	7.44	8.93	4.52	3.12	−2.08
1928	43.61	39.69	2.84	0.10	0.92	3.56	−0.97
1929	−8.42	−51.36	3.27	3.42	6.01	4.75	0.20
1930	−24.90	−38.15	7.98	4.66	6.72	2.41	−6.03
1931	−43.34	−49.75	−1.85	−5.31	−2.32	1.07	−9.52
1932	−8.19	−5.39	10.82	16.84	8.81	0.96	−10.30
1933	53.99	142.87	10.38	−0.07	1.83	0.30	0.51
1934	−1.44	24.22	13.84	10.03	9.00	0.16	2.03
1935	47.67	40.19	9.61	4.98	7.01	0.17	2.99
1936	33.92	64.80	6.74	7.52	3.06	0.18	1.21
1937	−35.03	−58.01	2.75	0.23	1.56	0.31	3.10
1938	31.12	32.80	6.13	5.53	6.23	−0.02	−2.78
1939	−0.41	0.35	3.97	5.94	4.52	0.02	−0.48
1940	−9.78	−5.16	3.39	6.09	2.96	0.00	0.96
1941	−11.59	−9.00	2.73	0.93	0.50	0.06	9.72
1942	20.34	44.51	2.60	3.22	1.94	0.27	9.29
1943	25.90	88.37	2.83	2.08	2.81	0.35	3.16
1944	19.75	53.72	4.73	2.81	1.80	0.33	2.11
1945	36.44	73.61	4.08	10.73	2.22	0.33	2.25
1946	−8.07	−11.63	1.72	−0.10	1.00	0.35	18.16
1947	5.71	0.92	−2.34	−2.62	0.91	0.50	9.01
1948	5.50	−2.11	4.14	3.40	1.85	0.81	2.71
1949	18.79	19.75	3.31	6.45	2.32	1.10	−1.80
1950	31.71	38.75	2.12	0.06	0.70	1.20	5.79
1951	24.02	7.80	−2.69	−3.93	0.36	1.49	5.87
1952	18.37	3.03	3.52	1.16	1.63	1.66	0.88
1953	−0.99	−6.49	3.41	3.64	3.23	1.82	0.62
1954	52.62	60.58	5.39	7.19	2.68	0.86	−0.50
1955	31.56	20.44	0.48	−1.29	−0.65	1.57	0.37
1956	6.56	4.28	−6.81	−5.59	−0.42	2.46	2.86
1957	−10.78	−14.57	8.71	7.46	7.84	3.14	3.02
1958	43.36	64.89	−2.22	−6.09	−1.29	1.54	1.76
1959	11.96	16.40	−0.97	−2.26	−0.39	2.95	1.50
1960	0.47	−3.29	9.07	13.78	11.76	2.66	1.48
1961	26.89	32.09	4.82	0.97	1.85	2.13	0.67
1962	−8.73	−11.90	7.95	6.89	5.56	2.73	1.22
1963	22.80	23.57	2.19	1.21	1.64	3.12	1.65

Year	Large company stocks	Small company stocks	Long-term corporate bonds	Long-term government bonds	Intermediate-term government bonds	US Treasury bills	Inflation
1964	16.48	23.52	4.77	3.51	4.04	3.54	1.19
1965	12.45	41.75	−0.46	0.71	1.02	3.93	1.92
1966	−10.06	−7.01	0.20	3.65	4.69	4.76	3.35
1967	23.98	83.57	−4.95	−9.18	1.01	4.21	3.04
1968	11.06	35.97	2.57	−0.26	4.54	5.21	4.72
1969	−8.50	−25.05	−8.09	−5.07	−0.74	6.58	6.11
1970	4.01	−17.43	18.37	12.11	16.86	6.52	5.49
1971	14.31	16.50	11.01	13.23	8.72	4.39	3.36
1972	18.98	4.43	7.26	5.69	5.16	3.84	3.41
1973	−14.66	−30.90	1.14	−1.11	4.61	6.93	8.80
1974	−26.47	−19.95	−3.06	4.35	5.69	8.00	12.20
1975	37.20	52.82	14.64	9.20	7.83	5.80	7.01
1976	23.84	57.38	18.65	16.75	12.87	5.08	4.81
1977	−7.18	25.38	1.71	−0.69	1.41	5.12	6.77
1978	6.56	23.46	−0.07	−1.18	3.49	7.18	9.03
1979	18.44	43.46	−4.18	−1.23	4.09	10.38	13.31
1980	32.42	39.88	−2.76	−3.95	3.91	11.24	12.40
1981	−4.91	13.88	−1.24	1.86	9.45	14.71	8.94
1982	21.41	28.01	42.56	40.36	29.10	10.54	3.87
1983	22.51	39.67	6.26	0.65	7.41	8.80	3.80
1984	6.27	−6.67	16.86	15.48	14.02	9.85	3.95
1985	32.16	24.66	30.09	30.97	20.33	7.72	3.77
1986	18.47	6.85	19.85	24.53	15.14	6.16	1.13
1987	5.23	−9.30	−0.27	−2.71	2.90	5.47	4.41
1988	16.81	22.87	10.70	9.67	6.10	6.35	4.42
1989	31.49	10.18	16.23	18.11	13.29	8.37	4.65
1990	−3.17	−21.56	6.78	6.18	9.73	7.81	6.11
1991	30.55	44.63	19.89	19.30	15.46	5.60	3.06
1992	7.67	23.35	9.39	8.05	7.19	3.51	2.90
1993	9.99	20.98	13.19	18.24	11.24	2.90	2.75
1994	1.31	3.11	−5.76	−7.77	−5.14	3.90	2.67
1995	37.43	34.46	27.20	31.67	16.80	5.60	2.54
1996	23.07	17.62	1.40	−0.93	2.10	5.21	3.32
1997	33.36	22.78	12.95	15.85	8.38	5.26	1.70
1998	28.58	−7.31	10.76	13.06	10.21	4.86	1.61
1999	21.04	29.79	−7.45	−8.96	−1.77	4.68	2.68
2000	−9.11	−3.59	12.87	21.48	12.59	5.89	3.39
2001	−11.88	22.77	10.65	3.70	7.62	3.83	1.55
2002	−22.10	−13.28	16.33	17.84	12.93	1.65	2.69

Fundamentals of portfolio analysis

Investment in the News 7

FT

Fund managers cautious over equities

Uncertainty over a war with Iraq has seen fund managers around the world adopt 'extreme' levels of risk aversion, a survey has found. Merrill Lynch said its monthly survey of fund managers showed they were now even more risk averse than in the aftermath of the September 11 attacks. While holdings of the safer investment havens of cash and bond investments had risen sharply, exposure to equities continued to slide to low hits only three times in the last four years.

This was despite a widespread perception that global equities were undervalued. Half of 308 fund managers, who collectively oversee some $714 bn, surveyed by Merrill Lynch thought global equities were undervalued – the highest level since the investment bank started carrying out the survey on a global basis in April 2001. A quarter thought stock markets were undervalued by more than 15 per cent.

Mark Hartnett, Merrill chief strategist for Europe, said macro-economic concerns had contributed to the uncertainty but geopolitical risks appeared to overhang sentiment. 'The most glaring factor is Iraq,' he said. Mr Hartnett said the pessimism may presage a stock-market rally, given cash holdings had increased. However, it was questionable whether this rally would be sustainable until the geopolitical risks had been resolved. 'When you see things like Nato might break up on the front page, that is a significant geopolitical risk to take into account,' he said.

The Merrill survey showed a net balance of respondents saying they were currently running a lower-than-normal risk strategy in deciding what investments to make rose from 25 per cent in January to 34 per cent in February. A net 25 per cent of funds said they were overweight in cash compared with 12 per cent a month earlier. The average cash holding was 4.9 per cent of a portfolio in February compared with 4.2 per cent in January. One in six funds were holding more than 12 per cent in cash. Funds were underweight in bonds at a net 11 per cent but this was well below the 30 per cent seen in January. Asset allocators also reported being more underweight in equities than overweight in shares, only the third time in four years.

The cautious stance by investors towards equities contrasted strongly with optimism on earnings and economic growth. Sixty-two per cent of respondents expect a stronger world economy over the next 12 months with an average nominal GDP growth rate for the G7

▶

countries of 3 per cent. Average global earnings-per-share growth was expected to be 7 per cent over the next year. Seventy-one per cent of respondents said the main contributor to profit growth would be lower costs. 'If risk aversion were to lift for whatever reason, some of the conditions are in place for a tactical bounce in world equities,' said David Bowers, Merrill chief investment strategist.

Source: Tony Tassell, 'Fund Managers Cautious Over Equities', *Financial Times*, 19 February 2003.

Learning objectives

After studying this chapter, you should be able to:

1 Explain the basic concepts of the portfolio possibilities set, the probability distribution of returns and the utility function.

2 Explain the maximum expected utility criterion for portfolio selection.

3 Explain what a risk-averter is.

4 Explain why a risk-averter typically diversifies his or her portfolio and why he or she charges risk premiums over and above the riskless rate.

5 Explain why the expected utility criterion is not operational. Explain also why the criterion is still important.

In early 2003, the geopolitical risks related to the 11 September 2001 terrorist attacks, the following 'war on terrorism' and the uncertainty over the business cycle made it hard for investors to be brave. Indeed, Investment in the News 7 reports on a survey of global fund managers by Merrill Lynch that pointed to heightened risk aversion and unusually short time horizons. Also, the survey revealed that despite the high level of risk aversion, a majority of fund managers had optimistic expectations about future earnings and economic growth.

As is clear from this article, investment decisions are determined to a large extent by the perceived risks of investment and the aversion to risk. Another important determinant is investment restrictions. Many investors face restrictions such as limits on the amount invested in risky investments (e.g. stocks, junk bonds and derivatives) and social and environmental screens (socially responsible investment). Such restrictions are imposed on investors by, for example, regulators, investment mandates and industry codes of ethical conduct.

Indeed, financial economists typically model investment as a problem of constrained optimisation under uncertainty. There are three elements to such a problem: optimisation, uncertainty and constraints. Investors try to optimise some objective function in a situation characterised by uncertainty and subject to the investment restrictions imposed on them. In brief, investment is seen by financial economists as an attempt by investors to invest as good as possible, given their expectations, objectives and restrictions. To implement this general approach, financial economists frequently use three fundamental concepts: a utility function to describe the investor's objectives, a probability distribution to describe the investor's subjective expectations about the possible future returns and the probabilities of those returns, and a portfolio possibilities set to describe the possibilities and restrictions faced by the investor. Below, we will discuss these concepts in more detail. For the sake of exposition, it is useful to discuss the concepts in reverse order, beginning with the portfolio possibilities set and ending with the utility function. After discussing the concepts, we will combine them in the expected utility criterion, which states that investors select the portfolio that yields the highest possible expected value for the utility function. Finally, we will use the expected utility framework to shed light on two important economic phenomena: the diversification of investment portfolios and the premium of risky assets over the riskless rate.

7.1 The portfolio possibilities set

Suppose the investor can invest in n different assets, associated with uncertain rates of return $R_1, \ldots, R_n$. The investor chooses a portfolio that combines the assets in a variety of proportions, or portfolio weights. The weights are nothing but the proportion of wealth invested in each available asset. Throughout the text, we will use $w_1, \ldots, w_n$ to denote the weights. The investor does not have to diversify in all available assets. If an asset is not in the portfolio, then its proportion is zero ($w_i = 0$). Recall from Chapter 3 that short sales occur when an investor sells securities that he or she does not already own. If you have a short position in a security, then that security effectively has a negative weight in your portfolio ($w_i < 0$), i.e. you hold a negative amount of this security. The rate of return on a portfolio is given as the weighted average of the rates of return of the individual assets:

$$R_p = \sum_{i=1}^{n} w_i R_i = w_1 R_1 + \ldots + w_n R_n \tag{7.1}$$

Generally, the weights are not fully free, and constraints are placed on the portfolio weights. The most elementary restriction is that an investor cannot invest more than his or her entire wealth. This restriction can be represented by the constraint that the portfolio weights must add up to one, or 100%:

$$\sum_{i=1}^{n} w_i = w_1 + \ldots + w_n = 1 \tag{7.2}$$

Another frequently encountered restriction is the condition that short sales are not allowed. Short-selling typically is difficult to implement in practice due to margin requirements and explicit or implicit restrictions on short-selling for institutional investors.[1] Short-selling can be excluded by restricting all weights to be greater than or equal to zero, or

$$w_i \geq 0 \tag{7.3}$$

for all $i = 1, \ldots, n$. These are just two examples of portfolio restrictions. Other examples includes restrictions on the deviations from a benchmark index or from a long-run asset

---

[1] See, for example, Sharpe (1991).

| Exhibit 7.1 | Example portfolio possibilities sets for two different sets of investment restrictions |

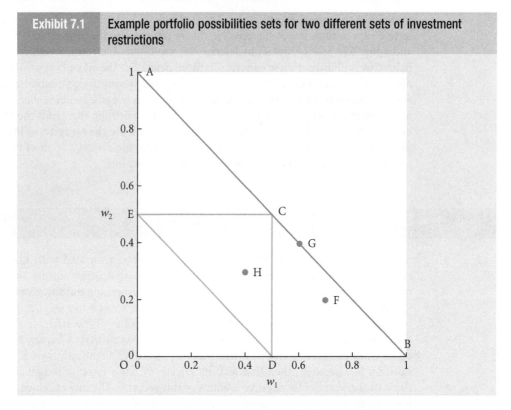

allocation, restrictions on the amount invested in individual stocks, sectors, countries and asset types, and the exclusion of firms involved in the production and/or distribution of tobacco, alcohol and weapons.

Exhibit 7.1 displays the portfolio possibilities set for an investor who can invest in three different stocks: stock 1, stock 2 and stock 3. This exhibit shows the contours of the portfolio possibilities sets associated with two different sets of restrictions. The triangle OAB gives the contour of the possibilities if two restrictions are imposed: (1) the portfolio weights should sum to 100% ($w_1 + w_2 + w_3 = 1$) and (2) short sales are not allowed ($w_1, w_2, w_3 \geq 0$). For example, portfolio F consists of 70% invested in stock 1, 20% invested in stock 2 and 10% invested in stock 3. Similarly, portfolio G consists of 60% invested in stock 1, 40% invested in stock 2 and 0% invested in stock 3. Note that the exhibit shows only the weights for stock 1 and stock 2. Since the portfolio weights must add up to 100%, the weight of stock 3 is found as $1 - w_1 - w_2$. This explains why portfolio G, with 0% invested in stock 3, is on the contour of the possibilities set OAB; the short sales restriction is binding for this portfolio ($w_3 = 0$). The triangle CDE represents the portfolio possibilities set if we add the third restriction that each portfolio weight should be smaller than or equal to 50% ($w_1, w_2, w_3 \leq 0.5$). Note that portfolios F and G lie outside this possibilities set, because the weight of stock 1 exceeds 50%. By contrast, portfolio H, with 40% invested in stock 1, 30% invested in stock 2 and 30% invested in stock 3, is feasible.

Generally speaking, imposing investment restrictions reduces the investment possibilities and makes investors worse off by limiting their choices. (Of course, society as a whole may benefit from restrictions that prevent investors from pursuing illegal or unethical investment strategies.) Similarly, lifting investment constraints expands the investment possibilities set and makes investors better off. For example, Connecting Theory to Practice 7.1 reports on the relaxing of restrictions on equity ownership and international investment by pension funds.

Equity investments by pension funds projected to surge

Equity investments by pension funds will show 'exceptional growth' over the next decade with much of the new investment going into non-domestic markets, according to a new study prepared by Birinyi Associates, the stock market research firm. The study, 'Pension Reform and Global Equity Markets', represents an attempt to analyse and quantify the impact of changes in pension arrangements in 41 nations on both mature and emerging stock markets. If correct, the findings suggest that institutional investors are likely to play an even more crucial role in supporting equity prices in the longer term and reversing the losses of the last two years. They also imply that the shift towards more balanced 'world' portfolios and greater cross-border investment by pension funds will accelerate.

The study points out that during the 1990s, global pension fund assets grew, on average, 15 per cent a year, from Dollars 4600 bn to Dollars 15 900 bn. At the same time the equity holdings of pension funds increased from Dollars 1600 bn to Dollars 8000 bn – or from 35 per cent to 51 per cent of total assets. By 1998, pension fund equity holdings represented 27.4 per cent of global equity market capitalisation, up from 17 per cent in 1990, but slipped back to 22.9 per cent in 1999 as internet mania took hold and market valuations expanded dramatically. This growth was driven mainly by the big three pension markets – the US, Japan and the UK, which together account for over 80 per cent of global assets. The US alone accounts for 60 per cent. From 1995 to 1999, US pension assets grew by an average rate of 21 per cent while the UK grew at 16 per cent per year and Japan by nearly 10 per cent. The report predicts that this decade-long expansion in pension fund equity holdings will continue in the next decade, fuelled by three main factors:

First, pension reforms have been adopted since the mid-1990s across Europe, Latin America and Asia as governments have moved to supplement or replace under-funded pay-as-you-go pension systems with funded schemes. In most cases, governments are following the US model of individual savings accounts such as IRAs and 401(k) plans. In Sweden, which has moved fastest among the European nations, a new system based on mandatory individual retirement accounts is expected to funnel Dollars 16 bn into equity funds in its first year of operation. In Germany new legislation will lead to the creation of tax-advantaged pension accounts this year that are expected to generate Dollars 30 bn in new pension savings by 2008. China's pension scheme is also operating in serious deficit and is likely to be further strained as more state-run industries are shut down as part of economic reforms. In response, the government is considering reforms that would include mandatory employer-based savings plans that, if adopted, might generate as much as Dollars 1600 bn in pension assets by 2030.

At the same time, restrictions on equity ownership by pension funds are gradually being relaxed as bond yields drop and investors become more comfortable with the risks associated with equities. The marked trend towards equity investments is particularly apparent in Europe where looser investment restrictions and strong efforts to diversify fund portfolios have led to big changes in equity allocations. In addition, government reserve funds around the world are shifting their asset allocations from government bonds to equities. This is happening in Japan where over Dollars 90 bn is to be shifted into equities before 2010, Korea, Canada, Ireland, France and Belgium.

Finally, restrictions on foreign investment by pension funds are also being reconsidered as financial markets mature and the benefits of risk diversification are more widely recognised. This trend is increasingly apparent in Ireland, Belgium, Spain and Iceland. In the US one study of the top 200 defined pension plans found that their foreign equity holdings increased from 12.1 per cent in 1998 to 14.2 per cent in 1999 alone.

Birinyi Associates notes: 'Increased equity purchases by pension funds will impact both mature and emerging markets and are likely to be sustained over the long term.'

Source: Paul Taylor, 'Equity Investments By Pension Funds Projected To Surge', *Financial Times*, 5 March 2002.

7.2 The probability distribution

For most assets, the future rate of return is uncertain, i.e. there is more than one possible outcome. There is one asset, however, that is very close to being a certain asset: US short-term Treasury bills (T-bills). It is true that, over time, the yield on T-bills changes. However, when one purchases a given T-bill, the rate of return he or she earns is fixed if he or she holds it to maturity (ignoring inflation and the chance of a revolution in the USA). Also, because it is a short-term asset, changes in interest rates do not significantly affect the price before maturity. Therefore, it is common to refer to T-bills as the riskless asset and to the yield on T-bills as the riskless interest rate.

For other assets, such as stocks, long-term debt, options, investments in real estate, and so forth, the future rate of return is highly uncertain. (See Section 2.4 for a list of the various risks that stock and bond investors face, and see Section 6.5 for the historical variations in the return of these assets.) In fact, if these assets involved no risks, then their rate of return should be equal to the rate of return on T-bills; otherwise, investors would sell the asset with the lowest rate of return and switch their investment to the asset with the highest rate of return. To understand this, suppose two assets exist, A and B, each with a market price of $100. We know with certainty that asset A's future price will be $110 and asset B's future price will be $120, and no dividend or interest is paid on these assets. Is the market in equilibrium? No, it is not. Since assets A and B have the same current price of $100, and asset B provides a higher certain future return, then an investor currently holding asset A should sell it and buy asset B. The investor would be sure of earning $10, or $120 − $110, in the future with no investment. This type of trading strategy, in which profits are made with no risk and no investment, is known as arbitrage. This arbitrage trading will cause the price of asset A to fall (because there will be a glut of asset A on the market) and the price of asset B to rise (because it will be in great demand) until the two assets yield the same certain rate of return. Hence, the fact that stocks and bonds have historically yielded higher average rates of return than the riskless interest rate in a way proves that stocks and bonds are risky.

Formally, we have to distinguish between the concepts of uncertainty and risk. If investors know the probability of each possible outcome, then they face risk. If the probability of each outcome is unknown to investors, then they face uncertainty.[2] Note that in both uncertainty and risk, more than one future value is possible. Actual probabilities that are known (as in a coin-flipping experiment) are called objective probabilities. In actual decision-making by investors, the true probabilities are rarely known. Normally, to estimate the probabilities of possible future rates of return on the stock of a firm, the investor can collect a set of historical rates of return on the stock asset or comparable assets (for example, stocks of firms of the same size and from the same industry), and based on these data estimate the future probabilities. Also, he or she can adjust the historical probability estimates to reflect information about the firm, the industry and the economy that is not included in past returns. The resulting estimates are called subjective probabilities. Thus, even if the objective probabilities are unknown, an investor can attach subjective probabilities to each possible future value of an asset. By doing so, he or she faces a situation defined as risk rather than uncertainty. Since an investor can always assign subjective probabilities to the various possible outcomes, the rest of this book uses the words 'uncertainty' and 'risk' interchangeably to mean that there are multiple possible outcomes.

---

[2] This distinction was first proposed by Knight (1921).

The investor's subjective expectations about the possible future returns and the probabilities of those returns can be described by a probability distribution. A probability distribution is a mathematical function that assigns a probability to every possible outcome of a random variable or a set of random variables. The probability distribution of asset returns is sometimes referred to as the return-generating process. A univariate distribution considers the possible outcomes of individual random variables separately. By contrast, a multivariate distribution considers the joint distribution of several random variables.

In the context of portfolio choice, it is important to consider the joint probability distribution of all available assets. The univariate distribution considers the possible outcomes of an individual asset in isolation. By contrast, the multivariate probability distribution gives the possible outcomes of all assets together. We must consider the joint distribution in order to evaluate the probability distribution of portfolios that are composed of multiple assets. For example, an asset offers greater diversification possibilities if there is a high probability that the asset zigs when other assets zag. Hence, to evaluate an asset, we have to account for its dependency on the other assets in the portfolio in addition to its own probability distribution. The univariate distributions do not give information on the degree of dependency between assets; the multivariate distribution does give this information.

We will represent here the multivariate probability distribution by a discrete set of m possible different states of the world. For example, a possible state of the world is the scenario of an economic expansion of the US economy but a stagnation in the rest of the world. Associated with these states are the probabilities $P_1, \ldots, P_m$. These probabilities are positive $(P_1 \geq 0)$ and they sum up to one, or 100% $(\sum_{j=1}^{n} P_j = 1)$.[3] For the jth scenario, the rates of return on the assets are denoted by $R_{1,j}, \ldots, R_{n,j}$.[4]

Exhibit 7.2 displays an example probability distribution for three different stocks: stock 1, stock 2 and stock 3. In the example, there are ten economic scenarios, each associated with an equal probability of 10%. Exhibit 7.2(a) shows the multivariate probability distribution of the three stocks, while Exhibit 7.2(b) shows the univariate distributions by means of histograms.[5] Exhibit 7.2(c) displays the dependency between each pair of assets (stock 1 and stock 2, stock 1 and stock 3, and stock 2 and stock 3).

Exhibit 7.2(a) includes two common statistics for summarising the (univariate) return distribution: mean and variance. The expected return or mean return measures the central tendency of the return distribution or where the distribution is centred.[6] The mean of the ith asset is computed as the weighted average of the returns to the ith asset in all possible states of the world:

$$E(R_i) = \sum_{j=1}^{m} P_j R_{i,j} \tag{7.4}$$

[3] This requires that the states of the world are exhaustive (all possible scenarios are covered) and exclusive (the scenarios do not 'overlap').

[4] In practice, the number of scenarios typically is too large to apply this approach. Section 7.2.1 discusses how this problem can be circumvented by using a continuous distribution that is described by only a few shape parameters.

[5] A histogram is the graphical representation of a probability distribution. The advantage is that we can see quickly which outcomes are most likely. The probability of an outcome is represented by the height of the corresponding bar. Many return levels have a zero probability and, hence, they do not have height in the histogram.

[6] Other measures of central tendency include the mode and the median.

Exhibit 7.2(a)	Multivariate probability distributions for stock 1, stock 2 and stock 3			

Scenario	Probability	Stock 1	Stock 2	Stock 3
1	0.1	0.120	0.060	0.080
2	0.1	0.180	0.080	0.090
3	0.1	0.080	0.100	0.090
4	0.1	0.080	0.030	0.100
5	0.1	0.120	0.100	0.070
6	0.1	0.080	0.060	0.080
7	0.1	0.040	0.080	0.080
8	0.1	−0.020	0.130	0.060
9	0.1	0.080	0.080	0.070
10	0.1	0.040	0.080	0.080
Mean ($E(R)$)		0.080^a	0.080	0.080
Variance (σ^2)		0.0026^b	0.0007	0.0001
Standard deviation (σ)		0.051^c	0.026	0.011
Covariances	Stock 1	0.0026	−0.0005	0.0003
	Stock 2	$−0.0005^d$	0.0007	−0.0002
	Stock 3	0.0003	−0.0002	0.0001
Correlations	Stock 1	1	−0.3788	0.4619
	Stock 2	$−0.3788^e$	1	−0.7107
	Stock 3	0.4619	−0.7107	1

[a] $0.080 = 0.1 \times 0.120 + 0.1 \times 0.180 + \ldots + 0.1 \times 0.040$.
[b] $0.0026 = 0.1 \times (0.120 - 0.080)^2 + 0.1 \times (0.180 - 0.080)^2 + \ldots + 0.1 \times (0.04 - 0.08)^2$.
[c] $0.051 = 0.0026^{1/2}$.
[d] $\sigma_{1,2} = 0.1 \times (0.120 - 0.080) \times (0.080 - 0.060) + 0.1 \times (0.180 - 0.080) \times (0.080 - 0.080) + \ldots$
$\quad + 0.1 \times (0.040 - 0.080) \times (0.080 - 0.080) = -0.0005$.
[e] $\rho_{1,2} = -0.0005/(0.051 \times 0.026) = -0.3788$.

where E is the expectation operator. Note that $E(R_i)$ is an ex-ante return measure, i.e. it refers to the future. By contrast, the sample mean $\bar{R}_i$ discussed in the previous chapter is an ex-post measure that is computed from a sample of past returns. To distinguish between these two measures, $E(R_i)$ is commonly referred to as the population mean. In this case, all three stocks have the same mean (0.080).

The population variance of returns is a measure of the dispersion around the central tendency and is used as a measure of risk.[7] The variance of the possible returns is denoted by σ^2 and is calculated as follows:

$$\sigma_i^2 = E(R_i - E(R_i))^2 = \sum_{j=1}^m P_j (R_{i,j} - E(R_i))^2 \qquad (7.5)$$

Thus, the variance is the sum of the probability multiplied by the squared deviations from the mean. As can be seen from this equation, the higher the uncertainty as measured by deviations

---

[7] Variance is not the only measure of risk, but it is the most widely used. Other risk measures include the range, mean absolute deviation, skewness, kurtosis, probability of loss, expected loss and semivariance.

Exhibit 7.2(b) Univariate probability distributions for stock 1, stock 2 and stock 3

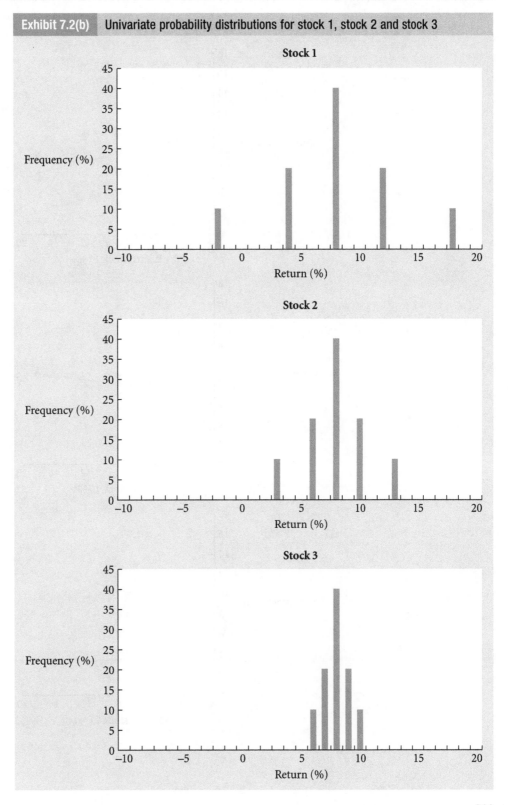

Exhibit 7.2(c)   Dependence between stock 1, stock 2 and stock 3

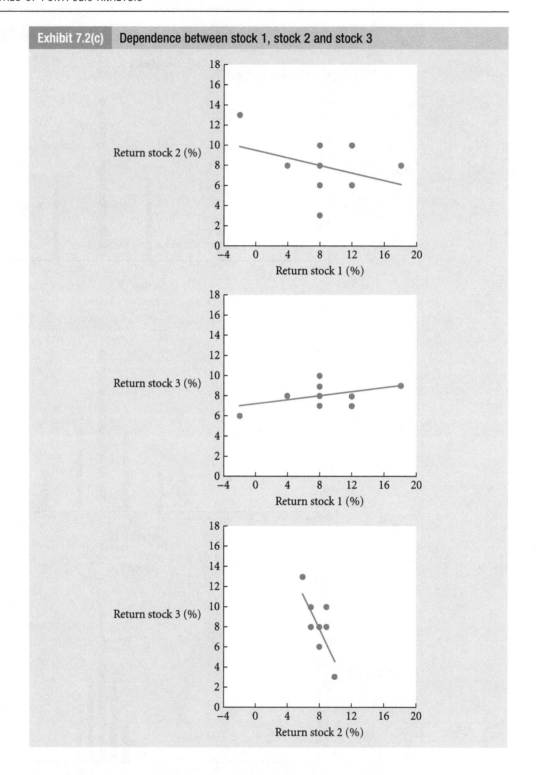

from the mean, the higher the variance. Sometimes, the following equivalent expression is more convenient:[8]

$$\sigma_i^2 = E(R_i^2 - E(R_i))^2 = \sum_{j=1}^{m} P_j R_{i,j}^2 - E(R_i)^2 \tag{7.5a}$$

Since the rates of return are expressed in percentage figures or dollar figures, the unit of variance is percentage squared or dollars squared. Since these terms can be difficult to interpret, it is common to take the square root of the variance, or σ_i, which is called the population standard deviation; this measure is stated in percentages or dollars. Note that σ_i^2 is an ex-ante risk measure, i.e. it refers to the future. By contrast, the sample variance $\hat{\sigma}_j^2$ measures the dispersion of past returns. In this case, stock 1 has the highest variance (0.0026) and stock 3 has the lowest variance (0.0001).

Again, the univariate distributions provide information about the risk and return of the individual stocks. This information suffices for an investor who considers holding any of the three stocks in isolation. However, an investor who considers holding a combination of the three stocks needs information on the dependence between the stocks. Chapter 6 introduced two common measures for summarising the dependency between a pair of random variables: covariance and correlation. That chapter showed how these measures can be computed from historical data. The resulting measures $\hat{\sigma}_{i,j}$ and $\hat{\rho}_{i,j}$ are the sample covariance and sample correlation. By contrast, Exhibit 7.2a includes the population covariance and population correlation, which are computed relative to the future return distribution.

Formally, the population covariance between the ith asset and the sth asset is given by the following formula:

$$\sigma_{i,s} = E((R_i - E(R_i))(R_s - E(R_s))) = \sum_{j=1}^{m} P_j R_{i,j} - E(R_i))(R_{s,j} - E(R_s)) \tag{7.6}$$

This equation shows that covariance is the expected value of the product of deviations from the mean. If both stock returns are above their mean or both stock returns are below their mean at the same time, then the product will be positive and, hence, the covariance will be positive. However, if one stock return is above its mean when the other stock return is below its mean, then the product will be negative; if this occurs frequently, then the covariance will be negative. Sometimes, the following equivalent expression is more convenient:[9]

$$\sigma_{i,s} = E(R_i R_s) - E(R_i)E(R_s) = \sum_{j=1}^{m} P_j R_{i,j} R_{s,j} - E(R_i)E(R_s) \tag{7.6a}$$

By analogy to the discussion of the sample covariance in Chapter 6, the population covariance of an asset with itself is simply its own population variance. From Equation 7.6a, we have

---

[8] The following equalities show that these expressions are equivalent:
$$\sigma_i^2 = E(R_i - E(R_i))^2 = E(R_i^2 - 2R_i E(R_i) + E(R_i)^2) = E(R_i^2) - 2E(R_i)^2 + E(R_i)^2 = E(R_i^2) - E(R_i)^2.$$

[9] The following equalities show that these expressions are equivalent:
$$\sigma_{i,s} = E([R_i - E(R_i)] [R_s - E(R_s)]) = E(R_i R_s - R_i E(R_s) - E(R_i)R_s + E(R_i)E(R_s))$$
$$= E(R_i R_s) - E(R_i)E(R_s) - E(R_i)E(R_s) + E(R_i)E(R_s) = E(R_i R_s) - E(R_i)E(R_s).$$

(substituting i for s) $\sigma_{i,i} = \sum_{j=1}^{m} P_j R_i^2 - E(R_i)^2 = \sigma_i^2$. Also, $\sigma_{i,s} = \sigma_{s,i}$; the covariance of assets i and s is equal to the covariance of assets s and i.

The dependence measured by covariance can also be seen in the graph of Exhibit 7.2(c), which shows the rates of return for all three pairs of stocks. Each point represents the returns for a pair of stocks in a given scenario. Clearly, there is a negative co-movement or negative covariance between stock 1 and stock 2. When one stock is doing relatively well, the other generally is doing poorly, and vice versa. For example, in scenario 8, stock 1's rate of return is −2% and stock 2's rate of return is +13%. Conversely, when stock 1's rate of return is high, stock 2's rate of return generally is low. Notice that the pattern moves downwards as you look from left to right. This downward pattern characterises a negative covariance. By contrast, there is a positive covariance between stock 1 and stock 3.

Positive and negative covariances imply that the assets either move together or move in opposite directions, but they are silent on the strength of this association. By dividing the covariance by the standard deviations of each asset, we can determine the strength of their dependency, or their correlations. The number we obtain is called the population correlation coefficient:

$$\rho_{i,s} = \frac{\sigma_{i,s}}{\sigma_i \sigma_s} \tag{7.7}$$

Like the sample correlation coefficient (see Chapter 6), the population correlation coefficient ranges between −1 and +1, and the population correlation coefficients can be compared directly across different pairs of assets. For example, the correlation of rates of return between stocks 1 and 2 is −0.3788 and the correlation between rates of return between stocks 2 and 3 is −0.7107; hence, we can state that stocks 2 and 3 have a stronger negative dependency than stocks 1 and 2. In Exhibit 7.2(c), the strong dependency between stocks 2 and 3 is reflected by the small dispersion of the points around the straight line, while the weaker dependency between stock 1 and stock 2 shows up in more dispersion around the line. If there is a perfect positive association between rates of return, then the correlation is +1. If there is a perfect negative association, then the correlation is −1. If the rates of return are unrelated (i.e. uncorrelated), then the correlation is zero. As in Chapter 6, the correlation of an asset with itself is always +1, as $\rho_{i,i} = \frac{\sigma_{i,i}}{\sigma_i \sigma_i} = \frac{\sigma_i^2}{\sigma_i^2} = 1$. Also, $\rho_{i,s} = \rho_{s,i}$; the correlation of assets i and s is equal to the correlation of assets s and i.

7.2.1 The normal distribution

The probability distribution shown in Exhibit 7.2 involves a countable number of states of the world ($m = 10$). Such a distribution is called a discrete distribution. By contrast, we cannot count the number of possible outcomes of a continuous distribution. For such a distribution, we cannot describe the possible outcomes by a countable set $R_1, \ldots, R_n$, because the outcome $(R_1 + R_2)/2$, not in the set, would always be possible. This implies that the probability assigned to any outcome is infinitely small. Related to this, continuous distributions are typically described in terms of their probability density functions. The probability density of an outcome is the probability after rescaling such that the area under the function is one. Due to the rescaling, the density measures the probability not in absolute terms but in relative terms. For example, if the probability density for $R = 0$ is 0.397 and for $R = 1$ it is 0.242, this does not mean that there is a 39.7% probability that $R = 0$ or a 24.2% probability that $R = 1$. Rather, it means that the probability of $R = 0$ (which is infinitely small) is $39.7/24.2 = 1.64$ times as high as the probability of $R = 1$ (which is also infinitely small).

In principle, the return distribution of assets can be modelled using a discrete distribution, as we frequently do not need an uncountable number of scenarios. Still, the number of scenarios generally is so large that the information and computation burden becomes too high, especially if we consider hundreds or thousands of assets. In this respect, certain continuous distributions are helpful, because they can be described by a small number of shape parameters. The most important continuous distribution in investment work is the two-parameter normal distribution.[10] This distribution plays an important role in mean–variance analysis (see Chapter 8), which underlies many asset-pricing theories and practical investment tools.

Formally, the normal probability density at R is given by

$$f(R) = \frac{1}{\sigma \times \sqrt{2\pi}} \times \exp\left(-\frac{1}{2} \times \left(\frac{R - E(R)}{\sigma}\right)^2\right) \tag{7.8}$$

where $E(R)$ and σ denote the mean and standard deviation, respectively, and exp stands for exponential, i.e. e to the power of.

Exhibit 7.3(a) shows three examples of normal distributions (A, B and C). Like these examples, the normal distribution in general has a number of characteristic properties:

▪ The distribution is characterised completely by its mean and variance (or its square root, the standard deviation). For example, distribution A corresponds to $E(R_A) = 0$ and $\sigma_A = 1$. Distribution B has the same central tendency ($E(R_B) = 0$) but a higher standard deviation $\sigma_B = 2$. Clearly, this distribution is more spread out than distribution A. Finally, distribution C has a mean of $E(R_C) = 2$ and a standard deviation of $\sigma_C = 2$. This distribution is the same as distribution B, except for its central tendency, which is higher. Distribution A (with a zero mean and a unit variance) is called a standard normal distribution. All other normal distributions are simple linear transformations of the standard normal one. Specifically, if a random variable obeys a normal distribution with mean $E(R)$ and standard deviation σ, then the standardised random variable $Z = \dfrac{R - E(R)}{\sigma}$ (or the Z-score) obeys a standard normal distribution.

---

[10] The normal distribution was first introduced by a French mathematician, Abraham de Moivre (1667–1754). Much of the appeal of the normal distribution comes form the so-called central limit theorem (CLT), which states that the sum or the mean of a large number of independent random variables is approximately normally distributed, provided the random variables obey the same probability distribution (which need not be normal). The CLT is one of the cornerstones of econometrics; it is used to derive the large-sample properties of various statistical estimators. However, despite the usefulness of the CLT, we need to be careful in applying it to real-life economic data, because real-life data frequently do not obey the assumptions underlying the CLT. For example, the return on a well-diversified portfolio of assets is a weighted average of the returns on a large number of individual assets. Still, we cannot apply the CLT and conclude that portfolio returns obey a normal distribution, because the individual assets are not independent and they do not have the same return distribution. Similarly, the portfolio return over a long period of time is a weighted average of the portfolio returns over many short time intervals. Still, we cannot apply the CLT and conclude that the portfolio returns obey a normal distribution, because the return distribution may change over time (for example, the variances and the correlations may increase during a crisis situation) and the returns may be correlated through time (for example, if asset prices do not immediately and completely adjust when new information arrives). This does not mean that portfolio returns do not obey a normal distribution; rather, it merely means that we cannot use the CLT to justify normality. The portfolio returns are still distributed normally if the indidivual assets obey a normal distribution.

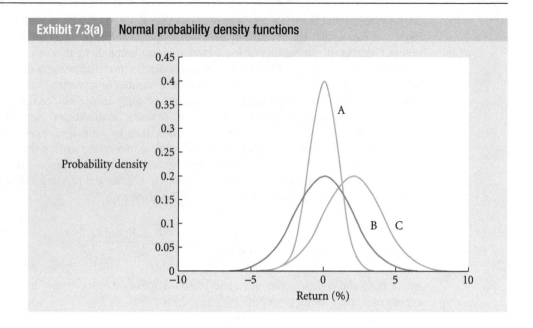

Exhibit 7.3(a) Normal probability density functions

- The possible outcomes range from minus infinity to plus infinity; the tails of the normal distribution extend without limits to the left and to the right.
- The distribution is symmetric around the mean; the probability density for an outcome of $E(R) + x$ is exactly equal to the density for an outcome of $E(R) - x$. The symmetry can be seen from Exhibit 7.3(a). Also, the symmetry can be seen from Equation 7.8. The value $f(R)$ is the same for $R = E(R) + x$ and $R = E(R) - x$; in both cases, we have $\left(\dfrac{R - E(R)}{\sigma} \right)^2 = \dfrac{x^2}{\sigma^2}.$
- The larger the distance of an outcome from the mean, the lower the probability density assigned to that outcome. In addition, for small deviations from the mean, the density falls at an increasing rate, while a decreasing rate applies for large deviations. This gives the distribution a characteristic bell-like shape.

Again, for a continuous random variable, the probability of individual outcomes is infinitely small, and typically we are not interested in such probabilities. Rather, typically we wish to know the probability that a variable falls within a specific range, falls below a critical value or exceeds some threshold. For this purpose, we need to consider the cumulative distribution function. The cumulative distribution function gives the probability that a random variable takes a value that is smaller than or equal to a specified value. Mathematically, it represents the area below the probability density function from minus infinity to the specified value. Recall that the total area under the density function (from minus infinity to plus infinity) is one and, hence, the value for the cumulative distribution function goes to one for large values. Exhibit 7.3(b) displays the cumulative distribution functions for the three normal density functions shown in Exhibit 7.3(a). For distribution A, the probability that the return falls below −1% is 15.9%. For distribution B, which has a higher variance, the probability is 30.9%. For distribution C, which has a higher mean, the probability is 6.7%.

Unfortunately, there exists no close-form solution for computing the probabilities of cumulative normal distribution functions. However, the values can be approximated by means

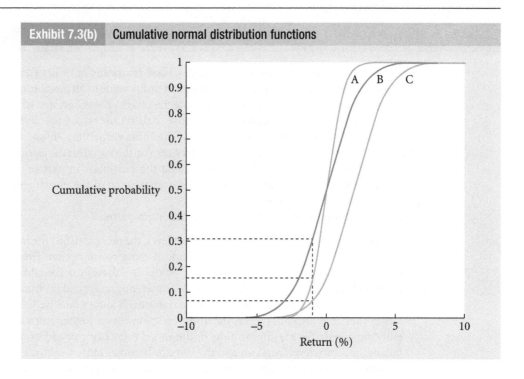

Exhibit 7.3(b) Cumulative normal distribution functions

of computer-simulation techniques or numerical integration techniques. Appendix 7 contains a table with probabilities of the standard normal distribution. The values for a normal random variable with a non-zero mean and a non-unit variance can be computed by transforming the variable to a standard random variable. Again, for this purpose, we compute the standardised scores $Z = \dfrac{R - E(R)}{\sigma}$. So, if an asset obeys distribution C, with $E(R) = 2$ and $\sigma = 2$, then the probability that the return will fall below $R = -1\%$ is found by computing the standardised score $\dfrac{-1\% - 2\%}{2\%} = -1.5$ and finding the associated probability in the standard normal table shown in Appendix 7. In this case, the resulting probability is 0.0668, or 6.7%.

Note that the above examples are univariate normal distributions. To describe the joint distribution of multiple normal random variables, we have to consider the multivariate normal distribution. Apart from the means and variances of the individual variables, the multivariate distribution also accounts for the degree of dependency between assets. For normal distributions, the relevant dependency measure is the covariance (or the correlation, which is a standardised version of covariance). Hence, a multivariate normal distribution is described by the means and variances of all individual assets, as well as the covariances (or correlations) of all pairs of assets.

Interestingly, a weighted average of two or more random variables with a normal distribution is also distributed normally. Hence, when a group of assets has a (joint) normal distribution, then a portfolio of those assets also has a (univariate) normal distribution. Chapter 8 will demonstrate how the mean and the variance of a portfolio can be computed from the means, variances and covariances (or correlations) of the individual assets.

7.3   The utility function

The objectives of investors are frequently described by means of utility functions. A utility function is a mathematical function that assigns a utility value to all possible portfolio returns. Throughout the text, we will use $u(R)$ to denote the utility value associated with return R. This utility value measures the degree of subjective satisfaction associated with return R. The satisfaction may come from several sources. The most elementary source of satisfaction is the additional consumption of goods and services (or the social status associated with those goods and services) that is possible after selling the portfolio (in part or in whole). Also, some investors may derive satisfaction from the excitement of the investment game or from outperforming other investors.

Utility functions in general have four important properties:

- Utility is increasing, i.e. the higher the return level, the more satisfied the investor becomes, for the simple reason that he or she can afford more consumption. Even if the investor does not wish additional consumption, he or she can always use the additional money to give it to his or her relatives or to charity. Put differently, marginal utility, or the additional satisfaction derived from a unit of additional return, is always positive.[11]
- Utility functions are concave, i.e. the utility function curves to the return axis.[12] Put differently, marginal utility is diminishing, or the added value from an additional unit of return falls as the return level increases and the investor becomes more wealthy. Utility is concave, because consumers typically satisfy their most basic needs first, so every additional unit of wealth is used for less essential goods and services.

  For example, if you learn that upon graduation your annual salary will double from $30 000 to $60 000 a year, does this mean your satisfaction will double as well? Most likely, the answer is no. With the first $30 000, you must buy the most important goods and services (for example, food, clothing and shelter), while the second $30 000 is used for less important goods and services (for example, a car or a holiday). Hence, your salary will increase your satisfaction but it will not double it. Put differently, a five-course dinner after a heavy lunch yields less satisfaction than a similar dinner when one is hungry.

  As we will see below, diminishing utility generally implies that the investor is risk-averse. If presented with two portfolios with the same average return but with different levels of risk, then the investor will choose the least risky one. The risky alternative involves a higher probability of high gains and a higher probability of high losses. If the investor loses money, then he or she has to sacrifice goods and services that are more important than those he or she can afford if he or she wins money. Again, this is because the investor first satisfies his or her most essential needs. In brief, the pain from losses is greater than the pleasure from equivalent gains. Consequently, the investor will prefer the least risky alternative, i.e. he or she is risk-averse. Put differently, investors with diminishing marginal utility avoid the honey (higher return) not because they do not like honey but because they know that there is a probability that they could get stung! The curvature of the utility function, or the rate at which marginal utility decreases, determines the degree of risk-aversion.

---

[11] Formally, marginal utility is defined as the first-order derivative or $u'(R) = \dfrac{\partial u(R)}{\partial R} \geq 0$.

[12] In other words, the second-order derivative is negative or $u''(R) = \dfrac{\partial^2 u(R)}{\partial R^2} \leq 0$.

■ Different investors have different utility functions, depending on, among other things, their wealth, income, education and age. For example, if an investor with a modal income loses a given percentage of his or her wealth, then he or she may have to give up some of his or her essential goods and services (for example, sell his or her house or cut expenses for food and clothing). By contrast, a high-net-worth individual may experience less pain from losing a similar percentage of his or her wealth, because he or she can still satisfy his or her most basic needs. Similarly, the shape of the utility function of a given investor changes through time, as the investor goes through different stages of his or her life or as the state of the economy changes.

■ A utility function, for a given investor and for a given point in time, is not unique. In fact, if we add a constant term to the utility function and/or multiply utility by a positive constant term, then exactly the same ordering is obtained for all choice alternatives.[13] For this reason, we cannot directly compare the level of utility and marginal utility of different utility functions associated with different investors or different points in time.

Exhibit 7.4(a) shows two example utility functions, possibly the utility function of two different investors or the functions of a single investor at two different points in time. The first utility function is given by $u_A(R) = 1 - \exp(-6R)$. This type of utility function is called a negative exponential utility function. The exponent -6 determines the curvature (and, hence, the degree of risk-aversion) of the investor. If we use a more extreme value of, for example, -10, then the curvature increases. By contrast, a less extreme value of, for example, -2 yields a lower curvature. The second utility function is linear; it takes the form $u_B(R) = 10R$. Exhibit 7.4(b) shows the marginal utility functions associated with these utility functions, which are constructed by taking the first-order derivative of the utility functions. For the first utility function, marginal utility or $u'_A(R) = 6 \times \exp(-6R)$ is diminishing.[14] By contrast, the marginal utility of the second function or $u'_B(R) = 10$ is constant.[15]

7.4 The expected utility criterion

Thus far, we have discussed the three key elements of investment: the possibilities set, the probability distribution and the utility function.[16] The expected utility criterion combines these three elements in a single decision rule. Specifically, the expected utility criterion states that the investor will select the portfolio that yields the highest possible expected value for his or her utility function. Expected utility is computed as the weighted average of the utility of portfolio return in all possible states of the world, where every state is weighted by its probability:

$$E(u(R_p)) = \sum_{j=1}^{m} P_j u(R_{p,j}) = \sum_{j=1}^{m} P_j u\left(\sum_{j=1}^{n} w_i R_{i,j} \right) \tag{7.9}$$

---

[13] Formally, utility is invariant to linear transformations; $a + b \times u(R)$ gives exactly the same ordering as $u(R)$, for all a and $b > 0$.

[14] The rules of differential calculus imply that the first-order derivative of $u(R) = a + b \times \exp(c \times R)$ is given by $u'(R) = b \times c \times \exp(c \times R)$. In our case, we have $a = 1$, $b = -1$ and $c = -6$.

[15] The rules of differential calculus imply that the first-order derivative of $u(R) = a + b \times R$ is given by $u'(R) = b$. In our case, we have $a = 0$ and $b = 10$.

[16] The maximisation of expected utility was first proposed as a criterion for decision-making under uncertainty by Cramer (1728) and then Bernouilli (1738). Much later, the axiomatic justification for this criterion was provided in an appendix to the classic work by Von Neumann and Morgenstern (1944).

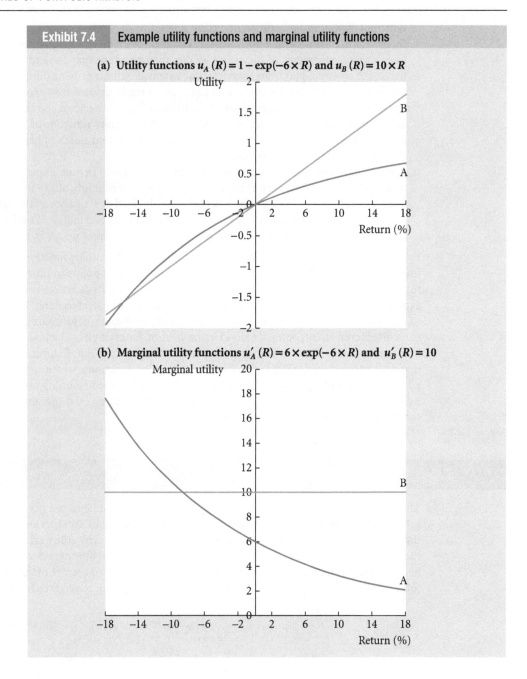

Exhibit 7.4 Example utility functions and marginal utility functions

(a) Utility functions $u_A(R) = 1 - \exp(-6 \times R)$ and $u_B(R) = 10 \times R$

(b) Marginal utility functions $u'_A(R) = 6 \times \exp(-6 \times R)$ and $u'_B(R) = 10$

Thus, the expected utility rule can be summarised as follows:

$$\text{Maximise } E(u(R_p))$$

subject to all investment restrictions placed on the weights $w_1, \ldots, w_n$.

Exhibit 7.5 illustrates this rule using the two possibilities sets from Exhibit 7.1 (a possibilities set with no short sales and one with no short sales and a maximum weight of 50%), the probability distribution from Exhibit 7.2 and the two utility functions from Exhibit 7.4 (a risk-neutral utility function and a risk-averse utility function). Parts (a)–(c) give the expected

Exhibit 7.5	Computation of expected utility

(a) Stock 1

Scenario	Probability	Return	Utility function A	Utility function B
1	0.1	0.120	0.513	1.200
2	0.1	0.180	0.660	1.800
3	0.1	0.080	0.381	0.800
4	0.1	0.080	0.381	0.800
5	0.1	0.120	0.513	1.200
6	0.1	0.080	0.381	0.800
7	0.1	0.040	0.213	0.400
8	0.1	−0.020	−0.127	−0.200
9	0.1	0.080	0.381	0.800
10	0.1	0.040	0.213	0.400
Expected utility			0.351	0.800

(b) Stock 2

Scenario	Probability	Return	Utility function A	Utility function B
1	0.1	0.060	0.302	0.600
2	0.1	0.080	0.381	0.800
3	0.1	0.100	0.451	1.000
4	0.1	0.030	0.165	0.300
5	0.1	0.100	0.451	1.000
6	0.1	0.060	0.302	0.600
7	0.1	0.080	0.381	0.800
8	0.1	0.130	0.542	1.300
9	0.1	0.080	0.381	0.800
10	0.1	0.080	0.381	0.800
Expected utility			0.374	0.800

(c) Stock 3

Scenario	Probability	Return	Utility function A	Utility function B
1	0.1	0.080	0.381	0.800
2	0.1	0.090	0.417	0.900
3	0.1	0.090	0.417	0.900
4	0.1	0.100	0.451	1.000
5	0.1	0.070	0.343	0.700
6	0.1	0.080	0.381	0.800
7	0.1	0.080	0.381	1.800
8	0.1	0.060	0.302	0.600
9	0.1	0.070	0.343	0.700
10	0.1	0.080	0.381	0.800
Expected utility			0.380	0.800

Exhibit 7.5 continued

(d) Optimal portfolio with short sales constraint (27.1% stock 2, 72.9% stock 3)

Scenario	Probability	Return	Utility function A	Utility function B
1	0.1	0.075[a]	0.361	0.746
2	0.1	0.087	0.408	0.873
3	0.1	0.093	0.427	0.927
4	0.1	0.081	0.385	0.810
5	0.1	0.078	0.374	0.781
6	0.1	0.075	0.361	0.746
7	0.1	0.080	0.381	0.800
8	0.1	0.079	0.377	0.790
9	0.1	0.073	0.354	0.727
10	0.1	0.080	0.381	0.800
Expected utility			0.381	0.800

(e) Optimal portfolio with short sales constraint and maximum weight of 50% (8.2% stock 1, 41.8% stock 2, 50.0% stock 3)

Scenario	Probability	Return	Utility function A	Utility function B
1	0.1	0.075[b]	0.362	0.749
2	0.1	0.093	0.429	0.932
3	0.1	0.093	0.429	0.934
4	0.1	0.069	0.340	0.691
5	0.1	0.087	0.405	0.867
6	0.1	0.072	0.349	0.717
7	0.1	0.077	0.369	0.767
8	0.1	0.083	0.391	0.826
9	0.1	0.075	0.362	0.750
10	0.1	0.077	0.369	0.767
Expected utility			0.380	0.800

[a] $0.075 = 0.271 \times 0.060 + 0.729 \times 0.080$.
[b] $0.075 = 0.082 \times 0.120 + 0.418 \times 0.060 + 0.500 \times 0.080$.

utility associated with investment in stock 1, stock 2 and stock 3. These expected utilities are found as the sum of the products of the probabilities in column 2 and the expected utilities in columns 4 and 5, respectively, for the two utility functions. For the curved utility function (utility function A), stock 1 has the lowest expected utility and stock 3 has the highest expected utility. Hence, presented with a choice from these three stocks, an investor with this utility function would choose stock 3. The reason is simple. Recall from Exhibit 7.2(b) that all stocks have the same expected value of 8%. However, stock 1 has the highest dispersion and stock 3 has the lowest dispersion. For an investor with diminishing marginal utility, the higher the risks, all else equal, the lower the expected utility. Again, this is because the pain from losses is greater than the pleasure from equivalent gains, as investors first satisfy their most essential needs. For example, from Exhibit 7.5(a), we can infer that the utility of 8% return is 0.381 and that utility increases by 0.132 (0.513 − 0.381) if 4% return is added (so the return becomes 12%). However, utility decreases by 0.168 (0.381 − 0.213) if 4% return is subtracted (so the return becomes 4%).[17] Hence, the investor is risk-averse; all else equal, he or she prefers the alternative with the lowest dispersion around the mean.[18] By contrast, for the linear utility function (utility function B), all three stocks achieve the same expected utility level. An investor with this type of preferences is risk-neutral; he or she forms decisions solely on the basis of expected return, and he or she is indifferent between choice alternatives with the same mean.

We have thus far compared the expected utilities for stock 1, stock 2 and stock 3, and we have concluded that stock 3 is preferred to stock 1 and 2 by the risk-averter. However, this does not mean that stock 3 is the optimal solution to the expected utility maximiser. After all, the portfolio possibilities set also includes combinations of the three stocks in addition to holding the stock in isolation. As discussed in Section 7.1, the possibilities set depends on the investment restrictions that are imposed. As it turns out, if we impose the first set of restrictions (the weights should add up to 100% and they should be positive), then the optimal portfolio for the risk-averter (utility function A) consists of 27.1% invested in stock 2 and the remainder (72.9%) invested in stock 3.[19] Exhibit 7.5(d) shows that the expected utility of this optimal portfolio (0.381) is, indeed, greater than the expected utility of investing everything in stock 3 (0.380). Thus, although the expected utility of stock 2 (0.374) is smaller than that for stock 3, stock 2 is still included in the optimal portfolio. The reason is that stock 2 performs relatively well if stock 3 yields low returns. For example, in scenario 8, stock 2 yields a 13% return while stock 3 yields only 6%. Hence, by investing part of the wealth in stock 2, the risk-averter reduces risk and hence increases expected utility. For example, in scenario 8, the return to the optimal portfolio is 7.9% rather than only 6%. Again, the risk-neutral investor is indifferent between all possible portfolios, because they all offer the same expected return of 8% and hence the same expected utility (0.800).

Exhibit 7.5(e) shows the results for the second set of restrictions (the weights should add up to 100% and should lie between 0 and 50%). In this case, the optimal portfolio of the risk-averter assigns weights of 8.2%, 41.8% and 50.0% to stock 1, stock 2 and stock 3, respectively. Notice that the expected utility in this case is lower than in the case without the additional restriction (0.380 versus 0.381). This illustrates the principle that investment restrictions

---

[17] Specifically, $1 - \exp(-6 \times 0.12) = 0.513$, $1 - \exp(-6 \times 0.08) = 0.381$ and $1 - \exp(-6 \times 0.04) = 0.213$.

[18] We use a loose definition of risk and we use the terms 'risk' and 'dispersion' interchangeably. In general, we may define a risk-averter as somebody who dislikes so-called mean-preserving spreads. A mean-preserving spread transfers weight from the centre of the density function to its tails without changing the mean. For example, consider two lotteries. The first lottery gives a 10% probability of winning $1000 and the second lottery gives a 1% probability of winning $10 000. In this case, the latter lottery is a mean-preserving spread of the former. In both cases, the mean is $100. However, the second lottery has more probability mass in the tails than the first one. All investors who follow the expected utility rule and have a concave utility function will choose the first lottery, for the simple reason that the probability of winning is ten times higher, while the utility of $10 000 is less than ten times higher than the utility of $1000 (marginal utility is diminishing). Interestingly, the second lottery can be seen as a compound lottery where the lottery player first plays the first lottery (a 10% probability of winning $1000) and, if he or she wins the $1000, he or she then plays a follow-up lottery with a 90% probability of losing the $1000 and a 10% probability of winning an additional $9000. The follow-up lottery has a zero-mean and all risk-averters will choose to avoid it.

[19] The proof that this is the optimum is beyond the scope of this book, as it requires non-linear constrained optimisation. The interested reader is referred to Bazaraa et al. (1993). The reader who is already familiar with optimisation should note that objective function (expected utility) is concave (provided the utility function is concave) and the feasible set (the portfolio possibilities set) is convex (provided we include only linear equalities and inequalities, such as in Equations 7.2 and 7.3). Hence, the first-order optimality condition is necessary and sufficient to determine the optimum.

generally make the investor worse off (ignoring the beneficial effect that restrictions may have on society as a whole by preventing illegal or unethical investment strategies). Again, the risk-neutral investor is indifferent between all possible portfolios.

7.5 Risk-aversion, diversification and risk premiums

In the previous section, we saw that diminishing marginal utility yields risk-aversion in the expected utility framework. Risk-averters, other things being equal, are investors who dislike risk or dispersion. They always prefer a certain investment to an uncertain investment as long as the expected returns on the two investments are identical. Investors who are risk-neutral completely ignore an investment's risk and make investment decisions based only on the asset's expected return. Investors are defined as risk-seekers if they like risk or dispersion.

There is ample evidence that some people are risk-seekers, at least during some periods of time and for small dollar amounts. For example, most gambling activities, such as state lotteries, have expected payoffs that are less than the cost to play, and yet many people still buy lottery tickets.[20] Similarly, without accounting for risk-seeking, it may seem difficult to understand why many individual investors hold highly underdiversified portfolios.[21] After all, portfolio diversification reduces risk (if the assets have a low degree of dependency) and risk-reduction increases the expected utility of risk-averters (all else equal). Also, it is difficult to understand excessive trading (incurring more transaction costs than justified by the additional risk-adjusted return) by individual investors.[22]

However, for several reasons, risk-aversion is the standard assumption. First, there exist many other explanations (other than risk-seeking) for gambling, underdiversification and excessive trading, including the errors of judgement and errors of preference that are discussed in Chapter 12. Second, many (institutional) investors do seek to diversify their investment portfolios and use risk-management instruments (such as derivative securities) so as to reduce risk. Also, the number of households investing in mutual funds, as well as the growth in the number of mutual funds, has increased markedly over the past two decades. Presumably, this growth is caused by the desire for low-cost diversification. Third, the historical average return on risky asset classes (such as stocks and junk bonds) includes a sizeable risk premium above the average return on risk-free assets such as T-bills (see Chapter 6). This is another indication that financial markets are dominated by risk-averters.

Asset-pricing theories try to explain the level of the risk premiums of different assets and the evolution of the risk premiums through time. Chapters 10 and 11 discuss two of the basic asset-pricing theories: the capital asset-pricing theory (CAPM) and the arbitrage pricing theory (APT). These theories use an important insight that is also illustrated in this chapter. Specifically, to evaluate the risk of an asset, we need to account for its degree of dependency on the other assets in the investor's portfolio in addition to its risk when held separately.

---

[20] See, for example, Friedman and Savage (1948), Markowitz (1952) and Hartley and Farrell (2002).

[21] See, for example, Blume and Friend (1975). Chapter 8 discusses underdiversification further.

[22] See, for example, Barber and Odean (2000). This study found that the average household turns over 80% of its common stock portfolio each year. The associated transaction costs, such as commissions running and a spread between the bid and ask prices, substantially reduces the average net return below the levels of a passive strategy of holding an index fund. 20% of the households sported a 283% average annual turnover rate; investors in this group basically swapped out their entire portfolios three times a year. Adjusted for risk, the net return of this high-turnover group lagged the market by as many as 10.9 percentage points per year.

In general, the higher the degree of dependency of a particular asset with other risky assets included in a portfolio, the higher will be this asset's contribution to the portfolio's risk, and the less attractive the asset becomes. Hence, investors will require a high-risk premium for assets that strongly covary with other assets and a low premium for assets with a low or negative codependence.

As discussed above, the historical record shows that risky assets carry a premium above the riskless rate. In this respect, asset-pricing theories are qualitatively correct. However, the magnitude of the risk premiums is more difficult to understand. For example, Connecting Theory to Practice 7.2 discusses the so-called equity premium puzzle.

The equity premium is the difference in the expected rate of return between stocks and Treasury bills (sometimes, Treasury bonds are used as the benchmark). This figure is of central importance in portfolio-allocation decisions and estimates of the cost of capital. Also, it is central to the debate about investing social security funds in the stock market. There is a wealth of evidence that for more than a century, stock returns have been considerably higher than those for Treasury bills. The average annual real return (i.e. the inflation-adjusted return) on the US stock market over the past 110 years has been about 7.9%. Over the same period, the return on T-bills was a paltry 1%. The equity premium – the difference between these returns – is 6.9%. The difference is even more pronounced since the Second World War, with the premium being almost 8%. Further, this pattern of excess returns on equity holdings is not unique to US capital markets. Equity returns in other countries also exhibit this historical regularity. For example, the equity premium in the UK stock market was 4.6% since the war, and similar differentials are documented for France, Germany, Italy and Spain.[23]

Again, the size of the equity premium suggests that risk-aversion is the dominating preference in the marketplace; if all investors were either risk-neutral or risk-seeking, there would be no positive risk premium. However, the size of the historical equity premium seems far greater than can be justified using reasonable assumptions about the risk of stocks and the risk-aversion of investors. Even during the Depression of 1929–39, a well-diversified investor who continued to reinvest his or her dividends in the stock market would have seen his or her stock portfolio fall by only 18%; this implies that it is hard to come up with plausible scenarios with catastrophic losses for well-diversified shareholders. Given this limited risk of stocks, we need an unreasonably high degree of risk-aversion to explain the magnitude of the historical equity premium. For this reason, the size of the equity premium has puzzled academics and practitioners for decades.[24]

Some claim that current asset-pricing models do not account properly for the risk perception and the risk attitude of investors.[25] Others claim that the historical average rates of return have been overstated. For example, the computations typically assume that dividend payments to stocks are reinvested and no taxes are paid. Still others claim that the historically observed average rates of return are not representative for the returns that investors actually expected in the past (for example, due to unexpectedly few catastrophic events such as world wars) and also they are not representative for the returns that investors currently expect for the future (for example, because investment vehicles such as index funds and ETFs make low-cost, low-risk equity portfolios available even for small individual investors). This debate is likely to continue for a long time.

---

[23] See, for instance, Ibbotson Associates (2001).
[24] See, for instance, Mehra and Prescott (1985) and Kocherlakota (1996).
[25] See, for instance, Benartzi and Thaler (1995).

A puzzle at the heart of equities

The past three years has not been kind to those in the business of selling equities. As the global bear market progressed, their 'models' showing equities to be cheap fell by the wayside one after another. Government bonds have outperformed equities over the past 16 years. The heady days when books were published with titles such as *Dow 36 000* or *Dow 100 000* are long gone.

With so much stock market gloom around, it may seem odd that economics is still struggling to explain why equities have produced such high investment returns. But the figures are clear: over long periods of 40 years or more, equities have significantly outperformed other investments. Estimates vary but whatever long time period, measuring technique or country you choose, the total return on equities far exceeds that of a riskless asset, such as a government bond. Perhaps the most careful analysis, by Elroy Dimson, Paul Marsh and Mike Staunton*, calculates that this equity risk premium was 4.9 percentage points a year in the US over the past century and 4.6 percentage points globally. The power of compound interest over very long periods implies that even though equity markets have roughly halved over the past three years, calculated equity risk premiums remain high. The US premium since 1900, for example, would still be well above 4 percentage points.

What has surprised economists since the mid-1980s is not that equities have higher returns – they are riskier assets than bonds so investors require higher returns – but that the size of the equity risk premium cannot be justified by the additional risk.

One of the authors of the original 1980s work, Rajnish Mehra of the University of California, has recently published a paper examining whether economic theory has been able satisfactorily to explain the 'equity premium puzzle' in the 20 years since it became widely discussed**. Since equities and bonds perform similarly in various economic scenarios, he calculates that equities should command only a 1 percentage point annual premium over riskless assets. His answer is that none of the theoretical explanations adequately explains the discrepancy. Some academics have constructed models that mirror the data but their assumptions about human behaviour, especially regarding risk aversion and prudence, 'become improbably large'. A potential upward bias in the equity return data because the US market has survived the past century also fails because government bonds are as vulnerable to financial implosion owing to war or revolution. Other explanations similarly fail, according to Prof Mehra, leaving the equity premium puzzle intact. He draws the conclusion that since economic theory has failed to answer his puzzle, and since the data on long-run equity returns are better than almost any other economic series, there is every reason to expect equity returns to keep outperforming bonds significantly over the next century.

Others disagree. They tend to the view that since the size of the equity premium has been a genuine puzzle, there is little reason to expect it to remain high. Writing in the Financial Analysts Journal last year, Robert Arnott and Peter Bernstein made a distinction between the historical real stock market return relative to riskless bonds and the prospective risk premium that investors could have expected when committing their money***. They contended that equity investors in the early part of the 20th century never expected a long-term premium of 5 per cent over government bonds but were simply fortunate that equities performed so well. Such performance could not have been predicted. Partly it was due to economic policy changes that led to the re-emergence of inflation after the second world war, decreasing real bond returns but not those on equities. A second reason was the rise in equity values relative to dividends paid, particularly since the mid-1980s. This could not have been forecast at the beginning of the century. Third, the improvement in company regulation after the 1920s helped equity returns.

▶

If equity investors were simply lucky, rather than being compensated for additional risk, there is no reason, according to Arnott and Bernstein, to expect the same equity premium in the future. Moreover, the recent high valuations of equities relative to prospective dividend payments led them to believe the prospective short-term equity premium 'may well be near zero, perhaps even negative'.

The good news for equity investors is that if the 'normal' level of the equity premium is lower, current market values can be better justified by dividend levels and their likely growth. But the bad news is that equities are unlikely to perform as well in the current century as in the last. If Prof Mehra is right and the historic 5 percentage point equity premium is here to stay over the very long term, the prospects for equity investors seem brighter. But the crucial phrase is 'over the very long term'. Right now, a prospective higher risk premium suggests US equities remain overvalued because only with lower stock prices could equities start to yield the required 5 percentage point premium over government bonds.

* Triumph of the optimists, Princeton University Press
** The equity premium: why is it a puzzle? www.nber.org/papers/w9512
*** What Risk Premium is Normal? Financial Analysts Journal, March/April 2002, published by AIMR

Source: Chris Giles, 'A Puzzle At the Heart of Equities', FT.com site, 18 March 2003.

7.6 Looking forward: from expected utility to mean–variance analysis

The expected utility criterion provides an elegant and theoretically sound approach to modelling investment decisions. However, an individual or corporation seeking investment advice will not be grateful for the suggestion to maximise expected utility. The expected utility criterion is not operational; in general, we do not know the shape of the utility function and the shape of the probability distribution of returns, and hence we cannot calculate expected utilities. Moreover, corporations typically have many shareholders, each presumably with a different utility function. Consequently, the expected utility criterion generally cannot be applied in practice. Still, the criterion is useful, because it shows the theoretically correct link between investor objectives, expectations and constraints. Also, many operational investment tools rely on the principles of the expected utility framework.

Chapter 8 discusses mean–variance analysis, which can be seen as an approximation to expected utility analysis. In the mean–variance framework, investors make a trade-off between the expected return or mean and the risk as measured as variance or standard deviation (the square root of variance). This greatly simplifies the problem of estimating the preferences of investors and the probability distribution of assets. Under particular assumptions about the shape of the utility function and the probability distribution, mean–variance analysis gives a good approximation to expected utility analysis; under more general assumptions, it is a useful approximation. In contrast to the expected utility framework, mean–variance analysis is operational. In fact, currently it is the most popular model for structuring investment decisions. It is used widely for applications of portfolio selection, performance evaluation and risk management. In addition, mean–variance analysis forms the basis of many theoretical asset pricing models, such as the CAPM (discussed in Chapter 10). Still, we stress that it is an approximation to the theoretical expected utility framework and that it intends to capture the theoretical relationships between investors' objectives, expectations and constraints that were discussed in this chapter. Knowledge of the expected utility framework is required in order to

227

understand the limitations of mean–variance analysis and in order to develop operational alternatives for mean–variance analysis.[26]

Summary

Explain the basic concepts of the portfolio possibilities set, the probability distribution of returns and the utility function.

Financial economists typically model investment as a problem of constrained optimisation under uncertainty. To implement this general approach, three fundamental concepts are used: a utility function to describe the investor's objectives, a probability distribution to describe the investor's subjective expectations about the possible future returns and the probabilities of those returns, and a portfolio possibilities set to describe the possibilities and restrictions faced by the investor.

Explain the maximum expected utility criterion for portfolio selection.

The expected utility criterion states that an investor chooses his or her investment portfolio by solving the following problem of constrained optimisation under uncertainty:

$$\text{Maximise } E(u(R_p)) = \sum_{j=1}^{m} P_j u\left(\sum_{i=1}^{n} w_i R_{i,j} \right)$$

subject to all investment restrictions placed on the weights $w_1, \ldots, w_n$.

Investors differ in the following respects:

- They have different objectives or utility functions $u(R)$; some are more risk-averse than others.
- They have different expectations about the future return distribution, denoted here by the probabilities $P_1, \ldots, P_m$.
- They face different sets of restrictions on the weights $w_1, \ldots, w_n$; investors may face, for example, short-selling constraints, restrictions on the deviations from a benchmark index or from a long-run asset allocation, restrictions on the amount invested in individual stocks, sectors, countries and asset types, or social and environmental screens.

Explain what a risk-averter is.

A risk-averter, all else equal, dislikes volatility. Such an investor will always prefer a certain investment over an uncertain investment as long as the expected returns on the two investments are identical. In the expected utility framework, risk-aversion arises from diminishing marginal utility. The investor first satisfies his or her most basic needs by buying the most essential goods and services (shelter, food, clothing). Every additional dollar yields less utility

---

[26] If mean–variance analysis is considered too restrictive, then the framework of stochastic dominance offers an alternative. In contrast to mean–variance analysis, stochastic dominance analysis does not require a quadratic utility function or normally distributed returns. Rather, stochastic dominance analysis relies on a general set of assumptions about the preferences of the investor and the statistical distribution of asset returns. The following classic works provide the theoretical foundation for stochastic dominance analysis: Hadar and Russell (1969), Hanoch and Levy (1969), Rothschild and Stiglitz (1970) and Whitmore (1970). Since its conception, stochastic dominance analysis has seen considerable theoretical development and empirical application in various areas of economics. Useful surveys of the topic can be found in Levy (1992) and Levy (1998). Finally, an empirical methodology for applying stochastic dominance analysis to portfolio selection and portfolio evaluation is found in Post (2003).

as it is spent on less essential goods and services. For this reason, the pain experienced from a loss exceeds the pleasure from an equivalent gain, and the investor prefers a certain investment over an uncertain investment, all else equal.

Explain why a risk-averter typically diversifies his or her portfolio and why he or she charges risk premiums over and above the riskless rate.

A risk-averter will diversify his or her portfolio across many different assets because diversification reduces the risk of an investment portfolio, provided the assets are not correlated strongly. Investor risk-aversion also results in a risk premium over and above the riskless rate of return. The risk premium is the additional average return required to compensate the investor for the risk exposure of risky assets. The risk premium is required because a risk-averter will choose the riskless asset rather than the risky assets if the risky assets have the same expected rate of return.

Explain why the expected utility criterion is not operational. Explain also why the criterion is still important.

We generally cannot apply the expected utility framework in practice, because we do not know the precise shape of the utility function and the probability distribution. Still, the framework captures the basic principles of investment (the portfolio possibilities set, the return distribution and the utility function). Many operational tools, such as the mean–variance framework, rely on the principles of the expected utility framework.

Key terms

Arbitrage 208	Multivariate probability distribution 209	Probability distribution 205
Constrained optimisation under uncertainty 204	Objective probability 208	Risk 208
Constraint 204	Optimisation 204	Riskless asset 208
Continuous distribution 214	Population correlation 229	Riskless interest rate 208
Cumulative distribution function 216	Population correlation coefficient 214	Risk-neutral 223
Discrete distribution 214	Population covariance 213	Risk-seeker 224
Equity premium 225	Population mean 210	Standard normal distribution 215
Equity premium puzzle 225	Population standard deviation 213	Subjective probability 208
Expected return 209	Population variance 210	Uncertainty 204
Marginal utility 218	Portfolio possibilities set 205	Univariate probability distribution 209
Mean 209	Portfolio weights 205	Utility function 204
Mean return 209	Probability density 214	Variance 209
Mean–variance analysis 215	Probability density functions 214	

Review questions

1   To model investor behaviour, economists refer to three fundamental concepts – utility functions, probability distributions, and portfolio possibilities sets:

   a. Name the main three properties of utility functions that describe investors' objectives.
   b. What is the purpose of probability distributions?
   c. What is the effect of investment restrictions on the portfolio possibilities set?

2   Suppose an investor with utility function $u(R) = E(RP)0.5$, where $E(RP)$ is the expected return on the portfolio P. The investor wishes to invest in a portfolio that combines the three stocks from Exhibit 7.2a. Will he or she prefer an equal weighted average of the three stocks to holding stocks 2 and 3 only, with corresponding portfolio weights $(0; {}^1/_4; {}^3/_4)$?

3   Suppose an investor with a logarithmic utility function $u(R_p) = \exp^{Rp}$. Initial wealth of the investor equals EUR 1000. The investor can make an investment and gain 10% return with a probability of 25%, or lose 5% with a probability of 75%:

   a. Will the risk-averse investor undertake this investment possibility?
   b. Given that the investor can either gain 10% or lose 5% of his investment's value, what's the probability of success at which the investor will prefer to take a risk rather than avoid investing?

4   Although the size of the equity premium suggests that risk-aversion is the dominating preference in the marketplace (i.e. if all investors were either risk-neutral or risk-seeking there would be no positive risk premium), the size of the historical equity premium seems far greater than can be justified using reasonable assumptions about the risk of stocks and the risk aversion of investors. Give some of the explanations for the magnitude of the historical equity premium that have been provided by academics and practitioners.

5   Although the expected utility criterion is not operational, the criterion is still useful. Explain why.

For an extensive set of review and practice questions and answers, visit the Levy–Post investment website at www.booksites.net/levy

Selected references

Arrow, K. J., 1951, 'Alternative Approaches to the Theory of Choice in Risk-Taking Situations', *Econometrica*, **19** (4), 404–437.

Arrow, K. J., 1964, 'The Role of Securities in the Optimal Allocation of Risk-Bearing', *Review of Economic Studies*, **31** (1), 91–96.

Barber, B. M. and T. Odean, 2000, 'Trading is Hazardous to Your Wealth: The Common Stock Investment Performance of Individual Investors', *Journal of Finance*, **55**, 773–806.

Bazaraa, M. S., H. D. Sherali and C. M. Shetty, 1993, *Nonlinear Programming Theory and Algorithms*, 2nd edn, New York: John Wiley & Sons.

Benartzi, S. and R. H. Thaler, 1995, 'Myopic Loss Aversion and the Equity Premium Puzzle', *Quarterly Journal of Economics*, **110**, 73–92.

Bernouilli, D., 1738 (trans. L. Sommer, 1954), 'Specimen Theoriae Novae de Mensura Sortis' (Exposition of a New Theory on the Measurement of Risk), *Econometrica*, **21** (1), 23–36.

Blume, M. E. and I. Friend, 1975, 'The Asset Structure of Individual Portfolios and some Implications for Utility Functions', *Journal of Finance*, **30**, 585–603.

Cramer, G., 1728, Letter to Nicolas Bernouilli; extracts printed in Bernouilli (1738) and in Sommer's (1954) translation.

Fama, E. and K. French, 2001, 'The Equity Premium', working paper 522, Chicago: University of Chicago, http://gsbwww.uchicago.edu/fac/finance/papers/newequity.pdf

Friedman, M. and L. J. Savage, 1948, 'The Utility Analysis of Choices Involving Risk', *Journal of Political Economy*, **56**, 279–304.

Good, R. W., 1994, 'Yes, Virginia, there is a Risk Premium, But . . .', *Financial Analysts Journal*, **50** (1), 11–12.

Hadar, J. and W. R. Russell, 1969, 'Rules for Ordering Uncertain Prospects', *American Economic Review*, **59**, 25–34.

Hanoch, G. and H. Levy, 1969, 'The Efficiency Analysis of Choices Involving Risk', *Review of Economic Studies*, **36**, 335–346.

Hartley, R. and L. Farrell, 2002, 'Can Expected Utility Theory Explain Gambling?', *American Economic Review*, **92**, 613–624.

Hirshleifer, J. H., 1958, 'On the Theory of Optimal Investment Decision', *Journal of Political Economy*, **66**, 329–352.

Ibbotson Associates, 2001, *Stocks, Bonds, Bills and Inflation: 2000 Yearbook*, Chicago: Ibbotson Associates.

Knight, F. H., 1921, *Risk, Uncertainty and Profit*, Boston, MA: Houghton Mifflin.

Kocherlakota, N. R., 1996, 'The Equity Premium: It's Still a Puzzle', *Journal of Economic Literature*, **34**, 42–71.

Levy, H., 1992, 'Stochastic Dominance and Expected Utility: Survey and Analysis', *Management Science*, **38** (4), 555–593.

Levy, H., 1998, *Stochastic Dominance*, Norwell, MA: Kluwer Academic Publishers.

Levy, H. and A. Cohen, 1998, 'On the Risks of Stocks in the Long Run: Revisited', *Journal of Portfolio Management*, **24**, 60–69.

Markowitz, H. M., 1952, 'The Utility of Wealth', *Journal of Political Economy*, **60**, 151–158.

Mehra, R. and E. C. Prescott, 1985, 'The Equity Premium: A Puzzle', *Journal of Monetary Economics*, **15**, 145–162.

Post, G. T., 2003, 'Empirical Tests for Stochastic Dominance Efficiency', *Journal of Finance*, **58** (5), 1905–1932.

Rothschild, M. and J. E. Stiglitz, 1970, 'Increasing Risk I: A Definition', *Journal of Economic Theory*, **2**, 225–243.

Sharpe, W. F., 1965, 'Risk Aversion in the Stock Market: Some Empirical Evidence', *Journal of Finance*, **20**, 416–422.

Sharpe, W. F., 1991, 'Capital Asset Prices With and Without Negative Holdings', *Journal of Finance*, **64**, 89–509.

Von Neumann, J. and O. Morgenstern, 1944, *Theory of Games and Economic Behavior*, Princeton, NJ: Princeton University Press.

Whitmore, G. A., 1970, 'Third-Degree Stochastic Dominance', *American Economic Review*, **60**, 457–459.

APPENDIX 7 Cumulative standard normal distribution

Z-score	Second decimal of Z-score									
	0.00	0.01	0.02	0.03	0.04	0.05	0.06	0.07	0.08	0.09
−3.00	0.0013	0.0013	0.0013	0.0012	0.0012	0.0011	0.0011	0.0011	0.0010	0.0010
−2.90	0.0019	0.0018	0.0018	0.0017	0.0016	0.0016	0.0015	0.0015	0.0014	0.0014
−2.80	0.0026	0.0025	0.0024	0.0023	0.0023	0.0022	0.0021	0.0021	0.0020	0.0019
−2.70	0.0035	0.0034	0.0033	0.0032	0.0031	0.0030	0.0029	0.0028	0.0027	0.0026
−2.60	0.0047	0.0045	0.0044	0.0043	0.0041	0.0040	0.0039	0.0038	0.0037	0.0036
−2.50	0.0062	0.0060	0.0059	0.0057	0.0055	0.0054	0.0052	0.0051	0.0049	0.0048
−2.40	0.0082	0.0080	0.0078	0.0075	0.0073	0.0071	0.0069	0.0068	0.0066	0.0064
−2.30	0.0107	0.0104	0.0102	0.0099	0.0096	0.0094	0.0091	0.0089	0.0087	0.0084
−2.20	0.0139	0.0136	0.0132	0.0129	0.0125	0.0122	0.0119	0.0116	0.0113	0.0110
−2.10	0.0179	0.0174	0.0170	0.0166	0.0162	0.0158	0.0154	0.0150	0.0146	0.0143
−2.00	0.0228	0.0222	0.0217	0.0212	0.0207	0.0202	0.0197	0.0192	0.0188	0.0183
−1.90	0.0287	0.0281	0.0274	0.0268	0.0262	0.0256	0.0250	0.0244	0.0239	0.0233
−1.80	0.0359	0.0351	0.0344	0.0336	0.0329	0.0322	0.0314	0.0307	0.0301	0.0294
−1.70	0.0446	0.0436	0.0427	0.0418	0.0409	0.0401	0.0392	0.0384	0.0375	0.0367
−1.60	0.0548	0.0537	0.0526	0.0516	0.0505	0.0495	0.0485	0.0475	0.0465	0.0455
−1.50	0.0668	0.0655	0.0643	0.0630	0.0618	0.0606	0.0594	0.0582	0.0571	0.0559
−1.40	0.0808	0.0793	0.0778	0.0764	0.0749	0.0735	0.0721	0.0708	0.0694	0.0681
−1.30	0.0968	0.0951	0.0934	0.0918	0.0901	0.0885	0.0869	0.0853	0.0838	0.0823
−1.20	0.1151	0.1131	0.1112	0.1093	0.1075	0.1056	0.1038	0.1020	0.1003	0.0985
−1.10	0.1357	0.1335	0.1314	0.1292	0.1271	0.1251	0.1230	0.1210	0.1190	0.1170
−1.00	0.1587	0.1562	0.1539	0.1515	0.1492	0.1469	0.1446	0.1423	0.1401	0.1379
−0.90	0.1841	0.1814	0.1788	0.1762	0.1736	0.1711	0.1685	0.1660	0.1635	0.1611
−0.80	0.2119	0.2090	0.2061	0.2033	0.2005	0.1977	0.1949	0.1922	0.1894	0.1867
−0.70	0.2420	0.2389	0.2358	0.2327	0.2296	0.2266	0.2236	0.2206	0.2177	0.2148
−0.60	0.2743	0.2709	0.2676	0.2643	0.2611	0.2578	0.2546	0.2514	0.2483	0.2451
−0.50	0.3085	0.3050	0.3015	0.2981	0.2946	0.2912	0.2877	0.2843	0.2810	0.2776
−0.40	0.3446	0.3409	0.3372	0.3336	0.3300	0.3264	0.3228	0.3192	0.3156	0.3121
−0.30	0.3821	0.3783	0.3745	0.3707	0.3669	0.3632	0.3594	0.3557	0.3520	0.3483
−0.20	0.4207	0.4168	0.4129	0.4090	0.4052	0.4013	0.3974	0.3936	0.3897	0.3859
−0.10	0.4602	0.4562	0.4522	0.4483	0.4443	0.4404	0.4364	0.4325	0.4286	0.4247
0.00	0.5000	0.5040	0.5080	0.5120	0.5160	0.5199	0.5239	0.5279	0.5319	0.5359
0.10	0.5398	0.5438	0.5478	0.5517	0.5557	0.5596	0.5636	0.5675	0.5714	0.5753
0.20	0.5793	0.5832	0.5871	0.5910	0.5948	0.5987	0.6026	0.6064	0.6103	0.6141
0.30	0.6179	0.6217	0.6255	0.6293	0.6331	0.6368	0.6406	0.6443	0.6480	0.6517
0.40	0.6554	0.6591	0.6628	0.6664	0.6700	0.6736	0.6772	0.6808	0.6844	0.6879
0.50	0.6915	0.6950	0.6985	0.7019	0.7054	0.7088	0.7123	0.7157	0.7190	0.7224
0.60	0.7257	0.7291	0.7324	0.7357	0.7389	0.7422	0.7454	0.7486	0.7517	0.7549
0.70	0.7580	0.7611	0.7642	0.7673	0.7704	0.7734	0.7764	0.7794	0.7823	0.7852
0.80	0.7881	0.7910	0.7939	0.7967	0.7995	0.8023	0.8051	0.8078	0.8106	0.8133

Z-score	Second decimal of Z-score									
	0.00	0.01	0.02	0.03	0.04	0.05	0.06	0.07	0.08	0.09
0.90	0.8159	0.8186	0.8212	0.8238	0.8264	0.8289	0.8315	0.8340	0.8365	0.8389
1.00	0.8413	0.8438	0.8461	0.8485	0.8508	0.8531	0.8554	0.8577	0.8599	0.8621
1.10	0.8643	0.8665	0.8686	0.8708	0.8729	0.8749	0.8770	0.8790	0.8810	0.8830
1.20	0.8849	0.8869	0.8888	0.8907	0.8925	0.8944	0.8962	0.8980	0.8997	0.9015
1.30	0.9032	0.9049	0.9066	0.9082	0.9099	0.9115	0.9131	0.9147	0.9162	0.9177
1.40	0.9192	0.9207	0.9222	0.9236	0.9251	0.9265	0.9279	0.9292	0.9306	0.9319
1.50	0.9332	0.9345	0.9357	0.9370	0.9382	0.9394	0.9406	0.9418	0.9429	0.9441
1.60	0.9452	0.9463	0.9474	0.9484	0.9495	0.9505	0.9515	0.9525	0.9535	0.9545
1.70	0.9554	0.9564	0.9573	0.9582	0.9591	0.9599	0.9608	0.9616	0.9625	0.9633
1.80	0.9641	0.9649	0.9656	0.9664	0.9671	0.9678	0.9686	0.9693	0.9699	0.9706
1.90	0.9713	0.9719	0.9726	0.9732	0.9738	0.9744	0.9750	0.9756	0.9761	0.9767
2.00	0.9772	0.9778	0.9783	0.9788	0.9793	0.9798	0.9803	0.9808	0.9812	0.9817
2.10	0.9821	0.9826	0.9830	0.9834	0.9838	0.9842	0.9846	0.9850	0.9854	0.9857
2.20	0.9861	0.9864	0.9868	0.9871	0.9875	0.9878	0.9881	0.9884	0.9887	0.9890
2.30	0.9893	0.9896	0.9898	0.9901	0.9904	0.9906	0.9909	0.9911	0.9913	0.9916
2.40	0.9918	0.9920	0.9922	0.9925	0.9927	0.9929	0.9931	0.9932	0.9934	0.9936
2.50	0.9938	0.9940	0.9941	0.9943	0.9945	0.9946	0.9948	0.9949	0.9951	0.9952
2.60	0.9953	0.9955	0.9956	0.9957	0.9959	0.9960	0.9961	0.9962	0.9963	0.9964
2.70	0.9965	0.9966	0.9967	0.9968	0.9969	0.9970	0.9971	0.9972	0.9973	0.9974
2.80	0.9974	0.9975	0.9976	0.9977	0.9977	0.9978	0.9979	0.9979	0.9980	0.9981
2.90	0.9981	0.9982	0.9982	0.9983	0.9984	0.9984	0.9985	0.9985	0.9986	0.9986

To find the cumulative probability for the value R for a random variable with mean $E(R)$ and standard deviation σ, first compute the standardised value $Z = (R - E(R))/\sigma$. Next, enter the row with the first decimal of the Z-score and the column with the second decimal. For example, if a variable has $E(R) = 2$ and standard deviation $\sigma = 4$, then the Z-score for $R = 6$ is $(6 - 2)/4 = 1$ and the cumulative probability is 0.8413, or 84.13%. This table was generated using Microsoft® Excel™.

CHAPTER 8

Mean–variance analysis

Investment in the News 8

FT

The enlightening struggle against uncertainty

Chronology of risk

- **1654** French mathematicians Blaise Pascal and Pierre de Fermat analyse games of chance, providing for the first time a formal and mathematical basis for the theory of probability.

- **1662** English merchant John Graunt publishes tables of births and deaths in London using innovative sampling methods. He estimates the population of London by the technique of statistical inference.

- **1687** Edward Lloyd opens a coffee house in Tower Street, London. In 1696 he launches Lloyd's List, giving information on aspects of shipping from a network of European correspondents.

- **1696** English mathematician and astronomer Edmund Halley shows how life tables can be used to price life insurance at different ages.

- **1713** Swiss mathematician Jacob Bernoulli's 'Law of Large Numbers' is published posthumously, showing how probabilities and statistical significance can be identified from limited information.

- **1733** French mathematician Abraham de Moivre proposes the normal distribution, the pattern in which a series of variables distribute themselves around an average, from which he also derives the concept of standard deviation.

- **1738** Jacob Bernoulli's nephew Daniel introduces the idea of utility: decisions relating to risk involve not only calculations of probability but also the value of the consequences to the risk-taker.

- **1885** English scientist Francis Galton discovers regression to the mean, the tendency of extremes to return to a normal or average.

- **1944** In Theory of Games and Economic Behavior, US academics John von Neumann and Oskar Morgenstern apply the theory of games of strategy (in contrast to games of chance) to decision-making in business and investing.

- **1952** US economist Harry Markowitz demonstrates mathematically that risk and expected return are directly related but that investors can reduce the variance of return on their investments by diversification without loss of expected return.

- **1970** US academics Fischer Black and Myron Scholes publish a mathematical model for calculating the value of an option.

Source: Peter L. Bernstein, 'The Enlightening Struggle Against Uncertainty', *Financial Times*, 25 April 2000.

Learning objectives

After studying this chapter, you should be able to:

1 Summarise the mean–variance criterion.

2 Explain the economic meaning of the mean–variance framework.

3 Discuss two approaches for computing the mean and variance of a portfolio of assets.

4 Locate the efficient and inefficient investment strategies.

Investment in the News 8 gives a chronology of the scientific advances in understanding risk, measuring it and weighing its consequences. The first breakthrough came in 1654, when Blaise Pascal and Pierre de Fermat used mathematics to analyse a simple game of chance and created the basis for probability theory. This chapter focuses on the mean–variance framework, which originated from the work by Nobel Laureate Harry Markowitz.

In Chapter 7, we explained that financial economists typically model investment as a problem of constrained optimisation under uncertainty. The expected utility framework shows the theoretical relationship between the elements of this problem: the portfolio possibilities set, the probability distribution of asset returns (describing the investor's subjective expectations about the future) and the investor's utility function (describing the investor's investment objectives). As discussed in Chapter 7, generally we cannot apply the expected utility framework in practice, because we do not know the precise shape of the utility function and the probability distribution. The mean–variance framework is a popular approximation to the expected utility framework. In fact, it is currently the most popular model for structuring investment decisions. It is used widely for applications of portfolio selection, performance evaluation and risk management. Among other things, it helps investors to select optimally diversified (or mean–variance-efficient) portfolios.

To guide one through our analysis, it is useful to summarise briefly the key ingredients of mean–variance analysis. In the mean–variance framework, the utility function and the return distribution are expressed in terms of two parameters: the expected return or mean return of the investment portfolio and the variance (or the square root of variance, standard deviation). In the mean–variance framework, the investment possibilities are represented by the mean–variance possibilities set, which gives the set of combinations of portfolio mean and variance that are feasible given the return distribution of the individual assets and the investment restrictions faced by the investor. Further, the investor's subjective trade-off between risk and return is represented by mean–variance indifference curves that connect the combinations of mean and variance that yield the same level of expected utility. Unfortunately, as is true for the expected utility framework, typically we do not know the precise shape of the mean–variance indifference curves. However, we do know that investors prefer more return to less return and that they are risk-averse (see Chapter 7). Hence, every investor, irrespective of the shape of his or her indifference curves, prefers a high mean and a low variance. This allows us to develop the mean–variance efficiency criterion: an asset or portfolio of assets is mean–variance-efficient if there exists no other asset or portfolio that yields a higher mean and a lower variance. Using this criterion, we can identify the efficient mean–variance frontier, which is the part of the mean–variance possibilities set that includes the efficient portfolios. Every investor, irrespective of the shape of his or her indifference curves, will select a portfolio from this efficient frontier. This insight greatly simplifies the investment problem; rather than having to consider all possible portfolios, each investor needs to consider only the efficient portfolios.

The remainder of this chapter is structured as follows. Section 8.1 explains the link between mean–variance analysis and the general expected utility framework (discussed in Chapter 7) and elaborates on mean–variance indifference curves and the mean–variance criterion. Section 8.2 turns to computing the mean and variance of investment portfolios. The portfolio mean can be computed simply as the weighted average of the means of the individual assets in the portfolio. By contrast, computing portfolio variance is more complicated, as we have to account for the degree of dependency between the invidual assets. Finally, Section 8.3 discusses the mean–variance portfolio possibilities set and the mean–variance-efficient frontier.

8.1 Fundamentals of mean–variance analysis

In the mean–variance framework, investors care only about the mean and the variance of their portfolio. The expected utility, or $E(u(R))$, of mean–variance investors can be written as a function of mean $E(R)$ and variance σ only, say $f(E(R), \sigma)$. Since investors are assumed to prefer a high return and a low risk (see Chapter 7), expected utility is assumed to be an increasing function of the mean and a decreasing function of the variance. A natural first question is can we link mean–variance analysis to the general expected utility framework? Basically, there are two possible justifications for mean–variance analysis:

- The return distribution can be approximated by a normal distribution.[1]
- The utility function can be approximated by a quadratic function.

8.1.1 A normal return distribution

First, as discussed in Chapter 7, if the asset returns obey a normal probability distribution, then the entire distribution of a portfolio is described by the mean and the variance only. Unfortunately, the assumption of normality can be very restrictive in practice.[2,3] For example, a problem in most return series is the 'fat tails' problem; given the mean and the standard deviation, the probability of extremely high or extremely low returns is much higher than it is according to the normal distribution. In other words, the 'tails' of the distribution are 'fatter' than according to the normal distribution.[4] For example, in the week of 19 December 1994, the Mexican peso depreciated by 40%. Assuming a normal distribution and given the

---

[1] More generally, mean–variance analysis is consistent with expected utility analysis for all so-called elliptical distributions; such distributions can be expressed in terms of their mean and variance alone. The normal distribution is one example of an elliptical distribution.

[2] The Jarque–Bera statistic is one way of testing the null hypothesis that a series is distributed normally (i.e. has skewness of zero and kurtosis of three); see Bera and Jarque (1981).

[3] A selection of studies of the statistical distribution of actual asset returns includes Fama (1965), Arditti (1971), Simkowitz and Beedles (1978), Singleton and Wingender (1986) and Chunhachinda et al. (1997).

[4] This phenomenon is called 'leptokurtosis'. Kurtosis is a statistical measure for the thickness of the tails. This measure is defined as $E(R - E(R))^4$. For extreme returns (far below or far above the mean), the term $(R - E(R))^4$ takes very large positive values. Hence, if a distribution has a high probability of such returns, then it will have a high kurtosis.

historical mean and variance of the peso, we would conclude that a move of this magnitude was to be expected perhaps once during the life of the universe. However, even during the relatively short time span of the past two decades, several of these 'one-in-a-million events' have occurred: the US equity crash of October 1987; the breakdown of the European exchange rate mechanism (ERM) in 1992; the plunge in copper prices in 1996; the devaluation of the peso in 1994, of the Thai baht, Philippine peso and Malaysian dollar in 1997, and of the Turkish lira in 2001; and so forth. One possible explanation for this phenomenon is that asset returns appear to be correlated positively over time: if a negative return is likely to be followed by another negative return, then the probability of a large negative return is higher than with zero correlation.[5] Another explanation is that the variance of asset returns changes substantially over time; if we ignore these changes and assume that the variance is constant, then extreme returns will occur more frequently than expected.[6]

Another persistent departure from normality in most asset-return series is that the returns are not symmetric. Many assets have 'positive skewness', in which case the probability of large gains is higher than the probability of equivalent losses.[7] Examples of assets with high positive skewness include stocks of firms that have high growth potential, bonds with conversion features, and long positions in options. By contrast, negative skewness occurs when the probability of large gains is lower than the probability of equivalent losses. For example, an investor who writes options is exposed to large possible losses and limited gains (also see Chapter 19). Paradoxically, well-diversified portfolios typically exhibit a high negative skewness, even if the individual assets in the portfolio are skewed positively. (This is a paradox, because investors diversify to avoid a high probability of large losses or negative skewness.) A possible explanation for this phenomenon is that correlations tend to increase during crisis situations, reducing the effectiveness of diversification when it is needed most. This implies that large negative returns will occur more frequently than large positive returns. For example, Exhibit 8.1 compares the historical distribution of monthly returns on the S&P 500 index for the period from February 1939 to October 2003 with a normal distribution that has the same mean and variance.[8] Clearly, the left tail of the actual distribution is 'too fat', and extreme negative returns occur with a much higher frequency than according to the normal distribution.

For these reasons, the normal distribution generally does not fully capture the risks and returns of assets and investment portfolios.

---

[5] The central limit theorem does not apply if the random variables are not independent.

[6] The central limit theorem does not apply if the random variables have a different distribution.

[7] The skewness of a distribution is measured as $E(R - E(R))^3$. For returns far below the mean, the term $(R - E(R))^3$ takes very large negative values. Hence, if a distribution has a high probability of such returns, then it will have a negative skewness.

[8] The shape of the return distribution depends on the investment horizon and the graph looks different if we use, for example, daily returns or yearly returns. One obvious reason is the effect of compounding returns. To see this, consider the hypothetical case where there is a 50% probability of a negative return of -10% and 50% probability of a positive return of $+10\%$ for a stock in each and every period. This return distribution is perfectly symmetrical around the mean of zero. If we consider the total return over two periods, then there is a 25% probability of two negative returns, yielding a total return of $0.9 \times 0.9 - 1 = -0.19$, a 50% probability of one positive return and one negative return, yielding a total return of $1.1 \times 0.9 - 1 = -0.01$, and a 25% probability of two positive returns, yielding a total return of $1.1 \times 1.1 - 1 = 0.21$. Clearly, this distribution is not symmetric around the mean of zero $(0.25 \times (-0.19) + 0.5 \times (-0.01) + 0.25 \times 0.21 = 0)$; the maximum upside deviation of 21% is larger than the maximum downside deviation of -19%. Similarly, over very many time periods, the minimal possible return is -100%, while there is no upper limit.

Exhibit 8.1	Histogram of monthly rates of returns to the S&P 500 index (February 1939–October 2003)

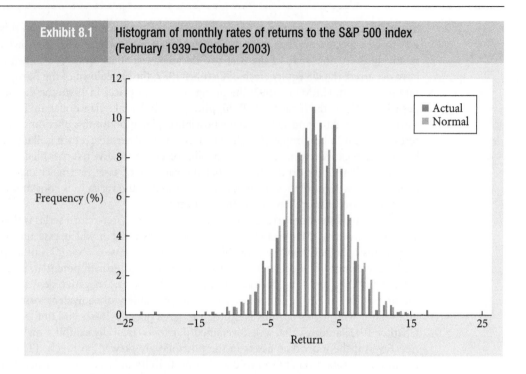

8.1.2 A quadratic utility function

Second, if the investor's utility function is 'smooth' (i.e. it does not exhibit any 'kinks', or marginal utility does not exhibit 'jumps') and concave (i.e. marginal utility is diminishing), then it can well be approximated by a quadratic utility function over the typical range of investment returns.[9,10] A quadratic utility function takes the following form $u(R) = a + bR + cR^2$, where a, $b > 0$ and $c < 0$ are parameters that determine the shape of the utility function.[11] For this type of utility function, we can write expected utility as:[12]

$$E(u(R)) = a + (b + cE(R))E(R) + c\sigma^2 \tag{8.1}$$

---

[9] See, for example, Tsiang (1972) and Levy and Markowitz (1979).

[10] It is common to refer to the mean and the variance as the first two central moments of the return distribution. If the range of returns is very wide, then higher-order central moments (such as skewness and kurtosis) may become relevant in addition to mean and variance. See, for example, Kraus and Litzenberger (1976). If the utility function exhibits kinks, then the investor cares about lower partial moments (such as expected loss and semivariance) in addition to the central moments. See, for example, Bawa and Lindenberg (1977).

[11] The parameter determines the intercept of the utility function; b determines the slope at $R = 0$; and c determines the curvature of the function. To guarantee that the utility function is increasing (over a range), we must have $b > 0$. (Notice that the function is increasing for $R < -b/2c$ and it is decreasing for $R > -b/2c$.) Also, we need $c < 0$ so as to impose risk-aversion.

[12] To see this, we first use the following chain of equalities: $E(u(R)) = \sum_{j=1}^{m} P_j u(R_j) = \sum_{j=1}^{m} P_j(a + bR_j + cR_j^2) = a + b \times \sum_{j=1}^{m} P_j R_j + c \times \sum_{j=1}^{m} P_j R_j^2 = a + bE(R) + cE(R^2)$. Next, using $\sigma^2 = E(R^2) - E(R)^2$, the last equality can be rewritten as $E(u(R)) = a + (b + cE(R))E(R) + c\sigma^2$.

Exhibit 8.2	Quadratic approximation to a utility function

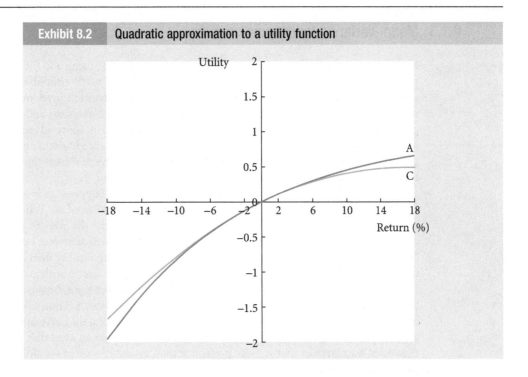

which is a function of mean and variance only. In addition, expected utility increases as the mean increases and as the variance decreases.[13] To illustrate this point, Exhibit 8.2 shows a quadratic utility function that approximates the negative exponential utility function $u_A(R) = 1 - \exp(-6R)$ used in Exhibit 7.4.[14] Clearly, the quadratic function gives a good approximation over the relevant range (−2% is the minimum and 18% the maximum return in Exhibit 7.2). Hence, in this case, we can assume safely that the investor cares about mean and variance only. Indeed, comparing Exhibits 7.2 and 7.5, we can see that the mean–variance criterion gives exactly the same ordering as the expected utility criterion; the lower the variance of an asset or portfolio, the higher the expected utility. Note that this is true while the probability distributions in Exhibit 7.2(b) clearly do not satisfy the assumption of normality.

The exhibit displays the negative exponential utility function $u_A(R) = 1 - \exp(-6R)$ and the quadratic utility function $u_C(R) = 1 + 4R - 8R^2$.

In many cases, at least one of these conditions is satisfied by approximation (the return distribution is approximately normal or investor utility is approximately quadratic), and hence mean–varaince analysis gives a good approximation to the general expected utility framework.[15]

---

[13] We assumed $c < 0$ in order to impose concavity. Hence, expected utility in Equation 8.1 is decreasing in variance. Also, we assumed that utility is increasing or $u'(R) = b + 2cR > 0$. Taking the expectation of both sides of the equation, we find $E(u'(R)) = b + 2cE(R) > 0$ or $c > -b/(2E(R))$. This implies that the term $b + cE(R)$ in Equation 8.1 is greater than $b/2$. Hence, expected utility is increasing in the mean.

[14] This particular quadratic utility function is obtained by a second-order Taylor series approximation around $R = 0$. Specifically, we set $a = u_A(0) = 1$, $b = u'_A(0) = 4$ and $c = u''_A(0)/2 = -8$.

[15] Again, if these conditions are considered too restrictive, then the framework of stochastic dominance offers an alternative to mean–variance analysis. See the references in Section 7.6 for more information.

8.1.3 Mean–variance indifference curves

In the mean–variance framework, investors care only about the mean and the variance of their portfolio; they like a large mean and a small variance. This greatly simplifies the investment problem. Still, we need to specify the subjective trade-off that each investor makes between mean and variance. Timid investors have a high degree of risk-aversion, and they will be prepared to accept risk only in exchange for a high expected return. More adventurous investors have a low degree of risk-aversion and will accept a high variance in exchange for a small risk premium. A useful instrument for representing the subjective trade-off that investors make between risk and return is mean–variance indifference curves.

Exhibit 8.3 illustrates the concept of indifference curves. Suppose an investor holds asset A that has an expected return of $E(R_A)$ and a standard deviation of σ_A. Will this investor be better off exchanging asset A for asset A_1? We can safely say that the investor would not prefer asset A_1 to asset A because asset A_1 has the same expected return as asset A but has higher risk $(\sigma_{A1} > \sigma_A)$. Hence, asset A represents a higher level of expected utility than asset A_1, because investors like high returns and low risks. Now let us compare asset A with asset A_2. Would the investor be willing to exchange asset A for asset A_2? The answer is yes, because asset A_2 offers a higher expected return, $E(R_{A2}) > E(R_A)$, with the same risk as asset A. Thus, asset A is preferable to asset A_1, and asset A_2 is preferable to asset A. If we move along the curve in Exhibit 8.3 from asset A_1 to asset A_2, we follow an investor who is moving from an asset that is less preferable than asset A to an asset that is more preferable than asset A. As we move along this curve, we pass through a point, A_3, where the investor is indifferent between asset A and asset A_3. We can present the same argument that asset B_2 is preferable to A, whereas asset B_1 is less desirable than asset A. Hence, there must be a point, B_3, where the investor is indifferent between asset A and asset B_3. We can repeat this exercise for other points that are closer to or further away from point A, and we will obtain a curve consisting of all points of indifference, such as B_3, A and A_3. This curve, I, is called an indifference curve, because the investor who viewed each asset on the curve as equivalent in risk and return would be indifferent to exchanging one asset on the curve for another; every investment on the indifference curve represents the same level of expected utility. Moving along the curve, an investor either takes on more risk for greater

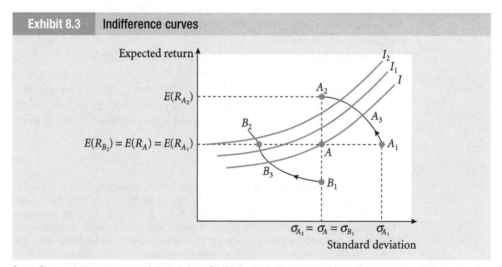

Exhibit 8.3   Indifference curves

expected return or incurs less risk for lower expected return. Either way, the investor has the same preference for these various assets, as long as they lie on the same indifference curve.

If we repeat the same exercise but start with a point vertically above point A, we get another indifference curve, I_1, that is higher than I. The higher the indifference curve, the higher the level of expected utility and the better off investors are, because they can attain a higher expected return for a given level of risk. Similarly, indifference curve I_2 represents a higher level of expected utility than I_1.

The basic characteristics of indifference curves are as follows:

- All combinations $(E(R), \sigma_R)$ lying on a given indifference curve provide the investor with the same level of expected utility.
- Investors prefer a high mean and a low variance. Hence, the indifference curves are upward-sloping; if we increase the variance, then we must also increase the mean in order to achieve the same level of expected utility. The slope reflects the trade-off between risk and return or the risk premium required for accepting an additional unit of risk.
- The indifference curves are convex, i.e., they curve towards the expected return axis. That is, extra units of risk will have to be compensated by ever increasing levels of expected return. Most investors will be prepared to accept some risks, even if the risk premium is small, but hardly any investor will be prepared to accept very large risks, even if the risk premium is large.[16]
- Moving to a higher indifference curve (for example, a shift from I to I_1 or from I_1 to I_2) increases the investor's expected utility. Hence, seeking to reach the highest possible indifference curve is tantamount to reaching the highest possible expected utility.
- Like utility functions, indifference curves are subjective, and their shapes differ from one investor to another; for a given investor, they may also differ from one point in time to another.

8.1.4 Mean–variance efficiency

Unfortunately, as is true in the expected utility framework, we typically do not know the precise shape of the indifference curves (representing the investor's objectives). Also, we may wish to develop investment tools that apply for all investors rather than one specific investor with one specific utility function. Fortunately, we do know some general properties that apply for all investors: all investors prefer more return to less return and they are risk-averse (the indifference curves are upward-sloping). Put differently, investors prefer (1) the lowest

---

[16] To understand this, it is useful to rewrite Equation 8.1 as $\sigma^2 = -E(u(R))/c - a/c - (b/c)[E(R) - E(R)^2]$. If we fix the level of expected utility $E(u(R))$, then this expression gives the variance σ^2 as a function of the mean $E(R)$; it gives the indifference curve for $E(u(R))$. By taking the first-order derivative of σ^2 with respect to $E(R)$, we find $\dfrac{\partial \sigma^2}{\partial E(R)} = -b/c - 2E(R)$, which is the slope of the indifference curve or the additional units of variance that the investor will accept for a unit of additional expected return. By taking the first-order derivative of σ^2 with respect to $E(R)$, we find $\dfrac{\partial^2 \sigma^2}{\partial (E(R))^2} = -2$, which is the curvature of the indifference curve. The curvature is negative, which means that the additional units of variance that the investor will accept for a unit of additional expected return decrease. Put differently, the additional units of expected return required to compensate for a unit increase of variance increase. Note that variance is a concave function of mean return (the second-order derivative is negative), or the mean is a convex function of the variance (the second-order derivative is positive).

Exhibit 8.4	Mean–variance dominance relationships and efficiency classifications						
Asset	A	A_1	A_2	A_3	B_1	B_2	B_3
Dominated by A	–	Yes	No	No	Yes	No	No
Dominated by A_1	No	–	No	No	No	No	No
Dominated by A_2	Yes	Yes	–	Yes	Yes	No	No
Dominated by A_3	No	Yes	No	–	No	No	No
Dominated by B_1	No	No	No	No	–	No	No
Dominated by B_2	Yes	Yes	No	No	Yes	–	Yes
Dominated by B_3	No	No	No	No	Yes	No	–
Efficient	No	No	Yes	No	No	Yes	No

variance for the same (or higher) expected return or (2) the highest expected return for the same (or lower) variance. This allows us to develop the mean–variance efficiency criterion: investment A dominates investment B if either of the following two conditions holds:

$$E(R_A) \geq E(R_B) \text{ and } \sigma_A^2 < \sigma_B^2$$

or

$$E(R_A) > E(R_B) \text{ and } \sigma_A^2 \leq \sigma_B^2$$

If investment A dominates investment B, then all risk-averse investors will prefer A to B. An investment that is not dominated by any other investment is called mean–variance-efficient. For every efficient investment, we can think of a risk-averse investor for whom the investment is optimal (it puts him or her on the highest possible indifference curve, or it maximises his or her expected utility). By contrast, an inefficient investment is dominated by at least one other investment, and it is not optimal for a risk-averse investor.

Exhibit 8.4 shows the dominance relationships and the efficiency classifications for the seven assets that were included in Exhibit 8.3. In this case, only asset A_2 and asset B_2 are efficient; these assets are not dominated by any other asset. The other five assets are inefficient, because there exists at least one other asset with a more favourable mean and a more favourable variance.

Note that the mean–variance efficiency criterion allows only for a partial ordering of the alternatives. The criterion does not yield a ranking for all investment options, and it does not forward the 'best' (or the 'worst') option. Rather, the efficiency criterion distinguishes only between a group of efficient alternatives (alternatives that are not dominated by any other alternatives) and inefficient alternatives (alternatives that are dominated by at least one other alternative). The strength of this criterion is that it applies for all risk-averse investors. Its weakness is that it generally cannot identify the optimal investment; to select the optimal investment for a given investor from the efficient alternatives, we need further information on the preferences of that investor (his or her subjective trade-off between risk and return).

8.2 The mean and variance of a portfolio

Now that we have seen how the mean–variance criterion works and why it is economically meaningful, we turn to the question of computing the mean and variance for a portfolio of assets. We distinguish between two alternative methods: the direct method and the indirect method. Conceptually, the direct method is the simplest. However, this method cannot be applied unless we have full information about the returns of all individual assets in all possible states of the world. The indirect method circumvents this problem because it requires not the individual returns but rather the means, variances and covariances of the individual assets. As it turns out, the indirect approach of computing the portfolio mean is rather simple; we can compute the portfolio mean as a simple weighted average of the individual means. By contrast, the indirect approach of computing the portfolio variance is more complicated. The reason is that we cannot compute the portfolio variance as a simple weighted average of the variance of the individual assets. Rather, we have to account for the dependence between the individual assets in the portfolio, as measured by the covariance or correlation. Despite the computational burden, the information requirement is lower (we do not need the individual return observations). Also, the indirect method offers useful insights into the determinants of portfolio variance and the effectiveness of portfolio diversification.

8.2.1 The direct method for computing portfolio mean and variance

The simplest approach to computing the mean and variance of a portfolio is to compute, for each possible scenario, the portfolio return as the weighted average of the returns of the individual assets, or

$$R_{p,j} = \sum_{i=1}^{n} w_i R_{i,j} \tag{8.2}$$

where w_i is the portfolio weight for the ith asset and $R_{i,j}$ is the return to the ith asset in the jth state of the world. Equations 7.4 and Equation 7.5 (see Chapter 7) then yield the following expressions of the portfolio mean and portfolio variance:

$$E(R_{p,j}) = \sum_{j=1}^{m} P_j R_{p,j} \tag{8.3}$$

$$\sigma_p^2 = \sum_{j=1}^{m} P_j (R_{p,j} - E(R_p))^2 \tag{8.4}$$

This approach is known as the direct approach for computing portfolio means and variances. The required computations are straightforward, because the portfolio is treated like any other single asset. Exhibit 8.5 shows the computations for the optimal portfolio from Exhibit 7.5(d). Recall that this portfolio uses the investment weights $w_1 = 0$, $w_2 = 0.271$ and $w_3 = 0.729$.

In this example, the direct approach is simple because there are only a small number of scenarios ($m = 10$) with known returns and probabilities. Unfortunately, individual scenarios and the returns in those scenarios generally are not known, or the number of scenarios is very large (for a continuous return distribution, the number is infinitely large). To circumvent this problem, we may use the indirect approach.

Exhibit 8.5	Direct approach of computing the mean and variance for a portfolio consisting of 27.1% stock 2 and 72.9% stock 3

Scenario	Probability	Stock 1	Stock 2	Stock 3	Portfolio
1	0.1	0.120	0.060	0.080	0.075[a]
2	0.1	0.180	0.080	0.090	0.087
3	0.1	0.080	0.100	0.090	0.093
4	0.1	0.080	0.030	0.100	0.081
5	0.1	0.120	0.100	0.070	0.078
6	0.1	0.080	0.060	0.080	0.075
7	0.1	0.040	0.080	0.080	0.080
8	0.1	−0.020	0.130	0.060	0.079
9	0.1	0.080	0.080	0.070	0.073
10	0.1	0.040	0.080	0.080	0.080
Weight (w_i)		0.000	0.271	0.729	
Mean ($E(R)$)					0.080[b]
Variance (σ^2)					0.00003[c]
Standard deviation (σ)					0.006[d]

[a] $0.075 = (0.271 \times 0.060) + (0.729 \times 0.080)$.
[b] $0.080 = (0.1 \times 0.075) + (0.1 \times 0.087) + \ldots + (0.1 \times 0.080)$.
[c] $0.0003 = 0.1 \times (0.075 - 0.080)^2 + 0.1 \times (0.087 - 0.080)^2 + \ldots + 0.1 \times (0.080 - 0.080)^2$.
[d] $0.006 = 0.00003^{1/2}$.

8.2.2 The indirect method

The indirect approach to computing the portfolio mean is straightforward. Specifically, if we substitute Equation 8.2 in Equation 8.3, then we will find

$$E(R_p) = \sum_{j=1}^{m} P_j R_{p,j} = \sum_{j=1}^{m} P_j \sum_{i=1}^{n} w_i R_{i,j} = \sum_{i=1}^{n} w_i \sum_{j=1}^{m} P_j R_{i,j} = \sum_{i=1}^{n} w_i E(R_i) \qquad (8.5)$$

Thus, the portfolio mean is simply the weighted average of the means of the individual assets, weighted by the portfolio weights. Obviously, the higher the proportion of wealth (w_i) invested in the ith security, the higher its individual effect on the portfolio's mean. In the extreme, when all the wealth (100%) is invested in only one security, the portfolio's mean rate of return is simply the mean of that security.

For example, the mean of the portfolio in Exhibit 8.5 (0.080) can be found as a weighted average of the means of the individual assets:

$$w_1 E(R_1) + w_2 E(R_2) + w_3 E(R_3) = (0 \times 0.080) + (0.271 \times 0.080) + (0.729 \times 0.080) = 0.080$$

In summary, the expected rate of return on a portfolio can be calculated in two ways:

■ First calculate all possible returns on the portfolio (using the portfolio weights as the weights), and then calculate the weighted average across all scenarios, using the probabilities of the scenarios as the weights.

■ First calculate the means of all individual assets (using the probabilities of the scenarios as the weights), and then calculate the weighted average across all assets, using the portfolio weights as the weights.

The indirect approach to computing the portfolio variance is more complicated. The reason is that we cannot compute the portfolio variance as a simple weighted average of the variances of the individual assets. We have to account for the dependence between the individual assets in the portfolio. Still, the indirect method is useful because it does not require the individual return observations. Also, the indirect method gives insight into the determinants of portfolio variance and the benefits of portfolio diversification.

First, by substituting Equation 8.2 in Equation 8.4, we obtain

$$\sigma_p^2 = E(R_p - E(R_p))^2 = E\left(\sum_{i=1}^{n} w_i R_i - \sum_{i=1}^{n} w_i E(R_i)^2\right)$$

$$= E(w_1 R_1 + \ldots + w_n R_n - (w_1 E(R_1) + \ldots + w_n E(R_n)))^2$$

$$= E(w_1(R_1 - E(R_1)) + \ldots + w_n(R_n - E(R_n)))^2$$

Opening the bracket, it can be shown that it includes the product of each pair of terms inside the brackets, as well as the product of each term with itself. Thus,

$$\sigma_p^2 = E\left(\sum_{i=1}^{n} \sum_{s=1}^{n} w_i w_s (R_i - E(R_i))(R_s - E(R_s))\right)$$

$$= \sum_{i=1}^{n} \sum_{s=1}^{n} w_i w_s E((R_i - E(R_i))(R_s - E(R_s)))$$

The last equation follows from w_i and w_j being constants and not random variables, and hence $E(w_i w_s (R_i - E(R_i))(R_s - E(R_s))) = w_i w_s E((R_i - E(R_i))(R_s - E(R_s)))$. Since $\sigma_i^2 = E(R_i - E(R_i))^2$ and $\sigma_{i,s} = E((R_i - E(R_i))(R_s - E(R_s)))$, we get:

$$\sigma_p^2 = \sum_{i=1}^{n} \sum_{s=1}^{n} w_i w_s \sigma_{i,s} \tag{8.6}$$

Sometimes, the portfolio's variance is written in an equivalent way that breaks the portfolio's variance into two terms:

$$\sigma_p^2 = \sum_{i=1}^{n} w_i^2 \sigma_i^2 + \sum_{i=1}^{n} \sum_{\substack{s=1 \\ s \neq 1}}^{n} w_i w_s \sigma_{i,s} \tag{8.6a}$$

The first term is a weighted sum of all the individual variances. The second term sums up all the covariances. To guarantee that we will not have double counting of the variance terms, we add to the second term the constraint $s \neq i$; namely, sum all terms except the variance terms (recall that $i = s$ means that a term is a variance term). Note that in the second term, each term appears twice. For example, we have $w_1 w_2 \sigma_{1,2}$ and $w_2 w_1 \sigma_{2,1}$, but because $\sigma_{1,2} = \sigma_{2,1}$, these two terms are equal. This is true for all covariance terms in the equation. Therefore, the variance formula can also be written as

$$\sigma_p^2 = \sum_{i=1}^{n} w_i^2 \sigma_i^2 + \sum_{i=1}^{n} \sum_{\substack{s=1 \\ s > 1}}^{n} w_i w_s \sigma_{i,s} \tag{8.6b}$$

We multiply the second term of the variance by two, indicating that each term appears twice. However, we must also add the constraint $s > i$ to the second summation operator. For example, if $i = 1$ and $s = 2$, then we have the term $w_1 w_2 \sigma_{1,2}$. Because $s > i$, we do not count the term $w_2 w_1 \sigma_{2,1}$. However, not counting this term specifically is correct, because we multiply the first term, $w_1 w_2 \sigma_{1,2}$, by two, which takes care of the missing term.

Finally, because $\rho_{i,s} \sigma_i \sigma_s = \sigma_{i,s}$, we can substitute $\rho_{i,s} \sigma_i \sigma_s$ for $\sigma_{i,s}$ in Equations 8.6, 8.6a and 8.6b and express the portfolio's variance in terms of correlations $\rho_{i,s}$ rather than covariances $\sigma_{i,s}$. For example, substituting $\rho_{i,s} \sigma_i \sigma_s$ for $\sigma_{i,s}$ in Equation 8.6 yields

$$\sigma_p^2 = \sum_{i=1}^{n} \sum_{s=1}^{n} w_i w_s \rho_{i,s} \sigma_i \sigma_s$$

Equations 8.6, 8.6a and 8.6b can be illustrated by considering the simple case with just two individual assets ($n = 2$). In this case, the formulae reduce to

$$\sigma_p^2 = (w_1^2 \sigma_1^2) + (w_2^2 \sigma_2^2) + (2 w_1 w_2 \sigma_{1,2}) = (w_1^2 \sigma_1^2) + (w_2^2 \sigma_2^2) + (2 w_1 w_2 \rho_{1,2} \sigma_1 \sigma_2) \quad (8.7)$$

This expression clarifies the factors that affect the portfolio variance: the variances σ_1^2 and σ_2^2, the covariance $\sigma_{1,2}$ or the correlation coefficient $\rho_{1,2}$, and the weights w_1 and w_2. Although Equations 8.6, 8.6a and 8.6b look much more complicated (due to the double summation), the message is the same, namely that the variance of a portfolio of assets is determined by the variances of the underlying assets (σ_i^2), the covariances ($\sigma_{i,s}$) or the correlations ($\rho_{i,s}$), and the choice of weights (w_i). Similarly, the contribution of an asset to the portfolio risk depends on its variance, its covariance with the other assets, its weight in the portfolio and the weights of the other assets. Hence, a risky asset (i.e. an asset with a high variance) can actually lower the portfolio variance if it has a low covariance with the assets that have a high weight in the portfolio. For example, stock 2 in our example (see Exhibit 7.2a) is more risky than stock 3. Still, by including stock 2 in the portfolio with a 27.1% weight, we can achieve a lower variance than by investing in stock 3 alone. In Chapters 10 and 11, we will see that a fair risk premium for an asset depends on its covariance with other assets.

In contrast to the direct method for computing portfolio variance (see Equation 8.4), Equations 8.6, 8.6a and 8.6b can be used if we do not have information on the returns of the individual assets in all relevant scenarios (there may be infinitely many scenarios) but we have information on the variance and covariance terms of the individual assets. A drawback is that the number of variance–covariance terms increases rapidly as the number of assets (n) increases. In the special case when $n = 2$, we need only two variances, σ_1^2 and σ_2^2, and a single covariance $\sigma_{1,2}$ or correlation coefficient $\rho_{1,2}$. In general, we need n variances (one for each asset) and $(n^2 - n)/2$ covariances or correlation coefficients (one for each pair of assets).[17] Hence, for a large n, the number of variance–covariance terms becomes very large. For example, if $n = 25$, then the total number of terms is $25 + 300 = 325$. For this reason, it is useful to use spreadsheet software for the practical implementation of the indirect method (see Appendix B at the end of the book).

---

[17] Each of the n assets can be combined with all other $(n - 1)$ assets, giving a total of $n(n - 1)$ combinations. The combination of the ith asset and the jth asset gives the same pair as the combination of the jth asset and the ith asset. Hence, to avoid double counting, we must divide the number of combinations by two in order to arrive at a total number of pairs of $(n^2 - n)/2$. In mathematical terms: $\binom{n}{2} = \dfrac{n!}{(n-2)! \times 2!}$
$$= \frac{n(n-1)(n-2) \ldots \times 2 \times 1}{((n-2) \ldots \times 2 \times 1)(2 \times 1)} = \frac{n(n-1)}{2}.$$

Exhibit 8.6	Direct approach for computing the mean and variance for a portfolio consisting of 27.1% stock 2 and 72.9% stock 3

(a) Variances and covariances of three assets

	Asset(s)		
Asset i	1	2	3
1	0.0026	−0.0005	0.0003
2	−0.0005	0.0007	−0.0002
3	0.0003	−0.0002	0.0001

(b) Product of the investment weights and variances and covariances

	Asset(s)		
Asset i	1	2	3
1	0.0026×0^2	$-0.0005 \times 0 \times 0.271$	$0.0003 \times 0 \times 0.729$
2	$-0.0005 \times 0 \times 0.271$	0.0007×0.271^2	$-0.0002 \times 0.271 \times 0.729$
3	$0.0003 \times 0 \times 0.729$	$-0.0002 \times 0.271 \times 0.729$	0.0001×0.729^2
Sum of columns	0.00000	0.00001	0.00002
Sum of sums	0.00003		

Exhibit 8.6 illustrates the implementation of the indirect method for the portfolio that was also used in Exhibit 8.5. Recall that this portfolio is constructed as a weighted average of the three stocks from Exhibit 7.2(a); the investment weights are $w_1 = 0$, $w_2 = 0.271$ and $w_3 = 0.729$. Exhibit 8.6(a) gives the variance–covariance terms $\sigma_{i,s}$ of the individual stocks, as taken from Exhibit 7.2(a). Exhibit 8.6(b) multiplies these terms by the product of the relevant investment weights, or $w_i w_j$. Then, the portfolio's variance is nothing but the sum of all elements in this exhibit, which in this case is $\sigma_p^2 = 0.00003$. As expected, the outcome is exactly equal to the result of the direct approach in Exhibit 8.5. Obviously, using the basic data of Exhibit 8.6(a), one can calculate the variance of portfolios with investment weights (w_i) simply by substituting the weights in Exhibit 8.6(b).

8.3 Efficient and inefficient investment strategies

The previous section discussed two ways to compute the mean and variance of a given investment portfolio: the direct method and the indirect method. In this section, we will introduce the set of all feasible mean–varaince combinations, or the mean–variance possibilities set. Obviously, the shape of the mean–variance possibilities set will depend on the restrictions that are placed on the portfolio weights or the portfolio possibilities set (see Section 7.1): the more restrictions, the smaller the mean–variance possibilities set. The mean–variance possibilities set includes all possible portfolios. Generally, we cannot identify a single 'optimal portfolio', because different investors have different indifference curves and the shape of their indifference curves is not known. Still, the mean–variance criterion derived in Section 8.1.4 predicts that investors prefer (1) the lowest variance for the same (or higher) expected return or (2) the highest expected return for the same (or lower) variance. Using this criterion, investors will choose their portfolio from a subset of the mean–variance possibilities set called the efficient mean–variance frontier. Since investors prefer the lowest variance for the same (or higher) expected return, they will focus on the set of portfolios with the smallest variance for a given mean or the mean–variance frontier. The mean–variance frontier can be divided into parts: an efficient frontier and an inefficient frontier. The efficient part includes the portfolios with the highest mean for a given variance. To introduce these concepts, this section first considers portfolios composed of two assets with a zero correlation and then extends the discussion to non-zero correlation and portfolios composed of n assets.

8.3.1 Efficient and inefficient frontiers in the two-asset case

Exhibit 8.7 shows the means and variances of two assets, A and B, whose correlation is assumed to be zero. These means and variances are computed using the indirect method (i.e. using Equations 8.5 and 8.6); we cannot use the direct method, as the returns in the individual scenarios are not known in this case. As Exhibit 8.7 shows, by decreasing the proportion invested in the asset with the lowest expected return (asset A), the portfolio's expected return increases. This result is obvious, because one invests a higher proportion in the asset with the higher expected return (asset B). Thus, the effect of a reduction in w_A on the portfolio's mean is unambiguous: the higher the proportion invested in asset B, the higher the expected return on the portfolio. In the extreme case where $w_A = 0$ and $w_B = 1$, the portfolio's mean return is 20%, because the portfolio is composed of asset B alone.

Exhibit 8.7	Efficient- and inefficient-frontier zero correlation

(a) The two assets

	Asset A	Asset B
Mean return (%)	10	20
Variance (%)	10	15

(b) Efficient and inefficient strategies

w_A	w_B	Mean[a]	Variance[b]	Is the portfolio efficient?
1	0	10	10	No
0.9	0.1	11	8.25	No
0.8	0.2	12	7	No
0.7	0.3	13	6.25	No
0.6	0.4	14	6 MPV	Yes
0.5	0.5	15	6.25	Yes
0.4	0.6	16	7	Yes
0.3	0.7	17	8.25	Yes
0.2	0.8	18	10	Yes
0.1	0.9	19	12.25	Yes
0	1	20	15	Yes

[a] $E(R_p) = w_A(10) + (1 - w_A)20$.
[b] Because $\rho_{A,B} = 0$, we have $\sigma_p^2 = (w_A^2 10) + (1 - w_A)^2 15$.

Source: From *Introduction to Investments*, 2nd edn, by Levy. © 1999. Reprinted with permission of South-Western, a division of Thomson Learning: www.thomsonrights.com. Fax 800 730-2215.

Exhibit 8.8	Portfolio combinations of two securities

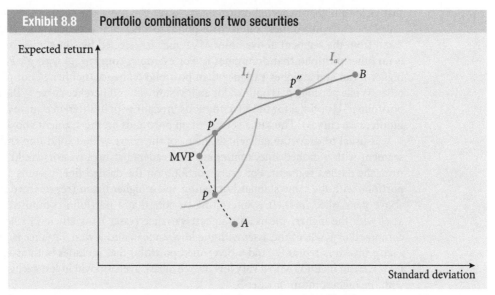

Source: From *Introduction to Investments*, 2nd edn, by Levy. © 1999. Reprinted with permission of South-Western, a division of Thomson Learning: www.thomsonrights.com. Fax 800 730-2215.

The variance column does not show such unambiguous results. The portfolio variance first decreases as w_A decreases (and w_B increases); it reaches its minimum at proportion $w_A = 0.60$, and then it starts to increase. The portfolio corresponding to $w_A = 0.60$ is called the minimum variance portfolio (MVP). The MVP is the portfolio with the smallest variance from the mean–variance frontier. The relationship between the portfolio's variance and the investment proportion is quite general, bending toward the vertical axis (apart from the extreme cases of $\rho_{A,B} = -1$ and $\rho_{A,B} = +1$, or if one of the assets is perfectly riskless). By combining the mean column with the variance column, we can see that not all diversification strategies are inefficient. Specifically, all investment strategies with $w_A > 0.60$ are inefficient because lower expected returns and higher variances can be achieved by strategies with $w_A \leq 0.60$. For example, the investment strategies with $w_A = 0.70$, $w_A = 0.80$, $w_A = 0.90$ and $w_A = 1.00$ all have a lower mean and a higher variance than the MVP with $w_A = 0.60$.

Exhibit 8.8 shows the results of Exhibit 8.7 graphically. The curve AB describes the expected returns and standard deviations of portfolios composed of various combinations of assets A and B, where point B corresponds to 100% investment in asset B and point A corresponds to 100% investment in asset A. As the investment proportion in asset A decreases, the portfolio mean is always increasing. The variance, however, decreases only up to point MVP; then it starts increasing. It is obvious from this graph that no investor would select portfolios from the segment below point MVP, because for each portfolio on this segment there is at least one portfolio taken from the segment above point MVP that will offer a higher expected return and a lower variance (for example, the MVP). To illustrate, consider portfolio p: portfolio p' dominates portfolio p, because it has a higher portfolio mean and the same variance. Portfolio p' is optimal for an investor with indifference curve I_t, a timid investor (with very steep indifference curves). Clearly, investing in portfolio p puts this investor on a lower indifference curve and makes him or her worse off than investing in portfolio p'.

Although AB is the mean–variance frontier, only a portion of it is the efficient frontier. The segment below point MVP is called the inefficient frontier, which corresponds to inefficient investment strategies. That is, there is at least one portfolio on the segment above point MVP that yields a higher expected return and a lower variance. The segment above point MVP is called the efficient frontier, and it corresponds to efficient investment strategies. Any portfolio taken from the segment above point MVP may be selected by some investors, because there is no other portfolio that dominates it. For example, compare p' with p''. Portfolio p'' has a higher mean and a higher variance than portfolio p'; hence, neither p' nor p'' dominates the other. While portfolio p' is optimal for an investor with indifference curve I_t (the timid investor), portfolio p'' is optimal for the adventureous investor with indifference curve I_a (with less steep indifference curves). The same is true for all portfolios on the segment above point MVP.

It is usual to draw the efficient segment of the curve with a solid line and the inefficient segment with a dashed line, reminding the reader that no investor would select portfolios from the dashed segment. For every portfolio on the dashed line, there is another available portfolio with the same standard deviation and a higher mean (represented by the solid line above the dashed line). It is interesting to note that a portfolio composed of 100% of the asset with the highest mean and highest variance (asset B) is efficient, whereas a portfolio composed of 100% of the asset with the lowest mean and lowest variance is inefficient. Risk-averse investors typically hold a diversified portfolio that includes both asset A and asset B. However, an investor with a very low degree of risk aversion will invest exclusively in the asset with the highest mean or asset B.

Exhibit 8.9	Two-asset portfolio mean and variance for various levels of correlation

(a) Basic inputs – the assets' mean and variance

	Asset A	Asset B
Mean return (%)	10	20
Variance (%)	10	15

(b) Portfolio mean[a] and variance[b] for various weights and asset correlations

Invested weights		Correlation ($\rho=-1$)		Correlation ($\rho=-0.5$)		Correlation ($\rho=+0.5$)		Correlation ($\rho=+1$)	
w_A	$w_B = 1 - w_A$	Mean	Variance	Mean	Variance	Mean	Variance	Mean	Variance
1.0	0.0	10.0	10.00	10.0	10.00	10.0	10.00	10.0	10.00
0.9	0.1	11.0	6.05	11.0	7.15	11.0	9.35	11.0	10.45
0.8	0.2	12.0	3.08	12.0	5.04	12.0	8.96	12.0	10.92
0.7	0.3	13.0	1.11	13.0	3.68	13.0	8.82	13.0	11.39
0.6	0.4	14.0	0.12	14.0	3.06	14.0	8.94	14.0	11.88
0.55	0.45	14.5	0.00	14.5	3.03	14.5	9.09	14.5	12.12
0.5	0.5	15.0	0.13	15.0	3.19	15.0	9.31	15.0	12.37
0.4	0.6	16.0	1.12	16.0	4.06	16.0	9.94	16.0	12.88
0.3	0.7	17.0	3.11	17.0	5.68	17.0	10.82	17.0	13.39
0.2	0.8	18.0	6.08	18.0	8.04	18.0	11.96	18.0	13.92
0.1	0.9	19.0	10.05	19.0	11.15	19.0	13.35	19.0	14.45
0.0	1.0	20.0	15.00	20.0	15.00	20.0	15.00	20.0	15.00

[a] The mean is calculated as $E(R) = w_A 10 + (1 - w_A)20$.
[b] The variance is calculated as $\sigma_p^2 = w_A^2 10 + (1 - w_A)^2 15 + 2w_A(1 - w_A)\rho\sqrt{10}\sqrt{5}$ where ρ is the assumed correlation and $\sqrt{10}$ and $\sqrt{5}$ are the standard deviations of the two assets, respectively.

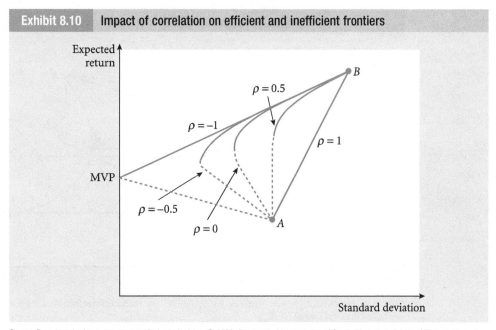

Exhibit 8.10 Impact of correlation on efficient and inefficient frontiers

Source: From *Introduction to Investments*, 2nd edn, by Levy. © 1999. Reprinted with permission of South-Western, a division of Thomson Learning: www.thomsonrights.com. Fax 800 730-2215.

8.3.2 Two assets with different correlations

This section examines how the correlation coefficient influences the mean–variance frontier for the two-asset case. Exhibit 8.9 is the same as Exhibit 8.7 except that it compares four different correlations of assets A and B: $\rho_{A,B} = -1, -0.5, +0.5$, and $+1$, respectively. The results for $\rho_{A,B} = -0.5$ and $\rho_{A,B} = 0.5$ are very similar to the case of $\rho_{A,B} = 0$. The only difference is that the gain from diversification is smaller for $\rho_{A,B} = +0.5$ than for $\rho_{A,B} = 0$, and it is larger when $\rho_{A,B} = -0.5$. For example, in a portfolio with a mean of 12%, when $\rho_{A,B} = -0.5$ the variance is 5.04, and when $\rho_{A,B} = +0.5$ the variance is 8.96, whereas when $\rho_{A,B} = 0$ the variance is 7. In general, the higher the value of $\rho_{A,B}$, the smaller the gain from diversification, all other things remaining equal.

Exhibit 8.10 uses the results of Exhibits 8.7 and 8.9 to demonstrate the effect of the prevailing correlation on the efficient and inefficient segments. For $\rho_{A,B} = +1$, the efficient frontier is a straight line, *AB*. All investment strategies lying on this line are efficient. For correlation $\rho_{A,B} = -1$, the line from *B* to point MVP is the set of all efficient investment strategies, and the line from MVP to *A* is the inefficient set. The two straight lines touch the vertical axis, which implies that for some investment proportions, a perfectly risk-free portfolio (zero variance) can be achieved. Any correlation between −1 and +1 yields a curved efficient frontier. However, as the correlation declines, the curve bulges to the left, which implies larger risk reduction because of diversification.

8.3.3 Efficient and inefficient frontiers with many assets

So far, the gain from diversification has been demonstrated in the case where only two assets are available. In this case, the mean–variance frontier is the same as the set of all possible

Exhibit 8.11	Efficient and inefficient frontier with many assets

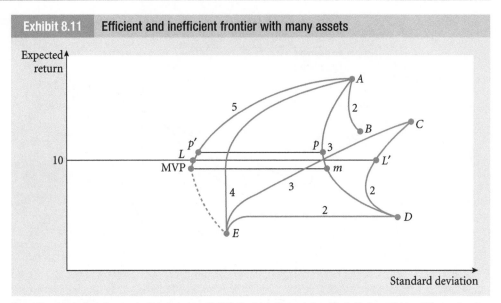

Source: From *Introduction to Investments*, 2nd edn, by Levy. © 1999. Reprinted with permission of South-Western, a division of Thomson Learning: www.thomsonrights.com. Fax 800 730-2215.

combinations of mean and variance (or the mean–variance possibilities set); every possible portfolio that could be constructed is a member of the mean–variance frontier. Actual portfolio choices are more complicated because they typically involve more than two assets. In actual portfolio choices, we first have to find the mean–variance frontier and then identify its efficient and inefficient parts.

With many assets, an investor may find some investment strategies that are on the mean–variance frontier and some investment strategies that are interior to the frontier, lying to the right of the frontier. Exhibit 8.11 shows five assets labelled A–E. An investor can benefit by diversifying in any combination of two, three, four or five of these assets. The graph shows three such diversification strategies, *AB*, *CD* and *DE*; all are labelled '2', indicating that two-asset portfolios are created. Of course, there are other two-asset portfolio possibilities (e.g. *AE*), which, for simplicity, are not shown in the exhibit. Similarly, the curves labelled '3', '4' and '5' stand for three-asset, four-asset and five-asset portfolios, respectively. There is an infinite number of possible diversification strategies.[18]

Curve 5 in this case, for a given mean rate of return, has the lowest standard deviation when compared with the other curves. Therefore, it is the mean–variance frontier. Note that for any point, *p*, there is on curve 5 a point *p'* that yields the same mean return and lower standard deviation. Only part of the A–MVP–E curve is mean–variance-efficient, however. The segment from MVP to *E* of the frontier is mean–variance-inefficient, whereas the segment from MVP to *A* is the efficient segment.

Unlike the case with two assets, with many assets other investment strategies are feasible but are not on the mean–variance frontier – for example, point *D*, curves 2, 3 and 4, and so forth. All these strategies are interior to the frontier. Because no investor would choose a portfolio that was interior to the mean–variance frontier, the best way to find an optimal portfolio is first to locate the mean–variance frontier and then to identify its efficient and inefficient segments.

---

[18] The more assets considered, the more likely it is that the mean–variance frontier could be improved and shifted further to the left.

8.3.4 Finding the mean–variance frontier

Whereas the graphical demonstration of the efficient frontier in this chapter is quite simple, finding the portfolio weights corresponding to the frontier and its efficient segment is not an easy task. Still, the computations can be performed with standard spreadsheet software.

Finding the efficient frontier requires solving the following problem: find the portfolio weights $w_1, w_2, \ldots, w_n$ that minimise the portfolio's variance

$$\sigma_p^2 = \sum_{i=1}^{n} \sum_{s=1}^{n} w_i w_s \sigma_{i,s}$$

subject to the constraints

$$E(R_p) = \sum_{i=1}^{n} w_i E(R_i) = \mu \text{ (a given expected return)}$$

and

$$\sum_{i=1}^{n} w_i = 1 \text{ (fully invested portfolio)}$$

and possibly additional constraints, such as short sales constraints (see below).[19]

For example, suppose an investor desires a portfolio that yields a mean return of $E(R_p) = 10\%$. All diversification strategies that lie on the line LL' (see Exhibit 8.14) yield this mean return. By minimising the portfolio's variance σ_p^2, we find the investment strategy corresponding to point L, which is a point on the mean–variance frontier. Namely, there is no other portfolio with a mean return of 10% and a lower variance. Hence, point L represents a frontier portfolio.

Solving the problem once again for another value of $E(R_p)$ – say, 11% – we get another point on the frontier, point p'. By changing $E(R_p)$, we identify the whole mean–variance frontier, as well as the efficient set of investment strategies; in our specific case, it is the segment MVP to A (see Exhibit 8.11).

It should be clear by now that the shape of the mean–variance frontier depends on the means, variances and covariances of the individual assets. The shape of the frontier also depends on the investment restrictions that are placed on the portfolio weights, i.e. the portfolio possibilities set discussed in Section 7.1. Of course, if more restrictions are placed on the weights, then the investor has fewer investment strategies to choose from and, hence, the frontier deteriorates, i.e. the highest possible mean (given the variance) decreases and the lowest possible variance (given the mean) increases. Similarly, the lifting of investment constraints improves the mean–variance frontier by making more favourable mean–variance combinations feasible. For example, Chapter 10 shows how allowing investors to lend and borrow at a risk-free rate widens the investment opportunities. Exhibits 8.12–8.14 demonstrate the effect of lifting short-selling restrictions (allowing investors to short assets).

---

[19] At first sight, this problem looks rather complex because the objective (variance) is a non-linear function of many variables (the weights), and the problem involves constraints. However, from a mathematical programming perspective, the problem is relatively simple, because the objective function is concave and the portfolio possibilities set is convex; the problem is a so-called convex quadratic programming problem. Spreadsheet software can solve such problems (see Appendix B at the end of this book). Note, however, that the problem becomes more complex if we add non-linear constraints such as the constraint that the number of assets should be less than or equal to some fixed number. In this case, the portfolio possibilities set is no longer convex. For such cases, we generally need specialised software.

Exhibit 8.12	Historical estimate of five major US asset groups (based on annual rates of return from 1926 to 1996)

Asset group	Mean (%)	SD (%)	Large company	Small company	Correlation		
					Long-term corporate bonds	Long-term government bonds	Intermediate-term government bonds
Large-company stock	12.7	20.3	1	0.81	0.25	0.18	0.01
Small-company stock	17.7	34.1		1	0.11	0.03	−0.03
Long-term corporate bonds	6.0	8.7			1	0.94	0.9
Long-term government bonds	5.4	9.2				1	0.91
Intermediate-term government bonds	5.4	5.8					1

Source: Ibbotson Associates, 1997, *Stocks, Bonds, Bills, and Inflation, Annual Yearbook*, Chicago, IL: Ibbotson Associates

Exhibit 8.13	Efficient frontier: with and without short sales

(a) Without short sales

	Global MVP	Efficient portfolios								
Mean (%)	5.8	7.1	8.5	9.8	11.1	12.4	13.7	15.1	16.4	17.7
Standard deviation (%)	5.7	6.7	9.1	12.1	15.3	18.7	22.1	25.6	29.6	34.1
Investment weights (%)										
Large-company stock	1.9	11.2	20.4	29.6	38.9	48.1	56.6	52.8	26.4	0
Small-company stock	2.3	7.6	12.8	18.1	23.3	28.5	33.7	47.2	73.6	100
Long-term corporate bonds	0.0	0.0	0.0	0.0	0.0	0.0	9.6	0.0	0.0	0
Long-term government bonds	0.0	0.0	0.0	0.0	0.0	0.0	0.0	0.0	0.0	0
Intermediate-term government bonds	95.7	81.3	66.8	52.3	37.8	23.3	0.0	0.0	0.0	0

(b) With short sales

	Global MVP	Efficient portfolios								
Mean (%)	5.8	7.1	8.4	9.7	11.0	12.3	13.6	14.9	16.2	17.5
Standard deviation (%)	4.5	5.7	8.1	11.1	14.2	17.4	20.7	24.0	27.3	30.6
Investment weights (%)										
Large-company stock	6.2	13.9	21.7	29.4	37.2	44.9	52.7	60.5	68.2	76.0
Small-company stock	1.0	5.2	9.5	13.8	18.0	22.3	26.6	30.8	35.1	39.3
Long-term corporate bonds	−31.2	4.4	40.0	75.6	111.2	146.8	182.4	218.0	253.6	289.2
Long-term government bonds	−50.5	−78.2	−105.9	−133.6	−161.3	−189.0	−216.7	−244.4	−272.1	−299.8
Intermediate-term government bonds	174.6	154.7	134.8	114.8	94.9	75.0	55.1	35.1	15.2	−4.7

Source: From *Introduction to Investments*, 2nd edn, by Levy. © 1999. Reprinted with permission of South-Western, a division of Thomson Learning: www.thomsonrights.com. Fax 800 730-2215.

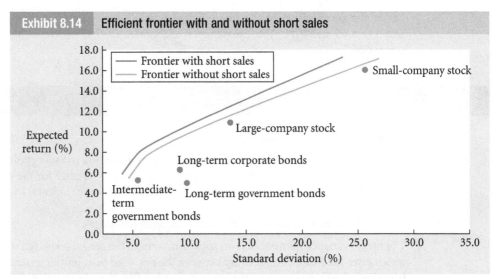

Exhibit 8.14 Efficient frontier with and without short sales

Source: From *Introduction to Investments*, 2nd edn, by Levy. © 1999. Reprinted with permission of South-Western, a division of Thomson Learning: www.thomsonrights.com. Fax 800 730-2215.

Exhibit 8.12 provides historical estimates of the expected returns, standard deviations and correlation coefficients for five major asset groups (large-cap stocks, small-cap stocks, long-term corporate bonds, long-term government bonds and intermediate-term government bonds).

The values in Exhibit 8.12 are used to determine the efficient frontiers with and without short sales. As discussed in Section 7.1, short sales can be excluded by adding the condition that all weights should be greater than or equal to zero ($w_i \geq 0$). Exhibit 8.13(a) shows the composition of several efficient portfolios when short sales are not allowed. Exhibit 8.13(b) shows the results when short sales are allowed. Exhibit 8.14 compares graphically the mean–variance frontier with and without short sales. As this graph shows, the efficient frontier with short sales dominates that with no short sales, i.e. the frontier with short sales is located to the left of the no-short-sales frontier, because the investor has more investment opportunities when w_i is allowed to be negative (he or she can always select $w_i \geq 0$ if preferred). For example, with a mean of 7.1%, when short sales are allowed, the lowest possible standard deviation is 5.7%; in contrast, when short sales are not allowed, this increases to 6.7%. Clearly, short-selling substantially improves the efficient frontier.

The above example shows that the shape of the mean–variance frontier depends heavily on the restrictions that are placed on the portfolio weights. It also shows that low-yield asset classes can be attractive investments if they are correlated weakly or negatively with other asset classes. Exhibit 8.12 shows that bonds had very low mean returns over the historical period. Still, investors should consider these securities for their portfolios because of the associated diversification benefits. For example, in Exhibit 8.13(a), where there are no short sales, consider a target return of 11.1%. In addition to investing 38.9% in large-cap stocks and 23.3% in small-cap stocks, the efficient portfolio invests 37.8% in intermediate bonds, which had a mean of only 5.4%. Exhibit 8.13(b) provides similar results, except that short sales are allowed.

Finally, it is important to remember that the efficient frontier in this example is constructed based on historical estimates of means, standard deviations and correlations. The actual means, standard deviations and correlations may be very different in future periods;

hence, the composition of the true efficient portfolios may be very different from that in Exhibits 8.13 and 8.14. The next chapter elaborates further on the subject of parameter estimation.

Summary

Apply the mean–variance criterion in asset selection.

The mean–variance criterion (MVC) provides a simple method to make choices between risky assets. The MVC states that investors prefer (1) the lowest variance for the same (or higher) expected return or (2) the highest expected return for the same (or lower) variance.

Explain the economic meaning of the mean–variance framework.

The mean–variance framework is an approximation to the general expected utility framework, which gives the general relationship between the portfolio possibilities set, the probability distribution of asset returns and the investor's utility function. In practice, the expected utility framework is not operational, and the mean–variance framework provides an operational approximation. The approximation is good if the return distribution is approximately normal or if the utility function can be approximated by a quadratic function; in both situations, the investor cares only about the mean and the variance of his or her investment portfolio. In many cases, at least one of these conditions is satisfied and, hence, mean–variance analysis gives a good approximation to the general expected utility framework.

Discuss two approaches for computing the mean and variance of a portfolio of assets.

The simplest method for computing portfolio means and variances is the direct method. This method calculates the portfolio returns in all possible states of the world using the returns to the individual assets and the portfolio weights as inputs, and then it calculates the portfolio mean and variance in the same way as the means and variances for individual assets. Unfortunately, the direct method cannot be applied unless we have full information about the returns of all individual assets in all possible states of the world. The indirect method circumvents this problem. This method computes the portfolio mean as a weighted average of the means of the individual assets, and it computes the portfolio variance as a combination of the variances of the individual assets and the covariances of all pairs of assets. The indirect approach of computing the variance is more complicated than the direct approach. However, the information requirement is lower; we don't need the individual return observations. Also, the indirect method offers useful insights into the determinants of portfolio variance and the effectiveness of portfolio diversification.

Locate the efficient and inefficient investment strategies.

Using the mean–variance criterion, investors will choose their portfolio from a subset of the mean–variance possibilities set called the efficient mean–variance frontier. Since investors prefer the lowest variance for the same (or higher) expected return, they will focus on the set of portfolios with the smallest variance for a given mean, or the mean–variance frontier. The mean–variance frontier can be divided into two parts: an efficient frontier and an inefficient frontier. The efficient part includes the portfolios with the highest mean for a given variance. To find the efficient frontier, we must solve a quadratic programming problem, for example by using spreadsheet software.

Key terms

Covariance 243
Direct approach 243
Efficient frontier 248
Expected utility framework 235
Indifference curve 240
Indirect approach 243
Inefficient frontier 248
Mean–variance efficiency criterion 242

Mean–variance-efficient 242
Mean–variance framework 235
Mean–variance frontier 248
Mean–variance-indifference curve 240
Mean–variance possibilities set 247
Minimum variance portfolio (MVP) 249
Normal distribution 236

Normal probability distribution 236
Portfolio mean 243
Portfolio variance 243
Quadratic function 236
Quadratic utility 238
Standard deviation 236
Variance 243

Review questions

1 a. Summarise the mean–variance efficiency criterion.
   b. What is the connection between this criterion and the mean–variance-efficient frontier?

2 a. Describe how the expected rate of return, and the variance of a portfolio are calculated.
   b. Describe an asset's risk when held with other assets in a portfolio.
   c. Explain what 'covariance' means.
   d. What is the role of correlation within a portfolio?

3 What are the two methods to compute the mean and variance for a portfolio of assets? In which circumstances is each of them used?

4 The following table gives the probability distributions of returns for Stock H and Stock I.

State of economy	Probability	Stock H	Stock I
Terrifying	0.2	−30%	−12%
Bothersome	0.3	−10%	0%
Pleasant	0.5	6%	20%

Use both the direct method and the indirect method to calculate the standard deviation of a portfolio that is formed by investing $5000 in Stock H and $15 000 in Stock I.

5 How do you expect the efficient frontier to change, given the following events?:

   ■ Allowing for short-selling (assume first short sales were forbidden).
   ■ Introduction of additional assets.
   ■ Increased correlation between the assets.

For an extensive set of review and practice questions and answers, visit the Levy–Post investment website at www.booksites.net/levy

Selected references

Arditti, F. D., 1971, 'Another Look At Mutual Fund Performance', *Journal of Financial and Quantitative Analysis*, **6**, 909–912.

Bawa, V. S. and E. B. Lindenberg, 1977, 'Capital Market Equilibrium in a Mean-Lower Partial Moment Framework', *Journal of Financial Economics*, **5**, 189–200.

Bera, A. K. and C. M. Jarque, 1981, 'An Efficient Large-Sample Test for Normality of Observations and Regression Residuals', *Australian National University Working Papers in Econometrics*, **40**, Canberra, Australia.

Bigelow, J. P., 1993, 'Consistency of Mean–Variance Analysis and Expected Utility Analyses: A Complete Characterization', *Economic Letters*, **43**, 187–192.

Chunhachinda, P., K. Dandapani, S. Hamid and A. J. Prakash, 1997, 'Portfolio Selection and Skewness: Evidence from International Stock Markets', *Journal of Banking and Finance*, **21**, 143–167.

Fama, E. F., 1965, 'The Behavior of Stock Market Prices', *Journal of Business*, **38**, 34–105.

Hanoch, G. and H. Levy, 1970, 'Efficient Portfolio Selection with Quadratic and Cubic Utility', *Journal of Business*, **43** (2), 181–189.

Kraus, A. and R. Litzenberger, 1976, 'Skewness Preference and the Valuation of Risk Assets', *Journal of Finance*, **31**, 1085–1100.

Levy, H. and G. Hanoch, 1970, 'Relative Effectiveness of Efficiency Criteria for Portfolio Selection', *Journal of Financial and Quantitative Analysis*, **5** (1), 63–76.

Levy, H. and H. Markowitz, 1979, 'Approximating Expected Utility by a Function of Mean and Variance', *American Economic Review*, **69**, 308–317.

Markowitz, H. M., 1952, 'Portfolio Selection', *Journal of Finance*, **7** (1), 77–91.

Markowitz, H. M., 1959, *Portfolio Selection*, New York: John Wiley & Sons.

Markowitz, H. M., 1987, *Mean–Variance Analysis in Portfolio Choice and Capital Markets*, New York: Basil Blackwell.

Samuelson, P. A., 1970, 'The Fundamental Approximation Theorem of Portfolio Analysis in Terms of Means, Variances, and Higher Moments', *Review of Economic Studies*, **37**, 537–542.

Simkowitz, M. A. and W. L., Beedles, 1978, 'Diversification in a Three-moment World', *Journal of Financial and Quantitative Analysis*, **13**, 927–941.

Singleton, J. C. and J. Wingender, 1986, 'Skewness Persistence in Common Stock Returns', *Journal of Financial and Quantitative Analysis*, **21**, 335–341.

Tobin, J., 1958, 'Liquidity Preferences as Behaviour Toward Risk', *Review of Economic Studies*, **25**, 65–86.

Tsiang, S. C., 1972, 'The Rationale of the Mean-Standard Deviation Analysis, Skewness Preference and the Demand for Money', *American Economic Review*, **62**, 354–371.

Investment in the News 9

Pension plans under scrutiny

US policymakers are likely to step up their scrutiny of company pension plans following allegations that Enron, the bankrupt energy trader, forced employees into massive 401(k) plan losses.

The US Department of Labor late on Wednesday opened an investigation into Enron's handling of its Dollars 2.1 bn pension fund. Fund administrators had allowed 60 per cent of the 401(k) pension plan's assets to be held in Enron stock and temporarily halted trading when the company's shares fell sharply in October.

Two subcommittees from the House of Representatives' financial services committee will also consider Enron's pension plan when it meets next week to discuss the effect of the company's collapse on investors.

Although the investigations are limited to Enron, they could have broader implications. 'It looks to me like a bunch of innocent people got crushed here,' Rep Richard Baker, chairman of the House subcommittee on capital markets, said in a statement. 'What I'd like to know is how this happened, how it could have been avoided . . . and how do we avoid a similar collapse in the future.'

In 1974, Congress set a 10 per cent cap on the amount of company stock that could be held in a defined benefit plan, an older type of company-sponsored pensions plan. But limits were never set on 401(k) plans, which were introduced in 1984. These are flexible pension plans which allow the employee to choose a spread of investments including a company share purchase plan. However, about 2000 companies match their employee contributions with company stock, rather than cash, according to the Employee Benefit Research Institute.

About 120 of the largest US companies hold at least one-third of their employees' 401(k) assets in their own stock, according to the Committee on the Investment of Employee Benefit Assets. General Electric's plan, for example, contains 75 per cent GE stock. Coca-Cola's plan holds 78 per cent.

Employee lawsuits against Enron, filed last month, argue that company pension fund managers are breaching their fiduciary duty by holding such a large concentration of company stock because they are ignoring prudent principles of diversification. Eli Gottesdiener, a plaintiff attorney in one of the lawsuits, hopes that the Labor Department

Investment in the News 9 continued

and Congressional inquiries into Enron will prompt lawmakers to cap company stock in 401(k) funds.

'The Department of Labor would . . . want to study this to determine whether or not there is any basis for legislation to be proposed, but a Republican-led administration is naturally not inclined to suggest legislation,' said Geoff Bobroff, a former Securities and Exchange Commission attorney and financial industry consultant.

Any rule that might dilute the concentrations of company stock in 401(k) plans would take time to be realised, he said.

Also, Congress would be inclined to defer to the Labor Department in the case of retirement plan regulations. 'It's hard for them to adopt a law telling GE or Coca-Cola to do anything,' Mr Bobroff said.

Source: Alison Beard and Elizabeth Wine, 'Pension Plans Under Scrutiny', *Financial Times*, 7 December 2001.

Learning objectives

After studying this chapter, you should be able to:

1 Explain how an investor can find uncorrelated assets.

2 Discuss the effectiveness of international portfolio diversification.

3 Explain how many assets are needed to achieve the benefits of portfolio diversification.

4 Discuss possible barriers to portfolio diversification.

5 Discuss the effect of estimation risk on portfolio diversification.

6 Discuss the actual portfolio diversification by households and mutual funds.

Investment in the News 9 discusses the poor diversification of Enron's pension plan and the public discussion about the diversification of company pension plans that followed Enron's collapse, which left thousands of employees out of work and with lost retirement savings.[1] The basic notion of diversification involves spreading a portfolio over many investments to avoid excessive exposure to a few sources of risk. In simple English this means 'Don't put all your eggs into one basket'. At the very minimum, investors should avoid investing in only one particular risky stock. This is where many investors get burned. What happens if the stock turns out to be a second Enron? Your hard-earned money becomes scrambled eggs! By spreading your portfolio among a variety of assets, you ensure that a single bad investment won't wipe out your portfolio.

---

[1] See Section 2.7 of Chapter 2 for some further details on the Enron case.

Diversification is the 'free lunch' of finance. The 'lunch' is 'free' because through diversification, you can achieve a higher average return for the same risk or a lower risk for the same average return. However, in practice, investors encounter various difficulties in constructing efficient portfolios. This chapter discusses several practical aspects of portfolio diversification. How can an investor find weakly correlated assets? How many assets are needed to achieve the benefits of diversification? Do investors actually diversify their portfolios? This chapter answers these and related questions. Our discussion is phrased in terms of the mean–variance framework that was introduced in Chapter 8.

9.1 Finding uncorrelated assets

As discussed in Chapter 8, the lower the covariance or correlation between the assets, the lower the portfolio variance (provided the portfolio weights are chosen correctly). How can an investor find weakly correlated assets? Basically, there are three ways to diversify:

■ diversification across sectors and industries (technology, utilities, real estate and so on);
■ diversification across asset classes (stocks, bonds, commodities and so on);
■ international diversification or diversification across regions and countries (see Section 9.2).

If you invest in a single country, a single asset class or a single industry, for example US technology stocks, then you are still putting all your eggs into one basket, no matter how many different stocks you choose.

Exhibit 9.1 shows a correlation matrix for various regions, sectors and asset classes.[2] Each cell contains the correlation coefficient between two market indices, computed using monthly US dollar returns over the period 1994–2003. Correlations are computed from the viewpoint of a US investor. Returns are converted to US dollars at the prevailing exchange rates before correlations were calculated. Each cell contains the correlation coefficient between two types of assets. For example, the correlation between the UK and the US stock market is 75%, and the correlation between the US stock market and Japanese Government bonds is 8%. The shaded cells include correlation coefficients below 40%, which are attractive for the purpose of diversification. In fact, 40% is the typical correlation for two individual US stocks. Note that the correlations in the exhibit are computed using market indices, and the correlations between individual assets can be expected to be much lower. As can be seen from this exhibit, uncorrelated assets can be found by considering various sectors, asset classes and countries.

Connecting Theory to Practice 9.1 discusses a number of asset classes that have recently attracted attention as they are correlated very weakly with stocks and bonds: hedge funds, catastrophe bonds, fine art and venture capital.

---

[2] The cells above the diagonal are not filled, because the correlation matrix is symmetric. For example, the correlation between US and UK stock markets (second row, first column) is identical to the correlation between UK and US stock markets (first row, second column).

Exhibit 9.1 Correlation matrix for regions, sectors and asset classes (1994–2003)

	Equity US	Equity Europe except UK	Equity Japan	Equity UK	Equity emerging markets	Consumer	Manufacturing	High-tech	Health	Other	US Treasury	UK Gilts	Bonds Japan	Bonds Germany
Equity US	1.00													
Equity Europe except UK	0.75	1.00												
Equity Japan	0.43	0.41	1.00											
Equity UK	0.74	0.81	0.44	1.00										
Equity emerging markets	0.68	0.63	0.48	0.56	1.00									
Consumer	0.89	0.71	0.41	0.73	0.61	1.00								
Manufacturing	0.79	0.65	0.41	0.71	0.63	0.79	1.00							
High-tech	0.85	0.67	0.41	0.57	0.64	0.64	0.52	1.00						
Health	0.64	0.39	0.21	0.39	0.38	0.56	0.53	0.45	1.00					
Other	0.87	0.63	0.31	0.71	0.59	0.87	0.82	0.57	0.57	1.00				
US Treasury	−0.10	−0.18	−0.12	−0.06	−0.24	−0.11	−0.06	−0.16	0.04	−0.08	1.00			
UK Gilts	−0.06	0.02	0.01	0.23	−0.16	−0.07	0.00	−0.12	0.05	−0.06	0.54	1.00		
Bonds Japan	0.08	0.09	0.45	0.20	0.04	0.11	0.14	0.05	−0.02	0.02	0.07	0.23	1.00	
Bonds Germany	−0.19	0.05	0.02	0.10	−0.18	−0.18	−0.07	−0.19	−0.10	−0.16	0.38	0.65	0.44	1.00

The equity indices are MSCI indices. The sector indices are monthly return indices based on the five industry classification of the Kenneth French homepage (data come from the CRSP database and are average value-weighted returns). The bond indices are MSCI indices.

Source: mba.tuck.dartmouth.edu/pages/faculty/ken.french/

→ **Connecting Theory to Practice 9.1**

Investors seek escape from ties that bind

From 1926 to 1969, returns from stock markets and bond markets were hardly correlated, making portfolio diversification a fairly simple task. Today's investors do not have it so easy. The connection between the equity and fixed income markets grew tenfold from 1970 to 1980, then jumped another 65 per cent from 1981 to 1998, according to research from Ibbotson Associates. The trend was of little concern during the 1990s bull market, when moving in lockstep with the soaring stock market was a good thing. Now, investors are scrambling to balance out their equity positions.

Finding investments with a low correlation to the stock market is tricky. Most investments depend on the economy, which ensures at least some connection to the stock market. Assets that usually do not correlate can move together when the financial system is shocked. And correlations may change over time owing to factors like inflation and market participation. 'It is not a black and white issue,' said Eli Combs, an adviser to high net worth clients at Goldman Sachs. But that has not stopped money management firms from coming up with some interesting ideas. Here are some of them.

▶

■ **Managed futures funds.** Most hedge funds claim to protect investors from stock declines but managers who buy and sell commodity contracts make a better case than most. The funds can be volatile, particularly if they are placing big, leveraged bets in a few markets. But their average returns show low correlation to equities, even when compared with other hedge fund strategies. Perhaps the best evidence of this trend is an index created by Mt Lucas Asset Management, a firm with $600 m in investor assets. Instead of tracking managers, the MLM index tracks 25 futures markets – four energy, six currencies, three metals, five grains, three US interest rates, coffee, cotton, sugar and cattle – all with equal weighting. Since 1982, the correlation between the index and the Standard & Poor's 500 has been −0.14. (Correlation ranges from −1 to 1, with 0 signifying no relationship.) In negative stock market quarters, the index gained 3.1 per cent against a 9.4 per cent loss for the S&P. In quarters where equities gained, the index rose by 0.5 per cent, on average. 'We're not hurting you in positive years and we're helping you a great deal in negative ones,' said Ray Ix, senior vice-president at Mt Lucas.

■ **Catastrophe bonds.** Another option available to institutional and wealthy investors is catastrophe bonds. Insurance companies, such as Swiss Re, sell them to investors to offload their natural disaster risk, issuing about $2 bn worth each year. Catastrophe bonds yields are significantly higher than similarly rated bonds because investors risk total loss if a flood or earthquake hits the geographic area on which the bonds are based. But, to date, no 'Cat' bond buyers have lost their principal. Natural disasters have no correlation to the economy. And, because issuers create special-purpose vehicles to sell the bonds, investors are not exposed to any company credit risk. 'You're dealing with something exotic, so demand has not been very high but sophisticated investors – hedge funds and mutual funds – have always thought they were a good investment,' said James Doona, a director at Standard & Poor's.

■ **Old Masters paintings.** Few financial advisers recommend fine art as an investment. But subsectors of the market can provide low correlation to equities. According to Jianping Mei and Michael Moses, professors at New York University, prices for Old Masters paintings – by Rembrandt, for example – have shown a 0.04 correlation to the S&P 500 since 1950, compared with 0.23 and 0.24 for American and Impressionist art. Measuring the variation in S&P returns against Old Masters, the correlation is 0.02, compared with 0.05 for American Art and 0.28 for the Impressionists. 'Old Masters have never in recent times been a faddish commodity,' Prof Moses explained. 'They're less volatile and they have lower returns' than the S&P and other main art categories. Impressionist prices are more affected by equity swings because it is a more popular, more expensive market. 'If there is a substantial downdraft in the S&P, it makes people hesitant about buying those multi-million dollar paintings,' Mr Moses said.

■ **Venture capital.** The correlation between VC funds and US equities does not seem low but it is, according to an Ibbotson study of the 148 venture capital funds that liquidated between 1960 and 1999. With a compounded average annual return of 13 per cent and a standard deviation of 115 per cent, the funds show only a small correlation to stocks. VCs depend on a strong economy and equity market for their exit strategies but they are also able to wait out downturns. Funds' annual 'returns' can be judged through appraisals but the Ibbottson study used liquidation values – a more accurate way of judging returns. 'At first glance, it may appear that the correlation . . . between VC investment and public equities is too low,' Mr Ibbotson acknowledged. But 'VC investments are typically concentrated in a small number of products or ideas. The long-term pay-off . . . depends heavily on the success of these products or ideas, which are often independent of the overall stock market performance.'

Source: Alison Beard, 'Investors Seek Escape From Ties That Bind', *Financial Times*, 22 November 2002.

Exhibit 9.2	Biggest one-day percentage declines in DJIA			
Rank	Date	Close	Net change	% change
1	19 October 1987	1738.74	−508.00	−22.61
2	28 October 1929	260.64	−38.33	−12.82
3	29 October 1929	230.07	−30.57	−11.73
4	6 November 1929	232.13	−25.55	−9.92
5	18 December 1929	58.27	−5.57	−8.72
6	12 August 1932	63.11	−5.79	−8.40
7	14 March 1907	76.23	−6.89	−8.29
8	26 October 1987	1793.93	−156.83	−8.04
9	21 July 1933	88.71	−7.55	−7.84
10	18 October 1937	125.73	−10.57	−7.75

Through proper diversification across assets from different countries, asset classes and industries, an investor can eliminate a substantial part of the risk of individual assets. Still, diversification cannot eliminate the risk that comes from the broad capital market as a whole. Even if you hold a well-diversified portfolio, you cannot avoid the fluctuations of the whole market. For example, on 19 October 1987, the whole US stock market went down by more than 20%. Exhibit 9.2 shows the ten biggest one-day declines of the Dow Jones Industrial Average in terms of the percentage change. No matter how well diversified your portfolio was on 19 October 1987, or any of the other days shown in Exhibit 9.2, you could not have avoided this loss.

The risk that can be diversified away is called non-systematic risk, diversifiable risk or asset-specific risk. The risk that remains after extensive diversification is called systematic risk, non-diversifiable risk or market risk. This is the part of risk that comes from the common exposure of assets to economy-wide risk factors, such as the business cycle, interest rates and exchange rates. Market risk generally can be reduced or eliminated only by shifting to low-yielding assets (for example, T-bills and CDs) or by using derivatives (which also lower the expected rate of return because they require a premium).

9.2 International diversification

As discussed above, international investment is one method of portfolio diversification. The benefits of international portfolio diversification have been well-documented since the 1960s.[3] The correlations between US stock indices and stock indices of other countries range from 43% (Japan) to 75% (Europe except the UK). For bonds, the correlations between US bond indices and bond indices of other countries are between 7% (Japanese government bonds) and 54% (UK Gilts). These values are very low compared with correlations between US stock indices and between US bond portfolios, which typically are 95% or higher. In fact, the correlations are comparable to those of individual US stocks: the correlation between a pair of US common

---

[3] See, for example, Grubel (1968), Levy and Sarnat (1970), Solnik (1973, 1974), Bergstrom (1975), Lessard (1976), Solnik and Noetzlin (1982), Jorion (1985), Levy and Lerman (1988), Black and Litterman (1992), Hatch and Resnick (1993), Eun and Resnick (1994), Michaud *et al.* (1996) and Shawky *et al.* (1997).

stocks typically ranges from 30 to 50%. The correlation across both countries and asset types is even smaller. For example, the correlation between US stock and foreign bonds lies between −19% and 8%, and the correlation between US bonds and foreign stocks ranges from −24% to −6%. Since international markets are not correlated perfectly with each other or with the US market, investors can achieve reductions in risk beyond those achieved by investing in a variety of US securities. This is true for US investors, and even more so for investors in small countries. For example, the top 15 companies account for more than three-quarters of the relevant FTSE index in Austria, Belgium, Denmark, Germany, Italy, the Netherlands, Norway, Portugal, Spain and Switzerland. In Australia, Canada, France and the UK, they account for over half. This limits the diversification benefits that can be obtained within a domestic portfolio.

Of course, correlations are only part of the story. Recall from Chapter 8 that the composition of efficient portfolios is determined also by the means and variances of the assets. The basic argument for international diversification is that international assets raise the Markowitz mean–variance-efficient frontier above that for portfolios with only domestic assets. In other words, by investing abroad, a higher average return can be achieved for a given level of risk and a lower level of risk can be achieved for a given level of average return.

Exhibit 9.3 illustrates this point. The exhibit shows various efficient frontiers constructed from MSCI bond and equity indices for Austria, Australia, Hong Kong, Italy, Belgium, Canada, Germany, Finland, France, Japan, the Netherlands, New Zealand, Spain, Sweden, Switzerland, the USA and the UK.[4] The frontiers are constructed using monthly returns in excess of the one-month US T-bill for the ten-year period from January 1994 to December 2003, a total of 120 months.

Exhibit 9.3(a) illustrates the improved efficient frontiers for bond portfolios with international investing. For example, a portfolio of US bonds had an average return of 2.73% and a standard deviation of 4.40%. In this case, the US bond portfolio is efficient; it is not possible to achieve a higher average return and a lower standard deviation. Still, by diversifying internationally, other efficient risk–return combinations are achievable. For example, an adventurous investor with a low degree of risk aversion can combine US and UK bonds to achieve a higher average return.

Exhibit 9.3(b) focuses on international diversification in the equity market and illustrates the efficient frontiers derived from various combinations of country portfolios. The US stock portfolio is very close to the frontier. Again, it is hard to achieve a higher average return and a lower standard deviation. Still, a higher average return can be achieved (at the cost of a higher standard deviation) by investing in foreign stock markets.

Exhibit 9.3(c) illustrates efficient frontiers for an international bond portfolio combined with an international stock portfolio. A global portfolio of both bonds and stocks results in an efficient frontier that is superior to the portfolios of either just bonds or just stocks. For example, investing in US stocks exclusively yields an average return of 4% and a standard deviation of about 16%. This combination is highly inefficient, because combining international stocks and bonds can yield an average return of about 10% at the same level of risk. Also, an average return of 4% can be achieved with a standard deviation of only 5%. Overall, this is a strong case for global diversification across both asset classes and countries.

The early research on international diversification demonstrated convincingly the gains from investing in oversees capital markets. In 1990, a 20-year history of global indices showed that international equities had generated higher returns than US stocks, while the low correlation

---

[4] For Hong Kong, we included only the MCSI equity index. For New Zealand, we included only the MSCI bond index.

Exhibit 9.3   Various efficient frontiers

(a) International bond portfolios

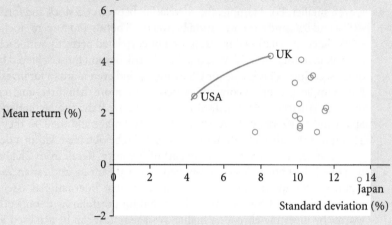

(b) International equity portfolios

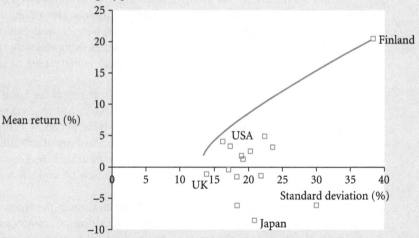

(c) International bond and equity portfolios

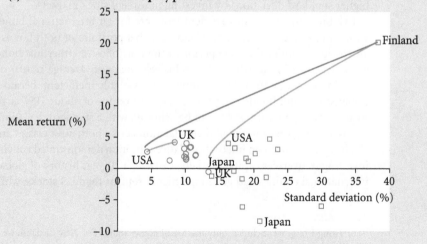

with the US created diversification benefits. In brief, international diversification seemed a 'free lunch', offering higher returns and lower risks.

During the next decade, three phenomena changed the perspective:

- **Superior returns in US markets:** During the 1990s, the US stock market soared and the Japanese and other foreign markets lagged behind. Further, emerging markets were hit hard between 1995 and 1996, with crises in Latin America, Asia and eastern Europe. In fact, the S&P 500 outperformed the MSCI EAFE index by 217% in the period 1991–2001.
- **Increasing correlation between developed countries:** Correlations between developed countries have been increasing over the years, hence reducing the benefits of international diversification.[5] Macroeconomic convergence between the USA and Europe, the effect of European monetary union on intra-European correlations and the cross-listing of stocks have eroded easy diversification gains. Also, many of the dominant industries have become global. When national markets are segmented, a particular market will be influenced primarily by national factors and will not be influenced strongly by factors in other national markets. However, as economies become more integrated, a particular market will be influenced by external factors to a greater extent than when markets are segmented. As national economies are becoming linked more closely, there is greater potential for their stock markets to become more highly correlated, thus reducing the benefits of international diversification. The globalisation of economies has tied stock markets closer together. This has meant that many stock markets around the world take their cue from the USA and move in tandem.

  In Europe, the process of economic and monetary integration significantly increased the correlations between national stock indices, hence reducing diversification opportunities within Euro-land, in the 1990s. The increased conformity of stock returns implies that those diversification opportunities on a purely geographical basis are better if extended outside the European region. Indeed, the evidence suggests that country factors now appear to be dominated by the factors associated with industry or sector.[6]
- **Increasing correlation during international market crises:** Recent evidence indicates that correlations among international security markets tend to increase during crisis situations, thus reducing the efficacy of international diversification at the time it is needed most.[7] Unfortunately, when US stocks get really pounded, it seems that foreign shares also tend to tumble. During all the regular market crises in recent memory, there was no hiding outside the USA. Average correlations between the S&P 500 and the EAFE increased by 30% in months when the S&P was down by more than 5%.

The turmoil in capital markets following the recent Asian financial crisis provides a vivid illustration of the phenomena. The devaluation of the Thai baht in July 1997 was generally unexpected and caught many global investors off guard. The Thai devaluation brought other South-East Asian countries under closer scrutiny, resulting in speculative attacks against the currencies of several of those countries. The subsequent devaluations in Indonesia, Malaysia, South Korea and other countries in the region created a significant amount of turbulence in the region's financial markets. In the aftermath, volatility spread throughout the world. Russia devalued its currency and defaulted on its foreign debt in the late summer of 1998, and

---

[5] See, for instance, Solnik *et al.* (1996), Shawky *et al.* (1997), Longin and Solnik (1995, 1998), Hanna *et al.* (1999) and Solnik (2000).

[6] See, for example, Beckers *et al.* (1996), Griffin and Karolyi (1998), Rouwenhorst (1999), Baca *et al.* (2000), Brooks and Catão (2000), Cavaglia *et al.* (2000) and Isakov and Sonney (2003).

[7] See Erb *et al.* (1994).

Brazil was forced to devalue the real early in 1999.[8] Combined, high domestic returns for US invetsors, structurally higher correlations between developed markets and higher correlations during market crises have weakened the case for international diversification. In fact, a superficial review of the data would suggest that US investors no longer benefit from investing in overseas markets.[9] Note that this is not true for investors in other countries (if only because of the superior returns in US markets). However, a more sophisticated analysis reveals that international diversification is still useful for improving the risk–return characteristics of investment portfolios, even for US investors.

First, with hindsight it is easy to say that, for a given period, investors from some countries (say, the USA in the 1990s) would have been better off without foreign investing. With hindsight, they would probably have been better off selecting the best-performing single stock in their own market. But this would hardly have been a wise decision ex ante. If we consider a longer period, say 1960–2000, then the picture looks rosier.

Second, the analysis considers the isolated effect of international diversification. Diversification across both countries and sectors, however, remains the much superior investment strategy.[10] Some industries are correlated across countries, and some are not. For example, iron and gold-mining stocks are highly correlated, regardless of their home country, because they are all exposed to the price of iron and gold. Giant multinational corporations, no matter their origin, also tend to be correlated, as they depend on the same global economy. On the other hand, many industries are affected primarily by local conditions, and their stocks tend to have little correlation across borders. For example, retailers, restaurants, real estate and local banks have few common factors across borders, especially if a small size limits their geograhic spread. Given this, if you want effective diversification, then consider buying small-cap stocks that are owned mostly by local (foreign) investors and that are affected mostly by local business conditions. Also, for smaller countries, not all industries are represented in their domestic capital market. For example, if UK investors stick with British stocks, they may find it hard to achieve exposure to the global economy. The UK market is heavily biased towards certain sectors such as oil, gas, pharmaceuticals, telecommunications and financials, but it underweights electronics, cars and information technology. This means that UK investors could still find a role for 'geographic' diversification so that they can gain exposure to sectors not heavily represented in the UK, such as technology in the USA and luxury goods in France.

Third, it is true that the correlations among most developed markets have increased during the past decades and also that the correlations between emerging markets have increased. However, the correlation between the USA and emerging markets has remained quite low. Since the market capitalisation of these emerging markets has grown more rapidly than total world market capitalisation, especially in Asia, their share in world indices has increased. The average correlation between the US market and the MSCI World Ex-US index, therefore, has not increased over the past decades, based on monthly readings of rolling five-year periods (see Exhibit 9.3).

While Roll (1992) attributes the low correlation among country indices particularly to the diverse national industry structures, Heston and Rouwenhorst (1994) decompose stock-return

---

[8] The spreading of currency crises is also known as the tequila effect. Following the December 1994 decline in the Mexican peso, Mexican interest rates spiked and the equity market fell. Investors, rationally or otherwise, pulled out of countries that they felt resembled Mexico. As a result, equity markets fell in Brazil and Argentina.

[9] See, for instance, Hanna et al. (1999). This study has shown that in the 1990s, from the point of view of an American investor, returns from six foreign developed countries were lower than those in the USA, and international diversification by American investors into these markets could not result in any diversification gain.

[10] A similar argument applies for diversification across different asset classes.

volatility into pure country and industry sources of variation and clearly document the pre-valence of country-specific effects (the ratio of country to industry variances is 4.5). In a later study, Griffin and Karolyi (1998) found that when emerging markets were included in the analysis, the proportion of country portfolios variance explained by the time series variation in pure country effects was higher than documented previously, which again reinforced the suggestion that one would be better off – in terms of risk reduction – by pursuing a geo-graphical approach, rather than an industrial one, to international investing. Conversely, recent work by Cavaglia *et al.* (2000) and Baca *et al.* (2000), among others, found evidence that industry factors grew in importance in recent years. Also, Brooks and Catão (2000) showed that industry sectors are becoming more important in explaining country portfolio risk and that a global industry factor associated with information technology has been growing in importance since 1995. In addition, there is increased consensus among the investment community and in the financial press that the industrial dimension of diversification is more important nowadays than the geographic dimension.

9.3 A little diversification goes a long way

The larger the number of assets in the portfolio, the lower the portfolio variance that can be achieved. It is often the case that adding more securities to your portfolio will make the port-folio more diversified. But this is not always the case. For example, if your portfolio is already weighted heavily towards telecom stocks, then adding another telecom stock might make your total portfolio less diversified. To enjoy the benefits of diversification, the portfolio weights have to be selected correctly, i.e. they should reflect the means, variances and covariances of the assets. In this case, adding more securities will indeed reduce risk. However, generally, the benefit of including additional assets decreases rapidly as more assets are included. To under-stand this, assume that all assets are equally risky, i.e. each asset has the same variance of σ^2 and the covariance between each pair of assets is $\rho\sigma^2$, where ρ is the correlation coefficient between each pair of assets. In this case, the variance is minimal if we assign all assets the same weights, i.e. $w_i = 1/n$.[11] Using these weights, the portfolio variance can then be written as

$$\sigma_p^2 = \sum_{i=1}^{n} w_i^2 \sigma^2 + \sum_{i=1}^{n} \sum_{\substack{s=1 \\ s \neq i}}^{n} w_i w_s \rho\sigma^2 = \sum_{i=1}^{n} \left(\frac{1}{n}\right)^2 \sigma^2 + \sum_{i=1}^{n} \sum_{\substack{s=1 \\ s \neq i}}^{n} \left(\frac{1}{n}\right)\left(\frac{1}{n}\right)\rho\sigma^2$$

$$= n\left(\frac{1}{n}\right)^2 \sigma^2 + n(n-1)\left(\frac{1}{n}\right)^2 \rho\sigma^2 = \frac{1}{n}\sigma^2 + \frac{n-1}{n}\rho\sigma^2$$

As the number of assets (n) increases, the first term, $\frac{1}{n}\sigma^2$, goes to zero. However, the rate at which this term decreases falls as the number of assets increases. In addition, the second term, $\frac{n-1}{n}\rho\sigma^2$, converges to $\rho\sigma^2$. No matter how many assets are included, this term always remains; this is the market risk shared by all assets.

---

[11] This approach is known as the $1/n$ heuristic, or naive diversification. This approach is optimal if all assets are considered to be equally risky. However, if different assets have different variance and covariance terms, then the weights should reflect these differences. Generally speaking, it will be desirable to assign the highest weight to the asset with the lowest variance and covariance with other assets.

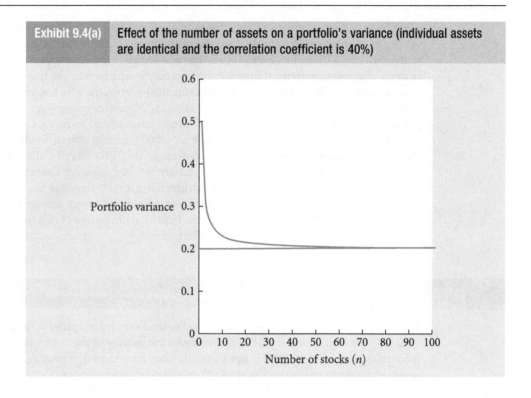

Exhibit 9.4(a)   Effect of the number of assets on a portfolio's variance (individual assets are identical and the correlation coefficient is 40%)

Exhibit 9.4(a) displays the portfolio variance for different numbers of assets (n), assuming that $\rho^2 = 0.5$ and $\rho = 0.4$. Clearly, increasing the number of assets in the portfolio lowers the portfolio variance. However, as the number of assets increases, the incremental contribution to the reduction in the portfolio's variance becomes smaller and smaller. If we move from $n = 1$ to $n = 2$, the portfolio variance drops from $\sigma_p^2 = 0.5$ to $\sigma_p^2 = 0.35$, a reduction of 0.15. An increase in the number of assets from four to five further reduces the variance from $\sigma_p^2 = 0.275$ to $\sigma_p^2 = 0.26$, a reduction of only 0.015, or one-tenth of 0.15. With a larger number of assets, the marginal reduction in the variance is minimal. Most of the gain is achieved by diversifying in a relatively small number of assets as a little diversification goes a long way. In the limit, when the number of assets becomes very large, the variance approaches $\rho\sigma^2 = 0.4 \times 0.5 = 0.2$. This illustrates that we generally cannot diversify away all risk, because there are few assets with negative correlation.

Exhibit 9.4(b) shows the results for different values for the correlation coefficient (ρ). Clearly, the correlation coefficient determines the amount of non-systematic risk that can be diversified away and the amount of systematic risk that cannot be eliminated. However, for every value of ρ, the potential benefits of diversification fall quickly as additional assets are included, and the majority of the potential benefits is achieved with a relatively small number of assets.

Unlike the above example, actual assets rarely have identical variance and covariance terms, and holding an equal-weighted portfolio does not minimise variance. However, the principle still holds even when the variances and covariances differ across assets. When the correlation is about 0.3 to 0.5 (which is typical for many stocks in the US market), it can be shown that about 90% of the maximum potential benefit of the risk reduction is achieved with a portfolio composed of 12–18 securities. This number is surprisingly small, considering that the financial markets trade several thousand securities.

Exhibit 9.4(b)	Effect of the number of assets and the correlation coefficient on a portfolio's variance (individual assets are identical)

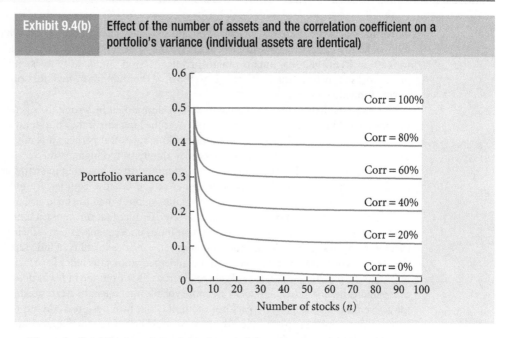

These findings are very important in portfolio management, especially for small investors. Suppose you have $100 000 to invest. Investing in all available securities would yield the lowest possible portfolio variance. However, to diversify $100 000 in several thousand securities is impossible, because the transaction costs would be prohibitively high. Fortunately, an investor can reap most of the gain of risk reduction by investing in a much smaller number of securities.

→ Connecting Theory to Practice 9.2

FT

Why enough is never enough

Do you have enough companies in your portfolio? New research shows that, to get a properly diversified portfolio, you may need more shares than you think. Indeed, the implication of the research is that small investors who buy shares in just one or two companies are taking very big risks.

A study by four US academics – John Campbell, Martin Lettau, Burton Malkiel and Yexiao Xu* – has found that individual stocks have become significantly more volatile since the 1960s. The authors break down share price volatility into three sections: market-related, industry-related and company-related. Over the period 1962–97, there was a significant increase in company-related volatility. But there was no significant trend in that related to the market as a whole or to industries. (The figures refer to the US, but there seems no reason why the same trends should not have applied in the UK.) Company volatility accounted for 65 per cent of total volatility in 1962, but that had risen to 76 per cent by 1997. Although this may sound like jargon, what it means is fairly simple; the market may go up by 10 per cent a year on average but the movement of individual stocks has become more widespread. In the old days, most stocks would move in, say, the minus 10 per cent to 30 per cent range. Now the range is minus 30 per cent to 50 per cent.

The result is it is much harder to construct a well-diversified portfolio. In a properly diversified portfolio, the ups and downs of individual stocks should cancel out so that fluctuations in the value of the portfolio are reduced. As the authors note, the conventional wisdom is that a portfolio of 20 stocks or so will bring all the benefits of diversification. But the correlations between individual stocks has decreased sharply. The authors found that, in the period 1986–97, a portfolio as large as 50 stocks was needed to create the same level of risk that could be achieved with 20 stocks in 1962–85. But how many private investors could afford to assemble a portfolio of 50 stocks? Whatever the answer, it is well below the number of investors now involved in buying individual stocks.

This suggests that some more conventional wisdom might be wrong. It is generally believed that individual investors are always better off, over the long run, if they buy equities. This would still seem to be the case if they buy an index-tracking fund. But perhaps it is not the case if they own only one or two stocks – the volatility may simply be too high. At the very least, it should suggest that investors demand a higher 'risk premium' from investing in shares as opposed to bonds or cash. (They should demand a higher return because equities are more risky.) But current calculations indicate that the risk premium is lower than the historical average.

The second implication is at the institutional level. Groups that run pension fund and unit trust money have to perform well if they are to retain funds under management – their greatest risk is to underperform significantly the index. Because of the greater volatility of individual stocks, however, the risks of an actively managed portfolio underperforming the index have increased. That has increased the pressure on fund managers to divert as little from the index as possible. There is a nice paradox here. If individual stocks are more volatile, that ought to create greater opportunities for active fund managers to outperform the index. But business pressures are forcing them to become 'closet trackers' instead. And the process could be self-reinforcing. A closet tracker will be forced to pile into stocks with small free floats but large market weightings, pushing up the volatility of those stocks. That will create more pressure for funds to become closet trackers and so on.

Why have individual stocks become more volatile? The academics have no definitive answer but they have several suggestions. More companies are now traded on the market; the smaller companies that have been floated are more likely to be dependent on one customer or one product, and thus more volatile. Companies are also joining the market at a far earlier stage of their development, when there is greater uncertainty about their long-term prospects. Old-style conglomerates have broken themselves up into businesses focused on specific industries (and thus more volatile than a diversified group such as Hanson). And changes to executive compensation – mainly, the greater use of share options – may have increased managements' incentive to take risks.

One final issue emerges from the paper. In the past, periods of stock market volatility (at the market, industry and individual company level) have shown a marked tendency to precede recessions. So the recent surge in stock market volatility is not very good news at all.

* Have Individual Stocks Become More Volatile? An Empirical Exploration of Idiosyncratic Risk. To be published in the Journal of Finance.

Source: Philip Coggan, 'Why Enough Is Never Enough: A New Study Shows That You May Need More Shares In Your Portfolio Than You Think', *Financial Times*, 24 June 2000.

→ Making the connection

According to Campbell *et al.* (2001), individual stocks have become more volatile in recent history. Indeed, something is going on when the stock price of Computer Associates plunges by 44% in one day and wireless giant Nokia loses a quarter of its market value. At the same time, the correlation between assets dropped, leaving the overall market volatility more or less unchanged. As discussed above, the convention is that owning 12–18 stocks offers the bulk of the benefits of diversification in an equity portfolio. Decreasing correlations imply that this number has recently become even smaller (a little diversification goes a long way). Still, the heightened volatility means that we need many more stocks to achieve the same level of risk as before.

9.4 Barriers to diversification

When you are a small investor, maintaining a diversified portfolio can be difficult and costly. Collecting and analysing information can be a full-time job. It is very difficult for any small investor to monitor over a dozen of stocks. Also, diversification can involve significant transaction costs. To add to the problem, to remain optimally diversified, a portfolio needs to be rebalanced periodically, which further increases the transaction and information costs. Recall that an investor's optimal portfolio depends on the means, variances and correlations of the assets and the portfolio weights. It is important to note that these parameters generally change through time (see Section 9.5) and hence the portfolio needs to be rebalanced periodically in order to maintain the desired level of diversification.

However, in order to avoid this problem, investors can invest in mutual funds, which pool together the funds of many small investors to achieve economies of scale in information-processing and transaction costs.[12] But such diversification does not come free of cost: mutual funds put charges over and above their transaction costs (see Chapter 4). The cost of diversification through mutual funds can be anything between 1 and 3% per annum. Further benefits of having a diversified portfolio by such professionals are doubtful, as returns from mutual funds generally lag the overall market return (see Chapter 22). This may help to explain the current popularity of passive index funds and exchange-traded funds (ETFs), which offer diversification at lower costs. Further, as discussed in Connecting Theory to Practice 9.3, the evolution of online trading has substantially reduced the barriers to diversification. Consequently, according to the author of this newspaper article, your excuses for not diversifying no longer add up.

→ Connecting Theory to Practice 9.3 **FT**

Diversifaction: your excuses don't add up

Mentioning 'diversification' when the FTSE 100 stands at a seven-year low might seem odd, but it isn't. Excuses for failing to diversify are unacceptable. Yet, most traders have probably not realised that heeding this simple fact could save them thousands in the coming months.

■ **Excuse 1: Diversification is only for long-term investors.** Diversification is not just about having a wide variety of stocks in your long-term portfolio to iron out individual stock volatilities. It is useful even for short-term active traders.

One form of diversification is cross-hedging. I always try to hold simultaneously various long (buying in anticipation of a price rise) and short positions (selling in anticipation of buying back more cheaply to close the trade). Say that at the start of this month you had bought Emap and 3i and had sold short WPP and Friends Provident. You did not have a strong feeling which way the broader market would move. As it transpired, the market moved lower, the FTSE dropping 6 per cent, making it more likely to profit from falling stocks (short sales). You would have made

---

[12] It may be possible to achieve full diversification with only one mutual fund. If you are already holding a fully diversified fund, you will not achieve additional diversification by going into a second fund, unless the second fund covers other asset classes, sectors or regions.

gains from the 17 per cent drops in WPP and Friends Provident. Emap and 3i also fell, and you would have held or sold them.

How do you know on which stocks to go long and which to sell short? Use the same techniques you use in your usual stock picking, such as charting or fundamentals. Going short is not a problem; many online trading products allow the private investor to do that as easily as going long.

A more sophisticated version of this strategy examines the beta of the stocks. A stock that moves in tandem with the market, say the FTSE 100, has a beta of 1. If the market goes up 10 per cent, the stock is expected to go up 10 per cent. A low-beta share tends to move less than the index, while one with a high beta tends to make bigger moves than the index. These calculations give me an idea of the likely effect on my positions of a move by the broader market. Thankfully, websites calculate beta for us.

This strategy certainly allows protection from the J. Pierpont Morgan adage: 'The market will go up and it will go down, but not necessarily in that order.'

■ **Excuse 2: Diversification is too complicated.** Effective diversification often comes from holding international securities because they don't move in line with domestic ones. Investments with low correlations (whose prices move less in tandem with each other) reduce the chance that all your investments will fall together. Harry Markowitz won a Noble Prize for that discovery, and new research confirms the finding*. Moreover, holding stocks in foreign currency (itself an asset with a low correlation to UK stocks) should further reduce portfolio risk. But this requires multiple accounts with different brokers in different currencies and consequently expensive transaction costs.

None of these excuses applies today. A typical CFD, spread bet or stock futures broker offers access to global stocks such as Nokia, Microsoft and Sony. Indeed, online brokers increasingly allow such access from one account. So, if you expect Microsoft to rise in the next fortnight, you look for a foreign stock, such as Sony, that is likely to fall in the same period. Again, that way you make an immediate gain on one and wait to make the gain on the other.

■ **Excuse 3: I don't just invest in stocks.** Diversification benefits are not solely applicable to stock traders. If you are one of the increasing number of traders using spread bets, stock futures or contracts for difference, these simple rules can assist: first, don't invest more than 10 per cent of your portfolio in a particular industry. Second, have a variety of long and short trades. Third, mix international holdings with domestic ones.

Moreover, those online financial products originally designed for short-term traders are now increasingly being modified for long-term investing as stock substitutes. Their benefits include gearing (a small amount of money controls a lot of stock) and tax efficiency. There is no stamp duty, for example, with spread bets, CFDs or stock futures.

■ **Excuse 4: Diversification is for the unskilled.** Admittedly Warren Buffett, the legendary 'sage of Omaha', believes in 'putting all your eggs in one basket, and watching the basket'. Nevertheless, in a volatile, uncertain market where direction is difficult to predict, diversification offers two bites at the cherry for active traders. You can make a profit on the stocks you shorted as the market falls and a gain on the ones you bought as it rises again.

Clearly then, Pierpont Morgan's statement does not mean that the online trader in search of a fortune is a hostage to fortune.

* Smooth Transition Regression Models in UK Stock Returns; Nektarios Aslanidis, University of Crete; September 2002. www.soc.uoc.gr/econ/ seminars/Aslanidis_2002a.pdf

Source: Alpesh B. Patel, 'Diversification: Your Excuses Don't Add Up', *Financial Times*, 15 March 2003.

→ **Making the connection**

This article lists a number of excuses for failing to diversify. The author argues that online access to short-selling, international securities and derivatives greatly simplifies diversification. Note: CFDs (contracts for difference) and spread bets are contracts with a broker to exchange the difference between the opening price and the closing price of a security (a stock, a bond, a derivative) over a specific period. Like futures, such contracts allow the investor to trade without having to buy the underlying security.

The author also argues that short-term active traders should diversify. This is an important message. The flip side of having a well-diversified portfolio is reducing the chances of becoming extremely rich. Warren Buffet did not get rich with a highly diversified portfolio. You might think that accepting greater risk gives you the opportunity for greater gains. Perhaps that is why some active investors make huge bets on a few volatile technology stocks. However, for the most part, this reasoning is wrong. Diversification does not exclude active investment strategies (e.g. picking winners and timing the market), and active strategies do not exclude diversification. In fact, you are free to enter any expected rate of return – high or low – in the formulas for finding the efficient diversification strategies. The fact is that even for the most optimistic forecasts about a single asset, diversification will remain useful. For instance, in the example shown in Section 8.3.5, low-yielding intermediate bonds were assigned a very high weight in the optimal portfolio, simply because they offered high-diversification benefits. Of course, the higher the mean of a specific asset (for example, a biotech stock), the higher the optimal weights assigned to that asset (all else equal). Still, the computations will show that it will still pay off to also invest in other assets.

Suppose you believe in the biotechnology industry; you are convinced that these innovative companies will eventually develop a cure for cancer, AIDS and other diseases, which will translate into big business. You could buy a few biotechnology company stocks and pray that you picked right. Or you could spread your investment over many biotechnology company stocks, thinking – quite reasonably – that the long-term winning stocks will mute the effects of the losing stocks. Further, you could include some highly uncorrelated sectors or asset classes, even if their expected return is much lower. If you invest in just a few stocks, no matter how much research you have done, then you are taking on a lot of unnecessary risk. You can diversify your portfolio without sacrificing your portfolio's expected returns, even if you think you can pick the winners and the moment to move in or out of the market.

International diversification is more complex than domestic diversification. For example, investing in foreign securities has two additional risks: foreign-exchange risk and political risk. Recall from Chapter 6 that rates of return on international investments are influenced by movements in foreign exchange. Political risk, discussed in Chapter 2, refers to the possibility that a country will take over a publicly held firm. This sometimes occurs when a country is at war or in severe economic or political crisis. In addition, part of the perceived risk results from a simple lack of information. Investors are more comfortable investing in domestic firms with which they are familiar, namely firms from which they buy products, about which they read in their newspaper on a daily basis, and with which they can communicate in their own language. Also, crossborder security analysis is complicated by differences in accounting standards. Many other countries do not follow the same general accepted accounting procedures (GAAP) that firms in the USA do. There can be substantial differences regarding issues such as valuation, depreciation, reserves, consolidation and treatment of taxes.

On the other hand, several ongoing changes in the global capital markets have stimulated international investing. For example, the governments of several countries have been adopting more flexible exchange-rate regimes. One of the main reasons for restrictions on crossborder capital flows had been to mitigate the pressure that capital outflows would place on a fixed or pegged exchange rate. With exchange rates now generally more flexible, there is less need to control capital flows. Furthermore, privatisation of government-owned enterprises and/or the relaxing of restrictions on the percentage of foreign ownership in domestic firms in many countries are creating new opportunities for investors worldwide. For example, after the collapse of the USSR and Communism in 1989–91, there are now some 20 additional capitalist economies, each with corporate stock investment possibilities, where a decade ago there were none. In addition, nations that have never been communist, such as Mexico, are privatising governmental bureaucracies at an accelerating pace. Mexico has, for instance, already privatised its telephone system (TELMEX) and will soon privatise a portion of its petroleum industry (PEMEX). In addition to regulatory barriers, non-regulatory barriers to capital movement are diminishing as well. Perceived political risk is declining as governments worldwide are becoming more fiscally prudent and are responding to demands for more transparency in financial reporting. In the euro-area, investment funds (money market, bond and equity funds) and institutional investors (pension funds and insurance companies) have, to some extent, seized the opportunities opened by the disappearance of currency risk with the advent of the euro and, related to that, the disappearance of currency-matching restrictions (institutional investors were restricted to investing only a small fraction of their wealth in foreign currencies).[13]

In addition, advances in information technology are enhancing the ability of investors to make well-researched investment decisions in the international arena, and new investment vehicles are making these investment opportunities more readily accessible to more investors. An investor who wishes to invest internationally can use several instruments. A straightforward method is to purchase foreign securities directly in foreign capital markets. This approach, however, is not simple because it requires multiple accounts with different brokers in different currencies and consequently expensive transaction costs. Also, operating directly in foreign capital markets involves complications such as foreign currency transactions, foreign taxes and foreign regulations. In practice, this approach is available primarily to larger institutional investors. However, as discussed in Chapter 2, even small individual investors can take advantage of international diversification by means of foreign ordinaries and ADRs, crossborder investment funds and WEBS and by using derivative securities that are written on foreign-market indices or foreign currencies.

The lifting of regulatory and non-regulatory investment restrictions makes benefits of international diversification feasible for many investors. Indeed, both institutional and individual investors worldwide are finding it increasingly attractive and convenient to engage in international portfolio diversification. Still, as discussed in Section 9.7, investors seem to suffer from a home bias, and they could achieve greater diversification benefits by investing more in international equity and debt.

---

[13] See, for instance, Galati and Tsatsaronis (2001) and Adam *et al.* (2002).

9.5 Estimation error

To repeat, the construction of efficient portfolios requires the means, variances and covariances of all assets considered. In Chapter 7, these parameters were as follows:

$$E(R_i) = \sum_{j=1}^{m} P_j R_{i,j} \qquad (7.4)$$

$$\sigma_i^2 = \sum_{j=1}^{m} P_j (R_{i,j} - E(R_i))^2 \qquad (7.5)$$

$$\sigma_{i,s} = \sum_{j=1}^{m} P_j (R_{i,j} - E(R_i))(R_{s,j} - E(R_s)) \qquad (7.6)$$

where P_j denotes the probability that the jth state of the world will occur. In practice, these parameters are not known, because we do not know the future return distribution. Rather, we typically have a sample of T historical returns (a time series data set). For example, we may have a sample of monthly returns during the period from January 1993 to December 2002, a total of 120 observations. Using the historical returns, we can obtain estimates for the unknown population means, variances and covariances. In general, the best way to estimate these population parameters depends on the historical evolution of the probability distribution of returns.

One possibility is to assume that the return distribution did not change during the sample period and that the returns in one period did not depend on the previous returns and that they did not affect subsequent returns. If these assumptions are satisfied (by approximation), then we may estimate the population mean, variance and covariance by their sample equivalents, the sample mean, sample variance and sample covariance (introduced in Chapter 6):

$$\bar{R}_i = \frac{1}{T} \times \sum_{t=1}^{T} R_{i,t} \qquad (6.15)$$

$$\sigma_i^2 = \frac{1}{T} \times \sum_{t=1}^{T} (R_{i,t} - \bar{R}_i)^2 \qquad (6.17)$$

$$\sigma_{i,s} = \frac{1}{T} \times \sum_{t=1}^{T} (R_{i,t} - \bar{R}_i)(R_{s,t} - \bar{R}_s) \qquad (6.18)$$

Comparing the formulas for the population statistics (Equations 7.4–7.6) with the formulas for the sample statistics (Equations 6.15, 6.17 and 6.18) reveals that the sample statistics are nothing but the population statistics if we use the historical observations as the possible future scenarios ($j = t$ and $m = T$) and we assign an equal weight of $P_t = 1/T$ to every scenario. Clearly, this approach makes sense if the return distribution did not change through time and if the returns did not depend on previous returns and did not affect subsequent returns. In that case, all observations contain an equal amount of unique information and all observations should be weighted equally.[14] Still, this approach involves three problems:

■ In practice, the return distribution does change and the returns in one period do depend on past returns and do affect future returns. For example, there are prolonged periods with persistently high volatilities and high correlations, known as volatility clusters. A volatility cluster may occur, for example, after a catastrophic event such as the 11 September 2001 terrorist attack. During a volatility cluster, it makes little sense to estimate variance and covariance parameters using an equal-weighted average of the historical scenarios, because we know that the actual variances and covariances are much higher than the historical averages. For this reason, more advanced time series estimation methods are needed, including so-called autoregressive integrated moving average (ARIMA) and generalised autoregressive conditional heteroskedasticity (GARCH) methods.[15] These methods are beyond the scope of this book, but the reader should be aware of their existence and the reasons for adopting them.

■ If the number of observations, T, is sufficiently large (and the correct estimation method is used), then the estimates are statistically good, i.e. it is very likely that the estimates are very close to the true population values. However, if the sample is small, then the estimates generally have a low quality. Note that even the most advanced estimation method simply extrapolates from the past and it will yield imperfect estimates. To add to the problem, increasing the sample size by including additional observations comes at the risk of adding observations that are not comparable, because the economies, industries and individual companies can change dramatically over time. In practice, it is fairly easy to arrive at good estimates for variances and correlations (provided we use the appropriate estimation method). By contrast, coming up with a good estimate for future expected returns has been almost impossible.[16]

■ The construction of efficient portfolios is very sensitive to estimation errors in the means, variances and covariances. Relatively small errors in inputs can produce large errors in the portfolio selected. In fact, the addition of a few observations may cause the optimal weights to change dramatically. One approach to quantifying the effect of estimation error is to construct confidence intervals for the optimal weights.

In other words, the problem with calculating the efficient frontier for future investments is not that the mathematics is too complicated; the problem has always been that users estimate the input parameters incorrectly. One ad hoc method for controlling for estimation risk is to assign all available assets and equal weight (see Section 9.3). Still, estimation error is not a valid argument for adopting this naïve approach. There is no simple remedy for estimation error. However, the point is that generally we can still do better than to completely ignore the

---

[14] Formally, the sample statistics (Equations 6.15, 6.17 and 6.18) are statistically consistent estimators for the population statistics (Equations 7.4–7.6) if the historical returns are distributed identically and independently.

[15] Harvey (1993) provides a useful introduction to time series models.

[16] Sharpe (1990) writes: 'While results vary from asset class to asset class and from time period to time period, experience suggests that for predicting future values (expected returns), historic data appear to be quite useful with respect to standard deviations, reasonably useful for correlations and virtually useless for expected returns.'

problem of estimation and use a simple equal-weighted portfolio. A more sensible approach is to collect data that are as reliable as possible, to use the most advanced estimation methods available and to account explicitly for the estimation error by constructing confidence intervals for the optimal weights. Sometimes, the confidence intervals will be so wide that the equal-weighted portfolio is included. However, in cases where the estimates are more reliable, we generally will be able to identify portfolios that are better diversified and that dominate the equal-weighted portfolio.

9.6   Human capital and property holdings

We have thus far assumed that investors diversify their portfolios of financial assets. Recall from Chapter 7 that investment is not an end to itself but rather a means to the end of funding future consumption. By portfolio diversification, an investor wishes to reduce risk so that his or her future consumption level becomes less uncertain. To reduce consumption risk, the investor should account for all of his or her sources of consumption, not just the financial assets.

The single most important asset that most people have is their human capital, developed through investments in education and experience. The fruits of those investments are a stream of future wages and salaries, or dividends and capital gains on privately held businesses. These cash flows typically are quite variable and may be highly correlated with stock and bond market returns. For example, for corporate executives and small-business owners, the value of their human capital tends to decline with stock prices during recessions. Unlike a portfolio of securities, diversifying human capital risk can be expensive. Establishing a speciality maximises the value of experience but also puts workers at risk if their skills lose value. For entrepreneurs, investing heavily in their own businesses may be the only alternative when outside financing is extremely costly or unavailable. Grants of shares and share options are valuable in helping to align an executive's incentives with those of other shareholders, but they put executives doubly at risk to the extent that their job security and investments are highly correlated.

Ideally, an investor will find a portfolio of securities that tends to pay a high return in states of the world in which his or her human capital is likely to decline, hence diversifying his or her human capital risk. For example, an entrepreneur specialising in support services to Internet start-ups may want to hold a portfolio that avoids shares of high-tech companies. This reduces the probability of a decline in portfolio value just when the demand for the entrepreneur's services falls. By contrast, a tenured university professor with an assured income stream will still be in a relatively secure financial position if he or she decides to invest in high-tech stocks.

A similar argument applies for property holdings. For many investors, a large part of their wealth is invested in their own property, and property forms a large component of their overall consumption. In many cases, property is funded in part or in whole by means of a mortgage loan. For this reason, most investors – even if they adopt a low-risk investment strategy – have a natural exposure to property prices and interest rates. Hence, most investors probably are well-advised to avoid financial assets that further increase their exposure to these risk factors. Perhaps this is why a typical investment portfolio includes less real-estate (for example, Real-Estate Investment Trusts; REITs) than would be expected based on the historically high risk–reward ratio of real estate and the low correlation of real estate with other asset classes (see, for instance, Webb and Rubens (1987) and Kullman (2001)).

9.7 Actual diversification by households and mutual funds

As discussed above, the potential benefits of diversification are large, and a little diversification goes a long way in capturing those benefits. Yet, the empirical evidence indicates that an individual's portfolios are not well diversified. Blume and Friend (1975) appear to have been the first to document that equity portfolios of most US households of the 1960s and early 1970s were highly concentrated (or grossly underdiversified).[17] Stock-market participation has increased since the 1970s, and mutual funds and pension plans have played an important role in this process by providing low-cost access to well-diversified portfolios for the average investor. Still, a large fraction of households keeps a non-negligible share of their total financial resources in undiversified portfolios of individual stocks and often hold such portfolios jointly with well-diversified funds.

For example, Goetzmann and Kumar (2002) examined the portfolios of more than 40 000 equity investment accounts from a large discount brokerage during a six-year period (1991–96). Using the historical performance for the equities in these accounts, they estimated the volatility and risk characteristics of their portfolios. They also found that a vast majority of investors in the sample were underdiversified. More than 25% of investor portfolios contained only one stock, more than 50% of them contained fewer than three stocks, and in any given month only 5–10% of the portfolios contained more than ten stocks. Consequently, investor portfolios had extremely high volatility (more than 75% of investor portfolios had higher volatility than the market portfolio), and they exhibited even worse risk–return trade-off than randomly constructed portfolios.

The degree of diversification also seems to depend on an investor's age, education, occupation and income.[18] The degree of diversification is higher for old investors than for young ones, as older people are supposed to be more mature and risk-averse. It is also found that the proportion of investors with undiversified portfolios is higher among people with low levels of education than among people with high levels of education. Further, investors in the professional category have a higher average diversification level than those in the non-professional category, while investors in the retired category have the highest average diversification level. It is also found that investors with higher incomes hold more diversified portfolios in comparison with those with low incomes.

Academics have forwarded several explanations for underdiversification by individual investors, but this phenomenon remains a puzzle, as the potential gains of diversification are large, the costs of diversification are falling, and mutual funds, index fund and ETFs offer low-cost diversification. Apart from information and transaction costs (discussed in Section 9.4), underdiversification may be explained by the fact that the retirement plans of many investors include large holdings of current or former employers' stock. For example, as reported in Investment in the News 9, Enron's fund administrators had allowed 60% of the 401(k) pension plan's assets to be held in Enron stock. At the time of writing, the pension plans of General Electric and Coca-Cola were even less diversified, with 75% and 78%, respectively, invested in own-company stock. Similarly, the personal portfolios of corporate executives are typically weighted heavily with company stock (in order to align the executives' incentives with those of other shareholders). Also, various psychological factors, such as overconfidence,

---

[17] Other studies on this subject include Cohn *et al.* (1975), Kelly (1995), Guiso *et al.* (1996), Bertaut (1998), Heaton and Lucas (2000), Perraudin and Sorensen (2000) and Goetzmann and Kumar (2002).

[18] See, for instance, Cook and Clotfelter (1991) and Goetzmann and Kumar (2001).

familiarity with certain stocks and gambling instinct, are believed to explain underdiversification. Many investors believe that a few carefully selected stocks, such as a few lottery tickets, provide a chance for becoming rich but that a well-diversified portfolio of stocks, such as a well-diversified portfolio of lottery tickets, gives only mediocre results. Also, investors may develop an illusory sense of control because they are involved directly in the investment process and they make their own choices instead of relying on others (as in the case of mutual funds) for their investment decisions. Familiarity with a certain set of stocks may exacerbate further the illusion of control, where investors may fail to realise that more information does not necessarily imply control over the returns earned by the portfolio. Chapter 12 discusses the psychology of investment ('behavioural finance') further.

In contrast to households, mutual funds typically hold hundreds of different securities. Why do these funds hold so many securities if a much smaller number would do just as well? Two reasons can be given. First, even though the benefit from including more assets in the portfolio diminishes, it is still positive and there is some gain. An individual investor who faces relatively large information and transaction costs cannot study and buy thousands of firms. For a large fund, however, the cost of data and information collection and transaction costs per dollar invested are so small that it is still worthwhile to increase the number of assets in the portfolio and enjoy the little ensuing benefit from risk reduction. Second, large funds, with billions of dollars in assets, cannot concentrate on only a few securities, because the fund's buying and selling would greatly affect the price of those securities. For example, buying 200 000 shares of a stock that typically has a daily trading volume of only 5000 shares would exert upward price pressure on the stock. To avoid this, mutual funds must diversify in many stocks.[19]

→ **Connecting Theory to Practice 9.4**

Investors get a lesson in home economics

European investors should radically reduce their holdings of domestic equities if they are to maximise returns while minimising risk, according to a report to be released today.

Under recommendations, put forward by the Centre for European Economic Research, a German-based think-tank, German investors should take the most radical action of all: selling all their domestic equities.

UK investors should reserve only 10 per cent of their portfolio for domestic equities, while French investors should weight theirs 70:30 in favour of Paris-listed companies. Only US investors cannot do any better than buy domestic equities.

The scale of the ideal investment outside domestic markets will surprise even seasoned investors familiar with the theory that diversification improves returns.

So too will the scale of the missed opportunity caused by 'home bias'. If the new advice had been followed over the past 20 years, German investors would have seen their returns rise by 82 per cent and UK investors by 54 per cent.

French investors would have made only a small improvement: some 0.7 per cent. This is why French investors would not need to make such a radical shift in their portfolios. French investors did better because France has a broader balance of companies, with large capitalisation businesses in oil, pharmaceuticals and TMT.

---

[19] Mutual funds are required by Regulation M of the Internal Revenue Service not to own more than 5% of any company's stock. Clearly, this requirement influences billion-dollar funds such as Fidelity Magellan.

Michael Schroder, author of the report, produced these figures by comparing the returns of different equity and bond portfolios to a risk-free interest rate and expressing the result as a so-called Sharpe ratio. Under this, the higher number represents better performance. For German investors with domestic equities, the ratio is 0.085, whereas for German investors with a global portfolio, it is 0.136.

The report says 'home bias' is caused by an 'information asymmetry': where investors know more about local companies than they do about foreign ones.

The Benefits of Diversification and Integration for International Equity and Bond Portfolios, by Michael Schroder of the Centre for European Economic Research in Mannheim, Germany.

Source: James Mawson, 'Investors Get A Lesson In Home Economics', *Financial Times*, 25 February 2002.

→ Making the connection

This article reports on a study that found that European investors should invest a larger fraction of their portfolios in foreign securities so as to receive the full benefits of international diversification. As discussed in Section 9.2, many studies yield similar results; foreign stocks and bonds are correlated relatively weakly with domestic securities and, hence, investors can improve the risk–return characteristics of their portfolios by investing in overseas markets. This is true for US investors and even more so for investors in smaller countries. Still, despite the potential gains of international diversification and the lifting of regulatory and non-regulatory investment restrictions (see Section 9.4), most investors still invest largely in domestic stocks.[20] For example, the US equity market currently represents about 60% of the world equity market. However, International Monetary Fund (IMF) statistics show the proportion of the US equity market owned by foreigners is only about 7%. This phenomenon is commonly referred to as the home-bias puzzle.[21] The contrast between the apparent benefits of international diversification and the actual portfolios that many investors hold raises the question of whether there are negative aspects of international investment that offset these benefits.

Summary

Explain how an investor can find uncorrelated assets.

Uncorrelated assets can be found by diversifying across asset classes, sectors and regions. However, market risk or the risk that comes from the broad capital market as a whole cannot be diversified away.

Discuss the effectiveness of international portfolio diversification.

Since international markets are not correlated perfectly with each other or with the US market, investors can achieve reductions in risk beyond those achieved by investing in US securities alone. Recently, high domestic returns for US investors, higher correlations between developed markets and higher correlations during market crises seem to have weakened

---

[20] See, for instance, French and Poterba (1991), Lewis (1996) and Baxter and Jermann (1997).
[21] Even at home there often is a home bias in the sense that local investors tend to invest mostly in companies that are located close by; see, for example, Coval and Moskowitz (1999).

the case for international diversification. However, international diversification is still useful, especially if combined with diversification across industries and asset classes and if international small caps and emerging markets are taken into consideration. This is true for US investors and even more so for investors in small countries.

Explain how many assets are needed to achieve the benefits of portfolio diversification.

A little diversification goes a long way; about 90% of the potential risk reduction from diversification is achieved with a portfolio of 12–18 securities. However, in practice, households generally hold far fewer securities in their portfolios, while institutional investors hold far more securities.

Discuss possible barriers to portfolio diversification.

Many barriers to diversification have disappeared with evolution of mutual funds, index funds and ETFs and, recently, with the availability of low-cost online trading. International investors face several additional regulatory and non-regulatory barriers. However, many of these barriers have been swept away by deregulation and privatisation abroad and by the availability of international investment vehicles, such as foreign ordinaries and ADRs, crossborder investment funds, WEBS and derivatives on foreign-market indices and foreign currencies.

Discuss the effect of estimation risk on portfolio diversification.

The construction of efficient portfolios is very sensitive to the estimates for the means, variances and covariances of the assets, and the investor can account for estimation error by constructing confidence intervals for the optimal weights. In the extreme case in which the investor cannot distinguish between the various assets and all assets are seen as equally risky, the investor should hold an equal-weighted portfolio.

Discuss the actual portfolio diversification by households and mutual funds.

Individuals' portfolios are not well-diversified. This underdiversification may be explained in part or in whole by the fact that the retirement plans frequently include large holdings of current or former employers' stock and by psychological factors, such as overconfidence, familiarity with certain stocks and gambling instinct. By contrast, mutual funds appear overdiversified, because they enjoy economies of scale in transaction and information costs. Also, they cannot concentrate on only a few securities, because of liquidity effects and regulatory restrictions.

Key terms

Asset-specific risk 264	Human capital 279	Non-systematic risk 264
Diversifiable risk 264	Information costs 273	Property holdings 279
Diversification 260	Market risk 264	Systematic risk 264
Estimation risk 278	Mutual funds 273	Transaction costs 271
Home bias 282	Non-diversifiable risk 264	Volatility clusters 278

Review questions

1 a. What is the basic argument for international diversification?
   b. Discuss recent developments in international diversification possibilities.
   c. Discuss possible diversification strategies.

2   Explain how the number of stocks in a portfolio affects the portfolio's risk.

3   What are the two additional risks of international diversification compared to the risks associated with domestic diversification?

4   'Diversification across different mutual funds does not lower risk, because mutual funds are already diversified.' Evaluate this statement.

5   You hear a discussion between an individual investor (with $100 000 to invest) and a money manager (with $10 million to invest). The individual investor claims that investing in five to seven securities is sufficient diversification, whereas the money manager claims that it takes at least one hundred securities to diversify effectively. How do you reconcile these two viewpoints?

For an extensive set of review and practice questions and answers, visit the Levy–Post investment website at www.booksites.net/levy

Selected references

Adam, K., T. Jappelli, A. Menichini, M. Padula and M. Pagano, 2002, *Study to Analyze, Compare and Apply Alternative Indicators and Monitoring Methodologies to Measure the Evolution of Capital Market Integration in the European Union*, Brussels: Commission of the European Communities, Internal Market Directorate General.

Baca S. P., B. L. Garbe and R. A. Weiss, 2000, 'The Rise of Sector Effects in Major Equity Markets', *Financial Analysts Journal*, **56** (5), 34–40.

Baxter, M. and U. J. Jermann, 1997, 'The International Diversification Puzzle is Worse than You Think', *American Economic Review*, **87**, 170–180.

Beckers S., G. Connor and R. Curds, 1996, 'National versus Global Influences on Equity Returns', *Financial Analysts Journal*, **52** (2), 31–39.

Bergstrom, G. L., 1975, 'A New Route to Higher Returns and Lower Risks', *Journal of Portfolio Management*, **2**, 30–38.

Bertaut, C. C., 1998, 'Stockholding Behavior of US Households: Evidence from 1983–1989 Survey of Consumer Finances', *Review of Economics and Statistics*, **80**, 263–275.

Black, F. and R. Litterman, 1992, 'Global Portfolio Optimization', *Financial Analysts Journal*, **48** (5), 28–43.

Blume, M. E. and I. Friend, 1975, 'The Asset Structure of Individual Portfolios and some Implications for Utility Functions', *Journal of Finance*, **30**, 585–603.

Brooks R. and L. Cato, 2000, 'The New Economy and Global Stock Returns', IMF Working Paper 216.

Campbell, J. Y., M. Lettau, B. G. Malkiel and Y. Xu, 2001, 'Have Individual Stocks Become More Volatile? An Empirical Exploration of Idiosyncratic Risk', *Journal of Finance*, **56**, 1–43.

Cavaglia S., C. Brightman and M. Aked, 2000, 'The Increasing Importance of Industry Factors', *Financial Analysts Journal*, **56** (5), 41–54.

Chunhachinda, P., K. Dandapani, S. Hamid and A. J. Prakash, 1997, 'Portfolio Selection and Skewness: Evidence from International Stock Markets', *Journal of Banking and Finance*, **21**, 143–67.

Cohn, R. A., W. G. Lewellen, R. C. Lease, and G. G. Schlarbaum, 1975, 'Individual Investor Risk Aversion and Investment Portfolio Composition', *Journal of Finance*, 30, 605–620.

Cook, C. and P. Clotfelter, 1991, *Selling Hope*, Boston, MA: Harvard University Press.

Coval, J. D. and T. J. Moskowitz, 1999, 'Home Bias at Home: Local Equity Preference in Domestic Portfolios', *Journal of Finance*, 54 (6), 2045–2073.

Erb, C., C. Harvey and T. Viskantas, 1994, 'Forecasting International Correlation', *Financial Analysts Journal*, 50 (6), 32–45.

Eun, C. S. and B. G. Resnick, 1994, 'International Diversification of Investment Portfolios: US and Japanese Perspective', *Management Science*, 40, 140–161.

French, K. R. and J. M. Poterba, 1991, 'Investors Diversification and International Equity Markets', *American Economic Review*, 81 (2), 222–226.

Galati, G. and K. Tsatsaronis, 2001, 'The Impact of the Euro on Europe's Financial Markets', Working Paper 100, BIS Monetary and Economic Department, Bank for International Settlements Information, Press and Library Services, Basel.

Goetzmann, W. N. and A. Kumar, 2001, 'Equity Portfolio Diversification', Working Paper 8686, NBER Working Paper Series, National Bureau of Economic Research, Cambridge, MA.

Goetzmann, W. N. and A. Kumar, 2002, 'Equity Portfolio Diversification', Working Paper, Yale International Center for Finance, National Bureau of Economic Research, Cambridge, MA.

Griffin, J. M. and A. G. Karolyi, 1998, 'Another Look at the Role of the Industrial Structure of Markets for International Diversification Strategies', *Journal of Financial Economics*, 50, 351–373.

Grubel, G. H., 1968, 'Internationally Diversified Portfolios: Welfare Gains and Capital Flows', *American Economic Review*, 58, 1299–1314.

Guiso, L., T. Japelli and D. Terlizze, 1996, 'Income Risk, Borrowing Constraints and Portfolio Choice', *American Economic Review*, 86, 158–172.

Hanna, M. E., J. P. McCormack and G. Perdue, 1999, 'A Nineties Perspective on International Diversification', *Financial Services Review*, 8, 37–45.

Harvey, A. C., 1993, *Time Series Models*, Hemel Hempstead, Harvester Wheatsheaf.

Hatch, B. and B. G. Resnick, 1993, 'A Review of Recent Developments in International Portfolio Selection', *Open Economies Review*, 4, 83–96.

Heaton, J. and D. Lucas, 2000, 'Portfolio Choice and Asset Prices: The Importance of Entrepreneurial Risk', *Journal of Finance*, 55, 1163–1198.

Heston S. and K. G. Rouwenhorst, 1994, 'Does Industrial Structure Explain the Benefits of International Diversification?', *Journal of Financial Economics*, 36, 3–27.

Huberman, G., 2001, 'Familiarity Breeds Investment', *Review of Financial Studies*, 14, 659–680.

Isakov, D. and F. Sonney, 2003, 'Are Practitioners Right? On the Relative Importance of Industrial Factors in International Stock Returns', Working Paper, HEC-University of Geneva no 2003.04 and FAME Research Paper no 69, HEC-University of Geneva/International Centre of Fame, Geneva.

Jorion, P., 1985, 'International Portfolio Diversification with Estimation Risk', *Journal of Business*, 58, 259–278.

Kelly, M., 1995, 'All their Eggs in One Basket: Portfolio Diversification of US households', *Journal of Economic Behavior and Organization*, 27, 87–96.

Kroll, Y., H. Levy and A. Rapoport, 1988, 'Experimental Tests of the Separation Theorem and the Capital Asset Pricing Model', *American Economic Review*, 78, 500–519.

Kullmann, C., 2001, 'Real Estate and its Role in Asset Pricing', Working Paper, New York: Columbia University.

Lessard, D. R., 1976, 'World, Country and Industry Factors in Equity Returns: Implications for Risk Reductions through International Diversification', *Financial Analysts Journal*, **32**, 32–38.

Levy, H. and M. Sarnat, 1970, 'International Diversification of Investment Portfolios', *American Economic Review*, **60** (4), 668–675.

Levy, H. and Z. Lerman, 1988, 'The Benefits of International Diversification in Bonds', *Financial Analysts Journal*, **44** (5), 56–64.

Lewis, K. K., 1996, 'What Can Explain the Apparent Lack of International Consumption Risk Sharing?', *Journal of Political Economy*, **104** (2), 267–297.

Longin, F. and B. Solnik, 1995, 'Is the Correlation in International Equity Returns Constant: 1960–1990?', *Journal of International Money and Finance*, **14**, 3–26.

Longin, F. and B. Solnik, 1998, 'Correlation Structure of International Equity Markets During Extremely Volatile Periods', *Les Cahiers de Recherche 646*. Jouy-en-Josas cedex: Groupe HEC, HEC Business School.

Michaud, R. O., G. L. Bergstrom, R. D. Frashure and B. K. Wolahan, 1996, 'Twenty Years of International Equity Investing: Still a Route to Higher Returns and Lower Risks?', *Journal of Portfolio Management*, **23**, 9–22.

Perraudin, W. R. M. and B. E. Sorensen, 2000, 'The Demand for Risky Assets: Sample Selection and Household Portfolios', *Journal of Econometrics*, **97**, 117–144.

Roll, R., 1992, 'Industrial Structure and the Comparative Behavior of International Stock Market Indices', *The Journal of Finance*, **47**(1), 3–41.

Rouwenhorst, K. G., 1999, 'European Equity Markets and the EMU', *Financial Analysts Journal*, **55** (3), 57–64.

Sharpe, W. F., 1990, 'Asset Allocation', in J. L. Maginn and D. L. Tuttle, editors, *Managing Investment Portfolios*, 2nd edn, Boston, MA: Warren Gorham and Lamont.

Shawky, H. A., R. Kuenzel and A. D. Mikhail, 1997, 'International Portfolio Diversification: A Synthesis and an Update', *Journal of International Financial Markets, Institutions and Money*, **7**, 303–27.

Solnik, B. H., 1973, *European Capital Markets: Towards a General Theory of International Investment*, Lexington, MA: Lexington Books, D.C. Heath and Company.

Solnik, B. H., 1974, 'Why Not Diversify Internationally Rather Than Domestically?', *Financial Analysts Journal*, **30** (4), 48–54.

Solnik, B. H., 1991, *International Investments*, 2nd edn, Reading, MA: Addison-Wesley.

Solnik, B. H., 2000, 'Dispersion as Cross-Sectorial Correlation', *Financial Analysts Journal*, January–February, **56** (1), 54–61.

Solnik, B. H., C. Boucrelle and Y. Le Fur, 1996, 'International Market Correlation and Volatility', *Financial Analysts Journal*, **52** (5), 17–34.

Solnik, B. H. and B. Noetzlin, 1982, 'Optimal International Asset Allocation: Lessons from the Past', *Journal of Portfolio Management*, **9**, 11–21.

Statman, M., 1987, 'How Many Stocks Make a Diversified Portfolio?', *Journal of Financial and Quantitative Analysis*, **22**, 353–363.

Statman, M., 2002, 'How Much Diversification is Enough?', Working Paper, Santa Clara University, Santa Clara, CA.

Sumit, P. C., 1998, 'Taking Care of Correlation', *Risk*, **1** (4), S2–S9.

Webb, J. R. and J. H. Rubens, 1987, 'How Much in Real Estate? A Surprising Answer', *Journal of Portfolio Management*, **13**, 10–14.

Part 3

CAPITAL MARKETS IN EQUILIBRIUM

CHAPTER 10

The capital asset-pricing model

Investment in the News 10

A model weighting game in estimating expected returns

Overstating the importance of expected returns in investments is difficult. For money managers, expected returns on assets are important inputs to portfolio decisions. For corporate managers, the expected return on their company's stock is central to the company's cost of capital and thereby affects which projects the company decides to undertake. Expected return estimates also affect consumers. Charges set by utility companies are set to ensure the utility earns a 'fair rate of return', defined by regulators as the utility's cost of capital. Our energy bills partly depend on how regulators estimate expected returns on utility stocks. Unfortunately, expected returns are elusive as well as important. Finance professionals differ on how they should be estimated. This article compares the relative merits of common approaches to this challenging task and argues that the best estimates are produced by combining theory with historical returns data and judgment.

Looking to history

'I know of no way of judging the future but by the past,' said American revolutionary Patrick Henry. One simple estimator of an asset's expected return is a sample average of its historical returns. Unless we suspect that expected return changes in a non-trivial way over time, the sample average return is an unbiased estimator of expected future return – that is, it is not systematically higher or lower than the true expected value. The unbiased nature of this method is its main advantage. However, getting things right on average is not the only objective. You might have overheard a joke about three econometricians who went hunting and came across a deer. The first one fired a shot and missed by 10 metres to the left. The second one missed by 10 metres to the right. Instead of firing, the third one shouted in triumph: 'We got it!' The main disadvantage of the sample average is its imprecision. Suppose we want to estimate expected return on the stock of General Motors, traded on the New York Stock Exchange. Using monthly returns from January 1991 to December 2000, the sample average return on GM is 14 per cent a year. The standard error, the usual statistical measure of imprecision, is huge: 10 per cent a year. With 95 per cent confidence, the true expected return is within two standard errors of the sample average, or between –6 per cent and 34 per cent a year. We want to be more confident than that!

Investment in the News 10 continued

Would the precision increase if we used weekly instead of monthly data? No. Although higher-frequency data helps in estimating variances and covariances of returns, it does not help in estimating expected returns. Intuitively, what matters for expected return is the beginning and ending prices over a given period, not what happens in between. The only way to get a more precise average is to collect more data. For example, if we use GM returns back to December 1925, the historical average is 15.5 per cent and the 95 per cent confidence interval narrows to between 8.7 per cent and 22.3 per cent. However, the gap is still too wide. Moreover, GM today is very different from 70 years ago, so the estimate could be contaminated by old data. In general, as we add older data, we gain precision at the expense of introducing potential bias. Striking a balance is difficult and needs sound judgment. Despite its drawbacks, the long-run average return is a popular estimator for expected returns on aggregate market indices. Unfortunately, we have no theory for what the expected market return should be. Luckily, for individual stocks and most portfolios, we can rely on estimates produced by theoretical asset pricing models. Those estimates tend to be substantially more precise than sample averages.

Source: Lubos Pastor, 'A Model Weighting Game In Estimating Expected Returns', *Financial Times*, 21 May 2001.

Learning objectives

After studying this chapter, you should be able to:

1 Understand the capital market line (CML), which contains only efficient portfolios.

2 Explain the separation property.

3 Understand why the security market line (SML) describes the capital asset-pricing model (CAPM) equilibrium relationship between risk and expected rate of return.

4 Explain the two-pass regression method for testing the CAPM.

5 Understand why it is extremely difficult to test whether the CAPM gives a good description of capital markets.

6 Understand how practitioners use the CAPM.

Chapter 8 discussed mean–variance analysis as a framework for structuring investment decisions. In that chapter, we considered the problem of investment given the expected rates of return, variances and covariances of the individual assets. However, we haven't said much about how expected rates of return are determined. Asset-pricing theories try to understand why certain capital assets have higher expected returns than others and why the expected returns are different at different points in time. For example, recall from Chapter 6 that stocks historically have produced much higher average returns than bonds and bills. How can we explain such differences?

Asset-pricing theories try to explain the equilibrium rates of return of assets. What do we mean by 'equilibrium rates of return'? First, expected rates of return are simply convenient ways to express the relative prices of assets. For example, in contrast to the actual stock prices, expected stock returns are not affected by the absolute level of prices and the number of stocks that the firm has outstanding. For example, when a stock splits two-for-one, the stock price typically falls by about 50% but the expected returns will stay the same. Like any good or service, the prices and expected returns of capital assets are determined by demand and supply. If many investors decide to sell a stock, then, all other things remaining equal, the price will fall (and the expected return will increase) in order to match demand and supply. The capital market is in equilibrium if all asset prices (or expected returns) are such that demand equals supply for all capital assets. Put differently, market equilibrium prevails if all investors hold their optimal portfolio and hence there is no reason for further transactions. If some investors do not hold their optimal portfolio, for example because they adjust slowly to new economic circumstances, then they still want to buy or sell assets, hence changing the demand and supply of assets and the prices (and rates of return).

Asset-pricing theories help one to understand the most important forces behind capital markets. In addition, the theories are used widely for practical applications of portfolio selection, performance evaluation, risk management and capital budgeting. In Investment in the News 10, Lubos Pastor, an assistant professor of finance at the Chicago Graduate School of Business, explains that theoretical asset-pricing models can be used for estimating expected stock returns. The resulting estimates tend to be substantially more precise than simple sample averages of historical returns.

There are many different asset-pricing theories, each based on a different set of assumptions. This chapter focuses on the capital asset-pricing model (CAPM), which is the most basic asset-pricing theory. The model was developed independently by Sharpe (1964), Lintner (1965a,b) and Mossin (1966). The CAPM is based on very simplified assumptions. Basically, the theory asks the following question: what are the equilibrium rates of return if all investors apply the mean–variance criterion to an identical mean–variance-efficient set? There is an ongoing debate on whether this theory gives an accurate description of equilibrium rates of return and whether alternative theories are more appropriate. Nevertheless, the CAPM is used widely in practice. In addition, many alternative asset-pricing models (including the general capital asset-pricing model (GCAPM), the intertemporal capital asset pricing model (ICAPM) and the consumption-based capital asset-pricing model (CCAPM) discussed later in this chapter) can be seen as generalisations of the CAPM. Hence, the CAPM forms a natural starting point for studying asset-pricing theory.

Our discussion of the CAPM will use the terminology and notation of mean–variance analysis that was introduced in Chapter 8. Further, we use two additional concepts: the risk-free asset and the market portfolio of risky assets.

In contrast to the discussion thus far, the CAPM adds a risk-free asset to the investment universe. Investors can borrow and lend at a risk-free interest rate, where 'risk-free' means that the return is known with certainty (with probability 1). It is common among practitioners to use the rate of return on short-term Treasury bills as a proxy for the risk-free interest rate. Here we will denote the risk-free rate by r. When investors lend money, they effectively hold a long position in the risk-free asset and they receive a rate of return of r on the investment. Similarly, when they borrow money, they effectively short the riskless asset, and they pay r. Since r is obtained (or paid) with certainty, the asset's expected return is $E(r) = r$. In addition, the variance of the risk-free asset, as well as the covariance with other assets, is zero.[1]

---

[1] The variance of the riskless asset is $\sigma_r^2 = E(rr) - E(r)E(r) = r^2 - r^2 = 0$. Similarly, the covariance of the riskless asset with the ith asset is $\sigma_{r,i} = E(rR_i) - E(r)E(R_i) = rE(R_i) - rE(R_i) = 0$.

The market portfolio is a portfolio that includes all available risky capital assets and that weights the assets by their relative market value (the market value of the asset divided by the total market value of all assets). The market portfolio has three important properties:

- The market portfolio includes all risky capital assets in the world. It includes not only stocks and bonds but also non-financial assets such as real-estate holdings, commodities and human capital (the present value of future labour income). Of course, in practice, we do not have full information on the returns and the market value of all assets in the world, and we need a proxy for the market portfolio. Frequently, the proxy is a stock index such as the S&P 500 index. We stress that such proxies are narrow-market portfolios, because they exclude, for example, small caps, preferred stocks, bonds, housing, commodities, non-financial assets and non-US assets.
- Since assets cannot have a negative market value, all assets enter with a positive weight in the market portfolio. Hence, in order to replicate the market portfolio, an investor does not need to short-sell any asset.
- Since every capital asset appears in the portfolio of some investor, the market portfolio can also be seen as the sum of the investment portfolios of all investors. Specifically, the relative market capitalisation of an asset equals the proportion of that asset in the total portfolio of all assets. Of course, since all capital assets in the world are included in the market portfolio, the terms 'investment portfolio' and 'investor' should be interpreted in a general way. In fact, even a newborn baby who has never read a financial newspaper or watched business news on TV classifies as an investor with an investment portfolio of human capital.

The remainder of this chapter is structured as follows. Section 10.1 introduces the theory behind the CAPM. Section 10.2 examines the empirical research regarding the validity of the CAPM. Does the CAPM describe historical rates of return accurately? Is the theory testable at all? Section 10.3 discusses practical applications of the CAPM.

10.1 The theory

This section introduces the theory behind the CAPM. To guide in the analysis, we provide the three most important implications of the CAPM:

- In equilibrium, all investors, irrespective of their risk preferences, hold the market portfolio of risky assets. Still, different investors hold different combinations of the market portfolio and the riskless asset. This property is referred to as the separation principle.
- Since everybody holds the market portfolio, the risk of an individual asset is characterised by its covariance with respect to the market; the remaining risk is diversified away. A standardised measure of covariance with the market is known as market beta. Beta is the correct measure of risk for individual assets and portfolios alike, regardless of whether these portfolios are efficient. However, for efficient portfolios (combinations of the market portfolio and the riskless asset), the investor can use either beta or variance (or standard deviation) to size up risk without affecting the ranking of the portfolios by their risk.
- Since non-systematic risk is diversified away, investors need to be compensated for bearing systematic risk (as measured by market beta) but not for non-systematic risk. The security market line (SML) formalises this principle by linking the expected return of an asset to its market beta.

10.1.1 The assumptions behind the capital asset-pricing model

■ The capital market is characterised by perfect competition. There are a large number of investors, each with wealth that is small relative to the total market value of all capital assets. Hence, the portfolio choice of individual investors has no noticeable effect on the prices of the securities; investors take the price as given.

■ All investors choose their portfolio according to the mean–variance criterion, i.e. each investor selects the optimal portfolio from the mean–variance efficient that is optimal given his or her expectations about the means, variances and covariances of the assets and given his or her preferences (the personal mean–variance indifference curves). Notice that the mean–variance criterion ignores practical considerations such as transaction costs and taxes.

■ All investors have the same expectations regarding the future in terms of means, variances and covariances (homogeneous expectations). Hence, every investor faces the same mean–variance portfolio possibilities set and the same mean–variance-efficient set. This assumption requires that all investors have access to the same information. Also, it assumes that all investors have the same investment horizon, as the shape of the return distribution typically differs for different investment horizons.

■ Investors can borrow and lend at a risk-free interest rate. Again, the variance of the risk-free asset, as well as the covariance with other assets, is zero. As we will see below, this property greatly simplifies the shape of the mean–variance-efficient frontier with riskless borrowing and lending.

Under these assumptions, all investors face an identical efficient frontier. The only difference between investors is the amount of wealth they must invest and the personal trade-off they make between portfolio mean and portfolio variance (the shape of their mean–variance indifference curves).

10.1.2 The opportunity line

Recall from Chapter 8 that the mean–variance-efficient set of risky assets is generally a curve in the expected return–standard deviation space. The degree of curvature is determined by the variances and covariances of the individual assets. If riskless borrowing and lending is possible, then the efficient set becomes a straight line instead of a curve. All efficient portfolios are a mix of the riskless asset and a single portfolio of risky assets.

To see how the efficient set changes when the investor can borrow or lend at the risk-free rate, let us start by assuming that the investor has only one risky asset available, denoted by A, with an expected return of $E(R_A)$ and a standard deviation of σ_A. In addition to A, the investor can lend and borrow at the riskless rate r. The rate of return (R_p) on a mix of asset A and the risk-free asset is

$$R_p = w_r r + (1 - w_r)R_A \tag{10.1}$$

where w_r is the investment weight of the risk-free asset in the portfolio. The expected return is

$$E(R_p) = w_r r + (1 - w_r)E(R_A) \tag{10.2}$$

The variance of R_p is given by

$$\sigma_p^2 = w_r^2 \sigma_r^2 + (1 - w_r)^2 \sigma_A^2 + 2w_r(1 - w_r)\sigma_{r,A} = (1 - w_r)^2 \sigma_A^2$$

The second equation follows from the fact that the variance of the riskless asset (σ_r^2) and its covariance with asset A ($\sigma_{r,A}$) are zero. Taking the square root of both sides to obtain the standard deviation, we get

$$\sigma_p = (1 - w_r)\sigma_A \qquad (10.3)$$

Thus, by adding a positive amount of a risk-free asset to an asset, we lower the risk of that asset. The higher the proportion invested in the risk-free asset, the lower the portfolio risk. Unfortunately, when we lower the overall risk of a portfolio, we lower its expected return as well. Equations 10.2 and 10.3 can be used to show how the portfolio return is related to the portfolio risk. From Equation 10.3, we can solve for the proportion of wealth invested in the risky asset to obtain

$$w_r = 1 - \frac{\sigma_p}{\sigma_A} \qquad (10.3a)$$

Substituting for w_r in Equation 10.2 yields

$$E(R_p) = \left(1 - \frac{\sigma_p}{\sigma_A}\right)r + \left(\frac{\sigma_p}{\sigma_A}\right)E(R_A)$$

or

$$E(R_p) = r + \frac{[E(R_A) - r]}{\sigma_A}\sigma_p \qquad (10.4)$$

Thus, the portfolio expected return, $E(R_p)$, is related positively to its standard deviation, σ_p. Moreover, this association is linear, as is evident from Equation 10.4, which yields a straight line. This line is known as the opportunity line. The opportunity line describes all available portfolios created by mixing r with A (see Exhibit 10.1(a)). Adding the risk-free asset to asset A creates an indefinitely large number of portfolios all lying on the straight line ra, which is the opportunity line. Investors can move along this line by varying the proportion of the risk-free asset according to their preferences.

Exhibit 10.1(b) shows that the risk-free asset allows investors a range of possible portfolios with different risk and expected return characteristics that allow them to reach higher indifference curves. Without the risk-free asset, only asset A is available; with the risk-free asset, all portfolios lying on line ra are attainable. When risk-free borrowing and lending are added, this point is expanded to the straight line ra. The more adventurous investors borrow and invest heavily in the risky asset, A. The more timid investors lend a large proportion of their portfolio at the risk-free rate and invest only a small portion in the risky portfolio. Exhibit 10.1(b) illustrates these two types of investors, where the indifference curve I_t denotes the timid investor and I_a denotes the adventurous investor. Note that the indifference curves representing the investors' preferences do not change when the risk-free asset is added. However, as the feasible set changes, the tangency point changes too (see Exhibit 10.1(b)). With a risk-free asset, both investors are able to reach a higher indifference curve – the adventurous through borrowing, and the timid through lending. Thus, the availability of the risk-free asset increases the investor's utility. Investors can always refuse to borrow and lend, a case where they confine themselves to point A. However, unless the indifference curve is exactly tangent at point A, a higher utility can be achieved by borrowing or lending.

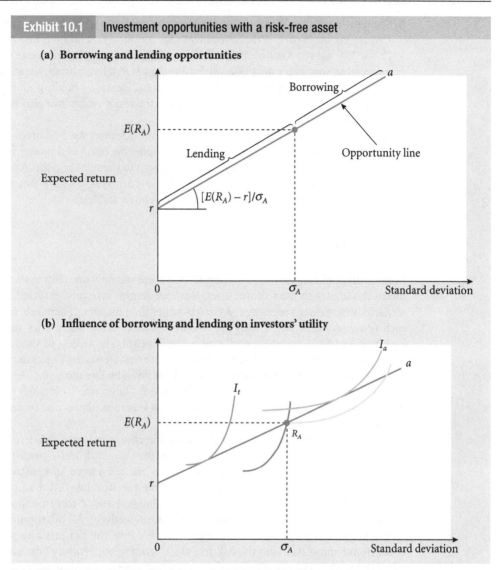

Exhibit 10.1 Investment opportunities with a risk-free asset

(a) Borrowing and lending opportunities

(b) Influence of borrowing and lending on investors' utility

Source: From *Introduction to Investments*, 2nd edn, by Levy. © 1999. Reprinted with permission of South-Western, a division of Thomson Learning: www.thomsonrights.com. Fax 800 730-2215.

The opportunity line has the following characteristics:

■ The intercept of the opportunity line is r. Thus, if an investor wants a portfolio with zero risk ($\sigma_p = 0$), then the return will be r. This result is achieved simply by investing 100% in risk-free assets ($w_r = 1$) so that risk is eliminated completely.

■ The slope of the opportunity line is $(E(R_A) - r)/\sigma_A$, where $E(R_A)$ and σ_A are the mean return and standard deviation of risky portfolio A, respectively. Clearly, the higher the expected portfolio rate of return or the lower the portfolio standard deviation, the steeper the slope. The slope is also known as the Sharpe ratio, and it is used widely as a portfolio performance measure (see Chapter 22).

■ If we choose a degree of risk to be equal to σ_A ($\sigma_p = \sigma_A$), then Equation 10.4 shows that we obtain an expected return of $E(R_P) = E(R_A)$. In this case, the portfolio has mean $E(R_A)$ and risk σ_A, as given by point A in Exhibit 10.1.

- The portfolios that lie on the segment rA are constructed by lending (investing in risk-free assets) some part of the investment (i.e. $0 < w_r < 1$), and investing the remainder or $(1 - w_r)$ in asset A. Assuming that $E(R_A) > r$ (because investors are averse to risk), then the mean return on such a portfolio will be less than $E(R_A)$. In addition, the standard deviation $(1 - w_r)\sigma_A$ (see Equation 10.3) will be less than σ_A. Hence, by holding some positive investment weight in the risk-free asset, we reduce the mean return but also reduce the risk of the portfolio.
- An investor can construct a portfolio from the segment Aa by borrowing (i.e. $w_r < 0$, $(1 - w_r) > 1$)) and investing their own money plus the borrowed money in the risky portfolio. This is a strategy of leveraging. The segment to the right of point A in Exhibit 10.1(a) represents these levered portfolios, which are portfolios that are financed partially by borrowing and have relatively high expected returns and high risk.

10.1.3 The capital market line

In the analysis of Exhibit 10.1, we assumed that there was only one risky asset and the investors mixed this asset with the risk-free asset. Now, we analyse investors' choices in a more realistic scenario, where there are many risky assets rather than just one. Therefore, investors can mix each of the available assets with the risk-free asset, creating many lines such as that given by Equation 10.4. Nevertheless, all risk-averse investors, regardless of their preferences, will choose the same risky portfolio and mix it with the risk-free asset. The chosen portfolio is the one that maximises the slopes of the straight lines given by Equation 10.4. As we shall see later in this chapter, this choice is important because it allows one to identify the risk measure of each asset (the beta) and, given the asset's risk measure, allows one to derive equilibrium rates of return.

Exhibit 10.2 represents the investor's available choices when a risk-free asset and many risky assets are available. Segment LZ represents the efficient frontier consisting of only risky assets.[2] We assume that all possible risky assets are considered in constructing curve LZ. The dots located to the right of curve ALZ and the two dots labelled A and Z (which are on the line ALZ) represent individual risky assets. Points A and Z correspond to the individual assets with the lowest and highest mean returns, respectively. All other points on the curves represent portfolios. As shown in Exhibit 10.1, the investor can mix any portfolio or asset taken from Exhibit 10.2 with the risk-free asset, creating opportunity lines such as lines 1 and 2 in Exhibit 10.2. The question is, of course, which opportunity line puts the investor on the highest indifference curve?

In Exhibit 10.2, line ra has the highest slope. By choosing this line, the investor can reach the highest possible indifference curve (for example, indifference curve I_2 rather than I_1). The portfolios that fall along line ra, which is tangent to the curve LZ, are achieved by mixing portfolio m with the risk-free asset. Portfolio m, which maximises the slope of the opportunity line, is called the tangency portfolio, or the optimal portfolio of marketable risky assets. The tangency portfolio provides all investors, regardless of their preferences, the highest utility they can achieve when risk-free borrowing and lending are available. Note that the tangency portfolio is a portfolio and not an individual asset, and by mixing it with the risk-free asset we end up holding a portfolio of risky assets and the risk-free asset.

---

[2] Curve LZ represents the set of all points between L and Z on the mean–variance frontier. The segment AL represents the inefficient part of the frontier.

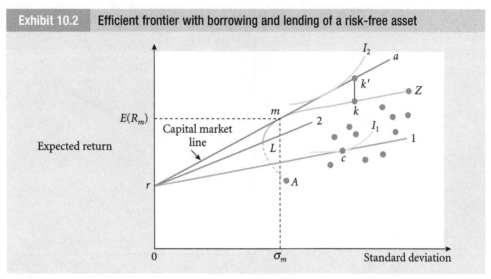

Exhibit 10.2 Efficient frontier with borrowing and lending of a risk-free asset

Source: From *Introduction to Investments*, 2nd edn, by Levy. © 1999. Reprinted with permission of South-Western, a division of Thomson Learning: www.thomsonrights.com. Fax 800 730-2215.

The straight line *ra* is composed of all possible combinations of the tangency portfolio (point *m* in Exhibit 10.2) and the risk-free asset (*r*). We can employ Equation 10.4 for portfolio *m* to obtain the formula for this line:

$$E(R_p) = r + \frac{[E(R_m) - r]}{\sigma_m} \sigma_p \qquad (10.5)$$

This line is called the capital market line (CML). In the absence of borrowing and lending, the mean–variance efficient frontier is given by the curve *LZ* (see Exhibit 10.2). By adding the possibility of borrowing and lending, the efficient frontier now becomes the straight line *ra*, or the CML. The CML clearly dominates the set of risky assets *LZ* because, for any portfolio on curve *LZ*, there is a better portfolio on line *ra* (except for portfolio *m*, which lies on both *LZ* and *ra*). For example, portfolio *k′* on line *ra* is superior to portfolio *k* on curve *LZ*, because it has the same risk but a higher mean return. Thus, by allowing borrowing and lending at *r*, the efficient frontier is expanded or improved. Also, note that no portfolio taken from line *ra* dominates another portfolio taken from this line. Thus, line *ra* includes all efficient portfolios. All portfolios on the CML are efficient by the mean–variance criterion (MVC), and all other portfolios (and individual assets) are inefficient.

To summarise, the straight line obtained by mixing the tangency portfolio (*m*) with borrowing and lending of the risk-free asset is called the CML. Any such mix of *m* and *r* creates a portfolio that includes all the risky assets composing the tangency portfolio. Because all the portfolios lying on line *ra* are efficient, the linear risk–return relationship given by Equation 10.5 is appropriate only for efficient portfolios consisting of various combinations of *r* and *m*.

10.1.4 The portfolio separation principle

The CAPM assumes that all investors face the same riskless rate and the same efficient set of risky assets. Hence, all investors face the same CML. As discussed above, the CML yields an opportunity line steeper than any other possible lines attained by mixing the risk-free asset with other risky portfolios; by mixing the tangency portfolio and the riskless asset, investors can

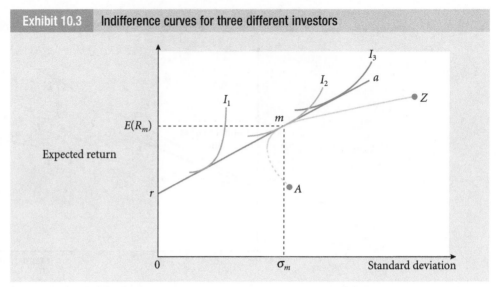

Source: From *Introduction to Investments*, 2nd edn, by Levy. © 1999. Reprinted with permission of South-Western, a division of Thomson Learning: www.thomsonrights.com. Fax 800 730-2215.

achieve the highest possible expected return for a given risk level. Consequently, all investors, regardless of their preferences, will choose a portfolio from the CML or mix the tangency portfolio (m) with the risk-free asset (r).

Exhibit 10.3 illustrates the indifference curves of three possible investors. Investor 1, a lender, puts some proportion of his or her money in the riskless asset and some in the risky tangency portfolio. Investor 3 borrows money and invests all of his or her own wealth, plus the amount borrowed, in portfolio m. Investor 2 follows the old adage, 'Neither a borrower nor a lender be.' All three investors have one common strategy: they invest in the same portfolio m of risky assets.

Since all investors hold the tangency portfolio, this portfolio must equal the market portfolio; after all, the market portfolio is simply a mix of the portfolios of all individual investors.

The possibility of borrowing and lending at interest rate r allows a separation of the investment process into two stages:

1. At stage 1, we find portfolio m, which is located at the point where the CML and the efficient frontier of risky assets are tangent. Since all investors hold the same portfolio, this portfolio corresponds to the market portfolio. Hence, we can also locate portfolio m by weighting all assets by their relative market value. Notice that this stage is objective and common to all investors; there is no need to know each investor's unique preference (i.e. the indifference curves) in order to find portfolio m.

2. At stage 2, all investors maximise their utility by mixing the market portfolio determined in stage 1 and the risk-free asset to adjust the portfolio's risk and return characteristics according to their preferences. An investor who wishes to achieve a higher expected return than the market portfolio (by taking more risk than the market portfolio) can do so by borrowing money and investing the borrowed amount plus his or her own wealth in portfolio m. Similarly, an investor who wishes to achieve a lower risk than the market portfolio (by accepting a lower expected return than the market portfolio) can do so by lending part of his or her wealth and by investing the remainder in portfolio m. This stage is subjective, and each investor's preference needs to be known; it is determined by indifference curves that vary from one investor to another.

This separation of the investment decision into two stages is called the separation principle. This principle follows directly from the assumptions listed in Section 10.1.1. Specifically, all investors face the same mean–variance-efficient frontier. This frontier takes the form of a straight line from the riskless asset through the tangency portfolio (the CML) and it includes only a single portfolio of risky assets (the tangency portfolio). Since all investors select a portfolio from this frontier, every investor holds the risky assets in the same proportion (the weights of the tangency portfolio). Hence, the market portfolio, which is the weighted average of the individual portfolios, also has the same composition as the tangency portfolio.

10.1.5 Market risk and non-market risk

Recall from Chapter 7 that an asset's risk is determined by its contribution to the risk of the entire portfolio. In turn, this contribution is determined by the variance of the asset and the covariances with the other assets in the portfolio. In Chapter 7, the optimal portfolio was not known; in fact, we had to consider the entire variance–covariance matrix in order to delineate the mean–variance-efficient set from which each investor chooses his or her optimal portfolio (depending on his or her personal risk–return trade-off). By contrast, under the assumptions of the CAPM, the optimal portfolio of risky assets is known; the separation principle implies that all investors will hold the market portfolio. It follows naturally that the relevant risk measure for individual assets is the contribution to the risk of the market portfolio or the covariance between the return of the asset and the market return.

The variance of the market portfolio is given by (see Chapter 7)

$$\sigma_m^2 = \sum_{i=1}^{n} \sum_{s=1}^{n} w_i^* w_s^* \sigma_{i,s}$$

where w_i^* denotes the weight of the ith asset in the market portfolio or its relative market value, and $\sigma_{i,s} = E(R_i R_s) - E(R_i)E(R_s)$ denotes the covariance between the ith and the sth asset. The contribution of the ith individual asset to the variance of the market portfolio is determined by the covariance between the return of the asset and the market return:[3]

$$\sigma_{i,m} = E(R_i R_m) - E(R_i)E(R_m)$$

Since the market portfolio is a mix of all risky assets, i.e. $R_m = \sum_{s=1}^{n} w_s^* R_s$, the covariance $\sigma_{i,m}$ effectively captures the covariances with all assets. Specifically, $\sigma_{i,m} = \sum_{s=1}^{n} w_s^* \sigma_{i,s}$.[4] In the general mean–variance framework, we had to consider all individual covariances $\sigma_{i,s}$ separately. By contrast, in the CAPM, the weights of the optimal portfolio (the market portfolio) are known, and we weigh the individual covariances accordingly to arrive at the covariance with the market portfolio.

---

[3] Using differential calculus, we can show that the first-order derivative of the variance of the market portfolio with respect to the weight of the ith asset is $\dfrac{\partial \sigma_m^2}{\partial w_i} = 2 \sum_{s=1}^{n} w_s \sigma_{i,s} = 2\sigma_{m,s}$. Hence, the covariance with the market measures the sensitivity of the variance of the market portfolio to small changes in the portfolio weights.

[4] Specifically, this follows from the following chain of equalities:

$$\sigma_{i,m} = E(R_i R_m) - E(R_i)E(R_m) = E\left(R_i \sum_{s=1}^{n} w_s^* R_s \right) - E(R_i)E\left(\sum_{s=1}^{n} w_s^* R_s \right) = \sum_{s=1}^{n} w_s^* E(R_i R_s) - E(R_i)E(R_s) = \sum_{s=1}^{n} w_s^* \sigma_{i,s}.$$

For an investor who holds the market portfolio, the covariance with the market portfolio ($\sigma_{i,m}$) is the relevant risk measure, because the remaining risk is diversified away. Related to this, investors need to be compensated for bearing systematic risk but not for non-systematic risk. We will return to this issue later. First, we introduce a standardised version of the covariance with the market.

In practice, the covariance with the market is typically standardised by dividing it by the variance of the market portfolio:

$$\beta_i = \frac{\sigma_{i,m}}{\sigma_m^2} = \frac{E(R_i R_m) - E(R_i)E(R_m)}{E(R_m^2) - E(R_m)^2} \tag{10.6}$$

This measure is known as the market beta. Beta measures the (systematic) risk of an asset relative to that of the market portfolio. What is the beta of the market portfolio? Recall from Chapter 7 that the covariance of an asset with itself is simply its variance. Thus, the beta of the market portfolio (from Equation 10.6) is one, because

$$\beta_m = \frac{\sigma_{i,m}}{\sigma_m^2} = \frac{\sigma_m^2}{\sigma_m^2} = 1$$

Thus, if $\beta_i > 1$, then the asset has more (systematic) risk than the market. Such assets are commonly referred to as aggressive assets. Technology stocks, for example, tend to have high betas; many technology funds have betas of 2.0 or more. Similarly, defensive assets have less (systematic) risk than the market ($\beta_i < 1$) and neutral assets have a market beta of 1.

Apart from a measure of relative riskiness, the market also measures the sensitivity of an asset to market movements. Note that β_i is simply the slope of the regression line given by[5]

$$R_i - r = \alpha_i + \beta_i[R_m - r] + e_i \tag{10.7}$$

where α_i is the intercept of the regression line or the asset's 'alpha' and e_i is the deviation from the line, called the error term. This error term is a random variable with mean $E(e_i) = 0$ and variance $\sigma_{e_i}^2$.[6] The regression line describing the relationship between R_i and R_m is called the characteristic line.[7] The regression line uses returns in excess of the riskless rate, or excess returns. This does not affect the definition of beta. However, it does affect the definition of alpha. The reason for using excess returns will become clear later; the alphas can then be interpreted as 'pricing errors'.[8]

Thus, beta measures the sensitivity of the ith stock or the portfolio rate of return to changes in the market portfolio rate of return. The larger the beta, the higher the sensitivity to the market and the riskier the asset to investors who hold the market portfolio. For example, if

---

[5] See Appendix A at the end of this book for an introduction to regression analysis.

[6] Section 10.1.6 will show that alpha (α) has an economic meaning; it measures the return in excess of the risk-adjusted return, as implied by the CAPM, and therefore is called the abnormal return.

[7] The characteristic line measures the expected excess return on the ith asset for a given R_m. Thus, for any R_m, a point on the line is given by $R_i = \alpha_i + \beta_i R_m$. If R_m is, say, 10% and $\beta = 2$ and $\alpha = 5\%$, we have $R_i = 5\% + 2 \times 10\% = 25\%$. However, if R_m changed from 10% to 14%, then the expected excess return on the stock would be $R_i = 5\% + 2 \times 14\% = 33\%$, and the change in the expected excess return would be 8%, as a beta of 2 would predict.

[8] By taking expectations of both sides of the characteristic line (Equation 10.7) and using $E(e_i) = 0$, we find $E(R_i) - r = \alpha_i + [E(R_m) - r]\beta_i$ or $\alpha_i = E(R_i) - r - [E(R_m) - r]\beta_i$. By contrast, if we use $R_i = \alpha_i' + \beta_i R_m + e_i$ for the characteristic line, then we find $\alpha_i' = E(R_i) - E(R_m)\beta_i$. The two alphas are related in the following manner: $\alpha_i' = \alpha_i - (1 - \beta_i)r$.

Exhibit 10.4   Examples of the characteristic line

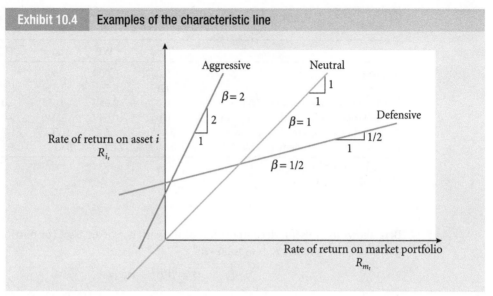

$\beta_i = 2$ (an aggressive asset) and the market rate of return increases by 1%, then this asset's rate of return is expected to go up by 2% on average. However, when the market rate of return falls by 1%, the asset's rate of return is expected to fall by 2%. This asset fluctuates twice as much as the market portfolio. Similarly, if $\beta_i = 0.5$ (a defensive asset), then the asset fluctuates half as much as the market and is considered to be relatively safe. A defensive asset 'defends' the investor from large losses but also denies the investor a high expected return. Finally, a neutral asset ($\beta_i = 1$) moves exactly with the market on average.

Exhibit 10.4 describes characteristic lines corresponding to aggressive, defensive and neutral assets. The stocks of computer firms, such as Apple Computer and Microsoft, are considered to be aggressive stocks. When the market goes up by x%, they usually go up by more than x%; when the market falls by x%, they are usually down by more than x%. The stocks of utilities, such as Florida Gas and Florida Power and Light, are considered to be defensive. When the market is up by x%, the demand for gas or electricity increases, but by less than x%. When the market goes down by x%, the demand for gas and electricity goes down less sharply than the overall demand for other products; hence, the stocks of these firms decrease by less than x%.

Interestingly, the beta of a portfolio is a simple weighted average of the individual betas; if $R_p = \sum_{s=1}^{n} w_s R_s$, then[9]

$$\beta_p = \sum_{s=1}^{n} w_s \beta_i$$

---

[9] This follows from the following chain of equalities:

$$\beta_p = \sigma_{p,m}/\sigma_m^2 = [E(R_p R_m) - E(R_p)E(R_m)]/\sigma_m^2 = \left[E\left(\sum_{s=1}^{n} w_s R_s R_m\right) - E\left(\sum_{s=1}^{n} w_s R_s\right)E(R_m)\right]/\sigma_m^2$$

$$= \left[\sum_{s=1}^{n} w_s[E(R_i R_m) - E(R_i)E(R_m)]\right]/\sigma_m^2 = \sum_{s=1}^{n} w_s \sigma_{i,m}/\sigma_m^2 = \sum_{s=1}^{n} w_s \beta_i.$$

Exhibit 10.5	Breakdown of monthly variances (market standard deviation = 0.047)				
	Dow	CWE	Exxon	GE	IBM
Alpha	0.002	0.004	0.007	0.001	−0.001
Beta	1.17	0.55	0.73	1.12	0.80
Standard deviation of stock (σ_i)	0.076	0.055	0.053	0.067	0.059
Standard deviation of the error term (σ_{e_i})	0.052	0.049	0.040	0.041	0.045.
Proportion of systematic risk (%)	52.4[a]	22.1	41.9	61.7	40.6
Proportion of unsystematic risk (%)	47.6[b]	77.9	58.1	38.3	59.4

[a] $[(1.17^2 \times 0.047^2)/0.076^2]100 \cong 52.4\%$.
[b] $(0.052^2/0.076^2)100 \cong 47.6\%$.

Beta allows for a useful decomposition of the variance of an asset (or portfolio of assets). In particular, the variance R_i is as follows:[10]

$$\sigma_i^2 = \beta_i^2 \sigma_m^2 + \sigma_{e_i}^2 \qquad (10.8)$$

Thus, the variance σ_i^2 can be broken down into two terms. The first term, $\beta_i^2 \sigma_m^2$, is the firm's systematic risk component, or market risk, which represents the part of the asset's variance that is attributable to overall market volatility. The second term, $\sigma_{e_i}^2$, is the firm's unsystematic risk component, or non-market risk, which represents the part of the asset's variance that is not attributable to overall market volatility. The unsystematic risk component is related to the firm's specific volatility. If all price movements of the asset are related to the movements of the market, then the error term e_i is always zero and $\sigma_{e_i}^2 = 0$. The greater the number of important firm-specific factors, the larger is $\sigma_{e_i}^2$, which measures the dispersion of the points around the regression line.

If we divide both sides of Equation 10.8 by σ_i^2, we get the following:

$$1 = \frac{\beta_i^2 \sigma_m^2}{\sigma_i^2} + \frac{\sigma_{e_i}^2}{\sigma_i^2}$$

where the first term is the proportion of the total risk of a security that is systematic and the second term is the proportion that is unsystematic.

Exhibit 10.5 illustrates the variance broken down into systematic and non-systematic risk for five securities using monthly data over a 20-year period. Notice that the beta coefficient is 1.17 for Dow and 0.55 for CWE. The exhibit also reports the proportions of systematic and unsystematic risk (where, of course, the sum of these two components is one). Firms such as CWE that specialise in power production (which is highly regulated) have a low proportion of systematic risk. Alternatively, GE, which is a diversified conglomerate, is very sensitive to market conditions and thus has a high proportion of systematic risk.

In Exhibit 10.5, the standard deviation of GE is 0.067, while that of CWE is 0.055. Hence, GE is riskier in terms of total risk (σ). However, the standard deviation of the error term for GE (0.041) is lower than that for CWE (0.049). Thus, the proportion of the total risk that can be diversified away is higher for CWE than it is for GE.

---

[10] This expression follows from the variances and covariances of the terms in the right-hand side of Equation 10.7. Since α_i and β_i are constant, their variances and covariances are zero. Also, in regression analysis, the regressor (R_{m_t}) is independent of the error term (e_{i_t}). Hence, $\sigma_i^2 = \mathrm{Var}[\alpha_i + \beta_i R_{m_t} + e_{i_t}] = \beta_i^2 \sigma_m^2 + \sigma_{e_i}^2$.

10.1.6 The security market line

As discussed above, under the assumptions of the CAPM, all investors hold the market portfolio. In addition, for investors who hold the market portfolio, the relevant risk of an individual asset is the market risk, as measured by market beta (which is a standardised version of the covariance with the market). The remaining non-market risk is not relevant, because it is diversified away. Related to this, investors need to be compensated for bearing systematic risk (but not for non-systematic risk) in the form of a risk premium above the riskless rate. More specifically, under the assumptions of the CAPM, the following linear risk–return relationship should hold:

$$E(R_i) \quad = \quad r \quad + \quad [E(R_m) - r]\beta_i \qquad (10.9)$$

Expected rate of return $\qquad$ Risk-free rate $\qquad$ Risk premium

This linear relationship is called the security market line (SML).[11] The SML asserts that the expected rate of return on asset i is equal to the risk-free rate plus a risk premium, namely the expected return the investor requires above and beyond what can be earned on the risk-free asset, or $(E(R_i) - r)$. This risk premium is equal to the market risk premium, or $[E(R_m) - r]$, multiplied by the asset's beta.[12] Since $[E(R_m) - r] > 0$ (investors are assumed to be risk-averse and hence require a positive risk premium), we conclude that the higher β_i is, the greater the risk and thus the higher the required risk premium. Recall that β_i reflects only market risk; only the systematic part of the firm's variance is relevant in determining the required risk premium and hence the expected rates of return. By contrast, the CAPM does not account for the component $\sigma_{e_i}^2$, which can be eliminated by holding the market portfolio.

We stress that the SML follows directly from the fact that the market portfolio is positioned on the efficient frontier. In order for the market portfolio to be mean–variance-efficient, the individual assets should lie on the SML. Similarly, if at least one asset lies above or below the SML, then the market is inefficient. Put differently, the SML gives a necessary and sufficient condition for mean–variance efficiency of the market portfolio. Appendix 10 gives a formal proof of the SML that follows directly from this observation. We have already discussed the economic intuition behind the proof; in equilibrium, all investors hold the market portfolio, and hence investors require a risk premium for the market risk (as measured by beta) of individual assets but no premium for non-market risk (which is diversified away).

Note that the SML can also be stated in terms of the characteristic line (Equation 10.7). Specifically, taking the expectations of both sides of that equation and using $E(e_i) = 0$, we obtain

$$E(R_i) - r = \alpha_i + \beta_i[E(R_m) - r]$$

Next, we substitute Equation (10.9) for $E(R_i)$ to find

$$[E(R_m) - r]\beta_i = \alpha_i + \beta_i[E(R_m) - r]$$

or

$$\alpha_i = E(R_i) - r - [E(R_m) - r]\beta_i$$

---

[11] Appendix 10 contains a formal proof of the SML.

[12] The market risk premium is the expected excess return on the market portfolio, or $[E(R_m) - r]$. This premium is sometimes referred to as the **beta premium** or the **equity premium**.

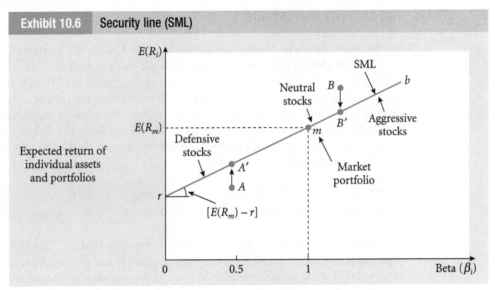

Exhibit 10.6 Security line (SML)

Source: From *Introduction to Investments*, 2nd edn, by Levy. © 1999. Reprinted with permission of South-Western, a division of Thomson Learning: www.thomsonrights.com. Fax 800 730-2215.

To summarise, alpha measures the difference between an asset's expected return $E(R_i)$ and the equilibrium rate of return given the asset's beta or $r + [E(R_m) - r]\beta_i$. Hence, the alpha measures the abnormal return or pricing error above and beyond the rate of return expected by the CAPM (or the normal return). The SML implies that all alphas should equal zero:

$$\alpha_i = 0 \qquad\qquad (10.9a)$$

If $\alpha'_i > 0$, then the asset lies above the SML and it has a positive pricing error. In other words, the asset is underpriced; the expected return is too high and the price should rise. By contrast, if $\alpha'_i < 0$, then the asset lies below the SML and it is overpriced.

Exhibit 10.6 demonstrates the SML. Note first that if $\beta_i = 0$, then we obtain $E(R_i) = r$. Thus, as expected, the return of an asset with no systematic risk equals the riskless rate r. Second, if $\beta_i = 1$, then $E(R_i) = E(R_m)$. In this case, the asset's price fluctuates, on average, in tandem with the market. Therefore, the asset has the same market risk as the market and hence yields, on average, the same rate of return as the market portfolio, $E(R_m)$. When $\beta_i > 1$, the asset is aggressive, i.e. it has more systematic risk than the market portfolio. Therefore, in equilibrium, the aggressive asset will be characterised by a higher expected return than the market $[E(R_i) > E(R_m)]$. If the asset is defensive ($\beta_i < 1$), then the expected return will be smaller than $E(R_m)$. Note that Exhibit 10.6 does not show the expected return for assets with a negative beta. Such assets are very uncommon; most assets have a positive correlation with the market. Nevertheless, we can obtain a negative beta by short-selling assets and by using derivative securities (for example, by selling futures contracts). The SML implies that assets with a negative beta have an expected return that is lower than r because $[E(R_m) - r] > 0$, and it may even be negative. Does this result make sense? Of course, it doesn't make sense to hold a risky portfolio with a negative beta if that portfolio yields a lower expected return than the riskless rate. However, it does make sense to include assets with a negative beta in a portfolio, because such assets stabilise the whole portfolio's return (i.e. they reduce the portfolio's risk) and hence investors will accept a relatively low return on these assets. Hence, the SML also applies when beta is negative.

The SML represents equilibrium, i.e. the situation where all investors hold their optimal portfolio and hence there is no reason to further demand or supply assets. If some assets deviate from the SML, then the market is in disequilibrium. For example, in Exhibit 10.6, asset A lies below the SML, i.e. its expected return is too low relative to its beta, while the expected return of asset B is too high. The vertical distance of the assets from the SML measures the alpha or the pricing error, i.e. the difference between the actual expected rate of return and the equilibrium rate. In this case, investors can improve the risk–return characteristics of their portfolio by selling asset A (which has negative alpha and is overpriced) and buying asset B (which has a positive alpha and is underpriced). By selling asset A, investors will lower the price and raise the expected return of asset A; by buying asset B, they will raise the price and lower the expected return of asset B. The selling and buying will continue until further transactions do not improve the risk–return characteristics of the investors' portfolios. In this case, all assets lie on the SML, the alphas are zero and the capital market is in equilibrium.

10.1.7 The link between the security market line and the capital market line

The SML, which is the relationship between mean and beta, applies to all individual assets as well as all portfolios, regardless of whether they are efficient. By contrast, the CML, which is the relationship between mean and standard deviation, applies only for efficient portfolios. The CML does not apply to individual assets or to portfolios that are inefficient, because investors do not require a compensation for non-systematic risk. To understand this, it is useful to rewrite Equation 10.8 as

$$\beta_i = \sqrt{(\sigma_i^2 - \sigma_{e_i}^2)/\sigma_m^2}$$

Substituting this equation in the SML (Equation 10.9) gives

$$E(R_i) = r + [E(R_m) - r] \times \sqrt{(\sigma_i^2 - \sigma_{e_i}^2)/\sigma_m^2}$$

Efficient portfolios have no non-systematic risk, i.e. $\sigma_{e_i}^2 = 0$, and hence the above expression reduces to the CML:

$$E(R_i) = r + \frac{E(R_m) - r}{\sigma_m} \times \sigma_i$$

To summarise, an efficient portfolio includes only systematic risk, i.e. $\sigma_{e_i}^2 = 0$ and $\sigma_p^2 = \beta_p^2 \sigma_m^2$. Hence, we can measure risk as beta (SML) or as variance or standard deviation (CML). However, for inefficient portfolios ($\sigma_{e_i}^2 > 0$), this is not true and only the SML applies.

Exhibit 10.7 shows the CML. Notice that the slope of the CML is $[E(R_m) - r]/\sigma_m$, whereas the slope of the SML is $E(R_m) - r$. If we invest in an efficient portfolio whose standard deviation is σ_m (the market portfolio), we receive, by employing the CML, an expected return of $E(R_m)$. This is consistent with the SML, because for the market portfolio we have $\beta_m = 1$ and the expected return of $E(R_m)$. Also, because all portfolios and the CML are simply a mix of m and the risk-free asset, by increasing the proportion invested in portfolio m, one also increases β.[13]

To continue our earlier example in Exhibit 10.6, Exhibit 10.7 also includes asset A and asset B. Note that, in equilibrium, both assets (A′ and B′) lie below the CML. Apparently, both assets

---

[13] For a mix of the riskless asset and the market portfolio, $R_p = w_r r + (1 - w_r)R_m$, where w_r is the investment proportion in the risk-free asset. In this case $\sigma_p = (1 - w_r)\sigma_{R_m}$ and $\beta_p = (1 - w_r)\beta_m = (1 - w_r) \times 1$. Thus, as w_r decreases, both σ_p and β_p increase at the same rate.

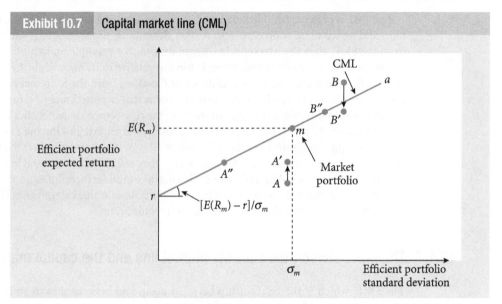

Exhibit 10.7 Capital market line (CML)

are inefficient. The horizontal distances of the assets from the CML (A′A″ and B′B″) measure the non-systematic risk of these assets (i.e. $\sigma_{e_A}^2$ and $\sigma_{e_B}^2$). We stress that such deviations from the CML do not imply that the market is in disequilibrium. It means merely that the assets are inefficient and the investor should not hold them in isolation. Nevertheless, all investors should hold the assets in their portfolio with a weight that is equal to their relative market value. To check whether the market is in equilibrium, we have to see whether all assets lie on the SML rather than the CML. Of course, in equilibrium, assets cannot lie above the CML. For example, in Exhibit 10.7, asset B lies above the CML. This means that investors can improve the risk–return characteristics of their portfolio by buying asset B. By buying asset B, investors will increase the price and lower the expected return of asset B. In equilibrium, asset B′ lies on the SML and below the CML.

10.1.8 Estimating the characteristic line with historical data

Recall from Section 10.1.5 that beta is the slope of the characteristic line

$$R_i - r = \alpha_i + \beta_i[R_m - r] + e_i$$

where α_i is the intercept of the regression line and e_t is a firm-specific factor with mean $E(e_i) = 0$ and variance $\sigma_{e_i}^2$. In practice, the coefficients α_i and β_i are not known, because we do not know the future return distribution. Rather, we typically have a sample of T historical returns (a time series data set) on the individual assets. For example, for each asset, we may have a sample of monthly returns during the period from January 1993 to December 2002, a total of 120 observations. Throughout the text, we will denote the return on the ith asset in the tth period by $R_{i,t}$, the return on the market portfolio is denoted by $R_{m,t}$ and the return on the riskless asset by r_t. Such data allow for estimating the characteristic line with regression analysis, the statistical tool that is described in Appendix A at the end of this book. This tool is included in many statistical software packages and spreadsheet software and even in more advanced pocket calculators.

Roughly speaking, regression analysis estimates the characteristic line by finding the estimators that give the statistically best fit to the relationship between the $R_{i,t}$ and $R_{m,t}$. There exist several different regression methods, and the appropriate method depends on the statistical distribution of the observations. A common assumption is that the true (unknown) return distribution (the intercept α_i, the beta β_i and the non-market risk $\sigma_{e_i}^2$) does not change over time, so that the observations all obey the same characteristic line, i.e.

$$R_{i,t} - r_t = \alpha_i + \beta_i[R_{m,t} - r_t] + e_{i,t}$$

for all $t = 1, \ldots, T$. Another common assumption is that the different return observations are independent from each other. If these two assumptions hold (by approximation), then we can use the ordinary least squares (OLS) regression method described in Appendix A. This yields coefficient estimates for alpha and beta, denoted by $\hat{\alpha}_i$ and $\hat{\beta}_i$. These estimates give information about the shape of the line of best fit. However, the shape says nothing about how reliable the estimators are. To assess the accuracy of the estimates, we also have to consider the standard errors of the coefficients. In addition, the R-squared (a goodness measure that ranges from 0 to 1) gives the percentage of the total variance that is market risk; the remaining percentage is non-market risk. An asset that moves randomly against the market will still have a beta value assigned to it, but the power of it to predict the asset's return for a given return of the market will be strictly limited. This will be reflected in a high standard error for the beta estimate and a low (near zero) R-squared.

Appendix A gives more details on how to compute standard errors and R-squared. The appropriate statistics for estimating the characteristic line of the ith asset are obtained by substituting $(R_{i,t} - r_t)$ for y_i and $(R_{m,t} - r_t)$ for $x_{1,i}$. For example, the estimated beta is computed from

$$\hat{\beta}_i = \frac{\dfrac{1}{T} \times \sum_{t=1}^{T} (R_{i,t} - r_t)(R_{mt} - r_t) - (\bar{R}_i - \bar{r})(\bar{R}_m - r_t)}{\dfrac{1}{T} \times \sum_{t=1}^{T} (R_{m,t} - r_r)^2 - (\bar{R}_m - \bar{r})^2} \tag{10.10}$$

where $\bar{r}$ denotes the average riskless rate over the sample period. Similarly, the estimated alpha is computed as

$$\hat{\alpha}_i = \bar{R}_i - \bar{r} - \hat{\beta}_i[\bar{R}_m - \bar{r}] \tag{10.11}$$

Appendix A demonstrates the computations for Microsoft stock using monthly excess returns for the period from January 1991 to December 2000 (120 monthly observations). Exhibit 10.8 summarises the results. This shows a scatter diagram that plots the returns of Microsoft stock against the return on the CRSP all-share index, a value-weighted average of all common stocks listed on the NYSE, AMEX and NASDAQ. Also, Exhibit 10.8 includes the estimated regression line, or the line of best fit. The coefficient estimates, standard errors and R-squared are given in the lower right-hand corner. In this case, the estimated alpha is 1.248% (a positive abnormal return) and the estimated beta is 1.535 (an aggressive stock). Unfortunately, these estimates are highly inaccurate, as can be seen from the standard errors (the numbers within brackets), which are high (0.877 and 0.216, respectively). Appendix A shows that we can state with 95% confidence that Microsoft's true alpha ranges from $-/-0.506$ to 3.002 ($1.248 \pm 2 \times 0.877$), a very wide interval. Similarly, the 95% confidence interval for beta ranges from 1.103 to 1.967 ($1.535 \pm 2 \times 0.216$). As discussed in Appendix A, this degree of inaccuracy is typical for estimating the characteristic line for individual assets. The problem

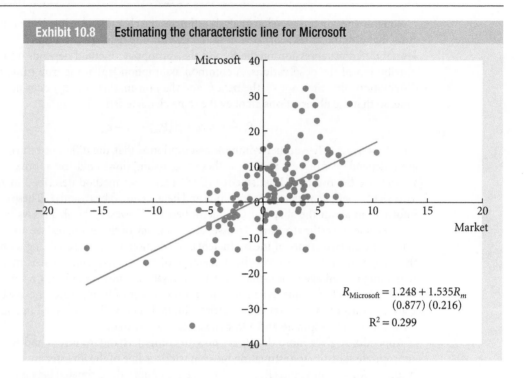

Exhibit 10.8 Estimating the characteristic line for Microsoft

$$R_{\text{Microsoft}} = 1.248 + 1.535R_m$$
$$(0.877) \ (0.216)$$
$$R^2 = 0.299$$

is that the return on individual assets is determined to a large extent by asset-specific factors, which makes it difficult to estimate the contribution of market risk. For example, the R-squared is 0.299 for Microsoft stocks, which means that only about 30% of the return volatility can be attributed to fluctuations of the market return; the remaining 70% is due to non-market factors. For portfolios, the problem generally is less severe, because asset-specific returns of individual assets cancel out in the context of a portfolio.

Exhibit 10.9 includes the alphas and betas for 30 industry portfolios for the 120-month period January 1993–December 2002.[14] This exhibit also includes the standard errors of the coefficients and the R-squared. The results are ranked by the size of the beta. The industry with the highest beta was business equipment; the lowest-beta industry was beer and liquor. Note the good performance of the alcohol and tobacco industries. During the 1990s, these industries showed the highest risk-adjusted returns as measured by alpha: 0.81 and 0.59, respectively

There is a caveat in estimating the characteristic line from historical data. Alphas and betas can change through time. For example, the beta of a firm's stock will increase if the firm starts investment projects that are more risky than the projects in place or if the firm issues new debt claims (which are senior to equity claims). This is true even for whole sectors. For example, the technology sector has changed beyond recognition in recent years: entirely new industries have emerged, and companies have come to the public markets at a much earlier (and riskier) stage in their evolution. For these reasons, it is frequently recommended for estimating characteristic lines not to use data beyond the most recent ten years. Also, as is explained in Connecting Theory to Practice 10.1, the best estimates are produced by combining theory with historical returns data and judgment.

---

[14] The market return, the industry definitions and industry returns used to compute the results are obtained from the homepage of Kenneth French (www.mba.tuck.dartmouth.edu/pages/faculty/ken.french/). The risk-free rate is obtained from Ibbotson.

Exhibit 10.9	Betas of different industries						
Portfolio	Mean	Standard deviation	α	se(α)	β	Se(β)	R^2 (%)
Beer and liquor	0.89	4.63	0.81	0.42	0.17	0.09	3
Utilities	0.20	4.56	0.08	0.40	0.27	0.09	7
Tobacco	0.75	7.96	0.59	0.72	0.36	0.16	4
Food products	0.55	4.81	0.36	0.40	0.44	0.09	17
Coal	0.50	7.97	0.27	0.70	0.53	0.15	9
Other	0.04	5.30	−0.20	0.43	0.55	0.09	23
Petroleum and gas	0.55	4.98	0.31	0.39	0.56	0.09	26
Healthcare	0.77	4.80	0.50	0.36	0.61	0.08	34
Mines	0.04	6.86	−0.25	0.57	0.66	0.12	19
Textiles	−0.42	5.99	−0.72	0.47	0.67	0.10	26
Business supplies	0.35	5.08	0.05	0.37	0.68	0.08	37
Publishing	0.71	4.26	0.40	0.26	0.70	0.06	55
Chemicals	0.35	4.89	0.04	0.34	0.70	0.07	42
Consumer goods	0.82	4.55	0.52	0.30	0.70	0.07	49
Restaurants and hotels	0.20	5.10	−0.11	0.36	0.72	0.08	41
Transport equipment	0.90	5.98	0.57	0.45	0.75	0.10	33
Wholesale	0.48	4.47	0.15	0.26	0.75	0.06	59
Apparel	−0.07	6.17	−0.40	0.47	0.76	0.10	31
Construction	0.36	4.82	0.02	0.30	0.78	0.07	54
Transportation	0.40	5.25	0.05	0.34	0.82	0.07	50
Financial sector	0.83	4.99	0.47	0.30	0.82	0.07	56
Retail	0.50	5.47	0.13	0.35	0.86	0.08	51
Automobiles	0.31	6.76	−0.10	0.48	0.93	0.11	40
Machinery	0.51	6.34	0.01	0.34	1.13	0.07	66
Recreation	0.26	6.84	−0.23	0.41	1.14	0.09	57
Steel works	0.24	6.88	−0.27	0.41	1.16	0.09	59
Communication	0.17	6.91	−0.36	0.39	1.21	0.08	63
Electrical equipment	0.68	8.32	0.08	0.50	1.38	0.11	57
Services	0.69	8.52	−0.01	0.40	1.62	0.09	75
Business equipment	1.00	9.45	0.24	0.48	1.73	0.11	70
Market portfolio	0.44	4.55	0.00	0.00	1.00	0.00	100

10.1.9 Theoretical extensions of the capital asset-pricing model

In Section 10.1.1, we summarised the most important assumptions of the CAPM. By relaxing these assumptions, we can obtain generalisations of the CAPM. Below, we summarise briefly four of the most important generalisations of the CAPM: the zero-beta model, the GCAPM, the ICAPM and the CCAPM. A detailed discussion of these models is beyond the scope of this book, and the interested reader is referred to the references listed at the end of this chapter.

The generalised models relax various assumptions regarding the possibility of borrowing at the riskless rate. They do not deal with the assumptions about short-selling. Note that Section 10.1.1 made no assumptions about short-selling. Nevertheless, the examples have implicitly assumed that short-selling is not allowed. Interestingly, short-selling constraints do not affect the CAPM. Recall that all investors in the CAPM hold the market portfolio and that the market portfolio weights the assets by their relative market value, which is always positive.

Hence, no investor would short-sell assets, even if they were allowed to do so. In other words, a short-selling constraint would not be binding.

Zero-beta model

The CAPM assumes that investors can borrow and lend at the risk-free interest rate. As discussed in Section 10.1.3, this assumption implies that the mean–variance-efficient set is a straight line in mean–standard deviation space. Related to this, all investors will hold the same portfolio of risky assets (the market portfolio). In reality, investors can indeed lend at the riskless rate by buying government bonds with a duration that equals the length of their investment horizon. However, investors generally cannot borrow at the riskless rate. For example, individuals generally pay a large premium over the risk-free interest rate for an unsecured bank loan (without collateral), so as to compensate the bank for accepting credit risk. Hence, investors generally can lend but not borrow at the riskless rate. The zero-beta model formulated by Black (1972) takes this observation as a starting point.

In the zero-beta model, the efficient set is no longer a straight line. Rather, it consists of two components: (1) a linear line segment from the riskless asset to the tangency portfolio and (2) a curve from the tangency portfolio. This means that different investors generally will not hold the same portfolio of risky assets (the market portfolio); the two-fund separation principle no longer applies. In fact, a three-fund separation principle now applies. All investors will hold a combination of the riskless asset, the tangency portfolio and the market portfolio. Nevertheless, all investors will hold an efficient portfolio; no investor will select a portfolio that is dominated in terms of mean and variance.

Interestingly, if all investors hold efficient portfolios, then the market portfolio, which is a weighted average of the individual portfolios, will also be efficient.[15] By analogy to the analysis in Appendix 10, the optimality conditions for portfolio optimisation imply that in equilibrium there exists a linear relationship between assets' expected rate of return and their market beta that is similar to the SML in Equation 10.9. However, contrary to the original CAPM, the intercept or the zero-beta rate can exceed the riskless rate r, and the slope or the beta risk premium may be smaller than the equity premium $[E(R_m) - r]$.

The general capital asset-pricing model

The CAPM ignores transaction costs. In general, the larger the number of shares bought, the lower the percentage paid in transaction costs. Investors and, in particular, small investors hold only a relatively small number of stocks in their portfolios; hence, they do not invest in the market portfolio. For the case in which there is only a limited number of stocks in the optimum portfolio, Levy (1978), Markowitz (1990), Merton (1987) and Sharpe (1991) suggest an alternative model that is similar to the CAPM but that allows investors to hold a relatively small number of assets in their portfolios. This model is called the general capital asset-pricing model (GCAPM); it is 'general' in the sense that once the transaction costs are eliminated from the model, the CAPM is obtained as a specific case of the GCAPM. Under this model, each investor holds a different portfolio; therefore, each portfolio has a different beta (which is measured against the portfolio held). The beta of the ith asset is obtained as a weighted average of all these betas, where the weights depend on the wealth invested in the asset by the different investors.[16]

---

[15] The mean–variance-efficient set is 'convex', i.e. if two (or more) portfolios are efficient, then a weighted average of those portfolios is also efficient.

[16] A problem in testing and implementing the GCAPM is the need for information on the portfolio composition and the wealth level of each investor.

The intertemporal capital asset-pricing model

The CAPM is a single-period model, i.e. it assumes that investors choose a portfolio at the beginning of the period, wait for time to pass and uncertainty to resolve, and liquidate the portfolio at the end of the period. In reality, the problem of many investors is better described by a multiperiod model, where the return distribution (means, variances and covariances) and hence the mean–variance-efficient frontier changes through time and investors revise their portfolios accordingly. Merton's (1973) intertemporal capital asset-pricing model (ICAPM) was developed to capture this multiperiod aspect of financial market equilibrium. Merton basically asked the following question: how should investors choose an initial portfolio so that it is optimal not just over one period but over the investor's entire investment horizon? In academic terms, how can one determine a portfolio that is dynamically optimal? The main insight of the ICAPM is that the portfolio chosen at the initial date must not only lie on the efficient frontier but also provide the best hedge against unfavourable changes in the set of future investment opportunities (such as decreasing interest rates and risk premiums or increasing variances and correlations).

For individual securities, the implication is that assets carry two types of premiums. The first risk premium compensates for exposure to period-by-period fluctuations in the value of the market portfolio; this is similar to the beta premium in the CAPM. The second premium compensates for exposure to deteriorations of the efficient frontier. If a particular security tends to have high returns when bad things happen to the investment opportunity set, then investors would want to hold this security as a hedge. This increased demand would result in a higher equilibrium price for the security (all other things remaining equal). One of the main insights of the ICAPM is the need to reflect this hedging demand in the asset-pricing equation.

The ICAPM generalises the CAPM, because the CAPM is obtained as a specific case of the ICAPM if investors behave as single-period investors and do not revise their portfolios when the frontier shifts or, alternatively, if the return distribution does not change through time and the efficient frontier does not shift.[17]

The consumption-based capital asset-pricing model

The CAPM assumes that the expected utility of investors can be formulated in terms of the mean and the variance of the return to their investment portfolio. In reality, generally investors derive satisfaction not directly from investment but rather from current and future consumption of goods and services (see Chapter 7). Of course, an investment portfolio is a possible source of financing future consumption, and hence investors derive utility indirectly from the return on their investment portfolios. However, for several reasons, we cannot simply equate portfolio return with consumption. For example, apart from investment portfolios, there are other sources of consumption, such as human capital and property. Also, consumers look beyond a single period. A loss in a single period, no matter how catastrophic, does not imply that consumption is immediately adjusted accordingly. For example, October 1987 was one of the worst months in recent history for shareholders. However, the overall effect of the crash on consumption was surprisingly small. By contrast, the prolonged bear markets of the early 1970s did have a significant effect on consumption, even though the

---

[17] The ICAPM can be difficult to test and implement because it requires detailed information on the way that the return distribution changes through time or the return dynamics. Unfortunately, economic theory does not put forward strong predictions on this topic.

returns in the individual months were not nearly as catastrophic as those in October 1987. For this reason, looking at stock returns may give a wrong impression of the consumption risks involved in investing. In the consumption-based capital asset-pricing model (CCAPM) of Breeden (1979), the equity premium is proportional to a single beta, which is the covariance with consumption growth per capita rather than the return to the market portfolio. In the CCAPM, an asset is more risky if it pays less when consumption is low. Risk-averse investors will choose assets with the highest expected value of returns weighted by the value placed by investors on additional funds. This model is based directly on the intuition that an extra dollar of consumption is worth more to a consumer when the level of aggregate consumption is low. When things are going really well and many people can afford a comfortable standard of living, another dollar of consumption does not make one feel very much better off. But when times are hard, a few extra dollars to spend on consumption goods is very welcome. Based on this diminishing marginal utility of consumption, securities that have high returns when aggregate consumption is low will be demanded by investors, bidding up their prices (and lowering their expected returns). In contrast, stocks that covary positively with aggregate consumption will require higher expected returns, since they provide high returns during states of the economy where high returns are valued least.

The standard CAPM is the special case of the CCAPM if per-capita consumption growth equals the return on the market portfolio.[18]

The three-moment capital asset-pricing model

The CAPM is based on the mean–variance framework, where the expected utility of investors increases with the expected return on the investment portfolio and decreases with the portfolio variance. Moments other than mean and variance, such as skewness, are assumed to be irrelevant for the investor. However, since financial assets show asymmetry and fat tails in the return distributions (see Chapter 8), preference over higher moments may become relevant. Other things being equal, decision-makers generally like positive skewness (the probability of large gains is higher than the probability of equivalent losses) and dislike negative skewness (the probability of large gains is smaller than the probability of equivalent losses). For example, lottery tickets are bought because of the positively skewed payoff pattern. Kraus and Litzenberger (1976) have extended the mean–variance-based CAPM into a three-moment or mean-variance-skewness capital asset-pricing model (3M CAPM). In this framework, a stock is selected based on its mean, covariance and co-skewness (contribution to the skewness of the market portfolio). As in the standard CAPM, the price of a stock depends on its contribution to the risk of the market portfolio, but now risk consists of both variance and skewness. In this framework, stocks with high negative co-skewness will be less attractive and hence will have higher expected returns. For example, small stocks tend to exhibit negative co-skewness, which makes them riskier than the covariance would suggest (Harvey and Siddique, 2000). This adjustment for risk, based on skewness, may help to explain the historically high returns of these stocks. The standard CAPM is a special case of the 3M CAPM if returns are distributed normally or if investors are indifferent with respect to skewness.

---

[18] Despite the intuitive appeal of the consumption-based model, empirical tests have not supported its predictions (see Breeden *et al.*, 1989). Accordingly, consumption-based asset pricing has not received as much attention in practice as the CAPM. One difficulty in using this model is problems in measuring the rate of growth in per-capita consumption. Consumption data generally are substantially less reliable than transaction data on financial assets. For example, statistics are reported on expenditures rather than consumption, which ignores the important effects of consumption from durable goods and storage of non-durables.

A model weighting game in estimating expected returns

Theory is good

Finance theory says riskier assets must offer higher expected returns and asset pricing models quantify this. The Capital Asset Pricing Model (CAPM) says a stock is riskier the more closely its price moves with prices in the market as a whole. The appropriate measure of risk is therefore the degree of a stock's co-movement with the market, which is summarised by a measure called beta (b). Expected return, E(r), on a given stock is linearly related to the stock's beta. Specifically, the expected stock return in excess of the risk-free rate rf ('expected excess return') can be expressed using: $E(r) - rf = b \times E(rm - rf)$. The constant of proportionality, E(rm − rf), is the expected excess return on the market as a whole. It is often called the equity premium. The value we choose for the risk-free rate rf depends on our objectives. To forecast expected stock returns over the next month, the appropriate risk-free rate is the yield to maturity on a Treasury bill that matures in one month. If we want to estimate a company's cost of capital to value the company's future cash flows, the risk-free rate should be derived from a longer-term Treasury bond. The bond's duration should be close to the duration of the company's cash flows. Very long-term bonds should be avoided, because their yields might also reflect premiums for risks such as inflation.

Does the above equation solve all our problems? Not quite. The elements on the right side, beta and the equity premium, need to be estimated. Beta is typically estimated by regressing monthly stock returns on market returns over the most recent five to 10 years. For example, the estimate of GM's beta using its monthly data from January 1996 to December 2000 is 1.11. How much data should we use to estimate beta? The trade-off is similar to that involved for sample averages: the further we go back in time, the higher the statistical precision of the estimate, but the bigger the possibility of introducing bias from old data. Unlike sample averages, however, here it often pays to use more frequent data. For example, whereas the 95 per cent confidence interval for GM's beta based on the monthly data is 0.65 to 1.57, this interval based on weekly data is tighter, 0.69 to 1.08. GM's beta estimated using weekly data is 0.88. However, going from monthly to weekly data is recommended only for the most liquid and volatile stocks. For other stocks, some week-to-week price changes are simply movements between the bid and ask prices around the true price, which introduces additional error. Also, it may take time for market-wide news to affect the prices of illiquid stocks, which biases the usual beta estimates downward. Conveniently, betas of illiquid stocks can be estimated using an alternative approach developed by economists Myron Scholes and Joseph Williams.

It is clear from the GM example that estimates of beta contain a fair amount of noise. A useful way of reducing that noise is to 'shrink' the usual estimates to a reasonable value, such as 1. This is reasonable because the average beta across all stocks is 1, by construction. The 'shrinkage' estimate of beta is the weighted average of the usual sample estimate and of the shrinkage target. For example, the 'adjusted' betas reported by Merrill Lynch put a 2/3 weight on the sample estimate and a 1/3 weight on the value of 1. The adjusted beta for GM is therefore: $(2/3) \times 0.88 + (1/3) \times 1 = 0.92$. Shrinkage betas can be justified as 'Bayesian' estimators, named after the 18th century English mathematician Thomas Bayes. They reflect not only data but also prior knowledge or judgment. Bayesian estimators have solid axiomatic foundations in statistics and decision theory, unlike many other estimators used by statisticians. Before seeing data on GM, we know it is a stock, so a good prior guess for GM's beta is 1. Also, we know more about the company; for example, we know which industry it operates in. Since the average beta among carmakers is about 1.2, a reasonable prior guess for GM's beta is 1.2. How much weight we put on the guess and how much on the estimate depends on the precision of the sample estimate and on the strength of our prior beliefs. Those beliefs can be based for example on the dispersion of betas among carmakers: the stronger the concentration around 1.2, the more weight we put on the prior guess. With equal weights on the prior guess and the weekly sample estimate, GM's industry-adjusted beta is: $(1/2) \times 0.88 + (1/2) \times 1.2 = 1.04$.

Unfortunately, the CAPM says nothing about expected market return and estimating the equity premium is more difficult than estimating betas. More frequent data does not help and there is no obvious prior guess. The most common approach is to average a long series of excess market returns, which leads to equity premium estimates of 5–9 per cent a year, depending on the sample period. A recent equity premium study by Robert Stambaugh and the author puts the current premium in the US at 4.8 per cent a year. This estimate comes from a model in which the premium changes over the past 165 years. Combining this estimate with GM's industry-adjusted beta and a 6 per cent risk-free rate, the CAPM estimates GM's annual expected return (its cost of equity capital) at 6 per cent plus $(1.04 \times 4.8$ per cent$)$, which comes out at 11 per cent.

Source: Lubos Pastor, 'A Model Weighting Game In Estimating Expected Returns', *Financial Times*, 21 May 2001.

10.2 Empirical tests of the capital asset-pricing model

The empirical validity of the CAPM can be tested in two ways:

- By checking whether the underlying assumptions of the model are realistic and fit actual investors' behaviour.
- By testing empirically the degree to which the CAPM explains the actual behaviour of security prices.

The CAPM rests on a number of very simplifying assumptions. Obviously, many of these assumptions (for example, no transaction costs, homogeneous expectations regarding the future, uniform investment horizons, etc.) are violated in the real world. However, one should not reject the CAPM solely on these grounds. Perhaps these deviations from reality are not crucial, so that the CAPM may still explain price behaviour. As Friedman (1953) has emphasised, the realism of a theory's assumptions can be judged only by the degree to which the theory provides valid and meaningful explanations and predictions, and this requires an examination of the logical consequences of the theory against observed reality. In fact, to be meaningful and useful, the assumptions must be descriptively unrealistic in the sense that they must abstract from a complex reality. Few would argue that the hair colour of the president of the NYSE is germane to the problem of explaining asset prices. But how unrealistic can the assumptions be? We have no recourse but to test the model's predictions empirically.

Recall from the previous section that the central prediction of the CAPM is that the market portfolio is positioned on the mean–variance-efficient frontier. Again, this prediction is equivalent to the prediction that all assets lie on the SML given in Equation 10.8. The bulk of the empirical research on CAPM focuses on this prediction.

Notice that the CAPM is formulated in terms of investors' expectations about future returns or the ex-ante return distribution. If the ex-ante return distribution were known, then one could directly test the CAPM simply by checking whether the market portfolio is indeed positioned on the efficient frontier. However, in practice, the ex-ante distribution is not known, because we cannot read the minds of investors. Empirical research typically uses a series of historical or ex-post returns for a set of assets to approximate the ex-ante distribution. From the ex-post returns, we can compute historical means, variances and covariances, construct an historical efficient frontier and determine the location of the market portfolio relative to the frontier.

Unfortunately, data sets almost always give an imperfect representation of the true ex-ante return distribution, a problem known as sampling error. This problem is especially severe if the number of time-series observations is small relative to the number of assets. Due to sampling error, the ex-post efficiency classification (efficient or inefficient) does not logically imply anything about the true efficiency classification relative to the ex-ante distribution. In fact, the market portfolio will almost always be ex-post mean–variance-inefficient, even if the market portfolio is ex-ante efficient. The market will be ex-post inefficient relative to portfolios that assign a higher weight to assets that performed better than expected and that assign a lower weight to assets that performed worse than expected.

To deal with the problem of sampling error, one may use statistical tests. Such tests generally use a test statistic that measures the degree to which the data set violates the hypothesis that the market portfolio is efficient. One example is the R-squared found if one regresses ex-post means on ex-post betas (see below). The test statistic can be used for statistical inference about the null hypothesis, i.e. for computing the probability that the market portfolio is efficient or inefficient. If this p-value is smaller than the desired level of significance, for example 5%, then the market portfolio is significantly inefficient and we must reject CAPM as a valid theory.

We cannot possibly collect and process information on all available assets in the investment universe. Also, if we use a large number of assets, then we need an extremely large number of time-series observations in order to obtain reliable estimates for the joint return distribution. For this purpose, assets are typically grouped into a small set of benchmark portfolios based on a particular attribute of the stocks. Market capitalisation or size, estimated beta, book-to-market equity ratio, momentum and industry classification are some of the most common attributes used in sorting stocks. Empirical studies typically include 10–100 benchmark portfolios.

The CAPM has been subject to rigorous empirical testing for more than three decades. One important stimulus for the empirical research has been the availability of large-scale, high-quality data sets for the US stock market, most notably from the Center for Research in Security Prices (CRSP). This financial research centre at the University of Chicago Graduate School of Business creates and maintains historical US databases for individual stock (NASDAQ, AMEX, NYSE), indices, bond and mutual fund securities. This high-quality database is updated continuously and is free of any survivorship and delisting (since 1999) biases.

We cannot possibly survey all individual empirical studies here. This is because the studies differ greatly with respect to the data sets and the research methodology. The differences reflect the many choices empirical researchers have to make. A partial list of choices that empiricists have to make includes the following:

- the assets that are included in the analysis (for example, all US common stocks listed on the NYSE);
- the method for grouping assets into portfolios (for example, sorted by book-to-market equity ratio);
- the proxy for the market portfolio (for example, the S&P 500 index);
- the return frequency (for example, monthly returns);
- the sample period (for example, 1926–2003);
- the statistical methods (for example, the two-pass regression method discussed below).

The approach we adopt is to discuss briefly one frequently employed empirical methodology: the so-called two-pass regression methodology. We then turn to several persistent patterns in historical returns series of the stock market that seem inconsistent with the CAPM. These patterns are sometimes referred to as stock market anomalies. Next, we discuss a few of the problems inherent in empirical tests of the CAPM. These problems cast serious doubt on the meaning of empirical tests of the CAPM and call into question whether the CAPM is testable to begin with.

10.2.1 The two-pass regression methodology

There exist many different ways to test the predictions of the CAPM. One popular approach is the so-called two-pass regression methodology. This methodology basically involves the following four steps:

1. **Establish sample data.** The first step is to collect a data set of historical returns for a set of benchmark portfolios, a proxy for the market portfolio (for example, the S&P 500 index) and a proxy for the riskless rate (for example, a T-bill). Data are collected for a particular return frequency (for example, daily, monthly or yearly frequency) and over a particular sample period. This will results in T time-series observations on n benchmark portfolios, the market portfolio and the riskless rate.

2. **Estimate characteristic lines.** The second step estimates, for every benchmark portfolio separately, the characteristic line (Equation 10.7) using time-series regression analysis. The time-series regressions to estimate the characteristic lines are sometimes referred to as the first-pass regressions, because their output is used in a second-pass regression (see below). Frequently, the OLS regression estimator given in Equation 10.10 is used.

3. **Estimate the SML.** The third step is directed at empirically estimating the SML. Specifically, this estimates the cross-sectional relationship between the ex-post market betas (obtained from the above time-series regression) and the ex-post mean excess returns, which are treated as estimators of the ex-ante expected excess returns. For this purpose, the following regression model is used:

$$\bar{R}_i - r = \gamma_0 + \gamma_1 \hat{\beta}_i + u_i \qquad (10.12)$$

where $\bar{R}_i$ is the historical average return on the ith benchmark portfolio, γ_0 is the historical intercept, $\hat{\beta}_i$ is the historical estimate of the beta for the ith benchmark portfolio, γ_1 is the historical slope coefficient for market risk, and u_i is the deviation from the line. The output of the regression model will include coefficient estimates $\hat{\gamma}_0$ and $\hat{\gamma}_1$, standard errors and an R-squared. The appropriate statistics for estimating the SML are obtained by substituting $\bar{R}_i$ for y_i and $\hat{\beta}_i$ for $x_{1,i}$ in the general expressions in Appendix A.[19]

In order to test the predictions of the CAPM, we may also include variables that should not affect expected returns. One example is beta squared, or $\hat{\beta}_i^2$. If the CAPM holds, then this variable should have no explanatory power, as the CAPM predicts a linear relationship between mean and beta. An example includes non-market risk, or $\hat{\sigma}_{e_i}^2$, i.e. exposure to

---

[19] Note that this estimation method assumes that the errors for the different assets have the same distribution and that they are mutually independent. In many cases, this assumption is violated and other estimation methods are needed; see Section 10.2.3.

non-market factors or purely firm-specific risk. According to the CAPM, non-market risk should have no explanatory power, as only systematic risk is priced:

$$\bar{R}_i = \gamma_0 + \gamma_1\hat{\beta}_i + \gamma_2\hat{\beta}_i^2 + \gamma_3\hat{\sigma}_{e_i}^2 + u_i \tag{10.13}$$

where γ_2 measures the effect of beta squared and γ_3 measures the effect of non-market risk.

4. **Test predictions of the CAPM.** The final step is to determine whether the properties of the estimated SML are in accord with the predictions of the CAPM. If the CAPM is true, then the intercept of the SML is zero, i.e. $\gamma_0 = 0$, and the slope of the SML should equal the equity premium, i.e. $\gamma_1 = [E(R_m) - r]$. We can test this by checking whether the estimated regression coefficients are significantly different from the hypothesised values.[20] Further, the CAPM requires that beta is the only variable explaining expected returns, i.e. there should exist an exact fit between mean and beta. If all pairs of expected rates of return and beta lie on one line, the SML, then the market is in equilibrium. However, when historical data are used to estimate the expected rate of return and beta, generally some assets plot above or below the SML, indicating either disequilibrium or a statistically insignificant deviation from the line (because of sampling errors). Test whether the R-squared for the empirical SML is not significantly lower than unity.

Further, terms related to non-linear market risk, such as beta squared, or non-market risk should have no explanatory value, and the regression coefficients should not be significantly different from zero.

Example application

To demonstrate this procedure, we apply it to a sample of US stock returns. Specifically, we use the value-weighted CRSP all-share index as the market portfolio and the one-month US T-bill as the riskless asset. The investment universe is summarised by ten value-weighted benchmark portfolios based on market beta. Each year, at the end of December, all individual stocks are ranked on the basis of their historical beta, and ten beta portfolios are formed. The 10% of stocks with the lowest beta go into portfolio 1, and so on, through portfolio 10, which includes the 10% of stocks with the highest beta (Exhibit 10.10). For these portfolios, we collect data on the monthly returns from January 1935 to June 1968, exactly the same data period as Fama and Macbeth (1973) used.[21,22]

Exhibit 10.11 illustrates the results graphically. Exhibit 10.11(a) shows the mean–standard deviation diagram, including the individual benchmark portfolios (the clear dots) and the market portfolio (M). This diagram is constructed using the sample means and variance–covariance terms. The dashed line represents the efficient frontier of risky assets (without the riskless asset). Clearly, the market portfolio is very close to the efficient frontier. By contrast, the market portfolio is far away from the efficient frontier with the riskless asset (the black line). It seems possible to achieve a better risk–return trade-off with riskless borrowing and using the proceeds to invest in the tangency portfolio (T).

---

[20] For this purpose, we can use the *t*-test and F-test discussed in Appendix A at the end of this book.

[21] The market return is obtained from the homepage of Kenneth French (www.mba.tuck.dartmouth.edu/pages/faculty/ken.french/). The risk-free rate is obtained from Ibbotson. The beta portfolios are taken from the data library of Pim van Vliet at www.finance-on-eur.nl

[22] Using more recent data, the relationship between mean and beta is much weaker and the market portfolio seems mean–variance-inefficient relative to beta-sorted portfolios.

Exhibit 10.10 Descriptive statistics for ten beta-sorted portfolios

Portfolio	Mean	Standard deviation	α	se(α)	β	se(β)	R^2 (%)
Low β	0.74	3.16	0.20	0.09	0.57	0.02	66
2	0.82	3.32	0.20	0.08	0.65	0.02	77
3	0.85	3.91	0.10	0.08	0.79	0.02	82
4	0.80	4.34	−0.05	0.08	0.89	0.02	86
5	1.00	4.54	0.09	0.08	0.95	0.02	88
6	0.96	4.93	−0.02	0.09	1.03	0.02	88
7	0.95	5.24	−0.10	0.09	1.10	0.02	90
8	1.07	5.57	−0.05	0.08	1.18	0.02	91
9	1.09	6.12	−0.15	0.09	1.31	0.02	92
High β	1.23	7.23	−0.22	0.12	1.52	0.03	90

Exhibit 10.11 Empirical results for ten beta-sorted portfolios

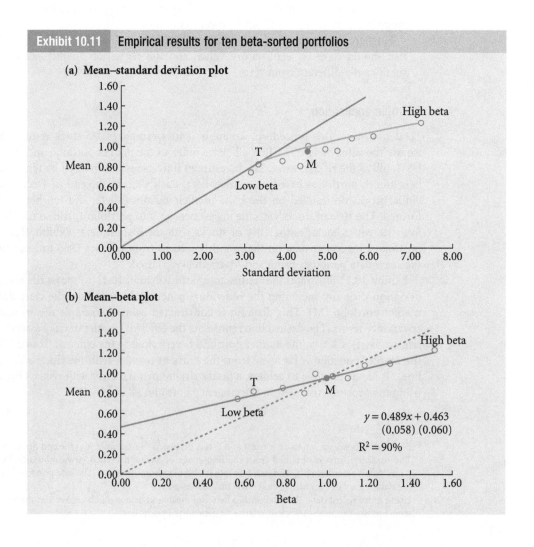

(a) **Mean–standard deviation plot**

(b) **Mean–beta plot**

$$y = 0.489x + 0.463$$
$$(0.058) \quad (0.060)$$
$$R^2 = 90\%$$

Exhibit 10.11(b) displays the mean–beta diagram. The straight line represents the regression line, i.e. the line that gives the best fit between means and betas. The regression line has three important properties:

■ There exists a positive relationship between expected return and market risk, as measured by beta; that is, high risk is associated with high return.
■ The relationship is linear; that is, for every unit increase in beta, there is the same increase in expected return. The intercept of the estimated SML is 0.463, reflecting an expected excess return on a zero-beta portfolio of 0.463 per month, or 5.5% per year. The slope of the empirical SML is 0.489, reflecting a market risk premium of 0.489% per month, or 5.9% per year.
■ The relationship is nearly exact; that is, apart from beta, there is nothing that determines expected return. The adjusted R-squared is roughly 90%; that is, there is a near-perfect fit. Nearly all the cross-sectional differences in average return on the portfolios can be explained by differences in the market betas.

These three properties reflect the fact that the market portfolio is close to the efficient frontier of risky assets. Note, however, that the intercept of the regression line is 0.463%. The intercept is an empirical estimate for the expected excess return on a zero-beta portfolio. In this case, the intercept is significantly higher than zero, meaning that the zero-beta portfolio yields a significantly higher expected return than the riskless rate. In addition, the slope of the regression line (0.489%) is significantly lower than the average excess return on the market portfolio (0.953%). This reflects the fact that the market portfolio is far away from the efficient frontier with riskless borrowing. The dotted line represents the SML that is expected if riskless lending and borrowing are allowed.

To summarise, based on this data set, there appears to be a near-perfect, positive, linear relationship between mean return and market beta, with the intercept significantly different from the riskless rate and the slope lower than the equity premium.

10.2.2 Capital asset-pricing model anomalies

Many researchers have performed similar tests. Early tests appeared consistent with the CAPM.[23] However, the intercept of the relationship was too high and the slope too flat to be consistent with the original Sharpe–Lintner model. However, as above, the results were consistent with Black's zero-beta model, where riskless borrowing is not allowed. The CAPM gained much support among academics as well as professionals after the publication of their results. However, shortly thereafter, several phenomena were discovered that seemed inconsistent with the CAPM. The following three stock market anomalies are well-documented:

The size effect

Firms with a low market capitalisation (small caps) seem to earn positive abnormal average returns, while large caps earn negative abnormal returns.[24] The size effect generally is not very strong if we sort portfolios only on size. This is because size and beta are correlated very strongly: small firms typically have high betas. However, the size effect generally appears if we

---

[23] Black et al. (1972), Friend and Blume (1973) and Fama and MacBeth (1973), among others.
[24] See, for example, Banz (1981) and Fama and French (1992).

perform a double sort, first on beta and then on size. Small caps generally outperform big caps of comparable beta. Estimates for the abnormal return on small caps are around 2–4% per annum. The size premium was most pronounced during the 1960s and 1970s.

The value effect

Chapter 15 discusses some popular valuation multiples for valuing stocks, such as the price-to-earnings ratio (P/E), dividend-to-price ratio (D/P) and book-to-market ratio (B/M). Stocks with a high market value relative to firm fundamentals (earnings, dividend, book value) are referred to as 'growth stocks'. Such funds have a high P/E and a low D/P and B/M. By contrast, 'value stocks' have a low market value relative to firm fundamentals, i.e. low P/E and high D/P and B/M. The value effect denotes the fact that value stocks seem to earn abnormal high average returns while growth stocks earn negative abnormal returns.[25] The abnormal return on value stocks is estimated at about 4–6% per annum.

The momentum effect

As discussed in Chapter 12, the efficient market theory predicts that we cannot predict abnormal returns. However, it seems that we can predict abnormal returns from past returns. Roughly speaking, in the short run, i.e. for periods up to a year, losers in the past continue to lose while winners continue to gain.[26] The momentum effect is even stronger than the size and value effects; estimates for the abnormal return range from about 4 to 6% per annum. However, the momentum effect is also likely to be exaggerated to some extent. Consider the following facts:

- Pure-momentum strategies involve very high turnover. Consequently, transaction costs and taxes can significantly erode momentum profits.
- Most of the return to the 'winner-minus-loser' momentum portfolio is due to the poor performance of the losers. So, in order to capture the bulk of the momentum effect, short positions are necessary. This is not feasible for some investors.
- The momentum effect is stronger among small-cap stocks, which tend to be less liquid. Trying to implement a high-turnover strategy with small-cap stocks is unrealistic.

These points suggest that momentum strategies probably do not represent a real opportunity for investors to earn abnormal returns, at least not to the extent implied by recent studies.

Interestingly, the momentum effect is reversed for longer periods of time, i.e. multiple years. Specifically, stocks that do well for a long time tend to do poorly subsequently; stocks that do poorly for a long time tend to come back and do well later on.[27]

To summarise, common market proxies seem significantly mean–variance-inefficient relative to portfolios that include more small caps, value stocks and past winners and fewer large caps, growth stocks and past losers. Related to this, market covariance seems to explain only a small portion of the cross-sectional variation in mean return, while size, BE/ME and momentum appear to have substantial explanatory power.

---

[25] See, for example, Basu (1977), Basu (1983), Jaffe et al. (1989), Rosenberg et al. (1985), Chan et al. (1991) and Fama and French (1992).
[26] See, for example, Jegadeesh (1990), Jegadeesh and Titman (1993) and Fama and French (1996).
[27] See, for example, DeBondt and Thaler (1985) and Chopra et al. (1992).

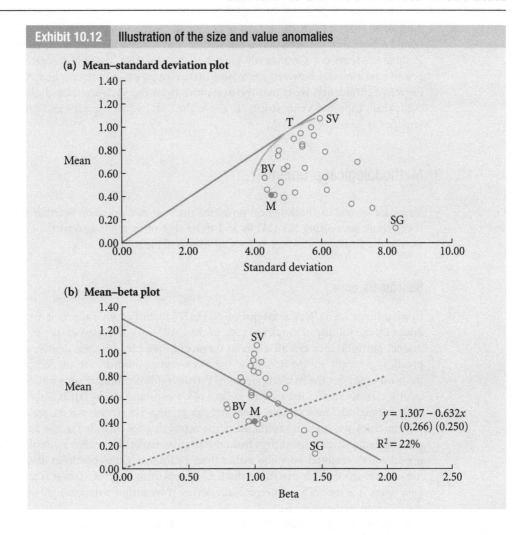

Exhibit 10.12   Illustration of the size and value anomalies

(a) **Mean–standard deviation plot**

(b) **Mean–beta plot**

$$y = 1.307 - 0.632x$$
$$(0.266)\ (0.250)$$
$$R^2 = 22\%$$

We may illustrate these problems using historical returns for US stock portfolios that are formed on size and BE/ME. Specifically, we will again proxy the market portfolio by the CRSP all-share index and the riskless asset by the one-month US Treasury bill. For the individual risky assets, we use the so-called Fama and French portfolios formed on size and BE/ME. These portfolios are formed by placing all individual stocks listed on the AMEX, NYSE and NASDAQ in five size categories, ranging from the smallest stocks to the largest stocks, and five B/M categories, ranging from low B/M (growth stocks) to high B/M (value stocks), giving a total of 25 portfolios. We use 474 monthly returns from July 1963 to December 2002.[28]

Exhibit 10.12(a) shows the mean–variance diagram for this data set. Clearly, the market portfolio is highly inefficient in terms of mean–variance analysis. This result violates the central prediction of the mean–variance CAPM: mean–variance efficiency of the market portfolio. Exhibit 10.12(b) shows the mean–beta diagram for the 25 benchmark portfolios. The relationship between mean and beta is very weak. The R-squared is only 22%; that is, only

[28] The data on the market portfolio and the benchmark portfolios are taken from the homepage of Kenneth French (www.mba.tuck.dartmouth.edu/pages/faculty/ken.french/). The Treasury bill data are from Ibbotson.

22% of the variance in the means is explained by the betas. If the CAPM holds, then we would expect an R-squared that is not significantly smaller than unity. By contrast, the actual R-squared seems not significantly greater than zero! Also, there is a negative rather than a positive relationship between mean and beta. Hence, we may reject the CAPM with a high degree of confidence. Note that the deviations from the SML are related directly to size and B/M; small caps and value stocks lie above the SML, while big caps and growth stocks systematically lie below the SML.

10.2.3 Methodological problems

There are several methodological problems that call into question whether the existing tests (both those supporting the CAPM and those that offer proof against the CAPM) are really tests of the CAPM, and whether the CAPM is testable to begin with.

Benchmark error

In what is known as 'Roll's critique', Roll (1977) identified logical problems that cast serious doubt on the validity of empirical tests of the CAPM. As discussed earlier in this chapter, the market portfolio includes all assets in the world, weighted by their relative market value. In practice, generally we do not know the exact composition of the market portfolio; rather, we use a proxy for the market portfolio. Proxies typically include only a subset of assets. For example, many studies use narrow indices of US common stocks (such as the S&P 500 index) and they exclude, for example, preferred stocks, non-US stocks, bonds, real-estate holdings, commodities and human capital. Also, the assets that are included in the analysis frequently are assigned a weight that differs from the relative market value. For example, several studies use an equal-weighted portfolio rather than a value-weighted portfolio. Roll shows that the use of a subset of assets can make the CAPM appear to be true when it is false, or to appear false when it is true. The same problem occurs if we assign wrong weights to the assets that are included in the analysis.

Again, the CAPM predicts that the market portfolio is mean–variance-efficient or, equivalently, that there exists a perfect fit between means and market betas (the SML). Roll made two important observations.

First, we will always find a perfect fit between means and market betas if the betas are computed relative to a market proxy that includes all individual assets and that is mean–variance-efficient, irrespective of whether the true market portfolio is efficient. Thus, empirical studies that find a perfect fit between means and market betas indicate only that an efficient portfolio (a portfolio situated on the efficient frontier) has been selected as a proxy to the market portfolio. Conversely, empirical studies that show less than perfect association indicates only that an inefficient portfolio (a portfolio interior to the efficient frontier) has been selected as a proxy.

Second, to test whether the market portfolio is efficient, we need to include all assets, weighted by their market value. Since we do not know the exact composition of the market portfolio, the CAPM is untestable. Tests of CAPM really are tests for the efficiency of the market proxy rather than the true market portfolio. To summarise, it is possible to accept the CAPM if it is not true (if we use an efficient market proxy), and it is possible to reject the CAPM if it is true (if we use an inefficient market proxy). Hence, we can test the CAPM only if the composition of the true market portfolio is known.

Unfortunately, small deviations from the true market portfolio, for example by excluding assets or by assigning wrong weights, can be sufficient to produce a poor fit between means and betas, even if the CAPM holds and the true market portfolio is fully efficient. Conversely, small deviations are sufficient to produce a good fit between means and betas, even if the CAPM does not hold and the true market portfolio is highly inefficient. The problem is that small changes in the portfolio weights can yield large changes in the betas of the individual assets. Roll and Ross (1994), Kandel and Stambaugh (1995) and Grauer (1999) show that this phenomenon occurs also for plausible return distributions.

The point is that we cannot logically derive the efficiency classification of the market portfolio from the efficiency classification of a proxy portfolio, because the efficiency classification is highly sensitive to the portfolio composition. Hence, we need to know the exact composition of the market portfolio (the identity of all assets and the exact relative market value). Unfortunately, in practice, we never know the exact market portfolio. For financial assets that are traded on exchanges, we may compute the market value from information on the number of assets issued and the market prices. However, for non-traded assets, such as human capital, we generally do not have accurate information on quantities and prices. For this reason, there is substantial uncertainty regarding their weight in the market portfolio. Hence, the CAPM is, in practice, an untestable theory.

We stress that the sensitivity to the market proxy is a problem of logical inference rather than statistical inference. The problem is not that we have an insufficient number of observations to derive statistically good estimates for the betas, but rather that small changes in the portfolio weights can cause large changes in the betas. Hence, Roll's critique applies even in the hypothetical case where the true population means and betas are known or if the sample is sufficiently large to derive accurate estimates for the betas.

Roll's critique casts serious doubt on much of the empirical research on the CAPM. For example, suppose that some empirical studies do not reject the null hypothesis that the S&P 500 index is mean–variance-efficient, because there is a very strong relationship between the means and betas of individual stocks included in the index. This does not prove that the market portfolio is efficient, because the S&P 500 index excludes, for example, small-cap stocks, non-US stocks, bonds, real estate, commodities, currencies and human capital, and including these asset classes may produce very different results. Similarly, rejection of efficiency of the S&P 500 index does not provide evidence against the CAPM.

One possible response to benchmark error is to try to identify the omitted asset classes, to find a proxy variable for their return, and to add the proxy in the analysis. For example, Jagannathan and Wang (1996) used a proxy for changes in the value of human capital based on the rate of change in aggregate labour income. In addition to the beta for the value-weighted stock market index, their model also includes a beta for labour income growth.

Similar problems occur because of the use of benchmark portfolios rather than individual assets. Specifically, even if the benchmark portfolios are priced correctly, then we still cannot be sure that the individual assets are also priced correctly. In addition, if the individual assets are priced correctly, then the benchmark portfolios may still appear mispriced if the portfolio weights are not equal to the relative market value. Unfortunately, there is no simple solution to this problem, as we cannot possibly obtain reliable estimates for the joint return distribution of a large number of individual assets.

Time variation of the return distribution

Again, we generally do not know the true ex-ante return distribution, and so we use ex-post observations to proxy the ex-ante distribution. The conclusions that we can draw from ex-post data depend on the statistical distribution of the observations. One possibility is to assume that the observations are random draws from the ex-ante distribution and that the composition of the market portfolio does not change. In this case, the historical return distribution is a statistically good estimate of the ex-ante return distribution. We may then test market efficiency by examining the relationship between ex-post means and ex-post betas. This relationship allows for statistical inference on the true ex-ante relationship.

Cheng and Grauer (1980, 1982) develop a powerful argument against assuming that betas are constant even if the return distribution of the assets remains constant. We know that different assets yield different ex-post returns. These differences translate into changes in the relative market value of the assets or changes in the composition of the market portfolio. In addition, changes in the composition of the market portfolio yield changes in the betas. We already know that even small changes in the composition of the market can cause large changes in beta.

Further, there is a wealth of evidence to suggest that the return distribution (expected returns, variances, correlations) changes over time. Part of the change in the return distribution is related to the business cycle. For example, the risk premiums typically are high during a recession period. This may reflect the simple fact that when times are hard, the subjective pain of losing dollars to spend on consumption goods is very high. Conversely, the market risk premium typically is low during periods of economic expansion. Also, the relative riskiness of assets generally changes through time. For example, the stocks of firms that are highly leveraged, i.e. with high debt-to-equity ratios, become more risky and more correlated during a recession. Ignoring the time-variation of the riskless rate, the market risk premium and the betas can seriously bias the regression results and lower the goodness of fit.

What exactly is the problem if the return distribution changes over time? If the distribution changes over time, then every observation on the market portfolio represents the solution to a different optimisation problem relative to a different conditional return distribution. However, the market portfolio generally does not represent the optimal solution relative to the unconditional distribution. Put differently, if investors are allowed to alter their portfolios depending on the state of the economy, then generally they will not choose a fixed portfolio composition for all states. If investors use the information on the state of the economy and base their investment decisions on the conditional distribution, then generally they will be better off, i.e. achieve a more favourable trade-off between risk and return, than if they ignore all available information and use the unconditional distribution. In a similar way, we make better decisions if we listen to the weather forecast before we leave the house. If we ignore the weather forecast, then we may have to carry a coat and an umbrella with us all year, even if clear skies and high temperatures are expected. Surely this is not an optimal solution. If the market portfolio does not represent the optimal solution relative to the unconditional distribution, then there is no reason to expect an exact positive linear relationship between unconditional mean and unconditional beta. In fact, we may find any type of relationship between means and betas – both strong and weak relationships and both positive and negative relationships. Assets with positive correlation between market risk premium and beta, i.e. that have a high beta when the market risk premium is high, will appear to earn positive abnormal returns if we focus on the unconditional distribution. For example, Lettau and Ludvigson (unpublished paper) show that value stocks have a high beta during recessions (when the market risk premium is high) and that failure, due to this cyclical time variation, results in a spurious value effect; see Chapter 17 for further details.

One possible response to time variation is to use a moving window of a small number of observations, so as to account for structural changes in the return distribution over time. For example, Fama and MacBeth (1973) regress, for every monthly observation separately, the excess returns of the benchmark portfolios on the betas that are estimated from the previous 60 monthly observations. This approach leaves one with a difficult trade-off. If the window size is large, then the problem of time-variation may still be relevant. For example, a five-year period may include both recession and expansion observations. Conversely, if the window size if small, then we may not have sufficient observations to reliably estimate the return distribution.

Another possible solution is to model the return dynamics. Specifically, we may try to estimate a relationship between the betas and the market risk premium on the one hand and indicators of the business cycle on the other hand. Popular examples of such indicators are the T-bill rate, the credit spread and the term spread. This approach effectively tries to recover the conditional portfolio possibilities. This allows for testing if the market portfolio is efficient relative to the conditional return distribution at every point in time.

A drawback of this approach is that economic theory gives minimal guidance for specifying the return dynamics. There are some general predictions, such as a low riskless rate and a high market risk premium during a recession. However, there is no exact model for describing the return dynamics. Another problem is that data on macroeconomic variables that describe or forecast the business cycle generally are of lesser quality than financial-market data: the data are available less frequently and they are prone to revisions and changes in definitions. Finally, the link between the business cycle and the return distribution itself may change over time. In fact, Ghysels (1998) finds that ill-specified conditional asset-pricing models in many cases yield greater pricing errors than unconditional models.

Another problem related to the shape of the return distribution relates to the choice of the relevant investment horizon. Levhari and Levy (1977) show that beta coefficients estimated with monthly returns are not the same as betas estimated with annual returns. Since they are different, the results of empirical studies will depend upon which beta estimation convention is used. Kothari et al. (1995) argue that annual betas are more appropriate than monthly betas, since the investment horizon for a typical investor is probably closer to a year than a month. They show that the relation between beta and return is stronger when betas are estimated using annual returns.

Statistical problems with the test methodology

There exist many different statistical techniques for testing the predictions of the CAPM. Each technique aims to find the statistically best estimators given a set of assumptions about the statistical distribution of the return observations. If the assumptions are wrong, then the estimation results may turn out be completely unreliable, even if the model itself suggests that the results are perfectly reliable. Some of the empirical results on the validity of the CAPM – both the evidence in support of the CAPM and the evidence against the CAPM – may reflect the use of inappropriate statistical techniques.

The two-pass regression method that we outlined earlier suffers from at least two possible econometric flaws. First, the procedure relies on OLS regression. This regression method assigns an equal weight to every observation. Econometrically, this makes sense if all error terms have the same variance (homoskedasticity) and if they are mutually independent (no serial correlation). In economic terms, for the second-pass regression, this means that we have to assume that the non-market risk is the same for all assets and the non-market risk of every asset is independent of the non-market risk of all other assets. In many cases, these assumptions are violated. For example, assets with high market risks (betas) generally also have high non-market risks, and the non-market risk of different assets includes a common exposure to industry trends, exchange rates, interest rates and commodities prices.

In such cases, we should not assign the same weight to all observations. Rather, the statistical techniques should assign a high weight to the asset with little non-market variance and little non-market covariance with the remaining assets. Conversely, we should assign a low weight to the asset with high non-market variance and high non-market covariance with the remaining assets.

Another problem is that we treat the estimation of the betas in the first-pass regression independent of the estimation of the empirical SML in the second-pass regression. In this way, the second-pass regression ignores the errors that result from the first pass. Econometrically, this is problematic, because the test procedure will confuse measurement error for beta with pricing errors or deviations from the SML. The line that minimises the sum of both errors generally does not minimise the sum of pricing errors, i.e. give the best approximation to the SML. In fact, we may prove that this problem causes the estimated intercept of the second-pass regression to be biased away from zero and the estimated slope to be biased towards zero, with the bias depending on the relative importance of errors in variables relative to other sources of deviations from the true regression line. Also, if beta is measured with error, then non-market factors may appear to have a significant influence if they are correlated with the true (unknown) beta. Miller and Scholes (1972) show by means of a well-controlled simulation experiment that this problem can lead to very misleading estimation results if we use individual assets. This is an important reason for using well-diversified benchmark portfolios rather than individual assets. For well-diversified portfolios, many of the errors in the beta estimates of individual assets cancel out and the portfolio betas are more accurate.

Ignoring these statistical problems can lead to seriously biased estimation results. To circumvent these problems, we may use more sophisticated statistical techniques, such as Hansen's (1982) generalised method of moments (GMM). The GMM technique effectively considers the problems of estimating the betas and estimating the SML simultaneously. In addition, the technique can account for differences and dependencies in non-market risk.

Ultimately, the appropriate statistical techniques depend on the assumptions that we make about the statistical distribution of the return observations. Unfortunately, the CAPM does not forward strong predictions about this distribution, as it does not specify the means and variance–covariance terms of the observations and the way in which these evolve through time.

Data-mining, data-snooping and sample-selection bias

Data-mining is the practice of finding patterns by the extensive searching through models and data sets. In empirical research, we always have to accept a probability of wrongly rejecting a hypothesis. The significance level gives the accepted probability of wrongly rejecting a hypothesis for a given model and a given data set. If we try a sufficiently large number of models and data sets, then surely some significant pattern will appear just by chance. Data-mining problems arise when a researcher does not report how many different models and data sets were tested before finally reporting the successful one. Also, hundreds of researchers, in an attempt to write publishable papers, spend a great deal of time looking for relationships between stock returns and other variables. Only the successful tests are submitted for publication; the unsuccessful ones never see the light of day.

Data-snooping is prying into past empirical results to guide future research. The result is that what may be chance patterns in the data can appear to be very significant. Data-snooping can be a collusive activity of chasing patterns that may be illusory as several analysts study the same data. The antidote is to examine new data. Unfortunately, data-snooping is difficult to avoid, because empirical research is based on historical data and because asset markets are highly correlated. Hence, all researchers essentially look at the same data set or very similar data sets that overlap in time and with assets that are highly correlated with previously studied assets. Some research has shown that the magnitude of bias from data-snooping can be substantial. Specifically, the benchmark portfolios are formed on firm characteristics (size and BE/ME) that are, a priori, known to be correlated with expected returns (see, for example, Lo and Mackinlay (1990)). For example, the size and BE/ME effects were well known before the influential Fama and French studies (see, for example, Banz (1981) and Rosenberg et al. (1985)).[29] In addition, sorting the portfolios on these firm characteristics artificially inflates the differences in return between the portfolios.

Sample-selection bias may occur if data availability leads to certain assets being excluded from the analysis. For example, it is well-known that the Compustat database suffers from a survivorship bias, due to the way in which firms are added to the database. As described by Banz and Breen (1986), Breen and Korajczyk (1994) and Kothari et al. (1995), firms are typically brought into the Compustat files with several years of historical data. Since the firms that are added to the database during a given year are firms that still exist, the backfilling of historical data for the previous several years biases the database toward firms that survived through those years. The firms that died during those years and that were not already in the database are never included. This ex-post selection bias can have a significant effect on cross-sectional studies of stock returns. Again, many studies in finance have found an abnormally high average return for stocks with a low market value relative to accounting measures of firm fundamentals. If the data set that we use to collect accounting data excludes failing companies, then sample selection bias may arise. Kothari et al. (1995) investigated this question and argued that failing stocks would be expected to have low returns and high B/M ratios. If we exclude failing stocks, then those stocks with high B/M ratios that are included will have returns that are higher on average than if all stocks with high B/M ratios were included. They suggested that this bias is responsible for the previous findings on the relationship between mean return and B/M ratio. Adding the firms that are excluded from Compustat to the database would reduce the explanatory power of B/M, and possibly even eliminate it.

A sample can also be biased because of the removal (or delisting) of a company's stock from an exchange. For example, the Center for Research in Security Prices (CRSP) at the University of Chicago is a major provider of return data in academic research. When a delisting occurs, CRSP tries to collect returns for the delisted company, but often CRSP cannot collect these returns and it must list them as missing. A recent study by Shumway and Wharter (1999) documented the bias caused by delisting for CRSP NASDAQ return data. The authors showed that delistings associated with poor company performance (e.g. bankruptcy) are missing more often than delistings associated with good or neutral company performance (e.g. a merger or moving to another exchange). In addition, delistings occur more frequently for small companies.

---

[29] Black (1993a, 1993b) suggested that the results of the famous Fama and French (1992) study of the size and B/M effects were likely an artefact of data-mining. Since Fama and French chose their explanatory variables based on the results of earlier empirical studies, the observed explanatory power of these variables could be due to a massive data-mining exercise on the part of the authors of these earlier studies. Based on this, Black contended that some of the statistical tests in Fama and French (1992) were not specified properly. He also suggested that since the relations between returns and size and B/M were likely an artefact of data-mining, then they would disappear if another time period or another data source were analysed. Mackinlay (1995) also mentions data-mining as a potential cause of the observed results.

10.3   Conclusion: dead or alive?

Many researchers have tried to test the empirical validity of the CAPM. The bulk of the research focuses on the prediction that the value-weighted market portfolio is mean–variance-efficient or, equivalently, that all individual assets lie on the SML (there exists an exact, positive, linear relationship between assets means and betas). Early research for the US stock market suggested that there indeed exists such a relationship. The intercept of the relationship was too high and the slope was too flat to be consistent with the original Sharpe–Lintner model. Nevertheless, the results were consistent with Black's zero-beta version of the CAPM, which does not allow for riskless borrowing (see Section 10.2.1). However, in the past three decades, a number of insights have emerged that call these findings into question. First, a number of empirical stock-market anomalies have been found; it seems that we can beat the market (achieve a more favourable trade-off between risk and return) by overweighting small caps, value stocks and past winners relative to their market value (see Section 10.2.2). Second, there are several methodological problems that call into question whether the existing tests are really tests of the CAPM, and whether the CAPM is testable at all. These methodological problems include the choice of the appropriate market portfolio and benchmark portfolios, the time variation of the return distribution, the choice of the appropriate statistical methods, and data problems such as data-mining, data-snooping and sample-selection bias (see Section 10.2.3). Based on these insights, we cannot draw an unambiguous conclusion about the empirical validity of the CAPM. Some researchers think that the CAPM is dead, and they have turned to other asset-pricing models, including the GCAPM, the ICAPM, the CCAPM, the arbitrage pricing theory (APT) (see Chapter 11) and models of behavioural finance (see Chapter 12). Some think that the CAPM is still alive, possibly after including human capital in the market portfolio and after accounting for the cyclical variation of the return distribution. Others await more meaningful tests, and still others think that the CAPM is principally non-testable because it does not specify key aspects such as the composition of the market portfolio and the return dynamics over time.

It seems that this controversy is not going to end soon. Despite the controversy, the CAPM is one of the cornerstones of investment theory and it forms the basis for deriving many alternative asset-pricing models, as well as the benchmark for gauging the empirical validity of those alternatives.

Also, the CAPM is applied widely in practice for purposes of portfolio selection, performance evaluation, risk management and capital budgeting. The chapters of this book that deal with these subjects will clarify the importance that practitioners assign to the CAPM. For example, alpha and beta are used widely for portfolio selection. Beta is a popular measure of market timing. For example, if an investor wants to stay invested in shares but is worried that the market might fall in the short term, then the best strategy would be to invest in shares that have low betas. Conversely, high betas should give an investor better-than-average returns when the market is on the up. Alpha is useful for security selection because it indicates which stocks are likely to yield abnormal return above and beyond a fair compensation for the risk involved.

Similarly, alpha and beta are useful for performance evaluation. While portfolio selection looks at the future, performance evaluation looks at the past. In the case of a mutual fund, the fund's alpha and beta allow an investor to assess whether a fund manager is earning his or her pay (a high alpha) or simply riding on the market's coat tails (a high beta during a bull market or a low beta during a bear market).

Beta is used frequently as a measure of (systematic) risk for risk management, for example in the value-at-risk framework discussed in Chapter 21. One of the attractions of beta is that it measures the dependency of an asset on the other available assets by a single number. By contrast, in the mean–variance framework of Chapter 8, this dependency was measured by $(n-1)$ covariances. Beta weights the covariance of each asset by its relative market value, which is a sensible thing to do for a well-diversified portfolio. In this respect, the CAPM is a useful instrument for reducing the burden of information and computation of the full mean–variance framework.

Apart from portfolio selection, performance evaluation and risk management, the CAPM is also useful as a decision-support tools for corporate finance. Firms need to estimate their cost of capital to evaluate new investment projects (capital budgeting). Financial managers can use the CAPM to calculate the cost of equity, which constitutes a major component in the cost of capital. In addition, costs of capital estimates are needed in situations where market valuations are absent, either because the equity is privately held or because the proposed publicly traded entity has not yet been created (for example, IPOs, mergers and spinoffs).

To summarise, practitioners think that the CAPM is alive. Nevertheless, most practitioners also think that the CAPM is not well; they know that it is difficult to obtain reliable estimates of alpha and beta (estimation error) and that the CAPM is a simple model that excludes many real-life considerations. Therefore, despite the wide use of the CAPM, and the use of beta as a measure of risk and alpha as a measure of excess return, practitioners use additional tools in choosing, monitoring and managing their investment portfolios, as we will see in the remainder of this book.

→ **Connecting Theory to Practice 10.2**

A model weighting game in estimating expected returns

Imperfect models

The CAPM is just a model, not a perfect description of reality. Indeed, many academic studies reject its validity because some stock return patterns seem inconsistent with the model. Does this mean we should throw the model away and rely only on model-free estimators, such as the sample average return? No! Every model is 'wrong', almost by definition, because it makes simplifying assumptions about our complex world. But even a model that is not exact can be useful. It is again helpful to adopt a Bayesian perspective and combine what the data tell us with our best prior guess. While the data speak to us about expected return through the sample average return (14 per cent a year for GM), our prior guess can be based on finance theory such as the CAPM (11 per cent a year for GM). The resulting estimate is a weighted average of the two numbers. The weights depend on how strongly we believe in the model and on how well the model compares with the data. This Bayesian approach is developed in another study by Robert Stambaugh and the author. The study finds that even if we have only modest confidence in a pricing model such as the CAPM, our cost of capital estimates should be heavily weighted towards the model. Average stock returns are noisy, so they should receive small weights. In other words, theory is more powerful than data when estimating expected stock returns.

To make the water muddier, the CAPM is not the only theoretical model of expected returns. Competition comes from multifactor models, in which expected return depends on the stock's betas with respect to more factors than just the market. The factors can be either macroeconomic variables (for example, a five-factor model developed by Nai-fu Chen, Richard Roll and Stephen Ross), or portfolios formed based on companies' characteristics (for example, a three-factor model of Eugene Fama and Ken French), or even return series constructed using statistical techniques such as factor analysis. Opinions vary on which model is best and the jury is still out.

Meanwhile, what are we to do? A sensible solution is to construct a weighted average of expected return estimates from all models that we are willing to consider, including the 'no-theory' model that produces the sample average estimate. Each estimate should be weighted by the probability that its parent model is correct. Where do we get these probabilities? It helps to be aware of the relevant research, but in the end this is a matter of judgment. The author believes that, despite its weaknesses, the CAPM has the strongest theoretical foundation and should receive the largest weight. Other models should be weighted according to their theoretical support and empirical success.

Uncertainty

Although pricing models generally produce expected return estimates that are significantly more precise than sample averages, uncertainty remains. Research by Fama and French shows standard errors of more than 3 per cent a year are typical for estimates of industry costs of equity based on common pricing models. Where does the uncertainty come from? Is it more important that we do not know the true beta, the exact value of the equity premium, or that we do not know the right model?

Interestingly, not knowing which model is right turns out to be less important on average than not knowing the parameters within each model. That is one conclusion from the author's cost of capital study mentioned earlier. We should therefore spend less time searching for the right model and more time trying to improve estimates within each model. In addition, uncertainty about the premium is bigger than uncertainty about betas, which makes the intangible equity premium the biggest source of uncertainty in the companies' cost of capital estimates.

As popular as they are, asset pricing models are not the only option for estimating the cost of capital. Another approach that is often used for regulated utilities in the US is based on the Gordon growth model, described by M. J. Gordon in 1962. This gives the cost of equity as equal to the sum of the current dividend yield and the long-term dividend growth rate. This approach is generally favoured less by academics, for several reasons. It makes the strong assumption that dividends will grow forever at the same rate. Besides, there is no theory to help us estimate the dividend growth rate, which is unfortunate because the cost of equity estimate is very sensitive to that rate. This approach therefore strongly reflects opinions about a company's prospects.

A moving target

There is an emerging consensus in academia that expected returns vary over time. For example, expected stock returns seem to be related to the business cycle – they tend to be higher in recessions and lower in expansions. Among the variables that have been found useful in explaining the time-variation in expected stock market returns are the aggregate dividend-price ratio (D/P) and earnings-price ratio (E/P). Low values of these ratios have historically predicted low returns. In other words, when prices are high relative to the fundamentals, future returns are on average low, especially at longer horizons such as 10 years ahead. The predictive power of the D/P and E/P ratios was reinforced last year, when the Standard & Poor's 500 index lost 10 per cent of its value while the ratios were at their historical lows. However, these predictors worked poorly in the 1990s, when low D/P and E/P peacefully coexisted with high stock market returns.

'If you torture the data long enough, Nature will confess,' said the Nobel Prize winning economist Ronald Coase. If you search enough variables, you will find a variable that appears to predict returns. However, this apparent predictability exists by chance and such 'data-mined' variables will not work in the future. An interesting example of data mining was provided in an article by Peter Coy, who quoted David Leinweber, managing director of First Quadrant, a money-management company. Leinweber 'sifted through a United Nations CD-Rom and discovered that historically, the best predictor of the S&P 500 was butter production in Bangladesh.' Good luck if you try to make money on this – you'll need it.

Fortunately, economists have come up with reasons for D/P and E/P having predictive power. Difficult questions remain, though. Is the predictive relation linear? What is the best way to estimate the unknown parameters of this relation? What other predictors should we include?

If it is hard to estimate expected returns when they are constant, it is even harder when they change with time. There is no simple recipe for estimating expected returns. Since data are noisy and no theory is flawless, judgment enters the process at several points. There is nothing wrong with that. After all, economic theories themselves ultimately reflect our judgment about how the world behaves. Given the importance of expected returns and the huge uncertainty associated with them, the finance profession clearly needs to invest more in their estimation. Such an investment will undoubtedly provide a high expected return. But please don't ask me for an exact number.

Further reading

Chen, N., R. Roll and S. Ross, 1986, 'Economic Forces and the Stock Market', *Journal of Business*, 59, 383–403.

Coy, P., 1997, 'He Who Mines Data may Strike Fool's Gold', *Business Week*, 16 June.

Fama, E. F. and K. R. French, 1997, 'Industry Costs of Equity', *Journal of Financial Economics*, 43, 153–193.

Pastor, L. and R. F. Stambaugh, 1999, 'Costs of Equity Capital and Model Mispricing', *Journal of Finance*, 54, 67–121.

Pastor, L. and R. F. Stambaugh, 'The Equity Premium and Structural Breaks', *Journal of Finance*, 56, 1207–1239.

Scholes, M. and J. Williams, 1977, 'Estimating Betas from Nonsynchronous Data', *Journal of Financial Economics*, 5, 309–327.

Source: Lubos Pastor, 'A Model Weighting Game In Estimating Expected Returns', *Financial Times*, 21 May 2001.

→ Making the connection

This text is the third and final part of the article used in this chapter's Investment in the News. In this part, Lubos Pastor discusses the use of asset-pricing theories, including the basic CAPM, for the purpose of estimating expected rates of return in practice. Pastor concludes that theory allows for more precise estimates than simple sample averages of historical returns. The best estimates are produced by combining theory with historical returns data and judgement.

Summary

Understand the capital market line (CML), which contains only efficient portfolios.

An investor can mix any risky asset with a risk-free asset, creating a large set of investment opportunities, all lying on the opportunity line. All investors, regardless of their indifference curves, will choose a portfolio from the opportunity line with the highest slope. This line is called the capital market line (CML). All portfolios lying on the CML are efficient, and all are composed of various mixes of the market portfolio and the risk-free asset.

Explain the separation property.

The portfolio selection procedure can be divided into two stages: (1) choosing the best portfolio of risky assets and (2) choosing the optimal mix of the portfolio selected in stage 1 with the risk-free asset. In stage 1, no information regarding the indifference curve is needed. All investors choose the same portfolio (the market portfolio). In stage 2, information on the indifference curve is needed.

Understand why the security market line (SML) describes the capital asset-pricing model (CAPM) equilibrium relationship between risk and expected rate of return.

In equilibrium, all assets, individual stocks and portfolios lie on a straight line called the security market line (SML). According to the CAPM, the higher the asset risk (beta), the higher the expected rate of return will be; all assets lie on the SML. In equilibrium, all assets are priced correctly and one cannot find 'bargains'. Any deviation from the SML implies that the market is not in the CAPM equilibrium.

Explain the two-pass regression method for testing the CAPM.

A popular approach to test the empirical validity of the CAPM is the two-pass regression methodology. This methodology uses a first-pass time-series regression to estimate the characteristic line for every benchmark asset or portfolio separately, and a second-pass cross-section regression to estimate the SML for all assets or portfolios jointly. Using the two-pass regression methodology, some researchers have found empirical support for the CAPM. However, others have found patterns that seem to systematically contradict the CAPM. Among these patterns are the stock-market anomalies related to market capitalisation, book-to-market equity ratio and momentum.

Explain why it is extremely difficult to test whether the CAPM gives a good description of capital markets.

There are several methodological problems that call into question whether the existing tests are really tests of the CAPM, and whether the CAPM is testable at all. These methodological problems include the choice of the appropriate benchmark portfolios and market portfolio, time variation of the return distribution, the choice of the appropriate statistical methods, and data problems such as data-mining, data-snooping and sample-selection bias. Based on the current empirical results, we cannot draw unambiguous conclusions about the empirical validity of the CAPM. Some researchers think that the CAPM is dead, and they have turned to other models, including the APT, GCAPM, ICAPM and CCAPM. Some think that the CAPM is still alive, possibly after including human capital in the market portfolio and after accounting for the cyclical variation of the return distribution. Others await more meaningful tests, and still others think that the CAPM is principally non-testable.

Understand how practitioners use the CAPM.

Many practitioners think that the CAPM is still alive but not well. The CAPM is applied widely in practice for purposes of portfolio selection, performance evaluation, risk management and capital budgeting. Nevertheless, most practitioners also think that the CAPM is not well: they know that it is difficult to obtain reliable estimates of alpha and beta (estimation error) and that the CAPM is a simple model that excludes many real-life considerations. Therefore, despite the wide use of the CAPM and the use of beta as a measure of risk and alpha as a measure of excess return, practitioners use additional tools in choosing, monitoring and managing their investment portfolios.

Review questions

1 Explain the following issues of the Capital Asset Pricing Model:

   a. Explain the separation theorem of the CAPM.
   b. What does the beta (β) measure of risk measure?
   c. What is the alpha (α) of a stock?
   d. Describe the security market line (SML).
   e. Describe the capital market line (CML).

2 Suppose you have the following data for Stock A and the market portfolio:

Year	Rate of return on Stock A	Rate of return on the Market
1	5%	8%
2	3%	−2%
3	20%	30%

   a. Calculate β_A.
   b. Calculate σ_A^2.
   c. Calculate the systematic and non-systematic risk component. Discuss these risks in pro-
      portional terms.

3 Suppose the market portfolio has the following parameters: $E(R_m) = 10\%$, and $\sigma_m = 10\%$. You hold an efficient portfolio with $\sigma_p = 20\%$, and the mean return on your portfolio is 15%:

a. Do you borrow or lend? How much?
b. What is the risk-free interest rate?

4 Despite the fact that the CAPM has unrealistic assumptions and that it is difficult to test empirically, the CAPM is widely applied in practice. Discuss for which purposes the CAPM is applied.

5 Discuss the three most documented inconsistencies with the CAPM, also known as stock market anomalies, observed in capital markets.

For an extensive set of review and practice questions and answers, visit the Levy–Post investment website at www.booksites.net/levy

Selected references

Banz, R. W., 1981, 'The Relationship between Return and Market Value of Common Stock', *Journal of Financial Economics*, **9**, 3–18.

Banz, R. W. and W. J. Breen, 1986, 'Sample-Dependent Results Using Accounting and Market Data: Some Evidence', *Journal of Finance*, **41**, 779–793.

Basu, S., 1977, 'Investment Performance of Common Stocks in Relation to their Price–Earnings Ratios: A Test of the Efficient Market Hypothesis', *Journal of Finance*, **32**, 663–682.

Basu, S., 1983, 'The Relationship between Earnings Yield, Market Value and Return for NYSE Common Stocks: Further Evidence', *Journal of Financial Economics*, **12**, 129–156.

Black, F., 1972, 'Capital Market Equilibrium with Restricted Borrowing', *Journal of Business*, **45**, 444–455.

Black, F., 1993a, 'Beta and Return', *Journal of Portfolio Management*, **20**, 8–18.

Black, F., 1993b, 'Estimating Expected Return', *Financial Analysts Journal*, **49**, 36–38.

Black, F., M. C. Jensen and M. Scholes (1972), 'The Capital Asset Pricing Model: Some Empirical Tests', In: Jensen, M. C., editor, *Studies in the Theory of Capital Markets*, New York: Praeger, 79–121.

Breeden, D., 1979, 'An Intertemporal Asset Pricing Model with Stochastic Consumption and Investment Opportunities', *Journal of Financial Economics*, **73**, 265–296.

Breeden, D., M. Gibbons and R. Litzenberger, 1989, 'Empirical Tests of the Consumption-Oriented CAPM', *Journal of Finance*, **44**, 231–262.

Breen, W. J. and R. A. Korajczyk, 1994, 'On Selection Biases in Book-to-Market Based Tests of Asset Pricing Models', Working Paper 167, Northwestern University, Chicago, IL.

Campbell, J. Y., 2000, 'Asset Pricing at the Millenium', *Journal of Finance*, **55**, 1515–1567.

Chan, L. K. C., Y. Hamao and J. Lakonishok, 1991, 'Fundamentals and Stock Returns in Japan', *Journal of Finance*, **46**, 1739–1789.

Cheng, P. L. and R. R. Grauer, 1980, 'An Alternative Test of the Capital Asset Pricing Model', *American Economic Review*, **70**, 660–671.

Cheng, P. L. and R. R. Grauer (1982), 'An Alternative Test of the Capital Asset Pricing Model: Reply and Further Results', *American Economic Review*, 2, 1201–1207.

Chopra, N., J. Lakonishok and J. R. Ritter, 1992, 'Measuring Abnormal Performance: Do Stocks Overreact?', *Journal of Financial Economics*, 31, 235–268.

DeBondt, W. F. M. and R. H. Thaler, 1985, 'Does the Stock Market Overreact?', *Journal of Finance*, 40, 557–581.

Fama, E. F., 1996, 'Multifactor Portfolio Efficiency', *Journal of Financial and Quantitative Analysis*, 31, 441–465.

Fama, E. F. and K. R. French, 1992, 'The Cross-Section of Expected Stock Returns', *Journal of Finance*, 47, 427–465.

Fama, E. F. and K. R. French, 1996, 'Multifactor Explanations of Asset Pricing Anomalies', *Journal of Finance*, 51, 55–84.

Fama, E. F. and J. Macbeth, 1973, 'Risk, Return and Equilibrium: Empirical Tests', *Journal of Political Economy*, 81, 607–636.

Friedman, M., 1953, 'The Methodology of Positive Economics', in *Essays in Positive Economics*, Chicago, IL: University of Chicago Press.

Friend, I. and M. Blume, 1973, 'A New Look at the Capital Asset Pricing Model', *Journal of Finance*, 28, 283–299.

Ghysels, E., 1998, 'On Stable Factor Structures in the Pricing of Risk: Do Time-Varying Betas Help or Hurt?', *Journal of Finance*, 53, 549–573.

Grauer, R. R., 1999, 'On the Cross-Sectional Relation between Expected Returns, Betas and Size', *Journal of Finance*, 54, 773–789.

Grundy, K. and B. Malkiel, 1996, 'Reports of Beta's Death Have Been Greatly Exaggerated', *Journal of Portfolio Management*, 23, 36–45.

Hansen, L. P., 1982, 'Large Sample Properties of Generalized Methods of Moments Estimators', *Econometrica*, 50, 1029–1064.

Harvey, Campbell R. and Akhtar Siddique, 2000, 'Conditional Skewness in Asset Pricing Tests', *Journal of Finance*, 55, 1263–1295.

Jaffe, J., D. B. Keim and R. Westerfield, 1989, 'Earnings Yields, Market Values, and Stock Returns', *Journal of Finance*, 44, 135–148.

Jagannathan, R. and Z. Wang, 1996, 'The Conditional CAPM and the Cross-Section of Expected Returns', *Journal of Finance*, 51 (1), 3–53.

Jegadeesh, N., 1990, 'Evidence of Predictable Behavior of Security Returns', *Journal of Finance*, 45, 881–898.

Jegadeesh, N. and S. Titman, 1993, 'Returns to Buying Winners and Selling Losers: Implications for Stock Market Efficiency', *Journal of Finance*, 48, 65–91.

Kandel, S. and R. F. Stambaugh, 1995, 'Portfolio Inefficiency and the Cross-Section of Mean Returns', *Journal of Finance*, 50, 157–184.

Kothari, S. P., J. Shanken and R. G. Sloan, 1995, 'Another Look at the Cross-Section of Expected Returns', *Journal of Finance*, 50, 185–224.

Kraus, Alan and Robert H. Litzenberger, 1976, 'Skewness Preference and the Valuation of Risk Assets', *Journal of Finance*, 31, 1085–1100.

Lettau, M. and S. Ludvigson, 2002, 'Time-Varying Risk Premia and the Cost of Capital: An Alternative Implication of the Q Theory of Investment', *Journal of Monetary Economics*, 49 (1), 31–66.

THE CAPITAL ASSET-PRICING MODEL

Lettau, M. and S. Ludvigson, 'Expected Returns and Expected Dividend Growth', unpublished paper.

Levhari, D. and H. Levy, 1977, 'The Capital Asset Pricing Model and the Investment Horizon', *Review of Economics and Statistics*, **59**, 92–104.

Levy, H., 1978, 'Equilibrium in an Imperfect Market: A Constraint on the Number of Securities in a Portfolio', *American Economic Review*, **68**, 643–658.

Lintner, J., 1965a, 'Security Prices and Maximal Gains from Diversification', *Journal of Finance*, **20**, 587–615.

Lintner, J., 1965b, 'The Valuation of Risk Assets and the Selection of Risky Investments in Stock Portfolios and Capital Budgets', *Review of Economics and Statistics*, **47**, 13–37.

Lo, A. W. and A. C. Mackinlay, 1990, 'Data-Snooping Biases in Tests of Financial Asset Pricing Models', *Review of Financial Studies*, **3**, 431–467.

Lucas, R., 1978, 'Asset Prices in an Exchange Economy', *Econometrica*, **46** (6), 1426–1445.

Mackinlay, A. C., 1995, 'Multifactor Models Do Not Explain Deviations from the CAPM', *Journal of Financial Economics*, **38**, 3–28.

Maginn, J. L. and D. L. Tuttle, 1990, *Managing Investment Portfolios: A Dynamic Process*, 2nd edn, New York: Warren, Gorham & Lamont.

Markowitz, H. M., 1990, 'Normative Portofolio Analysis: Past, Present, and Future', *Journal of Economics and Business*, **42** (2), 99–103.

Merton, R. C., 1973, 'An Intertemporal Capital Asset Pricing Model', *Econometrica*, **41**, 867–887.

Merton, R. C., 1987, 'A Simple Model of Capital Market Equilibrium with Incomplete Information', *Journal of Finance*, **42**, 483–510.

Miller, M. and M. Scholes, 1972, 'Rates of Return in Relation to Risk: A Re-examination of Some Recent Findings', in M. Jensen, ed., *Studies in the Theory of Capital Markets*, New York: Praeger, 47–78.

Mossin, J., 1966, 'Equilibrium in a Capital Asset Market', *Econometrica*, **34**, 768–783.

O'Neal, E. S., 1997, 'How Many Mutual Funds Constitute a Diversified Mutual Fund Portfolio?', *Financial Analysts Journal*, **53** (2), 37–46.

Roll, R., 1977, 'A Critique of the Asset Pricing Theory's Tests, Part 1: On Past and Potential Testability of the Theory', *Journal of Financial Economics*, **4**, 129–176.

Roll, R. and S. A. Ross, 1994, 'On the Cross-Sectional Relation Between Expected Returns and Betas', *Journal of Finance*, **49**, 101–121.

Rosenberg, B., K. Reid and R. Lanstein, 1985, 'Persuasive Evidence of Market Inefficiency', *Journal of Portfolio Management*, **11**, 9–17.

Ross, S. A., 1976a, 'The Arbitrage Theory of Capital Asset Pricing', *Journal of Economic Theory*, **13**, 341–360.

Ross, S. A., 1976b, 'Risk, Return, and Arbitrage', In: I. Friend and J. Bicksler, editors, *Risk and Return in Finance*, Cambridge, MA: Ballinger, 189–218.

Rudd, A. and H. K. Clasing, Jr, 1988, *Modern Portfolio Theory: The Principles of Investment Management*, 2nd edn, Orinda, CA: Andrew Rudd.

Sharpe, W. F., 1964, 'Capital Asset Prices: A Theory of Market Equilibrium', *Journal of Finance*, **19**, 425–442.

Sharpe, W. F., 1991, 'Capital Asset Prices with and without Negative Holdings', *Journal of Finance*, **46**, 489–510.

Shumway, T. and V. Wharter, 1999, 'The Delisting Bias in CRSP's NASDAQ Data and its Implications for the Size Effect', *Journal of Finance*, **54**, 2361–2379.

APPENDIX 10 A formal proof of the capital asset-pricing model

By the separation principle, all investors hold the same efficient portfolio (the market portfolio). Since this portfolio is efficient by the mean–variance criterion, it is the solution to the following problem:

$$\text{Minimise} \sum_{i=1}^{n} \sum_{s=1}^{n} (w_i w_s \sigma_{i,s}) \tag{10A.1a}$$

$$\text{subject to} \sum_{i=1}^{n} w_i E(R_i) = E(R_m) \tag{10A.1b}$$

$$\sum_{i=1}^{n} w_i = 1 \tag{10A.1c}$$

To summarise, this problem looks for the portfolio that minimises the variance (10A.1a) subject to the mean of the market portfolio (10A.1b) and subject to the restriction that all wealth is invested (10A.1c).[30]

We could solve this problem directly and show that the SML represents the optimal solution. However, to simplify the exposition, it is useful to consider the following equivalent problem:

$$\text{Minimise} \sum_{\substack{i=1 \\ i \neq r}}^{n} \sum_{\substack{s=1 \\ s \neq r}}^{n} (w_i w_s \sigma_{i,s}) \tag{10A.2a}$$

$$\text{subject to } r + \sum_{\substack{i=1 \\ i \neq r}}^{n} w_i (E(R_i) - r) = E(R_p) \tag{10A.2b}$$

This problem excludes the weight of the riskless asset and includes only the weights of the risky assets. This means that we can exclude the restriction that the weights should sum to one (10A.1c). If the sum of the weights of the risky assets is greater than one, then the investor simply borrows the difference; if the sum is less than one, then the investor simply lends the difference. Excluding restriction 10A.1c simplifies the problem. However, we have to change the objective function (10A.1a) and the restriction on the mean (10A.1b) by substituting $w_r = 1 - \sum_{\substack{i=1 \\ i \neq r}}^{n} w_i$. This yields the adjusted objective function 10A.2a and the adjusted restriction 10A.2b.

---

[30] Apart from requiring full investment, we could also exclude short-selling by imposing the additional constraint $w_i \geq 0$ $i = 1, \ldots, n; i \neq r$. However, this constraint would not affect the solution, because we know a priori that the optimal solution involves only positive weights, as the market portfolio weights the assets by their relative market value, which is always positive. Hence, no investor would short-sell assets, even if they were allowed to do so. In other words, a short-selling constraint would not be binding.

Now that we have simplified the problem, let us turn to solving it. The problem 10A.2a–b is a so-called convex quadratic programming problem. For such problems, we can find the optimal solution by solving the first-order optimality conditions. For this purpose, we can set up the following Lagrange function:

$$L = \sum_{i=1}^{n} \sum_{s=1}^{n} (w_i w_s \sigma_{i,s}) - \lambda(\sum_{i=1}^{n} w_i(E(R_i) - r) - E(R_m)) \qquad (10A.3)$$

where λ is a Lagrange multiplier that represents the shadow price of the restriction on the mean (10A.2b); it measures the increase of the optimal portfolio's variance if we increase the required mean. The first-order derivative of the Langrage function with respect to portfolio weight w_i is:

$$\frac{\partial L}{\partial w_i} = 2 \times \sum_{s=1}^{n} (w_s \sigma_{i,s}) - \lambda(E(R_i) - r) \qquad (10A.4)$$

The first-order condition states that the optimum is found by choosing the weights for which all first-order derivatives equal zero, i.e. $\frac{\partial L}{\partial w_i} = 0$ for all $i = 1, \ldots, n$. Hence, the market portfolio with portfolio weights w_i^*, $i = 1, \ldots, n$, is optimal if and only if

$$2 \times \sum_{s=1}^{n} (w_s^* \sigma_{i,s}) - \lambda(E(R_i) - r) = 0$$

Since $\sum_{s=1}^{n} w_s^* \sigma_{i,s} = \sigma_{i,m} = \beta_i \sigma_m^2$, the previous equation can be written as

$$2\beta_i \sigma_m^2 - \lambda(E(R_i) - r) = 0$$

or

$$\lambda(E(R_i) - r) = 2\beta_i \sigma_m^2 \qquad (10A.5)$$

Since the equation applies to all assets, it must also hold for the market portfolio, which has $\beta_m = 1$. Hence,

$$\lambda(E(R_m) - r) = 2\sigma_m^2$$

or

$$\lambda = \frac{2\sigma_m^2}{(E(R_m) - r)} \qquad (10A.6)$$

Substituting for λ in (10A.5) yields:

$$\frac{2\sigma_m^2}{(E(R_m) - r)} \times (E(R_i) - r) = 2\beta_i \sigma_m^2$$

Dividing both sides of the equation by $\dfrac{2\sigma_m^2}{(E(R_m) - r)}$ yields the SML:

$$E(R_i) = r + (E(R_m) - r)\beta_i \tag{10A.7}$$

which completes the proof. To summarise, the SML is simply the first-order optimality condition for mean–variance efficiency of the market portfolio.

In search of money for nothing

Arbitrage is one of the most important concepts in modern finance theory. An arbitrage opportunity is an investment that requires no net outflow of cash and carries no chance of losing money, yet has some probability of yielding a positive return. The classic example of an arbitrage opportunity occurs when two assets offer the same returns, but trade at different prices. Faced with this situation, an arbitrageur will buy the cheaper asset and short-sell the more expensive one. Doing this provides an immediate benefit of cash (the difference in prices) and there is nothing to pay for in the future, because the cash flows associated with the long and the short positions offset each other. Thus the investor gets money for nothing.

What about a strategy that requires an initial investment, but guarantees a profit that exceeds this investment at some time in the future? Is this an arbitrage opportunity? After all, the investor knows no money will be lost. In fact, comparing an initial investment with a future return is like comparing apples with oranges and we cannot describe this investment as an arbitrage opportunity without additional information. For example, suppose a default-free government bond is trading at par and will pay a fixed coupon rate at maturity. Buying this bond requires an initial investment but gives a guaranteed higher return at maturity. This is not an arbitrage opportunity as the investor is just receiving a fair compensation for lending money.

The no-arbitrage principle and the law of one price
In the economists' world of perfect markets, arbitrage opportunities are ruled out in equilibrium, if we make the plausible assumption that there exists at least one investor who wants more wealth. Suppose an arbitrage opportunity does exist: one stock becomes overpriced relative to another combination of assets that generates exactly the same future cash flows. Then, all rational investors in search of more wealth will hold a short position in this stock and a long position in the alternative assets. These investors make money immediately and are fully hedged. Yet by following this strategy, the rational investors will bid down the price of the expensive asset and bid up the price of the alternative assets, until the two have converged and the arbitrage opportunity is eliminated. Therefore we can rule out arbitrage opportunities just by assuming market equilibrium and the existence of rational investors who want more. As the economists put it: 'There is no free lunch.'

The absence of arbitrage implies the law of one price: two perfect substitutes must trade at the same price. (Perfect substitutes are products or instruments that are identical in their investment characteristics.) This result is extremely helpful, because it allows us to price complicated financial instruments by replication, that is, instead of trying to measure an instrument's true value directly we just need to find a portfolio of perfect substitutes whose price we can directly observe.

One application of the law of one price is the famous Black–Scholes option pricing formula, derived by professors Fischer Black, Robert Merton and Myron Scholes, which constitutes the basis of modern option pricing theory. They were faced with the task of pricing financial options, which are financial instruments with complicated cash flow structures. They solved the problem by identifying a specific portfolio of stocks and bonds that acted as a perfect substitute for the option. Because we know the prices of the stocks and the bonds, we can easily compute the price of the option. Another application came from the work of academics Franco Modigliani and Merton Miller. They used the arbitrage principle to establish their capital structure irrelevance proposition: in perfect capital markets, making changes to the capital structure of the company does not change the value of the company.

Risk arbitrage

As mentioned above, under perfect capital markets, the condition required for ruling out arbitrage opportunities is that just one investor wants more wealth. Recently, however, financial economists have begun to study a slightly different concept – risk arbitrage. In most financial markets, as pointed out by academics Andrei Shleifer and Robert Vishny, if assets are mispriced and therefore fail to trade at their fundamental value, then this does not generate pure arbitrage, but 'risk arbitrage'.

Suppose that an arbitrageur knows that a given asset is overpriced. To take advantage of this opportunity, the arbitrageur must simultaneously sell the asset, and buy a perfect substitute that is 'correctly priced' – in more technical terms, the perfect substitute is trading at its fundamental value. This perfect substitute must be an asset or (replicating) portfolio that will deliver exactly the same cash flows in the future, so the arbitrageur is fully hedged.

In reality, though, such a substitute might be hard to find, depending on the asset one wants to mimic. For example, a perfect substitute for US three-month Treasury bills is easier to find than a perfect substitute for shares of Amazon.com.

When perfect substitutes do not exist, arbitrageurs must face the idiosyncratic risk associated with both the long and the short positions: these positions no longer cancel each other out exactly. The concept of arbitrage relies on the notion of price convergence: the price of the expensive asset will eventually converge to the fundamental price given by the price of the replicating portfolio and when this happens the arbitrageur will make money. If the replicating portfolio is not a perfect substitute, then the investment strategy is not a pure arbitrage opportunity. The two prices might not converge, or they might diverge much more before they converge, and the investor might end up losing money.

Even when it is possible to find a perfect substitute, the opportunity for arbitrage might still be limited in certain markets because of restrictions placed on short-selling. And even if there are no such restrictions, short positions are more risky for investors, because they carry margin requirements that force them to put down collateral payments. These payments are marked-to-market, which means that every day investors must cover their losses. If the price gap widens, they will be required to increase the margin deposit.

Investment in the News 11 continued

As a result, arbitrageurs might need capital to finance their strategies, otherwise they will be forced to liquidate their position at a loss. This is therefore an example of risk arbitrage. Investors do not make money with absolute certainty and may need to invest significant capital before the price convergence eventually occurs.

The technology bubble

Imagine an investor in April 1999 who believes the NASDAQ is substantially overvalued. The tracking stock of the NASDAQ 100 Index (known as 'The Qs' for its ticker symbol QQQ) climbs to Dollars 60 by July 1999 and the investor decides to sell it short. This immediately presents a problem: what is a perfect substitute for the NASDAQ? How can the position be hedged? One way is to take a position in US Treasury bills, if stocks appear overvalued relative to government bonds. Alternatively, if technology stocks appear overpriced relative to other stocks, the investor can take a position in a value fund – a mutual fund that invests predominantly in 'old economy stocks'.

Either way will present some idiosyncratic risk. If the investor kept the position until April 2001, there would have been a substantial return as the tracking stock was trading at close to Dollars 35. However, before this correction took place, the NASDAQ 100 index was substantially higher, reaching a peak of close to Dollars 120 by March 2000. At this point, the investor would have been faced with substantial margin calls, and would probably have been required to liquidate the position at a heavy loss. [...]

Source: Gomes Francisco, 'In Search of Money for Nothing', *Financial Times*, 11 June 2001.

Learning objectives

After studying this chapter, you should be able to:

1 Explain factor risk models and why they simplify the computations required for mean–variance analysis.

2 Explain the arbitrage pricing theory (APT), its assumptions and the resulting linear equilibrium relationship.

3 Compare and contrast the CAPM and the APT.

4 Summarise the results of the empirical research of the APT.

In Chapter 10, we discussed the strengths and weakness of the CAPM. In this chapter, we examine another basic asset-pricing model, the arbitrage pricing theory (APT) developed by Ross (1976). Moving away from construction of mean–variance efficient portfolios, Ross derived relations among expected rates of return that would rule out riskless profits by any investor in well-functioning capital markets. The two key concepts of APT are arbitrage and factor risk models.

In Investment in the News 11, Francisco Gomes, an assistant professor of finance at London Business School, explains the concept of arbitrage. Basically, arbitrage is an umbrella term for strategies that construct a zero-investment portfolio that will yield positive returns. Zero-investment means investors need not use any of their own money in an initial investment. The APT is built on the concept that arbitrage opportunities do not exist for very long. When arbitrage opportunities do exist, a few large traders can take advantage of the opportunity until prices return to equilibrium.

Factor risk models relate the common movements of asset prices to a series of common risk factors, such as interest rates, stock-market indexes, exchange rates and commodity prices. These models are useful in order to decompose an asset's risk into components of systematic risk and unsystematic risk. Also, factor risk models reduce the numerical complexity of mean–variance analysis relative to Markowitz's full mean–variance analysis.

In this chapter, we examine both the single index model (SIM), a model with a single common risk factor, and the multiple index model (MIM). Then we turn to the APT, the relationship between the APT and the CAPM, as well as some of the empirical evidence on the relative merits of the APT.

11.1 Factor risk models

11.1.1 The single index model

The SIM uses some basic assumptions about the probability distribution of asset returns (or the return-generating process). According to the SIM, two factors are responsible for a given asset's rate of return: the percentage change in a common risk factor and changes related to asset-specific events. The common risk factor could be any variable that is correlated with security returns, such as the inflation rate, GDP or the S&P 500 index. Examples of asset-specific news might be Microsoft's success in developing a new version of Windows software, the development of the new drug Viagra by Pfizer Pharmaceuticals in 1998, the resignation of the chair of General Motors, or a fire at an uninsured factory.

Formally, the SIM assumes that the rate of return on asset i is given by:

$$R_i = \alpha_i + \beta_i I + e_i \qquad (11.1)$$

where R_i is the rate of return on asset i, I is the percentage change in the common risk factor, and e_i is the asset-specific component. Like the market beta used in the characteristic line of the CAPM, β_i measures the sensitivity of the ith asset's return to changes in the common risk factor. This sensitivity coefficient is commonly referred to as the factor loading or the beta. Note that the common risk factor in the APT need not be the market portfolio; it can be any variable that is correlated with security returns. The beta is calculated formally as $\beta_i = \sigma_{i,I}/\sigma_I^2$, where $\sigma_{i,I}$ is the covariance between asset i and the risk factor and σ_I^2 is the variance of the risk factor.

For example, if $\beta_i = 2$ and I is the GDP, then the SIM beta tells us that if the GDP goes up by 1%, then R_i, on average, will go up by 2%. The intercept α_i represents the expected return on an asset or portfolio with $\beta_i = 0$, as well as the expected return when $I = 0$. The term e_i is the random deviation from the straight line given by $R_i = \alpha_i + \beta_i I$. It can be either positive or negative, depending on whether the asset-specific news is good or bad.

The straight line in Exhibit 11.1 has an intercept of α_i and a slope of β_i. If all points (R_i) are exactly on the line, then all deviations (e_i) are zero. However, in general, some points are located above the line and some below it due to asset-specific factors.

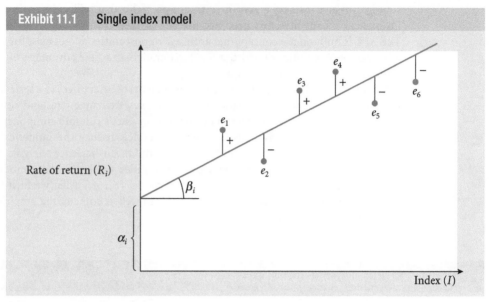

Exhibit 11.1 Single index model

Source: From *Introduction to Investments*, 2nd edn, by Levy. © 1999. Reprinted with permission of South-Western, a division of Thomson Learning: www.thomsonrights.com. Fax 800 730-2215.

→ **Connecting Theory to Practice 11.1**   **FT**

Dow inches forward into the black

Wall Street opened slightly higher on Wednesday, building on the previous session's gains as investors began to view dollar weakness as a positive for US equities.

Shortly after the opening bell, the Dow Jones Industrial Average was up 0.2 per cent at 9590.85, while both the NASDAQ Composite and the S&P 500 started flat.

With no economic data due, investors focused on corporate events, particularly Cisco Systems, the world's leading networks company, which said after the close on Tuesday that its board had authorised the company's plans to expand its $13 bn stock buyback programme by a further $7 bn. Cisco stock gained 1 per cent at the open.

In Europe, stocks were firm after Vivendi Universal reported narrower losses than had been expected, and issued an upbeat outlook on the full year. The Franco-US media giant also said that it was committed to a speedy resolution of its plans to merge its entertainment business with General Electric's NBC. Vivendi's Paris-listed stock was up 3 per cent in European morning trade. General Electric meanwhile, gained 0.4 per cent.

Drugs companies were also expected to be in focus as Swiss manufacturer Novartis said it may have to delay the launch of its arthritis and pain killing drug Prexige. The US Food and Drug Administration said it needed more information on the drug. Pfizer was down 0.3 per cent, while Eli Lilly fell 0.2 per cent.

Viacom, the entertainment group, was down 3.5 per cent after it cut its profit and revenue forecasts for the year. The company, which owns television networks CBS and MTV, said local advertising remained slow, but the economic recovery had translated into robust national advertising sales growth.

Source: Neil Dennis, 'Dow Inches Forward Into the Black', FT Online, 24 September 2003.

→ **Making the connection**

This article lists several examples of corporate events on 24 Septermber 2003: the expansion of the buyback programme of Cisco, the upbeat outlook and merger plans by Vivendi, the delay of the launch of a drug by Novartis and a cut of the profit and revenue forecasts by Viacom. These corporate events moved the stock prices of these corporations, but not the stock market as a whole. Hence, they represent asset-specific risk rather than common risk factors.

Practice box

Problem   When Hurricane Andrew hit the Florida and Louisiana coasts, it caused a big loss for many insurance companies. Is this an asset-specific surprise or a common-factor surprise?

Solution   If there was only one insurance firm in the country, then only this firm would be affected, and the loss due to the hurricane would be considered an asset-specific surprise. However, because there are many insurance firms, the loss would be considered an industry factor, which is a common factor rather than an asset-specific factor.

In addition to the linear factor structure in Equation 11.1, the SIM imposes three assumptions about the statistical distribution of the asset-specific factor e_i. First, the asset-specific factor is expected to be zero:[1]

$$E(e_i) = 0 \qquad (11.2)$$

for all $i = 1, \ldots, n$. Second, the SIM assumes that asset i's specific news is independent of the specific news for asset s. For example, this means that if some success or failure occurs at Microsoft, then it does not affect the chance of success or failure at Pfizer Pharmaceuticals. In statistical terms, this assumption implies that

$$E(e_i e_s) = 0 \qquad (11.3)$$

for all $i = 1, \ldots, n$ and $s = 1, \ldots, n$. Third, the asset-specific term is assumed to be independent of the common factor. For example, this means that a recession or a bear stock market does not affect the probability of damage caused by natural disasters such as fires, floods and hurricanes. Formally,

$$E((I - E(I))e_i) = 0 \qquad (11.4)$$

for all $i = 1, \ldots, n$, where $E(I)$ denotes the expected percentage change in the common factor.

_____

[1] If $E(e_i)$ is not zero, we can always add $E(e_i)$ to α_i; then the mean of the deviations left is, by construction, zero. Also, when we run a regression to estimate β_i, the sample mean $\bar{e}_i$ will be zero.

These three assumptions simplify the return distribution relative to the mean–variance framework that underlies the CAPM in several ways.[2] First, it follows that the expected return of asset i is given by

$$E(R_i) = \alpha_i + \beta_i E(I) \tag{11.5}$$

where $E(R_i)$ denotes the expected rate of return on asset i, and $E(I)$ denotes the expected percentage change in the common factor. Note that the common factor I and the factor sensitivity coefficient β_i determine the expected return on asset i. For example, if the SIM beta of an asset is positive, then we can predict that when the common risk factor I goes up, the asset's return will go up on average, and when the common risk factor goes down, the rate of return will go down on average. Note that we say that *on average* the return will go up or down. This is different from saying anything about the actual change in returns. In determining the actual rate of return, we must include the asset-specific event e_i. It is possible for the common risk factor to go up but an asset-specific event to cause the actual return to be negative.

Second, it can be shown that the variance of asset i is given by

$$\sigma_i^2 = \beta_i^2 \sigma_I^2 + \sigma_{e_i}^2 \tag{11.6}$$

where $\sigma_I^2 = E(I - E(R))^2$ is the variance of the common factor and $\sigma_{e_i}^2 = E(e_i^2)$ is the variance of the asset-specific factor. The term $\beta_i^2 \sigma_I^2$ is the risk that is due to the common factor. This part is called the systematic risk; it is undiversifiable risk that cannot be eliminated simply by including many assets in the portfolio. This risk can be eliminated by choosing the portfolio weights such that $\beta_p = 0$, but it can't be eliminated by diversification. For example, if I is the GDP, then no matter how large our portfolio, we cannot avoid the variability in the portfolio's return that is due to the variability of GDP; hence, the risk caused by this factor cannot be eliminated. By contrast, the term $\sigma_{e_i}^2$ is called unsystematic risk (risk not related to the common factor), or diversifiable risk. This risk can be virtually eliminated if the investor holds a large portfolio of assets. Specifically, for a portfolio with weights $w_1, \ldots, w_n$, then the asset-specific factor is $\sum w_i e_i$. Since the asset-specific factors of individual assets are assumed to be independent (Equation 11.3), we expect some e_i to be positive and some to be negative, and on average they cancel each other out. Hence, $\sum w_i e_i$ goes to zero if many assets are included (and the individual weights become very small).

Exhibit 11.2 illustrates the relationship between the portfolio variance and its components, systematic and unsystematic risk. For example, if there are only two assets in the portfolio and the systematic risk is 10 and the unsystematic risk is 11, then the portfolio variance is 21. By adding more assets to the portfolio, the variance of the unsystematic component, $\sum w_i e_i$, goes down (because the e_i of some assets cancels the e_i of others). For example, if systematic risk remains 10 in our example, then for $n = 30$, the unsystematic risk is reduced to only 1, and the portfolio variance is 11. For a very large n, the unsystematic risk is reduced to zero.

Third, the SIM greatly simplifies the computation of covariance. Chapter 8 showed that in order to solve for the mean–variance-efficient set, we have to minimise the portfolio's variance for a given mean return. The portfolio's variance, in turn, is a function of the covariance

---

[2] Section 11.1.2 generalises the analysis to the general multiple index model (MIM) with multiple common risk factors. In that section, footnotes formally derive the means, variances and covariances of the assets from the assumptions about the return generating process. This analysis also applies for the SIM discussed in this section; the appropriate results are obtained by setting the number of common factors (K) equal to 1.

Systematic and unsystematic risk as a function of the number of assets in the portfolio

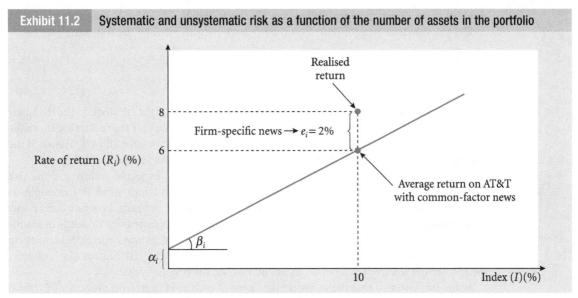

Source: From *Introduction to Investments*, 2nd edn, by Levy. © 1999. Reprinted with permission of South-Western, a division of Thomson Learning: www.thomsonrights.com. Fax 800 730-2215.

of all possible pairs of assets.[3] If we have n assets, then the number of pairs of assets and hence the number of covariance terms is $(n^2 - n)/2$. If $n = 100$, then $(n^2 - n)/2 = 4950$, which is quite a large number to handle. Under the assumptions of the SIM, the covariance of asset j and asset s is reduced to the following:

$$\sigma_{i,s} = \beta_i \beta_s \sigma_I^2 \tag{11.7}$$

Therefore, we have to estimate only 100 betas to get all 4950 covariance terms needed without the assumptions of the SIM. Thus, the assumptions of the SIM greatly reduce the number of estimates needed for the derivation of the efficient frontier.

11.1.2 The multiple index model

So far, we have assumed that only one factor generates the return on the various assets. It is possible, however, that several common factors generate the return on the assets, such as the term spread (the difference between the long-term government bond yield and the T-bill rate), unexpected inflation, the credit spread (the difference between the yield on corporate bonds and government bonds) and the growth rate of industrial production.[4] MIMs are an attempt to capture the non-market influences that cause securities to move together. They introduce extra indexes (or external factors) in the hope of capturing additional information. The cost of introducing additional indexes (or factors) is the chance that they are picking up

---

[3] We use the 'indirect method' for computing portfolio variance rather than the 'direct method' (see Chapter 8). In contrast to the indirect method, the direct method does not require information on the variances and the covariances of the assets. However, the direct method requires even more information, as it requires the returns of all individual assets in all possible states of the world (the number of states can be infinitely large).

[4] Chen *et al.* (1986) identified these four common risk factors for the US stock market. However, there currently is no consensus on the relevant set of risk factors.

random noise rather than real influences. Denoting the jth factor by I_j, the multifactor risk model assumes that rates of return on the ith asset are generated by the following process:

$$R_i = \alpha_i + \sum_{j=1}^{K} \beta_{ij} I_j + e_i \qquad (11.1a)$$

where there are K factors, and β_{ij} is the sensitivity of the return of the ith stock to the jth factor ($j = 1, 2, \ldots, K$). It is convenient though unnecessary to assume that the factors are mutually independent. Formally, this implies $E((I_j - E(I))(E(I_k - E(I_k)))) = 0$ for all $j \neq k$. Hence, if the first factor goes up or down, then this implies nothing about the second factor.[5]

Note that the MIM assumes that the relationship between expected return and the risk factors is linear. In some cases, we know that this assumption is not valid. For example, as we will see later in this book, the return to long-run bonds depends in a non-linear way on interest rates (the so-called convexity effect), and the return to options depends in a non-linear way on the return on the underlying asset (the so-called gamma effect). Still, in these cases, we can employ the MIM by using transformations of the risk factors (for example, the risk factors squared) instead of, or in addition to, the original values.

Again, it is assumed that the asset-specific factor of each asset is zero on average, or $E(e_i) = 0$ for all $i = 1, \ldots, n$, that the asset-specific factors of different assets are independent of each other, or $E(e_i e_s) = 0$ for all $i = 1, \ldots, n$, and $s = 1, \ldots, n$, and that the asset-specific terms are independent of the common factors, or $E((I_j - E(I_j))e_i) = 0$ for all $i = 1, \ldots, n$ and $j = 1, \ldots, K$. Using these assumptions, we can write the means in the following manner:[6]

$$E(R_i) = \alpha_i + \sum_{j=1}^{K} \beta_{ij} E(I_j) \qquad (11.5a)$$

Further, variances can be expressed as follows:[7]

$$\sigma_i^2 = \sum_{j=1}^{K} \beta_{ij}^2 \sigma_{I_j}^2 + \sigma_{e_i}^2 \qquad (11.6a)$$

---

[5] In practice, factors such as GDP, inflation, interest rates and exchange rates are correlated. However, we can always convert a set of correlated factors into a set of uncorrelated factors using a statistical technique called orthogonalisation. Independent factors are convenient, because it simplifies the expressions for variance and covariance.

Specifically, if $E((I_j - E(I))(E(I_k - E(I_k)))) = 0$ for all $j \neq k$, then $E\left(\sum_{j=1}^{K} \beta_{ij}(I_j - E(I_j))\right)^2 = \sum_{j=1}^{K} \beta_{ij}^2 E(I_j - E(I_j))^2$ and $E\left(\left(\sum_{j=1}^{K} \beta_{ij}(I_j - E(I_j))\right)\left(\sum_{j=1}^{K} \beta_{sj}(I_j - E(I_j))\right)\right) = \sum_{j=1}^{K} \beta_{ij}\beta_{sj} E(I_j - E(I_j))^2$. Both equalities are needed to derive Equations 11.6a and 11.7a.

[6] Using Equation 11.1a, we can write $E(R_i) = E\left(\alpha_i + \sum_{j=1}^{K} \beta_{ij} I_j + e_i\right) = \alpha_i + \sum_{j=1}^{K} \beta_{ij} E(I_j) + E(e_i)$. Since $E(e_i) = 0$, we find $E(R_i) = \alpha_i + \sum_{j=1}^{K} \beta_{ij} E(I_j) + e_i$.

[7] Using Equation 11.5a, we find $(R_i - E(R_i)) = \sum_{j=1}^{K} \beta_{ij}(I_j - E(I_j)) + e_i$. Hence, we can rewrite variance as follows:

$\sigma_i^2 = E(R_i - E(R_i))^2 = E\left(\sum_{j=1}^{K} \beta_{ij}(I_j - E(I_j)) + e_i\right)^2 = \sum_{j=1}^{K} \beta_{ij}^2 E(I_j - E(I_j))^2 + 2\sum_{j=1}^{K} \beta_{ij} E((I_j - E(I_j))e_i) + E(e_i^2)$. Since $\sigma_{I_j}^2 = E(I_j - E(I_j))^2$, $E((I_j - E(I_j))e_i) = 0$, and $\sigma_{e_i}^2 = E(e_i^2)$, we find $\sigma_i^2 = \sum_{j=1}^{K} \beta_{ij}^2 \sigma_{I_j}^2 + \sigma_{e_i}^2$.

Finally, we can write the covariances as:[8]

$$\sigma_{i,s} = \sum_{j=1}^{K} \beta_{ij}\beta_{sj}\sigma_{I_j}^2 \qquad (11.7a)$$

11.1.3 Estimating a multifactor risk model

In practice, the factor loadings are not known. However, using historical observations of the asset's returns and the factors, we can estimate the loadings using regression analysis (see Appendix A at the end of this book for an introduction to regression analysis). Specifically, for each asset, we can estimate the following time-series regression model,

$$r_{i,t} = \alpha_i + \beta_{i,1}I_{1,t} + \ldots + \beta_{i,K}I_{K,t} + \varepsilon_{i,t} \qquad (11.8)$$

where $r_{i,t}$ is the return on the ith asset in the tth period, α_i is the expected return to the ith asset if all factors take the value zero, $\beta_{i,1}, \ldots, \beta_{i,K}$ are the factor loadings, $I_{1,t}, \ldots, I_{K,t}$ are the factors in the tth period, and $\varepsilon_{i,t}$ is the return that is not explained by the factors.

We may estimate this model using regression analysis. The regression output includes estimates $\hat{\alpha}_i, \hat{\beta}_{i,1}, \ldots, \hat{\beta}_{i,K}$, standard errors for the coefficients and the R-squared (a measure of percentage variance explained by the factors).

To illustrate this approach, we estimate the factor loadings for a set of 25 US stock portfolios. The portfolios are the so-called Fama and French benchmark portfolios based on market capitalisation (size) and book-to-market equity ratio (B/M) of the stocks. These benchmark portfolios were also used in Chapter 10 to illustrate the empirical anomalies of the CAPM.

We use the so-called three-factor model developed by Fama and French (1996):

$$r_{i,t} = \alpha_i + \beta_{i,m}r_{m,t} + \beta_{i,SMB}r_{SMB,t} + \beta_{i,HML}r_{HML,t} + \varepsilon_{i,t}$$

which includes the following risk factors:

Factor	Measured by
Market factor	Return on market index minus risk-free interest rate
Size factor	Return on long position in small-capital stocks less return on large capital stocks (small minus big, SMB). The size breakpoint is the median NYSE market equity
Book-to-market factor	Return on long position in high B/M stocks (value stocks) less return on short position in low B/M stocks (high minus low, HML). The BE/ME breakpoints are the 30th and 70th NYSE percentiles

---

[8] Using equation 11.5a, we find $(R_i - E(R_i)) = \sum_{j=1}^{K} \beta_{ij}(I_j - E(I_j)) + e_i$ and $R_s - E(R_s) = \sum_{j=1}^{K} \beta_{sj}(I_j - E(I_j)) + e_s$. Hence, using

some algebra, we find $\sigma_{i,s} = E((R_i - E(R_i))(R_s - E(R_s))) = E\left(\left(\sum_{j=1}^{K} \beta_{ij}(I_j - E(I_j)) + e_i\right)\left(\sum_{j=1}^{K} \beta_{sj}(I_j - E(I_j)) + e_s\right)\right) =$

$\sum_{j=1}^{K} \beta_{ij}\beta_{sj}E(I_j - E(I_j))^2 + \sum_{j=1}^{K} \beta_{ij}E((I - E(I))e_s) + \sum_{j=1}^{K} \beta_{sj}E((I - E(I))e_i) + E(e_i e_s) = \sum_{j=1}^{K} \beta_{ij}\beta_{sj}\sigma_{I_j}^2$. The ultimate equality

follows directly from the fact that the last three terms in the penultimate equation are assumed to be zero, i.e. $\beta_{ij}E((I_j - E(I_j))e_s) = 0$, $\beta_s E((I_j - E(I_j))e_i) = 0$, and $E(e_i e_s) = 0$, for all $i = 1, \ldots, n$, $s = 1, \ldots, n$, and $j = 1, \ldots, K$.

| Exhibit 11.3 | Factor loading for the Fama and French (1996) three-factor model |

Size	B/M	α_i	standard error	$\beta_{i,m}$	standard error	$\beta_{i,SMB}$	standard error	$\beta_{i,HML}$	standard error	R^2 (%)
Small	Low	−0.45	0.11	1.06	0.03	1.38	0.03	−0.33	0.04	92
Small	2	0.00	0.08	0.97	0.02	1.32	0.03	0.07	0.03	94
Small	3	0.04	0.07	0.93	0.02	1.12	0.02	0.29	0.02	95
Small	4	0.21	0.06	0.90	0.02	1.04	0.02	0.46	0.02	94
Small	High	0.15	0.07	0.98	0.02	1.09	0.02	0.68	0.02	95
2	Low	−0.19	0.08	1.12	0.02	1.00	0.03	−0.40	0.03	95
2	2	−0.12	0.07	1.03	0.02	0.89	0.02	0.18	0.03	94
2	3	0.08	0.07	0.99	0.02	0.76	0.02	0.42	0.02	94
2	4	0.09	0.06	0.98	0.02	0.72	0.02	0.59	0.02	94
2	High	−0.03	0.06	1.09	0.02	0.84	0.02	0.77	0.02	95
3	Low	−0.07	0.07	1.08	0.02	0.73	0.02	−0.45	0.03	95
3	2	0.01	0.08	1.06	0.02	0.52	0.03	0.22	0.03	90
3	3	−0.07	0.08	1.02	0.02	0.44	0.02	0.51	0.03	90
3	4	0.01	0.07	1.00	0.02	0.39	0.02	0.67	0.03	90
3	High	0.02	0.08	1.11	0.02	0.53	0.03	0.83	0.03	90
4	Low	0.14	0.07	1.05	0.02	0.38	0.02	−0.45	0.03	94
4	2	−0.17	0.08	1.10	0.02	0.21	0.03	0.26	0.03	88
4	3	−0.07	0.08	1.08	0.02	0.16	0.03	0.51	0.03	88
4	4	0.03	0.08	1.04	0.02	0.20	0.02	0.62	0.03	89
4	High	−0.05	0.10	1.18	0.02	0.26	0.03	0.84	0.04	86
Big	Low	0.21	0.06	0.96	0.01	−0.26	0.02	−0.38	0.02	94
Big	2	−0.02	0.07	1.04	0.02	−0.24	0.02	0.15	0.03	90
Big	3	−0.03	0.08	0.99	0.02	−0.23	0.03	0.29	0.03	85
Big	4	−0.09	0.07	1.01	0.02	−0.20	0.02	0.64	0.03	88
Big	High	−0.24	0.11	1.05	0.03	−0.11	0.03	0.82	0.04	79

The latter two factors do not follow directly from a theoretical model, but they are motivated by the empirical anomalies related to size and B/M (see Chapter 10). At present, the economic interpretation of these factors is not entirely clear.

We estimate this model using OLS regression analysis for a sample of monthly returns over the period from July 1963 to December 2002. Exhibit 11.3 shows the results. From the magnitude of the standard errors, we can see that, apart from the stock market portfolio, the size and B/M hedge portfolios have a significant effect on the stock returns.[9] Apparently, small caps, big caps, value stocks and growth stocks are exposed to common risk factors other than market risk alone. Combined, the three factors explain about 79–95% of the return variations (the R-squared ranges between 79 and 95%). Note that the benchmark portfolios with small caps generally have a high positive factor loading for the SMB portfolio. For example, the first

[9] As a rule of thumb, a variable has a significant effect at a level of significance of 95% if the magnitude of the standard error is smaller than one-half of the magnitude of the coefficient estimate; in this case, the t-statistic (or the absolute value of the ratio of the coefficient estimate to the standard error) is larger than two. For example, for the first benchmark portfolio, the SMB beta is 1.384, with a standard error of 0.034, giving a t-statistic of 1.384/0.034 = 40.71, which is highly significant. For more details about hypothesis testing, refer to Section A.5 of Appendix A at the end of this book.

benchmark portfolio of small growth stocks ('Small' and 'Low') has a size beta of 1.384. This makes sense, because the SMB portfolio captures the return difference between small caps and large caps. Similarly, growth stocks generally have negative betas for the HML factor, which captures the difference between value stocks and growth stocks.

11.2 The arbitrage pricing theory

Resembling the CAPM, the APT is an equilibrium pricing model; it reaches conclusions about what determines the equilibrium rates of return of capital assets. However, the APT is based on a different set of assumptions. Recall that in deriving the CAPM, we assumed that all investors make their investment decisions by a mean–variance rule. In deriving the APT risk–return relationship, Ross does not assume risk aversion or rely on the mean–variance rule. Rather, he explains the linear relationship between expected return and risk as arising because there are no arbitrage opportunities in security markets. It is based on the law of one price: two items that are the same cannot sell at different prices. The strong assumptions made about utility theory in deriving the CAPM are not necessary. An assumption of homogeneous expectations is necessary. In fact, the APT description of equilibrium is more general than that provided by a CAPM-type model because pricing can be affected by influences beyond simply means and variances. The assumption of investors utilising a mean–variance framework is replaced by an assumption of the process generating security returns. APT requires that the returns on any stock be related linearly to a set of inexes.

Arbitrage is a strategy that makes a positive return without requiring an initial investment. For example, opportunities for arbitrage arise from differences in an asset's price when this asset is traded on two or more markets.[10] A profit with zero investment is made by buying the asset at the low price and simultaneously selling the asset at the high price. All investors would prefer such a strategy independent of their risk attitude (risk-averse, risk-neutral or risk-seeking). Furthermore, the more money they can make in this way, the better off they are.[11] To have an arbitrage opportunity, the returns can be certain or uncertain, as long as with a zero investment the returns are non-negative and there is at least one positive potential return.

If investors can find a strategy that earns a positive return with a zero net initial investment, then all investors will try to follow this strategy. As a result, the price of the assets will change until, in equilibrium, the positive return drops to zero and the arbitrage opportunity vanishes from the market. The APT is the return–risk relationship that applies in the equilibrium situation with no arbitrage opportunities.

11.2.1 Examples of arbitrage

Consider first the simplest case of arbitrage, where you can borrow $100 at bank A at 5%, and you can deposit the money in a second fully insured bank B to earn 6%. The cash flow from these two transactions is shown in Exhibit 11.4. In this simple example, you have a zero out-of-pocket investment at t_0 and a profit of $1 at the end of the year (t_1). If such a financial

---

[10] The 'law of one price' states that two items that are the same should sell at the same price. Violations of the law of one price create opportunities for arbitrage if short-selling is possible.

[11] We need only to assume that investors prefer a higher return to a lower return. Put differently, the utility of return must be increasing (see Chapter 7).

Exhibit 11.4	A simple case of arbitrage with bank interest (in $)				
Strategy		Time t_0	Strategy		Time t_1
Borrow from bank A		+$100	Withdraw deposit from bank B		+$106
Deposit in bank B		−100	Pay back bank A		−105
Net cash flow		0			+1

Source: From *Introduction to Investments*, 2nd edn, by Levy. © 1999. Reprinted with permission of South-Western, a division of Thomson Learning: www.thomsonrights.com. Fax 800 730-2215.

Exhibit 11.5	Profit and loss on an investment		
State of the economy	Securities		
	A	B	C
Recession	−$2	−$4	$0
Stable	6	4	10
Boom	10	16	6

Source: From *Introduction to Investments*, 2nd edn, by Levy. © 1999. Reprinted with permission of South-Western, a division of Thomson Learning: www.thomsonrights.com. Fax 800 730-2215.

situation existed, it would be an arbitrage opportunity. If you could borrow an unlimited amount of money at 5% and lend it at 6%, then the potential profit would be infinite. Such a case is called a money machine; one has a machine, so to speak, to create money.

Although in general such situations do not exist in the market, this simple example illustrates the concept of an arbitrage opportunity. You create a financial transaction such that with zero net investment, you earn a positive return. If such a situation exists, arbitrage profit is available, and the financial transaction by which this profit is achieved is called an arbitrage transaction.

A more realistic example, which is essential to the derivation of the APT, involves the short-selling of risky securities. Recall that when investors sell a security short, they sell shares that they do not own. The process of short-selling is as follows: the investor borrows the shares from a broker and then sells the shares in the market to receive the proceeds from the sale. At some future date, the investor must buy the stocks in the market to replace the shares borrowed.

To illustrate how an investor can create an arbitrage profit using short-selling transactions, suppose you have three securities, A, B and C, with returns as given in Exhibit 11.5. For simplicity, assume that each share is trading at $100, so the profit or loss in dollars is also the percentage return on your investment. For example, making $10 on a $100 investment means a +10% rate of return. It is obvious from Exhibit 11.5 that stock B does not always earn a better return than stock A – stock B yields a lower return in a recession and in a stable economy than does stock A. In addition, stock C does not always earn a better return than stock A – stock C yields a lower return than stock A when the economy booms.

Although neither stock B nor stock C is always better than stock A, you can create a port-folio of stocks B and C such that arbitrage opportunities are available. Suppose you sell short two shares of stock A for $200, take the $200 proceeds from the short sale and buy one share of stock C for $100 and one share of stock B for $100. The return from the transaction, in dollars, is given in Exhibit 11.6. If a recession occurs, then stock A will lose −$2. However, you were short two shares of stock A, and you have a gain of 2($2) = $4, as illustrated in the

Exhibit 11.6	Arbitrage profit with short sales		
State of the economy	Short sale of two shares of stock A	Portfolio of one share of stock B and one share of stock C	Total net return from the arbitrage transaction
Recession	2($2) = $4	(1 × −$4) + 1 × $0 = −$4	+$4 − $4 = $0
Stable	2(−$6) = −$12	(1 × $4) + (1 × $10) = $14	−$12 + $14 = $2
Boom	2(−$10) = −$20	(1 × $16) + (1 × $6) = $22	−$20 + $22 = $2

Source: From *Introduction to Investments*, 2nd edn, by Levy. © 1999. Reprinted with permission of South-Western, a division of Thomson Learning: www.thomsonrights.com. Fax 800 730-2215.

second column of Exhibit 11.4. Buying one share of stocks B and C in a recession will result in a $4 loss on stock B and no profit or loss on stock C, as illustrated in the third column of Exhibit 11.4. A similar calculation shows a profit of $14 on stocks B and C in a stable economy and a profit of $22 if the economy booms. Hence, the total net return from the arbitrage transaction is +$4 − $4 = $0 if recession occurs. Following similar logic, you have a $2 gain if either a stable or a boom economy exists.

The initial investment on the transaction described in Exhibit 11.6 is zero (ignoring any trading costs), because the investor sells short two shares of stock A, gets the $200 proceeds, and invests $100 in stock B and $100 in stock C. The investor's future net return is always non-negative, regardless of the state of the economy. The investor gains either nothing (in a recession) or $2 (in a stable or boom economy). This is clearly an arbitrage opportunity. Why not double the transaction to $400 and make a potential profit of $4 (or $0), or invest $2000 to make a profit of $20 (or $0), or even invest $1 million to make an arbitrage profit of $10 000 (or $0)? The investor will continue to sell stock A short and buy stocks B and C to earn arbitrage profits.

With many such transactions in large amounts, there will be selling pressure on stock A and buying pressure on stocks B and C. Therefore, the price of stock A will fall, and the price of stocks B and C will go up, until eventually no arbitrage opportunities are available. The market mechanism that eliminates the arbitrage profit is as follows. Assume that as a result of the selling pressure on stock A, its price falls from $100 to $90. Similarly, the price of stock B rises to $105 due to buying pressure, and the price of stock C likewise rises to $110. Selling two shares of stock A will provide proceeds of only 2 × $90 = $180. This is not sufficient to buy one share of stock B and one share of stock C. Suppose you split the $180 proceeds between stocks B and C; hence, you buy only $90/$105 ≅ 0.857 of a share of stock B and $90/$110 ≅ 0.818 of a share of stock C. The proceeds in dollars given in Exhibit 11.6 are per one share; you now get a fraction of these proceeds, because you hold a fraction of stocks B and C. This strategy would not result in an arbitrage profit. For example, during an economic boom, you lose $20 from short-selling two shares of stock A but gain from buying a fraction of Stock B [$16(90/105) ≅ $13.71] and from buying stock C [$6(90/110) ≅ $4.91]. Thus, the net profit on such a transaction is −20 + 13.71 + 4.91 = −$1.38. Note that the net profit is negative, implying that given the new market prices, this transaction no longer represents an arbitrage opportunity.

Investors will continue to search for another possible arbitrage opportunity, for example by splitting the $180 short-sales proceeds in various proportions in stocks B and C. If investors search for all possible financial transactions and find that none can guarantee a positive return in all states of the economy (returns can be zero in some states of the economy but positive at least for one state of the economy) with a zero investment, then we say that arbitrage opportunities are not available.

When the prices of stocks are such that no arbitrage profit is available, the linear relationship between the mean return and risk of each asset is a main result of the APT. For example, if prices change such that a portfolio composed of short-selling asset A and holding assets B and C (with zero initial investment) yields returns of −$2 in recession, +$5 in a stable economy and +$4 in a boom economy, then we say that the arbitrage opportunity disappears because there is a chance of loss.

In practice, small investors may not get the proceeds from the short sale to take advantage of arbitrage opportunities, because the proceeds are held with the broker. However, large investors, particularly institutional investors, do get the short-sale proceeds. All investors do not have to make the arbitrage transaction; it is enough to have even one large investor who can create this money machine to move the stocks to the APT line – a property that makes the model more intuitively appealing than the CAPM. The ability of money managers to trade vast sums of money is beneficial to small investors because it ensures that the securities will be trading close to their equilibrium price.

 Connecting Theory to Practice 11.2

The curious case of Palm and 3Com

Former US Treasury secretary Lawrence Summers once described finance professors as practitioners of ketchup economics: 'They have shown that two quart bottles of ketchup invariably sell for twice as much as one quart bottle of ketchup except for deviations traceable to transaction costs . . . Indeed, most ketchup economists regard the efficiency of the ketchup market as the best established fact in empirical economics.' Summers was right. Arbitrage, defined as the simultaneous buying and selling of the same security for two different prices, is the central concept of modern finance. The absence of arbitrage is the basis of most modern financial theory, including option pricing and corporate capital structure.

In capital markets, the law of one price says that identical securities must have identical prices, otherwise investors could make unlimited profits by buying the cheap one and selling the expensive one. It does not require that investors be rational or sophisticated, only that they are able to recognise arbitrage opportunities. Because arbitrageurs can make profits by enforcing this law, it should be almost impossible to break in a well-functioning capital market. The law of one price is a basic, common-sense condition, so theorists have used it as a minimal condition, a starting point that leads to other implications.

Market disturbance

Unfortunately, something very disturbing happened in US capital markets during the recent technology stock mania. The law of one price was violated. A prominent example is the price of Palm relative to 3Com. On March 2 2000, 3Com sold part of its stake in handheld computer maker Palm. In this transaction, called an equity carve-out, 3Com sold about 4 per cent of its stake in Palm in an initial public offering and about 1 per cent to a consortium of companies. It kept 95 per cent of the shares. Palm shares were issued at Dollars 38. On the first day of trading, Palm immediately went to Dollars 150 and later rose to Dollars 165, before ending the day at Dollars 95.06.

Based on the relative number of shares of Palm and 3Com, a holder of one share of 3Com stock indirectly owned 1.5 shares of Palm stock. Based on 3Com's ownership of Palm alone, at the end of the first day of trading, 3Com shares were worth at least Dollars 142.59. 3Com, in addition to owning Palm, held cash and securities worth more than Dollars 10 a share, and ran a substantial and profitable network business. Thus one might expect 3Com to trade substantially above Dollars 142.59.

In fact, 3Com's value was Dollars 81.81 (3Com's stock price actually fell 21 per cent during the day). The 'stub value', or implied value of 3Com's non-Palm assets and businesses, is the difference between the lower bound of Dollars 142.59 and observed price Dollars 81.81, or – Dollars 60.78. The equity market gave a negative implied value to 3Com's other assets, which is puzzling since stock prices cannot be negative.

Most puzzling of all, 3Com had announced its intention to spin off its remaining shares of Palm, pending a decision from the US Internal Revenue Service on the tax status of the spin-off. The spin-off was expected to take place by the end of the year and a favourable ruling was highly likely. To profit from the mispricing, an arbitrageur would need to buy one share of 3Com, short 1.5 shares of Palm and wait less than a year. In essence, the arbitrageur would be buying a security worth at least zero for – Dollars 60.78, and would not need to wait long to realise the profits . . . This strategy (if one had been able to implement it with no transaction costs) would have been very profitable. The stub value of 3Com gradually rose until the distribution took place.

This mispricing was not in an obscure corner of capital markets, but in an IPO that attracted frenzied attention. On the day after the issue, the mispricing was discussed in several newspaper articles.

The 3Com example is not unique. In 1923, for instance, the young Benjamin Graham, later to co-author a classic book on security analysis, became the manager of what would now be called a mutual fund. Graham noticed that Du Pont's market capitalisation was about the same as the value of a stake it owned in GM. Du Pont had a stub value of about zero, despite the fact that it was a major company with many valuable assets. Graham bought Du Pont, short-sold GM, and profited when Du Pont later rose in value.

Something is terribly wrong here. This negative implied 'stub value' should not be happening. Economists have known about other apparent violations of the law of one price for many years. But these cases have special features that might explain the discrepancy between price and value. While one might be able to dismiss such cases as freakish anomalies, large capitalisation stocks trading in NASDAQ should not be mispriced.

Correcting prices

In understanding any violation of the law of one price, there are two questions. First, why don't arbitrageurs correct the mispricing by selling the overpriced security and buying the underpriced security? Second, even if something prevents the arbitrageurs from correcting the mispricing, why would anyone ever buy the overpriced security when they can buy the under-priced security?

The answer to the first question lies in transaction costs. To implement the arbitrage trade, one needs to sell short shares of Palm. Transaction costs arise in two ways: finding shares to short and the cost of holding the short position over time. To be able to sell short a stock, one must borrow it; for institutional reasons borrowing shares can be difficult or impossible for many equities, especially on the day of the IPO. Even weeks after the IPO, shorting can be difficult.

To borrow shares, an investor needs to find a willing lender. Much of this borrowing is typically done through financial institutions, such as mutual funds, trusts or asset managers, who lend their securities. In the case of Palm, retail investors rather than institutions held most of the shares, making Palm hard to borrow. For short sellers who could find shares to borrow, lenders demanded a high payment. This comes in the form of a daily cost to those shorting the stock. In the case of Palm, there were reports of very high holding costs, in the order of 40 per cent a year.

Thus the arbitrage opportunity is more apparent than real, since it is difficult and expensive to sell Palm short. Although not an easily exploitable arbitrage opportunity, this is a case of blatant mispricing. And it's worth noting that some investors did make substantial profits. While these investors did not make infinite arbitrage profits, they were making very high returns on near-arbitrage opportunities. For example, a young finance professor who took advantage of negative stub situations used the proceeds to buy a new car. Finance professors are not generally

▶

known for their market savvy or stock-picking success. Compared with institutional investors, they certainly have higher information-gathering and trading costs. So the apparent ability of professors to earn excess returns is troubling for the efficient markets hypothesis.

Evidence from the level of short-selling is consistent with the idea that Palm was overpriced. The level reached an amazing 148 per cent of floating shares, meaning that more than all the available shares had been sold short. This is possible if shares are borrowed, then sold short to an investor who permits the shares to be borrowed again. But it takes time to build this supply of shares, because this shorting market works sluggishly . . .

Why buy Palm?

Putting aside the failure of arbitrage, the second question is why anyone would buy a share of Palm for Dollars 95.06 when they could buy a share of 3Com (embedding 1.5 shares of Palm) for Dollars 81.81. One superficially appealing explanation for the mispricing is that the price of Palm is high because demand for shares outstrips supply. While undoubtedly true, this does not explain much. Why were Palm shareholders content to pay so much more when cheaper choices where available (such as 3Com stock or Palm options)? At one point when the stub value of 3Com was negative, investors worth more than Dollars 2.5 bn thought that Palm was a better buy than 3Com.

While it is impossible to say what, if anything, was going through these investors' minds, there are clues. Numerous press reports mentioned that without Palm, 3Com's future growth was expected to be lower. For example, in the week after the IPO, a headline from The Wall Street Journal read '3Com faces bleaker future without Palm'. Investors may have simply pursued the idea that Palm was good and 3Com was bad, without pausing to do the calculations.

More generally, early 2000 was a time of great optimism about technology stocks. Between February 1999 and February 2000, the tech-heavy NASDAQ Composite Index more than doubled. One dramatic illustration of this optimism occurred in Hong Kong. In February 2000, chaos erupted when crowds gathered at 10 banks and police were called. Some branches closed and others extended their hours to accommodate the mob. A bank run? Sort of. But instead of fighting to get their money out, people were fighting to get their money in. They were applying to subscribe to the IPO of tom.com, an internet company. According to some sources, 300 000 people queued to apply and more than 453 000 applications were submitted, so that almost 7 per cent of the population subscribed to the IPO.

Market implications

There are two important implications of the efficient market hypothesis. The first is that it is not easy to earn excess returns. The second is that prices are 'correct' in the sense that they reflect fundamental value. This latter implication is, in many ways, more important than the first. Do asset markets offer rational signals to the economy about where to invest real resources? If some companies have stock prices that are far from intrinsic value, they will attract too much or too little capital.

While important, this aspect of the efficient market hypothesis is difficult to test because intrinsic values are unobservable. That is why the example of 3Com and Palm is important. It demonstrates that market prices can be wrong when transaction costs prevent arbitrageurs from correcting market mistakes. The example casts doubt on the claim that market prices reflect only rational valuations because it is a case that should be particularly easy for the market to get right. If markets are failing this easy test, what else are they getting wrong?

Stock market prices affect the real world. When prices are wrong, the world suffers. The technology stock mania that peaked in 2000 had real consequences. Money, time and talent were poured into ventures that gave little return.

Financial economists have regarded 'frictions', such as transaction costs, as minor concerns. Using an analogy from physics, the trajectory of a ball thrown in the air can be predicted using a simple formula that ignores complications such as wind resistance; one can pretend the ball has been thrown into an airless vacuum. While all agree that transaction costs, like wind resistance, exist, the traditional view is that these minor deviations are safe to ignore.

This is a misleading analogy. The case of 3Com and Palm shows that frictions are not minor details, but are central to understanding how market prices are determined. It is as if the ball, rather than being thrown into a vacuum, were hurled into a tornado. Although one is sure that the ball will eventually return to earth, ignoring complications is not a good idea.

Further reading

Lamont, O. A. and Thaler, R. H. (2003) 'Can the market add and subtract? Mispricing in tech stock carve-outs', Journal of Political Economy, 111 (2), 227–268.

Ross, S. A. (1987) 'The interrelations of finance and economics: theoretical perspectives', American Economic Review, May, 77 (2): 29–34.

Summers, L. H. (1985) 'On economics and finance', Journal of Finance, July, 40 (3): 633–35.

Source: Owen Lamont, 'The Curious Case of Palm and 3Com', *Financial Times*, 18 June 2001.

→ Making the connection

On 2 March 2000, the value of Palm exceeded the value of 3Com, while one share of 3Com entitled the shareholder to 1.5 shares of Palm plus a part of 3Com's other assets. Apparently, there was a possibility for making riskless profits by short-selling 1.5 shares of Palm and buying one share of 3Com. Owen Lamont, an associate professor of finance at the University of Chicago Graduate School of Business, offers several explanations for this puzzling phenomenon.

11.2.2 The arbitrage pricing theory: assumptions and risk–return relationship

Recall that by the definition of an arbitrage opportunity, with a zero investment, the future return on the portfolio must be non-negative. Ross employs this argument to derive the APT. To be more specific, he explores what asset prices should be in order to eliminate arbitrage opportunities, because prices change when arbitrage exists. The mean return and risk of each asset also change until arbitrage opportunities disappear. In short, when arbitrage transactions are available, the economy is not in equilibrium. This is why the APT is an equilibrium pricing model. Thus, the APT investigates the market equilibrium prices when all arbitrage transactions are eliminated. This section examines the assumptions and resulting model of the APT.

The assumptions of the arbitrage pricing theory

The assumptions underlying the APT are as follows:

■ The capital market is characterised by perfect competition. There are a large number of investors, each with wealth that is small relative to the total market value of all capital assets. Hence, the portfolio choice of individual investors has no noticeable effect on the prices of the securities; investors take the price as given. Also, capital market imperfections such as transaction costs and taxes do not occur.

- All investors have the same expectations regarding the future in terms of mean, variance and covariance terms (homogeneous expectations). The expectations are captured by a return distribution that is described by a factor risk model (SIM or MIM); rates of return depend on some common risk factors and some random asset-specific factor. The asset-specific factor has a zero mean, is uncorrelated across assets and is uncorrelated with the common factors.
- Investors prefer more wealth to less wealth. Note that no assumptions are made regarding risk attitude; investors may be risk-average, risk-neutral or even risk-seeking.
- A very large number of capital assets exist in the economy. The number of assets is sufficiently large to create portfolios with no non-systematic risk and with any desired values for the factor sensitivity coefficients (the betas). For example, for every risk factor I_j, it is possible to create a factor portfolio, i.e. a well-diversified portfolio with zero non-systematic risk ($\sigma_{e_p}^2 = 0$), a unity beta for the risk factor under consideration ($\beta_{pj} = 1$) and a zero beta for all other risk factors ($\beta_{ps} = 0, s \neq j$).
- Short-sales are allowed, and the proceeds are available to the short-sellers.

Interestingly, these assumptions imply a linear equilibrium relationship between expected return and the factor sensitivities or betas. To examine this risk–return relationship, we first consider the case where the returns obey a SIM and subsequently move the general MIM.

Arbitrage portfolios

Essential to deriving the APT is the use of a well-diversified portfolio that has a zero beta and requires no investment due to short-selling. Such a portfolio is called an arbitrage portfolio. In general, when using the SIM, the return of a portfolio is given by

$$R_p = \alpha_p + \beta_p I + e_p \tag{11.1b}$$

where $\alpha_p = \sum_{i=1}^{n} w_i \alpha_i$ and $\beta_p = \sum_{i=1}^{n} w_i \beta_i$ are the portfolio alpha and beta, respectively, which are the averages of all the assets' alphas and betas weighted by their proportion (w_i) in the portfolio. Further, we know that the expected return and variance of the portfolio are given by:

$$E(R_p) = \alpha_p + \beta_p E(I) \tag{11.5a}$$

$$\sigma_p^2 = \beta_p^2 \sigma_I^2 + \sigma_{e_p}^2 \tag{11.6a}$$

where $\sigma_{e_p}^2 = \sum_{i=1}^{n} w_i^2 \sigma_{e_i}^2$ is the portfoloio's specific risk due to asset-specific factors. For a very large portfolio composed of many securities (that is, n is very large), the noise factors (e_i) tend to cancel each other, so we can assume safely that $\sigma_{e_p}^2 = 0$. Therefore, for a very large portfolio, Equation 11.6a can be rewritten as follows:

$$\sigma_p^2 = \beta_p^2 \sigma_I^2 \tag{11.6b}$$

Now suppose you can create a portfolio with zero investment and with zero risk, namely, $\sum w_i = 0$ and $\sum w_i \beta_i = 0$. From Equation 11.6b, if beta is zero and the portfolio is well-diversified, then the risk of the portfolio is zero, i.e. $\sigma_p^2 = 0$. Since by assumption this is a zero-investment portfolio, the expected return must be equal to zero, otherwise we have an arbitrage opportunity. For example, if the zero-beta, zero-investment portfolio had positive returns, then this would be a money machine. Alternatively, if this portfolio had negative returns, then an investor could construct another portfolio with exactly opposite weights that would result in positive dollar returns.

To summarise, arbitrage portfolios have three key properties: (1) they require no net investment, (2) their betas are equal to zero or they have no systematic risk, and (3) they are well-diversified or they have no non-systematic risk. Due to these properties, the expected return on arbitrage portfolios must be equal to zero, otherwise arbitrage possibilities arise.

The linear risk–return relationship

Using the zero beta and zero investment portfolio, Ross demonstrated that in order to exclude arbitrage opportunities, the mean return on the ith asset, $E(R_i)$, is related to β_i in a linear fashion as follows:[12]

$$
\underset{\text{Expected rate of return}}{E(R_i)} \quad = \quad \underset{\text{Zero beta rate}}{E(R_Z)} \quad + \quad \underset{\text{Risk premium}}{(E(I)} \quad - \quad \underset{\text{Factor beta}}{E(R_Z))\beta_i} \qquad (11.9)
$$

Hence, in APT equilibrium, when all arbitrage possibilities are vanished, there exists a linear relationship between expected return, $E(R_i)$, and the sensitivity to the common risk factor, β_i. The intercept, $E(R_Z)$, is the expected return on a portfolio with a zero beta, or the zero-beta rate. As discussed in Chapter 10, if a riskless asset is available (such as T-bills), then the zero-beta rate must equal the riskless rate ($E(R_Z) = r$). The reason for this is that when $\beta_i = 0$, there is no risk (remember, we are considering well-diversified portfolios with no non-systematic risk), and to avoid arbitrage, the return on an investment with no risk must be equal to the risk-free rate. The slope, $E(I) - R_Z$, is the expected return on the common risk factor in excess of the zero-beta rate. This term is the risk premium required to compensate investors for the exposure to the common risk factor (which cannot be diversified away).

The basic idea behind the APT equilibrium equation can be illustrated with the following three well-diversified portfolios. (For simplicity, assume each portfolio has the same market price.)

	Portfolio		
	A	B	C
Mean return ($E(R_i)$)	8%	13%	?
Beta (β_i)	1	2	3
Specific risk ($\sigma^2_{e_i}$)	0	0	0

Our goal is to select a mean rate of return on portfolio C such that no arbitrage opportunities exist. Exhibit 11.7 plots A and B and connects them by a straight line. The APT holds if point C also lies on this line. We will show that this is required to exclude arbitrage opportunities.

Suppose we selected investment proportions $w_A = -1$, $w_B = 2$ and $w_C = 0$, then $\sum w_i = -1 + 2 = 1$ and $\sum w_i \beta_i = (-1 \times 1) + (2 \times 2) = 3$. Thus, we constructed a portfolio with exactly the same beta as portfolio C. Since all portfolios have zero specific risk ($\sigma^2_{e_p} = 0$), the combination of A and B has the same risk as portfolio C. Hence, the two portfolios must also have the same expected

---

[12] Appendix 11 formally derives the APT equilibrium relationship from the maintained assumptions. The proof focuses on the general MIM with K risk factors. The proof for the single-factor APT is obtained simply by setting $K = 1$.

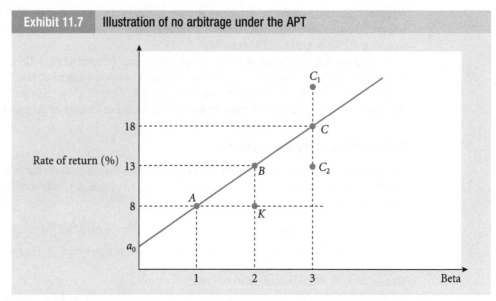

Exhibit 11.7 Illustration of no arbitrage under the APT

Source: From *Introduction to Investments*, 2nd edn, by Levy. © 1999. Reprinted with permission of South-Western, a division of Thomson Learning: www.thomsonrights.com. Fax 800 730-2215.

return. The combined portfolio has an expected return of $\sum w_i E(R_i) = (-1 \times 8) + (2 \times 13) = 18$. If the expected return of portfolio C deviated from 18%, then arbitrage opportunities exist. Let us elaborate. Suppose that $E(R_C) = 23\%$. Then we can select investment proportions $w_A = 1$, $w_B = -2$ and $w_C = 1$, then $\sum w_i = 1 - 2 + 1 = 0$ and $\sum w_i \beta_i = (1 \times 1) + (-2 \times 2) + (1 \times 3) = 0$. Thus, we constructed a portfolio with zero beta and zero investment. The expected return of this portfolio is $\sum w_i E(R_i) = (1 \times 8) + (-2 \times 13) + (1 \times 23) = 5\%$. Hence, there are arbitrage opportunities. Holding such a portfolio creates a positive certain profit with no investment. This is impossible in equilibrium, because it constitutes a 'money machine'. Similarly, if $E(R_C)$ is lower than 18% – say, 13% – with zero investment and risk, we get a negative return of $\sum w_i E(R_i) = (1 \times 8) + (-2 \times 13) + (1 \times 13) = -15\%$. Then, by short-selling such a portfolio with zero investment, we get a positive return, which is again a money machine.[13]

Now, what is left to show is that the point given by $E(R_C) = 18\%$ and $\beta_C = 3$, which characterises portfolio C when there are no arbitrage opportunities, lies on the same straight line as portfolios A and B, as asserted by the APT. Exhibit 11.7 demonstrates the straight line connecting points A and B with the relevant parameters taken from the example. The slope of the line (or $(E(I) - R_Z)$) is $[(13\% - 8\%)/(2 - 1)] = 5\%$, which is the line KB (the rise) divided by the line KA (the run). The intercept of this line $E(R_Z)$ can be found by inserting the parameters of point A (or point B) and employing the straight line formula with a slope of 5%:

$$E(R_i) = E(R_Z) + (5\% \times \beta_i)$$

Since for portfolio A we have $E(R_A) = 8\%$ and $\beta_A = 1$, we get $8\% = E(R_Z) + (5\% \times 1)$; thus, $E(R_Z) = 3\%$. The straight line connecting portfolios A and B is given by $E(R_i) = 3\% + (5\% \times \beta_i)$, where $E(R_Z) = 3\%$ and $E(I) - R_Z = 5\%$.

If $E(R_C)$ is greater than 18% (say, 23%), then the point is above the line (see point C_1 in Exhibit 11.7). If $E(R_C)$ is lower than 18% (say, 13%), then the point is below the line (see point

---

[13] This boils down to using the weights $w_A = 1$, $w_B = -2$ and $w_C = 1$. In other words, we need to short-sell two times portfolio B and use the proceeds to buy portfolio A and portfolio C.

C_2 in Exhibit 11.7). Since a mean return of exactly 18% for portfolio C eliminates an arbitrage possibility, and all three stocks lie on the same straight line, we conclude that when arbitrage opportunities are eliminated, we get a linear relationship between expected return and beta (Equation 11.9).

The APT linear relationship has been illustrated with three portfolios, but the same principle holds with any number of assets or portfolios of assets. As long as one of the stocks is not on the straight line, an arbitrage profit can be made. To eliminate such an arbitrage profit, all $[E(R_i), \beta_i]$ points must lie on the one straight line.

Practice box

Problem

Suppose there are three portfolios on the APT straight line with the following parameters:

	A	B	C
Mean (%)	5	10	15
Beta	1	2	3
Specific risk	0	0	0

1. What is the zero-beta rate $(E(R_Z))$ and what is the risk premium $(E(R_I) - E(R_Z))$?
2. Show that every combination of the three portfolios is also on the line.

Solution

1. The APT line can be written as

$$E(R_i) = E(R_Z) + (E(R_I) - E(R_Z))\beta_i$$

The slope of the line is given by the rate of change between any two of the assets:

$$(E(R_I) - E(R_Z)) = \frac{10\% - 5\%}{2 - 1} = \frac{15\% - 10\%}{3 - 2} = \frac{15\% - 5\%}{3 - 1} = 5\%, \text{ or } 0.05$$

Then, the intercept is given by

$$E(R_Z) = E(R_i) - (E(R_I) - E(R_Z))\beta_i = E(R_i) - 0.05\beta_i$$

If we take portfolio A, we get

$$E(R_Z) = 0.05 - (0.05 \times 1) = 0.0$$

If we take portfolio B, we get

$$E(R_Z) = 0.1 - (0.05 \times 2) = 0.0$$

If we take portfolio C, we get

$$E(R_Z) = 0.15 - (0.05 \times 3) = 0.0$$

Thus, the APT line with these figures is given by

$$E(R_i) = 0 + 0.05\beta_i$$

2. Since the beta of a portfolio, β_p, and the mean of a portfolio, $E(R_p)$, are linear functions, we know

$$\beta_p = \sum_{i=1}^{n} w_i \beta_i$$

and

$$E(R_p) = \sum_{i=1}^{n} w_i E(R_i)$$

and any combination must also be on the line. For example, take a portfolio of one-third invested in each of the three portfolios. Then

$$\beta_p = \frac{1 + 2 + 3}{3} = 2$$

and

$$E(R_p) = \frac{0.05 + 0.1 + 0.15}{3} = 0.1$$

This combination is also on the straight line, because $0.1 = 0 + (0.05 \times 2)$.

Multifactor arbitrage pricing theory model

So far, we have assumed that only one factor, I, generates the return on the various assets. It is possible, however, that several factors generate the return on the assets, such as the inflation rate, the unemployment rate and exchange rates. In these cases, the MIM (Equation 11.1a) rather than the SIM (Equation 11.1) applies. The same no-arbitrage-opportunity approach can be used where we have zero investment ($\sum w_i = 0$) with zero betas for each of the above factors. Thus, $\sum w_i \beta_{i1} = 0$, $\sum w_i \beta_{i2} = 0$, and so forth, and there is no arbitrage opportunity. Following this procedure, we get a linear relationship similar to the one-factor APT of the following form:

$$E(R_i) \quad = \quad E(R_Z) \quad + \quad (E(I_1) \quad - R_Z)\beta_{i1} + \ldots + \quad (E(I_K) \quad - E(R_Z))\beta_{iK} \quad (11.9a)$$

| Expected rate of return | Zero beta rate | Risk premium of first factor | First beta | Risk premium, Kth factor | Kth beta |

which is a generalisation of the APT when K factors, rather than one factor, are generating the returns. The intercept is the rate of return expected if all betas are zero (the risk-free rate), $(E(I_j) - E(R_Z))$ is the market price of the risk related to factor j on a per-unit basis, and β_{ij} is the sensitivity of security i to factor j. Appendix 11 at the end of this chapter formally derives the APT equilibrium relationship.

11.3   The arbitrage pricing theory and the capital asset-pricing model

There exists a strong analogy between the APT equilibrium relationship in Equation 11.9a and the security market line (SML) of the CAPM in Equation 10.9 of Chapter 10. In both cases, asset expected returns are a linear function of one or more sensitivity coefficients that measure risk. In fact, when asset returns obey the SIM, the market portfolio (m) is the common risk factor, and a riskless asset is available, then the APT equilibrium relationship reduces to

$$E(R_i) = r + (E(R_m) - r)\beta_{im} \quad (11.9b)$$

which is identical to the SML. However, it is important to stress that the CAPM is not a special case of the APT and the APT is not an extension of the CAPM. Both models are based on completely different sets of assumptions. Still, in some cases, the two models predict exactly the same risk–return relationship, and in these cases we cannot distinguish between the two models.

Recall that in Chapter 10 we identified the major assumptions of the CAPM. Primarily, the CAPM is built on the assumption that investors are risk-averse and they select a mean–variance-efficient portfolio from the same mean–variance-efficient frontier. In turn, as discussed in Chapter 8, the mean–variance rule requires assumptions about investor preferences (investor utility takes a quadratic form) or the return distribution (returns obey a joint normal distribution). The APT does not require these assumptions. Thus, the APT is considered to be much less restrictive. That is, the APT can apply to markets where investors are not risk-averse or where more than portfolio mean and variance matter. Related to this, the CAPM predicts that all investors will hold the market portfolio and that the market beta explains fully the differences in expected return across assets; there is no such prediction with the APT. On the other hand, the APT assumes that it is possible to short-sell risky assets with no additional costs, while the CAPM does not require this assumption; in the CAPM, all investors hold the market portfolio, which includes only long positions. Also, the flexibility to account for multiple risk factors has a flip side; while the CAPM predicts that the relevant risk factor is the market portfolio, the APT fails to tell us exactly what the common factors are. Also, the APT does not say anything about the size or signs of the risk premiums.

Still, the two models are not mutually exclusive. For example, the CAPM is not inconsistent with the assumption that returns are generated by a MIM with multiple risk factors. The CAPM states merely that the sensitivity to a single risk factor (the market portfolio) determines the equilibrium expected rates of return. This statement allows for multiple risk factors, provided they are not 'priced', i.e. the exposure to these factors does not affect the equilibrium expected rates of return. Hence, it it not true that the CAPM assumes that returns are generated by a SIM with the return to the market portfolio as the only common risk factor. Practitioners and empirical researchers sometimes do make this assumption when they try to estimate betas; however, it is neither an assumption nor a prediction of the CAPM.[14] Consequently, the finding in Section 11.1.3 that US stocks are affected by size and B/M factors in addition to the market factor does not violate the CAPM.

Even the finding that multiple risk factors are priced does not necessarily violate the CAPM. For example, the general APT equilibrium relationship in Equation 11.9a is identical to the CAPM/SML in Equation 11.9b if the risk factors, $I_1, \ldots, I_K$, obey the CAPM, i.e.

$$(E(I_j) - r) = (E(R_m) - r)\beta_{I_j m}$$

where $\beta_{I_j m}$ is the market beta of the jth risk factor. Substituting this expression in Equation 11.9a, and using $E(R_Z) = r$, yields:

$$E(R_i) = r + (E(R_m) - r)\beta_{i_1}\beta_{I_1 m} + \ldots + (E(R_m) - r)\beta_{iK}\beta_{I_K m}$$
$$= r + (E(R_m) - r)(\beta_{i_1}\beta_{I_1 m} + \ldots + \beta_{iK}\beta_{I_K m}) = r + (E(R_m) - r)\beta_{im}$$

or the SML (Equation 11.9b).[15] The relevant question to test the CAPM is not whether multiple risk factors are priced but whether risk factors other than the market portfolio are priced.

---

[14] Note that the equation $R_i = \alpha_i + \beta_i I + e_i$ is always true as long as we do not specify the statistical distribution of the errors. To repeat, the SIM assumes that the errors have a zero mean and that they are uncorrelated with each other and with the common risk factor. These assumptions are violated in case of multiple common risk factors. The CAPM does not assume $R_i = \alpha_i + \beta_i R_m + e_i$ with the above conditions for the error terms. By contrast, practitioners and empirical researchers sometimes do make this assumption, which is needed to justify the use of OLS regression analysis (see Appendix A at the end of this book).

[15] The final equation follows from the fact that $\beta_{im} = (\beta_{i_1}\beta_{I_1 m} + \ldots + \beta_{iK}\beta_{I_K m})$.

11.4 Empirical tests of the arbitrage pricing theory

Like the CAPM, the APT rests on a number of simplifying assumptions (see Section 11.2). In many ways, the assumptions of the APT are less restrictive than those of the CAPM; for example, the APT does not assume that investors are risk-averse and that they obey the rules of mean–variance analysis. Still, many of the remaining assumptions (for example, no transaction costs and taxes, homogeneous expectations, etc.) are violated in the real world. However, as discussed in Chapter 10, to be useful, a theory must be descriptively unrealistic in the sense that it must abstract from a complex reality, and the usefulness must be judged by the degree to which the theory provides valid and meaningful explanations and predictions. Empirical tests of the APT typically focus on testing the predicted equilibrium risk–return relationship in Equation 11.9a. Assuming that a riskless asset exists ($E(R_Z) = r$), this relationship is given by:

$$E(R_i) = r + (E(I_1) - r)\beta_{i1} + \ldots + (E(I_K) - r)\beta_{iK} \qquad (11.9c)$$

We cannot possibly survey all individual empirical studies here.[16] This is because the studies differ greatly with respect to the data sets and the research methodology. The differences reflect the many choices empirical researchers have to make, including the following:

- the assets that are included in the analysis (for example, all US common stocks listed on the NYSE);
- the method for grouping assets into portfolios (for example, sorted by book-to-market equity ratio);
- the relevant set of common risk factors (for example, a default risk factor and a general stock market risk factor);
- the factor portfolios used to proxy the relevant risk factors (for example, the spread between B-rated corporate bonds and A-rated bonds as a proxy for the default risk factor);
- the return frequency (for example, monthly returns);
- the sample period (for example, 1926–2003);
- the statistical methods (for example, the two-pass regression method discussed below).

Note that similar choices have to be made for testing the CAPM. Related to this, empirical tests of the APT suffer from similar problems as tests of the CAPM, including time variation of the return distribution, the choice of the appropriate statistical methods, and data problems such as data-mining, data-snooping and sample-selection bias (see Section 10.2.3 in Chapter 10). The most important difference is identifying the relevant set of common risk factors. The CAPM predicts that the market portfolio is the only priced risk factor (although we may use multiple risk factors to proxy for the market portfolio; see Section 11.3). By contrast, the APT gives no clues as to the appropriate number of factors and the identity of the factors. In this respect, any test of the APT is a joint test of the hypothesis that the APT is a correct equilibrium model and the hypothesis that the set of risk factors is correct. In other words, we may wrongly reject the APT if some relevant risk factors are excluded from our tests or if we use poor proxies, and we may wrongly accept the model if we include irrelevant risk factors.

11.4.1 Two-pass regression method

One popular approach to test the APT is analogous to the two-pass regression method used to test the CAPM. Applied to the APT, this approach involves the following four steps:

---

[16] The references at the end of this chapter include an extensive list of empirical studies of the APT.

Step 1: establish sample data

The first step is to collect a data set of historical returns for a set of benchmark portfolios to proxy the investment universe, a set of factor portfolios to proxy for the common risk factors (for example, the S&P 500 index to proxy for the stock-market risk factor and the credit spread to proxy for the credit risk factor) and a proxy for the riskless rate (for example, the T-bill rate). Data are collected for a particular return frequency (for example, daily, monthly or yearly frequency) and over a particular sample period. This will result in T time-series observations on n benchmark portfolios, K factors portfolios and the riskless rate.

As discussed above, selecting the risk factors is a key problems in testing the APT. Roughly speaking, there exist three approaches to this problem, each with its own strengths and weaknesses. The first approach is to use economic knowledge to specify a priori the relevant risk factors. Unfortunately, economic theory yields very few predictions about the return distribution of assets. Rather, financial economists typically deal with the behaviour of investors given the return distribution. Still, we do know that the intrinsic value of an asset is determined as the present value of its expected future cash flows to the investor, where the expected cash flows are discounted to the present with a discount rate that includes an appropriate risk premium (see Chapters 13–18 for more details). Hence, variables that predict future cash flows and discount rates are likely 'economic' candidates as risk factors. A second approach uses econometric specification tests to select the set of factors that best describes a given data set from a set of prespecified factors (this approach effectively combines steps 1 and 2). The most important limitation of this approach is that there is a high probability of data-mining or finding spurious patterns by the extensive searching through different model specifications. Finally, we may use a statistical method known as factor analysis to jointly identify the relevant risk factors (which are weighted averages of the benchmark portfolios) and estimate the factor loadings of the benchmark portfolios.[17] The most important drawback of this method is that there is no economic interpretation for the factors, which are simply a weighted average of the individual assets, selected to create the best fit in the sample. Also, the sign and the magnitude of the risk factors are not determined uniquely, and hence the sign and the magnitude of the factor loadings and risk premiums also become arbitrary.

Step 2: estimate the multi-index models

The second step estimates, for every benchmark portfolio separately, the MIM (Equation 11.1a) using the time-series regression model in Equation 11.8 (see Section 11.2.3). The time-series regressions used to estimate the MIMs are sometimes referred to as the first-pass regressions, because their output (regression estimates of the factor loadings or betas) is used in a second-pass regression (see below).

---

[17] See, for instance, Lawley and Maxwell (1963) for a detailed treatment of factor analysis. Roughly speaking, the technique determines a set of common risk factors and factor loadings such that the covariance between the residual returns (the returns after correcting for the risk factors, e_i) is minimal. The number of factors is determined by a predetermined probability (say, 5 or 10%) that including additional factors will further improve the explanatory power of the model. Until Chen *et al.* (1986), empirical applications of APT were based on this technique. Roll and Ross (1980) is among the many studies that use factor analysis. Chen *et al.* (1986) tested the APT using a set of prespecified macroeconomic factors (term spread), credit spread, unexpected inflation and growth rate of industrial production.

Step 3: estimate the risk–return relationship

The third step is directed at empirically testing the equilibrium risk–return relationship in Equation 11.9a. Specifically, it estimates the cross-sectional relationship between the estimated factor loadings (obtained from the above time-series regression) and the ex-post mean returns, which are treated as estimators of the ex-ante expected returns. For this purpose, the following cross-sectional regression model is used (with n observations, one for each benchmark portfolio):

$$\bar{R}_i = \gamma_0 + \gamma_1\hat{\beta}_{i1} + \ldots + \gamma_K\hat{\beta}_{iK} + u_i \tag{11.10}$$

where $\bar{R}_i$ is the historical average return on the ith benchmark portfolio, γ_0 is the historical intercept, $\hat{\beta}_{ij}$ is the historical estimate of the sensitivity of the ith benchmark portfolio for the jth risk factor, γ_j is the historical slope coefficient for the jth beta, and u_i is the deviation from the line. The output of the regression model will include coefficient estimates $\hat{\gamma}_0, \ldots, \hat{\gamma}_K$, standard errors and an R-squared.

Step 4: test predictions of the arbitrage pricing theory

The final step is to determine whether the properties of the estimated risk–return relationship are in accord with the predictions of APT. If the APT is true, then we should find that the intercept of the SML equals the riskless rate, i.e. $\gamma_0 = r$, and that the risk premium equals the equity premium, i.e. $\gamma_j = [E(I_j) - r], j = 1, \ldots, K$. We can test this by checking whether the estimated regression coefficients are significantly different from the hypothesised values.[18] Further, the APT requires that the betas are the only variable explaining expected returns, i.e. there should exist an exact fit between mean and beta. If all combinations of expected rate of return and betas lie on the equilibrium line, then the market is in equilibrium. However, when historical data are used to estimate the expected rate of return and betas, generally some assets plot above or below the line, indicating either disequilibrium or a statistically insignificant deviation from the line (because of sampling errors). Test whether the R squared for the risk–return relationship is not significantly lower than unity.

11.4.2 Example application

To demonstrate the two-pass regression procedure, we apply it to the sample of 25 benchmark portfolios used in Section 11.2.3. That section estimated the factor loadings of these portfolios relative to the three Fama and French factors (the market portfolio and the SMB and HML hedge portfolios). This effectively completed step 2 of the procedure. We now turn to step 3, using the output of step 2 as input.

To test the APT, given the three-factor model, we use regression analysis to estimate the following relationship:[19]

$$\bar{R}_i = \gamma_0 + \gamma_m\hat{\beta}_{i,m} + \gamma_{SML}\hat{\beta}_{i,SML} + \gamma_{HML}\hat{\beta}_{i,HML} + u_i$$

---

[18] For this purpose, we can use the t-test and F-test discussed in Appendix A at the end of this book.

[19] Note that the Fama and French three-factor model is not an APT model. In fact, the model is not derived from any economic model. Rather, the model is motivated by the empirically observed size and B/M anomalies. Currently, the economic interpreting of the three-factor model is unclear. Apart from interpeting the model as an APT model, some think it is a conditional version of the CAPM that corrects for the variation of market betas during the business cycle (see Chapters 10 and 17); others think it is an intertemporal CAPM (see Chapter 10).

where $\bar{R}_i$ is the average return on the ith asset, $\hat{\beta}_{i,m}$ is the estimated market beta, $\hat{\beta}_{i,SML}$ is the estimated SML beta, $\hat{\beta}_{i,HML}$ is the estimated HML beta, and ε_i is an error term that measures the deviation from the equilibrium line. If the three-factor model is correct, then we would expect a very good fit for this regression equation.

The estimation results are as follows (standard error between brackets):

$$\bar{R}_i = 1.270 - 0.831\,\hat{\beta}_{i,m} + 0.165\,\hat{\beta}_{i,SML} + 0.465\,\hat{\beta}_{i,HML} + u_i \quad R^2 = 0.76$$
$$\quad\; (0.434)\;\, (0.413) \qquad (0.053) \qquad (0.062)$$

Several results should be noted. First, contrary to the predictions of the CAPM, market beta carries a negative premium (-0.831), which is hardly significant, and the size and B/M factors carry highly significant, positive risk premiums (0.165 and 0.465). Second, contrary to the CAPM, the three-factor model gives a very good fit (R-squared is 76%).

11.4.3 Striking the balance

Based on the empirical tests of the APT, there are strong indications that risk factors other than the market portfolio affect expected returns. For example, the size and B/M factors found in the previous section have been found in data sets of various assets, periods and countries. This result is of theoretical and practical significance. The size and B/M premiums cast serious doubt on the validity of the theoretical CAPM as well as on financial management applications (e.g. capital budgeting and performance evaluation) that are based on the CAPM. Still, we stress that tests of the APT, like tests of the CAPM, are joint tests of the equilibrium theory (APT), the research methodology and the quality of the data (including the choice of the benchmark portfolios and the factor portfolios). For this reason, we may never be able to find unambiguous empirical evidence in favour of or against the APT, or establish its value relative to the CAPM. For example, the APT may appear wrongly to outperform the CAPM if the risk factors are nothing but proxies of the (true but unobserved) market portfolio, or if the risk factors capture the time-variation of the (true but unobserved) equity premium and the (true but unobserved) market betas of the benchmark portfolio. Still, the APT is very useful, because it shows the theoretical implications of arbitrage without requiring strong assumptions about the risk attitude of investors and the return distribution of assets. This insight greatly improves our understanding of how capital markets work.

Summary

Explain factor risk models and why they simplify computations required for mean–variance analysis.

The single index model (SIM) and the arbitrage pricing theory (APT) were originally developed for different purposes, but they are very similar. The SIM was developed to reduce the computational problems in calculating the efficient frontier. The APT was developed as an alternative to the CAPM.

The SIM drastically reduces the inputs needed in solving for the optimum portfolios in the efficient frontier, because the covariances can be calculated as follows:

$$Cov(R_i, R_j) = \beta_i \beta_j \sigma_I^2$$

Thus, the investor needs only to estimate the betas for each stock rather than all possible covariances. This reduction is the result of the assumption that returns are generated by a single factor (say, I) and firm-specific factors. Specifically, the SIM assumes that

$$E(R_i) = \alpha_i + \beta_i E(I) + e_i$$

where $Cov(I, e_i) = 0$, and that for any two stocks $Cov(e_i e_j) = 0$.

With the SIM, risk can be broken down easily into its systematic and unsystematic components. Systematic risk cannot be diversified; unsystematic risk can be diversified. With a large number of assets in a portfolio, unsystematic risk can be virtually eliminated.

Explain the arbitrage pricing theory, its assumptions and the resulting linear equilibrium relationship.

The primary assumption of the APT is that security returns are generated by a linear factor model. The APT is based on a no-arbitrage condition. That is, an investor should not be able to build a zero-risk, zero-investment portfolio that has positive returns. However, the APT assumes that there are many assets in the economy and that there is some specific return-generating process. In general, the expected return on a security under the APT with multiple factors is given by

$$E(R_i) = a_0 + a_1\beta_1 + a_2\beta_2 + \ldots + a_K\beta_K$$

where a_0 is the risk-free interest rate, β_i is the security's sensitivity to each factor, and a_i is the market price per unit of sensitivity.

Compare and contrast the CAPM and the APT.

The APT is an alternative equilibrium pricing model that is built on different assumptions to the CAPM. Specifically, the APT does not assume that investors make decisions according to the mean–variance rule; also, investors do not have to be risk-averse.

Summarise the results of the empirical research of the APT.

The most important complication in testing the APT is identifying the relevant set of common risk factors. While the CAPM predicts that the market portfolio is the only priced risk factor, the APT gives no clues as to the appropriate number of factors and the identity of the factors. In this respect, any test of the APT is a joint test of the hypothesis that the APT is a correct equilibrium model and the hypothesis that the set of risk factors is correct. Due to this problem, and other problems related to data and methodology, we may doubt whether it is possible to ever find unambiguous empirical evidence in favour of or against the APT. Still, the APT is very useful, because it shows the theoretical implications of arbitrage without requiring strong assumptions about the risk attitude of investors and the return distribution of assets.

Key terms

Arbitrage 342
Arbitrage opportunities 351
Arbitrage portfolio 358
Arbitrage pricing theory
(APT) 351
Arbitrage profit 352
Asset-specific events 343
Beta 343

Common risk factor 343
Factor loading 343
Factor portfolio 358
Factor risk models 342
Law of one price 351
Money machine 352
Multiple index model
(MIM) 347

Single index model (SIM) 343
Systematic risk 346
Three-factor model 349
Unsystematic risk 346
Zero-beta rate 359
Zero-investment portfolio 343

Review questions

1. Why does the single index model (SIM) reduce the inputs needed for solving the optimum portfolios on the efficient frontier?

2. Suppose the SIM holds true, where the common factor is the gross national product: the following table contains annual returns for Stock F and annual percentage changes in the gross national product (I):

Year	R_F	I
1	10%	3%
2	22%	2%
3	18%	−1%
4	−5%	−2%
5	12%	5%

Suppose $E(I)$ for year 6 is 4%, estimate $E(R_F)$ for the same year based on the historical returns.

3. **a.** Explain the arbitrage pricing theory (APT). What are its assumptions?
   b. How does the APT differ from the CAPM?

4. Suppose there are three portfolios on the APT straight line with the following parameters:

	A	B	C
Mean	4%	8%	12%
Beta	1	2	3
Specific risk	0	0	0

What is the zero-beta rate ($E(R_Z)$) and what is the risk premium ($E(R_I) − E(R_Z)$)?

5. What are both the similarities and the differences in the difficulties encountered when empirically testing the validity of the CAPM and the APT?

For an extensive set of review and practice questions and answers, visit the Levy–Post investment website at www.booksites.net/levy

Selected references

Bansal, R. and S. Viswanathan, 1993, 'No Arbitrage and Arbitrage Pricing: A New Approach', *Journal of Finance*, **48**, 1231–1262.

Bansal, R., D. A. Hsieh and S. Viswanathan, 1993, 'A New Approach to International Arbitrage Pricing', *Journal of Finance*, **48**, 1719–1747.

Berry, M. A., E. Burmeister and M. B. McElroy, 1988, 'Sorting Out Risks Using Known APT Factors', *Financial Analysts Journal*, **44** (2), 29–42.

Brown, S. J., 1989, 'The Number of Factors in Security Returns', *Journal of Finance*, **44**, 1247–1262.

Brown, S. J. and M. I. Weinstein, 1983, 'A New Approach to Testing Asset Pricing Models: The Bilinear Paradigm', *Journal of Finance*, **38**, 711–743.

Burmeister, E. and M. B. McElroy, 1988, 'Joint Estimation of Factor Sensitivities and Risk Premia for the Arbitrage Pricing Theory', *Journal of Finance*, **43**, 721–733.

Burmeister, E. and K. Wall, 1986, 'The Arbitrage Pricing Theory and Macroeconomic Factor Measures', *Financial Review*, **21**, 1–20.

Chamberlain, G., 1983, 'Funds, Factors and Diversification in Arbitrage Pricing Models', *Econometrica*, **51**, 1305–1323.

Chang, Eric C. and Wilbur, G. Lewellen, 1985, 'An Arbitrage Pricing Approach to Evaluating Mutual Fund Performance', *Journal of Financial Research*, **8** (1), 15–30.

Chen, N.-F., 1983, 'Some Empirical Tests of the Theory of Arbitrage Pricing', *Journal of Finance*, **38**, 1393–1414.

Chen, N.-F. and J. Ingersoll, 1983, 'Exact Pricing in Linear Factor Models with Finitely Many Assets: A Note', *Journal of Finance*, **38**, 985–988.

Chen, N.-F., R. R. Roll, and S. A. Ross, 1986, 'Economic Forces and the Stock Market', *Journal of Business*, **59**, 383–404.

Connor, G., 1984, 'A Unified Beta Pricing Theory', *Journal of Economic Theory*, **34**, 13–31.

Connor, G. and R. A. Korajczyk, 1986, 'Performance Measurement with the Arbitrage Pricing Theory: A New Framework for Analysis', *Journal of Financial Economics*, **15**, 373–394.

Connor, G. and R. A. Korajczyk, 1988, 'Risk and Return in an Equilibrium APT: Application of a New Test Methodology', *Journal of Financial Economics*, **21**, 255–290.

Connor, G. and R. A. Korajczyk, 1993, 'A Test for the Number of Factors in an Approximate Factor Model', *Journal of Finance*, **48**, 1263–1291.

Dhrymes, P., I. Friend, and M. Gultekin, 1984, 'A Critical Re-Examination of the Empirical Evidence on the Arbitrage Pricing Theory', *Journal of Finance*, **39**, 323–346.

Dybvig, P. H., 1983, 'An Explicit Bound on Deviations from APT Pricing in a Finite Economy', *Journal of Financial Economics*, **12**, 483–496.

Dybvig, P. and S. A. Ross, 1985, 'Yes, the APT is Testable', *Journal of Finance*, **40**, 1173–1188.

Ehrhardt, M. C., 1987a, 'Arbitrage Pricing Models: The Sufficient Number of Factors and Equilibrium Conditions', *Journal of Financial Research*, **10**, 111–120.

Ehrhardt, M. C., 1987b, 'A Mean–Variance Derivation of a Multi-Factor Equilibrium Model', *Journal of Financial and Quantitative Analysis*, **22**, 227–236.

Fama, E. F. and K. R. French, 1996, 'Multifactor Explanations of Asset Pricing Anomalies', *Journal of Finance*, **51**, 55–84.

Gehr, A., 1975, 'Some Tests of the Arbitrage Pricing Theory', *Journal of Midwest Finance Association*, **7**, 91–105.

Geweke, J. and G. Zhou, 1996, 'Measuring the Pricing Error of the Arbitrage Pricing Theory', *Review of Financial Studies*, **9**, 557–587.

Gilles, C. and S. F. LeRoy, 1991, 'On the Arbitrage Pricing Theory', *Economic Theory*, **1**, 213–229.

Grinblatt, M. and S. Titman, 1983, 'Factor Pricing in a Finite Economy', *Journal of Financial Economics*, **12**, 497–507.

Grinblatt, M. and S. Titman, 1985, 'Approximate Factor Structures: Interpretations and Implications for Empirical Tests', *Journal of Finance*, **40**, 1367–1373.

Huberman, G., 1982, 'A Simple Approach to Arbitrage Pricing Theory', *Journal of Economic Theory*, **28**, 183–191.

Ingersoll, J., 1984, 'Some Results in the Theory of Arbitrage Pricing', *Journal of Finance*, **39**, 1021–1039.

Jarrow, R. and A. Rudd, 1983, 'A Comparison of the APT and CAPM: A Note', *Journal of Banking and Finance*, **7**, 295–303.

King, B. F., 1966, 'Market and Industry Factors in Stock Price Behavior', *Journal of Business*, **39**, 139–190.

Lawley, D. N. and M. A. Maxwell, 1963, *Factor Analysis as a Statistical Method*, London: Butterworths.

Lehmann, B. and D. Modest, 1988, 'The Empirical Foundations of the Arbitrage Pricing Theory', *Journal of Financial Economics*, **21**, 213–254.

Mei, J., 1993, 'A Semiautoregression Approach to the Arbitrage Pricing Theory', *Journal of Finance*, **48**, 599–620.

Merton, R., 1973, 'An Intertemporal Capital Asset Pricing Model', *Econometrica*, **41**, 867–880.

Nawalkha, S. K., 1997, 'A Multibeta Representation Theorem for Linear Asset Pricing Theories', *Journal of Financial Economics*, **46**, 357–381.

Robin, A. J. and R. K. Shukla, 1991, 'The Magnitude of Pricing Errors in the Arbitrage Pricing Theory', *Journal of Financial Research*, **14**, 65–82.

Roll, R., 1977, 'A Critique of the Asset Pricing Theory's Tests, Part I: On Past and Potential Testability of the Theory', *Journal of Financial Economics*, **4**, 129–176.

Roll, R. and S. A. Ross, 1980, 'An Empirical Investigation of the Arbitrage Pricing Theory', *Journal of Finance*, **35** (5), 1073–1103.

Roll, R. and S. A. Ross, 1983, 'A Critical Reexamination of the Empirical Evidence on the Arbitrage Pricing Theory: A reply', *Journal of Finance*, **39**, 347–350.

Ross, S. A., 1976, 'The Arbitrage Theory of Capital Asset Pricing', *Journal of Economic Theory*, **12**, 341–360.

Ross, S. A. (1977), 'Return, Risk and Arbitrage', In: Friend, I. and J. L. Bicksler, editors, *Risk and Return in Finance*, Cambridge, MA: Ballinger.

Shanken, J., 1982, 'The Arbitrage Pricing Theory? It is Testable', *Journal of Finance*, **37**, 1129–1140.

Shanken, J., 1992a, 'The Current State of the Arbitrage Pricing Theory', *Journal of Finance*, **47**, 1569–1574.

Shanken, J., 1992b, 'On the Estimation of Beta-Pricing Models', *Review of Financial Studies*, **5**, 1–33.

Sharpe, W. F., 1963, 'A Simplified Model for Portfolio Analysis', *Management Science*, **9**, 277–293.

Shleifer, A. and R. W. Vishry, 1997, 'The Limits of Arbitrage', *Journal of Finance*, **52**, 35–55.

Shukla, R. K. and Charles A. Trzcinka, 1990, 'Sequential Tests of the Arbitrage Pricing Theory: A Comparison of Principal Components and Maximum Likelihood Factors', *Journal of Finance*, **45**, 1541–1564.

Trzcinka, C. A., 1986, 'On the Number of Factors in the Arbitrage Pricing Model', *Journal of Finance*, **41**, 347–368.

Varian, H., 1987, 'The Arbitrage Principle in Financial Economics', *Journal of Economic Perspectives*, **1**, 55–72.

Wei, K. C. J., 1988, 'An Asset-Pricing Theory Unifying CAPM and APT', *Journal of Finance*, **43**, 881–892.

APPENDIX 11   A formal proof of the arbitrage pricing theory

Under the assumptions of the APT, we can form an arbitrage portfolio with the following properties:

$$\sum_{i=1}^{n} w_i = 0 \qquad (11A.1)$$

$$\sum_{i=1}^{n} w_i \beta_{i1} = 0 \qquad (11A.2a)$$

$$\vdots \qquad\qquad\qquad\qquad \vdots$$

$$\sum_{i=1}^{n} w_i \beta_{iK} = 0 \qquad (11A.2K)$$

$$\sum_{i=1}^{n} w_i e_i \approx 0 \qquad (11A.3)$$

The first condition (Equation 11A.1) states that the portfolio requires no investment: the portfolio weights sum to zero. Mathematically, this condition states that the weight vector $(w_1, \ldots, w_n)$ is orthogonal to the unity vector $(1, \ldots, 1)$. The subsequent K conditions (11A.2a to 11A.2K) state that the portfolio has no systematic risk: the portfolio's betas are all equal to zero. Mathematically, these conditions state that weight vector is orthogonal to the vectors of betas $(\beta_{1j}, \ldots, \beta_{nj})$, $j = 1, \ldots, K$. Finally, the portfolio includes practically no non-systematic risk (11A.3).

Since the arbitrage portfolio involves no net investment and no risk, it must yield a zero expected return:

$$\sum_{i=1}^{n} w_i E(R_i) = 0 \qquad (11A.4)$$

If the expected return were positive, then arbitrageurs can make riskless profits by buying this portfolio; if the expected return were negative, then arbitrageurs can make riskless profits by short-selling this portfolio. Mathematically, condition 11A.4 states that the weight vector $(w_1, \ldots, w_n)$ is orthogonal to the vector of expected returns $(E(R_1), \ldots, E(R_n))$.

A well-known theorem in linear algebra states that if orthogonal to a set of vectors implies orthogonal to another vector, then the latter vector can be expressed as a linear combination of the former vectors. In our case, the $(K + 1)$ orthogonal conditions 11A.1 and 11A.2a to 11A.2K imply the $(K + 2)$ orthogonal condition 11A.4. Hence, the theorem implies that we can express the expected returns as a linear function of the sensitivities:

$$E(R_i) = a_0 + a_1 \beta_{i1} + \ldots + a_K \beta_{iK} \qquad (11A.5)$$

In this expression, a_0 is the expected return to a zero-beta portfolio, or $E(R_Z)$. We can find each risk premium a_j, $j = 1, \ldots, K$, by forming a well-diversified portfolio that has a unity sensitivity for the jth risk factor and a zero beta for the remaining risk factors, or $\beta_{pj} = 1$ and $\beta_{ps} = 0$ for all $s \neq j$. Such a portfolio effectively replicates the jth risk factor, because it is equally risky (recall that well-diversified portfolios have no non-systematic risk). Hence, the expected return of the portfolio must equal the expected return of the risk factor, $E(I_j)$. Substituting $E(R_p) = E(I_j)$, $\beta_{pj} = 1$ and $\beta_{ps} = 0$ for all $s \neq j$ in Equation 11A.5, we find

$$E(I_j) = E(R_Z) + a_j$$

Solving for the risk premium a_j gives $a_j = (E(I_j) - E(R_Z))$, and hence

$$E(R_i) = E(R_Z) + (E(I_1) - R_Z)\beta_{i1} + \ldots + (E(I_K) - E(R_Z))\beta_{iK} \qquad (11A.6)$$

373

Investment in the News 12 **FT**

Markets behaving badly

Are the financial markets, and their participants, of sound mind? Over the years, perhaps naively, I have generally given them at least the benefit of the doubt, in aggregate. True, the stock market's boom-and-crash sequence of 1987 was hard to explain on any basis except that of mass hysteria; and now, after the strange events of the past two years or so, it may be time to conduct a post mortem examination on the corpse of rationality.

One of the fundamental concepts is market efficiency. This implies that prices accurately reflect information generally known and understood (although the quality of that knowledge may vary). There is also a more general economic hypothesis of rational expectations, that individuals anticipate the future in a coherent way. In the stock market this implies that values can be modelled statistically in terms of factors like expected earnings per share growth, interest rates and the equity-risk premium.

Set against these hypotheses, however, are the behavioural theories. These explore much less rational possibilities, such as that people will follow fashions and be influenced by peer group pressures. The explanation for financial manias may be psychological, or even chemical: indeed, recently an American doctor sent me a paper that seriously discussed the possibility that Wall Street's bubble reflected the ever-rising consumption of Prozac which, he said, fuelled over-optimism.

Setting the pill bottle aside, how can we interpret the markets' recent gyrations? After all, the Nasdaq – at its peak the world's biggest exchange – has crashed in value by two-thirds within 13 months. This week it was down 6 per cent on Tuesday, up 9 per cent on Thursday; on Friday it was tumbling again. Cisco Systems, which for just a day or two during mad March last year was the world's most valuable company, worth $550 bn, has since (at the recent low point) suffered a share-price collapse of 84 per cent. The drop at Deutsche Telekom has been 70 per cent. These are not speculative minnows but widely-owned giants subjected to high levels of reporting and analysis.

Clearly, confidence in rationality has been shaken although, as is usual in the aftermath of a big fall, the puzzling aspect is not why values have tumbled but why they ever got so high in the first place. From a selfish point of view the distortions have made it easier to predict the future: it is possible to forecast price trends in an inefficient market but in a completely efficient one you never have a better than 50 per cent chance of getting the up-or-down decision right.

Investment in the News 12 continued

However, looking at the markets from an economic point of view, they have become distorted and maybe dangerous: capital has been allocated wrongly, with vast sums now being dissipated before our very eyes in ill-conceived internet projects and telecoms over-expansion.

There have been problems at three levels. The one that received the most publicity during the bubble was the enormous increase in stock market speculation during the late 1990s by private individuals; millions were lured into the more fashionable sectors of the equity markets, notably technology. Improved access to information and dealing facilities through the internet fuelled this expanded participation, often by so-called 'day traders'. Rational valuation took an extended holiday.

Second, professional investors have failed to provide a proper balance. Portfolio managers have been drawn towards relative performance, with the help of increasingly varied and complicated stock market indices, and risk-control models. Thus Vodafone, which accounted for 13 per cent of London's All-Share Index at one stage, was generally regarded as a low-risk holding relative to the index, whereas in absolute terms it actually carried a high risk, though with a share price down 'only' 51 per cent it has not turned out to be as risky as some (not yet, anyway). Fund managers who held out against the irrational fashions of 1999 and early 2000 faced a big risk of being washed away by the tide, although if they survived they will have performed very well recently.

Thirdly, the market's institutional structures have become unstable. Investment banks, and their executives, became irresponsibly greedy, a trend that culminated in the wave of flotations of immature companies, often scarcely past the start-up stage. Stock exchanges, sometimes themselves new, competed aggressively for the quotations of these unproven and risky enterprises, degrading their own listing standards in the process. Quality was abandoned. Now we read that the Neuer Markt is having trouble persuading some of its listed companies to report their results within its three-month time limit. Accounting standards have become seriously distorted, in the US technology sector at any rate, by the huge handouts of stock options. Many of those options are presumably worthless, but that poses the problem that workforces no longer locked in will crumble away.

Amid all the hysteria the community of investment analysts, with some honourable exceptions, was focused on keeping the bubble inflated. In the technology sector, earnings forecasts were hoisted higher and higher. Just how crazily optimistic they had become is pointed out this week by a Goldman Sachs investment strategy report: consensus estimates of global technology earnings in 2001 have collapsed by one-third in just six months, and probably have further to fall. Again, as with portfolio managers, an important problem is that analysts are chasing relative accuracy: in this case, how far their forecasts diverge from the consensus, rather than whether they turn out to be right or not in absolute terms. Only the ones who stray away from the herd feel vulnerable.

A nasty bear market has been needed to resolve these many distortions. And, of course, it has all happened before. Perhaps it is disappointing that better information and technology have not really helped the capital markets to operate more reliably. Perversely, facts and analysis, however vast the quantity, can easily be brought to bear to justify wrong prices than to generate correct ones.

A full post mortem on rationality will have to wait until the dust has settled. My interim report is that human nature, often dominated by short-sightedness and greed, will always be the most important factor. The efficient market hypothesis must co-exist with behavioural theory.

Source: 'Markets Behaving Badly', FT.com site, 6 April 2001.

Investment in the News 12 questions whether the stock market is efficient, i.e. whether market prices accurately reflect the information available to investors. The author believes that the psychology of investors causes the market to be inefficient.

Many successful managers also do not believe in efficient market theory. The best summary of their strong view appeared in *Fortune*:

> What do Sequoia Funds' William Ruane, Berkshire Hathaway's Charles Munger and Warren Buffett, and money manager Walter Schloss have in common? They don't believe in efficient markets. Says Buffett: 'I'd be a bum on the street with a tin cup if the market were efficient.'[1]

This chapter considers ways in which investors can use information on stock prices to earn better returns. It looks at the information that investment professionals use to make their selections. The focus is on the way that the markets process information and how that information influences security prices. Although this chapter focuses primarily on the stock market, the analysis is applied easily to the bond market and other markets.

In studying the impact of information on stock prices, we work with the efficient market theory (EMT).[2] Basically, this theory predicts that stock prices reflect all information that is relevant for the stock and that no investor can profit by earning an abnormal return (or an excess return after adjusting for risk) by trying to find buying or selling opportunities in the market. For example, if an investor could analyse the historical prices of IBM stock and develop a buy–sell rule that will yield a positive, risk-adjusted return, then this would contradict the EMT. This chapter explores the various ways to interpret the EMT.

In general, academics support the EMT, whereas practitioners do not. Recently, however, some academics who preached for decades in support of the EMT have found empirical evidence favouring market inefficiency.[3] Some academics have turned to 'behavioural finance', which seeks to combine financial economics with the psychology of decision-making under uncertainty (see Section 12.7). Because practitioners use investment strategies that rely on market inefficiency, Parts 4 and 5 of this book describe some widely used valuation methods (based on technical analysis and fundamental analysis) that assume market inefficiency, at least to a certain degree.

---

[1] Terence P. Paré (1995), 'Yes, You Can Beat the Market', *Fortune*, 3 April 69.

[2] The EMT is also referred to widely as the efficient market hypothesis (EMH).

[3] See Fama and French (1992).

Your own perception of the EMT will govern, in large part, the particular investment philosophy you adopt. The objective of this book is not to persuade you to adopt one school of thought over another but rather to give you the analytical tools needed to reach your own conclusions. This chapter examines the investment implications and appropriate strategies to use if markets are efficient or, alternatively, inefficient. It also surveys the available empirical evidence regarding market efficiency.

12.1 Efficient market defined

How efficiently do markets process information? An investigation of the effect of information on security prices must begin with a definition of an efficient market. A well-functioning financial market in which prices reflect all relevant information is said to be an efficient market. Another way to state this is that the EMT claims that security prices reflect all relevant information; that is, the current market price of a security incorporates all relevant information. If a financial market is efficient, then the best estimate of the true value of a security is given by its current market price.

In an efficient market, it is assumed that a large number of analysts are assessing the true value of firms. The analysts try to find stocks whose market prices are substantially different from their true values. If the analysts find such 'mispriced' securities, they buy or sell them, driving the market price instantaneously towards the true value of the security. Thus, competition in the stock market pushes prices to their 'true' value. Thus, stock prices change every day, every hour, even every second, as new information flows into the marketplace.

To demonstrate how information influences stock prices, consider Tropicana, a corporation that produces citrus products in Florida. If analysts who study weather patterns anticipate a hard freeze that would be devastating to citrus crops, they will try to make large profits by selling short Tropicana stock. This selling pressure drives the stock price down toward its 'true' value. Thus, the information changes the stock price. If doctors at a prominent research hospital release a study that shows that people who drink three glasses of orange juice a day reduce their risk of cancer, then the price of orange juice stocks should rise because the demand for orange juice will increase. Thus, the results of trading by the weather predictors, which would force the stock price down, would be reversed by the actions of investors who think the demand for orange juice (and the profits of juice manufacturers) will rise. This constant assimilation of information causes the prices of securities to change as investors react to all relevant information.

Is the market efficient? Actually, it is almost impossible to test purely whether the market is efficient, which explains why there are no clear winners in the market efficiency dispute. Most of the tests of market efficiency are joint tests – that is, one is testing whether the model measuring returns is appropriate and the other whether markets are efficient. If the market is efficient, there are no 'bargains' in the market, because all assets are priced correctly. In such a case, most of the work done by analysts who try to find bargains in the market is worthless. Thus, one of the reasons for the market-efficiency dispute is that tests of market-efficiency are joint tests of the assumed model and the market efficiency.

To illustrate this, suppose that an analyst claims to observe the historical price movement of IBM stock; based on these historical figures, the analyst reaches the conclusion that IBM stock is a bargain (that is, it is underpriced). Suppose the analyst buys IBM stock, and their annual realised rate of return on the stock is 12%. Can we then conclude that the market is inefficient? Did the analyst succeed in exploiting the information on historical prices to make an extraordinary return? To reach such a conclusion, we first need to find out the risk involved with the investment in IBM stock and figure out whether there is an abnormal return adjusted for this risk. For example, suppose that we use the CAPM and IBM's beta to estimate the expected rate of return on IBM to be 11%. In such a case, the analyst has an extraordinary profit of 1%. This extraordinary profit is also called an abnormal return. It seems that based on this result, we might claim that the market is inefficient. However, what if the CAPM is an incorrect model, and therefore the 11% estimate of the required expected return was wrong? Then we may come to the wrong conclusion regarding market efficiency, because we employed an incorrect model to measure the 'normal' rate of return.

Thus, in testing for market efficiency, first we should estimate what should be the normal rate of return on an asset, which is also called the risk-adjusted rate of return. For that purpose, we need a model asserting what the risk is and what the corresponding risk premium should be. Then we compare the return realised by the analyst's investment policy to this normal return. If the realised return is significantly higher than the normal return, researchers generally assert that the market is inefficient, because the analyst made abnormal or excess returns.

However, by this procedure, we see that we have a joint hypothesis and therefore should conduct a joint test of the model and of market efficiency. To illustrate, suppose that the CAPM is wrong, and the variance of the rate of return, rather than beta, is the correct measure of risk. We may conclude that with this risk measure, the required rate of return is 12% in the IBM example. Now the analyst does not make any profit after adjusting for risk. Thus, testing market efficiency is based on a normal return as a benchmark. Because this normal return is deduced from some model, empirical tests are joint tests of the model and of market efficiency.

12.2 What constitutes the appropriate information set?

A great deal of information is available in the stock market: historical stock prices, earnings and dividends, macroeconomic data, private information known only to insiders, and other information that seems irrelevant for stock valuation (for example, the age and eye colour of a firm's chief executive officer). Exhibit 12.1 illustrates this idea. At one extreme, it might be argued that all information is useful in earning an abnormal return. An investor can use all available information and make an extraordinary profit. In other words, it pays to analyse available information in making a security selection.

At the other extreme, it might be argued that prices reflect all information that exists; that is, everything that can be known about a security is already incorporated in its price. For example, even the poor health of an important member of upper management would be reflected in the stock price. From this point of view, any data collection or economic analysis is a waste of time.

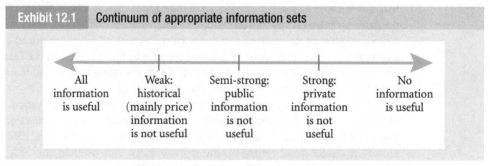

Exhibit 12.1 Continuum of appropriate information sets

| All information is useful | Weak: historical (mainly price) information is not useful | Semi-strong: public information is not useful | Strong: private information is not useful | No information is useful |

Clearly, these two extremes are irrational and probably irrelevant in price determination. However, somewhere between these two extremes lies a reasonable set of the information employed in determining stock prices. Along the journey across the continuum from 'no information' to 'all information' lie three milestones or information sets: historical, public and private information. The EMT, which describes the impact of information on the market prices of securities, can be analysed in terms of these specific information sets and their impact on price determination. Thus, there are three forms of the EMT: the weak, the semi-strong and the strong EMT.

12.2.1 Weak form of the efficient market theory

The first form of the EMT is the weak form.[4] According to the weak form of the EMT, today's stock prices reflect all information about the historical prices of the stock, so historical prices are not useful for investment decisions. If this is true, then an investor could not use historical stock price information to find mispriced stocks and thus profit from buying or selling these stocks. The stock prices would have adjusted already for this information. Technical analysts try to use historical price information to locate mispriced stocks. Therefore, under the weak form of the EMT, we would not expect them to find opportunities that generate abnormal returns using these techniques. Investors would just earn the normal profit for the risk taken.

If the weak form of the EMT holds, and thus prices are independent of the pattern of historical stock prices, we say that price changes will appear to follow a random walk when examining just the historical series.[5] A random walk is a statistical concept that predicts that the next outcome in a series does not depend on its previous outcomes. A simple example that illustrates the random walk notion is the flipping of a coin. Although the first three tosses may be heads, heads and tails, these outcomes do not affect the probability of head or tail in the next toss, i.e. the result in the next toss does not depend on previous results.

Because risky securities offer positive expected returns, we would anticipate stock prices to rise over time. Despite this trend, price changes may still follow a random walk. For example, suppose we have a security presently trading at $100. We know that in each period, the price will rise by 12% with a 75% probability or fall by 10% with a 25% probability. In this case, three out of four times (75%) the return will be 12%, whereas only one out of four times (25%) the return will be −10%. The expected return in this case is

$$E(R) = 0.75(12\%) + 0.25(-10\%) = 6.5\%$$

Although the expected return is 6.5%, the particular outcome observed in a given year is random. Hence, even in this case, we say that the security follows a random walk.

Going back to the coin-tossing example, suppose you flip a biased coin with a probability of heads of three in four and a probability of tails of one in four.[6] Do the results of the first three tosses affect the result of the next toss? Absolutely not. This process has no memory, and the probabilities are still three in four for heads and one in four for tails.

---

[4] See Roberts (1967). In 1991, Fama suggested broadening this category to include other variables used in determining return predictability.

[5] Technically, stocks, on average, will move up by the stocks' expected return. Hence, the random walk concept is applied after adjusting for the expected return.

[6] A biased coin is typically heavier on one side. Hence, tossing it results in outcomes different from 50–50.

Exhibit 12.2 presents monthly rates of returns over a recent period for three stocks: Commonwealth Edison, General Electric (GE) and Dow Chemical. Can you spot any trends? It seems that monthly stock returns appear to follow a random walk.[7] Notice that although the next outcome for all three companies is unpredictable, it is apparent that Commonwealth Edison is less volatile than GE, and GE is less volatile than Dow Chemical. Hence, random walks can occur with varying magnitudes of volatility. Also, note that these firms have more points above than below the zero horizontal line, which reflects that, on average, investors get a positive profit on such risky investments. There is one school of thought that the financial markets are not weak-form efficient (thus, they believe that they can learn from the historical data and improve their investment decisions). Trading strategies based on historical market data (mainly stock prices) are known as technical analysis (which will be discussed in Chapter 18).

12.2.2 Semi-strong form of the efficient market theory

The second form of the EMT is the semi-strong form. According to the semi-strong form of the EMT, prices reflect all relevant publicly available information. In addition to historical stock prices, publicly available information includes financial statements, notes to the financial statements, and supplementary information required by accounting regulations. Publicly available information also includes other external financial and regulatory filings such as property taxes paid, as well as market-related data such as the level of interest rates and the stock's beta.

According to the semi-strong form of the EMT, an investor could not earn abnormal returns on trading strategies built on publicly available information. Thus, if the market is semi-strong efficient, then a diligent study of financial statements is of no economic value. The idea behind this is that once this information becomes public, all investors react instantaneously and push the price to reflect all public information. Thus, when you read your newspaper with your morning coffee and see some public information, such as a new drug discovery or a financial crisis in Asia, it is too late for you to earn an abnormal profit. The price at which you can buy or sell the stock already reflects this information.

In contrast to proponents of the semi-strong form of the EMT, there are investors who think they can profit from a careful study of publicly available data – particularly accounting data. These investors practise fundamental analysis and use the information in financial statements and other public sources to identify mispriced stock. The two factors commonly employed to identify underpriced stock in a fundamental analysis are the price/earnings (P/E) ratio and the market-to-book-value (M/B) ratio, where M is the market value (stock price) and B is the book value per share. These techniques will be discussed in Part 4.

12.2.3 Strong form of the efficient market theory

The third form of the efficient market theory is the strong form. This form states that current prices already reflect all publicly and privately available information. Thus, the strong form includes all relevant historical price information and all relevant publicly available information, as well as information known only to a select few such as management, the board of directors and private bankers. For example, suppose a member of the board of directors of Intel knows that the firm has decided to take over another firm. The board member's spouse

---

[7] Of course, some quantitative methods are needed to measure the random walk, such as serial correlation, runs tests, and so forth. These quantitative methods are beyond the scope of this book.

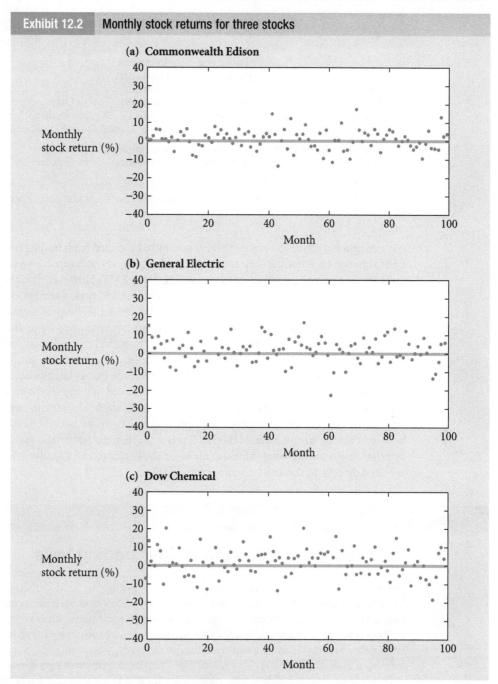

Exhibit 12.2   Monthly stock returns for three stocks

Source: From *Introduction to Investments*, 2nd edn, by Levy. © 1999. Reprinted with permission of South-Western, a division of Thomson Learning: www.thomsonrights.com. Fax 800 730-2215.

then buys shares of Intel stock before the takeover becomes public information. This would be considered trading on inside information, and it is illegal.

If the strong EMT form were true, then insiders would not profit from trading on their information. As Connecting Theory to Practice 12.1 illustrates, however, the market is clearly

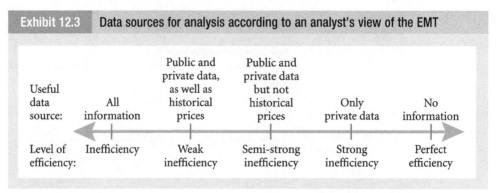

Exhibit 12.3	Data sources for analysis according to an analyst's view of the EMT

Source: From *Introduction to Investments*, 2nd edn, by Levy. © 1999. Reprinted with permission of South-Western, a division of Thomson Learning: www.thomsonrights.com. Fax 800 730-2215.

not strong-form efficient, because there is money to be gained from trading on inside information (although such trading is illegal). Insiders who know about future takeovers or acquisitions can earn large profits, contradicting the strong-form EMT. However, it is illegal to trade on private information, and many inside traders have received prison sentences for doing so.

Exhibit 12.3 summarises the discussion thus far from the viewpoint of an analyst. If an analyst believed that the weak form of the EMT was not true, then he or she should be able to systematically earn abnormal returns based on historical price data as well as public and private data. If an analyst believed that the weak form, but not the semi-strong form, of the EMT was true, then he or she should be able to earn excess returns based on public and private data but not historical prices. If an analyst believed that the semi-strong form, but not the strong form, of the EMT was true, then he or she should be able to earn excess returns only based on private information (which is illegal to trade upon). Finally, if an analyst believed that the strong form of the EMT was true, then no systematic excess returns would be possible, no matter what information he or she could access. Clearly, investment strategy is linked directly to the analyst's view of the EMT.

→ **Connecting Theory to Practice 12.1**

Few countries enforcing insider trading laws

Nearly 85 per cent of the world's stock markets have laws against insider trading but only one-third have enforced them. And in countries where no insiders have been prosecuted, companies pay an average of 5 per cent extra to raise capital, according to a new study.

'That is the price of honesty,' said Utpal Battacharya, a finance professor at Indiana University's Kelley School of Business and co-author of the study, which will soon be published in the Journal of Finance. 'Countries have to pay 5 per cent extra to their shareholders.'

In a market where insiders with non-public information can trade freely, broker-dealers protect themselves by increasing their sell price and decreasing their buy price. This bumps up transaction costs, forcing traders to demand better returns. Mr Battacharya also argues that 'controlling large shareholders could easily be tempted by management to make profits from stock tips rather than . . . from hard-to-do monitoring. Knowing this, [other] shareholders would demand a higher return on equity.' But laws are not enough, he said. Capital-raising costs go down and a country's credit rating goes up only after the first prosecution.

Mr Battacharya began his investigation of the world's 103 markets, with PhD student Hazem Daouk, after conducting similar research in Mexico. In that study, he found that A shares, which are held by only Mexicans, including corporate executives, were traded heavily before an important company announcement, while B shares, which are held by foreigners, saw less activity. 'In the US, when a takeover is announced the stock jumps up. It may have already gone up because there is about a 50 per cent leakage rate in the US, but in Mexico, it's 100 per cent,' Mr Battacharya said.

Emerging markets mutual fund managers criticised the study, however, arguing that insider trading was not a significant problem. Mr Battacharya acknowledges that he set out to prove them wrong. He spent one year gathering information from every world market – including the youngest (Tanzania), the oldest (Germany), the largest (the New York Stock Exchange) and the smallest (Guatemala). 'I faxed, e-mailed, voice-mailed, slow-mailed each and every country to ask if they had insider trading laws and if they had enforced them,' he said.

Controlling for other factors, such as company risk and market liquidity, he found that listed companies saved 5 per cent in countries where insiders had been prosecuted.

'You probably need one big insider trading case every year – someone getting caught,' Mr Battacharya said, pointing to the US as a model. The Securities and Exchange Commission prosecutes about 40 to 50 insider trading cases a year. 'They don't always succeed but they try very hard to keep it away,' Mr Battacharya said. 'And the US becomes the most liquid market in the world. It's a virtuous circle that more than pays for the enforcement costs.'

In Europe, the situation is varied. Germany, which established its stock market in 1585 but only outlawed insider trading in 1994, has had only a few prosecutions. In France, many of the cases are politically motivated, Mr Battacharya said.

But the US has influenced other markets. 'In the 1990s, the SEC has entered into some sort of club with the other securities commissions,' Mr Battacharya said. 'They are telling them, "This is what you need to do to attract foreign capital."'

The 81 emerging markets are slowly coming around, he said. 'In the markets where only a few stocks are trading, they are just learning the institutional details. A few countries asked "What is insider trading?"' A copy of The World Price of Insider Trading can be found at www.ssrn.com.

Source: Alison Beard, 'Few Countries Enforcing Insider Trading Laws', *Financial Times*, 12 April 2001.

→ Making the connection

In some countries, inside traders are not prosecuted, either because there are no laws against insider trading or because the existing laws are not enforced. Not surprisingly, the cost of capital for issuers of securities is substantially higher in these countries than in countries that do prosecute insider trading, reflecting the additional risk to outside investors.

12.3 Investment strategy in an efficient market

It seems reasonable that markets do process historical and public data with relative efficiency, and this is the view of many academic investment theorists. Thus, this section examines how to structure a successful investment strategy in the semi-strong form of the EMT. It first examines how resources are allocated in this market. Next, it examines portfolio selection and the usefulness of employing the expected return–risk trade-off when markets are efficient. It also distinguishes between passive and active portfolio management strategies.

12.3.1 Resource allocation and the efficient market theory

If relatively more money is allocated to firms that have good capital budgeting projects and relatively less money is allocated to firms with poor projects, then we say that money is allocated in an effective manner. Efficient allocation of capital is also referred to as the 'invisible hand'. Hayek (1945) notes that the invisible hand works as a huge continuous polling mechanism that records the updated votes of millions of investors in the continuously changing current price. In efficient markets, resources are allocated to the various firms in an effective manner, because those firms with good prospects will be able to raise additional capital in the primary market on relatively good terms. That is, in constructing their portfolios, investors will allocate more money to those firms that they deem a relatively good investment. For example, suppose IBM has a reliable and powerful new computer, or Pfizer develops a new drug such as Viagra. When this information becomes public, investors will allocate more of their money to IBM stock or to Pfizer stock, and the stock price will go up instantaneously.

Thus, a firm with good prospects will have a higher stock price and can issue stocks on better terms in the market. In contrast, a firm with poor prospects (one that is expected to go bankrupt) would be unable to raise money through either a stock issue or a bond issue. Thus, the information on the firm's prospects is reflected in the stock prices; the rosier the estimated future, the higher the stock price.

This observation regarding the link between resource allocation and the EMT illustrates a seeming paradox. In order for markets to be efficient, new firm information should affect the stock price. Hence, some investors have to be paying attention to firm information. However, the EMT suggests that there is no benefit in monitoring firm information. In practice, those with the least costly access to information capitalise on minor mispricing, which drives prices to reflect swiftly all relevant information. Hence, the practical application of the EMT focuses on trading costs and speed. This helps explain why some trading firms are willing to invest heavily in super-computers and high-speed information highways. For most investors, however, the new information is worthless, because the price is adjusted instantaneously to reflect it.

12.3.2 Portfolio selection and the efficient market theory

Is there a contradiction between the EMT and portfolio selection? If financial markets are efficient under the semi-strong form of the EMT, is there any need to burden ourselves with portfolio diversification? Under the semi-strong form of the EMT, the analysis conducted by technicians (who do technical analysis) and fundamentalists (who do fundamental analysis) will not generate excess returns. There are no 'bargains' in the market, and stock-selection techniques are worthless. What is left for portfolio managers is portfolio diversification, which pays off even in efficient markets.

To demonstrate this idea, suppose that two stocks, 1 and 2, each trade for $10. You flip two coins, one corresponding to each stock. If a head comes up, the stock price increases to $13; if a tail appears, the stock price falls to $9. Of course, these stock-price changes conform to semi-strong form market efficiency, because the price changes are dependent on a random coin toss and do not depend on historical or public information. If you do not diversify between the two stocks, for your $10 investment, the future mean and variance of each stock is as follows:

$$\text{Mean: } (0.5 \times \$13) + (0.5 \times \$9) = \$11$$

$$\text{Variance: } 0.5(13 - 11)^2 + 0.5(9 - 11)^2 = 4, \text{ and } \sigma = \$2.$$

Can you gain from diversification in such a market that obeys the EMT? The answer is yes. To see why, assume you invest $5 in stock 1 and $5 in stock 2. Because the two stocks are independent (you toss two coins, separately, one for each stock), you get the following returns:

Stock 1	Stock 2	Portfolio
$0.5 \times \$13 +$	$0.5 \times \$13 =$	$13 (with a probability of 0.25)
$0.5 \times \$13 +$	$0.5 \times \$9 =$	$11 (with a probability of 0.25)
$0.5 \times \$9 +$	$0.5 \times \$13 =$	$11 (with a probability of 0.25)
$0.5 \times \$9 +$	$0.5 \times \$9 =$	$9 (with a probability of 0.25)

where 0.5 is the proportion of investment in each stock ($5/$10 = 0.5). The portfolio mean return is

$$(0.25 \times 13) + (0.25 \times 11) + (0.25 \times 11) + (0.25 \times 9) = \$11$$

which is exactly the same as investing in just stock 1 or stock 2 alone. Note, however, that the variance of the portfolio is lower:

$$0.25(13 - 11)^2 + 0.25(11 - 11)^2 + 0.25(11 - 11)^2 + 0.25(9 - 11)^2 = 2, \text{ and } \sigma \cong \$1.41$$

Thus, you reduce the risk by diversifying.

Some believe that the semi-strong form of the EMT implies that all stocks are priced correctly and therefore you can select stocks at random – for example, by throwing a dart at a list of stocks obtained from the financial pages (see Investment in the News 12). This is not correct. Although you cannot predict which stock will go up and which will go down in the future, by diversification you can reduce your risk. If you ignore this diversification, you are exposing yourself to higher risk with no compensation in the form of a higher expected return. Note that in the previous example, your variance decreased through diversification, but your expected return remained the same, at $11.

The previous example can be extended to many assets with positive and negative correlations. For example, suppose you have a stock with a high variance but a low beta (for example, $\beta_i = 0.5$). According to the CAPM, the mean rate of return on the stock will be relatively low, because this stock has a low correlation with other securities and, hence, portfolio risk is reduced. If you do not diversify and thus hold only one stock (or only a few stocks), you pay a relatively high price for the stock; you expose yourself to high risk and do not enjoy the benefits of the risk-reduction possibilities that are due to the negative correlation.

In summary, if the semi-strong form of the EMT holds, then technical and fundamental analysis are economically worthless. However, portfolio analysis remains important; in fact, more effort should be allocated to portfolio analysis. If the market is inefficient, then both security analysis (to find 'bargains' in the market) and portfolio analysis (to reduce risk) are economically important.

12.3.3 Passive versus active portfolio management

Portfolio managers face two difficult tasks:

- How to diversify among the various assets. Finding the desired investment proportions and adhering to them is called passive investment strategy.
- When to change the investment proportions in the various assets. Managers try to predict whether the stock market or the bond market will be stronger, say, next month, and actively

change the investment proportions according to their predictions. Such a management strategy is called active investment strategy. Managers may increase the proportion of stocks from 40 to 60% today, and reverse this proportion next month, reducing the stock proportion to 40% or even less.

If the market is efficient, only the passive management strategy is relevant, because according to the semi-strong form of the EMT, publicly available information (for example, the budget deficit, the amount of money in the market, reported earnings by firms, or unemployment) is not useful in predicting whether stocks or bonds will be better in the future. In such a case, portfolio managers do not have 'timing ability', or the ability to predict the best time to move from heavy bond investment to more stock investment, or vice versa. Nearly all investors know that when interest rates go down, the stock market typically rallies. However, can they predict what the interest rate will be next month? If you believe in the semi-strong form of the EMT, you cannot benefit from active investment strategies. The best investment strategy is simply to find some investment proportions and adopt a passive investment strategy; a portfolio manager should not try to outsmart the market.

Funds known as index funds do not engage in active rebalancing strategies. For example, the Vanguard Index 500 Portfolio holds stocks in the same proportions as the Standard & Poor's 500 stock price index. Thus, if you buy this fund, you really buy the index, and the manager does not make any attempt to outperform the S&P 500 index. Because stock index funds do not involve high trading/transaction costs and do not need to spend money on economic analyses, they incur expenses of about 0.2%; for managed funds (funds that invest not only in indexes but also in stocks, bonds, options, futures, currencies, etc., thus offering the investor the advantage of professional management), these fees are much higher (usually around 1.3%).

→ **Connecting Theory to Practice 12.2**

'I'm a tracker punter and proud of it'

First, a declaration of interest: I own a tracker fund. Worse than that, I have lost almost a fifth of the money invested in the tracker – Legal & General's UK Index fund – because since 1998 the market has plummeted. Am I frustrated? Sure. But I remain convinced that trackers are still the best way for the average punter to bet on the stock market.

Trackers are pretty simple funds to understand. They try to follow an index – typically the FTSE All-Share or FTSE 100 – which measures the performance of all or part of the stock market. If the market does well, the tracker does well. If it does badly the tracker does badly, as I discovered. The managers, helped by computers, do not try to outperform, do not make any big bets, they concentrate on doing what the market does. As a result, they are cheap: at about 0.5 per cent a year, the typical tracker charges around a third of an actively managed fund (do not pay more than 0.5 per cent, and shop around for less). Of course, this means there is no chance of beating the market. Investors in a 'passive' tracker are buying boredom; they will not double their money in a year.

Buy an 'active' fund and you are also unlikely to double your money, at least in one year. But some of the gamblers trusting a fund manager to pick the winning shares will make more money than the investors in trackers. Anyone who bought Fidelity's Special Situations fund, managed by the legendary Anthony Bolton, four years ago has made a 44 per cent profit, even as the markets dived.

This, broadly, is the choice facing investors: picking an active fund is gambling on the chances of the fund manager doing better than the norm. But gamblers may find the odds stacked against them when they try to select a fund manager. According to research for Virgin by WM Company, the specialist performance analysts, three-quarters of all active funds failed to beat the index in the average five-year period over the past 20 years. Last year almost two-thirds failed to beat the index, even though it was falling – just the conditions where active managers ought to find life easier. In general, active managers will do better when smaller companies are doing well, and under-perform in bull markets when the blue-chips are leading the index upwards. Because outperformance does not usually last very long, the best performers of the past five or 10 years are no more likely than any other fund to continue topping the tables. The odds, in fact, are almost exactly even. As the regulators warn, past performance is no guide to the future.

There are selection methods that are slightly more scientific than throwing darts at a dartboard, however. Funds that simply got lucky on one bet can be filtered out by looking for consistency: did the fund do well every year? Pull in calculations of volatility and the probability is slightly improved. Interview the fund manager about their investment style and read their guide to investment process. Some analysts believe three in four of their recommendations will beat the average. Not bad odds. Sadly, few ordinary investors have access to this data or the time or inclination to study it. 'Identification of likely future outperformance requires highly sophisticated and time-intensive analysis of performance data and fund managers' styles,' Ron Sandler, former chief executive of the Lloyd's insurance market, concluded in a recent study for the government. 'Only a tiny minority of consumers have access to this sort of analysis.' He also found that there is no link between charge and future performance. So the argument from some champagne-swilling fund managers that you have to pay up to get the best should be dismissed.

William Carey, joint chief executive of Liontrust, which runs active and passive funds, recommends taking advice to choose an active fund. 'Trying to select funds that persistently outperform an index is pretty hard,' he said. The problem with advice is that finding a good independent financial adviser is not easy. If you have one you trust to do the research for you, go ahead and buy an active fund. But if all you want is to bet on the stock market, a cheap index tracker is the quickest, easiest and surest way to do so.

Source: James Mackintosh, 'I'm A Tracker Punter and Proud Of It', *Financial Times*, 17 August 2002.

→ Making the connection

This article elaborates on two important reasons for investing in index funds: (1) low expenses and (2) difficulty of finding an active fund that will beat the market.

12.4　Investment strategy in an inefficient market

In an inefficient market, the appropriate investment strategy is different from when the market is efficient. The particular strategy to pursue depends on the level of efficiency (or inefficiency). Investors who believe in the weak form of the EMT but not the semi-strong form might locate mispriced securities using fundamental analysis. Hence, the investors with the lowest cost per investment dollar for conducting fundamental analysis and those who are the best at analysing the data will earn the greatest returns.

Similarly, investors who do not believe in the weak form of the EMT would even benefit from some technical trading rules based on historical prices as well as fundamental analysis. Finally, investors who believe in the strong form of the EMT believe that they cannot benefit, even if they are insiders. Those who do not believe in the strong form of the EMT can earn abnormal profits. However, they have to consider the risk–return profile, and they risk being sent to prison!

→ Connecting Theory to Practice 12.3

Hewitt Bacon recommends 'blindfolded monkey' way

One of the world's biggest investment consultancies is recommending that pension funds measure themselves against the investment acumen of a 'blindfolded monkey'. It could spell the end of the traditional index benchmark.

Hewitt Bacon & Woodrow, the Anglo-American consultancy, said it was in 'advanced discussions' with several UK pension funds – and their fund managers – about its new idea: the 'unconstrained' benchmark. Instead of being tied to stock market indices, equity portfolios could be measured against an artificially generated peer group. This would include hundreds of randomly constructed portfolios – put together using a tool that mimics the stockpicking skills of a blindfolded monkey throwing darts at a list of stocks.

In the wake of the stock market downturn, fund managers have come under fire for their tendency to design portfolios that look like their benchmarks. This is largely because managers are given tightly constrained performance targets that are pegged to an index. Nicola Horlick, the head of SG Asset Management in the UK, recently found herself at the centre of a row over 'not being an active manager'. Hewitt Bacon & Woodrow believes that an 'unconstrained' benchmark would force fund managers to take truly active bets, putting an end to 'index hugging'.

Kerrin Rosenberg, investment consultant at Hewitt Bacon & Woodrow, said: 'Fund managers interpret [portfolio] risk as the divergence from the index weighting of stocks. As a result, they end up putting a large part of the portfolio into a small number of big stocks.' For example, five UK banking groups presently account for 20 per cent of the market capitalisation of the FTSE All Share index. During the technology boom, stocks such as Vodafone, the UK mobile phone giant, accounted for a big part of pension funds' portfolios.

Mr Rosenberg points to the role of the pension fund trustees, who unwittingly influence stock selection through their traditional reliance on index benchmarks. 'We would be perfectly happy for a UK fund manager to hold 10 per cent of a portfolio in BP if he were choosing to do that on pure investment grounds.' Mr Rosenberg believes that index hugging has helped to push frustrated pension fund clients into the arms of equity long/short hedge fund managers. He says that unconstrained benchmarks lead to the same result – active management – at a lower risk.

Source: Florian Gimbel, 'Hewitt Bacon Recommends "Blindfolded Monkey" Way', FT.com site, 16 June 2003.

→ Making the connection

According to Hewitt Bacon & Woodrow, the practice of benchmarking investment performance relative to a stock market index has motivated pension fund managers to adopt a passive strategy of simply tracking the index. While this strategy minimises the risk diverging from the index, it may actually be very risky, because some indexes (such as the FTSE All Share index) are poorly diversified portfolios with heavy weights for a few large-cap stocks. To stimulate active management, Hewitt Bacon & Woodrow proposes to measure investment performance relative to a randomly generated peer group ('blindfolded monkeys throwing darts at a list of stocks'). Presumably, this boils down to using an equal-weighted index rather than a value-weighted index, which would stimulate pension fund managers to invest more in small-cap funds.

12.5 Empirical evidence related to the efficient market theory

Does actual price behaviour support the EMT? The existing evidence is vast; this text will survey only a few studies to answer this question.

However, before we look at the empirical tests of the various forms of market efficiency, it is worth noting another set of classifications that has been suggested by Fama (1991). His classifications are derived from the empirical tests conducted to figure out whether the market is efficient. The first category includes tests for return predictability, which includes historical prices and other variables such as dividends, interest rates, firm size, and so on. If one can use these variables to predict stock price or to make an abnormal return, then we say that the market is inefficient. The second category includes event studies, which test whether an abnormal rate of return exists because of an announcement of an event such as an increase in dividends or a merger. Once again, if one can make an abnormal return using this information, then the market is inefficient. The third category includes tests for private information, which are similar to the tests for insider information discussed earlier.

This chapter will adhere to the original classifications of market efficiency. Nevertheless, keep in mind that these classifications are arbitrary and can be changed without changing the empirical tests for market efficiency. The names change, but the content of the tests does not.

The objective of this section is to assess how efficient the market actually is in practice. To organise our investigation, we categorise the evidence according to how it is related to the three forms of the EMT (weak, semi-strong and strong).

12.5.1 Evidence related to the weak form of the efficient market theory

Many investment rules are based on historical prices. For example, one trading rule suggests buying stocks that are trading at their 52-week low. A large number of empirical studies have tested the weak form of the EMT; some are summarised in Exhibit 12.4. In general, the early research provides strong evidence in favour of markets being weak-form-efficient. More recent evidence has uncovered many anomalies, which are events that are not anticipated and that offer investors a chance to earn abnormal profits. Researchers were so convinced that the EMT was true that they felt any contrary evidence must be an anomaly; some of these findings were referred to as enigmas.

Two primary techniques are used to test the validity of the weak form proposition: analysis of technical trading rules for abnormal rates of return and statistical tests on historical data to locate significant patterns.

Analysis of technical trading rules for abnormal rates of return

Technical trading rules can be examined to determine whether they generate abnormal rates of return after trading cost (technical trading rules are covered in detail in Chapter 18). Abnormal rates of return, as defined earlier, are the rates of return that are above what we would expect to earn given the level of risk taken.

To calculate abnormal returns, we must first determine normal returns. We can use, for example, the CAPM, the SIM or the APT to find normal returns. With the CAPM, recall that the expected return on asset i (a security or a portfolio) is

$$E(R_i) = r + [E(R_m) - r]\beta_i \qquad (12.1)$$

Exhibit 12.4	Summary of evidence related to the weak form of the efficient market theory

Author(s)	Year	Assets studied	Weak-form-efficient?	Comments
Bachelier	1900	French securities	Yes	Tried to test whether the French government securities options and futures market was efficient
Roberts	1959	US stocks	Yes	Found that stock prices resemble random patterns
Osborne	1959	US stocks	Yes	Found that stock prices are similar to random movement of physical particles in water (Brownian motion)
Granger and Morgenstern	1963	US stocks	Yes	Employed spectral analysis (a powerful statistical tool that identifies patterns), but still found no significant patterns
Fama	1965	US stocks	Yes	Examined serial correlations and other statistical tools to check for patterns, and found no significant patterns
Fama and Blume	1966	US stocks	Yes	Examined technical trading rules and found no abnormal profits
Levy	1967	US stocks	Yes/No	Discovered high returns on momentum investment rules; did not test for abnormal profits
Solnik	1973	Stocks in nine countries	Yes	Used serial correlations and found no profitable investment strategies
Merton	1980	US stocks	No	Found that changes in variance are somewhat predictable from past data
French	1980	US stocks	No	Identified a weekend effect
Keim	1983	US stocks	No	Identified a January effect
Gultekin and Gultekin	1983	International markets	No	Identified seasonal patterns
Jaffe and Westerfield	1985	International markets	No	Identified seasonal patterns
DeBondt and Thaler	1985	US stocks	No	Identified the reversal effect
Lehmann	1990	US stocks	No	Identified more reversal effects
Jegadeesh and Titman	1993	US stocks	No	Identified momentum effect
Serletis and Sondergard	1995	Canadian stocks	Yes	Using tests of the 1980s, found that efficiency holds for Canadian stocks
Masih and Masih	1996	Daily spot exchange rates	No	Tested spot rates and found that they suggest violation of market efficiency
McQueen and Thorley	1997	Gold	No	Found that previous returns on an equally weighted portfolio of gold stocks predict gold returns
Fama	1998	US stocks	Yes	Apparent overreaction is about as common as underreaction; long-term return anomalies tend to disappear with reasonable changes in technique
Niarchos and Alexakis	2003	Athens stock exchange	No	Possibility of profitable intraday stock price patterns not only more profitable than 'buy and hold strategy' but also more safe

Source: From *Introduction to Investments*, 2nd edn, by Levy. © 1999. Reprinted with permission of South-Western, a division of Thomson Learning: www.thomsonrights.com. Fax 800 730-2215.

where r is the risk-free interest rate, $E(R_m)$ is the expected rate of return on the market portfolio, and β_i is the beta coefficient (defined as $\sigma_{i,m}/\sigma_m^2$). Thus, the normal expected rate of return is given by $E(R_i)$. The abnormal rate of return (AR_i) is defined as

$$AR_i = R_i - E(R_i) = R_i - \{r + [E(R_m) - r]\beta_i\} \tag{12.2}$$

or, in words,

Abnormal rate of return = Actual rate of return − Normal rate of return

where R_i is the realised or actual return on the ith stock. Because $E(R_m)$ and β_i are unknown parameters, they are usually estimated by using historical data. Hence, the normal return is estimated first, and then the abnormal return is estimated. This technique is commonly employed in the event studies explained next.

Many research studies of market efficiency examine the behaviour of these abnormal rates of return over time. Researchers measure this using the cumulative abnormal rate of return (CAR_i), the sum of all abnormal rates of return for the whole investment period, which is calculated for a particular trading strategy as follows:

$$CAR_i = \sum_{t=1}^{m} AR_{i,t} \tag{12.3}$$

where m is the number of periods (usually days). If the cumulative abnormal rates of return are significantly positive, then we conclude that abnormal returns are possible following some strategy, and the EMT is wrong. An alternative conclusion would be that the risk of the portfolio was not estimated appropriately by its beta. Therefore, as discussed before, we face a joint hypothesis regarding the EMT and the model used to measure the normal rate of return. In order to check whether the abnormal return is solely a consequence of the strategy used and not of the model used, we can use a technique called event study.

An event study is a technique used to measure the impact of a particular event on a firm's stock price. It measures the response of the stock price to the event – for example, an announcement of an increase in cash dividends. Suppose that a firm announces an increase in cash dividends, and the stock price on the same day goes up by 2%. Is it an abnormal profit? The answer is not clear, because many other economic phenomena that may affect the stock price may occur on the same day – an announcement of a decrease in the interest rate, a new peace treaty, and so on. The aim of event-study methodology is to measure the increase in price that is due solely to the event itself.

Because β_i is unknown, we cannot directly employ Equation 12.2 to measure AR_i. Therefore, in an event study, we commonly employ the SIM (see Chapter 11) when the factor is some stock index (for example, the S&P 500 index). The event date is denoted by t. Then the abnormal rate of return on day t (see Equation 12.2) is estimated by e_t, given by the equation

$$R_t = a + bR_{m,t} + e_t$$

Namely, the abnormal return is estimated by e_t, given by

$$e_t = R_t - a - bR_{m,t}$$

where R_t and $R_{m,t}$ are the rates of return on the announcement date of the firm's stock and on the market portfolio (for example, the S&P 500 index), respectively, and a and b are the intercept and the slope, respectively, of the regression line of R_t regressed against $R_{m,t}$. In order not to contaminate the estimates of a and b by the event itself, generally some period before the announcement date is taken – for example, 60 months (starting 65 months before the announcement date) – and a regression of R_t on $R_{m,t}$ is conducted in this period to estimate a and b. Also, because there may be leaks of information before the event and a continuing effect after the event, it is common to measure the abnormal return corresponding to a few days surrounding the event date as well.

To make sure that e_t measures the abnormal rate of return and not another economic factor occurring on the same date, many firms that increase the cash dividends from different dates in the past are excluded in the study. Thus, by having various periods, the effects of other economic factors tend to cancel each other. Thus, $\bar{e}_t$, which is the average of e_t across many firms, is the estimate of the abnormal return, AR_i, across all firms on the various announcement dates (t). Having the average abnormal return of all the firms included in the study on the announcement date (which differs across firms but is still denoted by t) allows us to employ Equation 12.3 to calculate the average cumulative abnormal rate of return.

If the average abnormal return $(\bar{e}_t)$ (or the average cumulative abnormal rate of return) is significantly different from zero, we say that the announcement itself provides an abnormal return, and the market is semi-strong inefficient. If the average abnormal return is significant before the announcement date as well, we conclude that information was leaked before the announcement date. Finally, if the average abnormal return is significant after the event, we conclude that investors can earn an abnormal rate of return after the information is in the public domain for a few days, which strongly contradicts the market semi-strong efficiency. However, do not forget that the event study has a joint test, and the commonly strong conclusion may be misleading, because the model employed to measure the normal return may be wrong!

The empirical evidence generally rejects the notion that abnormal returns are generated from simple trading rules. However, there are many trading rules, some of which are held privately; hence, not all rules have been tested.

Statistical tests of historical data for significant patterns

A second way to test the validity of the weak form of the EMT is to conduct statistical tests on historical data to locate significant patterns. For example, autocorrelations or serial correlations can be examined to assess whether past returns had predictive power in determining future returns.[8] Alternatively, non-parametric tests can be employed to assess whether negative returns are followed by positive returns, or vice versa.[9] Although some evidence suggests that weak patterns do exist, they are not strong enough to profit when transaction costs are taken into consideration.

An important caveat in detecting patterns in historical return series is that not every pattern implies that the market is weak-form inefficient. Specifically, as discussed in Sections 10.2 and 17.2, the return distribution (the riskless rate, the betas and the equity premium) changes through time, as the economy evolves through different stages of the business cycle. For example, during a recession period, we can expect the equity premium to be high and the betas of financially distressed firms also to be high. Apart from the cyclical variation, the return distribution also changes structurally as capital markets evolve through different stages

---

[8] Autocorrelations or serial correlations look at how correlated past changes are with current changes. Positive serial correlation means that positive returns tend to be followed by positive returns (momentum); negative serial correlation means that negative returns follow positive returns (reversal). If past changes are highly correlated (positive or negative), they can be used to predict future changes.

[9] Non-parametric tests are statistical techniques that seek to determine whether patterns exist in a given set of data without specifying the shape of the relationship at forehand. In many cases, the researcher does not know whether the relationship has, for example, a linear or a curvilinear shape. Non-parametric tests avoid this problem, but this comes at the cost of requiring large data sets in order to conclude that a pattern is statistically significant.

of their lifecycles. For example, the introduction of derivatives and mutual funds, index funds and exchange traded funds (ETFs) may have structurally lowered the risk of equity and the equity premium (see Section 7.5). In part, these changes are predictable using historical data. For example, it is well known that variables such as the dividend yield and the earnings yield of stocks and the credit spread of bonds can predict the level of stock market returns.[10] However, the patterns are typically interpreted as evidence for cyclical variation of the equity premium rather than as evidence against weak-form efficiency of the stock market; the dividend yield, earnings yield and credit spread predict the stage of the business cycle and the equity premium associated with that stage rather than abnormal returns or deviations from the normal return given the stage of the business cycle. In brief, finding a predictable pattern in the normal returns is something other than predicting abnormal returns.

Looking again at Exhibit 12.4, one pattern is clear. Early evidence appears to support the weak form of the EMT, but more recent evidence appears to reject it. Numerous patterns have been identified that suggest that markets do not even adhere to the weak form of the EMT. This evidence will be discussed in detail in Section 12.6.

Practice box

Problem

Suppose you know that the expected daily rate of return of Morgan, Inc. common stock is 0.0453%. You also observe the following daily rates of return around day 3. Assume that the firm announced an increase in dividends on day 3.

Day	Rate of return (%)
1	−0.5
2	0.3
3	5.0
4	3.0
5	0.05

Calculate the cumulative abnormal rates of return.

Solution

Given that $E(R_i) = 0.0453\%$, construct the following table:

Day	Rate of return (%)	$AR_{i,t}$ (%)	$CAR_{i,t}$ (%)
1	−0.5	−0.5453	−0.5453
2	0.3	0.2547[a]	−0.2906[b]
3	5.0	4.9547	4.6641
4	3.0	2.9547	7.6188
5	0.05	0.0047	7.6235

[a] $0.2547 = 0.3 − 0.0453$.
[b] $−0.2906 = −0.5453 + 0.2547$.

The main implication of these results is not that there was a 5% return on day 3 when the dividends announcement is made. The main implication is that there was a 3.0% return the day after, which could have resulted in abnormal profits. Thus, investors can buy the stock on day 3 and still make money on day 4. This example illustrates the concept of abnormal returns. However, five observations of one security are not enough to draw any conclusions.

---

[10] See, for instance, Fama and French (1988), Campbell and Shiller (1988) and Keim and Stambaugh (1986).

12.5.2 Evidence related to the semi-strong form of the efficient market theory

When investigating whether the semi-strong form of the EMT is true, researchers try to determine whether investors using fundamental analysis could earn abnormal returns. If these investors cannot earn abnormal returns consistently, then the semi-strong form is true. Exhibit 12.5 lists some studies of the semi-strong form of the EMT and their conclusions.

The evidence related to the semi-strong form of the EMT investigates information obtained through fundamental analysis. Part 4 of this book describes fundamental analysis techniques in greater detail. Fundamental analysis focuses on the analysis of a firm's specific information

Exhibit 12.5		Summary of evidence related to the semi-strong form of the efficient market theory		
Author(s)	Year	Assets studied	Semi-strong-form-efficient?	Comments
Fama *et al.*	1969	US stocks	Yes	Stock splits – no gains after announcements
Scholes	1972	US stocks	Yes	Large secondary offerings – price decline is permanent when insiders are selling
Jaffe	1974	US stocks	No	Insiders can profit from public information about insider trading
Ball	1978	US stocks	No	Earnings-announcement reactions take considerable time
Basu	1977	US stocks	No	Stocks with low price/earnings (P/E) ratios earn abnormal profits
Banz	1981	US stocks	No	Stocks with low market caps (P) earn abnormal profits
Rendleman *et al.*	1982	US stocks	No	Similar results to Ball (1978)
Roll	1984	Orange juice futures	Yes/no	Inefficient due to exchange limits; otherwise efficient
Seyhun	1986	US stocks	Yes	Insiders cannot profit from public information about insider trading
Fama and French	1992	US stocks	No	Empirical extention of Basu (1977) and Banz (1981)
Peterson	1995	US stocks	Yes	Abnormal returns associated with 'stock highlights' published by Value Line found consistent with EMT
Bernard and Seyhun	1995	US stocks	No	Using a stochastic dominance approach to test market efficiency following earnings announcements showed the market to be inefficient
Kanto *et al.*	1998	Helsinki stock exchange	No	Adjustment of share prices to unexpected reported interim earnings found to be delayed by statistically significant period
Post and van Vliet	2004	US stocks	Yes	Market is efficient; size, value and momentum anomalies can be explained by downside risk

and its stock prices. The most common information analysed is the reported earnings per share (EPS). Thus, fundamental analysis seeks to determine whether there is a link between basic information about a company (such as earnings per share) and its stock price.

The key to understanding the relationship between earnings per share and stock prices lies in what was expected by the market. That is, we should ask how different the earnings are from what was expected. Rendleman *et al.* (1982) used this measure to analyse the validity of the semi-strong form of the EMT, examining the cumulative abnormal rates of return for ten groups of stocks. The stock groups were constructed by rankings based on the following equation:

$$SUE = \frac{EPS - E(EPS)}{SEE} \tag{12.4}$$

where SUE is the standardised unexpected earnings, EPS is the earnings per share, E(EPS) is the expected earnings per share,[11] and SEE is the standard error of the estimate. The denominator helps adjust for some industries having more or less volatility than other industries. For example, utility firms have a fairly predictable EPS, whereas software firms have a very unpredictable EPS. Thus, a 5% difference in the actual EPS from the expected EPS may be interpreted as dramatic by investors in a utility firm's stock but interpreted as insignificant by investors in software companies. The SEE would be greater for the software firm, reducing the SUE. After adjusting for this difference in earnings volatility, ten groups of stocks were formed, where group 1 represents firms with the lowest SUE, group 2 represents firms with the next-to-lowest SUE, and so forth. Thus, group 10 represents stocks with the highest SUE.

Exhibit 12.6 illustrates the results. Clearly, market prices react to unexpected earnings announcements as cumulative average excess returns move up or down due to the announcements. In contradiction to the EMT, however, the best (group 10) and worst (group 1) continue to move up and down, respectively, after the announcement. Thus, the information on the surprise in the past can be employed to make profits in the future. This is good evidence against the semi-strong form of the EMT.

12.5.3 Evidence related to the strong form of the efficient market theory

The evidence against the strong form of the EMT is irrefutable; some of this research is summarised in Exhibit 12.7. Several studies found that insiders can profit significantly from the valuable information they possess. Exactly where you draw the line between private information and public information may influence your position on the strong form of the EMT. For example, Liu *et al.* (1990) found significant price changes on stocks discussed in the 'Heard on the Street' column in the *Wall Street Journal*. When reporters find this information, is it private or public at that point? Clearly, after publication, it is public information. However, reporters know this information before it is published, yet they are not insiders. Technically, however, it is inside information prior to publication.

If the strong form of the EMT is correct, then insiders should not be able to generate abnormal returns from their trading decisions. The evidence presented in this section is very convincing: insiders (but not mutual funds managers) can generate abnormal profits, and hence the strong form of the EMT is not supported. However, recall that it is illegal to trade on insider information.

---

[11] E(EPS) is estimated by Rendleman *et al.* (1982) using an 'extrapolative trend model with seasonal dummies'. Basically, the forecasts were made based on projecting historical data.

Exhibit 12.6	Cumulative abnormal rates of return for unexpected earnings announcements

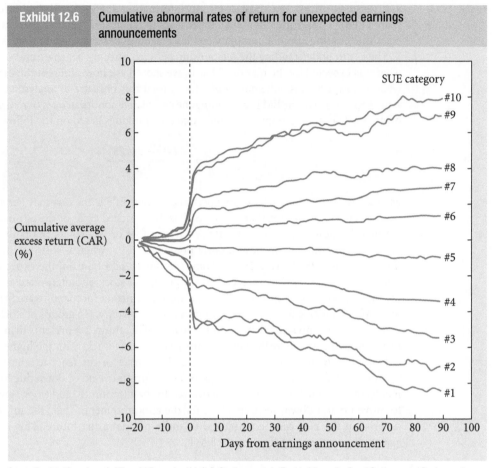

Source: Reprinted from *Journal of Financial Economics*, Vol. 3, R. Rendleman *et al.*, 'Empirical Anomalies Based On Unexpected Earnings and the Importance Of Risk Adjustment', pp. 285–6, copyright 1982, with permission from Elsevier.

12.6 Market anomalies

The EMT has some widely known and well-documented violations. Recall that a market anomaly is any event that can be exploited to produce abnormal profits. Anomalies exist in any form of the EMT but in most cases relate to the semi-strong form of the EMT.

Market anomalies imply market inefficiency. However, because all market-efficiency tests are joint tests, it is possible that these anomalies are actually not anomalies but rather that we do not have a powerful model to explain them. This explanation is convincing, particularly in cases where anomalies persist for a long time. Why don't they disappear, as investors are very familiar with them? Typically, these observations of anomalies have been extensively back-tested by researchers – that is, they have examined how historical prices behaved in response to some observation or some event. For the results of back-testing to be significant, the pattern identified must persist for some time.

Exhibit 12.8 identifies four categories of anomalies: firm, accounting, calendar and event anomalies. Firm anomalies are anomalies that result from firm-specific characteristics. For example, small firms tend to outperform large ones on a risk-adjusted basis, an anomaly called

Exhibit 12.7	Summary of evidence related to the strong form of the efficient market theory			

Authors	Year	Assets studied	Strong-form-efficient?	Comments
Cowles	1933	Money managers*	Yes	Professionals do not do any better than the market as a whole
Friend *et al.*	1962	Mutual funds*	Yes	Average mutual fund does not outperform market as a whole
Neiderhoffer and Osborne	1966	NYSE specialist	No	Specialists generate significant profits
Jensen	1968, 1969	Mutual funds*	Yes	Risk-adjusted performance of mutual funds is not any better
Scholes	1972	Insiders	No	Insiders have access to information not reflected in prices
Jaffe	1974	Insiders	No	Insiders can profit
Henriksson	1984	Mutual funds*	Yes	Before load fees but after other expenses, mutual funds do about average
Seyhun	1986	Insiders	No	Insiders can profit
Ippolito	1989	Mutual funds	No	Before load fees but after other expenses, mutual funds do slightly better than average
Liu *et al.*	1990	US stocks	No	Prices change with publication of articles in the 'Heard on the Street' column in the *Wall Street Journal*
Halil Kiymaz	2002	Turkish stocks	No	Positive significant abnormal returns are observed days before the publication date

* Many assumed that money and mutual fund managers were in possession of inside information. Hence, examining the performance of mutual fund managers was a test of strong-form efficiency. The evidence suggests that mutual fund managers are not in possession of material inside information (or at least they cannot profit from it if they have it).

Source: From *Introduction to Investments*, 2nd edn, by Levy. © 1999. Reprinted with permission of South-Western, a division of Thomson Learning: www.thomsonrights.com. Fax 800 730-2215.

the size effect. A similar anomaly is the neglected firm effect: the fewer the analysts tracking a particular security, the larger the average return. This anomaly may be an instance of the size effect, because neglected firms tend to be small.

Accounting anomalies are changes in stock prices that occur after the release of accounting information. For example, after an announcement of unusually high earnings, a firm's stock price continues to rise, as discussed earlier. Another accounting anomaly is the P/E ratio anomaly. Stocks with low P/E ratios tend to have higher returns. An anomaly that has attracted a lot of attention lately is the earnings momentum anomaly, in which stocks of firms whose growth rate of earnings has been rising tend to outperform other similar securities. Reinganum (1988) and Fama and French (1992) analyse the market-to-book-value (M/B) ratio of stocks as a predictor of returns across securities. The terms 'book value' and 'market value' relate to the book value and market value of the firm's equity. Fama and French classify all the stocks included in their sample into ten deciles, according to the M/B ratio. They found that the decile with the lowest M/B ratio had an average monthly rate of return of 1.65%, whereas the decile with the highest M/B ratio had a return of only 0.72% per month. Exhibit 12.9 shows their findings regarding the M/B anomaly.

Exhibit 12.8	Summary of market anomalies

Anomaly	Description/implication
Firm anomalies	
Size	Returns on small firms tend to be higher, even on a risk-adjusted basis
Closed-end mutual funds	Returns on closed-end funds that trade at a discount tend to be higher
Neglect	Firms that are not followed by many analysts tend to yield higher returns
Institutional holdings	Firms that are owned by few institutions tend to have higher returns
Accounting anomalies	
Price/earnings ratio	Stocks with low P/E ratios tend to have higher returns
Earnings surprises	Stocks with larger-than-anticipated earnings announcements tend to continue to rise even after the announcement
Price/sales ratio	If the price/sales ratio is low, then the stock tends to outperform
Market-to-book ratio	If the market-to-book value (M/B) ratio is low, then the stock tends to outperform
Dividend yield	If the dividend yield is high, then the stock tends to outperform
Earnings momentum	Stocks of firms whose growth rate of earnings is rising tend to outperform
Calendar anomalies	
January	Security prices tend to be up in January, especially in the first few days (as well as in the last days of December)
Weekend	Securities tend to be up on Fridays and down on Mondays
Time of day	Securities tend to be up in the first 45 minutes and the last 15 minutes of the day
End of month	Last trading day of the month tends to be up
Seasonal	Firms with highly seasonal sales tend to be up during high sales periods
Holidays	Returns tend to be positive on the last trading day before a holiday
Event anomalies	
Analysts' recommendations	The greater the number of analysts recommending purchase of a stock, the more likely it will go down
Insider trading	The greater the number of insiders buying a stock, the more likely it is to go up
Listings	Security prices rise after it is announced that a firm will be listed on an exchange
Value Line rating changes	Security prices continue to rise after Value Line places a security in its number-one category

Source: From *Introduction to Investments*, 2nd edn, by Levy. © 1999. Reprinted with permission of South-Western, a division of Thomson Learning: www.thomsonrights.com. Fax 800 730-2215.

A calendar anomaly is an anomaly that depends solely on time. For example, the January anomaly (or January effect) is the tendency for stock prices to be abnormally up in January (and late December).

Exhibit 12.10 demonstrates the January effect for various assets for the periods 1926–96 and 1987–96. For the period 1926–96 (Exhibit 12.10a), the January effect is striking for small stocks, which had an average monthly rate of return of about 7% in January and less than 2% in most other months. For the S&P 500 index, there is no January effect; a larger rate of return is recorded in July and August, and a similar rate of return is recorded in December. For the

| Exhibit 12.9 | Average monthly rate of return as a function of the ratio of market value to book value |

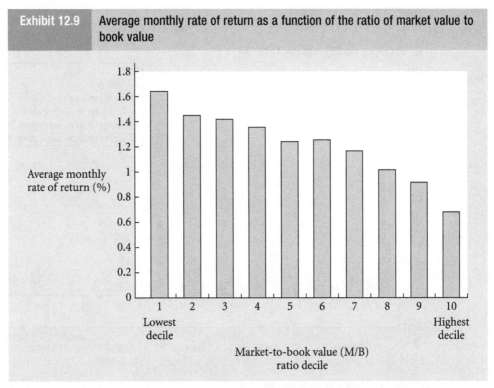

Source: From 'The Cross Section of Expected Returns', *Journal of Finance*, Vol. 47, pp. 427–65. Reproduced with permission of Blackwell Publishing Ltd (Fama, E. F. and French, K. R., 1992).

other assets categories (Treasury bills, long-term corporate bonds, long-term government bonds and intermediate-term government bonds), there is no January effect.

Exhibit 12.10b is the same as Exhibit 12.10a, except that the averages of the rates of return are for only ten years, i.e. 1987–96. Although the rate of return on small stocks in January is higher than in any other month, the January effect was reduced dramatically. The January effect does not exist for the other assets. It is possible that investors, being more aware of the January effect in the recent period, bought the stocks earlier in the year (in December) in an attempt to gain in January. This possibility provides only a partial explanation for the reduction in the January effect in the last decade, because in February, May and December there is also a relatively high rate of return on the S&P index and on small stocks, which is not explained by this argument. Whether the January effect disappears or not remains to be seen.

Several reasons have been offered for this stock price pattern. The size effect is the phenomenon that smaller firms tend to outperform larger firms on a risk-adjusted basis. Several studies have linked the January effect to the size effect. Although it is unclear why, smaller firms have a much more pronounced January effect. There also is some empirical support for the January effect being related to tax-loss selling in December. By selling in December stocks that have fallen during the year, an investor is able to realise his or her losses and these are deductible from income taxes.

Another anomaly is the weekend anomaly, the observation that securities tend to be up on Fridays and down on Mondays. This anomaly is even more pronounced on holiday weekends.

Finally, event anomalies are price changes that occur after some easily identified event, such as a listing announcement. Security prices of firms rise after it is announced that the

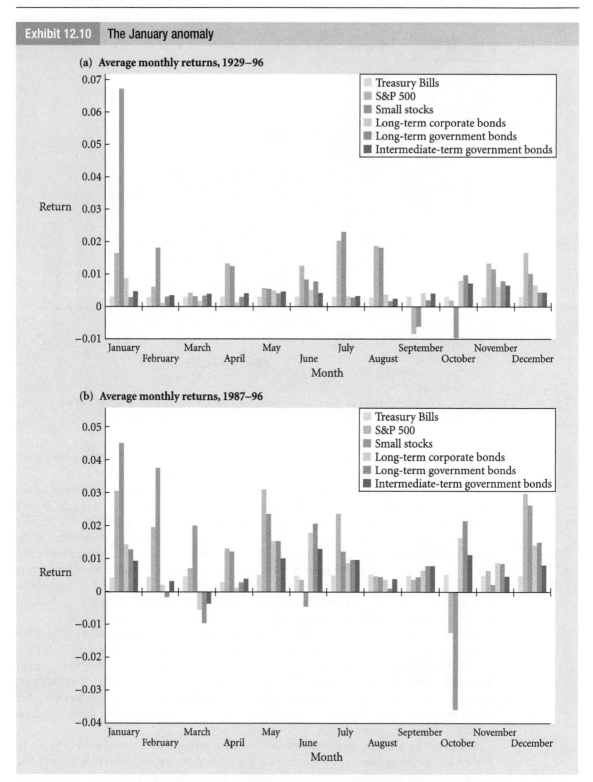

Exhibit 12.10 The January anomaly

(a) **Average monthly returns, 1929–96**

(b) **Average monthly returns, 1987–96**

firm's stock will be listed on a major stock exchange like the NYSE. Another event anomaly is analysts' recommendations. The more analysts there are recommending a particular security, the more likely it is that the security's price will fall in the near future. This puzzling result can be explained as follows. When one or two analysts discover an undervalued stock they recommend it to their clients, and when the clients buy the stock the price is driven up. This price increase attracts the attention of other analysts who subsequently recommend it, pushing the price even higher. This upward price pressure continues until some analysts start changing their buy recommendations to sell recommendations, and the price subsequently falls.

What can we conclude about market efficiency? As was stated at the beginning of the chapter, the purpose is not to place one position over another but rather to leave the final conclusion to the reader. The following are a few quotations that show what others have concluded:

> It's very hard to support the popular academic theory that the market is rational [that is, that the EMT is true] when you know somebody who just made a twentyfold profit in Kentucky Fried Chicken, and furthermore, who explained in advance why the stock was going to rise. My distrust of theorizers and prognosticators continues to the present day.

(Lynch, 1989).

> Event studies are the cleanest evidence we have on efficiency. . . . With few exceptions, the evidence is supportive.

(Fama, 1991).

> It takes a lot of data and perhaps a better theoretical idea of what to look for, before researchers can finds persuasive evidence against EMH. Therefore it took so long before a new area of research was created: behavioral finance.

(Shleifer, 2000)

> Often people ask me whether I coined the term irrational exuberance, since I (along with my colleague John Campbell and a number of others) testified before Greenspan and the Federal Reserve Board only two days before his famous speech before the American Enterprise Institute, on December 3, 1996, and I had lunch with him on that day. I did testify that markets were irrational. But, I very much doubt that I am the origin of the words irrational exuberance.

(Shiller, 2001)

> For the past 40 years, a total of approximately one million unsuspecting MBA students have been thoroughly indoctrinated by business schools with the belief that stock markets are efficient.

(Haugen, 2002)

> You can't predict them by divining Wall Street's crowd psychology; or by charting trends in stock prices; or by doing lots of research on companies' business prospects. Also, you still can't beat the market by buying companies even with '.com' in the name . . .

(Malkiel, 2004)

As you can see, disagreement regarding market efficiency still exists.

12.7 Behavioural finance

Since traditional investment theories seem unable to explain market inefficiency and market anomalies, some researchers have turned to theories of 'behavioural finance' (BF).[12] Traditional theories assume that investors process all available investment information in a rational

---

[12] Shefrin (2000) provides a good general starting point for studying behavioural finance.

manner to form expectations and that they act according to the predictions of expected utility theory (EUT).[13] EUT predicts that decision-makers will choose the alternative that provides the highest expected utility (given the expectations derived from the available information) (see Chapter 7). By contrast, BF assumes that the psychology of decision-making under uncertainty may lead to market-inefficiency and market anomalies. This section discusses some of the arguments used in BF theories, as well as the counter-arguments provided by traditional financial economists. BF is very controversial. Its proponents claim that it can explain market-inefficiency and market anomalies, while its opponents claim that these phenomena arise merely due to methodological problems of empirical tests.

12.7.1 Arguments of behavioural finance

BF is a relatively new field, and currently there is no unified theory. However, a common theme is that decision-makers suffer from 'errors of judgement' and 'errors of preference'. Errors of judgement, or cognitive biases occur if the decision-maker systematically overestimates or underestimates the true probability of chance events. This typically happens for choice problems of high complexity and high uncertainty, especially if the decision-maker has little prior experience with the problem. If the decision-maker makes these errors, then he or she does not process all available information in a rational manner. Typical examples of such errors include the following:

- Representativeness means that decision-makers tend to judge the more representative outcome to be more likely, independent of the true probabilities. Further, they see patterns where perhaps none exists; people are biased to adopt the hypothesis that a causal factor is at work behind any notable sequence of events.
- Overconfidence is the tendency of people to be far more secure in their judgements than they should be and to overestimate their predictive skills. For example, someone may claim that he or she is '99% sure' that an event will occur, while the actual probability is only 85%. To illustrate this, in one famous survey, 90% of Swedish car drivers classified their own driving skills as 'better than average'.
- Anchoring refers to the tendency of people to make judgements that are 'anchored' in their own experience. For example, if you ask a resident of a small village to give an approximation of the number of people who live in Albany, NY, that resident will probably give a low estimate, since his or her idea of a city begins at home. Someone born in New York City would probably give an estimate that is too high.
- Gamblers' fallacy arises when people predict inappropriately that a trend will reverse. This can be considered to be an extreme belief in regression to the mean. Regression to the mean implies that an extreme trend will tend to move closer to the mean over time. Sometimes, regression to the mean is interpreted incorrectly as implying that, for example, an upward trend must be followed by a downward trend in order to satisfy a law of averages.
- Availability bias emerges when people place undue weight on easily available information in making a decision.

Errors of preference refer to 'mistakes' that people make in assigning values to future outcomes or from improper combinations of probabilities and values. Strictly speaking, errors of preference are not mistakes. If we explain to people that they make errors of preference,

---

[13] Examples of these traditional theories are the CAPM and the APT, which are discussed in Chapters 10 and 11, respectively.

then typically they will continue to make these errors. Rather, these errors mean that people systematically deviate from the predictions of EUT. These errors occur even if the true probabilities of chance events are known to the decision-maker. Hence, they are different from errors of judgement, which are errors made in using the available information from expectations. The most important errors of preference are summarised by the prospect theory, which was developed by Kahneman and Tversky (1979). These errors include:

- Framing in terms of gains and losses. There is evidence that decisions are framed in terms of deviations (gains and losses) from a subjective reference point (for example, the original price at which a good was purchased) rather than in terms of total wealth or total return.
- Loss aversion, or the phenomenon that decision-makers are distinctly more sensitive to losses than to gains of the same size; the 'pain' experienced from a loss is two to three times the 'pleasure' from an equivalent gain.
- Risk-seeking for losses. There is evidence that people play safe when protecting gains but are willing to take chances in an attempt to escape from a losing position.
- Subjective probability distortion. Traditional theories of decision-making assume that decision-makers use the true probability distribution. By contrast, experimental evidence suggests that decision-makers use subjective decision weights that overweight small probabilities of large gains and losses and underweight large probabilities of small gains and losses.

These errors of judgement and preference occur in a systematic way in controlled psychological experiments. This has led many economists to believe that rationality and EUT do not adequately describe decision-making under uncertainty. BF theorists believe that investors also suffer from these errors and that accounting for these errors will lead to a better understanding of financial markets. Errors of judgement can cause market prices to deviate from fundamental values or market inefficiency. For example, DeBondt and Thaler (1985) argue that because investors rely on the representativeness heuristic, they could become overly optimistic about past winners and overly pessimistic about past losers and that this bias could cause prices to deviate from their fundamental level. Similarly, investor overconfidence may lead to excessive trading and slow revisions of expectations about the future when new information arrives, and anchoring can lead investors to expect a share to continue to trade in a defined range or to expect a company's earnings to be in line with historical trends, leading to possible underreaction to trend changes. Errors of preference can also affect market prices. For example, Benartzi and Thaler (1995) argue that the historically high-equity premium (the average return on stocks in excess of the riskless rate) can be explained by 'myopic loss aversion', i.e. the fact that investors have a relatively short evaluation horizon (for example, one year) and that they are loss-averse; the equity premium serves as a compensation for the high downside risk at short evaluation horizons. More generally, the combined effect of the four errors of preference (see above) is that investors will like investments that combine downside protection with upside potential.[14] In contrast to errors of judgement, errors of preference do not cause the market to be inefficient, because the investors process all available information in a rational manner. Still, investors process the information in a way that is different from the traditional theories, leading to different market prices and market anomalies.

---

[14] Shefrin and Statman (2000) provide a behavioural portfolio theory in which investors are driven by the 'twin desires of hope and fear' and they seek investments that 'avoid poverty' and offer 'a chance at riches'. Post and Levy (2004) demonstrate that this model could explain the stock-market anomalies related to firm size, price/book ratio and stock-price momentum: stocks that appear overvalued or yield abnormally low average return in terms of CAPM (large caps, growth stocks and past losers) generally lower the downside risk and/or increase the upside potential of a portfolio.

12.7.2 Counter-arguments of traditional financial economists

Traditional financial economists have criticised BF on both a theoretical and a methodological level. For example, there are good reasons to expect that errors of judgement are much less severe for real-life aggregate investor behaviour than for individual behaviour in laboratory choice experiments. For example, investors can extract information about the true return distribution from historical return data and from fundamental economic data. In addition, if large amounts of money are at stake, then there is a large incentive to gather and process such data so as to eliminate systematic errors of judgement. Further, one may wonder why competition between professional investors does not eliminate systematic errors of judgement. In this respect, the EMT does not require that all investors necessarily act in a rational manner. The principles of arbitrage, if arbitrage can be undertaken efficiently, would quickly drive prices to their 'correct' level if one of the parties was rational. Unfortunately, the behaviour of markets that are composed of both rational and irrational traders is not well understood.

Fama (1998) argues that apparent overreaction to information (e.g. reversal) is about as common as underreaction (e.g. momentum), which is consistent with the efficient market hypothesis. Also, it has been suggested that observed market anomalies may arise, not because of behavioural issues but rather because of mis-specified systematic risk (for example, through the use of incorrect asset-pricing models) or because of 'data-snooping' (chasing patterns that may be illusory as several analysts study more or less the same data with the same random patterns).

12.7.3 What is the balance?

At this point, the balance of the above arguments is unclear. Behavioural factors undoubtedly play a role in the decision-making processes of individual investors. However, it is not clear that these factors also play a significant role at the aggregate market level and that they can explain market-inefficiency and market anomalies. In fact, we may never be able to test whether the market is efficient. One of the critics of behavioural finance, for example, reminds us that 'market efficiency per se is not testable' (Fama, 1991). Market efficiency must be tested jointly with an asset-pricing model that predicts the normal rates of return (see Section 12.1). Consequently, there is no way to disprove conclusively the claims of either the traditional or the behavioural theories.

Summary

Define an efficient market.
A well-functioning financial market in which prices reflect all relevant information is said to be efficient.

Identify the types of information related to security prices in each form of the efficient market hypothesis.

The efficient market theory (EMT) has three forms: the weak, the semi-strong and the strong forms. The weak form of the EMT states that stock prices reflect information revealed by the historical price sequence. The semi-strong form of the EMT states that stock prices reflect all relevant publicly available information. The strong form of the EMT states that prices reflect all publicly and privately available information.

Compare investment strategies in efficient markets with investment strategies in inefficient markets.

The existence of efficient capital markets has several important implications. Most important is that scarce resources are allocated in an efficient manner. Also, technical analysis is useless if at least the weak form of the EMT is true, and fundamental analysis is useless if at least the semi-strong form of the EMT is true. Finally, no matter what form of the EMT an investor adheres to, portfolio-selection benefits still hold. Thus, even under the EMT, portfolio selection is still important.

Describe the findings of researchers who tested each form of the efficient market theory.

Researchers have gathered empirical evidence related to the weak, the semi-strong and the strong forms of the EMT. The evidence against the strong form is the most conclusive; some insiders are clearly able to make abnormal returns. The evidence related to the weak and the semi-strong forms is mixed. The weak form of the EMT is not supported completely because of anomalous results, such as the January effect. The semi-strong form of the EMT is not supported completely because of large anomalous results, such as trading based on the size effect and the market-to-book-value ratio.

Define 'anomaly' and identify the common types of anomalies.

An anomaly offers investors a chance to earn abnormal profits. Most of the anomalies that have been documented can be categorised in one of the following groups: firm, seasonal, event and accounting anomalies.

Describe the explanations of behavioural finance for market-inefficiency and market anomalies.

Behavioural-finance theorists believe that investors suffer from 'errors of judgement' and 'errors of preference' and that these errors can help explain market-inefficiency and market anomalies. Behavioural factors certainly play a role in the decision-making processes of individual investors. However, it is not clear that these factors also play a significant role at the aggregate market level and that they can explain market inefficiency and market anomalies.

Key terms

Abnormal rate of return 378	Efficient market theory (EMT) 376	Index fund 386
Accounting anomaly 397	Errors of judgement 402	Passive investment strategy 385
Active investment strategy 386	Errors of preference 402	Random walk 379
Anomaly 389	Event anomaly 399	Semi-strong form of the EMT 380
Behavioural finance 401	Expected utility theory (EUT) 402	Strong form of the EMT 380
Calendar anomaly 397	Firm anomaly 396	Technical analysis 380
Cumulative abnormal rate of return (CAR) 391	Fundamental analysis 380	Weak form of the EMT 379
Efficient market 377		

Review questions

1 **a.** What is an efficient market? Describe some important implications of the efficient market theory for technical and fundamental analysis.
   b. Briefly define the three forms of the efficient market theory.

2 Describe the empirical evidence of each form of the efficient market theory.

3 'One piece of evidence of inefficient markets can be found in the volume of trading activity. The volume of trading always increases before a takeover announcement.' Evaluate this statement.

4 Define 'anomaly' and describe four common types of anomalies.

5 **a.** Which two types of errors are specific to the Behavioural Finance Theory?
   b. Which of the above are not really errors, and why?
   c. If an investor reads on the Internet that a particular firm has sold more products this year and, as a result, he buys stock in this firm, which type of error in judgment does he make?
   d. An investor did not earn the return he wanted this year; in fact, he even lost money. He receives information about a firm that may soon be quoted on a stock exchange. Based on this information he decides to buy stock in this firm in the hope he will improve his poor financial position. Which type of error of preference does he make?

For an extensive set of review and practice questions and answers, visit the Levy–Post investment website at www.booksites.net/levy

Selected references

Ariel, R. A., 1987, 'A Monthly Effect in Stock Returns', *Journal of Financial Economics*, **18**, 161–174.

Bachelier, L., 1900, 'Théorie de la spéculation', *Annales Scientifiques de l'École Normale Supérieure*, **3** (17), 21–86.

Bachelier, L., 1967, '*Theorie de la speculation: Annales de l'Ecole Normale Superieure*', transl. A. J. Boness. In: Cootner, P. H., editor, *The Random Character of Stock Market Prices*, Cambridge, MA: MIT Press.

Ball, R., 1978, 'Anomalies in Relationships between Securities' Yields and Yield-Surrogates', *Journal of Financial Economics*, **6**, 103–126.

Banz, Rolf W., 1981, 'The Relationship between Return and Market Value of Common Stocks', *Journal of Financial Economics*, **9**, 3–18.

Basu, Sanjoy, 1977, 'Investment Performance of Common Stocks in Relationship to their Price–Earnings Ratios: A Test of the Efficient Market Hypothesis', *Journal of Finance*, **32**, 663–682.

Bernard, V. L. and H. N. Seyhun, 'Does Post-Earnings-Announcement Drift in Stock Prices Reflect a Market Inefficiency? A Stochastic Dominance Approach', *Review of Quantitative Finance and Accounting*, **9** (1), 17–34.

Bernard, V. L. and J. K. Thomas, 1990, 'Evidence that Stock Prices Do not Fully Reflect the Implications of Current Warnings for Future Earnings', *Journal of Accounting and Economics*, **13**, 305–340.

Benartzi, S. and R. H. Thaler, 1995, 'Myopic Loss Aversion and the Equity Premium Puzzle', *Quarterly Journal of Economics*, **110**, 73–92.

Bhardwaj, R. K. and L. D. Brooks, 1992, 'The January Anomaly: Effects of Low Share Price, Transaction Costs, and Bid–Ask Bias', *Journal of Finance*, **47**, 553–575.

Campbell, J. Y. and R. Shiller, 1988, 'Stock Prices, Earnings and Expected Dividends', *Journal of Finance*, **43**, 661–676.

Chan, K. C. and N.-F. Chen, 1991, 'Structural and Return Characteristics of Small and Large Firms', *Journal of Finance*, **46**, 1467–1484.

Cochrane, J. H., 1991, 'Volatility Tests and Efficient Markets: A Review Essay', *Journal of Monetary Economics*, **27**, 463–485.

Connolly, R. A., 1989, 'An Examination of the Robustness of the Weekend Effect', *Journal of Financial and Quantitative Analysis*, **24**, 133–169.

Cowles, A. 1933, 'Can Stock Market Forecasters Forecast?' *Econometrica*, **1** (3), 309–324.

Cowles, A. and H. E. Jones, 1937, 'Some Posteriori Probabilities in Stock Market Action', *Econometrica*, **5** (3), 280–294.

DeBondt, W. F. M. and R. Thaler, 1985, 'Does the Stock Market Overreact?', *Journal of Finance*, **40**, 793–805.

Fama, E., 1965, 'The Behavior of Stock Market Prices', *Journal of Business*, **38** (1), 34–105.

Fama, E. F., 1998, 'Market Efficiency: Long-term Returns and Behavioural Finance', *Journal of Financial Economics*, **49**, 228–306.

Fama, E. F., 1991, 'Efficient Capital Markets: 2', *Journal of Finance*, **46**, 1575–1617.

Fama, E. F. and Blume, M. E., 1966, 'Filter Rules and Stock Market Trading – Part 2: Supplement on Security Prices', *Journal of Business*, **39**, 226–241.

Fama, E. F. and K. R. French, 1988, 'Dividend Yields and Expected Stock Returns', *Journal of Financial Economics*, **22**, 3–25.

Fama, E. F. and K. R. French, 1992, 'The Cross-Section of Expected Stock Returns', *Journal of Finance*, **47**, 427–466.

Fama, E., L. Fisher, M. Jensen and R. Roll, 1969, 'The Adjustment of Stock Prices to New Information', *International Economic Review*, **10** (1), 1–21.

French, K., 1980, 'Stock Returns and the Weekend Effect', *Journal of Financial Economics*, **8**, 55–69.

Friend, I., F. E. Brown, E. S. Herman and D. Vickers, 1962, *A Study of Mutual Funds*, Washington, DC: US Government Printing Office.

Granger, D. and O. Morgenstern, 1963, 'Spectral Analysis of New York Stock Market Prices', *Kyklos*, **16**, 1–27.

Gultekin, M. and S. Gultekin, 1983, 'Stock Market Seasonality: International Evidence', *Journal of Financial Economics*, **12** (4), 469–481.

Haugen, R. A., 2002, '*The Inefficient Stock Market: What Pays off and Why*', 2nd edn, Upper Saddle River, NJ: Pearson Education.

Haugen, R. A. and J. Philippe, 1996, 'The January Effect: Still There after All These Years', *Financial Analysts Journal*, **52** (1), 27–31.

Hayek, F. A. von, 1945, 'The Use of Knowledge in Society', *American Economic Review*, **35** (4), 519–530.

Henrikisson, R. D., 1984, 'Market Timing and Mutual Fund Performance: An Empirical Investigation', *Journal of Business*, **57** (1), 73–96.

Huberman, G. and S. Kandel, 1990, 'Market Efficiency and Value Line's Record', *Journal of Business*, **63**, 187–216.

Ippolito, R. A., 1989, 'Efficiency with Costly Information: A Study of Mutual Fund Performance', *Quarterly Journal of Economics*, **104**, 1–23.

Jaffe, J., 1974, 'Special Information and Insider Trading', *Journal of Business*, **47**, 410–428.

Jaffe, J. and R. Westerfield, 1985, 'The Weekend Effect in Common Stock Returns: The International Evidence', *Journal of Finance*, **40** (2), 433–454.

Jegadeesh, N., 1990, 'Evidence of Predictable Behavior of Security Returns', *Journal of Finance*, **45**, 881–898.

Jegadeesh, N., and S. Titman, 1993, 'Returns to Buying Winners and Selling Losers: Implications for Stock Market Efficiency', *Journal of Finance*, **48**, 65–91.

Jensen, M., 1968, 'The Performance of Mutual Funds in the Period 1945–64', *Journal of Finance*, May 1968, 389–416.

Jensen, M., 1969, 'Risk, the Pricing of Capital Assets, and the Evaluation of Investment Portfolios', *Journal of Business*, **42**, 167–247.

Jersen, G. R., R. R. Johnson and J. M. Mercer, 1997, 'New Evidence on Size and Price to Book Effects', *Financial Analysts Journal*, **53** (6), 37–42.

Kahneman, D., and A. Tversky, 1979, 'Prospect Theory: An Analysis of Decision Making Under Risk', *Econometrica*, **47**, 263–291.

Kanto, A. J., H. A. Kahra, D. R. Blevins, and H. J. Schadewitz, 1998, 'An Explanation of the Unusual Behavior of Some Market Model Residuals', *Finnish Journal of Business Economics*, **47** (3), 288–300.

Keim, D. B., 1983, 'Size-related Anomalies and Stock Return Seasonality: Further Empirical Evidence', *Journal of Financial Economics*, **12**, 13–32.

Keim, D. B. and R. F. Stambaugh, 1986, 'Predicting Returns in the Stock and Bond Markets', *Journal of Financial Economics*, **17**, 357–390.

Kendall, M., 1953, 'The Analysis of Economic Time Series, 1: Prices', *Journal of the Royal Statistical Society*, **96** (1), 11–25.

Kiymaz, H., 2002, 'The Stock Market Rumours and Stock Prices: A Test of Price Pressure and the Size Effect in an Emerging Market', *Applied Financial Economics*, **12**, 469–474.

Lakonishok, J. and E. Maberly, 1990, 'The Weekend Effect: Trading Patterns of Individual and Institutional Investors', *Journal of Finance*, **45**, 231–243.

LeBaron, D., 1983, 'Reflections on Market Inefficiency', *Financial Analysts Journal*, **39** (3), 16–17, 23. Reprinted in: Ellis, C. D., editor, *Classics 2: Another Investor's Anthology*, Homewood, IL: AIMR and Business One Irwin.

Lehmann, B., 1990, 'Fads, Martingales and Market Efficiency', *Quarterly Journal of Economics*, **105**, 1–28.

Levy, Robert A., 1967, 'Relative Strength as a Criterion for Investment Selection', *Journal of Finance*, **22** (4), 595–610.

Liu, P., S. D. Smith and A. A. Syed, 1990, 'Stock Price Reactions to the *Wall Street Journal*'s Securities Recommendations', *Journal of Financial and Quantitative Analysis*, **25**, 399–410.

Lynch, P., 1989, *One Up on Wall Street*, New York: Penguin Books.

Malkiel, B. G., 1989, 'Efficient Market Hypothesis', In: Eatwell, J., M. Milgate and P. Newman, editors, *The New Palgrave: Finance*, New York: Macmillan Press.

Malkiel, B. G., 2003, 'The Efficient Market Hypothesis and Its Critics', *Journal of Economic Perspectives*, **17** (1), 59–82.

Malkiel, B. G., 2004, *A Random Walk Down Wallstreet*, 8th edn, New York: W. W. Norton and Company.

Masih, A. M. M. and R. Masih, 1996, 'Common Stochastic Trends, Multivariate Market Efficiency and the Temporal Causal Dynamics in a System of Daily Spot Exchange Rates', *Journal of Applied Financial Economics*, **6** (6), 495–504.

McQueen, G. and S. Thorley, 1997, 'Do Investors Learn? Evidence from a Gold Market Anomaly', *The Financial Review*, **32** (3), 501–526.

Merton, R., 1980, 'On Estimating the Expected Return on the Market: An Exploratory Investigation', *Journal of Financial Economics*, **8** (4), 323–361.

Moy, R. L. and A. Lee, 1991, 'A Bibliography of Stock Market Anomalies', *Journal of Financial Education*, **17**, 41–51.

Niarchos, N. A. and C. A. Alexakis, 2003, 'Intraday Stock Price Patterns in the Greek Stock Exchange', *Applied Financial Economics*, **13** (1), 13–22.

Niederhoffer, V. and M. F. M. Osborne, 1966, 'Market Making and Reversals on the Stock Exchange', *Journal of the American Statistical Association*, **61**, 897–916.

Ogden, J. P., 1990, 'Turn-of-Month Evaluations of Liquid Profits and Stock Returns: A Common Explanation for the Monthly and January Effects', *Journal of Finance*, **45**, 1259–1272.

Osborne, M., 1959, 'Brownian motion in the Stock Market', *Operations Research*, 7, 145–173.

Peterson, D., 1995, 'The Informative Role of the Value Line Investment Survey: Evidence from Stock Highlights', *Journal of Financial and Quantitative Analysis*, **30**, 607–618.

Post, G. T. and H. Levy, 2004, 'Does Risk Seeking Drive Stock Prices? A Stochastic Dominance Analysis of Aggregate Investor Preferences and Beliefs', *Review of Financial Studies*, forthcoming.

Post, G. T. and P. van Vliet, 2004, 'Downside Risk and Asset Pricing', ERIM working paper.

Reinganum, M. R., 1988, 'The Anatomy of a Stock Market Winner', *Financial Analysts Journal*, **44**, 272–284.

Rendleman, R. J., Jr, C. P. Jones and H. A. Latane, 1982, 'Empirical Anomalies Based on Unexpected Earnings and the Importance of Risk Adjustments', *Journal of Financial Economics*, **10**, 269–287.

Roberts, H., 1959, 'Stock Market "Patterns" and Financial Analysis: Methodological Suggestions', *Journal of Finance*, **44**, 1–10.

Roberts, H. V., 1967, 'Statistical Versus Clinical Prediction of the Stock Market', unpublished manuscript, CSRP, University of Chicago, Chicago, IL.

Roll, R., 1984, 'Orange Juice and Weather', *American Economic Review*, **74** (5), 861–880.

Scholes, M., 1972, 'The Market for Securities: Substitution vs. Price Pressure and the Effect of Information on Share Price', *Journal of Business*, **45**, 179–211.

Seyhun, N., 1986, 'Insiders' Profits, Costs of Trading and Market Efficiency', *Journal of Financial Economics*, **16**, 189–212.

Seyhun, H. N., 1993, 'Can Omitted Risk Factors Explain the January Effect? A Stochastic Dominance Approach', *Journal of Financial and Quantitative Analysis*, **28**, 195–212.

Shefrin, H., 2000, *Beyond Greed and Fear*, Boston, MA: Harvard Business School Press.

Shefrin, H. and M. Statman, 2000, 'Behavioral Portfolio Theory', *Journal of Financial and Quantitative Analysis*, **35**, 127–151.

Shiller, R. J., 2000, *Irrational Exuberance*, Princeton, NJ: Princeton University Press.

Shiller, R. J., 2001, *Bubbles, Human Judgment, and Expert Opinion*, Cowles Foundation Discussion Papers No. 1303, Stanford, MA: Yale University.

Shiller, R. J., 2003, 'From Efficient Markets Theory to Behavioral Finance', *Journal of Economic Perspectives*, **17** (1), 83–104.

Shleifer, A., 2000, *Inefficient Markets: An Introduction to Behavorial Finance*, New York: Oxford University Press.

Part 4

SECURITY ANALYSIS

CHAPTER 13

Interest rates and bond valuation

Funds get caught in a bond bubble bind

I was recently asked by a fund management trade association to write an analysis of why there was such a dramatic boom and bust in equities. I started by discussing why stocks rose so high. As an order of magnitude, share prices rose to twice the price level that was reasonably justified at the end of the 1990s. The TMT [technology, media and telecom] sector rose to more like four times the justified level. Sell-side analysts attempted to explain this by pointing to a projected acceleration of corporate earnings growth. But this never happened; in fact, earnings fell.

The question now is whether something similar has happened in bonds. After all, since the March 2000 peak in equities, the aggregate total return in dollars of the JP Morgan Global Government Bond Index has reached 33 per cent, mostly since early 2002. As in the equity boom, the biggest recent gains have been concentrated in some of the riskiest sectors, such as high-yield corporate bonds. These have delivered a total return of 19 per cent in the first half of 2003, while emerging market bonds have returned 36 per cent over the past 12 months.

The justification for the bond boom is said to be the threat of deflation. Indeed, falling prices would bring a bonus to bond yields by adding an extra real return. But it remains to be seen whether deflation proves to be any more of a real event for bonds than the corporate profits boom was for equities. In any case, deflation would surely be compatible with a widening of credit spreads rather than the narrowing that we have seen in recent times [falling prices lower the profitability and creditworthiness of corporate issuers].

James Foster, a prominent bond fund manager at ISIS Asset Management in London, has surprised investors (and probably his marketing director) by warning of a bubble in some of his own bond sectors. Investors, he said, should switch to equities. On the website of Pimco, the US bond giant, Lee R Thomas has just put out a similar message. 'You cannot rationalise long-maturity bond yields where they are today. Sell bonds.'

The peak [in bonds] coincided with some provocative new issues. For example, General Motors' $13.5 bn blockbuster to plug a hole in its pension plan (not the kind of motivation normally favoured by the bond market). There was also the UK Treasury's opportunistic move to exploit, through a $2^{1}/_{4}$ per cent dollar bond issue, what it clearly viewed as an anomalous bubble in the US fixed income market.

Investment in the News 13 continued

Modern marketing methods attract vast sums into the latest high-returning assets. The UK unit trust sector has been dominated this year – for the first time – by net inflows into corporate bond funds. The purchases have been made largely by intermediaries.

For most fund groups, the response is to retrain – or hire – some bond managers and launch a range of focused products, just as technology equity funds were being created in numbers in the late 1990s. The problem is that investors are likely to wind up being the losers and will become disillusioned with an investment industry that peddles illusions.

For the fund management industry, the problem remains that its appetite for volatility is greater than that of most of its clients.

Source: 'Funds Get Caught In A Bond Bubble Bind', *Financial Times*, 8 July 2003.

Learning objectives

After studying this chapter, you should be able to:

1 Use the bond-pricing equation to find bond prices and bond yields.

2 Interpret a yield curve.

3 Summarise the theories that explain the shape and level of yield curves.

4 Describe the behaviour of the spread over Treasuries.

5 Describe the impact of the call feature and the convertible feature on bond prices.

I nvestment in the News 13 reports on large recent gains and large potential future losses for investors in bonds. As discussed in Chapter 2, bonds are fixed-income securities that offer periodic coupon payments plus a promise of the payment of the par value at maturity. If we ignore default risk and call and conversion features, then the cash flows to bond investors are fully predictable. Hence, at first sight, bonds may seem perfectly safe investments. However, the market price of a bond is determined in large part by market interest rates. Changes in the interest rates can cause large bond-price fluctuations.

This chapter and the next focus on the risk and return associated with investing in bonds and on managing an investment in bonds in a climate of volatile interest rates. Section 13.1 first discusses the relationship between bond prices and interest rates. It also discusses various ways of measuring the return on bonds or bond yields. Section 13.2 introduces the yield curve, which is the relationship between the yield on zero-coupon government bonds and the time to maturity. In addition, it discusses several hypotheses that explain the shape of yield curve. The yield on zero-coupon Treasury bonds is a benchmark for determining the yield on non-Treasury bonds. Yields on defaultable bonds are computed by adding a credit spread to the Treasury yields. Section 13.3 discusses the spread over Treasuries. Finally, Section 13.4 discusses the impact of embedded options (such as conversion and call features) on the prices and yields of bonds.

This book uses the terms 'price' and 'value' interchangeably. It is assumed implicitly that the bond market is efficient; that is, the intrinsic bond value is equal to its market price.

Although there may be disagreement on whether the bond market is efficient, this assumption is a clear starting point for understanding bond market prices. Thus, unless indicated explicitly, in this text a bond's market price is the same as its value.

13.1 Bond prices and yields

13.1.1 Bond prices

A bond represents a claim to future cash flows (coupon payments and par value). The current market value of a bond is the present value of the cash flows if every cash flow is discounted by the current market interest rate for the maturity of the cash flow. Formally, the price of a bond can be computed using the following bond-pricing equation:

$$P = \sum_{t=1}^{n} \frac{C}{(1 + R_t)^t} + \frac{Par}{(1 + R_n)^n} \tag{13.1}$$

where C is the coupon payment each period, n is the number of periods to maturity, Par is the face value of the bond (payment at maturity), P is the current market price of the bond, and R_t is the interest rate that applies for cash flows that are received after t periods.

We stress that this bond-pricing equation applies only for straight bonds without significant default risk (for example, a US Treasury bond). For such bonds, the cash flows can be predicted with full accuracy and the bonds are exposed only to the risk of changing market interest rates. The equation does not apply for bonds with embedded options (such as call and converison features) or for bonds with significant default risk (speculative bonds). Such bonds are exposed to risks other than interest rate risk, for example risks related to the financial health of the issuing municipality or company. The effect of default risk and call and conversion features are discussed later in this chapter.

Every cash flow is discounted by the current market interest rate for the maturity of the cash flow. This interest rate is the relevant discount factor because it represents the opportunity cost for the cash flow; a bond investor could sell the cash flow in the market for its present value discounted against this rate. Hence, changes in market interest rates cause changes in bond prices. Since interest rates change all the time, bond prices also fluctate all the time. If an investor purchased a five-year, $1000 par, 5% coupon bond for $1000 and interest rates doubled, then the value of his or her bond would decline. Who would still pay $1000 for his or her bond when bonds that pay 10% coupon sell at the same price? No one would, and thus the bond would decline in value.

13.1.2 Yield to maturity

There exist various alternative measures for the expected rate of return on bonds. The most common measure is yield to maturity. Yield to maturity is the annualised discount rate that makes the present value of the future cash flows (coupon payments and par value) just equal to the current price of the bond. Formally, the yield to maturity (y) is the internal rate of return of the bond that is calculated from the following equation:

$$P = \sum_{t=1}^{n} \frac{C}{(1 + y)^t} + \frac{Par}{(1 + y)^n} \tag{13.2}$$

Two special cases are worth noticing. For zero-coupon bonds ($C = 0$) with n years to maturity, the yield to maturity is given by the value y that solves the following equation:

$$P = \frac{Par}{(1 + y)^n}$$

The solution to this problem is:

$$y = \left(\frac{Par}{P}\right)^{1/n} - 1$$

For a perpetuity bond ($n = \infty$) with an annual coupon of C, the yield to maturity is given by the value y that solves the following equation:[1]

$$P = \frac{C}{y}$$

Thus, the yield to maturity is given by

$$y = \frac{C}{P}$$

It is useful to compare Equation 13.2 with Equation 13.1. While Equation 13.1 involves multiple discount rates (every cash flow is discounted at different market interest rates), Equation 13.2 applies a single discount rate to all cash flows. The yield to maturity effectively is a weighted average of the different market interest rates used to discount the different cash flows. We stress, however, that the weights that are assigned to the different market interest rates are not fixed. Rather, the weights change over time, as the market interest rates change and as time left before receiving the cash flow shortens. Also, the weights are different for different bonds, because different bonds have different cash-flow patterns.

The yield to maturity is given on an annual basis. If coupons are paid annually, then y is the yield to maturity. If coupons are paid semiannually, then the yield to maturity is $(1 + y)^2 - 1$. This expression corrects for the effect of compounded interest. Still, practitioners commonly ignore the compounding effect when they switch from semiannual yields to annual yields; they typically compute the yield to maturity on semiannual bonds simply as $2y$.[2]

Equation 13.2 can also be used to value a given bond if we know the relevant yield. Since the yield to maturity y is a weighted average of the individual interest rates R_t, applying Equation 13.2 might seem like an awkward way to apply Equation 13.1; if first we have to determine the individual interest rates in order to compute the yield to maturity, then we could just as well apply Equation 13.1 directly. However, if comparable bonds are traded in the market, then we may use their yield to maturity to compute the value of the bond. This approach does not require full information on the individual market interest rates.

Appendices 13A–C at the end of this chapter contain several useful tools for applying Equation 13.2 in practice. Appendix 13A provides a simple equation for bond pricing that is easier to work with in spreadsheets (see, specifically, Equation 13A.2). Further, Equation 13.2 assumes that the next coupon is paid exactly one period from now (the valuation moment); hence, the equation assumes that we are now at a coupon payment date. Appendix 13B presents

---

[1] See Appendix 13A for formal derivation.

[2] Yields annualised using this simple interest method are also called bond-equivalent yields. The yield that accounts for compound interest is known as effective annual yield.

a more general equation for the valuation of bonds at any date, not necessarily a coupon date. Finally, Appendix 13C discusses the various compounding methods used in the bond market.

13.1.3 Other measures of bond yields

This text uses the term 'yield' to mean 'yield to maturity'. Among investors and in the financial media, the term 'yield' has various meanings. This section introduces four other definitions.

The coupon yield or nominal yield is the promised annual coupon rate:

$$ny = \frac{C}{Par}$$

For example, if the annual coupon payment is $120 and the par value is $1000, then the coupon or nominal yield is 12%.

Current yield is found by taking the stated annual coupon payment and dividing it by the current market price of the bond:

$$cy = \frac{C}{P}$$

Current market prices for bonds can be found in any financial newspaper or through a broker. A 12% coupon bond selling at $900, for example, has a current yield of $120/$900 \cong 13.33\%$ (where $120 is 12% of $1000 par).

Recall from Equation 13.2 that the yield to maturity is a more complex yield than the coupon yield and the current yield. However, for some bonds, these different yields are approximately the same. First, as discussed in Section 13.1.2, the yield to maturity of a perpetual bond is just $y = C/P$ or the current yield. More generally, for long-term bonds, because of discounting, the value of $Par/(1 + y)^n$ approximates zero and the yield to maturity approximates the current yield. By contrast, for short-term bonds, the yield to maturity approximates the coupon yield. For example, the value of a bond with one year to maturity is

$$P = \frac{C + Par}{1 + y}$$

Solving for y gives the yield to maturity:

$$y = \frac{C + Par}{P} - 1$$

Since a short-term bond's price will be close to its par value, that is $P \cong Par$, the yield to maturity is

$$y \cong \frac{C}{Par}$$

which is equal to the coupon yield. The yield to call is similar to the yield to maturity, except that it assumes the bond will be called at the first possible call date. The call feature essentially allows a firm to buy back bonds at a specified price. In this case, instead of using the par value at maturity as the final payment, we use the amount to be paid to bondholders when the bond is called. Specifically,

$$P = \sum_{t=1}^{nc} \frac{C}{(1 + yc)^t} + \frac{call\ price}{(1 + yc)^{nc}} \qquad (13.3)$$

where yc is the yield to call and nc is the number of coupon payments until the first call date. The call price typically is in excess of the par value. For example, the call price may be set at par plus one year's interest. However, the investor is not assured that the bonds will in fact be called on this date.

Finally, the realised yield refers to the holding period rate of return actually generated from an investment in a bond. While the yield to maturity, coupon yield, current yield and yield to call refer to the future, the realised yield refers to the past. In addition, the holding period rate of return generally is related inversely to changes in the interest rates, as rising interest rates lower bond prices.[3] In fact, falling bond prices may cause the holding period rate to be negative. Chapter 6 discussed past bond yields in greater detail.

When referring to yield, one should be careful to specify exactly which yield calculation is meant. The most common yield quoted is the yield to maturity. However, there are no set standards in interest rate quotations and, as is shown in the box below, the yield calculation does make a difference in the returns.

Practice box

Problem

Calculate the five different yields given the following information. The bond is a two-year, 8% annual coupon, and it has $1000 par. The bond is currently trading for $1030 and is callable at $1050 (without interest included) in one year. After one year, the bond is trading for $1010 (without interest).

Solution

The current yield is

$$C/P = \$80/\$1030 \cong 7.77\%$$

The coupon or nominal yield is

$$C/Par = \$80/\$1000 = 8.0\%$$

The yield to maturity is found using computer software or a pocket calculator by solving the following equation:

$$\$1030 = \sum_{t=1}^{2} \frac{\$80}{(1+y)^t} + \frac{\$1000}{(1+y)^2}$$

Using a financial calculator, we get 6.36%.

The yield to call is found by solving this equation:

$$\$1030 = \sum_{t=1}^{1} \frac{\$80}{(1+yc)^t} + \frac{\$1050}{(1+yc)^1} = \frac{\$1130}{1+yc}$$

Thus, the yield to call is 9.71%.

---

[3] This is true if the holding period is shorter than the 'duration' (weighted average maturity of the coupons and par value) of the bond; in this case, the 'price effect' dominates the 'reinvestment effect'. However, if the holding period is longer than the duration, the reinvestment effect dominates, and rising interest rates increase the holding period return. Chapter 14 elaborates on this subject.

Finally, assuming that the bond has not been called, the realised yield if the bond was actually held for one year is

$$R = (\$1010 + \$80)/\$1030 - 1 \cong 5.83\%$$

Thus, we see that the yield calculation does make a difference in the returns.

13.2 The yield curve

13.2.1 Interest rates and the demand and supply of money

As discussed in the previous section, bond prices are related inversely to market interest rates. What determines interest rates? Interest rates are the price for borrowing or lending money for a specified maturity. If money is considered to be a commodity like any other good, then interest rates are determined by the supply and demand for money. Changes in the supply and demand for money cause interest rates to vary. The actors in the economy – individuals, businesses, governments and foreign investors – influence the supply and demand for money.

The relationship between supply and demand of money is complex. The amount individuals are willing to save, which is part of the money supply, is determined in part by interest rates, the individuals' current incomes and wealth levels. Higher savings result in a greater supply of money and hence a lower interest rate. The relationship between the amount people save and interest rates is not immediately transparent, however. An increase in interest rates may be an incentive for people to save, because their savings earn a higher rate of return. Investors substitute, so to speak, consumption today for savings that allow for future consumption – a phenomenon called the substitution effect. Alternatively, an increase in interest rates may actually result in a decrease in savings, because people now have to save less in order to achieve a fixed level of consumption in the future – a phenomenon called the income effect. There is also a wealth effect, a phenomenon in which an increase in interest rates implies a decrease in current wealth levels, which may affect people's investment behaviour. For example, if an investor holds a bond portfolio and the interest rate goes from 8 to 10%, then the value of the investor's portfolio goes down.

Money is demanded by groups similar to those who supply it: individuals, businesses, governments and foreign borrowers. For example, an increase in the demand for home mortgages will cause interest rates to rise. An increased demand for loans by businesses will also cause rates to rise. However, the reverse is also true: the lower the interest rate, the lower a firm's cost of capital, the more projects are expected to have positive net present values, and the more the firm is willing to borrow.

We do not intend to explain the complex forces of demand and supply for money in this book; this is the subject of advanced macroeconomics. Rather, we use interest rates as summary measures for the relative strength of demand and supply for bonds with different maturities. A high interest rate for ten-year bonds means that there is a relatively high supply or a relatively low demand for ten-year bonds (for whatever underlying reason) and hence that the prices of ten-year bonds are relatively low compared with bonds with a different maturity. We stress that the relationship between market interest rates and bond prices is not causal, i.e. high interest rates are not the cause of low bond prices, and low interest rates are not the cause of high prices. Rather, the relationship is tautological. Interest rates are derived from bond prices as their yield to maturity (the discount rate that equates the market price with the discounted value of the cash flows). Hence, bond prices and market interest rates are determined simultaneously by the underlying economic forces that drive the supply and demand for money. So, if we write 'bond prices fall *because* the interest rates rise', then we really mean 'bond prices fall *and* interest rates rise because of an unfavourable shift in the underlying demand and supply forces for money'.

13.2.2 The yield curve

The market generally has various interest rates for various maturities. Apparently, the demand and supply for different maturities should be seen as the demand and supply for different goods. We may ask why this is true. A bond represents borrowing by the bond's issuer and saving by the bond's purchaser. The interest rate represents the percentage investment revenue for the bond buyer and the percentage funding cost to the bond seller if the bond is held to its maturity. It seems that lenders should choose to lend for the maturity with the highest interest rate, because by such a lending policy they obtain the highest percentage investment revenue. Similarly, borrowers should choose to borrow for the maturity with the lowest interest rate, because by such a borrowing policy they obtain the lowest percentage funding costs. Hence, in order for demand and supply to be equal, the interest rates for all maturities should be equal. Although this is a tempting conclusion, it is generally wrong for at least three reasons:

■ Interest rates change over time, for example because of changes in inflation. If short-term interest rates are expected to rise in the future, then we may expect long-term interest rates to be higher than short-term rates. Otherwise, lenders could increase their investment revenues by investing at short-term maturities, wait for interest rates to rise, and then reinvest their money at the higher rates. Similarly, borrowers could lower their funding costs by borrowing at long-term maturities. If lenders offer short-term funds and borrowers demand long-terms funds, then the market does not clear. For the market to clear, the long-term interest rates would have to rise above the short-term rates. Conversely, if short-term interest rates are expected to fall in the future, then long-term interest rates would have to fall below the short-term rates in order for the market to clear. Hence, interest rates for different maturities differ because of different market expectations about the future interest rates at different time horizons.

■ Lending or borrowing at different maturities involves different risks. The risks are a function of the time horizon of the issuer or investor. To illustrate these risks, we first consider the lender's viewpoint. The lender must choose between investing in short-term bonds or long-term bonds. Consider the choices facing young parents who want to invest or lend their money to ensure that their children will have funds to attend college in 15 years. If the parents invest over a period that is shorter than 15 years, then they may have to reinvest the money in the near future at a different interest rate, which may be lower. This risk of declining interest rates is known as reinvestment risk – the risk to bondholders that in the future they will not be able to reinvest the cash flows they receive from their investment at the same rate they receive today. By contrast, if the parents invest over a period that is longer than 15 years, then they may have to sell the bond before maturity at a low price as a result of a higher interest rate. This exposure to price declines is known as price risk. Bond investors experience price risk because increases in interest rates decrease a bond's price. Let's turn to the borrower's viewpoint. Assume that a borrower – maybe a corporation – needs money for long-term investment projects. The corporation faces the choice of borrowing for either a short-term or a long-term period. If a corporation chooses a short-term bond, it may have to refinance the bond at higher interest rates. Note that this is exactly the opposite of the problem faced by lenders. If the corporation chooses the long-term bond and interest rates fall, then the corporation is paying a higher borrowing rate than would have been required if the financing had been short-term. The fact that lending and borrowing at different maturities involves different risks causes different interest rates for different maturities.

■ Market imperfections may prevent some lenders and borrowers from lending or borrowing at a particular maturity. For example, asset-liability constraints, either regulatory or self-imposed, may prevent institutional investors from investing too much money at maturities that do not match the maturity of their liabilities.

For these reasons, the market generally has various interest rates for various maturities. Lenders and borrowers want to lend and borrow for varying lengths of time, because of different expectations, risks and restrictions. These varied needs within the economy create the demand and supply for bonds of varying maturities. In addition, the needs of borrowers and lenders change over time. Thus, there are loans of different maturities (such as one month, one year or ten years), different interest rates may prevail for the different maturities, and these rates change over time.

The relationship between the market interest rate and the time to maturity is known as the yield curve, or the term structure of interest rates. The yield curve generally refers to the yield on government bonds, which are default-free. Yields on defaultable bonds are computed by adding a risk premium to the Treasury yields (see Section 13.3). In addition, the yield curve generally refers to zero-coupon bonds, computed either from existing zero-coupon bonds (so-called stripped Treasury bonds) or by inferring the implied zero-coupon yields from a series of existing Treasury coupon bonds with different maturities (the so-called bootstrapping approach). The reason for focusing on zero-coupon bonds is that the resulting yields can be used directly for discounting the cash flows of other bonds, regardless of their coupon rate and maturity; all we need to do to find the appropriate discount rate for a future cash flow is to find the yield on a zero-coupon Treasury bond with maturity equal to the time of receipt of the cash flow. In this way, we obtain an instrument that can be used for pricing all possible bonds, regardless of their coupon rates and maturities.

Exhibit 13.1 illustrates some recent yield curves for US Treasury securities. Exhibit 13.1a shows the yield curve for US Treasury securities on 5 August 1997, when the yield curve was upward-sloping. The horizontal axis is time to maturity (n) and the vertical axis is yield to maturity (y). Exhibit 13.1b shows a flat yield curve observed on 29 December 1989, and Exhibit 13.1c shows an inverted yield curve observed on 31 December 1980, where the yield decreases as the maturity increases. These graphs show that the yield curve can have a wide variety of shapes.

It is interesting to note that in May 2000, the yield curves in the USA and Europe were inverted. Connecting Theory to Practice 13.1 attributes this pattern to reduced government bond supply due to the decreased need of governments to borrow as their budget deficits fell or moved into surplus.

Researchers and analysts try to determine what factors influence the shape of the yield curve. Put differently, they analyse why bonds of different maturities have different yields to maturity (or why equilibrium interest rates are different for different maturities). Several hypotheses have been developed in an attempt to explain the shape of the yield curve. Each hypothesis assigns different weights to the reasons for why interest rates at different maturities differ. We will review each hypothesis and briefly highlight its strengths and weaknesses. However, first it is necessary to define and explain several concepts related to bonds that are used in the explanation of the shape of the yield curve.

Exhibit 13.1 Examples of actual yield curves

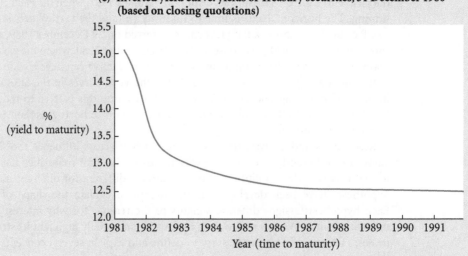

(a) **Upward-sloping yield curve: yields of Treasury securities, 5 August 1997 (based on closing quotations)**

%
(yield to maturity)

Year (time to maturity)

(b) **Flat yield curve: yields of Treasury securities, 29 December 1989 (based on closing quotations)**

%
(yield to maturity)

Year (time to maturity)

(c) **Inverted yield curve: yields of Treasury securities, 31 December 1980 (based on closing quotations)**

%
(yield to maturity)

Year (time to maturity)

Euro-zone yield curve on inversion course

The first signs that euro-zone government yield curves could follow their US and UK counterparts and become inverted were seen this week as the yield gap between 10-year and 30-year German bunds fell to its lowest ever. Analysts said this development, which has resulted in the yield difference between these two maturities falling from 40 basis points last month to only 20 bp now, might open the way for 30-year yields falling below 10-year paper. Further inversion along the yield curve, such as the temporary flip between 10-year and seven-year bunds seen this week, is also not ruled out.

The driving force behind inverted yield curves in the US, UK and, most recently, Sweden have been expectations of sharply reduced government bond supply. This reflects the decreased need of governments to borrow as their budget deficits fall and some move into surplus. The US yield curve inverted in January, when the Treasury announced plans for buying back long-dated bonds. The 30-year long bond now yields less than all other maturities. This year, the long bond yield has fallen by 90 bp to its current 6.2 per cent, despite rising inflation expectations which would normally push yields higher. The perception of government bond scarcity is spreading to the euro-zone, with Germany's plans to use the proceeds of its mobile phone licences later this year to repay debt bringing forward expectations for reduced debt.

The rise in economic growth is generating higher tax revenues for governments pushing deficits lower or into surplus. The deficit-to-gross domestic product ratio for the euro-zone countries is expected to fall to one per cent this year and to 0.6 per cent in 2001, ABN Amro said. The combination of improved tax revenues, unexpected bonuses from mobile phone licence sales and from privatisation is fuelling the supply arguments in Europe. Britain raised an unexpectedly high Pounds 22.5 bn (Dollars 33.75 bn) from its sale of third-generation phone licences, and Germany is expected to raise more than that. Licence sales will follow in France, Italy and the Netherlands. The impact of the improved government finances will already be felt in terms of reduced supply from Germany this year, analysts at J. P. Morgan said. In a recent report, they estimated that from Euros 49 bn (Dollars 44 bn) in the first half of this year, Germany could issue just Euros 30 bn in the second half. Previous forecasts were for Euros 50 bn of supply.

Source: Aline van Duyne, 'Euro-zone Yield Curve On Inversion Course', *Financial Times*, 19 May 2000.

13.2.3 Spot rates, forward rates and forward contracts

The spot rate is the yield to maturity of a zero-coupon bond that has a stated maturity, where zero-coupon bonds are sold at a discount from their par value and pay no coupons. For example, if a one-year bond is trading at $90.9 with $100 par value, we say the spot rate is about 10%, or [($100 − $90.9)/$90.9] × 100.

The forward rate is the yield to maturity of a zero-coupon bond that an investor agrees to purchase at some future specified date. For example, an investor agrees today to purchase in one year at $89.286 a bond that has one year to maturity with a par value of $100. In this case, there is no cash flow today, and in one year the investor will pay $89.286 for the bond (regardless of its current market price in a year) and will receive $100 two years from today (or one year from the bond purchase date). The forward rate is about 12%, or [($100 − $89.286)/ $89.286] × 100. The forward rates can be used in interpreting the information contained in the yield curve, as will be shown later.

A concept related to the forward rate is the forward contract, which is an agreement between a buyer and a seller to trade something in the future at a price negotiated today. A forward contract is obligatory to both the buyer and the seller. For example, a forward contract to buy $1 million of par value of Treasury bills at a 6% discount rate (which determines the bond's price) in six months obligates the buyer to purchase the T-bills at a 6% discount rate; it also obligates the seller to sell the T-bills at the same price. Suppose T-bills are selling for a 7% discount rate in six months when the forward contract matures and the buyer delivers the bills. This means that the T-bills have a lower market price. Recall that when interest rates are up, bond prices are down (that is, there is an inverse relationship between bond prices and yields). The seller will profit from this transaction, and the buyer will lose, because the buyer is obligated to purchase the T-bills at 6% despite the fact that a 7% rate is available in the market. At a 7% rate, the buyer could purchase the T-bills at the lower market price, but the buyer must buy them at the 6% rate (a higher price) to comply with the forward contract. A range of actively traded forward contracts is available in interest rates, currencies and energy products (such as crude oil and natural gas).

The forward interest rates can be derived from the spot rates of bonds with various maturities.[4] To understand this, consider the following example. Suppose we wish to invest for two years. Consider the following investment strategies:

Strategy 1: invest in a two-year zero-coupon bond and earn 5.8% (the two-year spot rate).

Strategy 2: invest in a one-year zero-coupon bond and earn 5%. Also enter into a one-year forward rate agreement (FRA) to invest in one year.

What interest rate on the FRA will make strategies 1 and 2 equivalent?

It will be the forward rate that results in an overall annual rate of return of 5.8% for two years. To understand this, consider investing $1 in each bond, and let R_i denote the spot rate and f_i denote the forward rate for each year, $i = 1, 2$.

Strategy 1: $\$1(1 + R_2)^2 = \$1(1 + 0.058)^2 = \$1.119364$.

Strategy 2: $\$1(1 + R_1) = \$1(1 + 0.05) = \$1.05$. Then invest $1.05 in the FRA.

The forward rate that makes strategies 1 and 2 equivalent is $\$1.05(1 + f_2) = \$1.119364$, or $f_2 = 0.06606$, or 6.606%. Thus, in equilibrium we have

$$(1 + R_2)^2 = (1 + R_1)(1 + f_2)$$

Note that if f_2 is higher than 6.606%, then all investors will be better off not buying the two-year bond. Its price will fall, and R_2 will go up until the equation $(1 + R_2)^2 = (1 + R_1)(1 + f_2)$ holds. The opposite is true if f_2 is smaller than 6.606%. Similarly, for a three-year period there are three alternative strategies:

Strategy 1: invest in a zero-coupon bond with three years to maturity and earn 6.3% (the three-year spot rate).

Strategy 2: invest in a one-year zero-coupon bond, enter into a one-year FRA to invest in one year, and enter again into a one-year FRA to invest in two years.

Strategy 3: invest in a two-year zero-coupon bond and enter into a one-year FRA to invest in two years.

---

[4] A market exists for contracts based on forward interest rates. These contracts are known as forward-rate agreements, and they are traded in the over-the-counter market primarily between banks.

Following the same analysis as before, the return on all of these strategies must be the same. Hence, we arrive at the following equilibrium:

$$(1 + R_3)^3 = (1 + R_1)(1 + f_2)(1 + f_3)$$

However, because in equilibrium, as we have seen before, $(1 + R_2)^2 = (1 + R_1)(1 + f_2)$, this can be rewritten as

$$(1 + R_3)^3 = (1 + R_2)^2(1 + f_3)$$

and for the given spot rates R_2 and R_3, f_3 can be determined.

This type of analysis could be conducted for n periods in order to arrive at the following general expression of equilibrium:

$$(1 + R_n)^n = (1 + R_1)(1 + f_2)(1 + f_3) \ldots (1 + f_n) \tag{13.4}$$

or

$$(1 + R_n)^n = (1 + R_{n-1})^{n-1}(1 + f_n) \tag{13.4a}$$

We can use Equation 13.4a to calculate the equilibrium forward rate. If we know that the four-year spot rate is 6.4% and the five-year spot rate is 6.45%, then we can solve for the forward rate over the fifth year as follows:

$$(1 + 0.0645)^5 = (1 + 0.064)^4(1 + f_5)$$

Solving for f_5, we find the forward rate to be 6.65%.

The numerical example in Exhibit 13.2 calculates forward rates for different maturities. The data in the table are spot and forward rates for annually compounded, zero-coupon bonds.[5] A yield curve plotted from these data would be upward-sloping from 5% for one-year bonds to 6.45% for five-year bonds.

From Equation 13.4, we see that spot interest rates can be thought of as a portfolio of agreements for forward contracts. If the yield curve is upward-sloping, then the implied forward rates are higher than the short-term spot rate. Indeed, in the example, we have an upward-sloping yield curve, and we found $f_5 > R_4$, which confirms this assertion. Similarly, if the yield curve is downward-sloping, then the implied forward rates are lower than the short-term spot rate. For a flat yield curve, the forward rates are equal to the spot rate.

Exhibit 13.2   Spot and forward rates for annually compounded, zero-coupon bonds

Maturity (years)	Spot rate (R_m) (%)	Forward rate (f_n)[a] (%)
1	5	–
2	5.8	6.606
3	6.3	7.307
4	6.4	6.701
5	6.45	6.650

[a] $f_2 = (1 + R_2)^2/(1 + R_1) - 1 = (1 + 0.058)^2/(1 + 0.05) - 1 \cong 0.06606$.
$f_3 = (1 + R_3)^3/(1 + R_2)^2 - 1 = (1 + 0.063)^3/(1 + 0.058)^2 - 1 \cong 0.07307$
$f_4 = (1 + R_4)^4/(1 + R_3)^3 - 1 = (1 + 0.064)^4/(1 + 0.063)^3 - 1 \cong 0.06701$
$f_5 = (1 + R_5)^5/(1 + R_4)^4 - 1 = (1 + 0.0645)^5/(1 + 0.064)^4 - 1 \cong 0.06650$

Source: From *Introduction to Investments*, 2nd edn, by Levy. © 1999. Reprinted with permission of South-Western, a division of Thomson Learning: www.thomsonrights.com. Fax 800 730-2215.

[5] The following analysis could be conducted with coupon-bearing bonds but would be slightly more complex.

Practice box

Problem	Suppose the ten-year spot interest rate was 8% and the 11-year spot interest rate was 7.9%. What is the equilibrium forward rate for the eleventh period?
Solution	Using Equation 13.4a and solving for f_n, we have

$$f_n = \frac{(1+R_n)^n}{(1+R_{n-1})^{n-1}} - 1$$

Substituting for the spot interest rates, we have

$$f_n = \frac{(1+R_{11})^{11}}{(1+R_{10})^{10}} - 1 = \frac{(1+0.079)^{11}}{(1+0.08)^{10}} - 1 \cong \frac{2.3080}{2.1589} - 1 \cong 0.069, \text{ or } 6.9\%$$

Once again, notice that the forward rate is less than the ten-year spot rate because the 11-year spot rate is less than the ten-year spot rate.

These basic bond and interest rate concepts can help investors to understand the various hypotheses that have been developed to explain yield curves. The discussion begins with the expectations hypothesis.

13.2.4 The expectations hypothesis

The expectations hypothesis, as its name implies, predicts that investors' expectations determine the course of forward interest rates. There are two main competing versions of this hypothesis: the local expectations hypothesis and the unbiased expectations hypothesis.

The local expectations hypothesis (LEH) states that all bonds (similar in all respects except for their maturities) will have the same expected holding period rate of return. That is, a one-month bond and a 30-year bond should, on average, provide the same rate of return over the next period. Thus, by this hypothesis, if an investor wants to invest for one month, then, on average, he or she will get the same rate of return if he or she buys a one-month bond and holds it to maturity or buys a 30-year bond and sells it after one month. The LEH doesn't specify the length of the next period.

Empirical evidence consistently rejects this hypothesis. Specifically, holding period returns on longer-term bonds are, on average, significantly different than holding period returns on shorter-term bonds. On average, the holding period rates of return on longer-term bonds are higher and have higher volatility. Hence, longer-term bonds offer greater rewards yet have higher risk. The LEH doesn't match our observations that investors are risk-averse and require higher returns, on average, to take the higher risk related to long-term bonds. Investor risk aversion implies, in turn, that the yield curve, on average, will be upward-sloping.

The unbiased expectations hypothesis (UEH) states that the current implied forward rates are unbiased estimators of future spot interest rates. Therefore, if the yield curve is upward-sloping, the UEH states that the market expects the spot rates to rise. For example, from Exhibit 13.2 and the UEH, our best estimate in year 1 of year 2's spot rate is for it to rise to 6.606% (the implied forward rate). In contrast, if the yield curve is downward-sloping, the UEH states that the market expects rates to fall.

The empirical evidence shows consistently that forward rates are biased predictors of future interest rates. Specifically, forward rates generally overestimate future spot rates.[6] This evidence leads to the next hypothesis, the liquidity preference hypothesis.

13.2.5 The liquidity preference hypothesis

According to the expectation hypothesis, the only determinant of the yield curve is the markets' expectations about the future direction of market interest rates. The liquidity preference hypothesis (LPH) also accounts for the risks associated with lending or borrowing at different maturities (reinvestment risk and price risk). According to the LPH, the yield curve includes risk premiums for maturities that present the highest risks to lenders and borrowers. As discussed in Section 13.2.2, these risks are a function of the time to maturity of bonds relative to the time horizon of the issuer or investor. To complicate matters, different borrowers have different time horizons, as do different lenders. For example, commercial banks have short-term liabilities in the form of deposits. For these institutions, long-run bonds are risky because of the price risk. On the other hand, pension funds and life insurance companies have long-run liabilities, and they view short-term bonds as risky investments because of the reinvestment risk. Despite these differences, advocates of the LPH typically assume that the holding period of lenders is shorter than that of borrowers. Hence, short-term bonds are more risky to borrowers than to lenders. Therefore, borrowers will borrow short-term funds only if short-term yields are relatively low and investors are willing to accept such low yields. Similarly, long-term bonds are more risky to lenders than to borrowers. Hence, investors will demand a risk premium for long-term bonds, and issuers are willing to pay this premium. Briefly, the LPH states that the yield curve normally should be upward-sloping, reflecting investors' preference for the liquidity and lower risk of shorter-term securities and issuers' preference for long-term funding.

In its purest form, the LPH is not supported by observation of the historical behaviour of the term structure. In fact, on numerous occasions the yield curve has been inverted; see, for example, Connecting Theory to Practice 13.1. Note that an inverted yield curve does not necessarily contradict the LPH when that hypothesis is combined with the UEH. If nothing is known regarding the future (interest rates can go up or down with an equal probability), then an upward-sloping yield curve should be expected. Suppose, however, that inflation is so high that it pushes the interest rate to 15% (which, in fact, occurred in 1980, when interest rates were very high, as shown in Exhibit 13.1c). Thus, for short-term bonds, the yield is 15%. However, no one expects this rate of inflation to continue at such a high level for a long period. Hence, for ten-year bonds, the yield is only 12.5%, and we observe a decreasing yield curve. Taking these yields and dividing them by the expected inflation rate, the yield curve can be stated in real terms. The resulting real yield curve may be increasing and consistent with the LPH. Thus, the LPH may hold even if there is a decreasing nominal yield curve.

A combination of the UEH and the LPH is therefore a possible explanation of the shape of the yield curve. That is, both hypotheses, when combined, may be valid. Specifically, the UEH may account for part of the shape of the yield curve, with the LPH accounting for the rest. Exhibit 13.3 illustrates this idea. The yield curve by UEH is based on expectations. For example, analysts could be surveyed about their expectations for the future course of interest rates. Suppose the market is anticipating a sharp decline in interest rates over the next few years,

---

[6] See Fama (1976, 1984) and Levy and Brooks (1989).

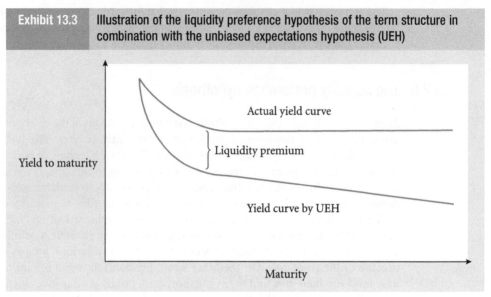

| Exhibit 13.3 | Illustration of the liquidity preference hypothesis of the term structure in combination with the unbiased expectations hypothesis (UEH) |

Source: From *Introduction to Investments*, 2nd edn, by Levy. © 1999. Reprinted with permission of South-Western, a division of Thomson Learning: www.thomsonrights.com. Fax 800 730-2215.

and therefore the forward rates are declining with time. The UEH would suggest a downward-sloping yield curve, as shown in Exhibit 13.3. However, the LPH may cause the curve to be less steep (see the actual yield curve in Exhibit 13.3) because of risk premiums that have to be offered to investors to induce them to take the risk of investing in longer-term securities. If the risk premium increases as the length to maturity increases, then the gap between these two curves increases.

The difference between the yield curve under the UEH and the actually observed yield curve is sometimes called the liquidity premium. This name reflects the idea that shorter-term bonds have greater marketability than long-term bonds. Unfortunately, it is very difficult to estimate the magnitude of the liquidity premium, because it changes over time. Thus, breaking down the existing term structure into its component parts – expectations and liquidity premiums – is virtually impossible. However, these theoretical hypotheses help explain why the yield curve has the shape it does.

13.2.6 The market segmentation hypothesis

The last hypothesis, the market segmentation hypothesis (MSH), evaluates the yield curve from a slightly different perspective. This hypothesis states that bonds of different maturities trade in separate segmented markets. For example, banks tend to participate exclusively in the short-maturity bond markets, whereas insurance companies tend to participate exclusively in the long-maturity markets. The yield curve shape is a function of these different preferences. Thus, the supply and demand preferences of participants within each maturity segment determine the equilibrium interest rate without regard to the equilibrium interest rate in neighbouring maturities. Also, speculators will take risky positions across the term structure if it gets out of perceived equilibrium.

A modified version of the MSH, the preferred habitat hypothesis, states that different participants have preferred locations on the yield curve, but with sufficient incentive they can be induced to move. Thus, segmentation in the bond market affects the term structure, because short-term bonds that are riskless for banks may be risky for insurance firms, which have long-term obligations. If a bank invested in long-term bonds, then it would be taking considerable price risk. If an insurance company invested in short-term bonds, then it would be taking considerable reinvestment risk. Different segments have different risk premiums, but they are ready to take less preferable bonds once the price of the bonds falls below a certain level.

In summary, no theory provides a complete description of what we actually observe. Each hypothesis offers insight into what may drive the current shape of the yield curve. Expectations and risk clearly play a role in determining the shape of the yield curve.

13.3 Spreads over Treasuries

So far, this chapter has discussed only one type of risk: the risk associated with changes in the interest rate and its effect on the price of a bond. With government bonds, this is the only real risk that investors face. With corporate bonds, however, there is an additional risk factor: credit risk, or the risk that the issuing company will fail to pay the coupon payments and/or the par value in a timely way. If investors believe that there is a possibility of default on corporate bonds, then they will demand a higher yield than on Treasury bonds with similar characteristics. This difference is known as the spread over Treasuries, and it is a measure of credit risk.

13.3.1 Bond ratings

The firms that assess the credit risk of bonds are known as rating agencies, because they seek to 'rate' bonds on a scale from low credit risk to high credit risk. The most familiar rating services are Moody's Investors Service, Standard & Poor's and Fitch Investors Services. Corporations issuing bonds pay a rating fee ranging from a few thousand dollars to over $50 000.

Exhibit 13.4 lists the categories the rating agencies use. The highest-rated bonds are known as prime-rated bonds (Aaa by Moody's and AAA by the other two firms). These bonds are referred to as triple A and are perceived to have very little credit risk; they are described as being of high credit quality. The next level down in credit quality is a high-quality rating, or double A (Aa by Moody's and AA by the other two firms). The main difference between double A and triple A is the amount of cushion available to avoid default. Double A bonds have a smaller cushion, but they are still very strong and have relatively low credit risk. Double A and triple A bonds are sometimes called high-grade bonds.

Single A bonds are the third level down on the rating scale, indicating slightly higher credit risk than double A. These bonds are referred to as upper-medium-grade bonds, and they may suffer under circumstances such as an economic downturn in the firm's industry.

The next rating category is medium-grade bonds, which is denoted as Baa by Moody's and BBB by the other two firms. These bonds are more vulnerable to default if the firm encounters hard times.

Triple A through triple B bonds fall under the classification of investment grade. Many professionally managed funds are restricted to investing solely in investment grade securities. For example, the Vanguard Bond Market mutual fund must invest in investment-grade bonds.[7]

---

[7] See American Association of Individual Investor's Staff, Liszkowski, R. J. and Craig, B. (eds), (1991) *The Individual Investor's Guide to No-Load Mutual Funds*, 10th edn, Chicago, IL: International Publishing, p. 433.

Exhibit 13.4	Bond rating categories by company

Category	Moody[a]	S&P[b]	Fitch[b]	Description
Prime	Aaa	AAA	AAA	Best quality, extremely strong
High-quality	Aa	AA	AA	Strong capacity to pay
Upper medium	A	A	A	Adequate capacity to pay
Medium	Baa	BBB	BBB	Changing circumstances could affect the ability to pay
Speculative	Ba	BB	BB	Has speculative elements
Speculative	B	B	B	Lacks quality
Default	Caa	CCC	CCC	Poor standing
Default	Ca	CC	CC	Highly speculative
Default	C	C	C	Low quality, may never repay
Default	D	D	DDD[c]	In default
			DD	
			D	

Moody, Moody's Investors Services, Inc.; S&P, Standard & Poor's, Inc.; Fitch, Fitch Investors Services, Inc.

[a] Applies numerical modifiers 1, 2 and 3 to indicate relative position within rating category. For example, Baa may be Baa-1, Baa-2 or Baa-3.

[b] Uses + or − to indicate relative position within the rating category. For example, BBB may be either BBB+, BBB or BBB−.

[c] Different degrees of default, with D being worse than DD and DDD.

Because of these restrictions, firms strive to keep the ratings on their bonds at or above triple B in order to maintain greater demand for their bonds and hence also maintain a lower required yield to maturity.

Bonds rated below investment grade (below triple B) are referred to as speculative grade bonds or junk bonds. At the upper end of speculative grade bonds are Ba, BB or double B. These bonds are considered to have 'major ongoing uncertainties'. That is, these bonds face considerable risks in an economic downturn. Single B bonds are slightly more risky than double B. Bonds in categories CCC and below are bonds nearing default or in default. Also, triple C and double C sometimes refer to bonds that are subordinated to bonds holding B ratings that are not already in default (the term 'subordinated bonds' means bonds that stand behind senior bonds in the credit line in the event of default). Junk bonds are discussed in detail later in this chapter.

To enhance the credit quality of their bonds (to improve the rating and reduce the interest cost), firms agree to abide by certain restrictions and requirements that are spelled out in the bond indenture agreement. The bond indenture is a legal agreement between the bond issuer and the bondholders covering all the terms of the issue. It includes stipulations such as type of bond issued and amount of the issue, sinking fund provisions, restrictions on financial ratios and call features.

A sinking fund is money put into a separate custodial account that is used to reduce the outstanding principal through repurchases. An independent third party manages the sinking fund. The effect of a sinking fund is to reduce the likelihood of default at the time of bond maturity.

Restrictions on financial ratios are established in an effort to ensure that the firm has the ability to meet its interest payments, as well as its sinking fund requirements. For example, there may be a restriction that requires the current ratio (the ratio of current assets divided by

Exhibit 13.5	Value-weighted average recovery rates (%) for defaulted North American and European debt instruments (1982–2003)[a]

Instrument	1982–2002		2002	
	North America[b]	Europe[c]	North America	Europe
Secured bank loans	56.90	52.70	54.20	NA
Bonds				
Senior secured	52.00	48.50	55.10	44.80
Senior unsecured	33.50	15.50	27.90	16.30
Senior subordinated	28.00	10.20	21.50	NA
Subordinated	28.70	8.60	33.50	2.70
Junior subordinated	16.50	NA	NA	NA
All bonds	33.30	16.80	28.10	17.10
Preferred stock	6.70	7.90	5.20	NA
All instruments	34.80	21.40	31.60	17.10

[a] Value-weighted recovery rates represent the average of recovery rates on all defaulted issuers, weighted by the face value of those issues.

[b] USA and Canada.

[c] European Union countries, Latvia, Liechtenstein, Lithuania, Moldova, Norway, Poland, Romania, Russia, Slovak Republic, Slovenia, Switzerland, Bulgaria, Croatia, Cyprus, Czech Republic, Estonia, Guernsey, Hungary, Iceland and Isle of Man.

current liabilities) to be greater than two. The purpose of this restriction is to ensure that the issuing firm has the liquidity necessary to make the bond's coupon payment. Indeed, financial analysts examine the financial ratios of some items taken from the firm's financial statements as indicators of the firm's financial strength.

The credit rating measures the probability that the bond issuer will default on its obligations to the bondholder. In case of default, bondholders can incur substantial losses. However, they generally will not lose their entire investment, because bondholders have a legal claim on the assets of the issuer. The recovery rate is the percentage of the face value that can be expected to be recovered in case of default. Exhibit 13.5 displays the historical recovery rates during the period 1982–2002, taken from a study of the credit experiences of over 16 000 corporate issuers that sold long-term public debt at some time between 1919 and 2003. In the study, the recovery rate is measured by the market price of the defaulted instrument observed 30 days after the date of default as a percentage of the face value.

The recovery rates are strongly dependent on seniority or the priority that the claimholder has relative to other claimholders in the event of default. We can distinguish between secured bonds and unsecured bonds. Secured bonds are backed by the guarantee of collateral (which may be in the form of land, buildings or even equipment). The title to this collateral will be transferred to the bondholders in the case of default. The most common type of a secured bond is a mortgage bond. Unsecured bonds, known as debentures, are backed only by the 'full faith and credit' of the issuing firm. We can also distinguish between senior bonds and junior bonds. Senior debt has the priority over junior debt in the case of default. Finally, subordinated bonds are subordinated to all other creditors in the case of financial distress.

The effect of seniority is substantial. For example, in North America, senior secured bonds have a recovery rate of 52%, while junior subordinated bonds have a recovery rate of 16.5%. Note also that the European recovery rates tend to be consistently lower than US recovery rates. In Continental Europe, bond indentures typically impose fewer restrictions on borrowers, giving lenders less control when things begin to go wrong. Further, bankruptcy laws are less slanted towards the investors than in Anglo-American markets, leaving investors comparatively out in the cold in the event of default. Most notably, French bankruptcy law is focused primarily on the preservation of employees and the borrower, with investors coming in third place.

Credit ratings measure the probability of default and recovery rates measure the severity of loss in case of default (given the seniority of the bond). Apart from default risk, the bondholder also faces credit migration risk, or the risk that the credit quality falls and the credit rating is lowered. For example, if a bond is downgraded from upper-medium grade (A) to medium grade (BBB or Baa), then the price will fall and the yield will rise (all other things remaining equal) to reflect the increased credit risk. Note that such downgrades can happen even though the bond issuer continues to meet its current obligations. To assess credit migration risk, rating agencies also issue rating transition matrices. A rating transition matrix is a matrix that gives the estimated probability that a bond with a given grade will migrate to another grade.

Exhibit 13.6 shows an example of a rating transition matrix for Standard & Poor's credit ratings. The matrix shows the historical frequencies of credit migrations (upgrades, downgrades and defaults) over a one-year period.[8] For example, the relative frequency of US bonds migrating from upper-medium grade (A) to medium grade (BBB) is 5.39%. Note that for most credit ratings, the most likely outcome is that the credit rating will not change. However, the probability of remaining in the same grade decreases with credit quality. The probability of staying prime grade (AAA) over a year is around 88%, while it is around 47% for a CCC/C rating. Note also that the probability of being upgraded more than one grade (for instance, from BBB to AA) is virtually zero, while the probability of being downgraded tends to decline more slowly, so that the probability of moving down two or three grades is substantial. Thus, higher credit grades are less subject to up- and downgrades, and upgrade probabilities tail off more quickly than downgrades.

Despite the important role of credit ratings, the quality of the ratings done by rating agencies is sometimes questioned. Some people question the information that ratings, upgradings and downgradings contain about the future likelihood of bonds to default and about the volatility of the market prices of bonds. Further, some claim that when downgrading occurs, it is too late; the market already knows the firm is in trouble, and the bond's price has already fallen. Thus, if the market reacts to the financial stress of a firm before the rating agencies downgrade the firm's bond, what service do the rating agencies provide? Indeed, during many major crises in the market, the rating agencies caught on after the fact. Connecting Theory to Practice 13.2 illustrates the growing concern about the quality of credit ratings and exactly what they mean.

---

[8] These historical frequencies may involve considerable uncertainty if they are measured based on a small number of issues (for example, downgrades from AAA to BBB are very rare and, hence, we cannot obtain a reliable estimate for the probability of such downgrades) or if they are computed during a different stage of the business cyle (for example, the probability of a downgrade during a recession period is higher than during a period of economic expansion).

Exhibit 13.6	The average one-year global, US and European rating transition matrix (1981–2003)

(a) Global transition rates (%)

From/To	AAA	AA	A	BBB	BB	B	CCC/C	D	NR[a]
AAA	88.07	6.81	0.60	0.14	0.06	0.00	0.00	0.00	4.33
AA	0.59	87.37	7.50	0.57	0.07	0.10	0.02	0.01	3.77
A	0.05	2.01	87.42	5.54	0.43	0.16	0.03	0.05	4.31
BBB	0.03	0.19	3.91	84.46	4.56	0.84	0.22	0.37	5.41
BB	0.03	0.07	0.37	5.09	76.32	7.53	1.02	1.36	8.21
B	0.00	0.07	0.24	0.31	4.88	73.88	4.42	6.08	10.12
CCC/C	0.08	0.00	0.25	0.51	1.36	9.32	46.27	30.85	11.36

(b) US transition rates (%)

From/To	AAA	AA	A	BBB	BB	B	CCC/C	D	NR[a]
AAA	88.31	5.83	0.70	0.08	0.08	0.00	0.00	0.00	5.00
AA	0.59	87.27	7.22	0.64	0.07	0.13	0.03	0.01	4.04
A	0.07	2.03	87.39	5.39	0.50	0.18	0.04	0.06	4.34
BBB	0.04	0.21	4.25	84.17	4.59	0.81	0.17	0.32	5.44
BB	0.04	0.09	0.42	5.46	75.83	7.98	0.82	1.31	8.03
B	0.00	0.08	0.24	0.31	4.83	74.42	4.39	5.90	9.84
CCC/C	0.10	0.00	0.31	0.62	1.55	8.67	47.47	29.41	11.87

(c) EU transition rates (%)

From/To	AAA	AA	A	BBB	BB	B	CCC/C	D	NR[a]
AAA	87.93	8.43	0.50	0.33	0.00	0.00	0.00	0.00	2.81
AA	0.23	87.18	9.06	0.40	0.06	0.00	0.00	0.00	3.08
A	0.00	2.06	88.22	5.28	0.24	0.04	0.00	0.00	4.17
BBB	0.00	0.19	4.18	84.31	2.60	0.74	0.19	0.56	7.24
BB	0.00	0.00	0.00	2.75	77.80	6.41	0.69	1.14	11.21
B	0.00	0.00	0.72	0.36	4.66	68.46	5.73	7.17	12.90
CCC/C	0.00	0.00	0.00	0.00	0.00	7.14	28.57	60.71	3.57

[a] NR, rating withdrawn.

Source: From *Corporate Defaults in 2003 Recede from Recent Highs*, copyright 2004 by Standard & Poor's, material reproduced with permission of Standard & Poor's, a division of The McGraw-Hill Companies, Inc. (Brady, B., 2004).

→ **Connecting Theory to Practice 13.2**

Bond and rating agencies: scores are often junk, say critics

As corporate bonds grow in popularity, fears are increasing that investors are relying too much on credit ratings – and on the agencies that issue them.

Over the past 30 years, says Professor Jonathan Macey of Cornell Law School, the agencies have evolved into a 'quasi-governmental' authority that 'dramatically and artificially' increases the power of their ratings in the marketplace.

Without a rating a bond will not be considered by most fund managers. But regulatory moves to restrict links between equity analysts and investment bankers have added weight to claims that the big three agencies – Standard & Poor's, Moody's and Fitch – face a similar conflict of interest because they rely on fees paid by the companies they rate for about 90 per cent of their income.

The ratings are crucial for companies because they determine the cost of debt. The higher the rating, the lower the cost to the company. The difference between BBB- and BB+ can change the fixed interest rate by as much as 1 percentage point. For a company issuing £500 m of bonds, that means paying an extra £5 m of interest annually.

Glenn Reynolds, president of CreditSights, a credit research firm in New York, says the agencies' fee-paying arrangements encourage complacency in ratings assessments. 'The fact that the rating agencies have a business model that allows them to get paid regardless of the quality of product they deliver makes for a great equity story, but not necessarily a very good market watchdog.'

Reynolds, an outspoken critic of the rating agencies, is one of many experts who have given evidence to a US Securities and Exchange Commission inquiry into the rating process following the collapse of Enron, whose bonds retained their investment-grade rating until four days before the company declared bankruptcy.

The agencies vehemently deny any conflict of interest. 'We are nothing like the research arm of an investment bank that is interested in future mandates or banking fees,' says Martin Winn of S&P. Fitch acknowledges the potential for conflict, but defends its fee system, comparing itself to 'journalists and other members of the media who derive revenue from subscribers and advertisers that include companies they cover'.

Martin Weiss, chairman of Weiss Ratings, a New York-based credit research firm, says this is a false parallel. If Which? magazine accepted money from the providers of products that it rates for consumers, it would be a laughing stock, he says. Yet 'here you have major Wall Street firms doing just that'.

Critics also deplore the system under which bond issuers pay only for the ratings they decide to use, which they claim encourages the agencies to rate bonds more leniently. Once the bonds are issued – and the agencies have been paid their fees – ratings can be downgraded, potentially leaving investment managers and pension funds with bonds that no longer suit their investment criteria.

Three years of jittery markets have put pressure on all levels of credit quality. However, critics say that record number of so-called 'fallen angel' downgrades – companies whose ratings have fallen from investment grade to junk status – suggests that the agencies have little financial incentive to revise their rating strategy until bonds have reached the marketplace and bond-holders are at risk.

Last year saw a record number of fallen angels in the European Union, affecting $88 bn (£56.4 bn) of outstanding bonds, according to S&P. This year, Ahold, the Dutch supermarket retailer, and ThyssenKrupp, the German steel conglomerate, have already fallen, and there are signs that others will follow.

Investment bankers also complain that rating agencies are understaffed with analysts, who are therefore forced to cover too many issuers. 'Whereas equity analysts spend their lives monitoring three or four companies each, the rating agency guys cover entire industries,' says a senior executive in the credit department at Morgan Stanley. 'When big news breaks in the markets, it's usually the equity guys who find the dirt. It just makes you question why the rating agencies get such special treatment and how much you can rely on ratings.' The executive points to examples such as France Telecom, whose bonds were downgraded in June last year – months after equity researchers expressed concern over the company's debt burden. Since that downgrade, the agencies have come under fire for failing to spot broader trends. When problems are spotted, the result can be a random and sudden rash of downgrades on several issuers at once, causing havoc for fund managers.

This was what happened recently when S&P revised its treatment of unfunded pension liabilities. Its downgrade of ThyssenKrupp was accompanied by 11 changes in the ratings for other debt issuers, including Sainsbury, BAE Systems and Rolls-Royce. Equity researchers had been pointing to the pension gap problem for months, but the rating downgrade took the markets and ThyssenKrupp's management by surprise.

For investors, the best advice may be to avoid relying on ratings alone. 'Rating agencies are in the business of taking a long-term view and assessing the possibility of [companies] defaulting on their debt,' says Ted Bacon, who manages the Sterling Investment Grade Corporate Bond Fund at Threadneedle Investments. 'They do not look at day-to-day changes that might resolve themselves. The last thing they want to do is downgrade a bond and then have to change it back when they get it wrong.'

Source: Jamie Felix, 'Bond and Rating Agencies: Scores Are Often Junk, Say Critics', *Financial Times*, 8 March 2003.

13.3.2 Credit spreads over Treasuries and the economy

We have seen that bond ratings influence bond prices and bond yields. The spread over Treasuries or credit spread for similar bonds varies over time. For example, Exhibit 13.7 gives the yield to maturity for ten-year corporate bonds rated Baa by Moody's and for ten-year Treasury bonds from 1954 to 2002. Clearly, the difference in yield between Baa bonds and Treasuries has changed substantially over time, reaching lows of about 0.3% and highs of about 3.8%.

The investor who was considering purchasing medium-grade bonds (BBB or Baa) would want to know whether the yields on Treasury bonds were expected to rise and also whether the credit spreads were expected to widen. A combination of both of these effects could result in a sharp fall in prices.

For example, consider the years 1978–82, when the interest rate increased sharply and bondholders incurred relatively large losses. An investment in ten-year Treasury bonds at $1000 par in 1978 had fallen to $824 in 1982 because of the increase in interest rates.[9] This is a 17.65% loss. Since the spread also widened, an investment in Baa bonds at a $1000 par in 1978 would have fallen to $764, a 23.57% loss.[10] Thus, the widening of the spread from 1.08% in 1978 to 3.11% in 1982 resulted in an additional 5.92% loss.

The health of the economy influences the size of the credit spread. In recessions, bondholders tend to move out of lower-rated bonds into higher-rated bonds – a phenomenon known as 'the flight to quality'.[11] For example, in 1978 inflation-adjusted growth in the GDP

---

[9] The value $824 was calculated using the standard bond-pricing equation with the bond now being a six-year bond (four years have elapsed); the yield to maturity has risen.

[10] These computations are based on semiannual bonds with ten years to maturity initially (Treasury bonds with 8.41% coupon and Baa bonds with 9.49% coupon) and then six years to maturity left in 1982 to calculate the losses.

[11] The link between the health of the economy and the yield to maturity is less clear. The yield is affected by both inflation and the risk of default. In a recession, the risk of default goes up; this increases the yield to maturity. However, inflation may go up or down. When inflation is up (e.g. in the early 1980s) in a recession, the two forces of inflation and default risk join each other, and bond prices plummet. When the inflation and the economy are down (e.g. in the early 1990s), there are conflicting forces and bond prices are relatively stable.

Exhibit 13.7	History of yields on ten-year US Baa corporate bonds and ten-year US Treasury bonds (1954–2002)

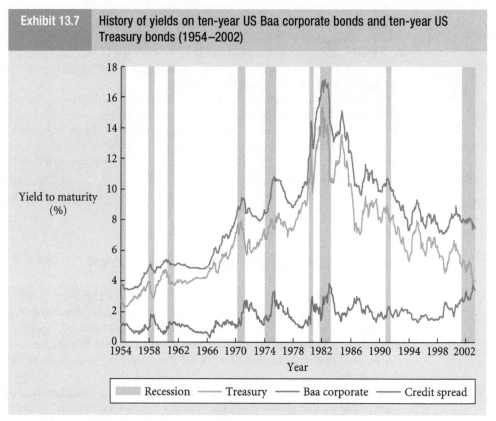

was 6.1%, but by 1982 it had fallen to −3%. At the same time, the credit spread had risen from 1.08 to 3.11%, an increase of 203 basis points. Exhibit 13.7 shows that this flight to quality is a general property of recession periods. Specifically, during recession periods, which are coloured grey in Exhibit 13.7, the credit spread peaks. Thus, the credit spread shows a highly cyclical pattern.

Note that we have thus far ignored taxes. The yield to maturity published in the financial media is the pretax yield. Since investors pay income tax on regular interest and capital gain tax on realised profit from the sale of the bonds, the published yields do not reflect the investor's after-tax rate of return. Municipal bonds (bonds issued by a state or local government) are exempt from income tax, whereas all other bonds are taxable. Hence, a comparison of the pretax yields on various types of bonds may be misleading.

If a particular bond receives a favourable tax treatment, then its (before-tax) yield may be lower than that of a Treasury bond with the same maturity, even if they involve default risk. For example, the yield on US municipal bonds, which involve default risk, commonly is smaller than the yield on US Treasury bonds. For example, on 22 September 1997, the yield to maturity on Florida Ports Financing was 5.52%, whereas the yield to maturity on US Treasury bonds (with the same 30 years to maturity) was 6.36%. The reason that municipals offer such low yields is that they are exempt from Federal income tax, not because their risk is lower than that of Treasury bonds. Still, if we correct for taxes, then we would find that municipals have significantly higher after-tax yields than Treasuries, which reflect their default risk premium.

13.3.3 Junk bonds

Junk bonds or speculative-grade bonds are lower-rated corporate bonds (below BBB or Baa). Although junk bonds have a considerable amount of credit risk, they have two attractive features. First, their yields are relatively high, which implies a high realised rate of return if bankruptcy does not occur. In fact, junk bonds can have yields in excess of 30% – this is why they also go by the name of high-yield bonds. Second, junk bonds are very sensitive to the overall health of the issuing firm and hence their price moves more with information related to the firm than with changes in overall interest rates. It turns out that a diversified portfolio of junk bonds with a relatively low correlation is less volatile than a diversified portfolio of US Treasury securities. Recall from Chapter 9 that securities that have low correlations can be used to form portfolios with relatively low overall volatility. Combined, these effects mean that a diversified portfolio of junk bonds can have a relatively high risk-adjusted return.

Still, the popularity of junk bonds is a relatively recent phenomenon. Until the late 1970s, all public issues of corporate bonds involved investment-grade bonds. The only publicly traded junk bonds were fallen angels or bonds that originally carried investment-grade ratings but had fallen from grace because of a decline in credit quality as a result of adverse changes in business conditions or the assumption of too much financial risk. For these fallen angels, the interest yields at face value had not been very high, but with the bonds selling at a fraction of face value, the yield for secondary purchasers was quite high. Companies with ratings below investment grade raised new money by borrowing from banks, through private placements of bonds or through stock offerings.[12,13] One factor explaining this situation is that regulators restrict investing in investment grade bonds by pension funds and insurance companies.

The debt market in the USA changed dramatically after 1977, when Bear Stearns and Company, a New York investment house, underwrote the first IPO of a junk bond, giving a substantially larger coupon to investors than was otherwise available on the market. Soon thereafter, Drexel Burnham Lambert financed seven companies that had previously been shut out of the corporate bond market. By 1983, over a third of all corporate bond issues were non-investment grade, two-thirds of which were new issues. Three factors help to explain this explosion of new junk bond issues.

First, junk bonds held enormous appeal for issuing firms because publicly issued bonds typically carry lower interest rates than bank loans and private placements (because they are more liquid), they tend to impose fewer restrictions on the actions of the borrowers (covenants), and also they do not dilute the value of the outstanding stock, contrary to stock offerings.

Second, the advent of modern portfolio theory meant that financial researchers soon began to observe that the credit risk of junk bonds was more than compensated for by their higher yields, suggesting that the actual credit losses were exceeded by the higher interest payments. In other words, someone who bought a diversified portfolio of these risky bonds would do better than someone who bought investment-grade bonds, even after deducting losses on the bonds that defaulted.

---

[12] A private placement is the sale of bonds directly to an investor such as an insurance company. Because private placements are not registered with the Securities and Exchange Commission, the original purchasers cannot easily resell them to other investors.

[13] Only the bonds of a small minority of large US companies have an investment grade. Thus, before the rise of the junk bond market, the large majority of companies were, in effect, denied an important means to finance growth and business development.

Third, investment banks ran an aggressive marketing campaign to push junk bonds to investors, with stunning success. Michael Milken of Drexel Burnham Lambert, the brokerage that dominated the high-yield market, became famous by marketing junk bonds on an unprecedented scale (and earning hundreds of millions of dollars for himself in the process).

By the early 1980s, investment banks were underwriting nearly as many junk bonds as investment-grade ones. And investors, who were starved for good investment avenues at the time, were only too eager to make the leap of faith. Early successes and massive profits for investors in junk bonds led to what can be described only as a frenzy, as the promoters aggressively pushed junk bonds. Investors accepted increasingly worse terms (including zero-coupon junk bonds) and demanded higher yields.

The golden age of junk bonds lasted roughly a decade and built to a frenzy of new bond issues in 1988 and 1989. That resulted, in 1989 and 1990, in an unprecedented number of defaults by junk bond issuers, the bankruptcy of Drexel Burnham Lambert and the conviction of Michael Milken.[14] Almost overnight, the market for newly issued junk bonds disappeared, and no significant new junk issues came to market for more than a year.

Despite this, the variety and number of junk bond issues recovered in the 1990s and at the time of writing is currently thriving. In fact, as discussed in Connecting Theory to Practice 13.3, junk bonds have recently become very popular again. Many mutual funds have been established that invest exclusively in high-yield bonds, which have continued to have high risk-adjusted returns.

In Europe, the junk market is relatively small compared with that of the USA. One reason for this is the lack of a single legal system in Europe, which makes it hard for bondholders to work out what share of a company's assets they are entitled to in the case of a bankruptcy. In Europe, each country has its own system, and there are still few case studies. European investors have been burnt by guessing risks wrongly and only agreed to buy some recent deals after documentation and protection was improved.

→ **Connecting Theory to Practice 13.3**

A fad for junk bonds

Wall Street witnessed the mutual fund equivalent of a man-bites-dog story this month when US fund group Vanguard, which oversees $610 bn in assets, said it would stop accepting contributions for its $9.2 bn corporate high-yield bond fund.

Vanguard imposed the cooling-off period on June 12 because a junk-bond rally had attracted the wrong crowd: short-term players who could be expected to withdraw their money at the first sign of trouble, raising trading costs for Vanguard's more sober investors.

'There was a bit of panic buying,' said Gus Sauter, chief investment officer at Vanguard. 'It's a frequent pattern after a fund performs quite well. Nothing sells like performance and you see a quick rush of money into the fund.'

---

[14] In 1989 a federal grand jury indicted Milken for violations of federal securities and racketeering laws. He pleaded guilty to securities fraud and related charges in 1990, and the government dropped the more serious charges of insider trading and racketeering. Milken was fined and sentenced to prison for ten years and barred from the industry for life.

The investor thirst for junk bonds reflects the shortage of palatable alternatives. Stocks still make many feel queasy. At the same time, the Federal Reserve's efforts to push down interest rates mean safer fixed-income investments offer tiny yields.

Sit by the pool at any US retirement community and the resident experts will tell you the score: junk bonds offer the only appetising yields around.

The result has been a buying binge of historic proportions. About $16 bn flowed into US high-yield mutual funds last month – more than the total for the previous two years combined, according to Lipper. Vanguard's high-yield fund alone raised $1.4 bn in the first five months of the year.

'There is good money and bad money,' says Sauter. 'When you take bad money, it hurts your returns. A lot of people are willing to take it because it pumps up your assets.' The danger is that this short-term money is setting up the end game that Vanguard wants to avoid. Chuck Clough, the former Merrill Lynch strategist who warned about the dangers of overheated markets during the 1990s, sees a familiar pattern.

'A lot of good high-yield investors are probably not very active right now,' Mr Clough said. 'There is so much money seeking yield, and so much money has gone into corporate bond funds, that liquidity is chasing yields down.'

Consider the numbers. The average high-yield bond fetched 99 cents on the dollar last week, compared with 78 cents in October, Merrill says. The difference in interest rates on junk bonds and 10-year Treasuries – the spread – has narrowed to 5.56 percentage points from 10.15 percentage points in October and 7.34 this time last year.

Merrill's models suggest the spreads between junk bonds and 10-year Treasuries should be where they were last year, about 7.5 percentage points. This view is supported by Moody's KMV, a risk measurement company whose work is widely followed by regulators. Tim Kasta, Moody's KMV managing director, said the median expected default rate for US non-investment-grade companies is *higher* now than it was a year ago.

The tightening in junk bond spreads suggests investors are growing too casual. High-yield bonds tend to trade more like stocks than other fixed-income securities. If the economy slows – and this risk is causing the Fed to keep rates low – junk-bond investors could get hammered.

'They [high-yield investors] probably think they are diversifying and they are not,' said Rich Bernstein, Merrill's current investment strategist. 'High-yield has much more sensitivity to the economy. It's positively correlated with the economy, whereas most bonds are negatively correlated.'

Newcomers to the high-yield market, in other words, should sober up. If Vanguard doesn't have the heart to take investors' money, they should think twice before parting with it.

Source: Gary Silverman, 'A Fad For Junk Bonds', *Financial Times*, 28 June 2003.

→ **Making the connection**

In early 2003, a weak stock market and low returns on other fixed-income securities encouraged many investors to turn to retail junk bond funds. A record demand for high-yield debt securities narrowed yield spreads on junk bonds to around 5.6% over US Treasuries, and it prompted a surge in issuance of corporate high-yield bonds. Some feared that investors may have underestimated the default rate and the high correlation with the economy of junk bonds. If investors sober up, they may want to withdraw their money and the junk bond market may collapse. For this reason, at some point, the large US fund group Vanguard actually stopped accepting further contributions for its high-yield bond fund.

13.3.4 Inflation-indexed bonds

This section analyses inflation-indexed bonds. When issued by governments, these bonds are also known as Treasury inflation-protected securities (TIPS). As discussed earlier, a bond investor is exposed to various risks, including interest-rate risk, liquidity risk and, possibly, default risk. In addition to these risks, the investor faces uncertainty regarding the future price level. After all, the bond issuer promises to pay fixed dollar amounts of coupons and principal, and inflation erodes the purchasing value of those fixed dollar amounts. Inflation-indexed bonds avoid purchasing power risk by linking the coupon and par payments to the inflation rate. Like most other US Treasury bonds, TIPS are usually sold in initial amounts of $1000. However, the principal is adjusted semiannually, based on changes in the consumer price index (CPI) three months earlier.

To illustrate how TIPS work, it is useful to consider an indexed bond with a coupon rate of 3% that is issued at 1 January 2004. If the CPI increases from 127 at 1 October 2003 (three months earlier) to 129 at 31 March 2004 (three months later), the principal is adjusted to $1000 \times (129/127) \cong $1015.75 and the investor receives a first coupon of $1015.75 \times 0.03/2 \cong$ $15.24 at 1 July 2004 (six months later). If the CPI increases further to 132 at 30 September 2004 (nine months later), the principal will be adjusted to $1000 \times (132/127) \cong 1039.37$ and the investor receives a second coupon of $1039.37 \times 0.03/2 \cong $15.59 at 1 January 2005 (12 months later).

TIPS should appeal primarily to investors who are wary of rising inflation. Long-run investors such as pension funds who are worried about inflation eroding the value of their investments relative to their pension liabilities can use TIPS to protect their portfolios against inflation.[15] In turn, these investors may accept a lower yield than for otherwise similar (non-indexed) government bonds, which may lower the funding costs of the government. However, TIPS are not as successful as was thought previously. The yield on TIPS generally is not lower, or not substantially lower, than for otherwise similar government bonds. Sometimes, the yield is even higher, which suggests that TIPS possess some unattractive features. The following two factors may help to explain the limited success of TIPS thus far:

- The trading volume of TIPS is relatively low, which makes TIPS illiquid investments relative to conventional government bonds. In part, this reflects the fact that TIPS are buy-and-hold instruments for long-run investors. Unlike speculators, these buy-and-hold investors do not seek to sell at the next profitable opportunity. Illiquid assets carry a liquidity premium to compensate for the risk that they cannot be sold quickly and without price concessions.
- As with conventional bonds, the semiannual interest payments on inflation-indexed bonds are taxable. Investors are also required to report as income every year any increase in the value of the principal that arises because of inflation, even though the increase in principal is not received until the bond matures or is sold.[16] Because of this tax treatment, the after-tax yield on indexed bonds held in taxable accounts is not fully insulated from inflation. For this reason, indexed bonds are relatively unappealing to investors in high tax brackets. Indeed, they are most useful for tax-exempt investors such as pension funds and tax-deferred retirement funds such as IRAs and 401k plans.

---

[15] Recall from Chapter 4 that defined-benefit pension plans are typically linked to the wage level and, hence, the liabilities are denominated in real terms rather than fixed in nominal terms. Also, the pensions in payment to pensioners are typically indexed to correct for inflation.

[16] Treasury press release, 'Questions and Answers on Marketable Inflation-Protection Securities', 16 May 1996.

Outside the USA, the governments in the UK, New Zealand and many other countries also issue indexed bonds. For example, the French treasury has issued euro-denominated inflation-indexed bonds that are indexed to the Eurozone CPI.

Since the introduction of TIPS, corporations have also issued inflation-indexed bonds. Some of these private-sector bonds are structured differently from TIPS. The principal amount of TIPS grows every six months by the most recent CPI figure, and the entire inflation-adjusted amount is paid out at maturity. The principal amount can grow to an uncomfortably large proportion. This might conflict with the investor's need for diversification. To address this problem, some private issuers have structured their indexed bonds so that inflation adjustment is paid out as part of the coupon payment. Thus, under this 'current pay' structure, the coupon rate actually floats.

13.4　The impact of embedded options

Issuers often add provisions to bonds to protect themselves from interest-rate changes or to make the bonds more attractive to investors. Many features in corporate bond issues are essentially options. Recall from Chapter 2 that an option gives its holder the right, but not the obligation, to do something in the future. Both callable and convertible bonds contain option-like features. The option to call a bond and the option to convert a bond to stock dramatically change the fundamental price behaviour of bonds.

13.4.1　The call feature

Most corporate bonds are callable by the issuing firm. That is, the issuer has the right to buy back the bonds at a stated redemption price. The bondholders face the risk that the bonds will be called at a time when they would prefer to hold them.[17]

For example, in 1979, Duke Power Company issued a 10% coupon bond at $1000 par that had a stated maturity of 1 March 2009.[18] The bonds were rated Aa by Moody's and thus contained little credit risk.

Suppose these bonds were purchased with the idea of holding them until 2009. As interest rates fell in the late 1980s and early 1990s, these bonds should have experienced a dramatic rise in price, except that they were callable at 105.65% of par, or $1056.50. Thus, even though yields on comparable bonds reached the mid-8% level, these bonds never rose much above $1056.50. Thus, the call provision put a ceiling on the possible profit due to a fall in interest rates. On 23 December 1991, Duke Power Company called back the bonds and paid $1056.50 (plus accrued interest).

The investor then had the problem of what to do with the $1056.50 proceeds per bond. Unfortunately, the investor had to replace a $10\frac{1}{8}$% coupon bond with an 8.5% bond (the yield available at the time), resulting in an annual coupon loss of $1\frac{5}{8}$%, or $16.25 (0.01625 × $1000), per bond per year.

Exhibit 13.8 illustrates the impact of the call feature on bond price behaviour with respect to yield to maturity, assuming everything else about the bonds is the same (maturity, coupon,

---

[17] Nevertheless, callable bonds typically come with a period of call protection, an initial period during which the bonds are not callable.
[18] From Moody's (1991), *Corporate Bond Guide*, New York: Moody's Investors Service, p. 69.

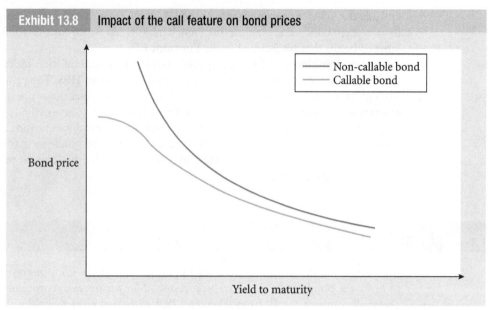

| Exhibit 13.8 | Impact of the call feature on bond prices |

Source: From *Introduction to Investments*, 2nd edn, by Levy. © 1999. Reprinted with permission of South-Western, a division of Thomson Learning: www.thomsonrights.com. Fax 800 730-2215.

and so forth). If the callable and the non-callable bonds were priced the same, which bond would an investor rather own? An investor would prefer the non-callable bond, of course, because he or she could gain more if there were a large increase in price because of falling interest rates. Thus, for similar bonds, a non-callable bond is always worth more. Indeed, Exhibit 13.8 demonstrates this property. This exhibit also shows that as yields to maturity get progressively higher, the difference in prices gradually declines. An investor would not expect too great a threat from a call feature at 105% of par when the bond is trading at, say, 70% of its par value. Thus, the market value of the call feature declines as yields to maturity rise.

Exhibit 13.8 also highlights the divergence in price when interest rates fall. Specifically, the callable bond usually does not trade much above the price at which the firm can call the bonds. Notice the left-hand side of Exhibit 13.8. As rates fall, the non-callable bond's price continues to rise. However, the callable bond levels off at the value of the bond if it were called.

Why, then, do investors buy callable bonds? The reason is that issuing firms offer 'sweeteners' in the form of higher coupon rates in return for the call feature. The issuing firm of callable bonds offers the investor a higher yield to maturity. However, should the yield to maturity fall, the investor will miss out on a sizeable run-up in price. Once again, there is a trade-off between risk (the call feature) and return (the higher initial yield to maturity).

Why do firms issue callable bonds? The call feature allows firms some flexibility in their financing policies. In particular, the firm is not locked into an expensive debt issue. When interest rates fall, the bonds can be refinanced at a lower rate.

13.4.2 The conversion feature

When firms want to reduce their required coupon rate, they sometimes offer to make their bonds convertible to common or preferred stock. One advantage from the issuing firm's viewpoint is that it will issue new common stock at a relatively high price when the conversion takes place in the future. Typically, the conversion price (which equals the par value of the bond divided by the conversion ratio) is set significantly above the current common stock price. If the firm raised capital through a new issue of common stock, it would have to offer the new issue at a price slightly less than the current stock price. Therefore, convertible bonds provide a way to achieve, albeit in the future, an equity issue at a higher price.

Consider the Cray Research Inc. (makers of super-computers) $6^{1}/_{8}$% coupon, semiannual convertible bonds, maturing 1 February 2011, with a rating of Baa-2 by Moody's. The conversion ratio is 12.82, which means that for every bond converted, the firm will issue 12.82 shares of common stock. Thus, the conversion price is about $78 (par/conversion ratio = $1000/12.82).

On 24 July 1992, the bonds closed at 73.5% of par, and the common stock closed at $29.38. These bonds offer a yield to maturity of approximately 9%. At the time, the Cray Research bonds offered a yield to maturity that was indistinguishable from that of comparable non-convertible bonds. The conversion feature had very little value. The stock price must rise by 165.53% before the conversion price is reached [($78 − $29.375)/$29.375]. Thus, these bonds offer a strong 9% yield to maturity, and they also contain an 'equity kicker'. If the common stock price goes up considerably, then these bonds will likewise rise (and yields fall).

Convertible bond price behaviour is quite different from the price behaviour of regular bonds. The conversion value is the value of the bond if it is immediately converted into stock. Hence, as the stock price rises, so does the conversion value. The reason for the low value of the Cray Research bonds is that the common stock price lost over 50% of its value (the super-computer industry is very sensitive to recessions). If it had been a straight bond, its price would have gone up (because interest rates decreased); however, the conversion value went down more, which explains the loss. Exhibit 13.9 illustrates this price behaviour. Notice that the straight (non-convertible) bond is almost insensitive to stock price changes, except when the firm's stock price gets very low. The straight line represents the conversion value, which equals the conversion ratio times the current stock price. Clearly, as the stock price rises, so does the conversion value. Thus, when Cray Research stock began its fall, the convertible

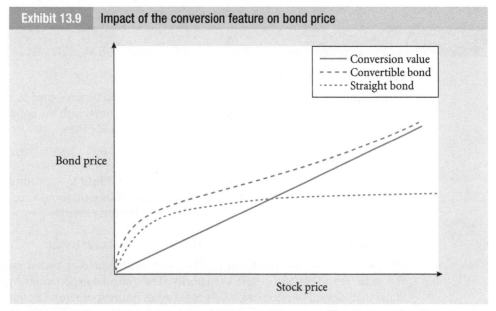

Exhibit 13.9   Impact of the conversion feature on bond price

Source: From *Introduction to Investments*, 2nd edn, by Levy. © 1999. Reprinted with permission of South-Western, a division of Thomson Learning: www.thomsonrights.com. Fax 800 730-2215.

bond followed suit. Notice that the convertible bond price always exceeds the straight bond price, even for low stock prices, because the ability to convert the bonds to stock is always worth something (although it may not be worth very much at low stock prices). The higher price of convertible bonds relative to straight bonds implies that their yield must be lower.

→ **Connecting Theory to Practice 13.4**

Telephone exchanges

Difficult capital markets call for innovative financing products. This season's favourite: the exchangeable bond. France Telecom is breaking new ground by using a bond exchangeable into Orange stock as part of the Orange flotation – while Hutchison Whampoa yesterday sold a further tranche of bonds exchangeable into Vodafone stock.

It would be more straightforward just to sell these shares in the market. But telecoms valuations have sunk and equity investors are loath to swallow any more stock. By issuing exchangeables, sellers can raise capital against their equity holdings from non-equity investors – debt funds, specialist convertible funds and arbitrageurs. France Telecom has an additional motive, to play off convertible investors against equity investors to maximise the proceeds from Orange.

An exchangeable is much like a convertible – a low-coupon bond bundled with a call option – only exchange takes place into another company's shares. These are not new shares, the impact is on the free float, which increases over the lifetime of the bond (assuming the underlying shares rise above the strike price). The overall impact should be to reduce volatility in the underlying stock – though only at the margin – and by less than a convertible issue.

As a tool for dealing with overhangs exchangeables have merit. But part of the proceeds are hedged immediately by arbitrageurs, and the equity market discounts the future supply of paper. As Vodafone's share fall yesterday demonstrates, there is no free lunch.

Source: 'Lex Column: Telephone Exchanges', *Financial Times*, 9 January 2001.

Summary

Use the bond-pricing equation to find bond prices and bond yields.

When the bond's price is given, the yield to maturity can be computed as the discount rate that equates the present value of the bond's future cash flows with the bond's price. There is an inverse relationship between yield to maturity and bond prices.

Interpret a yield curve.

The yield to maturity is the interest earned on a bond if held to its maturity. A yield curve is a relationship between a bond's time to maturity and its yield to maturity. The yield curve provides some clues regarding the future course of interest rates.

Summarise the theories that explain the shape and level of yield curves.

The local expectations hypothesis (LEH) states that the holding period rates of return are the same, regardless of the time to maturity. The unbiased expectations hypothesis (UEH) states that forward rates are unbiased predictors of future spot rates. The liquidity preference hypothesis (LPH) states that investors have a preference for securities with shorter maturities; hence, longer-term bonds will have a higher yield to maturity. The market segmentation hypothesis (MSH) is based on investors and borrowers having specific preferences regarding time to maturity. Supply and demand in these segments of the yield curve will govern the yield to maturity. Finally, the preferred habitat hypothesis is similar to the MSH, except that investors and borrowers can be induced to change their maturity preferences when yields to maturity are sufficiently different.

Describe the behaviour of the spread over Treasuries.

Bond-rating agencies classify the credit risk inherent in bonds. Over time, the additional yield required for bearing this credit risk – the spread over Treasuries – varies. During economic downturns, the spread over Treasuries widens to compensate investors for the additional risk of default.

Describe the impact of the call feature and the convertible feature on bond prices.

The call feature causes bond prices not to rise as much as a comparable non-callable bond when interest rates fall. The option to call a bond held by the issuer becomes more valuable when interest rates fall, because the bonds can be refinanced at a lower rate. The conversion feature causes bonds to behave like the underlying stock after the stock price has risen sufficiently.

Key terms

Bond indenture 430
Coupon yield 417
Credit quality 429
Credit risk 429
Credit spread 435
Current yield 417
Debenture 431
Fallen angel 437
Forward contract 424
Forward rate 423
High grade 429
Holding period rate 418
Inflation-indexed bonds 440
Investment grade 429
Junior bonds 431
Junk bond 430

Liquidity preference hypothesis
  (LPH) 427
Liquidity premium 428
Local expectations hypothesis
  (LEH) 426
Market segmentation hypothesis
  (MSH) 428
Nominal yield 417
Preferred habitat hypothesis 428
Price risk 420
Rating agency 429
Rating transition matrix 432
Realised yield 418
Recovery rate 431
Reinvestment risk 420
Secured bonds 431

Senior bonds 431
Seniority 431
Sinking fund 430
Spot rate 423
Spread over Treasuries 429
Subordinated bonds 431
Term structure of interest
  rates 421
Treasury inflation-protected
  securities (TIPS) 440
Unbiased expectations
  hypothesis (UEH) 426
Unsecured bonds 431
Yield curve 421
Yield to call 417
Yield to maturity 415

Review questions

1 'If the yield to maturity is zero, no matter what the maturity is, the par value of the bond must be equal to its market value.' Evaluate this statement. Is there a specific type of bond for which this is true?

2 Assuming a flat yield curve and a bond that is trading at par, why does the yield to call exceed the yield to maturity?

3 Identify and discuss the various theories related to the behaviour of the yield curve.

4 Due to financial stress, the bonds of Intelo have been downgraded by Moody's from A to BBB. What is the predicted effect on the bonds' price? What is the predicted effect on the bonds' yield to maturity?

5 A PLC has issued a 10-year zero-coupon bond that can be converted into five of their shares. Comparable straight bonds have a yield to maturity of 10%. The firm's share is currently trading at $25. Use a face value of $100 in your calculations:

   a. Calculate the conversion value and the conversion price of the bond.
   b. If you had to convert now or never, what would you do?
   c. If the convertible bond is trading at $52, what is the value of the call option?
   d. What happens to the value of the convertible bond if the riskiness of the firm's assets increases?

For an extensive set of review and practice questions and answers, visit the Levy–Post investment website at www.booksites.net/levy

Selected references

Altman, E. I., 1989, 'Measuring Corporate Bond Mortality and Performance', *Journal of Finance*, 44, 909–922.

Altman, E. I., 1990a, *The High-Yield Debt Market: Investment Performance and Economic Impact*, Homewood, IL: Dow Jones–Irwin.

Altman, E. I., 1990b, 'Setting the Record Straight on Junk Bonds', *Journal of Applied Corporate Finance*, 3, 82–95.

Altman, E. I., 1992, 'Revisiting the High-Yield Bond Market', *Financial Management*, 21 (2), 78–92.

Altman, E. I. and D. L. Kao, 1992, 'The Implications of Corporate Bond Ratings Drift', *Financial Analysts Journal*, 48 (3), 64–75.

American Association of Individual Investor's Staff, Liszkowski, R. J. and Craig, B. (eds), 1991, *The Individual Investor's Guide to No-Load Mutual Funds*, Chicago, IL: International Publishing.

Asquith, P., D. W. Mullins, Jr and E. D. Wolff, 1989, 'Original Issue High-Yield Bonds: Aging Analysis of Defaults, Exchanges and Call', *Journal of Finance*, 44, 923–952.

Best, P., A. Byrne and A. Ilmanen, 1998, 'What Really Happened to U.S. Bond Yield', *Financial Analysts Journal*, 54 (3), 41–49.

Blume, M. E., and D. B. Keim, 1987, 'Low Grade Bonds: Their Risks and Returns', *Financial Analysts Journal*, 43, 26–33.

Blume, M. E. and D. B. Keim, 1991a, 'Realized Returns and Defaults on Low-Grade Bonds: The Cohort of 1977 and 1978', *Financial Analysts Journal*, 47 (2), 63–72.

Blume, M. E. and D. B. Keim, 1991b, 'The Risk and Return of Low-Grade Bonds: An Update', *Financial Analysts Journal*, 47 (5), 85–89.

Cornell, B., 1991, 'Liquidity and the Pricing of Low-Grade Bonds', *Financial Analysts Journal*, 47 (1), 63–67, 74.

Cottle, S., R. F. Murray and F. E. Block, 1988, *Graham and Dodd's Security Analysis*, 5th edn, New York: McGraw-Hill.

Fabozzi, F. J., 1990, *The New High-Yield Debt Market: A Handbook for Portfolio Managers and Analysts*, New York: HarperCollins.

Fama, E. F., 1976, 'Forward Rates as Predictors of Future Spot Interest Rates', *Journal of Financial Economics*, **3**, 361–377.

Fama, E. F., 1984, 'The Information in the Term Structure', *Journal of Financial Economics*, **13**, 509–528.

Fons, J. S. and A. E. Kimball, 1991, 'Corporate Bond Defaults and Default Rates 1970–1990', *Journal of Fixed Income*, **1**, 36–47.

Fridson, M. S. and C. Garman, 1998, 'Determinants of Spreads on New High Yield Bonds', *Financial Analysts Journal*, **54** (2), 28–39.

Fridson, M. S., M. A. Cherry, J. A. Kim and S. W. Weiss, 1992, 'What Drives the Flows of High-Yield Mutual Funds?', *Journal of Fixed Income*, **2**, 47–59.

Geanuracos, J. and B. Millar, 1991, *The Power of Financial Innovation*, New York: Harper Business.

Lederman, J. and M. P. Sullivan, 1993, *The New High-Yield Bond Market: Investment Opportunities, Strategies and Analysis*, Chicago: Probus Publishing.

Levy, H. and R. Brooks, 1989, 'An Empirical Analysis of Term Premiums Using Stochastic Dominance', *Journal of Banking and Finance*, **13**, 245–260.

Livingston, M., 1990, *Money and Capital Markets: Financial Instruments and Their Uses*, Englewood Cliffs, NJ: Prentice Hall.

Ma, C. K., R. Rao and R. L. Peterson, 1989, 'The Resiliency of the High-Yield Bond Market: The LTV Default', *Journal of Finance*, **44**, 1085–1097.

Roach, S., 1989, 'Living with Corporate Debt', *Journal of Applied Corporate Finance*, **2**, 19–29.

Ryan, P. J., 1990, 'Junk Bonds – Opportunity Knocks?', *Financial Analysts Journal*, **46** (3), 13–16.

APPENDIX 13A Simple equations for bond pricing

In this appendix, we develop bond-valuation formulas that can be programmed easily in a spreadsheet. Since we present bond-pricing equations that can be placed in a single cell of a spreadsheet, sensitivity analysis (such as the graphs presented in this chapter and the next) can be performed easily.

When we have a bond that never matures (for example, the British Consol or preferred stock), we can employ the Geometric Series Theorem,[19] which states that the present value of an infinite stream of $1 payments discounted at y is worth $1/y$. That is,

$$P_p = \sum_{t=1}^{\infty} \frac{1}{(1+y)^t} = \frac{1}{y} \qquad (13A.1)$$

where P_p is the price of a perpetual bond or perpetuity (a bond with no maturity) and y is the yield to maturity.

Thus, a perpetuity, which is a security that offers an infinite stream of cash flows (such as preferred stock or consol bonds), is worth the payment amount divided by the yield to maturity.

Using the geometric series theorem, the n period bond-pricing equation can be rewritten as:[20]

$$P = C\left\{\frac{1}{y} - \frac{1}{y}\left[\frac{1}{(1+y)^n}\right]\right\} + \frac{Par}{(1+y)^n}$$

Factoring $1/y$, we have

$$P = \frac{C}{y}\left[1 - \frac{1}{(1+y)^n}\right] + \frac{Par}{(1+y)^n} \qquad (13A.2)$$

Using Equation 13A.2, we can compute, for instance, the bond price of a $1000 par, 10% coupon bond with 30 years to maturity when yield to maturity is 12%:

$$P_{30\text{-year, }12\%\text{ yield}} = \frac{\$100}{0.12}\left[1 - \frac{1}{(1+0.12)^{30}}\right] + \frac{\$1000}{(1+0.12)^{30}}$$

$$= \$833.3333(1 - 0.03338) + \$33.37792 \cong \$838.90$$

Equation 13A.2 applies to annual coupon bonds at a coupon payment date. Using a similar approach for the more popular semiannual bonds and also finding the price at times other than the coupon payment date, we have the following bond-pricing equation:[21]

---

[19] Formally, the geometric series theorem states $\sum_{t=1}^{\infty} ax^t = a\dfrac{x}{1-x}$, where $x < 1$. In the case of bonds, $x = 1/(1+y)$.

[20] The first summation sign of Equation 13A.1 can be viewed as two infinite series, one starting today less one starting at period n.

[21] Writing Equation 13A.3 in this manner facilitates developing spreadsheet applications because the price of the bond can be input in a single cell of a spreadsheet. The alternative way to express this same price is as given in Equation 13.1. However, Equation 13.1 cannot be programmed easily into spreadsheets.

$$P = \left(1 + \frac{y}{2}\right)^{f} \left\{ \frac{2C}{y} \left[1 - \frac{1}{\left(1 + \frac{y}{2}\right)^{n}} \right] + \frac{Par}{\left(1 + \frac{y}{2}\right)^{n}} \right\} \tag{13A.3}$$

where f is the fraction of the semiannual period since the last coupon payment, n is the number of coupon payments, C is the semiannual amount of coupon paid, and y is the annualised yield to maturity.

For example, consider using closing prices observed on 4 October 1994 for the 9% coupon, 15 November 1996, US Treasury notes with ask yield of 6.00% and quoted asked price of 105.27. The coupon is paid semiannually on 15 May and 15 November. Thus, we have the following inputs:

$C = \$45$, namely $0.5 \times 0.09 \times \$1000$;
$y = 0.06$;
$n = 5$, number of coupon payments left from 4 October 1994 up to 16 November 1996;
$f = 142/184 \cong 0.77$, where 142 is the number of days from 15 May through 4 October and 184 is the number of days from 15 May through 15 November;
$Par = \$1000$.

Working through Equation 13A.3, we have

$$P = \left(1 + \frac{0.06}{2}\right)^{142/184} \left\{ \frac{2 \times \$45}{0.06} \left[1 - \frac{1}{\left(1 + \frac{0.06}{2}\right)^{5}} \right] + \frac{\$1000}{\left(1 + \frac{0.06}{2}\right)^{5}} \right\}$$

$$\cong 1.023074 \left[\$1500 \left(1 - \frac{1}{1.159274} \right) + \frac{\$1000}{1.159274} \right]$$

$$= 1.023074(\$206.0867 + \$862.6088) = \$1093.35$$

APPENDIX 13B Incorporating accrued interest and partial periods

In this appendix, we illustrate how to calculate the bond price by a variation of Equation 13A.3 and show how accrued interest affects the value of the bond. We also explain the difference between the quoted price of a bond and its value, namely the amount of cash one has to pay when one buys the bonds.

Suppose that for the popular semiannual bonds we need to price bonds on days other than a coupon payment date; the following bond-pricing equation is then required:[22]

$$P = \sum_{t=1}^{n} \frac{C}{\left(1 + \frac{y}{2}\right)^{t-f}} + \frac{Par}{\left(1 + \frac{y}{2}\right)^{n-f}} \tag{13B.1}$$

---

[22] Equation 13B.1 can be written in a manner that facilitates developing spreadsheet applications because the price of the bond can be input in a single cell of a spreadsheet. See Appendix 13A (Equation 13A.3) for this formulation.

where f is the fraction of the semiannual period since the last coupon payment, n is the number of coupon payments (namely, if we have four years with semiannual coupons, then $n = 8$), C is the semiannual amount of interest paid, and y is the annualised yield to maturity.

The factor, f, reflects the fact that two bonds that are entitled to the same future coupons and par value are not priced the same. This can happen if one bond pays its next coupon in a week and the other pays its coupon in five months. Thus, the closer the next coupon, the larger is f, and the smaller the discount factor, the larger the bond price.

Suppose $n = 4$ and we evaluate the bond exactly one second after the last coupon was paid. Then $f = 0$ and Equation 13.5 is

$$P = \sum_{t=1}^{4} \frac{C}{\left(1 + \dfrac{y}{2}\right)^{t-0}} + \frac{Par}{\left(1 + \dfrac{y}{2}\right)^{n-0}}$$

Now suppose three months have elapsed and we want to price this bond. Then, since three months is one-half of a half year ($f = 0.5$) we get

$$P = \sum_{t=1}^{4} \frac{C}{\left(1 + \dfrac{y}{2}\right)^{t-1/2}} + \frac{Par}{\left(1 + \dfrac{y}{2}\right)^{n-1/2}}$$

Thus, we see that incorporating the fractional periods alters the original formulation in a minor way. Note that for a given number of remaining coupons, the closer we are to the next coupon payment date, the larger the value of f, and, as expected, the price of the bonds goes up, since there is less discounting.

Let us illustrate this calculation with a US Treasury note used in Appendix 13A. Consider using closing prices observed on 4 October 1994, for the semiannual 9% coupon note that matures on 15 November 1996. The time line for this bond shows that the last coupon was paid on 15 May 1993, and the next coupon will be paid on 15 November 1993.

The yield was 6.00% and the quoted price was 105.27. The ask yield is the yield to maturity based on the asked price and is reported in the financial press. Thus, we have the following inputs:

$C = \$45$, namely, $0.5 \times (0.09 \times \$1000)$;
$y = 0.06$;
$n = 5$, number of coupon payments left;
$f = 142/184$, where 142 is the number of days from 15 May 1994 to 4 October 1994, and 184 is the number of days from 15 May through 15 November 1994;
$Par = 1000$

Working through Equation 13B.1, we have

$$P = \sum_{t=1}^{5} \frac{\$45}{\left(1 + \dfrac{0.06}{2}\right)^{t-142/184}} + \frac{\$1000}{\left(1 + \dfrac{0.06}{2}\right)^{5-142/184}}$$

$$P = \frac{\$45}{\left(1 + \dfrac{0.06}{2}\right)^{1-142/184}} + \frac{\$45}{\left(1 + \dfrac{0.06}{2}\right)^{2-142/184}} + \frac{\$45}{\left(1 + \dfrac{0.06}{2}\right)^{3-142/184}}$$

$$+ \frac{\$45}{\left(1 + \dfrac{0.06}{2}\right)^{4-142/184}} + \frac{\$45 + \$1000}{\left(1 + \dfrac{0.06}{2}\right)^{5-142/184}}$$

Calculating the present value of each component, we get

$$P = \$44.6974 + \$43.3955 + \$42.1316 + \$40.9045 + \$922.2256 = \$1093.35$$

This is slightly different from what we calculated in Appendix 13A, due to rounding.

Note that if we made this calculation one second before 15 November 1994, $f = 184/184 = 1$ and $t - f = 1 - 1 = 0$ (when $t = 1$), and we immediately get the $45. On the other hand, if we make the calculation one second after 15 May 1994, $f = 0/182$ and $t - f = 1$ ($n = 4$), and we get a simple discounting with no correction for f.

How do we reconcile this result with the quoted asked price of 105.27 reported in the *Wall Street Journal*? The answer is accrued interest. Bond prices are quoted without accrued interest, whereas the pricing formula incorporates accrued interest. To get the quoted price we have to deduct accrued interest. Accrued interest is found by multiplying the fraction of the semiannual coupon period that has elapsed (f) by the coupon amount (C). Therefore, the quoted price will be as follows:

$$\text{Quoted price} = P - \text{accrued interest} = P - fC = \$1093.35 - [(142/184) \times \$45]$$
$$= \$1093.35 - (0.77 \times \$45) = \$1093.35 - 34.65 = \$1058.70$$

Again, how can we reconcile this with the 105.27 quoted price? Bonds are quoted based on $100 par and in 32nds. Converting the ask quote, we have

$$\text{Actual quoted price} = 10(105 + 27/32) = \$1058.44$$

(where 10 is a figure that makes the bonds based on $1000 par rather than $100 par). The remaining differences are attributed to the rounding of the yield to maturity.

Exhibit 13B.1 illustrates the effect of accrued interest on the market value of a bond. This pattern has important ramifications on bondholders. The bond value goes up (assuming no other changes) as each semiannual coupon payment approaches (and maturity gets shorter – moving from right to left). The bond value is increasing due to the accruing of interest. In this case, the quoted price remains the same because we assumed no change in interest rates, and bonds are quoted without accrued interest. To avoid the gyrations in price due simply to the accruing of interest, prices are quoted without accrued interest, and thus changes in bond prices better reflect changes in market conditions. When a coupon payment is made, the economic value of the bond declines by the amount of the coupon payment, but the quoted price does not change. When trading bonds, we need to account for both the quoted price as well as the accrued interest.

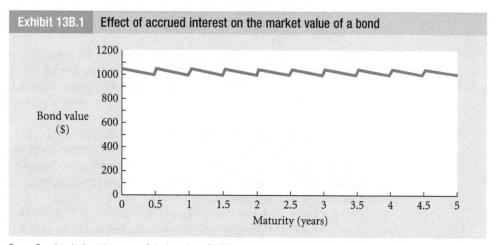

Exhibit 13B.1 Effect of accrued interest on the market value of a bond

APPENDIX 13C Methods of compounding interest rates

Suppose one bank lends at 10% a year compounded annually and another bank lends at 9.5% compounded quarterly. Which bank offers a better deal? The different methods used to compute interest and quote bond prices make bond management difficult. Computing interest might seem straightforward. Interest is just equal to the principal or initial price (P) multiplied by the interest rate (R) multiplied by the time (t). That is, simple interest (Int) is calculated as follows:

$$Int = PRt$$

For example, if one borrows $10 000 at 8% for two years, does the borrower have to pay $Int = \$10\ 000 \times 0.08 \times 2 = \$1600$ in interest? If the lender agrees to be paid by the simple interest method then the borrower pays $1600 in interest; the total loan amount to be repaid is $11 600 ($10 000 borrowed + $1600 interest).

If the lender specified that interest is compounded annually, then the loan amount or Par value (Par) to be repaid is

$$Par = P(1 + R)^t = \$10\ 000(1 + 0.08)^2 = \$11.664$$

Notice in this case that the borrower has to pay an additional $64 ($11 664 − $11 600) in interest due to compounding (for a review of compounding, see Appendix 1A). In effect, the $64 is the interest earned in the second year on the $800 interest payment made at the end of the first year.

If the lender specified multiple compounding within one year, then the loan amount to be repaid is

$$Par = P\left(1 + \frac{R}{n_p}\right)^{tn_p}$$

where n_p is the number of compounding periods within one year. For example, using the data above for the two-year loan, if the compound frequency is monthly, then the loan amount to be repaid is

$$Par = \$10\ 000\left(1 + \frac{0.08}{12}\right)^{2 \times 12} = \$11\ 729$$

Unfortunately, the differences in compounding methods are not the only characteristics separating the various methods actually employed in practice. Exhibit 13C.1 provides a brief summary of the most common compounding methods. Clearly, in order to compare the various rates quoted on different bonds, it is important to know which compounding method is being used.

For example, suppose an investor wants to invest $50 000 for six months (more specifically, 182 days) in a safe investment. A previously issued US Treasury bond with six months to maturity is offering 6% semiannual yield. A bank offers a 6%, six-month CD where interest is compounded daily on a 360-day basis. Which would the investor prefer, ignoring his or her preferences for cash flow and transaction costs?

From Exhibit 13C.1, we know the compound method for US Treasury bonds is semiannual yield (y) and for daily, 360-day CDs is the daily yield (denoted by b) with 360 rather than 365. Because we assume that the initial investment is the same, the security prices, P, are the same for all expressions. Hence, the appropriate pricing equations are

Exhibit 13C.1	Different compounding methods used in the bond market	

Compound method[a]	Pricing equation[b]	Securities using this method
Discount (d)	$P = Par_d \left(1 - \dfrac{dt}{360} \right)$	US Treasury bills
Add-on or money market (m)	$P = \dfrac{Par_m}{1 + \dfrac{mt}{360}}$	Eurodollar CDs
Bond equivalent (r)	$P = \dfrac{Par_r}{1 + \dfrac{rt}{365}}$	Makes discount or add-on rate comparable to semiannual rates
Annual (a)	$P = \dfrac{Par_a}{[1 + a]^{t/365}}$	Not used widely outside academia
Semiannual (y)	$P = \dfrac{Par_y}{\left(1 + \dfrac{y}{2} \right)^{2t/365}}$	US Treasury bonds, corporate bonds
Daily[c] (b)	$P = \dfrac{Par_b}{\left(1 + \dfrac{b}{365} \right)^{t}}$	Bank securities and mortgages
Continuous (c)	$P = Par_c \times e^{-c(t/365)}$	Bank securities such as CDs are used with options

[a] Letters in parentheses denote the interest rate, which is expressed in decimal terms.
[b] P represents the current price or the amount of the original loan, Par represents the par value of the bond or the amount that has to be paid back at the end of the period (the subscript just denotes the compounding method), t is the number of calendar days in the loan period, and d, m, r, a, y, b and c all represent quoted interest rates by various methods.
[c] Sometimes 360 is used instead of 365.

Source: From Livingston, Miles, *Money and Capital Markets: Financial Instruments and their Uses*, 1st edn, © 1990. Reprinted by permission of Pearson Education, Inc., Upper Saddle River, NJ.

$$P = \frac{Par_y}{\left(1 + \dfrac{y}{2} \right)^{2t/365}} \quad \text{Treasury bond}$$

$$P = \frac{Par_b}{\left(1 + \dfrac{b}{360} \right)^{t}} \quad \text{360-day CDs}$$

Since we invested $50 000 in both contracts in this example, our preference will depend on which security will have the largest payoff at the end. Restating both equations in terms of par value and recalling that these are six-month securities ($t = 182$), we have

$$Par_y = P \left(1 + \frac{y}{2} \right)^{2t/365} \quad \text{Treasury bond}$$

$$Par_b = P \left(1 + \frac{b}{360} \right)^{t} \quad \text{360-day CDs}$$

where Par_y is the amount paid back at the end of the period with semiannual compounding, Par_b is the amount paid back at the end of the period with compounding on a daily basis with a 360-day year, P is the price paid today, y is the semiannual compounding interest rate, and b is the compounding on a daily basis with a 360-day year.

In our example, $y = b$ and is 6%. Computing the future value of these two investments, we have

$$Par_y = \$50\ 000\left(1 + \frac{0.06}{2}\right)^{2\times182/365} = \$51\ 496$$

$$Par_b = \$50\ 000\left(1 + \frac{0.06}{360}\right)^{182} = \$51\ 540$$

Thus, although the quoted rates are the same, the proceeds from the investment in the bank CD are $44 higher, indicating a clear preference for the bank CD. We see that the quoted interest rate must be accompanied by a statement regarding how interest is being compounded, otherwise the rate is not precise.

CHAPTER 14

Bonds: analysis and management

Investment in the News 14

Balancing risk and return in volatile market conditions

Bond funds may be among the best plays around with their short-term versions offering the best balance between returns and risk associated with eventual economic recovery.

According to Morningstar, the mutual fund research firm, domestic equity funds over the past 12 months are down an average of 15.26 per cent. However, the average bond fund is up a solid 7.89 per cent. The Investment Company Institute, the mutual fund industry clearing house, reports that investors poured a net Dollars 36.08 bn into bond funds in the first half of the year compared with a net outflow of more than Dollars 40 bn during the same period last year. But with debt securities having already rallied for the better part of the past year, the overlying concern is how much steam do they have left?

Bond rallies are driven by interest rate cuts, and the Fed Funds rate currently stands at a low level of 3.75 per cent. The last time they broke below 3 per cent was at the end of 1993. But with rates having dropped so precipitously since the beginning of the year, the Fed may be inclined to wait a while before priming the economy any further. Long-term yields even suggest that we may not be far from a monetary tightening. Since the end of March, 10-year Treasury rates have risen nearly 50 basis points. While their August 3 yield was 24 basis points below the July 5 peak of 5.44 per cent, the overall trend on the long end of the yield curve is startling in contrast with the Fed's aggressive moves. 'At this stage I don't expect the Fed to cut rates by more than another 25 basis points,' explains Gerlad Thunelius, director of the taxable fixed income group at Dreyfus in New York, 'suggesting that we are now seeing the bearish flattening of interest rates which typically precedes a recovery.'

If the bottom of the economic cycle is near, then short-term bond funds would be the preferred place to be. The reasons are simple. The shorter duration of a bond or bond fund, the lower the volatility. While this is not of particular importance when rates are stable, it is when rates begin to rise. While the price of all fixed-income instruments will decline as interest rates increase, a shorter-term maturity will keep a bond's price closer to par. And because a portfolio of short-term bonds matures more rapidly than bonds in a longer-term fund, short-term bond fund managers are sooner able to reload with higher-yielding debt.

Source: Eric Uhlmeyer, 'Balancing Risk and Return In Volatile Market Conditions', *Financial Times*, 21 August 2001.

After studying this chapter, you should be able to:

1 List the basic principles of bond pricing.

2 Explain how duration is used to minimise interest-rate risk and to quantify interest rate risk.

3 Explain why, for some bonds, convexity is needed in addition to duration for managing interest-rate risk.

4 Describe passive bond-management strategies.

5 Describe active bond-management strategies.

As discussed in the previous chapter, bond prices are determined by market interest rates, and interest-rate fluctuations generally cause bond prices to change. Investment in the News 14 reports on the large gains to bond investors due to falling interest rates during the economic recession at the beginning of the 2000s. To limit the risk of losing money if interest rates rise when the economic recovers, investors may want to invest in bonds with a shorter-term maturity; such bonds have a relatively low interest-rate sensitivity. The goal of this chapter is to analyse the risk associated with changes in the interest rates and to find out how investors can develop strategies to manage interest-rate risk. The investigation begins by introducing some basic bond-pricing principles. Next, these principles are used to explain duration and convexity, two risk measures that are commonly used in the process of managing the interest-rate risk of bond portfolios. Finally, we discuss various bond-management strategies that employ the duration and convexity measures.

14.1 Bond-pricing principles

This chapter's investigation of bond-pricing principles begins with the basic bond-pricing equation that was introduced in the previous chapter. The price of a bond is the present value of all future coupon payments plus the par value discounted to the present at the yield to maturity:

$$P = \sum_{t=1}^{n} \frac{C}{(1+y)^t} + \frac{Par}{(1+y)^n} \tag{14.1}$$

where P is the current market price of the bond, n is the number of coupon payments left, C is the coupon paid each period, Par is the face value of the bond (payment at maturity), and y is the *periodic* yield to maturity.[1] Equation 14.1 can be used to identify specific relationships among the factors that determine interest rate risk. In Section 14.2, these bond-pricing principles will be used to develop two risk measures that are commonly used in interest-rate risk management: duration and convexity.

---

[1] For example, if this is a semiannual bond with an annual yield to maturity of 10%, then the semiannual yield is $y = 0.1/2$, or 5%. Note that the precise semiannual yield is $\sqrt{1.1} - 1 = 0.048809$, or roughly 4.88%. However, because practitioners commonly ignore the compounding effect when they switch from semiannual yields to annual yields, we adhere to their simple method of calculating periodic yields.

We stress that Equation 14.1 applies for straight bonds without significant default risk (Treasuries and investment-grade corporate bonds). For such bonds, the cash flows (coupon payments and par value) are fully predictable and the bonds are exposed only to the risk of interest-rate changes. The equation does not apply for bonds with embedded options (such as call and conversion features) and for bonds with significant default risk (speculative bonds). Such bonds are exposed to risks other than interest-rate risk, for example risks related to the financial health of the issuing company.

14.1.1 Principle 1: bond prices change with the passage of time

The first bond-pricing principle is that the price of a bond – not just its quoted price but also its value including accrued interest – changes with the passage of time. That is, bond prices change as the number of coupon payments left (n) falls and as the time left to receiving the payments shortens. Exhibit 14.1 illustrates the change in bond price that occurs with three different assumed yields to maturity. All three bonds are characterised by a 10% semiannual coupon rate, $1000 par value and 20 years to maturity. For simplicity, assume that the yield to maturity does not change over the 20-year period. These bonds differ in their yield to maturity; they have 8, 10 and 12% yields to maturity. These various yields could be due to differences in risk. The 10% yield bond is the essentially flat line at the par value. This bond's price moves up because of the accruing of interest. At a coupon payment date, the price drops back to $1000. When a bond has a coupon rate of 10% and a yield to maturity of only 8%, it trades at a premium above par, because the coupon rate is higher than the yield to maturity.

| Exhibit 14.1 | Bond prices and the passage of time for different yields to maturity (spikes due to the coupon accrual) |

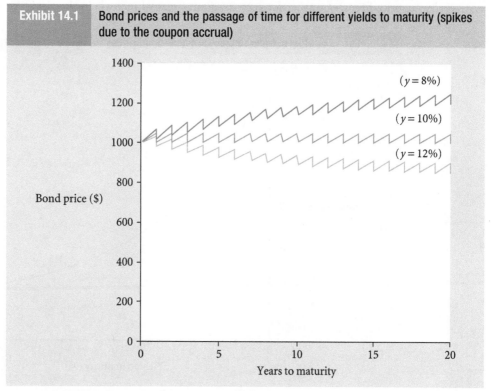

Source: From *Introduction to Investments*, 2nd edn, by Levy. © 1999. Reprinted with permission of South-Western, a division of Thomson Learning: www.thomsonrights.com. Fax 800 730-2215.

That is, the price is greater than the par value. As time to maturity becomes shorter, there are fewer coupon payments to be paid, and the premium declines. Indeed, this bond's price drifts downward over time, and it is redeemed at the par value. Similarly, a bond trading at a discount (when $C = 10\%$ and $y = 12\%$) drifts upward over time. Hence, bond prices change with the passage of time. Of course, the 10% yield, 10% coupon-paying bond has a par value equal to the bond price; the price is constant, apart from the small spikes reflecting the accruing of interest.

Investors analysing a particular bond must assess the trade-off between a bond's current price and its coupon rate. Premium bonds with high coupon rates experience declining prices in the future, whereas discount bonds with low coupon rates experience rising prices in the future.

14.1.2 Principle 2: bond prices are related inversely to the yield to maturity

After a bond is issued, the interest rate in the economy may change (for example, because of a change in the rate of inflation) and, thus, the yield on bonds changes. As discussed in the previous chapter, for a given coupon rate and a given time to maturity, bond prices are related inversely to the yield to maturity. Exhibit 14.2 illustrates this relationship for a $1000 par bond having a 20-year length to maturity and a 10% semiannual coupon rate. The resulting curve is convex – that is, it is curved away from the origin. As yields to maturity fall below 10%, the price rises at an increasing rate; as yields to maturity rise above 10%, the price falls at a decreasing rate.

The data in Exhibit 14.3 also show the convex relationship graphed in Exhibit 14.2. Consider the data for the bond with 20 years to maturity. Notice that the decline in the bond price becomes smaller for each 2.5% incremental increase in the yield. For example, when

| Exhibit 14.2 | Convex relationship between bond prices and yield to maturity |

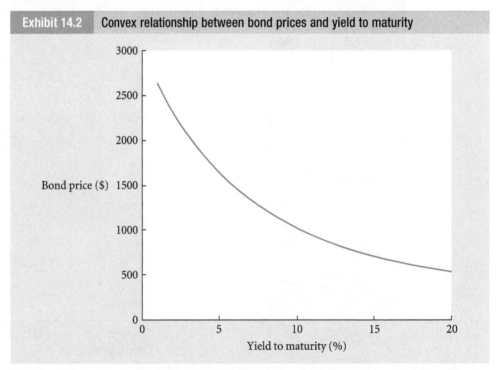

Exhibit 14.3	Prices ($) of a 10% coupon bond for different maturities and yields to maturity				
Years to maturity	Yield to maturity (%)				
	5	7.5	10	12.5	15
1	1048	1024	1000	977	955
2	1094	1046	1000	957	916
3	1138	1066	1000	939	883
4	1179	1085	1000	923	854
5	1219	1103	1000	909	828
10	1390	1174	1000	859	745
15	1523	1223	1000	832	705
20	1628	1257	1000	818	685
25	1709	1280	1000	810	676
30	1773	1297	1000	805	671
∞	2000	1333	1000	800	667

Source: From *Introduction to Investments*, 2nd edn, by Levy. © 1999. Reprinted with permission of South-Western, a division of Thomson Learning: www.thomsonrights.com. Fax 800 730-2215.

the yield rises from 5 to 7.5%, the price falls by $371 ($1 628 − $1 257). However, when the yield rises from 12.5 to 15%, the price falls by only $133 ($818 − $685). The explanation for this is that the percentage change in interest rates from 5 to 7.5% (a 50% increase) is much greater than the percentage increase from 12.5 to 15% (a 20% increase). Thus, the price–yield relationship is convex – that is, it has the kind of curve shown in Exhibit 14.2.

14.1.3 Principle 3: the longer the maturity, the more sensitive the bond's price to changes in the yield to maturity

The relationship between bond prices and changes in yield to maturity is different for various bond maturities. Specifically, for a given coupon at a given yield to maturity, the prices of longer-maturity bonds are more sensitive than the prices of short-maturity bonds to changes in the yield to maturity.[2] Exhibit 14.4 illustrates the differences in price for bonds having 10-year, 20-year and 30-year maturities. (Here $n = 20$, 40 and 60, where n is the number of coupon payments with semiannual coupons.)

Notice that all three bonds trade at par (the coupon rate on all three bonds is 10%) when the yield to maturity is 10%. Thus, we assume that the coupon rate is constant and consider the effect of different maturities (n) for changing yields to maturity. As yields change in either direction from $y = 10\%$, the 30-year ($n = 60$) bond's price experiences the largest price change. In contrast, the 10-year ($n = 20$) bond experiences the least amount of price change. Notice in Exhibit 14.3 that when the yield falls from 10 to 5%, the price of the 30-year bond rises to $1773, whereas the price of the 10-year bond rises to only $1390. We can conclude that short-term bonds are less volatile than long-term bonds for equivalent changes in yield to maturity.

The explanation for this phenomenon is straightforward: the longer an investor is locked in a contract (the bond's maturity) that pays, say, 10% a year when the market interest rate is

---

[2] This is true as long as the coupon is unchanged. If two bonds have different coupons, then their duration rather than their maturity measures the sensitivity of the bonds' price to changes in the interest rate. See the discussion in Section 14.2.

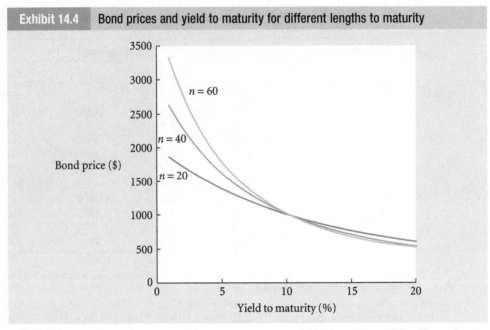

Exhibit 14.4 Bond prices and yield to maturity for different lengths to maturity

Source: From *Introduction to Investments*, 2nd edn, by Levy. © 1999. Reprinted with permission of South-Western, a division of Thomson Learning: www.thomsonrights.com. Fax 800 730-2215.

only 8%, the larger the gain in present value terms (the price of the bond). Similarly, the longer the investor is locked in a contract that pays 10% when the market interest rate is 12%, the larger the loss.

Practice box

Problem   Suppose you have a bond with $n = 10$ years to maturity that pays an annual coupon of $100 every year. The par value is $1000. Determine the bond's price for the following yields to maturity: 2.5%, 5.0%, 7.5%, 10%, 12.5%, 15.0% and 17.5%. How would you change your answer if the bond is a zero-coupon bond?

Solution   Using Equation 14.1, the following bond prices can be determined when $n = 10$, $Par = 1000 and $C = 100:

Yield to maturity (%)	Price of coupon bond ($)	Price of zero-coupon bond ($)
2.5	1656.40	781.20
5.0	1386.09	613.91
7.5	1171.60	485.19
10.0	1000.00	385.54
12.5	861.59	307.95
15.0	749.06	247.18
17.5	656.87	199.35

We see from this example that the higher the yield to maturity, the less sensitive the bond price to the changes in the yield to maturity.

14.1.4 Principle 4: the sensitivity of the price of a bond to changes in the yield to maturity increases at a decreasing rate with the length to maturity

Although longer-term bonds are more sensitive to changes in yield to maturity, this sensitivity declines for longer maturities. Exhibit 14.5 compares the price difference between five-year and ten-year bonds with the price difference between 25-year and 30-year bonds for various yields to maturity. Initially, the bonds had 10% yields. Now check the price difference of two bonds when the interest rates change (see Exhibit 14.3). Note that the price difference between a five-year bond and a ten-year bond, with a yield to maturity of 15%, is $83 ($828 − $745), whereas the price difference between a 25-year bond and a 30-year bond is only $5 ($676 − $671). Notice that when moving from a 30-year bond to a perpetuity, the price difference for a 5% yield to maturity is $227 ($2000 − $1773), whereas when moving from a one-year bond to a ten-year bond, the price difference is $342 ($1390 − $1048). In Exhibit 14.5, the dark blue line represents the price difference between 10% coupon bonds that have five and ten years to maturity – namely, $P(\text{ten-year}) - P(\text{five-year})$. The pale blue line represents the price difference between 10% coupon bonds that have 25 and 30 years to maturity, i.e. $P(\text{30-year}) - P(\text{25-year})$. Thus, the price difference is much more sensitive to changes in yield to maturity for shorter-term bonds.

What can we learn from this pattern? Suppose that you are considering investing in either relatively short-term bonds (five to ten years to maturity) or long-term bonds (25–30 years to maturity). You expect changes in the interest rate, but you are uncertain of the direction of the changes. It is recommended that you devote more analysis to whether to invest in

Exhibit 14.5	Difference between bond prices for different yields to maturity for bonds of different maturities

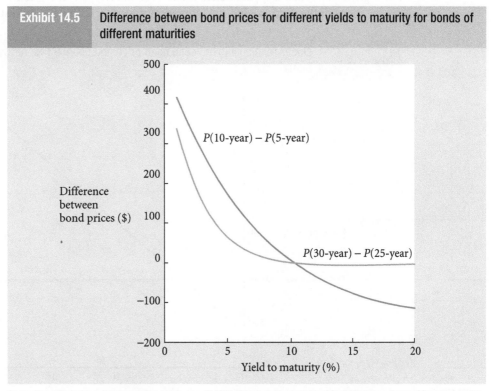

Source: From *Introduction to Investments*, 2nd edn, by Levy. © 1999. Reprinted with permission of South-Western, a division of Thomson Learning: www.thomsonrights.com. Fax 800 730-2215.

five-year or ten-year bonds than to 25-year bonds or 30-year bonds (see Exhibit 14.5). The reason is that any error in your decision has a greater impact for relatively short horizons.

14.1.5 Principle 5: there is a linear relationship between a bond's coupon rate and its price

A bond price can be formulated as a line in relation to the bond's coupon payment. As will be described below, this linear relationship is useful in creating a portfolio of bonds and in taking advantage of arbitrage opportunities in the bond market. Equation 14.1 can be rearranged to express the bond price as a linear function of the coupon payment:

$$P = aC + b \qquad (14.2)$$

where

$$a = \sum_{t=1}^{n} \frac{1}{(1+y)^t}$$

and

$$b = \frac{Par}{(1+y)^n}$$

Equation 14.2 shows that there is a linear relationship between the bond's price and its coupon. For a given par value, the parameters a and b of the straight line given in Equation 14.2 are functions of the yield (y) and the number of years (n). Exhibit 14.6 illustrates the linear

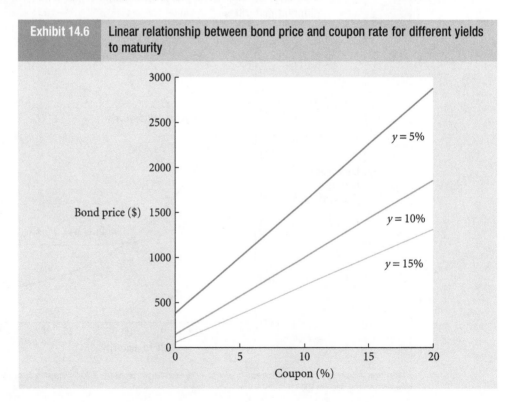

| Exhibit 14.6 | Linear relationship between bond price and coupon rate for different yields to maturity |

relationship between price and coupon for a semiannual bond with a $1000 par value and 20 years to maturity. The relationship is shown for yields to maturity of 5, 10 and 20%. Clearly, the relationship is linear for every yield level. However, the relationship is very different for different yield levels. For high yields, the intercept (the price of a zero-coupon bond or the present value of the par value) and the slope (the present value of the additonal coupon payments from increasing the coupon rate by 1%) are lower than for low yields.

Practice box

Problem

Suppose you are monitoring the US Treasury bond market, and you notice the following information about three bonds with identical maturities. The par value of the three bonds is $1000.

Bond (%)	Coupon (%)	Yield to maturity
A	3	5
B	5	4.5
C	7	5

Are there opportunities for arbitrage profits?

Solution

Note that bonds A and C have the same yield to maturity. This observation can be used to identify opportunities for arbitrage profits as long as these yields to maturity are available. Since the yield to maturity of bonds A and C is 5%, any combination of the two still yields 5%. If we can create a portfolio from bonds A and C that provides the same coupon as bond B, then we can profit by short-selling bond B and buying the portfolio of bonds, because the future cash flows are the same (the same coupon and par value). Also, the yield of bond B is lower, which implies a higher price for bond B relative to the portfolio, and hence the arbitrage profit. Namely, we get more money from the short-sale than what we need for investing in the portfolio.

To elaborate, suppose we consider investing 50% in bonds A and C and short-selling bond B. We denote the pricing equations for these bonds as follows:

$$P_A = a_A C_A + b_A$$

$$P_B = a_B C_B + b_B$$

$$P_C = a_C C_C + b_C$$

Because $y_A = y_C$ and the bonds have identical maturities, we know that $a = a_A = a_C$ and $b = b_A = b_C$. If we invest 50% ($w_A = 0.5$) in bond A and 50% ($w_C = 0.5$) in bond C, the value of the bond portfolio is

$$P = w_A P_A + w_C P_C = w_A a_A C_A + w_C a_C C_C + w_A b_A + w_C b_C$$

Therefore,

$$P = a(w_A C_A + w_C C_C) + b(w_A + w_C)$$

Because $w_A + w_C = 1$ and $w_A C_A + w_C C_C = 0.5 \times 3\% + 0.5 \times 7\% = 5\%$, we have 'synthetically' created a 5% coupon bond (or portfolio of bonds) with a yield to maturity of 5% (recall that both bonds initially had 5% yields to maturity). Bond B has the same coupon rate as the portfolio, but a lower yield to maturity of 4.5%. Thus, bond B will sell at a higher price. If we short-sell bond B and use the proceeds to buy the portfolio described previously, we will capture the difference in prices between bond B and the portfolio. The gain from the arbitrage will depend on the maturity of the bonds. (If we assume ten-year bonds, then the gain will be $40. The $40 gain reflects the price of a 4.5% yield bond minus the price of a 5% yield bond, i.e. $1040 – $1000.) At the same time, all future cash flows required from short-selling bond B will be provided by the portfolio (the 5% coupon payments and the par value). Thus, the net future cash flow is zero at all dates, and the current cash flow is positive, which implies that an arbitrage profit is feasible. In equilibrium, this profit will vanish, because the price of bond B will fall, and the price of bonds A and C will rise. However, quick investors can benefit from a temporary disequilibrium in the bond market.

Note that we decided to invest 50% in bond A and 50% in bond C, thus making the average coupon rate 5%, the same as with bond B. If bond C had had a coupon rate of 8%, then we would have had to invest different proportions in bonds A and C to get 5%. Specifically, we would have to solve

$$5\% = w_C \times 8\% + (1 - w_C) \times 3\%$$

which works out to be an investment of 40% in bond C and 60% in bond A. Thus, in this case there is an opportunity for arbitrage profits.

Exhibit 14.7 presents a numerical example demonstrating the relationship between the percentage change in the bond price and the change in the yield to maturity for various coupon levels. The percentage change in the bond's price for given changes in yield is lower for higher-coupon bonds. For example, for the 5% coupon bond, when the yield to maturity falls

| Exhibit 14.7 | Effect of changes in yield to maturity for different coupon levels for 20-year, semiannual bonds |

Annual yield to maturity	Coupon rate					
	5%		10%		15%	
	Price ($)	Change[a] (%)	Price ($)	Change[a] (%)	Price ($)	Change[a] (%)
0	2000	100	3000	84	4000	77
5	1000	75	1628	63	2255	58
10	571	54	1000	46	1429	43
15	370	39	685	34	1000	32
20	267		511		756	

[a] Change is the percentage change in the price for a given change in the yield to maturity. Thus, the percentage figures correspond to a decline from 20% yield to 15% yield, then to a decline from 15 to 10%, and so on. Because we start with a 20% yield, all percentage changes are positive.

from 5 to 0%, the percentage change is 100% (i.e. ($2000 − $1000)/$1000). Recall that for a 5% coupon, 20-year bond, you receive $50 × 20 = $1000 in coupon payments. Hence, with 0% yields, the price of the bond is $2000 ($1000 interest plus the $1000 par value). For a 15% coupon bond, the percentage price change is 77% for the same change in the yield from 5 to 0%.

Thus, if you were anticipating a decline in interest rates, you would buy lower-coupon bonds. (Compare any given line in Exhibit 14.7.) The reason for this decision is that for lower-coupon bonds, you receive your payments further in the future, and changes in interest rates will have a greater impact. Alternatively, for higher coupon rates, you are 'paid back' sooner, and hence changes in rates do not have as great an impact.

In summary, bond prices change just with the passage of time; that is, they 'drift' toward their par value. Bond prices also are related inversely to changes in interest rates, and this relationship is more pronounced for longer maturities. However, the percentage change in bond prices in response to changes in yields declines for longer and longer maturities. Bond prices are also related linearly to coupon rates, which allows for arbitrage trading and the synthetic creation of the coupon an investor desires. Of course, in equilibrium, the arbitrage profit vanishes. Finally, the higher the coupon rates, the less sensitive the bond is to changes in yield to maturity.

Hence, if bond investors forecast an increase in overall yields, then they will first want to move into short-term bonds, because the prices of short-term bonds depreciate less than long-term bonds if yields rise. In addition, investors will want to invest in high-coupon bonds – perhaps synthetically creating the coupon level they desire – because the higher the coupon rate, the lower the capital loss on bonds due to an increase in the interest rate. Of course, for bond issuers, the situation is the reverse. Expecting increasing yields, they will want to buy back their outstanding low-coupon, long-maturity bonds, and they will want to issue new low-coupon, long-maturity bonds. After all, if yields rise, then the present value of their liabilities will depreciate more if the liabilities are more sensitive to yield changes. Connecting Theory to Practice 14.1 illustrates this point.

→ **Connecting Theory to Practice 14.1**

Low rates prompt bond buybacks

With costs of borrowing close to record lows and investors hungry for new corporate bond issues, European companies are taking advantage of the market conditions to extend the maturity of their debt and lock in the lower interest rates. One result of this has been an increase in the number of bond buybacks. Several companies have announced buybacks in the past few weeks including Deutsche Telekom, the oilfield services company Schlumberger and the telcos group Alcatel. Behind the scenes, bankers also report an increase in repurchase activity in the open market.

'Rating agencies like seeing maturities pushed out, particularly in the case of investment grade companies with lower credit ratings,' said May Busch, a managing director at Morgan Stanley. 'From an issuer standpoint this is a very good time to do it, because of how low rates are on an absolute basis, and how much demand there now is in the euro market for longer duration.' With yields as low as they are, investors are increasingly hungry for debt in the 10 to 20 year maturity range, because it pays more than shorter dated debt.

Buybacks do not always result in an immediate boost to the financial statements. If a heavily indebted company has junk bonds trading at 50 cents on the dollar but carried on the balance

▶

sheet at 100, buying them back can have a dramatic impact on its debt to equity ratio. But the pattern is often different for the healthier borrowers. Low interest rates mean most companies have seen their bond prices rise. And investors require a premium to persuade them to part with the paper. A buyback above par usually means recognising a loss on the income statement at first, with the cost benefits kicking in later years. Still, 'most investors would view that sort of loss very differently from some unexpected loss on the operating side. Usually investors will recognise that it's a smart thing for the company to be doing if the overall impact is justified,' said Michael Saron, director of fixed income at CSFB.

Source: Adrienne Roberts, 'Low Rates Prompt Bond Buybacks', FT.com site, 19 June 2003.

→ Making the connection

This article reports on a recent trend among corporate bond issuers to buy back their out-standing low-coupon, long-maturity bonds, and to issue new low-coupon, long-maturity bonds, so as to exploit the currently low market interest rates. Of course, if the bond market is efficient, then such restructuring of debt does not increase the value of the companies (in fact, the value may decrease due to the transaction costs involved in buying back and issuing bonds). After all, the firms will have to pay a relatively high market price for the outstanding bonds since the interest rates are low. In addition, if the new bonds have a longer duration, then the yield is generally higher than for the outstanding bonds (recall that the yield curve is typically upward-sloping). Hence, the proceeds of issuing the bonds will be relatively low. However, the companies may think that the market is inefficient and that they can exploit their superior view of future interest rates. Alternatively, as discussed in this article, the restructuring of debt may be a means to improve financial statements for some companies.

14.2 Duration

How can we quantify the interest-rate risk of a given bond portfolio for a given bond investor? Is there a way to reduce or eliminate this risk? To answer these questions, we have to take a closer look at the effect of an interest-rate change on the value of bond portfolios at different points in time. We need to distinguish between two competing effects, the price effect and the reinvestment effect. The relative importance of these two effects depends critically on the length of the holding period of the bond investor. In fact, there is a holding period for which the two effects cancel each other out and the interest rate risk is zero. The length of this hold-ing period is known as the duration of the bond portfolio.

An increase in interest rates has the immediate effect of reducing the price of a bond, a phenomenon known as the price effect. However, when interest rates rise, investors can make more money on the new opportunities offering a higher interest rate. Investors who own coupon bonds can reinvest the coupon payments at a higher rate even though the bond's price falls. Thus, a rise in the interest rate results in a higher reinvestment rate for the coupon payments, a phenomenon known as the reinvestment effect. (This reinvestment effect does not exist for zero-coupon bonds.) In contrast, a fall in interest rates causes bond prices to rise. Reinvest-ment opportunities offer less attractive rates. In this case, the price and reinvestment effects have the opposite effects on bond investments than they do when market interest rates rise.

The holding period determines whether the price effect is greater than the reinvestment effect, regardless of the direction of the change in market interest rates. An investor who plans to hold the bond for only one day would be concerned exclusively with the price effect. For a one-day holding period, the investor does not reinvest any cash flow and therefore does not gain or lose from the reinvestment effect. However, if an investor plans to hold the bond until it matures, then only the reinvestment effect matters. The higher the coupon rate, the greater the reinvestment effect. (Because the investor will receive the par value of the bonds at maturity, assuming no default risk, there is no concern about the path the price takes to maturity, and the investor is concerned solely with the reinvestment of the coupons.) Finally, if an investor holds the bond until it matures and it pays no coupon, the investor is not concerned with either the price effect or the reinvestment effect. Thus, the planned holding period and the bond's dispersion of future cash flows are crucial in measuring the effect of changes in the interest rate.

To illustrate the evaluation of price and reinvestment effects, suppose you purchase a four-year annual coupon bond that pays $100 each year, has a yield to maturity of 10% and has a par value of $1000. Because the coupon rate equals the yield to maturity, you know the bond is currently trading at $1000. Suppose interest rates immediately jump to 12% after you purchase the bond. Are you glad or disappointed? If your holding period is only a day, you will be disappointed, because the price will fall to $939.25 – a loss of approximately 6.1%. If you hold the bond for two years (and rates do not change again), then your $1000 investment will be worth $100 coupon payment at the end of year 2 plus $100 × (1 + 0.12) = $112 for the coupon payment paid at the end of the first year (reinvested at 12% for one year) plus $966 (the price of a two-year, 10% coupon bond with a 12% yield). The total value of the bond holding at the end of the second year is thus $1178 (i.e. $100 + $112 + $966), for an annualised rate of return of 8.5% (i.e. ($1178/$1000)$^{1/2}$ − 1). If you hold the bond for four years, then at the end of the fourth year the bond holdings will be worth

$$\$1000 + \$100 + \$100 \times (1 + 0.12) + \$100 \times (1 + 0.12)^2 + \$100 \times (1 + 0.12)^3 = \$1477.93$$

The annualised rate of return is 10.26% (i.e. ($1477.93/$1000)$^{1/4}$ − 1), which exceeds the original 10% yield. Here, we see the benefits of the additional interest with no loss due to the increase in interest rate.

Thus, for a one-day holding period, you are worse off. For a four-year holding period, you are better off. The opposite is true if interest rates decline rather than increase. Because you do not know in advance the direction of the changes in the interest rate, you are exposed to interest-rate risk. Can you eliminate this risk? Yes, you can. The price effect is strongest for short holding periods, while the reinvestment effect (which works in the opposite direction) is strongest for long holding periods. Somewhere between a holding period of one day and a holding period of the maturity of the bond, you would intuitively expect a holding period where the price effect and the reinvestment effect just offset one another. At this holding period, you should have little, if any, interest-rate risk. When rates rise, you benefit enough from the reinvestment effect to just offset the cost encountered from the price effect, provided that indeed you hold the bonds for the full holding period.

Let us examine the offsetting of price and reinvestment effects with an example. Exhibit 14.8a lists information about three bonds. The yield curve is upward-sloping, because the yield of the shortest-maturity bond (bond A) is less than the yield of the middle-maturity bond (bond B), which is less than the yield of the lowest-maturity bond (bond C): $y_A < y_B < y_C$.

Suppose you have money to invest, and you know that you will need the money back in exactly four years. What is relevant for you is the final change in your wealth at the end of four years. This is crucial in selecting your investment strategy. If you select bond A, then you incur considerable reinvestment risk; this bond matures in one year, and you will have to reinvest the cash available at the end of the first year in another bond at an unknown rate. If you select

Exhibit 14.8 **Illustration of duration and its impact on a bond's volatility**

(a) Parameters of three semiannual, default-free, $1000 par bonds

Bond	Coupon rate (%)	Yield to maturity (%)	Years to maturity	Market price ($)
A	9	9	1	1000
B	10.68	10.68	5	1000
C	11	11	10	1000

(b) Immediate price effect

Yield to maturity	Bond	Price effect (%)
Decline of 3%	A	2.87
	B	12.26
	C	20.39
No change	A	0.00
	B	0.00
	C	0.00
Rise of 3%	A	−2.75
	B	−10.61
	C	−15.89

(c) Annualised holding period annual rates of return (%)

Yield to maturity	Bond	Holding period		
		1 year	4 years	7 years
Decline of 3%	A	8.94	6.73	6.42
	B	20.05	10.71	9.40
	C	28.22	12.88	10.77
No change	A	9.00	9.00	9.00
	B	10.68	10.68	10.68
	C	11.00	11.00	11.00
Rise of 3%	A	9.06	11.26	11.58
	B	2.02	10.70	11.97
	C	−3.74	9.42	11.37

(d) Mean (%) and standard deviation of annual rate of return, assuming each scenario is equally likely

	Bond	Holding period		
		1 year	4 years	7 years
Mean	A	9.00[a]	9.00	9.00
	B	10.92	10.70	10.69
	C	11.83	11.10	11.05
Standard deviation	A	0.05[b]	1.85	2.11
	B	7.36	0.01	1.05
	C	13.06	1.41	0.25

[a] The mean for bond A is $\frac{1}{3}(8.94\%) + \frac{1}{3}(9.00\%) + \frac{1}{3}(9.06\%) = 9.00\%$.

[b] The variance for bond A is $\frac{1}{3}(8.94\% - 9.00\%)^2 + \frac{1}{3}(9.00\% - 9.00\%)^2 + \frac{1}{3}(9.06\% - 9.00\%)^2 = 0.0024$; the standard deviation is $(0.0024)^{1/2} \cong 0.05\%$.

Source: From *Introduction to Investments*, 2nd edn, by Levy. © 1999. Reprinted with permission of South-Western, a division of Thomson Learning: www.thomsonrights.com. Fax 800 730-2215.

bond C, which has a ten-year maturity, you incur considerable price risk, because you will have to sell the bond after four years. The price at the end of four years is affected greatly by the prevailing interest rates at that time (this bond will have six years left to maturity). What about bond B? In four years, bond B will have only one year left to maturity, so it will have some price risk. However, you have four years in which to incur reinvestment risk. Recall that these risks have offsetting effects.

Exhibit 14.8b shows the immediate price effect of yield changes for these three bonds under three different scenarios. Assume that the yield curve either immediately shifts down by 3%, stays the same, or immediately shifts up by 3%. A 3% shift down means that bond A now has a yield to maturity of 6% (i.e. 9% − 3%). The price risk is smallest for the one-year bond and largest for the ten-year bond. However, this does not mean that the the ten-year bond has the highest interest-rate risk. To determine the full interest-rate risk, we have to consider the reinvestment risk during the holding period in addition to price risk.

Exhibit 14.8c displays the annual holding period rates of return (the combination of the price effect and the reinvestment effect) for the three bonds and the three scenarios for three alternate holding periods: one year, four years and seven years. The yield curve shift is assumed to be immediate and permanent.[3] To compute these returns, we assume that the coupons received are reinvested in the identical yield to maturity of the bond prevailing when the coupons are received. That is, coupons from the ten-year bond are reinvested in the same ten-year bond.

Exhibit 14.9 gives the detailed calculations of one cell in Exhibit 14.8c; it calculates the rate of return of about 10.7% for bond B when rates fall by 3%. There are two parts to Exhibit 14.9.

Exhibit 14.9	Illustration of the rate-of-return calculation for a 10.68% coupon bond held for four years with a rate decline of 3%				
Time to cash flow	Value of coupons due to first four years ($)		Time to cash flow	Value of coupon of fifth year and par value ($)	
	Semiannual coupon[a]	Future value[a] (at end of 4th year) of coupon		Cash flow	Present value[b] (at end of 4th year) of coupon and par
0.5	53.40	69.5175	4.5	53.4	51.4253
1.0	53.40	66.9467	5.0	1053.4	976.9311
1.5	53.40	64.4710		Total	1028.3564
2.0	53.40	62.0869			
2.5	53.40	59.7909			
3.0	53.40	57.5799			
3.5	53.40	55.4506			
4.0	53.40	53.4000			
	Total	489.2435			

[a] Coupons are reinvested at (10.68% − 3%) = 7.68%, and on a semiannual basis at 7.68%/2 = 3.84%. For example, $53.4(1.0384) \cong 55.4506$. Similarly, $53.40 interest for seven half-year periods is worth $53.40(1.0384)^7 \cong 69.5175.
[b] Calculated at 3.84% on a semiannual basis. For example, $1053.4/(1.0384)^2 \cong 976.9311$.

[3] In practice, interest rates change every day. To simplify the analysis, we assume that interest rates change only once – immediately after the bond is purchased. We ignore any potential changes that may occur during the bond's maturity. Hence, the initial yield to maturity is earned over the entire life of the bond.

The first three columns are used to calculate the future value of the coupons received out to four years. A 10.68% coupon bond with a par value of $1000 has a semiannual coupon payment of $53.4, or $0.1068 \times 0.5 \times 1000$. The last three columns are used to calculate the present value of the cash flows received after the fourth year. The value after four years is $1517.60, or $489.2435 + $1028.3564. Hence, the semiannual rate of return is $(\$1517.60/\$1000)^{1/8} - 1 = 0.0535$, or 10.7% on an annual basis (0.0535×2), which is approximately 10.68%, the original coupon yield.

Exhibit 14.8c shows that if there is no change in the yield to maturity, then the holding period rate of return exactly equals the initial yield to maturity. If yields fall by 3%, then for a one-year holding period the ten-year bond experiences a rate of return of 28.22% due to the large appreciation in price. However, the one-year bond actually has a rate of return of 8.94% less than the original 9%, because the semiannual coupon had to be reinvested at 6% rather than 9%. If yields rise by 3%, then exactly the opposite effect occurs for the one-year holding period.

For the seven-year holding period, the reinvestment effect is more prevalent. For example, if rates fall by 3%, then the one-year bond (bond A) has to be reinvested at a lower rate. Hence, the rate of return is 6.42%.

Notice what happens at year 4 for bond B. The rates of return under all three scenarios are almost identical, at around 10.7%. Exhibit 14.8d presents the mean and standard deviation, assuming the yield curve shifts are equally probable. Notice that the standard deviation for only bond B for a four-year holding period was almost 0. The reason for this is that at four years, the price effect and reinvestment effect just offset each other for a five-year bond.

In summary, investors with a well-defined holding period should be able to invest in a bond or construct a bond portfolio that will have minimal overall interest-rate risk. Investors accomplish this result by balancing the price effect against the reinvestment effect.

To find the investment strategy that minimises the interest-rate risk, we need to consider the bond's duration. The concept of duration and its definition was first suggested by Macaulay (1938). Duration takes into account the fact that the bond's par value is paid at maturity, whereas coupon payments are paid during the life of the bond. For example, if an investor has a coupon bond with a five-year maturity, he or she does not wait five years to receive the money back; the investor receives some of it earlier as coupon payments. Duration is the average number of years investors have to wait to get their money back (in the form of coupon payments and/or par value). It is not a simple average, because the further away the cash inflow, the less weight investors give it, because it has a lower present value in comparison with the same amount of money received earlier.

The formal definition of duration is a present value-weighted average of the number of years investors wait to receive cash flows. The duration is calculated as follows:[4,5]

$$D = \sum_{t=1}^{T} t w_t \tag{14.3}$$

---

[4] Appendix 14A contains an alternative expression for duration that is easier to program in spreadsheets.

[5] Various alternative definitions of duration exist. We adhere to Macaulay's definition in this chapter. According to this definition, duration is computed using Equation 14.3a. Two commonly used alternatives are modified duration $MD = \sum_{t=1}^{T} t \times \dfrac{CF_t/(1+y)^{t+1}}{P}$ and dollar duration $DD = \sum_{t=1}^{T} t \times CF_t/(1+y)^{t+1}$. The rules for Macaulay duration can be adapted to these alternative definitions, by using the following relationship: $D = MD(1+y) = DD(1+y)/P$.

where the weight w_t is given by $w_t = PV(CF_t)/P$, and $PV(CF_t)$ is a present value,

$$PV(CF_t) = \frac{CF_t}{(1+y)^t}$$

and CF_t is the cash flow received (coupon payment or both coupon and par) at time t, P is the current market price of the bond, y is the periodic yield to maturity, and T is the bond's time to maturity (that is, the number of periods to maturity measured generally in years or half years – see next examples).

Substituting the formula for the weight w_t in Equation 14.3, we obtain the following equivalent formulation of duration:

$$D = \sum_{t=1}^{n} t \times \frac{CF_t/(1+y)^t}{P} \qquad (14.3a)$$

Because $P = \sum PV(CF_t)$, we see that duration is a weighted average of the time t when cash flows are received (where $PV(CF_t)/P$ serves as the weight). Note that for a zero-coupon bond, there is only one future cash flow; hence, $P = PV(CF_t)$, and the duration is just the time to maturity. Moving from a zero-coupon bond to a coupon-paying bond, the duration declines.

Interestingly, duration represents the length of the holding period that minimises the interest-rate risk or, put differently, the holding period that balances the price effect against the reinvestment effect. Appendix 14B provides a formal proof of this result. Hence, to minimise interest-rate risk, a bond investor should structure his or her portfolio in such a way that the duration exactly matches the length of the holding period.

Recall from the above discussion that the interest-rate risk for bond B in Exhibit 14.8 (a five-year bond with ten semiannual coupon payments of $C = \$53.40$ and a yield to maturity of $y = 0.1068/2$) is almost zero for a four-year holding period. The following computation shows that the duration for this bond is indeed roughly four years (or eight half-year periods):

$$D = \sum_{t=1}^{10} t \left[\frac{CF_t \Big/ \left(1 + \frac{0.1068}{2}\right)^t}{\$1000} \right] = \left[\frac{1}{\$1000} \sum_{t=1}^{10} \frac{tC}{(1.0534)^t} + \frac{1}{\$1000} \times \frac{10Par}{1.0534^{10}} \right]$$

$$= \left\{ 0.001 \left[\frac{1 \times 53.4}{(1.0534)^1} + \frac{2 \times 53.4}{(1.0534)^2} + \ldots + \frac{10 \times 53.4}{(1.0534)^{10}} \right] + \frac{1}{\$1000} \times \frac{10 \times \$1000}{1.0534^{10}} \right\}$$

$$\cong 0.001(\$2058 + 5944) \cong 8$$

Similar calculations reveal that the semiannual duration for the one-year bond is 1.957 years, and the duration for the ten-year bond is 12.757 half-year periods.

Exhibit 14.10 further illustrates the concept of duration for bond B. For holding periods shorter than four years, the price risk is more dominant than the reinvestment risk. The price risk declines as we increase the holding period, becasue the present value (at the end of the holding period) of the cash flows (coupon payments and par value) beyond the end of the holding period becomes smaller. For holding periods of more than four years, the reinvestment risk is more dominant. This reinvestment risk increases as we increase the holding period, because the future value (at the end of the holding period) of the coupon payments before the end of the holding period increases. For a four-year holding period, the two risks almost offset each other; hence, the standard deviation is almost zero.

Exhibit 14.10	Duration as a measure of the holding period that minimises interest-rate risk measured as the standard deviation of rates of return (holding period is assumed to be four years)

Practice box

Problem

Calculate the duration of the following two bonds. Bond A is a two-year, zero-coupon bond trading at $850 ($Par$ = $1000). Bond B is a two-year, 5% annual coupon bond trading at par (Par = $1000).

Solution

For a zero-coupon bond, the duration is equal to the maturity. Hence, the duration for bond A equals two years. For bond B, Equation 14.3 shows the following:

$$D = \left[\sum_{t=1}^{2} t\left(\frac{CF_t/(1+0.05)^t}{\$1000} \right) \right] = \frac{1}{\$1000}\left[1\left(\frac{\$50}{1+0.05} \right) + 2\left(\frac{\$1050}{(1+0.05)^2} \right) \right]$$

$$\cong \frac{1}{\$1000}(\$47.619 + \$1904.762) \cong 1.95 \text{ years}$$

Thus, the coupon payments are shown to reduce the value of duration.

Apart from the holding period that minimises interest-rate risk, duration has another application. Duration is a direct measure of the sensitivity of a bond's rate of return to changes in the yield to maturity. Thus, duration can be used as a measure of the overall sensitivity or riskiness of a bond or a bond portfolio. The following can be shown mathematically using a first-order Taylor series approximation of the relationship between price and yield to maturity:

$$D \cong -\frac{\Delta P}{P} \times \frac{(1+y)}{\Delta y} = -R(\Delta y) \times \frac{(1+y)}{\Delta y}$$

where $R(\Delta y)$ is the rate of return on the bond induced by a given change in yield to maturity (Δy).[6] Note that this is just an approximation. Rearranging the above expression yields

$$R(\Delta y) \cong -\frac{D\Delta y}{(1+y)} \tag{14.4}$$

Clearly, the larger the duration, the greater the risk due to changes in interest rates. When using duration for this purpose, Δy is assumed to be a small constant, such as ten basis points. The larger the value of Δy, the less accurate the approximation. For large changes in interest rates, we can obtain a more accurate approximation by accounting for convexity (see Section 14.3).

For example, we saw in Exhibit 14.8c that for one-year holding periods, ten-year bonds were more sensitive to interest-rate changes than were one-year bonds. We can reach the same conclusion by observing that the one-year bond has a semiannual duration of 1.957, and the ten-year bond has a duration of 12.757 half-year periods. For example, if we increase the semiannual yield by 1.5%, i.e. $\Delta y = 0.015$, then for the one-year bond and the ten-year bond we have (from Equation 14.4):[7]

$$R_{1\text{-year}}(0.015) \cong -\frac{1.957 \times 0.015}{1 + 0.045} = -0.0281$$

$$R_{10\text{-year}}(0.015) \cong -\frac{12.757 \times 0.015}{1 + 0.055} = -0.1814$$

Notice that the approximation is accurate for the one-year bond; the predicted price effect of −2.81% is very close to the actual price effect of −2.75% (see Exhibit 14.8c). However, for the ten-year bond, the approximation is less accurate; the predicted effect is −18.14%, while the actual price effect is −15.89%. This reflects that duration is not an accurate measure if the yield change is large (as is true in this example) and if the duration of the bond changes rapidly as the yield changes (as is true for the ten-year bond).

Recall that using duration as a measure of price sensitivity is just one function of duration. Duration is also used to identify the holding period at which interest-rate risk is minimised.

14.2.1 Duration principles

The following are well-known duration principles:

---

[6] Formally, duration is defined as the interest-rate elasticity of the bond price (multiplied by −1 to obtain a positive number); that is,

$$D = -\left(\frac{dP}{dy}\right)\left[\frac{(1+y)}{P}\right]$$

In this equation, $\frac{dP}{dy} = -\sum_{t=1}^{T} tCF_t/(1+y)^{t+1}$ represents the first-order derivative of the price–yield relationship.

[7] Notice that these figures include only the price effect that occurs immediately after the yield changes. To compute the change in holding period return (as in Exhibit 14.8), we also have to account for the reinvestment effect.

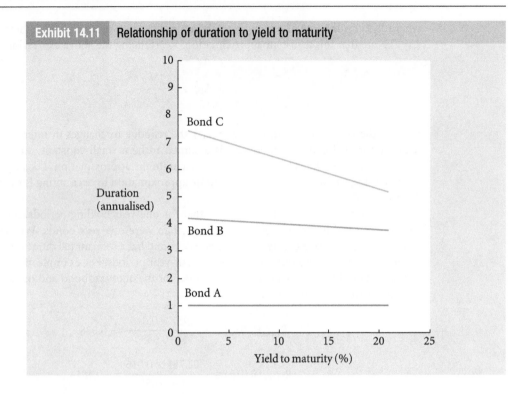

Exhibit 14.11 Relationship of duration to yield to maturity

Principle 1

Normally, duration is related inversely to yield to maturity. Recall that duration is the present value-weighted average of the number of years that investors wait to receive cash flows. For higher yields, the present value of more distant cash flows will be discounted by a greater amount. Hence, those cash flows will receive less weight, resulting in a lower duration. To illustrate the inverse relationship between duration and yield, Exhibit 14.11 shows the relationship for bonds A, B and C (as introduced in Exhibit 14.8). Note that the relationships are different for the three bonds, as the bonds have different lengths to maturity and different coupon rates. The effects of maturity and coupon are discussed below.

Principle 2

Normally, duration depends positively on the length to maturity. The longer the maturity, the more sensitive the present value of the par value becomes to yield changes. In addition, lengthening the maturity adds 'remote' coupon payments, with present values that are also very sensitive to the yield. Hence, for long maturities, duration generally is higher than for short maturities. However, there are exceptions to this rule. To understand this, recall that duration is a weighted average of the cash flows, and that the weights equal the relative discounted value of the cash flows. 'Early' inflows are not discounted so heavily as 'late' inflows, and hence the weight of the early inflows increases relative to the weight of the late outflows as the maturity increases. This effect slows the increase of duration for coupon bonds. If the yield to maturity is higher than the coupon rate, then duration will actually fall beyond some critical point. Exhibit 14.12 illustrates this point further using three five-year semiannual bonds with a 10.68% yield to maturity. Curve 1 describes the relationship between duration

Exhibit 14.12	Relationship of duration to length to maturity for bonds with different coupon rates

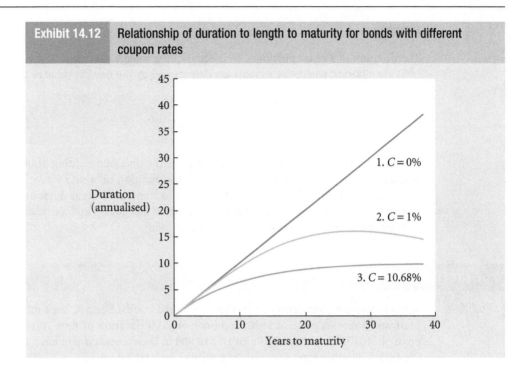

and maturity for a zero-coupon. In this case, duration is equal to maturity. Curve 2 describes a bond with a coupon that is equal to the yield to maturity (10.68%). In this case, duration is shorter than maturity; hence, curve 2 is completely below curve 1. However, the curve is still increasing. Curve 3 represents a bond whose coupon rate is 1%, far below the yield to maturity. At the beginning, as the years to maturity increase, the duration also increases. However, beyond some critical point, the weight of the par value decreases drastically, and the weight of the coupons increases (in particular, the early coupons, which are not discounted so heavily). Hence, the duration decreases.

Since duration decreases as the length to maturity decreases, the duration of a given bond portfolio normally declines over time, a pattern called the duration drift. Hence, for a given investment period, bond portfolios employing duration-based strategies must be rebalanced periodically to minimise the risk.

Principle 3

Normally, duration is related inversely to the level of coupon payments. The higher the coupon rate, the greater the weight given to the earlier cash flows (the coupon payments). Hence, the higher the coupon rate, the shorter the duration. Exhibit 14.12 illustrates this effect. For the zero-coupon bond (bond 1), duration equals maturity. For the 1% coupon bond (bond 3), duration is smaller. This effect is strongest for longer maturities, as the weight of the early cash flows then becomes very high. The duration of the 10.68 coupon bond (bond 2) is even smaller.

Principles 1, 2 and 3 are useful when an investor is altering the bond portfolio's duration. The investor who wishes to lengthen the duration should move to lower-yield, lower-coupon and longer-maturity bonds.

Principle 4

The duration of a bond portfolio, D, is equal to the weighted average of the durations of the individual bonds, where the weights are determined by the market value of the bonds:

$$D = \sum_{i=1}^{n} w_i D_i \qquad (14.5)$$

where $w_i = MV_i/MV$, MV_i is the market value of the portfolio holding of bond i, MV is the market value of the total bond portfolio, D_i is the duration of bond i, and n is the number of bonds in the portfolio. Therefore, an investor who wants a five-year duration (to manage the interest-rate risk) can mix several bonds to achieve this goal. Thus, duration can be used to manage the interest rate sensitivity of bond portfolios.

Practice box

Problem

Suppose you are considering an investment in two bonds. Bond A has a duration of eight years and a market price of $950, and bond B has a duration of four years and a market price of $1050. How should you invest $10 000 in these bonds if you have a desired holding period of seven years and wish to minimise interest-rate risk?

Solution

The duration of the bond portfolio can be found using Equation 14.5:

$$D = w_A D_A + w_B D_B = w_A D_A + (1 - w_A)D_B$$

Substituting for w_A yields

$$D = (MV_A/MV)D_A + (1 - MV_A/MV)D_B$$

Solving for MV_A yields

$$MV_A = [MV(D - D_B)]/(D_A - D_B)$$

Using the data given in the problem yields

$$MV_A = [\$10\ 000(7.0 - 4.0)]/(8.0 - 4.0) = \$7500$$

Hence, $7500 should be invested in bond A, and $2500($10 000 − $7500) should be invested in bond B.

In summary, the four principles state clearly the separate effect of each factor on duration. However, when more than one factor is changed simultaneously (for example, for a given yield, the coupon decreases and the maturity increases), the relationship between duration and years to maturity is more complex.

As discussed above, duration is not a precise measure of interest-rate sensitivity. Interest-rate risk is minimised against small changes in interest rates. The measure can be very imprecise for large yield changes. Due in part to this weakness, an additional measure known as convexity has been developed.

14.3 Convexity

As discussed above, duration can be used to measure the slope of a bond's price–yield relationship (see Exhibit 17.2). Convexity is a measure of the curvature of the price–yield relationship. It measures the degree by which the duration changes as the yield to maturity changes. For a single cash inflow CF_t that is received at time t, the duration is given by t. The convexity of the cash inflow is given by:[8]

$$\frac{t(t+1)}{(1+y)^2}$$

The formal definition of convexity is a present value-weighted average of this number:

$$C = \sum_{t=1}^{T} \frac{t(t+1)}{(1+y)^2} w_t \qquad (14.6)$$

where the weight w_t is again given by $w_t = PV(CF_t)/P$. Substituting the formula for the weight w_t in Equation 14.6, we obtain the following equivalent formulation of convexity:

$$C = \sum_{t=1}^{n} t(t+1) \frac{CF_t/(1+y)^{t+2}}{P} \qquad (14.6a)$$

For example, for bond B in Exhibit 14.8 (five years to maturity, ten semiannual coupon payments of \$53.4 and a yield of 10.68%), we may compute convexity as follows:

$$C = \sum_{t=1}^{10} \frac{t(t+1)}{(1.0543)^2} \left[\frac{CF_t \bigg/ \left(1+\dfrac{0.1068}{2}\right)^t}{\$1000} \right] = \left[\frac{1}{\$1000} \sum_{t=1}^{10} \frac{t(t+1)C}{(1.0534)^{t+2}} + \frac{1}{\$1000} \times \frac{10 \times 11 \times Par}{1.0534^{12}} \right]$$

$$= 0.001 \left\{ \left[\frac{1 \times 2 \times 53.4}{(1.0534)^3} + \frac{2 \times 3 \times 53.4}{(1.0534)^4} + \ldots + \frac{10 \times 11 \times 53.4}{(1.0534)^{12}} \right] + \frac{10 \times 11 \times \$1000}{1.0534^{12}} \right\}$$

$$\cong 0.001(\$14\ 235.397 + 58\ 921.381) = 73.157$$

Notice that this figure measures the convexity for changes of the semiannual yield. To obtain the annual convexity, we need to divide the figure by four, i.e. $73.157/4 = 18.289$.[9] Similar calculations reveal that the convexity for the one-year bond is 5.336 years, and the convexity for the ten-year bond is 202.359 years.

Recall from Equation 14.3 that duration can be used to approximate a bond's rate of return following changes in the yield to maturity. The duration-based approximation generally is accurate only for small changes in the yield. Convexity can be used to obtain a more accurate

---

[8] This term effectively is the second-order derivative of $PV(CF_t) = 1/(1+y)^t$ with respect to y, expressed as a percentage of $PV(CF_t) = CF_t/(1+y)^t$. Specifically, the second-order derivative is given by $\dfrac{d^2PV(CF_t)}{dy^2} = t(t+1)CF_t/(1+y)^{t+2}$. Dividing this term by $PV(CF_t)$ gives $\dfrac{d^2PV(CF_t)}{dy^2}/PV(CF_t) = \dfrac{t(t+1)}{(1+y)^2}$.

[9] To see this, we need to look at the term $C(\Delta y)^2$ in Equation 14.7. Define $y_a = 2y$ as the annual yield and C_a as the annual convexity. The semiannual convexity C and the annual convexity C_a are related in the following manner: $C(\Delta y)^2 = C_a(\Delta y_a)^2 = C_a(2\Delta y)^2 = 4C_a(\Delta y)^2$ or $C_a = C/4$.

approximation for large changes. The following can be shown mathematically using the first-order derivative and the second-order derivative of the bond price with respect to yield:[10]

$$R(\Delta y) \cong -\frac{D\Delta y}{(1 + y)} + \frac{1}{2} C(\Delta y)^2 \qquad (14.7)$$

Recall from our earlier discussion that the bond price is a convex function of the yield. Put differently, duration decreases as the yield increases. Therefore, convexity, or the degree of curvature of the price–yield relationship, is always positive. Hence, it follows from Equation 14.7 that the return from a yield change is always more favourable than we would expect based on duration alone.

For example, in Section 14.2, we used duration to estimate the price decrease of a one-year bond and a ten-year bond (bond A and bond C in Exhibit 14.8) following a 1.5% increase of the semiannual yield ($\Delta y = 0.015$). Combining duration with convexity, we can obtain the following estimates:

$$R_{1\text{-year}}(0.015) \cong -\frac{1.957 \times 0.015}{1 + 0.045} + \frac{1}{2} \times 5.336 \times 0.015^2 = -0.0275$$

$$R_{10\text{-year}}(0.015) \cong -\frac{12.757 \times 0.015}{1 + 0.055} + \frac{1}{2} \times 202.359 \times 0.015^2 = -0.1586$$

These computations show how convexity improves the approximation. Most notably, for the ten-year bond, the actual price change is −15.89%. Using duration only, the estimated price change is −18.14% or 2.25% lower than the actual change. Correcting for convexity yields an estimated change of −15.86, or only 0.03% lower than the true value. Corrections like these are generally needed if the yield change is large (as is true in this example) and if the duration of the bond is very sensitive to the yield level (as is true for the ten-year bond, which has a very high convexity).

As with bond prices and duration, there are some basic principles related to convexity:

Principle 1

Convexity is related inversely to yield to maturity. Recall from Exhibit 14.2 that the curvature was greater for lower yields than for higher yields. Exhibit 14.13 illustrates this point further. This exhibit shows the relationship between convexity and yield for bonds A, B and C (as introduced in Exhibit 14.8). Again, the relationships are different for the three bonds, as the bonds have different lengths to maturity and different coupon rates. The effects of the maturity and coupon are discussed below.

Principle 2

Convexity is related positively to length to maturity. Recall from Exhibit 14.4 that the curvature is greater for longer-maturity bonds. Exhibit 14.13 illustrates this point further. This exhibit shows the relationship between convexity and maturity for bonds 1, 2 and 3 (as introduced in Exhibit 14.12). For all three bonds, convexity increases as maturity increases. However, for bond 1, with a 1% coupon rate and a 10.68% yield, convexity decreases beyond a point.

---

[10] This relationship is based on taking a second-order Taylor series of the relationship between price and yield to maturity. See any standard calculus book for more information on the Taylor series.

| Exhibit 14.13 | Relationship of convexity to yield to maturity |

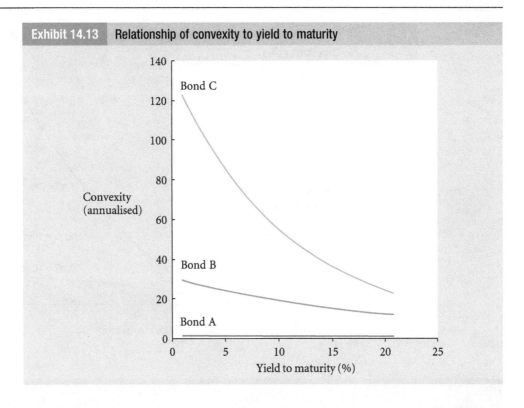

Principle 3

Convexity is related inversely to the coupon. Recall from Exhibit 14.10 that the curvature was flatter for higher-coupon bonds. Exhibit 14.14 illustrates this point further. This exhibit shows the relationship between convexity and maturity for the bonds 1, 2 and 3 (as introduced in Exhibit 14.12). The zero-coupon bond (bond 1) has the highest convexity, while bond 2, with a 10.68% coupon rate, has the lowest convexity.

These principles are useful for bond management. For example, if you wanted to lengthen duration and raise the convexity, you could move to lower-yield, lower-coupon, longer-maturity bonds.

Principle 4

The convexity of a bond portfolio, C, is equal to the weighted average of the convexity of the individual bonds, where the weights are determined by the market value of the bonds:

$$C = \sum_{i=1}^{n} w_i C_i \tag{14.8}$$

where $w_i = MV_i/MV$, MV_i is the market value of the portfolio holding of bond i, MV is the market value of the total bond portfolio, C_i is the convexity of bond i, and n is the number of bonds in the portfolio. Therefore, an investor who wants a given convexity (to manage the interest-rate risk) can mix several bonds to achieve this goal.

The tools of duration and convexity can be used in bond-portfolio management. Because these techniques are used primarily by institutional portfolio managers, we refer to them as bond managers rather than bond investors.

Exhibit 14.14	Relationship of convexity to length to maturity for bonds with different coupon rates

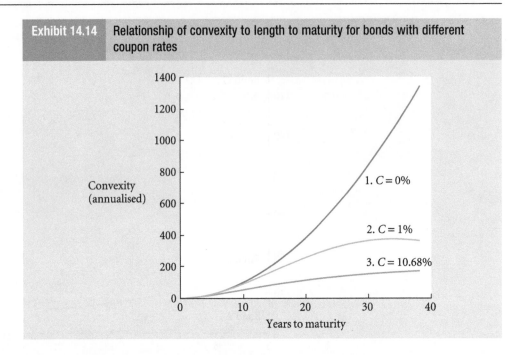

14.4 Passive bond-management strategies

Bond management can be either passive or active. In case of passive bond management, the manager does not attempt to time the market by making predictions about future interest rates and does not attempt to indentify bonds that are underpriced or overpriced. Rather, the passive manager is concerned with ensuring that the portfolio is well-diversified and/or matches the liabilities. Also, passive management tries to avoid liquidity problems and keep transaction costs to a minimum. Recall that if the bond market is efficient, and thus all bonds are fairly priced, then the process of bond-portfolio selection could be managed passively. By contrast, active bond management assumes implicitly that the bond market is not efficient and, hence, that there are excess returns to be pursued by predicting future interest-rate moves and identifying overpriced bonds and underpriced bonds.

There exist two broad classes of passive bond-management strategies: indexing strategies, which seek to replicate well-diversified bond indexes, and immunisation strategies, which construct bond portfolios in order to match the interest-rate risk of a liability portfolio. Since passive bond managers take market prices as given, they can devote most of their energy to refining the indexation or immunisation technique that they adopt.

14.4.1 Indexing

Indexing strategies create a bond portfolio to mirror the composition of a well-diversified bond market index. Recall from Chapter 6 that there are three major bond indices in the USA: the Lehman Brothers Aggregate Index, the Merrill Lynch Domestic Master Index and the Salomon Brothers Broad Investment Grade (BIG) index. While indexing is a passive strategy, assuming that bonds are priced fairly, it is by no means a simple strategy. Each of the broad bond indexes contains thousands of individual bonds. The market indices are continually rebalanced as newly issued bonds are added to the index and existing bonds are dropped from the index as their maturity falls below one year. Information and transaction costs make it practically impossible to purchase each bond in proportion to the index. The fact that bonds generate considerable cash flows (coupon and par payments) that must be reinvested further complicates the task of tracking an index. Rather than replicating the bond index exactly, indexing typically uses a stratified sampling approach. The bond market is stratified into several subcategories based on, for instance, maturity, industry and credit quality. For every subcategory, the percentage of bonds included in the market index that fall in that subcategory is computed. The bond manager then constructs a bond portfolio with a similar distribution across the subcategories. In this way, bond managers hope to match the general characteristics of the market index, without the burden of having to replicate the exact composition of the index. To measure the goodness of this approach, tracking error measures are used. The tracking error in a given period is the difference in the return of the market index and the bond portfolio tracking the market index. The lower the tracking error, the better the approximation obtained by stratified sampling.

14.4.2 Immunisation

Indexed bond managers do not try to eliminate interest rate risk but try to track a bond market index as closely as possible. An set of alternative passive bond-management strategies are known as immunisation strategies or duration-matching strategies. These strategies try to neutralise or 'immunise' the effects of interest-rate changes by creating a bond portfolio with a duration that is equal to the investment horizon. Recall from Section 4.2 that this approach ensures that the price effect and the reinvestment effect of interest-rate changes offset each other. Immunisation frequently is adopted by pension funds and life insurance companies who have to meet fixed obligations for future payment to pensioners and other beneficiaries. These institutional investors have a well-defined investment horizon: the duration of their liabilities. By contrast, indexing frequently is adopted by passive mutual funds and open-end funds who don't have such fixed obligations. This section discusses two categories of immunisation strategies: income-immunisation and price-immunisation.

In principle, all that is required for immunisation is the matching of the duration of the assets with the investment horizon. For example, one way to construct an immunised portfolio would be to purchase only zero-coupon bonds that had a maturity exactly equal to the investment horizon. However, this strategy has an important drawback. Specifically, any cash disbursements before the maturity of the zero-coupon bond (for example, payments of retirement benefits or insurance claims) may have to be paid out by selling bonds at temporarily depressed prices during periods of low market liquidity. Income immunisation strategies ensure that adequate resources are available to meet cash disbursement needs.

One appealing income-immunisation strategy is to invest in a bond portfolio that has coupon and principal payments that exactly meet the future cash needs. This approach is known as a cash-matching strategy. This strategy is totally unaffected by changes in the interest rates. However, in practice, exact cash matching is impossible because we cannot predict the cash disbursements with full accuracy, and even if we could, it would still be impossible or too expensive to buy bonds with cash flows that match exactly all individual disbursements. Also, a cash-matching strategy is very restrictive and allows very little flexibility; cash-matching may eliminate many otherwise attractive bonds because they do not have the desirable cash-flow properties.

For this reason, the horizon-matching strategy has been developed. In a horizon-matching strategy, the manager designs a portfolio that is duration-matched over the full period but cash-matched only over the short horizon. For example, the manager could cash-match only over the next 12 months to avoid having to sell during a liquidity crisis and then duration-match the remaining liabilities. Thus, the horizon-matching strategy provides the liquidity benefits for short-term liabilities of cash-matching, while avoiding the problems of implementation for long-term liabilities.

The income-immunisation strategies ensure that sufficient resources are available to meet future cash needs, regardless of changes in the interest rates. However, these strategies ignore the impact of interest-rate changes on the current market value of the bond portfolio. The current market value of the portfolio is a critical concern for bank portfolio managers, who must maintain certain levels of capital for regulatory reasons. Also, the performance of fund managers is commonly judged by the market value of the assets managed. Managers who are concerned with the preservation of the original market value of the portfolio may consider price-immunisation techniques.

Price-immunisation includes those strategies that ensure that the market value of the bond portfolio always exceeds the market value of liabilities by a specified amount. Price-immunisation strategies use convexity in addition to duration. These strategies seek to develop a portfolio that not only is duration-matched but also has the convexity of its assets exceeding the convexity of its liabilities. As long as the convexity of the assets exceeds the convexity of the liabilities, then the difference between the market value of the assets and the liabilities will grow with changes in interest rates. Also, the greater the convexity, the greater will be the gains from changes in interest rates.

It is useful to illustrate the difference between income-immunisation and price-immunisation by means of a numerical example. Consider a pension fund that has $3 million in cash and has to pay retirement benefits worth $1 million after six months, 12 months and 18 months. To meet these liabilities, the pension fund could, of course, simply hold the $3 million in cash until the benefits have to be paid out. However, this strategy is not optimal, because the yield on cash money is zero. By investing in an immunised bond portfolio, the pension fund can achieve a higher yield without additional risk. Suppose that the three zero-coupon Treasury bonds shown in Exhibit 14.15a are available in the bond market.

As before, T is used for the maturity measured in semiannual period, D is the duration, C is the convexity, P is the price and y is the yield to maturity.

To create an immunised bond portfolio for the pension fund, we must first evaluate the value and the duration of the retirement liabilities. Given the yields in Exhibit 14.15a, we can compute these figures as follows:

$$P = \$1\ m(1.05)^{-0.5} + \$1\ m(1.055)^{-1} + \$1\ m(1.06)^{-1.5} \cong \$2.84\ m$$

$$D = 1 \times \frac{\$1\ m(1.05)^{-0.5}}{\$2.84\ m} + 2 \times \frac{\$1\ m(1.055)^{-1}}{\$2.84\ m} + 3 \times \frac{\$1\ m(1.06)^{-1.5}}{\$2.84\ m} \cong 1.98$$

The objective of immunisation is to eliminate interest-rate risk by equalising the duration of the bond portfolio and the duration of the retirement liabilities. This is why the pension fund cannot simply buy the bonds with the highest yield, or bond C, which has a duration of three. What bond portfolio should the pension fund construct in order to eliminate interest rate risk? Exhibit 14.15b compares the cash-matching strategy and the price immunisation strategy.

Cash-matching in this case boils down simply to purchasing 1000 bonds of type A, 1000 bonds of type B and 1000 bonds of type C. The costs of this strategy are $1000 \times (\$975.90 + \$947.87 + \$916.31) = \$2.84$ million, leaving $3 million $-\$2.84$ million $= \$0.16$ million in cash. The future

Exhibit 14.15	Examples of immunisation strategies

(a) Available bonds

Bond	Par ($)	T	D	C	P ($)	y (%)
A	1000	1	1	1.814	975.90	5.0
B	1000	2	2	5.391	947.87	5.5
C	1000	3	3	10.680	916.31	6.0

(b) Cash-matching versus price immunisation

	Cash flow after ($)			P ($)	y (%)	D	C
	6 months	12 months	18 months				
Liabilities	1 million	1 million	1 million	2.84 million	5.66[1]	1.98	5.88[2]
Cash-matched bond portfolio	1 million	1 million	1 million	2.84 million	5.66	1.98	5.88
Price-immunised bond portfolio	1.486 million	0	1.517 million	2.84 million	5.74	1.98	6.15

[1] The yield is found by solving $\$1\, m(1+y)^{-0.5} + \$1\, m(1+y)^{-1} + \$1\, m(1+y)^{-1.5} = \$2.84\, m$ for y.

[2] $C = 1 \times 2 \times \dfrac{\$1\, m(1.05)^{-0.5}}{\$2.84\, m} + 2 \times 3 \times \dfrac{\$1\, m(1.055)^{-1}}{\$2.84\, m} + 3 \times 4 \times \dfrac{\$1\, m(1.06)^{-1.5}}{\$2.84\, m} \cong 5.88.$

par payments of the cash-matched bond portfolio are identical to the future retirement payments.[11] Hence, the cash-matching strategy involves no interest-rate risk at all; the pension fund will be able to pay the retirement benefits, irrespective of the future interest-rate levels.

In our case, price-immunisation boils down to holding 1486 bonds of type A and 1517 bonds of type B.[12] The costs of this strategy are identical to those of cash-matching: 1486 × $975.90 + 1517 × $917.31 = $2.84 million, again leaving $0.16 million in cash. Also, the duration of the bond portfolio again equals the duration of the liabilities. While the value and the duration of the price-immunised portfolio, the cash-matched portfolio and the retirement liabilities are identical, the bond-price-immunised portfolio has a higher yield. Thus, the price-immunised portfolio achieves a benefit compared with the cash-matched portfolio. Convexity is the key to understanding this result: the price-immunised portfolio has a higher convexity than the price-immunised portfolio and the liabilities. Duration measures the sensitivity to small interest-rate moves. Since the assets and liabilities have the same duration, the pension fund is protected from such interest-rate moves.[13] This is true for both the cash-matched portfolio and the price-immunised portfolio, which have the same duration. However, due to the more favourable convexity, the price-immunised portfolio enjoys a benefit in case of large interest-rate moves. Specifically, if interest rates rise, then the duration of the price-immunised portfolio will fall less than the duration of the liabilities (and the cash-matched portfolio), causing a smaller loss for the price-immunised portfolio. Similarly, if interest rates fall, the duration of the price-immunised portfolio will rise more, causing a larger gain.

---

[11] Not surprisingly, the duration and convexity of the bond portfolio are also identical to those of the liabilities; if the cash flows are identical, then the value of the cash flows will be indentical, irrespective of the interest-rate levels.

[12] This portfolio was identified by maximising the convexity subject to the constraints that the duration of the portfolio equals that of the liabilities, $2.84 million is invested, and no short positions are taken.

[13] Specifically, any fall in the value of the bonds due to an interest-rate rise will be offset by an equivalent increase in the reinvestment return during the holding period.

Note that we are still assuming that bond markets are efficient. In an efficient bond market, it is not possible that two bond portfolios with exactly the same cash flow patterns trade at different yields. Nevertheless, efficient markets do not require two bond portfolios with different cash-flow patterns to have the same yield, even if the portfolios have the same duration. In this case, the cash-matched portfolio is inferior to the price-matched portfolio for managers who seek to maximise the market value of the assets. The downside is that the price-matched portfolio creates liquidity problems for the pension fund: after six months, the cash inflow is $1.486 million but the cash outflow is only $1 million. Hence, $0.486 million has to be reinvested until the next period. Similarly, after 12 months, the $0.486 million (plus any reinvestment return) and the initial cash balance of $0.16 million will fall short of the $1 million of benefit payments and hence part of the 1517 bonds of type C will have to be liquidated. The transaction costs associated with these buy and sell transactions are an important consideration for adopting some sort of income immunisation.

14.5 Active bond-management strategies

Recall that if the bond market is efficient, and thus all bonds are priced fairly, then the process of selecting bonds could be managed passively. By contrast, active management assumes implicitly that the bond market is not efficient and, hence, that excess returns can be achieved by forcasting future interest rates and identifying overpriced bonds and underpriced bonds. In an efficient market, this is impossible, so bond managers will use indexation or immunisation strategies.

There are many different speculative bond-management strategies. One strategy involves selling bonds that are believed to be relatively overpriced and buying bonds with similar characteristics that are believed to be relatively underpriced. This strategy is called a substitution swap.[14] Another strategy, called a pure yield pickup swap, involves buying bonds with a higher yield to maturity and selling bonds with a lower yield to maturity, which also typically implies longer-duration bonds. Speculating on the spread between two different bond markets, such as Eurodollar bonds and domestic bonds, is known as an intermarket spread swap.[15] Finally, a rate-anticipation swap involves positioning a bond portfolio such that maximum gains are achieved if a perceived rate change occurs.

Active bond managers are faced with a dilemma. How can they pursue active bond-management strategies without exposing a bond fund to excessive interest-rate risk? One solution is known as contingent immunisation, which can be seen as a combination of active bond management and passive immunisation. Contingent immunisation is an investment strategy designed to accommodate both the desire to pursue active strategies and the desire to minimise the effect of adverse movements in interest rates. A bond manager using this approach pursues timing strategies or duration mismatches in an attempt to profit from forecasted moves in interest rates. Alternatively, a bond manager may actively trade bonds that are believed to be mispriced by selling overpriced bonds and buying underpriced bonds.

The bond manager can act unimpeded as long as his or her performance is good. However, when he or she begins to experience relatively poor performance, he or she must move towards immunising strategies. Hence, the pension fund can establish a 'floor' on the active manager's

---

[14] The names given to these active strategies originated in Homer and Leibowitz (1972).
[15] Recall that Eurodollar bonds are bonds that pay in US dollars but are issued outside the USA.

performance. If the active manager performs well, then there are very few restrictions regarding exposure to interest-rate risk. As the active manager's performance declines, there are increasing restrictions. Specifically, the manager must increasingly immunise the bond portfolio.

→ **Connecting Theory to Practice 14.2**

Vanguard's investment grade bond fund

In the Investment Grade Bond Portfolio, we used the weakness in the market to add to bond positions and reduce cash reserves. The average maturity is now 24.8 years, up from 21.9 years six months ago. The Portfolio's duration is now 9.1, up from 8.6 on January 31. Swaps were made into issues that provide better call protection, improving the sustainability of the Portfolio's income. Utility investments were reduced in favor of industrial issuers, as the possibility of event risk now appears to be lower. We maintain nearly 20% of the Portfolio in U.S. government securities, which provide excellent quality, liquidity, and call protection. The average quality of our corporate holdings is between 'A' and 'Aa.' The Portfolio is well diversified with over 60 different corporate issuers. It is aggressively structured to provide solid returns if interest rates trend lower, as we expect over the next year.

Source: Semi-Annual Report of the Vanguard Fixed Income Securities Fund, 31 July 1990, p. 2.

→ **Making the connection**

This report indicates that the managers of Vanguard's Investment Grade Bond Portfolio pursued active bond management strategies. Clearly, these managers believed they had superior forecasting abilities. Specifically, they forecasted lower interest rates and a stronger economy. Their reference to 'event risk' shows a reduced concern about a recession. Public utility bonds are safer than industrial bonds in recessions. Of course, industrial bonds offer a higher yield. Believing that interest rates will 'trend lower' and the economy will strengthen, the managers lengthened the duration and accepted more default risk with industrial bonds.

Summary

List the basic principles of bond pricing.

The price of a bond is the present value of all future coupon payments plus the par value discounted to the present at the required rate of return (the yield to maturity). Bond prices change with the passage of time. Bond prices are related inversely to the yield to maturity. Longer-term bonds are more sensitive to changes in yield to maturity. The sensitivity to changes in yield to maturity increases at a decreasing rate with maturity. There is a linear relationship between a bond's coupon rate and its price. Finally, higher-coupon bonds are less sensitive to changes in yield to maturity than lower-coupon bonds.

Explain how duration is used to minimise interest-rate risk and to quantify interest-rate risk.

A bond portfolio's duration corresponds to the holding period at which the portfolio's interest-rate risk is minimised. Duration can also be used as a measure of relative bond-price volatility.

Explain why, for some bonds, convexity is needed in addition to duration for managing interest-rate risk.

For bonds with a low yield, a low coupon rate and/or a long maturity, the duration is very sensitive to yield changes. Convexity measures this sensitvity or the curvature of a bond's price–yield relationship. When a large yield change occurs, the change in a bond price is predicted more accurately with the use of convexity.

Describe passive bond-management strategies.

A passive bond manager does not attempt to time the market by making predictions about future interest rates and does not attempt to indentify bonds that are underpriced or overpriced. There exist two broad classes of passive bond-management strategies: indexing strategies and immunisation strategies. Indexing tries to mirrors the composition of a well-diversified bond market index. Immunisation techniques protect both income streams and the current market value of the assets and liabilities from the effects of changing interest rates. Income-immunisation protects future income needs. Income-immunisation strategies include cash-matching, duration-matching and horizon-matching. Price-immunisation uses convexity and seeks to protect current market values.

Describe active bond-management strategies.

The overall objective of active bond-management strategies is to make superior bond selections. Prudent bond-trading strategies require the ability to forecast future events such as changing interest rates and overall economic activity. Default risk should always be of utmost concern. Contingent immunisation is an investment strategy designed to accommodate both the desire of bond managers to trade actively and the desire of investors to minimise interest-rate risk. Several bond-trading strategies are designed to enhance returns, including substitution swaps, pure yield pickup swaps, intermarket swaps and rate anticipation swaps.

Key terms

Active bond management 480	Horizon-matching	Price effect 466
Cash-matching strategy 481	strategy 482	Price-immunisation 482
Contingent immunisation 484	Immunisation strategies 480	Pure yield pickup swap 484
Convexity 456	Income-immunisation	Rate-anticipation swap 484
Duration 456	strategy 481	Reinvestment effect 466
Duration drift 475	Indexing 480	Stratified sampling 481
Duration-matching	Intermarket spread swap 484	Substitution swap 484
strategy 481	Passive bond management 480	Tracking error 481

Review questions

1 Suppose that the yield on a 30-year junk bond is 9.13% and the yield on a short-term 5-year bond is 5.9%. Suddenly, inflation (accompanied by rapid expansion) hits the economy. The yield on the short-term bond goes up from 5.9% to 7.9%, and the yield on the junk bond goes up from 9.13% to 9.2%. Calculate the capital loss on these two bonds, assuming that before inflation, the two bonds sold at par, which is $1000.

In light of your results, explain the argument that 'some junk bonds with long maturities have the interest-rate sensitivity of shorter investments. If you are worried more about inflation than a depression, junk is a very attractive alternative to long Treasures.' (Hint: consider the risk of bankruptcy.)

2 Suppose you have two bonds with the following characteristics: bond A, P_A = $900 and 8 years; bond B, PB = $1100 and DB = 15 years. You have a holding period of 12 years. What bond portfolio mix will suit your holding period, assuming you wish to minimise interest-rate risk? (Assume a $500 000 portfolio.)

3 Calculate the annual convexity for bond M, which has three years to maturity and a yield of 9.6%. The semiannual coupon rate is 4.8%. The market price of bond M is $1000. Why is convexity needed in addition to duration for managing interest-rate risk?

4 Several income immunisation strategies were discussed in this chapter. Rank each immunisation strategy from the least flexible to the most flexible. Explain your rankings.

5 **a.** When are active bond strategies used?
  b. How can an active bond manager avoid excessive interest rate risk?

For an extensive set of review and practice questions and answers, visit the Levy–Post investment website at www.booksites.net/levy

Selected references

Barber, J. R. and M. L. Copper, 1997, 'Is Bond Convexity a Free Lunch?', *Journal of Portfolio Management*, **24**, 113–119.

Bierwag, G. O., 1987, *Duration Analysis: Managing Interest Rate Risk*, Cambridge, MA: Ballinger.

Bierwag, G. O., I. Fooladi and G. S. Roberts, 1993, 'Designing an Immunized Portfolio: Is M-Squared the Key?', *Journal of Banking and Finance*, **17** (6), 1147–1170.

Christensen, P. O. and B. G. Sorensen, 1994, 'Duration, Convexity, and Time Value', *Journal of Portfolio Management*, **20** (2), 51–60.

Dybrig, P. H. and W. Marshall, 1996, 'Pricing Long Bonds: Pitfalls and Opportunities', *Financial Analysts Journal*, **52** (1), 32–39.

Fabozzi, F. J., 1988, *Fixed Income Mathematics*, Chicago: Probus Publishing.

Fabozzi, F. J. and T. D. Fabozzi, 1989, *Bond Markets, Analysis and Strategies*, Englewood Cliffs, NJ: Prentice Hall.

Homer, S. and M. L. Liebowitz, 1972, *Inside the Yield Book: New Tools for Bond Market Strategy*, Englewood Cliffs, NJ: Prentice Hall.

Kahn, R. N., 1998, 'Bond Managers Need to Take More Risk', *Journal of Portfolio Management*, **24**, 70–76.

Kritzman, M., 1992, 'What Practitioners Need to Know . . . about Duration and Convexity', *Financial Analysts Journal*, **48** (6), 17–20.

Longstaff, F. A. and E. S. Schwartz, 1993, 'Interest Rate Volatility and Bond Prices', *Financial Analysts Journal*, **49** (4), 70–74.

Macaulay, F. R., 1938, *Some Theoretical Problems Suggested by the Movements of Interest Rates, Bond Yields, and Stock Prices in the United States since 1856*, New York: National Bureau of Economic Research.

Mehran, J. and G. Homaifar, 1993, 'Analytics of Duration and Convexity for Bonds with Embedded Options: The Case of Convertibles', *Journal of Business, Finance and Accounting*, **20** (1), 107–113.

Thomas, L. and R. Willner, 1997, 'Measuring the Duration of an Internationally Diversified Bond Portfolio', *Journal of Portfolio Management*, **24**, 93–101.

Computational equation for duration

This appendix develops a duration equation that can be placed in a single cell of a spreadsheet; hence, sensitivity analysis can be performed easily. The approach developed here is primarily beneficial for students who want to analyse duration using a spreadsheet.

The following equation is flexible enough to accommodate compounding other than just semiannual compounding. The computational equation for duration, which can be programmed easily into a spreadsheet, is as follows:

$$D = \frac{C\left[\left(1 + \frac{y}{np} - f\frac{y}{np}\right)\left(1 + \frac{y}{np}\right)^n - \left(1 + \frac{y}{np}\right) - \frac{y}{np}(n-f)\right] + \left(\frac{y}{np}\right)^2 Par(n-f)}{C\frac{y}{np}\left[\left(1 + \frac{y}{np}\right)^n - 1\right] + \left(\frac{y}{np}\right)^2 Par} \quad (14A.1)$$

where C is the coupon payment in dollars per period, f is the fraction of the coupon period elapsed since the last payment, n is the total number of remaining coupon payments, Par is the par value of the bond y is the current yield to maturity, and np is the number of coupon payments per year (for example, mortgages are typically paid monthly, so $np = 12$).

Although Equation 14A.1 looks fairly complicated, it is much easier to program into a spreadsheet than is Equation 14.3, because Equation 14.3 requires setting up summations of differing lengths. For example, the spreadsheet to compute a 30-year, semiannual coupon bond requires 60 cash flows to be discounted. Equation 14A.1 can be placed in a single cell and used for a bond of any maturity (as well as any payment frequency).

For example, according to Exhibit 14.8, the inputs for the five-year bond are as follows: $C = \$53.40$, or $1000 \times 0.1068 \times \frac{1}{2}$; $y = 0.1068$; $f = 0$; $np = 2$ (semiannual bond); $Par = 1000$; and $n = 10$ (five-year bond with two payments per year). Thus,

$$D = \frac{\$53.4\left[\left(1 + \frac{0.1068}{2}\right)\left(1 + \frac{0.1068}{2}\right)^{10} - \left(1 + \frac{0.1068}{2}\right) - \frac{0.1068}{2}(10)\right] + \left(\frac{0.1068}{2}\right)^2 1000(10)}{53.4\frac{0.1068}{2}\left[\left(1 + \frac{0.1068}{2}\right)^{10} - 1\right] + \left(\frac{0.1068}{2}\right)^2 1000}$$

Working through the calculations yields $D = 8.0$ semiannual periods, or 4.0 years.

Duration as the holding period that minimises interest-rate risk: a formal proof

As discussed in Section 14.2, duration represents the length of the holding period for which interest-rate risk is minimal. This appendix provides a formal proof of this result.

The future value of the cash flow from a bond portfolio, as computed at the end of a holding period, is

$$FV_T(y) = \sum_{t=1}^{n} \frac{CF_t}{(1+y)^{t-T}} \tag{14B.1}$$

where n is the maturity of bond portfolio, CF_t is the cash flow at the end of the tth period, T is the length of the holding period, and y is the current yield to maturity. If the yield changes from y to $y + \Delta y$, then the future value changes by

$$FV_T(y + \Delta y) - FT_T(y) = \sum_{t=1}^{n} \frac{CF_t}{(1+y+\Delta y)^{t-T}} - \sum_{t=1}^{n} \frac{CF_t}{(1+y)^{t-T}} \tag{14B.2}$$

$$= \sum_{t=1}^{n} CF_t \left[\frac{1}{(1+y+\Delta y)^{t-T}} - \frac{1}{(1+y)^{t-T}} \right] \tag{14B.2a}$$

For small yield changes Δy, the following can be shown mathematically (using a first-order Taylor series approximation):

$$\left[\frac{1}{(1+y+\Delta y)^{t-T}} - \frac{1}{(1+y)^{t-T}} \right] \cong \left[\frac{T-t}{(1+y)^{t-T+1}} \right] \Delta y \tag{14B.3}$$

Substituting the right-hand side for the left-hand side in Equation 14B.2a, we find

$$FV_T(y + \Delta y) - FT_T(y) \cong \sum_{t=1}^{n} CF_t \left[\frac{T-t}{(1+y)^{t-T+1}} \right] \Delta y \tag{14B.4}$$

$$= \left[T \sum_{t=1}^{n} \frac{CF_t}{(1+y)^{t-T+1}} - \sum_{t=1}^{n} t \frac{CF_t}{(1+y)^{t-T+1}} \right] \Delta y \tag{14B.4a}$$

This expression equals zero if

$$T = \frac{\displaystyle\sum_{t=1}^{n} t \frac{CF_t}{(1+y)^{t-T+1}}}{\displaystyle\sum_{t=1}^{n} \frac{CF_t}{(1+y)^{t-T+1}}} = \frac{\displaystyle\sum_{t=1}^{n} t \frac{CF_t}{(1+y)^{t}}}{\displaystyle\sum_{t=1}^{n} \frac{CF_t}{(1+y)^{t}}} \tag{14B.5}$$

$$= \sum_{t=1}^{n} t \frac{CF_t/(1+y)^t}{P} = D \tag{14B.5a}$$

Hence, the future value at the end of the holding period is not affected by yield changes if the duration of the bond portfolio equals the length of the holding period, i.e. if $D = T$. This means that the holding period return is completely predictable and that the interest-rate risk is zero. Notice however, that the first-order approximation in Equation 14B.3 is accurate only for small yield changes. If large yield changes occur, then duration changes (the convexity effect) and the bond portfolio need to be rebalanced in order to match the duration and the length of the holding period.

CHAPTER 15　Stocks: valuation and selection

Investment in the News 15　FT

Markets/yields

If investors concerned about US earnings quality are paying less attention to price/earnings ratios, one option is to look at the dividend yield. It is relatively easy to inflate earnings, but it is hard to fake a dividend.

Rearranging the Gordon growth model, the market's warranted yield is the cost of equity minus the dividend growth rate. Very roughly, assume a real cost of equity of 6 per cent for US companies. Subtract the trend economic growth rate (profits cannot outgrow the economy in the long run) of say 3-1/4 per cent and it suggests the warranted dividend yield is about 2-3/4 per cent. The current dividend yield on the S&P 500 is still only 1.9 per cent. But it is necessary to adjust for share buybacks since, especially in the US, this has become an important way of returning cash to shareholders. Federal Reserve economists estimate that a 0.5 per cent net repurchase retirement yield is sustainable in the long run. Comparing a 2.4 per cent adjusted yield with the 2-3/4 warranted yield suggests stocks are still about 10 per cent overvalued.

If you assume that distributions to shareholders rise faster than earnings in the next year or two (and no re-rating of shares) things look better. Investors are likely to demand higher payouts, given the concerns over earnings quality and the fact that long-term real equity returns are likely to be mid-single digits rather than the double digits of recent history. If 'reformers' in Washington want to do something useful, they could end the differential tax treatment of capital gains and dividend income.

Source: 'Markets/Yields', FT.com site, 26 July 2002.

Learning objectives

After studying this chapter, you should be able to:

1 Explain how investors use stock-valuation models.

2 Describe the assumptions underlying the constant dividend growth model (CDGM).

3 Describe how to estimate the input parameters of the CDGM.

4 Value firms that are presently experiencing super growth.

5 Explain how the free cash flow model (FCFM) is employed.

6 Explain why dividend discount models must be used with caution.

7 Explain why valuation multiples must be used with even greater caution.

8 Discuss the estimates and valuations by professional analysts.

Investment in the News 15 questions whether the US stock market was overvalued in July 2002. The analysis uses the so-called Gordon growth model as well as the so-called price/earnings ratio and dividend yield. This chapter introduces methods that investors can use to value and select stocks. Most of the methods are based on the economically sound principle of computing the value of a stock by discounting its expected future dividends at an appropriate risk-adjusted discount rate. While this principle is economically sound, it is extremely difficult to apply in practice, because future dividends are highly uncertain due to various risks at the level of the economy, the industry and the company. Still, the discounted cash flow principle can be made tractable by imposing particular simplifying assumptions on the future growth rates of the dividends. For example, the Gordon growth model makes the simplifying assumption that dividends grow at a constant rate for perpetuity. If we impose even more simplifying assumptions, then we obtain valuation multiples such as the price/earnings ratio and the dividend yield. These multiples are easy to compute, easy to understand and easy to communicate. However, they should be applied with care, because they are economically sound only under very restrictive assumptions.

Before we discuss these valuation methods, it is useful to first connect the discussion to the CAPM and the EMT.

This chapter evaluates stocks in isolation rather than as part of a broader portfolio of assets. Does this contradict the CAPM, which advocates that each asset should be evaluated in a portfolio context because asset-specific risks are 'diversified away' in a portfolio? The answer is no, because the discount rate used to discount an individual stock's expected future dividends is determined in the marketplace, and it takes into account the stock's specific risk as well as the covariance with other assets. If investors hold stock of a single firm, then the variability of the future dividends of that firm determines the value of the discount rate. If, as in the CAPM, investors hold many assets in their portfolios, then the beta (or the covariance) of the future dividends with the market portfolio determines the discount rate. Thus, the valuation method presented in this chapter does not contradict the portfolio analysis studied in the previous chapters, and, in particular, it does not contradict the CAPM.

The valuation methods discussed in this chapter generally use publicly available information. If we assume that capital markets are efficient in the semi-strong form, then all such information should already be reflected in stock prices. Hence, the valuation methods cannot systematically yield abnormal returns. Still, there are at least three compelling reasons for studying these methods. First, the popularity of the valuation methods suggests that the market is not efficient in semi-strong form, or at least there are many investors who believe so. Even though you may not believe that stock-valuation models can identify mispriced stocks, you must include other people's opinions in your assessment of stock prices. After all, if a group of believers in a valuation model predict that prices will move in a given direction, then their actions could affect stock prices, even though there is no economic foundation for this price change. Indeed, the economist John Maynard Keynes (1936) describes the Stock Exchange as a place where successful investing is the art of what people think other people think about stock prices. Second, even if the market is efficient, then it is still useful to understand the mechanism that leads to efficiency, i.e. to understand the valuation methods that practitioners use to analyse publicly available information. Third, the valuation methods are also useful as decision-support tools for corporate finance. Firms need to estimate their costs of capital to evaluate new investment projects (capital budgeting). Financial managers can use stock-valuation models to calculate the cost of equity, which constitutes a major component in the cost of capital. In addition, valuation techniques are needed in other situations where market valuations are absent, either because the shares are held privately or because the proposed publicly traded entity has not yet been created (for example, IPOs, mergers and spinoffs).

15.1 The intrinsic value of stocks

Many asset-valuation models have their roots in the discounted cash flow (DCF) principle, which states that the intrinsic value of any asset is the present value of all its expected future cash flows to the investor, discounted at the appropriate risk-adjusted discount rate. In the previous chapters, we applied this principle to bonds and computed the intrinsic value as the present value of all expected future coupon payments and the par value, discounted at the yield of Treasury bonds plus a risk premium for the credit risk of corporate bonds. For stocks, the relevant cash flows are cash dividends during the holding period and the sales revenue after selling the stocks at the end of the holding period.[1] Hence, the intrinsic value of a stock is the present value of these expected future cash flows. Valuation models that are based on this principle are called dividend discount models (DDMs).

To illustrate DDMs, suppose you forecast that Ford Motor Company will pay a $4 cash dividend per share (DPS) at the end of the next year and a $5 cash DPS at the end of the second year. Furthermore, you estimate that you will be able to sell the shares of Ford two years from now for $130. Since these are only estimates, they are uncertain; and like any uncertain cash-flow stream, you discount the cash flows at the proper discount rate (k), composed of the risk-free interest rate (which represents the time value of money) and a risk premium (which represents the risk-aversion of investors). Suppose the discount rate is $k = 15\%$. The current stock price is $P_0 = \$100$. Should you buy the Ford stock? Like any other capital budgeting project, your decision rules are these (where PV is the present value of the expected cash flows and NPV is the net present value):

If $PV > P_0$, buy the stock ($NPV > 0$).
If $PV < P_0$, do not buy the stock ($NPV < 0$).
If $PV = P_0$, you are indifferent as to whether to buy or not to buy the stock ($NPV = 0$).

---

[1] We need to distinguish between cash dividends and stock dividends, because the latter do not represent a cash flow to the investor. Stock dividends do lower the dividends per share. However, this generally is compensated for by the number of shares held by each investor. Hence, the 'dividend per investor' is not affected.

Exhibit 15.1	Present value of $4 dividend per share (DPS) in year 1 and $5 DPS and $130 stock price in year 2	
	End of first year (t_1)	End of second year (t_2)
Expected dividends ($)	4	5
Expected price ($)		130
Total expected cash flow ($)	4	135
Discount factor	1/1.15	$1/1.15^2$
Contribution to present value	$4/1.15 \cong $3.48	$135/1.15^2 \cong $102.08
Present value of the total cash flows	$3.48 + $102.08 = $105.56	

Source: From *Introduction to Investments*, 2nd edn, by Levy. © 1999. Reprinted with permission of South-Western, a division of Thomson Learning: www.thomsonrights.com. Fax 800 730-2215.

Exhibit 15.2	Present value of $4 dividend per share (DPS) in year 1 and $5 DPS and $120 stock price in year 2		
Beginning of first year (t_0)	End of first year (t_1)	End of second year (t_2)	
Expected dividends ($)		4	5
Expected price ($)			120
Total expected cash flow ($)		4	125
Discount factor for each year		1/1.15	$1/1.15^2$
Contribution to present value		$4/1.15 \cong $3.48	$125/1.15^2 \cong $94.52
Present value of the total cash flows		$3.48 + $94.52 = $98.00	

Source: From *Introduction to Investments*, 2nd edn, by Levy. © 1999. Reprinted with permission of South-Western, a division of Thomson Learning: www.thomsonrights.com. Fax 800 730-2215.

The present value of Ford's $4 DPS paid at the first year is $3.48 (see Exhibit 15.1). At the end of the second year, $5 DPS are paid; however, the stock is also expected to be sold at $130, making the total expected cash flow $135, with a discounted value of $102.08. Therefore, the present value of all expected cash flows is $PV = $105.56. Since $105.56 is greater than the current price ($P_0 = $100), the net present value ($NPV = PV - P_0 = $105.56 - $100 = $5.56) is positive. If you expect these cash flows, then you should buy the stock.

Who, then, sells Ford stock? Other investors in the market may have different predictions of the cash flows and, hence, a different future stock price. Suppose another investor believes, as you do, that the DPS will be $4 next year and $5 in two years; but, unlike you, this investor believes that at the end of the second year, the Ford stock will be selling at only $120. Even if this investor also uses a 15% discount rate, the present value of these cash flows is $98, as shown in Exhibit 15.2.

Suppose the second investor owns Ford stock. Since the present value in his or her opinion is $98, which is less than the current stock price ($P_0 = $100), this investor should sell the stock for $100. Investors who believe that a stock is undervalued ($P_0 < PV$) buy their stock, and investors who believe that a stock is overvalued ($P_0 > PV$) sell their stock. Since investors have differing opinions, the stock of Ford, as well as the stocks of other firms, change hands. However, despite the differences of opinion, both investors used the discounted cash flow principle.

When investors buy and sell stocks, they generally affect prices. When no one wants to execute any more transactions, the present value of cash flows for all investors who hold the stock (or those considering buying it) must be equal to the market stock price (P_0). To illustrate this, assume that for some investors $PV = \$120$ and $P_0 = \$100$. Then investors will continue to buy until the market price has gone to a point where $PV = P_0$. Similarly, if $PV < \$100$, investors will sell the stock, and the price will go down until $PV = P_0$.

Generalising the results for Ford Motor Company to any stock held for any holding period, we obtain the following general valuation equation:

$$P_0 = \sum_{t=1}^{n} \frac{E(DPS_t)}{(1+k)^t} = \frac{E(DPS_1)}{1+k} + \frac{E(DPS_2)}{(1+k)^2} + \ldots + \frac{E(P_n)}{(1+k)^n} \qquad (15.1)$$

where $E(DPS_t)$ is the expected DPS paid at the end of year t, n is the length of the holding period in years, and $E(P_n)$ is the expected selling price at the end of the holding period.

At first sight, Equation 15.1 seems difficult to implement in practice, because it requires the length of the holding period (n). Unfortunately, different investors have different holding periods; in addition, for most investors, the length of the holding period is not known in advance. However, as it turns out, we can use an arbitrary (positive) number for n, as Equation 15.1 is invariant to the length of the holding period. The explanation of this is that the expected stock price at the end of the holding period is nothing but the present value (discounted to year n) of the expected future dividends beyond year n, i.e.

$$E(P_n) = \sum_{t=1}^{\infty} \frac{E(DPS_{n+t})}{(1+k)^t} = \frac{E(DPS_{n+1})}{1+k} + \frac{E(DPS_{n+2})}{(1+k)^2} + \frac{E(DPS_{n+3})}{(1+k)^3} + \ldots$$

After all, if the stockholder sells the stock in year n, then the value to the buyer of the stock will be simply the present value of the dividends beyond the end of the holding period. Hence, the present value of the expected stock price is nothing but the present value (discounted to year 0) of the expected future dividends beyond year n, i.e.

$$\frac{E(P_n)}{(1+k)^n} = \sum_{t=n+1}^{\infty} \frac{E(DPS_t)}{(1+k)^t} = \frac{E(DPS_{n+1})}{(1+k)^{n+1}} + \frac{E(DPS_{n+2})}{(1+k)^{n+2}} + \frac{E(DPS_{n+3})}{(1+k)^{n+3}} + \ldots$$

Substituting the right-hand side of this equation into Equation 15.1, we find

$$P_0 = \sum_{t=1}^{\infty} \frac{E(DPS_t)}{(1+k)^t} = \frac{E(DPS_1)}{1+k} + \frac{E(DPS_2)}{(1+k)^2} + \frac{E(DPS_3)}{(1+k)^3} + \ldots \qquad (15.2)$$

which does not depend on the length of the holding period.

Most stockholders have a finite holding period and plan to sell the stock at some future moment. At that future moment, they will make a capital gain or capital loss, depending on whether the share price has fallen or risen. In fact, for short-term investors, the capital gain or capital loss generally is much more important than the dividend payments. Still, in principle, every stockholder, regardless of the holding period, is entitled to an infinite stream of cash dividends. Hence, we can value stocks 'as if' investors have an infinite holding period and ignore capital gains or losses. Consequently, we can compute the intrinsic value as the present value of all expected future dividends.

Discounting expected future dividends is a theoretically sound approach to stock valuation. Unfortunately, this approach is extremely difficult to apply in practice. Specifically, the investor must forcast all future dividends over an infinite horizon, while future dividends are highly uncertain. Dividends are the part of the firm's earnings that are distributed to the shareholders or

$$DPS_t = d_t \times EPS_t \qquad (15.3)$$

where EPS_t is the earnings per share in year t and d_t is the dividend payout ratio, or the percentage of EPS that is distributed as dividend in year t.[2] Both EPS and the payout ratio can be difficult to predict. For example, the firm's earnings are exposed to various risks at the level of the economy, the industry and the company. Also, the dividend payout ratio can be difficult to predict. If the payout ratio were a constant, then dividends would be just as volatile as earnings. However, most companies try to smoothe dividends levels (rather than the payout ratio) by defining a long-run target payout ratio and by making slow adjustments towards that ratio. In fact, investors typically perceive sudden large changes in the dividend level (such as the recent dividend cut by DaimlerChrysler; see Connecting Theory to Practice 15.1) as information that the fundamental long-run prospects of the company have changed. The target payout ratio is determined in a complex way by factors such as the tax treatment of dividends and capital gains, debt convenants imposed by banks, and the availability of profitable investment projects and external funding (for example, bank loans or issuing new stocks or bonds) for those projects.[3] A change in any of these factors can cause changes in the target payout ratio. Specifically, a firm may cut the payout ratio and reinvest the retained earnings if it encounters a profitable investment opportunity and external funding is too expensive.

Despite the difficulties in predicting future dividends, the general DDM in Equation 15.2 provided a useful framework for structuring the process of stock valuation. The model can be made tractable by imposing particular assumptions on the future growth rate of the dividends. Section 15.2 discusses the constant dividend growth model (CDGM), which assumes that dividends grow at a single constant growth rate for perpetuity. Section 15.3 discusses the validity of this model if the growth rate changes over time, for example due to changes in the profitability of the firm's investment projects or changes in the firm's dividend policy. Section 15.4 generalises the single-stage CDGM model to a multiple-stage growth model, which uses multiple growth rates for multiple periods.

→ **Connecting Theory to Practice 15.1**　　　　　　　　　**FT**

DaimlerChrysler board poised to make its first dividend cut

The management board of DaimlerChrysler is this week expected to recommend the first dividend cut since the 1998 merger of Daimler-Benz and Chrysler following a sharp fall in profits at the German-US automotive group.

A board meeting on Wednesday is due to consider cutting the annual pay-out by more than one-third to about Euros 1.50 a share, down from Euros 2.35 last year. The move is expected to save DaimlerChrysler more than Euros 1 bn (Pounds 607 m). But company insiders claim its net cash position and promising operating outlook this year does not justify a deeper cut. Some observers, including the automotive team at UBS Warburg, have called for the dividend to be more than halved.

The dividend has yet to be formally agreed by the management board. But Jurgen Schrempp, its chairman, is likely to describe a cut as prudent. He has already warned that last year's profits

---

[2] The **ploughback ratio** or **earnings retention ratio** or $(1 - d_t)$ is the fraction of the earnings that is retained and reinvested in the firm.

[3] The optimal dividend policy is one of the central problems of corporate finance. Miller (1986) reviews the research on this subject.

would be at the lower end of the company's Euros 1.2 bn–Euros 1.6 bn range compared with Euros 5.17 bn in 2000. Nevertheless, the company is expected to report slightly better-than-expected operating profits of about Euros 1.3 bn following a strong performance at Mercedes-Benz and cost-cutting at Chrysler. The chairman will reiterate that the outlook for 2002 is considerably better than last year when Chrysler restructuring involved 26,000 job losses and six plant closures. Chrysler is expected to post losses of about Euros 2.2 bn–Euros 2.3 bn for 2001. Although the company will not strip out divisional results in its release on Wednesday, senior managers have insisted that Chrysler will achieve a break-even this year. Most industry analysts, however, expect the company to reduce its profits forecasts for the year from the previous Euros 5.5 bn–Euros 6.5 bn range to about Euros 4 bn–Euros 5 bn. In a recent meeting with investors and analysts in Stuttgart, Mr Schrempp said 2002 could be difficult for carmakers and that luxury brands, including the group's Mercedes flagship, would not be immune to volatile demand.

The company will make clear this week the dividend has to be approved by the supervisory board. The board of non-executive directors and labour representatives is due to meet this month to consider the dividend and financial results, shortly before DaimlerChrysler unveils detailed figures on February 20. Supervisory boards in Germany rarely overturn management board recommendations.

Source: Tim Burt, 'DaimlerChrysler Board Poised To Make Its First Dividend Cut', Tim Burt, *Financial Times*, 4 February 2002.

→ **Making the connection**

This article discusses a recent dividend cut by DaimlerChrysler. The dividend cut reflects the worsening of the business conditions for car makers and analysts have revised their forecasts for future earnings accordingly. This example illustrates that dividends can be volatile and difficult to estimate.

We have thus far assumed that the firm pays out cash to its shareholders by declaring cash dividends. As discussed in Investment in the News 15, firms can also return cash to shareholders by share buybacks, or repurchasing part its own stock. One reason to prefer share buybacks to cash dividends is the different tax treatment between dividend income and capital gain; in the USA, stockholders who sell shares back to the firm are taxed only on their capital gain. However, the IRS may decide that regular or large repurchases should be treated as disguised dividend payments. In some other countries, share buybacks are not allowed or they are taxed as regular cash dividends. Share buybacks can also be used to return excess cash if few profitable investment projects remain or to change the firm's capital structure. In principle, for stock valuation, share buybacks should be treated in a similar way as cash dividends; their present value should be added to the present value of the cash dividends. However, in practice, buybacks occur only irregularly, and generally they cannot be predicted sufficiently accurately to be included in the analysis. Also, there is a risk of double-counting cash flows if we include buybacks in the analysis. If an investor sells back his or her share, then he or she obviously doesn't receive the cash dividends in the following years. Also, by repurchasing stock, the firm will have less money left to distribute as dividends to the investors who do not sell their shares. In fact, the reduction in the total dividends generally cancels the reduction in the number of shares outstanding, leaving the DPS unchanged. For these reasons, share repurchases typically are not included in valuing stocks, and we forecast dividends 'as if' no share repurchase occurs.

Note that we do not claim that the announcement of a share buyback does not affect stock prices. Indeed, such announcements can have a large impact on prices. For example, an unexpected announcement of a share buyback may signal that, contrary to investors' expectations, the firm has no profitable investment projects left. In this case, stock prices may fall sharply following the announcement. The point is that we could model this effect equivalently by lowering the expected future dividends.

15.2 The constant dividend growth model

The CDGM or Gordon growth model is a popular simplification of the general DDM given in Equation 15.2.[4] The model assumes that the firm's expected earnings per share (EPS) grows every year by a constant growth rate denoted by g, where g is expressed as a percentage:

$$E(EPS_t) = EPS_0(1 + g)^t \qquad (15.4)$$

In addition, the firm is expected to employ a constant dividend payout ratio, denoted by d. Under these assumptions, the firm's expected DPS also grows at the constant rate g:[5]

$$E(DPS_t) = DPS_0(1 + g)^t \qquad (15.5)$$

Similarly, the share price is also expected to grow at the same constant rate g:[6]

$$E(P_t) = P_0(1 + g)^t \qquad (15.6)$$

Further, the general DDM in Equation 15.2 reduces to the following simplified valuation equation:[7]

$$P_0 = DPS_0 \frac{(1 + g)}{(k - g)} = \frac{E(DPS_1)}{(k - g)} \qquad (15.7)$$

One good feature of this model is that all future dividends do not have to be estimated directly. We need estimate only the growth rate (g) and the discount rate (k); Sections 15.2.1 and 15.2.2 discuss this issue.

Exhibit 15.3 illustrates Equation 15.7 for a stock that paid a DPS of $1.5 in the last period. This exhibit shows the relationship between the share price and the discount rate (k) for three different growth rates (0, 1 and 2%). Obviously, the greater the growth rate (g) and the lower the discount rate (k), all other things being the same, the larger the discounted expected future dividends will be, resulting in a higher stock price (P_0).

---

[4] This model was originally developed by Gordon (1959).

[5] This follows from the following chain of equations: $E(DPS_t) = dE(EPS_t) = d \times EPS_0(1 + g)^t = DPS_0(1 + g)^t$.

[6] To see this, we first substitute Equation 15.5 into Equation 15.2: $P_0 = \sum_{t=1}^{\infty} E(DPS_t)/(1 + k)^t = \sum_{t=1}^{\infty} DPS_0(1 + g)^t/ (1 + k)^t$. Next, we do the same for the expected share price in Year t: $E(P_t) = \sum_{s=t+1}^{\infty} E(DPS_s)/(1 + k)^s = \sum_{s=1}^{\infty} DPS_0(1 + g)^{s+t}/(1 + k)^s$. Dividing the last expression by the first one, we obtain $E(P_t)/E(P_0) = (1 + g)^t$.

[7] Substituting $E(DPS_1) = EPS_0(1 + g)$ and $n = 1$ into Equation 15.1 yields $P_0 = DPS_0(1 + g)/(1 + k) + E(P_1)/(1 + k)$. Substituting $E(P_1) = P_0(1 + g)$ (from Equation 15.6) into this equation gives $P_0 = DPS_0(1 + g)/(1 + k) + P_0(1 + g)/ (1 + k)$. Multiplying both sides of this equation by $(1 + k)$ yields $P_0(1 + k) = DPS_0(1 + g) + P_0(1 + g)$ or $P_0(k - g) = DPS_0(1 + g)$ or $P_0 = DPS_0(1 + g)/(k - g)$.

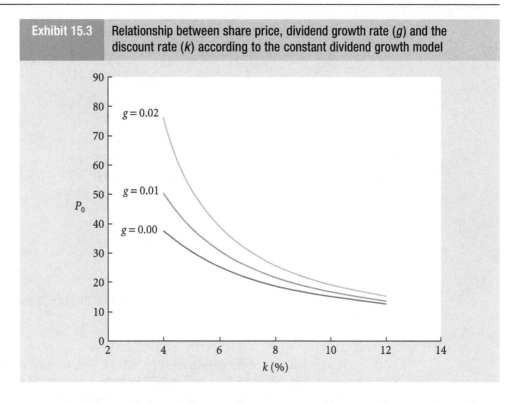

Exhibit 15.3 Relationship between share price, dividend growth rate (g) and the discount rate (k) according to the constant dividend growth model

Note that this formula holds only when the growth rate (g) is smaller than the discount factor (k). If $g > k$, then dividends grow faster than the discount rate, and the DCF of an infinite stream of dividends yields an infinite price. However, this situation cannot continue forever, because a company that exhibits such growth for perpetuity would eventually encompass the entire economy! We can therefore assume safely that $g < k$, or at least that $g > k$ cannot continue forever. The case where $g > k$ for a limited period of time is discussed later in this chapter.

15.2.1 Estimating the dividend growth rate

One method of estimating the appropriate growth rate (g) is historical extrapolation, or extrapolating the past growth pattern of dividend to the future. According to Equation 15.5, the relationship between the expected values of the two dividends in periods t and $t - 1$ is

$$E(DPS_t) = E(DPS_{t-1})(1 + g)$$

or

$$g = \frac{E(DPS_t)}{E(DPS_{t-1})} - 1$$

Suppose we have a series of $S + 1$ historical observations on the dividend per share, say $DPS_{-S}, DPS_{-S+1}, \ldots, DPS_1, DPS_0$. In its simplest form, historical extrapolation boils down simply to computing the sample average of the growth rates:

$$\hat{g} = \frac{1}{T} \sum_{t=-S+1}^{0} \left(\frac{DPS_t}{DPS_{t-1}} - 1 \right) \tag{15.8}$$

Exhibit 15.4	Hypothetical data for estimating g for ABC, Inc.	
Year	DPS_t	$DPS_t/DPS_{t-1} - 1$
1994	0.95	
1995	0.99	0.042
1996	1.04	0.051
1997	1.13	0.087
1998	1.16	0.027
1999	1.18	0.017
2000	1.24	0.051
2001	1.28	0.032
2002	1.40	0.094
2003	1.43	0.021
Average		0.048

Exhibit 15.4 illustrates this method with 1994–2003 data for ABC, Inc., a hypothetical transportation company. In this case, we find

$$\hat{g}_{ABC} = 0.048$$

Thus, the regression estimate of the growth rate of dividends over the past ten years is 4.8%.

Notice, however, that past growth of EPS and DPS can be a poor guide to future growth, especially for forecasts beyond one year. In fact, the classic 'higgledy-piggledy growth' studies reported that earnings changes over time appear to be distributed almost randomly.[8] For this reason, investors generally make subjective modifications to the historical record based on additional information about the prospects of the general economy, the industry and the firm (see Section 15.8).

An alternative approach is to compute the 'implied' growth rate. In this case, we assume the stock price to be the 'correct' or equilibrium market price and solve for the unknown value of g. Specifically, we can rewrite the CDGM (Equation 15.7) as follows:

$$g = \frac{kP_0 - DPS_0}{P_0 + DPS_0}$$

Hence, if we have an estimate for the discount rate ($\hat{k}$), for example using Equation 15.10 below, then we can estimate the implied growth rate as

$$\hat{g} = \frac{\hat{k}P_0 - DPS_0}{P_0 + DPS_0} \tag{15.9}$$

Obviously, if we plug this estimate into Equation 15.7, then we will find that the market price is 'fair'. Still, an investor can use the implied growth rate to compare it with his or her own estimate of the growth rate; if the implied rate is smaller than the investor's estimate, then the stock is 'undervalued' and the investor should buy the stock. Alternatively, the investor can apply Equation 15.9 to a firm that is comparable with the evaluated firm (for example, a firm

---

[8] The 'higgledy-piggledy growth' studies include the four classics by Little (1962), Rayner and Little (1966), Brealey (1967) and Lintner and Glauber (1967).

from the same industry and of comparable risk) and plug the resulting growth rate estimate into Equation 15.7 for the evaluated firm.

Notice that the implied growth estimate in Equation 15.9 is related directly to the dividend yield and P/E ratio (these valuation multiples are discussed in Section 15.7). Indeed, these valuation multiples are used frequently as indicators of future growth potential. There exists evidence that such implied growth rates indeed have predictive value for corporate earnings. For example, a US study by Fuller *et al.* (1992) revealed that portfolios based on E/P ratios rank-order future earnings growth for a number of years ahead; in other words, low P/E stocks tend subsequently to generate low earnings growth whilst high P/E stocks provide high future earnings growth.[9]

We stress that altering the growth rate can have a dramatic effect on estimated stock values. In addition, estimates in many cases are highly inaccurate. For this reason, it is recommended that you invest in obtaining estimates that are as accurate as possible, and in addition that you assess the robustness of the results with respect to several alternative assumptions about the growth rate.

15.2.2 Estimating the required rate of return

You will recall from Chapter 9 that one method used to estimate the required rate of return (k) is to use the CAPM:

$$\hat{k} = r + \beta[E(R_m) - r] \tag{15.10}$$

where r is the riskless rate, β is the stock's market beta and $[E(R_m) - r]$ is the expected future equity risk premium (the expected future return on the market portfolio minus the riskless rate).

Suppose ABC's estimated beta is 1.25. If we use $r = 6\%$ as before and estimate $E(R_m)$ to be 10%, then

$$\hat{k}_{ABC} = 0.06 + 1.25(0.10 - 0.06) = 0.11, \text{ or } 11\%$$

Unfortunately, this approach is much more difficult than it seems at first sight. First, the estimated beta may be unreliable. As discussed in Chapter 10, it is difficult to estimate betas for individual stock from historical data. For example, the stock prices of most firms are affected highly by firm-specific factors, which makes it difficult to estimate the betas (which reflect only systematic risk); in addition, the beta may change over time because the assets and the liabilities of the firms change. Also, betas depend heavily on the choice of the market index, and there is no consensus about the relevant index. Estimating the equity risk premium is also difficult. Connecting Theory to Practice 15.2 illustrates the range of opinions. The average historical equity risk premium in the USA has been about 4%. However, some analyses suggest that the expected risk premium has been as low as 1% at some points in time. Assuming a risk-free rate of 3%, then the historical average yields an estimated cost of equity of 7% for the average US company. By contrast, the estimate is only 4% if we assume an expected risk premium of 1%. This means a difference of 3% in the estimated cost of equity for the average company! In addition to issues of estimating the beta and the equity risk premium, the validity of the CAPM has been debated (see Chapter 9). Under other models, such as APT (see Chapter 10), calculations of the cost of equity may include multiple macroeconomic factors or company characteristics.

---

[9] Two related studies are Ou and Penman (1989) and Penman (1996).

Another method is to compute the 'implied' cost of capital. In this case, we assume the stock price to be the 'correct' or equilibrium market price and solve for the unknown value of k. Specifically, we can rewrite the CDGM in Equation 15.7 as follows:

$$k = \frac{DPS_0(1 + g)}{P_0} + g$$

Hence, if we have an estimate for the expected growth rate g (for example, using Equation 15.9), then we can solve for the expected rate of return by the stockholders:

$$\hat{k} = \frac{DPS_0(1 + \hat{g})}{P_0} + \hat{g} \qquad (15.11)$$

Based on our calculation of g using historical hypothetical data for ABC (and assuming that ABC was trading for $62 per share at this time), we could estimate

$$\hat{k}_{ABC} = \frac{\$1.52(1 + 0.047)}{\$62} + 0.047 \cong 0.0727$$

Therefore, investors who determine the stock price in the market are expecting (or requiring) to earn 7.27% on their investment. Obviously, if we plug the result into Equation 15.7, we will find that the market price of $62 is 'fair'. However, an investor can use this implied discount rate to compare it with his or her required rate of return given the risk of the stock. If an investor's required rate of return is greater than 7.27%, then the investor should avoid this investment. However, if the investor's required rate of return is lower than 7.27%, then the stock seems an attractive investment. Alternatively, an investor can apply Equation 15.11 to a firm that is comparable with ABC (for example, another transportation company with comparable risk) and plug the resulting discount rate into Equation 15.7 for ABC.

As is true for the growth rate, altering the discount rate can have a dramatic effect on stock prices. In addition, estimates generally are highly inaccurate. For this reason, we again recommend that you invest in obtaining accurate estimates and analysing the robustness with respect to several alternate assumptions.

15.3 Normal-growth and super-growth firms

Recall that the CDGM is a simplified version of the general DDM. Specifically, the CDGM assumes that the firm's EPS grows every year by a constant growth rate and that the dividend payout ratio is constant. Very few firms fit neatly into these assumptions. The growth rate of earnings and the payout ratio of many firms change as their business conditions change over time. This section examines how such changes affect the validity of the CDGM.

Generally, the CDGM applies only for the special case of normal-growth firms, or firms with investment projects that yield a rate of return that is exactly equal to the investors' required rate of return.[10] As we will see below, for such firms, the payout ratio is irrelevant for the value of the shares. Hence, the CDGM applies even if the dividend policy changes over time. For example, an increase in the growth rate caused by a cut in dividends does not lead

---

[10] Paradoxically, normal-growth firms are the exception rather than the rule. Most firms exhibit super growth at some stage of their lifecycle.

to an increase in the stock price if the retained earnings are reinvested in a project that yields the required rate of return.

By contrast, super-growth firms have investment projects that yield a rate of return that exceeds their cost of capital (projects with positive NPVs).[11] For these firms, the CDGM valuation is no longer valid if the payout ratio changes. For example, an increase in the growth rate caused by a cut in dividends leads to an increase in the stock price if the retained earnings are reinvested in a project with extraordinary returns. Also, for such firms, the growth rate will change over time, as abnormal investment returns generally attract new competitors. For these reasons, the CDGM generally does not apply for super-growth firms, and corrections are needed.

15.3.1 Normal-growth firms

Consider a normal-growth firm, i.e. a firm with no extraordinarily profitable projects. Given the riskiness of the firm, the stockholders require $k\%$ return per year on their investment. Suppose the firm reinvests the retained earnings in projects yielding $k\%$, exactly as required by the stockholders. Can the firm's earnings and dividends grow ($g > 0$) in such a case? Yes, they can, because the firm pays only a portion of its earnings as dividends and has some funds left to reinvest in the firm. Reinvesting these funds leads to higher future earnings and dividends. In this case, the increase in investment is financed by internal sources, namely by cutting the current dividends. The lower the portion of earnings paid out as dividends, the greater the firm's future growth rate.

Exhibit 15.5a gives an example of a normal-growth firm with EPS of $10 in the first year and a payout ratio of 50%. The firm earns a return of $y = 10\%$ on its investments, and the stockholder's required cost of equity is $k = 10\%$. In the second year, the earnings grow to $10.5, because $5 per share earned in the first year is reinvested at 10%, yielding an additional $5 \times 0.1 = \$0.5$ EPS. Since the firm distributes 50% of its earnings as dividends, in the second year it pays DPS of $5.25. Thus, the EPS, DPS and, hence, the firm's stock price grow from the first year to the second year at a 5% growth rate. Note that although this firm earns $y = 10\%$ on its investment, the growth rate is only 5%, because only 50% of the EPS is retained.

By this process, the EPS, DPS and stock price are expected to continue to grow at this rate in all other years. For example, the earnings of the third year are $10.5(1.05) = \$11.025$. Similarly, the dividend grows at 5%; hence, in the third year, the DPS is $5.25(1.05) = \$5.5125$. Employing Equation 15.7, the stock price is given by

$$P_0 = \frac{DPS_1}{k - g} = \frac{\$5}{0.10 - 0.05} = \frac{\$5}{0.05} = \$100$$

Exhibit 15.5b still assumes the same normal-growth firm – namely $k = 10\%$ – but the firm now reinvests 90% of its retained earnings in projects yielding 10%. The only difference between this case and the previous case is that the firm distributes only $1 (out of $10) as cash dividends and reinvests the retained earnings of $9 per share. The $9 per share is invested in projects yielding, as before, 10%; therefore, the dollar return on this reinvestment of the retained earnings is $0.90 (given by $9 \times 0.1 = \$0.90$) per share. Let us continue these computations for the second year; 10% of the EPS, or $0.1 \times 10.9 = \$1.09$, is paid out as dividends in the second year. What is left is once again reinvested at 10%. Since the growth rate is 9% for all years, the EPS in the third year is $10.9 \times 1.09 = \$11.881$, and the DPS is $1.09 \times 1.09 = \$1.1881$; this growth rate

---

[11] Theoretically, a firm can also have investment projects with negative NPVs. However, in this case, the firm should liquidate the project and invest the proceeds in positive NPV projects or pay out cash dividends.

Exhibit 15.5	Expected growth rate in dividends, earnings and stock prices for normal-growth firms

(a) Growth rate of $g = 5\%$ with $5 first-year dividends

Year (t)	E(EPS$_t$)	E(DPS$_t$)	Stock price
0			$P_0 = 100$
1	$10	$5	$P_0(1.05)$
2	$10.5	$5.25	$P_0(1.05)^2$
3	$11.025	$5.5125	$P_0(1.05)^3$

(b) Growth rate of $g = 9\%$ with $1 first-year dividends

Year (t)	E(EPS$_t$)	E(DPS$_t$)	Stock price
0			$P_0 = 100$
1	$10	$1	$P_0(1.09)$
2	$10.9	$1.09	$P_0(1.09)^2$
3	$11.881	$1.1881	$P_0(1.09)^3$

Source: From *Introduction to Investments*, 2nd edn, by Levy. © 1999. Reprinted with permission of South-Western, a division of Thomson Learning: www.thomsonrights.com. Fax 800 730-2215.

continues forever. Comparing parts a and b of Exhibit 15.5, it is easy to see that by decreasing the dividends that are paid to the stockholders in the first year, more money is left to be reinvested. Hence, earnings and dividends grow at a rate of $g = 9\%$ rather than $g = 5\%$. Therefore, when only 10% of earnings is paid out as dividends, the stock price at the end of the first year (P_1) should grow at 9% over the original price (P_0). Note that the increase in the stock price is not due to the availability of extraordinary projects. The firm reinvests, as before, in projects yielding 10%. However, by cutting the dividends from $5 per share to $1 per share, the dollar volume of the investment in projects increases and, hence, the dividend growth increases.

Does the increase in the growth rate by moving from 5 to 9% affect the current stock price (P_0)? To answer this question, use Equation 15.7 in the case described in Exhibit 15.5b to obtain

$$P_0 = \frac{DPS_1}{k - g} = \frac{\$1}{0.10 - 0.09} = \frac{\$1}{0.01} = \$100$$

Thus, the increase in the growth rate of the dividends does not increase the current stock price (P_0). It is true that in Exhibit 15.5b, the future dividends grow at a faster rate than in Exhibit 15.5a (9% versus 5%). However, for the faster-growth case (9%), there is also a lower dividend base – a $1 first-year dividend versus a $5 first-year dividend. These two factors cancel each other out exactly, and the stock price remains unchanged at $P_0 = \$100$. The price ($P_1$) at the end of the first period increases faster in Exhibit 15.5b than in Exhibit 15.5a because, as less dividends are consumed, the money is kept in the firm. This higher future stock price does not mean that the investor is better off, however; the investor in Exhibit 15.5a receives higher current dividend and he or she can achieve the same future wealth by reinvesting these dividends at 10%.

The intuitive economic explanation for this result is that stockholders require a $k = 10\%$ return on their investment. If the firm invests the retained earnings at 10%, then by investing more or less (that is, by changing the dividend level), the stockholders cannot be worse off or better off. To illustrate this argument, suppose you invest for two years in one of the two alternate firms given in Exhibit 15.5. If the firm pays out 50% of its earnings as dividends, after two years you obtain $P_0(1.05)^2 = \$110.25$ plus the second-year dividend of $5.25. Further, assuming you can reinvest for a year at 10%, the value of the $5 dividend received after one year is $5(1.1) = \$5.50$ after two years. Hence, you obtain $110.25 + $5.25 + $5.50 = $121 altogether. Now, suppose that the firm pays out only 10% of its earnings as dividends. At the end of two years, you obtain $P_0(1.09)^2 = \$118.81$ plus $1.09 (the second-year dividend) plus the first-year dividends that you can invest at 10%, $1(1.1) = \$1.10$ – again, $121 altogether. As you can see, the sum is the same in both cases; hence, the current price will be the same.

Let us now generalise the discussion. For a normal-growth firm, the expected return on investment equals the required rate of return (k). Hence, if the payout ratio is constant at d, then the growth rate of EPS, DPS and share price is

$$g = k(1 - d) \tag{15.12}$$

For example, in Exhibit 15.5a, $k = 0.10$, $d = 0.5$ and $g = 0.10(1 - 0.5) = 0.05$, and in Exhibit 15.5b, $k = 0.10$, $d = 0.1$ and $g = 0.10(1 - 0.1) = 0.09$.

Substituting Equation 15.12 into Equation 15.7, we obtain

$$P_0 = \frac{E(DPS_1)}{(k-g)} = \frac{dE(EPS_1)}{(k-k(1-d))} = \frac{dE(EPS_1)}{kd} = \frac{E(EPS_1)}{k} \tag{15.13}$$

That is, the value of a normal-growth firm's stock equals the present value of an annuity equal to next year's expected EPS. As in the above example, this value does not depend on the dividend payout ratio d. In fact, next year's expected EPS represents the maximum level of dividend that can be sustained throughout the lifetime of the firm; the firm can pay out this amount of DPS while leaving its capital stock and earning capacity unchanged.

The conclusion is that the CDGM applies for all normal-growth firms, even if they change their dividend policy through time. The bottom line is that the firm cannot create value by retaining earnings because the expected return on reinvested earnings equals the required return, and hence the dividend policy is irrelevant for valuing the firm's stock. If earnings are paid out as dividend, then the investor can reinvest the dividends at k%. If the earnings are retained in the firm, then the firm can reinvest at k%. In both cases, the shareholders' wealth is the same.

15.3.2 Super-growth firms

In contrast to a normal-growth firm, a super-growth firm can increase the growth rate of the EPS and the DPS with no change in their dividend policy – that is, without reducing the current dividends. Such a firm reinvests the retained earnings in projects yielding more than the required rate of return (positive NPV projects). Since the firm earns extra profits on these projects, it experiences increased growth in earnings and dividends.

It might seem as though super-growth firms will always have a larger growth rate than normal-growth firms, but this is not always true. To illustrate this, consider the following example. One firm may reinvest 90% of its profit at the required rate of return k and grow at $g = 10$%, whereas another firm may reinvest only 20% of its profit in projects with extraordinary profits (those with a rate of return greater than k) and grow only at $g = 8$%. The relatively low growth rate of the second firm results from the low proportion of the earnings retained. However, the firm with a 10% growth rate is classified as a normal-growth firm, whereas the firm with an 8% growth rate is classified as a super-growth firm. In other words, the actual growth rate is determined by the rate of return on reinvested earnings as well as the proportion of earnings reinvested in the firm. However, only the first factor – the profit on projects – determines whether the firm is classified as a normal-growth or a super-growth firm.

In general, for super-growth firms, the valuation in Equation 15.13 does not apply, because $g > k(1 - d)$ (contrary to Equation 15.12). Rather, the following equation applies:

$$P_0 = \frac{E(EPS_1)}{k} + PVGO \qquad (15.14)$$

The first part of the right-hand side is commonly referred to as the value of assets in place, or the no-growth value. This is the firm's value if we ignore its super-growth possibilities. The second part is called the present value of growth opportunities (PVGO). This part of the firm's stock value is derived from exceptional returns on retained earnings.

A super-growth firm can be valued using the CDGM, provided the return on investment (y) and the dividend payout ratio (d) are constant. In that case, the growth rate of EPS, DPS and share price is

$$g = y(1 - d) \qquad (15.15)$$

Substituting this equation into Equation 15.7, we obtain

$$P_0 = \frac{E(DPS_1)}{k - y(1 - d)} \qquad (15.16)$$

Since $y > k$, this equation will of course yield a higher value than Equation 15.13. Still, the CDGM also applies in this case.

To illustrate this point, Exhibit 15.6 gives an example of a super-growth firm with a constant dividend growth rate. The example is identical to that in Exhibit 15.5a, with the exception that the firm can invest its retained earnings at 18% rather than 10%. In this case, the second-year EPS will be $10 + (\$5 \times 0.18) = \$10.90$. The second-year DPS is $5.45. Similarly, the EPS and DPS grow at 9% in all other years.[12] Since dividends and earnings grow at $g = 9\%$ per year, the stock price should also grow at 9% per year. Equation 15.7 in this case yields:

$$P_0 = \frac{DPS_1}{k - g} = \frac{\$5}{0.10 - 0.09} = \frac{\$5}{0.01} = \$500$$

Exhibit 15.6	Expected growth rate in dividends, earnings and stock prices for a super-growth firm: 9% with $5 first-year dividends		
Year (t)	E(EPS$_t$)	E(DPS$_t$)	Stock price
0			$P_0 = 500$
1	$10	$5	$P_0(1.09)$
2	$10.90	$5.45	$P_0(1.09)^2$
3	$11.88	$5.94	$P_0(1.09)^3$

Source: From *Introduction to Investments*, 2nd edn, by Levy. © 1999. Reprinted with permission of South-Western, a division of Thomson Learning: www.thomsonrights.com. Fax 800 730-2215.

_____

[12] Reinvestment at 18% of 50% of the EPS induces a growth rate of $18\% \times 0.5 = 9\%$.

Unlike the comparison of stock prices in Exhibit 15.5, a comparison of stock prices in Exhibit 15.5a and Exhibit 15.6 (in both cases, 50% of earnings is paid as dividends) reveals a dramatic jump in the current stock price (P_0) from \$100 to \$500. How can we account for this large price increase? By shifting from Exhibit 15.5a to Exhibit 15.5b, we saw that the change in the growth rate (from 5 to 9%) was due to a change in the dividend policy. The firm reduces its dividend and reinvests more in projects (at 10%); hence, the growth rate increases from 5 to 9% at the expense of a reduction in the base dividend from \$5 to \$1. As a result, no gain in the stock price is achieved, and it remains $P_0 = \$100$. However, in the comparison of Exhibit 15.5a and Exhibit 15.6, the growth rate increases, once again, from 5 to 9%, not at the expense of a reduction in the base dividend, which is kept in the first year at \$5.

The key difference between the normal-growth firm and the super-growth firm is that with the normal-growth firm, both the stockholders and the firm can reinvest at $k = 10\%$. The super-growth firm, in contrast, can reinvest in the real markets at 18%, whereas stockholders can reinvest the dividends in the financial markets at only 10%. The availability of projects with a positive NPV yields a PVGO of \$400 in addition to the value of assets in place of \$100.

We have seen that the CDGM still applies for super-growth firms if we assume a constant return on investment and a constant dividend payout. However, these assumptions generally do not make sense for a super-growth firm, and the CDGM does not apply. Most super-growth firms cannot enjoy extraordinary investment opportunities forever, because extraordinary profits attract new competitors. When Apple and IBM first entered the personal computer market, for example, prices were very high and these firms enjoyed extraordinary profits. After a few years, many competitors were attracted to this profitable business, the prices of personal computers fell dramatically, and the extra profit disappeared. Such firms are super-growth firms for a few years. When the accelerated growth levels off, they become normal-growth firms, with earnings and dividends growing at normal, rather than abnormal, rates. Similarly, firms involved in the research and development of a new drug (e.g. the recent Viagra pill) often achieve super growth for a limited period. If a firm's research is successful, then the firm can obtain a patent on the drug for a limited number of years, during which super growth prevails. After the patent expires, competitors will be allowed to produce the drug, and the original firm becomes a normal-growth firm. Also, most super-growth firms change their dividend policy through time. Specifically, the incentive to retain earnings disappears if no extraordinary investment projects remain. For many super-growth firms, it seems more reasonable to assume that the firm evolves through three stages during their lifecycles:

1. Growth stage. This stage is characterised by the introduction of new products, rapid growth of sales, high profit margins and abnormally high growth in EPS. Still, due to extraordinary profit opportunities, the dividend payout ratio remains low. (In many cases, all earnings are retained and reinvested in the firm. In these cases, the CDGM predicts that the firm's stock has no value (see Equation 15.7), because the model ignores the increase in dividend growth in the subsequent stages.) The extraordinary profits attract competitors, leading to the second stage.
2. Transition stage. In this stage, increasing competion reduces profit margins and earnings growth begins to subside. With fewer new extraordinary investment opportunities, the firm begins to pay out a larger percentage of earnings as dividend. (In this stage, we still cannot apply the CDGM, because the return on investment and the dividend payout ratio change.)
3. Maturity stage. Eventually, the firm reaches the third stage, in which investment opportunities offer, on average, only the required rate of return. The earnings growth rate, payout ratio and return on equity stabilise for the remainder of the firms's life. In addition, EPS,

507

DPS and the share price grow only because the firm retains part of its earnings. (In this stage, we may apply the CDGM using Equation 15.13.)

If the growth rate of a super-growth firm changes according to this three-stage model, or according to some other pattern, then the CDGM no longer applies and we need a valuation model that accounts for changing growth rates.

15.4 Multiple-stage growth models

Multistage growth models account for the fact that firms may grow at different growth rates during different stages of their lifecycles. The basic idea behind multistage models is to simplify Equation 15.2 by assuming growth patterns for the various stages of the firm's lifecycle. In principle, there are infinitely many options; we can specify any number of stages and any growth pattern within every stage. Since there exist no general rules for selecting the appropriate growth pattern, we will not provide a general valuation model. Still, most multistage growth models assume that the firm eventually enters a normal growth stage in some future period $t = N + 1$, either because competition is expected to eliminate extraordinary profits or because the investor simply cannot make accurate long-run predictions of future growth. Hence, the models assume that, for $t = N + 1$ and thereafter, the dividends will grow according to the pattern

$$E(DPS_t) = E(DPS_N)(1 + g)^{t-N}$$

with $g = k(1 - d)$. Hence, we know from Equation 15.7 that the expected share price at $t = N$ is given by

$$E(P_N) = \sum_{t=1}^{\infty} \frac{E(DPS_{N+t})}{(1 + k)^t} = E(DPS_N)\left(\frac{1 + g}{k - g}\right)$$

Substituting this equation and $n = N$ in Equation 15.1 gives

$$P_0 = \sum_{t=1}^{N} \frac{E(DPS_t)}{(1 + k)^t} + \frac{E(DPS_N)}{(1 + k)^N}\left(\frac{1 + g}{k - g}\right) \tag{15.17}$$

This expression is a simplified version of the general DDM in Equation 15.1. It requires only information on the expected dividends before the normal growth stage and the normal growth rate g.

We can directly insert estimates for the individual dividends in Equation 15.17 and compute the intrinsic value. Alternatively, we may try to further simplify Equation 15.1 by specifying growth patterns in the periods before normal growth. The most common multiperiod growth models are two-stage growth models and three-stage growth models.

15.4.1 Two-stage growth models

Two-stage growth models assume that the firm first experiences super growth at the super-growth rate g^* during a period that lasts from $t = 1$ to $t = N$. During this period, the dividends are expected to grow according to the pattern

$$E(DPS_t) = DPS_0(1 + g^*)^t \tag{15.18}$$

Exhibit 15.7	Super-growth firm: expected growth rate of $g_1 = 9\%$ for the first year and $g_2 = 5\%$ thereafter with $5 expected first-year dividend per share (DPS)		
Year (t)	E(EPS$_t$)	E(DPS$_t$)	Stock price
0			$P_0 = 103.64$
1	$10	$5	$P_0(1.09)$
2	$10.90 $P_0(1.09)(1.05)$	$5.45	
3	$11.44 $P_0(1.09)(1.05)^2$	$5.72	

Source: From *Introduction to Investments*, 2nd edn, by Levy. © 1999. Reprinted with permission of South-Western, a division of Thomson Learning: www.thomsonrights.com. Fax 800 730-2215.

After the super-growth period, the firm enters a period of normal growth at the normal growth rate g. During this period, the dividends grow according to the pattern

$$E(DPS_t) = E(DPS_N)(1 + g)^{t-N} = DPS_0(1 + g^*)^N(1 + g)^{t-N}$$

If the super-growth rate (g^*) and the length of the super-growth period (N) are known, then we can use Equation 15.18 to estimate the dividends in the super-growth period. These estimates and the normal growth rate (g) are then plugged into Equation 15.17 to find the stock's value.[13]

To illustrate the two-stage model, Exhibit 15.7 extends the earlier example from Exhibit 15.6. Suppose that in the first year, the firm can again reinvest the retained earnings at a super-growth rate of 18%. This high rate of return is only for one year. The earnings retained from all subsequent years are invested at the firm's normal rate of 10%. In this example, the expected DPS grows at 9% in the first year and at the normal growth of 5% thereafter. Therefore, using Equation 15.17, we find

$$P_0 = \frac{5}{1.10} + \frac{5 \times 1.09}{1.10^2} + \frac{5 \times 1.09}{1.10^2} \times \frac{1.05}{0.10 - 0.05} \approx 103.64$$

Hence, due to the super growth in the first period, the PVGO is only $3.64. This result is quite different from the PVGO of $400 when the extra profit of 18%, and hence the super growth of 9%, were assumed to continue forever.

15.4.2 Three-stage growth models

Recall that many firms evolve through three stages: growth, transition and maturity. Three-stage growth models account for this growth pattern. The model again uses a constant growth rate g^* for the initial super-growth stage. After the super-growth period, the firm enters a transition stage, during which the super-growth rate falls. Finally, the normal growth rate g applies for the maturity stage. There exist many variations to this theme. For example, some models assume a constant rate during the transition stage, while others assume that the growth rate gradually shifts from g^* to g. Still, irrespective of the precise growth pattern, we can apply Equation 15.18 if we first predict the dividends in the super-growth and transition stages using the appropriate growth rates.

---

[13] In this particular case, we can also obtain a single valuation equation (a simplification of Equation 15.17 and a generalisation of Equation 15.7); see Appendix 15.

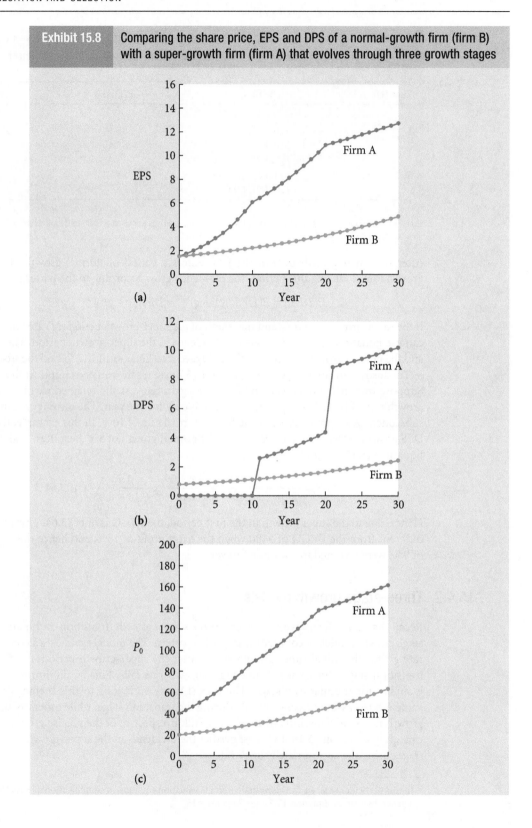

Exhibit 15.8 Comparing the share price, EPS and DPS of a normal-growth firm (firm B) with a super-growth firm (firm A) that evolves through three growth stages

Recall that in the CDGM, the share price, DPS and EPS grow at the same constant rate (g). For multistage growth models, this generally is not true. Exhibit 15.8 illustrates this point using a hypothetical super-growth firm ('firm A') that is expected to evolve through three stages. The initial growth stage lasts for ten years. During this stage, the firm faces extraordinary profitable investment opportunities and the firm's EPS is expected to grow at a rate of 15% per year, starting with a value of 1.5 in the first year. The firm distributes no dividends and retains all earnings, because the return on investments far exceeds the required rate of return of 8%. During the transition stage, which also lasts ten years, the rate of return on investment falls gradually and the firm increases the dividend payout ratio from zero to 40%. The lower return on investment and the higher dividend reduce the growth rate of EPS from 15 to 6%. Finally, in the maturity stage, the return on investments drops to the required rate of return of 8% and the payout ratio rises to 80%, leaving an EPS growth rate of only 1.6%. For the sake of comparison, we have also included the results for firm B, which is a normal-growth firm that also starts with a EPS of 1.5 and that also has a required rate of return of 8%. Firm B pays out 50% of its earnings as dividend. In this case, the CDGM applies and the share price, DPS and EPS all grow at 8%. By contrast, for the super-growth firm, the share price, EPS and DPS have very different patterns.

You will have noticed that multistage growth models require more information than the single stage CDGM (see Equation 15.7). For example, the two-stage model requires two additional input parameters, the length of the super-growth period (N) and the super-growth rate (g^*). More general models require even more input parameters. Of course, estimating these input parameters can be very difficult. However, in many cases, even inaccurate estimates will outperform the naive solution of completely ignoring changing growth rates (that is, using the CDGM).

15.5 Implementing discounted cash flow models in practice

Discounted dividend models are a theoretically sound way of thinking about the value of stocks. Still, in practice DDMs should be used with caution. A close examination of the DDMs (and related models) reveals several baffling problems.[14] The purpose of this section is not to destroy confidence in DDMs but to identify some of the weaknesses of these models. Most alternative valuation models (such as the free cash flow method and the valuation multiples discussed below) also suffer from these problems.

■ DDMs do not explain why mispricing occurs or when it will be corrected. After the exercise of calculating stock values based on the DDM has been completed, what can you do with the results? For example, suppose you determine that a stock is 10% undervalued according to the DDM. What should you do? At first glance, you may say, 'Buy it, of course!' The answer, however, is not that clear-cut. A first problem is determining whether the stock is really mispriced or whether you are just missing some crucial information. For example, your estimate of the dividend growth rate (g) may be too high or your discount rate (k) may be too low. Second, if we use a DDM to identify mispriced stocks, we are assuming that although a stock is not now valued appropriately, some day soon its value will return to its appropriate level. However, the factors that caused the price to be 10% undervalued may well drive it to be 20% undervalued before it begins to turn around. That is, the DDM would be of no use if the stock did not revert back to its fair

---

[14] The following sections are based in part on Nagorniak (1985).

value soon. For these reasons, an analysis of the forces driving the (temporary) mispricing (for example, institutional selling because of a legal constraint) is required when assessing the appropriate action to be taken.

■ The discount rate may change over time. DDMs assume that the discount rate (k) is constant over time. In practice, this may not be the case. As discussed in Section 15.3, firms go through a lifecycle as they move from infancy to maturity. Most firms have a rapid-growth phase, when they pay no dividends; then an expansion phase, when they begin to pay dividends; and finally a maturity phase, when they exhibit little or no growth. A DDM incorporates the changing dividends as the firm progresses through its lifecycle. When discounting dividends through these different phases, why should we believe that the investor's required rate of return remains the same? After all, the risk of the firm also changes over the lifecycle, so k should change with the firm's lifecycle. Intuitively, we would anticipate that k would be lower when the firm is in maturation, because less risk is involved. Thus, to estimate value accurately, we need to allow for changes in both dividends and the investor's required rate of return.

■ Again, the results of DDM generally are highly sensitive to the choice of the input parameters, such as the growth rate (g) and the discount rate (k), in the CDGM. Unfortunately, the estimates for these parameters in many cases are highly inaccurate (see Sections 15.2.1 and 15.2.2). For this reason, investors must assess the robustness of their results with respect to several alternative assumptions about the parameters.

■ The DDM is a forward-looking equation, yet most investors rely on history to establish initial estimates. They combine history with current events to estimate future events. One difficult job of an investor is to make the appropriate alterations to historical estimates. The alterations should include management's current strategy. Clearly, such alterations require skills in evaluating things that are not quantifiable. For example, assessing the current quality of management and the impact it will have on the current stock price is difficult to quantify. A final difficulty lies in establishing how long it will take for a firm to move from one phase to another. For example, how long can a firm remain in the super-growth phase? How can this be estimated? Although not entirely impossible, it is a difficult task.

■ The final problem is determining how to assess the performance of the DDM. The critical question is whether the predicted DDM performance leads to abnormal returns. The DDM may lead to a successful result on some stocks and to a failure on other stocks. Also, the DDM may work only during some time period or under certain conditions. Thus, we need statistical tools to evaluate the extra profit made if we employ this method on many investments and in many time periods. One can, for example, employ the CAPM on many decisions made by the DDM and test whether the return on such a portfolio is significantly higher than the return on a random portfolio with the same risk.

Despite these problems, DDMs remain a useful theoretical framework for stock valuation. Indeed, discounted dividend models are used widely in practice. Connecting Theory to Practice 15.2 gives an example of a recent application by the Bank of England. The bank used a discounted dividend model to analyse the US stock market and concluded that the equity risk premium in July 2001 was extremely low (1 or 2%), even if after accounting for higher future dividend growth due to retained earnings and super growth. Note that the bank assumed implicitly that the market was efficient, and it adjusted the equity risk premium in order to rationalise the high stock market prices. By contrast, if we fix the equity risk premium at, for example, its historical average of 4%, then we may conclude that the stock market was highly overvalued. In fact, Investment in the News 15 takes this approach.

Equities in wonderland

In *Alice Through the Looking Glass*, the Queen believed as many as six impossible things before breakfast. According to the Bank of England's latest financial stability review, the US equity markets may be attempting a similar feat.

The Bank uses the standard dividend discount model, the basis for all equity valuation methods, to see what assumptions investors are making. In the model, equity prices are based on the present value of expected future dividends (and other cash flows). Those future dividends are discounted by a risk-free rate (normally the real yield on government bonds) and the equity risk premium (the excess return demand by investors for holding a risky asset such as equities).

Assume dividends grow in the future at an annual real rate of 2.5 per cent – just above the historical average of 2.2 per cent – and the risk-free rate is 3 per cent. On that basis, the equity risk premium fell to about zero in early 2000 and is still less than 1 per cent. That compares with a historical average for the risk premium of 4 per cent.

No doubt, new era enthusiasts will laugh at the idea of real dividend growth as paltry as 2.5 per cent a year. But the Bank has anticipated such an objection. The report points out: 'Even if investors now expect real dividend growth to be 4 per cent annually as a result of higher trend productivity growth, the premium would have had to fall to about 2 per cent.' In order to make the equation work with the historical risk premium of 4 per cent, investors would have to assume a real dividend growth rate of 6 per cent a year.

Is that possible? One reason why the real dividend growth rate might be set to rise is that the dividend payout ratio in the US has fallen sharply from 50.9 per cent in 1990–93 to 28.5 per cent in the second quarter of 2001.

If companies are retaining more of their earnings and reinvesting the proceeds, that could point to higher profit – and dividend – growth. So the Bank's statisticians have duly calculated the implied return on equity required to justify current share prices. Assuming a risk premium of 4 per cent and a risk-free rate of 3 per cent, the return on equity would have to rise to 8 per cent compared with the historic average of 7 per cent.

But, given the assumption that the US corporate sector as a whole is increasing the amount of capital invested, how realistic is it to assume a rise in the return on equity? Surely a greater level of competition should lead to a reduction in the rate of return? Furthermore, the Bank argues that this scenario would still require a real dividend growth rate of 6 per cent a year.

Of course, there are occasions on which dividends can grow significantly faster than gross domestic product – when, for example, profits are recovering from a cyclical slump. But that is not the case at the moment. The profit share of GDP is about 12 per cent of GDP compared with a long-term average of 10 per cent.

So how else might the current level of the market be justified? One answer could be a fall in the risk-free rate. But the Bank points out that, if the US index-linked bond market is any guide, the risk-free rate has been rising, not falling.

Some will disdain the Bank's focus on dividends, pointing to the increased use of share buy-backs to return cash to shareholders. But buying back shares from some investors is not the same as returning cash to all investors – and, in any case, if share buy-backs are accounted for, so should rights issues, placings and executive option plans.

In the end, we are remorselessly driven back to a lower equity risk premium as the most plausible explanation for the level of US equity markets. And the Bank points to some reasons why the premium might have fallen: greater opportunities for portfolio diversification, increased participation in the markets, falling trading costs.

▶

But if the equity risk premium is very low, presumably investors should expect similar future rates of return from equities and bonds. Surveys show little sign such a view is widespread. And if the risk premium is very low, equity issuance should represent a very cheap method of finance for companies. However, they are issuing bonds by the bucketful.

So either equity investors are being incredibly optimistic or corporate finance directors are missing a golden opportunity. Curiouser and curiouser, said Alice.

Source: Philip Coggan, 'Equities in Wonderland', FT.com site, 1 July 2001.

15.6 The free cash flow model

As discussed above, only expected future dividends are needed for stock valuation. However, estimating future dividends can be very difficult. If the earnings per share grow at a constant rate and the firm regularly pays a given portion of its earnings, then future dividends can be estimated using, for example, Equation 15.10. In practice, however, relying on future dividends presents an estimation problem for firms that do not pay cash dividends, firms that pay irregular dividends, and firms that change their payout ratio over time. For example, how can we evaluate firms such as Microsoft, which as of 2003 had never paid cash dividends and had announced no intention to do so in the future? In fact, currently only about a fifth of public companies pay dividends; 'fallen angels' can no longer afford to pay dividends, and small-growth firms retain earnings to internally fund their future growth.[15] The free cash flow model (FCFM) applies in such cases.

The FCFM is based on a priciple that was discussed in Section 15.3.1; for normal-growth firms, the dividend policy does not affect the valuation of the stock, because the firm simply reinvests all retained earnings at the required rate of return. Hence, we can value the stock 'as if' the firm decided to distribute the maximum sustainable amount of dividend, even though the firm may actually pay no dividends at all. This maximum amount is called the free cash flow (FCF) of the firm. For example, if a firm invests all its earnings because it expands, then this does not mean that it does not have FCF. The FCF in this case is all that is invested for growth rather than for maintaining current operations. It follows from Equation 15.13 that the value of a normal-growth firm can be computed as

$$P_0 = \frac{E(FCF_1)}{k} \qquad (15.19)$$

where $E(FCF_1)$ is the next period's expected FCF per share. Notice three things:

- As in Equation 15.13, only next year's expected FCF is relevant for stock valuation, and any increase in the expected FCF in the future should be ignored, even though in fact the FCF is expected to grow over time (because part of the FCF is retained, and even if deposited in the bank will add income to the firm).
- Equation 15.13 uses $E(EPS_1)$, while Equation 15.19 uses $E(FCF_1)$. In some cases, FCF and EPS are equivalent, but this is not true in general, as we will see below.

---

[15] See Fama and French (2001).

■ It follows from the discussion in Section 15.3.2 that this approach does not apply for super-growth firms, because maximising dividend payments would destroy the PVGO of super-growth firms. Indeed, for super-growth firms, the FCFM calculates only the value of assets in place.

Before defining FCF, a definition of the firm's cash flow (CF) from operations is in order. The firm's annual cash flow is the cash flow received from operations in a given year, after interest and taxes have been paid. For simplicity, assume that all the firm's expenses and revenues are for cash (this issue will be discussed later). Then, the cash flow from operations is simply the earnings plus the depreciation, denoted by D_p. We add the depreciation to the earnings, because depreciation is not a cash outflow. Thus,

$$CF = EPS + D_p$$

where CF, EPS, and D_p are all per share.

The CF has a clear-cut definition and is easy to measure, but the definition of the FCF, which we need for stock valuation, is more ambiguous. The most common definition of FCF is the cash flow that the firm has after deducting the capital expenditure needed to maintain the ongoing operation of the firm at its current level. To illustrate this, suppose the firm's CF is $50 million. It needs to invest $10 million to maintain its operation at the current level, but it invests $20 million because it wants to expand. After deducting the cash outlay on investment, the firm actually has only $30 million; however, according to the previous definition, its FCF is $40 million. It could distribute $40 million as dividends without affecting its current level of operation. If the firm needs to reinvest the depreciation to maintain the current level of operation (a reasonable assumption), then (once again assuming that all operations are for cash) the FCF equals the EPS, because

$$FCF = CF - D_p = EPS + D_p - D_p = EPS$$

Thus, if we adopt the FCFM as the model for stock valuation, the value of the stock is simply the present value of next year's expected EPS (as in Equation 15.13). In other words, the expected EPS is the maximum amount that the firm can pay as dividends without affecting its current level of operation.

Since the accounting principles are not on a cash basis (see Chapter 16), we generally cannot assume that the depreciation is what the firm needs to invest to maintain its operation at the current level. Hence, next period's expected EPS is not precisely the relevant measure of FCF per share, and adjustments are needed in employing the FCFM. The FCF is estimated by taking the CF from operations and subtracting the capital expenditures needed for the firm to maintain its current level of operation. These adjustments are very tricky. The capital expenditures must be analysed carefully and added back to the CF if they are not necessary for the firm's continuing operation at its current level.

Another version of the FCFM commonly employed by practitioners discounts the firm's gross operating cash flow, which is the cash flow before interest and taxes are paid. This method avoids the distorting effects of changing taxes and debt over time. (Note that when the proportion of debt changes, the cost of equity (k) also changes, which complicates the analysis.) By discounting the gross free cash flow, the value of the firm that belongs to the stockholders, bondholders and the IRS (taxes) is obtained.

In summary, for a normal-growth firm, the PV of all expected future dividends is equal to the PV of an annuity of next period's expected FCF. Thus, next period's expected FCF can be used to evaluate a firm, even if no dividends have been paid in the past. Using the FCFM, there is no need to forecast when the firm will start paying dividends or whether the firm's payout rate will change in the future.

Practice box

Problem   Suppose that next year's expected FCF is $10. The firm invests the depreciation in such a way that it can maintain its operation at the current level forever. The discount rate is $k = 10\%$.

1. What is the value of the stock if the entire $10 per share is expected to be paid as cash dividends each year?
2. What is the value of the stock if the firm does not intend to pay dividends in the first year and invests the entire FCF in a perpetuity at k? (Assume that from year 2 and thereafter, all earnings are paid as dividends.)
3. Assume that the characteristics in part 2 apply, and we discount the expected future FCF rather than next year's expected FCF. What is the PV of all expected future earnings?

Solution   1. The value of the stock is given by the present value of the $10 annual expected FCF: $10/0.1 = $100.
2. If dividends are not paid in the first year, then $10 is expected to be reinvested, yielding an expected $10 \times 0.1 = $1 in each of the following years. Thus, $11 is expected from year 2 onward, and the present value of expected future dividends is as follows:

$$\frac{0}{1.1} + \frac{\$11}{(1.1)^2} + \frac{\$11}{(1.1)^3} + \ldots = \frac{1}{1.1}\left[\frac{\$11}{1.1} + \frac{\$11}{(1.1)^2} + \ldots\right] = \frac{1}{1.1}\left(\frac{\$11}{0.1}\right) = \$100$$

We see that by the DDM, the value of the stock is $100, regardless of the dividend policy of the firm. Thus, even though free cash flows (and dividends) are $11 per share (from year 2), the value of the stock can be obtained by dividing the next year's expected FCF ($10) by the discount rate and ignoring the future growth in FCF.

3. In this case, the PV of earnings is given by

$$\frac{\$10}{1.1} + \frac{\$11}{(1.1)^2} + \frac{\$11}{(1.1)^3} + \ldots = \frac{\$10}{1.1} + \$100 \cong \$109.09$$

which is higher than the true value as obtained by the DDM.

The box above illustrates that the DDM implies that we can either discount all expected future dividends or simply discount the next year's expected FCF (i.e. $10 in our example) and ignore the future growth in FCF. Thus, using the FCFM, we discount the maximum dividends that the firm could pay next year, not the dividends it actually will pay. Although the firm will have $11 FCF from year 2 and thereafter, we look at the next year's FCF of $10 and assume it will be at this level forever. The fact that stockholders did not get the $10 in the first year does not affect the value of the stock, because it is offset by the fact that the $10 is invested by the firm and more will be paid to the stockholders in the future. Thus, assuming that the $10 was obtained in year 1 (even though no cash was distributed to the stockholders), and ignoring the increase in future earnings (or FCF) that is due to the reinvestment of the retained earnings, the same present value of future cash flows is obtained. In other words, the following two hypothetical cash flows have the same present value of $100:

■ $10, $10, $10, . . . (next year's expected FCF).
■ $0, $11, $11, . . . (expected future DPS).

Thus, although the second scenario represents the actual expected cash flows to the stockholder and the first scenario does not, we can switch from scenario 2 to scenario 1 without changing the present value. This is exactly what the FCFM does. It relies on next year's expected FCF ($10) and ignores the growth in next year's FCF (+$1). If we discount the expected future FCF, rather than next year's expected FCF, we get an overvaluation, as in part 3 of the previous box. Since we do not know the cash flow given by scenario 2 or when the firm will stop reinvesting its earnings and start paying cash dividends (for example, the firm may also skip the $11 in year 2 and pay more dividends from year 3 onward), we can use the FCF given by scenario 1 to calculate the value of the stock. Thus, by using the FCFM, we can get the PV of future dividends without knowing what these dividends will actually be. This is true as long as the firm reinvests at k.

15.7 Valuation multiples

DDMs provide a useful framework for valuing stocks, because they account for the return and risk to stockholders in a consistent manner. Still, DDMs are not a panacea. Section 15.5 discussed some practical problems (associated with valuation methods in general – not just DDMs). In addition, despite their theoretical elegance, DDMs require considerable computational effort (as you may well have discovered by now!), and their results can be difficult to understand and to communicate to others. For these reasons, practioners frequently employ simpler valuation methods based on valuation multiples. Generally, multiples are the ratio of the market price of a share or the total market value of a firm's equity to a value driver, i.e. a variable that is supposed to measure the intrinsic value of the share or the firm's equity. Examples of value drivers include dividends, earnings, cash flows and sales. Practitioners use many different valuation multiples. We cannot possibly review all existing valuation multiples in this section. Indeed, as Connecting Theory to Practice 15.3 reports, during the great technology bubble of 1999–2000, many investors valued stocks using multiples that were based not on traditional value drivers but rather on 'market opportunity' and 'concept'. Rather than giving a complete review, we will focus on three popular multiples: the price/earnings ratio,

> ### → Connecting Theory to Practice 15.3   **FT**
>
> ## Conceptual
>
> Never underestimate Wall Street's ingenuity when it comes to justifying the latest share price bubble. Internet stocks – now somewhat deflated – taught everyone to study multiples of revenues rather than multiples of earnings (because there were none). Then came internet infrastructure companies, such as Akamai Technologies, which wasn't even generating sales, so analysts switched neatly to assessments of the 'market opportunity' – measured in billions of dollars. Now the money men are being confronted by companies such as Corvis, which went public without earnings, without revenues and with a product that no one was allowed to see. Even so, the business still managed to soar initially to a Dollars 37 bn market capitalisation and is currently worth a handy Dollars 28 bn. But have no fear: 'It's not a multiple on revenue, it's a multiple of concept,' explains a Wall Street soothsayer. Got that?
>
> Source: 'Conceptual', *Financial Times*, 28 August, 2000.

the dividend yield and Tobin's q. The strength of these measures (essentially, the simplicity in computing, understanding and communicating them) and their weaknesses (essentially, their incorrect or incomplete representation of the risk and return to investors) also carry over to many other multiples.

15.7.1 Price/earnings ratio

Probably the most popular multiple is the price/earnings (P/E) ratio. This multiple is generally computed as the ratio of the current stock price to the current year's annual EPS:

$$P/E = \frac{P_0}{EPS_0}$$

The reciprocal of the P/E ratio, the earnings/price (E/P) ratio or earnings yield, is also used frequently:

$$E/P = \frac{EPS_0}{P_0}$$

A low P/E ratio (or high E/P ratio) is typically interpreted as evidence that the stock is attractive. After all, if the share price is low relative to the EPS, then we may expect relatively high dividends; also, we may expect capital gains once other investors discover this. Are investors justified in using the P/E ratio? Is the P/E ratio an economically meaningful measure for identifying underpriced and overpriced stocks?

The P/E ratio can be seen as an extremely simplified DDM. After all, dividends are paid from earnings and earnings are in the denominator of the P/E ratio. The P/E ratio is linked closely to the CDGM for normal-growth firms (super-growth firms are discussed below). As discussed in Section 15.3.1, the intrinsic value of the stocks of such firms is given by Equation 15.13. We may rewrite that equation in the following manner:

$$\frac{E(EPS_1)}{P_0} = k \tag{15.20}$$

Consequently, the reciprocal of the P/E ratio is related directly to the expected rate of return for normal-growth firms. A low P/E ratio suggests a high expected rate of return and, hence, the stock seems attractive.

However, this conclusion is generally wrong for at least three reasons: estimation error, super-growth opportunities and risk.

Estimation error

Equation 15.20 uses next year's expected EPS, while the P/E ratio is generally computed using the current year's EPS. As discussed earlier in this chapter, estimating corporate earnings generally is extremely difficult because corporations are exposed to various risks at the level of the economy, the industry and the firm. Using a single observation (last year's EPS) is likely to provide a very inaccurate estimate. Hence, firms with a high P/E ratio may simply be firms whose EPS is temporarily inflated, and low P/E firms' EPS may temporarily lie above the expectations.

Indeed, the financial media sometimes publish not only the P/E ratio with the current year's earnings per share but also the P/E ratio with next year's expected EPS. This P/E ratio is commonly referred to as the forward P/E ratio. The 'normal' P/E ratio and the forward P/E ratio can differ substantially. For example, as of 5 January 1997, the P/E ratio of Boeing using the EPS over 1997 was 74.2. By contrast, Boeing's P/E ratio was 19.9 if we used the analyst earnings estimates for 1998.[16]

Still, even if we use estimates of next year's EPS, then we should remember that estimates may be inaccurate and that 'abnormal' P/E ratios may simply reflect estimation error. This problem is highly relevant, for example, if we compare firms from different countries with different accounting methods for computing earnings.

Super-growth opportunities

Equation 15.20 applies for normal-growth firms but not super-growth firms. Super-growth firms are expected to grow at a higher rate than the required rate of return after correcting for dividend payments (which are rare for super-growth firms). EPS measures the value of assets in place, but it does not measure the PVGO of super-growth firms. To see this, we may rewrite Equation 15.14 as follows:

$$\frac{E(EPS_1)}{P_0} = k\left(1 - \frac{PVGO}{P_0}\right) \tag{15.21}$$

The term $\left(1 - \dfrac{PVGO}{P_0}\right)$ is smaller than 1 for firms with PVGO. Hence, the E/P ratio will underestimate the expected return on super-growth stocks. Consequently, firms with a low P/E ratio may simply be firms with no extraordinary investment opportunities, while a high P/E ratio may simply measure super-growth possibilities. Indeed, small-growth stocks generally have high P/E ratios, and the P/E ratio is used frequently as a measure for future (abnormal) growth.

To illustrate this point, it is useful to return to the two normal-growth firms in Exhibit 15.5. These two cases have the following expected rates of return:

$$\text{(a)} \quad k = \frac{E(DPS_1)}{P_0} + g = \frac{\$5}{\$100} + 0.05 = 0.05 + 0.05 = 0.10$$

$$\text{(b)} \quad k = \frac{E(DPS_1)}{P_0} + g = \frac{\$1}{\$100} + 0.09 = 0.01 + 0.09 = 0.10$$

Thus, the future profitability to the investor is expected to be 10%. Indeed, $E/P = 0.10$ in both cases, as $\$10/\$100 = 0.10$. However, employing the P/E ratio (or the E/P ratio) for super-growth firms is misleading. Comparing Exhibits 15.5a and 15.6 yields

$$\text{For normal-growth firm: } \frac{E}{P} = \frac{\$10}{\$100} = 0.10$$

$$\text{For super-growth firm: } \frac{E}{P} = \frac{\$10}{\$500} = 0.02$$

Using the P/E ratio, we indeed get a precise figure for a normal-growth firm but a distorted figure for super-growth firms. (Note that $k = 10\%$, not 2%; see Exhibit 15.6.) The reason for the distortion is that for the super-growth firm, the future earnings, which grow at an accelerated rate, are ignored in the calculation based on E/P, because that calculation is based fully on current earnings.

---

[16] Source: *Barron's*, 5 January 1998, p. MW97.

Exhibit 15.9	Comparing the price/earnings (P/E) ratio of a normal-growth firm (firm B) with a super-growth firm (firm A) that evolves through three growth stages

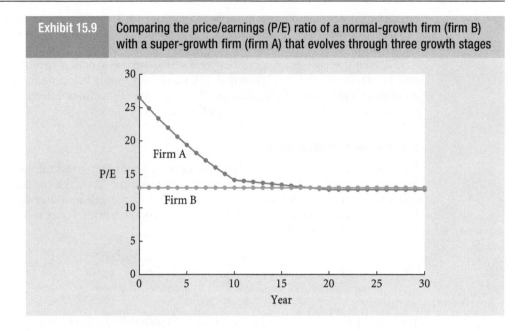

To illustrate our point further, Exhibit 15.9 displays the expected path of the P/E ratio for the super-growth firm A and the normal-growth firm B from Exhibit 15.8. Initially, during the growth stage, firm A has a substantially higher P/E ratio than firm B. However, the difference becomes smaller as firm A moves to the transition period. Finally, in the maturity stage, firm A's PVGO has disappeared and the P/E ratios of the two firms are equal.

Risk

Even if we value normal-growth firms and we use accurate estimates of expected EPS, then the P/E ratio still is not a valid valuation measure. In this (rare) case, we know from Equation 15.19 that the P/E is the reciprocal of the expected return. The expected return generally is not a valid measure for ranking stocks, because it ignores risk. Hence, the P/E ratio may measure nothing but differences in risk between stocks; risky stocks will require a high expected return and hence a low P/E ratio (see, for example, Equation 15.10), and 'safe' stocks will tend to have a high P/E ratio. Similarly, we need to be careful if we compare P/E ratios from different time periods. After all, the expected rate of return, and hence the 'normal' P/E ratio, changes as the riskless rate, the riskiness of stocks and the market risk premiums change through time.

For these reasons, the P/E ratio generally does not measure the degree by which the market price of stocks differs from the intrinsic value. The P/E ratio may confuse undervalued stocks with stocks that report temporarily inflated earnings, lack profitable investment opportunities and/or are highly risky. Conversely, overvaluation may be confused with temporarily deflated earnings, super-growth opportunities and low risk. Of course, there is no simple remedy for the above problems, and all valuation methods suffer from inaccurate earnings estimates and inadequate corrections for risk. However, the point is that we can do better than to completely ignore these problems.

Still, we do not claim that the P/E ratio is useless or that investors who use the P/E ratio are mistaken. It makes perfectly good sense to use (forward) P/E ratios to compare firms from a peer group, provided that the peer group consists of 'comparable' companies (for example, the same industry, the same size and the same degree of financial leverage), and provided that the estimates of next period's EPS are 'reasonably' accurate. This approach effectively tries to control for the above problems.

→ **Connecting Theory to Practice 15.4**

The great technology bubble has been purged

One of the favourite charts of the bears on Wall Street is a historical graph of the price/earnings ratio of the stock market. Historical data permit us to calculate this all-important yardstick all the way back to 1871 for the Standard & Poor's 500 index, or a similar group of high-capitalisation stocks.

Until the past decade, the ratio fluctuated between the high single digits and the low 20s, with a mean of about 15. But during the past bull market and the recession of 2001 the ratio soared to 47 and, even with stock prices down about 40 per cent from their peak, the ratio stands today at 29 times the average reported earnings of the past 12 months of $29.94.

These data make it easy to convince investors that the market may have to fall substantially more before this bear market ends. But there are two counters to this pessimism.

First, p/e ratios always spike higher in recessions, since earnings are temporarily depressed. The latest recession took a severe toll on profits, particularly in the technology sector, where earnings have slumped. Over the next 12 months, reported earnings are expected to rise – using a conservative methodology – to $37.79.

Second, there is no reason why the current p/e ratio should equal the historical average, unless one believes that the economy and the financial markets are the same now as over the past 130 years. But this is clearly not the case. The sharp drop in transaction costs makes it quite easy for investors to diversify their portfolio completely and thereby reduce their risk in equities, if they choose to do so. This action would have been quite costly and practically impossible to achieve throughout most of the 19th and early 20th centuries. Throughout history, liquid assets have always commanded higher prices than less liquid assets. Given the explosive increase in share trading volume, it cannot be denied that stocks have become much cheaper to trade than in the past. Furthermore, extreme events that have been so detrimental in the past, such as banking panics, the Great Depression and double-digit inflation, are extremely unlikely in the future as modern central banks can both keep the financial system solvent and inflation under control. Last, as investors become better educated about superior long-term returns on equity (which have averaged between 6.5 and 7 per cent a year after inflation in the US and are only a bit lower in the UK), shareholders should bid up stock prices to higher multiples than those that prevailed in the past. My research suggests low inflation, favourable taxes on equities and low transaction costs justify a p/e ratio in the low 20s for the S&P 500 index. It is quite possible that from these higher levels of valuation, stockholders will receive a somewhat lower return than they have in the past. The 6.7 per cent real historical return on stocks is quite generous, given the relative long-term stability of stock returns, and is an adequate premium for investors who endure the short-term vicissitudes of the market. A forward-looking prospective real return of 5.5 per cent on equities is still about 3 percentage points above the return that is available from risk-free, inflation-indexed government bonds.

One should note that, although I have taken 'reported earnings' as my yardstick, Standard and Poor's has just released estimates of 'core earnings' of S&P 500 firms. Core earnings are a tough new standard that accurately reflect the profitability of a company's core businesses and should become the new standard for determining what its stock is worth. Over the past 12 months, these core earnings fell considerably below reported earnings owing primarily to the full expensing of

▶

options and the decline in pension portfolios backing defined-benefit plans. However, if the return on stocks is a modest 7.8 per cent next year, S&P reports that pension costs will not be a negative factor in next year's earnings. Furthermore, with the decline in the equity market, stock options are becoming a far less popular form of employee compensation. Therefore, 2003 core earnings should be much closer to reported earnings than over the past 12 months.

All these factors suggest that the sharp decline in US stock prices has purged the excesses of the great technology bubble of 1999–2001. Valuations are higher than they usually are at the end of a bear market but they are close to those justified by favourable economic and market factors. From these levels, stocks should give investors long-term forward-looking returns that not only are near their historical levels but also substantially outstrip returns on fixed-income assets.

Source: Jeremy Siegel, 'The Great Technology Bubble Has Been Purged', FT.com site, 28 October 2002.

→ Making the connection

In this article, Professor Siegel, a professor of finance at the Wharton School of the University of Pennsylvania, argued that the high P/E ratios of US stocks did not imply that the stock market was (still) overvalued at the time of writing (October 2002). Rather, he explained the high P/E ratios by a temporary depression of earnings due to the economic recession and a structurally lower required return on equity (due to various factors discussed in the article). With hindsight, we know that the 'technology bubble' was not fully 'purged' by October 2002. Still, the article points out some important limitations of the P/E ratio.

15.7.2 Dividend yield

The dividend yield is generally computed as the current year's cash dividend per share divided by the current stock price:

$$DY = \frac{DPS_0}{P_0}$$

Like a low P/E ratio (or a high E/P ratio), a high dividend yield typically is interpreted as evidence that the stock is attractive. However, the dividend yield suffers from limitations that are similar to those for the P/E ratio. Specifically, it follows from Equation 15.7 that the dividend yield for normal-growth firms can be expressed as follows:

$$DY = \frac{DPS_0}{\left(\dfrac{E(DPS_1)}{k-g}\right)} = \frac{DPS_0}{\left(\dfrac{(1+g)DPS_0}{k-g}\right)} = \frac{(k-g)}{(1+g)} \qquad (15.22)$$

Hence, the dividend ratio depends on the growth rate (g). For firms with high growth, we may expect a low dividend yield, even if the price is fair. There are two reasons for this. First, high-growth firms have low values for the numerator $(k - g)$, or the discount rate that the CDGM applies to next year's DPS. Second, high-growth firms have high values for the denominator $(1 + g)$; the current year's DPS underestimates next year's DPS (which enters the CDGM). Similarly, for firms with high risk, the discount rate (k) is high and, hence, the dividend yield is also high.

Also, like the P/E ratio, the dividend yield is affected by super-growth possibilities. Specifically, super-growth possibilities tend to lower the dividend yield, because they drive up the stock price relative to the current earnings and may also reduce the current dividends (because the firm retains earnings for profitable reinvestment).

Briefly, a high dividend ratio may reflect any of the following: (1) the stock is undervalued, (2) last year's dividend was temporarily inflated, (3) the firm has no profitable investment opportunities, (4) the payout ratio is high, and (5) the stock is highly risky.

Still, as is true for the P/E ratio, it can be sensible to use the dividend yield, provided we use a homogeneous peer group and provided we use a forward dividend yield with a sufficiently accurate estimate of next period's DPS. In this case, the dividend yield is consistent with the discounted cash flow principle.

One other interesting application of the dividend yield is in measuring the duration of stocks. Recall from Chapter 14 that the duration of a bond portfolio measures the length of the holding period for which the portfolio can be 'immunised' against adverse movements in the investor's required rate of return. If the length of holding period equals the duration of the bond portfolio, then the reinvestment effect exactly cancels the price effect. A similar analysis is possible for stocks. That is, at least conceptually, by equating the duration of the stock portfolio with the investor's holding period, a stock portfolio can be 'immunised' against adverse movements in the investor's required rate of return (k).[17] If k rises, then stockholders will suffer capital losses. However, if the duration of a stock portfolio is matched with the length of the holding period, then the effect of reinvesting future dividends at a higher rate of return will cancel the initial capital losses.

If we start from the CDGM (Equation 15.7), then we can use the mathematics of infinite series to demonstrate that a stock's duration is given by

$$D_s = \frac{\sum_{t=1}^{\infty} t \frac{E(DPS_t)}{(1+k)^t}}{P_0} = \frac{\sum_{t=1}^{\infty} t DPS_0 \frac{(1+g)^t}{(1+k)^t}}{DPS_0 \left(\frac{1+g}{k-g}\right)} = \left(\frac{1+k}{k-g}\right) \quad (15.23)$$

For example, if $k = 14\%$ and $g = 10\%$, then $D_s = (1 + 0.14)/(0.14 - 0.10) = 28.5$ years. By the definition of duration, a holding period of 28.5 years would minimise the risk of a change in k. The 28.5-year holding period is the point where the price and reinvestment-rate risks are just offset. Suppose another firm has the same k but a higher growth rate $(g = 11\%)$. Then, the duration of the firm's stock is $D_s = (1 + 0.14)/(0.14 - 0.11) = 38$ years. Thus, the common stock of this firm has a longer duration. This makes sense, because with a higher growth rate, relatively more cash flow is obtained in the more distant future, which increases the duration. This analysis demonstrates why insurance companies and other investors who have long-term horizons should consider stocks with a low dividend yield; high-dividend stocks entail a relatively high reinvestment risk for these investors.

Duration can be approximated by the reciprocal of the dividend yield in Equation 15.22, i.e.

$$D_s = \frac{1+k}{k-g} \cong \frac{1+g}{k-g}$$

---

[17] Of course, the investor is not immunised against changes in the expectations about future EPS and DPS. Also, duration applies only for small changes of the discount rate and the portfolio needs to be rebalanced periodically to match its duration with the length of the holding period.

For example, as of 6 July 1998, Texaco's dividend yield was 2.9%, implying a duration of $1/0.029 \cong 34.48$ years. For utility firms, which typically have dividend yields of about 6%, the duration is about $1/0.06 = 16.67$ years.

15.7.3 Tobin's q

Connecting Theory to Practice 15.5 discusses the strengths and weaknesses of another popular valuation multiple, Tobin's q. This multiple is computed as the ratio of the market value of a company to the replacement cost (that is, the cost of replicating the firm's assets and liabilities). In the long run, competition will force the market value and the replacement to be approximately equal (that is, Tobin's q will approximately equal 1). If the market value exceeds the replacement cost, then new competitors will enter the market, which will lower the market value of the company. Conversely, if the market value falls short of the replacement cost, then existing competitors will exit the market, hence increasing the market value of the company.

 Connecting Theory to Practice 15.5

Getting the measure of Wall Street

The challenge of stock market investment is to identify value ahead of the competition, to buy stocks when they are 'undervalued'. The trouble is that traditional indicators of value have always been somewhat unreliable, and have become even more so in the current bull market.

In the old days when dividends averaged around 4.5 per cent of share prices, as they did until the 1950s, the dividend yield gave a useful indication. In recent decades, however, companies have retained more of their earnings for re-investment and paid out more through stock buybacks. The dividend yield has not reverted to its long-term average, and its use as a measure of value is doubtful. Because corporate earnings are volatile, depressed in bad years and inflated in boom times, the price-earnings multiple – the ratio of share price and earnings-per-share – is another poor indicator. Even more discredited is the notion that the ratio of share price to 'book value', measured by dividing the number of outstanding shares by net assets on the balance sheet, has anything meaningful to say. Not only is book value corrupted by inflation and takeovers, but many high technology companies achieve high earnings with little capital. Another valuation tool involves comparing either corporate earnings or dividends to the yield on government bonds. Unfortunately, there appears to be no stable relationship between share prices and bonds. Finally, stocks are valued using a dividend discount model which puts a present value on future dividends. Although theoretically correct, this method produces wildly varying results depending on the discount rate and other assumptions fed into the model.

Some economists claim that investors have no need for valuation tools since shares are always priced efficiently by the market and there is never a discrepancy between share price and intrinsic value. All investors need do is buy an index fund, regardless of price, knowing that the best financial brains are unlikely to do better. This is the so-called 'efficient market hypothesis'. The weakness of this theory is that it fails to explain how shares become efficiently priced, since this situation could only come about if someone were already applying an effective yardstick of value. Furthermore, at times shares become so overpriced that they subsequently underperform other investments for lengthy periods. Thus investors who bought shares blindly in the summer of 1929 waited quarter of a century for the stock market to regain its peak. In today's heady market how can one be sure that a similar period of under-performance is not around the corner?

Before despairing, the prudent investor might consider a valuation method that is currently being touted by Andrew Smithers, a City economist with his own research firm, and Stephen Wright of Cambridge University. In their forthcoming book, Valuing Wall Street*, Smithers and Wright claim that intrinsic value can be identified by dividing the market capitalisation of companies by their replacement cost (i.e. what it would cost to build the companies from scratch). This measure is known as 'Tobin's "q"' after the American Nobel-prize winning economist, James Tobin, who devised it in the late 1960s.

The inspiration for 'q' came from a comment in Keynes' General Theory: 'The daily revaluations of the Stock Exchange,' wrote Keynes, 'inevitably exert a decisive influence on the rate of current investment. For there is no sense in building up a new enterprise at a cost greater than that at which a similar enterprise can be purchased; whilst there is an inducement to spend on a new project what may seem an extravagant sum, if it can be floated on the Stock Exchange at an immediate profit.' In other words, Keynes was arguing that the value of a company in the stock market must be related to the cost of establishing a new company. For Tobin, the relationship between the market value of companies and their replacement cost has a profound influence on corporate investment.

Smithers and Wright observe that 'q', the ratio of market capitalisation to corporate net worth, rises and falls but reverts over the long run to a stable average. While Tobin claims the reversion of 'q' comes about through changes in corporate investment, Smithers and Wright argue that the process operates mainly through movements in share prices. Their conclusion is axiomatic: when 'q' is above its long-term average share prices are destined to fall; and when 'q' is below average shares offer good value. The reversion of 'q' occurs because in a free market the cost of capital (what companies pay for their capital) must, in the long run, equal the returns on capital (the total returns investors receive from their stock market investments). If the return on shares is higher than the cost of capital new capital will flood into the stock market. This explains why bull markets are accompanied by a boom in flotations, a tendency witnessed recently in the internet sector. Conversely, when shares cost less than the replacement cost of the assets they represent, they will be bought up by other companies or purchased for their break-up value. This process was at work during the leveraged buy-out boom of the mid-1980s when the stock market was undervalued on a replacement-cost basis. According to Smithers and Wright, '"q" acts like a piece of elastic, it pulls the stock market back towards its proper value when it gets too high or too low'.

During the twentieth century, Tobin's 'q' successfully indicated several periods of extreme overvaluation: in the late 1920s, in 1937, and in the early 1970s. On the other hand, 'q' also identified good times to buy stocks: most notably in 1932, during the depth of the depression when corporate earnings were severely depressed. Smithers and Wright claim that investors can earn higher returns with less risk by following the investment dictates of 'q' than by holding a portfolio of stocks through thick and thin.

Before getting too excited, investors must brace themselves for the bad news.

First, 'q' cannot be used an indicator of value for individual companies, since some companies are worth more than their replacement cost and others are worth less. It is only useful for valuing the market as a whole.

Second, 'q' gives no indication of short-term market movements. Smithers and Wright have been arguing since 1995 that the US market has been severely overvalued according to 'q'. Anyone who followed their advice would have sat on the sidelines during the greatest bull market on record.

Third, some commentators allege that 'q' has become less relevant in the information age when companies require less tangible capital and seem, therefore, to earn extraordinarily high returns with what little capital they do employ. At first glance, this is a persuasive argument. But Smithers and Wright deny it vehemently. They claim there is no evidence that modern companies are, on average, less capital intensive than in the past. Some companies, they say, earn high rates of

▶

return on their capital and others earn below average returns: goodwill accruing to some should be offset by the 'ill will' of less successful ones.

James Tobin, now in semi-retirement at Yale University in the US, agrees. 'It's hard to apply "q" theory to valuations of firms that have very little physical capital, where what is being valued is human skill and ingenuity,' he says. 'The problem is that slavery is illegal, and there is no way a firm can keep a superb team of employees from grabbing all the rents.' In other words, it is difficult for companies reliant on 'human capital' to earn high rates of return. Thus investment banks are forced to pay out huge bonuses, even when they make no profits; and high tech companies, such as Microsoft, dish out billions of dollars worth of stock options to their employees.

Smithers and Wright say that 'q' would cease to function properly only if there were a rise in monopolies, which have barriers to entry and pricing power to earn excessive returns. However, they see no evidence that monopolies are increasing. On the contrary, the internet is characterised by low barriers to entry and therefore should offer companies, and investors, only average returns.

Smithers and Wright conclude that the US stock market is currently two and a half times over-valued, and that the reversion of 'q' will cause stock prices to fall by around 60 per cent. The British market is also overvalued but not so grossly. Although they do not know when the market will turn, they predict there is less than a 5 per cent chance that US stocks will outperform US inflation-protected bonds over the next 15 years. James Tobin is more cautious and prefers not to use 'q' to identify stock market bubbles or predict crashes. Of course, he adds, bubbles occur, and then reversion occurs when psychology changes and the bubble bursts.

Fund managers will ignore the message of 'q', since it requires them to be underweight in stocks, a suicidal position in the current bull market. Private investors have greater freedom of manoeuvre. They will be glad not to have heard of 'q' these past few years. But can they afford to ignore its message now?

* *Valuing Wall Street* will be published by McGraw-Hill in late March 2005.

Source: Edward Chancellor, 'Getting the Measure of Wall Street', *Financial Times*, 19 February 2000.

15.8 How analysts value stocks

All valuation methods discussed thus far (DDMs, the FCFM and multiples) require estimates of future earnings or dividends. Again, obtaining accurate estimates is extremely difficult, because the firm's earnings are exposed to various risks at the level of the economy, the industry and the company. Clearly, valuation requires a careful analysis of, for example, general economic prospects, competition, and the quality of management. This section examines the different approaches to security analysis. Also, we discuss the earnings forecasts and valuations of professional analysts.

15.8.1 Different approaches to security analyis

In general, we may distinguish between the following three approaches to security analysis:[18]

---

[18] Another popular approach to security analysis is technical analysis (see Chapter 18), which uses graphs and charts of historical market data rather than fundamental values such as company financial statements and sector and macroeconomic data. We ignore technical analysis in this section, because technical analysis does not use the discounted cash flow framework; it does not try to estimate and discount future earnings and dividends.

Firm-level analysis

At the firm level, the investor can analyse the financial statements issued by the firm (most notably, the balance sheet, the income statement and the cash flow statement). Chapter 16 discusses further financial statements and their use for security analysis. Apart from the quantitative information contained in the financial statements, investors also assign a high value to qualitative information such as the quality and depth of a company's management. Is the firm run by one super-star, or are there numerous highly qualified people managing the firm? How can investors measure something like this? The most relevant assessment media are (1) the performance record of management, (2) interviews, meetings and presentations of management to analysts, and (3) evidence of management's strategic planning and ability to meet stated objectives.

Industry analysis

Many investors believe that industries go through lifecycles. A lifecycle is a discernible pattern for an industry in which it is first born, then goes through an expansion phase of rapid growth, and finally reaches a period of maturation. Each industry is unique in how it progresses through each phase. Some industries, such as the biotechnology industry, develop rapidly; others, such as the natural gas industry, develop slowly. It is important for investors to understand where in the industrial lifecycle a particular industry is located, as future prospects depend on the remaining life of the industry.

External forces greatly influence a particular industry's progression through its lifecycle. Political and regulatory changes influence the growth or decline of a given industry. For example, environmental legislation has spurred the growth of industries engaged in reducing pollution and cleaning toxic waste sites. Social and demographic forces also play an important role. For example, as the US population grows older with the ageing of the baby boomers, the pharmaceutical industry probably will experience stronger sales.

When analysing a particular industry, it is helpful to break down the analysis based on factors that influence demand for the industry's products as well as factors that influence the supply of the industry's raw materials. On the demand side, investors try to identify who the end users of products are and how they may change their behaviour in the future. Investors are ever watchful for technological innovations that may have dramatic influences on demand for an industry's products. For example, a recent technological innovation is the ability to send interactive television signals via telephone wires. If this technology develops, then the cable television industry will suddenly have a competitor – the telephone industry – which already has a direct connection to most homes.

On the supply side, investors try to identify the degree of concentration within an industry. The concentration ratio is a measure of how much of the industry is dominated by the largest firms. How do these firms compete? Is the competition based on price, quality or warranties? For example, software firms and airline firms are both notorious for their price-cutting wars. Clearly, when a group of firms is willing to cut its prices enormously to gain market share, then this could have an adverse impact on share prices.

Investors try to assess the future profitability of an industry. They use supply and demand analysis in an effort to understand how these different factors interact. Will any cost factors get out of control? Will price wars erupt that will seriously dampen profitability? What technological innovations are on the horizon that may redefine the entire industry? Will future governmental regulations dramatically alter how a particular industry functions? These are some of the important questions that investors must address when examining an industry.

Macroeconomic analysis

Economy-wide factors affect the prices, risks and returns of almost all securities in all industries, because they influence the expected future cash flows to investors (for example, dividends and coupons), the risks of the cash flows (for example, market risk and default risk), and the interest rates and risk premiums (for example, the equity premium and the default premium) used to discount the cash flows. Therefore, it is useful for security analysis to understand the forces behind economy-wide factors such as interest rates, the business cycle and exchange rates. Chapter 13 focused on interest rates and credit spreads. Chapter 17 will deal with the business cycle and exchange rates.

15.8.2 The analysts' forecasts

How do professionally trained security analysts evaluate common stocks? A survey of members of the Financial Analysts Federation by Chugh and Meador (1984) shed some light on this question.[19] The survey focused on the investment horizon that security analysts have. The investment horizon determined the characteristics the analysts used to select superior stocks. The survey results indicated overwhelmingly that analysts examine the long-run economic and financial outlook of the company. In the long run (more than one year), analysts attached the greatest importance (in this order) to (1) expected changes in EPS, (2) expected return on equity, and (3) prospects of the relevant industry. In the short run (less than one year), analysts attached the greatest importance (in this order) to (1) prospects of the relevant industry, (2) expected change in EPS, and (3) general economic conditions.

Arriving at the valuation of these factors, and in particular the valuation of changes in EPS, requires a detailed analysis of the firm. Based on their survey results, Chugh and Meador (1984) conclude the following:

> No single operating ratio from the company's financial statements, nor any single product or market event, captures for the analyst the long-term prospective value of the stock. Analysts appear to view a company in its entirety – its history, capabilities and position in the industry . . . [Analysts] attached more importance to the regularity of new product introduction and product refinement, for example, than to anticipated introduction of a new product . . . [Analysts also] look to qualitative factors such as quality and depth of management, market dominance and strategic credibility to validate quantitative financial and economic variables.[20]

Exhibit 15.10 illustrates the stock-valuation process as inferred from the results of the survey of the Financial Analysts Federation. Standard information sources are combined with assessment media to develop predictors of financial performance. The predictors of financial performance are combined with the environment in which the firm operates to develop a systematic or well-ordered view of the company. From this systematic view, analysts develop long-term financial performance forecasts of EPS and return on equity (ROE), or net income/book value of equity. Finally, based on these long-term forecasts of EPS and ROE, analysts arrive at the value of the common stock.

---

[19] The Financial Analysts Federation is now a part of the Association for Investment Management and Research.

[20] Chugh and Meador (1984), pp. 42, 43.

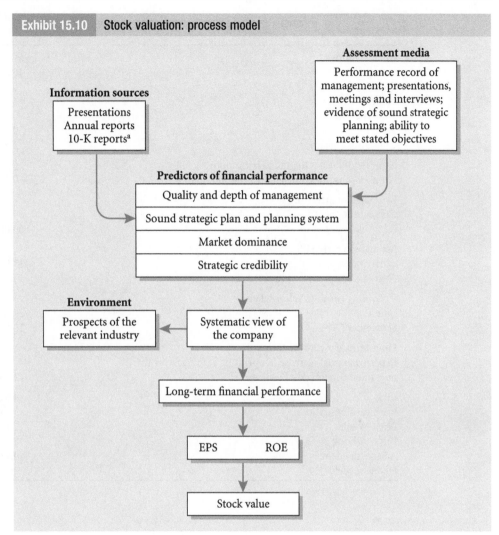

Exhibit 15.10 Stock valuation: process model

Source: L. C. Chuch and J. W. Meador (1984) 'Break the Barrier Between You and Your Analyst', *Financial Executive*, September, p. 19.

Nowadays, with a click of a button on your computer, you can get an estimate of the future growth of earnings as estimated by the analysts and the buy–hold–sell recommendation.[21] Exhibit 15.11 illustrates the analysts' view of IBM stock in mid-1999.

First, all the analysts considered IBM stock to be a good investment: 13 recommended 'strong buy', ten recommended 'buy' and four recommended 'hold'. None recommended selling the stock. Ranking their recommendations from 1 (strong buy) to 5 (sell), the consensus mean is 1.667, which implies a very strong optimistic view regarding investment in IBM's stock.

We also see from Exhibit 15.11 that IBM is neither upgraded nor downgraded in its rating. Then, we have the estimated EPS for 1999 and 2000. Probably the most important figure is the growth in earnings estimate for the next three to five years, which is 13% per year for IBM.

---

[21] There are several sources for obtaining estimates of future EPS. For example, Zack's Earnings Estimates, Institutional Brokerage Estimate System (I/B/E/S) and Value Line are information services that provide these figures.

Exhibit 15.11	Financial analyst forecast and recommendation for IBM stock

Analyst ratings	
Strong buy	13
Buy	10
Hold	4
Underperform	0
Sell	0
Consensus (mean)	1.667[a]
Number of ratings upgraded last month	0
Number of ratings downgraded last month	0
Estimated quarterly EPS	
Current (06/1999)	$0.88
Next (09/1999)	$0.88
Estimated yearly EPS	
Current (1999)	$3.99
Next (2000)	$4.60
Upcoming earnings release dates	
June 1999	21 July 1999
September 1999	20 October 1999
Long-term growth-rate forecast	
Expected annual increase in operating earnings over the next full business cycle (3–5 years)	13.00%
EPS	3.52
Price/earnings ratio	35.44 (December)
Price-to-sales	2.77
Price-to-book	12.665
Annual dividend	0.48
Dividend yield	0.30

[a] 1 = strong buy, 5 = sell.

Source: www.Quicken.com

One can use this analysts' estimate and contrast it with the statistical growth-rate estimate, which is based on historical series of EPS. Probably, the analysts have more information (due to recent changes in the firm) and the historical EPS series does not represent well the future growth. Thus, a large deviation between the analysts' estimate and the 'statistical' estimate calls for more investigation and a future analysis of recent changes (e.g. change in management, spinoff, merger, etc.) that have occurred in the firm.

Analysts rely on a wealth of information in addition to historical growth rates; hence, their forecasts may be expected to be superior to those found by means of historical extrapolation. Several studies have examined the accuracy of analyst growth forecasts. Generally, analysts seem to yield slightly better short-term forecasts due to the additional information they can use. However, the long-run forecasts (forecasts beyond a year) are equally as inaccurate as those found by means of historical extrapolation (see Section 15.3.2).[22] Also, there is little if any

---

[22] See, for example, Cragg and Malkiel (1968), Crichfield *et al.* (1978), Collins and Hopwood (1980) and O'Brien (1988).

evidence that investors can systematically earn abnormal returns by security analysis using publicly available information or by following the recommendations of analysts (see Chapter 12).

Summary

Explain how investors use stock-valuation models.

Stock-valuation models can be useful for assessing investment opportunities and for estimating a firm's cost of equity for capital budgeting decisions. Stock-valuation models are also useful in situations where market valuations are absent, either because the equity is held privately or because the proposed publicly traded entity has not yet been created (for example, IPOs, mergers and spinoffs). A sound valuation method must rely on discounting cash flows to investors at an appropriate risk-adjusted discount rate.

Describe the assumptions underlying the constant dividend growth model (CDGM).

The most popular valuation model is the CDGM, which assumes that every year the earnings grow at a constant rate and the firm pays a constant percentage of its earnings as dividends. The model applies more generally for normal-growth firms. Such firms invest the retained earnings at the required cost of equity and, hence, the retention ratio does not affect the current stock price.

Describe how to estimate the input parameters of the CDGM.

The input parameters are the dividend growth rate (g) and the discount rate (k). Methods for estimating g include the historical extrapolation method and the implied growth rate. Methods for estimating k include the CAPM and the implied discount rate. No method is always appropriate for estimating g and k. Part of the skill an investor requires is knowing which method to use at what time.

Value firms that are presently experiencing super growth.

Although the constant dividend growth model can be employed for normal-growth and super-growth firms, economic logic and historical data tell us that constant super growth cannot continue forever. (IBM, for example, was a symbol of super growth for many years, but it faced a decline in profit and even had negative earnings in 1992 and 1993.) Therefore, in the case of a super-growth firm, a more reasonable assumption is that the super growth will last only for a given number of years. Then competitors will reduce the firm's growth, and finally normal growth will characterise the firm. Hence, for super-growth firms, multistage growth models are more appropriate than the CDGM. One task facing an investor is to forcast the growth path of super-growth firms.

Explain how the free cash flow model (FCFM) is employed.

Not paying dividends or paying irregular dividends induces a difficulty in applying the CDGM. For normal-growth firms, the FCFM provides exactly the same value as the CDGM but has the advantage that there is no need to estimate future dividends.

Explain why dividend discount models must be used with caution.

Some empirical results indicate that dividend discount models can be used to build stock portfolios that outperform the market. However, investors must be cautious when implementing DDMs. Using DDMs to identify mispriced stocks assumes implicitly that stocks are not priced correctly at present but that they will one day soon move towards the correct price. Further, DDMs assume that the discount rate is constant over time, which is not necessarily true. Also, valuation generally is very sensitive to the input parameters (such as the growth rate and the discount rate), while the input parameters cannot be determined with high precision. Finally, investors must modify historical parameter estimates in light of current conditions and develop statistical tools to determine whether the DDM yields investment returns that are significantly better than the market after correcting for risk.

Explain why valuation multiples must be used with even greater caution.

Valuation multiples in many cases rely on the same logic as DDMs. However, they are simplified versions of DDMs that are more simple to compute, understand and communicate to others. In general, the limitations of valuation multiples are (1) they are sensitive to estimation error by relying on a few past numbers, (2) they do not account properly for future growth and super-growth opportunities, and (3) they do not account properly for risk. For these reasons, multiples frequently confuse undervalued stocks with stocks that report temporarily inflated perform-ance, lack future growth opportunities and/or are highly risky. Conversely, overvaluation may be confused with temporarily deflated performance, high future growth and low risk.

Discuss the estimates and valutions by professional analysts.

Analysts consider a wide range of firm-level, industry and macroeconomic data sources to estimate corporate earnings and to arrive at recommendations for buying or selling stocks. Despite this, there is little if any evidence that analysts' earnings estimates are more accurate than estimates found by means of historical extrapolation and that investors can systematic-ally earn abnormal returns by following the recommendations of analysts.

Key terms

Constant dividend growth model (CDGM) 496	Growth rate 492	Super-growth firm 503
Discount rate 492	Multistage growth models 508	Three-stage growth model 509
Dividend discount model (DDM) 493	Normal-growth firm 502	Tobin's q 524
Dividend yield 522	P/E ratio 518	Two-stage growth model 508
Duration 523	Present value of growth opportunities (PVGO) 506	Valuation multiples 517
		Value of assets in place 506

Review questions

1 The P/E ratio of a normal-growth firm is 10. The dividend is $DPS_1 = \$10$, and the stock price is $20. What is the growth rate (g)?

2 The Sugar Corporation's dividends have been growing at 6% per year for the past 15 years. The firm currently pays an annual dividend of $5 per share. Determine the current value of a share of the firm's common stock to investors with the following required rates of return:

a. 12%

b. 14%

c. 6%

d. 4%

3   In 1990, the stock of IBM traded for $P_0 = \$100$ with $E(DPS_1) = \$6$ per share, $k = 12\%$ and $g = 6\%$. Because of sharp competition in the computer industry, and mismanagement, the market revised the estimate of the growth rate, making it only 4%. What should be the effect on the stock price?

4   According to the CDGM, which of the following factors cause higher P/E ratios? For each response, assume that all other variables remain constant. In each case, explain your answer carefully:

   a. Greater growth prospects for the company.
   b. Greater risk.
   c. Higher payout ratio.

5   'If a dividend discount model indicates that a stock is undervalued, investors should buy the stock.' Is this statement always true, only sometimes true, or never true? Explain your answer carefully.

For an extensive set of review and practice questions and answers, visit the Levy–Post investment website at www.booksites.net/levy

Selected references

Bower, R. S., 1992, 'The N-Stage Discount Model and Required Return: A Comment', *Financial Review*, **27** (1), 141–149.

Brealey, R. A., 1967, 'The Statistical Properties of Successive Changes in Earnings', paper presented to seminar on the analysis of security prices, May 1967, University of Chicago, Chicago.

Chugh, L. C. and J. W. Meador, 1984, 'The Stock Valuation Process: The Analysts' View', *Financial Analysts Journal*, **40** (6), 41–48.

Collins, W. and W. Hopwood, 1980, 'A Multivariate Analysis of Annual Earnings Forecasts Generated from Quarterly Forecasts of Financial Analysts and Univariate Time Series Models', *Journal of Accounting Research*, **18** (2), 390–406.

Cragg, D. and B. Malkiel, 1968, 'Consensus and Accuracy of the Predictions of the Growth of Corporate Earnings', *Journal of Finance*, **23**, 67–84.

Crichfield, T., T. Dyckman and J. Lakonishok, 1978, 'An Evaluation of Security Analysts Forecasts', *Accounting Review*, **53**, 651–668.

Danielson, M. G., 1998, 'A Simple Valuation Model and Growth Expectation', *Financial Analysts Journal*, **54** (3), 50–57.

Fama, E. F. and K. R. French, 2001, 'Disappearing Dividends: Changing Firm Characteristics or Lower Prospensity to Pay?', *Journal of Financial Economics*, **60**, 3–43.

Farrell, J. L., Jr, 1985, 'The Dividend Discount Model: A Primer', *Financial Analysts Journal*, **41** (6), 16–25.

Fuller, R. J., L. C. Huberts and M. Levinson, 1992, 'It's not higgledy-piggledy growth!', *Journal of Portfolio Management*, **18** (2), 38–45.

Gehr, A. K., Jr, 1992, 'A Bias in Dividend Discount Models', *Financial Analysts Journal*, **48** (1), 75–80.

Good, W. R., 1991, 'When Are Price/Earnings Ratios Too High – or Too Low?', *Financial Analysts Journal*, **47** (4), 9–12.

Gordon, M. J., 1959, 'Dividends, Earnings and Stock Prices', *Review of Economics and Statistics*, **41**, 99–105.

Higgins, H. N., 1998, 'Analyst Forecasting Performance in Seven Countries', *Financial Analysts Journal*, **54** (3), 58–62.

Horvath, P. A., 1993, 'A Further Comment on the N-Stage Discount Model and Required Return', *Financial Review*, **28** (2), 273–277.

Keynes, J. M., 1936, *The General Theory of Employment and Money*, New York: Harcourt Brace.

Leibowitz, M. L. and S. Kogelman, 1994, 'The Growth Illustration: The P/E "Cost" of Earnings Growth', *Financial Analysts Journal*, **50** (2), 36–48.

Lintner, J. and R. Glauber, 1967, 'Higgledy-Piggledy Growth in America', paper presented to seminar on the analysis of security prices, University of Chicago. In: Lorie, J. and R. Brealey, editors, *Modern Developments in Investment Management*, 2nd edn, Hinsdale, IL: Dryden Press, 594–611.

Little, I. M. D., 1962, 'Higgledy-piggledy growth', *Oxford Bulletin of Statistics*, 387–412.

Miller, M. H., 1986, 'Behavioural Rationality in Finance: The Case of Dividends', *Journal of Business*, **59**, s451–s468.

Nagorniak, J. J., 1985, 'Thoughts on Using Dividend Discount Models', *Financial Analysts Journal*, **41** (6), 13–15.

O'Brien, P., 1988, 'Analyst's Forecasts as Earnings Expectations', *Journal of Accounting and Economics*, **10**, 53–83.

Ou, J. A. and S. H. Penman, 1989, 'Accounting Measurement, Price-Earnings Ratio, and the Information Content of Security Prices', *Journal of Accounting Research*, **27**, 111–152.

Penman, S. H., 1996, 'The Articulation of Price-Earnings Ratios and Market-to-Book Ratios and the Evaluation of Growth', *Journal of Accounting Research*, **34** (2), 235–259.

Rayner, A. C. and I. M. D. Little, 1966, *Higgledy-Piggledy Growth Again: An Investigation of the Predictability of Company Earnings and Dividends in the UK*, Oxford: Blackwell.

Rozeff, M. S., 1990, 'The Three-Phase Dividend Discount Model and the ROPE Model', *Journal of Portfolio Management*, **16**, 36–42.

Sorensen, E. H. and D. A. Williamson, 1985, 'Some Evidence on the Value of Dividend Discount Models', *Financial Analysts Journal*, **41** (6), 60–69.

Tuttle, D. L., *et al.*, 1993, *Equity Security Analysis and Evaluation*, Charlottesville, VA: AIMR.

The two-stage growth model: a single valuation equation

Substituting $E(DPS_t) = DPS_0(1 + g^*)^t$ for $t = 1, \ldots, N$ and $E(DPS_t) = DPS_0(1 + g^*)^N(1 + g)^{t-N}$ for $t = N + 1, N + 2, \ldots$ in Equation 15.17 yields

$$P_0 = \sum_{t=1}^{N} \frac{DPS_0(1 + g^*)^t}{(1 + k)^t} + DPS_0\left(\frac{1 + g}{k - g}\right)\left(\frac{(1 + g^*)^N}{(1 + k)^N}\right) \tag{15A.1}$$

The first term on the right-hand side represents the present value of the dividends during the super-growth period. This term consists of the difference between two infinite series. Using Equation 15.7 twice, and discounting all cash flows to the present, we can rewrite this term as follows:

$$\sum_{t=1}^{N} \frac{DPS_0(1 + g^*)^t}{(1 + k)^t} = \sum_{t=1}^{\infty} \frac{DPS_0(1 + g^*)^t}{(1 + k)^t} - \sum_{t=N+1}^{\infty} \frac{DPS_0(1 + g^*)^t}{(1 + k)^t}$$

$$= DPS_0\left(\frac{1 + g^*}{k - g^*}\right) - DPS_0\left(\frac{1 + g^*}{k - g^*}\right)\left(\frac{(1 + g^*)^N}{(1 + k)^N}\right)$$

$$= DPS_0\left(\frac{1 + g^*}{k - g^*}\right)\left(1 - \frac{(1 + g^*)^N}{(1 + k)^N}\right) \tag{15A.2}$$

Substituting Equation 15A.2 in Equation 15A.1, we obtain:

$$P_0 = DPS_0\left\{\left(\frac{1 + g^*}{k - g^*}\right)\left(1 - \frac{(1 + g^*)^N}{(1 + k)^N}\right) + \left(\frac{1 + g}{k - g}\right)\left(\frac{(1 + g^*)^N}{(1 + k)^N}\right)\right\} \tag{15A.3}$$

From this equation, we can see that the value of the stock is a weighted average of $DPS_0\left(\frac{1 + g^*}{k - g^*}\right)$ and $DPS_0\left(\frac{1 + g}{k - g}\right)$. The first term represents the stock value if we assume that the super-growth rate g^* applies for the entire period. Since $g^* > g$, this would overestimate the true value. Similarly, the second term uses a growth rate that is too low for the first n periods and, hence, it underestimates the true stock value. Consequently, the true stock value must lie somewhere between these two figures. Indeed, if the CDGM applies, i.e. $g^* = g$, then Equation 15A.3 reduces to $P_0 = DPS_0\left(\frac{1 + g}{k - g}\right)$.

Notice that Equation 15A.3 applies only for a two-stage model with a constant super-growth rate. The model does not apply if there are multiple stages or if the super-growth rate shifts gradually from g^* to g. For this reason, we focus on Equation 15.17, which applies in general.

True diligence

Xerox had an unorthodox but effective way of matching or beating analysts' earnings forecasts in the late 1990s. When operating results looked as if they would fall short – which was often, because the US group was struggling to adapt to a more competitive market for its copiers – executives would 'close the gap' using off accounting tricks.

That is the central allegation – neither admitted nor denied by the company – of the Securities and Exchange Commission's recent complaint against Xerox, a case that its officials say is one of the largest financial frauds they have seen. Xerox formally settled the case last week, with the payment of a record Dollars 10m (Pounds 7m) civil penalty, but investors in other companies are having a hard time putting the implications of this and other SEC probes behind them.

The collapse of Enron, the indictment of its former auditor Arthur Andersen, and publicity for SEC probes of Xerox and a clutch of technology and telecoms companies, have jolted the confidence of US investors in the usefulness, accuracy and even legality of corporate data.

As the season of first-quarter earnings and shareholder meetings gets into full swing, disclosure is the buzzword on Wall Street. But more information is not necessarily reassuring investors.

The Xerox settlement, and publication of the SEC's damning analysis of the alleged fraud, came last Thursday. On the same day, the market knocked down the shares of General Electric, in spite of its efforts to improve transparency, and battered the stock of International Business Machines on rumours, denied by the SEC, of a new probe.

It is not a coincidence that both GE and IBM are blue-chip companies, for which steady growth in reported earnings was vital in the 1990s. Such companies now top a list of US groups that investors are scrutinising for signs that their success in the past decade was built on weak foundations.

Meanwhile, regulators are pressing for even tighter standards in governance, accounting and disclosure. The SEC is urging stock markets to tighten listing standards to exclude or penalise companies with poor governance. Last Thursday, the agency approved proposals that would accelerate the speed at which companies publish financial data, and increase the amount of information they release about loans to, or share trades by, officers and directors.

Investment in the News 16 continued

'There is a cost of capital to an inefficient system, a less transparent system, a system in which people have less confidence,' adds Barry Melancon, president and chief executive of the American Institute of Certified Public Accountants. He is one of many who believes accounting scandals will force companies to produce more timely data, including current information on performance.

Optimism about change is tempered with caution. Risks include, for example, over-hasty implementation of new rules. John Biggs, chairman and chief executive of TIAA-Cref, is a former member of the body that oversees the private-sector Financial Accounting Standards Board. After the Enron scandal, critics attacked FASB for its sluggish procedures, which led to indefinite deferral of new principles that might have forced the energy trader to reveal more. But Mr Biggs says: 'All I heard then was that we were going too fast and people didn't have a chance to respond.'

He warns that, in the short-term, directors may also try to micro-manage companies, lest they inadvertently approve practices such as those that brought down Enron or tainted Xerox.

Most importantly, there is a risk that new rules, possibly backed by legislation, and a new culture of openness might lull investors into a false sense of security. As one Wall Street accounting analyst puts it: 'Companies are saying that because they have added 45 pages to the annual report they are now much more transparent – and that's clearly not the case.'

Confirmation of economic recovery and a stock market rally could also soften the aggressive scrutiny to which US companies are now subject. And, as repeated scandals around the world demonstrate, improved disclosure and stronger rules are no shield against an intelligent financial fraudster.

'We must never forget that you can't legislate impeccably,' warned Richard Grasso, chairman of the NYSE, last week. 'No matter what you put on the books you can't force dishonest people to be honest.'

Source: Andrew Hill, 'True Diligence', *Financial Times*, 15 April 2002.

Learning objectives

After studying this chapter, you should be able to:

1 Discuss the four basic financial statements commonly used in security analysis.

2 Identify the most important ratios used in financial statement analysis, discuss how these ratios are used, and describe what to be cautious about.

3 Explain how analysts assess the quality of reported earnings.

In 2002, a wave of accounting scandals broke in the USA. A number of prominent companies, including Enron, HealthSouth, Xerox, Tyco and Worldcom, admitted to misstating their books and, thus, giving a misleading impression of their financial health. In public companies, this practice amounts to fraud, and a series of investigations have been launched by the Security and Exchange Commission (SEC). In several cases, the sums involved are in the billions of dollars.

In the wake of these scandals, many of the companies saw their equity values plummet dramatically and experienced a decline in credit ratings of their debt issues, often to junk bond status. Many of them were forced to file for Chapter 11 bankruptcy protection from creditors.

Apart from the effect on stock and bond prices, several major changes have taken place in response to the widespread outcry that followed these scandals. The Enron scandal has so far resulted in the criminal conviction of auditor Arthur Andersen, formerly one of the Big 5 audit firms, who subsequently went out of business. Three of the remaining Big 4 audit firms have either divested or publicly announced plans to divest their consulting businesses, so as to avoid conflicts of interest between their activities as auditor and consultant.

Also, wide-ranging legislative and regulatory changes were adopted or proposed. In July 2002, President George W. Bush signed the Sarbanes–Oxley Bill (also known as the Corporate Oversight Bill) into law. This law imposes a number of corporate governance rules on all public companies with stock traded in the USA. Similarly, in August 2002, the NYSE proposed an additional set of corporate governance rules. If approved by the SEC, these rules will become part of the NYSE's listing requirements and apply to most companies with stock listed on the NYSE. Among their many provisions, the new law and the NYSE proposal together require that the board of a publicly traded company be composed of a majority of independent directors and the board's audit committee consist entirely of independent directors and have at least one member with financial expertise. They also require a company's officers to certify that information in the financial report is correct and they impose restrictions on the types of services that outside auditors can provide to their audit clients (see Connecting Theory to Practice 5.2 in Chapter 5 for more details).

Obviously, these accounting scandals cast serious doubt on the information contents of financial statements. Still, for investors, financial statements are one of the primary sources of information about the economic situation of a firm. Stockholders can use these statements to form expectations about future earnings and dividends (which are the inputs for the valuation models discussed in Chapter 15). Bondholders can use the statements to assess the financial health of the firm (liquidity and solvency) so as to assess the risk of default (and the relevant default premium for the firm's bonds; see Chapter 13).

A detailed treatment of accounting rules is beyond the scope of this book; this topic merits a book in its own right. Rather, we try to develop a general understanding of the basic financial statements that firms issue and their possible uses by investors. Section 16.1 introduces four basic financial statements: the balance sheet, the income statement, the cash flow statement and the statement of shareholders' equity. Section 16.2 turns to the issue of the financial ratio analysis and Section 16.3 to the quality of reported earnings, i.e. the question of whether reported earnings adequately represent economic earnings.

16.1 Financial statements

Financial statements contain the basic accounting data that help investors to understand a firm's financial history. Firms provide four major financial statements for investors:

- The income statement reports the firm's sales, cost of goods sold, other expenses, earnings, and so forth during a given accounting period, usually a quarter or a year.
- Unlike the income statement, the balance sheet provides a snapshot of the firm's assets and liabilities at a given moment, for example on 31 December 2002.

Exhibit 16.1	Basic accounting concepts
Concept	**Explanation**
Business entity	Entity is separate from owners
Going concern	Statement reflects an ongoing firm (not liquidation)
Monetary	Events are measured only in monetary terms
Accounting period	Flow of activity is divided into periods
Consistency	Statement reports similar transactions in the same way
Historical cost	Transactions are measured in price paid (not value today)
Realisation	Revenues are realised when services or goods are exchanged, not when cash is exchanged
Matching costs and revenues	Statement uses accrual accounting method that attempts to match costs and revenues to when they are incurred rather than when they are paid
Dual aspect	Assets = liabilities + owners' equity
Reliability of evidence	Transactions are based on evidence
Disclosure	Statement provides enough information so that informed readers will not be misled
Conservatism	Accountant is sceptical and estimates value on the low side
Materiality	Statement reports items that have 'significant' economic value
Substance over form	Accounting emphasises economic substance of events, not legal form

Source: From *Financial Statement Analysis: Theory, Application and Interpretation*, 4th edn, Homewood, IL, Irwin (Bernstein, L. A., 1989), reproduced with permission of The McGraw-Hill Companies.

■ The statement of cash flows is based on actual cash inflows and outflows rather than on accrual accounting (see Exhibit 16.1), which forms the basis of the income statement. From this statement, analysts can learn about the sources of a firm's cash flow and how these cash flows are used to pay for capital expenditures, dividends, interest expenses, and so forth.

■ The statement of shareholders' equity reports the amounts and sources of changes in equity from capital transactions with owners. Here, analysts can find, for instance, the number of shares outstanding and the amount of retained earnings.

16.1.1 Financial accounting concepts

Accountants follow specific rules when collecting, organising and reporting financial information about a company. The concepts and assumptions that form the framework for these rules are listed in Exhibit 16.1.

In adhering to these concepts, accountants may report values on financial statements for items or activities that overstate or understate their economic worth. Accountants assume that the business entity – an enterprise separate from its owners – is a going concern. Under the going concern assumption, they value amounts that will be paid or received at their future expected values (rather than, for example, the liquidation value). For example, accounts receivable are reported as the amount expected to be received eventually. This procedure ignores the time value of money. In the balance sheet, accounts receivable due in three months are valued in the same way as accounts receivable due in six months. Another example is that machines and equipment are valued at book value, not market value.

Financial statements record only events that are measurable in monetary terms. However, not all events affecting a firm's value are monetary. For example, a scientific discovery by an employee can be converted into profit in the years ahead, but it is not included as an asset on the balance sheet. Similarly, the financial statements do not account for the effect of the business cycle or the industry competition on the firm's prospects.

Firms are required to report their financial data in a consistent fashion. For example, they cannot constantly change their method of valuing inventory. Firms should adopt one method and stick with it. However, if there are changes, they should be reported in the footnotes to the financial statements.

Most accounting statement items are valued using historical cost, not current market value. This method can result in dramatic differences between the recorded value of an asset on the balance sheet and its actual current market value. Thus, a security analyst must be very cautious when using accounting statements for the purpose of establishing market value. In most cases, valuing assets and liabilities at historical cost is an obvious source of problems for investors. Investors want to know the value of the assets and liabilities today, not what price was paid for them in the past. For example, an eastern Florida railroad company may not have much growth potential in moving cargo, but if it holds many acres of land on the east coast of Florida that were bought 40 years ago, then it may be a valuable company in terms of the market value of its assets.

When accountants apply the concept of conservatism to value assets and revenues, they may underestimate their actual worth. Similarly, they may overestimate liabilities and expenses. Firms apply conservatism in different degrees, which may make it difficult for investors to compare accounting data across different firms and across different years.

The following sections will examine in detail the four financial statements: the balance sheet, the income statement, the statement of cash flows and the statement of shareholders' equity. They use the financial statements of Pfizer, Inc., a leading drug company, to identify the information contained in financial statements and to show how investors can interpret these data. Pfizer discovers, develops, manufactures and sells pharmaceuticals, medical devices, surgical equipment and healthcare products. Probably the most well-known drug produced by Pfizer is Viagra, which was introduced to the market in 1998.

16.1.2 Balance sheet

A balance sheet shows the assets, liabilities and equity of a firm on a specific date. The balance sheet is based on the following equality:

$$\text{Assets} = \text{liabilities} + \text{owners' equity}$$

This equation holds because the assets reported on the balance sheet are generated or purchased by the firm and are financed by the creditors and the owners. The information contained in the balance sheet helps answer questions such as these: What is the firm's capital structure? How is the capital being invested? Are most assets current or fixed?

Exhibit 16.2 presents Pfizer's balance sheet, which contains data for three consecutive years (1994, 1995 and 1996). Notice that Pfizer holds a large portion of its assets in current assets and property, plant and equipment. One risk that a company such as Pfizer has is that some inventory may become obsolete or outdated. A new drug discovery, for example, may result in the need to destroy the stock of existing drugs.

Exhibit 16.2	Pfizer 1996 annual report: quarterly consolidated balance sheet (in $ millions, except per-share data)

	31 December		
	1996	1995	1994
Assets			
Cash and cash equivalents	1 150	403	1 458
Short-term investments	487	1 109	560
Accounts receivable, less allowances for doubtful accounts: 1996, $58; 1995, $61; 1994, $44	2 252	2 024	1 665
Short-term loans	354	289	361
Inventories			
Finished goods	617	564	528
Work in process	695	579	535
Raw materials and supplies	277	241	202
Total inventories	1 589	1 384	1 265
Prepaid expenses, taxes and other assets	636	943	479
Total current assets	6 468	6 152	5 788
Long-term loans and investments	1 163	545	829
Property, plant and equipment, less accumulated depreciation	3 850	3 473	3073
Goodwill, less accumulated amortisation: 1996, $115; 1995, $79; 1994, $48	1 424	1 243	326
Other assets, deferred taxes and deferred charges	1 762	1 316	1 083
Total assets	14 667	12 729	11 099
Liabilities			
Short-term borrowings, including current portion of long-term debt	2 235	2 036	2 220
Accounts payable	913	715	525
Income taxes payable	892	822	731
Accrued compensation and related items	436	421	419
Other current liabilities	1 164	1 193	931
Total current liabilities	5 640	5 187	4 826
Long-term debt	687	833	604
Post-retirement benefit obligation other than pension plans	412	426	433
Deferred taxes on income	253	166	212
Other noncurrent liabilities	671	564	661
Minority interests	50	47	39
Total liabilities	7 713	7 223	6 775
Owner's equity	6 954	5 506	4 324

See Notes to Consolidated Financial Statements, which are an integral part of these statements.

Source: www.pfizer.com/are/mn_investors.cfm

Probably the most notable changes in the balance sheet are the reduction in cash and cash equivalents in 1995 relative to 1994. Also, accounts receivable have risen. This increase in accounts receivable may signal lower credit standards in an effort to sell more products. In 1996, Pfizer reported an increase in its cash ($1150 million versus $403 million in 1995) and an increase in accounts receivable and inventory. These increases may indicate a much greater sales volume (as we will soon discover from the income statement). On the liability side, the most notable change is the increase in total current liabilities.

Financial analysts investigate these changes. Are the changes in cash and marketable securities a signal that something is wrong, or are they due to a temporary demand for cash? Why are accounts receivable increasing? To answer these questions, the analyst must look at the explanations to the balance sheet that are normally part of the financial statements. If satisfied by the explanations, the analyst can conclude that this is a firm with very low long-term liabilities. Hence, it is mostly an equity firm with regard to its long-term financial policy. Thus, Pfizer has relatively little financial risk. Also, Pfizer seems quite stable, because this firm has had no drastic changes in the past few years. Most balance-sheet items have grown steadily over time. It seems that creditors are quite safe, because most of them are short-term creditors, and the current liabilities are covered by the current assets.

One valuable exercise is to convert the balance-sheet items into market values. Many clues as to the current market values of various balance-sheet items are hidden in the financial statements. The analyst must search diligently through the reported financial statements to find these clues. This exercise helps the analyst to assess the current stock price and whether it is reasonable. The following sections examine selected balance-sheet items.

Inventory evaluation: FIFO, LIFO and average cost

Inventory is a relatively large item on the balance sheet; it can represent more than 50% of the assets of department stores such as J. C. Penney and Sears. Financial analysts, therefore, should analyse carefully changes in a firm's inventory level.

Recall that the balance sheet reports assets at book value or historical cost, not at market value. How can an investor convert book values of assets and liabilities to their corresponding market values? Sometimes, the book value equals the market value of the assets. For most firms, however, this is not the case. In particular, the book value of the stock is generally different from its market value. To convert the balance sheet from book value to market value, the analyst must make several adjustments. For example, receivables are listed as the amount anticipated to be collected. Clearly, the current market value is lower (due to the time value of money).

The 'Notes to Financial Statements' section of most annual reports discusses how inventories, raw materials, work in progress and finished goods are carried on the balance sheet. For example, a recent annual report of Pfizer, Inc., includes the following:

> Inventories are valued at cost or market, whichever is lower. Except as noted below, raw materials and supplies are valued at average or latest actual costs and finished goods and work in process are average actual costs.
>
> Substantially all of the Company's U.S. sourced pharmaceuticals, animal health and specialty chemicals inventories are valued utilizing the last-in, first-out (LIFO) method.

The concept of conservatism applies to inventory valuation. Inventory is valued at cost or market, whichever is less. Pfizer uses the last-in, first-out (LIFO) method to value certain US product inventories. Alternative methods to LIFO for valuing inventories are the first-in, first-out (FIFO) and the average cost methods. Although LIFO is the most popular method in the USA, it tends to understate inventories during inflationary periods, as will be shown below. For this reason, it is forbidden to use in some countries; it doesn't give a true and fair valuation. In Europe, it will be allowed to report using LIFO only if the firm also states what the impact of this will be on the value of the inventory; with these numbers, analysts will be able to recalculate the financial statements for FIFO or average costs.

Let us compare these three methods with a simple example.[1] Suppose we are given the following information regarding the inventory of Birmingham Steel Tubing Retailers, Inc.:

		Total cost ($)
Inventory on 1 January	1000 tubes at $500	500 000
First purchase in year	3000 tubes at $550	1 650 000
Second purchase in year	3000 tubes at $600	1 800 000
Third purchase in year	2000 tubes at $650	1 300 000
Total available for sale	**9000 tubes**	**5 250 000**
Inventory on 31 December	3000 tubes	

To understand inventory accounting methods better, we examine the impact of each method on the income statement. A more thorough examination of the income statement is covered below. Our interest here is in the appropriate value for ending inventory, because ending inventory valuation plays a critical role in determining the cost of goods sold on the income statement. Recall that the cost of goods sold can be calculated as follows:

Cost of goods sold = beginning inventory + purchases − ending inventory

The value of beginning inventory is given as $500 000, and three purchases were made totalling $4 750 000 (i.e. (3000 × $550) + (3000 × $600) + (2000 × $650)). The problem of calculating ending inventory remains.

With the FIFO method, the goods first placed in inventory are the ones sold first. Thus, the ending inventory would be valued at the cost of the latest purchases. In our example, the ending inventory by the FIFO method would be $1 900 000 (i.e. (2000 × $650) + (1000 × $600)) and the cost of goods sold would be $3 350 000 (i.e. $5 250 000 − $1 900 000).

The LIFO method bases the cost of goods sold on the most recent costs incurred. To illustrate, think of inventory as a pile of sand. The last goods purchased are poured on to the inventory pile, and any sales are taken from the top of the pile. Based on the LIFO method, the ending inventory would be $1 600 000 (i.e. (1000 × $500) + (2000 × $550)), and the cost of goods sold would be $3 650 000 (i.e. $5 250 000 − $1 600 000). If prices go up because of inflation, then the cost of goods sold by the LIFO method will be higher than that by the FIFO method. Indeed, the goal of the LIFO method is to better align the revenues with current costs during inflation. (See also the Practice box below.)

The average cost method spreads cost fluctuations over time. A weighted-average cost is employed in valuing inventories and charging cost of goods sold. Thus, the average cost of all purchases and beginning inventories is $583.33 (total cost/number of units = $5 250 000/9000). Thus, the ending inventory would be valued at $1 749 990 (i.e. 3000 × $583.33), and the cost of goods sold would be $3 500 010 ($5 250 000 − $1 749 990).

---

[1] For a more detailed discussion of valuing inventories, see Bernstein (1989).

The following table summarises the results of the three inventory accounting methods. Clearly, the method used influences both the cost of goods sold reported on the income statement and the ending inventory carried on the balance sheet.

	FIFO	LIFO	Average cost
Ending inventory ($)	1 900 000	1 600 000	1 749 990
Cost of goods sold ($)	3 350 000	3 650 000	3 500 010

A firm's adoption of an inventory valuation practice is accompanied by some tax considerations. In the previous example, the FIFO method would report the lowest cost of goods sold and hence result in the highest reported earnings. This method subjects the firm to higher taxes. For tax reasons, therefore, this firm would want to adopt the LIFO method, which would result in lower reported earnings.[2]

Firms are not allowed to constantly switch their inventory accounting practices. This switching would violate the basic accounting concept of consistency. Although the IRS does allow firms to change inventory accounting policies, the firm must document valid reasons for the switch. The box below illustrates an inventory example that has rising prices.

Practice box

Problem

Suppose you are given the following information about EMI/Micro Computer Retailers, Inc.:

		Total cost ($)
Inventory on 1 January	100 PCs at $1000	100 000
First purchase in year	300 PCs at $900	270 000
Second purchase in year	200 PCs at $800	160 000
Total available for sale	**600 PCs**	**530 000**
Inventory on 31 December	50 PCs	

What is the value of the ending inventory and the cost of goods sold by the FIFO, LIFO and average cost methods? Which method is preferred for tax purposes?

Solution

By the FIFO method, the ending inventory is $40 000 (i.e. 50 × $800). Recall that according to the FIFO method, the first PCs in are assumed to be sold first. The cost of goods sold is $530 000 − $40 000 = $490 000.

By the LIFO method, the ending inventory is $50 000 (i.e. 50 × $1000). Recall that according to the LIFO method, the last PCs in are assumed to be sold first. The cost of goods sold is $480 000 (i.e. $530 000 − $50 000).

By the average cost method, the average cost of PCs available for sale is $530 000/600 $\cong$ $883.33. Thus, the ending inventory is valued at 50 × $883.33 = $44 166.50, and the cost of goods sold is $530 000 − $44 166.50 = $485 833.50.

---

[2] A recently enacted US tax policy requires that firms be consistent in their use of inventory valuation methods. The method used for tax purposes must be the method used for financial reporting.

The FIFO method gives the highest cost of goods sold. Hence, it will produce the lowest taxable profits (as the following table illustrates), so it is preferred for tax reasons. However, the FIFO method also results in the lowest reported earnings to shareholders. (The table assumes that each PC was sold for $1000 and that the income tax rate is 31%.)

Income statement	FIFO	LIFO	Average cost
Sales ($)	550 000	550 000	550 000
Cost of goods sold ($)	490 000	480 000	485 833.50
Earnings before tax	60 000	70 000	64 166.50
Tax	18 600	21 700	19 891.615
Net income	41 400	48 300	44 274.885

Inventory is at the very heart of most corporations. High inventories are an early warning sign that a firm is unable to sell its products. In early 1998, for example, Compaq Computers announced that it was significantly reducing the retail price of its computers because of low inventory turnover (see Exhibit 16.6 later in this chapter). When inventory turnover drops considerably during a quarter, analysts often react very negatively and dump the stock, believing that trouble lies ahead for the firm. Inventory is a closely watched item on the balance sheet.

Property, plant and equipment

Property, plant and equipment (PPE) are reported on the balance sheet at cost less depreciation. Investors seek current values for these assets. For older firms, this value is especially difficult to determine. For example, a firm may have a physical plant that has been fully depreciated but is worth hundreds of millions of dollars. Investors might have to work with other sources to find estimates of the current values for these assets. One source is the property tax assessments for the firm. Although this information is publicly available, it is usually difficult to acquire (because it is buried in some public tax collector's office). Another method used to determine the value of the firm's property is to examine how much the firm pays for fire insurance. A value for the property can be inferred from fire insurance expenses. Firms may or may not provide this information.

Another way to get a glance of what is happening is to calculate the average age of the PPE. This is calculated by accumulated depreciation (if reported) divided by depreciation expense. This makes comparison between industries and in the time possible. If the average age of the PPE gets higher, it will mean that the company waits longer before buying new equipment. This can be useful in two ways: (1) the analyst can estimate when large capital requirements will come to replace the old equipment; (2) if the age gets higher, then the efficiency will go down. This will make the firm uncompetitive.

Intangibles

Intangible assets are non-monetary assets without physical substance. Examples of intangible assets include goodwill, patents, copyrights, trademarks, franchises, licences, human capital, and organisation and development expenses.

The basic problem with evaluating intangibles stems from the fundamental attributes of intangible assets. If the intangibles are generated inside the firm, then it is almost impossible to calculate accurately the costs incurred by the development of these assets. For instance, how much of the overall costs (for instance, informational and administrative expenses) must be put to the development of a new brand name? Calculating the value by measuring the potential benefits has the problem that these benefits are not easy to calculate and it is almost impossible to calculate the economic life of intangibles. In the EU, it is required to expense research costs but capitalise the development costs when specific requirements are met (see International Accounting Standards (IAS) 39). In the USA, imbursements for intangible assets are not treated as assets; that is, they are not activated on the balance sheet. Rather, the imbursements are treated as costs that are expensed through the income statement of the period in which they are made. However, in case of acquisitions, the rules in the USA and Europe are identical: intangibles can be activated under the heading of the asset 'goodwill' or the difference between the market price of the aquired firm and the accounting value of the individual assets and liabilities. In brief, intangibles are activated on the balance sheet only when a business is sold (acquired) and therefore are not valued for firms that have not been acquired. This does not, of course, imply that the latter firms do not own any intangible assets.

For example, Procter and Gamble has developed strong brand names internally, and these costs have been expensed through the income statement. The value of these brand names does not appear on the balance sheet. On the other hand, RJR Nabisco has acquired strong brand names through outside purchases. When purchased, RJR Nabisco reported the costs on the balance sheet as goodwill. Thus, the uninformed investor could easily reach radically different conclusions when comparing these two firms. Economically, in both cases, costs have been incurred to increase future cash flows and add value to the firm; but from an accountant's point of view, only acquired intangibles can be activated as an asset on the balance sheet; self-generated intangibles cannot.

The overall effect of the accounting perspective is that a corporation that invests in intangibles will look weak in the financial statements: profits are low because the outlays cannot be capitalised. This effect helps to explain why many corporations nowadays report their earnings in terms of EBITDA,[3] an acronym for earnings before interest, taxation, depreciation and amortisation. Under such reporting schemes, corporations report the profit before interest costs, the outlays or costs for taxes, depreciation of certain assets, and amortisation of goodwill paid. The flip side of EBITDA is the inflation of the depicted profits, because if a company acquired another company with goodwill, it would include the consolidated earnings in the income statement, but it would exclude the price it paid for the earnings of the party it took over.

Future developments in the field of financial accounting must find a middle way to correct the current accounting inconsistency; otherwise, confusion about the real state of affairs and non-relevant numbers are here to stay.

Liabilities

On the liability side of the balance sheet, current liabilities typically are listed at what will be paid rather than at their present value. Hence, the analyst must discount the current liabilities to determine their market value. To assess the market value of long-term debt, the analyst

---

[3] An analyst joke is that EBITDA stands for Earnings Before I Tricked the Dumb Auditors, indicating that net earnings are not reliable because of the many accounting tricks that companies use to get the earnings number they want. EBITDA is more reliable because there are fewer tricks to change this number.

should adjust the debt for changes in interest rates. For example, if a firm issued 30-year bonds at 6.5% and rates moved up to 12%, then the book value stays the same but the market value of the 30-year bonds is much less than what the firm received (hence, the firm has benefited from this issue).

Equity

An analyst can adjust equity to market value fairly easily by taking the number of shares outstanding and multiplying it by the current market price. Unlike accounting requirements, the exercise of converting the balance sheet to market value does not require assets to exactly equal liabilities and owners' equity. In fact, the differences that arise are the basis on which analysts determine whether to buy or sell the firm's stock.

Practice box

Problem Suppose a firm's current assets are $100 million and current liabilities are $50 million. The long-term liabilities are $25 million. The firm issued ten million shares, whose current market price is $2 per share. Based on the book value, is this stock underpriced or overpriced? Why?

Solution Even if we completely ignore the firm's fixed assets, the firm can use the current assets to pay all its liabilities and still have $100 million − $50 million − $25 million = $25 million left. Because there are only ten million shares, the firm can liquidate itself and pay $2.5 per share ($25 million/10 million). Thus, based on this information, the stock trading for $2 is underpriced. However, before buying it, we should learn who manages the firm, how much of the profit is taken in compensation to managers, whether there is any pending litigation, and so forth.

16.1.3 Income statement

The income statement shows the flow of sales, expenses and earnings during a specified period. The income statement is also known as the profit and loss (P&L) statement. It provides a summary of the revenues, cost of goods sold and expenses of a firm for an accounting period.

The income statement helps investors to assess the abilities of management. Specifically, the income statement demonstrates how profitably the firm operated over a period of time. Related to profitability is management's ability to control expenses.

The information contained in the income statement helps answer several questions that investors may have: What were the revenues from the sales of goods and services, cost of goods sold and expenses? How much is invested in research and development? Does research and development produce income? What is the 'true' earning power of the firm, where 'true' implies actual benefits accruing to the firm? In particular, by comparing several years, what is the trend in revenues, costs and expenses, and profits? Answers to these questions are found in part in the income statement.

Exhibit 16.3 shows the income statement of Pfizer. The expense categories are cost of sales; selling, informational and administrative expenses; and research and development expenses.

Exhibit 16.3	Consolidated statement of income for Pfizer, Inc. and subsidiary companies (in $ millions, except per-share data)		
		Year ended 31 December	
	1996	**1995**	**1994**
Net sales	11 306	10 021	7977
Costs and expenses			
Cost of sales	2 176	2 164	1722
Selling, informational and administrative expenses	4 366	3 855	3184
Research and development expenses	1 684	1 442	1126
Other deductions – net[a]			
Income from continuing operations before provision for taxes on income and minority interests	2 804	2 299	1830
Provision for taxes on income	869	738	549
Minority interests	6	7	5
Income from continuing operations	1 929	1 554	1276
Discontinued operations – net of taxes on income	–	19	22
Net income	1 929	1 573	1298
Earnings per common share			
Income from continuing operations	2.99	2.47	2.05
Discontinued operations – net of taxes on income	–	.03	0.04
Net income	2.99	2.50	2.09
Weighted average shares used to calculate per share amounts	644	630	620

See Notes to Consolidated Financial Statements, which are an integral part of these statements.
[a] Interest expense was $165 million in 1996 and $193 million in 1995.

Source: www.pfizer.com/are/mn_investors.cfm

Investors seek to identify trends over time as well as across industries. Most items that appear on the income statement are stable, with reasonable growth every year. Nevertheless, there is a significant rise in earnings in 1996 (from $1573 million to $1929 million, an increase of more than 22.5%). The main item responsible for this increase is the increase in net sales from $10 021 million in 1995 to $11 306 million in 1996. In 1996, Pfizer managed to sell 15% more than in 1995 without a similar increase in the cost of sales. This item increased only 0.55% relative to 1995 and is the main reason for the more than 22.5% increase in 1996 net income. Also, notice that Pfizer managed to increase its net income by 22.63%.

We observe that Pfizer spends a significant amount on research and development ($1684 million in 1996). Note that the R&D expense is 87% of the company's net profit in 1996. What is the value of this research and development? Can we assume that just because a firm like Pfizer spends hundreds of millions of dollars on R&D, then this expenditure will necessarily add value to the firm? Are actual costs of R&D the best way to measure the usefulness of R&D expenditures? What is the best way to value R&D? R&D is one of the most difficult expense items to assess.[4] R&D expenses are viewed differently by investors and accountants. Typically, R&D expenses are treated as an expense and don't appear on the balance sheet. Depending on the type of R&D, investors may view R&D as an asset-generating expense. For

---

[4] Accounting policies require the expensing of research and development outlays when they occur (except for assets that have alternative uses, which are placed on the balance sheet as intangibles).

example, because of its R&D expenditures, Pfizer will be marketing several drugs over the next few years. Investors view these future drugs as income-generating assets and incorporate this information into their analysis.

It might seem that if the firm did not spend money on R&D, then this saving would dramatically increase the profit. Although this is true in the short run, in the long run, without R&D Pfizer would not have new products to offer, and its future earnings would decline. R&D expenditures are not necessary for some types of firms, but for Pfizer, which is in the pharmaceutical industry, they are essential. So when the R&D expenditures of Pfizer drop, it is a warning sign for investors that future growth can be lower for a better profit now.

Another major expense that requires close scrutiny is depreciation. The way an asset changes in value over time can be considerably different from how it is expensed on the income statement. Compounding the problem is the fact that firms can depreciate certain assets by different methods. Just like inventory valuation, there are different methods available to determine depreciation expense; for instance, they can depreciate large sums in the beginning to get higher profits in the future, or vice versa. Inflation also further distorts the difference between an asset's economic value and accounting value. Thus, some analysts attempt to determine the appropriate economic depreciation in trying to assess a firm's actual earnings abilities.

16.1.4 Statement of cash flows

Accounting principles are very different from valuation methods. By accounting principles a firm may be profitable, yet by valuation methods it could be near bankruptcy. Suppose Boeing sells 747 jumbo airplanes for $500 million each. The production costs, which are all paid in cash, are $470 million. Would Boeing be profitable? Your answer depends on the method you use to evaluate this firm. An accountant would report on the income statement $30 million in earnings for each plane sold. Suppose now that the planes are sold not for cash but on credit for one year. Does this affect accounting earnings? No: the earnings will be reported in the year of the transaction as $500 million in revenues, even though the $500 million has not yet been received. Thus, the $500 million will be on the balance sheet as accounts receivable. Now, suppose that the appropriate annual discount rate is 10%. Clearly, $500 million received one year from now is worth only $500 million$/(1 + 0.10) \cong \$454.5$ million (recall the time value of money). Because it cost $470 million to produce the planes, Boeing actually loses in economic terms (or in market value), even though the accounting statement shows a profit.

Although the reported earnings can be adjusted to reflect the true economic earnings, such distortions can be identified in the statement of cash flow that is also reported by the firm. In our example, if there are accounts receivable of $500 million, then this sum will be written as cash flow not this year but rather in the next year, when they are actually received.

The statement of cash flows tells us all the sources of cash for the firm (including borrowing or a new issue of stock) and how the firm uses this cash for expenses, investment, paying dividends, and so forth. The statement of cash flows has three components: operating activities, investing activities and financing activities. Operating activities include almost all items in the income statement as well as balance-sheet items that relate directly to earnings activities. Investing activities include buying or selling securities or revenue-generating assets as well as activities related to lending money. Financing activities include activities related to borrowing money as well as transactions related to owners' equity. The statement of cash flows is beneficial in assessing the ability of the firm to pay future dividends, fund future growth and service its debts.

Exhibit 16.4	Statement of cash flows for Pfizer, Inc. (in $ millions)		

	Year ended 31 December		
	1996	1995	1994
Operating activities			
Net income	1929	1573	1298
Adjustments to reconcile net income to net cash provided by operating activities:			
Depreciation and amortisation of intangibles	430	374	292
Deferred taxes	75	(12)	32
Other	14	76	(5)
Changes in assets and liabilities, net of effect of businesses acquired and divested:			
Accounts receivable	(255)	(290)	(160)
Inventories	(149)	(25)	(111)
Prepaid and other assets	(208)	(171)	(12)
Accounts payable and accrued liabilities	66	320	168
Income tax payable	23	88	121
Other deferred items	142	(112)	(135)
Net cash provided by operating activities	2067	1821	1488
Investing activities			
Acquisitions, net of cash acquired	(451)	(1521)	–
Purchases of property, plant and equipment	(774)	(696)	(672)
Proceeds from the sale of a business	353	–	–
Purchases of short-term investments	(2851)	(2611)	(1356)
Proceeds from redemptions of short-term investments	3490	2185	1245
Purchases of long-term investments	(820)	(151)	(162)
Purchases and redemptions of short-term investments by financial subsidiaries	(11)	(30)	44
Decrease in loans and long-term investments by financial subsidiaries	52	330	21
Other investing activities	75	151	40
Net cash used in investing activities	(937)	(2343)	(840)
Financing activities			
Proceeds from issuance of long-term debt	636	502	40
Repayments of long-term debt	(804)	(52)	(4)
Increase/(decrease) in short-term debt	259	(444)	1030
Stock option transactions	280	205	64
Purchases of common stock	(27)	(108)	(511)
Cash dividends paid	(771)	(659)	(594)
Other financing activities	45	37	37
Net cash (used in)/provided by financing activities	(382)	(519)	62
Effect of exchange rate changes on cash and cash equivalents	(1)	(14)	19
Net increase/(decrease) in cash and cash equivalents	747	(1055)	729
Cash and cash equivalents at beginning of year	403	1458	729
Cash and cash equivalents at end of year	1150	403	1458

Source: www.pfizer.com/are/mn_investors.cfm

Exhibit 16.4 presents Pfizer's statement of cash flows, which starts with net income and reconciles the change in the cash asset account on the balance sheet.

For example, the net earnings of Pfizer in 1996 were $1929 million. However, this does not mean that the firm obtained $1929 million in cash inflows. Cash inflows could be more or less. For example, the firm had depreciation of $430 million. This is not a cash outflow but an accounting allocation. Therefore, we add it to the $1929 million. If there are no more adjustments, this means that the cash inflow will be $1929 million + $430 million = $2359 million.

In practice, we see from Exhibit 16.4 that the cash-flow calculations are more complex. The firm makes these adjustments to get a net cash inflow from operations in 1996 of $2067 million. Similarly, the net cash flow was −$937 million from investing activities and −$382 million from financing activities. Of course, when the firm takes a loan, it increases the cash flow, and when the firm pays dividends, it decreases the cash flow.

Practice box

Problem   Suppose a firm reported a net income of $20 million. The depreciation for the period was $10 million and the firm paid $5 million in dividends. Finally, the firm raised $2 million in long-term debt. What was the net cash flow for the firm?

Solution   Starting with net income, we would add in depreciation, deduct dividend payments, and add in the long-term debt. Hence, the cash flow was $20 million + $10 million − $5 million + $2 million = $27 million.

It is interesting to see from this analysis that the firm has a policy of repurchasing its stocks. Stock buybacks can be interpreted by investors in one of two ways. Either management has run out of projects with positive NPVs and seeks to give investors capital gains rather than taxable dividends, or management believes the stock price is significantly underpriced. Instead of raising money by issuing more stock, Pfizer is using cash to repurchase its stocks. Because Pfizer's policy has been consistent for the past few years, it probably reveals significant information. It is possible that management thinks that its stock is underpriced, and it is a good investment to repurchase the stock. Also, this repurchasing signals a strong cash balance, because the repurchase is financed not by borrowing but from the firm's past earnings. The repurchasing may also mean that the firm lacks other profitable (NPV > 0) investment opportunities. It clearly indicates strong confidence in the stock by management and may be based on some positive information that management knows but investors do not.

16.1.5 Statement of shareholders' equity

The statement of shareholders' equity states some important things. For instance, it shows the number of shares that are issued, the amount of retained earnings and the size of the employee benefit trust.

The first point to look at is the preference upon liquidation. If the company goes bankrupt, the preferred stock will have priority for liquidation and dividends. As Exhibit 16.5 shows,

Exhibit 16.5	Pfizer 1996 annual report: shareholders' equity		

	31 December		
	1996	1995	1994
Preferred stock, without par value; 12 shares authorised, none issued			
Common stock, $.05 par value; 1500 shares authorised; issued: 1996, 689; 1995, 685; 1994, 681	34	34	34
Additional paid-in capital	1728	1235	651
Retained earnings	8017	6,859	5945
Currency translation adjustment and other	145	163	196
Employee benefit trust	(1488)	(1170)	(749)
Treasury stock, at cost: 1996, 44; 1995, 48; 1994, 52	(1482)	(1615)	(1753)
Shareholders' equity	6954	5506	4324

See Notes to Consolidated Financial Statements, which are an integral part of these statements.

Source: www.pfizer.com/are/mn_investors.cfm

Pfizer has no preferred stock outstanding, but it is authorised to do so. When it does, the amount recoverable by liquidation by holders of common stock will decline.

Analysts will pay most attention to the amount of common stock outstanding during a period. This is not only important for calculations about the profits per share; it can also tell something about the value of the stock in the eyes of the management. When management thinks the stocks are undervalued, they can choose to buy back stock instead of paying cash dividends. Another possible reason for a stock buyback is that the company runs out of positive NPV projects.

16.2 Financial ratio analysis[5]

Financial ratio analysis is a method used to compare financial statements across different firms and, for a given firm, across different periods and points in time. Ratio analysis is useful when converting raw financial statement information into a form that makes it easy to compare firms of different sizes.

Ratios typically are categorised into four groups: profitability ratios, liquidity ratios, debt ratios and activity ratios. Profitability ratios measure the earning power of the firm. Return on equity (net income/shareholders' equity) and earnings per share (net income/shares) are two popular profitability ratios. Liquidity ratios measure the ability of the firm to pay its immediate liabilities. For example, the current ratio (current assets/current liabilities) addresses the ability of the firm's current assets to pay for the firm's current liabilities. Because it is difficult to pay bills with inventory, analysts have devised other ratios, such as the quick ratio, which is similar to the current ratio, except that inventory and other non-marketable assets are first deducted from current assets. It is a 'quick' way to assess a firm's ability to meet current liabilities. Debt ratios measure the firm's ability to pay its debt obligations over time. For example, the fixed charge coverage ratio, which is given by

---

[5] Based on Cottle *et al.* (1988).

$$\frac{\text{income before tax} + \text{interest expense}}{\text{interest expense} + \text{leasehold payments}}$$

assesses how many times interest expense and leasehold payments can be paid with the current income.

Exhibit 16.6 lists the most important ratios for each category in order of importance based on the survey of chartered financial analysts (CFAs) quoted in Connecting Theory to Practice 16.1. The computation required for each ratio is shown in the second column of the exhibit and is illustrated briefly with Pfizer's 1996 data in the third column.

Exhibit 16.6   Ratios by category[a]

Ratio	Equation	Pfizer 1996 example
Profitability		
Return on equity	Net income/shareholders' equity	1929/6954 ≅ 27.7%
Earnings per share	Net income/shares	1929/644 ≅ $2.99
Net profit margin	Net income/net sales	1929/11 306 ≅ 17.06%
Return on assets	Net income/total assets	1929/14 667 ≅ 13.15%
Return on investment	(Net income + interest on long-term debt)/total capitalisation	(1929 + 165)/(6954 + 687) = 27.4%
Liquidity		
Quick ratio	(Current assets − inventory − other current assets)/current liabilities	(6468 − 1589 − 636)/5640 ≅ 0.752
Current ratio	Current assets/current liabilities	6468/5640 ≅ 1.147
Cash	(Cash + marketable securities)/current liabilities	(1150 + 487)/5640 ≅ 0.29
Debt		
Fixed charge coverage	(Income before tax + interest expense)/(interest expense + leasehold payments[b])	(2804 + 165)/(165 + 0) ≅ 17.99
Multiplied by interest earned	(Income before tax + interest expense)/interest expense	(2804 + 165)/165 ≅ 17.99
Debt to equity	Total liabilities/shareholders' equity	7713/6954 ≅ 1.11
Degree of financial leverage	(Income before tax + interest expense)/(income before tax − [preferred dividends/(1 − tax rate)])	(2804 + 165)/(2804 − 0) ≅ 1.06
Debt to assets	Total liabilities/total assets	7713/14 667 ≅ 0.526
Activity		
Days' sales in inventory	365(inventories/net sales)	(1589/11 306)365 ≅ 51.3
Inventory turnover	Cost of goods sold/ending inventory	(2176/1589) ≅ 1.37

[a] In order of importance according to a survey by Charles Gibson, *Financial Analysts Journal*, May–June 1987, pp. 74–76. Excerpted with permission from *Financial Analysts Journal*. © Copyright 1987, Association for Investment Management and Research, Charlottesville, VA. All rights reserved. All numbers are in millions and taken from previous tables, except where noted.
[b] Leasehold payments figures are in footnotes to the Annual Report.

Exhibit 16.7 shows some selected ratios over time for Pfizer, along with its industry averages. We see that the ROE has declined over time. However, Pfizer has remained above its industry averages for every year. Pfizer's above-average performance is due in part to its more aggressive use of financial leverage. For example, the current ratio for Pfizer is consistently at or below its industry averages. This indicates that other firms have more current assets available to pay for their current liabilities. We see also that Pfizer's debt-to-equity ratio is higher than its industry averages. Pfizer has more financial risk than its competitors. However, by taking this risk, Pfizer has outperformed other firms in the pharmaceutical industry based on ROE (except for the setback in 1991).

Percentage financial statements

Percentage financial statements help analysts to detect trends in time even when the size of the company changes constantly. Percentage financial statements (also known as common-size statements) are the balance sheet and income statement converted to percentages. Specifically, each item in the balance sheet is converted to a percentage of total assets (or total liabilities and equity), and each item in the income statement is converted to a percentage of net sales.

Exhibit 16.7	Comparison of Pfizer with its industry for selected ratios			
Ratio	Company/industry	1996	1995	1994
Return on investment	Pfizer	27.7	28.6	30.0
	Industry	17.4	16.9	17.6
Current ratio	Pfizer	1.1	1.2	1.2
	Industry	1.4	1.4	1.2
Debt to equity	Pfizer	111.0	131.0	157.0
	Industry	54.1	50.6	52.6

Source: © 2004, CCH INCORPORATED. All rights reserved. Reprinted with permission from *Almanac of Business and Industrial Financial Ratios* (Troy, L.), pp. 89–90.

With this information, an analyst can see easily how the relative composition of the financial statement is changing over time. Exhibits 16.8 and 16.9 provide this information based on Pfizer's financial statements.

These percentage financial statements reveal the amazing consistency of Pfizer over the past few years. For example, inventories have remained around 10 or 11% of assets and accounts receivable has stayed at 15% for these three years. Net property, plant and equipment has remained between 26 and 27% for these three years. The cost of goods sold has declined (from 21.6% in 1994 to 19.25% in 1996). Selling, general and administrative expenses have decreased steadily (from 39.91% in 1994 to 38.61% in 1996). Finally, we see that Pfizer is committed to research and development, and this expense is stable at around 14–15%.

Practice box

Problem

Suppose you are analysing two firms with the following attributes. Which firm is more attractive? Why?

	Firm A	Firm B
P/E ratio	3	3
EPS growth rate last year (%)	+10	−20
Debt-to-equity ratio	0.30	0.70
Sales ($ million)	100	100
Cash on balance sheet ($ million)	20	2

Solution

The low P/E ratio is a sign of a good investment. However, it may also be a sign of bankruptcy. We see from the financial data that firm A is strong. Firm A has a low debt-to-equity ratio, shows a +10% growth rate in EPS and holds a lot of cash. It is probably underpriced. These are not characteristics of firm B, whose low P/E ratio probably indicates a good chance of bankruptcy.

Using financial ratios for failure prediction

One of the important uses that can be made of financial ratios is the assessment of the probability that a firm will go bankrupt. Beaver (1968) and Altman (1968) pioneered the use

Exhibit 16.8 **Percentage balance sheet for Pfizer, Inc.**

Year	1996	1995	1994
Assets			
Cash (%)	7.84	3.2	13.1
Marketable securities (%)	3.33	8.7	5.0
Receivables (%)	15.4	15.9	15.0
Inventories (%)	10.83	10.9	11.4
Other current assets (%)	6.7	9.6	7.6
Total current assets (%)	**44.10**	**48.3**	**152.1**
Property, plant and equipment (%)	26.3	27.3	27.7
Other investments (%)	7.9	4.3	7.5
Intangibles (%)	9.7	9.8	2.9
Deposits, other assets (%)	12.0	10.3	9.8
Total assets (%)	**100**	**100**	**100**
Liabilities			
Accounts payable (%)	6.2	5.6	4.7
Accrued expenses (%)	3.0	3.3	3.8
Income taxes (%)	6.1	6.5	6.6
Other current liabilities (%)	7.9	9.4	8.4
Total current liabilities (%)	**38.5**	**40.7**	**43.5**
Deferred taxes on income (%)	1.7	1.3	1.9
Long-term debt (%)	4.7	6.5	5.4
Other long-term liabilities plus minority interest and post-retirement benefit obligations (%)	7.7	8.2	10.2
Total liabilities (%)	**52.6**	**56.7**	**61.0**
Common stock net (%)	2.3	0.3	0.3
Capital surplus (%)	11.8	9.7	5.9
Retained earnings (%)	54.7	53.9	53.6
Treasury stock (%)	(10.1)	(12.7)	(15.8)
Other liabilities (%)	1.0	1.3	1.8
Employee benefit trust (%)	(10.1)	(9.19)	(6.75)
Shareholders' equity (%)	**47.4**	**43.3**	**39.0**
Total liabilities and net worth (%)	**100**	**100**	**100**

Exhibit 16.9 **Percentage income statement for Pfizer, Inc.**

	1996	1995	1994
Net sales (%)	100.00	100.00	100.00
Cost of goods (%)	19.25	21.60	21.60
Gross profit (%)	80.75	78.40	78.40
R&D expenses (%)	14.90	14.40	14.11
Selling, general and administrative (%)	38.61	38.47	39.91
Other deductions – net (%)	2.44	2.60	1.44
Income before tax (%)	24.80	22.93	22.94
Tax and minority interests (%)	7.74	7.43	6.94
Net income (%)	17.06	15.50	16.00

of statistical analysis of financial ratios to predict corporate bankruptcy. Beaver (1968) used 14 financial ratios and tested for the differences in these ratios between failed and non-failed firms for as long as five years before failure. This kind of analysis is univariate: it does not consider the joint predictive power of multiple ratios at the same time. Of the variables that Beaver analysed, he concluded that cash flow/total debt was the single most important factor to consider in predicting failure. The debt ratio and the net income to total assets were also good predictors of corporate bankruptcy. Altman (1968) provides the first multivariate analysis. He combined multiple financial ratios using a statistic method known as discriminant analysis.[6] The predictive equation looks like a regression equation, and it produces an indicator of bankruptcy probability known as the 'Z-score'. Altman's original results are as follows:

$$Z = 0.012x_1 + 0.014x_2 + 0.033x_3 + 0.006x_4 + 0.999x_5$$

where x_1 is working capital/total assets, x_2 is retained earnings/total assets, x_3 is earnings before interest and tax/total assets, x_4 is market value of equity/book value of debt, and x_5 is sales/total assets. These results are based on a sample composed of 66 manufacturing companies with 33 firms in each of two matched-pair groups. The bankruptcy group consisted of companies that filed a bankruptcy petition under Chapter X of the US Bankruptcy Act from 1946 through 1965. Based on the sample, a Z-score below 1.81 indicates a high probability of failure, a Z-score above 2.99 indicates a high probability of non-failure, and a score between 1.81 and 2.99 represents cases where it is not possible to predict with confidence whether the firm will fail or not fail. This model was quite successful, as it classified correctly 80–90% of the failed firms one statement period before failure.

Many alternative bankruptcy prediction models have been developed since the work of Beaver and Altman. Lev (1974), Deakin (1977), Ohlson (1980), Platt and Platt (1990), Gilbert *et al.* (1990), and Koh and Killough (1990), among others, have continued to refine their seminal work.

Cautionary notes

Ratio analyses must always be the starting point rather than the endpoint for an analyst. After calculating the ratios, the analyst must look at the economic reality behind the figures. Some cautionary notes that must be checked before going any further are discussed below:

- ■ **Economic assumptions.** The objective of ratio analysis is to enable comparison across different firms and across different time periods. However, ratio analysis assumes implicitly that changes to the variable in the denominator cause a proportional change to the variable in the numerator. When, for instance, the cost of goods sold doubles and the ending inventory also doubles, than the inventory turnover will remain constant. However, will

---

[6] Discriminant analysis is used to determine which variables discriminate between two or more naturally occurring groups, in this case the group of failed firms and the group of non-failed firms. The basic idea underlying discriminant analysis is to combine the variables in such a way that the differences between the predefined groups are maximised. The procedure begins with a set of observations where both group membership and the values of the variables are known. The end result of the procedure is a model that allows prediction of group membership when only the variables are known. A second purpose of discriminant analysis is an understanding of the data set, as a careful examination of the prediction model that results from the procedure can give insight into the relationship between group membership and the variables used to predict group membership. See, for instance, Klecka (1980) for more details on this statistical technique.

the doubling of cost of goods sold actually yield a doubling of the ending inventory? Research shows that it doesn't. If cost of goods sold doubles, then the ending inventory will grow by only 40%, so the inventory turnover ratio will improve even when nothing substantial changes in the company (apart from the company size).

- **Timing and window dressing.** The balance sheet gives a snapshot of the state of the company at a particular time and, hence, financial ratios computed from the balance sheet will also give only snapshots. This can evoke window dressing, i.e. the practice of conducting certain transactions just before the ending of the accounting period so as to improve the balance sheet and the financial ratios. For example, Pfizer could improve the current ratio at the end of December by paying part of the short-term borrowings with the cash it has. The old current ratio was 1147; after window dressing, it will be 1184 (i.e. (6468 − 1150)/(5640 − 1150) = 1184) − a small improvement. This could be undone at the beginning of January by borrowing the same amount of $1150 million and holding that amount in cash.

- **Benchmarks.** After calculating the ratios, the analyst must compare the ratios of the firm with the ratios of a relevant benchmark. The selection of the appropriate benchmark is a difficult decision. For example, comparison with a firm of a different size, different country or different industry may be meaningless. For this reason, firms are frequently benchmarked against other firms of similar size and in the same home country and industry. However, such comparisons do not always reveal whether the company is buy-worthy, because the whole size category, country or industry may underperform.

- **Off-balance-sheet activities.** Financial ratio analysis looks at the information given in the financial statements. However, there exists lots of information that, due to accounting rules, is not mentioned in the statements but still is highly important for the financial condition of the firm. An example is the difference in accounting treatment of buying and leasing equipment. If the company buys, for instance, an expensive piece of machinery, then it will have to put the value of it on the balance sheet. The value of the balance-sheet item 'property, plant and equipment' will increase, and the amount of cash will decrease, because of the transaction. Another option for the company is to lease the same piece of machinery. The company will have the same machine for use, but the difference is that the company doesn't have to pay the whole amount for it in advance. The amount of cash on the balance sheet will not drop dramatically, and the value of 'property, plant and equipment' on the balance sheet will not change. Operationally, it makes no difference for the company whether they choose to lease or to buy the piece of machinery, but financially it can have big influences due to the way it is accounted for.

16.3 Quality of earnings

For the purpose of security valuation, analysts need to assess the future earnings ability of the firm. Unfortunately, financial accounting principles are not designed to yield the best possible estimate of future earnings; for example, the accounting principles of monetary, historical cost, realisation and conservatism (see Section 16.1.1) can distort the estimation of future earnings. Note that the issue is not whether the company adheres to the accounting principles, but rather that the accounting principles differ from economic valuation principles. Also, companies have considerable flexibility in implementing the accounting principles. For these reasons, the analyst generally needs to adjust the accounting figures to arrive at an unbiased estimate of the economic earnings.

How do the reported earnings differ from the actual earning ability of the firm? Reported earnings measures the past performance of the firm. Earning power, in contrast, refers to earnings per share that are sustainable in the future and that do not depend on accounting techniques. Many analysts use the income statement and reported earnings as a means to estimate the future earnings ability of a firm. When trying to arrive at the actual earning ability of a firm, the analyst must make several adjustments. For example, earnings attributable to non-recurring items, such as the sale of a subsidiary, should not be expected to be repeated. Therefore, they should not be included in the earnings calculation.

Earnings is an accounting number that can be manipulated by management. Management can manipulate these reports in many ways. To boost short-term earnings, for example, management can aggressively push merchandise on to distributors. By doing so, they increase accounting income and reduce total assets (inventories), thereby boosting the return on investment (see Exhibit 16.6). Similarly, management can depress earnings by adding to reserves (for example, for delinquent accounts). In 1999, Microsoft's accounting was under scrutiny by the SEC. The SEC investigated the company's accounting practices involving the status of the reserves. It was claimed that, in 1995, the chief financial officer of the company sent an email to Bill Gates saying: 'I believe we should do all we can to smooth our earnings and keep a steady state earnings model.'[7] While there are accounting rules asserting how a company should record revenue, there is a lot of flexibility given to the management to determine how to apply these rules. However, the purpose of the reserves is to reflect a company's true revenue – how much it will actually end up collecting in a given period if customers return merchandise or fail to pay their bills. But this flexibility opens up a door to smoothing earnings if not done correctly. In the specific case of Microsoft, the company may have reserved too much, which would mean that it may have understated its profit.

Analysts seek to establish their level of confidence in the reported earnings figure. Many analysts have devised ranking systems that are referred to as quality of earnings. Low quality implies that the reported earnings number differs greatly from the firm's actual operating earnings.

As analysts pore over financial statements, they seek information on the quality of earnings. They ask several questions about quality. For example, when managers can choose between different accounting procedures, do they select conservative or liberal procedures? Can a firm actually pay out the reported earnings, or is it not yet realised fully? Recall the preceding example of Boeing, where the $500 million in sales is in accounts receivable so cannot be paid as dividends. Over time, does the firm have stable earnings, or are the earnings volatile? How hard is it to forecast future earnings? Exhibit 16.10a summarises these and other issues involved in assessing quality.

Along with measures of quality, analysts have devised checklists for review, or red flags to look for, when assessing the quality of earnings. A sample checklist appears in Exhibit 16.10b. The first item on the checklist is typically the audit report. Auditors write a letter – known as the **independent auditor's report** – to shareholders and the board of directors, giving an opinion on the fairness of management's financial statements. If the auditor has reservations about the financial statements, then the auditor will express them in this letter. The independent auditor's report is a part of the annual report to shareholders required by the SEC.

---

[7] J. Markoff, 'Microsoft's accounting under scrutiny', *New York Times*, 1 July 1999, p. C6.

Exhibit 16.10	Issues in assessing the quality of earnings

(a) Measures of quality

High quality	Low quality
Conservative accounting	Liberal accounting
Earnings are distributable	Earnings are not realised
Stable earnings	Volatile earnings
Recent earnings good forecast of future	Recent earnings poor forecast of future
Related to ongoing business	Non-repeatable earnings
Reflect prudent, realistic view	Not economically realistic
No balance-sheet surprises	Overstated balance sheet
Earnings are from operations	Earnings are from financing
Earnings are domestic	Earnings are offshore
Earnings are understandable	Complex earnings

(b) Red flags related to quality of earnings

Long audit report
Reductions in managed costs, such as advertising
Changes in accounting policies
Increase in accounts receivable
Increase in intangible assets
One-time sources of income
Decline in gross margin percentage – price competition, high costs, or product mix is changing
Reduction in reserves for contingencies
Increase in borrowings
Increase in deferred tax portion of tax expense
Increase in unfunded pension liabilities
Low cash and marketable securities
Peak short-term borrowings at year end
Slowdown in inventory turnover

Source: From *Corporate Financial Reporting and Analysis*, 2nd edn, Homewood, IL: Irwin (Hawkings, D. F., 1989), reproduced with permission of The McGraw-Hill Companies.

→ **Connecting Theory to Practice 16.2**   FT

Ahold scandal stokes EU–US row over accounts regulation

The accounting scandal at Dutch retailer Ahold has deepened a dispute between the US and the European Union over the reach of the new US accountancy regulator.

US regulators believe the affair undermines European arguments against non-US accounting firms being forced to register with the new accounting oversight board.

European accountancy leaders admit that the Ahold scandal, revealed on Monday, has harmed their case but EU officials are privately threatening retaliation if non-US companies are not granted exemptions.

Controversy surrounding Ahold deepened yesterday after the Dutch ministry of justice said it would consider whether to investigate allegations of insider dealing. Separately, European stock market regulators said they would launch an inquiry into whether Ahold had complied with disclosure rules about market-sensitive information.

US regulators believe accountancy regulation in most of Europe is far weaker than in the US. They are determined to force many non-US accountants to register with the new Public Company Accounting Oversight board, opening them up to possible inspections and disciplinary action.

People within the SEC argue the board must have oversight of firms doing audits for companies with listings in the US – such as Deloitte Touche Tohmatsu's accountants in the Netherlands, responsible for Ahold's audit.

Senior Brussels officials point out that Ahold's problems seem mostly confined to its US operations. They have indicated the EU could retaliate against US-based accounting firms if America failed to give European firms a meaningful exemption from registration. 'We do not want our auditors to be under two sets of rules. We are discussing the principle of equivalence [between EU and US rules], if the US do not give us equivalence, there will be pressure not to give them equivalence,' said a Commission insider.

Frits Bolkestein, European financial services commissioner, is this week in the US lobbying the SEC.

Officially, the European Commission said only that so far it had had 'a very positive dialogue with the SEC' and was waiting for the US regulators' decisions.

David Devlin, president of the European Federation of Accountants, admitted the Ahold scandal might have a negative impact on its efforts to ensure European auditors were not monitored by the US accountancy regulator.

Source: 'Ahold Scandal Stokes EU–US Row Over Accounts Regulation', Adrian Michaels, Francesco Guerrera and Andrew Parker, *Financial Times*, 26 February 2003.

→ **Making the connection**

In 2003, a Dutch grocery conglomerate Ahold was hit by a series of accounting scandals. Among other things, its US subsidiary US Foodservice violated proper purchase accounting by treating the purchase discounts it received from its suppliers as revenue rather than as a reduction of cost and by recording the revenue in advance of the sale of the goods. This accounting scheme was allegedly designed to increase management performance bonuses. Also, Ahold had wrongly been booking all the revenue from various joint ventures in Europe and South America while it never owned more than 50% of these joint ventures. In sum, a total of about one billion dollars of accounting irregularities was discovered, requiring adjustments of the financial statements of 2002 and previous years. Ahold's chief executive and chief financial officer resigned, the shares tumbled, and investigations were started by European and US stock market regulators. As discussed in the newspaper article, the Ahold scandal also fuelled the discussion about forcing non-US accounting firms (such as Deloitte Touche Tohmatsu) and audit companies with US listings (such as Ahold) to register with the new US accounting oversight board, opening them up to possible inspections and disciplinary action.

Summary

Discuss the four basic financial statements commonly used in security analysis.

The primary financial statements used in security analysis are the balance sheet, the income statement, the statement of cash flows and the statement of shareholders' equity. The balance sheet presents the book value of assets and how the assets were financed. Many analysts convert the balance sheet into current market values. Important items to examine include inventory, property, plant and equipment, and intangibles. The methods of valuing these assets vary among firms in an industry, because they may use different accounting methods.

The income statement examines the flow of assets through the firm over a period of time. The income statement presents the sales, expenses and profits of the firm over a stated time period (usually a quarter or a year). Two major items that require close scrutiny are research and development and depreciation expense.

The statement of cash flows examines the flow of cash through a firm, specifically the sources of cash (financings and retained earnings) and the uses of cash (dividends, inventory and physical plant).

The statement of shareholders' equity shows the changes in equity from capital transactions with owners. It reports the number of outstanding shares by class and the amounts of retained earnings.

Identify the most important ratios used in financial statement analysis, discuss how these ratios are used and describe what to be cautious about.

Ratios allow investors to compare companies of various sizes and companies in time, even when they become smaller or larger. There are four major categories of ratios: profitability, liquidity, debt and activity. Profitability ratios measure the earning power of the firm. Liquidity ratios measure the ability of the firm to pay its immediate liabilities. Debt ratios measure the financial risk of a firm. Activity ratios are used to describe the relationship between the firm's level of operations and the assets needed to sustain operating activities. Among other things, financial ratios can be used to predict corporate bankruptcy. However, always be cautious about economic assumptions, timing and window dressing, benchmarks, and off-balance-sheet activities.

Explain how analysts assess the quality of reported earnings.

Analysts studying a firm's financial statements look for clues on how to assess the quality of the reported earnings number. For example, analysts assess whether the firm uses conservative or liberal accounting methods. Also, analysts seek to determine whether the earnings could actually be paid as dividends (as opposed to just accounting earnings that are not distributable). Analysts also examine specific items to identify red flags regarding the quality of earnings.

Key terms

Accounting scandals 537
Balance sheet 538
Common-size statement 554
Current ratio 552
Earnings per share 552
EBITDA 546

Failure prediction 557
Financial ratio analysis 552
Financial statement 538
Fixed charge coverage 552
Income statement 538
Percentage financial statement 554

Quality of earnings 559
Quick ratio 552
Return on equity 552
Statement of cash flows 539
Statement of shareholders' equity 538

Review questions

1 This year the R&C Corporation reported a net income of $190 million, depreciation of $100 million, and a dividend payment to stockholders of $10 million. If the firm paid off $15 million in long-term debt, what was the net cash flow for the firm?

What is the net cash flow if the company also repurchased $25 million in common stock and issued $5 million in preferred stock?

2 Ahold 'was recording revenue when it shipped products merely to its own warehouses' (see Connecting Theory to Practice 16.2). How does this accounting practice affect reported earnings and cash flows?

3 Suppose you are given the following information about the inventory of FRM, Inc., a maker of heating elements:

			Total cost
Inventory on 1 January	30	Elements at $750	$22 500
First purchase in year	85	Elements at $780	$66 300
Second purchase in year	55	Elements at $850	$46 750
Total available	170	Elements	$135 550

a. Calculate the value of inventory at the end of the year by the FIFO, the LIFO and the average cost methods if there are 60 elements in inventory on 31 December.
b. Calculate the cost of goods sold, given the information in Part a, by each inventory method.
c. If FRM Inc. sold each element for $900 and is in a 27% average tax bracket, what was the net income reported by each inventory method? (Assume no other costs.)

4 Explain the role of R&D within a corporation. Does more research and development automatically create shareholder value? Discuss your answer.

5 Consider the consolidated balance sheet for the XYZ company given below. What are the XYZ company's liquidity ratios?

2003
1 725	Cash and cash equivalents
7 31	Short-term investments
3 378	Accounts receivable
531	Short-term loans
2 384	Total inventories
954	Prepaid expenses, taxes and other assets
9 702	**Total current assets**
1 745	Long-term loans and investments
5 775	Property, plant and equipment, less accumulated depreciation
2 136	Goodwill
2 643	Other assets, deferred taxes and deferred charges
22 001	**Total assets**

3 353	Short-term borrowings
1 370	Accounts payable
1 338	Income taxes payable
654	Accrued compensation and related items
1 746	Other current liabilities
8 460	**Total current liabilities**
1 031	Long-term debt
618	Post-retirement benefit obligation other than pension plans
380	Deferred taxes on income
1 007	Other noncurrent liabilities
75	Minority interests
11 570	**Total liabilities**
10 431	**Owner's Equity**

 For an extensive set of review and practice questions and answers, visit the Levy–Post investment website at www.booksites.net/levy

Selected references

Accounting Standards Committee, 1989, *Statement of Standards Accounting Practice: SSAP22 Accounting for Goodwill*, Milton Keynes: ICAEW.

Altman, E. I., 1968, 'Financial Ratios, Discriminant Analysis, and the Prediction of Corporate Bankruptcy', *Journal of Finance*, **23**, 589–609.

Anonymous, 1992, 'Market Focus: All the World's a Ratio', *Economist*, **322** (7747), 72.

Beaver, W. H., 1968, 'Alternative Accounting Measures as Predictors of Failure', *Accounting Review*, **43**, 113–22.

Bernstein, L. A., 1989, *Financial Statement Analysis: Theory, Application, and Interpretation*, 4th edn, Homewood, IL: Irwin.

Bernstein, L. A., 1992, 'A Financial Analysts' Guide to Accounting Quality', *Business Credit*, **94** (2), 11–13.

Cottle, S., R. F. Murray and F. E. Block, 1988, *Graham and Dodd's Security Analysis*, 5th edn, New York: McGraw-Hill.

Deakin, E., 1977, 'Business Failure Prediction: An Empirical Analysis', in E. Altman and A. Sametz, editors, *Financial Crises: Institutions and Markets in a Fragile Environment*, New York: John Wiley & Sons.

Dennis, M. C., 1994, 'Understanding Cash Flow Statements', *Business Credit*, **96** (1), 40–42.

Evans, F. C., 1993, 'Analyzing a Financial Statement', *Management Review*, **82** (11), 52–53.

Gilbert, L. R., K. Menon and K. B. Schwartz, 1990, 'Predicting Bankruptcy for Firms in Financial Distress', *Journal of Business Finance and Accounting*, **17**, 161–171.

Jennings, R., M. J. Leclery and R. B. Thomson, II, 1997, 'Evidence on the Usefulness of Alternative Earnings per Share Measures', *Financial Analysts Journal*, **53** (6), 24–33.

Jensen, G. R., R. R. Johnson and J. M. Mercer, 1997, 'New Evidence on Size and Price/Book Effects in Stock Returns', *Financial Analysts Journal*, **53** (6), 34–42.

Johnson, H. Thomas, 1975, 'The Role of Accounting History in the Study of Modern Business Enterprise', *Accounting Review*, July, 444–450.

Klarman, S. A., 1991, *Margin of Safety: Risk-Averse Value Investing Strategies for the Thoughtful Investor*, New York: Harper Business.

Klecka, W. R., 1980, 'Discriminant Analysis', Sage University Paper Series on Quantitative Applications in the Social Sciences 07–019, Beverly Hills, CA: Sage Publications.

Knutson, P. H., 1993, *Financial Reporting in the 1990s and Beyond*, Charlottesville, VA: AIMR.

Koh, H. C. and Killough, L. N., 1990, 'The Use of Multiple Discriminant Analysis in the Assessment of the Going-concern Status of an Audit Client', *Journal of Business Finance and Accounting*, **17**, 179–192.

Kohler, E. L., 1975, '*A Dictionary for Accountants*', 5th edn, Englewood Cliffs, NJ: Prentice Hall.

Lev, B., 1974, *Financial Statement Analysis, A New Approach*, Englewood Cliffs, NJ: Prentice Hall.

Lynch, P., 1989, *One Up on Wall Street*, New York: Penguin.

Miller, B., 1994, 'Cause-and-Effect Ratio Analysis Adds Decision-Making Value to Credit Scoring Models', *Business Credit*, **96** (2), 27–29.

Ohlson, J. A., 1980, 'Financial Ratios and the Probabilistic Prediction of Bankruptcy', *Journal of Accounting Research*, **18**, 109–131.

Penman, S. H., 1992, 'Financial Statement Information and the Pricing of Earnings Changes', *Accounting Review*, **67** (3), 563–577.

Platt, J. D. and Platt, M. B., 1990, 'Development of a Class of Stable Predictive Variables: The Case of Bankruptcy Prediction', *Journal of Business Finance and Accounting*, **17**, 31–51.

Shivaswamy, M., J. P. Hobun, Jr and K. Matsumoto, 1993, 'A Behavioral Analysis of Financial Ratios', *Mid-Atlantic Journal of Business*, **29** (1), 7–25.

Speidell, L. S. and V. B. Bavishi, 1992, 'GAAP Arbitrage: Valuation Opportunities in International Accounting Standards', *Financial Analysts Journal*, **48** (6), 58–66.

Sveiby, K. E., 1997, *The New Organizational Wealth: Managing and Measuring Knowledge-Based Assets*, San Francisco, CA: Berrett-Koehler.

White, G. I., C. S. Sondhi and D. Fried, 1997, *The Analysis and Use of Financial Statements*, Hoboken, NJ: John Wiley & Sons.

Woelfel, C. J., 1993, 'Analysis Looks behind the Numbers', *Business Credit*, **95** (2), 4–5.

Job losses mean no end in sight to US recession

US job losses continued to rise at a worrying pace last month, extending what is either the country's longest recession or worst economic recovery since the second world war. The possibility the recession that officially began in 2001 persists or might have turned into a 'double dip' – a weak recovery followed by another recession – has kept the National Bureau of Economic Research, the academic group widely seen as the historian of US business cycles, from officially declaring the recession has ended.

The Labor Department reported yesterday that payrolls outside the agricultural sector fell by a seasonally adjusted 108 000 in March – the fifth drop in seven months and well above the 30 000 drop widely forecast. The job losses followed a 357 000 plunge in February, a figure revised sharply from an initial estimate of 308 000. The unemployment rate, based on a survey of households, held steady at 5.8 per cent because a large number of people who abandoned the search for work are not counted as unemployed. Only 62.3 per cent of the US population was employed in March, a nine-year low.

Equity markets took the bad news in their stride, apparently thankful it was not any worse. But the lengthy run of job losses has added to speculation about how severe the economy's troubles are.

US economists, on average, have underestimated the economy's weakness this year, consistently underforecasting big drops in employment, production, retail sales and home purchases. The gap between their predictions and the actual numbers is the widest in more than seven years – a development typical of turning points. 'Economists typically make enormous forecast errors when things change,' said Anirvan Banerji, research director for the Economic Cycle Research Institute. 'They use forecasting models that in some sophisticated way extrapolate from the recent past and fail to account for any possible change in the dynamic or any cascading effect.'

Employment generally lags behind the economy, and significant job losses have occurred in previous recoveries, only to give way to robust expansions. However, job losses during this recovery have so far surpassed, in size and duration, losses seen in previous post-recession periods, including the 'jobless recovery' after the 1990–91 recession. 'The current jobless recovery has lasted longer and is far worse,' said Charles McMillion, chief economist of MBG Information Services in Washington.

Investment in the News 17 continued

Because of the uncertainty, an end of the recession has yet to be officially declared. It could end up being recorded as the longest uninterrupted recession since 1945.

Traders in futures markets have been speculating on or hedging against the possibility the US economy remains sick. Futures markets began this week pricing in a rate cut of at least a quarter point by September as a certainty, but backed away from that yesterday.

Source: Peronet Despeignes, 'Job Losses Mean No End In Sight To US Recession', *Financial Times*, 5 April 2003.

Learning objectives

After studying this chapter, you should be able to:

1 Describe the key measure of the health of the overall economy, gross domestic product (GDP).

2 Describe the impact of government fiscal and monetary policy on the economy.

3 Explain the relationship between the overall economy and financial markets.

4 Describe the relationships between interest rates, exchange rates and inflation rates.

As discussed in Investment in the News 17, the economic outlook in the USA in mid-2003 was unclear to many analysts. Despite various signs of economic recovery from the recession that started in 2001, many feared that the recession would drag on. Among the sources of weaknesses that could short-circuit the recovery was the labour market situation. The recession had spawned the longest continuous decline in jobs in half a century; the monthly job reports for February and March alone showed a combined loss of almost half a million jobs. Job losses pose a direct threat to the economy, because there is a limit to how much consumers can spend when their jobs are disappearing and their pay cheques are under stress. Adding to the labour market situation were high consumer debts and high property prices. Low interest rates had made it easy for many cash-strapped consumers to borrow against their homes. In 2002, American homeowners raised $130 billion through home-equity loans, nearly double the amount they borrowed in 2001; in 2003, the home-equity borrowing binge continued. Homeowners were using the cash to buy all sorts of things they otherwise would not be able to afford – appliances, home repairs, new or used cars. Mainly, however, they were using it to pay off mounting credit-card debt.[1] As long as home values keep rising, borrowers are protected against a cash crunch. If they cannot make a payment, they can always take out another loan against the rising value of their home. However, when interest rates start heading up again (as is usual during a recovery), then mortgages will become more expensive, which means fewer people in the market to buy a home, and housing values will go down. Combined with the job losses, high consumer debts and falling property prices could cause a sharp drop in consumer spending. As Section 17.1.1 will show, consumer spending

---

[1] Interest rates on home-equity loans are only about half those on credit-card debt, and home-equity interest payments can be deducted from income taxes while interest on credit-card debt cannot.

accounts for around two-thirds of total US economic activity, meaning that the health of the consumer is a vital factor determining the health of the economy.

Economy-wide factors affect the profitability, liquidity and solvency of almost all companies. Also, they affect the trade-off that investors make between current consumption and future consumption and between risky and riskless investments; hence, it affects interest rates (the time-value of money) and risk premiums for risky assets. For these reasons, the overall economic situation affects the prices, risks and returns of almost all securities.

The most important economy-wide factors are interest rates, inflation rates, the business cycle and exchange rates. Chapter 13 dealt with interest rates, the yield curve and spreads over Treasuries. This chapter deals with the business cycle, inflation and exchange rates. Section 17.1 reviews some basic economic principles of overall economic activity and the business cycle. It also looks at the role that government policy plays in economic health. Section 17.2 then establishes the links between the economy and financial markets. Section 17.3 analyses some relationships between interest rates, inflation rates and (forward) exchange rates in the various markets – concepts that are helpful in analysing investment opportunities abroad.

17.1   Macroeconomic evaluation

This section reviews several economic series that indicate the overall strength of the economy. It first reviews the concept of gross domestic product (GDP) and other measures of economic health. It also reviews the most popular economic indicators used to analyse future economic trends. Finally, it examines various government policies, especially those of the Federal Reserve, and their role in stimulating economic activity.

17.1.1 Understanding gross domestic product

The most widely used measure of the health of the overall economy is the GDP. The GDP is typically measured both quarterly and annually, and the government issues preliminary estimates throughout the year. The GDP, or the nominal GDP, as it is sometimes called, is the value of all goods and services produced in an economy in a particular time period. The GDP is measured in monetary terms. Since inflation changes the value of money, economists adjust GDP values to include the effects of inflation. This inflation-adjusted measure, called the real GDP, allows economists and investors to compare the GDP over time, ignoring the impact of inflation. In the USA, statistics on the GDP and related measures of economic health are produced by the Bureau of Economic Analysis (BEA) of the US Department of Commerce.

A problem in measuring total output is how to count goods and services produced in a domestic country (say, the USA) by foreigners and how to count goods and services produced by nationals (say, Americans) in a foreign country. The solution to this problem is to have two measures of economic activity. Gross national product (GNP) counts goods and services produced by US nationals in a foreign country but does not include goods and services produced by foreigners in the domestic country. Thus, a factory built in Spain by US citizens would count in the US GNP but not in Spain's GNP. The GDP counts goods and services produced within the country's borders, ignoring who produced it. Thus, the factory built in Spain by US citizens would count as part of Spain's GDP but not as part of the US GDP.

One key to the successful use of macroeconomic data in investment analysis is an understanding of exactly how these data are published. Investors attempting to establish relationships

| Exhibit 17.1 | The procedure for reporting the GDP |

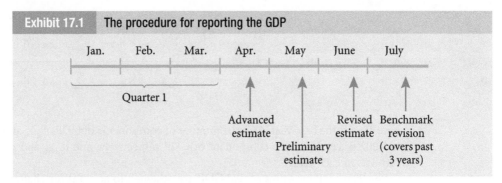

Source: 'The Procedure For Reporting the GDP', from *The Atlas of Economic Indicators*, by W. Stansbury Carnes and Stephen D. Slifer. Copyright © 1991 by HarperCollins Publishers, Inc. Reprinted by permission of HarperCollins Publishers, Inc.

between macroeconomic data and financial markets need to consider the revision process of reported macroeconomic data. Quarterly estimates of the GDP are first released during the last few days of the month following the end of the quarter. For example, for the first quarter ending 31 March, the advanced estimate of the GDP is released at the end of April (see Exhibit 17.1). Preliminary estimates are released a month later (May, in our example), followed by a revised estimate after another month (June, in our example). Finally after another month (July, in our example), benchmark revisions are made covering the past three years. Thus, advanced estimates may be altered several times before a final GDP figure is established, because of improvements in data collected over the particular time period. Thus, when examining historical data to establish relationships between financial markets and macroeconomic data, be sure to incorporate revised figures. The final reported GDP may be significantly different from the initial advanced estimate.

The GDP has four components: consumption, investment, government spending and net trade (exports less imports). The GDP is traditionally expressed as

$$GDP = C + I + G + (X - M) \qquad (17.1)$$

where C is consumption, I is investment, G is government spending and $(X - M)$ is net trade (that is, exports minus imports). In this equation, investment (I) includes spending for new capital goods and increases in corporate inventory, not financial investments. Investors watch the different components of the GDP closely, because some components tend to provide better information regarding the direction of the economy in the future. For example, in 2002, C = \$7303.7 billion, I = \$1593.2 billion, G = \$1972.9 billion, X = \$1014.9 billion and M = \$1428.5 billion.[2] Thus,

$$GDP = \$7303.7 + \$1593.2 + \$1972.9 + (\$1014.9 - \$1428.5) = \$10\,456.2$$

where all figures are in billions.

To compare real GDPs (adjusted for inflation), the BEA computes so-called chained (1996) dollar estimates. Focusing on the estimates for 2002, the chained (1996) dollar estimates are computed in the following way:[3]

---

[2] Data from the Bureau of Economic Analysis at www.bea.doc.gov/bea/dn/nipaweb/index.asp

[3] The square-root term is the so-called Fisher ideal quantity index. It is a geometric average of the so-called Laspreyes quantity index $\sum_{i=1}^{M} p_{i,1996}q_{i,2002} / \sum_{i=1}^{M} p_{i,1996}q_{i,1996}$, which uses base year prices, and the so-called Paasche quantity index $\sum_{i=1}^{M} p_{i,2002}q_{i,2002} / \sum_{i=1}^{M} p_{i,2002}q_{i,1996}$, which uses current prices.

$$realGDP_{2002} = GDP_{1996} \times \sqrt{\frac{\sum_{i=1}^{M} p_{i,1996} \times q_{i,2002}}{\sum_{i=1}^{M} p_{i,1996} \times q_{i,1996}} \times \frac{\sum_{i=1}^{M} p_{i,2002} \times q_{i,2002}}{\sum_{i=1}^{M} p_{i,2002} \times q_{i,1996}}} \qquad (17.2)$$

where 1996 is the base year, M is the number of components of GDP, $p_{i,1996}$ and $p_{i,2002}$ are 1996 and 2002 prices of the ith component of GDP respectively, and $q_{i,1996}$ and $q_{i,2002}$ refer to the quantities in each year.

The chain-type measures of real GDP are designed to account for changes in the relative prices of goods and services in addition to changes in the overall level of prices.[4] For example, during the past few decades, the relative price of computer equipment and components fell sharply. Relative price changes typically are related inversely to changes in relative quantities due to the substitution of expensive goods and services for inexpensive ones. For example, the falling price of computers is related to the automatisation process or the substitution of expensive human labour with inexpensive computers. When the relative price of a good or service is decreasing, but growth is measured using an earlier (higher) price, output of this good or service will receive an unwarranted high weight. Since the relative quantity of the good or service will increases if the price decreases (the substitution effect), we would underestimate the economic growth before the base year and overestimate the growth after the base year. The chained-dollar estimates do not suffer from this problem and produce unbiased estimates of economic growth because they are constructed using price weights that change continually as prices in the economy change.

Related to this, chained-dollar estimates of growth do not change every time the accounts are adjusted for a new base year (and hence different relative prices). Suppose the base year is changed from 1996 to 2000. In this case, the chained-dollar real GDP numbers for 2001 and 2002 will change, because the 2000 prices differ from the 1996 prices. However, the growth rate for 2001–02 will remain the same.

In chained (1996) dollars, the 2002 US GDP was $9439.9 billion.[5] Exhibit 17.2 gives the chained-dollar real GDP and its components for the years 1998–2002. This exhibit shows clearly that economic growth halted in 2001. While American consumers kept buying (see the entry 'Personal consumption expenditures'), corporations stopped buying capital goods (see the entry 'Gross private domestic investment') as the technology bubble burst. Also, companies ran down inventories (see the entry 'Change in private inventories'), subtracting from overall GDP growth. The exhibit also shows falling exports (due to slow growth abroad) and the propensity of US consumption to leak into imports. Clearly, US companies, and US GDP are not the beneficiaries of higher consumer expenditure.[6]

Several measures of economic activity provide clues on the magnitude and direction of the real GDP. Exhibit 17.3 lists some of these measures, the component of the GDP that they influence, and when these measures are announced. For example, the number of cars sold is announced every two weeks about three days following the end of the second week. Clearly,

---

[4] Chained-dollar estimates will soon be incorporated into other data series such as the Federal Reserve's index of industrial production and the Bureau of Labor Statistics' annual and quarterly measures of multifactor and labour productivity to reduce bias in these series.

[5] Recall that nominal GDP was $10 456.2 billion in 2002.

[6] As one joke doing the rounds in Washington has it, the US Federal Reserve is doing a great job of stimulating the economy – 'but it is China's economy they are stimulating'.

car sales represent consumption, and they help give early clues as to whether consumers are loosening their purse strings. Consumers tend to purchase cars when they have confidence in the overall economy.

Exhibit 17.2	US real gross domestic product (GDP) (1998–2002) (in billions of chained (1996) dollars)				
	1998	1999	2000	2001	2002
Gross domestic product	8508.9	8859.0	9191.4	9214.5	9439.9
Personal consumption expenditures	5683.7	5964.5	6223.9	6377.2	6576.0
Durable goods	726.7	812.5	878.9	931.9	999.9
Non-durable goods	1686.4	1765.1	1833.8	1869.8	1929.5
Services	3273.4	3395.4	3524.5	3594.9	3675.6
Gross private domestic investment	1558.0	1660.5	1762.9	1574.6	1589.6
Fixed investment	1480.0	1595.2	1691.9	1627.4	1577.3
Non-residential	1135.9	1228.4	1324.2	1255.1	1183.4
Structures	262.2	258.6	275.5	270.9	226.4
Equipment and software	875.4	975.9	1056.0	988.2	971.1
Residential	345.1	368.3	372.4	373.5	388.2
Change in private inventories	76.7	62.8	65.0	−61.4	5.2
Net exports of goods and services	−221.1	−320.5	−398.8	−415.9	−488.5
Exports	1002.4	1036.3	1137.2	1076.1	1058.8
Goods	722.9	750.0	834.7	785.2	756.9
Services	279.8	286.8	304.1	292.0	301.5
Imports	1223.5	1356.8	1536.0	1492.0	1547.4
Goods	1031.4	1157.5	1313.7	1270.5	1320.1
Services	192.2	200.3	223.6	222.4	227.2
Government consumption expenditures and gross investment	1483.3	1540.6	1582.5	1640.4	1712.8
Federal	525.4	537.7	544.4	570.6	613.3
National defence	341.6	348.8	348.7	366.0	400.0
Non-defence	183.8	188.8	195.6	204.4	213.3
State and local	957.7	1002.4	1037.4	1069.4	1099.7
Residual[7]	0.8	1.4	2.1	22.6	19.9

Source: From US Bureau of Economic Analysis, www.bea.doc.gov/bea/dn/nipaweb/index.asp

---

[7] A disadvantage of chain-type estimates is that the estimates of GDP and its components are not additive in real-dollar terms. That is to say, the sum of chained-dollar estimates of the components of GDP (for example, at the highest level of aggregation, consumption, investment, government spending and net exports) will not necessarily be the exact sum of GDP as an independently calculated aggregate. To acknowledge the loss of additivity, chained-dollar tables now include a residual entry, where the residual is defined as the difference between GDP or a component and the sum of the most detailed components of the table. Because the residual can be traced to price weights that are not the same as the base year, it can be expected that the residuals will be small for years close to 1996 (when the annual weights will likely be close in value to the 1996 weights). However, the size of residuals will increase dramatically for periods far from 1996. In general, comparisons of two or more different chained-dollar series and calculations of component contributions must be made with caution for periods away from the reference year. It is usually best to make comparisons of aggregate series in current dollars or to use BEA's estimates of contributions to percentage change.

Exhibit 17.3	Measuring inflation and components of the gross domestic product (GDP) and when they are reported

Component	Percentage of GDP (%)	Economic measures	When available[a]
Consumption	69	Car sales	After 3 days (biweekly)
		Retail sales	11th–14th
		Personal income/expenditures	22nd–31st
Investment	13	Housing starts/building permits	16th–20th
		Durable goods orders	22nd–28th
		New home sales	28th–4th
		Construction spending	1st (2 months prior)
		Factory orders/business inventories	30th–6th (2 months prior)
Government spending	19	Public construction	1st (2 months prior)
Net exports[b]	−0.5	Merchandise trade balance	15th–17th (2 months prior)
GDP	100[c]	Purchasing managers' index	1st
		Employment	1st–7th
		Industrial production capacity	14th–17th
Inflation		Producers' price index	9th–16th
		Consumer price index	15th–21st

[a] Unless stated otherwise the dates refer to the following month. See page 15 of the source.
[b] A negative figure implies that exports are smaller than imports.
[c] The sum is not exactly 100% because of rounding.

Source: 'The Procedure For Reporting the GDP', from *The Atlas of Economic Indicators*, by W. Stansbury Carnes and Stephen D. Slifer. Copyright © 1991 by HarperCollins Publishers, Inc. Reprinted by permission of HarperCollins Publishers, Inc.

The value of these published economic measures depends heavily on how soon they are available. Car sales, for example, are very valuable, because they are published after only three days (as well as biweekly). Factory orders are not as valuable, because they are published only several months after the order day.

17.1.2 The business cycle and economic indicators

A business cycle is a period of expansion and contraction of aggregate economic activity measured by the real GDP. Exhibit 17.4 illustrates the stages of a business cycle. The black line moving up through time represents long-run growth, which is determined by structural factors such as population growth and technological progress. As economic activity contracts, the real GDP dips below this growth rate. It reaches a low point known as the trough. Eventually, the economy expands until it reaches the high point of the business cycle, known as the peak. An economy is in an expansion phase between a trough and a peak; it is in a contraction phase after a peak and before a trough.

The National Bureau of Economic Research has constructed measures of business activity known as composite indexes, which are made up of selected economic data that vary depending on the purpose of the composite index. The three main indexes (also called indicators – a

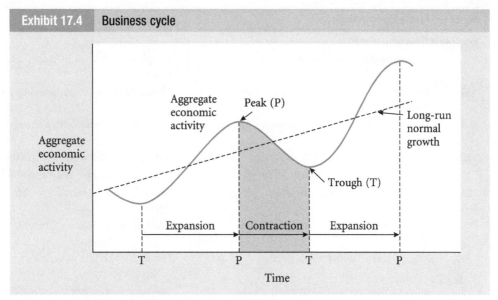

Exhibit 17.4 Business cycle

Source: Abel/Bernanke, *Macroeconomics*, Fig. 9.1. (p. 291), © 1995 by Addison-Wesley Publishing Company, Inc. Reprinted by permission of Pearson Education, Inc. Publishing as Pearson Addison Wesley.

technical measurement used to forecast the market's direction) are the leading, coincident and lagging indexes. Coincident indicators are indicators that are supposed to move directly with the business cycle. Leading indicators and lagging indicators are indicators that are supposed to lead and lag behind the business cycle. For example, the composite index of 11 leading indicators is a weighted average of 11 economic statistics that are supposed to lead the business cycle. Exhibit 17.5 gives these 11 components. Each index is given a specific reference number that helps analysts to keep track of how a particular index or a composite index is constructed. Thus, each index can be identified uniquely by its number. For example, the average weekly hours worked in manufacturing is Series 1.

From time to time, the composition of these composite indexes is changed. We see from Exhibit 17.5 that the 11 series making up the leading index are statistics that would be expected to change first with changes in the business cycle. For example, Series 1, the average weekly hours worked by manufacturing labour, would tend to rise as businesses perceive that the economy was entering an expansion phase and demand was rising. It is interesting to note that Series 19, the index of stock prices (which is actually the Standard & Poor's 500 index), is one of the best-performing leading indicators of the business cycle. This is consistent with the predictions of the EMT (see Chapter 12); all information about the future course of the business cycle is already reflected in current market prices.

17.1.3 Fiscal and monetary policy

The government uses fiscal policy and monetary policy to promote real GDP growth, relatively full employment and stable prices. The government can also intervene to avoid bankruptcy trends. For example, in November 1997, the fourth largest investment house in Japan declared bankruptcy. The Nikkei index dropped sharply, igniting fear of a bankruptcy chain reaction. The Japanese government immediately announced a reform plan to avoid the chain reaction and the Nikkei index recovered in response to this plan. Similarly, in September 1998, the US Federal Reserve organised a rescue of Long-Term Capital Management, a large and

Exhibit 17.5 Business cycle indicators and their components

Series	Type of index component	Explanation
Leading index components		
1	Average weekly hours, manufacturing	Length of work week increases with perceived future demand
5	Average weekly initial claims on unemployment insurance	Claims decline as economy rebounds
8	Manufacturers' new orders, consumer goods and materials	New orders increase with a stronger economy
32	Vendor performance, slower deliveries	Stronger demand will result in slower deliveries
20	Contracts and orders for plant and equipment	New orders increase as business outlook brightens
29	Index of new private housing units	People build houses based on forecast of future prospects
92	Change in manufacturers' unfilled orders, durable goods	Unfilled orders indicate future GNP growth
99	Change in sensitive materials prices	Demand for certain materials increases as economy expands
19	Index of stock prices, 500 common stocks	Stock prices are based on forecasted future performance
106	Money supply, M2 (M1, M2 and M3 are three measures of the money supply as defined by the Federal reserve: M1 represents all money that can be converted to cash immediately; M2 includes M1 plus savings accounts and time deposits; M3 is M2 plus the money market funds held by institutions)	Economies are sensitive to quantity of money available
83	Index of consumer expectations, University of Michigan	Consumers with bright expectations will spend more
Coincident index components		
41	Employees on non-agricultural payrolls	Number of people employed moves with business cycle
51	Personal income less transfer payments	Employee pay moves directly with business cycle
47	Index of industrial production	Production moves directly with demand for goods
57	Manufacturing and trade sales	Sales move directly with business cycle
Lagging index components		
91	Average duration of unemployment	Length of unemployment declines after economy rebounds
77	Ratio of manufacturing and trade inventories to sales	After economy rebounds, sales increase and inventories decline
62	Change in labour cost per unit of output	Labour costs rise after economy rebounds
109	Average prime rate charged by banks	Interest rates rise in response to business demand for funds
101	Commercial and industrial loans outstanding	Borrowing increases after economic rebounds
95	Ratio of consumer instalment credit outstanding to personal income	People borrow a greater percentage of their income after economic recovery
120	Change in Consumer Price Index for services	Price levels tend to rise only after an economy is expanding

prominent hedge fund on the brink of failure (see Investment in the News 19). The Federal Reserve intervened because it was concerned about possible dire consequences for world financial markets if it allowed the hedge fund to fail. Thus, governments, in implementing their policies, can affect the business environment as well as the financial markets.

The federal government and fiscal policy

Fiscal policy refers to the taxation and spending policies of the government. Governments can stimulate growth in real GDP with tax incentives for investment. For example, a reduction in the corporate capital gains tax rates may motivate businesses to make capital expenditures. This increase in investment directly increases the GDP. Personal tax rates also affect the stock market. For example, if investors had been able to forecast that the Clinton administration would reduce the capital gains tax from 28 to 20% (or even to 18% for a five-year holding period) in 1997, before this information was public or even before it was discussed publicly, then they could have made money by purchasing stocks, because such an announcement usually induces an increase in stock-market prices. Fiscal policy seeks to find the optimal strategy of taxation and spending that maximises GDP growth and employment and, at the same time, maintains stable prices.

The government can affect the unemployment rate in various ways. The most popular employment statistic monitored by governments is the civilian unemployment rate, which is the number of unemployed people as a percentage of the labour force (sum of civilians working and those actively seeking work). For example, in September 2003 there were 9.0 million unemployed people in the US, and the size of the civilian labour force was 146.5 million. Therefore, the civilian unemployment rate was

$$(9.0 \text{ million}/146.5 \text{ million})100 \cong 6.1\%$$

One method of stimulating a sluggish economy is for the government to hire unemployed people to perform various tasks, such as building roads. Without tax increases, however, this government spending will produce budget deficits. Similar to a personal budget deficit, a governmental budget deficit occurs when a government spends more in a given period than it takes in as tax revenues. For 2003 and 2004, the federal budget is expected to total more than $300 billion per annum. Over the next ten years, the federal deficit is expected to top $1500 billion. If President George W. Bush's proposed $730 billion tax cut is enacted, then the sum will be larger still. Large deficits generally push up long-term interest rates because the government will need to issue additional government bonds in the future (the demand for money increases) and because government spending may push up prices (the demand for goods and services increases).

These relationships are a good reason for assessing the fiscal soundness of a country's government and form a critical task for international portfolio analysis as well as analysis of domestic portfolios. Even good companies have difficulty remaining profitable if they operate in a country whose government is irresponsible. Hence, one key assessment criterion for international investment is the integrity of the foreign government's fiscal policy.

The Federal Reserve Bank and monetary policy

In 1913, Congress created the Federal Reserve Bank (the Fed) to carry out monetary policy. Monetary policy refers to actions by a central bank to control the supply of money and interest rates that directly influence the financial markets. Like fiscal policy, monetary policy aims to achieve growth in the real GDP, relatively full employment and stable prices. The Fed's primary focus is on interest rates and money supply. Additionally, the Fed acts as a lender of last resort (when there is a cash drain on a bank) and guards against severe currency depreciation.

The Fed will lend to banks, for example, when there are unusually large withdrawals. It will also try to support its currency in volatile foreign exchange markets. Generally, when the Fed announces an interest rate increase, the stock market falls; similarly, an interest-rate decrease is accompanied by an increase in stock prices.

The Fed regulates the volume of bank reserves, affects the pace of money creation, and sets the percentage of funds that banks are required to hold as reserves. It rarely uses bank reserves as a policy tool in its efforts to manipulate the economy. Bank reserves are the percentage of deposits that banks must hold in non-interest-bearing assets (cash). Reserve requirements set by the Fed are one of the key tools in deciding how much money banks can lend. The higher the reserve requirement, the tighter the money and, therefore, the slower the economic growth. In a recession, the Fed can decrease the reserve requirement to stimulate the economy. The tool used most often by the Fed to alter the money supply is its open market operations (these are activities by which the Federal Reserve Bank of New York carries out the instructions of the Federal Open Market Committee, which intends to regulate the money supply in the market). By buying and selling US Treasury securities directly in the bond market, the Fed can expand or contract the volume of bank reserves.

Exhibit 17.6 illustrates how the Federal Reserve system influences economic activity. Note that changes in bank reserves influence both the money supply and interest rates, which in turn influence both economic activity and inflation.

The Fed also establishes the bank discount rate, which is the rate the Fed charges banks when they borrow directly from it. Indirectly, the bank discount rate influences other interest rates. The amount borrowed varies widely and is seasonal. The federal funds rate is the rate charged for reserves borrowed between banks. The bank discount rate and the federal funds rate are highly correlated.

In many countries, the central banks that operate monetary policy are independent of the government. Examples are the Federal Reserve Bank, the European Central Bank and the Bank of England's Monetary Policy Committee. The reason for this independence is to ensure that monetary policy can be exercised quicker than fiscal policy (which must go through government)

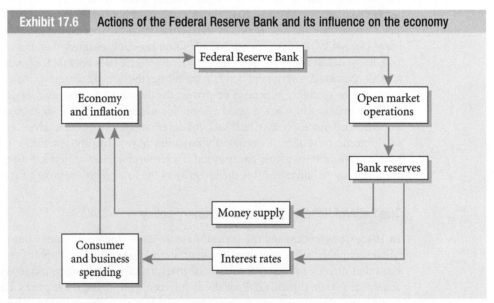

Exhibit 17.6 Actions of the Federal Reserve Bank and its influence on the economy

Source: 'The Actions of the Federal Reserve Bank and Its Influence On the Economy', from *The Atlas of Economic Indicators*, by W. Stansbury Carnes and Stephen D. Slifer. Copyright © 1991 by HarperCollins Publishers, Inc. Reprinted by permission of HarperCollins Publishers, Inc.

and, at the same time, remain independent of the political inclinations of an incumbent government. This is to make sure that economists who decide on monetary policy take into account the health of the economy as well as the effects their changes may have in the long run. Central bankers also enjoy longer terms in office (the chairperson of the Federal Reserve is appointed for a 14-year period) to make sure that investors find their policies and promises credible and reliable.

The ability of a central bank such as the Fed to maintain stable prices and stable interest rates is a key ingredient in providing an environment conducive to running business profitably. Thus, investors need to assess the current abilities of Federal Reserve Bank authorities as well as compare central bank operations across countries.

→ **Connecting Theory to Practice 17.1**

Undue pessimism is driving the eurozone's recession

There are intriguing parallels between the American boom of the second half of the 1990s and the present European recession. In both cases, policymakers decided that the economic conditions they observed were driven by structural factors.

In the US, the Federal Reserve attributed the great boom to a productivity miracle. In the eyes of the Fed, and of many others, the great economic expansion was driven by the new dynamics of the information technology revolution promising permanently higher growth rates. Acting on this diagnosis, the Fed felt unconstrained in providing ample liquidity.

It has now become obvious that this diagnosis was wrong. The US economy was experiencing a classic bubble led by the exaggerated expectations of believers in fairy tales. By providing all the extra liquidity, the Fed was fuelling the bubble, until it burst.

Surprisingly, something similar is happening in the eurozone, although the economic conditions are the opposite of those in the US in the 1990s. European policymakers, in particular the European Central Bank, have blamed the eurozone recession on structural factors. Labour market rigidities, above all, are seen as the root causes of the slowdown.

Acting on this diagnosis, policymakers have taken a wait-and-see attitude. The ECB has been slow in stimulating the economy and has blamed the eurozone politicians for doing nothing to liberalise labour markets and modernise welfare systems.

The eurozone governments have started to believe that nothing can be done to increase aggregate demand, and in any case their hands are tied by the stability pact, the European Union's public deficit limits.

The structural rigidities diagnosis of the downturn in the eurozone since 2000 is wrong. It is difficult to see how rigidities – a permanent feature of continental European economies for the past 30 years – can suddenly produce a drop in growth rates from more than 3 per cent in 1998–2000 to close to zero now. And why did the same rigidities not prevent a European economic boom in the second half of the 1990s?

It would be foolish to deny that there are market rigidities in Europe. Some welfare systems create disincentives to work and incentives to early retirement. Many countries place constraints on hiring and firing, while high taxation of labour and population ageing are widespread. But while they reduce the long-term growth potential of the eurozone, such rigidities barely affect business cycle conditions.

Economic growth in Europe has been known to move up and down, and will continue to do so irrespective of rigidities in labour, product and capital markets. By diagnosing the economic downturn as structural in origin, ECB officials and some governments have escaped their responsibility for stabilising the economy. In the US in the late 1990s and in the eurozone today, policymakers made the wrong diagnosis and applied the wrong policies.

▶

There is a second parallel between late 1990s America and the eurozone today. The US boom was driven by excessive optimism about economic prospects, which led American consumers and investors to embark on a spending spree. The eurozone recession is driven by excessive pessimism about the future of Europe. Pessimism leads consumers and investors to postpone spending on goods and services, and it becomes a self-fulfilling prophecy.

As it turned out, the US was not the miracle economy that policymakers and analysts believed it to be. In contrast, there is as yet no such consensus that the pessimism that pervades the eurozone is excessive. There is still a widely held view that Europe is sick and that its economic future is bleak. But the gloom is vastly exaggerated.

Productivity growth, when correctly measured, has been much the same in Europe and in the US over the last 10 years. The main difference is that European workers like to work fewer hours than their US counterparts. Several countries have embarked on reform programmes, even if progress is gradual. And unlike the US, the eurozone is not saddled with a consumer debt over-hang, a long-term imbalance that will be painful to correct.

There is a third parallel between booming America and gloomy Europe. This has to do with the talk that was once heard in Washington and is now common in Frankfurt, home of the ECB. During the late 1990s, Alan Greenspan, the Fed chairman, openly defended the idea that America was living through a productivity miracle. As a result, he convinced many doubters that the boom was not just some temporary demand upsurge, but was caused by structural changes in the American economy. It is likely that this gave a strong impetus to the bubble and allowed it to last longer than it would have without the exuberant talk.

Something similar has happened in Europe since the start of the economic slowdown. The lectures we hear from Frankfurt routinely stress the need for structural reform as a condition for getting out of the recession. Structural reforms, however, are very difficult to implement in democratic societies. They imply changes in the distribution of income and in economic security, and are resisted by those who are called upon to become more flexible. The implementation of these reforms will take many years. If they are a pre-condition for escaping from recession, there is no end in sight.

Thus, paradoxically, the endless criticism of structural rigidities emanating from Frankfurt serves to prolong the pessimism and therefore the weakness of demand. Europe is stuck in a sluggish state. Much as the Fed helped to fuel the great American boom of the late 1990s, the ECB is helping to sustain the recession by spreading the word that nothing can be done about it for the foreseeable future.

Pessimism is contagious. Fortunately, people become tired of it. That is why even modest signs of economic recovery can revive 'animal spirits'. That is also why policymakers can make a difference by providing even a small monetary or fiscal stimulus. Despite their reluctance to assume their responsibilities, there is no doubt that the economic upturn will become a reality in Europe as it has done so often in the past. Pessimism then will fade away, making place for a more sober diagnosis of Europe's economic problems.

Source: Paul De Grauwe, Undue pessimism is driving the eurozone's recession, *Financial Times*, 8 August 2003.

→ Making the connection

In this comment, Professor Paul de Grauwe of the University of Leuven, Belgium, gives a diagnosis of the 2003 recession in the eurozone. He argues that European policymakers, in particular the European Central Bank and European governments, are helping to deepen rather than to soften the recession by postponing actions to stimulate aggregate demand. According to De Grauwe, the policymakers assume wrongly that the recession is caused by structural factors such as the rigid labour market and the expensive welfare system. This is an example of the awareness that investors must possess regarding policy issues.

17.2 The economy and the financial markets

This section examines the relationship between the overall economy and the financial markets. Recall from Chapters 13 and 15 that the intrinsic value of a security is the present value of all expected future cash flows, discounted at appropriate risk-adjusted discount rates. Hence, the overall economy may impact security prices in the following ways:

- The overall economy affects the expected future cash flows. For example, a strong economy implies that firms are working near capacity, profit margins are high and, hence, the expected future dividends are high.
- The business cycle influences the risks of the cash flows. For instance, a weak economy may increase the risk of stocks of firms with a high degree of financial leverage (high interest costs) or a high degree of operational leverage (high fixed operational costs). In addition, the bonds of such firms become more risky due to an increased probability of default.
- The general economic situation affects interest rates, which form the basis of the discount rates (see Chapter 13).
- The risk premiums charged by investors for accepting risk depend on the overall economy. For example, the risk premiums typically are high during a recession period, which reflects that the subjective pain of losing dollars to spend on consumption goods is higher during bad times than during good times. Conversely, the market risk premium typically is low during periods of economic expansion.

Despite these effects on financial markets, generally it is difficult to beat the market using macroeconomic data. The semi-strong form of the EMT (see Chapter 12) predicts that such information, which is publicly available, cannot be used to systematically earn abnormal, risk-corrected returns. Indeed, as discussed in the previous section, the financial markets tend to move before the GDP, and although we would like to predict market moves by looking at GDP changes in earlier periods, we cannot. Still, this does not mean that macroeconomic analysis is useless for investors. For applications such as portfolio selection, risk management and performance evaluation, it is important to use good estimates for the risk–return characteristics of securities. As discussed above, these characteristics generally change during the business cycle. Much of these changes are predictable to some extent. For example, it is well known that variables such as the dividend yield and the earnings yield of stocks, the credit spread and the term spread of bonds, and measures for the stage in the business cycle can predict the level of future stock market returns.[8]

One possible measure for capturing the effect of the business cycle is the ratio of aggregate consumption to aggregate wealth or consumption-to-wealth ratio. Campbell and Mankiw (1989) provide a theoretical motivation for this ratio as a summary measure of expected returns on the market portfolio. Specifically, investors who want to maintain a flat consumption pattern over time will attempt to smooth out transitory movements in their wealth arising from time variation in expected returns. During an expansion period, investors expect a lower future market return (and, hence, a lower future growth rate of wealth) and they increase their current consumption by a smaller percentage than their wealth, thereby lowering the consumption-to-wealth ratio. Conversely, during a recession, investors expect a higher future market return and they increase the consumption-to-wealth ratio.

---

[8] See, for instance, Fama and Schwert (1977), Chen *et al.* (1986), Keim and Stambaugh (1986), Campbell and Shiller (1988) Fama and French (1988, 1989) and Ferson (1990).

Exhibit 17.7	Cyclical variation of the market risk premium

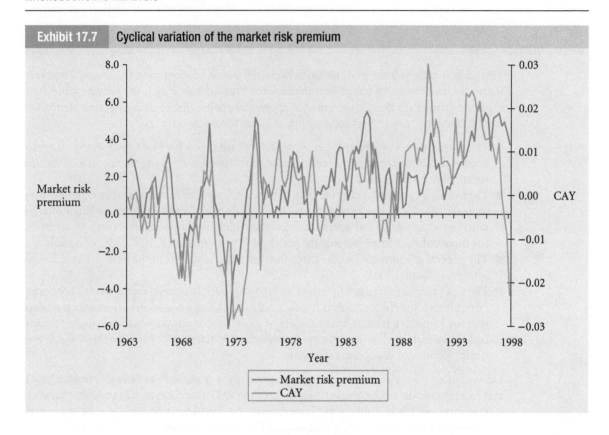

Lettau and Ludvigson (2001a) demonstrate convincingly that the consumption-to-wealth ratio has striking forecasting power for excess returns on aggregate stock market indexes and that it is the best univariate predictor among currently popular forecasting variables for horizons up to one year. To illustrate this pattern, Exhibit 17.7 shows the relationship between the consumption-to-wealth ratio (labelled 'CAY') and the average stock market return for the period from the third quarter of 1963 to the fourth quarter of 1998.[9] The graph includes a rolling window for the average quarterly return on the Fama and French US stock market index. For each quarter, the consumption-to-wealth ratio is compared with the average market return in the next two and a half years or ten quarters. Clearly, the market risk premium is high during recession periods (when the consumption-to-wealth ratio is high) and low during expansion periods (when the consumption-to-wealth ratio is low). For example, in the late 1990s, the stock market boomed, pushing up aggregate wealth. However, consumption was not adjusted accordingly and the consumption-to-wealth ratio fell sharply. This suggests that investors understood that the high stock market returns were only temporary. Indeed, the average return in the following period dropped quickly when the 2000–02 down market started.

---

[9] A difficulty with the consumption-to-wealth ratio is that the non-financial, human capital component of wealth is not observable. Lettau and Ludvigson (2001a) develop an observable version of this ratio, a cointegrating residual between log consumption, c, log asset (non-human) wealth, a, and log labour income, y (referred to as *cay* for short). Data on this proxy for the consumption-to-wealth ratio are available on a quarterly basis on the homepage of Martin Lettau at Stern School of Business, New York: http://pages.stern.nyu.edu/~mlettau/

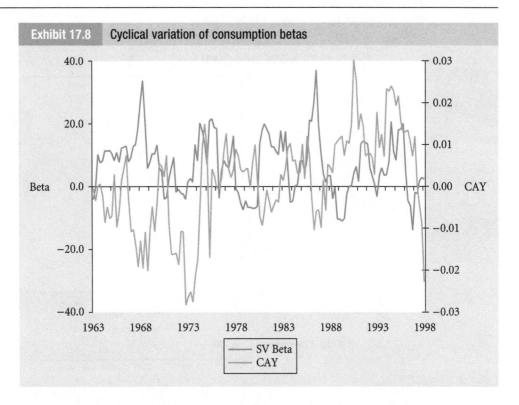

Exhibit 17.8   Cyclical variation of consumption betas

Further, Lettau and Ludvigson (2001b) showed that the betas of small-cap stocks (stocks with a small market capitalisation) and value stocks (stocks with a high book-to-market equity ratio) increase during a recession period, i.e. when the consumption-to-wealth ratio is high. To illustrate this pattern, Exhibit 17.8 shows the relationship between the consumption-to-wealth ratio and the five-year rolling beta of the Fama and French portfolio of US small-value stocks (SV). Note that we use the consumption beta or the beta relative to aggregate consumption rather than a stock market index. This is the beta that is used in the consumption CAPM (CCAPM) (see Chapter 10). Although the relationship is not perfect, the beta increases during an economic recession period (when the consumption-to-wealth ratio is high) and goes down during an expansion period (when the consumption-to-wealth ratio is low). Hence, the small-value stocks are riskiest when the degree of risk-aversion is highest (during a recession).

Note that these cyclical patterns in risk and return do not violate market efficiency; we can predict that the risks and the risk premiums change, but we cannot systematically earn returns in excess of the expected return given the risks and the risk premiums. For example, the knowledge that stocks earn higher expected returns during a recession than during an expansion does not suffice to earn abnormal returns, as the higher return simply may reflect higher risks or higher risk-aversion during a recession. Still, the cyclical patterns are very useful in order to obtain accurate estimates of the risk–return characteristics of securities. In fact, we may draw completely wrong conclusions if we ignore these patterns.

To demonstrate the effect of cyclical time variation, recall that the CAPM seems to fail to explain the return of benchmark portfolios formed on size (market capitalisation) and their book-to-market equity ratio (BE/ME) (see Section 10.2). Lettau and Ludvigson (2001b) showed that much of this evidence disappears if we correct for the cyclical variation of the expected return on the market portfolio and the market betas of the benchmark portfolios.

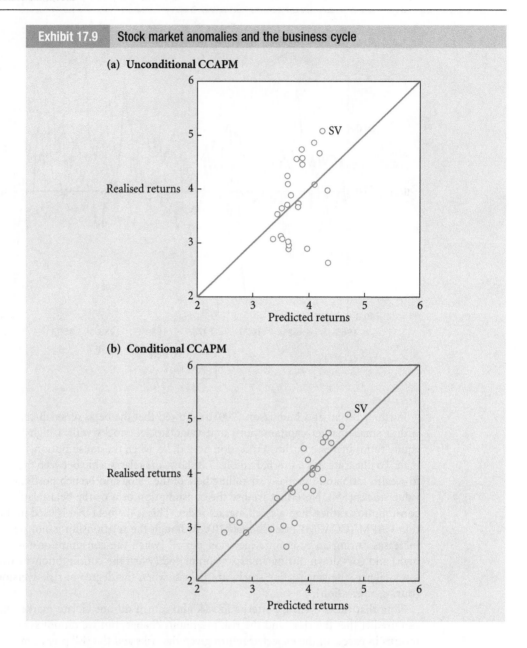

Exhibit 17.9   Stock market anomalies and the business cycle

(a) Unconditional CCAPM

(b) Conditional CCAPM

Exhibit 17.9 illustrates their point.[10] Exhibit 17.9a compares the actual average returns of the 25 Fama and French benchmark portfolios formed on size and BE/ME with the expected returns predicted by the CCAPM if we ignore the effect of the business cycle (a so-called unconditional model). If the CCAPM fits perfectly, then all the points in this exhibit would lie along the 45-degree line; however, the exhibit shows clearly that few points do. It seems that investors can beat the market with a strategy of buying small-cap stocks and value stocks, which yield much higher returns than expected based on their market betas.

---

[10] Exhibit 17.9 is a reproduced version of Figure 1 (parts a, b and d) in Lettau and Ludvigson (2001b).

Exhibit 17.9b shows similar results for a model that does correct for the cyclical variation of risk and return – a so-called conditional CCAPM model (conditional upon the consumption-to-wealth ratio). Interestingly, the conditional model performs far better than the unconditional specification, and it seems to explain the size and BE/ME effects; the points are much closer to the 45-degree line. From these results, Lettau and Ludvigson conclude that previous studies documenting the poor empirical performance of the CCAPM may have made inadequate allowances for time variation in the conditional moments of returns. At least, the results show that investors who ignore the information on the overall economic situation conclude that there are profit opportunities (in this case, by buying small caps and value stocks) when there are none.

17.3 International parity relationships[11]

Exchange rates are a key variable in determining returns from international investments. Also, exchange rates affect domestic economic growth via exports and imports. Investors rely on four parity relationships when they analyse future exchange rates: purchasing power parity, the international Fisher relationship, foreign exchange expectations, and interest-rate parity. We now look at these in turn.

17.3.1 Purchasing power parity

Purchasing power parity is the relationship between two countries' inflation rates and their foreign exchange rates. This parity relationship is used to estimate exchange rates based on expected inflation rates. To clarify the appropriate relationship between inflation rates and exchange rates, suppose we have an internationally traded good (say, aluminium) with no trading restrictions. That is, suppose we can trade aluminium internationally with no transportation or other costs. As in Chapter 6, let DC denote domestic currency ($ in the following example) and FC denote foreign currency (£ in the following example). Thus, $P_{0,DC}$ denotes the price of aluminium in the domestic currency today and $P_{0,FC}$ denotes the price of aluminium in the foreign currency today.

If we can trade internationally and costlessly, then we would expect aluminium to cost the same in either the domestic market or the foreign market, adjusted for the foreign exchange rate. That is,

$$P_{0,DC} = fx_0(DC/FC)P_{0,FC} \tag{17.3}$$

where $fx_0(DC/FC)$ is the foreign exchange rate today in terms of domestic currency per foreign currency. For example, if aluminium was selling for £0.65 and the foreign exchange rate today was $1.5385/£, then the price of aluminium in the USA should be

$$(\$1.5385/£)(£0.65) \cong \$1.00$$

If the cost of aluminium in the USA is any value other than $1, then arbitrage profits can be made. For example, if the actual price in the USA is $1.01 (still assuming that transactions are costless), then we can buy aluminium in the UK for £0.65 (with dollars exchanged at

---

[11] This section is based on Chapter 2 of Solnik (2000).

$1.5385/£) and sell it for $1.01, making a penny profit for each dollar of aluminium; with a large volume of such transactions, an investor can become rich at no risk.

Now suppose that over the next year, the USA experiences $h_{DC} = 3\%$ inflation and the UK experiences $h_{FC} = 5\%$ inflation. If inflation were the only influence on aluminium prices, then we would expect the following prices for aluminium:

$$P_{1,DC} = (1 + h_{DC})P_{0,DC}$$
$$= (1 + 0.03)\$1 = \$1.03 \tag{17.4}$$

$$P_{1,FC} = (1 + h_{FC})P_{0,FC}$$
$$= (1 + 0.05)£0.65 = £0.6825 \tag{17.5}$$

To maintain equilibrium in the international markets with no arbitrage possibilities, we know (according to Equation 17.3 but related to period 1) that at the end of the year, we must have

$$P_{1,DC} = fx_1(DC/FC)P_{1,FC} \tag{17.6}$$

In our case with aluminium, we must have

$$\$1.03 = fx_1(DC/FC)(£0.6825)$$

Solving for the foreign exchange rate, we have

$$fx_1(DC/FC) = \$1.03/£0.6825 \cong \$1.5092/£$$

Thus, we see that the higher inflation rate in the UK has the effect of lowering the foreign exchange rate (the pound is said to depreciate).

We can extend this analysis of the relationship between inflation and exchange rates with aluminium prices to the general level of inflation, because other goods can also be exported and imported. Up to this point, we have assumed that the rates of inflation are known. In practice, however, we do not know what the actual foreign exchange rates or inflation rates will be in a year. Hence, the relationship is based on expected values. The relationship between expected foreign exchange rates and expected inflation rates, known as purchasing power parity, can be expressed as follows:

$$[1 + E(h_{FC})]/[1 + E(h_{DC})] = E(fx_1(FC/DC) / fx_0(FC/DC))$$

where E denotes the expected rate. That is, the ratio of one plus the expected inflation rate is equal to the expected return on foreign exchange. The expression just given can be hard to interpret, so most analysts use the following linear approximation:

$$E(s_{fx}) = \frac{E[fx_1(FC/DC)]}{fx_0(FC/DC)} - 1 \cong E(h_{FC} - h_{DC}) \tag{17.7}$$

where E is the expected rate, s_{fx} is the rate of return in the spot market for foreign exchange expressed in foreign currency per domestic currency,[12] $fx_1(FC/DC)$ is the foreign exchange rate at the end of the year, $fx_0(FC/DC)$ is the foreign exchange rate at the beginning of the year, and h is the inflation rate for one year. This equation basically says that the expected rate of return on foreign exchange is approximately equal to the difference in the expected inflation rates.

---

[12] The spot market is where currency is exchanged today. However, usually there is a two-day settlement period. Hence, a trade made today in the spot market will actually result in currency trading in two days.

Let us see how well the approximation equation for purchasing power parity holds up using the data from the previous aluminum example. In the example,

$$fx_0(FC/DC) = 1/fx_0(DC/FC) = 1/(\$1.5385/\pounds) \cong \pounds0.65/\$$$

$$fx_1(FC/DC) = 1/fx_1(DC/FC) = 1/(\$1.5092/\pounds) \cong \pounds0.6626/\$$$

and we have

$$(\pounds0.6626/\$)/(\pounds0.65/\$) - 1 \cong 0.05 - 0.03$$

$$1.0194 - 1 \cong 0.02$$

$$0.0194 \cong 0.02$$

The precise figure is 2%, and the figure obtained by the approximation is 1.94%; hence, the approximation equation given by Equation 17.6 is very reasonable.

In principle, then, we should be able to look at the differences in expected inflation rates and get an estimate of future foreign exchange rates. In practice, however, there are two factors to consider. First, international trade is not costless, and there are actually significant trade barriers (such as tariffs and transportation costs). Second, purchasing power parity requires knowing the future inflation differential, but the actual inflation that will occur is unknown. Nevertheless, although far from perfect, purchasing power parity establishes a link between the foreign exchange market and the inflation differential that can be useful.

17.3.2 International Fisher relationship

The international Fisher relationship establishes a link between nominal interest rates and inflation rates in different countries. Specifically, if we know the nominal interest rates in two countries, then we can estimate expected inflation rates, which, as has been shown, can be used to estimate exchange rates.

We start with the observation that, in the presence of inflation, investors will demand a premium in excess of their compensation for the time value of money to compensate themselves for the reduction in the purchasing power of the currency. Specifically, the nominal interest rate will be related to the real interest rate and expected inflation as follows:

$$(1 + R_{n,DC}) = (1 + R_{r,DC})[1 + E(h_{DC})]$$

where R_n denotes the nominal interest rate on one-year bonds (default-free Treasury issues) and R_r denotes the real interest rate. This is the same as Equation 6.8 in Chapter 6, with the distinction that this equation uses expected inflation rather than historical inflation.

This relationship holds regardless of which country an investor is in and, thus, is the same for interest rates in a foreign currency. Hence, in 1930, Fisher established the following relationship:[13]

$$\frac{(1 + R_{n,DC})}{(1 + R_{n,FC})} = \frac{(1 + R_{r,DC})}{(1 + R_{r,FC})} \frac{(1 + h_{DC})}{(1 + h_{FC})}$$

Note that the inflation rates are actually expected inflation rates over the term of the interest rate.

We would expect the real rate of interest to be the same. Otherwise, money would move from the country with the lower real rate to the country with the higher real rate. If we assume

---

[13] See Fisher (1930).

that the real rate of interest is the same in both countries, then the above expression can be approximated by the following equation:

$$R_{n,FC} - R_{n,DC} \cong E(h_{FC} - h_{DC}) \qquad (17.8)$$

According to the international Fisher relationship, the difference between the nominal interest rates of two countries is approximately equal to the difference in the expected inflation rates. For example, if over the next year inflation is expected to be 5% in the UK and 3% in the USA, then we would anticipate approximately 2% difference in nominal one-year interest rates.

17.3.3 Foreign exchange expectations

Current foreign exchange expectations may be estimated from current forward foreign exchange rates. The forward foreign exchange rate is the exchange rate available today to exchange currency at some specified date in the future. The ability to convert one currency into another currency is critical for the successful management of international portfolios, because investors often know that they will have to exchange currencies at some future date.

For example, suppose a US investor has a yen-denominated certificate of deposit (CD) maturing in six months in Tokyo. In response to demand by investors to minimise the impact of currency swings on their portfolios, a forward market in foreign exchange has developed. A forward foreign exchange contract is a contract that obligates an investor to deliver a specified quantity of one currency in return for a specified amount of another currency. For example, if the US investor has a ten-million-yen CD maturing in six months, then the investor may enter into a forward foreign exchange contract to deliver ten million yen in return for $100 000. With a forward foreign exchange contract, the investor has eliminated any future risk related to changes in exchange rate.

Because the forward foreign exchange rate reflects investors' expectations regarding the future exchange rate, it is commonly asserted that the forward rate is an unbiased estimate of the future spot foreign exchange rate, i.e.

$$E[fx_1(DC/FC)] = F[fx_1(DC/FC)] \qquad (17.9)$$

where $F[fx_1(DC/FC)]$ denotes the forward foreign exchange rate today for foreign exchange at time 1 and $E[fx_1(DC/FC)]$ denotes the expected spot rate for foreign exchange at time 1.

If this assertion is true, then there is no benefit from bearing foreign exchange risk. On average, the return that is due to foreign exchange changes above or below the forward rate is zero. Thus, the expected return is zero for bearing foreign currency risk. Therefore, some argue that currency risk should be hedged.

17.3.4 Interest-rate parity

Assume that the interest rate is about 7% in Germany and less than 1% in Japan. It seems that an investor can take advantage of this situation and make a profit by borrowing money in Japan and investing it in Germany. Although such a transaction is default-free if the investor buys German government bonds, it is not free from foreign exchange risk. The Japanese investor may earn the interest difference but may lose money when the marks are converted to yen when the loan has to be paid back. To avoid such a risk, the investor can lock in a transaction in the forward market that essentially allows the exchange of German marks for

Japanese yen at the end of the period at an exchange rate that is determined today. If such a transaction with a forward risk protection yields a positive rate of return, then it represents an arbitrage opportunity. The demand for such transactions will affect interest rates and forward exchange rates until the arbitrage profit vanishes, because in equilibrium arbitrage opportunities do not exist.

To illustrate this point further, suppose that a Japanese investor borrows one million yen and invests the money in Germany. The Japanese investor will invest one million yen $\times$ $fx_0(FC/DC)$ marks and at the end of the year will obtain the following:

$$\text{one million yen} \times fx_0(FC/DC) \times (1 + R_{n,FC}) \text{ marks}$$

When this amount is sold in the forward market, the amount of yen obtained will be

$$\text{one million yen} \times fx_0(FC/DC)(1 + R_{n,FC})/F[fx_1(FC/DC)]$$

In equilibrium, when no arbitrage profit prevails, this must be equal to the amount of yen the borrower has to return to the lender in Japan, namely one million yen $\times (1 + R_{n,DC})$. Thus, in equilibrium, the following must hold:

$$fx_0(FC/DC)(1 + R_{n,FC}) = F[fx_1(FC/DC)](1 + R_{n,DC})$$

or

$$\frac{F[fx_1(FC/DC)]}{fx_0(FC/DC)} - 1 = \frac{1 + R_{n,DC}}{1 + R_{n,DC}} - 1 \cong R_{n,FC} - R_{n,DC}$$

Thus, no-arbitrage equilibrium is called interest-rate parity.

Interest-rate parity establishes a link between the forward foreign exchange rates and nominal interest rates where arbitrage profit does not exist. Specifically, interest rate parity can be expressed as follows:

$$F_{fx} = \frac{F[fx_1(FC/DC)]}{fx_0(FC/DC)} - 1 \cong R_{n,FC} - R_{n,DC} \tag{17.10}$$

where F_{fx} denotes the percentage difference in the forward foreign exchange rate relative to the prevailing current spot exchange rate. Thus, the percentage difference of the forward foreign exchange rate and the current exchange rate should be approximately equal to the prevailing difference between the nominal interest rates in the foreign and domestic countries. For example, if the British pound exchange rate with the US dollar is currently at £0.67/$ and the one-year forward rate is at £0.7/$, then we would expect the interest rate differential between the UK and the USA to be

$$(£0.7/\$)/(£0.67/\$) - 1 \cong 0.0448, \text{ or } 4.48\%$$

Specifically, we would anticipate that the British pound would weaken compared with the US dollar by about 4.48%, according to interest-rate parity.[14]

Exhibit 17.10 helps to clarify the interrelationships among the parity relationships discussed here. This exhibit shows that spot exchange rates, forward exchange rates, interest rates and inflation in different countries are interrelated. However, these interrelationships are theoretical.

---

[14] Note that we can also derive the interest-rate parity relationship by combining the main equations of the purchasing power parity relationship, the international Fisher relationship and foreign exchange expectations.

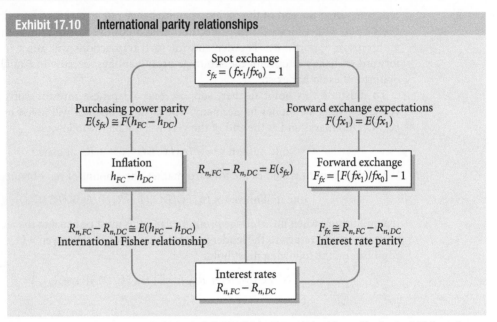

Exhibit 17.10 International parity relationships

Source: Solnik, B., *International Investments*, Exhibit 1.1. (p. 9), © 1991. Reprinted by permission of Pearson Education, Inc. Publishing as Pearson Addison Wesley.

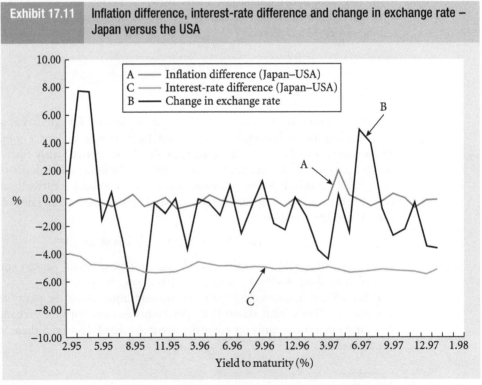

Exhibit 17.11 Inflation difference, interest-rate difference and change in exchange rate – Japan versus the USA

Source: From *Technical Analysis Explained*, New York, McGraw-Hill, p. 14 (Pring, M. J., 1991), reproduced with permission of The McGraw-Hill Companies.

Exhibit 17.11 reveals the relevant comparisons for Japan and the USA. Curve A denotes the inflation difference between Japan and the USA: $h_{Japan} - h_{USA}$. Curve B denotes the percentage change in foreign yen/dollar exchange rate: $f(x_1)/f(x_0) - 1$. Curve C denotes the difference in the annual short-term interest: $R_{n,Japan} - R_{n,USA}$. Of course, with ex-post data we employ the actual inflation rates and the actual foreign exchange rates rather than their corresponding expected values. However, on average, if the above theoretical relationships hold, then we would expect all three graphs in Exhibit 17.11 to coincide, or at least be close to each other. This is not the case. For example, in the period February 1995–January 1998, an American investor could borrow in Japan at a very low interest rate, deposit the money in the USA and make a profit, because the interest-rate difference was much bigger than the percentage change of the exchange rate (compare curves B and C). In the period January 1998–July 1998, the gain was enhanced because on top of the interest-rate difference, the yen depreciated, providing a double source of profit for the American investor: interest-rate differential as well as foreign currency profit. Thus, we see that the various relationships do not hold with actual ex-post data. Empirically, it is difficult to test the relationships with expectations data and so, in reality, even if the relationships hold, it is difficult to prove them. Academics argue about whether it is reasonable to assume that real interest rates are the same across countries. Also, debates arise about whether a given relationship holds in the short or long run. In practice, however, the relationships provide a framework for the investor to work from. Indeed, macroeconomic analysis is a complicated process for which most investment firms have in-house economist teams to formulate their views about the strength and direction of the economy.

→ **Connecting Theory to Practice 17.2**   **FT**

The costs of sterling

Opponents of UK membership of economic and monetary union have seized upon many arguments and strategies in recent years in their efforts to keep the pound alive. Some are clearly ludicrous – the news of the imminent release of a cinema advertisement featuring comic actor Rik Mayall dressed as Adolf Hitler declaring: 'Ein Volk! Ein Reich! Ein Euro' is the most recent – rather sick – example.

Other, more serious, arguments to keep sterling have made much of the alleged advantages of having a separate currency. On the surface, this claim seems logical. Indeed, a separate currency is widely supposed to provide an economy with a valuable source of flexibility that would be lost if the country entered a monetary union. Many who hold this view argue that the exchange rate acts as an automatic adjustment mechanism that can help the economy to absorb shocks, and that helps in the transmission of monetary policy to the real economy and to prices. Others who argue in favour of a separate currency say the exchange rate is an instrument of policy that the government can use in a more deliberate way to deal with shocks.

However, the UK's historical experience of a separate currency over the last 20 years suggests otherwise: fixing the exchange rate has not been successful for more than short periods of time; managing the exchange rate has been difficult, costly and ultimately unsuccessful; and letting the exchange rate float has led to recurring problems of misalignment. Indeed, the record indicates that the exchange rate is, in itself, a source of shocks and a separate currency is therefore not obviously worth retaining.

One way of trying to get a handle on the issue is to examine the historical evidence, with particular attention to the way the monetary authorities thought and behaved in different episodes. What comes out of such an analysis is surprisingly clear.

▶

First, the exchange rate has not generally acted as a useful automatic equilibrating mechanism. In fact, large exchange rate changes (identified as changes of more than 4 per cent between one quarter and the next) have typically not moved the real exchange rate back towards its long-run equilibrium level (identified in relation to past average levels). And in most such changes the exchange rate did not operate as a shock absorber or as part of a monetary transmission mechanism. Sometimes the exchange rate moved in what economists would consider the 'right' direction, but too fast and too far. At other times, it moved in the 'wrong' direction for reasons not connected with policy. And at others it has not moved at all when it would have been helpful if it had.

Second, the authorities have not in fact been able to use the exchange rate effectively as a policy instrument. The last 20 years included eight identifiably different monetary regimes, from the early Thatcher years of hard monetary targets through shadowing of the Deutsche Mark in 1987–1988 to inflation targeting with and without Bank of England control of interest rates in the 1990s. It turns out that in five of those phases the monetary authorities had some definite preferences over the level of the exchange rate – sometimes for stability, sometimes for controlled change in one direction or the other. But they were never able to make their preferences be realised for more than two or three years at a time. Furthermore, they had to accept exchange rates well away from their preferred levels for long periods.

Third, in nearly every one of these regimes there were significant movements of the exchange rate, or pressures upon it, that were both unexpected and unwelcome from the point of view of the authorities. In that sense, the exchange rate has indeed been for the UK a source of extraneous shocks – not so much short-term noise, which can be disregarded, but shocks of a kind that can have significant adverse effects on the structure, balance and ultimately size of the real economy. And there is no evidence that this problem has become smaller in the latest regimes.

Of course, there are many other things that need to be taken into account before deciding whether the UK should enter economic and monetary union. These include: the effectiveness of the European Central Bank; the nature of the asymmetric shocks that the UK might experience in the future if it were a member of the eurozone; the extent of prior cyclical convergence; and the appropriate rate of entry. But if the benefits of having a separate currency in the UK over the last 20 years have been so elusive, it is time to stop worrying about the costs of giving it up.

Source: David Cobham, 'The Costs of Sterling', FT.com site, 4 July 2002.

→ **Making the connection**

The author of this article argues that much of the alleged advantages of having a separate currency in the UK are elusive. Should the UK then enter the European monetary union and adopt the euro? This is a very difficult question, and we cannot possibly answer it here. Also, unfortunately, political considerations sometimes dominate economics. In this respect, many British politicians still have a painful memory of the newspaper headlines of 17 September 1992. At that time, the pound had crashed out of the European exchange rate mechanism (ERM) that preceded the current monetary union. The British government suspended membership of the ERM after a tidal wave of selling the pound on the foreign exchanges left them defenceless against international currency speculators. In the process, an estimated £10 billion from Britain's reserves was spent and interest rates were raised to 15%, causing further damage to an economy that was already deep in recession. The decision to suspend ERM membership represented a humiliating reversal for the chancellor (Norman Lamont) and the prime minister (John Major), who had staked enormous credibility on being able to resist devaluation. For Tony Blair, the prime minister at the time of writing, the legacy of the ERM is a massive obstacle in his path to take Britain into the euro.

Summary

Describe the key measure of the health of the overall economy, gross domestic product (GDP).

The GDP is composed of consumption, investment, government spending and net trade. Real GDP (GDP adjusted to include the effects of inflation) is used, because inflation changes the value of dollars. Analysts attempting to establish relationships between macroeconomic variables such as GDP and financial markets must incorporate a complex revision process into their analysis. Relationships that may appear based on final estimates of GDP may not appear based on advanced estimates of GDP.

Describe the impact of government fiscal and monetary policy on the economy.

Fiscal and monetary policy are key tools that governments use to achieve GDP growth, relatively full employment and stable prices. Fiscal policy includes taxation and spending policies, whereas monetary policy includes actions taken by a central bank, such as controlling the money supply and manipulating interest rates. The effectiveness of a government is a key factor to consider when analysing a country's financial market. Governments use both fiscal and monetary policies to stimulate economic growth, which affects financial markets directly.

Explain the relationship between the overall economy and financial markets.

Economy-wide factors affect the prices, risks and returns of almost all securities, because they influence the expected future cash flows to investors (for instance, dividends and coupons), the risks of the cash flows, and the interest rates and risk premiums used to discount the cash flows. According to the EMT, macroeconomic analysis cannot be used to systematically earn abnormal returns above and beyond what is required to compensate for risk. Indeed, stock market indexes are among the best-performing leading indicators for the business cycle; they react before we see the economic changes. Still, macroeconomic analysis is useful for predicting cyclical changes in interest rates, risks and risk premiums, simply because investors need accurate estimates of the risk–return characteristics of securities. In fact, ignoring macroeconomic information may lead investors to believe mistakenly that abnormal profit opportunities do exist.

Describe the relationships between interest rates, exchange rates and inflation rates.

Four important parity relationships that influence the international financial markets are purchasing power parity, the international Fisher relationship, foreign exchange expectations and interest rate parity. All of these are derived from certain non-arbitrage conditions between nominal interest rates, real interest rates, inflation rates and (forward) exchange rates between two countries. Although transaction costs may affect the accuracy of the relationships, and their true predictive power is empirically still under debate, the relationships provide a good framework for the macroeconomic analyst to work from.

Key terms

Advanced estimate 569
Bank discount rate 576
Bank reserves 576
Benchmark revision 569
Budget deficit 575
Business cycle 572
Chained (1996) dollar
  estimates 569
Civilian unemployment
  rate 575
Coincident indicator 573
Consumption-to-wealth
  ratio 579

Contraction 572
Expansion 572
Federal funds rate 576
Fiscal policy 575
Foreign exchange expectations
  586
Forward foreign exchange
  contract 586
Forward foreign exchange
  rate 586
Gross domestic product
  (GDP) 568
Interest-rate parity 587

International Fisher
  relationship 585
Lagging indicator 573
Leading indicator 573
Monetary policy 575
Open market operations 576
Peak 572
Preliminary estimate 569
Purchasing power parity 584
Real GDP 568
Recession 576
Revised estimate 569
Trough 572

Review questions

1 Suppose that consumption in the United States increased by $10 billion, and this increase was entirely in imported goods. How would this influence the United States' GDP?

2 'Leading indicators allow investors to predict whether the business cycle will expand or contract. Therefore, the market for cyclical stocks must not be semi-strong-form efficient.' Is this statement true? Explain your answer.

3 Explain the similarities and differences between fiscal policy and monetary policy.

4 Explain how the Fed can use open market operations to affect interest rates.

5 Take Europe as the domestic economy and the US as the foreign economy. Suppose the current exchange rate is $1.20/€. The expected inflation rates for the following year are 3% and 2.5% for the eurozone and the US, respectively:

   a. What is the expected exchange rate next period? (Suppose the nominal interest rate in the eurozone to be 2.5% and in the US to be 1%.)
   b. Is this consistent with the inflation data from the above? If not, where does the arbitrage opportunity lie?
       Recalculate the figures on the basis of a forward exchange rate for the next period of $1.15/€.
   c. According to interest-rate parity, what should the forward exchange rate for the next period be?
   d. Where do the arbitrage opportunities lie now?

For an extensive set of review and practice questions and answers, visit the Levy–Post investment website at www.booksites.net/levy

Selected references

Abel, A. B. and B. S. Bernanke, 1992, *Macroeconomics*, Reading, MA: Addison-Wesley.

Baker, H. K., 1992, *Improving the Investment Decision Process – Better Use of Economic Inputs in Security Analysis and Portfolio Management*, Charlottesville, VA: AIMR.

Black, F., 1981, 'The ABCs of Business Cycles', *Financial Analysts Journal*, **37** (6), 75–80.

Campbell, J. Y. and G. Mankiw, 1989, 'Consumption, Income, and Interest Rates: Reinterpreting the Time Series Evidence'. In: Olivier J. Blanchard and Stanley Fischer, editors, *NBER Macroeconomics Annual*, Cambridge, MA: MIT Press, 185–216.

Campbell, J. Y. and R. Shiller, 1988, 'Stock Prices, Earnings and Expected Dividends', *Journal of Finance*, **43**, 661–676.

Carnes, W. S. and S. D. Slifer, 1991, *The Atlas of Economic Indicators*, New York: Harper-Collins.

Chen, N. F., R. Roll and S. Ross, 1986, 'Economic Forces and the Stock Market: Testing the APT and Alternative Asset Pricing Theories', *Journal of Business*, **59**, 383–403.

Council of Economic Advisers, *Economic Report of the President*, Washington, DC: US Government Printing Office.

Donahoe, G. F., Parker, R. P., Seskin, E. P., *et al.*, 1996, 'Improved Estimates of the National Income and Product Accounts for 1959–95: Results of the Comprehensive Revision', *Survey of Current Business*, January–February, Washington, DC: US Department of Commerce.

Fama, E. F. and K. R. French, 1988, 'Dividend Yields and Expected Stock Returns', *Journal of Financial Economics*, **22**, 3–25.

Fama, E. and K. French, 1989, 'Business Conditions and Expected Return on Stocks and Bonds', *Journal of Financial Economics*, **25**, 23–49.

Fama, E. F. and K. R. French, 1996, 'Multifactor Explanations of Asset Pricing Anomalies', *Journal of Finance*, **51**, 55–84.

Fama, E. and G. W. Schwert, 1977, 'Asset Returns and Inflation', *Journal of Financial Economics*, **5**, 115–146.

Ferson, W., 1990, 'Are the Latent Variables in Time-Varying Expected Returns Compensation for Consumption Risk?', *Journal of Finance*, **45**, 397–430.

Fisher, I., 1930, *The Theory of Interest*, New York: Macmillan.

Jagannathan, R. and Z. Wang, 1996, 'The Conditional CAPM and the Cross-Section of Expected Returns', *Journal of Finance*, **51** (1), 3–53.

Keim, D. B. and R. F. Stambaugh, 1986, 'Predicting Returns in the Stock and Bond Markets', *Journal of Financial Economics*, **17**, 357–390.

King, B. F., 1966, 'Market and Industry Factors in Stock Price Behavior', *Journal of Business*, **39**, 139–190.

Lettau, M. and S. C. Ludvigson, 2001a, 'Consumption, Aggregate Wealth and Expected Stock Returns', *Journal of Finance*, **56**, 815–849.

Lettau, M. and S. C. Ludvigson, 2001b, 'Resurrecting the (C)CAPM: A Cross-Sectional Test When Risk Premia Are Time-Varying', *Journal of Political Economy*, **109**, 1238–1287.

Lowenstein, R., 1995, 'New Recipe for the GDP Leaves Sour Taste', *Wall Street Journal*, 12 December C1.

Prakken, J. L. and L. T. Guirl, 1995, 'Macro Modeling and Forecasting with Chain-Type Measures of GDP', *National Association of Business Economists News*, **113**, 7–13.

Solnik, B. H., 2000, *International Investments*, 4th edn, Reading, MA: Addison-Wesley.

US Bureau of the Census, *Statistical Abstract of the United States*, Washington, DC: US Government Printing Office.

The art and craft of reading the market

Over the past 30 years technical analysis has become an accepted part of making investment decisions. In dealing rooms, brokerage houses and fund companies, traders and sophisticated investors have access to charting packages, websites and proprietary software. Some colleges and universities have trading rooms and a few even have classes in the subject. Hedge funds use sophisticated technical approaches involving chaos theory and modelling. Many Wall Street investment banks arrange private courses on technical analysis for trainees. Traditional commodity markets have used technical analysis for decades; newer power and energy markets are following suit. The golden age of technical analysis may lie just ahead of us.

Source: Bruce Kamich, 'The Art and Craft Of Reading the Market', *Financial Times*, 9 July 2001.

After studying this chapter, you should be able to:

1 Define technical analysis and contrast it with fundamental analysis.

2 Explain the logic behind technical analysis.

3 Discuss the basic tools used by technical analysts.

4 Summarise the empirical evidence regarding the effectiveness of technical analysis.

Technical analysis of securities is based on graphs and charts of historical market data rather than on fundamental values such as company financial statements and sector and macroeconomic data. For example, a technical analyst would evaluate the past market prices, the amounts of short-selling and the volume of trading.

Financial economics generally has strong quantitative orientation; it makes extensive use of mathematical models and statistical tests. By contrast, technical analysis is as much art as science. Martin J. Pring (1991), President of the International Institute for Economic Research and a well-respected technical analyst, defines technical analysis thus:

> The technical approach to investment is essentially a reflection of the idea that prices move in trends which are determined by the changing attitudes of investors toward a variety of economic, monetary, political, and psychological forces. The art of technical analysis – for it is an art – is to identify trend changes at an early stage and to maintain an investment posture until the weight of the evidence indicates that the trend has reversed . . .
>
> Since the technical approach is based on the theory that the price is a reflection of mass psychology ('the crowd') in action, it attempts to forecast future price movements on the assumption that crowd psychology moves between panic, fear, and pessimism on one hand and confidence, excessive optimism, and greed on the other . . . [The] art of technical analysis is concerned with identifying these changes at an early phase, since these swings in emotion take time to accomplish. Studying these market trends enables technically oriented investors to buy or sell with a degree of confidence, on the principle that once a trend is set in motion it will perpetuate itself.

Pring thus views technical analysis as the art of being able to identify trends early.

In their popular book on technical analysis, Edwards and Magee (1992) define technical analysis as

> . . . the study of the action of the market itself as opposed to the study of the goods in which the market deals. Technical analysis is the science of recording, usually in graphic form, the actual history of trading (price changes, volume of transactions, etc.) in a certain stock or in 'the averages' and then deducing from that pictured history the probable future trend.

Whether technical analysis is an art (as Pring believes) or a science (as Edwards and Magee suggest), it is clear that it deals with making inferences about future price trends based on historical market information.

If we assume that markets are semi-strong-form-efficient (see Chapter 12), then all historical market information should already be reflected in the stock price. Consequently, adherents of the EMT would argue that these data cannot be used to systematically earn abnormal return above and beyond a fair risk premium to compensate for risk. Although many academics and practitioners dispute the value of technical analysis, it is used widely in practice. In fact, there are many professionals whose sole task is to examine historical market data to predict future price behaviour. Moreover, since many investors and traders follow the rules of technical analysis, this method may actually push prices up, at least in the short run, even if it is economically unjustified. Therefore, no matter how investors view the effectiveness of technical analysis, they should know how it works.

This chapter introduces some of the key concepts of technical analysis. First, we discuss the logic behind technical analysis. Much of the logic follows from the so-called Dow theory that originated from the work by Charles Dow, the grandfather of technical analysis. Next, the main tools used by technical analysts, such as charts and technical indicators, are discussed and illustrated. Although the focus is on stocks, these tools can also be applied to bonds, currencies, commodities and other financial assets. Finally, we discuss the empirical evidence regarding the effectiveness of technical analysis.

18.1 The logic behind technical analysis[1]

Most approaches to technical analysis assume that financial prices follow some sort of market cycle model. That is, overall prices tend to move through long trends of either rising or falling prices. Exhibit 18.1 illustrates a model of a market cycle. In theory, every 4–4.5 years, the market moves through a complete cycle. The broad double line, known as the primary trend cycle, represents this 4–4.5-year cycle. Technical analysts assert that such broad trends appear in currencies, stocks, bonds, commodities and other financial assets. The solid black line that has more wave is known as the intermediate trend, which has a much shorter duration (from three weeks to six months). Finally, the short-term trend, denoted by the dotted line, documents much more volatility and is more erratic.

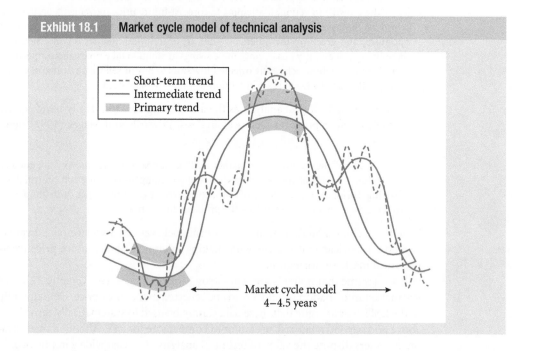

Exhibit 18.1 Market cycle model of technical analysis

- - - - Short-term trend
——— Intermediate trend
▨ Primary trend

◀—— Market cycle model ——▶
4–4.5 years

---

[1] This section is based in part on Colby (2003).

The first person to note these trends was Charles Dow (the founder of the Dow Jones news service), around 1900. In 1897, Charles Dow developed two broad market averages: the Industrial Average of 12 blue-chip stocks and the Rail Average of 20 railroad enterprises. Nowadays, these averages are known as the Dow Jones Industrial Average and the Dow Jones Transportation Average. The Dow theory resulted from a series of articles published by Charles Dow between 1900 and 1902 in the daily newspaper that he founded, the *Wall Street Journal*. The Dow theory forms the basis of many modern methods of technical analysis. Interestingly, the theory itself originally focused on the use of general stock market trends to indicate general business conditions rather than to forecast stock prices. However, subsequent work by analysts and writers has focused almost exclusively on forecasting.

The basic tenets of the Dow theory can be summarised as follows:

18.1.1 The averages discount everything

All available information is discounted by the Dow-Jones Industrial Average and the Dow-Jones Transportation Average. Since the averages reflect all information, experience, knowledge, opinions and activities of all stock market investors, everything that could possibly affect the demand for or supply of stocks is discounted by the averages.

18.1.2 The market is comprised of three trends

Three trends affect the stock market: the primary tide, secondary reactions and ripples. If the market is making successive higher highs and higher lows, then the primary tide is up (a bull market). If the market is making successive lower highs and lower lows, then the primary tide is down (a bear market). Sperandeo (1991) has quantified Dow theory definitions. He found that 75% of primary tide bear markets declined from 20.4 to 47.1% in price. Also, 75% of bear markets lasted between 0.8 and 2.8 years. Bull markets lasted much longer: 67% lasted between 1.8 and 4.1 years. Secondary reactions are intermediate, corrective reactions to the primary tide. Sperandeo found that 65% last from three weeks to three months, and 98% last from two weeks to eight months. Further, Sperandeo found that 61% retrace between 30 and 70% of the previous primary swing in price. Ripples are short-term movements lasting from one day to three weeks. Secondary reactions are typically comprised of a number of ripples. The Dow theory holds that, since stock prices over the short term are subject to some degree of manipulation (primary and secondary reactions are not), ripples are unimportant and can be misleading. Sperandeo found that 98.7% last less than two weeks.

18.1.3 Primary tides have three phases

The Dow theory says that the primary trend is made up of three phases. Bull markets typically unfold in three up moves in stock prices: scepticism, growing recognition and enthusiasm. Bear markets typically unfold in three down moves in stock prices: disbelief, shock and fear, and disgust. Combined, there are six phases of the full bull-through-bear cycle:

Scepticism

The first phase of a bull market is accumulation of stocks at bargain prices by the 'smart money' (the most knowledgeable and experienced investors). Meanwhile, the mass mood toward the stock market ranges from disgust to general scepticism. Stocks are depressed, and may have been for a long time. Still, some investors know that the cycle always turns up, even while fundamental business conditions still appear grim. The smart money begins to bid for out-of-favour stocks, which are selling at temptingly low bargain prices. Transactional volume, which has been low, starts to improve on rallies reflecting the entrance into the market by these forward-looking, patient investors.

Growing recognition

The second bull phase is known as the mark-up phase. Stock prices rise on increasing transactional volume. There is growing recognition that fundamental business conditions will improve. During this phase, stocks move up big, and it is a very rewarding time to be in the market.

Enthusiasm

The third bull phase is marked by popular enthusiasm and speculation. Sentiment indicators are near record levels. Fundamentals now appear extremely positive. There may even be widespread talk of a 'new era' of rapid economic growth and never-ending prosperity. Stories of speculators making millions in the market flood the media. Everybody is optimistic and is buying, so transactional volume is extremely heavy. Late in this third phase, however, volume starts to diminish on rallies, as greedy buyers shoot their wads and become fully invested, usually on margin. Also, the smart money has reminded itself that 'no tree grows to the sky' and all good things must eventually come to an end. Consequently, those knowledgeable investors, who bought early at wholesale prices, stop buying. Moreover, they begin the distribution phase, parcelling out their stocks at retail prices. Smart selling intensifies as the greedy but unsophisticated mob snaps up overvalued stocks at absurdly high prices. Late in this game, tell-tale bearish technical cracks start to appear under the obviously bullish surface. Technical divergences in stocks and groups are caused by irrational buying of the wrong stocks by unsophisticated players, while the smart money liquidates the best stocks. Stocks may begin to churn and make little net progress.

Disbelief

The first bear market phase is marked by clear and widespread technical deterioration, even while almost everybody is still feeling extremely bullish. But when everyone who is ever going to buy has already bought, there is only one direction for prices to go – down. When buying power is used up, there is insufficient demand to absorb the accelerating distribution of stocks by the smart money at current prices, so prices have to move lower. An ever increasing number of stocks already have stalled out and formed potentially bearish chart patterns. But even as stocks break critical chart support levels, this clear bearish technical evidence is ignored widely by the uninformed masses. After all, fundamental business conditions are still rosy, and 'buy the dips' is still the advice of the brokers and the dealers and their paid spokesmen in the media. The public hopes and believes that the conventional wisdom of all the highly compensated Wall Street analysts, strategists and economists is right. Besides, the public has been told that they bought for the long term, and over the long term stock prices always go up. So, stock-price declines are met with general disbelief. The public would buy more if only they were not already fully margined.

Shock and fear

The second bear phase is marked by a sudden mood change, from optimism and hope to shock and fear. One day, the public wakes up and sees, much to its surprise, that the emperor has no clothes. Actual fundamental business conditions are not panning out to be as positive as hoped previously. In fact, there may be a little problem. The smart money is long gone, and there is no one left to buy when the public wants out. Stock prices drop steeply in a vacuum. Fear quickly replaces greed. Repeated waves of panic may sweep the market. Transactional volume swells as the unsophisticated investor screams, 'Get me out at any price!' Sharp professional traders are willing to bid way down in price for stocks when prices drop too far too fast. The best that can be expected, however, is a dead-cat bounce that recovers only a fraction of the steep loss.

Disgust

The third bear phase is marked by discouraged selling and, finally, total disgust toward stocks. Fundamentals clearly have deteriorated and the outlook is bleak. Downward price movement continues, but the negative rate of change eventually begins to slow as potential sellers liquidate holdings at distress prices. Even the best stocks, which initially resist the down trend, succumb to the persistence of the bear marekt. Transactional volume, which was high in the panic phase, starts to diminish on price declines as liquidation runs its course. Eventually, after everyone who is capable of selling has sold already, the bear market is exhausted. The discouraged public lament is, 'never again'. After stocks are totally sold out, the stage is then set for the cycle to begin again. When everyone who is ever going to sell has already sold, there is only one direction for prices to go – up.

18.1.4 The averages must confirm each other

The industrials and transports must confirm each other in order for a valid change of trend to occur. To signal a primary tide bull trend, both averages must rise above their respective highs of previous upward secondary reactions. To signal a primary tide bear trend, both the Dow-Jones Industrial Average and the Dow-Jones Transportation Average must drop below their respective lows of previous secondary reactions. No matter how large a move in just one average, it would not be sufficient to indicate a change in the primary tide unless the other average confirmed. Non-confirmations (divergences where one average exceeds a preceding secondary reaction but the other average fails to confirm) function only as warnings to be alert for the possibility of an actual signal ahead. However, it is not necessary that both averages confirm on the same day or even the same month. The Dow theory does not stipulate any time limit on trend confirmation by both averages, although some writers believe the closer the better, and become more wary as the days pass without confirmation.

18.1.5 The volume confirms the trend

The Dow theory focuses primarily on price action. Volume is used only to confirm uncertain situations. Volume should expand in the direction of the primary tide. If the primary tide is down, then volume should increase during market declines. If the primary tide is up, then volume should increase during market advances.

18.1.6 A trend remains intact until it gives a definite reversal signal

An up trend is defined by a series of higher highs and higher lows. In order for an up trend to reverse, prices must have at least one lower high and one lower low (the reverse is true of a down trend). When a reversal in the primary tide is signalled by both the industrials and the transports, then the odds of the new trend continuing are at their greatest. However, as a trend continues, the odds of the trend remaining intact become progressively smaller.

Connecting Theory to Practice 18.1 presents a further discussion of the reasoning behind technical analysis. This discussion forms part of a larger survey article that was published in the *Financial Times*.

 Connecting Theory to Practice 18.1

The art and craft of reading the market

. . . Technical analysis is based on three or four underlying assumptions.

Market action or prices discount the future. While the market pays attention to day-to-day developments and unexpected events, it is also looks at what people believe will happen. The stock market is a leading indicator. The market has already discounted the news. One of the oldest sayings on Wall Street is 'Buy the rumour and sell the news.' The essence of this well-worn advice can also be seen in the lesser-known adage of 'News follows the tape.' If someone knows or believes something before most people, their buying or selling will show up in the marketplace. The share price will move before the news is reported. Sometimes news does break before prices react, but all too often a market moves and then you see the rush of the media and the business community to explain why. Often a move may happen without a news event because of a crystallisation of traders' thoughts and expectations. Consider movements in interest rates – how many times have you seen US Treasury bonds rally ahead of an expected interest rate cut by the Federal Reserve Bank, only to decline when the cut was announced?

History tends to repeat itself. When people are confronted with the same set of circumstances, they tend to react in similar ways. Things may not happen exactly as they did on previous occasions but human emotions swing from greed at the peak of a market cycle to fear at its trough. Patterns of supply and demand in the price action that technicians observed in 1901, 1951 and 2001 have played out in the same way.

Prices move in trends. A casual examination of charts of securities, commodities, interest rates or currencies will show many examples of prices forming discernible trends. A well-known upward trend is a long-term chart of the Dow Jones Industrial Average from the early 1920s, showing a clear upward slope with some minor dips from left to right on the chart. The chart is used in the sales literature of mutual funds and by financial planners to show the benefit of a buy and hold strategy. An upward trend is a succession of higher peaks and higher troughs. A downward trend is a succession of lower peaks and lower troughs. Before such trends begin, stocks go through periods of accumulation and distribution. Accumulation patterns occur at bottoms and distribution pattern at tops. During the accumulation phase, more informed and farsighted investors are accumulating stock, counting on better conditions six to nine months ahead. Investors tend to resist paying more for a stock than the price that others have recently paid unless the stock keeps going up – giving the investor the hope or confidence that it will continue to go up. In a downward trend, people will resist selling a stock for less than the price that other people have been getting unless the price keeps sliding and fear builds that it will continue to slide. Imagine you are reliably informed that a company's new product is a commercial success. If you are a shareholder, you are unlikely to sell your shares because the company is doing well. Or you may buy more shares because business is good. By not selling, or becoming a buyer, you keep shares off the market and reduce supply, so the share price tends to rise. At some point, news of the company's success spreads to brokers, other professional investors and perhaps a wider public. New buyers must pay more for the shares they want. This rationale underlies an upwardly moving trend.

Patterns have relationships. Commodity prices can make sharp moves from an unanticipated change in supply or a share price may jump up sharply from a takeover bid. However, large price moves are normally preceded by large sideways consolidations or trading ranges where the market trades up and down in a band and buyers slowly buy shares and reduce supply. These large consolidations represent the period when investors shift their views and alter their investments by gradually buying. Smaller sideways patterns tend to support only shorter rallies or falls and technicians have observed that the market movements have a relationship to one another. This assumption is important but not necessary to operate as a technician and is not a core belief like the first three.

Source: Bruce Kamich, 'The Art and Craft of Reading the Market', *Financial Times*, 9 July 2001.

18.2 Tools for technical analysis

To the technical analyst, the chart is the place to find clues regarding the future price direction of an asset. Technical analysts use several different charts, including bar charts, point-and-figure charts and candlestick charts. All these charts are based on historical prices. Thus, the users of these charts obviously do not believe in weak-form market efficiency. Charts typically are analysed using moving averages and relative strength indicators. In addition, technical analysis use technical indicators to interpret trends. Technical indicators typically draw from additional historical market-related data, such as volume of trading. Several technical indicators are believed to be leading indicators of future security price movements. These indicators can be classified as breadth indicators, which highlight overall market strength or weakness, and sentiment indicators, which highlight traders' opinions about the market. The users of these technical indicators apparently do not believe in semi-strong-form market efficiency, because the inputs to the analysis are publicly available information.

18.2.1 Bar charts

Bar charts are charts that illustrate each day's (or week's or month's) high, low and closing price movements for a specified time period. Exhibit 18.2 shows a bar chart of Coca-Cola Company stock price for one week (4–8 August 1997), and Exhibit 18.3 presents the data used to plot it. For example, on Tuesday, the high for Coke was $68.8125, while the low was $68, which was also that day's closing price. In Exhibit 18.2, the straight lines give the distance between the high and low prices, and the protruding horizontal nubs designate the closing prices.

Technical analysts use bar charts to determine trends and to observe when these trends will reverse themselves. The trendline is a line drawn on a bar chart to identify a trend where the angle of this line will indicate if it is an up or down trend line. For example, Exhibit 18.4 shows an up trendline and a down trendline.

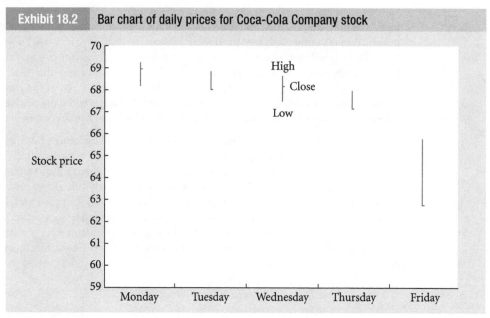

Exhibit 18.2   Bar chart of daily prices for Coca-Cola Company stock

Source: From *Introduction to Investments*, 2nd edn, by Levy. © 1999. Reprinted with permission of South-Western, a division of Thomson Learning: www.thomsonrights.com. Fax 800 730-2215.

Exhibit 18.3   Daily prices for Coca-Cola Company (4–8 August 1997)

Day	High	Low	Close
Monday	69.25	68.125	68.9375
Tuesday	68.8125	68	68
Wednesday	68.625	67.4375	68.125
Thursday	67.9375	67.125	67.125
Friday	65.75	62.6875	62.6875

Source: From *Introduction to Investments*, 2nd edn, by Levy. © 1999. Reprinted with permission of South-Western, a division of Thomson Learning: www.thomsonrights.com. Fax 800 730-2215.

In Exhibit 18.4a, an up trendline is drawn to touch the lowest prices over several days. Exhibit 18.4b shows a down trendline drawn to touch the two highest prices over several days.

Historical price data are used to draw trendlines. However, the precise manner in which technical analysts draw up and down trendlines is an art. That is, there is no widespread agreement about which criteria to use to establish when a trend has begun or about exactly how to draw the trendlines. Also, the number of days to check in order to select from the two lowest points is arbitrary.

Once analysts have drawn a trendline, they follow stock prices to identify changes in the trend. Exhibit 18.4a examines historical prices over the past *n* days and uses the lowest two points to draw the up trendline. Of course, other criteria could have been used.

A trendline is said to be penetrated when market prices move across it. This penetration is viewed as a sell signal for an up trendline and a buy signal for a down trendline. When a trendline is penetrated by a 'sufficient' magnitude, technical analysts say the trend has changed.

A channel is a pattern formed when two lines are drawn on a bar chart. Exhibit 18.5 illustrates up and down trend channels. An up trend channel (Exhibit 18.5a) is formed by

Exhibit 18.4 **Trendlines in technical analysis**

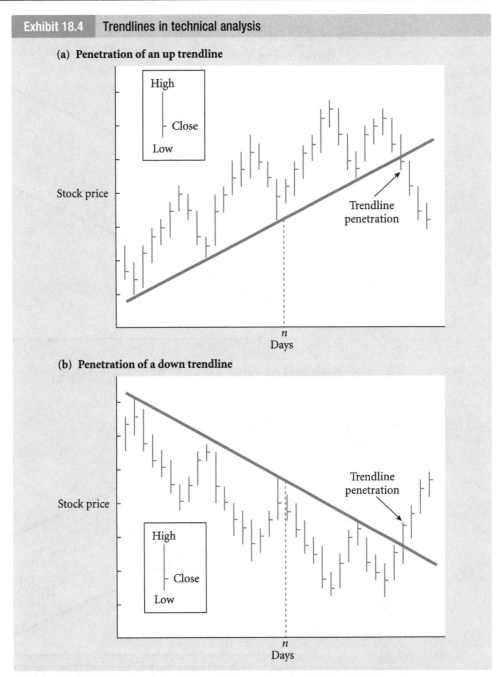

(a) Penetration of an up trendline

(b) Penetration of a down trendline

Source: From *The Technical Analysis Course*, Chicago, IL, Probus Publishing, pp. 102–3 (Meyers, T., 1989), reproduced with permission of The McGraw-Hill Companies.

first drawing the up trendline (the lower line) and then drawing another line near the two recent highs but also parallel with the up trendline. The line above the chart cannot touch the two recent highs, because channels require that the two lines be parallel. The down trendline is drawn in a similar fashion (Exhibit 18.5b).

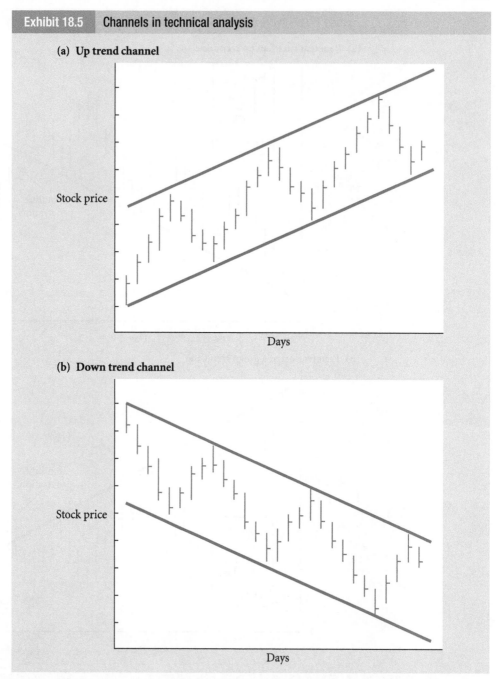

Exhibit 18.5 Channels in technical analysis

(a) Up trend channel

Stock price

Days

(b) Down trend channel

Stock price

Days

Source: From *The Technical Analysis Course*, Chicago, IL, Probus Publishing, pp. 109–10 (Meyers, T., 1989), reproduced with permission of The McGraw-Hill Companies.

Technical analysts believe that if stock prices do not reach the upper line of an up trend channel during a rally, then the price will fall below the lower trendline. They also assert that if stock prices do not reach the lower line of a down trend channel as prices fall, then the price will rise above the down trend channel.

Exhibit 18.6	Support and resistance in technical analysis

(a) Rising support and resistance

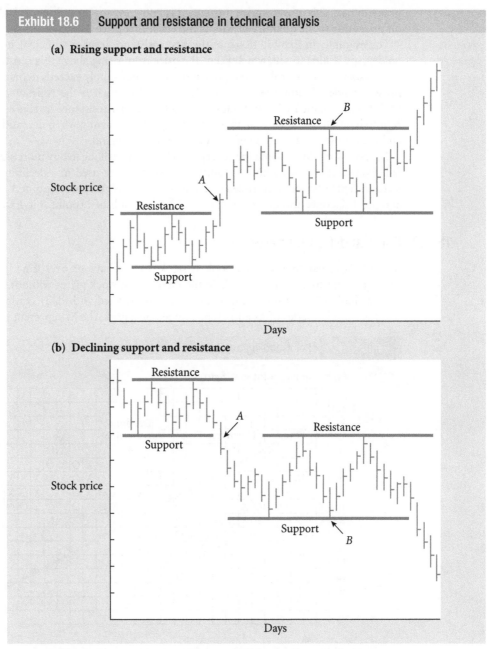

Source: From *The Technical Analysis Course*, Chicago, IL, Probus Publishing, pp. 120–1 (Meyers, T., 1989), reproduced with permission of The McGraw-Hill Companies.

Technical analysts also use bar charts to establish patterns of support and resistance (Exhibit 18.6). The idea behind these patterns is that within a certain price range, demand and supply factors influence a security's price movement. When prices rise, a number of sellers enter the market, causing the stock prices to fall. This downward price movement is known as resistance. Resistance is the upper bound on prices due to the quantity of willing sellers at that price level. When prices fall, a number of buyers enter the market, causing the stock

605

prices to rise. This upward price movement is known as support. Support is the lower bound on prices due to the quantity of willing buyers at that price level.

For example, in Exhibit 18.6a, at the first resistance level, a sufficient number of shareholders are willing to sell, which keeps the price from rising above this resistance level. Once the resistance level is broken, the price moves up until supply exceeds demand and the rising price is hindered. Some technical analysts would buy when the resistance level is broken (point A in Exhibit 18.6a) and sell when another higher resistance level is established (point B in Exhibit 18.6a). Technical analysts try to profit by buying when demand exceeds supply and then subsequently selling when supply exceeds demand.

Support works in the same way, except that buyers are willing to buy more shares when prices fall. Exhibit 18.6b shows how support and resistance are used in a declining market. Some technical analysts would short-sell when the support level is broken (point A in Exhibit 18.6b) and buy back once another lower support level is established (point B in Exhibit 18.6b).

18.2.2 Point-and-figure charts

In contrast to bar charts, which look at stock-price behaviour over time, point-and-figure charts attempt to identify reversals in the direction of stock prices without consideration of time. Exhibit 18.7 is a point-and-figure chart constructed with daily closing prices. Notice that the chart is a series of Xs and Os positioned on a grid. The Xs represent price increases of

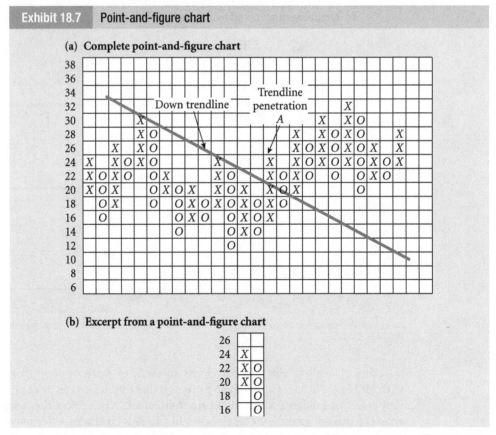

Exhibit 18.7 Point-and-figure chart

(a) Complete point-and-figure chart

(b) Excerpt from a point-and-figure chart

$2 or more, and the Os represent price decreases of $2 or more. For example, in Exhibit 18.7b, the stock price initially was at $18, and its first $2 move was up. Therefore, an X was placed in the first column by $20. Over the next few days, the stock finally surpassed the $22 mark (without first falling below $18), so another X was placed in the first column at $22. Once again, the stock rose to $24, so yet another X was added in the first column. After the price reached $24, the stock price fell by more than $2. To show this, an O was placed in the second column on the row at $22. In this case, the price continued to fall to $16.

All of the trendline analysis, channels, and support and resistance information used in bar charts can also be applied to point-and-figure charts. Compare the general pattern in Exhibit 18.7 with Exhibits 18.2, 18.4, 18.5 and 16.6. Clearly, bar charts and point-and-figure charts look generally similar. Thus, technical rules developed for bar charts are also applied to point-and-figure charts. For example, some technical analysts would draw a down trendline, as illustrated in Exhibit 18.7a. Point *A* shows a trendline penetration, and the technical analyst might view this as a bullish sign for this stock. Hence, point-and-figure charts are another popular tool of the technical analyst.

18.2.3 Candlestick charts

The candlestick chart, another tool of the technical analyst, was developed in Japan and has been used there for a long time. Only recently, however, has the candlestick chart become popular in the USA and other countries. Exhibit 18.8 shows a candlestick chart of the daily

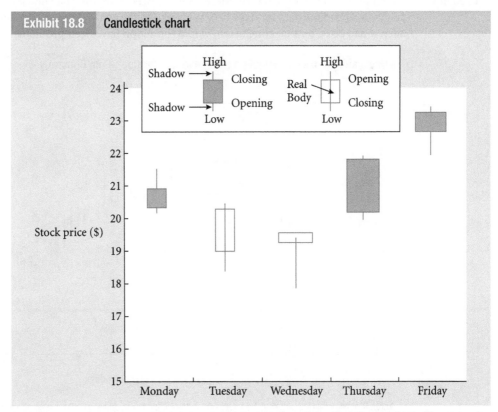

Exhibit 18.8   Candlestick chart

Source: From *Introduction to Investments*, 2nd edn, by Levy. © 1999. Reprinted with permission of South-Western, a division of Thomson Learning: www.thomsonrights.com. Fax 800 730-2215.

Exhibit 18.9	Daily prices for Borland International Inc. ($)			
Day	Open	High	Low	Close
Monday	20.375	21.5	20.25	20.875
Tuesday	20.25	20.5	18.125	19
Wednesday	19.5	19.5	17.75	19.25
Thursday	20.25	22	20	21.875
Friday	22.5	23.125	21.375	23

Source: From *Introduction to Investments*, 2nd edn, by Levy. © 1999. Reprinted with permission of South-Western, a division of Thomson Learning: www.thomsonrights.com. Fax 800 730-2215.

price data from Exhibit 18.9. The only piece of data used for candlestick charts that is not included in bar charts is the opening price. Each observation on a candlestick chart is based on a day's opening, high, low and closing prices. The candlestick chart is similar to the bar chart in many ways, in that it maps the price movement over time. For each day, the chart contains a candlestick line. There are two parts to the candlestick line. The real body is

Practice box

Problem   Examine the following data for Merck stock prices. Suppose that on day 6 a technical analyst analysed the data for days 1–6. What would the analyst most likely conclude? If the analyst had acted on that conclusion, would the action have been profitable?

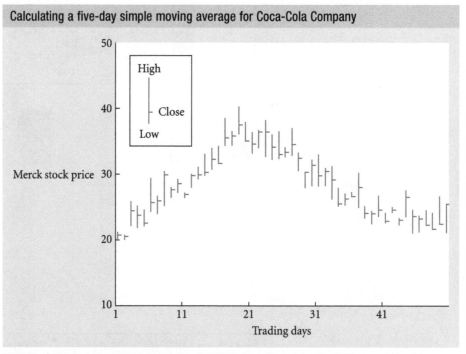

Calculating a five-day simple moving average for Coca-Cola Company

Source: From *Introduction to Investments*, 2nd edn, by Levy. © 1999. Reprinted with permission of South-Western, a division of Thomson Learning: www.thomsonrights.com. Fax 800 730-2215.

Solution

The technical analyst most likely would have identified an up trendline, as shown in the following chart. Notice that the trendline connects the two lowest points. In this particular case, the technical analysis would have proven to be very profitable. Suppose that Merck was purchased at $25 on day 7 after the up trendline was established on day 6. Merck was then sold at $32 on day 24 after the up trend was violated on day 23, and the sell signal was given on day 23. Hence, a profit of $7 per share (a rate of return of $7/$25 = 0.28, or 28%) was achieved over a period of eighteen days.

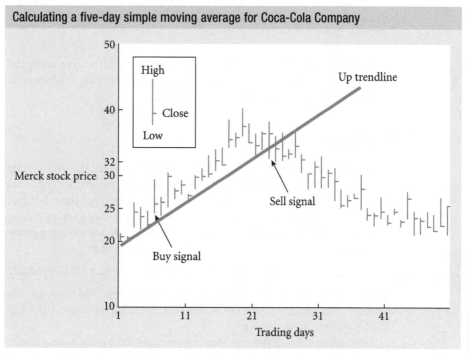

Calculating a five-day simple moving average for Coca-Cola Company

Source: From *Introduction to Investments*, 2nd edn, by Levy. © 1999. Reprinted with permission of South-Western, a division of Thomson Learning: www.thomsonrights.com. Fax 800 730-2215.

the broad part consisting of the difference between the opening and closing prices, and the shadows are the vertical thin lines above and below the real body. If the opening price is above the closing price, then the real body is shaded. Alternatively, if the opening price is below the closing price, then the real body is not shaded. Candlestick charts can also be constructed with intraday data, weekly data, and so forth.

The symbol shown for Wednesday in Exhibit 18.8 is called a hammer in a down market (hammering out a base) and a hanging man in an up market (the market is going to leave the investor hanging).[2] In Exhibit 18.8, Wednesday's result would be interpreted as a hammer and is considered by some technical analysts as a buy signal. There are many other interpretations of candlestick charts that are beyond the scope of this book.[3]

---

[2] Based on Nison (1991), p. 3.
[3] The interested reader can find several books on candlestick charts. The technical analysis books in this chapter's references all discuss candlestick charts.

Exhibit 18.10	Summary of charts		
	Bar chart	**Point-and-figure chart**	**Candlestick chart**
Data used	High, low, close	Close	Open, high, low, close
Time horizon	Days	None	Days
Applications	Trendlines (channels, support, resistance)	Trendlines (channels, support, resistance)	Depends on pattern and shapes

Source: From *Introduction to Investments*, 2nd edn, by Levy. © 1999. Reprinted with permission of South-Western, a division of Thomson Learning: www.thomsonrights.com. Fax 800 730-2215.

Although bar, point-and-figure and candlestick charts have vastly different applications, certain generalisations can be made about them. Exhibit 18.10 summarises the data, the time horizons and applications of each kind of chart.

18.2.4 Moving averages

One of the most popular tools of technical analysis is the moving average. A simple moving average is built by taking the arithmetic average of a stock price over the past predetermined number of days and graphing these results over a period of time. For example, Exhibit 18.11 gives the closing prices of a stock for 20 days. The five-day moving average is found by taking closing prices for the past five days, adding them up, and dividing by five. For example, on 8 August the five-day moving average can be calculated as

$$(68.9375 + 68 + 68.125 + 66.5625 + 62.6875)/5 = 66.8625$$

and on 11 August the earliest day (4 August) is dropped and the most recent one (11 August) is added. This process continues across the entire data set. Exhibit 18.12 illustrates graphically the five-day moving average.

Most technical analysts use moving averages for longer time periods. For example, one popular approach is that if the Dow Jones Industrial Average is above its 200-day moving average, then security prices should rise, and if it is below its 200-day moving average, then security prices should fall. Many technical analysts use moving averages in an attempt to identify the primary, intermediate and short-term trends.

Moving averages can also be used with individual stocks. For example, if a particular stock's price has been falling, then the moving average will typically be above the bar chart. If the stock's price subsequently rallies, breaking through the moving average line from below, then technical analysts view this as a bullish sign. Alternatively, if a particular stock's price has been rising, then the moving average typically will be below the bar chart. If the stock's price subsequently falls, breaking through the moving average line from above, then technical analysts view this as a bearish sign. As with other technical analysis tools, there are many possible interpretations of moving averages.

18.2.5 Relative strength

Many technical analysts use relative strength to assess a security. Relative strength measures the relationship between two historical series of financial assets' data (the rate at which one asset falls or rises relative to the second asset). Although relative strength can be expressed in

Exhibit 18.11	Calculating a five-day simple moving average for Coca-Cola Company		
Date	Closing price ($)	Five-day total (A) ($)	Five-day simple moving average (A/5) ($)
4/8/97	68.9375		
5/8/97	68		
6/8/97	68.125		
7/8/97	66.5625		
8/8/97	62.6875	334.3125	66.8625
11/8/97	63.75	329.125	65.825
12/8/97	60.9375	322.0625	64.4125
13/8/97	60.4375	314.375	62.875
14/8/97	60.125	307.9375	61.5875
15/8/97	58.75	304	60.8
18/8/97	60.375	300.625	60.125
19/8/97	60.8125	300.5	60.1
20/8/97	61.5	301.5625	60.3125
21/8/97	60.5625	302	60.4
22/8/97	60.6875	303.9375	60.7875
25/8/97	59.6875	303.25	60.65
26/8/97	59	301.4375	60.2875
27/8/97	58.625	298.5625	59.7125
28/8/97	58.25	296.25	59.25
29/8/97	57.3125	292.875	58.575

various ways, it is typically expressed as a ratio of the price performance of one asset or index to the price performance of another asset or index. For example, a technical analyst might use relative strength to compare the overall market performance as measured, for example, by the S&P 500 with the performance of a certain stock. This relative strength index (RSI) can range from 0 to 100%.[4] A high RSI value means that industry stock prices have been outperforming the market.

Exhibit 18.13 gives prices of IBM stock and the RSI level for this stock during the period July 1995–August 1996. The top curve of the chart shows the price of IBM stock. The bottom curve of the chart gives the RSI value for IBM. Thus, the RSI indicates how well IBM stock performed relative to the other stocks (represented by some stock index, such as the S&P 500). Exhibit 18.13 shows that it is possible that the price of the stock will rise sharply while its RSI value will fall (see March 1996), due to a sharper rise in the S&P 500 index price.

Some technical analysts believe that high RSI values indicate a sell signal and low RSI values indicate a buy signal. Many analysts are now using the RSI value of 20 for buy signals and 80 for sell signals (see Exhibit 18.13). Alternatively, some technical analysts believe that 'the trend is your friend'. That is, high values of RSI indicate a buy signal, because trends are believed to be persistent. In this view, an investor would sell only after the RSI value had fallen substantially.

---

[4] The actual numerical calculation is complex. RSI is widely available from data and analysis services such as Bloomberg.

Exhibit 18.12 Five-day simple moving average based on the closing price for hypothetical data

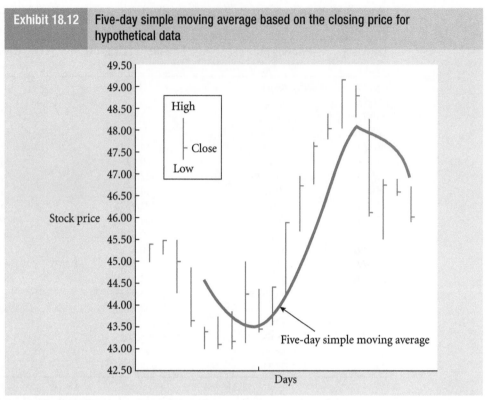

Source: From *The Technical Analysis Course*, Chicago, IL, Probus Publishing, p. 137 (Meyers, T., 1989), reproduced with permission of The McGraw-Hill Companies.

Exhibit 18.13 Relative strength of IBM stock (July 1995–August 1996)

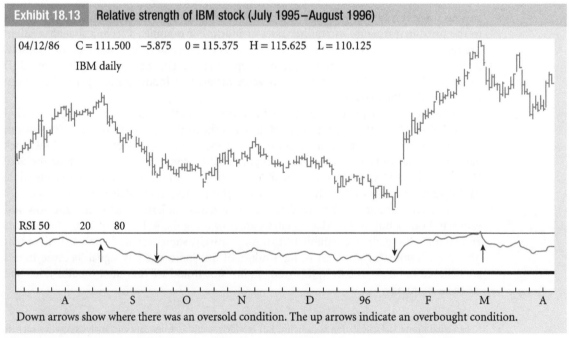

Down arrows show where there was an oversold condition. The up arrows indicate an overbought condition.

Source: Equity Analytics (1998) 'The Relative Strength of IBM Stock (July 1995–August 1996)', http://www.e-analytics.com/htm

FTSE rally gathers technical steam

Is it a bird? Is it a plane? No it's the FTSE! Since closing at a low for the year of 3287 only last Wednesday, London's blue-chip index has staged an impressive rebound, reaching an intra-day high at the time of writing on Tuesday of 3810. But is the FTSE's sharp 500-point plus advance since last Thursday another bear market rally or the start of a new bull trend? Unfortunately, the honest answer is that it is too early to tell, but from a technical analysis viewpoint the last week has thrown up some very positive developments.

Previous commentary suggested that, based on Elliott Wave Theory analysis, the FTSE was coming to the end of a 5-wave decline from the late November high at 4224.8, a fall that was expected to end between 3325 and 3118. In the event, the market dropped as low as 3277 on an intra-day basis on March 12, before March 13's 6 per cent rally started the current upswing. The rebound has also been accompanied by a divergence between price and momentum indicators. The Relative Strength Index (RSI) did not confirm the FTSE's fall beneath January's 3391 trough. January's low for the daily RSI was 8 while last week it fell only to 19. Divergence between price and momentum is an early indicator of a change in the direction of the trend. It was present last year between the July and September lows, helping to support October's sharp rebound.

The rally has made inroads into overhead resistance levels. On the daily FTSE chart a trend line can be drawn from the mid-May 2002 highs through the peak in early December 2002 and through this year's high in mid-January. February's attempted rally fell short of the trend line, but Monday's close at 3722 finished above the resistance. At the time of writing the move on an intra-day basis had surpassed both the February high at 3747 and a 50 per cent retracement of the November to March decline at 3751. If the FTSE closes above these levels, it will have taken the next positive technical step and will open up a move towards the 61.8 per cent Fibonacci retracement of the November-March drop at 3863. A close above 3747 would also mark a break in the bear pattern of successively lower lows and lower highs on the counter-trend rallies.

Technical analysts are now eyeing levels close to 4000 as the next significant area of resistance on the FTSE 100. The widely followed 200-day moving average currently provides resistance at 4027. Steve Hatton, a technical analyst with spread-betting service Deal4Free.com, highlights that a 78.6 per cent retracement of the November to March move, a retracement used by followers of Gann analysis, provides resistance at 4022. Chris Locke of Oystercatcher, a technical analysis consultancy based in the Netherlands, said that a rally of between 22 and 24 per cent would be consistent with historical precedent. A 22 per cent rebound from the recent low would take the FTSE 100 to 4010. On the question of whether the bear market was finally over Mr Locke suggested a prudent approach: 'Take it one step at a time and see how it unfolds from here.' He suggested that the 40-day moving average needed to cross above the 200-day moving average to signal a longer-term bull trend was developing.

The rebound is unlikely to unfold in a straight line and with the FTSE rallying more than 500 points in 4 trading sessions a very near-term pullback is highly likely. Even if the rebound is only a correction of the larger bear trend, Elliott Wave theory suggests that it should unfold in a three-wave zig-zag pattern. A 61.8 per cent retracement of the 3287 to 3810 move would take the market back to 3480, but unless the FTSE drops back through its recent low at 3287 the rebound cannot be pronounced dead in the water. Investors should expect further volatility in the days ahead.

The ferocity of the market's rebound has caught many retail investors unawares, while even the professionals will have struggled to make fresh profits from the rebound. Anecdotal evidence suggests that covering of short positions rather than the opening of new long positions has been the driving force behind the rally.

Chasing the market higher after a 500-point rally is not a prudent course of action. Short-term traders should use a near-term pullback to add to positions, but need to be prepared to withstand a move back below last week's low. For the longer-term investor, who may have missed out on the bounce so far, waiting to see if the market can clear the cluster of resistance levels near 4000 is the preferred course of action.

Source: Vince Heaney, 'FTSE Rally Gathers Technical Steam', FT.com site, 18 March 2003.

→ **Making the connection**

The author uses technical analysis to determine whether a series of recent gains on the FTSE index forms an early signal of a new bull market trend. The analysis uses the tools of moving averages and relative strength. In addition, the analysis relies on the so-called Elliott wave theory. This theory is an outgrowth of the original technical market analysis of Dow theory based on the belief that stock market movements can be predicted by observing and identifying a repetitive pattern of waves. Fibonacci numbers provide the mathematical foundation for the wave theory of technical analysis. Today, there are a number of websites that are designed to introduce investors to technical analysis, such as Elliott wave theory and Fibonacci numbers, or provide related services, including www.elliottwave.com, Elliott Wave International's site.

18.2.6 Breadth indicators

Breadth indicators include the advance–decline line, volume and new high/new low indicators. The advance–decline line is the number of advancing issues (stocks whose prices have gone up from the previous day) minus the number of declining issues (stocks whose prices have gone down from the previous day) on a particular day plus the cumulative total from the previous day (so trends can be monitored). We may illustrate this concept by using stock data from the NYSE Composite Index, a value-weighted index of all stocks traded on the NYSE. On 12 January 1998, advances (1343) were lower than declines (1710) by 367. Hence, the advance–decline line would be reduced by 367 on 12 January. The advance–decline line on day t (ADL_t) is the number of the advancing issues on day t (A_t) minus the number of declining issues on day t (D_t) plus the cumulative total from the previous day (ADL_{t-1}), i.e.

$$ADL_t = A_t - D_t + ADL_{t-1}$$

In this case, if $ADL_{1/11} = 1500$, then we have

$$ADL_{1/12} = 1343 - 1710 + 1500 = 1133$$

On 13, 14 and 16 January, the advances led the declines, so the advance–decline line would rise on each of these days by the difference between advances and declines. Most technical analysts view a falling advance–decline line in a rising market as bearish and a rising advance–decline line in a falling market as bullish.

Many breadth indicators are based on trading volume, because technical analysts interpret changes in trading volume as indicators of the size of future price changes in securities. Most financial media report the volume of trading in individual securities. For example, a sharp rise in volume of a stock whose price has been rising is interpreted as a signal of even more dramatic price increases in the future. Alternatively, a sharp rise in volume of a stock whose price has been falling is interpreted to signal even more dramatic price declines in the future.

The last category of breadth indicators to be described is related to the number of stocks hitting new 52-week highs when compared with the number of stocks hitting new 52-week lows. Breadth is typically measured as the ratio of new highs to new lows. When the breadth is declining in a rising market, it is thought to be a signal that the bull market is stalling. Hence, many technical analysts keep an eye on the trend in the ratio of new highs to new lows.

18.2.7 Sentiment indicators

Sentiment indicators attempt to gauge the overall mood, or sentiments, of investors. One measure of sentiment is a comparison of the number of stock-market newsletters that are bullish with the number of those that are bearish. Technical analysts typically believe that, on average, stock-market newsletters are wrong. Hence, when the majority of newsletters are bearish, analysts interpret this as a bullish sign.

Another sentiment indicator is based on the quantity of odd-lot trading. Recall that an odd lot is any transaction that is less than 100 shares (the trading in multiples of 100 is known as a round lot). Odd-lot trading is typically done by small investors, who, technical analysts believe, are usually wrong. Hence, technical analysts see odd-lot buying that exceeds odd-lot selling as a bearish signal, because they believe that small investors typically buy at the wrong time.

Another sentiment indicator is the put/call ratio, which is found by dividing the volume of put option trading by the volume of call option trading (see Chapter 19). Technical analysts view excessive put buying as a bearish signal and excessive call buying as a bullish signal. Investors buy put options, which give them the right to sell stocks in the future, when they believe that stock prices will fall. Alternatively, investors buy call options, which give them the right to buy stocks in the future, when they believe that stock prices will rise. Therefore, when the volume of put buying exceeds the volume of call buying, it indicates that option buyers in the aggregate are bearish.

Finally, technical analysts also monitor the amount of short-selling done by specialists. Recall that the specialist is the market maker on the NYSE. Specialists typically have superior information regarding a stock (they have the limit book; see Chapter 3) and are perceived as particularly good speculators. Hence, when specialists are selling short, it is a signal that the stock may decline. Specialists are also perceived as insiders, and investors want to mimic specialists' trading activities. Specialist short-selling indicates a bearish view on a stock; hence, technical analysts would view increases in specialist short positions as bearish.

18.3 Empirical evidence regarding technical analysis

Is there any empirical evidence to support the usefulness of technical analysis? Interestingly, several researchers have discovered patterns in security prices that suggest that technical analysis is useful. For example, by monitoring stock-price movements, Lehmann (1990) noted that when a stock price experienced a sizeable fall one week, the next week the stock would bounce back, and when a stock price experienced a sizeable rise one week, the next week the stock would fall back. These trends do not always occur, but historically they have occurred with sufficient frequency to create many profit opportunities. Jegadeesh (1990) also found predictable patterns in stock prices for monthly returns over a long period (1934–87). Specifically, Jegadeesh found strong evidence that the stocks with large losses in one month are likely to experience a significant reversal in the next month. Also, stocks with large gains in one month are likely to experience a significant loss in the next month. Finally, Jegadeesh documents clear seasonal patterns, a finding that supports the January effect mentioned in Chapter 12.

This evidence in favour of technical analysis is a direct challenge to the traditional view that markets are efficient and technical analysis is useless. Earlier research by Fama (1970) found evidence that markets are efficient. More recent research, including the above studies by Lehmann (1990) and Jegadeesh (1990), identifies patterns in historical stock prices.[5] This more recent empirical evidence gives merit to the use of technical analysis.

Still, the stock market anomalies do not imply that the stock market is in disequilibrium and that technical analysis is profitable. Rather, the anomalies may simply reflect that our asset-pricing models (such as the CAPM and APT) do not capture capital market equilibrium fully.

In Connecting Theory to Practice 18.3, Philip. Coggan raises another problem for assessing the effectiveness of technical analysis. According to Coggan, technical analysts fail to follow standard scientific procedure in presenting and evaluating their techniques and currently no scientific proof exists that technical analysis is profitable. Perhaps this is why technical analysis is frequently termed 'as much art as science'.

→ **Connecting Theory to Practice 18.3**　　　　　　　　　　　　　　　　**FT**

Technically, these methods don't work

It happens every couple of weeks. A letter arrives in my in-tray from someone, somewhere who has the answer. It may be that the Dow is heading to an all-time low. It may be that gold is heading to $1000 an ounce. But one thing is certain; it will contain some kind of chart, brightly coloured and covered with wiggly lines and arrows.

I have tried to keep an open mind about technical analysis. For some time, I regaled readers with news of the Coppock indicator, a technical measure that had the virtues of infrequent signals and a solid record. But I should have stuck to my natural cynicism. The Coppock indicator has signalled twice, during this bear market, that the FTSE 100 index was a buy. Each signal proved dead wrong. My view is now rather jaundiced. At best, technical analysts state the obvious; when the market's going up, they tell you it's going up; when it's falling, they tell you it's coming down. At worst, they generate a host of signals that cost small investors money through excessive trading costs.

It is true that highly intelligent people (including esteemed FT colleagues) believe in the stuff. And it is not, in principle, impossible that, at the core of technical analysis, there is some truth yet to be discovered. If one accepts that equity markets are not completely efficient and that

---

[5] See also French and Roll (1986), Fama and French (1988) and Lo and MacKinlay (1988), among many others.

investors can be biased, it is possible that the study of past price movements may be worthwhile. For example, academic studies show that, in the short term, price momentum appears to persist. Successful fund managers, such as Hugh Hendry of Odey Asset Management, use momentum as a check for their fundamental views; if the story is good, but the price is going down, there is probably something wrong with the story. But it is a big stretch from such analysis to the argument that all price movements follow a set pattern, or series of patterns.

As it happens, Victor Niederhoffer and Laurel Kenner, the authors of a new book*, have examined a host of different technical indicators, including head and shoulders patterns and Japanese candlestick measures such as 'three black crows'. None has passed the test of statistical significance; in other words, investors could not rely on them to provide signals to buy, or sell, stocks. Indeed, there is even a Federal Reserve paper on the issue of 'head and shoulders' patterns. Its author, Carol Osler, tested the patterns over 31 years and found that trading in individual equities based on such patterns is, on balance, unprofitable. As Niederhoffer and Kenner write:

'The problem with technical analysis is that practitioners and advocates fail to follow standard scientific procedure in presenting and evaluating its techniques. Technical analysis is so rife with subjective interpretations that it must be regarded as more of a religion than a method, complete with priests who bewilder the unwashed at high-priced seminars.'

One has to be even more suspicious of claims that financial markets move in long and short term patterns that can be found in nature. Take Elliott wave theory, which says that markets move in patterns of five and three – an up phase (itself consisting of three ups and two downs) and a down phase (comprising two downs and an up). Believers in Elliott wave theory argue that this is a 'fractal' pattern in which a small part replicates the whole. So Elliott waves can be found within a day's trading period and on a scale that spans centuries. Hence the belief in the 'long wave' or 'grand supercycle' that can be traced all the way back to the 18th century. The problem with such an ambitious theory is that it is completely unprovable. Financial data of the most rudimentary kind only date back around 300 years. So if there is a grand supercycle lasting centuries, we can only record one of them. And to date, the current bear market hardly demonstrates 'grand supercycle' strength – most indices dropped to six-year lows, not 60-year nadirs.

Economic students might recall the 'Kondratieff wave' that appeared to indicate a cycle of 54–56 years, after peaks in 1819, 1873 and 1929. When the 1987 crash came, some were quick to announce that Kondratieff had returned. But 1987 proved to be a blip. Maybe 2000 will turn out to be the latest Kondratieff peak, although the economic downturn to date is nothing like as bad as the previous examples. But if the 'regular' cycle has now extended to 71 years, maybe it's not that regular and maybe it's no more useful than saying 'economic dislocations occur from time to time but we can't tell when'.

It is human nature to look for patterns. Sometimes it can be useful; if dark clouds are above, it is likely to rain. But often we 'see' patterns that are not there, we can be 'fooled by randomness' to cite the excellent book of Nassim Nicholas Taleb**. Indeed, as people react to the patterns they perceive, their behaviour can change. Alas, that means there is no 'answer' – no universal law that can be divined from lines on a graph. Life is simply not that easy. Financial markets can also be affected by one-off events, such as September 11, that can totally alter investor attitudes. And if you believe that such events can be predicted by studying lines on a graph – there's a bridge in Brooklyn I'd like to sell you.

* *Practical Speculation* by Victor Niederhoffer and Laurel Kenner, published by John Wiley & Sons, 388pp, £20.95.
** *Fooled by Randomness*, published by Texere, 204pp, £18.99.

Source: Philip Coggan, FT Money: 'Technically, These Methods Don't Work', *Financial Times*, 7 June 2003.

Summary

Define technical analysis and contrast it with fundamental analysis.

Technical analysis is based on graphs and charts of historical market data (for example, market prices, the amounts of short-selling and the volume of trading) rather than on fundamental values such as company financial statements and sector and macroeconomic data.

Explain the logic behind technical analysis.

Most technical analysis procedures originate from the Dow theory, which is based on the idea that asset prices can be predicted by observing and identifying a repetitive pattern of primary, intermediate and short-term waves.

Discuss the basic tools used by technical analysts.

Technical analysts plot market data on charts, such as bar charts, point-and-figure charts and candlestick charts. The charts display historical information that enables technical analysts to extrapolate trends into the future. These trends are assessed using tools such as moving averages and relative strength. Moving averages are obtained by averaging the most recent past price data. Relative strength measures the price performance of one portfolio or index against another. Two popular technical indicators are the breadth and sentiment indicators. The breadth indicators include the advance–decline line, volume and new high/new low indicators. The advance–decline line measures the number of stocks that rose compared with the number of stocks that fell. Sentiment indicators include stock-market newsletters, odd-lot trading, the put/call ratio (a measure based on the volume of put and call option trading) and specialist short-selling.

Summarise the empirical evidence regarding the effectiveness of technical analysis.

There is no unambiguous proof for the effectiveness of technical analysis. There exist several empirical anomalies that asset-pricing models cannot explain. However, the anomalies may simply reflect that the asset-pricing models do not fully capture capital market equilibrium rather than that the capital market is in disequilibrium and that technical analysis is profitable. Also, assessing the effectiveness of technical analysis is complicated by the fact that many technical analysts fail to follow standard scientific procedure in presenting and evaluating their techniques.

Key terms

Advance–decline line 614
Bar chart 601
Breadth indicator 601
Candlestick chart 601
Candlestick line 608
Channel 602
Dow theory 597
Elliott Wave Theory 613
Intermediate trend 596

Moving average 601
Odd-lot trading 615
Point-and-figure chart 601
Primary tide 597
Primary trend 596
Put/call ratio 615
Real body 608
Relative strength 601
Resistance 605

Ripples 597
Secondary reactions 597
Sentiment indicator 601
Shadow 608
Short-term trend 596
Support 606
Technical analysis 595
Trendline 601

Review questions

1 Compare and contrast technical analysis and fundamental analysis.

2 What is the assumption on which technical theories are typically built?

3 How do technical analysts use charts to make inferences about future prices? Describe the candlestick chart.

4 Given the following price data, draw a point-and-figure chart using $1 gains and losses to determine when Xs and Os occur:

Day	High price ($)	Low price ($)	Closing price ($)
0	53.13	50.50	51.38
1	52.00	48.13	49.75
2	53.88	51.25	52.50
3	54.00	52.50	54.00
4	55.38	54.00	54.13
5	54.75	52.13	52.25
6	56.88	55.00	56.75
7	58.50	57.00	57.13
8	59.38	57.20	58.50
9	60.80	59.38	60.00
10	61.00	60.20	61.00

5 'All empirical research suggests that technical analysis is totally useless.' Evaluate this statement.

For an extensive set of review and practice questions and answers, visit the Levy–Post investment website at www.booksites.net/levy

Selected references

Brown, D. P. and R. H. Jennings, 1989, 'On Technical Analysis', *Review of Financial Studies*, **2** (4), 527–551.

Chance, D. M. and D. Rich, 2001, 'The False Teachings of the Unbiased Expectations Hypothesis', *Journal of Portfolio Management*, **27**, 83–95.

Clarke, R. G. and M. Statman, 1998, 'Bullish or Bearish', *Financial Analysts Journal*, **54** (3), 63–72.

Colby, R. W., 2003, *The Encyclopedia of Technical Market Indicators*, 2nd edn, New York: McGraw-Hill Publishing.

Darrat, E. F. and M. Zhong, 2000, 'On Testing the Random Walk Hypothesis: A Model-Comparison Approach', *Financial Review*, **35**, 105–124.

Edwards, R. D. and J. Magee, 1992, *Technical Analysis of Stock Trends*, 6th edn, New York: New York Institute of Finance.

Fama, E. F., 1970, 'Efficient Capital Markets: A Review of Theory and Empirical Work', *Journal of Finance*, 25, 383–417.

Fama, E. F. and K. R. French, 1988, 'Permanent and Temporary Components of Stock Prices', *Journal of Political Economy*, **98**, 247–273.

French, K. R. and R. Roll, 1986, 'Stock Return Variances: The Arrival of Information and Reaction of Traders', *Journal of Financial Economics*, **17**, 5–26.

Jegadeesh, N., 1990, 'Evidence of Predictable Behavior of Security Returns', *Journal of Finance*, **45**, 881–898.

Kroll, S. and M. J. Paulenoff, 1993, *The Business One Irwin Guide to the Futures Markets*, Homewood, IL: Business One Irwin.

Lehmann, B. N., 1990, 'Fads, Martingales, and Market Efficiency', *Quarterly Journal of Economics*, **105** (1), 1–28.

Lo, A. W. and A. C. MacKinlay, 1988, 'Stock Market Prices Do Not Follow Random Walks: Evidence from a Simple Specification Test', *Review of Financial Studies*, **1**, 41–66.

Meyers, T. A., 1989, *The Technical Analysis Course*, Chicago: Probus Publishing.

Morris, G. L., 1992, *Candle Power: Advanced Candlestick Pattern Recognition and Filtering Techniques for Trading Stocks and Futures*, Chicago: Probus Publishing.

Nison, S., 1991, *Introduction to Japanese Candle Charts*, New York: Merrill Lynch, Pierce, Fenner & Smith.

Pring, M. J., 1991, *Technical Analysis Explained*, New York: McGraw-Hill.

Sperandeo, V., 1991, *Trader Vic – Methods of a Wall Street Master*, New York: John Wiley & Sons.

Part 5

DERIVATIVE SECURITIES

CHAPTER 19 Futures, options and other derivatives

Investment in the News 19 — FT

The secret formula that saved Salomon North: Wall Street steps in to rescue the fund that thought it was too smart to fail

The faces gathered around the table in the 10th-floor boardroom of the New York Federal Reserve on Wednesday night were the elite of Wall Street. Few events are urgent enough to gather people such as David Komansky, chairman of Merrill Lynch, and Sandy Warner, chairman of JP Morgan, at a few hours' notice. But this was exceptional. The men were here to rescue one of their own – and save themselves from the effects of one of the most spectacular financial collapses of modern Wall Street. For Long-Term Capital Management, the elite hedge fund with $80 bn of assets, it was the moment of truth.

For four years, LTCM had produced spectacular and consistent returns on its capital base of up to $7 bn from its headquarters in Greenwich, Connecticut. The firm led by John Meriwether, one of Wall Street's legendary figures, had thrown down a gauntlet to Salomon Brothers, Mr Meriwether's former employer, and other financial institutions. But this all changed abruptly this summer when the Russian government defaulted on its debts in August.

The fall in value of its positions would not have mattered so much had it not been for its use of derivatives. Investors that buy futures and options through exchanges or banks have to post cash daily to cover any paper losses. These margin calls protect exchanges from the risk of default. As prices went awry, LTCM was forced to liquidate other assets in order to raise money for margin calls. The effect was devastating. In a letter to investors on September 2, Mr Meriwether confessed that the fund had lost 44 per cent of its net asset value in August alone, and was now down to $2.3 bn of capital.

When the banks, the Fed and the fund reconvened at around 1 pm that day, it was with a renewed sense of urgency. Among the key players in the discussions was Herb Allison, president and chief operating officer of Merrill Lynch, who drew up and presented the final rescue plan to bankers. 'By that time, nearly all of us realised that this was a deal that just had to be done,'* one person who was at the meeting says.

* Author note: actually, opinion is divided about whether the rescue operation of LTCM was such a great idea for the sector. Some suggest that it encouraged taking too much risk by large investors, by setting the precedent that the FED and the sector will come to your aid when things go wrong.

Source: John Gapper, 'The Secret Formula That Saved Salomon North: Wall Street Steps In To Rescue the Fund That Thought It Was Too Smart To Fail', *Financial Times*, 25 September 1998.

A derivative security is a financial asset that derives its value from another asset, hence the name 'derivative'. A derivative security is also called a contingent claim, because the value of the claim is contingent on characteristics of the underlying security, for example its price.[1] The underlying asset can be oil, wheat, British pounds, a bond or stock index, and so on.

Derivatives are important for both investors and firms. Hence, they are covered in courses on investments as well as corporate finance. First, they can be employed by firms to hedge risk on their corporate activities, enhancing the corporate finance policies. For example, derivatives can help to prevent financial distress. Second, derivatives can affect the risk of corporate projects, although their effect on cash flows might not show in financial reports.[2] For investors, they can mitigate risks on their portfolios or provide diversification benefits. They can also be a means to generate large returns, either by speculating or arbitrage. However, the risks of some of these strategies are equally large: if an investor has taken a position based on beliefs or assumptions that prove to be wrong (for example, one predicts the stock index will fall, but it actually rises), then the investor may lose a good deal. The example of LTCM, described in Investment in the News 19, is a stark reminder of this; they lost several billions of dollars in derivative transactions.[3] Given the great potential in both gains and losses, the future cash flow of derivatives should be known to anyone who uses them.

The two main categories of derivatives are (1) futures, forward and swap contracts and (2) option contracts. Options are distinctly different: with an option contract, the buyer has the *right* to buy or sell some asset in the future, such as common stocks, for an agreed price. With futures, swaps and forward contracts, the buyer is *obligated* to buy some asset in the future at a prespecified price, regardless of whether it is profitable at that time. (The seller always has an obligation to honour the terms of the contract, regardless of the type of derivative.) Both types of derivatives can be quite risky; the option holder has to pay a premium, which may not be recovered, and the futures contract creates an obligation to buy (or to sell) at a price that may be much higher (or much lower) than the value in the market, resulting in a

---

[1] A derivative is always a contingent claim, but the relation does not hold vice versa; a contingent claim does not have to be a derivative. In fact, some more advanced models in finance use claims that are not contingent on other assets but on 'the state of the world', for instance 'recession' or 'no recession'.

[2] To adress this issue, the US Financial Accounting Standards Board (FASB) requires that derivatives are 'marked to market' and put directly on the company balance sheet and income statements. Thus, any gain or loss on derivatives will be treated according to their current value ('mark to market') and will be reported, even if the result is not realised. For details, see Statement 133. On an international level, accounting standards are moving in the same direction; see, for example, IAS 32 and 39 from the International Accounting Standards Board (IASB).

[3] Further details on LTCM can be found in Connecting Theory to Practice 4.3, 21.1 and 21.2.

large loss. Therefore, the use of derivatives by fiduciary investors, such as mutual funds and pension funds, who invest on behalf of third parties, is strictly regulated.

This chapter starts by looking at reasons for the use of derivatives. Various derivative contracts are introduced, with a description of how firms and (individual and institutional) investors can gain or lose from investing in these securities. We start with forwards and swaps, the two instruments that are mainly used in corporate finance and between large institutional investors. These instruments are tailor-made and sold only in the over-the-counter (OTC) market. However, the focus of this chapter is on futures and options, because these derivatives are traded on financial exchanges. They are therefore easier to use, and information about them is publicly available. We survey the different markets and their organisational structures, and end with common strategies designed to alter payoff patterns.

Finally, the valuation of derivative assets is not a simple task. Indeed, Robert Merton and Myron Scholes were awarded the 1997 Nobel Prize in economics mainly for their contribution in the area of valuing derivatives, and this matter is deferred to the next chapter.

19.1 Reasons for using derivatives

In order to understand the reasons for investing in derivatives, let us first identify from a theoretical viewpoint what derivatives can and cannot contribute to investment possibilities.

First, derivatives can, at least in principle, be replicated by buying or short-selling the underlying asset and borrowing or lending money. Hence, at first sight, derivatives appear redundant.

Second, unlike stocks and bonds, derivatives are normally issued in the secondary market rather than the primary market. In other words, derivatives are not an instrument to fund the investment projects of corporations and governments.[4] Investing in a company (or buying government bills or bonds) presumably enables this company (or government) to produce goods or render services with greater value than the sum of the costs, including the costs to fulfil all obligations to the suppliers of capital (interest and principal to bondholders and dividends to stockholders). This process creates added value to society as a whole. However, it does not work this way with derivatives; in principle, derivative trading is a 'zero-sum game' – for every dollar made in the option market by a given investor, there is a dollar lost by another investor.

Using these two arguments, it seems that derivatives do not create new investment possibilities. How does this relate to the enormous popularity of derivatives? In the USA alone, investors create close to a billion contracts a year, with a notional value of over half a trillion (10^{12}) dollars. The above reasoning is correct, but it misses some more subtle points.

The first argument ('derivatives can be replicated by using the underlying asset and borrowing or lending') assumes perfect markets with no transaction costs or position limits. This assumption doesn't reflect reality; all brokers and exchanges enforce position limits to some degree, and most transactions entail a fee. Since it takes a great deal of transactions to mimic the behaviour of an option over time, these costs become prohibitive in many cases. Sometimes, it is even undesirable to trade the underlying asset, or it may even be impossible (for example, in the case of credit derivatives, selling a loan might give an adverse signal about the borrower, even if there were a functional market for second hand loans, which is often not the case). Derivatives therefore contribute to the investment possibilities by making payoff patterns available to a wider group of investors and at a lower cost.

---

[4] However, derivatives might be embedded in instruments that are issued in the primary market; for example, a convertible bond is, in fact, a combination of a bond and an option (or warrant).

The second argument ('derivatives are a zero-sum game') ignores that there can be a gain by reducing risk. A petrochemical company buys its calls on oil not because they expect to generate a profit from that transaction but because they generate payoffs in situations where these are needed most – that is, when there is a threat of a considerable loss, thereby preventing financial distress. Similarly, an investor may buy a put option on Microsoft stock not because he or she might gain from the transaction but to hedge against a sharp fall in the price of the Microsoft stock that he or she owns. So, it's not the expected gain but the situation in which the dollars are received or spent that matters. In brief, firms and investors may gain from risk reduction resulting from the usage of derivatives. Furthermore, issuers of primary securities can gain from the availability of derivatives. Specifically, investors may be willing to pay a premium for bonds and stocks if derivatives are available to manage the risk of these securities. Hence, the availability of derivatives may increase the proceeds of new issues of bonds and stocks or, put differently, lower the funding costs. This is the third reason why derivatives can add value to society as a whole.

Given these considerations, investors use derivative contracts in four basic strategies: hedging, speculating, arbitrage and portfolio diversification.

Hedging

Hedging strategies use derivative contracts to transfer price risk. One reason for trading derivative contracts is to transfer that price risk to another party who is willing to take it. Price risk arises in many different settings.

For example, suppose a firm purchases 100 000 MMBtu (million British thermal units) of natural gas each month. There is a six-month lag between the time prices rise and the moment the firm can pass on the price increase to its customers. Clearly, this firm could face significant risk if the price of natural gas rose. Therefore, the firm could lock in the price of natural gas for the next six months using natural gas futures contracts, effectively buying the gas today with delivery and payment in six months' time (details of how futures work can be found in the following sections). The firm benefits by eliminating the influence of natural-gas price swings on its earnings.

Derivatives are also useful when the quantity of the underlying assets to be hedged is uncertain. How does an investor hedge when there is uncertainty regarding the quantity of the underlying asset at risk? For example, when an investor owns foreign stocks and expects a dividend, there is uncertainty not only about the exchange rate but also about the amount of dividend that is to be received or the invested capital when you plan on selling the stock. An investor who hedges exchange-rate risk by selling currency futures could face unwanted consequences: if there is no dividend this year, the obligation of the futures contract still exists, a situation that may increase risk rather than decrease it. Futures contracts should be used as hedging vehicles only when the quantity to be hedged is fairly certain.

Whenever there is quantity risk, option contracts can be a good alternative; these give the investor the right to buy or sell, so if the markets take a turn for the worse, only the original value of the option can be lost.

Speculating

There are many ways to speculate with derivatives. Central to speculation is some belief about future prices. If investors believe that stocks will rise, then they buy index futures contracts or call options (they will take long positions in these instruments; see Sections 19.4 and 19.5). If they are wrong in their belief, as occurred with Nicholas Leeson of Barings Bank, then their loss can be devastating. (Leeson traded derivatives for speculative reasons. He was wrong in guessing the market direction, inducing a loss of more than $1 billion to Barings Bank, leading to the demise of this centuries-old investment bank.) While hedgers use derivative contracts to offset an existing long or short position, speculators seek to profit by exposing themselves to more risk. As described in Section 19.4.1, speculating using derivatives can yield far greater returns than just buying or selling the underlying asset. On the other hand, the potential for losses is usually also far greater; as we will see below, the buyers of options risk losing their entire investment (a return of −100%). Moreover, the buyers and sellers of futures and the writers of options are exposed to virtually unlimited losses (losing ten or sometimes a hundred times one's initial investment is quite possible).

Arbitrage

Arbitrage strategies involve re-creating a particular asset synthetically and trading the synthetic asset against the original asset, so as to exploit price differences between the two (see also Chapter 11). A synthetic security is a portfolio of securities that have payoffs identical to the original security. Arbitrage is different from speculation, because there should be no price risk accepted with arbitrage. The objective is to design a portfolio with no investment and positive cash flows in the future or positive cash flows today with no liabilities in the future. For example, with major market index (MMI) futures contracts, investors can synthetically take a position in the portfolio of 20 stocks in the MMI by buying an appropriate number of futures contracts.[5] Hence, an arbitrageur can monitor two portfolios – the synthetic portfolio with futures and the actual portfolio of 20 stocks – and buy and sell when discrepancies appear.

Portfolio diversification

Portfolio-diversification strategies use derivatives like any other assets to combine with a portfolio in order to gain further diversification (see also Chapter 9). The benefit of derivatives is that they can be used to create correlations with the portfolio that are otherwise difficult to obtain. For example, a portfolio that has sold (short) stock index futures contracts will be highly negatively correlated with a stock portfolio. (Unfortunately, the expected rate of return in equilibrium will be about equal to the risk-free interest rate.)

Let us illustrate the idea of portfolio diversification using managed futures funds to diversify a portfolio. Managed futures funds use derivatives to create a payoff profile that is very suited for portfolio diversification; many of these funds have managers who are actively buying and selling futures contracts. Hence, one week, a manager may be selling derivatives on the MMI; the next week, he or she may be buying the same derivatives on the MMI. Thus, the position held is very dynamic and not necessarily correlated with the general market. Another reason that futures portfolios are unrelated to stocks and bonds is that many are invested at least partially in commodity futures, whose prices do not move in the same direction as the stock and bond markets. An additional advantage of using derivatives is that on these markets, trading in the underlying often involves storage, transportation and other costs. Managed futures funds are especially convenient if investors lack the expertise to trade on these markets themselves.

---

[5] The MMI is a price-weighted index of 20 blue-chip stocks. It is very similar to the Dow Jones Industrial Average, which has 30 stocks (see Chapter 6).

Exhibit 19.1	Spot and forward exchange rates against the dollar			FT
	Closing	1 month	3 months	1 year
Eurozone (€)	1.2086	1.2075	1.2055	1.1979
UK (£)	1.7290	1.7249	1.7171	1.6799
Japan (¥)	108.970	108.850	108.645	107.275

Note that for the euro/dollar and pound/dollar rates, prices are quoted as dollars/euro and dollars/pound, while for the yen/dollar rate, the convention is yen/dollar, so one dollar buys 108.97 yen.

Source: *Financial Times*, 2 December 2003.

19.2 Forward contracts

In conducting a cash transaction, a buyer and a seller exchange goods for cash at the current market price, with delivery on short notice – usually 3 working days. In contrast, when the buyer and the seller sign a forward contract, they agree to exchange goods for cash at some future date (say, 1 January of the next year) at a predetermined price (the *delivery price*). The delivery price at which one can buy (or sell) a contract today is called the *forward price*. This means that there can be a substantial difference between the market price at the moment of delivery and the agreed delivery price. The seller of the contract is in a short position, which means that the investor has to deliver the good in exchange for the delivery price, whereas the buyer is in a long position, resulting in an opposite obligation: a commitment to receive the goods and pay the delivery price. Various forward contracts can be made, but the most common are foreign exchange forward contracts.

Exhibit 19.1 reports data on forward contracts. For example, on 2 December 2003, 1.2086 US dollars were needed to buy one euro. That was the exchange rate for cash transactions, also called the *spot rate*. The forward exchange rate – or, simply, the forward rate – between these two currencies depended on the delivery date. If you wished to buy or sell dollars for delivery one month later, on 2 January 2004, you could close a deal for 1.2075 dollars per euro. If you wished the delivery date 12 months later (December 2004), then the forward rate was 1.1979 dollar for each euro. The following Practice box demonstrates how foreign exchange forward contracts can be used to hedge foreign currency risk.

Practice box

Problem

A US investor buys $1 million stock in an IPO in the USA on behalf of a South African partner. The US investor pays now, in cash, but the contract with the partner is structured in such a way that payment is due in six months, when the South Africans have raised the 7.5 million rand they agreed to pay the US investor.

1. The discount rate is 5% for the six-month period. What will be the NPV if the future exchange rate remains at its current level of 7.39 rand per dollar?
2. What will be the NPV if the exchange rate six months from now is 6.50 rand per dollar? And if it is 10.00 rand per dollar?
3. Suppose also that the forward rate six months from now is 7.05 rand per dollar. Show how the US investor can guarantee a positive NPV by using a forward contract.

Solution

1. The investor will receive 7.5 million rand six months from now at the exchange rate of 7.39 rand per dollar. The investor will receive about $1 014 885 (7.5 million rand/ 7.39 rand per dollar). If the investor invests $1 million today, the NPV of this transaction is as follows:

$$\frac{\$1\ 014\ 885}{1.05} - \$1\ \text{million} \cong -\$33\ 443$$

2. If the exchange rate six months from now is 6.50 rand per dollar, the investor will receive $1 153 846 (7.5 million rand/6.50 rand per dollar). The NPV is

$$\frac{\$1\ 153\ 846}{1.05} - \$1\ \text{million} \cong \$98\ 901$$

If the exchange rate is 10.0 rand per dollar, then the investor will receive $0.75 million (7.5 million rand/10 rand per dollar). The NPV is

$$\frac{\$0.75\ \text{million}}{1.05} - \$1\ \text{million} \cong -\$285\ 571$$

Without hedging, the investor may profit ($98 901) or may lose ($285 714) if there are changes in the foreign currency exchange rate.

3. The investor cannot know the future exchange rate. Moreover, the investor does not want to take the risk associated with macroeconomic factors such as international trade and government monetary policy, which could render this deal unprofitable (or more profitable). Therefore, the investor can hedge the risk by buying a forward contract to sell rand at a predetermined price six months from now.

Suppose the investor buys a contract to sell 7.5 million rand at 7.05 rand per dollar six months from now. The investor will receive about $1 063 830 (7.5 million rand/7.05 rand per dollar). The NPV is

$$\frac{\$1\ 063\ 830}{1.05} - \$1\ \text{million} \cong \$13\ 171$$

If the investor uses a forward contract, he or she eliminates foreign currency risk.

The preceding practice box demonstrates how an investor can completely eliminate foreign exchange risk by using forward contracts. Who is taking this risk? An investor buys a forward contract from a bank. Does this mean that the bank is exposed to the risk? No, it does not; the bank is operating as a mediator. It finds another customer (say, a South African firm that exports to the US on credit) who wishes to sell dollars six months from now. Both sides eliminate risk through the transaction. This risk reduction is in effect as long as neither of the parties defaults. The exchange rate is set in such a way that no initial payment has to be made (except for some fees to the bank).

Forward contracts have a major deficiency. If prices change sharply, then one party has a strong incentive to default. For example, suppose Cone Mills has a forward contract to buy cotton from Cotton Corporation in July at 76.4 cents per pound. Suppose the current price of cotton is 75 cents per pound, but it falls in July to 40 cents per pound. Cone Mills can buy cotton in July at 40 cents in the market, but it is committed to pay 76.4 cents per pound to Cotton Corporation. Cone Mills has a strong incentive to default – to walk away from this

| Exhibit 19.2 | Payoff diagrams for a forward contract |

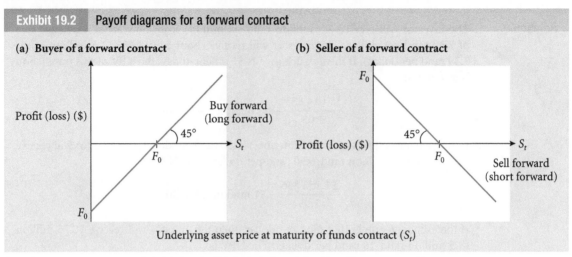

(a) **Buyer of a forward contract**

(b) **Seller of a forward contract**

Underlying asset price at maturity of funds contract (S_t)

Source: From *Introduction to Investments*, 2nd edn, by Levy. © 1999. Reprinted with permission of South-Western, a division of Thomson Learning: www.thomsonrights.com. Fax 800 730-2215.

transaction. Forward transactions require firms and institutions of high creditworthiness or that are willing to post collateral to mitigate the default risk.

Forwards are an OTC instrument, i.e. the contracts aren't listed on an exchange. The contracts are not standardised, and numerous kinds of conditions can be found. For example, a contract may stipulate that the underlying asset actually changes hands, but it may also say that the parties simply pay the difference between the delivery price and the market price in cash, leaving it to the buyer as to whether they actually want to buy the underlying assets in the market at that time. This is called cash settlement.

Forwards have a rather simple payoff structure: gains and losses are symmetric and move one for one with the price on the spot market. However, trading strategies can become quite complicated, especially when they involve many different derivatives, some with more complicated payoff structures. Therefore, it is convenient to construct a payoff diagram. The value of the underlying asset (S_t) is on the horizontal axis and the payoff (profit or loss, excluding elements that are investor-specific, such as taxes and transaction costs) is on the vertical axis. In this case, all payoffs are paid and received at maturity; the payoff diagrams for buying and selling forward contracts and holding them to maturity are represented by Exhibit 19.2.[6] Here we see why forwards are called *linear* instruments: the relation between the underlying asset and the payoff is linear throughout the domain of prices for the underlying assets. When a forward contract matures, it will be worth the price of the underlying asset minus the delivery price. A forward contract that expires immediately is the same as a spot contract at that date. Exhibit 19.2a shows that a trader profits or loses from buying futures when the underlying asset price changes to some value other than F_0, where F_0 is the forward price (the delivery price at the moment the contract was bought). The gain or loss equals the payoff of owning the underlying asset. (The losses are limited by the underlying asset price, which, at its worst, can drop to zero.)

Suppose one buys a forward contract on corn for F_0 = $2.07 per bushel (Exhibit 19.3a). If at maturity the spot corn price (S_t) is exactly $2.07 per bushel, then the investor will not profit or lose from the trade. Suppose, however, that the spot price at maturity is S_t = $2.17 per

---

[6] In this payoff diagram, we depict the payoff at maturity as a function of the value of the underlying asset at maturity. There is a difference between the payoff at maturity and the present value of this payoff because money has time value.

			Part a	Part b
	Price of the forward contract (F_0)	Spot price at maturity (S_t)	Buyer's payoff (loss)	Seller's payoff (loss)
1	2.07	2.07	0	0
2	2.07	2.17	2.17 − 2.07 = 0.10	2.07 − 2.17 = −0.10
3	2.07	1.97	1.97 − 2.07 = −0.10	2.07 − 1.97 = 0.10

Exhibit 19.3 Payoffs for forward contracts ($ per bushel)

bushel. Then, one can buy the corn for F_0 = $2.07 per bushel with the forward contract and sell it for S_t = $2.17 per bushel in the spot market, profiting $0.10 per bushel. Hence, in this case, for every dollar increase in the spot price at maturity, there is an additional dollar profit per bushel on the forward contract. In the same way, if the spot price is $1.97 at maturity and one has an obligation to buy at $2.07, he or she buys it for $2.07, sells for $1.97, and loses $0.10 per bushel. Therefore, the line in Exhibit 19.2 is at a 45-degree angle, passing through point $F_0 = S_t$, where neither loss nor profit occurs. Since the most that can be lost is F_0 – when S_T drops to zero – the line stops at the intersection with the vertical axis.

A similar example illustrates the dollar profits and losses from selling a forward contract. Suppose one sells a forward contract on corn for F_0 = $2.07 per bushel; there will be no profit or loss on the trade if the spot price at maturity equals $2.07 per bushel. If S_t = $2.17 per bushel, then the seller still has to fulfil his or her obligation and sell for the agreed price of $2.07 per bushel and bear losses of $0.10 per bushel. Similarly, if the spot price is S_t = $1.97 at maturity, one sells for F_0 = $2.07 with the forward contract and buys for S_t = $1.97, and thus the gain is $0.10 per bushel.

Therefore, the line has a negative 45-degree angle, passing through the point $F_0 = S_t$. Note that the loss of a forward contract seller is theoretically unlimited. The payoff diagram is similar to short-selling stock (see Exhibits 19.2b and 19.3).

19.3   Swaps

A swap is an agreement between two counterparties (the two sides of a swap) to exchange payments based on the value of one asset in exchange for payments based on the value of another asset. A simple example would be two bondholders – one holding a floating-rate bond and the other holding a fixed-rate bond – who agree to exchange coupon payments over the term of the bonds. This agreement can be seen equivalently as a bundle of long-term forward contracts – each payment on a coupon date is the result of a forward on the interest rate. If the floating rate differs form the forward rate (now called the swap rate), then one party pays the other the difference, as would be done with cash-settled forwards.

The four major types of swaps are interest-rate swaps, credit swaps, currency swaps and commodity swaps. Most swaps are cash-settled. For interest-rate swaps, the exchange of cash payments is based on the level of interest rates. Credit swaps base payments on whether defaults on loans or bonds occur. For currency swaps, the exchange of cash payments depends on the level of foreign exchange rates. For commodity swaps, the exchange of cash payments is based on the level of commodity prices.

The market for swaps is entirely over the counter, and one won't read quotes or volumes in financial pages of a newspaper. Nevertheless, the activity is enormous: by the end of 2002, close to a $100 trillion in notional principal was outstanding in currency and interest-rate swaps.[7] (Notional principal forms the basis on which the interest payments are calculated.) This was about 400 times the amount outstanding 15 years earlier. Furthermore, swaps are now available in other areas (ranging from energy products to equities) as well.

19.3.1 Interest-rate swaps

In an interest-rate swap, the counterparties exchange interest payments that depend on specified interest rates. For example, one counterparty typically exchanges fixed-rate interest payments for floating-rate interest payments. This particular swap is called a fixed-for-floating swap (or a plain vanilla swap). The two parties in a fixed-for-floating swap are the receive fixed counterparty and the receive floating counterparty. The receive fixed counterparty receives payments based on the fixed rate and makes payments based on the floating rate. The receive floating counterparty receives payments based on the floating rate and makes payments based on the fixed rate. Hence, when the floating rate exceeds the fixed rate, the receive fixed counterparty has to pay. When the fixed rate exceeds the floating rate, the receive fixed counterparty receives a payment. The currency of both payments is the same.

The actual sum that is exchanged can be computed as follows:[8]

Payment (receipt) = Payment based on the floating rate − Payment based on the fixed rate

$$= r_{fl}(NP)(t/360) - r_{fx}(NP)(t/360)$$

where r_{fl} denotes the floating rate (which typically is the London interbank offer rate; LIBOR), r_{fx} denotes the fixed rate, t is the number of days during which interest accrues (for example, for a semiannual paying swap, $t = 180$), and NP is the notional principal (the amount on which the dollar interest calculation is made, which is the same for both parties). For example, if the investor had a $1000 loan at 5%, then his or her annual interest payment would be $50, or $0.05 \times \$1000$. With swap payments, the notional principal is equivalent to the loan amount. We can rearrange the above expression as

$$\text{Payment (receipt)} = (r_{fl} - r_{fx})(NP)(t/360)$$

For example, a three-year LIBOR-based swap will have six future payments (one at the end of each semiannual period). If the fixed rate is 7% and the notional principal is $1 000 000, then the future cash flows will depend on the difference between 7% and the current LIBOR rate. If after six months the LIBOR rate is 8%, then the receive fixed counterparty must pay the receive floating counterparty $5000 [$5000 = (0.08 − 0.07)$1 000 000(180/360)]. An interest-rate swap is therefore equivalent to a package of forward contracts on the floating interest rate – each payment is equal to the payment on the expiration day that would result from a forward where the fixed interest rate serves as the forward rate. A swap contract lasts much longer than a typical forward, so swaps normally are used to hedge multiple exposures over a longer time period. Given the fact that swaps are rarely marked to market (see Section 19.4), the credit risk can be substantial. However, no principal is exchanged and payments are normally netted out – if party A owes party B $500 000, and party B owes

---

[7] Based on International Swap Dealers Association Survey, second half 2002.
[8] LIBOR is based on a 360-day year and an actual day count, which we assume here is 180 days. For credit-risk reasons, only the net cash flows are exchanged, rather than the receive fixed counterparty's paying 8% and the receive floating counterparty's paying 7%.

party A \$480 000, then only \$20 000 is transferred. The enormous turnover of the swap markets is therefore a rather poor indicator of the actual risks taken by participants.

Often, a financial intermediary – for instance, a bank – is involved in finding a counterparty. Obtaining a large swap without professional assistance is cumbersome and costly, especially because each party has to assess the other's default risk. The solution to this problem is that a bank acts as counterparty for both companies (for a fee of a few basis points). In that case, it's the creditworthiness of the bank that matters instead of the default risk of the original counterparty. Furthermore, a counterparty might not be available immediately. The bank will then agree to the swap and find a counterparty later on; this is known as warehousing swaps. Needless to say, banks will have to monitor their risks carefully. If they charge the wrong rates, they might never find a counterparty. Also, if a counterparty that is expected to pay more than it receives over the remainder of the swap defaults, the value is lost. If the situation is reversed (one has a liability towards a distressed company), then that company is likely to sell its rights under the swap agreement to obtain some cash. In other words, if default occurs, then it is very unlikely to be beneficial, but one stands a good chance of losing money.

Why are interest-rate swaps profitable for both parties? The answer is, again, credit risk. Suppose company A wants to borrow at a floating rate. Its bank gives the following quotes, based on A's credit risk: 7.20% fixed or six-month LIBOR + 35 basis points. (Recall that a basis point is 1/100 of a per cent, or a fraction of 0.0001; thus, 35 basis points = 0.35%.) Company B wants to borrow at a fixed rate. It is offered 8.50% fixed or LIBOR + 130 basis points floating. B's default risk is apparently greater than A's, but B still has a comparative advantage in borrowing at floating rates. B has to pay 1.30% extra if it takes a fixed loan, but only 0.95% more than A if it takes out a floating loan. They could agree to the following swap (see Exhibit 19.4):[9]

1. A borrows at the fixed rate (7.20%) but agrees to pay a floating interest of LIBOR + 0.95% to B. In exchange, A receives a fixed interest of 8.00% from B, which cancels the payments to the bank and some of the payments to B. In total, it has to pay LIBOR + 0.15% floating to others (the bank and B), which is 0.20% better than the bank's offer.
2. Now look at B. It pays LIBOR + 1.30% to the bank. But it receives LIBOR + 0.95% from A, so that leaves just 0.35%. It also has to pay 8.00% to A. In the end, it pays a fixed interest of 8.35% to external parties, regardless of LIBOR, or 0.15 % less than the initial offer.

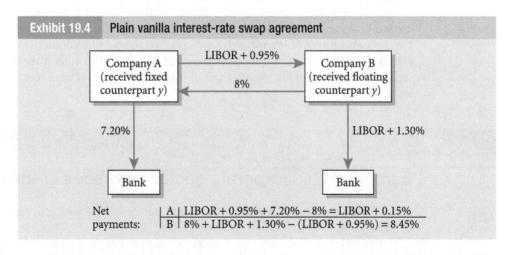

Exhibit 19.4   Plain vanilla interest-rate swap agreement

| Net | A | LIBOR + 0.95% + 7.20% − 8% = LIBOR + 0.15% |
| payments: | B | 8% + LIBOR + 1.30% − (LIBOR + 0.95%) = 8.45% |

---

[9] For ease of exposition, we assume that no financial intermediary is involved. If it was, then the total advantage of 35 basis points (20 + 15 in the example above) would be split between the three parties: A, B and the bank.

In this case, both companies reduce their funding costs. Apparently, there seems to be a free lunch for both companies. This would be the case if the differences in default premiums result from a debt market that isn't in equilibrium; for example, the default premium in the floating-rate market could be 'too low' or the fixed-rate market 'too high' due to a mismatch between demand and supply. However, another explanation is more credible: the difference in default premium simply may reflect differences in credit risk rather than market disequilibrium. Floating-rate contracts are reviewed more often, thereby reducing credit risk because the lender can adjust the conditions more often. So, company B's credit risk is higher, but the difference is smaller for floating-rate loans. Differing cash-flow patterns – profit from other activities might also have a correlation with the interest rate – might also be the basis for different conditions. So, we cannot conclude that this advantage must be due to a mispricing in the credit markets.

19.3.2 Credit swaps

A credit swap is designed to exchange default risk. For example, a bank might want to limit its exposure to a certain sector of the economy (fearing that its clients might default simultaneously) but to continue to provide its customers operating in that sector with the loans they request. This can be done by entering into a credit-swap agreement with a counterparty, who then agrees to reimburse any losses on the loans covered by the swap due to default, in exchange for a similar reimbursement for defaults on other loans owned by the counterparty, or a set of fixed payments. The reimbursement takes place only after a default.

Even if both sides exchange obligations to reimburse each other, they may profit because the probability of default has a lower correlation with their existing portfolios. Also, the counterparty need not be another bank: a non-bank investor could try to make money from assuming credit risk at a favourable price, treating the swaps as part of his or her investment portfolio.

There are two categories of credit swaps: default swaps, in which only default (= credit) risk is exchanged, and total return swaps, which combine interest-rate swaps and default swaps: both the risk of changing interest rates and default are exchanged. If a total return swap involves exchanging risks for fixed payments, then the deal will absorb all risk relating to that asset and replace it with counterparty risk (the risk that the counterparty will fail to honour its obligations). Sometimes, a default swap is combined with a bond: the investor seeking protection against default on a loan sells a new bond to the counterparty, receiving the notational principal immediately, and only has to redeem the bond to the extent that the loan is recovered. This construction is known as a credit-linked note. It should be noted that credit swaps are useful for various types of investors, as Connecting Theory to Practice 19.1 illustrates.

→ Connecting Theory to Practice 19.1

Euro markets: corporate sector embraces credit swaps

Banks are still the main users of credit derivatives but they are beginning to appeal to institutional investors.

In the past credit derivatives have been perceived purely as the domain of banks, which are the products' main users, hedging their considerable credit risks through impenetrable contracts with each other.

But these products are being slowly demystified and beginning to appeal to non-bank investors in Europe, keen to protect themselves against corporate event risk . . .

The growth of the corporate bond market in Europe has given credit default swaps a starring role. The heady pace of European M&A activity has often harmed the credit quality of the companies involved, and has led to a higher number of rating downgrades.

Credit default swaps allow investors to transfer the credit risk from a transaction to a third party, in return for a premium. Investors effectively buy protection against their counterparty defaulting on a payment, as the third party will cover the losses.

Unusually in the capital markets, the credit derivatives business is more developed in Europe than it is in the US. This is a reflection of the less developed state of the corporate bond market, and also the historical strength of Europe's asset swap market.

The European corporate bond market is still relatively undiversified and illiquid, although growing rapidly in size. Banks and financial institutions make up more than two-thirds of the corporate bond market, which does not reflect the full range of European companies. Credit default swaps can be created for any borrower, including those in the loan market . . .

As credit swaps guard against companies going bankrupt, one obvious use is in the growing European high-yield, or junk bond, market where default is more likely. However, most of the corporates in the market are investment grade. While only a fraction of contracts will end in default, the swaps also offer protection against less dramatic credit deterioration.

'Credit risk is everywhere, and credit swaps enable institutions to manage that credit risk efficiently,' says Tim Frost, head of credit derivative trading at J.P. Morgan. Banks are still the main users of credit derivatives but they are beginning to appeal to institutional investors, including insurance companies.

Credit swaps also allow investors to speculate on movements in the credit market, as they focus solely on a company's credit quality. The product removes the influence of movements in interest rates, swap spreads and currencies, the factors most commonly affecting values in the bond market.

Already this year several factors have moved the market forward and increased its accessibility to a wider pool of investors. This week saw the establishment of Creditex, an electronic trading platform for credit default swaps. Creditex hopes to enhance the transparency and liquidity of the market by making trading easier and providing a database of market information.

Last week, J.P. Morgan launched an index for credit default swaps in Europe, called the European Credit Swap Index (ESCI), containing 98 leading corporate names from the Eurotop 100 and the Eurostoxx 50. Two-thirds of the index are not-banks, but have an average rating of A/AA-. As the bond market tends to reflect movements in the swap rate . . . the index aims to track only changes in credit quality.

Source: R. Bream, 'Euro Markets: Corporate Sector Embraces Credit Swaps', *Financial Times*, 9 March 2000.

→ **Making the connection**

The market for credit risk has developed rapidly over the past few years. One of the reasons for these developments is the growing awareness that credit risk, like any other risk, can be traded and used for all four basic derivative strategies. Furthermore, credit risk is relevant for every investor in assets issued by corporations, and not just the banks that provide loans and underwrite bonds. The credit swap has proven to be the instrument of choice to trade credit risk.

19.3.3 Currency swaps

A currency swap involves the exchange of different currencies. The first currency swap occurred in August 1981, between IBM and the World Bank. The details of a currency swap are similar to those of an interest-rate swap, except that instead of interest payments, the notional amount is transferred and that these future exchanges are in different currencies.

For example, suppose British Petroleum (BP) expects to receive $900 000 from US sales each quarter for the next six years. BP would like to hedge this foreign exchange exposure, but exchange-traded futures contracts do not extend six years into the future. BP might find a company, such as PepsiCo (PC), that has UK sales and is headquartered in the USA. PepsiCo would like to convert its UK pounds into US dollars. A currency swap could hedge the foreign exchange risk for both parties. Specifically, based on current foreign exchange market conditions, a currency swap could be developed in which BP agrees to swap with PC $900 000 for £600 000 each quarter over the next six years. Thus, both BP and PC have locked in an exchange rate of $1.5/£ ($900 000/£600 000).

19.3.4 Commodity swaps

A commodity swap requires the exchange of cash based on the value of a specific commodity at specified points in the future. For example, a three-year crude-oil swap with quarterly payments would have 12 (four quarters × three years) cash exchanges. If the contract price in the swap for crude oil was $25 per barrel, then the cash exchange would be the difference between the current price of crude oil and $25. If crude oil was selling for $30 per barrel at a quarterly payment, then one counterparty would receive $5 ($30 − $25) per barrel from the other counterparty.

Another example is the jet-fuel price risk that airlines face. When jet-fuel prices rise, there is a lag in the airline's ability to pass this higher cost on to passengers in the form of higher ticket prices. Hence, airlines need a security that will be useful in managing future jet-fuel purchases. Commodity swaps fulfil this need. Airlines may use jet-fuel swaps to lock in their future purchase price of fuel, thus providing stability to their costs. Jet-fuel suppliers like commodity swaps because these swaps allow them to lock in a fixed sales price.

19.4 Futures contracts

Like a forward contract or a swap, a futures contract is a derivative security that can be used for all four basic derivatives strategies (hedging, speculation, arbitrage and diversification). All these contracts commit buyer and seller to exchange goods (or a variable amount of money) for an agreed amount of cash at some future date and at a predetermined price or rate.[10]

Futures contracts differ from forwards and swaps in several respects: they are traded on financial exchanges and have standardised conditions, which reduce the costs of these derivatives. This feature makes them more convenient for arbitrage and diversification. Moreover, unlike swaps or forwards, futures are typically marked to market and, hence, the cash-flow pattern is different. This procedure results in futures having less credit risk than forward or

---

[10] Note that the amount of cash to be paid varies in the case of some swaps, but the formula that determines the amount is always set in advance.

swap contracts. Further, futures contracts involve only one future transaction (as do forwards), whereas swaps typically have several future transactions. Finally, futures contracts are typically short-term and offer more flexibility in their delivery date, yet delivery of the underlying is uncommon; nearly all contracts cease to exist (are "closed out") before delivery becomes an issue or are settled in cash.

Futures contracts exist on a wide variety of items: agricultural products (corn, oats, wheat, livestock and meat, coffee, orange juice, cotton and sugar), metals and petroleum (gold, silver and crude oil) and financial assets (all major floating currencies, Treasury bonds and various stock indexes). Many financial institutions find interest-rate futures useful in managing their exposure to changes in interest rates. Multinational corporations and international investors use currency futures to manage their exposure to changes in foreign exchange rates. Equity investors find stock-index futures useful when managing the systematic risk of their portfolios.

Practice box

Problem

The settle price for the December natural-gas futures contract is $2.295. Suppose a firm that purchases 100 000 MMBtu of natural gas monthly buys ten December futures contracts (each for 10 000 MMBtu of natural gas.) Calculate the gains or losses for the firm if the futures price rises or falls by 20%.

Solution

The settle price for the December natural-gas futures contracts is

$$F_{\text{Dec}} = 2.295$$

If the futures price rises by 20%, then the price will be $1.2 \times \$2.295 = \$2.754$. If the futures price falls by 20%, then the price will be $0.8 \times \$2.295 = \$1.836$. Hence, if a firm purchases ten contracts at 10 000 units each, it profits as follows:

$$\text{Futures profit on price rise} = 10 \times 10\ 000(\$2.754 - \$2.295) = \$45\ 900$$

This profit would offset losses on the increased purchase price of natural gas. However, if the price falls, then the futures contract will experience losses of

$$\text{Futures loss on price fall} = 10 \times 10\ 000(\$1.836 - \$2.295) = -\$45\ 900$$

This loss in the futures market could offset gains that would be experienced in the spot market from falling prices. Thus, using futures contracts can reduce volatility. Or, a firm or investor might want to take a bet on the natural-gas price and take a profit or loss (in this case, the buyer would want to make sure that delivery won't take place). Arbitrage or even portfolio-diversification strategies are also possible.

19.4.1 Characteristics of futures contracts

Since there is an organised market, futures contracts are more liquid than forward contracts; buyers of futures contracts can 'net out' their position by selling a similar futures contract. For example, a buyer who has a July contract to buy cotton and a July contract to sell the same amount of cotton does not bear any risk.

The second difference between forward and futures contracts relates to delivery dates. Forward contracts specify precise delivery dates. With many futures contracts, the seller can choose any delivery date during the specified delivery month. If the seller of a July cotton futures contract notifies the exchange clearing house that he or she will deliver the cotton on July 15, then the clearing house notifies one of the contract buyers to be ready to receive the cotton in a few days. (The clearing house selects one of the many July buyers at random.) Choosing the delivery date during the delivery month gives the seller some flexibility. Most futures contracts are not settled by the delivery of the underlying asset. The settlement is done either for cash or by an offsetting trade (this is explained in detail in Section 19.4.2).

The most important characteristics, however, are marking to market and margin requirements.

Marking to market

With forward contracts, one party delivers the commodity and the other pays cash for it on the delivery date, and only then. Futures contracts, in contrast, are marked to market. With a marked-to-market cash settlement, cash flows in and out (between buyer and seller) on a daily basis whenever there are changes in the futures contract prices, as if the future was to be closed out and rewritten at the new price every day. As will be explained later, this marked-to-market daily cash settlement drastically reduces the risk of default. It was noted earlier that forward contracts should be conducted between parties with high creditworthiness. In contrast, futures contracts can be executed between strangers, because the incentive to default is relatively small. This feature makes futures contracts a better financial tool.

Exhibit 19.5 shows the cash flows to the buyer and the seller of a futures contract. Suppose that on 26 November Cone Mills buys a July futures contract (that is, for delivery July next

Exhibit 19.5	Cash flows to buyer and seller of cotton futures contracts: marked-to-market daily cash settlements			
Closing price (cents/pound)	24 November 90.75	1 March 93.75	1 May 90.25	16 July 90.25
Buyer	Buyer purchases cotton futures contracts at 90.75 cents per pound	Buyer receives 3 cents per pound from the clearing house within one business day	Buyer must pay the clearing house 3.50 cents per pound within one business day	Buyer pays 90.25 cents per pound and receives the cotton
Seller	Seller sells futures contracts at 90.75 cents per pound	Seller pays the clearing house 3 cents per pound within one business day	Seller receives from the clearing house 3.50 cents per pound within one business day	Seller receives 90.25 cents per pound of cotton and delivers the cotton to the buyer within one business day
Buyer's cash flow per 15 000-pound contract		3 cents per pound for 15 000 pounds = $450	3.50 cents per pound for 15 000 pounds = −$525	−90.25 cents per pound for 15 000 pounds = −$13 537.5
Seller's cash flow per 15 000-pound contract		−$450	$525	$13 537.5

Source: From *Introduction to Investments*, 2nd edn, by Levy. © 1999. Reprinted with permission of South-Western, a division of Thomson Learning: www.thomsonrights.com. Fax 800 730-2215.

year) at 90.75 cents per pound. Had it been a forward contract, then on 16 July the buyer would pay $13 612.5 (90.75 cents per pound × 15 000 pounds) per contract. Instead, with a futures contract, cash flows are involved each time the price changes. For simplicity, assume the price changes only twice. (In reality, the price is likely to change daily, and the same technique for determining the cash flow would be used on a daily basis.) Suppose that on 1 March the price rises to 93.75 cents. Being committed to sell at a lower, fixed price, the seller loses from such an increase. He or she must pay 3 cents per pound to a clearing house, which, in turn, pays the sum to the buyer. Then, on 1 May the price drops to 90.25 cents; the buyer pays the clearing house 3.50 cents per pound, which is passed on to the seller. Assuming no further changes in price, the buyer pays the seller 90.25 cents per pound on 16 July and the seller delivers the cotton. The total cash flow paid by the buyer for all dates is $13 612.50 ($450 − $525 − $13 537.50). This amount is exactly what the buyer would have paid in a forward contract. Similarly, the seller receives $13 612.50, just as much as in a forward contract.

However, there are two differences between the cash flows of forward and futures contracts. The first difference is that in futures contracts, the interim cash flows cannot be ignored, and the present value of interim cash flows in a futures contract may be different from the present value of cash flows in a forward contract. The more important difference is that the incentive to default is lower with futures contracts, because daily losses are not very large. With forward contracts, all losses are accumulated to one payment on the delivery date, producing a stronger incentive to default. As a consequence, the payoff diagram of a future is equal to that of a forward if we ignore the time value of money, but it becomes rather complicated if we want to take interest into account.

Margin and return

Recall from Chapter 3 that initial and maintenance margins are required for investors who borrow money to purchase stock. In the same way, initial and maintenance margins are required for both buyers and sellers of futures contracts. The actual margin requirements change frequently, but they are usually significantly lower than margins for stocks.

Exhibit 19.5 presents the marked-to-market cash flows between the buyer and the seller. On top of these cash flows, each trader establishes a margin account, typically of 5–10% of the contract value, that is paid to the clearing house. The margin is a security account consisting of near-cash securities to ensure that traders are able to satisfy their obligations under futures contracts. Since both parties are exposed to possible losses, both must post a margin. However, because the margin is in terms of interest-earnings securities, it does not impose a substantial cost on the traders.

Exactly how do margin requirements work? The initial margin is money that parties with a (possible) obligation send to the clearing house when they initially sell the futures. The maintenance margin is the dollar amount that must be kept with the clearing house throughout the term of the contract. If the amount of margin kept with the clearinghouse (which changes as asset prices change because of marking-to-market) falls below the maintenance margin, the party has to make an additional deposit so that the total is again equal to or exceeds the maintenance margin. For example, investors who buy futures contracts must place the initial margin with the clearing house. If prices move in the investors' favour, then the gains are received daily and some funds can be withdrawn from the margin account. However, if prices fall, then the investor does not have to post more margin until the maintenance margin level is reached.

Exhibit 19.6 illustrates an example of margin cash flow. On day 1, the futures price experiences a modest decline. There are no cash flows between the broker and the client. On day 4, the maintenance margin is hit, so the broker sends a margin call to the client to post additional monies (the client is a buyer) to bring the value of the account back to the initial margin level. On day 5, there is a gain, which the client can withdraw from the account immediately.

| Exhibit 19.6 | Margin cash flow over time |

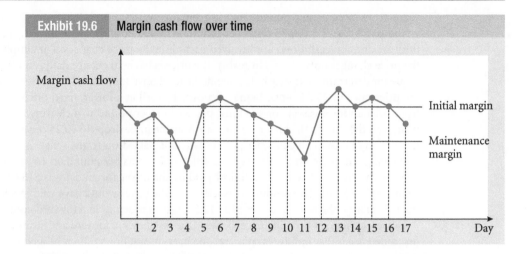

| Exhibit 19.7 | Calculating margins for a short position in one S&P 500 futures contract[a] |

Day	Futures price	Daily gain (loss) ($)	Cumulative gain (loss) ($)	Margin account balance ($)	Margin call ($)
	1124.5			14 000	
1 July	1125.5	(500)[b]	(500)	13 500	
2 July	1123.5	1000	500[c]	14 500[d]	
3 July	1126.5	(1500)	(1000)	13 000	
7 July	1129.5	(1500)	(2500)	11 500	2500
8 July	1128.5	500	(2000)	14 500	
9 July	1124.5	2000	0	16 500	

[a] The initial margin is $14 000 and the maintenance margin is $12 000. Each S&P 500 futures contract is for 500 times the index. The contract is entered on 1 July at 1124.5 and closed on 9 July at 1124.5.
[b] 500 = 500(1125.5 − 1124.5).
[c] 500 = (500) + 1000.
[d] The investor could withdraw $500, but we assume there was no withdrawal.

Exhibit 19.7 shows how the margin account changed over a period of six trading days. For simplicity, assume that this trader sold one S&P 500 futures contract at $1124.5 on the morning of 1 July and that the initial margin is $14 000 and the maintenance margin is $12 000. Each S&P 500 futures contract is cash-settled based on 500 times the index. By the end of the first day, the S&P 500 rises by 1 point, which results in a $500 loss. Recall that the investor is short one futures contract that pays at 500 times the index, and a 1 point change in the index results in $5040 change in payoff. The $500 loss reduces the margin balance to $13 500, but the investor doesn't receive a margin call, because the margin balance is still above maintenance level. When the price rises to $1129.50 on 7 July, the cumulative losses have now reduced the margin account so it is below the maintenance margin of $12 000. In this case, a margin call of $2500 is issued to restore the account balance to $14 000. In this simple case, the investor closes the futures position at exactly the original trade price for a net gain of zero. The margin account on 9 July is $2500 higher than it was at the time of the initial investment because of the margin call.

Margin requirements for futures contracts are the subject of controversy. Stock traders have to post a margin of at least 50%, whereas futures traders in the S&P 500 index have to post a margin at only approximately 5–10%. Thus, with the same investment, investors can take a larger speculative position with futures contracts than with the stocks themselves. This ability to take more speculative positions with futures contracts has concerned some people, because the high leverage (in this case, the relatively low amount of own money invested) in futures contracts may induce sharp changes[11] in the futures prices. Actually, some people blame the 1987 stock market crash on the high leverage in this market.

The effects of leverage on returns are profound and are caused by different margin requirements. Since margin requirements on futures contracts are lower than they are for stocks, investors are allowed to take larger positions with the same amount of margin (thus with the same investment). Consider the following example. Suppose the S&P 500 index is at 1134.67, and the nearest-maturity S&P 500 futures contract is trading at 1134.20. Also suppose the futures margin is 5% of the contract and the security margin is 50%. One unit of the S&P 500 futures contract would require a margin deposit of $56.71 ($0.05 \times 1134.20$), and one unit of the S&P 500 index contract would require $567.34 ($0.50 \times 1134.67$). Now, suppose that *both* markets rise by 10%; hence, the futures contract is at $1247.62 ($1.1 \times 1134.20$) and the S&P 500 index is at 1248.14 (1.1×1134.67). The rate of return on the invested sum in the futures contract (the margin) is

$$R_{Futures} = \text{profit/investment} = (1247.62 - 1134.20)/56.71 = 200\%$$

The rate of return on the margin for the S&P 500 is[12]

$$R_{S\&P\ 500} = \text{profit/investment} = (1248.14 - 1134.67)/567.34 = 20\%$$

Now, suppose that both markets fall by 15%; hence, the futures contract is at 964.07 (0.85×1134.20) and the S&P 500 index is at 964.47 (0.85×1134.67). In this case, the rate of return on the futures contract is

$$R_{Futures} = (964.07 - 1134.20)/56.71 = -300\%$$

and the rate of return on the S&P 500 is

$$R_{S\&P\ 500} = (964.47 - 934.67)/567.34 = -30\%$$

Clearly, the highly leveraged trading in futures contracts increases the volatility of returns on investments. In this example, the rates of return are magnified by a factor of ten. This might cause different trading patterns, because investors might panic in the face of a 150% loss, while a 15% loss has presumably less of an impact (a 150% loss also means that one has to find additional capital to meet one's obligations, which increases default risk).

There is a reason why futures margins are different from stock margins. Recall that the margin requirement for a stock is essentially a down payment for a security to be owned. The investor who trades on margin has all the rights and privileges of an outright owner. This is not true with futures contracts. When a stock is purchased, the new owner assumes control over the voting rights, whereas with futures contracts only price risk is transferred. Even more

---

[11] This mechanism works under the assumption that investors invest the same amount of money, regardless of the margin requirements. So, if one can buy 100 contracts instead of ten, then the changes in demand and, hence, prices will be much larger.

[12] Investors can buy the S&P index. Securities based on the S&P 500 trade on the AMEX and are known as SPDRS (spiders) (ticket symbol SPY), with a volume of around 40 million contracts a day. Also see section 4.4.2.

important, because of daily marking to the market, the need for collateral on futures contracts is minimised. A futures margin is just a performance bond that ensures that both parties will fulfil their obligations.

Practice box

Problem   Suppose a futures contract on palladium, a platinum alloy used as a catalyst and in dental products, is trading at $180 per troy ounce, and each contract is for 100 troy ounces. The margin requirement is $1350 per contract, and the spot market price is $190. Compute the rate of return both on buying one futures contract and on a cash purchase of 100 troy ounces if palladium rises to $216 per troy ounce or falls to $144 per troy ounce at the expiration of the futures contract.

Solution   Recall that the rate of return is profit divided by investment. For the futures contract, then,

$$R_{Futures} = 100(\$216 - \$180)/\$1350 = 267\%, \quad \text{i.e.} \quad \text{price goes up}$$

$$R_{Futures} = 100(\$144 - \$180)/\$1350 = -267\%, \quad \text{i.e.} \quad \text{price goes down}$$

For the cash purchase, note that the price at the expiration of the futures contract must be equivalent to the price in the spot market. A futures contract that will expire immediately is the same as a spot market purchase. Therefore,

$$R_{Cash} = 100(\$216 - \$190)/\$19\,000 = 13.7\%, \quad \text{i.e.} \quad \text{price goes up}$$

$$R_{Cash} = 100(\$144 - \$190)/\$19\,000 = -24.2\%, \quad \text{i.e.} \quad \text{price goes down}$$

where $\$19\,000 = 100 \times \$190$.

Thus, futures returns are much more volatile than spot market purchases, because futures contracts allow for highly leveraged transactions.

Drawbacks

The drawbacks of futures are primarily their qualities as a hedging instrument. As described in Section 19.1, futures do poorly in terms of hedging if there is quantity risk as well. Continuing the earlier example, Cone Mills has hedged its risk against an increase in the price of cotton by buying a futures contract at 90.75 cents per pound. But what happens if the price of a pound of cotton falls to 40 cents? Cone Mills is locked into this transaction and must pay 90.75 cents per pound.[13] Is there a way for Cone Mills to hedge possible increases in the cotton price while also enjoying the lower price of cotton if the price falls? As will be shown later on, options can provide Cone Mills a hedge against price increases and a benefit if the price falls. However, because there are no free lunches in the market, these options cost money.

---

[13] And to prove that corporate finance can be complicated, the competitors of Cone Mills who haven't hedged can buy their cotton much cheaper, lowering their costs. Cone Mills might therefore also face problems when selling its end products.

19.4.2 How to read financial data on futures

Futures contracts are traded on organised exchanges, and their prices are reported daily in the financial media, as shown in Exhibit 19.8.

The major types of commodity futures contracts are (1) precious metals, (2) energy, (3) grains and oilseeds, (4) food and fibre (also known as 'softs') and (5) meat and livestock. Futures on financial underlyings such as currencies, interest rates and stock indexes are also used widely.

The format for reporting futures trading information is to give the opening price at the beginning of the day followed by the high and low for the day (see Exhibit 19.8). Next, the settle price and the change from the previous day are given. For example, the futures contracts for May 2004 delivery of wheat on the LIFFE[14] settled at 118.65 pounds, being 0.85 pounds lower then the day before. During the day, prices reached a high of 120.20 pounds and a low of 118.50 pounds. The settle price is an average of the trading prices that occur during the last few minutes of the day. After this, today's volume is reported; for our example of May wheat, this was 270 contracts (for 100 tonnes each). Open interest, which is reported in the last column, is the number of contracts outstanding. It is half of the total number of positions both purchased and sold (which are the same). Open interest on this contract is 3860.

Settle prices and open interest deserve some more attention. Settle prices are used because a futures contract is marked to market and profits and losses are taken daily. Thus, if you buys a futures contract at $2.07 and the next day it rises to $2.09 (the settle price), then you will receive $0.02 (without having to sell the contract). If the next day the settle price is $2.05, then essentially the contract buyer would have to pay $0.04 ($2.09 − $2.05) to the seller of the futures contract (ignoring possible additional changes in required margin). Due to marking to market, large traders are tempted to drive up prices at the end of the day if they are long on futures contracts. The higher the price at the end of the day, the more profit futures buyers receive. Thus, settle prices were developed to avoid manipulation of futures prices at the end of the day. The settle price is an average of the trading prices occurring during the last few minutes of trading. Trading does not occur at the settle price, but the settle price is usually close to the price of the last trade of the day. Using settle prices rather than the last trade of the day makes it much more difficult to move the price.

Open interest is used as a measure of the liquidity of a futures contract. Higher open interest indicates that more buyers and sellers exist, which typically means a high volume of trading activity. The more trading activity there is, the easier and cheaper it will be to enter into a futures contract.

Most futures traders close their position rather than actually deliver or take delivery of the specified asset. A corn farmer in Kansas, for example, will find it less costly to close his or her Chicago delivery futures contract than to actually deliver corn in Chicago. Observe that the contract with the nearest maturity usually has less open interest. (See the futures contracts with December and January maturities in Exhibit 19.8; energy is the only exception because of its seasonal demand.) This confirms the previous statement that most futures investors close or offset their positions rather than hold them to maturity. Futures traders offset their positions when they take an opposite position from the position held. For example, suppose an investor purchased ten contracts of March 2004 wheat on the Chicago Board of Trade (CBT). The investor can offset this position by selling ten contracts of March 2004 wheat on the CBT. The ten contracts sold will automatically negate the ten contracts initially purchased.

---

[14] London International Financial Futures and Options Exchange.

Exhibit 19.8　Futures prices for 2 December 2003　　　**FT**

BASE METALS

LONDON METAL EXCHANGE

$/tonne	Cash Official	3 Mth Official	Kerb PM 3 Mth close	Day's High/Low (3 Mth)	Open interest (Lots)	Turnover (Lots)
Aluminium	1542.5–43	1549.5–50	1563–64	1564/1545	416,787	93,937
Alum Alloy	1420–25	1440–45	1443–45	1445/1435	8,612	4,165
Amer Alloy	1475–80	1503–5	1505–10	1505/1500	14,011	7
Copper	2120–22	2101–102	2127–28	2129/2088	235,121	48,679
Lead	647–7.5	641–2	647–49	647/636	64,315	11,367
Nickel	12560–65	12510–20	12550–60	12550/12440	46,147	6,705
Tin	5650–55	5590–600	5615–25	5620/5580	22,747	3,764
Zinc	948–9	965.5–6	979–80	980/957	168,515	32,127

Spot: 1.7214 3 mths: 1.7095 6 mths: 1.6985 9 mths; 1.6859. LME AM Official £/$ rate: 1.7214.
LME Closing £/$ rate:
Source: Amalgamated Metal Trading www.amt.co.uk.　　For further information see www.lme.co.uk

■ HIGH GRADE COPPER (COMEX)

	Sett price	Day's change	High	Low	Vol 000s	Open int
Dec	96.95	+1.40	97.30	95.10	2.22	5.77
Jan	97.10	+1.35	96.90	95.15	0.60	4.76
Feb	97.25	+1.30	96.50	95.60	0.02	0.80
Mar	97.40	+1.30	97.70	95.20	0.02	66.4
Total					**20.6**	**90.8**

■ LME WAREHOUSE STOCKS (tonnes)

Aluminium	+1,500	to	1.396m
Aluminium alloy	–140	to	59,000
Copper	–1,900	to	464,950
Lead	–550	to	133,325
Nickel	–48	to	34,344
Zinc	+23,325	to	745,250
Tin	–85	to	14,640

PRECIOUS METALS

■ GOLD COMEX (100 Troy oz; $/troy oz)

	Sett price	Day's chge	High	Low	Vol 000s	0 int 000s
Dec	403.7	+1.0	406.0	399.5	1.66	7.26
Feb	404.6	+0.8	407.0	400.3	51.9	192.8
Total					**56.2**	**276.2**

■ PLATINUM NYMEX (50 Troy oz; $/troy oz)

Jan	779.8	+5.8	780.5	768.5	0.96	8.55
Apr	772.8	+5.8	775.0	771.0	0.23	1.21
Total					**1.2**	**9.8**

■ PALLADIUM NYMEX (100 Troy oz; $/troy oz)

Dec	192.75	+3.75	193.50	190.00	0.43	0.92
Mar	194.60	+3.60	196.00	192.25	0.53	4.92
Total					**1.0**	**6.3**

■ SILVER COMEX (5,000 Troy oz; Cents/troy oz)

Dec	549.6	+5.1	551.0	543.0	0.92	3.26
Mar	552.0	+5.0	554.5	542.5	22.9	84.5
Total					**24.7**	**105.9**

■ LONDON BULLION MARKET

Gold (Troy oz)	$ price	£ equiv	€ equiv
Close	403.00–403.50		
Opening	401.00–401.50		
Morning fix	401.05	233.10	334.91
Afternoon fix	401.35	232.67	333.76
Day's High	405.25–405.75		
Day's Low	399.00–399.50		
Previous close	398.20–398.70		

Loco Ldn Mean Gold Lending Rates (v US$)			
1 mth......	1.09	6 mths......	1.10
3 mths......	1.09	12 mths......	1.25

Gold Leading Rates (v US$)			
1 mth......	0.08	6 mths......	0.18
3 mths......	0.09	12 mths......	0.37

Silver Fix	p/troy oz		US cts equiv.
Spot	317.72		546.00

Silver Lending Rates			
1 mth......	1.00	6 mths......	0.75
3 mths......	0.85	12 mths......	0.70

Source: N M Rothschild

ENERGY

■ CRUDE OIL NYMEX (1,000 barrels. $/barrel)

	Sett price	Day's change	High	Low	Vol 000s	0 int 000s
Jan	30.78	+0.83	30.97	29.80	67.1	157.5
Feb	30.62	+0.82	30.78	29.67	28.8	59.1
Mar	30.22	+0.75	30.33	29.35	9.17	45.5
Apr	29.81	+0.70	29.88	29.06	3.29	28.8
Total					**123.5**	**539.2**

■ CRUDE OIL IPE ($/barrel)

Jan	28.94	+0.69	29.20	28.11	48.1	76.4
Feb	28.75	+0.75	28.88	27.90	18.8	66.6
Mar	28.43	+0.66	28.55	27.70	5.23	22.8
Apr	28.15	+0.66	28.17	27.49	3.12	11.7
Total					**74.9**	**303.5**

■ HEATING OIL NYMEX (42,000 US galls; c/US galls)

Jan	86.26	+2.86	86.90	83.20	18.0	59.2
Feb	86.20	+2.63	86.65	83.40	7.00	22.5
Mar	84.05	+2.18	84.30	82.55	3.70	17.4
Apr	80.50	+1.83	81.00	80.25	0.76	7.71
Total					**32.7**	**136.0**

GRAINS & OIL SEEDS

■ WHEAT LIFFE (100 tonnes; £ per tonne)

	Sett price	Day's chge	High	Low	Vol 000s	0 int 000s
Jan	114.55	–0.95	116.25	114.55	0.05	0.86
Mar	116.65	–0.85	118.25	116.65	0.09	1.25
May	118.65	–0.85	120.20	118.50	0.27	3.86
Jul	120.00	–1.00		–118.25	0	0.23
Total					**0.4**	**8.5**

■ WHEAT CBT (5,000bu min; cents/60lb bushel)

Dec	395.75	+0.00	396.00	386.00	1.24	2.35
Mar	406.50	–2.25	408.00	399.00	15.1	95.0
May	398.00	–1.00	401.00	394.00	0.54	6.84
Jul	370.25	+0.75	372.00	365.50	1.42	10.5
Sep	374.00	+1.50	376.00	368.00	0.02	0.48
Dec	385.00	+0.50	386.00	381.00	0.04	0.79
Total					**18.4**	**116.0**

■ MAIZE CBT (5,000bu min; cents/56lb bushel)

Dec	245.75	–0.75	247.00	244.25	21.1	40.0
Mar	248.25	–1.00	249.50	247.25	48.1	284.5
May	250.75	–1.25	252.00	250.00	4.23	44.0

SOFTS

■ COCOA LIFFE (10 tonnes; £/tonne)

	Sett price	Day's change	High	Low	Vol 000s	0 int 000s
Dec	890	–9	916	888	2.02	27.5
Mar	923	–8	949	920	3.09	46.3
May	941	–7	966	841	0.30	18.0
Jul	961	–6	985	960	0.33	20.4
Sep	971	–5	989	970	0.18	20.1
Dec	978	–4	1000	975	0.11	40.2
Total					**6.0**	**190.1**

■ COCOA CSCE (10 tonnes; $/tonnes)

Dec	1535	–12	1550	1550	0.04	0.09
Mar	1540	–12	1580	1532	6.27	31.0
May	1534	–11	1570	1531	0.45	14.7
Jul	1534	–10	1567	1530	0.36	12.3
Sep	1536	–10	1567	1536	0.20	7.33
Dec	1546	–11	1577	1547	0.24	8.78
Total					**7.6**	**91.5**

■ COCOA (ICCO) (SDR's/tonne)

Dec 2		Price	Prev. day
Daily....................................		1087.46	1029.76

■ COFFEE LIFFE (5 tonnes; $/tonne)

Jan	696	+18	704	689	9.99	56.2
Mar	710	+17	718	704	6.29	36.5
May	726	+17	734	720	3.05	24.1
Jul	741	+16	749	739	0.31	12.6
Sep	755	+15	763	748	0.45	10.2
Nov	770	+16	776	769	0.27	5.89
Total					**20.4**	**146.7**

■ COFFEE 'C' CSCE (37,500lbs; cents/lbs)

Dec	62.00	+2.40	62.75	60.75	0.06	0.18
Mar	64.90	+2.50	65.50	63.40	14.0	57.6
May	66.70	+2.45	67.05	65.30	1.14	8.01
Jul	68.50	+2.45	69.00	67.40	0.19	5.20
Sep	70.25	+2.45	70.50	69.20	0.07	5.82
Dec	72.75	+2.35	73.00	71.90	0.05	3.20
Total					**15.6**	**81.8**

■ COFFEE (ICO) (US cents/pound)

Dec 2		Price	Prev. day
Comp. daily.............................		50.72	49.77

■ WHITE SUGAR LIFFE (50 tonnes; $/tonne)

Mar	194.1	+4.5	195.0	189.8	4.46	18.9
May	191.5	+2.4	192.0	190.0	0.69	7.46
Aug	189.8	+1.6	190.6	187.7	0.82	6.83
Oct	189.9	+1.3	190.0	188.6	0.87	3.60
Dec	192.4	+1.3	192.1	192.0	0.03	1.13
Mar	193.5	+1.1	192.4	192.4	0.04	0.10
Total					**6.9**	**38.1**

■ SUGAR '11' CSCE (112,000lbs; cents/lbs)

Jan	5.59	+0.09	5.70	5.60	0.02	0.20
Mar	6.38	+0.09	6.38	6.30	12.4	106.9
May	6.37	+0.06	6.37	6.32	1.82	23.7
Jul	6.21	+0.06	6.21	6.18	1.82	28.2
Oct	6.23	+0.05	6.24	6.21	0.96	18.1
Mar	6.37	+0.04	6.37	6.33	0.07	7.21
Total					**17.2**	**189.7**

■ COTTON NYCE (50,000lbs; cents/lbs)

Dec	68.50	+0.25	70.00	67.50	0.07	0.09
Mar	73.58	+0.49	73.90	72.25	7.85	55.8
May	74.39	+0.04	74.75	73.10	2.59	13.1
Jul	74.90	+0.16	75.70	73.80	0.97	5.69
Dec	67.00	+0.20	67.00	66.00	0.28	4.04
Total					**11.8**	**80.1**

■ ORANGE JUICE NYCE (15,000lbs; cents/lbs)

Jan	69.40	–1.20	71.30	69.30	2.48	16.6
Mar	72.80	–1.05	74.30	72.70	1.22	12.3
May	75.40	–0.95	76.80	75.40	0.06	5.44

Thus, the investor now has no position at all in CBT March 2004 wheat futures contracts. This action will reduce open interest only if both buyers and sellers are offsetting. In the next section, it is shown that each futures contract is actually two contracts: a contract between the buyer and the clearing house and a contract between the seller and the clearing house. Hence, when both buyer and seller are offsetting a position, the clearing house has no position with either buyer or seller, and the open interest declines. If one seller sells to a new trader, then the open interest remains the same.

Although not commonly reported in the media, an important piece of information is whether the market operates by cash settlement. When futures markets developed originally, physical delivery of the underlying commodity was required. For example, the investor who bought wheat futures contracts actually purchased the required quantity of wheat. Over time, however, market participants pressed for cash settlement instead to avoid the cost of storing commodities, feeding livestock and security measures for precious metals. Cash settlement is the payment of cash at the expiration of the futures contract based on the value of the spot asset rather than the physical delivery of the underlying asset. For example, it is much easier to make a cash settlement for an S&P 500 futures contract than to actually deliver 500 different securities (with different quantities of each security). Thus, the S&P 500 futures contract is strictly a cash-settled futures contract. Yet, most exchanges retain some sort of delivery possibility, because this helps arbitrage to prevent the price from moving too far away from its correct level. Someone with a long position in a non-cash-settled future has to accept delivery, but often he or she gets the possibility of finding another party with a long position to take delivery instead. To avoid any chance of having to take delivery, one should close the position before the first notice day, the earliest day at which traders with a short position can signal they are going to deliver (often around the beginning of the last month before expiration).

19.4.3 Buying and selling futures contracts

This section examines the process by which a futures trade is executed, explains the function of clearing houses and gives a brief overview of futures markets.

Trading a futures contract

All trading on futures exchanges is conducted by futures commission merchants (FCMs), who are equivalent to stock brokers. The typical order follows the sequence given in Exhibit 19.9a. First, the buyer and seller contact their brokers, who usually are futures commission merchants (step 1 in Exhibit 19.9a). A broker that is not an FCM typically works through an FCM. The FCM contacts its floor brokers regarding the buy or sell orders (step 2). A floor broker handles orders for several FCMs. The floor brokers have the trade executed in the pit, the part of the futures exchange where all buying and selling of futures contracts take place (step 3). There are also locals present who trade solely for their own accounts. They provide additional liquidity to the market.

If a buyer wants to acquire December corn futures at $2.21 per bushel and a seller wants to sell December corn futures at $2.22, then no transaction will take place. It is not until the buyer and seller reach a price acceptable to both that a transaction takes place. Once the buyer and seller reach a mutually acceptable price, trade can occur. The clearing house now enters the picture to effect the trade. Exhibit 19.9b shows the path of activity once the transaction has been made in the pit. The exact terms of the trade are sent back to the floor broker, who then contacts both the FCM and the clearing house.

Exhibit 19.9 Trading on a futures exchange

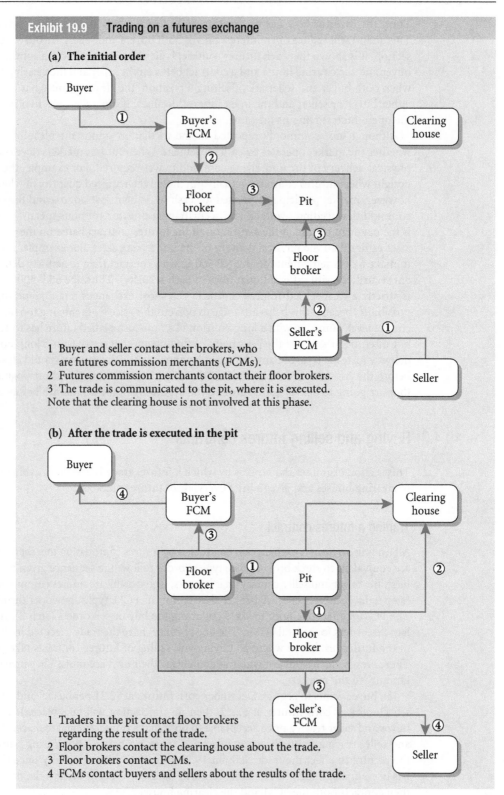

(a) The initial order

1 Buyer and seller contact their brokers, who are futures commission merchants (FCMs).
2 Futures commission merchants contact their floor brokers.
3 The trade is communicated to the pit, where it is executed.
Note that the clearing house is not involved at this phase.

(b) After the trade is executed in the pit

1 Traders in the pit contact floor brokers regarding the result of the trade.
2 Floor brokers contact the clearing house about the trade.
3 Floor brokers contact FCMs.
4 FCMs contact buyers and sellers about the results of the trade.

Source: M. J. Robertson (1990) *Futures Magazine Source Book 2003 and 2004*, Chicago, IL, Futures Magazine.

The clearing house

The clearing house plays a key role in futures trading. As with an option contract, the clearing house guarantees both sides of a futures contract. The clearing house not only helps to eliminate default risk but also guarantees the quality of the goods delivered. Most commodity futures contracts have a specified quality level, and the clearing house makes sure that the appropriate quality is delivered.

The clearing house also facilitates the exchange of daily cash flows between the winners and the losers. It makes sure that both the buyer and the seller of futures contracts provide adequate collateral.

The clearing house thus plays three vital roles:

- *Insurer*: the clearing house insures that the contract will be honoured.
- *Banker*: the clearing house provides for the exchange of profits and losses.
- *Inspector*: the clearing house guarantees good product delivery.

Margin monies are required by the clearing house so it can fulfil its first two roles. Exchanges compete with each other on these and other conditions, as Connecting Theory to Practice 19.2 illustrates.

→ **Connecting Theory to Practice 19.2**

Eurex makes inroads into US

With the outlines of its new US exchange emerging on Tuesday, Eurex has served notice to any doubters that it is serious about exporting its derivatives model to the world's largest capital market.

After months of talks, the German-Swiss exchange signed a deal with the Chicago-based Board of Trade Clearing Corporation under which BOTCC will act as the clearing organisation for Eurex's exchange, scheduled for launch in early 2004.

Customers will be able to trade both euro and dollar-denominated futures contracts on a 24-hour basis, using Eurex's electronic trading system, with trades being cleared on either side of the Atlantic for the first time.

It is the first significant transatlantic, cross-border clearing arrangement and brings closer the prospect of borderless derivatives trading and clearing.

However, with Eurex having secured arguably the most important building block in its US strategy, the development is now focusing minds on what it means for the future of Chicago's exchanges.

Eurex trades are carried out exclusively on cost-efficient electronic screens. Chicago's exchanges still maintain open outcry pits staffed with market-makers, which adds to their overall costs. The threat is that Eurex may draw trading in US interest rate and bond futures products away from the Chicago exchanges.

However, some brokers who are clearing members of the BOTCC and have long experience of trading on the Chicago exchanges say it will be no easy task, pointing out that it is hard to dislodge futures contracts from markets where there is already deep liquidity.

Most expect the Chicago exchanges to encourage traders to use their trading platforms by offering trading fee and clearing discounts, or even fee waivers.

The CBOT recently agreed to set up a 'common clearing link' with the CME that will include certain cross-margining arrangements that it believes will help attract business. 'I believe they have the staying power to meet the competitive threat,' says Mike Manning, president of Rand Financial.

Source: Jeremy Grant and Alex Skorecki, 'Eurex Makes Inroads Into US', FT.com site, 27 May 2003.

→ **Making the connection**

Exchanges are often companies with the objective of making a profit. From time to time, new entrants to the market seek to capture part of the trade in certain products or come up with new markets. Costs, margin requirements and liquidity are the issues that weigh heavily when customers can choose between markets. When the competition arrives, it is good to know how they shape their dealing process. For instance, a great advantage from linking margin between European and US markets is that investors don't have to keep margins for separate but offsetting positions on different sides of the Atlantic – which is especially important for arbitrage.

World derivative markets

Futures are traded in world derivative markets. Some believe that futures trading dates back as far as 2000 BC in India. In ancient Mesopotamia, futures contracts were inscribed in clay tablets around 1750 BC.[15] The ancient Greeks and Romans had comparable contracts. The futures and options market trading in the Netherlands flourished in the seventeenth century. Rice futures began trading in Osaka, Japan, in the 1730s.[16] The trade has expanded enormously since the 1970s. Exhibit 19.10 summarises the most important types of contracts traded on

Exhibit 19.10	World derivative exchanges	
Exchange	Futures	Options
American Stock Exchange (AMEX)		SI, S
Australian Options Market	SI, OG, SA	SI, PM
Bolsa de Mercadorias & Futuros (BM&F)	SA, IR, PM, FX	SA, IR, PM
Bourse de Montréal	IR, SI, S, OG, PM	IR, S, SI
Budapest Commodity Exchange (BCE)	FX, SA	FX, SA
Budapest Stock Exchange (BSE)	IR, S	S
Chicago Board Options Exchange (CBOE)		SI, S
Chicago Board of Trade (CBOT)	IR, SI, PM, SA	IR, SI, PM, SA
Chicago Mercantile Exchange (CME)	IR, FX, SI, SA	IR, FX, SI, SA
Coffee, Sugar & Cocoa Exchange (CSCE)	SI	SI
Commodity Exchange Inc.	IR, PM, BM	
Copenhagen Stock Exchange	SI	S, SI
Eurex (Frankfurt)	IR, SI	IR, S, SI
Eurex (Zurich)	IR, SI	S, SI
Euronext Amsterdam	IR, SI, S, FX	IR, SI, S, FX
Euronext Brussels	SI	S, SI
Euronext Lisbon	S, SI	S, SI
Euronext LIFFE	IR, FX, S, SI, SA	IR, FX, S, SI, SA
Euronext Paris	IR, SI, SA	IR, S, SI, SA

Source: M. J. Robertson (1990) *Futures Magazine Source Book 2003 and 2004*, Chicago, IL, Futures Magazine.

---

[15] See the extensive work on the history of derivatives by Swan (2000).
[16] See Robertson (1990).

Exhibit 19.10	continued

Exchange	Futures	Options
European Electricity Exchange (EEX)	OG	
Financial Instrument Exchange (FINEX)	IR, FX	IR, FX
Fukuoka Futures Exchange	SA	
Helsinki Exchanges	SI	S
Hong Kong Exchanges & Clearing	SI, S, IR	S, SI
Intercontinental Exchange (ICE)	OG, PM	OG, PM
International Securities Exchange (ISE)		S
International Petroleum Exchange (IPE)	OG	OG
Italian Derivatives Market (IDEM)	S, SI	S, SI
Kansas City Board of Trade (KCBT)	SI, SA	SI, SA
Korea Futures Exchanges (KOFEX)	IR, FX	IR, FX
Korea Stock Exchange (KSE)	SI	SI
London Metal Exchange	BM, PM	BM, PM
Malaysia Derivatives Exchange	SI, SA	SI
Mercado Español de Futuros Financieros (MEFF)	S, SI	S, SI
Mercado Mexicano de Derivados		
Mid-American Commodity Exchange	IR, FX, PM, SA	PM, SA
Midamerica Commodity Exchange (MIDAM)	SA	
Minneapolis Grain Exchange (MGE)	SA	SA
NASDAQ LIFFE Markets (NQLX)	S, SI	
National Exchange of India (NSE)	S, SI	S, SI
New York Board of Trade (NYBOT)	SI, SA, FX	SI, SA, FX
New York Mercantile Exchange (NYMEX)	SA, OG, PM, BM	SA, OG, PM
New Zealand Futures Exchange (NZFE)	IR, OG	IR, OG, S
OM Stockholm	IR, S, SI	IR, S, SI
OneChicago	S	
Osaka Securities Exchange	SI	SI
Osaka Mercantile Exchange	SA, BM	
Pacific Exchange (PCX)		S
Philadelphia Stock Exchange		S, SI, FX
Singapore (SGX-DX)	IR, FX, SI	IR, FX, SI
South African Futures Exchange (SAFEX)	S, SI, SA	S, SI, SA
Sydney Futures Exchange (SFE)	IR, SI, OG, SA	IR, SI, FX, OG
Tel-Aviv Stock Exchange	SI, FX	SI, FX
Tokyo International Financial Futures Exchange (TIFFE)	IR, FX	
Tokyo Commodity Exchange (TOCOM)	OG, BM, PM	
Tokyo Grain Exchange (TGE)	SA	SA
Tokyo Stock Exchange	IR, SI	IR, SI
Toronto Futures Exchange	IR, SI	IR, PM
Wiener Borse (WB)	SI	S, SI
Winnipeg Commodity Exchange (WCE)	SA	SA
Yokohama Commodity Exchange	SA	

BM, base metals; FX, foreign exchange or currencies; IR, interest rates; OG, energy, oil and gas; PM, precious metals; SA, softs (such as cotton) and agriculture; S, stocks; SI, stock indexes.
Note: options on futures are included under options, since they form a reasonably close substitute for options on the underlying asset. The major difference is the amount of leverage.

Source: M. J. Robertson (1990) *Futures Magazine Source Book 2003 and 2004*, Chicago, IL, Futures Magazine.

the world's derivatives exchanges, and these 62 exchanges are just the major ones. Notice that, while most exchanges used to specialise in one or two types of contracts, many exchanges have now started trading in a wide range of products. There has been a lot of merger and acquisition activity among the exchanges; for example, the Euronext operates exchanges in the UK, the USA, France, Belgium, Portugal and the Netherlands, which all used to be one or more separate exchanges (Euronext Paris is a combination of the Matif and Monep exchanges).

19.5 Options

An option gives its holder the right to buy or sell a specified amount of an underlying asset at a predetermined price. This right can be exercised at a specified future date or during a specific future period. There are two basic types of options: call options and put options. A call option gives its holder the right to *buy* a specified amount of the underlying asset during some period in the future at a predetermined price. If one holds a call option on IBM common stock and the option expires in three months with a predetermined strike price of $100, then it gives the right to buy IBM stock for $100 on or before the expiration date, regardless of the market price at that moment. Similarly, a put option gives its holder the right to *sell* a specified amount of the underlying asset during some period in the future at a predetermined price. Although puts and calls can be based on the same underlying asset, such as shares of IBM, they are separate securities. Note that if an investor buys a right, then someone else is selling an obligation. The investor who has bought the right to buy or sell is said to have a long position. The person who grants this right (writes the option) has a short position.

Put and call options trade on a vast array of underlying assets, including common stocks, Treasury bills, Treasury notes, Treasury bonds, futures contracts, commodities, stock indices and interest rates.

Although options can be considered as a simple bet, putting a value on such bets is complicated. In this chapter, only the characteristics of options (such as their cash flows) and of their markets, the terminology used in this field and the strategies for combining options to alter payoff structures are discussed. The next chapter studies the pricing of options and other derivatives.

19.5.1 Characteristics of options

An option buyer is the purchaser of an option contract. Recall that a call option gives its holder the right to buy the underlying asset at a predetermined price. Thus, if an investor bought a call option on Vodafone common stock, then by exercising the option contract, he or she would be purchasing Vodafone common stock at a predetermined price. This predetermined price is the strike price, or exercise price. Likewise, if an investor bought a put option on Vodafone common stock, then by exercising the option contract, he or she would be selling Vodafone's stock at the strike or exercise price. Note that the buyer who holds an option takes a long position in an option – whether it is a call or a put option.

To purchase call and put options, there must be people willing to sell the options. Option sellers are called option writers, and they can write both call and put options. The option writer is the person from whom the option buyer purchases the option contract; options trade between individual investors. The option writer is obligated to honour the terms of the option contract if the buyer decides to exercise the option.

It is worthwhile to distinguish between an option writer and a short-seller. A short-seller of a stock sells stock that is not owned but rather is borrowed from a broker. Therefore, the short-seller has an obligation to eventually repurchase the actual shares of stock so that the borrowed stock can be returned to the broker. An option writer, in contrast, may or may not have to actually supply or acquire the underlying asset; it all depends on whether the option is exercised and how it is settled.[17]

Some actual figures and possible transactions in call and put options will demonstrate how an option contract works. The relevant information on option prices is reported in several sources, including online services, newspapers and television. This section explains briefly how to read option quotes in newspapers such as the *Wall Street Journal* and the *Financial Times* and real-time quotes on the Internet.

Consider the example of options on the Nasdaq-100 index (an ETF with symbol QQQ, as discussed earlier) in Exhibit 19.11. The first column contains the option symbol, the expiration month and the strike price. The second column gives the last price of the option followed by the change in price that day in the next column. Note that the option prices listed are the prices for the last trade that occurred, which could have been hours before. The option prices are given on a per-share basis, although option contracts are written in multiples of 100 shares. Columns four to seven contain the bid price, the ask price, the volume traded on that day and the total open interest for that option, respectively. The last price can be outside the bid–ask range if the last trade was some time ago. The right-hand side of the table gives the same information for the put options.

To follow the demonstration of how to read an option quote, look at the March $33 call option ($33 being the strike price), with symbol QAVCG. This call option on QQQ shares last traded at $3.70. Since each option contract is for 100 shares of the stock, the cost of one option contract is $100 \times \$3.70 = \$370$. The price of the day before can be derived from the change column: the previous day's closing price was $3.70 + 0.20 = \$3.90$.

The expiration date, or maturity date, of an option contract is the date on which the option expires or ceases to exist if the option contract is not exercised. For most stock options, the expiration date is the Friday before the third Saturday of the expiration month. For example, a December 2003 stock option matured on 19 December, which was the Friday before the third Saturday. Options on underlying assets other than stocks, such as interest-rate options, have unique expiration dates. Eurodollar futures options expire on the Monday preceding the third Wednesday of the contract month. If the third Wednesday of March is 16 March, then the March contract expires on Monday, 14 March.

Stock options with maturity dates far into the future are sometimes referred to as LEAPS (long-term equity anticipation securities).[18] All options of the same type (puts or calls) with the same underlying asset are referred to as an option class. An option series is the part of a class with the same expiration date and strike price. Despite the plural term, this refers therefore to a particular traded contract, and is often referred to as just 'an option'.

The cost of purchasing an option contract is called the option premium. Specifically, the option premium is the price that the option buyer pays to the writer of the option. For

---

[17] The settlement is almost always done in cash.

[18] Another concept associated with options is the *option cycle*, which is the procedure with which new option contracts initiate trading. Some contracts have monthly cycles (for instance, each month for the next six months), and other contracts have quarterly cycles (say, each quarter for the next 2.5 years, such as Eurodollar futures options). Some contracts are a combination of both monthly and quarterly cycles. LEAPS generally follow a yearly cycle. Before actually trading options, investors must investigate which contracts are available.

Exhibit 19.11	QQQ option price quotes on the American Stock Exchange

MAR 04

Calls	Last Sale	Net Chg	Bid	Ask	Vol	Open Interest	Puts	Last Sale	Net Chg	Bid	Ask	Vol	Open Interest
MAR 04 20 QAVCS	$16.30	unch	$16.30	$16.50	171	315	MAR 04 20 QAVOS	$0.05	unch	$0.00	$0.05	N.A.	1 036
MAR 04 25 QAVCY	$11.30	0.60 ▼	$11.30	$11.50	171	826	MAR 04 25 QAVOY	$0.05	unch	$0.00	$0.05	N.A.	4 633
MAR 04 30 QAVCD	$6.40	unch	$6.40	$6.50	25	17 147	MAR 04 30 QAVOD	$0.05	unch	$0.00	$0.05	10	93 174
MAR 04 31 QAVCE	$5.50	0.20 ▲	$5.40	$5.50	834	7 578	MAR 04 31 QAVOE	$0.05	unch	$0.00	$0.05	20	46 662
MAR 04 32 QAVCF	$4.60	unch	$4.40	$4.60	1 809	54 227	MAR 04 32 QAVOF	$0.05	0.05 ▼	$0.00	$0.05	118	92 068
MAR 04 33 QAVCG	$3.70	0.20 ▲	$3.50	$3.60	522	36 688	MAR 04 33 QAVOG	$0.10	unch	$0.05	$0.10	752	60 469
MAR 04 34 QAVCH	$2.65	0.05 ▲	$2.60	$2.65	662	64 088	MAR 04 34 QAVOH	$0.20	unch	$0.15	$0.20	2 594	213 066
MAR 04 35 QQQCI	$1.85	unch	$1.80	$1.85	1 275	90 150	MAR 04 35 QQQOI	$0.35	0.05 ▼	$0.35	$0.40	6 235	190 169
MAR 04 36 QQQCJ	$1.15	0.05 ▲	$1.10	$1.15	11 232	121 866	MAR 04 36 QQQOJ	$0.70	unch	$0.65	$0.70	12 182	242 024
MAR 04 37 QQQCK	$0.65	0.05 ▲	$0.55	$0.60	26 432	262 946	MAR 04 37 QQQOK	$1.15	unch	$1.15	$1.20	26 867	286 177
MAR 04 38 QQQCL	$0.25	0.05 ▼	$0.25	$0.30	8 168	186 703	MAR 04 38 QQQOL	$1.85	0.05 ▲	$1.80	$1.90	15 718	118 933
MAR 04 39 QQQCM	$0.15	0.05 ▲	$0.10	$0.15	1 347	51 253	MAR 04 39 QQQOM	$2.70	unch	$2.65	$2.75	703	16 986
MAR 04 40 QQQCN	$0.05	unch	$0.00	$0.05	2 603	52 765	MAR 04 40 QQQON	$3.60	unch	$3.50	$3.70	191	14 679
MAR 04 45 QQQCS	$0.05	unch	$0.00	$0.05	N.A.	589	MAR 04 45 QQQOS	$7.60	unch	$8.50	$8.60	N.A.	194
MAR 04	$0.05	unch	$0.00	$0.05	N.A.	20	MAR 04	$11.70	unch	$13.50	$13.60	N.A.	230

Source: AMEX website (www.amex.com), 24 February 2004. Copyright American Stock Exchange LLC 2004. Reprinted with permission of the American Stock Exchange LLC.

example, if an option buyer pays $4.60 for the call option (for example, see the March 32 calls in Exhibit 19.11), the total premium would be $460 ($4.60 × 100), because each option contract is for 100 shares.[19] This $460 premium is not just a good-faith deposit or a down payment but rather a non-refundable fee. It is the reward for the risk that someone with a short position takes. Since an option is asymmetric (the holder only exercises if that would be beneficial) an up-front payment is required to compensate risk. The *option price* refers to the current market price of the option. The option premium and the option price are the same at the time of the option transaction ($400 in the example above). However, after the moment of purchase, the option premium is $400, whereas the option price can change with current market conditions. For example, if the stock price rallies, then the option price may rise to $800 per contract, whereas the option premium is still $400. The option premium refers to the option price when traded, not the current market price.

A distinction is made between the transactions that initiate an option contract and those that close the contract: an opening transaction occurs when a new position is established. A closing transaction occurs when an already established position is eliminated. For example, suppose an investor purchased one Vodafone April 25 call to open on 18 December for a premium of $0.85 per share. After two months, the investor decides to sell one Vodafone April 25 call for a market price that happens to be $3 per share. The opening transaction takes place when the investor purchases the Vodafone April 25 call. When the investor sells the call option, the transaction will be closed. Hence, after selling the options, one has no option position. The per-share profit before transaction costs is $2.15 ($3 − $0.85). Thus, after the sale of one Vodafone April 25 call, the investor would have zero net position, because the sale offsets the previous purchase.

Another distinction related to option contracts involves the date when the contract can be exercised: European-style versus American-style options. European-style options can be exercised only on specific dates – the maturity date. American-style options, in contrast, can be exercised any time on or before the expiration date of the contract. The holder of an American option has the freedom to decide when, if ever, the option contract will be exercised, as long as it is before the expiration date. Note that these terms do not refer to, or even reflect, geographic location (that is, Europe or the USA). For example, contracts that can be exercised only on the last day of the contract, such as foreign exchange options, are traded on the Philadelphia Stock Exchange, yet are of the European type. Most stock options are American-style options, and many index options and interest rate options are European-style options.

To illustrate options on interest rates, suppose that the last quoted price for a Treasury note maturing in August 2004 is $104.57. There is a call option to buy the bond at $101.50. The market price of this August 2004 call is $3.30. Note that an immediate exercise of the option yields $104.57 − $101.50 = $3.07. The call is traded for $3.30, and the difference between $3.30 and $3.07 reflects the chance that if the interest rate goes down before the end of August, then the bond's price will go up and the call option holder will have more profit. Note that these options are really on bonds, but they are called interest-rate options because investors are gambling on (or hedging) changes in interest rates. A change in interest rate induces a change in the bond's price and, hence, a change in the option price.

Options are categorised by the relationship that exists between the current market price of the underlying asset and the option's exercise price. Let S_0 represent the current market price of the generic underlying asset (for example, the stock price) and X represent the option exercise price. An in-the-money option is an option that would generate a positive cash flow

---

[19] The difference between ETF and 'normal' shares is not relevant for the current discussion.

if it were exercised now. That is, a call option is an in-the-money option if the market price of the underlying asset is greater than the strike price ($S_0 > X$) of the option contract. If the option is American style, then an investor could exercise the call option, pay X dollars for the stock, and sell the stock for S_0, generating a positive cash flow of $S_0 - X$. For put options, an in-the-money option is an option in which the price received for exercising the option (X) is higher than the current price of the stock ($X > S_0$). An out-of-the-money option is the exact opposite of an in-the-money option, i.e. for calls $X > S_0$ and for puts $X < S_0$. In the case of out-of-the-money options, there is no incentive to exercise the put or call. At-the-money options occur when the current price of the stock is exactly equal to the exercise price, i.e. $S_0 = X$.

Sometimes, option traders refer to *deep in-the-money options* or *deep out-of-the-money options*. The word 'deep' emphasises that the distance between S_0 and X is relatively large.

A call option written when the investor does not own the underlying asset is a naked position. A covered position is a call option written when the underlying asset is already owned. Writing a call option without owning the underlying asset is very risky, the potential loss is unlimited, and losses occur when the underlying asset rises.

Finally, we need to distinguish between options and warrants. The latter is simular to a regular option, but it is written by the firm of which the shares are the underlying asset. A regular option is written by an investor, independent from the company. Understandably, warrants are always call options. The differences between a regular call option and a warrant surface when the warrant is exercised: the company does not settle the contract in cash but in shares. Since these are the shares of the company itself, the company creates new shares to fulfil this obligation, so the number of outstanding shares rises. Given the fact that the warrants are paid for in advance, the only money the company receives for these new shares is the exercise price, which may be well below the current stock price. Therefore, warrants are considered to have a *dilutive effect*: the value of the company increases by a smaller amount than the value of the new stocks. Most of the money paid for the warrants has been received already, often years ago, and after the exercise there are more shareholders who have a right to part of the company's value.

Option values at expiration

To examine the value of options at expiration, it is again helpful to use *payoff diagrams*, which are also used in Section 19.6 to compare different option-based trading strategies. It should be noted, then, when constructing payoff diagrams for options, the option premium that is paid or received is included in the profit or loss.[20] Option prices can at any time be broken down into two components: intrinsic value and time value. We will deal with time value in the next chapter. The intrinsic value of an option is the value of the option if it would be exercised immediately, unless the value of immediate exercise is negative, in which case the intrinsic value is zero. Stated as a formula, the intrinsic value for calls (IV_c) is[21]

$$IV_c = \max(0, S_0 - X) \tag{19.1}$$

---

[20] Payoff diagrams can be used to illustrate option contracts, which are for 100 shares, or to illustrate an option on a single share. For simplicity, we illustrate payoff diagrams for an option on a single share. Payoff diagrams also ignore the time value of money and the ability to exercise early on American-style options. Note that excluding the option premium would result in a diagram of terminal cashflows, whereas payoffs = terminal cash flows – initial cash flows.

[21] Note that $\max(a, b)$ means to take the maximum of a or b. For example, if $y = \max(a, b)$ and if $a > b$, then $y = a$. We take the maximum because the option buyer has a right, which he or she won't exercise if it isn't as profitable as the alternative, which is doing nothing (and results in a cash flow of zero).

Exhibit 19.12   Payoff diagrams: buying a call option (long call)

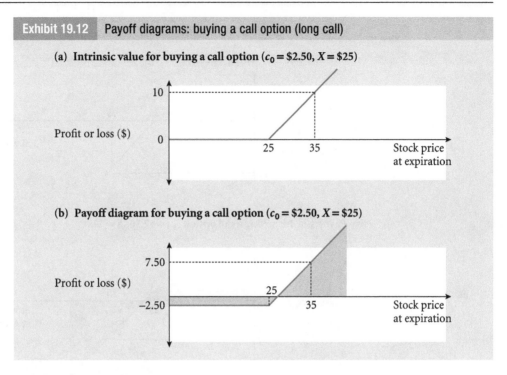

(a) **Intrinsic value for buying a call option ($c_0 = \$2.50$, $X = \$25$)**

(b) **Payoff diagram for buying a call option ($c_0 = \$2.50$, $X = \$25$)**

The intrinsic value for puts (IV_p) is

$$IV_p = \max(0, X - S_0) \tag{19.2}$$

If we look at European-style options, the intrinsic value is the same, even though immediate exercise is impossible.

As the stock price changes, the intrinsic value of the option may change as well. It remains zero if the option remains out of the money. The time value of an option is whatever value an option currently has above its intrinsic value. It is caused by the chance that the intrinsic value before expiration will be different from the intrinsic value at expiration. At this point, we look only at option payoffs at expiration, so the time value at that moment is always equal to zero. The payoff diagrams at expiration can therefore be constructed as follows:

1. Determine the intrinsic value of the option.
2. Add (or subtract) the option premium that has been received (paid).[22]

To illustrate, let us consider buying stock in Apple Computer Corporation. Exhibit 19.12a shows the various possible intrinsic values of a call option on Apple's stock at expiration.

Comparing Exhibit 19.12 with 19.2 one sees that, as opposed to forwards and the likes, options are *non-linear instruments*.

Now suppose that Apple stock was purchased for $25 per share. Exhibit 19.12b shows the profit or loss at the option expiration date. When Apple stock is at $35, the investor has a $10

---

[22] In constructing payoff diagrams, we ignore the fact that the premium has been received (paid) when the option was sold (bought), which could be long before the payoffs are received. Hence we should, strictly speaking, correct this amount for time-value effects. We ignore it here for ease of exposition. Yet this aspect is often omitted or overlooked, probably because of the fact that in calculating returns (the figure practitioners are usually more interested in) the option premium *should not* be discounted, as return = (profit or loss − investment)/investment.

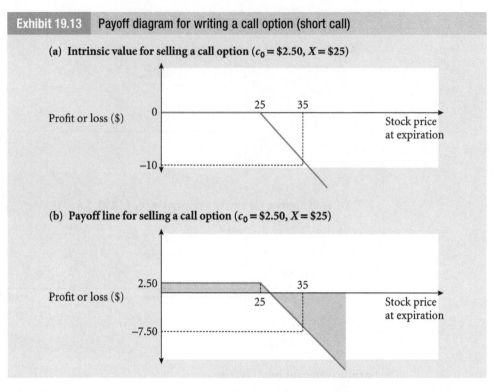

Exhibit 19.13   Payoff diagram for writing a call option (short call)

(a) Intrinsic value for selling a call option ($c_0 = \$2.50$, $X = \$25$)

(b) Payoff line for selling a call option ($c_0 = \$2.50$, $X = \$25$)

(i.e. $35 − $25) profit; when Apple stock is at $15, the investor chooses not to exercise and the option has no intrinsic value. Subtracting the option premium, this means a $7.50 gain and a $2.50 (the option premium) loss, respectively. So in terms of payoff, we break even on the call option investment if

$$IV_{c,T} = \max(S_T - X, 0) = c_0$$

or

$$S_T = X + c_0$$

where S_T represents the stock price at maturity.

We now examine the value of a call option at expiration from the call writer's point of view. Exhibit 19.13 illustrates the payoff diagram of writing a call option on Apple stock with a strike price of $25 and a call premium ($c_0$) of $2.50. Recall that when an investor shorts a call, he or she receives the cash flow c_0, which is the call premium. The value of this short-call position at expiration can be described as a minus 45-degree line going out from the horizontal axis at the strike price. The total payoff line is similar, except that it is shifted up by the $2.50 premium, which is received from writing each call. For example, if the stock price falls to $27.50, then the call writer keeps the call premium of $2.50 and has no obligations at maturity, because the option buyer will not exercise the call option. However, if the stock price rises to $35 at maturity, then the writer loses $10 at expiration and has a dollar loss of $7.50 (i.e. −$10 + $2.50).

In a similar fashion, Exhibit 19.14 presents the intrinsic value and payoff diagram lines for buying a put option (long put). Recall that buying a put option, in the case of stocks, gives the buyer the right to sell a stock at the strike price. Hence, a put option is more valuable as the price of the stock declines. In contrast, the value of the put option at expiration is zero if the put option expires out of the money (when the stock price is above $25, in this case). The intrinsic value at

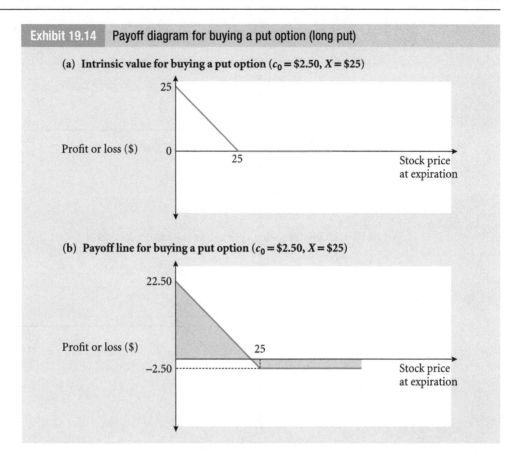

Exhibit 19.14 Payoff diagram for buying a put option (long put)

(a) Intrinsic value for buying a put option ($c_0 = \$2.50$, $X = \$25$)

Profit or loss ($) — 25, 0, 25, Stock price at expiration

(b) Payoff line for buying a put option ($c_0 = \$2.50$, $X = \$25$)

Profit or loss ($) — 22.50, 25, −2.50, Stock price at expiration

expiration is a 45-degree line rising as the stock price falls below $25 (−45-degree line), because for each $1 drop in the stock price, the value of the put option at maturity increases by $1.

The put payoff diagram can be viewed as the mirror image of the call payoff diagram, if the mirror is placed vertically on the strike price. (Note that there is no requirement that the put price equals the call price. We adopted these values to simplify the discussion.)

Exhibit 19.15 presents the intrinsic value and payoff lines for writing put options. Recall that put writing obligates an investor to buy a stock from the put buyer at a specified price. Hence, as the stock price falls, the put buyer will want to exercise the option and sell stock at the exercise price. Therefore, the put writer loses as the stock price declines. Note that from the put writer's viewpoint, the payoff line is above the intrinsic value line, because, by writing the put, the option writer receives the put price, which in our example is $2.50. Of course, the put price can be different from $2.50 (say, $3); then we add $3 to the value line to get the payoff line. The lines in Exhibit 19.15 are mirror images of those in Exhibit 19.14, where the mirror is placed on the horizontal axis.

The consequences of naked option trading (thus, without an offsetting position in other instruments) are demonstrated in a number of scandals, among them the case of LTCM described in Investments in the News 19.[23] Other examples are Barings (in which the naked

---

[23] In the case of LTCM, the problem was that the offsetting positions were insufficient, so that part of the portfolio could be considered as a naked derivative. The portfolio was also highly levered, so a small change in underlying values had a profound effect on the value of the hedge fund. LTCM exploited the large returns of derivatives to the fullest, but when it ran out of luck it also quickly ran out of money to meet the margin calls.

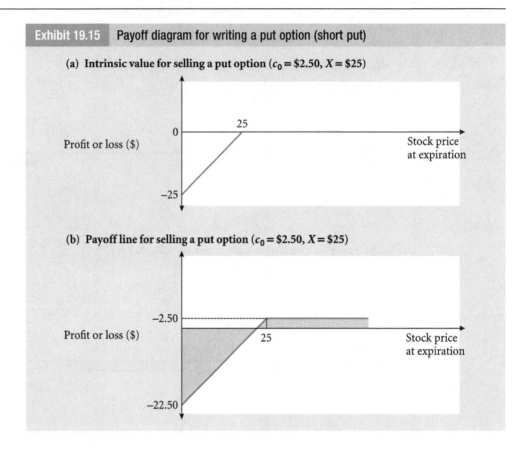

Exhibit 19.15 Payoff diagram for writing a put option (short put)

(a) **Intrinsic value for selling a put option** ($c_0 = \$2.50$, $X = \$25$)

(b) **Payoff line for selling a put option** ($c_0 = \$2.50$, $X = \$25$)

positions of Nicholas Leeson in the Japanese index ultimately led to the bankruptcy of the bank), Orange County and Metallgesellschaft who lost a considerable amount of money as well. Due to these cases – which mostly involve mismanagement to a certain degree as well as risk-taking trading – derivatives have had a bad name among many investors and companies for much of the 1990s. Clearly, investing in options can be very risky. However, practice demonstrates other uses of options as well – hedging to reduce losses and free up resources, as well as diversifying portfolios with derivatives. Banks have also discovered that fees from derivatives (and redistributing risk in general) can be a lucrative business opportunity. Connecting Theory to Practice 19.3 illustrates some of these issues.

→ **Connecting Theory to Practice 19.3**   **FT**

Overview: essential, controversial, popular and profitable

Derivatives have become essential tools for corporate treasurers, lenders and investors. But they have not lost their ability to generate controversy and debate.

Warren Buffett, the investment guru and chairman of Berkshire Hathaway, triggered the latest round with a stinging attack in March on derivatives as 'weapons of mass destruction'.

Mr Buffett warned: 'Large amounts of risk, particularly credit risk, have become concentrated in the hands of relatively few derivatives dealers. Derivatives are financial weapons of mass destruction, carrying dangers that, while now latent, are potentially lethal.'

Many in the financial services industry concluded that Mr Buffett's views were influenced by his frustration at being unable to extract Berkshire Hathaway from a portfolio of very long-dated 'exotic' derivatives products held by General Re Securities, part of an insurance company it owns.

Speaking two months after Mr Buffett's comments appeared, Alan Greenspan, chairman of the Federal Reserve Board, said: 'The benefits of derivatives, in my judgment, have far exceeded their costs.'

The Bank for International Settlements was equally supportive in its 2003 annual report. Until the emergence of credit derivatives, the credit markets had been among the least liquid, the most complicated to price and the most costly of financial markets in which to trade, it said. It certainly appears as though the reduction and dispersion of risk that supporters claim as the main advantage of derivatives has played a part in preventing the banking failures that have marked previous downturns. But the continuing rapid growth of both over-the-counter and exchange-traded derivatives remains a source of concern to many observers.

OTC derivatives trading is thought to amount to about 80 per cent of the total, indicating that the volume of exchange-traded derivatives was about $31,000 bn in the first six months of this year. The number of contracts traded between January and August rose 34 per cent from 3.87 bn in 2002 to 5.19 bn this year, according to Fow Tradedata, the market statistics group. As the derivative markets develop and contracts become commoditised, there could be a shift away from over-the-counter trading, involving bespoke contracts, to 'plain vanilla' contracts suitable for trading on an exchange.

'On a listed market you have transparency, uniformity and price competitiveness,' says Edward Condon, head of European listed derivatives at CSFB. 'And derivatives that are cleared through an exchange do not require the banks to carry the transaction on their balance sheet.' Overall trading volumes have been driven by recent sharp fluctuations in the bond and foreign currency markets.

In addition, banks and industrial companies have become more aware of the need to manage risk and have turned to derivatives for the cover they provide.

'The increase in interest rate derivatives outstanding reflects the need by market participants for risk management tools during a period of bond market and exchange rate volatility,' says Robert Pickel, ISDA chief executive.

Source: Charles Batchelor, 'Overview: Essential, Controversial, Popular and Profitable', *FT.com site*, 5 November 2003.

→ Making the connection

When options were first introduced, their risk and return structure was often misunderstood. This led to large losses because of the inappropriate use of options by investors – they were often blinded by the potential of huge returns and ignored the risk involved. As the article points out, however, options can be used to manage risk and may even improve market conditions in general. Furthermore – maybe because of the well-known, big losses – investors and companies are keeping a closer eye on their activities that expose them to risk. Derivatives are more and more the method of choice in order to shed various unwanted risks, and banks are accommodating this profitable trend.

19.5.2 Overview of option markets

The development of modern option trading

The earliest record of option trading is attributed to the ancient Greek scholar Thales around 550 BC.[24] Thales is said to have purchased call options (or reached a similar agreement) on the use of olive presses to benefit from his belief that the next olive harvest was going to be extremely good. When his prediction proved accurate, Thales exercised his call options and subsequently leased the olive presses to farmers at a considerable profit. A second account states that Thales anticipated a bad harvest and subsequently cornered the market by buying call-option contracts to buy olives at a predetermined price, profiting him when the market price rose.[25]

Option contracts (or *privileges*, as they were first called) appeared in the USA in the 1790s, shortly after the Buttonwood Tree Agreement – the agreement that established the NYSE. In the late nineteenth century, Russell Sage, the grandfather of modern option trading, organised a system for trading put and call options on an OTC market. Sage also introduced the idea of put-call parity – a concept that will be discussed in Chapter 20.

Organised option trading in the USA did not occur until the passage of the Investment Act of 1934, which legalised option trading. However, until 1973, option contracts had several limitations, including the following:

- Lack of standardised contracts: each transaction required a custom-designed contract.
- Lack of transferability between investors: it was difficult to get out of an options position.
- The requirement that the option holder had to take physical delivery of the underlying asset.
- The risk associated with the lack of collateral required by the seller of the option.
- The lack of market makers, which made transacting in options more difficult.

These concerns are very similar to those encountered in forward trading and were the motivation to create organised futures markets. To address these five concerns for options, the Chicago Board of Trade (CBOT) created the Chicago Board Options Exchange (CBOE). The CBOE began option trading on 26 April 1973. Initially, 16 call options were traded on common stocks (that is, the underlying assets were common stocks). Since 1973, the growth of the option market has been explosive. Exhibit 19.16 summarises the key events in development of the option market.

To get an impression of the current trading possibilities in options, see Exhibit 19.16. The most active option exchanges in the USA are the CBOE, the AMEX (in New York), the CBOT, the PHLX, the CME and the Pacific Stock Exchange (PSE, located in San Francisco). In Europe, London, Paris and Frankfurt are major derivatives markets; in Japan, Tokyo and Osaka are major derivatives markets. It should be noted that option trading occurs not only on exchanges but also over the counter and directly between buyers and sellers.

Option transactions are similar to stock transactions. For example, if John Q decides to buy call options on Boeing, then he would call his broker and state his desires. The broker would communicate this order to the appropriate option exchange, where the trade would occur with either an investor wanting to sell call options on Boeing or with the market maker (see Chapter 3).

---

[24] For a detailed history of options, see Chapter 1 of Options Institute (1990). A more recent work with a legal perspective is Swan (2000).

[25] Although it is questioned whether Thales actually participated in these transactions, the historical evidence does show that options trading existed centuries ago; see Copleston (1985).

Exhibit 19.16	Modern history of option trading

Year	Activity
1973	Chicago Board Options Exchange (CBOE) started, trading 16 call options. Thus, it introduced a standardised option contract for the first time
	Black and Scholes and Merton publish seminal option pricing papers
1975	American Stock Exchange (AMEX) and Philadelphia Stock Exchange (PHLX) start trading options
1976	Pacific Stock Exchange starts trading options
1977	Put options start trading; CBOE seeks approval to trade non-stock options
1978	European Options Exchange (Amsterdam) launched, the first in Europe
1979	US Labor Department declares that option use is not a breach of fiduciary duty. Comptroller of Currency eases restrictions on bank trust departments' use of options
1980	Volume of option trading exceeds New York Stock Exchange (NYSE) stock volume
1982	LIFFE (London) established, starts trading in financial futures and options
	Kansas City Board of Trade starts trading the options on Value Line Composite Average
	Chicago Mercantile Exchange (CME) starts trading the options on the S&P 500
	New York Futures Exchange starts trading the options on the NYSE Composite Index
	CBOE starts trading options on US Treasury bonds
	PHLX starts trading options on foreign exchange rates
1983	CBOE starts trading CBOE 100 stock index options
1984	International Money Market at the CME starts trading futures options (option contracts whose future value depends on the value of a futures contract) on foreign exchange
1985	CME starts trading Eurodollar futures options; NYSE introduces option trading
1986	MATIF (Paris futures exchange) opened
1987	Monep (Paris options exchange) founded
1989	Osaka Stock Exchange starts trading Nikkei 225 options
1996	NYSE sells option business to CBOE
1997	CBOE begins trading options on the Dow (DJX options)
1998	Eurex (joint venture of the Frankfurt and Swiss exchanges) starts trading
2000	Formation of the Euronext exchange
2003	CBOE shifts to (partial) electronic trading

An overview of the history of option trading isn't complete without a reference to the development of pricing models – one could argue that the theoretical knowledge gained over the years has greatly spurred trading in options (and vice versa). The advances made on the theoretical side are discussed briefly in Chapter 20.

Clearing

Because options are not marked to market, the clearing house (an organisation that facilitates the validation, delivery and settlement of security transactions and, most importantly, guarantees that obligations are met) plays a vital role in each options market. In the USA, the Options Clearing Corporation (OCC) maintains the records of option trades and is one of the major clearing corporations. The OCC is owned and backed by several exchanges (such as the CBOE, AMEX, NYSE and PHLX). The OCC is a very creditworthy corporation: it has a stable AAA rating. It issues all option contracts and guarantees both sides of the contracts. Thus, the option buyer does not have to evaluate the credit risk of the option writer. Also, all option contracts have standardised features that make them easier to resell, thereby enhancing the option contract's liquidity. The OCC provides a prospectus for each contract, which details the regulations related to trading options and processes all transactions related to option trading. All exchanges have a similar organisation, for example clearing in London on the Euronext Liffe (London International Financial Futures and Options Exchange) is handled by the London Clearing House (LCH).

Suppose that an investor purchases a call option with an exercise price of $50. The stock price subsequently increases to $200. Who guarantees that the call writer will pay the difference (i.e. $200 − $50 = $150)? The OCC requires that the call writer (as well as all other option writers) provides collateral, known as margin. The margin requirements, which are explained in detail in the next section, ensure that the option writer will pay the option buyer if the events indeed occur in the buyer's favour.

19.5.3 Margin requirements

Suppose an investor purchased 100 call option contracts for $5 per share (the total cost would be $50 000 = $5 × 100 shares per contract × 100 contracts). The seller has to post margin with the OCC. Suppose now the stock was in the money by $20 on the expiration date (i.e. $S_0 − X = \$20$). Then the 100 option contracts would be worth $200 000 (i.e. $20 × 100 shares per contract × 100 contracts). This means more margin is required to protect the OCC from too much default risk. How much will the call writer pay to the OCC as a result of the price increase?[26]

Exhibit 19.17 compares the initial and maintenance requirements for margin accounts for different types of contracts traded on the CBOE. Recall that margin accounts are required to keep securities (or cash) on deposit with the broker as collateral. In the options market, margin implies the money deposited by the option writer as collateral for the potential future liability. As Exhibit 19.17 illustrates, margin requirements are complex and differ across different types of securities and purposes (long, short and spreads). Margin requirements change with market conditions.

As an illustration, consider writing one call option on the S&P 100 stock index. The option contract is actually for 100 times the index. The formula for finding this margin requirement of the option writer based on Exhibit 19.17 (see Short calls, Index row and Initial margin column) is as follows:

$$\text{Margin} = \max(A, B)$$

where

$$A = c_0 + (0.15 \times 100 \times \text{index}) - [100 \times \max(0, X - \text{index})]$$

$$B = c_0 + (0.10 \times 100 \times \text{index})$$

---

[26] The risk of default is also related intimately to the volatility of the underlying asset. The more volatile the asset, the higher the risk of large losses and hence default by option writers.

		Exhibit 19.17	Initial and maintenance margin requirements

Position	Option type	Initial margin	Maintenance margin
Long (puts or calls)	All common underlying assets	Pay for option in full	None required
Short calls	Index (e.g. stock index options)	(100% of option premium + 15% of index − out-of-the-money amount (if any)) or (option premium + 10% of index) if this is greater	Same as initial margin
	Equities (e.g. stock options)	(100% of option premium + 20% of underlying asset − out-of-the-money amount (if any)) or (option premium + 10% of underlying) if this is greater	Same as initial margin
	Interest rates (e.g. options on Treasury bonds)	(100% of option premium + 10% of underlying asset − out-of-the-money amount (if any)) or (option premium + 5% of underlying) if this is greater	Same as initial margin
Short puts	Index (e.g. stock index options)	(100% of option premium + 15% of index − out-of-the-money amount (if any)) or (option premium + 10% of exercise price) if this is greater	Same as initial margin
	Equities (e.g. example, stock options)	(100% of option premium + 20% of underlying asset − out-of-the-money amount (if any)) or (option premium + 10% of the exercise price) if this is greater	Same as initial margin
	Interest rates (e.g. options on Treasury bonds)	(100% of option premium + 10% of underlying asset − out-of-the-money amount (if any)) or (option premium + 5% of exercise price) if this is greater	Same as initial margin
Combinations	Margin requirements for positions involving multiple options take the risk of the entire portfolio into account, which can lead to more complex formulas for margin requirements. For details, see the *Margin Manual* published by the CBOE (www.cboe.com).		

Source: Chicago Board Options Exchange (2000), *Margin Manual*, Chicago: CBOE.

where c_0 is the call price (per 100 units) and $100 \times \max(0, X - \text{index})$ is the out-of-the-money amount. For example, suppose we observe the S&P index at 1165 along with a call option contract with a strike price of 1200 and a call price (option premium) of $900. In this example,

$$A = \$1900 + (0.15 \times 100 \times \$1165) - \max[0, 100 \times (\$1200 - \$1165)]$$

$$= \$1900 + \$17\,475 - \$3500 = \$15\,875$$

$$B = \$1900 + (0.10 \times 100 \times \$1165) = \$1900 + \$11\,650 = \$13\,550$$

Hence, the margin is

$$\text{Margin} = \max(\$15\,875; \$13\,550) = \$15\,875$$

To write one call option contract on the S&P index, we are required to post a margin of $15 875. This margin is quite a bit more than the possible proceeds of $1900. The reason is that if stock prices rise, then the option writer must pay the option buyer the difference between the index value and the exercise price. Exhibit 19.17 shows that for short positions in options, the maintenance margin is the same as the initial margin. The equations for both A and B above are influenced directly by the value of the index. As the index rises, so does the margin required. For example, if the index rises to 1175 and the call price rises to $2500, then the required maintenance margin is

$$A = \$2500 + (0.15 \times 100 \times \$1175) - \max[0, 100 \times (\$1170 - \$1175)]$$

$$= \$2500 + \$17\,625 - 0 = \$20\,125$$

$$B = \$2500 + (0.10 \times 100 \times \$1175) = \$2500 + \$11\,750 = \$14\,250$$

Hence, the margin required is

$$\text{Margin} = \max(\$20\,125; \$14\,250) = \$20\,125$$

Thus, the option writer must place additional monies as margin. Specifically, $\$20\,125 - \$15\,875 = \$4250$ more must be placed as margin.

Practice box

Problem

Determine the required initial margin on selling an IBM call option contract that has a market value of $3 per share and is $5 out of the money; the stock is selling at $95.

Solution

From Exhibit 19.17 for equities, we can develop the following expression:

$$\text{Margin} = \max(A, B)$$

where

$$A = c_0 + (0.20 \times 100 \times S_0) - [100 \times \max(0, X - S_0)]$$

$$B = c_0 + (0.10 \times 100 \times S_0)$$

Recall that each contract is for 100 options, and $c_0 = \$300$, $S_0 = \$95$ and $X - S_0 = \$5$. Therefore,

$$A = \$300 + (0.20 \times 100 \times \$95) - [100 \times \max(0, \$5)] = \$300 + \$1900 - \$500 = \$1700$$

$$B = \$300 + (0.10 \times 100 \times \$95) = \$300 + \$950 = \$1250$$

Therefore,

$$\text{Margin} = \max(\$1700; \$1250) = \$1700$$

Thus, selling a call option valued at $300 will require $1700 in collateral.

Note that brokerage firms have the discretion to require higher margins if they wish. Note also that the focus is on default by option writers. Normally, option buyers must pay for the option in full; this totally eliminates the possibility of default by the option buyer. Thus, option buyers can never default on the contract, because option contracts give the option buyers the right, but not the obligation, to do something in the future. Specifically, an option buyer at worst could lose the option premium, but the buyer had to pay up front. Different regulations might apply for options with expiration dates that lie very far into the future.

19.6 Investment strategies using derivatives

When using derivatives, an investor generally has a certain desired payoff pattern, conditional on the underlying asset prices. Derivatives are an easy way to adjust or create payoff patterns and require relatively small up-front investments of capital. Usually, there are many strategies to achieve the same result. However, one type of derivative can be more suited for a certain goal than another type.

19.6.1 Futures versus options strategies

Investment strategies using forwards (and futures) do not need to be discussed here: the payoff pattern of a forward (and a futures) is similar to that of the underlying asset (see Exhibit 19.2). Hence, in principle, studying investment strategies for bonds and stocks is sufficient in order to learn about investment strategies for futures. The important difference in terms of the amount of payoffs is the amount of leverage: for the same investment, profits and losses in the futures market are much larger. Payoffs also differ slightly because of the timing of the cash flows (especially when derivatives are marked to market). Other differences include fewer restrictions on possible investments when using derivatives; going short is much easier using futures. However, when it comes to the actual pattern of payoffs, futures are very much like their underlying assets. In the remainder of this section, we will focus on options.

Options are a different story; they differ from most other securities because the profits and the losses are not symmetrical. For option buyers, losses are limited to the purchase price (which is relatively low), but profits can be virtually unlimited. Due to this asymmetry, options are well suited for investment strategies based on a prediction of the future stock price behaviour.

The simplest strategies involve buying or writing options of a single class in combination with a position in the underlying asset. More complex option strategies involve several options. For example, a spread involves holding both long and short positions on the same type of option (for example, calls on Exxon), but the options have different expiration dates and exercise prices. Straddles involve either buying or selling both puts and calls on the same underlying asset with the same exercise price and expiration date. Many other varieties exist, and almost any payoff pattern can be created if sufficient options (for instance, if the difference in strike prices is small enough) are available and one is willing to combine them in a complex way.[27] This is demonstrated at the end of the next section.

19.6.2 Option strategies

This section reviews several strategies using the data for Exxon Mobil stock listed in Exhibit 19.18.

Simple option strategies

Suppose an investor purchases Exxon stock for $50 per share and becomes concerned that its price might fall dramatically in the near future. However, he or she also believes that there is a strong chance that Exxon stock will double in the near future. (For example, there is a chance that a new offshore drilling site might yield gains and a chance that the site is worthless.

---

[27] Since exchange-traded options usually provide a rather limited choice in strike prices, one needs OTC deals with tailor-made conditions to make this a reality. Also see Payoffs 'à la carte' on p. 670.

Exhibit 19.18	Exxon Mobil stock data	
Strike price	Call price	Put price
$X_L = \$45$	$C_{0,L} = \$8$	$p_{0,L} = \$1.50$
$X = \$50$	$C_0 = \$5$	$p_0 = \$3.50$
$X_H = \$55$	$C_{0,H} = \$3$	$p_{0,H} = \$6.50$

Current stock price is $S_0 = \$50$.
H, higher strike price; L, lower strike price.

Likewise, the stock price of pharmaceutical companies will often change substantially in response to approval of a medicine by the Food and Drug Administration (FDA). The investor does not know for sure which of the two possibilities will be realised. What can he or she do? If the investor holds the stock, he or she is exposed to possible losses. If the investor sells the stock, he or she might miss out on an increase in price. One solution to this problem is to buy out-of-the-money put options on Exxon stock. Having the stock and at the same time buying a put option is called **protective put** buying. By buying a protective put option, investors can set a floor on their losses.

Exhibit 19.19 graphs the payoff diagrams of both buying the stock and buying a $45 strike, $1.50-per-share put option (see black payoff lines). If the stock price remains at $50 per share, then the investor has no profit or loss on the stock and has a $1.5-per-share loss on the put option, because it expired out of the money. At a stock price of $45, the investor has a total loss of $6.50, because the stock position has a loss of $5 (i.e. $50 − $45) and the put position is still not in the money, resulting in a $1.50-per-share loss. The bold blue payoff line in Exhibit 19.19 illustrates the net position for protective put buying. Note that for a stock price of $51.50, the net profit is zero, as $1.50 is earned on the stock but the investor loses $1.50, which is the premium on the put option.

Notice that the net position is very similar to the payoff diagram derived when simply buying a call option. The only actual difference relates to possible dividends.

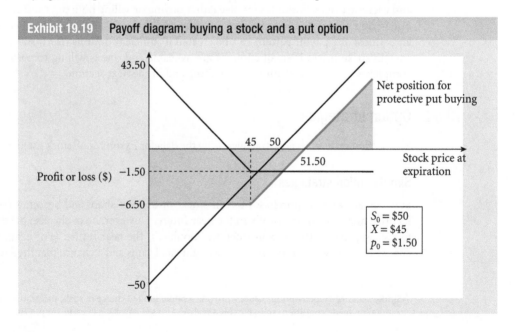

Exhibit 19.19 Payoff diagram: buying a stock and a put option

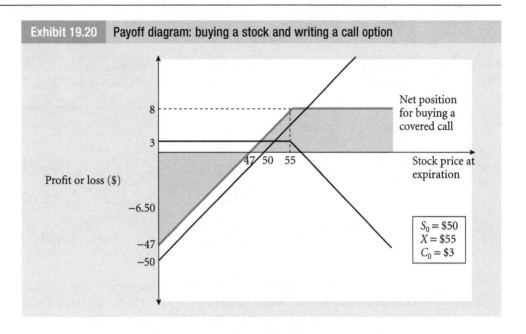

Exhibit 19.20   **Payoff diagram: buying a stock and writing a call option**

Now suppose an investor purchased Exxon stock for $50 per share, wanted to generate additional cash flow, and did not believe that Exxon's stock price had much potential for a substantial rise. What could he or she do? One solution to this problem is to write out-of-the-money call options on Exxon stock. Having the stock and writing a call option is called covered call writing.

Exhibit 19.20 illustrates the payoff of both buying the stock and writing a $55 strike, $3-per-share call option. Recall that a call buyer benefits when the stock price rises; hence, a call writer suffers a loss in this case. If the stock price rises to $55 (the strike price), then the investor has a $5 (i.e. $55 − $50) gain in the stock and a $3 (the call premium) gain on the call option, because it expired at the money. Notice in Exhibit 19.20 that above a $55 stock price, for every additional dollar gained on the stock position, the call option position loses a dollar. Investors are willing to accept this ceiling in return for receiving the call premium. Hence, the profit is greatest at $8 ($5 from the stock and $3 from selling the option). Below a $55 stock price, for every additional dollar reduction in the stock position, the call position's cash flow does not change. Hence, the net position loses a dollar.

The bold blue line in Exhibit 19.20 illustrates the net position of covered call writing. Notice that the net position is very similar in its shape to the payoff diagram derived when just writing a put option.

Spreads, straddles and strangles

Spreads, straddles and strangles add one layer of complexity: they involve the use of two options. Suppose the investor knows that Exxon will release its quarterly earnings soon and he or she expects a slight run-up in the stock price. The investor is also concerned that there may be a large negative earnings surprise. What can he or she do? Buying the stock would expose the investor to large potential losses. A bull spread is appropriate in this case. This strategy is designed to allow investors to profit if prices rise but to limit investors' losses if prices fall. For example, an investor employing a bull spread buys a call option with a low strike price (X_L) and sells a call option at a high strike price (X_H).

Exhibit 19.21	Profits and losses for a bull call spread		
Stock price at expiration (S_t) ($)	Long call[a] at $X_L = \$45$ ($)	Short call[b] at $X_H = \$55$ ($)	Bull spread[c] ($)
40	−8	3	−5
45	−8	3	−5
50	−3	3	0
55	2	3	5
60	7	−2	5
70	17	−12	5

[a] Profit on long call: $\max(0, S_t - X_L) - C_{0,L}$.
[b] Profit on short call: $-\max(0, S_t - X_H) + C_{0,H}$.
[c] Total profit is the sum of the profit on the call and the profit on the put.

Let us examine this bull spread.[28] Consider buying one call with a strike price of X_L ($45) at $8 and selling one call with a strike price of X_H ($55) at $3. Exhibit 19.21 shows the dollar profits and losses on the options at maturity for various stock prices. If the stock price falls below $45, then the most one can lose is $5 (an $8 loss on the call at X_L plus a $3 gain on the written call at X_H). Therefore, the investor loses only $5 on the bull spread. If the investor had just purchased the stock and the stock price fell to $40, then he or she would stand to lose $10 (i.e. $50 − $40). Hence, with the bull spread, the investor has less risk. Unfortunately, the potential return is also limited. The most one can gain is $5 if the stock price exceeds $55. To illustrate this claim, suppose the stock price rose to $70. The low strike price call value would be $25 (i.e. $70 − $45) and the profit on this option would be $17 (i.e. $25 − $8). The high strike price call is $15 in the money ($70 − $55); thus, the writer would lose $12 (i.e. −$15 + $3), so the total profit would be $17 − $12 = $5. For each additional dollar over $55, one has a $1 increase in the loss on being short the call at X_H. Also, the investor has a $1 increase in the gain on being long the call at X_L. Therefore, the net additional profit from the stock price increase is zero, and the maximum profit is $5 in this particular example.

The payoff diagram for a bull spread is shown in Exhibit 19.22. Notice that the investor profits if the price rises even slightly (which is not true if the investor merely purchases a call option, because the investor first has to recoup the call premium).

Once again, we see that there is no free lunch, even if the premiums that one pays and receives cancel out. The bull spread allows us to limit our losses, but it also limits the potential for large gains. Determining whether this strategy is optimal for an investor depends on the investor's risk preferences and future stock price expectations. Options offer a wider array of potential payoff patterns than an investor could earn solely from investments in stock.

There is more than one way to implement a bull-spread strategy. To be more specific, a bull-spread strategy can be achieved by the following possible investments:

- Buy a call at X_L and sell a call at X_H.
- Buy a put at X_L and sell a put at X_H.
- Buy a call at X_L, sell a put at X_H and sell short the stock.
- Buy a put at X_L, sell a call at X_H and buy the stock.

---

[28] Some reserve the word 'spread' for a strategy involving the sale and purchases of different options on the same underlying asset, and use the term 'collar' for a bull (or bear) spread.

Exhibit 19.22	Payoff diagram for a bull spread

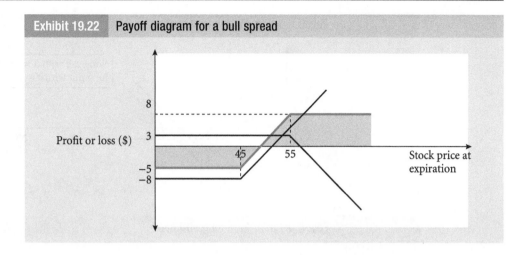

The next strategy, a straddle, is useful when an investor believes that something dramatic will happen to the stock price, but he or she is not sure exactly in which direction it will go. For example, the company might make a major research and development announcement, which can be either a major success or failure.

A straddle requires buying or selling both a single put and call on the same asset, with the same exercise price and expiration date. Investors employing a long straddle purchase options; those using a short straddle sell options. Let us consider a straddle with at-the-money Exxon options.

As shown in Exhibit 19.23, buying an at-the-money call ($X = \$50$) costs $5 per share and buying an at-the-money put costs $3.50 per share. Exhibit 19.23 illustrates the profits and losses for different possible stock prices at maturity. The most that can be lost is $8.50 when the stock price remains at $50, and both options have no value at maturity. When the stock moves either up or down, the long straddle increases in value, as illustrated graphically in Exhibit 19.24. At a stock price of either $58.50 or $41.50, the break-even on the total profit on the position exactly equals $8.50, which is the cost of the put and the call that were bought.

Exhibit 19.23	Profits and losses for an at-the-money long straddle		

Stock price at expiration date (S_t) ($)	Long call[a] at $X = \$50$ ($)	Long put[b] at $X = \$50$ ($)	Long straddle[c] ($)
0	−5	46.50	41.50
30	−5	16.50	11.50
41.50	−5	5	0
45	−5	1.50	−3.50
50	−5	−3.50	−8.50
55	0	−3.50	−3.50
58.50	3.50	−3.50	0
60	5	−3.50	1.50

[a] Profit on call: $\max(0, S_t - X) - c_0 = \max(0, S_t - \$50) - \$5$.
[b] Profit on put: $\max(0, X - S_t) - p_0 = \max(0, \$50 - S_t) - \$3.5$.
[c] Total profit is the sum of the profit on the call and the profit on the put.

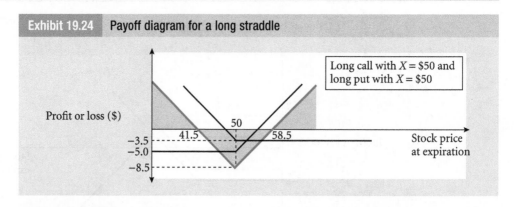

Exhibit 19.24 Payoff diagram for a long straddle

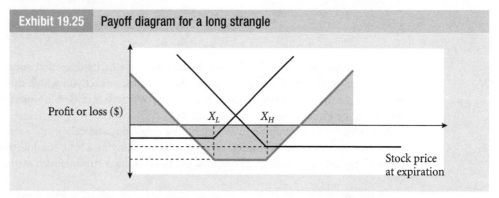

Exhibit 19.25 Payoff diagram for a long strangle

By the same procedure, we could also sell a put and a call, resulting in a payoff diagram that mirrors that of Exhibit 19.24 (with the mirror on the horizontal axis).

Yet another possibility is to invest in a strangle (see Exhibit 19.25). Again, the investor buys a call and a put, but the call has a higher exercise price (X_H). This results in an area where the movement of the stock price between X_L and X_H doesn't change the profit or loss. With a strangle, the downside risk is less than with a straddle. In the case of a short strangle, one sells a call and a put.

Payoffs 'à la carte'

The preceding sections showed that using more options opens up more possibilities. This is true generally and can be shown with a general result: any payoff pattern can be created if the appropriate options are available. This follows from a construction known as a butterfly. A long butterfly consists of buying two call options: one with a low strike price X_L and one with a high strike price X_H. Then one writes two calls with an intermediate strike price X. This results in a payoff pattern as shown in Exhibit 19.26. If X_L and X_H are chosen to be closer to each other, then this strategy results in a profit for a very limited and narrowing range of the value of the underlying asset and a very small loss in all other cases. If larger quantities of options are used (while keeping the ratios constant), then the slopes become steeper. Therefore we can, in the limit,[29]

---

[29] With this, we mean that we let the quantities of options approach infinity and let the difference between X_L and X_H approach zero. In reality, the transaction costs of this approach are prohibitive, resulting in the development of various exotic options and strategies to find a balance between desired payoff patterns and transaction costs.

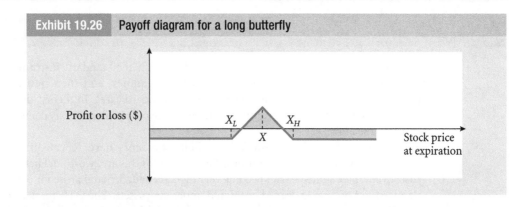

Exhibit 19.26 Payoff diagram for a long butterfly

Exhibit 19.27 Option strategies: costs, benefits and possible structure

Strategy name	Expected direction of stock	Profit potential limited	Loss potential limited	Option position			
				Calls, long	Calls, short	Puts, long	Puts, short
Long call	Up	No	Yes	X_H	–	–	–
Short call	Down	Yes	No	–	X_H	–	–
Long put	Down	No	Yes	–	–	X_L	–
Short put	Up	Yes	No	–	–	–	X_L
Bull spread	Up	Yes	Yes	X_L	X_H	–	–
Bear spread	Down	Yes	Yes	X_H	X_L	–	–
Long butterfly	Neither	Yes	Yes	$X_L + X_H$	2 at X	–	–
Short butterfly	Either	Yes	Yes	2 at X	$X_L + X_H$	–	–
Long straddle	Either	No	Yes	X	–	X	–
Short straddle	Neither	Yes	No	–	X	–	X
Long strangle	Either	No	Yes	X_H	–	X_L	–
Short strangle	Neither	Yes	No	–	X_H	–	X_L
Call ratio spread	Neither	Yes	No (+)*	X_L	2 at X	–	–
Put ratio spread	Neither	Yes	No (–)	–	–	X_H	2 at X
Call ratio backspread	Either	No (+)	Yes	2 at X	X_L	–	–
Put ratio backspread	Either	No (–)	Yes	–	–	2 at X	X_L

* No (+) indicates that potential is not limited on the positive side. No (–) indicates that potential is not limited on the negative side.

achieve a portfolio that results in a profit for a single value of the underlying asset. If we combine enough of these portfolios with different values for X, then we can create any payoff pattern we like.

Exhibit 19.27 illustrates some well-known strategies and how they might be generated. The 'expected direction of stock' column in Exhibit 19.27 is the direction that will produce the largest profits for the particular strategies. 'Neither' in this column indicates that the largest gains will be produced if the stock price does not move or moves only slightly. The 'profit potential limited' column indicates whether large profits are possible. The 'loss potential limited' column addresses whether the strategy produces the potential for large losses. The 'option position' columns provide one of many explicit trading strategies that could be implemented under the named strategy.[30]

---

[30] For the sake of brevity and clarity, only one potential trading strategy is provided here.

19.7 Financial engineering

The preceding chapters and sections have dealt with the standard instruments of investing: first money-market instruments, bonds and equities, and then futures and options (European calls and puts can be regarded as the standard case). In theory, these instruments can be combined to form an infinite number of payoff profiles, as was demonstrated in the preceding section.[31]

However, despite this theoretical flexibility, investors have repeatedly expressed their interest in more tailor-made solutions. The reasons for this are two-fold. First, the transaction costs of complex strategies can become very high; second, demand arose for contracts on non-standard and often non-traded or illiquid underlying assets. The OTC markets responded by creating large amounts of new, innovative financial instruments. Also, users implemented more traditional derivatives in new ways (for example, the managed futures funds mentioned earlier). These two processes taken together are most aptly described by the term 'financial engineering'.

Its extensive use in the 1980s and 1990s made it difficult to keep track of all developments and their efficacy – Steven Ross once spoke of a 'financial zoo'.[32] Yet, most innovations have been made to help investors reach their traditional goals as described in the beginning of this chapter: speculating, arbitrage, hedging and portfolio diversification. The innovations survive in the marketplace only if investors have a good reason to buy them – they must make speculating, hedging, and so on, easier, cheaper or more rewarding. This is done in several ways. Financial innovations:

- improve investment opportunities (and hence the allocation of capital, leading to a better return on assets);
- facilitate management of risks (some risks could not be hedged previously, or only at high cost);
- improve the monitoring of company executives and mutual fund managers (again, improving return);
- evade or react to tax and accounting regulations.

The remainder of this section will discuss briefly the major innovations that financial engineering has brought us.

The first reason why investors resort to financial engineering is prohibitive transaction costs. If an investor requires a strategy that consists of buying and selling standard instruments in continuously varying quantities or requires multiple non-standard expiration dates, then it is much cheaper to ask a large party whether they can provide the investor with this payoff pattern as a single package. Major examples are:

- *Exotic options* (a general term for complex options constructions):
  - *Compound options*: this is an option on an option, increasing the leverage even more.
  - *Barrier options*: these cease to exist if the price of the underlying asset hits a certain level (knock-out barrier option) or can only be exercised after that level is reached (knock-in barrier option).

---

[31] This should not be confused with the construction of a synthetic replica of an instrument for arbitrage. The section Payoffs à la carte, as well as this section, discuss ways to obtain payoff profiles that otherwise would not exist.

[32] Ross (1989).

- *Look-back and shout options*: these options have a payoff that is determined by the maximum (or minimum) of the price of the underlying asset during the life of the option (look-back option) or at a specific moment determined by the buyer (shout option). For example, a look-back call enables the buyer to buy the underlying asset at the lowest price reached during the life of the option.
- *Asian options*: the payoffs of these constructions depend on the average price of the underlying asset during the lifetime of the option.
■ *Options on futures and swaps*: as shown in the next chapter, trading in the underlying asset and borrowing or lending money in varying proportions can replicate the payoff of options, and this is true as well when the underlying asset is a derivative itself. However, it is much easier to ask a bank to write (or buy) a new option with another underlying asset, such as an existing option or swap.

The second reason (demand for contracts on non-standard or non-traded underlying assets) led financial engineers to (among others) the following derivatives:

■ *Credit spread options.* These are options on the difference between two interest rates, one for riskier bonds than the other, for example on the credit spread between corporate AA rated bonds and B rated bonds.
■ *CAT bonds.* These are bonds that have a changing interest rate (or where the principal has to be repaid only in part) if a certain catastrophe happens. These are useful for companies with assets in, for example, earthquake-prone areas, while investors benefit from higher interest rates and low correlations (as the effect of catastrophes generally is independent of the rest of the economy).
■ *Weather derivatives.* These are derivatives with a weather index as underlying value and are useful for clients with seasonal activities, such as farmers, manufacturers of winter-sports goods and ice-cream producers. Again, investors profit from low correlations.

Summarising, if there is any kind of derivative that may attract enough demand to be profitable for its developers, then a financial engineer is likely to create it. Overall, this process creates benefits in terms of more investment and hedging possibilities, but – as always – one has to keep track of where such risks end up.

Summary

Explain the basics of derivative contracts.

A futures contract is a marketable obligation to deliver a specified quantity of a particular asset on a given day (or during a given period). A forward contract is similar to a futures contract, except that a forward contract is not marketable. A swap contract is a bundle of forwards based on the exchange of payments. An option buyer has the right, but not the obligation, to buy (call option) or sell (put) the underlying asset in the future at a predetermined exercise price. Exhibit 19.28 provides an overview of some important characteristics of these basic derivatives.

Describe the process of buying and selling derivatives.

Forwards and swaps usually are tailor-made and are negotiated directly with a bank or the counterparty. Futures contracts are traded on exchanges; this trade is handled by futures commission merchants (FCMs). The clearing house guarantees performance by both sides

Exhibit 19.28	Characteristics of basic derivatives

Derivative	Markets	Value at purchase	Potential loss	Potential gain
Forward	OTC	0	Large[a]	Unlimited
Swap	OTC	Mostly 0	Unlimited[b]	Unlimited[b]
Future	Exchange	0	Large[a]	Unlimited
Long call option	Exchange, OTC	Positive, c_0	c_0	Unlimited
Long put option	Exchange, OTC	Positive, p_0	p_0	Large[a]
Short call option	Exchange, OTC	Positive, c_0	Unlimited	c_0
Short put option	Exchange, OTC	Positive, p_0	Large[a]	p_0

[a] The maximum loss (gain for long puts) occurs if the underlying asset becomes worthless.
[b] 'Unlimited' gains or losses in swaps occur only if the obligations of one party become 'infinitely' large and the receipts of the other stay stable or decline. If the obligations are fixed or limited (e.g. in a credit swap), this cannot occur – it requires a floating element of which the price explodes.
OTC, over-the-counter.

of the futures contract. It ensures that the futures contract buyer will deliver and the futures contract seller agrees to accept delivery. Options are also exchange-traded; the process is similar. In the USA, the OCC guarantees that the required payments will be made. It also issues option contracts, maintains appropriate records and processes all the necessary financial transactions.

Explain how derivatives traders can be protected from default.

Default protection is achieved through the clearing house, which acts as the counterparty. The clearing house is protected by margin requirements and marking to market (for futures). Margin is required from both sides of the contract. The initial margin amount is usually higher than the maintenance margin. When a losing position reduces the margin account balance below the required maintenance margin, then a margin call is placed to replenish the margin account to its initial margin level. With futures contracts, profits and losses are taken daily through a process known as marking to the market.

Describe the benefits of using derivatives and explain their risks.

Derivatives are easy-to-use and often exchange-traded instruments that can create payoff patterns or modify existing ones to reduce risk or profit from the realisation of expectations. They require relatively low initial investments. Selling futures or writing options (without owing the underlying asset) can expose one to an extremly large risk; for some instruments, the potential loss is almost unlimited.

Describe the basic strategies involving derivatives contracts.

Four basic strategies use derivative contracts: hedging, speculating, arbitrage and portfolio diversification. Hedging strategies use derivatives to offset an existing risk exposure, whereas speculating seeks to profit by taking more risk. Arbitrage strategies are based on equal pricing between various markets. Option strategies are used to create specific payoff patterns. Protective put buying sets a floor on potential losses, whereas covered call writing sets a ceiling on potential gains. Spreads are used when investors believe that the stock price will change by a small amount, straddles when they expect a large change. In theory, every payoff pattern can be constructed using options.

Key terms

American-style options 653
Arbitrage 626
At-the-money 654
Bull spread 667
Butterfly 670
Call option 650
Cash settlement 630
Closing transaction 653
Commodity swap 636
Contingent claim 624
Covered call 667
Covered position 654
Credit swap 634
Currency swap 636
Derivative security 624
European-style options 653
Exercise price 650
Exercising 650
Expiration date 651
Financial engineering 672
First notice day 645
Floor broker 645
Forward contract 628

Futures commission merchants
  (FCMs) 645
Futures contract 636
Hedging 626
Interest-rate swap 632
In-the-money 653
Intrinsic value 654
Locals 645
Long position 628
Margins 639
Marked to market 638
Maturity date 651
Naked position 654
Notional principal 632
Opening transaction 653
Open interest 643
Option 650
Option buyer 650
Option class 651
Option premium 651
Options Clearing Corporation
  (OCC) 662
Option series 651

Option writers 650
Out-of-the-money 654
Payoff diagram 630
Pit 645
Plain vanilla swap 632
Portfolio diversification 626
Protective put 666
Put option 650
Settle price 643
Short position 628
Short-seller 651
Speculating 626
Spread 665
Straddles 665
Strangle 670
Strike price 650
Swap 631
Underlying asset 624
Warehousing swaps 633
Warrants 654

Review questions

1 **a.** What are the three main reasons why derivatives can add value to society as a whole?
   b. What are the four basic strategies in which derivatives are used? Provide a brief description of each.

2 **a.** Explain the difference between an interest rate swap and a currency swap.
   b. If you were a financial manager for a large bank and you expected short-term interest rates to rise more than the market expects, what type of swap agreement should you engage in to try to make a profit based on this belief?

3 Suppose that the initial margin is $30,000 for an S&P 500 index futures contract, and that the maintenance margin is $27,000. Each S&P 500 index futures contract is for 500 times the index value. Suppose that on Day 0 you purchased one futures contract at 1218 points. Describe the cash flow to and from your account, given the following ten days of settle prices. Assume there is no withdrawal from the account, and the surplus remains in the account.

Day	Settle price	Day	Settle price
0		6	1222
1	1220	7	1217
2	1225	8	1210
3	1218	9	1215
4	1215	10	1220
5	1219		

4 Suppose that you are the chief financial officer in a company that produces chocolate and have just entered into a contract to deliver a large amount of candy to a large fast-food chain in six months. You know that your firm will be purchasing 2000 metric tons of cacao in five months and that a five-month futures contract on cacao is trading at $1000 per metric ton, and that each contract is for 10 metric tons. If the cost of cacao is $1000 per metric ton in five months, you anticipate a profit of $200 000 (based on a fixed revenue of $5.2 million, with $3.0 million in costs regardless of the price of cocoa, and $2.0 million in costs to purchase the cacao):

   a. Map the profit and loss from this contract with the fast-food chain with respect to future cacao prices.
   b. Illustrate the profit and loss from purchasing one five-month cacao futures contract in a graph.
   c. How could you completely hedge the cacao price risk? Demonstrate your results in a graph. Discuss the costs and benefits for your company of hedging with futures contracts.
   d. Suppose that your company was confident that cacao prices were going to be very stable, and that your assistant suggested not to hedge price movements but to speculate on a stable cacao price instead. Can this be done with futures? Can this also be done with options? If so, describe how.

5 Suppose that the stock price is $100 and the call price is $5 with a strike price of $105. What is the profit or loss on the following two strategies when the stock price goes up to $110? And when the stock goes down to $90?:

   a. Writing a call option.
   b. Writing a covered call option; that is, writing a call and buying the stock.

For an extensive set of review and practice questions and answers visit the Levy–Post investment website at www.booksites.net/levy

Selected references

Bookstaber, R. M., 1991, *Option Pricing and Investment Strategy*, 3rd edn, Chicago: Probus Publishing.

Chance, Don M., 2004, *An Introduction to Derivatives and Risk Management*, 6th edn, London: South-Western.

Chicago Board Options Exchange, 2000, *Margin Manual*, Chicago: CBOE.

Copleston, F. S. J., 1985, *A History of Philosophy*, Vol. 1, Garden City, NY: Image Books.

Cox, J. C. and M. Rubinstein, 1985, *Options Markets*, Englewood Cliffs, NJ: Prentice-Hall.

Dubofsky, D. A. and T. W. Miller, 2003, *Derivatives, Valuation and Risk Measurement*, New York: Oxford University Press.

Ehrhardt, M. C., J. V. Jordan and R. A. Walking, 1987, 'An Application of APT to Futures Markets: Test of Normal Backwardation', *Journal of Futures Markets*, **7** (1), 21–34.

Fabozzi, F. J., 1989, *The Handbook of Fixed-Income Options Pricing, Strategies & Applications*, Chicago: Probus Publishing.

Figlewski, S., W. L. Silber and M. G. Subrahmanyam, 1990, *Financial Options from Theory to Practice*, Homewood, IL: Business One Irwin.

Futures Magazine Source Book, 2003, 2004, Chicago, IL: Futures Magazine Group.

Gibson, R., 1991, *Option Valuation Analyzing and Pricing Standardized Option Contracts*, New York: McGraw-Hill.

Green, J. and E. Saunderson, 1998, 'No Room at the Top', *Risk*, 11.

Hull, J., 2003. *Fundamentals of Futures and Options Markets*, 4th edn, Englewood Cliffs, NJ: Prentice-Hall.

Konishi, A. and R. E. Dattatreya, 1991, *The Handbook of Derivative Instruments*, Chicago: Probus Publishing.

McLean, S. K. 1991, *The European Options and Futures Markets*, Chicago: Probus Publishing.

Options Institute, 1990, *Options: Essential Concepts and Trading Strategies*, Homewood, IL: Business One Irwin.

Robertson, M. J., 1990, *Directory of World Futures and Options*, Englewood Cliffs, NJ: Prentice-Hall.

Ross, S., 1989, 'Institutional Markets, Financial Marketing, and Financial Innovation', *Journal of Finance*, **64** (3), 541–556.

Smith, C. W., Jr, and C. W. Smithson, 1990, *The Handbook of Financial Engineering*, New York: Harper Business.

Smith, C. W., Jr, C. W. Smithson and D. S. Wilford, 1990, *Managing Financial Risk*, New York: Harper & Row.

Swan, E. J., 2000, *Building the Global Market: A 4000 Year History of Derivatives*, London: Kluwer.

Tsiveriotis, K. and N. Chriss, 1998, 'Pricing with a Difference', *Risk*, 11, 80–83.

Tyson-Quah, K., 1997, 'Clearing the Way', *Risk*, **10**, 8.

CHAPTER 20

Derivatives valuation

Investment in the News 20

FT

Press release by the Nobel committee

The Royal Swedish Academy of Sciences has decided to award the Bank of Sweden Prize in Economic Sciences in Memory of Alfred Nobel, 1997, to Professor Robert C. Merton, Harvard University, Cambridge, USA and, Professor Myron S. Scholes, Stanford University, Stanford, USA, for a new method to determine the value of derivatives.

Robert C. Merton and Myron S. Scholes have, in collaboration with the late Fischer Black, developed a pioneering formula for the valuation of stock options. Their methodology has paved the way for economic valuations in many areas. It has also generated new types of financial instruments and facilitated more efficient risk management in society.

This year's laureates, Robert Merton and Myron Scholes, developed this method in close collaboration with Fischer Black, who died in his mid-fifties in 1995. These three scholars worked on the same problem: option valuation. In 1973, Black and Scholes published what has come to be known as the Black–Scholes formula. Thousands of traders and investors now use this formula every day to value stock options in markets throughout the world. Robert Merton devised another method to derive the formula that turned out to have very wide applicability; he also generalized the formula in many directions.

Black, Merton and Scholes thus laid the foundation for the rapid growth of markets for derivatives in the last ten years. Their method has more general applicability, however, and has created new areas of research – inside as well as outside of financial economics. A similar method may be used to value insurance contracts and guarantees, or the flexibility of physical investment projects.

Black, Merton and Scholes' method has become indispensable in the analysis of many economic problems. Derivative securities constitute a special case of so-called contingent claims and the valuation method can often be used for this wider class of contracts. The value of the stock, preferred shares, loans, and other debt instruments in a firm depends on the overall value of the firm in essentially the same way as the value of a stock option depends on the price of the underlying stock. The laureates had already observed this in their articles published in 1973, thereby laying the foundation for a unified theory of the valuation of corporate liabilities.

Banks and investment banks regularly use the laureates' methodology to value new financial instruments and to offer instruments tailored to their customers' specific risks. At the same time such institutions can reduce their own risk exposure in financial markets.

Source: Press release: the Sveriges Riksbank (Bank of Sweden) Prize in Economic Sciences in Memory of Alfred Nobel for 1997. Used with permission.

This chapter covers the valuation of derivatives and how investors can determine whether derivatives are underpriced or overpriced. This has long been a theoretically daunting task, but one of great importance, which is illustrated by Investment in the News 20. Robert Merton and Myron Scholes received the 1997 Nobel Prize in economics for their contribution to option valuation. Fischer Black, who is a co-author of the work behind the Black–Scholes option valuation model, did not live to share the Nobel Prize for his contribution to the breakthrough option valuation model.

Derivative valuation relies heavily on the no-arbitrage rule – that is, in equilibrium, no arbitrage profits can be made. Recall that the same rule was used in Chapter 11 to derive the APT. This approach differs from the perspective we used in Chapter 13 on valuing bonds and Chapter 15 on valuing stocks, which was to discount future cash flows at a rate appropriate for the risk of these cash flows. We saw that when applying a discounted cash flow approach, we had two major tasks: estimate future cash flows (and, therefore, companies' earnings) and decide how to correct the discount rate for the risk of the cash flows. These tasks are already difficult for valuing bonds and stocks. For valuing derivatives, the problems are even more severe. First, derivatives' expected cashflows can be very volatile, and it can be very difficult to obtain accurate estimates for them, as they are very dependent on the price of the underlying asset – derivatives are often highly levered. Second, with derivatives, there is no constant risk-adjusted discount rate for the cash flows, because the risk of dervatives can change drastically as, for example, the value of the underlying asset or the time to maturity changes. For this reason, the research focused on a method that doesn't require discounting risky cash flows: valuation based on the no-arbitrage rule.

Hence, understanding the price behaviour of derivatives requires knowledge of derivatives arbitrage. Recall from Chapter 11 that an arbitrage opportunity means that with zero investment today, one will get only non-negative payments in the future.[1] In other words, there exists a chance for profit without risk of losing money, and it's available for free.[2] In equilibrium, arbitrage opportunities do not exist; the existence of arbitrage profit thus represents disequilibrium. Yet, when there are arbitrage opportunities available, they do not last long. With the computer technology available today, investors need to be quick to exploit arbitrage opportunities; everyone will want to take advantage of them, because arbitrage is basically

---

[1] Where at least one of these payments is non-zero.

[2] Note that this definition is rather general: an arbitrage opportunity also exists when a portfolio can be constructed that yields a cash inflow today and with no risk of future losses. By lending all the proceeds received today, one will receive a positive payoff in the future, again with zero net investment. So, this is also an arbitrage opportunity. See Section 11.2.1 for some examples.

a 'free lunch'. Derivative prices are determined for the most part by derivative traders eliminating arbitrage opportunities.

To understand this, let us look at the implications of a profitable arbitrage trade using derivatives: suppose a call option on a stock (exercise price is $21) is priced at $3.00. The stock is worth $15 and the put (exercise price also $21) is worth $7. The options are European and expire in one year. The interest rate is 5%. There is an arbitrage opportunity here. Specifically, an investor can make an abitrage profit if he or she (1) sells the call option, (2) borrows $20, (3) buys one stock and (4) buys one put option, The cash inflow today is $3 + $20 = $23 and the outflow today is $15 + $7 = $22, resulting in a net cash flow today of $23 − $22 = $1. But look at what happens at expiration: the net payoff is zero! One can check this using the payoff diagrams from Chapter 19.

Hence, the investor can earn a dollar without bearing any risk. Clearly, this investor will not use this strategy only once with a single contract but, rather, on as large a scale and as often as possible. The profit could be infinite – as long as these prices prevail. Clearly, a virtually infinite profit at no risk is highly desirable, so more investors will use this trading strategy. But as volumes increase, prices will adjust. The sale of large numbers of call options will cause downward pressure on the price, while the purchase of put options will raise the price (the other instruments may respond as well, but assume for a moment that only the option prices will adjust). As a result, the profit decreases. This process will continue for as long as there are any profits to be made, so in the end the prices will be the same. In practice, the adjustment process can be completed in merely a few minutes or seconds.

The example above shows that the concept of no arbitrage is a powerful tool for valuing securities. As long as an instrument can be replicated using investments with known prices, then arbitrage will ensure that the price of the instrument will be equal to that of the synthetic replica.[3] So, if we know the composition of this replicating portfolio, we know the value of any instrument. This approach is especially powerful for valuing derivatives, since they derive their value from an underlying asset, which is almost always traded. This makes constructing the replicating portfolio relatively easy – we need only the underlying asset and the ability to lend or borrow money, for which we use the risk-free instrument. Note that we do not use a discounted cash-flow approach and we thereby circumvent the problem of determining a risk-adjusted discount rate. Instead, we rely solely on the no-arbitrage rule, which says that the value of an instrument and its synthetic replica should be the same.

The remainder of this chapter will examine the valuation of various derivatives. We will first introduce some necessary terminology. Then we discuss the valuation of futures contracts, which also provides a blueprint for swaps and forwards (although these are not discussed explicitly). Futures valuation focuses on the so-called cost-of-carry model. In option valuation, we first examine the option valuation boundaries that all option prices must satisfy. Option prices remain within the boundaries because of arbitrage forces in the market. The chapter then develops the binominal model. Next, we shift to continuous time, and we discuss the Black–Scholes valuation approach to determine the equilibrium price of an option and its inputs. Finally, we examine empirical problems associated with the BS model.

Note that most of the illustrations in the sections on options relate to valuing stock options. However, the same principles demonstrated in this chapter apply to valuing options on any underlying asset, such as stock index options, options on futures, and foreign currency options.

---

[3] In the example above, the portfolio with a stock, a put and borrowed money is a synthetic replica for the call option.

20.1 Static and dynamic hedges

To help one understand the material in this chapter, it is helpful to make a distinction between two ways to conduct an arbitrage trade. The first uses a portfolio that remains riskless by construction (of the payoff pattern of the instruments involved) after the initial purchase, which is called a static hedge.[4] The initial portfolio remains riskless during the entire investment horizon, so a static hedge requires no further trades. The second way is a series of trades, creating a portfolio that must be rebalanced after each movement in price in order to remain riskless. The latter is a dynamic hedge.

We will encounter examples of a static hedge in futures valuation and both static and dynamic hedging in option valuation. The difference is no coincidence: dynamic hedging is required to create a 'synthetic derivative', where the payoff profile of the derivative is a non-linear function of the value of the underlying asset. If both derivative and underlying have similar payoff patterns (both patterns are linear), then a static hedge will suffice. If their patterns differ, such as in the case of options (compare the linear payoff of the stock and the asymmetrical pattern of the option depicted in Chapter 19), then a dynamic hedge is required. Every time the price of the underlying asset changes, one has to recalculate the proportions of stocks and bills that make up an arbitrage (or hedged) portfolio, and sell or buy assets accordingly. The only exception in option valuation is a case like that described in the example above, where one uses an option to create a static hedge for another option.

In practice, dynamic hedges are also used for risk management as alternatives or supplements to derivatives, as will be illustrated in Chapter 21. However, during the crash of October 1987, many investors using dynamic hedging were unable to trade the underlying assets at sufficient speed and quantities to maintain their hedges. Furthermore, the large amount of sales triggered by the dynamic hedges were – according to some observers – contributing to the crash, since they called for selling stocks when prices fell, causing them to fall even further. Current practice in many markets is that most investors use futures contracts rather than the underlying asset itself to create dynamic hedges – futures provide greater liquidity in case one needs large exposures.

20.2 Valuation of futures

This section develops general valuation models for futures contracts.[5] Futures prices rarely equal the current value of the spot asset. Most of the time, futures prices have a clear pattern when compared across maturities: futures prices on any underlying asset are almost always below or above the spot for all maturities. But why does this pattern differ for different underlying assets? How can we explain the fact that early-maturity futures of the S&P 500

---

[4] One should bear in mind that hedging and arbitrage are related, but different, strategies: in arbitrage, one tries to profit form pricing errors or differences in the market without taking on price risk, while hedging is intended to eliminate price risk on an existing exposure. However, since any arbitrage trade is supposed to be riskless, the positions taken should hedge each other, hence the use of the term 'hedge' in this context.

[5] Forward prices are often regarded as equivalent to futures prices. But, as the time to maturity increases the difference in the manner that the two contracts are settled (forwards at maturity, being an OTC product, and futures during the life of the contract as well as at maturity because they're marked to market) results in differences in the timing of the different cash flows involved, a difference that is often non-negligible for the amounts usually involved with these kinds of contracts.

index are consistently less than the S&P 500 index value? And what is the value that a futures contract should have, based on the no-arbitrage principle? The ability to value futures contracts is useful in many ways. Investors are able to assess whether the current futures prices are reasonable and adjust their portfolios accordingly. Also, even when futures are not being bought or sold by an investor, futures prices contain useful information on, for example, interest and exchange rates.

20.2.1 Valuing stock index futures

What should the value of a futures contract be before maturity? Let us look in detail at an S&P 500 index futures contract. Recall that the S&P 500 is a value-weighted index of 500 common stocks, and that the S&P 500 index futures contract is cash-settled, as described in Chapter 19.

One can create an arbitrage portfolio for this futures contract. Consider the following strategy: borrow $S_0 + m$, where m is the margin required on one futures contract and S_0 is the current stock price. Use this money to buy the stock (in our example, the S&P 500 index) and short a futures contract (requiring margin m), for a total initial cash flow of zero. The borrowing is for a predetermined period – until the futures contract matures. Let us see what happens at the end of this period. The cash flow required to repay the loan is $-(S_0 + m)(1 + r)$, where r is the relevant interest rate. The stock generates a cash flow $S_T + D$, where S_T is the stock price at the end of the period and D is the cash dividend paid.[6] The short futures contract required a margin of m, on which interest is earned, so the cash flow at the end of the period is $m(1 + r)$ plus the profit or loss from shorting the contract. At maturity, the spot price is equal to the futures price, so this latter part of the cash flow on the futures is $F_0 - S_T$, where F_0 is the current futures price.[7]

As Exhibit 20.1 reveals, the total cash flow today is zero by construction of the financial strategy. To avoid an arbitrage opportunity, the total future cash flow from the three investments (the loan, the stock and the futures contract) must be also zero, namely,

$$F_0 - S_0(1 + r) + D = 0$$

Exhibit 20.1	Determining the equilibrium price of stock index futures	
Strategy	**Cash flow today**	**Cash flow at end of one period**
Borrow $(S_0 + m)$	$S_0 + m$	$-(S_0 + m)(1 + r)$
Buy stock for S_0	$-S_0$	$S_T + D$
Sell one futures contract	$-m$	$(F_0 - S_T) + m(1 + r)$
Net position	0	$F_0 - S_0(1 + r) + D$

S_0 = current stock price, S_t = stock price at expiration, F_0 = current future price, m = margin required on one future contract, D = cash dividend paid, r = risk-free interest rate.

Source: From *Introduction to Investments*, 2nd edn, by Levy. © 1999. Reprinted with permission of South-Western, a division of Thomson Learning: www.thomsonrights.com. Fax 800 730-2215.

---

[6] For convenience, we assume that the dividend is paid at the end of the period. If not, we should correct for interest on the dividend.

[7] At maturity, futures and spot prices will always be equal. Buying a futures contract that matures immediately is no different than buying the asset on the spot market, see Chapter 19.

or

$$F_0 = S_0(1 + r) - D$$

Because D/S_0 (also denoted by d below) is the dividend yield, we obtain[8]

$$F_0 = S_0(1 + r) - S_0 \frac{D}{S_0} = S_0(1 + r - d) \tag{20.1}$$

In summary, the futures price is a function of the current index value, the risk-free interest rate, the dividend yield and the time to maturity. This means that the futures price is equal to the spot price plus the net benefits of owning the spot asset. That is, if the S&P 500 index is purchased by borrowing at the risk-free interest rate, then the cost of financing for the relevant period is r. However, actually owning the securities in the S&P 500 gives investors a dividend flow that reduces these financing costs. When the terminology was developed, these benefits where usually negative (as is true for commodity futures), and these net benefits are usually described as the cost of carrying the asset. For this reason, Equation 20.1 is often referred to as the cost-of-carry model.

It is interesting to note that the expectation regarding future prices does not enter the equation for futures valuation, except through S_0. Given current market conditions, the current price is the best estimate of the (discounted) future price, otherwise the price would change today – again, because of no arbitrage.[9]

All futures contracts can be priced using a similar approach. The only differences lie in the cost of owning (carrying) the underlying asset. In the case of the stock indices, the cost of owning the index is the risk-free rate (the financing cost) minus the dividend yield (the cash flow from the asset). For example, assume that the dividend yield on the MMI is 3% and the risk-free interest rate is 5%.[10] Also assume that the MMI is currently at 1045 and six-month futures are trading at 1085. Thus, $1085 > 1045(1 + 0.05 - 0.03)^{1/2} = 1055.4$, and an arbitrage profit is available. Consider the trading strategy that follows Exhibit 20.1. Buy the underlying MMI (either by direct purchase of the underlying securities or by purchasing a mutual fund that mimics the MMI); sell one futures contract that would require interest-bearing margin; and, finally, borrow the margin as well as the MMI price ($1045). Thus, the initial cash flow will be zero. From Exhibit 20.1, we know that this strategy produces a positive cash flow (for zero investment) in the future of $1085 - 1045(1 + 0.05 - 0.03)^{1/2} = 29.6$ per unit of the MMI.

This activity will drive the futures price down and the index value up. The arbitrageur plays an important role in making the securities market-efficient by trading on price discrepancies. Note that in practice, the arbitrageur does take some risks, such as the risk of mis-estimating the dividend yield or the current interest rate.

---

[8] If we have continuously compounded dividend and interest, then the equation can also be rewritten as $F_0 = S_0 e^{(r-d)t}$, where t is the fraction of a year between the two periods and $r - d$ is the total rate of return on the stock minus the dividend rate of return components – that is, the rate of return that is due to capital gains only.

[9] This might not hold when market conditions are expected to change in the future, for instance due to decreased supply (think of a major refinery closing for maintenance, diminishing oil products supply). These forecastable changes are a common occurrence in some markets.

[10] See Chapter 6 for a description of the MMI.

Exhibit 20.2	Determining the equilibrium price of foreign currency futures	
Strategy	**Cash flow today**	**Cash flow at expiration**
Borrow one British pound (convert to local currency)	S_0	$-S_1(1 + r_f)$
Lend $(S_0 - m)$ in the USA	$-(S_0 - m)$	$(S_0 - m)(1 + r_L)$
Purchase futures position to buy $(1 + r_f)$ pounds for F_0 dollars	$-m$	$(1 + r_f)(S_1 - F_0) + m(1 + r_L)$
Net position	0	$S_0(1 + r_L) - F_0(1 + r_f)$

S_0 = current exchange rate, S_1 = exchange rate at expiration, F_0 = current future price, m = margin required on one future contract, r_f = foreign risk-free interest rate, r_L = domestic risk-free interest rate.

20.2.2 Valuing currency futures

Currency futures can be evaluated in much the same way as index futures, except that the cost of carry is the difference between the domestic risk-free rate (r_L) and the foreign risk-free rate (r_f). Exhibit 20.2 illustrates the financial strategy by which one can derive an equilibrium price for futures on foreign currency. The primary difference between currency futures and index futures is that we assume that for currency futures, the foreign risk-free rate is earned, whereas in the index futures calculation, we assume the dividend yield is earned – when the spot currency is purchased, this sum is supposedly invested in foreign risk-free assets.

Exhibit 20.2 details the financial transactions, the cost of these transactions today, and the cash flows at contract expiration for the arbitrage strategy. Once again, a margin of m dollars is assumed on future transactions. This example uses British pounds for the foreign currency and US dollars for the local currency.

First we borrow £1, which at the current exchange rate (S_0) provides a cash flow of S_0 dollars. For example, if the exchange rate is 0.625 pounds to one dollar, then borrowing £1 will provide \$1.60 (= 1/0.625), and S_0 is 1.60. Then we have to pay $1 + r_f$ pounds, where r_f is the foreign risk-free interest rate that the British bank charges for the relevant transaction period. However, because in one year the exchange rate will be \$$S_1$ per pound, the cash payment in dollars will be \$$S_1(1 + r_f)$.

We lend $S_0 - m$ in the USA to obtain $(S_0 - m)(1 + r_L)$ in the future, where r_L is the interest in local currency for the relevant period. Finally, we purchase futures to buy $1 + r_f$ pounds; today we pay a margin of m, and next year we get an interest of $m(1 + r_L)$ plus a profit on the future transaction of $(1 + r_f)(S_1 - F_0)$.

With no arbitrage profit, the cash flow at the end of the period must be zero. Therefore,

$$F_0 = S_0 \left(\frac{1 + r_L}{1 + r_f} \right) \qquad (20.2)$$

where S_0 and F_0 are the spot and futures prices of one asset of foreign currency in terms of a local currency.[11] The cost of carry is $(1 + r_L)/(1 + r_f)$ for each dollar that the underlying asset

---

[11] With annualised continuous interest rates, this formula can be written as $F_0 = S_0 e^{(r_L - r_f)t}$ where t is the time, usually given as a fraction of a year.

is worth. Note that if the interest rate is given for a different time as the maturity of the contract (for instance, as an annual rate whereas the contract has only half a year left to maturity), then we need to correct the formula for this by taking $(1 + r_L)^t/(1 + r_f)^t$, where t is the time to maturity as the fraction of the period for which the rate is given.

Practice box

Problem

Suppose one is an arbitrage trader in the Swiss franc foreign exchange. After a major move in exchange rates, the following information is observed: $S_0 = \$0.65/\text{SwF}$ (the foreign exchange rate between US dollars and Swiss francs), $F_0 = \$0.64/\text{SwF}$ (foreign exchange futures price), $r_L = 3\%$ (the annual US risk-free rate), $r_f = 6\%$ (the annual Swiss risk-free rate), and $t = 0.5$ year. Are these prices in equilibrium? How will one profit if they are not in equilibrium?

Solution

To see whether these prices are in equilibrium, calculate the theoretical futures price and compare it with the actual futures price. Thus,

$$F_0 = S_0 \frac{(1 + r_L)^{1/2}}{(1 + r_f)^{1/2}} = (\$0.65/\text{SwF})\left(\frac{1.03}{1.06}\right)^{1/2} = 0.6407/\text{SwF}$$

which is higher than the current futures price of $0.64/SwF. Thus, the futures price is too low relative to the spot price. So, in this case, the arbitrage trade suggested in Exhibit 20.2 would result in the following cash flow today (see 'Net position' in the exhibit):

$$S_0(1 + r_L) - F_0(1 + r_f) = (\$0.65/\text{SwF})(1.03)^{1/2} - (\$0.64/\text{SwF})(1.06)^{1/2} \cong 0.00076$$

This strategy will result in a positive cash flow of 0.00076 and no cash flow in the future. (Note that both the buyer and the seller of futures contracts must place a margin.)

The futures market in foreign exchange is also useful to determine (implied) interest rate differentials, as the following practice box shows. Investors may take an interest in these markets if the implied interest rates differ from the observed rates (which might be due to a foreign exchange policy that cannot be maintained).[12]

Practice box

Problem

Assume that the British pound December 1997 futures contract settled at $1.6664/£ and the March 1998 contract settled at $1.6604/£. What is the implied interest-rate difference for this period between the pound and the dollar? (Assume that the yield curve is flat in both countries.)

Solution

We know from Equation 20.2 that

$$F_{\text{Dec97}} = S_0 \left(\frac{1 + r_L}{1 + r_f}\right)^{t_1} \tag{1}$$

---

[12] Readers interested in this subject are referred to L. S. Copeland (2000), *Exchange Rates and International Finance*, 3rd edn, Englewood Cliffs, NJ: Prentice-Hall. pp. 435–466.

$$F_{\text{Mar98}} = S_0 \left(\frac{1 + r_L}{1 + r_f} \right)^{t_2} \tag{2}$$

Dividing Equation 2 by Equation 1 yields

$$F_{\text{Mar98}} / F_{\text{Dec97}} = \left(\frac{1 + r_L}{1 + r_f} \right)^{(t_2 - t_1)}$$

Because these contracts are three months apart, we know that $t_2 - t_1 = 3/12 = {}^1/4$. Substituting for the futures prices yields the following:

$$1.6604/1.6664 \cong 0.9964 = \left(\frac{1 + r_L}{1 + r_f} \right)^{1/4}$$

Thus,

$$\left(\frac{1 + r_L}{1 + r_f} \right) \cong 0.9857, \text{ or } r_L - r_f \cong -1.43\%$$

The implied interest-rate difference between the USA and Britain is about -1.43%.

20.2.3 Valuing commodity futures

Exhibit 20.3 shows a transaction with commodity futures. To price commodity futures, we need to consider two parts of the cost of carry that are specific to commodities: storage costs and insurance costs, denoted by C. Here, S_0 is the current price of the commodity and F_0 is the price of the futures of the commodity. S_T is the future price of the commodity and m is the margin required on the futures transaction. Once again, no arbitrage profit implies the following:

$$F_0 = S_0(1 + r) + C \tag{20.3}$$

For commodity futures whose underlying assets are held purely for consumption (or production) purposes, as one can argue for pork-belly futures and such, Equation 20.3 changes slightly, to

$$F_0 \leq S_0(1 + r) + C$$

If $F_0 > S_0(1 + r) + C$, then the no-arbitrage argument still holds, as arbitrageurs can borrow the amount needed, at $1 + r$, to finance $S_0 + C$, and short a futures contract. But if $F_0 < S_0(1 + r) + C$, then one can make an arbitrage profit only by selling the underlying asset and acquir-

Exhibit 20.3	Determining the equilibrium price of commodity futures	
Transaction	Cash flows today	Cash flow at expiration
Buy asset at price S_0	$-S_0$	$S_T - C$
Borrow $S_0 + m$	$S_0 + m$	$-S_0(1 + r) - m(1 + r)$
Short futures position	$-m$	$F_0 - S_T + m(1 + r)$
Net cash flow	0	$F_0 - S_0(1 + r) - C$

S_0 = current currency price, S_t = currency price at expiration, F_0 = current future price, m = margin required on one future contract, C = cost of carry, r = risk-free interest rate.

Source: From *Introduction to Investments*, 2nd edn, by Levy. © 1999. Reprinted with permission of South-Western, a division of Thomson Learning: www.thomsonrights.com. Fax 800 730-2215.

ing futures contracts. Owners of the underlying asset will be reluctant to do this, because they own the underlying asset for consumption purposes, the value they derive from owning it might outweigh the possible arbitrage profit.

Recall that the investor who owned stock index futures received dividends, so the financing cost was reduced by the benefit of the dividends. With commodities, on the other hand, storage and insurance costs are an additional cost of carrying the asset.

20.2.4 Basis

Let us return to some of the questions at the beginning of this section: how can we explain the pattern in futures settle prices compared with the spot prices, especially when the futures price is below the spot? The above should make clear that the answer is the cost of carry. Let us use Equation 20.1, but interpret d as the total cost of carry: observing S_0 and r, and estimating d, the price of the futures, F_0, is given by

$$F_0 = S_0(1 + r - d)$$

If $r > d$, then $r - d > 0$ and $F_0 > S_0$, and the exact reverse is true if $r < d$. Since d can be positive or negative, depending on the underlying asset, we can explain futures prices both below and in excess of the spot price. Note that some writers consider the difference $(r - d)$ to be the cost of carry, implying that d is usually greater than r, which by no means needs to be the case.

But practitioners often look at the cost of carry in a slightly different way: they calculate the basis. The basis is the difference between the current spot price and the current futures price (it is totally different from the concept of a basis point). Specifically,

$$\text{Basis} = \text{spot price} - \text{futures price}^{13}$$

$$B_t = S_0 - F_{0,t}$$

where B_t denotes the basis using a futures contract maturing at time t, S_0 is the current spot price, and $F_{0,t}$ is the current futures price of a futures contract maturing at t. The basis changes during the life of a futures contract and may be positive or negative. The first situation is called (normal) backwardation (also known as a normal market); in the second situation, the futures market is said to be in contango (also known as an inverted market). There is one certainty, however: right before maturity, the basis will go to zero (there exists an arbitrage opportunity if the futures price at maturity differs from the spot price). This process is called convergence.

The basis can be used for various trading strategies because of this characteristic. One can speculate on the basis, which means that an investor shorts the more expensive instrument and buys the cheaper one. This generates an initial cash flow, but at maturity, the net cash flow will be zero. Such a strategy will be less profitable if the underlying asset has a non-negligible cost of carry (which the basis might merely be compensating for). In that case, such a strategy is better described as arbitraging on the cost of carry. Basis is also important in hedging, because if the contract must be liquidated prematurely, then the basis may cause unanticipated losses (or profits), thus lowering the quality of the hedge.

There is a relation between the basis and the cost of carry, but their effect is somewhat different: when we examine the cost-of-carry model, we see that the cost of carry is usually a multplicative term with respect to the spot price, whereas the basis is always an addititive term.

---

[13] Basis is computationally the same as the concept of intrinsic value used in options, introduced in Chapter 19. However, American-style options can be exercised immediately, so the intrinsic value can actually be received in cash. With the basis, this is impossible, because the settle date is fixed and is in the future.

This means that the basis might change (in dollars), while the cost of carry remains the same (per unit of the underlying asset). Furthermore, the actual cost of carry will differ between investors, because in reality not everyone faces the same interest rates or storage costs. The basis can be calculated from market data alone, while the cost of carry is (slightly) investor-specific, making it a less reliable measure on which to base a trading strategy.

20.3 Option valuation: bounds

Even if we evaluate option prices just by looking at their value at expiration, we can already conclude that options cannot have any value; their prices must lie between certain boundaries. These option value boundaries provide a helpful first step in the quest to understanding option prices, because if the prices wouldn't satisfy the boundaries, then investors could make an arbitrage profit. We demonstrated in the introduction to this chapter that arbitrage activity would quickly push the option price inside these bounds.

An aditional advantage is the fact that these bounds are not influenced by assumptions regarding the distribution of returns. Models that determine a value for options (instead of bounds) are always dependent on a distributional assumption, even if they are derived from the no-arbitrage rule. Option value boundaries are the best answers we can give without making additional assumptions.

To illustrate these bounds, consider Exhibit 20.4, which is a hypothetical quote sheet for a market maker in Unilever options. Are these reasonable prices? Are the options overpriced? Are they underpriced? Finding option boundaries gives a preliminary answer to these questions.

Exhibit 20.4   Closing prices, options based on Unilever

(a) Closing price quotes

		Calls			Puts		
		Time to maturity			Time to maturity		
Stock price	Strike price	31 days	91 days	182 days	31 days	91 days	182 days
50	40	10.18	10.66	11.54	0.01	0.17	0.56
50	45	5.40	6.43	7.74	0.21	0.87	1.63
50	50	1.85	3.27	4.81	1.64	2.67	3.58
50	55	0.35	1.42	2.79	5.12	5.74	6.43
50	60	0.04	0.52	1.52	9.78	9.78	10.04

(b) Example of the analysis of option boundaries: lower bounds for the options in (a)

		Calls			Puts		
		31 days	91 days	182 days	31 days	91 days	182 days
Stock price	Strike price	31 days	91 days	182 days	31 days	91 days	182 days
50	40	10.17	10.48	10.96	0.0	0.0	0.0
50	45	5.19	5.54	6.08	0.0	0.0	0.0
50	50	0.21	0.61	1.20	0.0	0.0	0.0
50	55	0.0	0.0	0.0	4.77	4.34	3.68
50	60	0.0	0.0	0.0	9.75	9.28	8.56

Exhibit 20.5	Lower boundary for call options: cash-flow table			

	Cash flows			
			At expiration	
Trading strategy	Today (0)		$S_t \geq X$	$S_t < X$
Buy one call option	$-c_0$		$S_t - X$	0
Sell short one share of stock	$+S_0$		$-S_t$	$-S_t$
Lend $X/(1 + r)^t$	$-X/(1 + r)^t$		X	X
Net cash flow	$-c_0 + S_0 - X/(1 + r)^t = ?$		0	$X - S_t$ (positive)

c_0 = current call price, S_0 = current stock price, S_t = stock price at expiration, X = strike price, r = risk-free interest rate, and t = time to maturity in fractions of a year.

Source: From *Introduction to Investments*, 2nd edn, by Levy. © 1999. Reprinted with permission of South-Western, a division of Thomson Learning: www.thomsonrights.com. Fax 800 730-2215.

20.3.1 Call option boundaries

For a call option, there is both an upper and a lower boundary for the current call price. First, the lower boundary: the prices of a European-style call option (c_0) must lie above the following value:[14]

$$c_0 \geq \max\left[0, S_0 - \frac{X}{(1 + r)^t} \right] \tag{20.4}$$

where S_0 is the price of the underlying asset today, X is the strike or exercise price, t is the time to maturity until the expiration date (in fraction of years), and r is the annual risk-free interest rate, which is assumed to be constant. So, for calls that are in the money or just out of the money $[S_0 > X/(1 + r)^t]$, the value is always strictly positive (since the expected stock price will be the current one plus a growth of r). If the option is so far out of the money that the expected value at expiration is still less than the strike price, the boundary is zero, simply because an optionholder has a right, not an obligation, to buy.

To demonstrate that Equation 20.4 holds, we consider the trading strategy presented in Exhibit 20.5. (We assume that any trade opened at 0 is closed at t.) Note that we separate the future into two possibilities: $S_t \geq X$ and $S_t < X$. More information on the exact value of S_t is not needed.

The first column of Exhibit 20.5 identifies the exact trading strategy to adopt at time 0. The second to fourth columns contain dollar cash inflows if positive (+) and outflows if negative (−); the amount is based on the trading strategy in the first column. Recall that when an investor short-sells the stock, he or she receives money. The net cash flow at the bottom of this column is found by summing the cash flows in the 'Today' column (the required investment). The question mark (?) indicates that we investigate whether the investment will be positive, zero or negative if arbitrage profits are absent. The third and fourth columns depict the cash flow when $S_t \geq X$ and when $S_t < X$. So, in the future we receive either zero (column 3) or a positive payoff (column 4). So if the question mark represents a positive

---

[14] We use the term 'price' rather than 'premium' because these boundaries apply throughout the life of the option, not just on the initial purchase date. Also, we ignore the possibility of the stock going ex-dividend during the lifetime of the option. In that case, one would have to adjust the formulas, as the buyer of a call doesn't receive the dividend, while the short-seller of a stock is obliged to pay the dividend. Also see section 20.3.3.

cash flow, we receive money now and in the future, which opens the possibility of very easy arbitrage. The same occurs when the question mark is zero: one pays nothing today, yet one gets cash in the next period. The conclusion is that under no-arbitrage conditions, the question mark must represent a negative number:

$$-c_0 + S_0 - \frac{X}{(1+r)^t} \leq 0$$

which implies that

$$c_0 \geq S_0 - \frac{X}{(1+r)^t}$$

We can conclude that the inequality given in Equation 20.4 holds. Exhibit 20.4b presents the lower boundaries where r is assumed to be 5%. Notice that all of the closing call prices are above the lower boundary. For example, the quote on the 91-day call with a strike price of 45 is 6.43, whereas its lower boundary is $\max[0,\ 50 - 45/(1 + 0.05)^{91/365}] \cong 5.54$ (see Equation 20.4). However, the amount by which the option price is above the lower boundary varies.

Using similar arguments, we can demonstrate that the price of a European-style call option must lie below an upper boundary, being the underlying stock price:

$$c_0 \leq S_0 \tag{20.5}$$

Intuitively, we would not pay more for an option to buy a security than we would pay for the underlying security if we purchased it directly. For example, why should we pay $50 for the right to buy the stock when we could buy it in the market for $S_t = \$40$? Thus, a call option is always worth less than the underlying security on which the option is written.

Exhibit 20.6 illustrates the boundaries for call options. Note that if we have an American-style call option and it is exercised, then the value is $S_0 - X$. Because $c_0 > S_0 - [X/(1 + r)^t] > S_0 - X$, it never pays to exercise the call option before maturity. (Investors are better off selling the option.) Thus, the boundaries of European-style call options also apply to American-style options. The only caveat is that the reasoning above doesn't apply when the underlying asset pays dividends; this situation is discussed in Section 20.4.

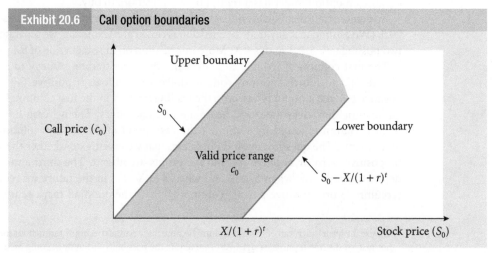

Exhibit 20.6 Call option boundaries

Source: From *Introduction to Investments*, 2nd edn, by Levy. © 1999. Reprinted with permission of South-Western, a division of Thomson Learning: www.thomsonrights.com. Fax 800 730-2215.

20.3.2 Put option boundaries

As with call options, European-style put options have value boundaries. The lower boundary for the put price (p_0) is

$$p_0 \geq \max\left[0, \frac{X}{(1+r)^t} - S_0\right] \qquad (20.6)$$

The trading strategy employed to demonstrate the lower boundary of a put option consists of three parts:

- borrowing the amount $X/(1+r)^t$;
- buying one share of stock;
- buying one put option.

Exhibit 20.7 illustrates the cash flows. The penultimate column of this table is non-negative by assumption ($S_t \geq X$). Therefore, if the cash flow today (0) is positive (? > 0), then this is an arbitrage opportunity. We are able to generate a positive cash flow today with no risk of future loss (and possibly a positive future cash flow). Thus, to avoid this arbitrage, we must find the cash flow today to be negative. This results in

$$-p_0 + X/(1+r)^t - S_0 \leq 0$$

which implies

$$p_0 \geq X/(1+r)^t - S_0$$

If we observe that $-p_0 + X/(1+r)^t - S_0$ is positive, everyone will want to buy put options, buy the stock and lend to create this money machine. Buying the stock and the put option will drive up the stock price and the put price, and eventually any arbitrage profits will vanish. Because the value of an option is never negative, Equation 20.6 holds.

The upper boundary is found by noting that the most an investor can lose from writing a put option (or earn by buying a put option) is the strike price. This occurs when the stock price falls to zero. Because this cash flow is paid at maturity and not on the day the put option is purchased, the put option price must be below the discounted value of the strike price:

$$p_0 \leq \frac{X}{(1+r)^t} \qquad (20.7)$$

Exhibit 20.7	**Lower boundary for put options: cash-flow table**		

	Cash flows		
		At expiration	
Trading Strategy	**Today (0)**	$S_t \geq X$	$S_t < X$
Buy one put option	$-p_0$	0	$X - S_t$
Borrow $X/(1+r)^t$	$+X/(1+r)^t$	$-X$	$-X$
Buy one share of stock	$-S_0$	$+S_t$	$+S_t$
Net cash flow	$-p_0 + X/(1+r)^t - S_0 = ?$	$S_t - X$ (positive)	0

p_0 = current put price, S_0 = current stock price, S_t = stock price at expiration, X = strike price, r = risk-free interest rate, and t = time to maturity in fractions of a year.

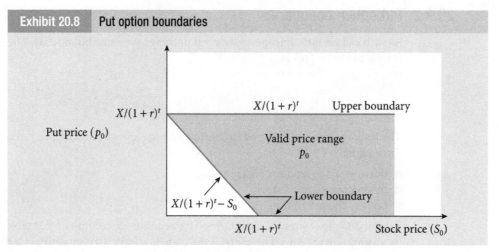

| Exhibit 20.8 | Put option boundaries |

Source: From *Introduction to Investments*, 2nd edn, by Levy. © 1999. Reprinted with permission of South-Western, a division of Thomson Learning: www.thomsonrights.com. Fax 800 730-2215.

Why would an investor pay more for an option than the present value of its maximum payoff? The answer is that they would not. For example, a one-year put option with a strike price of $50 at a 5% risk-free rate has an upper boundary of $47.62 [$50/(1 + 0.05)^1]. Investors will not pay more than $47.62 for a put option that gives them the right to make at most $50 one year from now. The only exception is an American-style option, which one can exercise today. For these options, the upper boundary is just the exercise price.

Exhibit 20.8 illustrates the boundaries for European-style put options. Again, the valid range of prices is still wide. We must investigate option valuation further to find out whether we can make a more precise assertion regarding the option price. We will now examine the relationship between stock, put option and call option prices.

Practice box

Problem

Based on the following information, verify that the closing prices of General Motors' put and call options satisfy the boundary conditions. The time to maturity is one month ($t = 1/12$), GM's stock price is $41.88, and the annual risk-free interest rate is 3%. Are there any arbitrage opportunities?

Expiration date and strike price	Closing price ($)
GM Oct 40 call	3.70
GM Oct 40 put	1.75
GM Oct 45 call	1.65
GM Oct 45 put	4.30
GM Oct 50 call	0.55
GM Oct 50 put	8.35

Solution

Clearly, none of these prices approaches the upper bounds ($41.88 for calls and $40, $45 and $50 discounted for one month at the risk-free rate for puts). We now examine the lower bounds. The discount factor is $1/(1 + r)^t = 1/(1 + 0.03)^{1/12} = 0.9975$. Thus, for $X = $40, we have $40 \times 0.9975 = \$39.90$; for $X = \$45$, we have $\$45 \times 0.9975 = \$44.8875$; and for $X = \$50$, we have $\$50 \times 0.9975 = \$49.875$.

Let us consider calls first. When $X = \$40$, we have a lower boundary of $\$41.88 - \$39.90 = \$1.98$, which is lower than the closing price of $3.70. When $X = \$45$, we note that $\$44.8875 > \$41.88$, and the lower boundary is zero. This is also true when $X = \$50$. In both cases, the lower boundary holds.

The boundaries for puts (using Equation 20.6) are as follows:

$X = \$40 \; p_0 = 0$
$X = \$45 \; p_0 = \$44.8875 - \$41.88 = \$3.0075$
$X = \$50 \; p_0 = \$49.875 - \$41.88 = \$7.995$

We see that each lower boundary is below the put option prices. Thus, based on these observations, there are no arbitrage opportunities.

20.3.3 Put–call parity

The notion of put–call parity (PCP) was first published by Russell Sage in the late nineteenth century. Put–call parity establishes an exact relationship among the current stock price, the call price and the put price at any given moment. In other words, put–call parity establishes the relationship among the underlying security, the risk-free interest rate, and call and put options that have the same strike price. Given any three of the following four securities – (1) underlying security, (2) zero-coupon bonds (borrowing or lending),[15] (3) a call option and (4) a put option – we can synthetically create the fourth. That is, by creating a portfolio of three assets, we can duplicate the cash flow of the fourth asset. Put–call parity can be written as follows:

$$c_0 = S_0 - \frac{X}{(1+r)^t} + p_0 \tag{20.8}$$

Intuitively, it helps to shift $-X/(1 + r)^t$ to the left-hand side, which shows that a call and a certain bond will be equivalent to a put and the underlying asset. If we draw a payoff diagram of these two combinations, one can see easily their equivalence. Again, we assume that any trade opened at time 0 is closed at the option maturity date (t). Exhibit 20.9 establishes the validity of Equation 20.8.

As before, the first column of Exhibit 20.9 identifies a trading strategy adopted at time 0 (today). The other three columns show the relevant cash flows. The net cash flows are simply the sums of all cash flows from the investment. Since the future cash flows are all zero, the value today should be zero as well (regardless of the discount rate used). Rearranging terms yields Equation 20.8. Any deviation from put–call parity will result in arbitrage opportunities, as was shown in the introduction to this chapter: the prices in that example violated put–call parity.

One can also adjust the formula for a stock that pays a dividend; we'll use this later on. If we assume that the dividend yield is a fixed percentage (so that the dividend depends on the value of the stock at the time it is paid), then put–call parity is given by

$$c_0 = \frac{S_0}{(1+q)^t} - \frac{X}{(1+r)^t} + p_0$$

---

[15] Buying a zero-coupon bond is equivalent to lending money, and selling a zero-coupon bond is equivalent to borrowing money.

Exhibit 20.9   Put–call parity: cash-flow table

		Cash flows	
		At expiration	
Trading strategy	Today (0)	$S_t \geq X$	$S_t < X$
Buy one call option	$-c_0$	$S_t - X$	0
Sell short one share of stock	$+S_0$	$-S_t$	$-S_t$
Lend $X/(1+r)^t$	$-X/(1+r)^t$	X	X
Sell (write) one put option	$+p_0$	0	$-(X-S_t)$
Net cash flow	$-c_0 + S_0 - X/(1+r)^t + p_0$	0	0

c_0 = current call price, p_0 = current put price, S_0 = current stock price, S_t = stock price at expiration, X = strike price, r = risk-free interest rate, and t = time to maturity in fractions of a year.

Source: From *Introduction to Investments*, 2nd edn, by Levy. © 1999. Reprinted with permission of South-Western, a division of Thomson Learning: www.thomsonrights.com. Fax 800 730-2215.

Practice box

Problem

Using the information in the previous problem on General Motors, evaluate whether the put–call parity holds when the strike price is $X = \$40$.

Solution

From Equation 20.8, we know that

$$c_0 - p_0 = S_0 - \frac{X}{(1+r)^t}$$

and we have $c_0 = \$3.70$, $p_0 = \$1.75$, $S_0 = \$41.88$, $X = \$40$, $r = 3\%$ and $t = {}^1/_{12}$. We need to evaluate whether the following equality exists:

$$\$3.70 - \$1.75 \stackrel{?}{=} \$41.88 - \$39.90$$

$$\$1.95 \neq \$1.98$$

Thus, put–call parity does not hold precisely. However, it would probably be impossible to profit from this discrepancy because of transaction costs. In practice, put–call parity holds very closely.

20.4   The binominal model

In this section, we discuss the first of two models that aim to give a valuation of options instead of a boundary condition. There is a reason why there are two models: we have seen in previous chapters that investments can be evaluated both with discrete interest and with continuously compounded interest. This difference – and the mathematical consequences of the choice – has led to two approaches concerning the valuation of derivatives and options in particular: a model in discrete time and one in continuous time. The first, called the binominal model, assumes that prices can change only at predetermined moments and stay constant in between; the latter (the Black and Scholes model) assumes that prices change continuously – not every second but all the time. These approaches are equivalent in their outcomes (given the same set of assumptions, and the continuous time approach often requires some additional assumptions to get a result), but they differ widely in their ease of use for different situations. In this section, we will first derive some basic results on option valuation using the discrete time approach. In the next section, we switch to the continuous time formulation, which is discussed at length. However, we must first deal with the relationship between the boundaries and the valuation models, a relation that involves time value.

20.4.1 Time value

Where does the option price lie within the boundaries? The answer is given by time value. Derivative prices can be broken down into two components: intrinsic value and time value. As we have seen in Chapter 19, the intrinsic value of a derivative is the value if the option would be exercised immediately and the stock would be sold by the party acquiring it. Even if an option is out of the money, the chance that the stock price may change and the option may end up in the money gives the option time value.[16] Let c_0 and p_0 represent the call and put premiums, respectively. Then, the time value of a call (TV_c) is

$$TV_c = c_0 - IV_c \tag{20.9}$$

The time value of a put (TV_p) is

$$TV_p = p_0 - IV_p \tag{20.10}$$

The chance that the option becomes in the money (or stays in the money if it is already so), and by how much, determines the time value of an option. In loose terms, we can identify the following factors (we make this more precise in a continuous time setting, in Section 20.5) influencing this chance and its value:

■ The amount the price of the underlying asset moves: if a stock's value changes regularly, then the chance that the price will move to the region where the option is in the money is larger than when the price of the stock hardly ever moves.
■ The discount rate for future payments: any future cash flow (including those resulting from an option that is in the money when it matures) has a present value that is lower than the nominal amount. How much lower is clearly important if we want to know the price of an option today.
■ The amount of time left before the option expires: this affects both the discounting and the chance that the price of the stock will end up in a favourable region.

The relative importance of these factors depends mainly on the ratio of the current share price and the exercise price.

---

[16] Most often, the term 'time value' refers to discounting future cash flows. When related to options, time value has a different meaning. It is the value of the option related to the chance that the option may go in the money (or further in the money, if it is already in the money).

Problem   Suppose the following option quotes for TotalFinaElf are given:

Option and NY Close	Strike price	Calls			Puts		
		Oct.	Nov.	Dec.	Oct.	Nov.	Dec.
154	150	4.25	7.50	8.25	0.35	2.25	3.00
154	155	0.80	3.85	5.00	1.75	4.50	5.30
154	160	0.15	2.00	2.45	6.10	7.75	8.25

Compute the intrinsic value and time value for each option.

Solution   The intrinsic value is the dollar amount of an in-the-money option. For calls, only the 140 strikes are $4 in the money. For puts, the 155 strikes are $1 in the money and the 160 strikes are $6 in the money. Thus, we can construct the following table for intrinsic value:

Intrinsic value strike price	Calls			Puts		
	Oct.	Nov.	Dec.	Oct.	Nov.	Dec.
110	4	4[a]	4	0	0	0
115	0	0	0	1	1	1
120	0	0	0	6	6[b]	6

[a] $IV_c = \max(0, S_0 - X) = \max(0, \$154 - \$150) = \$4$.
[b] $IV_p = \max(0, X - S_0) = \max(0, \$160 - \$154) = \$6$.

The time value is nothing but the option value minus the intrinsic value. We can construct the following table of time value:

Time value strike price	Calls			Puts		
	Oct.	Nov.	Dec.	Oct.	Nov.	Dec.
110	0.25	3.50[a]	4.25	0.35	2.25	3.00
115	0.80	3.85	5.00	0.75	3.50	4.30
120	0.15	2.00	2.45	0.10	1.75[b]	2.25

[a] $TV_c = c_0 - IV_c = \$7.50 - \$4 = \$3.50$.
[b] $TV_p = p_0 - IV_p = \$7.75 - \$6 = \$1.75$.

20.4.2 The binominal option valuation model

Option boundaries are useful in explaining option prices, but they are too wide; therefore, a more precise method of valuing an option is needed. The binominal option valuation model (or binominal model for short) is an elegant and relatively simple way to price options. It is called 'binominal' because, as with the binominal distribution in statistics, it is assumed that only two future stock prices (outcomes) are possible at the end of a period, given the value at the beginning of the period. It is the main tool for option valuation in a discrete time context.

Like any valuation model, the binominal model is based on several assumptions:

- The capital market is characterised by perfect competition.
- Short-selling is allowed, with full use of the proceeds.
- Investors prefer more wealth to less.
- Borrowing and lending at the risk-free rate is permitted.
- Future stock prices will have one of two possible values after a (single) period.

The first assumption is the same assumption as was made in Chapter 11 in developing the APT. For option pricing, the elements that matter most are a frictionless market (a market where trading is costless: there are no taxes, bid–ask spreads, brokerage commissions, and so forth) and the assumption that investors are price-takers (meaning that no single investor can significantly influence prices). As discussed in Chapter 3, short-selling is selling stock that one doesn't own with the understanding that one will return stock to the lender in the future. Note that the third assumption does not imply a risk attitude: investors may be risk-averse, risk-neutral or even risk-seeking. The fourth and fifth assumptions are required to construct the hedge portfolios.

The binominal model for call options is developed in five steps.

Step 1: determine stock price distribution

Assume that the price of a stock can change from its current level of S_0 to only one of two possible future values, S_u or S_d, where u implies that the stock went up and d implies that the stock went down. To express the future value of the stock in terms of its current value, we set $S_u = uS_0$ and $S_d = dS_0$, where u and d are constants. Our framework leads to the restriction – $d < 1 + r < u$.[17] Graphically, we have

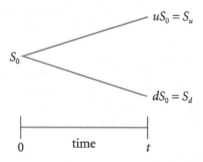

For example, assume that we have the following information: $S_0 = \$100$, $X = \$100$, $u = 1.10$, $d = 0.95$ and $r = 0.05$. With these data, $S_u = \$110$ and S_d is \$95. The model assumes that no other stock prices are possible; at expiration, the stock price will be either \$110 or \$95. However, as we shall see later on in this discussion, we can determine the equilibrium value of an option in this case without knowing the actual probabilities that S_u or S_d will occur.

---

[17] If $d > 1 + r$, then the stock will always yield more than the risk-free rate. In this case, everyone would borrow at r and invest in stock, yielding an arbitrage profit. If $u < 1 + r$, then the stock will always yield less than the risk-free rate. In this case, everyone would short-sell the stock and lend at r, yielding an arbitrage profit.

Step 2: determine the price distribution

Given step 1, we can now calculate the value of the call option at expiration. Specifically, the value of an option at expiration is just the dollar amount if it is in the money. That is, we can describe the call price distribution as follows:

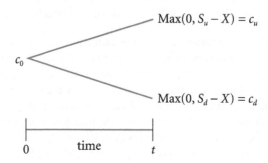

The data from our example result in the following situation: in state u, the value is the maximum of 0 and $(110 - 100)$, which is \$10. In state d, it is the maximum of 0 and $(95 - 100)$, which is 0.

Step 3: create a hedged portfolio

In this step, we construct a portfolio of a call option and a dynamic hedge of the option involving stock. However, we cannot yet determine the proportions of these two assets in the portfolio. In step 4, we tailor this portfolio to provide a future cash flow that is known with certainty – hence the term 'hedged portfolio'. Recall that the objective is to determine the call option price. This objective can be met by constructing a hedged portfolio. Consider the following strategy and the resultant cash flows depicted in Exhibit 20.10.

A hedged portfolio is constructed by first selling (i.e. writing) one call option. This action results in a positive cash flow today of the option price $(+c_0)$, but it requires paying out the option value (if any) at expiration $(-c_u$ or $-c_d)$ (see Exhibit 20.10). Next, an unspecified number of shares (h_c) of stock are purchased – the amount h_c will be specified in step 4. The proceeds from the sale of the shares will be either $h_c S_u$ or $h_c S_d$. The net cash flows are then found by adding the component cash flows from this trading strategy.

Step 4: solve for h_c

The number of shares we must buy for each call option we write (or sell) is given by h_c. At the start of step 4, we have net cash flows today (0) and at expiration (t) that depend on two unknown variables – the call price at 0 (c_0) and h_c, called the hedge ratio. It is a ratio because we are finding the number of shares of stock to buy for each call option that we write in order to eliminate future risks. That is, we find the ratio of calls written to stocks purchased that makes our future cash flows certain. To do this, we take the net cash flows of the hedged portfolio when S_u occurs and set that net cash flow equal to the net cash flows when S_d occurs:

$$-c_u + h_c S_u = -c_d + h_c S_d$$

In such a case, the portfolio's cash flow is certain, regardless of whether the stock's price rises or falls. Because all values are known apart from h_c, we can solve for h_c:

Exhibit 20.10 | **Hedged portfolio for a one-period binominal model to price a call option**

(a) Cash-flow table

		Cash flows	
		At expiration	
Trading strategy	Today (0)	$S_t = S_u = \$110$	$S_t = S_d = \$95$
Write one call option	$+c_0$	$-c_u$	$-c_d$
Buy h_c share of stock	$-h_c S_0$	$+h_c S_u$	$+h_c S_d$
Net cash flow	$+c_0 - h_c S_0 = ?$	$-c_u + h_c S_u$	$-c_d + h_c S_d$

(b) Example in which $S_0 = \$100$, $X = \$100$, $u = 1.10$, $d = 0.95$, $r = 5\%$ and $h_c = {}^2/_3$

		Cash flows	
		At expiration	
Trading strategy	Today (0)	$S_t = S_u = \$110$	$S_t = S_d = \$95$
Write one call option	$+c_0$	$-\$10$	$\$0$
Buy ${}^2/_3$ share of stock	$-({}^2/_3)\$100$	$+({}^2/_3)\$110$	$+({}^2/_3)\$95$
Net cash flow	$+c_0 - ({}^2/_3)\$100$	$-\$10 + ({}^2/_3)\$110$	$-\$0 + ({}^2/_3)\$95$
	$= +c_0 - \$66.67$	$= \$63.33$	$= \$63.33$

c_0 = current call price, c_u = call price at expiration when stock price goes up, c_d = call price at expiration when stock price goes down, S_0 = current stock price, S_t = stock price at expiration, S_u = stock price at expiration when it goes up, S_d = stock price at expiration when it goes down, and h_c = hedge ratio for a call.

Note that one has a positive cash flow at either state as well as an initial cash flow, whereas in an arbitrage strategy one preferably receives money without having to invest capital (on a net basis). This can be accomplished by shorting bonds at the risk-free rate, but this only adds unnecessary complexity.

$$h_c S_u - h_c S_d = c_u - c_d$$

$$h_c(S_u - S_d) = c_u - c_d$$

$$h_c^* = (c_u - c_d)/(S_u - S_d)$$

where h_c^* represents the selected hedge ratio. Substituting uS_0 for S_u and dS_0 for S_d, we have

$$h_c^* = \frac{c_u - c_d}{S_0(u - d)} \qquad (20.11)$$

Hence, the hedge ratio can be computed using data known at time $t = 0$. Using the data in the example, we have

$$h_c^* = (\$10 - \$0.0)/[\$100(1.1 - 0.95)] = 10/15 = {}^2/_3$$

So to create a hedged portfolio, we sell one call option for each ${}^2/_3$ shares of stock we buy. Alternatively, we sell three calls for each two shares we buy. Actually, because a contract has 100 shares as the underlying asset, we would sell three call option contracts for every 200 shares of stock purchased.

We have seen that with $h_c^* = {}^2\!/_3$, a riskless portfolio is created. This box demonstrates that when $h = {}^1\!/_2$ (that is, a value different from ${}^2\!/_3$), a risky portfolio is obtained.

Problem

Demonstrate that with $h = {}^1\!/_2$, a risky portfolio is obtained.

Solution

A hedge ratio of ${}^1\!/_2$ implies that for every call that is written, ${}^1\!/_2$ share of stock needs to be purchased. We can construct the following table of outcomes:

| | | Cash flows | |
| | | At expiration | |
Trading strategy	Today (0)	$S_t = S_u = \$110$	$S_t = S_d = \$95$
Write one call option	$+c_0$	$-\$10$	$\$0$
Buy ${}^1\!/_2$ share of stock	$-({}^1\!/_2)S_0$	$+({}^1\!/_2)\$110 = \$55$	$+({}^1\!/_2)\$95 = \$47.50$
Net cash flow	$+c_0 - ({}^1\!/_2)S_0 = ?$	$\$45$	$\$47.50$

We see that with this portfolio, the future outcomes are uncertain (either \$45 or \$47.50); hence, this portfolio is risky. Only the hedge ratio of $h_c^* = {}^2\!/_3$ creates a certain future cash flow, and only this hedge ratio is suitable for arbitrage strategies and option valuation.

Step 5: solve for the call price using net present value

We now have a standard net present value (NPV) problem. If we select h_c^* as the number of shares of stock to buy, then the future cash flows are certain. Our problem of changing discount rates therefore disappears on a portfolio level. With the future cash flows known with certainty, the appropriate discount rate is the risk-free interest rate (r).

The standard one-period NPV problem is written as follows:

$$NPV = \left[\frac{CF_1}{1+r}\right] - I \tag{20.12}$$

where CF_1 is the cash flow at time period 1, r is the discount rate and I is the required investment, which is taken to be a positive number. In equilibrium, the NPV must be zero. If NPV > 0, all investors will buy such a portfolio, driving its price up. If NPV < 0, all investors will sell such a portfolio short, driving its price down. In reality, prices rarely deviate dramatically from NPV = 0.

In our example (see Exhibit 20.10), the cash flow at the expiration date is

$$-c_u + (h_c^* S_u) = -c_d + (h_c^* S_d) = -\$0 + ({}^2\!/_3)\$95 = \$63.33$$

and

$$I = c_0 - (h_c^* S_0) = c_0 - ({}^2\!/_3)\$100 = c_0 - \$66.67$$

Substituting these results into Equation 20.12 yields the following:

$$\$63.33/(1 + 0.05) = \$66.67 - c_0$$

Solving for c_0, we have

$$c_0 = \$66.67 - (\$63.33/1.05) \cong \$6.36$$

The general expression for the binominal option valuation model for call options is

$$c_0 = h_c^* S_0 + \frac{c_d - h_c^* S_d}{1 + r} \tag{20.13}$$

Put options can be valued easily this way as well; the practice box below asks us to determine the formula for put options. One can use put–call parity too. In equilibrium, the call option in the example is worth $6.36. If the call price is any other value, then an opportunity to generate infinite profit at no risk will exist. (Demonstrate how one could generate unlimited profits if the call is worth $6 or $7.) Hence, in the simplified world depicted in this example, the equilibrium call price will be $6.36.

It is important to point out that we made no reference to the probabilities associated with the stock price moving up or down. Hence, we can infer correctly that for a given stock price today (S_0), option prices are independent of the future expected stock price. This puzzling result can be explained as follows: although the probabilities do not directly affect c_0, they do affect it indirectly. For example, if we increase the probability of S_u, we increase S_0 (otherwise we would again create an arbitrage opportunity – in short, this holds because the best estimate of the (discounted) future stock price is the current one) and an increase in S_0 will increase the value of c_0.

The more important issue is how to determine u and d – these variables do influence the call price through h_c^*, c_d and S_d. In fact, they determine the time value, since they implicitly assign a value to the chance that the option will be in the money and take into account the time to expiration. To obtain the best results, we should choose u and d to match the characteristics of the movements of the stock's price. A popular (but not the only) way of doing this is by looking at the volatility of the distribution of returns and set

$$u = e^{\sigma \sqrt{t}}$$

$$d = e^{-\sigma \sqrt{t}}$$

where σ is the standard deviation of the returns and t is the time to expiration (both should be measured using the same time scale, since it makes no sense to combine daily standard deviations with time measured in years). The ideas and mathematics behind this choice are beyond the scope of this book, but the interested reader should consult the references given at the end of this chapter.[18]

Practice box

We can also use the binominal model for put options.

Problem

Value a European put option on a stock with $S_0 = \$100$, $X = \$100$, $u = 1.10$, $d = 0.95$ and $r = 5\%$.

Solution

As always, we create a portfolio of put options and the underlying stocks whose cash flow in the future is certain. We first determine that the hedge ratio is $1/3$ (by equating the future cash flows) and then solve for p_0. Hence, exactly as with Exhibit 20.10, we can determine the put option value.

---

[18] In particular, see Hull (2003), *Options, Futures and Other Derivatives*, 5th edn, Englewood Cliffs, NJ: Prentice-Hall, pp. 355–358 and 369, and Cox *et al.* (1979), 'Option Pricing: A Simplified Approach', *Journal of Financial Economics*, 7, 229–263.

The hedge ratio for the put is

$$h_p^* = \frac{p_d - p_u}{S_u - S_d}$$

In our example,

$$h_p^* = \frac{5 - 0}{110 - 95} = {}^1\!/_3$$

The cash flows are as follows:

		Cash flows	
		At expiration	
Trading strategy	Today (0)	$S_t = S_u = \$110$	$S_t = S_d = \$95$
Buy one put option	$-p_0$	+\$0	+\$5
Buy h_p share of stock	$-(^1\!/_3)\$100$	$+(^1\!/_3)\$110 = \$36.67$	$+(^1\!/_3)\$95 = \$36.67$
Net cash flow	$-p_0 - (^1\!/_3)\,\$100 = -p_0 - \$33.33$		

all in the usual notation. Since $\$36.67/(1 + 0.05) = \$34.92$, which should equal $-(-p_0 - \$33.33)$, the price of the put option p_0 is $\$34.92 - \$33.33 = \$1.59$.

Extending the results to more than one period

There is no reason to limit the use of the binominal model to a single period: we can easily insert a second period beyond the first (or cut the existing period in two), which results in the following binominal tree:

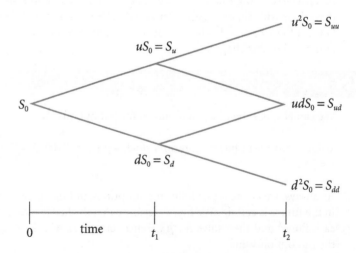

There are also two possible stock prices at the end of the second period, given the price at the beginning of that period. We see that two of these possibilities (a rise after a drop in the first period, and a drop after a rise in the first) give the same end result after the second period: the tree is said be to recombinant, and it is caused by the fact that we multiply by u or d in each period. This is a convenient (but not necessary) property of this binominal tree. Another matter that draws attention in the tree is that it appears that after two periods, there are two states in which the price of the underlying asset is back at its original value. However, we cannot say in general that $S_{ud} = S_0$ – although the difference often will be small. But if we use $u = e^{\sigma\sqrt{t}}$ and $d = e^{-\sigma\sqrt{t}}$, or any other set where d and u are each other's inverses, and consider a non-dividend-paying stock, any state involving an equal number of rises and drops will have a price $S = S_0$.

Our approach to solve the tree for c_0 is similar, but we must do this *recursively*, which means we start in the final period. We determine the value of the option at time t_2 for each outcome. Then we determine the hedge ratio in the last period for each set of outcomes. So, in our example, we calculate two hs for the last period, once starting from S_d and once starting from S_u. From this, we calculate the option values at time t_1: one value for S_u (denoted c_{1u}) and one for S_d (c_{1d}). Thus, S_0 in Equation 20.11 should be replaced by S_u or S_d, and S_0 and S_d in Equation 20.13 should be adjusted analogously. Then we can use c_{1u} and c_{1d} in the manner described above (calculating a third h) to calculate c_0, which is the answer. Note that all the hedge ratios (h) differ, reflecting the dynamic nature of a hedged portfolio.

In a similar fashion, we could split the time to expiration into even more periods, which results in a finer grid of possible outcomes. This is desirable, since in the one-period case the assumption is made that the underlying asset can assume only two values at expiration. If we use several subperiods, we allow for more possibilities, obtaining a better approximation. (The need for approximations is caused by the fact that we are using linear instruments to mimic a non-linear one. In section 20.5 it is shown that this problem can only be overcome if one makes certain assumptions and enlists the help of some mathematics.) However, the computational burden rises exponentially with the number of subperiods. Practitioners will use a computer model with dozens if not hundreds of subperiods. In Appendix B at the end of this book, an application is given that includes 50 subperiods. The reader is strongly encouraged to examine this spreadsheet.

20.4.3 The binominal model for other options

The binominal model can be applied to options other than European calls and puts. Because option values can be calculated at any time (by choosing an appropriate number of periods), the binominal model offers the flexibility required to value options with a value that depends on developments during the lifetime of the option. We'll discuss two examples: American options and a shout option, an exotic option described in Chapter 19.

Early exercise of American-style options

American options may derive value from their possibility of early exercise. The binominal-tree approach enables us to compare the value when exercised and the value of the option when it is not exercised at any point in time we choose. There are two cases where the value of an American-style option will be larger than that of its European-style counterpart:

■ A dividend is paid during the life of a call option. Recall from Chapter 15 that the intrinsic value of a stock falls immediately after a dividend payment. The exercise price is not corrected for this.[19] If the dividend is large enough, there is a chance that an in-the-money call will become out of the money overnight, depressing the value of the option. If the intrinsic value of the call right before the ex-dividend date is larger than the total value after the dividend is paid, then early exercise will take place. In a binominal tree,

---

[19] Unlike stock splits, which lead to a correction of the exercise price.

one has to correct all the share prices at the moment the stock goes ex-dividend. The most convenient way is to make sure that the ex-dividend date falls at the end of a subperiod. Then, calculate the price (starting backwards), until the ex-dividend date is reached. Then, add the dividend to the share price and recalculate the value at the ex-dividend date.

■ If one buys a put option on a firm that is under financial distress, and its stock price is, say, one cent. If the strike price is $10, one can better exercise the right of early exercise, get the cash flow (of $10 less one cent), and deposit the money in the bank to earn interest on this cash flow. The interest received may be more than the maximum additional profit from holding the put option until maturity (one cent at most if the stock price drops to zero). One doesn't have to change the binominal tree for this – just calculate the intrisic value at each point in time and multiply this by $(1 + r)^t$. If this is larger than the value of the option, then early exercise is warranted.

So, we see that American-style options may have a higher value than European-style options. For calls, the difference is present only if the underlying asset pays substantial dividends. For puts, the difference becomes larger if the chance of the underlying asset becoming worthless increases.

Shout option

The binominal model is well suited to evaluating exotic options with early exercise possibilities, changing strike prices, option values depending on the price of the underlying asset during the entire life of the option, and so on. If there is a change in the payoffs because of these variables, then the change can be taken into account in later periods.

A relatively easy example is a *shout option*. As mentioned in Chapter 19, a shout option has a payoff equal to that of a normal option. That is, unless the intrinsic value at which the buyer decided to *shout* in the past (in essence, making this value the minimum payoff on this option contract) isn't higher – in which case, this value is received by the buyer. If we denote the price of the underlying at the time of the shout by S^*, then the payoff at expiration is

$$\text{Max}(0, S_t - S^*) + (S^* - X)$$

The decision as to whether to shout at a certain stock price depends on the value of the option, but this value is in turn affected by the decision to shout. The solution to this problem is a binominal model: we calculate at each node the values if we were to shout at that point and if we were not to shout. The value of the option at that node is the larger of the two. An additional complication is that we can shout only once – after the shout, there is no opportunity to shout again, even if this would have been more profitable. The value of the option thus depends on an action taken earlier, but we have to solve the binominal model starting from the end. If we assume that the investor shouts at the moment that is most profitable to him or her, we must calculate the values for any moment one can shout, and then pick the most valuable.[20] We'll illustrate this briefly in the simplest possible context: a two-period binominal model. Again, any realistic application requires many more periods, in which case a computer becomes essential to perform the calculations.

Let us assume that $u = 1.1$, $d = 0.9$, the risk-free rate is 5.0% and S_0 is $100. Using the binominal model, one can calculate the value of a call option with an exercise price of $95. The option has the following structure (numbers above each node denote the value of S, the numbers below the node denote the intrinsic values of c).

---

[20] This assumes that the investor knows the parameters of the binominal model, and that this model is correct.

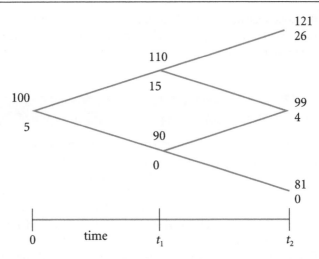

Given these assumptions, one can calculate the value of the option at each point in time if the investor never shouts:

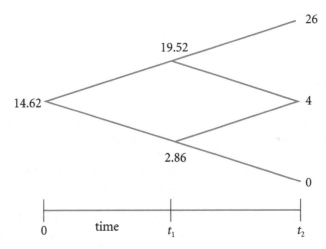

Now, examine the situation if an investor shouts at various moments. First of all, shouting at t_2 is pointless, since the investor will get the intrinsic value at this point anyway. If the investor shouts at t_1, then the minimum payoff at t_2 would be that intrinsic value (zero or 15). If there was an increase in price during the first period, then this would mean that the pay-offs at t_2 would be either 26 or 15. If we had S_d, it would be four or zero (since there is no intrinsic value at S_d). We now recalculate the value of the option assuming a shout at t_1 by replacing the payoffs: they become 26, 15, four and zero. Note that the payoff if the asset goes up and then down differs from S_{du}. Using this, we see that the value at t_0 given an investor that shouts at t_1 is $16.50. This is more than $14.62, so the investor is better off shouting at t_1 than if he or she never shouts.

Now look at the situation if the investor shouts at t_0. The intrinsic value at that moment is $5. The payoffs at t_2 would then become 26, five and five, respectively. The value at t_0 would become $15.25, which is less than if we shout at t_1. So, an investor would be better off shouting at t_1 if the stock price rises (whether or not one shouts at t_1 if the stock price decreased in the first period is irrelevant in this case). Given these parameters, the model assumes implicitly a high chance of a rise in stock prices, so in this example it pays to wait in

705

the hope that we can lock in a large intrinsic value at t_1 instead of locking in the $5 intrinsic value right away. So, despite being an approximation, if the number of periods is finite, then the binominal model is very convenient if options exhibit exotic characteristics.

20.5 Black–Scholes option-valuation model

The Black–Scholes option-valuation model (BS model) was developed in the now famous paper published by Fischer Black and Myron Scholes in 1973. Robert Merton developed, almost simultaneously, the Merton model, which proved to be a generalised version of the BS model. These models were distinct from other models proposed in the late 1960s and early 1970s because the option price does not depend on the expected returns on the underlying stock, an empirically unobservable variable.[21] Moreover, the model is based on the creation of a fully hedged, and therefore riskless, position. The riskless rate is thus employed to discount the future cash flows, and the price follows from the fundamental principle of no-arbitrage.

To better understand the usefulness and limitations of the BS model, let us examine the primary assumptions required for the BS model:

- The capital market is characterised by perfect competition.
- Short-selling is allowed, with full use of the proceeds.
- Investors prefer more wealth to less.
- Borrowing and lending occur at the risk-free rate.
- Price movements are such that past price movements cannot be used to forecast future price changes; the continuously compounded rate of return is distributed normally.

The first three assumptions are identical to those in the binominal option valuation model discussed in Section 20.4.2. Again, the elements that matter most are a frictionless market and the assumption that investors are price-takers.

The assumption that lending and borrowing take place at the risk-free interest rate conforms with standard practice. The assumption that it is compounded continuously is made for convenience and also serves to place the model in the framework of continuous time, as opposed to the discrete approach of the binominal model. There is no need for an approximation using many subperiods with the BS model: if the assumptions are true and the inputs are correct, then the result is the exact value of the option. (The real questions are, of course: are these assumptions realistic? What is the effect if they aren't correct? Do we have the correct input parameters? These issues are addressed in the next sections.) The fifth assumption determines the stock-price distribution. The assumption that the return in the future cannot be predicted from the past is used by Black and Scholes when obtaining the BS model. But they take this one step further: they assume that the continuously compounded rates of return are distributed normally. As a consequence, the returns have a probability distribution that is known in statistics as the log-normal distribution.[22]

Despite making different assumptions about the movement of stock prices over time, the BS model has a very intuitive link with the binominal model. If one breaks the period from 0

---

[21] However, one can derive an implicit expected return in the BS model, but the formula does not take it as an input: rather, it is a side result of the assumptions concerning the distribution.

[22] A log-normal distribution is skewed positively, in contrast to a normal distribution, which has no skewness. This reflects the fact that one can have returns of, for example, +200%, while the underlying asset cannot achieve a return below −100%. See, for instance, Hull (2003) and Kolb (2003), for more on this distribution and its place in the derivation of the BS model.

to t into an almost infinite number of subperiods and allows the stock price to move up or down by a small amount within each subperiod, then the resultant option price approaches the Black–Scholes price. In the limit (the number of subperiods goes to infinity), they give the same results.

20.5.1 The formula

Black, Scholes and Merton used the assumptions listed above and the same no-arbitrage argument given in the binominal option valuation model to develop a formula for valuing call options.[23] At first glance, the BS model looks rather complex. However, many problems tend to disappear after one has gained some familiarity with the symbols and steps required to systematically solve option-valuation problems. Moreover, software packages and spreadsheets (for example, those discussed in Appendix B at the end of this book) make the BS model easier to use.

The BS model for call options is as follows:[24]

$$c = Se^{-qt}N(d_1) - Xe^{-rt}N(d_2) \qquad (20.14)$$

where

$$d_1 = \frac{\ln(S/X) + [r - q + (\sigma^2/2)]t}{\sigma\sqrt{t}} \qquad (20.15)$$

$$d_2 = \frac{\ln(S/X) + [r - q - (\sigma^2/2)]t}{\sigma\sqrt{t}} = d_1 - \sigma\sqrt{t} \qquad (20.16)$$

S is, of course, the stock price and q is the continuously compounded dividend yield. Because dividends lower the value of the stock, the option value needs to be corrected for this. It is also the major difference between the publications of Black and Scholes and Merton: Merton included q, while Black and Scholes didn't. $N(d)$ is the cumulative area of the standard normal distribution.[25] For example, if $d_1 = 1.645$, then using the normal distribution, the cumulative area on the left of 1.645 is 95% – in other words, there is a chance of 95% that a random draw from a standard normal distribution will give a result of 1.645 or less (see Appendix 7). Hence, $N(d_1) = 0.95$. Thus, the area under the normal curve on the right-hand side of d_1 is 0.05. Let us consider a brief example: suppose that $\sigma = 24.5\%$, or 0.245, and $t = 1$. Then $d_2 = d_1 - \sigma\sqrt{t} = 1.645 - 0.245 = 1.400$ and the cumulative area up to $d_2 = 1.400$ is about 92%. Hence, $N(d_2) \cong 0.92$, and the area right of d_2 is about 0.08. Thus, the area between d_2 and d_1 is about 3%, or 0.03.

The other parameters of Equations 20.14, 20.15 and 20.16 are as follows: $\ln(\cdot)$ is the natural logarithm, σ is the continuously compounded, annualised standard deviation of stock

---

[23] Black and Scholes on the one hand, and Merton on the other, published their findings almost at the same time while they were working independently on option pricing. We will use the formulas proven by Merton, which are more general. However, Black and Scholes got their article published first, and hence the model is often referred to as the Black–Scholes model, even though for this version the term 'Merton model' is more appropriate. For the sake of brevity, and because of the general use of the term 'Black–Scholes model', we will use 'BS model' for Merton's extended model as well.

[24] Unless indicated otherwise, we drop the subscripts, i.e. $c = c_0$, $S = S_0$ and $p = p_0$ from here on, because we are no longer in a discrete time model.

[25] $N(d)$ is the area under the standard bell or normal curve up to point d. $N(d)$ can be solved using a computer or can be estimated using standard statistical tables, as discussed below.

returns, r is the continuously compounded, annual risk-free interest rate, t is the time to maturity as a fraction of a year (in the spreadsheet in Appendix B, we need to plug in t as the number of days to expiration), X is the strike price, S is the current stock price, and e is the base of natural logarithms and is roughly equal to 2.71828. Thus, we need six variables (σ, r, q, t, X and S) to calculate the price of a call option using the BS model.

Calculating the BS call option price is easy with software such as the Excel programs discussed in Appendix B. Section B.7 gives a number of excellent examples, which the reader is strongly encouraged to study. All we have to do in these programs is to insert S, X, σ, r, q and t, and c appears on the screen. But given some exercise, calculating them manually is not that difficult either; one just has to know how to work with tables of the standard normal distribution to calculate $N(d_1)$ and $N(d_2)$. We give an extensive example in Section 20.5.4.

Put options

The appropriate formula for put options can be found using the BS model for call options and put–call parity. Rearranging Equation 20.8 (with continuous compounding rather than discrete compounding) yields the following:

$$p = c - Se^{-qt} + Xe^{-rt} \tag{20.17}$$

Hence, we can price a put option by substituting into Equation 20.17 the call option-valuation equation (Equation 20.14):

$$p = Se^{-qt}N(d_1) - Xe^{-rt}N(d_2) - Se^{-qt} + Xe^{-rt}$$

Rearranging terms, we find:

$$p = Xe^{-rt}[1 - N(d_2)] - Se^{-qt}[1 - N(d_1)]$$

which can also be expressed as follows:[26]

$$p = Xe^{-rt}N(-d_2) - Se^{-qt}N(-d_1) \tag{20.18}$$

20.5.2 Varying input parameters

We are now ready to address the influence of changes in the input parameters: is the option price going to change greatly from rising interest rates, or from increasing volatility? Or is it decreasing? These answers are important, both theoretically and in practice. In the BS model, these parameters are assumed to be constant over time, but in reality they aren't. In this section, we'll derive what happens to the option price if an input parameter changes (or is mis-estimated). For easy reference, Exhibit 20.11 gives the conclusions in a qualitative sense.

Delta

To start with the share price, we can derive that the call price will move in the same direction as S. More specifically, this variable is called the delta and is given by

$$\Delta = e^{-qt}N(d_1) \tag{20.19}$$

---

[26] In general, $N(-d) = 1 - N(d)$ because of the symmetry of the normal distribution.

| Exhibit 20.11 | Reaction of option price to increases in input parameters |

Input parameter	Symbol	Sensitivity	Symbol	Effect on option prices	
				Calls	Puts
Stock price	S	Delta	Δ	+	−
Exercise price	X	–		−	+
Standard deviation	σ	Vega	V	+	+
Time to maturity	t	Theta	Θ	?	?
Interest rate	r	Rho	ρ	+	−
Dividend yield	q	–		−	+

This exhibit gives the effects of an increase in input parameters. In all cases, the effects are reversed if the parameter decreases. Note that the effect of S is discussed below using both delta and gamma (the exhibit mentions only the linear approximation delta) and that we do not discuss formulas for the exercise price, time to maturity or dividend yield. The effect of the passage of time – a decrease of the time to maturity – on the option price is usually negative (meaning we would place a '+' in the table), but there are some exceptions.

| Exhibit 20.12 | Delta-hedge |

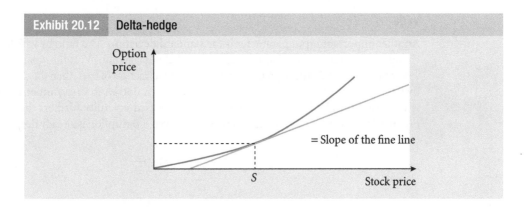

This means that if the share price rises by one dollar, then the price of a call option will increase by Δ dollar.[27] For a put, $\Delta = e^{-qt}[N(d_1) - 1]$. Delta's for calls are always positive, and delta's for puts are always negative. A word of caution: price changes calculated with Δ are only (linear) approximations. The thin line in Exhibit 20.12 represents this approximation. The larger the change in the share price, the more inaccurate the approximation becomes.

Delta is the continuous-time equivalent of the hedge ratio we encountered in the binominal model. For any given share price, a replicating (arbitrage) portfolio will consist of Δ shares and one short option. If the value of the total portfolio (that is, options and shares) does not change when S changes, then it is said to be delta-neutral. Dynamic hedges in options all start with delta-hedging, i.e. acquiring Δ shares to get a first approximation. The danger in this approach lies in large changes in stock prices; as can be seen in Exhibit 20.12, a doubling of S leaves the investor badly hedged.

---

[27] Formally, delta is the first derivative of c to S, dc/dS.

Gamma

The above leads investors with a dynamic hedge to consider another measure for the effect of price changes in the underlying on the call price as well. This is gamma (Γ); together with delta, this can form a quadratic approximation to the price curve in Exhibit 20.12. This reduces the error considerably. Technically, gamma is the ratio of the change in option price to the squared change in stock price.[28] The formula is the same for puts and calls:

$$\Gamma = \frac{e^{-qt-1/2(d_1)^2}}{S_0\sigma\sqrt{2\pi T}} \tag{20.20}$$

where e is Euler's number (the base of the natural logarithm, 2.71828), π is the number pi (3.14159), and d_1, S_0, σ and t are defined as before. The e and π enter because of the assumption that the BS model makes regarding the distribution of the returns.

When forming a quadratic approximation, this is done in the following way. Based on the old call price c_0, the new price c after a change in S (from S_0 to S) is

$$c = c_0 + \Delta(S - S_0) + \tfrac{1}{2}\Gamma(S - S_0)^2 \tag{20.21}$$

Vega

Another important input parameter is the standard deviation. The ratio by which the call price changes if the standard deviation changes is called vega, symbol V. If the volatility increases by 1% (assuming it is measured in per cent per year), or a fraction of 0.01, then the call price increases by $0.01V$ dollar. Note that vega is always positive; an option is an asymmetrical instrument, with greater upside than downside potential. Increased volatility furthers the chance that an option becomes in the money and raises its value (even if the option is already deep in the money).

The formula for vega is

$$V = \frac{S_0 e^{-qt-1/2(d_1)^2}\sqrt{T}}{\sqrt{2\pi}} \tag{20.22}$$

This value is usually high in comparison with other sensitivities. Estimating the correct standard deviation (which we will discuss below) is therefore important. Vega can also be seen as the error that one makes if the standard deviation is slightly mis-estimated: suppose we have estimated a standard deviation of 0.24, but we are concerned that the real standard deviation might be 0.26. The difference in option value based on these two estimates is given by $0.02V$ dollars.

Rho

The sensitivity of option prices towards changes in the interest rate is called rho, symbol ρ. Rho is different for calls and puts. For calls, it's given by

$$\rho = tXe^{-rt}N(d_2) \tag{20.23}$$

In case of a put option, it becomes

$$\rho = -tXe^{-rt}N(-d_2)$$

---

[28] Using calculus, it is the second derivative of the call price to the stock price.

Note that this formula assumes that interest rates are written as a fraction, so one basis point is 0.0001 and an increase in the risk-free rate of 25 basis points results in an increase of the call value of 0.0025ρ dollars. Note also that the equation does not take q as an argument (the formula is identical for dividend- and non-dividend-paying underlying assets), but that there will be a small difference in d_1 and d_2, which does depend on q.

Time decay

Even if no input parameter changes, the time value will still change, simply due to the passage of time. This is not as strange as it sounds: suppose one has made a bet that one's favourite (but disastrous) football team will win at least one out of the next five games. Would one still be willing to place this wager, with the same payoffs and for the same matches, after the team has already lost four of these five games? Just like this bet, options are subject to time decay: if they don't increase in intrinsic value, then part of their potential for profit is lost during this time, and so is part of their value.

Other aspects

After discussing delta, gamma, vega and rho, one might ask: are they the whole story, given that of the six input parameters, we gave formulas for only three types of sensitivities (relating to S, σ and r)?[29] One can indeed determine a sensitivity for the the dividend yield, which resembles that for the interest rate. One can also compute a formula (although it is a rather long expression) for the sensitivity of the option value to time decay. It is generally referred to as theta (Θ). Finally, there is little sense in estimating a sensitivity for X, since it is set in the option contract and cannot change for normal options.

So, theoretically, we can derive the (approximate) price changes if a single input parameter changes. Practioners also often look at a ratio of two input parameters, namely S/X, called the moneyness.[30] This is a term that describes whether the option is in the money or out of the money. A moneyness of one means that the option is at the money. Exhibit 20.13a–b shows the effect of changing moneyness on call and put prices, as well as the effects of time decay and volatility on the call and put prices.

Note that at expiration, the call price is either 0 or $S - X$. However, before the expiration date, the Black–Scholes formula shows the call price by a curved line that lies between the upper and lower bounds. Clearly, the call price is related positively to the moneyness. Exhibit 20.13a–b also shows the boundary conditions discussed earlier (see Equations 20.4–20.7). The exhibit shows that when the stock price either rises or falls by a large amount, the option converges to its lower boundary.

Note from Exhibit 20.13d that option prices are very sensitive to estimates of volatility (which are hard to obtain). For example, based on the initial estimates of $S = X = \$100$, $r = 5\%$, $t = 1$ and $\sigma = 30\%$, the BS model call price is \$13.58 and the put price is \$8.70. If it is subsequently determined that volatility is actually $\sigma = 25\%$, then the BS model call price is \$11.72 and the put price is \$6.85, yielding a decline in option price of 16% (i.e. (\$13.58 − \$11.72)/\$11.72) and 27% (i.e. (\$8.70 − \$6.85)/\$6.85), respectively. Hence, it is critical to have an accurate estimate of volatility before attempting to value an option.

---

[29] All sensitivities, except gamma, are based on linear approximations, but to limit the mistakes of these approximations, one can also look at higher-order approximations. Gamma is the most commonly used, but not the only one that large investors may want to look into.

[30] Some authors define it the other way around, namely X/S, and sometimes the difference between X and S is referred to as moneyness.

Exhibit 20.13 Sensitivity of option prices to changes in underlying parameters

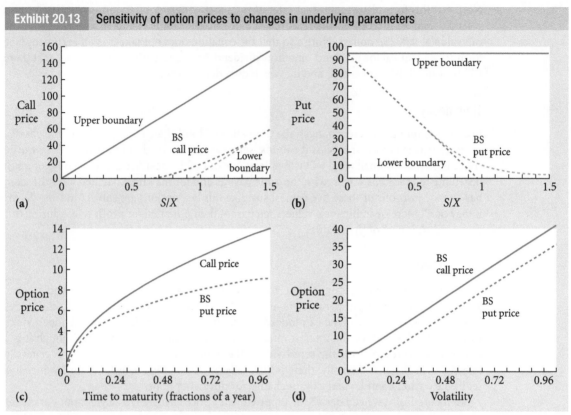

20.5.3 Estimating inputs to the Black and Scholes model

There are six input parameters in the BS model: S, X, t, r, q and σ. The current stock price (S) is easily obtainable by reading the financial media such as the *Wall Street Journal* and the *Financial Times*. One can also call a broker or subscribe to an information service, such as Reuters or Bloomberg. Last but not least, it can be found for free on the Internet as well, but usually with a short delay. The strike price (X) is specified in the options contract and published in the financial media.

Time to maturity (t) is the fraction of the year remaining until the option expires. There is some debate as to whether the year should be measured in business days (days when the market is open, which is approximately 250 days a year) or calendar days (365 or 366). For interest computations, the use of calendar days is relevant, but time to maturity also affects the chance of an option becoming in the money when we multiply $\sqrt{t}$ with the standard deviation. There are arguments to measure volatility (and, therefore, t, to maintain consistency) in business days. However, the consensus is to measure t in calendar days. Hence, if there are 73 calendar days before expiration, then $t = 73/365 = 0.20$, assuming that the year is not a leap year.

The risk-free interest rate (r) is slightly more difficult to estimate. We know that we should use fixed-income securities that are default-free, such as US Treasury bills. Thus, the appropriate rate to employ is the continuously compounded yield to maturity closest to the option maturity date. For example, if the option is for $t = \frac{1}{5}$ of a year, then we want a Treasury bill that pays $1 in one-fifth of a year that is trading now for P_B (the price of the bill). Mathematically, we have the following relationship:

$$P_B = 1e^{-r1/5} = e^{-r/5}$$

or

$$\ln(P_B) = -\frac{r}{5}$$

and, solving for r_c,

$$r = -\frac{\ln(P_B)}{t} = -\frac{\ln(P_B)}{\frac{1}{5}} \tag{20.24}$$

Thus, for the observed price P_B, we can solve for r. Chapter 6 elaborated on the relationship between the discrete and continuous interest rates. Recall from that chapter that US Treasury bills are quoted on a 360-day year and on a discount basis. That is, the prices are not reported widely. Calculating the continuously compounded interest rate based on the discount rate reported requires using the following formula:

$$r = \frac{\ln\left[1 + dt\left(\frac{365}{360}\right)\right]}{t}$$

where d is the quoted discount rate (in decimals) for bills (the average between the bid and ask rate), t is the fraction of the year, and $\ln[\cdot]$ is the natural log function.

The dividend yield, q, is the annualised percentage dividend paid on the stock during the life of the option. Again, the percentage is computed using continuous compounding.[31] However, Merton's model can also be applied to derivatives on other underlying assets, for instance on foreign currencies. In that case, q is not the dividend yield but the foreign interest rate. In case of an option on a commodity, q can be used to represent the cost of carry. Each of these applications requires a specific estimation procedure, so we will not discuss these here.

The last and most difficult parameter to estimate is the volatility of stock returns, which is measured by σ. There are several methods to estimate volatility, including the use of historical return data. Recall that the sample standard deviation of returns is calculated based on the following equation:

$$\hat{\sigma} = \sqrt{\frac{1}{n-1} \sum_{t=1}^{n} (R_t - \bar{R})^2} \tag{20.25}$$

where R_t is the continuously compounded rate of return during period t, $\bar{R}$ is the average rate of return on the underlying stock, and n is the number of historical observations. Chapter 6 presented the rate of return in discrete time. The only adjustment we need to make when calculating the standard deviation with continuous compounding is the equation to calculate R_t, which becomes

$$R_t = \ln\left(\frac{P_t + D_t}{P_{t-1}}\right) \tag{20.26}$$

where $\ln[\cdot]$ is the natural logarithm and D is the dividend (in dollars).

---

[31] In this respect, the continuously compounded dividend yield differs from the discrete dividend yield discussed in Chapter 15. If a dividend is paid m times a year and the discrete dividend yield is R_m per cent, the continuously compounded dividend yield is $q = m \ln(1 + R_m/m)$.

It can be shown that for sufficiently short time periods (or small changes in the stock price), the rates of return for either method of compounding are about the same. However, for long holding periods (longer than one week), the differences are more substantial.

Yet, this is not the end of the story: the most difficult problem is choosing n and t in Equation 20.25. Stock-market volatility is not constant over time, so if we calculate σ using the past five years, we probably get another answer than if we use just the past month.[32] The two main problems are volatility peaks and mean reversion, which are discussed next. Note that these problems are not specific to the BS model. In the binominal model, we also need to estimate the volatility to determine u and d.

Volatility peaks

Peaks in volatility are problematic if we fix the period that we use to calculate it. This is best illustrated by considering a crash that happened during this fixed period. As time passes, the crash drops out of the fixed period, and the volatility estimates become much lower. For example, if we use the past year to estimate volatility, then the estimates would be high on 10 September 2002 but much lower on 20 September 2002, simply because a few days with exceptional variance (11 September 2001, and the days afterwards) aren't included any more if we limit t to the past year.[33] Of course, it is not realistic that the variance should decrease by a large amount simply because a major event suddenly drops out of the estimation period. The variance on 10 September 2002 is unlikely to be different from the variance on 12 September 2002. This problem is not new (for example, the crash of 1987), and a number of solutions can be used. The easiest approach is to use an exponentially weighted moving average (EWMA). This works as follows: instead of giving every observation an equal weight and limiting ourselves to a certain period, we take all data into account, but the weight of data is decreased exponentially as they lie further in the past. So, the most recent data available get a weight of, say, w (with $w < 1$), the previous of w^2, and so on. Frequently used values for w are between 0.8 and 0.99. Of course, you have to divide the result by the sum of the weights, which is (approximately) $1/(1-w)$.

Consider a set of weekly observations of the variance of a stock index, and take w to be 0.9. If a week with a large variance (say, 0.2 instead of 0.01) occurred ten weeks ago, then this observation would have a weight that is just $0.9^{10} = 0.349$ times that of the current period. This means that an observation that is 20 times the average value still has great effect, which is desirable. But after 26 weeks, the ratio is 0.065, and after a year it is 0.004. So, the influence of extreme observations decreases gradually, preventing large jumps in the estimate of the variance.

Mean reversion

Reversion to the mean is a way of saying that despite the occasional (or somewhat prolonged) deviations, a certain parameter returns to a fixed average in the long run; variance tends

---

[32] Actually, this problem has two sides to it: on the one hand, we estimate the variance at this moment using historical data that may reflect a different variance from the current one. On the other hand, we assume that, once we've calculated the current variance, it remains constant for the rest of the life of the option. For options with long remaining maturities (especially LEAPS), the second problem needs to be addressed as well. This leads to econometric methods that are outside the scope of this book.

[33] It becomes even more problematic if trading was halted for some days, which is what happened on the New York exchanges in the aftermath of 11 September. There is no way of knowing what the returns and volatility would have been if trading in New York hadn't stopped. In this example, we assume that trading continued (e.g. stocks listed in Europe, Asia and Latin America).

to exhibit this type of behaviour. The EWMA model does not fit this empirical fact, since the immediate past gets the largest weight. So, if variance in the last periods has been above average, so will the estimate for the next period. Yet because of the mean reversion, this estimate is likely to be too high. Sometimes this matters in the field of option valuation, and even more advanced methods, such as a GARCH (Generalized Autoregressive Conditional Heteroscedasticity) model, offer the required flexibility. However, the computational and theoretical complexities are such that only large investors and researchers will regularly work with these types of models.

→ **Connecting Theory to Practice 20.1**

The varying nature of volatile forces

Volatility is a pervasive force in financial markets. On 14 April 2000, the Dow Jones index displayed a low of 10,202 and a high of 10,923, fluctuating by more than 700 points (7%) in a trading period of six-and-a-half-hours. This range was about five times the average daily range of about 1.5%. An investor in an index fund would have faced the alarming prospect of seeing the value of an investment fluctuate within a range of 7% in a day.

Is such an event uncommon or can we expect more of the same in the future? . . .

Forecasting

To forecast volatility it is important to know more about the way volatility changes over time. For example, is it related to past volatility? Does it increase on days that the market drops? Numerous empirical studies have been conducted using innovative statistical methods . . .

A simple method used by risk measurement specialists RiskMetrics is the 'exponential smoothing' method. It uses exponentially decaying weights, where more recent observations carry a higher weight than earlier ones. This method uses ad-hoc weights and does not take into account most of the phenomena mentioned above, such as mean reversion or the negative relationship between volatility and price changes.

The Arch-Garch class of models, pioneered by academic Robert Engle and extended by Tim Bollerslev, Daniel Nelson and others, builds on the fact that volatility varies over time and is persistent . . . Unlike the RiskMetrics model, it accounts for volatility reverting to the mean over time . . .

Implied volatility

Although these models attempt to incorporate all available statistical information, they do not use information from options markets. Option prices are determined by volatility, among other factors, so we can use the market price of the option to deduce the volatility implied by this price. In other words, the price of the option reflects the perception of market participants of the future volatility of the underlying asset. Since the introduction of option markets, implied volatility has been used extensively. Although it is derived from the Black–Scholes option-pricing model and relies on the assumptions of that model, it is used in various applications, including volatility forecasting . . . If implied volatility is strongly related to actual volatility, we should observe phenomena similar to those reported earlier. For example, the inverse relationship between volatility and price[34] has been examined by academic David Weinbaum using the S&P 100. He

---

[34] Author note: volatility is historically high and changing in times of economic crisis.

finds that an increase in implied volatility is strongly related to a decrease in market price and vice versa. Also, the volatility implied from long-term options is, most of the time, lower than the volatility implied from short-term options, which is consistent with mean reversion.

Options

In the past decade, the realization that volatility is itself volatile has not only affected forecasting, but also option valuation and risk management under such conditions. Little has been done to suggest how to manage risk under these conditions.

This author and Dan Galai have proposed making a volatility index and introducing volatility options and futures to hedge against changes. Recently, Monep, the French futures and options exchange, has introduced a volatility index based on this methodology.[35] The idea is to construct an index that implies the volatility that will prevail in the next 30 days by averaging across options with different maturities.

Another implied volatility index is VIX, introduced by the Chicago Board Options Exchange. The Financial Times publishes relative volatility indices from RiskMetrics for bond and equity markets from Tuesday to Friday.

The next step should be the introduction of options on volatility that could be useful to hedge against unexpected changes in the volatility of share and bond portfolios as well as option portfolios . . .

Source: Menachem Brenner, 'The Varying Nature of Volatile Forces', *Business Day (South Africa)*, 16 October 2001. Used with permission.

→ **Making the connection**

This article discusses several ways to estimate volatility. Apart from the EWMA already mentioned in the chapter, it also focuses on some alternative approaches, namely implied volatility (if we use the option price in the market as a starting point, we can turn around the BS model and calculate the volatility that is consistent with the current price; this volatility is called the implied volatility; the implied volatility of related options can be a good indication of the volatility one wants to estimate) and volatility indices (just like a stock index is an indication of the price of the most important shares on a market, a volatility index is an indication of the volatility on that market; some of these indices are also calculated using implied volatilities of index options). The latter have proven to be an interesting measure, but they are available for only a limited number of stock indices. These indices also illustrate the link between option-pricing work done in academia and trading developments.

20.5.4 An example

Let us now demonstrate the BS model. We could, of course, simply plug in the numbers in the Excel program described in Appendix B, but calculating an option value manually can be illuminating. We will also compare our answers with those of Excel to demonstrate the effects of rounding.

Suppose we wish to calculate the value of a call option with the following parameters: $S = \$102$, $X = \$100$, $\sigma = 30\%$, $r = 8\%$, $q = 1\%$ and $t = 182$ days, which is about $\frac{1}{2}$ year. We calculate the call price following these three steps:

---

[35] Author note: since this article was written, this exchange has been incorporated into Euronext Paris.

Step 1: given the parameters just listed and Equation 20.15, we have

$$d_1 = \frac{\ln\left(\dfrac{102.0}{100.0}\right) + \left[0.08 - 0.01 + \left(\dfrac{0.3^2}{2}\right)\right]\left(\dfrac{1}{2}\right)}{(0.3)\sqrt{^1/_2}} = \frac{0.0198 + 0.0575}{0.3 \times 0.7071} = 0.3644$$

Also, from Equation 20.16 we have

$$d_2 = 0.3644 - (0.3 \times \sqrt{^1/_2}) = 0.3644 - (0.3 \times 0.70711) = 0.1522$$

Now that we have d_1 and d_2, we are ready to compute $N(d_1)$ and $N(d_2)$.

Step 2: determine $N(d_1)$ and $N(d_2)$. Unfortunately, option prices are very sensitive to estimates of $N(d_1)$ and $N(d_2)$. Therefore, it is important to achieve a high level of accuracy. Appendix 7 presents values of $N(d)$ for given values of d accurate to four decimals. Our values for d_1 and d_2 are not given precisely here. Hence, we need to interpolate between the two nearest values for $N(d)$ in the exhibit:

$$d_{1H} = 0.365 \quad N(d_{1H}) = 0.6424 \qquad d_{2H} = 0.155 \quad N(d_{2H}) = 0.5616$$
$$d_{1L} = 0.360 \quad N(d_{1L}) = 0.6406 \qquad d_{2L} = 0.150 \quad N(d_{2L}) = 0.5596$$

Our estimates

$$d_1 = 0.3644 \quad N(d_1) = ? \qquad d_2 = 0.1522 \quad N(d_2) = ?$$

d_{1H}, d_{1L}, d_{2H} and d_{2L} are the values from Appendix 7 immediately above and below d_1 and d_2. H represents the value on the high side and L represents the value on the low side. The interpolation formula is

$$N(d) = N(d_L) + (d - d_L)\left[\frac{N(d_H) - N(d_L)}{d_H - d_L}\right]$$

Note that we simply add to the lower value $N(d_L)$ some portion of $N(d_H) - N(d_L)$, which becomes larger as $d - d_L$ increases. For example, if $d = d_H$, we get exactly $N(d) = N(d_H)$. If $d = d_L$, we get exactly $N(d) = N(d_L)$, as we would anticipate. Thus, for $N(d_1)$, we have

$$N(d_1) = 0.6406 + (0.3644 - 0.360)\left(\frac{0.6424 - 0.6406}{0.365 - 0.36}\right) = 0.6406 + (0.0044)(0.36) = 0.6422$$

Similarly, for $N(d_2)$,

$$N(d_2) = 0.5596 + (0.1522 - 0.150)\left(\frac{0.5616 - 0.5596}{0.155 - 0.150}\right) = 0.5596 + (0.0022)(0.40) = 0.5605$$

Now that we know $N(d_1)$ and $N(d_2)$, we are ready to calculate the option price.

Step 3: compute the call price.
    We now substitute the values of $N(d_1)$ and $N(d_2)$ into Equation 20.14:

$$c = (\$102.00e^{-0.01/2} \times 0.6422) - (\$100.00e^{-0.08/2} \times 0.5605) = \$65.18 - \$53.85 = \$11.33$$

Note that in using 182 days to expiration, the precise calculation done by the Excel program used in Appendix B is $c = \$11.31$. Strictly speaking, under the five assumptions of the BS model, we know that the call price has to be 11.31, or else there is arbitrage. Does it matter that in our example we were two cents off? Maybe not: in reality, one can doubt whether a difference of two cents is enough to compensate for transaction costs – a truly frictionless market does not exist.

Using the previous data and Equation 20.18, we can calculate the put price:

$$p = \$100.00 e^{-0.08/2} \times (1.0 - 0.5605) - \$102.00 e^{-0.01/2} \times (1.0 - 0.6422)$$

$$= \$100.00 \times 0.9608 \times 0.4395 - \$102.00 \times 0.9950 \times 0.3578 = \$42.23 - \$36.31 = \$5.92$$

Thus, the Black–Scholes put price is approximately \$5.92. Using the above parameters directly and 182 days to expiration, the computer program gets an outcome of \$5.91, again due to rounding.

Calculating the sensitivities is now a fairly easy job: the delta (and therefore the hedge ratio, should we want to create a dynamically hedged portfolio) is simply $e^{-qt}N(d_1)$ or $0.9950 \times 0.5605 = 0.5577$. So, if the stock price rises to \$103, the option value will become approximately $11.33 + 0.5577 = \$11.89$. A synthetic replica of this option would consist of (apart from borrowed money) 0.5577 shares. Likewise, the gamma of this option is

$$\Gamma = \frac{e^{-qt-1/2(d_1)^2}}{S_0 \sigma \sqrt{2\pi T}} = e^{-0.01/2-1/2(0.5605)^2} / [102 \times 0.3 \times \sqrt{2\pi \times 1/2}] = 0.8504/54.237 = 0.016.$$

So, if we want a quadratic approximation of the new option value after a rise of the stock price to \$103, it would be $c = c_0 + \Delta(S - S_0) + 1/2\Gamma(S - S_0)^2 = 11.33 + 0.5577(103 - 102) + 0.008(103 - 102)^2 = \$11.90$. Excel puts it at \$11.96, so we see that one has to be careful with approximations, even for such relatively small changes.

20.5.5 Empirical evidence and limitations of the Black–Scholes model

How accurate is the BS model in determining option values? We can calculate the theoretical value of an option as predicted by the BS model and compare it with the observed market price. If there is no significant difference, then the model works well. Several empirical studies have tested this model. Generally, these tests support the BS model. The BS model performs well for longer maturities (three months to one year), moderate volatilities and at-the-money options. However, in case of short-term options, extremely high or low volatilities, and options that are deep in or out of the money, the BS model does not perform well. Most of the known misvaluations by the BS model are not stable across time. For example, highly volatile stock options may be found to be overpriced by the BS model during one five-year period and underpriced during another five-year period.

Let us give a brief overview of some important empirical research into the BS model. Black and Scholes (1972) found that the BS model tends to overvalue options with high variance and to underprice options with low variance. Gultekin et al. (1982) found similar results, as well as finding that the BS model overestimates values of in-the-money options and underestimates values of out-of-the-money options. Macbeth and Merville (1979) found that the BS model predicted prices lower than the market for in-the-money options and predicted prices higher than the market for out-of-the-money options. The bias is more pronounced for shorter-term options. More recently, Long and Officer (1997) investigated the relationship between misvaluation in the BS model and the volume of trading. Their evidence indicates that call options that are traded heavily are priced more efficiently and have lower misvaluation errors than do thinly traded options.

Although researchers have found some biases, the BS model remains one of the best models for explaining an option's price behaviour. And not every deviation from the BS-value constitutes a bias: in general, there are three categories of explanations:

- There is a computational error in applying the model, or the wrong inputs were used.
- Observed market prices are out of line, violating the no-arbitrage rule.
- The assumptions underlying the BS model are violated.

In reality, individual investors might make a lot of errors in the first category. If we conclude that the third conclusion is indeed applicable, we can try to trace the error to a specific assumption of the BS model. We'll give some examples below, as research has unearthed some of the reasons for biases in the BS model. Current research focuses on three issues: the shape of the return distribution, the possibility of jumps in the stock price and non-constant volatility.

The first issue is discussed in the next section. With respect to jumps, we can say that the BS model assumes a continuous change in asset prices, meaning that if the underlying asset is worth $50 now, and $60 next month, then the stock price has been, at some point during that month, $50.01, $50.02 a bit later, and so on: all intermediate values between $50 and $60 should have occurred. It rules out that a stock's price is $50 at one moment and $60 the next. This is not realistic – if important new information reaches the market, then asset prices will exhibit a jump to their new value and skip all intermediate values. If there is a real possibility of such a jump – for instance, when an oil company is announcing whether a drill was successful – the BS model underestimates the chance of out-of-the-money options becoming in the money (both puts and calls). Non-constant volatility (or standard deviation) was mentioned in footnotes 32 and 34 of this chapter. When an option has three years left to expiration, it is unlikely that volatility will remain constant over that period, although it should be noted that uncertainty about volatility in the short term has little effect compared with the effect of jumps in the short term. Sometimes, models are used where the volatility itself is stochastic (random). This requires more advanced mathematics; the interested reader is referred to the references at the end of this chapter.

Volatility smiles

An alternative method of reviewing the effectiveness of the BS model is estimating the implied volatility of stock returns. The implied volatility is obtained basically by turning around the BS model and finding the volatility that gives the current market price of the option. So, we base our calculations on the actual expectations in the market. Under the assumptions of the BS model, the implied volatility of an option should not depend on the strike or stock price (or any other input parameter). By calculating the implied volatility for an option class with the same expiration date, one can investigate this easily. In practice, we see that the resulting pattern is not a straight line, but a 'smile' or 'sneer'. For stock and index options, the implied volatility is higher for options with a low strike price (deep out-of-the-money puts and deep in-the-money calls), resulting in the pattern in Exhibit 20.14a. Foreign exchange options behave differently: options with high and low strikes have higher implied volatilities, which is shown in Exhibit 20.14b (hence the name volatility smile).

We can explain part of the errors in the BS model depicted in Exhibit 20.14. We see that stock options with a low strike price are relatively expensive (remember that volatilty has a positive effect on option value, so a high implied volatility means a high value). These market prices imply a far higher chance of a crash in stock prices than is assumed under the BS model.[36] Rubinstein (1994) called this phenomenon 'crash-o-phobia'.

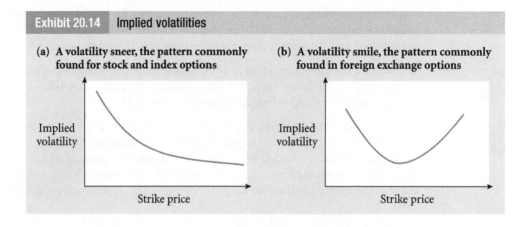

Exhibit 20.14 Implied volatilities

(a) A volatility sneer, the pattern commonly found for stock and index options

Implied volatility

Strike price

(b) A volatility smile, the pattern commonly found in foreign exchange options

Implied volatility

Strike price

The part of the fifth assumption of the BS model that postulates a log-normal distribution is often violated in practice. Another reason besides fear of crashes is *leverage*: leverage results in a more volatile equity value (and thus stock price) in response to a change in firm value. Assuming the debt of companies stays more or less constant relative to the total firm value, the leverage will increase when stock prices drop, increasing the volatility of the stock.

When we look at foreign exchange options (Exhibit 20.14b), we see that the implied distribution signals deviations from the log-normal distribution for both high and low strike prices. This is because extreme changes in exchange rates are more likely than under log-normality; regardless of the direction, exchange rates have a higher likelihood of exhibiting jumps (due to the pegging of some currencies – a policy that usually ends with a jump), and the volatility of exchange rates is even less constant than that of stocks. Yet despite these limitations, the BS model is still regarded as highly successful.

Summary

Use the futures valuation equations.

A futures contract can be priced by constructing a statically hedged portfolio, using the no-arbitrage principle. This portfolio creates exactly the same rights and obligations as the futures contract using assets with known prices, namely bonds and the underlying asset of the futures contract. The differences in value between futures on various underlying assets are caused by their different cost-of-carry.

Identify option boundaries and use put–call parity.

A call option will be worth at least the maximum of zero and the current share price minus the discounted exercise price. Its value will always be below that of the underlying asset. A put will be worth at least the maximum of zero and the discounted exercise price minus the current share price. Its value will always be below the discounted exercise price. Put–call parity

---

[36] More formally, we could derive an implied distribution from these data (calculate the distribution of returns from the stock prices). In other words, we can recover the market opinion about the chance of a certain S at maturity. This is a data-intensive matter, and requires some assumptions itself. See Rubinstein (1994) and Jackwerth and Rubinstein (1996).

establishes a relationship between the value of calls, puts, the underlying assets and bonds. A call option and a particular bond is equivalent to the underlying asset and a put option.

Calculate option prices with a binominal tree.

In summary, a five-step process is used to determine option prices. First, the stock prices are assumed to move to only one of two future values. Secondly, the option prices at maturity are determined from the future stock prices. Thirdly, a portfolio of the stock and the option is constructed. Fourthly, a specific number of stocks are traded, called the *hedge ratio*, such that the future payoff is certain. Fifthly, the option price is determined using a standard NPV approach. The model is easily extendable to multiple future stock prices. For a given stock price, the expected return on the stock does not directly influence the option price. The effect is only through the observed current stock price (S_0).

Use the Black–Scholes option valuation model to value both call and put options.

For a call option, the price according to the BS-model is:

$$c = Se^{-qt}N(d_1) - Xe^{-rt}N(d_2),$$

where $d_1 = \dfrac{\ln(S/X) + [r - q + (\sigma^2/2)]t}{\sigma\sqrt{t}}$ and $d_2 = d_1 - \sigma\sqrt{t}$. (20.16)

The price of a put option can be found using put–call parity. This applies only to European, non-dividend-paying options: American-style options, warrants and options on derivatives all require adaptations of the formula.

Discuss empirical evidence on option valuation.

The BS model is a successful model. But one has to be careful in its application: the model can only be as good as the estimates of its inputs. The estimate of the standard deviation has an especially large influence, the sensitivity to the estimated volatility (vega) is often very large compaired to the other sensitivities, and the estimate itself is often highly uncertain. The assumption of a log-normal distribution made by the BS model is questionable: there is evidence for 'crash-o-phobia', leverage effects in the return distribution of stocks, and a high frequency of extreme returns and jumps in currencies.

Key terms

Backwardation 687	Exponentially weighted moving average (EWMA) 714	Non-constant volatility 719
Basis 687		Option value boundaries 688
Binominal model 696	Frictionless market 697	Put–call parity (PCP) 693
Binominal tree 702	Gamma 710	Recombinant 702
Black–Scholes option valuation model (BS model) 706	Hedge ratio 698	Rho 710
	Implied distribution 720	Standard normal distribution 707
Contango 687	Implied volatility 716	Static hedge 681
Continuous time 694	Jump 719	Time decay 711
Cost-of-carry model 683	Log-normal distribution 706	Time value 695
Convergence 687	Mean reversion 714	Vega 710
Delta 708	Merton model 706	Volatility peaks 714
Discrete time 694	Moneyness 711	Volatility smile 719
Dynamic hedge 681	No-arbitrage 679	

Review questions

1 Assume that the spot price of gold is $340 per troy ounce. Suppose also that you observe the following gold futures prices:

Time to maturity (in years)	Futures price (in troy ounces)
$\frac{1}{4}$	$344.28
$\frac{1}{2}$	$348.61
$\frac{3}{4}$	$353.00
1	$357.43

a. Calculate the basis for each futures contract.
b. If the risk-free interest rate is 3%, what is the implied storage cost of gold (expressed as a per cent) for 1 year?

2 Using an arbitrage table, prove that the put option price must be below the discounted value of the strike price. That is, prove Equation 20.7:

$$p_0 \leq X/(1 + r)^t$$

3 Set up a binominal tree and price a put option using the following information: the option expires after two periods, and in each period $u = 1.20$ and $d = 0.75$; the current stock price is $100, and the exercise price is $92. The risk-free rate is 3% per period, and there are no dividends.

4 Suppose the standard deviation is $\sigma = 30\%$, $S_0 = \$100$, $X = \$100$, $r = 5\%$, $q = 3\%$ and $t = \frac{1}{2}$. Calculate the Black–Scholes call and put option prices.

5 Use the data in Question 4, but suppose the stock price increases by 1% to $101:

a. What are the new Black–Scholes call and put option prices? Compare your result with that of Question 4.
b. Calculate the changes in option prices using the formula for delta (see Equation 20.19).
c. Calculate the changes in option prices using the formula for both delta and gamma (see Equation 20.21).
d. Recalculate Parts a, b and c on the basis that the stock price increases by 10% to $110.

For an extensive set of review and practice questions and answers visit the Levy–Post investment website at www.booksites.net/levy

Selected references

Black, F. and M. Scholes, 1972, 'The Valuation of Option Contracts and a Test of Market Efficiency', *Journal of Finance*, **27** (2), 399–418.

Black, F. and M. Scholes, 1973, 'The Pricing of Options and Corporate Liabilities', *Journal of Political Economy*, **81**, 637–654.

Chance, Don M., 2004, *An Introduction to Derivatives and Risk Management*, 6th edn, London: South-Western.

Copeland, L. S., 2000, *Exchange Rates and International Finance*, 3rd edn, Englewood Cliffs, NJ: Prentice-Hall.

Cox, J. C., S. A. Ross and M. Rubinstein, 1979, 'Option Pricing: A Simplified Approach', *Journal of Financial Economics*, **7**, 229–263.

Ehrhardt, M. C., J. V. Jordan and R. A. Walking, 1987, 'An Application of APT to Futures Markets: Test of Normal Backwardation', *Journal of Futures Markets*, **7** (1), 21–34.

Green, J. and E. Saunderson, 1998, 'No Room at the Top', *Risk*, **11**.

Gultekin, N. B., J. Rogalski and S. M. Tinic, 1982, 'Option Pricing Model Estimates: Some Empirical Results', *Financial Management*, **11**, 58–69.

Hull, J., 2003, *Options, Futures and other Derivatives*, 5th edn, Englewood Cliffs, NJ: Prentice-Hall.

Jackwerth, J. C. and M. Rubinstein, 1996, 'Recovering Probability Distributions from Option Prices', *Journal of Finance*, **51** (5), 1611–1631.

Kolb, R. W., 2003, *Futures, Options and Swaps*, 4th edn, Malden, MA: Blackwell.

Long, D. and D. Officer, 1997, 'The Relation between Option Mispricing and Volume in the Black–Scholes Option Model', *Journal of Financial Research*, **20**, 1–12.

Macbeth, J. and L. Merville, 1979, 'An Empirical Examination of the Black–Scholes Call Option Pricing Model', *Journal of Finance*, **34** (5), 1173–1186.

Merton, R., 1973, 'Theory of Rational Option Pricing', *Bell Journal of Economics and Management Science*, **4**, 141–183.

Robertson, Malcolm J., 1990, *Directory of World Futures and Options*, Englewood Cliffs, NJ: Prentice-Hall.

Rubinstein, M., 1994, 'Implied Binominal Trees', *Journal of Finance*, **49** (3), 771–818.

Tyson-Quah, K., 1997, 'Clearing the Way', *Risk*, **10**, 8.

Part 6

PORTFOLIO MANAGEMENT

Investment in the News 21   FT

Banks wake up to risk management challenge

It has been billed as the biggest IT challenge to the banking industry since the Y2K scare. But while predictions of doom over the millennium bug did not materialise, the New Basel Capital Accord on risk management is set to pose more formidable technical and business challenges. Basel 2, as it is commonly known, will update and replace the 1988 'Basel 1' Accord from the Swiss-based Bank for International Settlements.

Due to be implemented at the end of 2006, it aims to make banks' assessment of their own investments and loans more sensitive to a range of risks – credit, operational and market-related. Operational risk, for instance, includes internal factors – people, processes and technology – and external risks such as terrorist threats.

The IT challenges posed by Basel 2 are vast, spanning data collection, systems integration and project management on a global scale. Analysts estimate that larger banks will have to spend between $30 m and $160 m to get their IT systems and business processes up to the standard required.

The revised accord from the BIS Basel committee – established in 1974 by the central bank governors of the G10 countries – does not have legal force. However, more than 100 countries are signatories to Basel 2 and are committed to enforcing it through legislation and market watchdogs. Industry observers have warned that failure to comply with the requirements of Basel 2 could damage a bank's share price, if markets believe it is more vulnerable to risk. The advantage of compliance for banks is that they should be able to set aside less capital to cover the various risks facing their business.

'Firms are waking up to Basel 2 with a renewed sense of urgency,' says PwC's Mr Venkat. 'I don't think non-compliance is an option.'

Source: Nick Huber, 'Banks Wake Up To Risk Management Challenge', FT.com site, 7 May 2003.

The reader should by now understand that risk and the trade-off between risk and return are essential to investment decision-making. Individual retail investors have strong incentives to manage the risk of their portfolio, because investment losses adversely affect their future expenses such as those for their children's college education or their own retirement income.[1]

Institutional investors also should have strong incentives to manage risk, because they are responsible for investing on behalf of their clients, who generally are risk-averse. Indeed, compensation schemes of investment managers frequently use risk-adjusted performance measures in order to link their income directly to the risk they take with their clients' money. Further, pension funds and insurance companies, which have fixed liabilities, generally will restrict the flexibility of (external) money managers that invest their funds. Finally, regulatory bodies may force institutional investors to adopt particular risk-management policies so as to mitigate systemic risk. For instance, Investment in the News 21 reports about the Bank of International Settlement's (BIS) new risk-management guidelines for banks. Banks are required by the BIS to keep a certain percentage of their assets in liquid, short-term securities so as to guarantee a minimum degree of solvency.

Risk management is the process of recognition, measurement and control of risks that an investor faces. Generally, the aim of risk management is not simply to reduce or even eliminate risk. Indeed, this may not be possible given various difficulties of measuring risk and the limitations of the instruments for controlling risk. Reducing risk also entails costs, for example the expected returns forgone by not investing in high-risk, high-return assets, the transaction and information costs of rebalancing a portfolio, and the premiums and transaction costs involved in trading derivatives. Rather than simply reducing or eliminating risk, the objective is to make informed decisions about the available trade-offs between risk and return. To ensure that those decisions are enacted in a consistent way, risk management must be a continuous process; the composition of the investor's portfolio and the risk of the assets therein, as well as the objectives and constraints of the investor, change over time.

Risk has always been a concern to investors. However, the need for risk management has increased sharply in the past three decades. The world economy has experienced oil shocks, currency crashes, commodity price fluctuations, country debt defaults and major corporate defaults. Some of these recent events are listed in Exhibit 21.1. The field of risk management has advanced rapidly as well. The innovations in financial theory on the one hand, and

---

[1] Chapter 7 formalises the risk-aversion of investors in terms of diminishing marginal utility of wealth.

Exhibit 21.1	Some recent market crashes, shocks, crises and debacles

Period	Event
1980–93	$300 billion in total loss made by US savings and loans associations. They made long-term loans (mainly mortgages with fixed rates) financed by short-term deposits, which paid variable rates. The industry faced problems after a sharp increase in interest rates
October 1987	Stock-market crash, also known as Black Monday (S&P lost 20% of its value)
1990	Financial crisis in Japan, leading to an estimated $500 billion of bad loans. Troubles resulted from the collapse of the real-estate bubble. The crisis hit the stock market as well, which, at the time of writing, has yet to attain its previous levels
September 1992	European Monetary System crisis. Negara (Malaysia's central bank) lost about $3 billion in 1992 and $2 billion in 1993 betting on exchange rates; the losses accrued after sterling left EMS
December 1993	Bankruptcy of the Spanish fifth largest bank Banesto ($4.7 billion of hidden losses, plenty of bad loans and doubtful investments)
1994	Up to the year 1994, Crédit Lyonnais was saved from bankruptcy by $10 billion support from the French Government. The problems accrued from unsuccessful action on the real-estate and film-production markets, unfettered expansion and lack of operational risk control
January 1994	Metallgesellschaft lost about $1.3 billion on oil futures
February 1994	Bond market crash. US banks were buying long-dated US bonds financed with (cheap) deposits. When the Fed unexpectedly raised rates by 25 basis points and further hikes where feared, yields on long bonds increased, deminishing their value and causing large losses to mainly investment banks
December 1994	Orange County's portfolio of reverse repurchase agreements (repos) lost about $1.7 billion. It was leveraged threefold. The loss occurred due to the unforeseen change in interest rates and high exposure to this risk of the portfolio
February 1995	Collapse of the Barings Bank, resulting from a $1.3 billion loss on unauthorised trading of futures and options by Nick Leeson
March 1995	Peso crisis resulting from the devaluation of the Mexican currency
September 1995	Japanese twelfth largest bank Daiwa announced a $1.1 billion loss, arising from rogue trading of Toshihide Igushi at Daiwa's New York branch
Summer 1997–98	Asian currency crisis. A currency and financial crisis that developed and spread across several Asian countries, many part of the East Asian Tigers, causing mounting economic and political uncertainty and triggering a heavy exodus of foreign money-market funds
August 1998	Russian credit crisis. Default on the debt resulted in a worldwide increase in the credit spread, low market liquidity and increased risks
September 1998	Long Term Capital Management hedge fund debacle following the Russian credit crisis: $3.7 billion loss
December 2001–March 2002	Bankruptcy of Enron and WorldCom due to rogue transactions and accountancy fraud
February 2004	Parmalat's accounting scandal connected with cumulative profit inflation and inability to meet its obligations

information and computer technology on the other, have led to a plethora of financial risk instruments. These instruments have been tested during recent tumultuous periods, and most professionals agree that the instruments ensured that the losses were not greater than anticipated and the financial system did not collapse.

This is not to say that the story has been all-perfect. Recent history has seen some major debacles leading to huge losses. This chapter will review some of the major debacles (e.g. Long Term Capital Management (LTCM) and Barings Bank) in terms of how influential they were in the development of risk-management instruments. These downfalls also provide an interesting probe into the reasons for risk management. LTCM, for example, was a hedge fund run by leading financial academics and practitioners. The debate continues as to whether LTCM failed to guard properly against its risks or whether its problems were caused solely by external events (the changes in market conditions following the Russian default).

This chapter elaborates on some concepts and tools that are useful for a wide group of investors, individual investors and institutional investors alike, and provides some insightful case studies. The discussion will adhere to the typology of risk that was developed in Section 2.7 of Chapter 2, which distinguished between market risk, credit risk and operational risk. Section 21.1 discusses market risk, or the risk resulting from unexpected adverse movements of market prices, volatility, correlations and liquidity. Next, Section 21.2 discusses credit risk, or the risk that a counterparty defaults on its obligations or the credit quality deteriorates. Section 21.3 discusses operational risk, which is an umbrella term for various investment risks other than market risk and credit risk, resulting from, for instance, a flawed organisational structure or the interruption of trading due to a terrorist attack. Finally, Section 21.4 discusses various instruments and strategies for managing these risks (diversification, derivatives and insurance).

21.1   Market risk

Market risk is the risk resulting from unexpected adverse movements of market prices. There are several different types of market risk. Interest-rate risk, foreign-exchange risk, equity risk and commodity risk all deal with market risk spurred by their respective risk factors: fluctuations in interest rates, exchange rates, stock indices and commodity prices (gold, oil, and so on). In addition, there is market liquidity risk: the risk that it could be very costly to the investor to sell the securities quickly.

Market risk can be measured as the potential loss in a portfolio that is associated with a price movement of a given probability over a specified time horizon. This is the value-at-risk (VaR) approach. Nowadays, many banks, brokerage firms and mutual funds use VaR methods to gauge their market risk. Bank regulators can force implementation of VaR methods because they can set capital adequacy requirements based on banks' VaR. In the USA, rating agencies such as Moody's and Standard and Poor's, the Financial Accounting Standard Board and the Securities and Exchange Commission have all announced their support for VaR.

21.1.1   The concept of value at risk

VaR is the maximum dollar loss that a portfolio may be expected to suffer over a given holding period, at a given level of confidence. If there is only a 5% probability that the portfolio will fall by more than $1 million in one trading day, then the VAR for one trading day and 95% confidence is $1 million. Thus, the VaR depends on two key parameters: the holding period T and the confidence level γ.[2] The usual holding period is one day or one month, but institutions can also use other holding periods.[3] One factor that determines the length of the holding period is the liquidity of the markets in which the investor operates. Ideally, the holding period is set equal to the length of time it takes to orderly liquidate the portfolio, i.e. to sell the portfolio without exerting abnormal price pressure and without incurring abnormal transaction costs. The confidence level is typically in the range 95–99%, so that VaR measures losses that occur with a small probability of 1–5%.

Throughout the text, we will use $VaR(\gamma, T)$ to denote the VaR as a function of γ and T. As we will see below, the VaR also depends on other factors, such as the composition of the portfolio and the risks of the assets in the portfolio. Hence, VaR is not a given number; it changes through time as the composition of the portfolio changes and as the risks of the assets in the portfolio change (for example, during the course of the business cycle). However, for a given portfolio and for given risks, the holding period and the confidence level determine the VaR.

Exhibit 21.2 illustrates the VaR for a hypothetical $100 million equity portfolio. Part a shows the probability distribution function for daily dollar gains and losses of this portfolio.[4] Suppose that we are interested in the VaR for one trading day and for 95% confidence. In other words, we intend to compute $VaR(0.95, 1/250)$.[5] This VaR is given by the negative of the point on the x-axis that cuts off the bottom 5% of the left tail of the distribution from the top 95% of the distribution.[6] In this case, the relevant value is -1.645, so the $VaR(0.95, 1/250)$ is $1.645 million.[7]

Again, the VaR depends on the level of confidence (γ). For example, the daily 99% confidence VaR, or $VaR(0.99, 1/250)$, is given by the negative of the cut-off between the top 99% and the bottom 1% of the distribution, which in this case is $2.326 million. In general, increasing the confidence level means that the cut-off point is located further to the left of the distribution, and the VaR will be higher. Exhibit 21.2b illustrates this point by showing how the VaR varies as we change the confidence level but keep all else constant. Note that the VaR increases with the confidence level at an increasing rate. This pattern is typical of many other cases.

Exhibit 21.2c shows the sensitivity of VaR to the length of the holding period. The panel shows the $VaR(0.95, T)$ for one trading day ($T = 1/250$) to 100 trading days ($T = 100/250$). Clearly, the VaR increases as the length of the holding period is increased. However, VaR increases at a decreasing rate. Again, this pattern occurs in most cases.

Exhibits 21.2b and c give only partial information about the effect of an isolated change to the confidence level or an isolated change to the holding period. Exhibit 21.2d gives a more

---

[2] The significance level α is the complement of the confidence level, i.e. $\alpha = 1 - \gamma$. At a confidence level of 95%, the VaR is not exceeded in 95% of cases. The significance level then is 5%, meaning that the VaR is exceeded in the remaining 5% of the cases.

[3] The BIS capital adequacy rules stipulate that banks use a holding period of two weeks or ten trading days.

[4] We assume that the daily dollar return on the portfolio is a normal random variable with a mean of zero and a standard deviation of $1 million. Hence, the value of the portfolio after one day is a normal random variable with a mean of $100 million and a standard deviation of $1 million.

[5] We express the investment horizon in years and assume 250 trading days in one year.

[6] Technically, the 95% cut-off point is known as the fifth percentile.

[7] Note that the VaR indicates the worst possible loss, which is a positive number, even though the value of the portfolio decreases.

Exhibit 21.2 Value at risk (VaR) for a hypothetical $100 million equity portfolio

(a) VaR and the probability distribution function

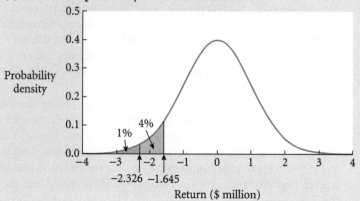

(b) Changing the confidence level while keeping the holding period fixed

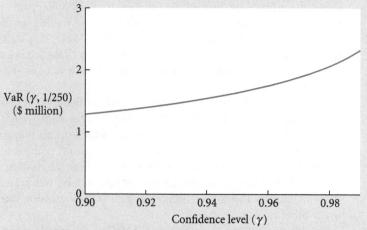

(c) Changing the holding period while keeping the confidence level fixed

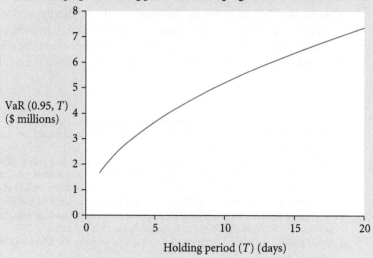

Exhibit 21.2   continued

(d) Changing the confidence level and the holding period simultaneously

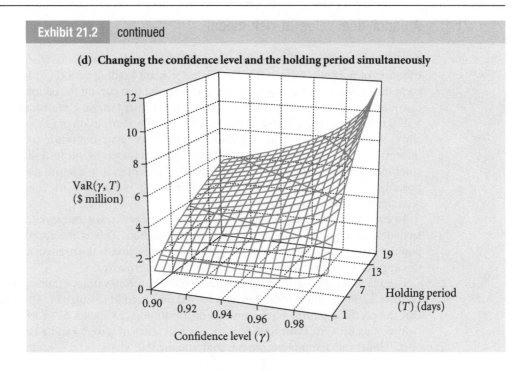

complete picture by considering simultaneous changes to the confidence level and the holding period. The resulting VaR surface allows us to determine the VaR for any combination of the confidence level and the holding period. Clearly, the VaR increases with both the confidence level (at an increasing rate) and the holding period (at a decreasing rate), and it culminates in a spike, which represents the point where the portfolio risk is highest (the combination of a confidence level of 99% and a holding period of 20 days).

Why is VaR so popular as a measure for market risk? The main advantage is that VaR captures market risk in a single measure that is conceptually simple to understand and simple to communicate to others (for instance, the clients or the senior managers of investment managers). VaR allows us to integrate the market risks from different types of assets (equities, bonds, derivatives, and so on), from different sources (equity markets, interest rates, exchange rates, commodity prices), and at different departments of a company (company-wide risk management).

Still, there are also drawbacks to VaR. One of the biggest problems with VaR is that, while it tells you what your maximum expected loss would be on, say, 95 days out of 100, it does not tell you whether your loss in the worst five days will be 1$ more or $1 million more than that maximum.[8] Also, while the concept of VaR is simple, estimating VaR can be difficult in practice (see Section 21.1.3), and different estimation methods can yield very different results. For this reason, it is important to report the exact procedure that was used to estimate VaR, the accuracy of the resulting VaR estimate and the sensitivity to the choice of the procedure. A VaR estimate is meaningless without such additional information.

---

[8] To circumvent this problem, some academics plead for using expected tail loss (ETL). While VaR tells us the most we can expect to lose if a tail event does not occur, ETL tells us what we can expect to lose if a tail event does occur.

21.1.2 An analytical value-at-risk model

As discussed in the previous section, the definition of VaR is relatively simple. If the distribution of portfolio gains and losses for the relevant holding period (T) is known, we can compute $VaR(\gamma, T)$ as the negative of the cut-off point that cuts off the bottom $(1 - \gamma)\%$ of the distribution from the top $\gamma\%$ of the left tail of the distribution. Unfortunately, computing VaR is much more complicated in practice, because the distribution of gains and losses generally is not known. In practice, typically we have to estimate the future return distribution information from a data set of historical returns for the assets in the portfolio and we have to combine the return distribution of the individual securities into a return distribution for the portfolio. Once the future portfolio return distribution is estimated, the computation of VaR is straightforward using the above cut-off rule.

To estimate VaR, several models are available. For brevity, we concentrate on the so-called analytical or variance–covariance model in this section. This is the approach used in the popular RiskMetrics framework.[9] We will subsequently discuss the strength and limitations of this approach and describe various extensions and alternatives.

The analytical approach is a direct extension of the mean–variance framework discussed in Chapter 8 and the multi-index models (MIMs) discussed in Chapter 11. The model assumes that the portfolio returns obey a normal distribution (see Chapter 6)[10] with a mean of zero (which is realistic for short time horizons such as a day or a week) and a standard deviation of σ_p. Under this assumption, we can compute the VaR as

$$VaR(\gamma, T) = z^{-1}(\gamma)\sigma_p\sqrt{T}P \qquad (21.1)$$

In this equation, $z^{-1}(\gamma)$ denotes the quintile of the standard normal distribution associated with the desired level of confidence (γ). The higher the desired level of confidence (or the lower the level of significance), the higher the VaR. After all, the maximum possible loss increases if we want to be more certain that the maximum loss is not exceeded. For example, for a confidence level of 95% the quantile is 1.645, but for a confidence level of 99% the quantile is 2.326.[11] Further, $\sqrt{T}$ is a correction for the time horizon.[12] Note that T is expressed in terms of the return interval used to measure the standard deviation. For example, if the standard deviation is computed using monthly returns and the time horizon is one day, then $T = 1/25$ and $\sqrt{T} \cong 0.2$ months. Similarly, if the standard deviation is computed using weekly data, then $T = 1/5$ and $\sqrt{T} \cong 0.447$ months.[13] Finally, P stands for the total value of the portfolio. The multiplication with P is required in order to move from the standard deviation of returns σ_p to the standard deviation of changes in portfolio value $\sigma_p P$.

---

[9] The RiskMetrics Group currently offers various methodologies for risk managament, as well as the technology and data required to apply the methodology. For example, DataMetrics offers tens of thousands of clean and synchronised historical time series ranging from prices for Intel to three-month gold forwards; from ten-year Australian government rates to Canadian/US dollar spot rates. The analytical approach discussed in this section is similar to the so-called RiskMetrics Classic methodology. For more details, see www.riskmetrics.com/mrdata.html

[10] This assumption is far from trivial: remember that, in practice, return distributions have 'fat tails', and VaR is concerned primarily with tail events.

[11] Other quantiles can be found in the standard normal table in Appendix 7 at the end of Chapter 7. With Excel spreadsheet software, the quantile can be found using the command NORMINV(γ; 0; 1) with γ for the desired level of confidence.

[12] If the standard deviation of a random variable is σ, then the standard deviation of the sum of T independent and identical random variables is $\sqrt{T}\sigma$.

[13] We assume that there are 25 trading days in one month and five trading days in a week.

Practice box

Problem
An investor buys a portfolio of $20 million of company A's shares and $30 million of company B's shares. The daily volatilities of stocks and their correlation ($\rho_{A,B}$) are as follows: $\sigma_A = 2\%$, $\sigma_B = 1.5\%$, $\rho_{A,B} = 0.2$.

1. What is the 99% daily VaR of the investment?
2. What is the 99% weekly VaR of the investment? Assume five trading days per week.
3. How will the results of 1 and 2 change if the correlation coefficient is −0.2 instead?

Solution
1. The total investment P in the portfolio equals $50 million ($20 million + $30 million), hence the weights of each type of shares are $w_A = 0.4$ ($20 million/$50 million) and $w_B = 0.6$ ($30 million/$50 million).

    Using Equation 8.6 from Chapter 8, it is possible to compute the portfolio's standard deviation:

$$\sigma_p = \sqrt{w_A^2 \sigma_A^2 + w_B^2 \sigma_B^2 + 2w_A w_B \sigma_{A,B}}$$

$$= \sqrt{w_A^2 \sigma_A^2 + w_B^2 \sigma_B^2 + 2w_A w_B (\rho_{A,B} \sigma_A \sigma_B)}$$

$$= \sqrt{0.4^2 \times 2^2 + 0.6^2 \times 1.5^2 + 2 \times 0.4 \times 0.6 \times 0.2 \times 2 \times 1.5}$$

$$= \sqrt{1.738} \cong 1.318\%$$

From the standard normal table in Appendix 7, we can infer that the quantile $z^{-1}(0.99)$ is 2.326. Further, $T = 1$, because we measure the daily VaR using the daily volatility. The portfolio's daily VaR is then

$$VaR(0.99, 1) = z^{-1}(\gamma)\sigma_p \sqrt{T} P = 2.326 \times 0.01318 \times 1 \times \$50 \text{ million} = \$1.533 \text{ million}$$

2. The weekly VaR of the investment can be computed by multiplying the daily VaR by $\sqrt{5}$, meaning there are five trading days in a week:

$$VaR(0.99, 5) = \$1.533 \text{ million} \times \sqrt{5} = \$3.428 \text{ million}$$

    It is logical that weekly VaR is greater then daily VaR, because during a longer period of time the investor can lose more money given the same probability.

3. If the correlation between stocks is negative ($\rho = -0.2$), then the investor will expect a lower VaR due to lower variance of the portfolio:

$$\sigma_p = \sqrt{0.4^2 \times 2^2 + 0.6^2 \times 1.5^2 + 2 \times 0.4 \times 0.6 \times (-0.2) \times 2 \times 1.5} = \sqrt{1.162} \approx 1.078\%$$

$$VaR(0.99, 1) = z^{-1}(\gamma)\sigma_p \sqrt{T} P = 2.326 \times 0.01078 \times 1 \times \$50 \text{ million} = \$1.254 \text{ million}$$

$$VaR(0.99, 5) = \$1.254 \text{ million} \times \sqrt{5} = \$2.804 \text{ million}$$

    A better portfolio diversification made the dollar amount of VaR lower.

A short history of LTCM

The fund began trading in February of 1994 and had stellar returns in its first two years – its investors earned 43 per cent in 1995 and 41 per cent in 1996. In 1997, the fund did substantially less well, earning 17 per cent. By December 1997, the fund's equity had grown to more than Dollars 7 bn. LTCM decided that it did not need so much equity in the fund and returned Dollars 2.7 bn to its investors.

At the beginning of 1998, the fund had capital of about Dollars 4.7 bn. Each dollar of capital was used to borrow funds, which brought the total assets of the fund roughly to Dollars 125 bn. The fund had derivatives positions in excess of Dollars 1250 bn of notional value. These positions were artificially high because LTCM's strategy was to get out of certain derivatives positions by taking new, off-setting positions rather than by terminating the existing contracts before maturity. In the summer of 1998, the fund had positions in a wide variety of markets: Danish mortgages, US Treasury bonds, Russian bonds, US stocks, mortgage bonds, Latin American bonds, UK bonds and US swaps. Under normal circumstances, these positions were mostly uncorrelated – the fund took advantage of diversification to reduce its risk in addition to hedging positions.

LTCM wanted the volatility of the fund to be roughly 20 per cent on an annualised basis. Before April 1998, its volatility was consistently below its target, averaging 11.5 per cent; the fund's volatility was very stable. After the fund's capital was reduced, its volatility was still substantially lower than 20 per cent. With capital of Dollars 4.7 bn, a monthly Value-at-Risk (VaR) of 5 per cent corresponding to a volatility of 20 per cent is Dollars 448 m. In other words, the fund was expected to lose in excess of Dollars 448 m in one month out of 20 at its target volatility.

On August 17, Russia defaulted on its domestic debt. This started a period of dramatic market movements that led to large losses for the fund.

On 21 August 1998, it lost Dollars 551 m, mostly in positions that had nothing to do with Russia, but many were adversely affected by it indirectly as discussed below. The loss on August 21 was more than 10 times the target daily volatility of the fund – computer spreadsheets return a probability of zero for such an event if returns follow the normal distribution.

By early September, the fund's investors had seen their investments reduced to half their January levels, and the fund was running out of capital. Meeting under the auspices of the Federal Reserve Bank of New York on September 23, the heads of 14 leading banks and investment houses decided to invest Dollars 3.65 bn in the fund and obtained a 90 per cent stake in LTCM. This was not a public money bail-out, since no public money was used. Rather, it was the equivalent of pre-packaged bankruptcy: the fund was restructured to avoid default.

In December 1999, the fund was dissolved. The above-mentioned banks and investment institutions made a profit of 10 per cent on their investment. The fund had about 100 investors who were not part of the management company. Out of these 100 investors, 88 made a profit on their investment. The typical investor's average annual return was 18 per cent.

Source: Rene Stultz, 'Why Risk Management Is Not Rocket Science', *Financial Times*, 27 June 2000.

The above text is a section taken from a larger survey article by Professor Rene Stultz of the Ohio State University that appeared in the *Financial Times*. Among other things, Stultz reviews the history of the hedge fund Long Term Capital Management (LTCM) up to and including the near-collapse of the fund in 1998.[14] According to this article, LTCM's monthly

95% VaR at the beginning of 1998 was \$448 million, and the \$551 million loss on 21 August 1998 was more than ten times the target daily volatility. Using the framework discussed in this chapter, we can replicate these numbers. First, using the information that the value of the capital is $P = 4.7$ billion, the relevant percentile is $z^{-1}(0.95) = 1.645$, the annual volatility is $\sigma_p = 0.2$ and the holding period is one month or $T = 1/12$, we arrive at the following estimate for the monthly 95% VaR:

$$\text{VaR}(0.95, 1/12) = 1.645 \times 0.2 \times \sqrt{1/12} \times \$4.7 \text{ billion} = \$446.34 \text{ million}$$

This figure is identical to that of Stultz, ignoring a small difference due to rounding. The above computation used the monthly target volatility of $0.2 \times \sqrt{1/12} \times \$4.7$ billion = \$271.36 million. Similarly, assuming 300 trading days per annum, the daily target volatility is $0.2 \times \sqrt{1/300} \times \$4.7$ billion = \$54.27 million. The actual loss of \$551 million is more than ten times this figure.

Thus far, we have assumed that the portfolio standard deviation σ_p is known. However, in practice, generally this figure is not known and has to be estimated by some estimation method. Recall from the mean–variance framework in Chapter 8 that σ_p can be computed from the portfolio weights and the variance–covariance terms of the assets in the portfolio (see Equation 8.6). Unfortunately, in practice, this approach involves an enormous information requirement, because we need information on the covariance between all pairs of assets, and the number of pairs increases rapidly as the number of assets in the portfolio increases. For example, for a portfolio of 100 assets, the number of covariance terms is 4950. For this reason, it is useful to employ the MIMs that were discussed in Chapter 11.

Recall that MIMs assume that the returns to the individual assets in the portfolio are linear functions of K common risk factors, such as equity indexes, interest rates, exchange rates and commodity prices. As discussed in Chapter 11, using regression analysis, we can estimate the factor sensitivities from historical observations of the asset's returns and the risk factors (see Appendix A at the end of this book for an introduction to regression analysis).[15] Using $\hat{\beta}_{ij}$ for the estimated sensitivity of the return of the ith asset ($i = 1, 2, \ldots, N$) to the jth factor ($j = 1, 2, \ldots, K$), the estimated sensitivity of the return of the portfolio p to the jth factor is given by

$$\hat{\beta}_{pj} = \sum_{j=1}^{K} w_i \hat{\beta}_{ij} \tag{21.2}$$

where w_i is the weight of the ith asset in the portfolio. An estimate for σ_p can be obtained by combining the estimated portfolio sensitivities $\hat{\beta}_{pj}$ ($j = 1, 2, \ldots, K$) with estimates of the variance–covariance terms for the risk factors. As discussed in Chapters 6 and 8, there exist various statistical methods for estimating the variance–covariance terms between the risk factors using historical data (the simplest method is using Equation 6.18). Using $\hat{\sigma}_{sj}$ for the estimated covariance between the jth factor ($j = 1, 2, \ldots, K$) and the sth risk factor ($s = 1, 2, \ldots, K$), we can estimate the portfolio standard deviation as:[16]

---

[14] Further details on LTCM can be found in Connecting Theory to Practice 4.3 and 21.2 and Investment in the News 19.

[15] Sometimes, the sensitivities can be computed directly from a formula, such as the formula for the duration (interest sensitivity) of bonds and the delta (sensitivity for the price of the underlying asset) of an option. However, this is possible only if we have a formula that links the price of the asset to the value of the risk factors.

[16] Note that we are ignoring asset-specific risk. This is possible only for a well-diversified portfolio. Further, in contrast to Chapter 11, we do not assume that the risk factors are mutually independent.

$$\hat{\sigma}_p = \sqrt{\sum_{j=1}^{K}\sum_{s=1}^{K}\hat{\beta}_{pj}\hat{\beta}_{ps}\hat{\sigma}_{s,j}} \tag{21.3}$$

Substituting this estimate for σ_p in Equation 21.1, we obtain the following estimator for VaR:

$$\widehat{VaR}(\gamma, T) = z^{-1}(\gamma) \times \sqrt{\sum_{j=1}^{K}\sum_{s=1}^{K}\hat{\beta}_{pj}\hat{\beta}_{ps}\hat{\sigma}_{s,j}} \sqrt{T}P \tag{21.4}$$

In brief, the estimated VaR depends on the following six factors:

- the estimated variance–covariance terms of the risk factors ($\hat{\sigma}_{s,j}$);
- the estimated sensitivity of the assets to the risk factors ($\hat{\beta}_{ij}$);
- the portfolio weights (w_i);
- the desired confidence level (γ);
- the desired holding period (T);
- the amount invested (P).

Practice box

Problem

We continue the example used in the previous practice box. An investor buys a portfolio of $20 million of company A's shares and $30 million of company B's shares. Both companies are exposed to two risk factors, a stock index I_1 and a bond index I_2. The daily volatilities of these indexes are estimated at 1.5% and 0.5%, respectively, and the estimated correlation is $\rho_{1,2} = 0.1$. The estimated sensitivities of company A shares are $\hat{\beta}_{A1} = 1.2$ and $\hat{\beta}_{A2} = 0.2$; for company B, they are $\hat{\beta}_{B1} = 0.1$ and $\hat{\beta}_{B2} = 1.4$.

1. Estimate the 99% daily VaR of the investment.
2. How can you explain the difference between this figure and the 99% daily VaR found in the previous practice box?

Solution

1. Using Equation 21.2, the estimated portfolio sensitivities are given by

$$\hat{\beta}_{p1} = w_A\hat{\beta}_{A1} + w_B\hat{\beta}_{B1} = 0.4 \times 1.2 + 0.6 \times 0.1 = 0.54$$

$$\hat{\beta}_{p2} = w_A\hat{\beta}_{A2} + w_B\hat{\beta}_{B2} = 0.4 \times 0.2 + 0.6 \times 1.4 = 0.92$$

Next, using Equation 21.3, the estimated portfolio standard deviation is

$$\hat{\sigma}_p = \sqrt{\hat{\beta}_{p1}^2\hat{\sigma}_1^2 + \hat{\beta}_{p2}^2\hat{\sigma}_2^2 + 2\hat{\beta}_{p1}\hat{\beta}_{p2}\hat{\sigma}_{1,2}} = \sqrt{\hat{\beta}_{p1}^2\hat{\sigma}_1^2 + \hat{\beta}_{p2}^2\hat{\rho}_2^2 + 2\hat{\beta}_{p1}\hat{\beta}_{p2}\hat{\rho}_{1,2}\hat{\sigma}_1\hat{\sigma}_2}$$

$$= \sqrt{0.54^2 \times 1.5^2 + 0.92^2 \times 0.5^2 + 2 \times 0.54 \times 0.92 \times 0.1 \times 1.5 \times 0.5} \cong 0.97\%$$

Finally, using Equation 21.4, the estimated VaR is

$$\widehat{VaR}(0.99, 1) = z^{-1}(\gamma)\hat{\sigma}_p\sqrt{T}P = z^{-1}(0.99)0.0097 \times 1 \times \$50 \text{ million} = \$1.129 \text{ million}$$

2. The estimated VaR is substantially lower than the figure in the previous practice box. Presumably, this reflects the use of a MIM, which ignores non-systematic risk. For a well-diversified portfolio, non-systematic risk can be ignored. However, for a portfolio of only two types of stocks, as in this example, non-systematic risk can be important. Another possible explanation is the use of estimated parameters rather than true parameters; perhaps the factor sensitivities, the volatilities or the correlation are underestimated.

21.1.3 Limitations, extensions and alternatives

The analytical VaR model offers a systematic framework for estimating market risk. Using modern computers and software, the computations are relatively straightforward. Also, since 1994, the RiskMetrics system volunteers a data feed for computing VaR (historical estimates for the variance and covariance terms of various risk factors).[17] However, the analytical VaR also has several shortcomings:

- The model assumes that the indices obey a normal distribution. However, as discussed in Chapter 8, asset returns typically do not obey the normal distribution. Specifically, for many assets, the risk of large losses is larger than predicted by the normal distribution; in other words, many asset-return distributions have fat left tails. For example, if the models were to be believed, the 1987 US equities crash and the 1994 Mexican peso crisis were once-in-a-millennium events. Section 21.2 will show the effect of fat left tails on the measurement of credit risk for corporate bonds.
- The model assumes a linear relationship between the returns of the assets and the risk factors. However, this assumption is not valid for some assets. For example, for long-maturity bonds we have to account for 'convexity' (see Chapter 14), and for options we have to account for 'gamma' (see Chapter 20). These assets involve a considerable non-linear exposure to risk factors.
- The estimated VaR is accurate only if the risk parameters (factor sensitivities and variance–covariance terms) are estimated in an accurate way. However, as discussed in Section 9.5 of Chapter 9, estimation error can arise from the use of small samples or the changing of the return distribution through time (time-varying risk parameters).
- The holding period used in the VaR computations should equal the length of time it takes to alter the risk profile at a reasonable cost. One limitation of VaR computations is that market liquidity is not constant over time. In fact, liquidity may dry up when the largest losses occur and, in turn, liquidity dry-up may cause or amplify the losses. Unfortunately, VaR models do not account for adverse changes in liquidity.
- In estimating the risk parameters (exposure coefficients, volatilities and correlations), it is typically assumed that the risks do not change through time. However, history teaches us that risk can change suddenly and dramatically. Chapter 9 discussed the effect of volatility clustering, or prolonged periods with persistently high volatility, and the effect of contagion, or the sudden increase of correlations during international market crises (such as that witnessed during and after the devaluation of the Mexican peso in 1994 and the devaluation of the Thai baht in 1997). The counterpart to contagion is correlation breakdown. If this happens, then previously reliable correlations cease to hold. For investors who hold long positions in assets, a correlation breakdown is good news, as the risk of their portfolio falls. However, for investors such as hedge funds that seek to offset the risk of assets by shorting other, highly correlated assets, a correlation breakdown can turn into a catastrophe.

The above limitations reduce the usefulness of market-risk modelling. Indeed, various financial institutions, including the hedge fund LTCM, have learned that 'risk management is not rocket science'. However, although modelling may carry its imperfections, it still represents an advance in quantifying and controlling risk over previous techniques. Also, the problems have stimulated the development of various extensions and alternatives to the analytical VaR model and improvements to the information feeding of the model:

---

[17] See www.riskmetrics.com.

■ Delta-gamma methods replace the linear relationship between asset returns and the risk factors with a quadratic relationship. For bonds, the non-linear exposure to interest rate risk is known as 'convexity' (see Chapter 14); for options, the non-linear exposure to the price of the underlier is called 'gamma'(see Chapter 20).

■ The analytical approach assumes a normal distribution and a linear factor structure. Under these assumptions, it is straightforward to derive a formula for the VaR (such as Equation 2.4). However, if we relax these assumptions, generally we cannot derive a formula in a simple way. Simulation methods are a solution to this problem. We can distinguish two different simulation methods. Historical simulation uses a sample of historical observations for the risk factors. For every observation, the portfolio return is determined, possibly according to a non-linear pattern or even according to explicit pricing functions such as discounted cash-flow models and option-valuation models. Finally, the VaR is computed as a percentile of the historical distribution of the portfolio returns. This approach does not require the specification of a statistical distribution but rather assumes that historical observations can approximate the true statistical distribution. Obviously, the results are very sensitive to sampling error.

Monte Carlo simulation (MCS) works in a similar way, but it uses a large number of random draws that are generated from a prespecified return distribution (possibly non-normal). The portfolio return is then determined for every random draw (possibly according to a non-linear pattern) and the VaR is computed as a percentile of the simulated distribution of the portfolio returns. While this approach does not require a normal distribution, some statistical distribution for the factor returns has to be specified in advance and, hence, specification error may arise. Although MCS does not use historical data, it is still exposed to sampling error. Specifically, there is a risk of running too few simulations to adequately capture the return distribution, and this could result in unreliable results. This is true especially if many risk factors are included in the model. Fortunately, calculation methods exist to estimate how far off a simulation is, so that one can decide whether or not to run more trials.

■ Advanced time-series estimation methods, including so-called autoregressive integrated moving average (ARIMA) and generalised autoregressive conditional heteroskedasticity (GARCH) methods, may be used to provide more accurate estimates for the risk parameters. Among other things, these methods can account for volatility clustering by allowing recent observations to have greater influence on volatility estimates than stale observations.

■ Despite the sophistication of the advanced time-series models, they can only extrapolate from past information. An alternative route to improved models is to enhance the quality of this information. Since option prices are forward looking, option-implied volatilities can yield more reliable estimates for future volatility. A good example is the behaviour of the implied volatilities of options on the US dollar–Thai baht exchange rate in the weeks before the baht peg to the dollar was broken on 2 July 1997. The spot rate hardly budged as the exchange rate came under pressure – after all, it was still pegged. However, implied volatilities rose sharply, indicating that the markets were distinctly aware of the possibility of a baht devaluation.

■ The limitations of the normal distribution for describing asset returns are well known. Unfortunately, it is not clear what alternative statistical distribution is appropriate, since any choice may involve specification error. However, the tail of return distribution (the probabilities of the largest market downturns) has the same shape for a wide range of statistical distributions (including non-normal distribution). A branch of statistics called extreme value theory (EVT) describes the tail behaviour. The estimation of the portfolio standard deviation, which describes the entire return distribution only in the case of a normal distribution, is replaced by the estimation of a tail index that describes the shape of the tail for a wide range of statistical distributions.

Further, the following tools are available for testing VaR models:

■ **Back-testing** is a method for assessing the validity of a VaR method by counting the number of times when the losses exceed the estimated VaR in an historical or simulated sample. The VaR model assumes that, for instance, a 95% VaR should, on average, be exceeded in just 5% of cases. If the actual relative frequency substantially exceeds the significance level (for example, 20% of cases fall below the 5% VaR), then the VaR method underestimates the true VaR. By contrast, if the frequency substantially exceeds the significance level (for example, 1% of cases exceed the 5% VaR), then the VaR method overestimates the true VaR.

■ **Sensitivity analysis** analyses the sensitivity of the VaR for the different modelling and estimation choices available. Sensitivity should be performed both across methods (for example, by comparing the results of the analytical VaR model with the results of MCS) and within methods (for example, by changing the data set used to estimate the risk parameters).

■ Back-testing verifies the accuracy of the VaR model under 'normal' market conditions; extraordinary situations are considered using **stress tests**. Stress tests examine a portfolio under a specific set of market events (scenarios) that are considered plausible, without developing a statistical model for such events. Stress tests should not be limited to quantitative exercises that compute potential losses or gains; they should also include more qualitative analyses of the actions that management might take under particular scenarios, for instance operating procedures and lines of communication.

Scenarios can be historical, in which case we would apply the market moves observed in a past crisis, for example the stock market crash of 1987 or the Exchange Rate Mechanism crisis of 1992. Historical scenarios are attractive because all relationships between markets are specified at once. On the other hand, no one believes that exactly the same combination of market moves will occur again. It is therefore common to specify hypothetical scenarios of events that are plausible but that have never occurred previously. Hypothesising a scenario for one market is straightforward; the difficulty arises in specifying relationships between markets that would be likely in such a crisis scenario. Market events, including the Asia crisis in 1997 and the aftermath of the Russia default in 1998, have taught us that relationships change in crises; ignoring these relationships when stipulating a scenario renders the exercise meaningless.

→ Connecting Theory to Practice 21.2　　　　　　　　　**FT**

Why risk management is not a rocket science

Between the time LTCM was created and 1998, the financial world changed dramatically, partly due to LTCM, partly due to regulatory actions. These changes explain much of what happened to LTCM.

LTCM was a spectacular financial innovation. The way it was structured was a marvel of financial engineering. Unfortunately for the partners, the world is a competitive place. It is hard to keep good ideas hidden. The enormous profits LTCM made early focused the attention of the financial sector on LTCM. This adversely affected LTCM for three reasons. First, it created a large number of imitators. Second, it put pressure on LTCM to keep pursuing high profits in an environment where this was no longer possible, leading it to create positions in which

▶

outsiders would not think it had a competitive advantage. Third, it made markets less liquid for LTCM.

Consider the impact of imitators on LTCM's strategies. Suppose that LTCM finds that yields are too high on a security. It goes and buys the security, while hedging the risk. When imitators do the same, the price of the security rises, eliminating the profit opportunity LTCM had first identified. This effect both reduced the size of the trades that LTCM could make and decreased the profits on those trades.

In 1997, the fund's investors earned 17 per cent, less than half what they earned the year before. Traditional positions exploiting yield spreads were becoming less profitable. To increase returns, LTCM reduced the fund's capital and went into areas that seem questionable: it took positions in Russian bonds; made volatility bets; and took positions in takeover stocks. LTCM thus took new positions the outcomes of which were more dependent on chance than its earlier positions. Nevertheless, it is important to note that the more traditional, fixed-income positions of LTCM explain the bulk of the August and September losses of 1998.

Imitators had another impact on LTCM. They changed the nature of the markets in which it was trading. Rather than acting in splendid isolation, LTCM became the lead steer of a herd. As it moved, all imitators moved. Thus the fund faced poor market conditions when it had to move out of positions because it did not do so alone. LTCM partly recognised this in its risk measurement by using correlations that were greater than historical correlations. It also meant that the value of the fund's positions was at the mercy of its imitators pulling out of their positions. In the summer of 1998, Salomon did just that – it closed its bond arbitrage department, leading to losses for LTCM.

LTCM's problems were compounded by regulations that required banks to use risk management models to set capital. Financial intermediaries make money out of providing liquidity. As investors want to get out of positions, financial intermediaries receive a liquidity premium to take on those positions. One would therefore have expected that in August 1998, financial intermediaries would make profits by scooping up positions that investors had to abandon. However, because their capital requirements increased with volatility, financial institutions had to dump positions themselves. Instead of being providers of liquidity, financial intermediaries became consumers of liquidity, forced to do so because of the regulatory environment. As a result, losses in Russia forced them to sell securities in other markets, propagating financial contagion.

In many ways, the events of August and September 1998 showed that risks can be managed. Despite dramatic changes in markets, no investment bank or bank in developed countries collapsed. Derivatives played a significant role in helping many of these institutions hedge their risks. None of the reasons that justified the award of Nobel prizes to Merton and Scholes were affected by the events of August and September 1998.

Yet, at the same time, these events showed brutally that risk management is part of the social sciences. What makes social sciences different is that their object of study changes continuously, in this case partly as a result of financial innovation. Understanding these changes and how they influence risk is critical in times of great uncertainty. Risk management is not rocket science – it cannot be, since the past does not repeat itself on a sufficiently reliable basis. Future risks cannot be understood without examining the economic forces that shape them – a skill that is not taught in physics departments or engineering schools. However, understanding risks makes sense only if that understanding is used to create value. This means that risk management cannot be done independently of an understanding of the profits that come from taking risks. Regulation that forces financial institutions to disregard profit opportunities in the name of risk control only ends up in making the financial system less stable.

Source: Rene Stultz, 'Why Risk Management Is Not Rocket Science', *Financial Times*, 27 June 2000.

> **→ Making the connection**
>
> The above text is another section taken from the survey article by Professor Rene Stultz. The author explains that the near-collapse of LTCM was caused not by a lack of risk management by LTCM but rather by the inherent limitations of risk-management models. Specifically, LTCM faced an unprecedented deterioration of correlations and liquidity due to the combined effect of a large number of imitators that copied its strategies ('copy cats') and regulatory capital requirements that forced financial institutions to close positions during volatile markets. Such unpredictable events explain why risk management is not a rocket science. Nevertheless, the near-collapse of LTCM has stimulated improvements in the methodology for measuring market risk. Hopefully, these improvements will help to prevent a similar event from happening again.

21.2 Credit risk

Credit risk is composed of default risk and credit-migration risk. Default risk is the risk that a counterparty will default on its obligations to the investor. For example, a bond issuer may fail to pay the coupons and par value in full or at the appropriate time.[18] Recall from Chapter 13 that rating agencies such as Moody's and Standard & Poor's assess the credit quality of bonds and issue credit ratings. Default risk is the risk that the credit quality deteriorates (or the default risk increases). For example, if an upper-medium-grade bond is downgraded to medium-grade (BBB or Baa), then the price of the bond will fall (all other things remaining equal) to reflect the lower credit quality. Hence, credit risk can materialise even though the counterparty continues to meet its current obligations. As discussed in Chapter 13, rating agencies publish transition matrices with the historical frequency of credit events (upgrades, downgrades and defaults).

Recall from Chapter 13 that the value of bonds also depends on the yield curve (interest rates on Treasury bonds) and the credit premiums (spreads over Treasuries). However, the risk of adverse changes of interest rates and default spreads is a form of market risk rather than credit risk. Thus, a credit risk model will predict that (default-free) US Treasury bonds involve no (credit) risk, even though US Treasury bonds can be very sensitive to interest-rate changes, especially when they have a long maturity and a low coupon rate (see Chapter 14). Thus, credit risk models generally do not give a complete picture of the risk of holding bonds.

21.2.1 Credit value at risk

In theory, measuring credit risk can be measured in the same way as market risk. Recall from the previous section that we can measure market risk by VaR. Similarly, we can compute credit risk by means of credit VaR or C-VaR. C-VaR is simply the maximum dollar loss that a bond

---

[18] Credit risk also occurs for OTC derivatives. By contrast, for exchange-traded derivatives, credit risk is mitigated by the role of mark-to-market procedures and clearing houses (see Chapter 19). For simplicity, we abstract from the credit risk for OTC derivatives and focus on the credit risk for bonds. Typical ways to control risk in the OTC market include the use of collateral and netting agreements (in which the trading partners agree to settle the net outstanding obligations rather than all individual outstanding obligations) – this is very similar to the procedure described for swaps in Chapter 19.

Exhibit 21.3	Illustration of credit value at risk five for a five-year, 6% coupon, BBB-rated bond

(a) Inputs required for deriving the value distribution

Credit rating	Yield to maturity (%)	Bond value ($)	Transition probability (%)
AAA	3.45	109.37	0.02
AA	3.50	109.19	0.33
A	3.63	108.66	5.95
BBB	3.92	107.55*	86.93
BB	5.42	102.02	5.30
B	6.56	98.10	1.17
CCC	11.31	83.64	0.12
Default	27.69	51.13	0.18

$$* P = \frac{6}{1.0392} + \frac{6}{(1.0392)^2} + \frac{6}{(1.0392)^3} + \frac{106}{(1.0392)^4} \cong 107.55$$

(b) Value distribution

portfolio may be expected to suffer over a given holding period, at a given level of confidence. If the distribution of portfolio gains and losses for the relevant holding period is known, we can compute C-VaR for γ% confidence as the negative of the cut-off point that cuts off the bottom $(1 - \gamma)$% of the distribution from the top γ% of the left tail of the distribution.

Exhibit 21.3 illustrates this point by using a simple example of a single BBB-rated bond with a 6% coupon rate and five years to maturity. Part a gives the input data required to derive the statistical distribution of the value of the bond after one year (that is, four years to maturity). The value of the bond (column 3) will depend on next year's credit rating (column 1) and next year's yield to maturity for the maturity and credit rating of the bond (Column 2).[19] If the

---

[19] The yield to maturity used here is a 'forward' yield to maturity rather than the current yield to maturity.

credit rating remains BBB, then the bond's value will be $107.55. The best possible outcome is an upgrade to AAA. In this case, the yield to maturity drops from 3.92 to 3.45% and the value of the bond rises from $107.55 to $109.37, a $1.82 gain. The worst possible outcome is default, associated with a rising yield from 3.92 to 27.69% and a falling price from $107.55 to $51.13, causing a loss of $56.42. Note that in the case of default, bonds generally do not lose all their value, because bondholders have a claim to the assets of the bond issuer and, hence, a substantial amount of the principal may still be recovered. In our case, the expected recovery rate is 51.13%. Column 4 gives the probabilities associated with the various credit events (upgrade, downgrade or default). For example, there is a 5.3% probability that the issuer will be downgraded to a BB rating. These migration probabilities may be taken from the transition matrices published by rating agencies.

Exhibit 21.3b gives the statistical distribution of the value of the bond after one year. Notice that this distribution differs in several ways from the normal distribution that was used in the analytical model for quantifying market risk in Section 21.2. First, the distribution is discrete rather than continuous; it involves a countable number of possible outcomes (eight different credit ratings). Second, the distribution is asymmetric or skewed; the probability of large losses far exceeds the probability of large gains. As discussed above, the best possible outcome is a $1.82 gain (upgrade to AAA), while the worst possible outcome is a $56.42 loss (default). Finally, the distribution has a fat left tail. The probability of large losses is much larger than under the normal distribution. For example, under the normal distribution, the probability of a loss exceeding $56.42 is 0.00%, while the actual probability is 0.18%.[20] These properties are typical of credit risk; credit risk has no upside potential, only downside risk.

To compute C-VaR for a confidence level of 99% and a holding period of one year, we must determine the first percentile of the distribution, or the cut-off point that cuts off the top 99% of the distribution from the bottom 1% of the left tail of the distribution. In our case, the first percentile is $92.29, which involves a loss of $15.26.[21] Hence, the C-VaR for a confidence level of 99% and a holding period of one year is $15.26.

Thus, we see that credit risk is conceptually not complex. More generally, the basic factors that determine the credit risk of a bond portfolio are as follows:

- The credit quality of the bonds, possibly measured by means of credit ratings. In turn, the credit quality is determined by factors such as the value of the assets and the degree of leverage of the issuer. A highly levered issuer will have a lower credit quality.
- The probability of deterioration of the credit quality, for instance measured by means of a transition matrix.
- The term structure of interest rates and credit spreads; these determine the current value of the bonds' losses in case of a future downgrade.
- The recovery rates, which determine the exposure in case of default. In turn, the recovery rates depend on the seniority of the bonds (see Chapter 13) and the underlying factors of the credit rating itself.
- The correlation between credit events (upgrades, downgrades and defaults) of the individual bonds. In general, the credit risk of a portfolio of assets will be less than the sum

---

[20] The standard deviation of the future bond value is given by $2.99. Hence, a loss of $56.42 amounts to a Z-value of $-\$56.42/\$2.99 = -18.87$. The P-value for this Z-value is about zero.

[21] This value is found using linear interpolation. Specifically, 0.30% (0.12% + 0.18%) of the probability mass lies at or below $83.64, and 1.47% (0.12% + 0.18% + 1.17%) of the probability mass lies below $98.10. Hence, the first percentile lies between $83.64 and $98.10. The exact value is found as $83.64 + ($98.10 − $83.64)(1.00% − 0.30%)/(1.47% − 0.30%) = $92.29.

of the credit risk of the individual assets, because of diversification effects. Diversification is very important because credit events predominantly are issuer-related and hence have very low correlations.

- The total dollar amount invested (P).
- The desired confidence level (γ). The higher the confidence level, the higher the C-VaR or the maximum loss at that level of confidence.
- The holding period (T). The longer the confidence level, the higher the C-VaR or the maximum loss during that period.

While the determinants of credit risk are known, computing C-VaR is a complex task in practice. For various reasons, modelling credit risk is more difficult than modelling market risk:

- For market risk, the normal distribution often gives a reasonable approximation to the return distribution of the assets (although there are important exceptions). By contrast, the normal distribution is not appropriate for describing credit risk. Exhibit 21.3 shows that the loss distribution for an individual bond involves negative skewness and fat left tails. This is generally true for bonds and for portfolios of bonds.
- Lack of reliable data on default and recovery rates. Credit-rating changes and defaults occur much less frequently than changes in market prices (which are used to model market risk). This problem is compounded by the use of a longer-term time horizon, usually one year rather than a few days or weeks as for market risk. The lack of reliable data complicates the estimation of default and recovery rates and also the back-testing required for measuring the accuracy of the model.
- For estimating the credit risk of a portfolio, we need to estimate the correlation between credit events (upgrades, downgrades and defaults) of different firms. This is even more difficult than estimating the migration probabilities of individual bonds.

21.2.2 Credit-risk models

The above problems have inspired the development of several sophisticated models and commercial software products for measuring portfolio credit risk. This whole area is currently subject to intensive research, and no 'superior' model has emerged thus far. Exhibit 21.4 compares the four portfolio credit-risk models that currently are used most commonly. The second column classifies the models as either default mode (DM) model or mark-to-market (MTM) model. A DM model focuses solely on the risk of default, while an MTM model considers both default risk and migration risk. The third column lists the source of credit risk and the fourth column indicates whether the model uses an analytical formula or relies on (MCS) to recover the credit-loss distribution. The last column gives a brief description of the model.

These models alleviate some of the problems associated with measuring credit risk. Specifically, they do not assume a normal distribution and allow for negatively skewed and fat-tailed loss distributions. Also, they offer various approaches to estimating credit correlations from the correlation of observable variables, such as the stock returns, industry and country classifications, and macroeconomic variables. However, they do not solve the problem associated with the lack of long-term data for exact estimation of default and recovery rates and for proper back-testing of the models. For this reason, the models should be used with care.

Exhibit 21.4	Comparison of portfolio credit-risk models			
Credit model (company)	DM/MTM	Sources of risk and correlations	Analytical/ MCS	Description
KMV (Moody's)	DM	Multivariate normal stock returns	Analytical	Computes the distance to default (DTD), the difference between the issuer's asset value – derived recursively via an option-pricing formula from the market value of equity – and the book value of liabilities. Next, the empirical default frequency (EDF), the historical default rate of firms below DTD, is computed
CreditMetrics (RiskMetrics Group)	MTM	Multivariate normal stock returns	MCS	Simulates issuer asset values by random draws from a multivariate normal distribution with correlations obtained from observed stock returns. The simulated asset values are then mapped to credit events via an historical migration matrix. The resulting migrations are mapped to bond prices with present-value computations using the term structure of interest rates and credit spreads
CreditRisk (Credit Suisse Financial Products)	DM	The default rate is stochastic (Poisson distribution with stochastic mean default rate (MDR) and loss given default (LGD))	Analytical	Actuarial model that requires data on MDRs and average LGDs of the bonds. The MDRs can be linked to economic factors giving rise to non-zero correlations between default probabilities of different issuers
CreditPortfolio view (McKinsey)	MTM	Multivariate distribution for macroeconomic (and country) variables	MCS	Econometric model that adjusts the migration matrix according to the prevailing macroeconomic situation. The intuition is that the credit cycle follows the economic cycle

Indeed, the BIS currently does not allow the use of portfolio credit-risk models for capital requirements of banks. By contrast, they do allow the use of portfolio models such as those described in Section 21.2 for measuring market risk. However, conceptually, the portfolio credit-risk models are superior to the simple credit-risk models used by regulators, although they are subject to greater computational complexity and data-collection costs. Specifically, the BIS sets minimum capital requirements of 8% of risk-weighted total assets (RWTA), a weighted average of the value of credit-risky bank assets. The weights are determined – in a rather crude fashion – by the type of credit instruments (and, in the Basel II accord, also by the credit rating). The major drawback of this approach is that it completely ignores correlations and diversification possibilities. It seems likely that, as with market risk, regulators will eventually allow some kind of portfolio credit-modelling approach to capital requirements for credit risk.

21.3	Operational risk

Operational risk is the least well defined of all the types of risk. In fact, the term 'operational risk' is usually used as an umbrella term for various investment risks other than market risk and credit risk. This risk category includes a wide variety of risk resulting from for instant malfunction of systems, flawed organisational structure, management failure, faulty control, fraud, human error and incorrect models. Additionally, it includes the risk that comes from the external environment, such as legal uncertainty.

Contrary to market risk and credit risk, these risks generally are difficult to quantify and control. How does one measure the probability and impact of fraud? How about legal risk? Or even natural disasters? The problems of measuring and controlling operational risk do not make operational risk less important. Indeed, many of the debacles listed in Exhibit 21.1 originated primarily from some sort of operational failure, where checks and controls within an organisation either have not existed or have failed and made fraud possible. For this reason, the field of operational risk management is receiving increasing attention by corporations, investors and regulators alike. For instance, the Basel II Accord, which defines capital adequacy requirements for banks, sets capital requirements for operational risk in addition to market risk and credit risk.

There is no better way to understand operational risk than to look at an example. A good illustration of operational risk is the collapse of Barings Bank. Barings Bank had a long history of success and was much respected as the UK's oldest merchant bank. But in February of 1995, this highly regarded bank, with $900 million in capital, was bankrupted by more than $1 billion of losses resulting from the unauthorised trading activities by one 'rogue trader', Nick Leeson, that went undetected as a consequence of management failure and lack of the most basic internal controls. Barings' collapse was finalised when the Dutch group ING purchased Barings for just one pound sterling and assumed all of its liabilities in March of 1995.

21.3.1 How Leeson broke Barings[22]

In 1993, Nick Leeson became general manager of Barings' futures subsidiary in Singapore, Barings Futures Singapore (BFS), running the bank's Singapore International Monetary Exchange (SIMEX) activities. Leeson was supposed to be exploiting low-risk arbitrage opportunities that would arise from price differences in the Nikkei 225 index futures on the SIMEX and the Osaka Stock Exchange (OSE). However, as will become clear in the following, Leeson did not conform to this strategy and finally caused the financial collapse of Barings. In fact, he was taking much riskier positions by buying and selling different amounts of the contracts on the two exchanges or buying and selling contracts of different types. As Leeson's losses mounted, he increased his bets. However, after an earthquake in Japan caused the Nikkei Index to drop sharply in January 1995, the losses increased rapidly, with Leeson's positions going more than $1 billion into the red. When Barings went into receivership on 27 February 1995, Barings, via Leeson, had outstanding notional futures positions on Japanese equities (Nikkei 225 index futures), interest rates (Japanese government bond futures) and currency (Euroyen futures) of $27 billion. Leeson also sold 70 892 Nikkei 225 index put and call options with a nominal

---

[22] Based on 'Not just one man – Barings', an extensive case study on the homepage of the IFCI Risk Institute, http://riskinstitute.ch

value of $6.68 billion. The nominal size of these positions is astounding when compared with the bank's reported capital of less than $1 billion.

The build-up of the futures positions took off after the Kobe earthquake of 17 January. Before the earthquake, with the Nikkei trading in a range of 19 000–19 500, Leeson had long futures positions of approximately 3000 contracts on the OSE. But Leeson's OSE position reflected only half of his sanctioned trades. If Leeson was long on the OSE, he had to be short the same amount of contracts on SIMEX.[23] After all, Leeson's official trading strategy was to take advantage of temporary price differences between the SIMEX and OSE contracts. This arbitrage required Leeson to buy the cheaper contract and simultaneously to sell the more expensive one, reversing the trade when the price difference had narrowed or disappeared. This kind of arbitrage activity has little market risk because positions are always matched. However, Leeson was long approximately the number of contracts he was supposed to be short. These were unauthorised trades, which he hid in an account named Error Account 88888.[24] He also used this account to execute all his unauthorised trades in Japanese government bond and Euroyen futures and Nikkei 225 options.

Exhibit 21.5 gives a snapshot of Leeson's unauthorised trades versus the trades that he reported. The most striking point of this exhibit is the fact that Leeson sold 70 892 Nikkei 225 options worth $6.68 billion without the knowledge of Barings London. The strategy of selling put and call options with the same strikes and maturities is known as creating a short straddle position (see Chapter 19). A short straddle on the Nikkei 225 index will generally

Exhibit 21.5   Leeson's reported versus actual positions as of 27 February 1995

| Type of contracts | Reported[a] | | Actual[b] | |
	Number of contracts	Nominal value ($)	Number of contracts[a]	Nominal value ($)
Nikkei 225 index futures	30 112	2809 million	Long 61 039	7000 million
Japanse government bond (JGB) futures	15 940	8980 million	Short 28 034	19 650 million
Euroyen futures	601	26.5 million	Short 6845	350 million
Nikkei 225 call options	Nil	Nil	Short 37 925	3580 million
Nikkei 225 put options	Nil	Nil	Short 32 967	3100 million

[a] Leeson's reported futures positions were supposedly matched because they were part of Barings' arbitrage activity, i.e. the number of contracts on the OSE, or the SIMEX, or the TSE.

[b] The actual positions refer to those unauthorised trades held in error account 88888.

[c] Expressed in terms of SIMEX contract sizes, which are half the size of those of the OSE and the TSE. For Euroyen, SIMEX and TIFFE contracts are of similar size.

Source: The Report of the Board of Banking Supervision Inquiry into the Circumstances of the Collapse of Barings, Ordered by the House of Commons, Her Majesty's Stationery Office, 1995. Crown copyright material is reproduced with the permission of the Controller of HMSO and the Queen's Printer for Scotland.

---

[23] In fact, he had to be short twice the number of contracts, because SIMEX contracts are half the size of OSE contracts.

[24] Error accounts are set up to accommodate trades that cannot be reconciled immediately. A compliance officer investigates the trade, records them on the firm's books and analyses how it affects the firm's market risk and profit and loss. Reports of error accounts normally are sent to senior officers of the firm. However, Barings London did not know of its existence since Leeson had asked a systems consultant, Dr Edmund Wong, to remove error account 88888 from the daily reports that BFS sent electronically to London.

be profitable when the Nikkei is trading near the options' strike price on expiry date, because the premium income more than offsets the small loss experienced on either the call (if the index rises) or the put (if the index falls). However, the seller faces the risk of unlimited losses if the Nikkei index crashes or rallies.

The strike prices of most of Leeson's straddle positions ranged from 18 500 to 20 000. He thus needed the Nikkei 225 to continue to trade in its pre-Kobe earthquake range of 19 000–19 500 if he was to make money on his option trades. The Kobe earthquake shattered Leeson's options strategy. On the day of the earthquake, 17 January, the Nikkei 225 was at 19 350. It ended that week slightly lower at 18 950, so Leeson's straddle positions were starting to look shaky. The call options that Leeson had sold were beginning to look worthless, but the put options would become very valuable to their buyers if the Nikkei continued to decline. Leeson's losses on these puts were unlimited and totally dependent on the level of the Nikkei at expiry, while the profits on the calls were limited to the premium earned.

This point is key to understanding Leeson's actions because before the Kobe earthquake, his unauthorised book, i.e. account 88888, showed a flat position in Nikkei 225 futures. Yet on Friday 20 January, three days after the earthquake, Leeson bought 10 814 March 1995 contracts. No one is sure whether he bought these contracts because he thought the market had overreacted to the Kobe shock or because he wanted to shore up the Nikkei to protect the position that arose from the option straddles. By buying Nikkei 225 futures, Leeson was increasing Baring's exposure to the Nikkei 225 rather than reducing it.

When the Nikkei dropped 1000 points to 17 950 on Monday 23 January1995, Leeson found himself showing losses on his two-day-old long futures position and facing unlimited damage from selling put options. There was no turning back; Leeson had to act. Leeson tried single-handedly to reverse the negative post-Kobe sentiment that swamped the Japanese stock market. On 27 January, account 88888 showed a long position of 27 158 March 1995 contracts. Over the next three weeks, Leeson doubled this long position to reach a high on 22 February of 55 206 March 1995 contracts and 5640 June 1995 contracts. However, the Japanese stock market did not recover, resulting in enormous losses for Leeson.

How was Leeson able to deceive everyone around him? How was he able to show a flat book when he was taking huge long positions on the Nikkei and short positions on Japanese interest rates? The Board of Banking Supervision (BoBS) of the Bank of England, which conducted an investigation into the collapse of Barings, believes that 'the vehicle used to effect this deception was the cross-trade'. A cross-trade is a transaction executed on the floor of an exchange by just one member who is both buyer and seller. If a member has matching buy and sell orders from two different customer accounts for the same contract and at the same price, then he or she is allowed to cross the transaction (execute the deal) by matching both client accounts. However, the member can do this only after he or she has declared the bid and offer price in the trading pit and no other member has taken it up. Under SIMEX rules, a cross-trade must be executed at market price. Leeson entered into a significant volume of cross-transactions between account 88888 and account 92000 (Barings Securities Japan – Nikkei and JGB Arbitrage), account 98007 (Barings London – JGB Arbitrage) and account 98008 (Barings London – Euroyen Arbitrage).

After executing these cross-trades, Leeson would instruct the settlements staff to break down the total number of contracts into several different trades and to change the trade prices thereon to cause profits to be credited to 'arbitrage' accounts referred to above and losses to be charged to account 88888. Thus, while the cross-trades on the exchange appeared on the face of it to be genuine and within the rules of the exchange, the books and records of BFS reflected pairs of transactions adding up to the same number of lots at prices bearing no relation to those executed on the floor.

The effect of these manipulations was to inflate reported profits in the arbitrage accounts at the expense of account 88888, which was also incurring substantial losses from the unauthorised trading positions taken by Leeson. In addition to crossing trades on SIMEX between account 88888 and the arbitrage accounts, Leeson also entered fictitious trades between these accounts, which were never crossed on the floor of the exchange. The effect of these off-market trades, which were not permitted by SIMEX, was again to credit the arbitrage accounts with profits whilst charging account 88888 with losses.

The bottom line of all these cross-trades was that Barings was counterparty to many of its own trades. Leeson bought from one hand and sold to the other, and in so doing did not lay off any of the firm's market risk. Barings was thus not arbitraging between SIMEX and the OSE but taking open (and very substantial) positions, which were buried in account 88888. It was the profit and loss statement of this account that represented correctly the revenue earned (or not earned) by Leeson. Details of this account were never transmitted to the Treasury or risk-control offices in London, an omission that ultimately had catastrophic consequences for Barings' shareholders and bondholders.

21.3.2 Lessons from Barings' collapse

There may be a temptation to view Barings' collapse as being caused by a single 'rogue trader' (Leeson). However, in reality, the fiasco should be attributed to the underlying structure of the firm. Since Barings' management failed to institute a proper managerial, financial and operational control system, the firm did not catch on in time to what Leeson was endeavouring to achieve. The lessons from the Barings collapse can be divided into four main headings:

Lesson 1: segregation of front and back offices

The management of Barings broke a cardinal rule of any trading operation: they effectively let Leeson settle his own trades by putting him in charge of both the front office (dealing desk) and the back office. This is tantamount to allowing the person who works a cash till to bank in the day's takings without an independent third party checking whether the amount banked in at the end of the day matches the till receipts.

The back office records, confirms and settles trades transacted by the front office, reconciles them with details sent by the bank's counterparties and assesses the accuracy of prices used for its internal valuations. It also accepts/releases securities and payments for trades. Some back offices also provide the regulatory reports and management accounting. In a nutshell, the back office provides the necessary checks to prevent unauthorised trading and to minimise the potential for fraud and embezzlement. Since Leeson was in charge of the back office, he had the final say on payments, ingoing and outgoing confirmations and contracts, reconciliation statements, accounting entries and position reports. He was perfectly placed to relay false information back to London.

Lesson 2: senior management involvement

Every major report on managing derivative risks has stressed the need for senior management to understand the risks of the business, to help articulate the firm's risk appetite and draft strategies and control procedures needed to achieve these objectives. Senior managers at Barings were found wanting in all these areas.

Barings' senior management had a very superficial knowledge of derivatives and did not want to probe too deeply into a subsidiary that was bringing in the profits. BFS alone ostensibly accounted for almost half of Barings' 1994 profits. The profitability of BFS was marvelled at by all senior managers, but it was never analysed properly. Senior managers did not even know the breakdown of Leeson's reported profits. They assumed erroneously that most of the profit came from Nikkei 225 arbitrage, which actually only generated profits of $7.36 million for 1994, compared with $37.5 million for JGB arbitrage. No wonder Peter Baring, ex-chairman of Barings, told the BoBS that he found the earnings 'pleasantly surprising', since he did not even know the breakdown. Senior management accepted naively that this business was a gold-mine with little risk, and they ignored the warning signals available in late 1994 and throughout January and February of 1995.

If Barings' auditors and top management had understood the trading business, they would have realised that it was not possible for Leeson to be making the profits that he was reporting without taking on undue risk, and they might have questioned where the money was coming from. Arbitrage is supposed to be a low-risk and, hence, low-profit business, so Leeson's large profits should have inspired alarm rather than praise. Also, Leeson was required to pay (or receive) daily margins and so needed funds from London. In January and February 1995 alone, he asked for $835 million. Given that arbitrage should be cash-neutral or cash-rich, alarms should have gone off as the bank wired hundreds of millions of dollars to BFS. Finally, Lesson could not hide his build-up of positions on the OSE because the exchange publishes weekly numbers. All his rivals could see his enormous positions, and many assumed that the positions were hedged because such naked positions were out of all proportion to the firm's capital base or even those of other players. His senior managers also assumed that Leeson's positions were hedged. But unlike outsiders who had to assume that these positions were hedged, Barings' management could and should have known better.

Lesson 3: proper internal control procedures

In many trading houses, there is not only a separation of operational duties between the front and back offices (absent in Barings) but also a risk-management unit independent of both to provide an additional layer of checks and balances.

As an example of the sloppy control procedures, Barings did not require Leeson to dis-tinguish between margin needed to cover proprietary in-house trades and customer trades; neither did it have a system to reconcile the funds that Leeson requested to his reported positions and/or that of its client positions. The London office would then have realised that the amount of money that Leeson was requesting was significantly more than that called for under SIMEX's margining rules. London simply remitted automatically to Leeson the sum of money he asked for. The fact that no one even asked Leeson to justify his requests is all the more astounding given the size of his demands.

A second example involves credit-risk management. The credit-risk implication of the client advances was significant if the total funds remitted to Singapore were needed to meet genuine client margin calls. Yet the credit-risk department did not question why Barings was lending over $500 million to its clients to trade on SIMEX and then collecting only 10% in return. It did not seem to have an idea of who these clients were; yet Barings' financial losses would have been significant if some of these clients defaulted. The credit committee under George Maclean insists that it was Barings' policy to finance client margins until they could be collected. But no limit per client or on the total advances was set. Indeed, clients who were advanced money in this way appear not to have undergone any credit-approval process. The credit committee never formally considered the credit aspects of the client advances, although it could see the growth of these advances as recorded on the balance sheets.

Lesson 4: clear lines of responsibility and accountability

All institutions should maintain an up-to-date organisational chart that shows clearly all reporting lines and who is accountable to whom and for what. Each individual in the institution should have a job description that identifies clearly his or her responsibilities and to whom and for what he or she is accountable.

Theoretically, Leeson had lots of supervisors; in reality, none exercised any real control over him. Barings operated a 'matrix' management system, where managers who are based overseas report to local administrators and to a product head (usually based at head office or the regional headquarters). This management system had responsibility for operations on a local basis and responsibility for products on a global basis. Leeson's Singapore supervisors were James Bax, regional manager, South Asia, and a director of BFS, and Simon Jones, regional operations manager, South Asia, also a director of BFS and chief operating officer of Barings Securities Singapore. Jones and the heads of the support functions in Singapore also had reporting lines to the group-wide support functions in London. Yet both Bax and Jones told the BoBS inquiry that they did not feel operationally responsible for Leeson. Bax felt that Leeson reported directly to Baker or Walz on trading matters and to Settlements/ Treasury in London for back-office matters. Jones felt that his role in BFS was limited only to administrative matters and concentrated on the securities side of Barings' activities in South Asia.

Leeson's reporting lines for product profitability were also not clear-cut. His ultimate boss was Ron Baker, head of the financial products group. But who had day-to-day control over him? Mary Walz, global head of equity financial products, insists that she thought Fernando Gueler, head of equity derivatives proprietary trading in Tokyo, was in charge of Leeson's intra-day activities, since the latter's arbitrage activities were booked in Tokyo. However, Gueler insists that in October 1994, Baker told him that Leeson would report to London and not Tokyo. He thus assumed that Walz would be in charge of Leeson. Walz herself still disputes this claim. Tapes of telephone conversations show that Leeson spoke frequently to both Gueler and Walz. (The bottom line, however, is that Gueler reported to Walz.)

21.4 Instruments for risk control

If an investor observes a discrepancy between the actual risk profile of his or her portfolio and the desired risk profile, then he or she may use one or more of the following instruments to alter the risk profile:

- diversification
- derivative securities
- insurance.

21.4.1 Diversification

As discussed in Chapter 9, the basic notion of diversification involves spreading a portfolio over many investments to avoid excessive exposure to a few sources of risk. In general, the effective means of risk reduction is to diversify across asset classes (stocks, bonds, commodities, and so on), sectors (technology, utilities, real estate, and so on) and regions (USA, Europe, Japan, emerging markets, and so on). If you invest in a single country, a single asset class and a single industry, for example in US technology stocks, then you are still putting all your eggs into one basket, no matter how many different stocks you choose.

Nowadays, many barriers to diversification, most notably transaction and information costs, have decreased substantially with the evolution of mutual funds, index funds and ETFs and, recently, with the availability of low-cost online trading. Also, many regulatory and non-regulatory barriers to international investment have been swept away by deregulation and privatisation abroad and by the availability of international investment vehicles such as ADRs, cross-border investment funds, WEBS and derivatives on foreign market indices and foreign currencies.

A generic limitation of diversification is that it cannot diversify away systematic or market risk. This is the part of risk that comes from the common exposure of assets to economy-wide risk factors, such as interest rates, exchange rates and commodity prices. Further, market risk tends to increase during international crisis situations, reducing the effectiveness of diversification when it is needed most. Market risk generally can be reduced or eliminated only by shifting to low-yielding assets (for example, T-bills and CDs) or by using derivatives (which also lower the expected rate of return because they require a premium). The latter are discussed in the section below.

21.4.2 Derivatives

As discussed in Chapter 19, derivatives such as forwards, swaps, futures and options are important instruments for altering the risk profile of an investment portfolio. An investor generally has a certain desired payoff pattern, conditional on the underlying asset prices. Derivatives are an easy way to adjust or create payoff patterns and require relatively small up-front investments of capital. Derivatives are used extensively to manage market risk. Recently, new forms of derivatives appeared to manage credit and operational risks as well (see also the final paragraphs of Section 19.7).

Exhibit 21.6 reviews the types of derivative that can be used to manage the different types of risk. Not all of these instruments may be familiar to the reader. However, most exotic derivatives are simply combinations or mixtures of basic derivatives; recall that Chapter 19 showed that, in theory, every payoff pattern can be created using the basic instruments. Since it's impossible to describe every possible derivative, this list is not exhaustive.

21.4.3 Insurance

Another effective tool for managing investment risk is insurance. In general, insurance means transferring the risk to a third party. In exchange for payments from the insured (called insurance premiums), the insurer agrees to pay the policyholder a sum of money upon the occurrence of a specific adverse event. In most cases, the policyholder pays part of the loss (called the deductible), and the insurer pays the rest.

Although market risk can be covered by insurance, derivatives are the main tool for managing this type of risk, due to the lower transaction costs and the better match to the market risk exposures. Also, the essence of insurance is the forecasting of the probability of the adverse event occurring. Market risks are extremely difficult to forecast if we assume that the financial markets are efficient by approximation.

Insurance is particularly useful for management of credit and operational risks. Credit insurance covers loss resulting from failure of debtors to pay their obligations to the insured.

Exhibit 21.6	Risk management using derivatives

Type of risk		Derivative with which the risk can be managed
Market risk	Equity risk	• Stock options • Index options • Index futures • Stock futures • Path-dependent options: options on average stock prices, look-back options, barrier options, contingent options • Multistock options: rainbow options, quanto options, basket options
	Exchange-rate risk	• FX forward contracts • FX futures • Currency swaps • Options on FX • OTC FX options • Break forwards, range forwards, participating forwards • Path-dependent options: options on average exchange rate, look-back options, barrier options, contingent options • Multifactor options: rainbow options, quanto options, basket options • Dual-currency bonds • Bonds with embedded foreign exchange options
	Interest-rate risk	• Floating-rate loans • Futures • Interest-rate swaps • Forward-rate agreements (FRAs) • Options • OTC options: caps, floors, collars • Hybrid securities: puttable bonds, convertible/exchangeable floating-rate notes, extendable bonds, inverse floating-rate notes • Swaptions (option on a swap), captions (options on the interest rate cap), futures on interest-rate swaps, diff swaps (swaps on differential between two interest rates)
	Commodity prices risk	• Oil futures contracts • Options on crude oil futures • Oil swap • Hybrid securities: petrobonds (straight debt plus long-dated forward contract on oil) • Oil-indexed notes (bonds with embedded oil warrants) • Gold-linked securities
Credit risk		• Total return swap • Credit default swaps • Options on debt instruments
Operational risk		• Catastrophe options • CAT bonds • Weather derivatives

Exhibit 21.7	Operational and credit risk insurance products

Credit risk insurance	Operational risk insurance
• **Mortgage guaranty insurance** Purchased by a lender to provide indemnification in case a borrower fails, for whatever reason, to meet required mortgage payments • **Municipal bond guarantee insurance coverage** Guarantees bondholders against default by a municipality; this form of financial guarantee was introduced in the early 1970s • **Mutual fund insurance** Form of financial guarantee insurance that guarantees the repayment of the principal invested in a mutual fund • **Investment return insurance** Insurance against the risk of loss for the value of the redeemable securities of an insured investor	• **Fidelity/bankers blanket bond** Designed to protect an employer against losses caused by dishonesty or default on the part of an employee as well as those that are caused by fraud and forgery • **Electronic computer crime** Provides cover against losses due to computer failure, viruses, data-transmission problems, forged electronic funds transactions, etc. • **Professional indemnity** Typically covers liabilities to third parties for claims arising out of employee negligence while providing professional services (e.g. investment advice) to clients • **Directors' and Officers' liability** Covers the personal assets of directors and officers against the expenses that might be incurred due to legal actions arising from the performance of their duties • **Employment practices liability** Covers liabilities that might arise due to breaches in employment law, such as harassment, discrimination, breach of contract, etc. • **Non-financial property** Covers the usual range of property risks (fire, weather damage, etc.) • **Unauthorised trading** Relatively new product that offers financial protection against unauthorised trading losses that were either concealed or recorded falsely • **General and other liability** Public liability, employer's liability, motor fleet • **Insolvency risk insurance** Provides a solution to liquidity risk

Generally, it provides coverage against all forms of debtor insolvencies and against non-payment of all past-due accounts filed with the insurer within, for example, 90 days after their original due date. Because of the increased awareness of operational risk and the threat of regulation, operational risk insurance products have also been developed. Exhibit 21.7 lists some of the common operational and credit risk insurance products.

As you can see from Exhibits 21.6 and 21.7, there has been a convergence between the insurance industry and the capital markets. Insurance companies now issue insurance contracts for financial risks that were previously managed using capital market instruments. One example of the insurance market invading the realm of the capital market is the much-touted Honeywell integrated insurance programme, a multi-line insurance programme that provided coverage for certain property-casualty risks as well as a basket of foreign currencies.[25] The

---

[25] C. T. Greer (1997), 'Who Needs Derivatives?', *Forbes*, 21 April.

insurance contract covered certain property-casualty losses and decreases in the value of the basket of foreign currencies above a predetermined level. Ideally, the programme will result in savings over the existing insurance costs for the property-casualty risks and the hedging costs for the foreign exchange risk. Similarly, investment banks are nipping at the market of insurance or reinsurance companies. For example, in recent years, a number of catastrophic insurance risks have been transferred to the capital markets through insurance-linked securities, such as the catastrophe (CAT) bond. The coupon and principal payments of a CAT bond are contingent on loss experience or the occurrence of a specified catastrophic event, such as an earthquake or a windstorm. If the CAT bond is triggered, the investor may lose the right to future coupon payments, principal payments, or both, depending on the type of bond. Examples of organisations employing CAT bonds or similar instruments are USAA, Tokio Marine, Swiss Re, Reliance and Winterthur.[26]

Summary

Define the purpose and scope of risk management.

Risk management is the process of recognition, measurement and control of risks that an investor faces. Risk management ensures that the risk-taking part of investing is being carried out in a controlled and understood manner. Risk management is a continuous process, because of the continuous change of the composition of the investor's portfolio, the risk of the assets in the portfolio, and the objectives and constraints of investors.

Discuss the value-at-risk framework for measuring market risk.

Value at risk (VaR) is the maximum dollar loss that a portfolio may be expected to suffer over a given holding period, at a given level of confidence. While the definition of VaR is straightforward, computing VaR generally is complicated in practice, because the probability distribution of future portfolio gains and losses generally is not known. In practice, we typically have to estimate the future return distribution from a data set of historical returns for the assets in the portfolio and we have to combine the return distribution of the individual securities into a return distribution for the portfolio. The so-called analytical or variance–covariance model does this by assuming a multi-index model (MIM) with normally distributed risk factors. The approach ignores the fat left tails of many risk factors and the non-linear exposure of many securities, may suffer from estimation error due to the use of small samples or time-varying risk parameters, and is sensitive to a possible dry-up of liquidity and increase of volatilities and correlations during crisis situations. Despite these imperfections, the model still represents an advance in quantifying and controlling risk over previous techniques. Also, the imperfections have stimulated the development of various extensions and alternatives, including delta-gamma methods, simulation methods and the use of implied volatilities, extreme value theory and advanced time-series estimation techniques.

Discuss the problems in measuring credit risk.

Credit risk is more difficult to measure because data on both defaults and recovery rates are not extensive, credit returns are highly skewed and fat-tailed, and longer-term time horizons and higher confidence levels are used in measuring credit risk. These problems have inspired

---

[26] *Investment Dealer's Digest*, 21 December 1998.

the development of several sophisticated models and commercial software products for measuring portfolio credit risk. Currently, the following four portfolio credit risk models are most popular: Credit Monitor of KMV Corporation, Credit Metrics of RiskMetrics Group, CreditRisk+ of CSFP and CreditPortfolioView of McKinsey.

Discuss four lessons learned from the case of Barings Bank for managing operational risk.

From the case study of Barings Bank, we can learn four lessons about how to control operational risk: (1) the front and back offices need to be seggregated to prevent unauthorised trading; (2) senior management needs to be involved in articulating the firm's risk objectives, drafting strategies and control procedures needed to achieve these objectives and to have knowledge of the type of trades that are conducted; (3) there needs to be a separate control layer that is independent of the front and back offices; and (4) the lines of responsibility and accountability need to be clearly defined and communicated.

Distinguish between three types of risk-management tools and recognise their possibilities and limitations.

Diversification refers to spreading a portfolio over many investments to avoid excessive exposure to a few sources of risk. This method reduces non-systematic risk or asset-specific risk. It cannot, however, diversify away systematic or market risk. Further, market risk tends to increase during international crisis situations, reducing the effectiveness of diversification when it is needed most. Derivative securities such as futures and options are one way to manage market risk. An investor generally has a certain desired payoff pattern, conditional on the underlying asset prices. Derivatives are an easy way to adjust or create payoff patterns and require relatively small up-front investments of capital. Insurance is a promise of compensation for specific potential future losses in exchange for a periodic payment (insurance premium). Insurance is used extensively for managing credit and operational risk. In recent years, there has been a convergence between insurance and capital markets, with investment banks invading the realm of insurance or reinsurance companies, and vice versa.

Key terms

Back office 751
Back-testing 741
Barings Bank 748
Catastrophe (CAT) bond) 757
Credit-migration risk 743
Credit risk 730
Credit value at risk (C-VaR) 743
Default mode (DM) model 746
Default risk 743
Delta-gamma methods 740

Derivatives 754
Diversification 753
Extreme value theory (EVT) 740
Front office 751
Historical simulation 740
Insurance 754
Long Term Capital Management (LTCM) 736
Market risk 730
Mark-to-market (MTM) model 746

Monte Carlo simulation (MCS) 740
Operational risk 730
Option-implied volatilities 740
Risk management 728
Sensitivity analysis 741
Simulation methods 740
Stress tests 741
Time-series estimation methods 740
Value-at-risk (VaR) 730

Review questions

1   Which types of investors practise risk management, and for what reason?

2   Consider a position consisting of a $200 000 investment in asset A and a $500 000 investment in asset B. Assume that the daily volatilities of the assets are 1.6% and 1.2%, respectively, and that the correlation coefficient between their returns is 0.3:

   a. What is the one-day 95% VaR for the portfolio?
   b. What is the five-day 99% VaR for the portfolio?
   c. Which conclusions can be drawn from the difference between the outcomes of Parts a and b?

3   Consider the table below, regarding joint rating change probabilities in one year's time for two obligors, a BB-rated and an A-rated obligor. The table is based on the approach of CreditMetrics, using an asset correlation of 20%.

Rating of first company	Rating of second company								
	AAA	AA	A	BBB	BB	B	CCC	Def	Total
AAA	0.00	0.00	0.03	0.00	0.00	0.00	0.00	0.00	0.03
AA	0.00	0.01	0.13	0.00	0.00	0.00	0.00	0.00	0.14
A	0.00	0.04	0.61	0.01	0.00	0.00	0.00	0.00	0.67
BBB	0.02	0.35	7.10	0.20	0.02	0.01	0.00	0.00	7.69
BB	0.07	1.79	73.65	4.24	0.56	0.18	0.01	0.04	80.53
B	0.00	0.08	7.80	0.79	0.13	0.05	0.00	0.01	8.87
CCC	0.00	0.01	0.85	0.11	0.02	0.01	0.00	0.00	1.00
Def	0.00	0.01	0.90	0.13	0.02	0.01	0.00	0.003	1.07
Total	0.09	2.29	91.06	5.48	0.75	0.26	0.01	0.06	100

   a. What is the probability that both the BB-rated and the A-rated obligor default in one year?
   b. What would this probability be if the asset correlation were zero rather than 0.20?

4   The Monte Carlo simulation is the most sophisticated method in calculating VaR in the view of many investors. However, this method also has disadvantages. Explain.

5   What are the lessons that can be learned from the debacle of Barings Bank?

For an extensive set of review and practice questions and answers, visit the Levy–Post investment website at www.booksites.net/levy

Selected references

Basel Committee on Banking Supervision, 1988, *International Convergence of Capital Measurement and Capital Standards*, www.bis.org/publ/bcbs04A.pdf

Basel Committee on Banking Supervision, 1996, *Amendment to the Capital Accord to Incorporate Market Risk*, www.bis.org/publ/bcbs24.pdf

Basel Committee on Banking Supervision, 2002, *Sound Practices for the Management and Supervision of Operational Risk*, www.bis.org/publ/bcbs91.pdf

Basel Committee on Banking Supervision, 2003, *Overview of the New Capital Accord*, www.bis.org/bcbs/cp3ov.pdf

Caouette, J. B., E. I. Altman and P. Narayanan, 1998, *Managing Credit Risk: The Next Great Financial Challenge*, Hoboken, NJ: John Wiley & Sons.

Credit Suisse First Boston, 1997, *CreditRisk+: A Credit Risk Management Framework*, www.csfb.com/institutional/research/assets/creditrisk.pdf

Crouhy, M., R. Mark and D. Galai, 2000, *Risk Management*, New York: McGraw-Hill Trade.

Crouhy, M., D. Galai and R. Mark, 2000, 'A Comparative Analysis of Current Credit Risk Models', *Journal of Banking and Finance*, **24**, 59–117.

Culp, C. L., 2001, *The Risk Management Process*, New York: John Wiley & Sons.

Cuthbertson, K. and D. Nitzsche, 2001, *Financial Engineering: Derivatives and Risk Management*, Hoboken, NJ: John Wiley & Sons.

Edwards, F. R., 1998, 'Hedge Funds and the Collapse of Long-Term Capital Management', *Journal of Economic Perspectives*, **13**, 189–210.

Embrechts, P., C. Kleppelberg and T. Mikosch, 1997, *Modelling Extremal Events*, Berlin: Springer Verlag.

Frenkel, M. and U. Hommel, 2000, *Risk Management: Challenge and Opportunity*, 1st edn, New York: Springer.

Hoffman, D. G., 2002, *Managing Operational Risk: 20 Firmwide Best Practice Strategies*, Hoboken, NJ: John Wiley & Sons.

Hull, J. C., 2002, *Options, Futures, and Other Derivatives*, 5th edn, Upper Saddle River, NJ: Prentice Hall.

Jorion, P., 2002, *Value at Risk: The New Benchmark for Managing Financial Risk*, New York: McGraw-Hill Trade.

Jorion, P., 2003, *Financial Risk Manager Handbook*, 2nd edn, Hoboken, NJ: John Wiley & Sons.

J.P. Morgan Inc., 1997, *CreditMetrics – Technical Document*, www.riskmetrics.com/techdoc.html

K.M.V. Corporation, 2001, *Modelling Default Risk*, www.moodyskmv.com/research/whitepaper/modeling default risk.pdf

K.M.V. Corporation, 2001, *Portfolio Management of Default Risk*, www.moodyskmv.com/research/whitepaper/portfolio management of default risk.pdf

Pearson, N. D., 2002, *Risk Budgeting: Portfolio Problem Solving with VaR*, Hoboken, NJ: John Wiley & Sons.

Schwartz, R. J. and C. W. Smith, 1997, *Derivatives Handbook: Risk Management and Control*, Hoboken, NJ: John Wiley & Sons.

Smithson, C. W., 1998, *Managing Financial Risk: A Guide to Derivative Products, Financial Engineering, and Value Maximization*, 3rd edn, New York: McGraw-Hill.

Long march into markets hell for a heavenly cause

To Dream the Impossible Dream. That first line of a song from *Man of La Mancha*, the musical based on *Don Quixote*, should really be the theme tune of active fund managers.

They are engaged in a doomed attempt to beat the stock market indices. But the index inevitably reflects the performance of the average investor *without costs.* Since fund managers do incur costs, beating the index becomes very difficult.

The latest evidence on the impossible dream comes from a report from WM, the investment performance measurement consultancy. It examined the performance of the UK All Companies unit trust sector and found that just 40 per cent of active managers beat the index last year. While these results are UK-based, academic studies have shown similar results elsewhere.

This report will disappoint active managers who have often claimed that their style gives them an advantage in bear markets. Index trackers, or passive managers as they are often known, are obliged to be fully invested at all times. In a bear market, active managers can hold small amounts of cash or bonds and thus sneak an advantage.

But not last year. Or in 2001, when only 36 per cent of active managers beat the index or in bear years such as 1990 (37 per cent) or 1994 (45 per cent). Only in 2000 did active managers succeed in their task, with 52 per cent beating the index.

So that is it. Victory to the index trackers and music to the ears of Virgin Money, which sponsored the study and runs an index fund. Not quite so fast. Index trackers also have costs, so they too underperform the index, usually by about 1 per cent a year. While only 40 per cent of active funds beat the index last year, 46 per cent beat the average index tracker.

If we go back over a longer period, 57 per cent of active funds beat the median tracker over five years and, over the 14 years covered in the survey, 48 per cent of funds beat the median tracker. That is as close to a statistical tie as makes no difference.

So does that mean investors should be indifferent between active and passive funds? Not necessarily. The WM survey shows the range of performances achieved by the various trusts. The performance of passive funds is clustered in a narrow range, just below the index. But active managers have a much wider range of results with many funds either beating the index or falling far short of it. For the investor, the decision to invest in an active fund is thus a risky one and *on average* that risk is not rewarded. The safe decision is thus to buy a tracker fund.

This trade-off would be different, of course, if it were possible to identify the active managers who can beat the index – the Peter Lynch of Fidelity Magellan or the Bill Miller of Legg Mason.

Academic studies have shown that there is little consistency in fund management performance, especially if risk is taken into account. Certain styles can succeed while they are in fashion – growth in the late 1990s and value in the past three years – but such managers will falter when the climate changes.

There may well be exceptional managers, but it is hard to identify them in advance. Even if one could the investor faces the additional danger that the fund manager may be poached by a rival firm. One can follow them when they move, of course, but that incurs switching costs.

Some in the fund management industry believe there are ways round the passive-active debate. One approach is to use 'enhanced indexation' – funds that track the index quite closely, but then take small 'side bets' in an attempt to enhance performance. The data so far seem quite encouraging; such approaches do seem to offer a good trade-off between risk and return.

Logic suggests, however, that enhanced indexation can only deliver attractive returns if it is a minority pursuit. If everyone adopted it the same old problem would arise; the average investor cannot beat the index.

Similar difficulties are attached to the idea of 'mixing and matching' – picking the best performers from different styles. One could do this by switching from, say, growth to value managers when fashions change. But there is little evidence that such fashion shifts can be predicted and the effort of switching may simply incur transaction costs.

Alternatively, one could own a portfolio of growth and value managers. But this approach runs into the difficulty of identifying the best managers in advance. WM suggests that 'the likeliest outcome is that the investor over-diversifies and ends up with what is, to all intents and purposes, an expensive tracker'.

This approach is even more likely to be frustrated if followed through the 'fund of funds' route where the investor pays two sets of fees, tilting the odds against outperformance. The WM report cites Roger Urwin of actuaries Watson Wyatt: 'I do not believe there is any reason that manager selection should be any more consistent in performance than the underlying performance records of the managers themselves.'

Professional managers will seek ever more sophisticated solutions to this dilemma and the fund management industry is having to respond in kind. Long gone are the days when one could simply trumpet 'stock-picking skills' and last year's performance numbers; nowadays it is all about process, risk management and information ratios.

Many retail investors may continue to believe in active fund managers, whether they believe they can beat the system or because trackers cannot deliver what they need, such as above-average income. But for most, trackers probably represent the safest long-term bet on equities because they avoid the risk of disastrous underperformance.

Source: Philip Coggan, 'Long March Into Markets Hell For A Heavenly Cause', *Financial Times*, 22 February 2003.

Learning objectives

After studying this chapter, you should be able to:

1 Calculate portfolio performance using four performance indices based on asset-pricing theory.

2 Explain style analysis and the most common approaches to style analysis.

3 Evaluate performance attribution as a means of identifying the sources of performance.

4 Summarise the empirical evidence regarding mutual fund performance.

5 Identify some problems with measuring investment performance in practice.

Performance evaluation is an essential part of the process of managing investment portfolios. Typical questions to be asked in evaluating performance include: How did the manager perform compared with a passive benchmark or index? What risk did the manager take to achieve a particular return? Were the securities chosen by the manager consistent with his or her mandate in terms of investment style? Did the manager deliver sufficient value-added or additional return to justify the fee for active management? What were the factors that determined portfolio performance?

The answers to these questions are of direct interest to investors seeking an appropriate mutual fund or choosing a financial planner. If the market is inefficient, then the best manager of the past may also turn out to be a successful performer in the future. However, 'Investment in the News' 22 states that very few actively managed funds have beaten the market index and passively managed index funds. Also, there is little consistency in the performance of funds from year to year. Indeed, if the efficient market theory (EMT) discussed in Chapter 12 is correct, then we would expect that, on average, a professional money manager would be unable to consistently earn abnormal profits. Still, many investors would like to identify the managers who have consistently outperformed the market in the past and hope that their performance continues to reap positive returns in the future.

Many other people and organisations also benefit from information on historical investment performance; examples include the following:

■ The compensation committee of the portfolio manager needs performance information. If a portfolio manager consistently outperforms an unmanaged portfolio of equivalent risk, then the manager should receive a bonus. If the manager consistently under-performs an unmanaged portfolio of equivalent risk, then the manager probably should be replaced.

■ Corporate financial officers need to evaluate the managers of their corporate pension plans.

■ Government agencies need to be able to assess the performance of public pension fund managers.

■ Large money-management firms need good evaluation tools to assess their employees' performance.

■ Bank trust departments need these tools to evaluate the performance of their various trust accounts.

This chapter surveys several techniques for evaluating managers and the portfolios they manage.

Chapter 6 discussed various ways to compute historical rates of return. We stress that performance evaluation entails much more than simply computing the rate of return over the evaluation period. Suppose that you learned that manager A realised a rate of return of −2% over the past year, while manager B earned +12%. What is the appropriate action? Replace manager A? Give manager B a large bonus? The answer is not clear, as the following examples demonstrate:

- The +12% earned by manager B is less impressive if he or she earned the money with an extremely risky strategy, such as buying a short-run, deep out-of-the-money call option (a very risky investment strategy). How could he or she take such risks with other people's hard-earned money? He or she could have lost it all just as easily as he or she had won it! Surely, then, manager B should not be rewarded. In general, performance evaluation must weigh the realised rate of return against the risk taken in order to achieve this return.
- Performance evaluation needs to separate investment skill from chance. For example, the performance of manager A is put in a different light if we know that he or she consistently outperformed the market in the previous ten years and that the poor performance in the last year is attributable solely to the unexpected bankruptcy of a company that was generally believed to have a high credit quality. Put differently, we need to determine whether the results are significantly better or significantly worse than expected.
- The −2% return of manager A looks very different if we know that the general market went down by 10%; in this case, manager A still outperformed the market by an impressive 8%. In other words, any analysis of investment performance needs to correct for the market conditions faced by the investment manager.
- What if the performance of manager B is attributable exclusively to a high allocation to foreign stocks, while manager A was restricted from investing in such assets? Performance evaluation needs to account for the investment restrictions imposed on the investment manager. Put differently, perhaps manager A succeeded in limiting the loss that may have been expected given the constraints imposed on him or her.
- Maybe manager A is extremely good in picking winners but failed to select the correct market, while manager B selected the correct market. Then, manager A shouldn't be replaced, but rather the two managers should collaborate and divide tasks: manager B could specialise in asset allocation and manager A could specialise in security selection. Performance evaluation needs to understand the performance drivers in order to determine the appropriate action.

Recall from Chapter 7 that investment can be seen as a problem of choice under uncertainty and under restrictions. Generally speaking, performance evaluation tries to assess whether and why a portfolio manager deviated significantly from optimising the investment objectives of the investor, given the investment restrictions that he or she faced. This is a difficult task, because objectives, opportunities and restrictions are not always defined clearly, the investment process consists of many different decisions, and many factors that affect investment performance are beyond the control of the manager. For these reasons, performance evaluation in many cases is as much art as it is science. Still, the following general tools have proven useful and they are used widely:

22.1.1 Risk-adjusted performance indexes

There exist various methods for correcting the realised return for risk. The methods reduce the risk–return trade-off to a single measure known as a risk-adjusted performance measure.

Generally, such measures are based on asset-pricing theories, such as the CAPM (see Chapter 10) and the APT (see Chapter 11), that predict how investors perceive risk and how risk affects asset prices. Section 22.2 discusses various popular risk-adjusted performance measures, including Sharpe's index, Treynor's index, Jensen's index and APT-based performance measures. Each measure is based on a different set of assumptions about the appropriate way to measure and correct for risk.

22.1.2 Benchmark portfolios

The simplest and most popular way to measure investment performance is to compare the realised return on the evaluated portfolio with the realised return on a general benchmark index. For example, it is commonplace for managers of US equity portfolios to see their performance compared with that of the Standard & Poor's 500 index, the Wilshire 5000 index or the Russell 3000 index. Similarly, US bond portfolios are commonly compared with the Lehman Brothers Aggregate Bond Index or the Merrill Lynch Aggregate Bond Index. Such comparisons can be useful as a rough gauge of a manager's results. However, general benchmark indexes generally do not match the objectives and constraints of many investors. For example, the performance of a manager of small-capitalisation stocks should not be compared with the performance of the S&P 500, which is a large-cap stock index. Instead, a small-cap index such as the Russell 2000 would be more appropriate. Also, a fixed-income manager can beat the general bond indices, which are filled with low-risk, low-yield government securities, by buying junk bonds. Normal portfolios and style benchmark portfolios circumvent this problem.

A normal portfolio is a customised passive benchmark portfolio that includes all the securities from which a manager 'normally' chooses, weighted as the manager would 'normally' weight them in a portfolio. 'Normally' means consistent with the long-term investment policy selected to control the overall risk and meet fund objectives. The problem is that good normals are hard to come by; only a couple of consulting firms are any good at it, and they charge high fees for their expertise. Finding the right mix of stocks with the right weights is what makes the normals so hard to construct.

A style benchmark portfolio is a benchmark portfolio that is designed to match the investment style of the fund. The portfolio typically is a blend of style indices. There are many families of style indices to choose from, including Russell, Wilshire and Standard & Poor's. For example, commonly used style indices for US small-cap stocks include the Russell 2000 index, the Wilshire Small Cap 1750 index and the S&P Smallcap 600 index. For bond indices, data providers include Lehman Brothers and Merrill Lynch. Examples of US non-investment grade bond indices are Lehman Brothers High Yield Bond Index and Merrill Lynch High Yield Master Index. Note, however, that a style portfolio need not be a stand-alone style index. Most managers appear to be a blend of styles. Not all growth managers are the same; some are smaller-company-oriented, some routinely hold value companies, etc. In addition, there are significant differences among style benchmarks of different vendors. It is common to win against a Russell index and lose against a comparable S&P index, for example. A lot of this has to do with reconstitution methodology. Russell reconstitutes its growth and value indices once a year; S&P does it twice a year. Suppose there is some major market movement between June and December. When the S&P indices reconstitute, they may have a whole different set of stocks than does Russell in the style indices. This has happened periodically in the past. For these reasons, style benchmark portfolios generally are a blend of style indices. 'Style analysis' is an umbrella term for a set of techniques used to determine the investment style of portfolios and the relevant style of benchmark portfolio. Section 22.3 discusses various approaches to style analysis and compares their strengths and weaknesses.

22.1.3 Performance attribution methods

Performance evaluation is not just about measuring past performance. Performance attribution attempts to understand what determined past performance in order to make better decisions in the future. The portfolio manager must make many decisions in building a portfolio, and performance attribution attempts to rate each of the portfolio manager's decisions. Did the investment manager add value by overweighting the portfolio in those industry sectors that perform better than the overall performance of the benchmark or by underweighting sectors that perform worse than the overall performance of the benchmark? For example, if the health-care sector had a return of 6% for the time period and the overall index had a return of 4% for the same time period, the manager would have added value by overweighting the health-care sector. Or, did the manager add value by selecting securities within an industry sector that perform better than the performance of the overall industry sector? For example, if the performance of the technology sector of a stock index was 2% for the time period, but the per-formance of an equity manager's technology stock selections was 3%, then the manager added value, although the technology sector underperformed the overall index. The understanding of what drove performance in the past can be used to improve future investment decisions. For example, investors can use the information to alter the constraints placed on a portfolio manager or the money allocated to the manager. Section 22.4 elaborates further on this subject.

22.1.4 Comparison universes

Benchmark portfolios are often not a good measure of competitive performance, or per-formance relative to the direct competitors; benchmarking against the S&P 500 index is not informative, even if the long-run objective is to invest in US large caps, when all competitors have large positions in small caps. Most investment consultants evaluate money managers and funds vis-à-vis a comparison universe of other money managers and funds. Various data providers provide a collection of performance universes for corporate defined-benefit pension plans, foundations, endowments, public funds and personal trust clients. There is a strong emphasis in each universe on direct data comparability, and only entirely comparable accounts are used.

→ Connecting Theory to Practice 22.1

Weighing up the risks

Ever so cautiously the WM Company, the UK's leading investment performance measurement consultancy for pension funds, is rolling out a risk measurement service.

Americans might ask why it has taken the UK so long. Lucky British pension fund trustees have until now been largely sheltered from the jargon of active risk, information ratios and interquartile risk ranges, even though such concepts have already been widely adopted by fund managers.

The generalist approach (I will not call it amateur) to the staffing of trustee boards in the UK has been an obstacle. Risk analysis, WM apologises in its introductory brochure, is 'too mathematical, too esoteric'. Investment professionals would mostly lap the subject up, but WM is clearly worried about baffling and alienating its clients.

Incidentally, the other UK measurement specialist, Caps, is also exploring risk, probably on a rather more ambitious and detailed basis, through Risk Reporting, a joint venture with Barra, the California-based risk modelling consultants. For its part, WM has collaborated with the Edinburgh risk consultants Barrie & Hibbert.

WM is not going so far as to devise risk-adjusted returns. They might be volatile, and anyway are too controversial for fund managers. It is focusing on relative risk, so that trustees can understand their overall level of risk against their benchmarks. Within that, the risk is allocated across different asset classes. An analysis of 'prospective risk' compares a fund's risk with that of the relevant WM universe of similar funds, and splits it between policy (or asset allocation) and stock selection.

One basic question is whether the amount of risk is appropriate in the context of performance targets. The median total fund risk in the WM50 Universe of the biggest funds seems to be quite modest, at about 1.5 per cent, this being the standard deviation of the individual's relative return against the universe. Policy risks are quite high, because of customised benchmarks, but stock selection risks are low, probably because of reliance on indexation.

Smaller funds in the WM2000 Universe often run lower policy risks, because of pressures to run with the herd. Stock selection risks in these smaller funds are higher, but in aggregate the interquartile range (from the 25th to 75th quartile) is more tightly bunched, and the median total risk is perhaps 1.4 per cent.

Arguably the range is too narrow. If a manager has been set an objective to beat the benchmark by 1 per cent a year then the relative risk should be at least 2 per cent. This is because it is unreasonable to assume an information ratio of more than 0.5, the latter ratio being defined as the relative return against the benchmark divided by the standard deviation of this relative return. It measures the manager's skill in adding value.

When informed about the risks the trustees can be more effective at monitoring. It is interesting to speculate about trustee behaviour over the past few years had they realised that increasing risks were often being incurred by leading external managers like Gartmore and Phillips & Drew, and even Mercury. These three managers have together lost mandates worth Pounds 9 bn net over the past twelve months, while index trackers have won Pounds 8 bn. Now, it is said, there is a risk-averse retreat to the benchmarks that will soon show up in the risk data.

The assessment of risks will be a challenge for generalist trustees. Risks cannot simply be added together, partly because of correlations. And there may be much more risk in, say, a small allocation to the Pacific ex-Japan region, as managers discovered in 1997, than in a much bigger divergence from the benchmark allocations between UK equities and UK bonds, which are more highly correlated.

So risk has finally arrived. Or rather, it was here all the time. Ignorance was bliss.

Source: 'Weighing Up the Risks', *Financial Times*, 2 December 1998.

→ Making the connection

This article reports on a risk-measurement service for UK pension funds by WM, a prominent UK investment performance measurement consultancy. The risk-measurement service includes many of the tools discussed in this section: benchmark portfolios, comparison universes and performance attribution. However, WM considers risk-adjusted performance measures too controversial. The next section discusses risk-adjusted performance measures and their strengths and weaknesses.

22.2 Risk-adjusted performance measures

As discussed above, performance evaluation must weigh the realised return of an investment portfolio against the risk of the portfolio. Hence, to develop a measure of performance quality of a portfolio, we must quantify risk and return. Return is easy to quantify; it can be estimated with rate-of-return methods described in Chapter 6. However, the appropriate measure of risk is not as obvious. Chapters 10 and 11 discussed two asset-pricing models that predict how investors perceive risk and how risk affects asset prices. Analysts use several performance measures or indices that are related to these asset-pricing models, including Sharpe's index (and the related M-squared measure), Treynor's index, Jensen's alpha (and the related appraisal ratio) and APT-based performance measures. As we will see, these measures are based on different sets of assumptions about how to measure portfolio risk and how to correct for risk. More specifically, the measures differ in the following respects:

- The relevant asset-pricing theory: some measures are based on the single-factor CAPM (Sharpe's index, Treynor's index and Jensen's alpha), while others are based on the APT which allows for multiple risk factors.
- The aggregation level: some measures are relevant for evaluating entire investment portfolios (Sharpe's index), while others are relevant for evaluating the contribution of individual assets or subportfolios (Treynor's index, Jensen's alpha and the APT-based measures) and they ignore asset-specific risks (these are assumed to be diversified away in the context of a broader portfolio).
- Some statistics measure risk-adjusted performance relative to the market (Jensen's alpha and the APT-based measures), so we know immediately by which percentage an asset or portfolio outperformed the market; other statistics do not benchmark against the market (Sharpe's index and Treynor's index).

To illustrate the different risk-adjusted performance measures, we will develop an example using three mutual funds: one that mirrors the market and two that are managed actively. We assume that the Vanguard Index Trust – 500 Portfolio is an adequate proxy for the market portfolio and hence has a beta of one. This fund is a passively managed index fund that seeks to mimic the performance of the S&P 500 stock index. Exhibit 22.1a lists the historical return information for a five-year period. All three funds have similar objectives: they seek growth and income. The returns in Exhibit 22.1a reveal no clear-cut preference for one fund over another. Fund B experienced the worst year, at −5.0%, in year 5. Vanguard had the best year, at 31.4%, in year 4. Fund A has a return higher than the other two funds' returns in year 2.

Exhibit 22.1b shows the mean returns, standard deviations and betas of these three funds. Fund A had the lowest average return, the lowest standard deviation and the lowest beta. The Vanguard fund was at the other extreme, having the highest average return, the highest standard deviation and the highest beta. Fund B was in the middle on both risk and return. Over the five years shown, which of these funds achieved the superior performance? Is it the Vanguard fund, because it had the highest return on average? Perhaps it was fund A with the lowest risk measures.

To illustrate further, suppose you wish to invest for one year and you believe that the distribution of ex-post performance will be repeated in the future.[1] You do not know which observation will be selected, but you know the set of possible outcomes. Which fund would you select? Performance indices provide a method of comparing funds with different risk–return

---

[1] Recall that ex-post data are historical data used to make inferences about the future.

Exhibit 22.1	Basic statistics for three mutual funds

(a) Actual annual rates of return (%) on three mutual funds after fees with reported betas

Year	Fund A	Fund B	Vanguard Index Trust – 500 Portfolio
1	16.3	15.4	18.3
2	8.6	3.1	4.7
3	8.7	17.9	16.2
4	23.6	28.7	31.4
5	−3.3	−5.0	−3.3

(b) Mean return (%), standard deviation (%) and beta based on part a

	Fund A	Fund B	Vanguard Index Trust – 500 Portfolio
Mean return	10.78	12.02	13.46
Standard deviation	10.03	13.17	13.33
Beta	0.64	0.85	1.0

Source: From *Introduction to Investments*, 2nd edn, by Levy. © 1999. Reprinted with permission of South-Western, a division of Thomson Learning: www.thomsonrights.com. Fax 800 730-2215.

characteristics. Thus, finding the best performer is what we hope performance indices will tell us. We will use the data from Exhibit 22.1 when we discuss and compare the performance measures.

22.2.1 Sharpe's performance index

Sharpe's (1966) performance index (PI_S) is based on the CAPM. Specifically, if we allow for riskless borrowing and lending at interest rate r, then the investment opportunities from a portfolio with expected return $E(R_i)$ and standard deviation σ_i are given by the following linear line:

$$E(R) = r + \frac{[E(R_i) - r]}{\sigma_i} \sigma_R \qquad (22.1)$$

The intercept of this line is the riskless rate and the slope is the ratio of excess return to standard deviation:

$$\frac{[E(R_i) - r]}{\sigma_i}$$

An investor would prefer the portfolio that produces the steepest slope, i.e. the portfolio that gives the highest average return for a given level of risk. Hence, Sharpe suggests we use the slope as a natural performance measure.

Of course, we do not know the values of the population parameters $E(R_i)$ and σ_i. Using ex-post data, we may estimate these parameters by their sample equivalents (see Chapter 6):

$$\bar{R}_i = \frac{1}{T} \times \sum_{t=1}^{T} R_{i,t} \qquad (6.15)$$

and

$$\hat{\sigma}_i = \frac{1}{T} \times \sum_{t=1}^{T} (R_{i,t} - \bar{R}_i)^2 / T \qquad (6.17)$$

Using these estimates, Sharpe's index ($PI_{S,i}$) for each portfolio i is given as follows:

$$PI_{S,i} = \frac{\bar{R}_i - r}{\hat{\sigma}_i} \qquad (22.2)$$

As the numerator and the denominator are given in percentages, Sharpe's index is a pure number.

For the example in Exhibit 22.1, the average short-term interest rate over this period was approximately 5%. Hence, Sharpe's index for the three mutual funds is calculated as follows:

$$PI_{S,Vanguard} = \frac{13.46\% - 5.0\%}{13.33\%} \cong 0.635$$

$$PI_{S,Fund\,A} = \frac{10.78\% - 5.0\%}{10.03\%} \cong 0.576$$

$$PI_{S,Fund\,B} = \frac{12.02\% - 5.0\%}{13.17\%} \cong 0.533$$

Consequently, using Sharpe's index, the best-performing fund for this period is Vanguard, followed by fund A. Fund B came in last, with the lowest value.

Note that the capital market line (CML) is found by replacing $E(R_i)$ and σ_i in Equation 22.1 with the expected return on the market portfolio $E(R_m)$ and the standard deviation of the market portfolio σ_m:

$$E(R) = r + \frac{[E(R_m) - r]}{\sigma_m} \sigma_R$$

According to the CAPM, the CML gives the set of all efficient portfolios, i.e. the market portfolio has the highest ratio of excess return to standard deviation (the Sharpe index). However, this need not be true if the CAPM does not apply. In addition, the market portfolio need not have the highest Sharpe index if we use empirical data. In this case, we use an empirical CML rather than the true CML.

Exhibit 22.2a illustrates the relationship between the Sharpe index and the empirical CML. On the line denoted A in Exhibit 22.2a are all possible combinations of fund A with borrowing or lending of the risk-free asset. Line B similarly denotes all possible combinations of fund B with borrowing and lending. The line denoted CML represents all possible combinations of the market portfolio (approximated by Vanguard) and the risk-free asset. Note that both fund A and fund B lie below the CML. Hence, the Vanguard fund outperformed both fund A and fund B. That is, the CML is steeper than the line that would be produced by either fund A or fund B and the risk-free asset.

Exhibit 22.2b illustrates Equation 22.2 for the Vanguard fund. Specifically, Sharpe's index is the 'rise over the run', or the slope, of the line where the denominator of Equation 22.2 (the run) is $\hat{\sigma}_{Vanguard} = 13.33\%$, and the rise is $E(R_{Vanguard}) - r = 13.46\% - 5\% = 8.46\%$. The rise measures the additional expected return (in addition to the risk-free rate of 5%) for taking the risk related to the Vanguard fund.

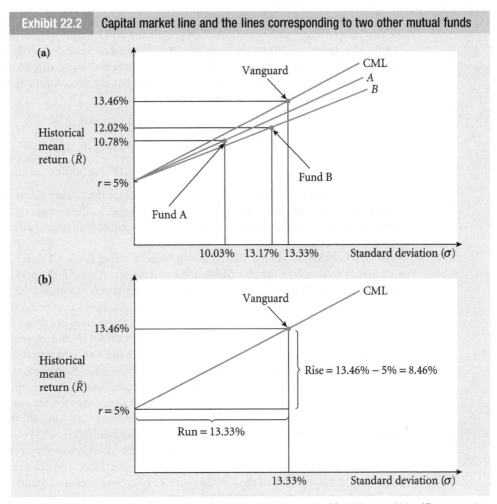

Exhibit 22.2   Capital market line and the lines corresponding to two other mutual funds

Source: From *Introduction to Investments*, 2nd edn, by Levy. © 1999. Reprinted with permission of South-Western, a division of Thomson Learning: www.thomsonrights.com. Fax 800 730-2215.

A closely related measure is known as M-squared.[2] M-squared measures the return that an investor would have earned if the portfolio had been altered by risk-free lending or borrowing so as to match the standard deviation of the market portfolio. We can compute this measure simply by substituting the sample standard deviation of the market portfolio $\hat{\sigma}_m$ in the ex-post version of Equation 22.1:

$$PI_{M^2,i} = r + \left[\frac{\bar{R}_i - r}{\hat{\sigma}_i} \right] \hat{\sigma}_m = r + PI_{S,i}\hat{\sigma}_m$$

From this equation, we can see that M-squared is nothing but a simple positive linear transformation of Sharpe's index. That is, Sharpe's index is multiplied by the positive constant $\hat{\sigma}_m$ and then the constant r is added. For this reason, M-squared and Sharpe's index will give

---

[2] This measure was first proposed by Graham and Harvey (1997). Later, the measure was popularised by Modigliani and Modigliani (1997) or 'M-squared'.

exactly the same assessment of a portfolio's performance relative to the market portfolio, and the two measures will also rank portfolios exactly the same.

Still, M-squared is a useful measure, because it can be compared directly with the average return on the market portfolio or $\bar{R}_m$ so as to see whether the portfolio outperformed or underperformed the market after correcting for risk. For example, for the three mutual funds in Exhibit 22.1, M-squared is calculated as follows:

$$PI_{M^2, Vanguard} = 0.05 + 0.635 \times 0.1333 = 0.1346$$

$$PI_{M^2, Fund\ A} = 0.05 + 0.576 \times 0.1333 \cong 0.1266$$

$$PI_{M^2, Fund\ B} = 0.05 + 0.533 \times 0.1333 \cong 0.1208$$

Clearly, the ranking of the funds is exactly the same as for the Sharpe index. Notice, however, that the M-squared of the market portfolio is exactly equal to the average return of the market portfolio (13.46%). Hence, comparison based on M-squared is simpler than comparison based on the Sharpe index.

To illustrate the Sharpe index and the M-squared measure further, Exhibit 22.3 applies these measures to well-known data for 34 US open-end mutual funds for the period 1954–63.[3] The first two columns display the averages and standard deviations of annual returns. The third and fourth columns show the Sharpe ratio and the M-squared measure, respectively, assuming a riskless rate of 3% and using the Dow-Jones Index as the market portfolio. The final column shows the ranking of the mutual funds, which is identical for both measures.

The Sharpe index and the M-squared measure use the standard deviation as the relevant risk measure. Standard deviation measures the total risk of the portfolio to the investor. This is not a relevant risk measure if we evaluate an individual asset or a portfolio that forms part of a broader portfolio of assets. In this case, we have to account for the correlation between the evaluated assets and the other assets in the broader portfolio. After all, the investor is not exposed to the part of the risk of the evaluated portfolio that is 'diversified away' in the context of the broader portfolio. The remaining measures discussed below try to measure the contribution of individual sets or portfolios to a broader portfolio. Treynor's index and Jensen's alpha use the market beta of the CAPM as the relevant risk measure. Standard deviation and beta stand at two extremes. Standard deviation is the appropriate measure of risk when the investor holds no other assets besides the mutual fund. Beta is the appropriate measure of risk of the mutual fund when the investor holds the entire market portfolio. In practice, neither extreme is realistic. However, if an investor has very limited holdings, then standard deviation may prove to be a more accurate measure of risk. If an investor has a wide array of holdings outside of this particular mutual fund, then beta may be a more accurate measure of risk. Another problem is that exposure to a market index as measured by beta may not be the only relevant risk factor. The APT-based performance measures address this problem.

22.2.2 Treynor's performance index

Treynor (1965) suggested evaluating portfolio performance based on the security market line (SML) rather than the CML (which is the basis for the Sharpe index). Treynor's performance index (PI_T) is the appropriate index to use in order to measure the performance of individual securities or a portfolio that forms part of a broader portfolio. Recall from Chapter 10 that the

---

[3] Data taken from Sharpe (1966).

| Exhibit 22.3 | Sharpe index, M-squared and ranking for 34 US open-end mutual funds, 1954–63 | | | | |

	Excess return	Standard deviation	Sharpe index	M-squared	Rank
Affiliated Fund	14.6	15.3	0.95	21.52	4
American Business Shares	10.0	9.2	1.09	24.10	3
Axe-Houghton, Fund A	10.5	13.5	0.78	18.10	29
Axe-Houghton, Fund B	12.0	16.3	0.74	17.29	30
Axe-Houghton, Stock Fund	11.9	15.6	0.76	17.81	27
Boston Fund	12.4	12.1	1.02	22.89	1
Broad Street Investing	14.8	16.8	0.88	20.10	7
Bullock Fund	15.7	19.3	0.81	18.79	14
Commonwealth Investment Company	10.9	13.7	0.80	18.44	26
Delaware Fund	14.4	21.4	0.67	16.06	31
Dividend Shares	14.4	15.9	0.91	20.58	6
Eaton and Howard, Balanced Fund	11.0	11.9	0.92	20.94	11
Eaton and Howard, Stock Fund	15.2	19.2	0.79	18.37	16
Equity Fund	14.6	18.7	0.78	18.15	21
Fidelity Fund	16.4	23.5	0.70	16.55	28
Financial Industrial Fund	14.5	23.0	0.63	15.24	33
Fundamental Investors	16.0	21.7	0.74	17.31	22
Group Securities, Common Stock Fund	15.1	19.1	0.79	18.35	18
Group Securities, Fully Administrated Fund	11.4	14.1	0.81	18.69	23
Incorporated Investors	14.0	25.5	0.55	13.66	34
Investment Company of America	17.4	21.8	0.80	18.49	13
Investors Mutual	11.3	12.5	0.90	20.55	12
Loomis-Sales Mutual Fund	10.0	10.4	0.96	21.66	10
Massachusetts Investors – Growth Stock	18.6	22.7	0.82	18.90	9
Massachusetts Investors Trust	16.2	20.8	0.78	18.12	17
National Investors Corporation	18.3	19.9	0.92	20.85	2
National Securities – Income Series	12.4	17.8	0.70	16.52	32
New England Fund	10.4	10.2	1.02	22.79	5
Putnam Fund of Boston	13.1	16.0	0.82	18.89	19
Scudder, Stevens & Clark Balanced Fund	10.7	13.3	0.80	18.62	25
Selected American Shares	14.4	19.4	0.74	17.41	24
United Funds – Income Fund	16.1	20.9	0.77	17.95	20
Wellington Fund	11.3	12.0	0.94	21.28	8
Wisconsin Fund	13.8	16.9	0.82	18.85	15

SML is the linear relationship between the expected return of a specific asset and its beta. Specifically, the SML is defined as follows:

$$E(R_i) = r + \beta_i(E(R_m) - r)$$

where β_i is the beta of the asset.

As with the CML, investors prefer the SML to be steeper. Of course, when the market is in equilibrium, all assets should lie on the SML. In actuality, however, some funds will be above the line and some funds will be below the line (either because the market is not in equilibrium or because we use estimated parameters rather than the true population parameters). Investors seek to achieve the highest return for a given beta or the lowest beta for a given return.

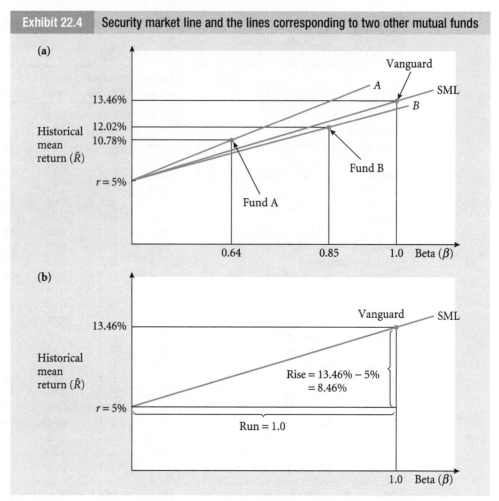

Exhibit 22.4 Security market line and the lines corresponding to two other mutual funds

(a)

Historical mean return ($\bar{R}$)

13.46%

12.02%
10.78%

$r = 5\%$

Vanguard

SML

A

B

Fund B

Fund A

0.64   0.85   1.0   Beta (β)

(b)

Historical mean return ($\bar{R}$)

13.46%

$r = 5\%$

Vanguard   SML

Rise = 13.46% − 5%
     = 8.46%

Run = 1.0

1.0   Beta (β)

Source: From *Introduction to Investments*, 2nd edn, by Levy. © 1999. Reprinted with permission of South-Western, a division of Thomson Learning: www.thomsonrights.com. Fax 800 730-2215.

Exhibit 22.4a illustrates the three mutual funds plotted using values from Exhibit 22.1. Fund A lies above the SML and hence 'beats the market'; that is, Fund A outperformed the market on a risk-adjusted basis.

Treynor suggested using the slope of the SML as a benchmark to assess performance. Treynor's performance index for a given portfolio, i, ($PI_{T,i}$), follows:

$$PI_{T,i} = \frac{\bar{R}_i - r}{\hat{\beta}_i} \tag{22.3}$$

where $\hat{\beta}_i$ is the estimated beta calculated from historical rates of return (see Chapter 10), i.e.

$$\hat{\beta}_i = \frac{\dfrac{1}{T} \times \displaystyle\sum_{t=1}^{T} (R_{i,t} - r_t)(R_{mt} - r_t) - (\bar{R}_i - \bar{r})(\bar{R}_m - r_t)}{\dfrac{1}{T} \times \displaystyle\sum_{t=1}^{T} (R_{m,t} - r_t)^2 - (\bar{R}_m - \bar{r})^2}$$

Exhibit 22.4b illustrates the calculations required for the Vanguard fund. This fund has a beta of 1.0, because we use this fund as a proxy for the market portfolio. Treynor's index compares the slope of the Vanguard fund with the slopes of other lines measuring other portfolios. Again, because this is a slope, we calculate the 'rise over the run'. For Vanguard, we find

$$PI_{T,Vanguard} = \frac{13.46\% - 5\%}{1.0} = 8.46\%$$

Note that because the numerator is given in percentages and beta is a pure number, Treynor's index is given in percentages.

Using Equation 22.3, we can calculate Treynor's performance indexes for the other two funds:

$$PI_{T,Fund\,A} = \frac{10.78\% - 5.0\%}{0.64} \cong 9.03\%$$

$$PI_{T,Fund\,B} = \frac{12.02\% - 5.0\%}{0.85} \cong 8.26\%$$

If a fund neither outperforms nor underperforms the market, then we expect it to lie on the SML – just as the Vanguard fund does – and to have a slope of 8.46%. If a fund has a line with a higher slope, then it outperformed the market. The opposite is true for a line with a slope lower than the SML. Thus, under the assumption that beta is the appropriate risk measure, we conclude that the best-performing fund for this period was fund A, followed by Vanguard. Fund B came in last again, with the lowest Treynor index.

A comparison of the results of Sharpe's index and Treynor's index shows that the choice of risk measure, standard deviation or beta affects the rankings. With Sharpe's index, we concluded that Vanguard is the best, whereas with Treynor's index, we concluded that fund A is the best. This finding is not a contradiction, because different results could be appropriate for different investors. Sharpe's index is more relevant for investors who do not hold any other portfolios, whereas Treynor's index is more relevant for investors who hold many other assets apart from the mutual fund.

The Treynor and Sharpe indices rank portfolios but do not indicate in terms of percentage return by how much a fund outperformed or underperformed the unmanaged portfolio. Thus, it is hard to understand intuitively the meaning of a PI_T of, for example, 8.26% per one unit of risk. However, there is an alternative performance index based on beta that allows us to answer the question: how much better did the fund do in terms of percentage return on a risk-adjusted basis? This method is Jensen's performance index.

22.2.3 Jensen's performance index

Jensen (1968) suggested a performance measure based on the CAPM that could assess, on a risk-adjusted, percentage basis, how well a portfolio performed.[4] Recall from Chapter 10 that the SML can be expressed equivalently in terms of 'alpha' or abnormal return or the pricing

---

[4] Jensen (1968).

error above and beyond the rate of return expected by the CAPM (or the 'normal return'). Specifically, the SML implies that an asset's alpha should equal zero:

$$\alpha_i = E(R_i) - r - \beta_i(E(R_m) - r) = 0$$

Jensen's performance index (PI_J) uses historical rates of return to estimate $E(R_i)$, $E(R_m)$ and β_i by $\bar{R}_i$, $\bar{R}_m$ and $\hat{\beta}_i$. Thus, Jensen's performance index, $\hat{\alpha}_i$, is as follows:[5]

$$PI_{J,i} = \hat{\alpha}_i = \bar{R}_i - \bar{r} - \hat{\beta}_i(\bar{R}_m - \bar{r}) \tag{22.4}$$

If $\hat{\alpha}_i > 0$, then we say that the fund earns more than is expected given its risk; the opposite holds for $\hat{\alpha}_i < 0$.

We find the following performance measures using Jensen's index on the three funds we have been tracking:

$$PI_{J,Fund\,A} = 10.78\% - [5\% + (13.46\% - 5\%)0.64] \cong 0.366\%$$

$$PI_{J,Fund\,B} = 12.02\% - [5\% + (13.46\% - 5\%)0.85] = -0.171\%$$

$$PI_{J,Vanguard} = 13.46\% - [5\% + (13.46\% - 5\%)1.0] = 0.0\%$$

These performance measures are expressed in percentages. Fund A earns an excess return of 0.366% compared with what it should earn given its beta. Notice that Jensen's performance index is zero for Vanguard. This is not a coincidence. We chose Vanguard as our market portfolio, hence $\hat{\beta}_i = 1$ and $PI_{J,i} = \bar{R}_m - [r + (\bar{R}_m - r)] = 0$. We find that the results using Jensen's measure are similar in some respects to the results using Treynor's measure. This, too, is no coincidence: both Treynor's and Jensen's indices use beta as their risk measure. As such, they both yield the same 'beat-the-market' assessment; that is, if Treynor's index for a fund indicates that it outperformed the market portfolio, then we know that Jensen's index must yield the same result.[6] This does not mean that Treynor's and Jensen's indices give the same fund rankings. In fact, the rankings generally will differ. That is, if, for example, we evaluate 100 funds, then both measures may show that 26 funds outperformed the market portfolio and 74 funds underperformed the market portfolio. However, Jensen's measure may show that fund 5 was the best, whereas Treynor's measure may rank fund 18 as the best.

A benefit of Jensen's index is its intuitive interpretation. We can conclude that fund A outperformed the Vanguard fund by 36.6 basis points (or 0.366%) and that fund B underperformed the Vanguard fund by 17.1 basis points (or 0.171%). Jensen's measure allows an investor to determine by how much one fund outperformed or underperformed another fund. Statistical tests can also be run to determine the significance of these results.[7]

---

[5] Formally, Jensen suggested running the following regression: $R_{i,t} - r_t = \hat{\alpha}_i + \hat{\beta}_i(R_{m,t} - r_t) + \hat{\varepsilon}_{i,t}$. Taking the average for both sides, we get $\bar{R}_i - \bar{r} = \hat{\alpha}_i + \hat{\beta}_i(\bar{R}_m - \bar{r}) + \hat{\bar{\varepsilon}}_i$ where the last term ($\hat{\bar{\varepsilon}}_i$) is zero. Therefore $\hat{\alpha}_i = \bar{R}_i - r - \hat{\beta}_i(\bar{R}_m - r)$.

[6] We ignore here the technical difficulties encountered with negative beta portfolios. Negative beta portfolios are very rare.

[7] See Appendix A on regression analysis at the end of this book. Among other things, this appendix estimates the alpha for Microsoft stocks and shows how to construct a confidence interval for alpha and how to test a hypothesis about alpha.

Still, Jensen's index does not inform us about the amount of non-systematic risk incurred in order to achieve the abnormal return. Jensen's index represents the average of the deviations from the SML, or

$$\varepsilon_{i,t} = R_{i,t} - [r + (R_{m,t} - r)\,\hat{\beta}_i]$$

A natural measure for non-systematic risk is the sample standard deviation of these errors, or[8]

$$\hat{\sigma}_{\varepsilon,i} = \sqrt{\sum_{t=1}^{T} (\hat{\varepsilon}_{i,t} - \hat{\alpha}_i)^2 / (T-2)}$$

The appraisal ratio or information ratio devides Jensen's index by this sample standard deviation:

$$PI_{I,i} = \frac{PI_{J,i}}{\hat{\sigma}_{\varepsilon,i}}$$

This ratio measures the amount of average abnormal return per unit of non-systematic risk. Of course, if the investor holds a well-diversified portfolio, then the residual risk of individual securities 'washes out' and the non-systematic risk of the portfolio is insignificant. In fact, for portfolios without non-systematic risk, $\hat{\sigma}_{\varepsilon,i} = 0$ and the appraisal ratio is not defined.

The performance indices of Sharpe, Treynor and Jensen are all based on the mean–variance framework. Still, as illustrated above, the three measures can give very different rankings. Using some algebra, we can formalise the relationship between the three measures in the following manner:

$$PI_{S,i} = \frac{\bar{R}_i - r}{\hat{\sigma}_i} = PI_{T,i} \times \frac{\hat{\beta}_i}{\hat{\sigma}_i} = \frac{PI_{J,i} + \hat{\beta}_i(\bar{R}_m - r)}{\hat{\sigma}_i}$$

→ Connecting Theory to Practice 22.2   **FT**

Sharpe's the word for risk and return

Since it was devised, the Sharpe Ratio has emerged as a widely accepted and useful tool for investment analysis and portfolio planning. Many research firms use the measure to compare a broad array of investment assets including mutual funds and other portfolio components.

But what happens if you apply the Sharpe Ratio to non-traditional investment options? A recent exhibition of the works of French Impressionist Edgar Degas at the Philadelphia Museum of Art, triggered the interest of Glenmede Trust, a local investment firm with offices across the US.

▶

---

[8] This expression is nothing but the standard error of regression found if we estimate the characteristic line by means of OLS regression; see Appendix A at the end of this book. Note that alpha is the average error or

$$\hat{\alpha}_i = \sum_{t=1}^{T} \hat{\varepsilon}_{i,t} / T.$$

Fine art has shown a durable record of price retention and a low correlation to more conventional asset classes. While Glenmede does not recommend investments in art, the firm speculated that these attributes could make art an interesting addition to a well-diversified portfolio, helping to reduce overall volatility while potentially generating long-term appreciation.

Compared with stocks, prices in the broad art market have held up relatively well during the downturn after the internet bubble. According to the Mei/Moses All Art index, set up by Jianping Mei and Michael Moses of New York University's Stern School of Business, fine art prices fell by about 8 per cent over the two years to the end of June 2002.

In contrast, the Standard & Poor's 500 declined 31 per cent over the same period. But over the longer term the Mei/Moses index has earned an average annual return of 8.2 per cent compared with an 8.9 per cent annual return for the S&P500. The Mei/Moses index is based on records of the main auction houses in New York and London and tracks sales of paintings that have come to market more than once since 1875.

Because fine art has shown a low correlation with stocks, values for art works and equities have tended to appreciate most strongly at different times, and portfolios that include both asset classes should be less volatile than those comprising one or the other asset class exclusively. When the Sharpe Ratios of bonds, stocks and fine art are calculated separately, and then in a diversified portfolio with or without a fine art component, this premise appears to be borne out.

Although a diversified portfolio with fine art comprising a 50 per cent allocation of stocks, 25 per cent bonds, 10 per cent cash and 15 per cent fine art might be expected to produce a slightly lower average return than fine art or stocks alone between 1926 and 2000, the diversified portfolio's value should be more stable from year to year.

Glenmede's calculations show that fine art produced an average return over that period of 13.19 per cent compared with a 12.9 per cent return from equities and an 11.25 per cent average annual return from a diversified portfolio with fine art.

However, the Sharpe Ratios for different types of asset class range from about 0.18 for bonds on their own, 0.33 for fine art and 0.47 for equities on their own. The Sharpe Ratio rises to about 0.48 for a diversified portfolio without fine art, but inches ahead to about 0.49 when fine art is added to the mix.

In other words, the figures suggest that adding fine art to a diversified portfolio produces a slightly greater return for each unit of risk, and a significantly better return with less volatility than most asset classes, including fine art, on their own.

There are, however, some caveats. Glenmede says that 'investment-quality art is a highly specialised asset class and should be included only as an adjunct to a traditional portfolio'.

In particular the report notes: 'As with other types of investment, fine art carries a number of unique risks. On a physical level, art typically requires a specially controlled environment where temperature, humidity and light are continuously monitored.

'On a financial level, prices for individual works may be unpredictable and difficult to compare. Investment horizons typically run for years or even decades, and the market is generally illiquid which significantly limits an investors' ability to convert a holding to cash if necessary.'

What is more, authenticating the ownership of individual works can be difficult and transactions may be costly involving sales commissions, appraisal fees and storage and shipping costs.

In spite of these challenges, the Philadelphia-based investment firm says: 'Art lovers through the centuries have pursued the avocation for the aesthetic and the potential economic reward that may come through an investment in fine art.'

Source: Paul Taylor, 'Sharpe's the Word For Risk and Return', *Financial Times*, 12 April 2003.

This article discusses including fine art in an investment portfolio. Over the period 1926–2000, the average return of fine art (13.19%) exceeded the average return on stocks (12.9%). However, due to its greater risk, the Sharpe index for fine art (0.33) was smaller than that for stocks (0.47). This means that investing in stocks alone gives a more favourable risk–return trade-off than investing in fine art alone. However, the return to fine art is not correlated strongly with the return on other asset categories and, hence, adding fine art to a portfolio can reduce risk through diversification. Indeed, a diversified portfolio with 50% stocks, 25% bonds, 10% cash and 15% fine art yields a Sharpe index (0.49) that is greater than that for a diversified portfolio without fine art (0.48) or with stocks only (0.47). This discussion shows that the Sharpe index is the appropriate performance measure for an investor's entire portfolio, but not for its individual components (stocks, bonds, cash, fine art). A similar conclusion could have been reached by computing Treynor's index or Jensen's index for the individual components; fine art yields a high average return and a low beta and, hence, its Treynor's index and Jensen's index are relatively high.

22.2.4 Performance indices with the arbitrage pricing theory

In principle, the notion of Jensen's performance measure can be applied within the APT framework. That is, the difference between the actual average return earned and the return expected under some single-factor or multifactor pricing model can be estimated. The basic idea of the APT performance index (PI_A) is to examine the difference between the actual average rate of return earned during the evaluation period compared with the average rate of return that is expected based on the APT.[9] The APT-based index is similar to Jensen's index, except that it uses the multifactor APT instead of the single-factor CAPM as the equilibrium model. In the APT, one or more factors are assumed to determine the risk, for example the market portfolio, inflation, the GNP, and so forth.

For example, after considering all risk factors, if the required expected rate of return is 10% but the fund actually earned 12%, then it outperformed 2% by the APT measure. Thus, the index is

$$\bar{R}_i - \hat{R}_{APT,i} = 12\% - 10\% = 2\%$$

We will further develop this multifactor approach in Sections 22.3 and 22.4. In these sections, a multifactor approach is useful because of its generality. Still, the single-factor model with the market portfolio as the sole risk factor (as in the CAPM) is embedded as a special case; in this case, the APT-based index reduces to Jensen's alpha.

Note that the choice between PI_S and the pair PI_T and PI_J depends on whether you hold only the asset under consideration or you hold many other assets in addition. The choice between these indices and the APT index depends on your belief about the process generating the returns. If, for example, you believe that, apart from the market portfolio, inflation also affects prices, then you should select the APT index.

---

[9] For more discussion of this concept, see Maginn and Tuttle (1990), Roll and Ross (1984), Brealey (1990), Sharpe (1992) and Kahn (1991).

22.3 Style analysis

→ **Connecting Theory to Practice 22.3** **FT**

Seeking out investment value in styles

A glance at the unit trust section of the *Financial Times* or the mutual funds section in the *Wall Street Journal* reveals that fund management companies tend to label products using a few common categories. Funds will frequently carry attributes such as small-cap, growth, value and international. Similarly, money managers tend to present themselves to institutional clients as, for example, an aggressive growth, a large-cap or a technology manager. Categorisations of this kind usually imply that a fund or a manager invests in a distinct group of stocks that share some characteristics. In recent years the term 'investment style' has become popular to describe this phenomenon.

Why classify?

There seems to be no compelling reason why a fund might, for example, restrict itself to growth stocks only. So why classify stocks into styles?

At a basic level styles may arise from a human desire for classification. Each day, stock market investors face an enormous flow of information and a diverse set of investment opportunities. Classifying assets may help investors to ease their burden in processing information and provide structure. Indeed, much of the variability in stock returns can be traced to variability of the asset classes to which a particular stock belongs. For example, when a small company shows a high return this often coincides with strong returns for other small companies.

The role of investment consultants may also contribute to the importance of investment styles. Investment consultants are hired to assess managers' skills on behalf of their clients. In measuring a manager's performance the consultant often wants to assess skill in selecting stocks relative to the performance of the style a manager follows. As a result style-based performance measurement and style-based benchmarks have become common.

How themes emerge

There seems to be some rationale for categorising stocks into styles. However, how do these styles arise? Why do investors perceive some asset characteristics to be of such importance that a style emerges?

An important factor in defining a style is the degree of co-movement of prices within a group of securities. In some cases the reason for the classification is obvious. This is true, for example, for styles defined by geographical location. Domestic stocks will move more with each other than with stocks traded abroad. Similarly, stocks within a particular industry tend to move more with each other than with stocks in other industries. An interesting example is the effect of the single currency on styles in the euro area. Many observers argue that the single currency will foster the co-movement of economic fundamentals across countries. As a result, a shift seems to have occurred, away from country styles towards pan-European industry styles.

Perhaps the most powerful contribution to the emergence of a style, however, comes from historical performance. In 1934, Benjamin Graham and David Dodd documented the superior performance of strategies that invested in high dividend yield stocks in the US. This gave rise to the value style (although it may not have been called a style then). The superior performance of the 'nifty-fifty' group of US blue-chip stocks, including IBM, Kodak and Xerox, in the early 1970s may have marked the emergence of the growth style. The popularity of this style was powerfully reinforced by the spectacular performance of growth stocks in the 1990s. In a similar vein, strong performance over several years gave rise to the new economy and TMT (technology-media-telecommunications) styles at the end of the 1990s.

In some cases, academic research contributed to the birth of a style. In 1981 a study by academic Rolf Banz at the University of Chicago showed that small-cap stocks had outperformed large-cap stocks in the US by a margin that could not be explained by conventional measures of risk. This led to the creation of Dimensional Fund Advisors, an investment company set up by Chicago graduates to capitalise on this finding. Its small-cap fund was the most successful launch in financial history. It sparked the creation of other small-cap funds and indices in the US, UK and other countries. A style was born. Similarly influential have been studies by Eugene Fama and Kenneth French in 1993, who documented a strong premium for value stocks, and Narasimhan Jegadeesh and Sheridan Titman in 1993, who reported high historical returns to momentum strategies.

Many style indices have been created to track style-based market segments. Style index mutual funds have emerged that give investors an alternative to actively managed funds, but without restricting their choices solely to tracking of market-wide indices.

Rotation

People who seek to diversify may wish to invest in a multi-style portfolio. Others who anticipate outperformance of a particular style, for example based on the historical performance record, might concentrate their investments. Active managers, whose specialisation is in some segment of the market, will also emphasise a specific style. A third possibility is to rotate styles and change the weight placed on a particular theme over time.

Style rotation is based on the idea that returns on particular styles may be predictable. This means that a model for forecasting style returns is needed to implement style rotation strategies. In the past decade a wide array of variables has been suggested for forecasting style returns. These include macroeconomic variables, recent style performance, measures of the spread in valuation ratios between styles and measures of investor sentiment. Armed with a model that has sufficient forecasting power, an investor may then be able to enhance portfolio performance by changing exposure to certain styles over time.

There are some reasons why one might be able, to some extent, to forecast style returns. For example, at least a part of the return differential in average returns between value and growth stocks appears to reflect differences in risk. Therefore, in times when investors demand high premia for bearing risk (for example when the economy is doing badly), future spreads between value and growth should tend be high. On the other hand, if investor sentiment plays a role in determining style returns, then a prolonged history of superior performance of a certain style could indicate sentiment-driven overvaluation, which would imply relatively low future returns on this style.

However, to be a viable investment approach, style rotation strategies need to earn the transaction costs they incur. Rotation requires considerably higher portfolio turnover than simple buy-and-hold strategies. Therefore, the question arises whether the predictability of style returns is high enough for rotation to be profitable after transaction costs. Empirical evidence is not encouraging. A study by Mario Levis and Manolis Liodakis in 1999 found that potential profits from style rotation between small and large or value and growth stocks were lost in transaction costs.

Performance

Nobel laureate William Sharpe has pioneered the application of style-based analysis of portfolio management problems. In an article in 1992 he observed that usually around 90 per cent of the variation in return on mutual funds can be explained by these funds' exposure to a few asset classes, such as bonds, bills, large-cap and small-cap stocks, value and growth stocks, and some others. In other words, to a large extent an investor could have replicated the performance of these funds by investing passively in a mixture of these asset classes or styles.

This raises two questions. First, if most of the funds' performance can be replicated by investing in passive portfolios one may be tempted to invest in the passive portfolios right away, without hiring a more expensive active manager. Second, if we are interested in an active manager's skill in picking stocks we may want to measure performance relative to a passive benchmark that replicates the style exposure of his portfolio. This would help determine how much the manager contributed to performance.

For unit trusts it has been common to compare managers with a peer group that follows a similar style. With style analysis this is becoming common practice for evaluating other portfolio managers, too. It is possible to estimate how much style exposure has contributed to a manager's performance and how much is due to skill in selecting individual stocks. Style-based performance evaluation has become widespread, with investment consultants providing detailed performance attribution services to clients.

Style analysis works well for managers whose style exposure is relatively constant. However, for managers who choose a style rotation approach, the methodology is not as successful. Such style rotators will insist that their skill lies in selecting the right style at the right time.

Conclusions

Are styles a passing fad or will they continue to be important in investment management? Currency union within Europe has accelerated the trend for analysing industries on a pan-European basis, and for some sectors, such as pharmaceuticals, oils and financials, a global perspective is needed. The relative performance of value and growth stocks appears to be increasingly aligned across countries, as shown by recent fluctuations of technology stocks. These developments suggest that co-movements of groups of stocks and the impact of investment styles have become permanent features of markets.

Source: Elroy Dimson and Stefan Nagel, 'Seeking Out Investment Value In Styles', *Financial Times*, 14 May 2001.

In Connecting Theory to Practice 22.2, Elroy Dimson, a professor of finance at London Business School, and one of his doctoral students report that investment styles (e.g. small-cap, value and international styles) have become essential in developing, analysing and evaluating investment strategies. Style analysis is an umbrella term for a set of tools for determining the investment style of portfolios and for measuring the performance of portfolios given their style. Money managers are often evaluated, in part, based on how well they stay within the bounds of a given investment style. In addition, investment style is often used as a proxy for risk, and the value of such an approach depends on a correct initial assessment of style.

The popularity of style analysis was aided by the Brinson *et al.* (1991) study. This study analysed the performance of 82 large, multiasset US pension fund portfolios from 1977 to 1987. Stated simply, they found that the investment policy or asset allocation to bills, bonds and stocks accounted for 91.5% of the portfolios' performance. Later studies found that as much as 98% or more of fund returns can be explained by asset allocation alone if we include additional asset classes (for example, real estate) or break down the asset classes (for example, value and growth stocks). Hence, the large majority of fund performance is attributable to its investment style – rather than investment strategy (market timing and security selection).

One of style analysis's most important outputs is the style benchmark for the managed portfolio, as of a certain date. The style benchmark is a weighted portfolio of reference indices whose return was as close as possible to that of the managed portfolio over a specified historical period. It thus expresses the apparent style over that period. A US fund manager's style might be represented on a certain date as:

40% domestic small-value stocks;
40% domestic large-value stocks;
20% domestic long-term, high-quality bonds.

The style benchmark in this case might be a weighted average of the Russell 2000 Value index (domestic small-value stocks), the Russell Top 200 Value index (domestic large-value stocks) and the Lehman Brothers US Government Long Bond index (domestic long-term, high-quality bonds). The performance of a portfolio can be measured relative to its style benchmark, either in terms of raw return comparisons or on a risk-adjusted basis (for example, using the Sharpe index or the Jensen index).

There exist two commonly used methods of style analysis: holdings-based style analysis (HBSA) and returns-based style analysis (RBSA).

22.3.1 Holdings-based style analysis

HBSA determines investment style by examining the characteristics of the individual securities in the portfolio. The style of each individual security is classified according to a set of rules, and then the securities are aggregated to arrive at the style of the portfolio.

One prominent example is the 'Current Investment Style' classification by Morningstar.[10] This classification is represented in a three-by-three matrix called the style box.

For domestic equity funds, the style box distinguishes between small-cap funds, mid-cap funds and large-cap funds, and between value funds, blended funds and growth funds.[11] The distinction between small-cap funds, mid-cap funds and larg-cap funds is based on the median of the market capitalisation of the fund's stocks. Morningstar ties market cap to the relative movements of the market. The top 5% of the 5000 largest domestic stocks in Morningstar's equity database are classified as large-cap, the next 15% of the 5000 are medium-cap, and the remaining 80% (as well as companies that fall outside the largest 5000) are small-cap. Morningstar then determines a fund's market cap by ranking the stocks in a fund's portfolio from the largest market-capitalised stock to the smallest, and then calculating the average weighted market capitalisation of the stocks in the middle quintile of the portfolio. After a fund's market cap has been determined, Morningstar places the fund in the large-cap, medium-cap or small-cap group. To make the distinction between value funds, blended funds and growth funds, Morningstar uses the price/earnings (P/E) and price/book (P/B) valuation multiples. Specifically, each stock in the Morningstar database receives a P/E score and a P/B score. This

---

[10] Morningstar, Inc., located in Chicago, is one of the most prominent providers of information about returns and characteristics of mutual funds. The homepage of Morningstar can be found at www/morningstar.com/

[11] Investment styles are determined differently for international-equity funds than they are for domestic-equity funds. Funds with medium market capitalisations of less than $1 billion are small-cap; funds with median market caps equal to or greater than $1 billion but less than or equal to $5 billion are medium-cap; and funds with median market caps greater than $5 billion are large-cap. Because earnings are reported in different ways in other regions, Morningstar uses price/cash flow, rather than price/earnings, for international investment-style data. Cash flow from operations takes into account net income and adds back all the adjustments that earnings accounting can make for non-cash expenses, such as depreciation and the use of reserve accounts, and subtracts out all cash payments. International funds' price/cash flow and price/book ratios are viewed in relation to the MSCI Europe Australia Far East index, rather than against the domestic S&P 500 index. Morningstar takes the stock portfolio's average price/cash-flow ratio relative to the MSCI EAFE index and adds it to the portfolio's average price/book figure relative to the MSCI EAFE index. (The MSCI EAFE average in each case is set equal to 1.00.) If the sum of the relative price/cash flow and the relative price/book is less than 1.75, the fund is defined as a value offering; if the sum lands from 1.75 to 2.25, the fund is classified as blend; and if the sum is greater than 2.25, the funds falls into the growth category.

is derived by dividing each stock's P/E and P/B ratios by the asset-weighted median P/E and asset-weighted median P/B of the stock's market-cap group. Next, Morningstar calculates the P/E valuation score and the P/B valuation score for each fund by ranking the stocks in a fund's portfolio by their median market caps and then calculating an average weighted P/E score and an average weighted P/B score from the stocks in the middle quintile of each fund's portfolio. These average weighted scores are the P/E valuation score and the P/B valuation score of the fund's portfolio. For each measure, 1.00 represents the market-cap group average. If the fund has a combined P/E score and P/B score that exceeds 2.25, then the fund is categorised as growth. The fund includes substantially more in growth stocks (which have a high price relative to fundamentals) than the market does. If the combined score is less than or equal to 2.25 but greater than or equal to 1.75, then the fund is categorised as blend. Finally, if the score is less than 1.75, then the fund is categorised as value. The fund then invests heavily in value stocks (which have a low price relative to fundamentals).

For fixed-income funds, the style box classifies funds based on interest-rate risk and default risk.[12] Morningstar distinguishes between short-term, intermediate-term and long-term funds based on the value-weighted average duration of the bonds in the portfolio. The average duration of short-term funds lies between one and 3.5 years; intermediate-term funds have an average duration between 3.5 and six years; for long-term funds, the duration is more than six years. In addition to interest-rate risk, fixed-income funds are classified based on credit risk as measured by the credit rating.[13] High-credit-quality funds have an average credit rating of at least AA; a medium classification is given if the average credit rating lies between BBB and A; low corresponds to an average less than BB.

Exhibit 22.5 displays example style boxes for a large-value equity fund and a fixed-income fund with intermediate-term duration and low credit quality.

Exhibit 22.5	Morningstar style boxes for a large-value equity fund (left box) and a fixed-income fund with intermediate-term duration and low credit quality (right box)

---

[12] For hybrid funds, both equity and fixed-income style boxes appear.

[13] US government securities are considered AAA bonds, non-rated municipal bonds generally are classified as BB, and all other non-rated bonds are considered B. If duration data are not available, Morningstar will use average effective maturity figures to calculate the fund's style box. Funds with bonds that have an average effective maturity of less than four years qualify as short-term. Funds with an average effective maturity greater than or equal to four years but less than or equal to ten years are categorised as intermediate, and those with maturity that exceeds ten years are long-term.

HBSA is a very useful tool for performance evaluation, because it enables analysts to design benchmarks that better fit the investment styles used by fund managers. However, the method has several drawbacks, the biggest being:

- Managers of mutual funds are required to disclose the exact composition of their portfolios only quarterly. Hence, for an actively managed fund, the last reported portfolio composition might no longer be relevant. In addition, portfolio managers are sometimes suspected of window dressing. This refers to trading activity immediately preceding the reporting data, with the sole intention of making it look as if the manager chose winner stocks.

- Investors need to keep track of and examine the portfolio composition and the properties of every stock in the portfolio, which – when done properly – will require a costly and time-consuming effort. Of course, there are professional data providers such as Morningstar that specialise in this task. However, these providers charge fees to cover their expenses. In addition, some investors may not agree with the way that the providers determine the investment styles.

- An HBSA requires the investor to evaluate all individual securities in the portfolio. Unfortunately, it can be very difficult to obtain reliable estimates for the characteristic of individual securities. For example, the P/E multiple (used by Morningstar to distinguish between growth stocks and value stocks) may suffer from temporarily inflated or deflated earnings (see Chapter 15).

For these reasons, the investor may consider returns-based style analysis (RBSA) in addition to or instead of HBSA.

22.3.2 Returns-based style analysis

RBSA is a method for determining the style of an investment portfolio by analysing its co-movements with indexes that proxy for different styles. The method builds on ideas proposed by Sharpe (1988, 1992). Essentially, the method tries to recover the asset allocation of a portfolio and to measure the performance given the asset allocation. RBSA recovers the asset allocation by identifying what combination of passive holdings across various asset classes would have replicated most closely the actual performance of the portfolio over a specified time period. For this purpose, a linear factor model is specified that links the portfolio return to a set of M style indices that represent the various asset classes. Formally, the factor model can be written as

$$E(R_i) = \beta_{0,i} + \beta_{1,i}E(I_1) + \ldots + \beta_{M,i}E(I_M) \tag{22.5}$$

where $E(I_1), \ldots, E(I_M)$ are the expected returns for the style indexes. The style coefficients $\beta_{1,i}, \ldots, \beta_{M,i}$ represent the exposure of the evaluated portfolio to the indexes. Combined, these coefficients represent the effective asset mix of the portfolio. The selection return $\beta_{0,i}$ is the part of expected return that is not related to general market movements, and it therefore measures the portfolio manager's stock-picking skills.

Using data on the historical returns of the evaluated portfolio and the indices, the coefficients can be estimated using regression analysis (see Appendix A at the end of this book). Specifically, we can estimate the following regression model:

$$R_{i,t} = \beta_{0,i} + \beta_{1,i}I_{1,t} + \ldots + \beta_{M,i}I_{M,t} + \varepsilon_{i,t} \tag{22.6}$$

Exhibit 22.6	Estimated style coefficients for Trustees' Commingled US Fund, January 1985 through December 1989

	Unconstrained	Coefficients sum to 100%	Coefficients positive and sum to 100%
Bills	14.69	42.65	0
Intermediate bonds	−69.51	−68.64	0
Long-term bonds	−2.54	−2.38	0
Corporate bonds	16.57	15.29	0
Mortgages	5.19	4.58	0
Value stocks	109.52	110.35	69.81
Growth stocks	−7.86	−8.02	0
Medium stocks	−41.83	−43.62	0
Small stocks	45.65	47.17	30.04
Foreign bonds	−1.85	−1.38	0
European stocks	6.15	5.77	0.15
Japanese stocks	−1.46	−1.79	0
Total	72.71	100.00	100.00
R-squared	95.20	95.16	92.22

Source: From 'Asset Allocation: Management Style and Performance Measurement', *The Journal of Portfolio Management*, Vol. 18, pp. 7–19, published by Institutional Investor, Inc., W. F. Sharpe (1992).

where $I_{1,t}, \ldots, I_{M,t}$ are the historical returns for the style indexes.[14] Methodically, regression analysis will choose the parameter values such that the indices can explain most of the return of the fund. Put differently, the style-attribution coefficients are determined in such a way that the variance of the excess return of the manager over the style benchmark becomes minimal. However, RBSA typically deviates from standard regression analysis by imposing constraints on the parameters. Since funds typically are barred from net short positions, the style coefficients are frequently restricted to positive values and they must sum to 100%.

For example, Exhibit 22.6 shows the estimated style coefficients for the Trustees' Commingled US Fund, estimated using monthly data from January 1985 through December 1989 (60 months) and using 12 different style indices. The results are shown with and without the restriction that all coefficients are between zero and one, and that the coefficients add up to one.

The results suggests that the fund yields returns that are similar to those achievable with a style portfolio with roughly 70% invested in a market-representative portfolio of value stocks and 30% in a market-representative portfolio of small stocks. The R-squared measures the part of the portfolio's return that is attributable to the asset allocation. In this case, over 92% of the month-to-month variation in the return on the fund can be explained by the variation in the return on the effective asset mix of value stocks and small caps. The proportion of return variability not explained by asset allocation, in this case about 8%, can be attributed to security selection within the asset classes. The selection return in this case is estimated to be $\hat{\beta}_{0,i} = -0.06\%$; and the portfolio manager has provided a monthly excess return of −0.06%

---

[14] Sometimes, the constant $\beta_{0,i}$ is not included. In this case, the objective is to minimise the error variance rather than the mean squared error. Both approaches effectively yield the same result. If the constant is excluded, then selection return is measured as the average value of the errors.

compared with the style index. Hence, the portfolio manager appeared to have no significant stock-picking skills. Notice that the selection return excludes the part of return that is attributable to small stocks and value stocks. An investor choosing Trustees' Commingled US Fund could and should have known that its style favoured small stocks and value stocks. Results (good or bad) associated with the choice of style should be attributed to the investor, not to the manager of a fund following that style.

RBSA is a very popular tool, and commercial software applications have made the method widely available.[15] The following features help explain its popularity:

- Mutual funds publish portfolio values on a daily basis, which means that the rate of return for each day is publicly available. By contrast, the composition of the portfolio (required for HBSA) is available only on a monthly basis.
- Investors need not examine every individual security in the portfolio; hence, RBSA is less costly and time-consuming. RBSA therefore is especially useful, or even preferable, in situations where current portfolio information is not readily available.
- The focus is on the style of the entire portfolio. Since portfolio data are less noisy than individual security data, the results may be more robust than HBSA. However, currently very little is known about the statistical goodness of the different approaches to style analysis.

Despite these attractive features, RBSA has a number of drawbacks:

- RBSA is a 'black box' because the regression can't explain why a particular blend of style indices gives the best fit. For example, if a US corporate bond portfolio yields poor returns in a period when US bond indices are flat (for example, due to downgrades of several bonds in the portfolio) and Japanese stocks fall in that period, then the analysis is going to say you have a portfolio with some Japanese stocks in it! Spurious loadings may also arise because of multicollinearity, which exists when the style indices used in the regression are highly correlated, so it becomes difficult to separate their effects. By contrast, with HBSA, the analyst can both observe the classification of every stock in the portfolio as well as question these classifications. In defence of RBSA, we may quote Sharpe (1988): '. . . returns-based style analysis is not going to dissect the creature to determine if its DNA belongs to that of a duck, but it will tell you if it has enough duck-like characteristics to qualify'.
- RBSA is very sensitive to style rotation, or changes in asset allocation over time. The technique essentially assumes a constant asset allocation over the evaluated time period. Hence, the style identified with RBSA is, in a sense, an average of potentially changing styles over the period covered. Month-to-month deviations of the fund's return from that of the style can arise from selection of specific securities within one or more asset classes, style rotation, or both security selection and style rotation. Also, RBSA can be a poor guide to the future in case of major changes to the portfolio composition. If there is a major change in the portfolio composition, then the historical returns will take a while to pick up that change. You will see the change a lot quicker if you use HBSA, which looks at the most recent data on the portfolio composition (even if those data are available only on a quarterly basis). For this reason, RBSA is applied frequently to a rolling window with a short time window. Unfortunately, the results become less reliable as the time period is shortened.

---

[15] RBSA has become a commodity that is quickly available and operated with a few points and clicks. Some websites offer free RBSA for a wide range of investment firms and products. Find the product, click on it, and out comes a style profile.

- A common problem for RBSA and HBSA is the selection of the appropriate set of styles and style indices. There currently exists no theory to guide in the selection, while the results can be very sensitive to the selection. Still, some rules of thumb result from practical experience with style analysis: (1) style indices should be mutually exclusive (no stock gets into more than one style, so as to minimise muticollinearity); (2) the style indices should be exhaustive (all stocks are classified); and (3) style indices should be rebalanced frequently, since things change rapidly: calling a cheap high-tech stock 'growth' because it had a high P/E a year ago doesn't make sense.

22.4 Performance attribution

Portfolio managers generally make three types of decisions:

- The investment-policy or asset-allocation decision involves deciding which asset classes to include and which to exclude from the portfolio and then deciding upon the normal, or long-term, weights for each of the asset classes allowed in the portfolio.
- Style rotation or market timing is the strategic under- or overweighting of an asset class relative to its normal weight to capture excess returns from short-term fluctuations in asset class prices. Timing is undertaken to achieve incremental returns relative to the policy return.
- Security selection is the active selection of investments within an asset class to achieve superior returns.

Overall performance measures provide no clues about which activities within the portfolio manager's domain are generating the superior (or inferior) performance; thus, it is not clear what the portfolio manager is doing well or not so well. Assessing the performance of the activities that make up portfolio management is known as performance attribution. If a manager is doing well in one area and badly in another, then performance attribution will identify areas where the manager can improve or identify tasks that should be taken from the manager and given to somebody else.

Performance attribution seeks to take the overall rate of return on a fund and break it down into its component parts, such as asset allocation and security selection. To attribute performance, we need to analyse the various management decisions. For example, Exhibit 22.7 illustrates the four layers of decisions that are typically made in the top-down approach used by portfolio managers.

First, the portfolio manager decides what percentages of the portfolio will be stocks, bonds and cash. This decision is known as asset allocation. (Other categories, such as real estate, could also be included.) For example, the manager may decide to place 40% of the portfolio in stocks, 30% in bonds and 30% in cash.

Next, the manager must decide how to allocate the 40% portion of stocks into various sectors, such as basic materials, conglomerates, and so forth. The sectors shown in Exhibit 22.7 are based on sector definitions provided in the *Wall Street Journal*. The decision to place 10% of the stock portion in utilities, for example, is known as the sector-allocation decision (how much of an asset to place in a specific sector). The sum of all the sector weights will equal 100%. Hence, sector weights denote the portion of the stocks held given to a certain sector category.

The next decision is how to allocate each of the sector portions into various industries. For example, the utilities sector can be broken down into four basic industries: telephone, electric, gas and water. The industry allocation is the allotment of investment dollars given to a sector's industry components. For example, the manager may decide to allocate 30% of the utilities sector to the water industry.

> **Exhibit 22.7** Flow chart of the top-down money-management process

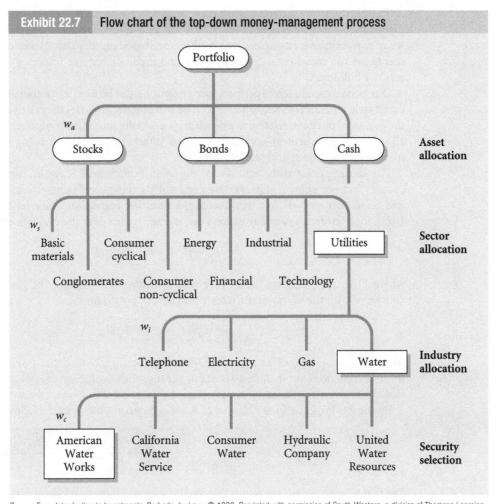

Source: From *Introduction to Investments*, 2nd edn, by Levy. © 1999. Reprinted with permission of South-Western, a division of Thomson Learning: www.thomsonrights.com. Fax 800 730-2215.

At this point, the manager is ready to select individual securities. For example, of the allocation given to the water industry, what portion should be invested in American Water Works (AWW)? This decision is known as security selection. The manager may decide to place 15% of the water industry allocation into American Water Works.

To attribute performance among the various management decisions, an index portfolio is needed for comparison. This index portfolio plays the role of a benchmark portfolio. The fund manager knows that the fund's performance will be compared with this benchmark portfolio. For example, suppose the fund outperformed the index portfolio by 250 basis points. Senior management wants to be able to determine which decisions generated the excess returns. Was it the asset-allocation decision to have less in stocks? Was it the sector-allocation decision, the industry-allocation decision and/or the security selections? The answer can be determined through the process of performance attribution.

Briefly, performance attribution decomposes the overall portfolio performance into components related to the different levels of the portfolio-selection process so as to understand the contribution that the various decisions made to the overall performance.

There exist many different attribution methods, based on different models of the invest-ment process (the four-layer model in Exhibit 22.7 is just one example), different models of security returns (for example, some methods are based on the CAPM) and different require-ments for the input data (for example, some methods require information on individual security holdings).

One popular approach to performance attribution can be used in combination with returns-based style analysis (see Section 22.3.2). The method decomposes the relative performance of the evaluated portfolio relative to a benchmark portfolio into three components related to asset allocation (investment policy), style rotation (market timing or deviating from the bench-mark asset allocation) and security selection.

The starting point is the multifactor model in Equation 22.5. Again, the coefficients $\beta_{0,i}$, $\ldots$, $\beta_{M,i}$ are not known. However, we can estimate these coefficients using historical returns and regression analysis. We will denote the resulting regression estimates by $\hat{\beta}_{0,i}, \ldots, \hat{\beta}_{M,i}$. Using these estimates, we may express the average return over the evaluation period as

$$\bar{R}_i = \hat{\beta}_{0,i} + \hat{\beta}_{1,i} \Gamma_1 + \ldots + \hat{\beta}_{M,i} \Gamma_M \qquad (22.7)$$

where $\Gamma_1, \ldots, \Gamma_M$ denotes the average return on the style indices. The average return $\bar{R}_i$ is compared with the average return on a benchmark portfolio:

$$\bar{R}^* = \beta_1^* \Gamma_1 + \ldots + \hat{\beta}_M^* \Gamma_M \qquad (22.8)$$

where $\beta_1^*, \ldots, \beta_M^*$ denotes the benchmark asset allocation. Notice that, unlike Equation 22.7, this equation does not include a constant, because the benchmark portfolio does not engage in security selection. Rather, it simply holds an exact combination of the style indexes.

By combining Equations 22.7 and 22.8, we can decompose $\bar{R}_i$ in the following manner:

$$\bar{R}_t = \underbrace{\bar{R}^*}_{\text{asset allocation}} + \underbrace{\hat{\beta}_{0,i}}_{\text{security selection}} + \underbrace{(\hat{\beta}_{1,i} - \hat{\beta}_1^*)\Gamma_1 + \ldots + (\hat{\beta}_{M,i} - \hat{\beta}_M^*)\Gamma_M}_{\text{style rotation}} \qquad (22.9)$$

The first term represents the return that would be earned if the portfolio manager did not engage in style rotation or security selection. This component is the result of the benchmark style coefficients and actual style index returns. The second term is the return due to security selection. This term is the result of deviations from the style index returns. The third term represents style rotation or deviation from the benchmark asset allocation. This component is the result of the deviations of actual style coefficients from the benchmark and actual style index returns. Combined, the effects of security selection and style rotation form the active return.

To demonstrate how this method works, we return to the example of Trustees' Com-mingled US Fund given in Exhibit 22.8. Using hypothetical data, this exhibit decomposes the overall portfolio return in components attributable to asset allocation, style rotation and stock-picking. We use the hypothetical returns to the style indices that are given in column 1. Further, we assume that Trustees' Commingled benchmark asset allocation is 50% invested in value stocks and 50% in growth stocks (column 4). Notice that this asset allocation differs substantially from the actual asset allocation given in column 1 (the values are taken from Exhibit 22.7). Clearly, Trustees' Commingled overweights value stocks and small stocks and underweights growth stocks. Column 3 displays the contribution of each of the style indices to the overall portfolio return; the values are found by multiplying the style index returns with the actual style coefficients. In this case, value stocks contribute 3.02% to the total portfolio return of 4.19%. The part not explained by the style indices (−0.06%) is attributed to stock-picking

Exhibit 22.8	Performance attribution with hypothetical data for Trustees' Commingled US Fund						

	(1)	(2)	(3)	(4)	(5)	(6)	(7)
	Return (%)	Actual weight (%)	Effect (1) × (2) (%)	Benchmark weights (%)	Effect (1) × (4) (%)	Weight difference (2)–(4) (%)	Differential effect (3)–(5) (%)
Bills	0.33	0	0	0	0	0	0
Intermediate bonds	0.72	0	0	0	0	0	0
Long-term bonds	0.82	0	0	0	0	0	0
Corporate bonds	1.13	0	0	0	0	0	0
Mortgages	1.33	0	0	0	0	0	0
Value stocks	4.32	69.81	3.02	50.00	2.16	19.81	0.86
Growth stocks	1.23	0	0	50.00	0.62	−50.00	−0.62
Medium stocks	3.80	0	0	0	0	0	0
Small stocks	4.12	30.04	1.24	0	0	30.04	1.24
Foreign bonds	−1.23	0	0	0	0	0	0
European stocks	−2.21	0.15	−0.00	0	0	0.15	0.00
Japanese stocks	−2.32	0	0	0	0	0	0
Security selection			−0.06		0		−0.06
Total		100.00	4.19	100.00	2.78	0.00	1.42

ability. Columns 4 and 5 show similar data for the benchmark portfolio. In this case, Trustees' Commingled outperforms the benchmark portfolio by 1.42%. Columns 6 and 7 decompose this difference and attribute it to the deviations from the benchmark asset allocation. The differences between the actual values of the style coefficients and the benchmark values are shown in column 6. Finally, the seventh column shows the differential effect, or the effect of deviating from the benchmark asset allocation. For example, the differential effect for small-value stock is 0.86%.

In this case, Trustees' Commingled achieved a total return of 4.19%. Has the fund been 'successful'? It has been successful in outperforming its benchmark, which achieved a return of only 2.78%. This difference was achieved by style rotation: the fund changed its asset allocation towards the better-performing asset classes (small stocks and value stocks). Hence, if the fund's style is to try and pick the asset classes with abnormal returns (style rotation), then the results support the fund's ability. However, the fund has not been successful at security selection, because the overall return is 0.06% lower than the return that could be expected given the actual asset allocation. Therefore, if the fund's style is to try and pick the securities with abnormal returns (security selection), then this is evidence of failure during this period.

22.5 Empirical evidence for the performance of open-end mutual funds

One of the first academic studies on mutual fund performance was the study by Sharpe (1966). He examined the performance of the US mutual funds used in Exhibit 22.3. He found that the major differences in their returns resulted from the expenses incurred by each mutual fund. Furthermore, as measured by Sharpe's index, the majority of these funds failed to outperform the Dow Jones Industrial Average based on Sharpe's index.

Exhibit 22.9	Mean–standard deviation diagram for 34 US open-end mutual funds, 1954–63

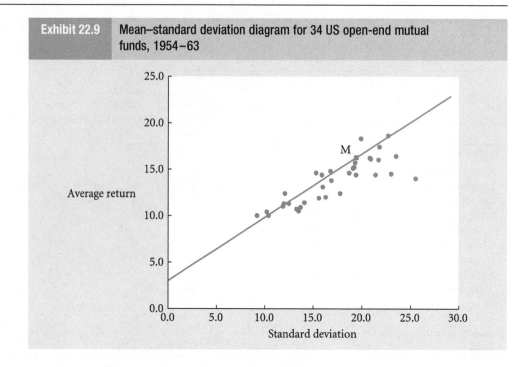

Exhibit 22.9 illustrates this finding using a mean–standard deviation diagram. The straight line connects the risk free fund with the Dow Jones Industrial Average (labelled 'M'). The slope of this line equals the Sharpe index for the Dow Jones. Clearly, the large majority of mutual funds has a lower Sharpe ratio.

Sharpe (1966, p. 138) concluded the following:

> The burden of proof may reasonably be placed on those who argue the traditional view – that the search for securities whose prices diverge from their intrinsic values is worth the expense required.

Sharpe's study, as well as the classic studies by Treynor (1965) and Jensen (1968), triggered a wide range of studies on the performance of mutual funds. As years have gone by, better techniques and larger and more specific data sets have become available to researchers, which has made it possible to get a new and more accurate perspective of the performance of mutual funds. Several different aspects of mutual fund performance have been examined. The three main questions are:

1. Are mutual funds on average able to beat the market? In other words, are mutual funds capable of stock-picking and/or timing the market?
2. Is there a relation between turnover, expenses and management fees incurred and the performance of mutual funds? Are turnover, expenses and management fees associated with superior or inferior performance?
3. Is there persistence in the performance of mutual funds? In other words, can we predict mutual fund performance based on past performance?

Exhibit 22.10 surveys some important studies. This exhibit displays the sample period, the number and type of funds examined, the performance benchmark(s), the type of performance measure and a short summary of the conclusions regarding the above three questions.

Exhibit 22.10   Overview of studies on mutual fund performance

Study	Sample period	Number/type of fund	Performance benchmark(s)	Performance measure(s)	Answers to questions 1–3
Sharpe (1966)	1954–65	34 US	DJIA	Sharpe ratio	Q1: MFs failed to outperform DJIA Q2: expenses of funds explain difference in returns
Jensen (1968)	1955–64	115 US	S&P 500	Jensen index	Q1: no outperformance
Ippolito (1989)	1965–84	143 US	S&P 500	Jensen index	Q1: MFs outperform the market, but not enough to offset load charges Q2: little or no correlation between turnover, fees, expenses versus inferior performance
Cumby and Glen (1990)	1982–88	15 International US	MSCI World and MSCI US index	Jensen index	Q1: outperformance of domestic benchmark but not of international benchmark
Eun *et al.* (1991)	1977–86	19 International US	S&P 500 and MCSI world index	Sharpe, Treynor and Jensen indices	Q1: outperformed S&P but not MCSI world index
Sharpe (1992)	1985–89	636 stock, bond and balanced US funds	12 style benchmarks	RBSA	Q1: MFs do not outperform their style benchmarks
Blake *et al.* (1993)	1979–88	361 bond funds	Several bond indices	Alphas on single and multiple index models	Q1: underperformance of bond funds Q2: underperformance and expense ratio are directly correlated
Elton *et al.* (1993)	1945–64/ 1965–84	115 US (45–64) 143 US (65–84)	S&P 500 and CRSP index (non-S&P stocks)	Jensen index	Q1: MFs underperform their benchmarks Q2: funds with higher fees and turnover underperform those with lower fees and turnover
Malkiel (1995)	1971–91	All US equity funds excluding international and sector funds	S&P 500, Wilshire 5000	Jensen index	Q1: MFs underperform benchmarks, also gross of expenses Q3: strong persistence during the 1970s, faded away during the 1980s.
Carhart (1997)	1962–93	1892 diversified US equity funds	CRSP index of all NYSE, AMEX, NASDAQ stocks	Alpha of four-factor model (market, size, value and momentum)	Q2: expenses and turnover have significantly negative impact on performance Q3: buying last year's winners and selling the losers yields a positive return; no long-term persistence
Daniel *et al.* (1997)	1975–94	2500 US general equity funds	Several, e.g. 125 HBSA benchmarks and Carhart four-factor portfolios	Several, e.g. HBSA and alpha of Carhart four-factor model	Q1: MFs outperform the style benchmarks, but excess returns are small, approximately equal to the average management fee; also, no timing ability found Q3: persistence can be explained by the prior year return anomaly
Wermers (2000)	1975–94	1788 diversified US equity funds	125 HBSA benchmarks	Daniel *et al.* methodology with attribution measures for selectivity and timing	Q1: MFs outperform style benchmarks, but net of expenses they underperform. MF managers outperform market almost enough to offset costs. Also, no timing ability was found Q2: high-turnover funds hold stocks with significantly higher average returns than low-turnover funds (gross of expenses)
Davis (2001)	1965–98	4686 US equity funds	Several style benchmarks	Alpha of Fama and French three-factor model	Q1: none of the styles generated positive abnormal returns Q3: some persistence among the best-performing growth funds and among the worst-performing small-cap funds

These studies are not always in agreement, and the results are also difficult to compare due to differences in data sets (sample period, number of funds, type of funds), performance benchmarks and performance measures. Still, we can draw the following general conclusions:

Most research shows that mutual funds on average underperform the market after correcting for costs. Before costs, some studies show that mutual fund managers have some stock-picking skills, but this is not enough to offset the expenses made by the funds. Mutual fund managers are on average not able to time the market. This means that they do not move into styles that turn out to perform better than expected or move out of styles that turn out to perform worse than expected.

Turnover, expenses and management fees have a negative impact on the performance of mutual funds, although some evidence is found that the funds with the highest turnover do earn significantly higher net returns than funds with the lowest turnover.

There is little consistency in performance of funds from year to year (see also Investment in the News 22 at the beginning of this chapter). Nevertheless, some short-term persistence is found among the best-performing funds and the worst-performing funds.

Recent studies point out that almost all previous studies have overstated true performance of mutual funds due to survivorship bias in their data sets.[16] Most of the data sets employed for mutual fund performance evaluation include the past records of all mutual funds currently in existence. Hence, when a fund merges or gets liquidated (ceases to exist), its past performance is deleted from the database, because today's investors are not interested in the records of funds that no longer exists. Thus, if mutual funds with bad performance are taken off the market, their bad records are buried with them. Therefore, the average performance of the surviving funds will overstate the success of the mutual fund industry as a whole (including the liquidated funds).

In response to the historically poor performance of actively managed mutual funds overall, many managers and investors have turned to indexing. Investors who follow an indexing strategy invest in a passively managed mutual fund that mirrors the market and incurs minimal expenses. The American equity mutual fund industry managed over $2500 billion in equities in 2002.[17] Every basis-point difference between the expense ratios of actively and passively managed funds results in hundreds of millions of extra costs for actively managed funds.

22.5.1 Evaluating socially responsible investing

As discussed in Chapter 5, socially responsible investing (SRI) accounts for the societal and environmental impact of investment decisions. An important issue in this respect is whether the socially responsible investor forgoes returns or diversification from using (positive or negative) social and environmental screens. After all, by putting up screens, the investment universe is reduced. However, there is some evidence that the actual financial cost of SRI in terms of opportunity costs is not substantial. For example, Guerard (1997) concludes that there was no statistically significant difference between the performance of a screened universe of 950 common stocks and an unscreened universe of 1300 stocks for the period 1987–96. D'Antonio et al. (1997) studied the returns of bonds from firms represented in the Domini 400 (an index for SRI) and compared these with the returns of the Lehman Brothers

---

[16] See Malkiel (1995) and Elton et al. (1996).
[17] ICI Factbook 2003.

Corporate Bond Index. They found no significant differences in average portfolio performance. Diltz (1995) concluded that there was no statistically significant difference in returns for 14 socially screened stock portfolios versus 14 unscreened stock portfolios generated from a universe of 159 securities during the period 1989–91. Given the outcomes of these studies, the conclusion seems justified that the returns of SRI portfolios are not statistically different from those of comparable investments.

22.6 A word of caution

As discussed in Section 22.1, performance evaluation generally tries to assess whether and why a portfolio manager deviated significantly from optimising the investment objectives of the investor, given the investment restrictions that the manager faced. This is a difficult task, because objectives, opportunities and restrictions are not always defined clearly, the investment process consists of many different decisions, and many factors that affect investment performance are beyond the control of the manager. In this chapter, we have discussed the strengths and weaknesses of several tools for performance evaluation. As a word of caution, we list several basic problems in applying these tools in practice:

- Performance evaluation is an historical exercise by its very nature; it tells us how well a manager did in the past (and possibly also why). However, for many purposes, our concern is how well the manager will do in the future. The link between past performance and future performance may be weak. For example, there seems to be little (if any) consistency in the performance of mutual funds from year to year. This lack of consistency over time greatly reduces the effectiveness of performance evaluation for selecting funds. However, it is clear that if a fund consistently charges too much for its services, then over time it will be outperformed by a similar fund with lower fees.
- Correcting for risk is very difficult, because there is no agreement on which asset-pricing model best describes the risk perception and risk attitude of investors. Do investors care only about systematic risk as in the CAPM and APT, or should we also account for non-systematic risk because many investors have poorly diversified portfolios? Should we use a single-factor model, or are multiple risk factors relevant, as in the APT? Theory provides little guidance in the selection of the appropriate set of risk factors. Another problem is the sensitivity of risk measures to the proxy for the risk factors. In this respect, Roll has argued that market beta is not a clear measure of risk.[18] For example, if we use a different proxy for the market (for example, a global stock index rather than the USA-based S&P 500 index), the betas may change considerably, and we may arrive at very different portfolio rankings. Moreover, if we employ any mean–variance-efficient portfolio to calculate beta, then all assets will show the same performance when adjusted for risk; this casts doubt on the Jensen and Treynor performance measures. Also, the calculated beta changes over time and depends on the time intervals used to compute rates of return. Thus, beta itself is not stable and depends on the market proxy used to calculate it.[19]

---

[18] See Roll (1978, 1980) and Roll and Ross (1984).

[19] Also, Roll (1977) shows that if an efficient portfolio is employed to calculate beta, then Jensen's measure will also be zero in the sample for all portfolios. Thus, the different performances that we observe may indicate only that an inefficient market portfolio was employed to calculate beta.

■ It is very difficult to obtain reliable estimates of the risk and return characteristics of individual securities. One reason is that individual securities are very volatile. Also, they are affected to a large extent by asset-specific factors that obscure their exposure to common risk factors. For this reason, we would need a large number of observations to obtain reliable estimates of exposure coefficients. Unfortunately, we cannot simply collect data over a long time period, because the return distribution changes as the assets and liabilities of individual firms change through time and as the economy goes through different stages of the business cycle.

■ Estimating the risk and return characteristics of a portfolio has the advantage that asset-specific factors and firm-specific changes cancel out in a portfolio context. However, an important problem for estimating the return distribution for portfolios is that the portfolio composition changes through time. For example, an active money manager may hold 80% stocks, 15% bonds and 5% cash one day and then 50% stocks, 45% bonds and 5% cash the next. (Such radical changes in allocations are now straightforward with the use of derivative securities.) If the stock portfolio is riskier than the bond portfolio, then the riskiness of the overall portfolio clearly has increased. There are ways to handle this problem, but they are very difficult to implement. For example, if beta is the appropriate risk measure, then we can calculate the betas of the stocks, bonds and cash portfolios and adjust the overall portfolio beta. That is, rather than compute the beta based on the historical behaviour of the portfolio, we can compute the beta based on the allocations among stocks, bonds and cash. Using this approach, Radcliffe *et al.* (1992–93) found that professional money managers with poor year-to-date returns at the end of the third quarter tend to have increased equity risk exposure during the fourth quarter of the calendar year. Apparently, managers tend to 'go for broke' by increasing their betas in the fourth quarter if they have not been doing well in the first part of the year. This higher-risk strategy will either dramatically improve the year-end performance or dramatically reduce the year-end performance. Thus, by calculating the portfolio beta as a weighted average of the securities' beta, we can detect changes in risk level as soon as portfolio changes are made. However, to implement this approach, we need timely information on the composition of the portfolio. Unfortunately, as discussed in Section 22.3, mutual funds typically report on their portfolio only on a quarterly basis and they may also engage in window dressing (this is why HBSA is so difficult to implement).

For these reasons, performance evaluation in many cases is as much art as it is science.

Summary

Calculate portfolio performance using four performance indices based on asset-pricing theory.

Performance indices provide a method of comparing funds with different risk–return characteristics. Four performance indices used to rank portfolio performance are Sharpe's index, Treynor's index, Jensen's index and an index based on the arbitrage pricing theory (APT). Sharpe's performance index compares fund performance where the standard deviation measures the risk, whereas Treynor's performance index compares fund performance where beta serves as the measure of risk. Sharpe's index is appropriate for portfolios in isolation, and Treynor's index is appropriate for portfolios in the context of the entire market portfolio. Jensen's performance index is also based on beta as a risk index, but it gives performance measure results in terms of rates of return. Because Treynor's and Jensen's indices are based on the CAPM framework, they both give the same assessment of outperformance or underperformance in relation to the market, but the indices can give different rankings within the two groups based on performance.

Explain style analysis and the most common approaches to style analysis.

'Style analysis' is an umbrella term for a set of tools for determining the investment style of portfolios and for measuring the performance of portfolios given their style. There exist two commonly used methods of style analysis: holdings-based style analysis (HBSA) and returns-based style analysis (RBSA). HBSA determines investment style by examining the characteristics of the individual securities in the portfolio and maps these characteristics into the style of the portfolio. RBSA does not use information on the individual securities but rather determines investment style by regressing the historical returns of the entire portfolio on a set of style indices.

Evaluate performance attribution as a means of identifying the sources of performance.

Performance attribution breaks down a fund's excess return into component parts. The component parts correspond with the layers of investment decisions, including asset allocation, market timing and security selection.

Summarise the empirical evidence regarding mutual fund performance.

The empirical evidence finds consistently that mutual fund managers on average lag behind the market if we correct for risk and costs. There seems to be little evidence for stock-picking and market-timing ability on behalf of mutual fund managers. Further, turnover, expenses and management fees seem to have a negative impact on the performance of mutual funds. Finally, there appears to be little (if any) consistency in the performance of funds over time, which greatly reduces the effectiveness of performance evaluation for selecting funds.

Identify some problems with measuring investment performance in practice.

Problems with measuring the performance of fund managers include the fact that historical performance is not an accurate forecast of future performance; the fact that theory provides little guidance for selecting the appropriate risk measures and risk factors; difficulties in estimating the exposure coefficients of individual assets due to high asset-specific risks and changes of the risk profiles of the underlying firms; and difficulties in estimating the exposure coefficients of portfolios due to changes in the composition of the portfolio and the lack of timely information about the portfolio composition.

Key terms

Review questions

1 **a.** The following data are for two mutual funds over a recent 10-year period. Determine which fund performed better, using Sharpe's and Treynor's index. (Assume a 6.5% risk-free rate.)

	Fund A	Fund B
Average return	14%	16%
Standard deviation	5.7	7.1
Beta	1.20	0.91

    b. Use Jensen's index to determine how mutual Funds A and B performed. The average return on the market for the period was 13.5%.

    c. If the required expected rate of return for a fund is 12% and the fund actually earned 13.7%, how much did the fund outperform as measured by the APT performance index?

2 Which is a better performance index, Sharpe's index or Treynor's index? Explain your answer carefully.

3 What are the four layers of decisions that are typically made in the top-down approach used by portfolio managers?

4 **a.** Explain what the difference is between the HBSA and the RBSA.
    b. What are the advantages of the RBSA?
    c. What are the disadvantages of the RBSA?
    d. What are the disadvantages of the HSBA?

5 Summarise the empirical findings for the performance of open-ended mutual funds.

For an extensive set of review and practice questions and answers, visit the Levy–Post investment website at www.booksites.net/levy

Selected references

Allen, G. C., 1991, 'Performance Attribution for Global Equity Portfolios', *Journal of Portfolio Management*, **17**, 59–65.

American Association of Individual Investors, *The Individual Investor's Guide to No-Load Mutual Funds*, Chicago: International Publishing Corporation.

Ankrim, E. M., 1992, 'Risk-Adjusted Performance Attribution', *Financial Analysts Journal*, **48** (2), 75–83.

Ankrim, E. M. and C. R. Hensel, 1994, 'Multicurrency Performance Attribution', *Financial Analysts Journal*, **50** (2), 29–35.

Bailey, J. V., 1992, 'Evaluating Benchmark Quality', *Financial Analysts Journal*, **48** (3), 33.

Blake, C. R., E. J. Elton and M. J. Gruber, 1993, 'The Performance of Bond Mutual Funds', *Journal of Business*, **66** (3), 371–403.

Blake, D., B. N. Lehmann and A. Timmermann, 1999, 'Asset Allocation Dynamics and Pension Fund Performance', *Journal of Business*, **72** (4), 429–461.

Bogle, J. C., 1992, 'Selecting Equity Mutual Funds', *Journal of Portfolio Management*, **18**, 94–100.

Brealey, R. A., 1990, 'Portfolio Theory Versus Portfolio Practice', *Journal of Portfolio Management*, **16**, 6–10.

Brinson, G., B. Singer and G. Beebower, 1991, 'Determinants of Portfolio Performance II: An Update', *Financial Analysts Journal*, **47** (3), 40–47.

Carhart, M. M., 1997, 'On Persistence in Mutual Fund Performance', *Journal of Finance*, **52**, 57–82.

Cumby, R. E. and J. D. Glen, 1990, 'Evaluating the Performance of International Mutual Funds', *Journal of Finance*, **45**, 497–521.

Daniel, K., M. Grinblatt, S. Titman and R. Wermers, 1997, 'Measuring Mutual Fund Performance with Characteristic-Based Benchmarks', *Journal of Finance*, **52**, 1035–1058.

D'Antonio, L., T. Johnson and B. Hutton, 1997, 'Expanding Socially Screened Portfolios: An Attribution Analysis of Bond Portfolios', *Journal of Investing*, **6** (4), 79–86.

Davis, J. L., 2001, 'Mutual Fund Performance and Manager Style', *Financial Analysts Journal*, **57** (1), 19–27.

Diltz, J. D., 1995, 'The Private Cost of Socially Responsible Investing', *Applied Financial Economics*, **5** (2), 69–77.

Elton, E. J., M. J. Gruber, S. Das and M. Hlavka, 1993, 'Efficiency With Costly Information: A Reinterpretation of Evidence from Managed Portfolios', *Review of Financial Studies*, **6** (1), 1–22.

Elton, E. J., M. J. Gruber and C. R. Blake, 1996, 'Survivorship Bias and Mutual fund Performace', *Review of Financial Studies*, **9** (4), 1097–1120.

Eun, C. S., R. Kolodny and B. G. Resnick, 1991, 'U.S.-Based International Mutual Funds: A Performance Evaluation', *Journal of Portfolio Management*, **17**, 88–94.

Fama, E. F., 1972, 'Components of Investment Performance', *Journal of Finance*, **27**, 551–567.

Farrell, J. L., Jr, 1983, *Guide to Portfolio Management*, New York: McGraw-Hill.

Graham, J. R. and C. R. Harvey, 1997, 'Grading the Performance of Market Timing Newsletters', *Financial Analysts Journal*, **53** (6), 54–66.

Grinblatt, M. and S. Titman, 1993, 'Performance Measurement Without Benchmarks: An Examination of Mutual Fund Returns', *Journal of Business*, **66**, 47–68.

Guerard, J. B., 1997, 'Is There a Cost to Being Socially Responsible in Investing: It Costs Nothing to Be Good?', *Journal of Investing*, **6** (4), 31–35.

Halpern, P., 1993, 'Investing Abroad: A Review of Capital Market Integration and Manager Performance', *Journal of Portfolio Management*, **19**, 47–57.

Henriksson, R. D., 1984, 'Market Timing and Mutual Fund Performance: An Empirical Investigation', *Journal of Business*, **57**, 73–96.

Henriksson, R. D. and R. C. Merton, 1981, 'On Market Timing and Investment Performance II: Statistical Procedures for Evaluating Forecasting Skills', *Journal of Business*, **54**, 513–534.

Hodgos, C. W., W. R. L. Taylor and J. A. Yoder, 1997, 'Stocks, Bonds, the Sharpe Ratio, and the Investment Horizon', *Financial Analysts Journal*, **53** (6), 74–80.

Investment Company Institute, 2003, *Mutual Fund Fact Book*, 43rd edn, Washington, DC: Investment Company Institute.

Ippolito, R. A., 1989, 'Efficiency with Costly Information: A Study of Mutual Fund Performance, 1965–1984', *Quarterly Journal of Economics*, **104** (1), 1–23.

Jensen, C. M., 1968, 'The Performance of Mutual Funds in the Period 1945–1964', *Journal of Finance*, **23**, 389–415.

Kahn, R. N., 1991, 'Bond Performance Analysis: A Multi-factor Approach', *Journal of Portfolio Management*, **17**, 40–47.

Karnosky, D. S. and B. D. Singer, 1994, *Global Asset Management and Performance Attribution*, Charlottesville, VA: Research Foundation of the Institute of Chartered Financial Analysts.

Khorana, A. and E. Nelling, 1997, 'The Performance Risk: A Diversification of Sector Funds', *Financial Analysts Journal*, **53** (3), 62–73.

Lehman, B. N. and D. M. Modest, 1987, 'Mutual Fund Performance Evaluations: A Comparison of Benchmarks and Benchmark Comparisons', *Journal of Finance*, **42**, 233–265.

Maginn, J. L. and D. L. Tuttle (eds), 1990, *Managing Investment Portfolios: A Dynamic Process*, New York: Warren, Gorham & Lamont.

Malkiel, B. G., 1995, 'Returns from Investing in Equity Mutual Funds 1971 to 1991', *Journal of Finance*, **50**, 549–572.

Metrick, A., 1999, 'Performance Evaluation with Transactions Data: The Stock Selection of Investment Newsletters', *Journal of Finance*, **54**, 1743–1775.

Modigliani, F. and L. Modigliani, 1997, 'Risk-Adjusted Performance', *Journal of Portfolio Managament*, **24**, 45–54.

Myers, M. M., J. M. Poterba, D. A. Shackelford and J. B. Shoven, 2001, 'Copycat Funds: Information Disclosure Regulation and the Returns to Active Management in the Mutual fund Industry', NBER Working Paper 8653, 18–24.

Radcliffe, R., R. Brooks and H. Levy, 1992–93, 'Active Asset Allocation Decisions of Professional Equity Managers', *Review of Financial Services*, **2** (1), 21–40.

Roll, R., 1977, 'A Critique of the Asset Pricing Theory's Tests, 1: On Past and Potential Testability of the Theory', *Journal of Financial Economics*, **6**, 129–176.

Roll, R., 1978, 'Ambiguity When Performance is Measured by the Security Market Line', *Journal of Finance*, **33**, 1051–1069.

Roll, R., 1980, 'Performance Evaluation and Benchmark Errors, 1', *Journal of Portfolio Management*, **6**, 5–12.

Roll, R., 1981, 'Performance Evaluation and Benchmark Errors, 2', *Journal of Portfolio Management*, **7**, 17–22.

Roll, R. and S. Ross, 1984, 'The Arbitrage Pricing Theory Approach to Strategic Portfolio Planning', *Financial Analysts Journal*, **40** (3), 14–26.

Sharpe, W. F., 1966, 'Mutual Fund Performance', *Journal of Business*, **39** (1), 119–138.

Sharpe, W. F., 1988, 'Determining a Fund's Effective Asset Mix', *Investment Management Review*, **2** (6), 59–69.

Sharpe, W. F., 1990, 'Asset Allocation'. In: Maginn, J. L. and D. L. Tuttle, editors, *Managing Investment Portfolios: A Dynamic Process*, 2nd edn, New York: Warren, Gorham & Lamont, pp. 1–71.

Sharpe, W. F., 1992, 'Asset Allocation: Management Style and Performance Measurement', *Journal of Portfolio Management*, **18**, 7–19.

Treynor, J., 1965, 'How to Rate Management of Investment Funds', *Harvard Business Review*, **43**, 63–75.

Treynor, J. and K. Mazuy, 1966, 'Can Mutual Funds Outguess the Market?', *Harvard Business Review*, **44**, 131–136.

Wermers, R., 2000, 'Mutual Fund Performance: An Empirical Decomposition into Stock-Picking Talent, Style, Transactions Costs, and Expenses', *Journal of Finance*, **55**, 1655–1690.

Zheng, L., 1999, 'Is Money Smart? A Study of Mutual Fund Investors' Fund Selection Ability', *Journal of Finance*, **54**, 901–933.

A.1   Introduction

Regression analysis is a statistical tool for analysing relationships between economic variables. It is an important tool for empirical research and practical applications of investment theory. For example, we may use this tool to estimate factor sensitivity coefficients, such as the market beta, of stocks. Also, we may use the tool to empirically test investment theories, such as the CAPM. The tool is included in many statistical software packages and spreadsheet software, and even in more advanced pocket calculators. There exist many different regression methods. We will focus here on the most elementary regression method: the ordinary least squares (OLS) method. Many more sophisticated methods are generalisations or adaptations of the OLS method.

A.2   Terminology of regression analysis

Suppose that a researcher has come up with the idea that there exists a linear relationship between a dependent variable or regressand and k independent variables or regressors. The relationship is assumed to be not deterministic or exact but rather stochastic, i.e. the regressand is also affected by factors beyond the regressors and that are treated as random errors. The errors capture the influence of factors that affect the regressand but that are not included in the model, for example because the researcher is not aware of their influence or because the researcher does not have reliable information on these factors. Examples of such factors include omitted regressors and measurement error. The stochastic relationship can be represented by the following regression equation:

$$y = \beta_0 + \beta_1 x_1 + \ldots + \beta_k x_k + \varepsilon \qquad (A.1)$$

where y is the regressand; β_0 is the intercept of the equation, measuring the expected value of the regressand y if the regressors equal zero; $x_1, \ldots, x_k$ are the regressors; $\beta_1, \ldots, \beta_k$ are the slope coefficients, measuring the expected increase in the regressand y from a unit increment in the regressors $x_1, \ldots, x_k$; and ε is the error term, measuring the influence of factors that affect the regressand but that are not included in the model.

For example, we may wish to estimate the characteristic line of Microsoft stocks by using the following regression equation:

$$R_{Micro} - r = \alpha_{Micro} + \beta_{Micro}[R_m - r] + \varepsilon$$

with R_{Micro} being Microsoft's stock return, r being the riskless rate, α_{Micro} being Microsoft's 'alpha', β_{Micro} being Microsoft's 'beta' and R_m being the market return.

We will refer to the intercept β_0 and the slope coefficients $\beta_1, \ldots, \beta_k$ as the regression coefficients. Generally, these coefficients cannot be determined using economic theory or practical knowledge. Rather, information is typically limited to a set of N observations on the regressand and the regressors. Indexing the observations by the index i, we represent the observations by

$$(y_i, x_{1,i}, \ldots, x_{k,i}) \quad i = 1, \ldots, N \tag{A.2}$$

Basically, there exist three types of data sets: time-series data, cross-section data and panel data sets. Time-series data refer to observations on a single object at different points in time or for different time periods. For example, the monthly returns of Microsoft from January 1993 to December 2002 form a time-series data set of 120 months. By contrast, cross-section data refer to observations on different objects during the same time period. For example, the means and betas of all stocks included in the S&P 500 index as computed over the period January 1993 to December 2002 form a cross-section data set of 500 stocks. Finally, panel data arise when data are available with both a time-series dimension and a cross-section dimension, i.e. a data set on different objects and different time periods; for example the monthly returns of all stocks included in the S&P 500 index during the period from January 1993 to December 2002 is a panel data set of $120 \times 500 = 60\,000$ returns. Panel data obviously contain more information than data with only a time-series dimension or only a cross-section dimension. However, it generally does not make sense to assume that the regression coefficients are constant across all periods and all observations. Also, the statistical properties of the errors for the time series may differ from the properties for the cross-section. Finally, the data for some combinations of the time periods and the cross-sectional objects may be missing, for example if stocks are listed or delisted during the sample period (an 'unbalanced panel'). For these reasons, we typically cannot simply pool all observations from a panel data set. Rather, we generally need special panel data regression methods to deal with panel data in an efficient manner. Therefore, we assume here that the data are either cross-section data or time-series data but not panel data.

The observations are assumed to obey the regression in Equation A.1, i.e.

$$y_i = \beta_0 + \beta_1 x_{1,i} + \ldots + \beta_k x_{k,i} + \varepsilon_i \tag{A.3}$$

where ε_i denotes the error term for the ith observation.

Regression analysis estimates the unknown regression coefficients by selecting the parameter values $\hat{\beta}_0, \hat{\beta}_1, \ldots, \hat{\beta}_k$ that provide the 'best fit' to the data.[1] The degree of fit for a particular observation is given by the regression residual:

$$\hat{\varepsilon}_i = y_i - \hat{\beta}_0 - \hat{\beta}_1 x_{1,i} - \ldots - \hat{\beta}_k x_{k,i} \tag{A.4}$$

or the distance of an observation from the estimated regression line $y_i = \hat{\beta}_0 + \hat{\beta}_1 x_{1,i} + \ldots + \hat{\beta}_k x_{k,i}$. The regression residual serves as an empirical estimator for the error term ε_i, which is unknown, because the true regression coefficients are unknown. In general, the estimated regression line gives a good fit if the residuals are 'as small as possible'.

For example, Exhibit A.1 shows the monthly excess returns of Microsoft stocks and a US stock market index (a value-weighted average of all common stocks listed on the NYSE, AMEX and NASDAQ exchanges) for the period from January 1991 to December 2000, a

---

[1] The 'hats' emphasise that these are estimates of the true but unknown parameters.

Exhibit A.1	Scatter plot of 120 monthly returns on Microsoft stocks and a US stock market index, 1991–2000

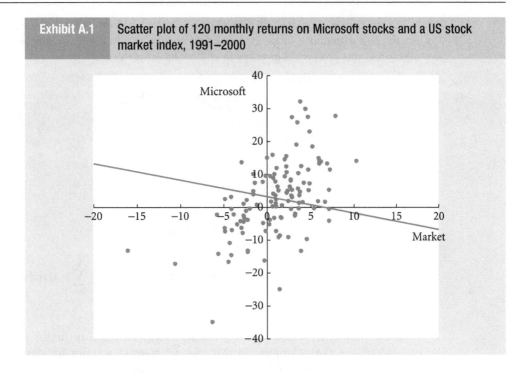

total of 120 monthly observations. A graph such as this is called a scatter plot. The set of observations is sometimes referred to as the scatter cloud. The graph also includes the line $R_{Micro} - r = 3.273 - 0.5(R_M - r)$. Obviously, this line gives a relatively poor fit to the data. The objective of regression analysis is to find the line of best fit.

A.3   The least squares principle

What measure should we take to aggregate the residuals of the different observations? Taking the sum of the residuals is not a good idea. Residuals can take positive and negative values. Hence, positive residuals for some observations may (partially) cancel out negative residuals for other observations. In fact, for any set of estimators for the slope coefficients $\hat{\beta}_1, \ldots, \hat{\beta}_k$, we can always find an intercept $\hat{\beta}_0$ such that the sum of positive residuals is exactly equal to the sum of negative residuals, and the total sum of residuals equals zero. In Exhibit A.1, we have selected the line $R_{Micro} - r = 3.273 - 0.5(R_M - r)$ such that the mean of the errors indeed equals zero. Obviously, in this case, the mean error gives a poor goodness measure.

A popular measure for goodness is the squares sum of residuals (SSR):

$$\sum_{i=1}^{N} \hat{\varepsilon}_i^2 = \sum_{i=1}^{N} (y_i - \hat{\beta}_0 - \hat{\beta}_1 x_{1,i} - \ldots - \hat{\beta}_k x_{k,i})^2 \tag{A.5}$$

The SSR measures the sum of squared deviations from the estimated regression line. Squared residuals are more informative than the residuals, because they always take a positive value and, hence, do not cancel out.

803

The ordinary least squares (OLS) method selects the parameters such that the SSR is minimal. For the case with only a single independent variable (that is, $k = 1$), or simple regression, the solution to this problem is given by the following estimators:[2]

$$\hat{\beta}_0 = \frac{\frac{1}{N}\sum_{i=1}^{N} x_{1,i}^2 \bar{y} - \bar{x}_1 \frac{1}{N}\sum_{i=1}^{N}(x_{1,i} y_i)}{\hat{\sigma}_{x_1}^2} \qquad (A.6)$$

and

$$\hat{\beta}_1 = \frac{\frac{1}{N}\sum_{i=1}^{N}(x_{1,i} y_i) - \bar{x}_1 \bar{y}}{\hat{\sigma}_{x_1}^2} \qquad (A.7)$$

where $\bar{x}_1 = \frac{1}{N}\sum_{i=1}^{N} x_{1,i}$ denotes the sample mean of $\bar{x}_1$, $\bar{y} = \frac{1}{N}\sum_{i=1}^{N} y_i$ stands for the sample mean of y, and $\hat{\sigma}_{x_1}^2 = \frac{1}{N}\sum_{i=1}^{N} x_{1,i}^2 - \bar{x}_1^2$ is the sample variance of x_1.

In the more general case with $k > 1$ independent variables, or multiple regression, the expressions are more complex. In this case, we have to account for possible correlation between the regressors, a problem also known as multicollinearity.

For our example, the estimates are $\hat{\alpha}_{Micro} = 1.248$ and $\hat{\beta}_{Micro} = 1.535$. Hence, if the market return is zero, then we expect a 1.248% return on Microsoft stocks. In addition, for every 1% return on the market, we expect 1.535% return on Microsoft stocks. Exhibit A.2 gives the associated regression line $R_{Micro} - r = 1.248 + 1.535[R_M - r]$. This regression line gives a substantially better fit than $R_{Micro} - r = 3.273 - 0.5[R_M - r]$. Specifically, the SSR drops from 17 921 to 10 234. In fact, the regression line is chosen such that the sum of squared residuals is minimal.

Again, the SSR measure is attractive, because squared residuals always take a positive value and, hence, do not cancel out. Still, it is difficult to interpret SSR, because it depends on the unit of measurement. Hence, we cannot compare the outcomes of different studies that use different units of measurement. For example, it is difficult to tell whether SSR = 5322 is high or low. To circumvent this problem, it is useful to use a standardised version, known as the coefficient of determination or R-squared:

$$R^2 = 1 - \frac{\sum_{i=1}^{N} \hat{\varepsilon}_i^2 / N}{\hat{\sigma}_y^2} \qquad (A.8)$$

with $\hat{\sigma}_y^2 = \frac{1}{N}\sum_{i=1}^{N} y_i^2 - \bar{y}^2$ being the sample variance of y. In this equation, the residual variance $\sum_{i=1}^{N} \hat{\varepsilon}_i^2 / N$ is standardised by the sample variance of the regressand. Hence, R^2 can be interpreted as the ratio of explained variance to total variance of the regressand. Since the regressand is measured in the same units as the residual, this measure is independent of the unit of

---

[2] A shortcut to computing $\hat{\beta}_0$ is to use $\hat{\beta}_0 = \bar{y} - \hat{\beta}_1 \bar{x}$.

Exhibit A.2	Regression line for Microsoft stocks

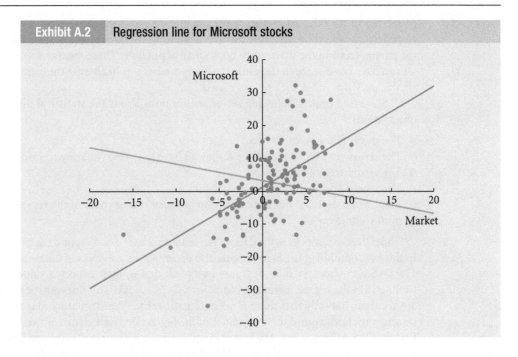

measurement and can be compared across different studies. In fact, the measure generally takes a value between zero (no explanatory power) and one (perfect explanatory power).[3] Again, the OLS method selects the estimators such that the SSR is minimal. Since R^2 is a simple transformation of SSR, this is equivalent to maximising R^2.

For our example of Microsoft stocks, the residual variance equals 85, while the sample variance of Microsoft return equals 122. Combining these two figures, we find $R^2 = 1 - (85/122) = 0.299$. This means that about 30% of the variability of Microsoft's return can be explained by the variability of the market return or, put differently, market risk constitutes 30% of the total risk of Microsoft stocks.

A.4   Statistical properties of ordinary least squares estimators

We know that a low SSR or a high R^2 means that the regression line gives a good description of the data set. We may be tempted to think that a low SSR or a high R^2 also implies that the parameter estimators are 'good', i.e. they are 'close to' the true values of the parameters. There is some truth in this line of thinking, as we will see below. However, in general, a good fit does not imply good estimators. For good estimators, we also need to know that the data are 'representative' of the (unknown) underlying relationship, i.e. the data should be scattered in a random way around the true regression line. Whether this is true depends on the statistical distribution of the observations. Given this distribution, we can determine the statistical

---

[3] Sometimes, an 'adjusted R-squared' is used. This statistic measures the statistical goodness of the regression model, after correcting for the number of regressors (k) in the model. Formally, the adjusted R-squared is defined as $\text{adj}R^2 = 1 - (1 - R^2)(N - 1)/(N - k)$. A limitation of the standard R-squared is that adding regressors to the model will always improve the R-squared and will never lower the R-squared, even if the regressor has a negligible effect. By contrast, the adjusted R-squared increases only if the t-value of the additional regressor exceeds one; if the t-value is smaller than one, then the adjusted R-squared will fall.

properties of the OLS estimators. For example, we can compute the mean and the variance. In general, it would be desirable for the mean to be as close as possible to the true values of the parameters and the variance to be as small as possible. These measures will tell us whether we can have confidence in the estimates and whether it is likely that the estimates will change significantly if another data set were used.

OLS is based on the following set of assumptions about the statistical distribution of the observations:

- The mean of the errors is zero, or $E(\varepsilon) = 0$.
- The errors are homoskedastic, i.e. they all have the same (unknown) error variance σ_ε^2.
- The errors are not correlated.
- The regressors are given (non-stochastic).
- There exists no exact linear relationship between two or more of the regressors (no perfect multicollinearity).

Under these assumptions, the data set is a random scatter cloud around the true regression line. In this case, optimising the fit to the data also optimises the goodness of the regression estimators. The OLS estimators $\hat{\beta}_0, \hat{\beta}_1, \ldots, \hat{\beta}_k$ are unbiased; that is, their expected value equals the true (unknown) values of the regression coefficients $\beta_0, \beta_1, \ldots, \beta_k$. This does not mean that estimators are accurate, but only that there is no systematic error. The estimators may still involve substantial variation around the true values of the regression coefficients. However, we can prove that the OLS estimates have the lowest possible variance among all unbiased linear estimators, i.e. the estimators are best linear unbiased estimators (BLUE). For simple regression (that is, $k = 1$), the standard deviation is estimated by the standard errors of the regression coefficients:

$$\hat{\sigma}_{\beta_0} = \sqrt{\frac{\sum\limits_{i=1}^{N} x_{1,i}^2}{N^2 \hat{\sigma}_{x_1}^2}} \, \hat{\sigma}_\varepsilon \tag{A.9}$$

and

$$\hat{\sigma}_{\beta_1} = \sqrt{\frac{1}{N \hat{\sigma}_{x_1}^2}} \, \hat{\sigma}_\varepsilon \tag{A.10}$$

where

$$\hat{\sigma}_\varepsilon = \sqrt{\sum\limits_{i=1}^{N} \hat{\varepsilon}_i^2 / (N - 2)} \tag{A.11}$$

is the standard error of regression. Under the maintained assumptions, this statistic serves as an unbiased estimator for the (unknown) standard deviation of errors σ_ε.[4] Related to this, the standard errors of the regression coefficients are unbiased estimators of the standard deviations of the regression coefficients.

---

[4] By dividing by $N - 2$ rather than N, we improve the statistical properties of the estimator. In statistical terms, the estimator is an unbiased estimator of σ_ε. Although this may seem counterintuitive, dividing by $N - 2$ is required because the true regression coefficients (β_0, β_1) are not known and estimating them by $(\hat{\beta}_0, \hat{\beta}_1)$ effectively reduces the number of observations left for estimating σ_ε from N to $N - 2$. Still, for large samples, it generally does not matter whether we divide by N or by $(N - 2)$, as $(N - 2)/N$ then converges to one.

The standard errors $\hat{\sigma}_{\hat{\beta}_0}$ and $\hat{\sigma}_{\hat{\beta}_1}$ measure the accuracy of the regression estimates $\hat{\beta}_0$ and $\hat{\beta}_1$. As a rule of thumb, in large samples, we can state with about 95% confidence that the true value of the intercept β_0 lies between a value of $\hat{\beta}_0 - 2\hat{\sigma}_{\hat{\beta}_0}$ and a value of $\hat{\beta}_0 + 2\hat{\sigma}_{\hat{\beta}_0}$. Put differently, there is a 5% probability that the estimates will lie outside this interval. The interval is known as the 95% confidence interval.[5] Similarly, the 95% confidence interval for the slope β_1 ranges from $\hat{\beta}_1 - 2\hat{\sigma}_{\hat{\beta}_1}$ to $\hat{\beta}_1 + 2\hat{\sigma}_{\hat{\beta}_1}$. The smaller the standard error of the regression coefficients, the smaller the interval and, hence, the more confident we are about the true value of the regression coefficients.

From Equations A.9 and A.10, we can infer the following determinants of the goodness of regression coefficients:

- The standard errors are smaller if the standard error of regression $\hat{\sigma}_{\varepsilon}$ is smaller. Hence, to obtain reliable estimates, we should make sure that no relevant regressors are excluded from the model and that the regressand is measured accurately (omitted variables and measurement errors are two sources of error).
- The standard errors are smaller if the sample size (N) is larger (provided all observations satisfy the above assumptions). In fact, if the data set is sufficiently large, then the standard errors equal zero and the estimators exactly equal the true parameters. Consequently, we should use the largest possible data set in order to obtain the most accurate estimates. Of course, enlarging the data set is recommended only if the data are of high quality and do not contain additional errors.
- The standard errors are smaller if the sample variance of the regressor $\hat{\sigma}_{x_1}^2$ is larger. Therefore, to improve the goodness of regression estimates, we need to find observations with the largest possible spread. Roughly speaking, it is better to include observations for which the regressor is far away from the mean than observations for which the regressor is close to the mean. Again, this recommendation assumes that all other things are equal and, hence, that the observations are of equal quality. This assumption is not valid if we have reasons to doubt the accuracy of extreme observations, such as observations during market crashes, when asset prices may be determined by panic rather than economic reasoning.

Again, for multiple regressions, the expressions are more complex in case of multicollinearity. In this case, there is a fourth determinant: the degree of mutual correlation between the regressors or multicollinearity. The standard errors are smaller if the correlation is weaker. If the regressors are correlated strongly, then it is 'difficult' to disentangle their effects. Perfect multicollinearity occurs if there exists an exact linear relationship between two or more regressors. In this case, it is impossible to compute the regression coefficients.

For our example of Microsoft stocks, the estimate for alpha was $\hat{\alpha}_{Micro} = 1.248$. How reliable is this estimate? To answer this question, we compute the standard error. In this case, the standard error of alpha is $\hat{\sigma}_{\hat{\alpha}_{Micro}} = 0.877$. Hence, we can state with 95% confidence that Microsoft's true alpha ranges from $1.248 - 2 \times 0.877 = -0.506$ to $1.248 + 2 \times 0.877 = 3.002$. Similarly, the standard error of Microsoft's beta is $\hat{\sigma}_{\hat{\beta}_{Micro}} = 0.216$ and a 95% confidence interval for beta ranges from $1.535 - 2 \times 0.216 = 1.103$ to $1.535 + 2 \times 0.216 = 1.967$. Clearly, the estimates

---

[5] The value '2' roughly equals the critical value of Student's t-distribution (see below) for a two-sided hypothesis, a significance level of 5% (or a confidence level of 95%), and a large number of observations relative to the number of regressors. In this case, the exact number is 1.96. For 90% and 99% confidence, the values are 1.65 and 2.48, respectively. In general, to determine the exact confidence interval associated with a significance level of α (or a confidence level of $1 - \alpha$), we need to find the critical value associated with a P value of $\alpha/2$ and a number of degrees of freedom that equals the number of observations (N) minus the number of regressors (k).

are not very accurate. Unfortunately, this degree of inaccuracy is typical for estimating the characteristic line for individual assets. The problem is that the returns on individual assets are determined to a large extent by asset-specific factors, which makes it difficult to estimate the contribution of market risk.[6] Unfortunately, there is no simple remedy for this problem. The above discussion suggests that we could improve the accuracy by including omitted variables, measuring the market return with higher precision or include additional observations, preferably for months where the market return was very high or very low. Unfortunately, none of these suggestions is very useful in this case. First, the characteristic line by definition includes only a single regressor (the market return) and, hence, there are no omitted variables. Second, the data are taken from a very reliable source, the CRSP data set and, hence, measurement errors are highly unlikely. Third, in principle we could extend the data set to include, for example, another 120 monthly observations. However, that also introduces additional errors, as the alpha and beta of a firm's stock can change substantially through time as the firm's assets and liabilities change. Therefore, it is frequently recommended for estimating characteristic lines not to use data beyond the most recent ten years.

A.5 Statistical inference and hypothesis tests

Often, economic theory will forward the null hypothesis (H_0) that certain regression coefficients should take on particular values or values within a given range. For example, the CAPM predicts that the alphas of all assets equal zero. Regression analysis is used frequently for testing whether the data support such predictions.

Under the maintained assumptions, the estimators $\hat{\beta}_0, \hat{\beta}_1, \ldots, \hat{\beta}_k$ are unbiased, but they still involve uncertainty. Hence, we cannot tell with full confidence from the estimators whether the true regression coefficients satisfy the null hypothesis. However, since the statistical distribution of the estimators is known, we can perform statistical inference; that is, we can make probabilistic statements about whether the hypothesis is true. Hypothesis tests generally use a test statistic that indicates the degree to which the estimation results violate the null hypothesis. They then derive the statistical distribution of the test statistic under the assumption that the null hypothesis is correct. From this null distribution, we compute the so-called probability of exceedance, or P-value. The P-value gives the probability that the test statistic takes a value that is equal to or greater than the observed value if the hypothesis was true. If this probability becomes very small, then we may question the hypothesis. After all, the test statistic then takes an improbable value given the null.

For example, consider the simplest possible case of a coin-flipping experiment. There are two outcomes to flipping a coin: heads or tails.[7] To test the null hypothesis that these outcomes are equally likely to occur, we could flip a coin 100 times and compute the number of tails flipped.[8] If the null hypothesis is true, then we expect the number of tails to be 50. Suppose that the actual number is 60. If the null hypothesis is true, then outcomes where the actual number of tails flipped is greater than or equal to 60 are unlikely to occur; the P-value in this case is about 3%.

---

[6] For portfolios, the problem generally is less severe, because asset-specific returns of individual assets cancel out in the context of a portfolio.

[7] We don't normally deal with the other two possibilities: flipping the coin so it lands on its edge, which is very hard to do, and flipping the coin so quickly that it gains orbit – even more difficult to accomplish.

[8] The number of tails flipped is a random variable that follows a so-called binomial distribution.

What conclusion can we draw from the P-value? In the coin-flipping experiment, does a P-value of 3% mean that the coin is biased towards tails? Or do we need a lower P-value? To answer this question, we have to trade off two possible errors:

- We may wrongly reject H_0 if it is true (a type I error).
- We may wrongly not reject H_0 if it is not true (a type II error).

The P-value gives the probability of making a type I error. Hence, rejecting the null only if the P-value equals zero minimises type I error. However, this comes at the cost of additional type II error. Hence, the correct interpretation of the P-value depends on the relative importance that we assign to wrongly rejecting the null if it is true (a type I error) and wrongly not rejecting the null if it is not true (a type II error). To strike this balance, we need to specify a significance level α. The significance level is the maximum acceptable frequency of type I error (wrongly reject the null if it is true). In practice, the significance level typically is set at a value between 1 and 10%. The complement of the significance level, that is, $1 - \alpha$, is referred to as the confidence level. If we reject the null if the P-value falls below α, then we can be at least $1 - \alpha\%$ confident about our conclusion. In the coin-flipping experiment, we can reject the null hypothesis that heads and tails are equally likely to occur against the alternative hypothesis that tails are more likely to occur than heads at a significance level of 3%, or a confidence level of 97%. This means that there is a 3% probability that we have wrongly rejected the null (heads and tails are equally likely).

An equivalent approach uses critical values. The critical value associated with significance level α is the value that the test statistic should take such that the P-value equals α. Hence, if the actual value of the test statistic exceeds the critical value associated with significance level α, then the actual P-value will be smaller than α and we can reject the null hypothesis with at least $1 - \alpha\%$ confidence. For example, in the coin-flipping experiment, we can show that that the critical value for a 10% significance level is about 56; there is a 10% probability that the number of tails is greater than or equal to 56 (if the null is true). Since the actual number of tails flipped (60) exceeds the critical value (56), we can reject the null with at least 90% confidence.

T-test for hypotheses about a single parameter

The simplest possible hypothesis deals with a single regression coefficient. One possibility is to test the hypothesis that the coefficient β_i is smaller than or equal to some value b or $H_0 : \beta_i \leq b$. This hypothesis would be rejected if the estimate $\hat{\beta}_i$ takes a value that is significantly larger than b. To determine whether the hypothesis is violated, we can compute the so-called t-statistic:

$$T = \frac{\hat{\beta}_i - b}{\hat{\sigma}_{\beta_i}} \qquad (A.12)$$

This statistic measures the deviation of the estimated regression coefficient $\hat{\beta}_i$ from the hypothesised value b, standardised by the standard error of the regression coefficient $\hat{\sigma}_{\beta_i}$.

Similarly, we can test the hypothesis that the coefficient β_i is greater than or equal to b or $H_0 : \beta_i \geq b$ by computing the t-statistic

$$T = \frac{b - \hat{\beta}_i}{\hat{\sigma}_{\beta_i}} \qquad (A.13)$$

These two hypotheses are one-sided hypotheses: the hypotheses are rejected if the estimate $\hat{\beta}_i$ takes a value that is either significantly larger than b (the first hypothesis) or significantly smaller than b (the second hypothesis). In some cases, we may wish to test whether β_i is equal to b or $H_0 : \beta_i = b$. This is a two-sided hypothesis: the hypothesis would be rejected if the estimate $\hat{\beta}_i$ takes a value that is significantly larger or significantly smaller than b. In these cases, the following t-statistic applies:

$$T = \left| \frac{\hat{\beta}_i - b}{\hat{\sigma}_{\hat{\beta}_i}} \right| \tag{A.14}$$

By taking the absolute value of the standardised deviation, this test statistic has a positive value also if the deviation is negative ($\beta_i < b$).

Under the assumptions made in Section A.4, the t-statistics A.12, A.13 and A.14 behave as random variables with a so-called Student t-distribution with $(N - k - 1)$ degrees of freedom (the number of observations minus the unknown regression coefficients).[9] We may test the hypothesis by comparing the P-values for observed values of the t-statistic with the desired significance level. Alternatively, we may compare the value of the t-statistic with the critical value associated with the desired significance level (α).

As a rule of thumb, in large samples and for a two-sided hypothesis, if the t-statistic is higher than 2, then the P-value is smaller than 2.5%, and we may reject the null hypothesis at the significance level of 2.5%, or a confidence level of 97.5 %. For other significance levels and/or for small samples, we can find the critical value from Exhibit A.3. Note that this table assumes that the hypothesis is one-sided. For two-sided hypotheses, the P-value is twice the P-value of a one-sided hypothesis. Similarly, the critical value is found by using $\alpha/2$ rather than α for the significance level. These corrections are needed because we reject a two-sided hypothesis if the estimated value is significantly greater or significantly smaller than the critical value; this doubles the probability of rejecting the null.

To illustrate the t-test, we apply it to our example of Microsoft stocks. We will consider the two-sided hypothesis that the beta equals one (the average market beta across all assets). The estimated value of beta equals 1.535, which is substantially greater than one. Does this mean that we can reject the null hypothesis that alpha equals zero and that the beta equals one if we use a 95% confidence level? To answer this question, we first compute the t-statistic by inserting $\hat{\beta}_{Micro} = 1.535$, $b = 1$ and $\hat{\sigma}_{\hat{\beta}_{Micro}} = 0.216$ in Equation A.14:

$$T = \left| \frac{\hat{\beta}_{Micro} - b}{\hat{\sigma}_{\hat{\beta}_{Micro}}} \right| = \left| \frac{1.535 - 1}{0.216} \right| \cong 2.48$$

Next, we determine the critical value of the t-distribution by entering the column with $\alpha = 0.05/2 = 0.025$ (the significance level) and the row with $(N - k - 1) = 118$ (the number of degrees of freedom). The relevant value in this case is 1.98. Since the observed value of the t-statistic 2.48 exceeds the critical value 1.98, we can reject the hypothesis that beta equals one with at least 95% confidence. Hence, although Microsoft's beta is estimated with a low degree of accuracy, we can be confident that Microsoft stocks are aggressive; their beta is significantly greater than one.

---

[9] The t-distribution was first published by William Gosset in 1908. His employer, Guinness Breweries, required him to publish under a pseudonym, so he chose 'Student'. Note that there is a different t-distribution for each sample size; in other words, it is a class of distributions. When we speak of a specific t-distribution, we have to specify the degrees of freedom, which is the number of observations minus the unknown regression coefficients. The t-density curves are symmetric and bell-shaped like the normal distribution and have their peak at zero. However, the spread (kurtosis) is more than that of the standard normal distribution; the distribution has 'fat tails'. The larger the degrees of freedom, the closer the t-density is to the normal density.

Exhibit A.3	Table of the Student's t-distribution (one-sided hypothesis)					
dfs ($N-k-1$)	$\alpha = 0.1$	$\alpha = 0.05$	$\alpha = 0.025$	$\alpha = 0.01$	$\alpha = 0.005$	$\alpha = 0.0025$
1	3.078	6.314	12.706	31.821	63.656	127.321
2	1.886	2.920	4.303	6.965	9.925	14.089
3	1.638	2.353	3.182	4.541	5.841	7.453
4	1.533	2.132	2.776	3.747	4.604	5.598
5	1.476	2.015	2.571	3.365	4.032	4.773
6	1.440	1.943	2.447	3.143	3.707	4.317
7	1.415	1.895	2.365	2.998	3.499	4.029
8	1.397	1.860	2.306	2.896	3.355	3.833
9	1.383	1.833	2.262	2.821	3.250	3.690
10	1.372	1.812	2.228	2.764	3.169	3.581
11	1.363	1.796	2.201	2.718	3.106	3.497
12	1.356	1.782	2.179	2.681	3.055	3.428
13	1.350	1.771	2.160	2.650	3.012	3.372
14	1.345	1.761	2.145	2.624	2.977	3.326
15	1.341	1.753	2.131	2.602	2.947	3.286
16	1.337	1.746	2.120	2.583	2.921	3.252
17	1.333	1.740	2.110	2.567	2.898	3.222
18	1.330	1.734	2.101	2.552	2.878	3.197
19	1.328	1.729	2.093	2.539	2.861	3.174
20	1.325	1.725	2.086	2.528	2.845	3.153
30	1.310	1.697	2.042	2.457	2.750	3.030
40	1.303	1.684	2.021	2.423	2.704	2.971
50	1.299	1.676	2.009	2.403	2.678	2.937
100	1.290	1.660	1.984	2.364	2.626	2.871
200	1.286	1.653	1.972	2.345	2.601	2.838
500	1.283	1.648	1.965	2.334	2.586	2.820
10 000	1.282	1.645	1.960	2.327	2.576	2.808

To find a critical value, enter the column with the appropriate significance level α and the row with the appropriate degrees of freedom ($N-k-1$). For example, the critical value for $\alpha = 0.05$ and ($N-k-1$) = 15 is 1.753. Note that the table assumes a one-sided hypothesis. For two-sided hypotheses, we need to use $\alpha/2$. Returning to the example, the critical value for a two-sided hypothesis with $\alpha = 0.05$ and ($N-k-1$) = 15 is 2.131. This table is generated using MS Excel spreadsheet software.

Similarly, we can test whether the alpha of Microsoft equals zero, as the CAPM predicts. In this case, the t-statistic is

$$T = \left| \frac{\hat{\alpha}_{Micro} - b}{\hat{\sigma}_{\hat{\alpha}_{Micro}}} \right| = \left| \frac{1.248 - 0}{0.877} \right| \cong 1.42$$

which is smaller then 1.98. Hence, we cannot reject the null that Microsoft is priced correctly.

A special case of the t-test occurs if we test the hypothesis that a parameter equals zero, i.e. $H_0 : \beta_i = 0$. If this hypothesis is rejected, then we conclude that the regressor has significant value for explaining the regressand; if the hypothesis is not rejected, the regressor has no significant explanatory value. This (two-sided) hypothesis can be tested using

$$T = \left| \frac{\hat{\beta}_i}{\hat{\sigma}_{\hat{\beta}_i}} \right|$$

This so-called t-value and/or the associated P-value is included in the standard output of most statistical software, and it is reported as standard output in empirical studies.

F-test for hypotheses about multiple regression coefficients

The t-test is useful for testing a single hypothesis about a single regression coefficient. However, it generally cannot be used for testing multiple hypotheses or hypotheses about multiple regression coefficients. A possible example is the joint hypothesis $H_0 : \beta_0 = 0$ and $\beta_1 = 1$. For example, we may wish to test whether the alpha of Microsoft stock equals zero and the beta equals one. At first sight, it seems that we can deal with this joint hypothesis simply by performing two separate t-tests; one for the hypothesis $H_0 : \beta_0 = 0$ and one for the hypothesis $H_0 : \beta_1 = 1$. However, this approach can yield erroneous conclusions. The problem is that the t-test accounts for the variability of the estimators, but not for their interdependence. The probability that two estimators exceed a critical value is larger (smaller) if the two estimators are correlated positively (negatively) than if they are uncorrelated. For example, if Microsoft stocks exhibited an extremely large return during a month when the market went up, then this return will increase both the alpha and the beta of Microsoft. The t-test does not account for such interdependencies. For testing hypotheses about multiple regression coefficients, we may use the so-called F-test.

Basically, the F-test checks whether R^2 decreases by a significant amount if we force the estimated regression coefficients to obey the restriction from the hypothesis. Recall from the discussion above that the OLS estimators are selected to maximise R^2. Hence, imposing restrictions on the estimators generally lowers R^2. However, if the hypothesis is correct, then we would expect only minimal changes to R^2.

If we impose the restrictions from the null hypothesis $H_0 : \beta_0 = 0$ and $\beta_1 = 1$ on the unrestricted model, then we obtain the following restricted model:

$$y = x_1 + \beta_2 x_2 + \ldots + \beta_k x_k + \varepsilon$$

The R^2 of this model is necessarily lower than or equal to the R^2 for the unrestricted model. The unrestricted model can set $\hat{\beta}_0 = 0$ and $\hat{\beta}_1 = 1$, and then both models have the same R^2. However, the unrestricted model can also select estimators (if any) that yield a higher value for R^2. The F-test tests whether the decrease of R^2 is sufficiently large to reject the null. The test statistic is the following standardised change of R^2:

$$F = \frac{(R_U^2 - R_R^2)/h}{(1 - R_U^2)/(N - k - 1)} \tag{A.15}$$

where R_U^2 is the R-squared for the model without restrictions, R_R^2 is the R-squared for the model with restrictions, N is the number of observations, h is the number of restrictions and k is the number of regressors.

Under the null hypothesis, the F-statistic is a random variable with a so-called f-distribution with h degrees of freedom for the numerator and $(N - k - 1)$ degrees of freedom for the denominator.[10] We can test hypotheses by comparing the P-value associated with the observed value of the test statistic with the desired level of significance.[11] Equivalently, we may compare the actual value of the F-statistic with the critical value associated with the desired significance level (α) and reject the null if the actual value exceeds the critical value. Exhibit A.4 gives the critical values for different values for the significance level (α), the number of hypotheses (h), the sample size (N) and the number of coefficients (k).

---

[10] Note that there is a different F-distribution for different numbers of observations (N), regression coefficients (k) and hypotheses (h).

[11] The F-test is always one-sided, because imposing restrictions cannot increase the R-squared.

Exhibit A.4   Table of the *F*-distribution

| | $\alpha = 0.10$ | | | | | $\alpha = 0.05$ | | | | |
($N - k - 1$)	$h=1$	$h=2$	$h=3$	$h=4$	$h=5$	$h=1$	$h=2$	$h=3$	$h=4$	$h=5$
1	39.86	49.50	53.59	55.83	57.24	161	199	216	225	230
2	8.53	9.00	9.16	9.24	9.29	18.51	19.00	19.16	19.25	19.30
3	5.54	5.46	5.39	5.34	5.31	10.13	9.55	9.28	9.12	9.01
4	4.54	4.32	4.19	4.11	4.05	7.71	6.94	6.59	6.39	6.26
5	4.06	3.78	3.62	3.52	3.45	6.61	5.79	5.41	5.19	5.05
6	3.78	3.46	3.29	3.18	3.11	5.99	5.14	4.76	4.53	4.39
7	3.59	3.26	3.07	2.96	2.88	5.59	4.74	4.35	4.12	3.97
8	3.46	3.11	2.92	2.81	2.73	5.32	4.46	4.07	3.84	3.69
9	3.36	3.01	2.81	2.69	2.61	5.12	4.26	3.86	3.63	3.48
10	3.29	2.92	2.73	2.61	2.52	4.96	4.10	3.71	3.48	3.33
11	3.23	2.86	2.66	2.54	2.45	4.84	3.98	3.59	3.36	3.20
12	3.18	2.81	2.61	2.48	2.39	4.75	3.89	3.49	3.26	3.11
13	3.14	2.76	2.56	2.43	2.35	4.67	3.81	3.41	3.18	3.03
14	3.10	2.73	2.52	2.39	2.31	4.60	3.74	3.34	3.11	2.96
15	3.07	2.70	2.49	2.36	2.27	4.54	3.68	3.29	3.06	2.90
16	3.05	2.67	2.46	2.33	2.24	4.49	3.63	3.24	3.01	2.85
17	3.03	2.64	2.44	2.31	2.22	4.45	3.59	3.20	2.96	2.81
18	3.01	2.62	2.42	2.29	2.20	4.41	3.55	3.16	2.93	2.77
19	2.99	2.61	2.40	2.27	2.18	4.38	3.52	3.13	2.90	2.74
20	2.97	2.59	2.38	2.25	2.16	4.35	3.49	3.10	2.87	2.71
30	2.88	2.49	2.28	2.14	2.05	4.17	3.32	2.92	2.69	2.53
40	2.84	2.44	2.23	2.09	2.00	4.08	3.23	2.84	2.61	2.45
50	2.81	2.41	2.20	2.06	1.97	4.03	3.18	2.79	2.56	2.40
100	2.76	2.36	2.14	2.00	1.91	3.94	3.09	2.70	2.46	2.31
200	2.73	2.33	2.11	1.97	1.88	3.89	3.04	2.65	2.42	2.26
500	2.72	2.31	2.09	1.96	1.86	3.86	3.01	2.62	2.39	2.23
10 000	2.71	2.30	2.08	1.95	1.85	3.84	3.00	2.61	2.37	2.21

| | $\alpha = 0.025$ | | | | | $\alpha = 0.01$ | | | | |
($N - k - 1$)	$h=1$	$h=2$	$h=3$	$h=4$	$h=5$	$h=1$	$h=2$	$h=3$	$h=4$	$h=5$
1	647.8	799.5	864.2	899.6	921.8	4052	4999	5404	5624	5764
2	38.51	39.00	39.17	39.25	39.30	98.50	99.00	99.16	99.25	99.30
3	17.44	16.04	15.44	15.10	14.88	34.12	30.82	29.46	28.71	28.24
4	12.22	10.65	9.98	9.60	9.36	21.20	18.00	16.69	15.98	15.52
5	10.01	8.43	7.76	7.39	7.15	16.26	13.27	12.06	11.39	10.97
6	8.81	7.26	6.60	6.23	5.99	13.75	10.92	9.78	9.15	8.75
7	8.07	6.54	5.89	5.52	5.29	12.25	9.55	8.45	7.85	7.46
8	7.57	6.06	5.42	5.05	4.82	11.26	8.65	7.59	7.01	6.63
9	7.21	5.71	5.08	4.72	4.48	10.56	8.02	6.99	6.42	6.06
10	6.94	5.46	4.83	4.47	4.24	10.04	7.56	6.55	5.99	5.64
11	6.72	5.26	4.63	4.28	4.04	9.65	7.21	6.22	5.67	5.32
12	6.55	5.10	4.47	4.12	3.89	9.33	6.93	5.95	5.41	5.06
13	6.41	4.97	4.35	4.00	3.77	9.07	6.70	5.74	5.21	4.86
14	6.30	4.86	4.24	3.89	3.66	8.86	6.51	5.56	5.04	4.69
15	6.20	4.77	4.15	3.80	3.58	8.68	6.36	5.42	4.89	4.56
16	6.12	4.69	4.08	3.73	3.50	8.53	6.23	5.29	4.77	4.44
17	6.04	4.62	4.01	3.66	3.44	8.40	6.11	5.19	4.67	4.34
18	5.98	4.56	3.95	3.61	3.38	8.29	6.01	5.09	4.58	4.25
19	5.92	4.51	3.90	3.56	3.33	8.18	5.93	5.01	4.50	4.17
20	5.87	4.46	3.86	3.51	3.29	8.10	5.85	4.94	4.43	4.10
30	5.57	4.18	3.59	3.25	3.03	7.56	5.39	4.51	4.02	3.70

| Exhibit A.4 | continued |

	$\alpha = 0.025$					$\alpha = 0.01$				
$(N-k-1)$	$h=1$	$h=2$	$h=3$	$h=4$	$h=5$	$h=1$	$h=2$	$h=3$	$h=4$	$h=5$
40	5.42	4.05	3.46	3.13	2.90	7.31	5.18	4.31	3.83	3.51
50	5.34	3.97	3.39	3.05	2.83	7.17	5.06	4.20	3.72	3.41
100	5.18	3.83	3.25	2.92	2.70	6.90	4.82	3.98	3.51	3.21
200	5.10	3.76	3.18	2.85	2.63	6.76	4.71	3.88	3.41	3.11
500	5.05	3.72	3.14	2.81	2.59	6.69	4.65	3.82	3.36	3.05
10 000	5.03	3.69	3.12	2.79	2.57	6.64	4.61	3.78	3.32	3.02

	$\alpha = 0.005$					$\alpha = 0.0025$				
$(N-k-1)$	$h=1$	$h=2$	$h=3$	$h=4$	$h=5$	$h=1$	$h=2$	$h=3$	$h=4$	$h=5$
1	16 212	19 997	21 614	22 501	23 056	64 850	79 989	86 457	90 003	92 208
2	198.5	199.0	199.2	199.2	199.3	398.5	399.0	399.2	399.3	399.3
3	55.55	49.80	47.47	46.20	45.39	89.58	79.93	76.06	73.95	72.62
4	31.33	26.28	24.26	23.15	22.46	45.67	38.00	34.95	33.30	32.26
5	22.78	18.31	16.53	15.56	14.94	31.41	24.96	22.42	21.05	20.18
6	18.63	14.54	12.92	12.03	11.46	24.81	19.10	16.87	15.65	14.88
7	16.24	12.40	10.88	10.05	9.52	21.11	15.89	13.84	12.73	12.03
8	14.69	11.04	9.60	8.81	8.30	18.78	13.89	11.98	10.94	10.28
9	13.61	10.11	8.72	7.96	7.47	17.19	12.54	10.73	9.74	9.12
10	12.83	9.43	8.08	7.34	6.87	16.04	11.57	9.83	8.89	8.29
11	12.23	8.91	7.60	6.88	6.42	15.17	10.85	9.17	8.25	7.67
12	11.75	8.51	7.23	6.52	6.07	14.49	10.29	8.65	7.76	7.20
13	11.37	8.19	6.93	6.23	5.79	13.95	9.84	8.24	7.37	6.82
14	11.06	7.92	6.68	6.00	5.56	13.50	9.47	7.91	7.06	6.51
15	10.80	7.70	6.48	5.80	5.37	13.13	9.17	7.63	6.80	6.26
16	10.58	7.51	6.30	5.64	5.21	12.82	8.92	7.40	6.58	6.05
17	10.38	7.35	6.16	5.50	5.07	12.55	8.70	7.21	6.39	5.87
18	10.22	7.21	6.03	5.37	4.96	12.32	8.51	7.04	6.23	5.72
19	10.07	7.09	5.92	5.27	4.85	12.12	8.35	6.89	6.09	5.58
20	9.94	6.99	5.82	5.17	4.76	11.94	8.21	6.76	5.97	5.46
30	9.18	6.35	5.24	4.62	4.23	10.89	7.36	6.00	5.25	4.78
40	8.83	6.07	4.98	4.37	3.99	10.41	6.99	5.66	4.93	4.47
50	8.63	5.90	4.83	4.23	3.85	10.14	6.77	5.47	4.75	4.30
100	8.24	5.59	4.54	3.96	3.59	9.62	6.37	5.11	4.42	3.97
200	8.06	5.44	4.41	3.84	3.47	9.38	6.17	4.94	4.26	3.82
500	7.95	5.35	4.33	3.76	3.40	9.23	6.06	4.84	4.17	3.73
10 000	7.88	5.30	4.28	3.72	3.35	9.15	6.00	4.78	4.11	3.68

To find a critical value, first find in the table the appropriate significance level α. Subsequently, find the column with the appropriate number of degrees of freedom for the numerator (h) and the row with the appropriate degrees of freedom for the denominator ($N - k - 1$). For example, the critical value for $\alpha = 0.05$, $h = 2$ and $(N - k - 1) = 15$ equals 3.68. This table is generated using MS Excel spreadsheet software.

For our example, the R-squared of the unrestricted model is 29.9%. If we impose the restriction that the alpha equals zero and that the beta equals one, then the R-squared drops to 26.3%. Does this mean that we can reject the null hypothesis that alpha equals zero and beta equals one if we use a 95% confidence level? To answer this question, we first compute the F-statistic by inserting $R_U^2 = 29.9\%$, $R_R^2 = 26.3\%$, $N = 120$ (the number of observations), $h = 2$ (the number of hypotheses) and $k = 1$ (the number of slope coefficients) in Equation A.15:

$$F = \frac{(29.9\% - 26.3\%)/2}{(1 - 29.9\%)/(120 - 1 - 1)} = 3.03$$

Next, we determine the critical value of the f-distribution by finding in the table with $\alpha = 0.05$ (the significance level), the column with $h = 2$ and the row with $(N - k - 1) = 118$. The relevant value in this case is 3.07. Since the observed value of the F-statistic (3.03) is smaller than the critical value (3.07), we cannot reject the hypothesis that alpha equals zero and beta equals one with 95% confidence. Given the fact that we did reject the simple hypothesis that beta equals one with a t-test (see the previous section), this result may seem surprising. If we reject the null that beta equals one, then doesn't it logically imply that we must also reject the null that beta equals one and alpha equals zero? The answer is no. In regression analysis, we generally do not reject hypotheses based on logic (that is extremely difficult due to estimation error); rather, we ask whether we can reject a hypothesis with a particular degree of confidence (in our case 95%). The point is that in computing confidence levels for a joint hypothesis, we have to account for the dependency between the estimators. Simple t-tests do not do this and, hence, may lead to wrong conclusions about the confidence levels for joint hypotheses.

A special case occurs if we test $H_0: \beta_1 = \ldots = \beta_k = 0$, i.e. the null hypothesis that none of the regressors has any explanatory value. This null is equivalent to testing whether R^2 is significantly different from zero. In this case, $R_R^2 = 0$, and the F-statistic reduces to

$$F = \frac{R_U^2/h}{(1 - R_U^2)/(N - k - 1)}$$

Again, this statistic and the associated P-value are included in the standard output of most statistical software and are reported as standard output in empirical studies.

A.6   Standard regression output

Regression analysis can be performed using any of a number of statistical packages. We will use the popular statistical software package called EViews to demonstrate the use of regression to calculate the beta of Microsoft.[12] We begin by opening the workfile that includes the data set, say 'EViews Regression.wf1.'[13] The window shown in Exhibit A.5 will appear.

In the upper left-hand corner, the workfile lists four icons (labelled 'c', 'ffm', 'micro' and 'resid'). These icons are links to spreadsheets containing the variables in the data set, in our case the returns on Microsoft ('micro') and the market ('ffm'), as well as two variables ('c' and 'resid') that EViews creates automatically in the event that the researcher wants to use them in a subsequent analysis, namely the coefficient estimates ('c') and the regression residuals ('resid').

To estimate a new regression equation in EViews, click 'Objects' and then 'New Objects.' Under the heading 'Type of object', select 'Equation.' The window shown in Exhibit A.6 will then appear.

---

[12] For information on how to purchase EViews software or to learn more about the most recently released version, visit www.eviews.com. For an elaborate step-by-step guide for regression using Eviews, see Seiler (2004) or go to www.prenhall.com/seiler

[13] An EViews workfile contains, among other things, the data set and the estimation and test results stored by the analyst. Workfiles are characterised by the extension .wf1. To keep the discussion compact, we assume that the data set is already included in the workfile. However, the analyst generally starts with an external data set, for example an MS Excel spreadsheet (with the extension .xls). In this case, the analyst first has to create a new EViews workfile and import the external data set into this workfile. The procedure for creating workfiles and importing data is described in the EViews help file as well as in Seiler (2004).

| Exhibit A.5 | Screenshot of the workfile 'EViews Regression.wf1' (I) |

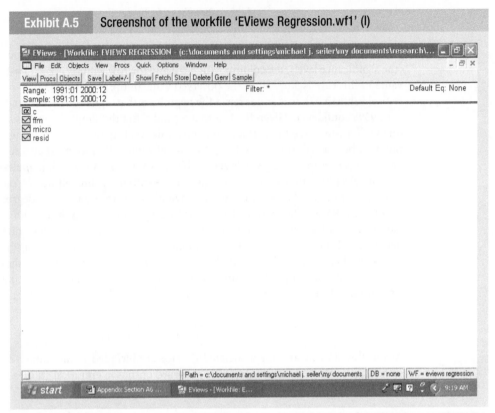

Source: Screenshot reprinted with permission from Microsoft Corporation.

Alternatively, you can reach this window by clicking 'Quick' and then 'Estimate Equation'. Under the box titled 'Equation specification,' you must convey to EViews the model you want to estimate. The dependent variable should be entered first, followed by the independent variables. EViews does not automatically include a constant in the equation, so if you wish to include one, you must enter the variable 'c' along with the independent variables. To measure the beta of Microsoft, we would specify the equation by entering the sequence 'micro c ffm'. Under the section titled 'Estimation settings,' we can leave the default values alone.[14] Click 'OK' to perform the regression. After maximising the resulting window, your screen should reveal the output shown in Exhibit A.7.

Most statistical software packages will yield similar output. Focusing on the results that are most relevant for this appendix, the interpretation of the output follows.[15] The coefficient

---

[14] The estimation settings allow for selecting the appropriate regression method. The default choice is ordinary last squares, the regression method discussed in this appendix. Also, we can select the sample of observations to be included in the analysis. Here, the default choice is the full sample.

[15] The interpretation of the remaining output is as follows. As discussed in Sections A.3 and A.4, the standard error of regression ('S.E. of regression') and the squares sum of residuals ('Sum squared resid') measure the goodness of fit of the estimated regression line. However, they are more difficult to interpret than R-squared, because they depend on the unit of measurement. The log likelihood measure is yet another goodness-of-fit measure: the smaller the value, the better the fit. The adjusted R-squared, Akaike criterion and Swartz criterion measure the trade-off between the goodness of fit and the number of variables included in the model. The Durbin–Watson statistic ('DW statistic') is a diagnostic test statistic for detecting serial correlation.

Exhibit A.6   Screenshot of the workfile 'EViews Regression.wf1' (II)

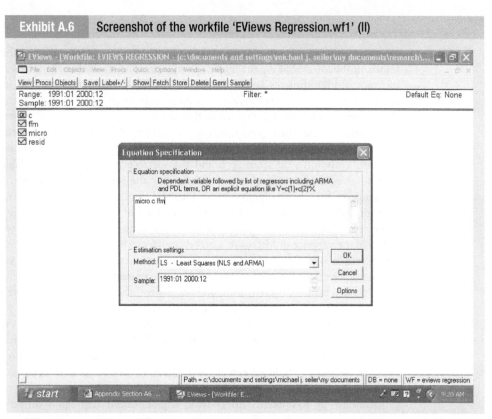

Source: Screenshot reprinted with permission from Microsoft Corporation.

Exhibit A.7   Screenshot of the workfile 'EViews Regression.wf1' (III)

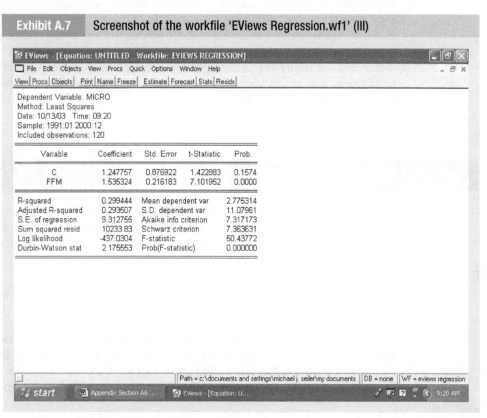

Source: Screenshot reprinted with permission from Microsoft Corporation.

estimates provide the best fit to the data set, where 'best fit' means that the regression line results in the lowest SSE or the highest R-squares. The standard errors measure the degree of accuracy of the estimates and allow for constructing confidence intervals for the regression coefficients. The *t*-value is the ratio of a coefficient estimate to the associated standard error. This is the relevant test statistic for testing the null hypothesis that the regression coefficient equals zero (or that the regressor has significant explanatory power). As a rule of thumb, for large sample sizes, we can reject the null if the *t*-value exceeds two. In this case, the coefficient is significantly different from zero and the variable has significant explanatory value. The *P*-value gives the exact level of significance for the same null hypothesis. In our example, we can reject the null that alpha equals zero at a significance level of 0.157, and we can reject the null that beta equals zero at a significance level of 0.001. (Note that this is not the earlier hypothesis that beta equals one.) The R-squared equals 0.299, or 29.9%, which means that 29.9% of the variance of Microsoft's excess return can be explained by variation in the market's excess return. The *F*-statistic tests the null hypothesis that the R-squared value equals zero. In general, this boils down to testing whether the regression coefficients of all regressors equal zero. In our example, there is only one regressor – the excess return on the market – so the null hypothesis reduces to the hypothesis that Microsoft's beta equals zero. For this reason, it is not surprising that we again find a *P*-value of almost zero, suggesting that we can be almost 100% certain that R-squared exceeds zero (and that beta is not equal to zero).

We stress that the coefficient estimates are meaningless if they are not complemented with the associated standard errors (or *t*-values or *P*-values) as indicators for the accuracy of the estimates. Also, we generally need to know the explanatory power of the regressors, as measured by R-squared. Apart from this standard regression output, it is generally recommended to include descriptive statistics that summarise the data set that was used to generate the regression output. How many observations were used? What was the variance of these variables? What was the correlation between these variables? It follows directly from our discussion in Section A.4 that the accuracy of regression results is determined by the answers to these questions. After all, we will not be surprised to find non-significant coefficients and failure to reject key hypotheses if the quality of data is poor (see Section A.7). In addition, it is generally recommended to include the outcome of diagnostic tests that determine whether the maintained assumptions of the OLS regression technique hold (see the next section).

A.7 Limitations of regression analysis

Regression analysis is a powerful statistical tool for uncovering and analysing economic relationships. Still, we stress that regression analysis is not a 'magical trick' that will automatically produce 'objective' or 'reliable' results. Basically, there are two types of limitations: poor data and methodological errors.

Poor data

Regression analysis aims to find the best possible estimators given the available data. If the data are of poor quality, then so will be the estimation results ('garbage in, garbage out'). Section A.4 discussed five assumptions that underlie OLS regression. We stress that these assumptions do not imply that the estimated regression coefficients are good. Rather, they imply that the estimators are the 'best' among a group of alternative estimators. How 'good' the 'best' is depends on the factors that were discussed in Section A.4: the importance of errors, the sample size and the sample distribution of the regressors. The conclusion we can draw is that the best guarantee for good results is to collect a high-quality data set. All other things remaining equal, 'high quality' is obtained by

- the largest possible data set;
- a data set that includes all relevant variables (minimal errors);
- the largest possible spread for the regressors;
- regressors that are mutually uncorrelated (no multicollinearity).

Another conclusion is that it is important when interpreting regression output to ask what data were used to generate the regression results. Again, we should not be surprised to find insignificant coefficients and failure to reject key hypotheses if the quality of data is low due to, for example, missing regressors, a small sample size, little variation for the regressors or a high correlation between the regressors.

Methodological errors

A high-quality data set is a prerequisite, but not a guarantee, for good results. In order to obtain good results, we must also use the appropriate estimation methodology. Different methodologies rely on different sets of assumptions about the relationship between the regressand and the regressor and about the statistical distribution of the error term. If the assumptions are incorrect, we will not use the information in the data set optimally. Hence, erroneous assumptions in the research methodology are a second limitation of regression analysis.

In this appendix, we restrict our attention to the OLS methodology. This methodology relies on the simplifying assumptions that were listed in Section A.4. These assumptions are convenient from a mathematical and statistical perspective. However, in many applications, the assumptions make little economic sense. Examples of violations of the assumptions of OLS regression include the following:

Functional specification error

OLS assumes that there exists a constant, linear relationship between the variables. This assumption is violated if the true relationship is non-linear, if the parameters change through time (in a time-series study) or if different objects involve different parameters (in a cross-section study). For example, the returns on bonds, especially bonds with a long maturity or a low coupon rate, generally are a non-linear function of interest rates ('the convexity effect'). In addition, the market beta of a stock changes over time if the financial leverage of the firm changes. Such functional specification errors are similar to omitting relevant regressors from the model. In this case, variables that capture the non-linear relationship or the changing parameters are omitted from the model. Omitting relevant variables generally lowers the goodness of fit relative to the fully specified model. The effect on the individual regression coefficients is difficult to assess in general, as it depends on, among other things, the correlation between omitted variables and the regressors that are included in the model. If the correlation is strong, then the regression coefficients generally are biased, because the effect of the omitted regressors will appear, wrongly, to be caused in part by the regressors that are included.

Heteroskedasticity

OLS assumes that all observations have the same error variance. Econometricians refer to this assumption as 'homoskedasticity'. Roughly speaking, it assumes that all observations are 'equally reliable' or contain an 'equal amount of information'. In some cases, this assumption is not realistic. For example, we may ask whether observations during stock-market crashes, such as the 1929 crash or the 1987 crash, are equally as reliable as 'regular observations'. During a crash, stock-market movements may reflect panic rather than a rational trade-off between risk and return. Similarly, the beta of a stock portfolio generally is more reliable if more stocks are included and if more observations are used to estimate the beta. Hence, heteroskedasticity occurs if we compare the beta of a poorly diversified portfolio that is evaluated over a short period with a well-diversified portfolio over a long period. In such cases, the errors are 'heteroskedastic'. OLS assigns an equal weight $(1/N)$ to all observations. This is not the most efficient way to extract information from the data if the observations are heteroskedastic.

Serial correlation

OLS assumes that there exists no correlation between the errors of the different observations (serial correlation). In other words, OLS assumes that every observation is completely unpredictable given the other observations and, hence, that the information in every observation is unique or not contained (in part or in whole) in the other observations. This assumption is violated in many cases. For example, serial correlation may occur if we compare the CAPM pricing errors of a set of assets from the same industry or the same country or, more generally, with a common exposure to non-market risk (exchange rates, interest rates, commodities prices, etc.). If we know that one asset from the set has a positive pricing error, for example due to a favourable change of exchange rates, then the other assets from the set can also be expected to yield abnormal returns. OLS assigns an equal weight to all observations. This is not the most efficient way to extract information from the data if the information that is contained in one observation is already included (in part or in whole) in the other observations.

Errors in variables

OLS treats the regressors as given (non-stochastic). This is reflected by the fact that OLS measures goodness by the vertical deviations from the regression line or the deviations of the regressand from the predicted value given the regressors. Unfortunately, for many economic problems, the regressors are measured with error. For example, consider again the two-pass regression methodology that is commonly used to determine the empirical validity of the CAPM. The first-pass, time-series regression estimates the characteristic line of each asset by regressing historical returns of the assets on historical returns of the market portfolio. Unfortunately, the exact composition of the market portfolio is unknown, for example because there is no reliable information on the return and the relative market value of human capital and real estate. Hence, the historical returns of the market portfolio are measured with error. The second-pass, cross-section regression estimates the security market line (SML) by regressing the historical average returns of assets on market betas. Since the true beta is not known, the true values are proxied by the estimated values from the first-pass regression, which evidently contain estimation errors. For example, in our example, the estimate of Microsoft's beta was very inaccurate; the 95% confidence interval ranged from 1.103 to 1.967. Econometrically, such measurement errors can seriously reduce the goodness of OLS estimators. In terms of the second-pass regression, the procedure will 'confuse' measurement error for beta with pricing errors or deviations from the SML. Hence, the line that minimises the sum of both errors generally does not minimise the sum of pricing errors; i.e. give the best approximation to the SML. In fact, we can prove that this problem can yield a positive bias for the estimated intercept and a negative bias for the estimated slope, with the magnitude of the biases depending on the relative importance of errors in variables relative to other sources of deviations from the true regression line. Miller and Scholes (1972) showed by means of a well-controlled simulation experiment that this problem can lead to very misleading estimation results if we use individual assets. This is an important reason for using well-diversified benchmark portfolios rather than individual assets. For well-diversified portfolios, many of the errors in the beta estimates of individual assets cancel out and the portfolio betas are more accurate.

We stress that these problems are not exotic phenomena that are purely of academic interest to theoretical econometricians, but rather real-life phenomena encountered in many economic problems. If these problems occur, then the OLS estimators may not be the best possible estimators and, even worse, they may be poor estimators, even if the data are of high quality. Consequently, it is recommended in order to obtain good results to use your economic insight (from theory or practice) as well as econometric diagnostic tests to detect violations of the basic assumptions of OLS regression. If violations are detected, then you should correct these (for example, by transforming the regression equation or by using alternative estimation techniques). For more details on diagnostic tests and extensions of OLS regression, we recommend taking an advanced econometrics course or consulting a textbook on econometrics, for example Campbell *et al.* (1997), Johnson and Dinardo (1997), Kennedy (1998) or Pindyck and Rubinfeld (1998). These investments generally pay off, because they enable you to more efficiently and effectively extract information from the data you have available. Also, they will enable you to better judge the regression results generated by others. Do the results really reflect an economic phenomenon or are they merely caused by methodological errors? To answer this question, you must use your economic insight as well as econometric diagnostic tests.

Selected references

Campbell, J. Y., A. W. Lo and A. C. MacKinlay, 1997, *The Econometrics of Financial Markets*, Princeton, NJ: Princeton University Press.

Johnson, J. and J. Dinardo, 1997, *Econometric Methods*, New York: McGraw-Hill.

Kennedy, P., 1998, *A Guide to Econometrics*, Cambridge, MA: MIT Press.

Miller, M. H. and M. Scholes, 1972, 'Rate of Return in Relation to Risk: A Reexamination of Some Recent Findings'. In: M. C. Jensen, editor, *Studies in the Theory of Capital Markets*, New York: Praeger Publishers, pp. 47–78.

Pindyck, R. S. and D. L. Rubinfeld, 1998, *Econometric Models and Economic Forecasts*, New York: McGraw-Hill.

Seiler, M. J., 2004, *Performing Financial Studies: A Methodological Cookbook*, Upper Saddle River. NJ: Prentice Hall.

Excel spreadsheet applications

Spreadsheets represent an extremely flexible means by which to create almost any formula or methodology imaginable. For more common procedures, Excel offers preprogrammed functions, called 'add-ins', which allow the user to circumvent the need to create procedures from scratch. Some of the most common add-ins include Analysis ToolPak, Analysis ToolPak VBA, Conditional Sum Wizard, Euro Currency Tools, Internet Assistant VBA, Lookup Wizard and Solver. For more information on add-ins or to order Microsoft Office products, visit http://office.microsoft.com/home/default.aspx

In this appendix, the Office XP version of Excel is used to demonstrate its ability to solve the following common financial applications (the corresponding chapters of this book are shown in brackets):

- margin calculations (Chapter 3);
- mean–variance analysis (Chapter 8);
- estimating an asset's market beta using regression analysis (Chapter 10);
- performing event studies (Chapter 12);
- bond valuation and yield-to-maturity calculation (Chapter 13);
- duration and convexity calculation (Chapter 14);
- calculating the price of a stock (Chapter 15);
- option valuation (Chapter 20).

For more information on these and many additional financial applications, we refer to Benninga (2000), Jackson and Staunton (2001), Walkenbach (2001a, 2001b) and Seiler (2004). This appendix is based on the excellent treatment by Seiler (2004). To download and use the data sets used in this appendix, you should visit www.prenhall.com/seiler

B.1 Margin calculations

Margin trading, discussed in Chapter 3 of this book, involves the use of leverage to magnify the returns associated with an investment. In this section, we will present the calculations needed for an investor to understand the financial ramifications associated with buying on margin. Begin by opening the Excel file 'Margin Calculations' (Exhibit B.1).

Values in red are those that you should fill in. All other cells should not be typed over. In cells A1 and A2, we need to know the price you paid for each share and the number of shares purchased. In cells A3 and A4, we need to know basic information about the account you set up with your brokerage firm. Specifically, you should enter the initial and maintenance margin percentages.

Cell A6 informs you as to the amount of cash you will need to establish your starting position. In cell A7, we show just how far the stock's price can drop before you receive a dreaded margin call. Based on our assumptions, the stock price can fall to as low as $62.22

Exhibit B.1	Screenshot of Excel file 'Margin Calculations'

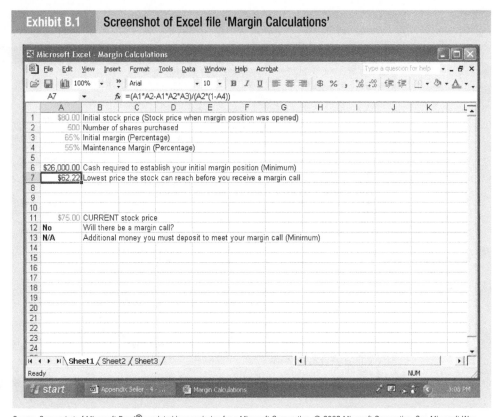

before you will have to deposit more money into your account. If the actual stock price falls below the minimum allowable stock price, you will want to know how much money you have to send to your broker. To answer this question, you need to enter the current stock price in cell A11. In cell A12, you will be informed as to whether this stock price will result in a margin call. In cell A13, you will be told exactly how much money you must send to your brokerage firm. If a margin call is not in effect, 'N/A' or 'not applicable' will be displayed.

B.2 Mean–variance analysis

As discussed in Chapter 8, mean–variance analysis is the most popular model for structuring investment decisions. It is used widely for applications of portfolio selection, performance evaluation and risk management. Among other things, it helps investors to select optimally diversified (or mean–variance-efficient) portfolios. The mean–variance-efficient frontier represents the set of portfolios that maximises the level of return for a given level of risk. At any point along the efficient frontier, optimal weights associated with each asset within the portfolio can be identified. Of course, every investor will potentially be at a different point along the efficient frontier, depending on his or her specific degree of risk-aversion.

The Excel file 'Mean-Variance Solver' demonstrates how to perform mean–variance analysis using Excel. The format used in this spreadsheet can easily be expanded to consider as many assets as you like. However, we have limited our spreadsheet to analyse four different

Exhibit B.2	Screenshot of Excel file 'Mean-Variance Solver' (I)

Source: Screenshot of Microsoft Excel® reprinted by permission from Microsoft Corporation. © 2003 Microsoft Corporation, One Microsoft Way, Redmond, Washington 98052-6399, USA. All rights reserved.

assets, simply to keep the presentation compact and manoeuvrability manageable. After opening the Excel file, you should see the screen shown in Exhibit B.2.

The first step in using the spreadsheet is to enter the names and returns associated with all the assets that you will consider in the analysis. The names of each asset should be entered into cells B3 through E3. The returns associated with each should be entered directly below starting in cells B4 through E4.[1] Note that in most cases mean–variance analysis will be performed using monthly, quarterly or, as in this case, annual data. Finally, if you like, you can enter the corresponding date in column A. The reporting of the date is strictly for the user's benefit; column A is not used anywhere else in the spreadsheet.

Expected return and standard deviation must be entered for each asset included in the analysis. If you have forecasted the level of expected return and/or standard deviation over this immediate future evaluation period, enter those values in cells I3 through J6. If not, then the historical data you entered in columns B through E will be used to calculate historical returns and standard deviations. In addition to the expected return and standard deviation, a

---

[1] The number of observations you can include is limited only by the length of the Excel spreadsheet. Excel can hold 65 536 rows of data, so from a practical standpoint this will not be a limiting factor.

[2] Note that the number of rows and columns of the covariance matrix (cells H10 through K13) must equal the number of assets. The example includes four assets and, hence, the covariance matrix has four rows and four columns, a total of 16 cells. If we add one additional asset, then the covariance matrix has five rows, five columns and 25 cells.

Exhibit B.3 Screenshot of Excel file 'Mean-Variance Solver' (II)

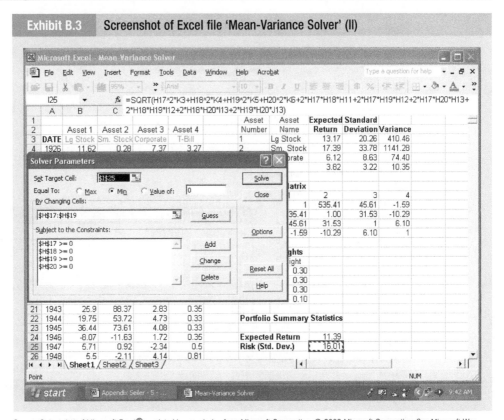

value for the covariance needs to be entered for each pair of asset combinations. If you have forecasts for the covariance terms, enter those values in cells H10 through K13.[2] If not, then the historical data you entered in columns B through E will be used to calculate historical covariances. In cells K11 through K14, initial portfolio weights are provided for each asset. It is not important what values you assign for now. What is important is that the last asset weight is programmed as being equal to one minus the weights of all the others. This ensures that the portfolio weights will always add up to one.

We are now ready to calculate the expected return and risk of the portfolio. Cell I21 contains the formula for the portfolio return. It is simply the weighted average of all the expected asset returns in the portfolio. In cell I22, the portfolio variance is shown, as computed using the formula in Equation 8.6 of Chapter 8.

The next step is to determine the risk and return of the minimum variance portfolio. We are now ready to use the Solver add-in from Excel. Click Tools and then Solver to view the screen shown in Exhibit B.3.

In the box titled 'Set Target Cell', type in I25. Since we want to find the portfolio with the lowest possible amount of risk, select 'Min.' In the box labelled 'By Changing Cells', indicate the range H17 through H19. We don't need to include H20 since it will change automatically. Finally, in the 'Subject to the Constraints:' box, we want to specify to Excel to keep all asset weights positive. In other words, this means we are not allowing assets to be sold short. As discussed in Chapters 7 and 8, this is a realistic and common assumption. We are now ready to solve for the minimum variance portfolio. Click on the Solve button to reach the solution.

Exhibit B.4   Screenshot of Excel file 'Mean-Variance Solver' (III)

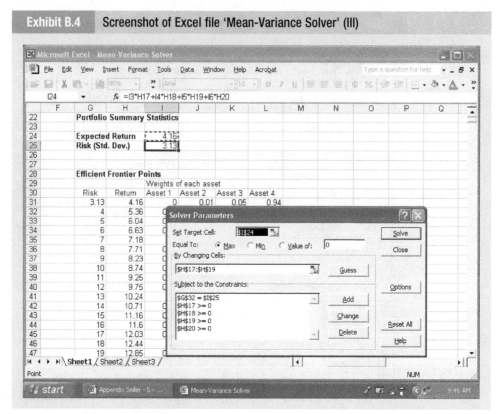

In cell I25, the value 3.13 appears. Correspondingly, the expected return on the minimum variance portfolio is equal to 4.16. Cells H17 through H20 have also changed. They now reflect the weights associated with each asset necessary to achieve the minimum level of risk. The minimum variance portfolio represents the left-most point on the efficient frontier. From here, we can learn of more points in the efficient set by providing Solver with the risk level and asking it to maximise return.

It is now our intension to identify various points along the efficient frontier. In addition to creating a running list of risk and return levels, we will also report the asset weights associated with each point. After repositioning within the spreadsheet and then selecting Tools and Solver, you should see the screen shown in Exhibit B.4.

In the box entitled 'Set Target Cell', type in I24. Since we want to find the highest return on the portfolio associated with a certain risk level, select 'Max.' In the box labelled 'By Changing Cells', indicate the range H17 through H19, just as you did before. In the 'Subject to the Constraints:' box, we again want to specify to Excel to keep all asset weights positive. The last step is to tell Excel that we already know the risk of our portfolio. We will specify the risk level at 4.0. To convey this to the program, we add the constraint that cell I25 = G32. We are now ready to solve for the maximum return. Click on the Solve button to reach the solution.

We see that the corresponding return is equal to 5.36. The associated asset weights for this portfolio are 0.08, 0.03, 0.14 and 0.74, respectively, for assets 1 through 4. We will repeat this process over and over again until we identify the ending point on the efficient frontier. For our case without short-selling, there is an easy way to determine just how far along the risk

Exhibit B.5 Screenshot of Excel file 'Mean-Variance Solver' (IV)

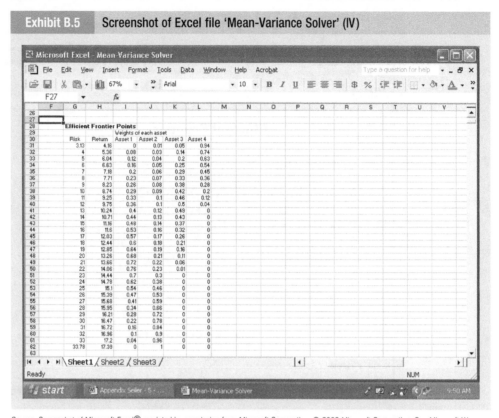

continuum we need to go. The highest return we can achieve in this portfolio without short-selling is to invest all of our money in the highest-return asset. Over our sample period, this means investing everything in small-capitalisation stocks. Correspondingly, the standard deviation associated with this asset is 33.78. This is the end of our efficient frontier. This observation can be demonstrated by examining the completed cells G62 and H62 (Exhibit B.5).

Another observation is worth discussing. If we examine the asset weights in cells I31 through L62, we see that at lower levels of risk, efficient portfolios assign a high weight to T-bills. As risk increases, corporate bonds show a presence. Eventually, both T-bills and corporate bonds are replaced by small- and large-capitalisation stocks. Ultimately, large-capitalisation stocks are overtaken by small-capitalisation stock, until small stocks are all that remain. This is very typical of what happens to various asset classes in mean–variance analysis.

It is sometimes of interest to graph the efficient frontier. To do so, highlight cells G32 through H62. After clicking on Chart Wizard, select XY (Scatter) and the second chart type. Label both axes, provide a chart title and then click Finish. Your final screen should look like that in Exhibit B.6.

B.3 Estimating an asset's market beta using regression analysis

As discussed in Chapter 10, an asset's market beta is used for empirical tests of asset-pricing theories as well as financial applications such as capital budgeting, portfolio selection, performance evaluation and risk management. In Appendix A, we showed how betas can be

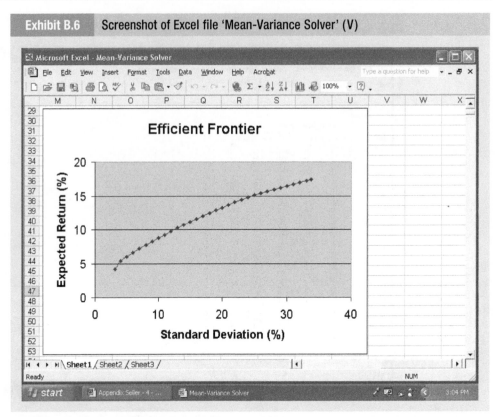

| Exhibit B.6 | Screenshot of Excel file 'Mean-Variance Solver' (V) |

computed using statistical software packages such as EViews. However, we can also calculate betas in Excel.[3] In fact, the procedure is simple. All we need are the excess returns on the asset and the excess returns on the market portfolio. Market betas can be calculated over any frequency. In our current example, we use monthly data for a stock. Begin by opening the file 'Calculating a Stock's Beta' (Exhibit B.7).

The date is shown in column A of the spreadsheet. The value of the S&P 500 index is shown in column B. Stock prices for the firm in question, Netegrity, are presented in column C, and T-bill yields are shown in column D.[4] The first step is to convert all these series into returns. This can be done simply by taking the natural log of the new value divided by the old value. For example, the return on the S&P 500 for February 1998 is equal to LN(B7/B6). Now that we have the return on all three series, the next step is to calculate the excess return on the market and the excess return on Netegrity. This is done by subtracting the T-bill return from each of the other two return series. This result is shown in columns H and I. In cell A2, we are now ready to report Netegrity's beta. Instead of performing a full-blown regression analysis, all we have to do is use the Excel function 'LINEST'. To be exact, we simply type in the

---

[3] Statistical software packages have the advantage of offering a wealth of different estimation techniques and diagnostic tests. The basic version of Excel does not include these features. However, the statistical software add-in called 'Analyse-it' does offer several useful additional statistical tools such as analysis of variance (ANOVA) and chi-squared tests. A free evaluation version can be downloaded at www.analyse-it.com/

[4] All prices have been adjusted fully for stock splits and dividends.

Exhibit B.7	Screenshot of Excel file 'Calculating a Stock's Beta'

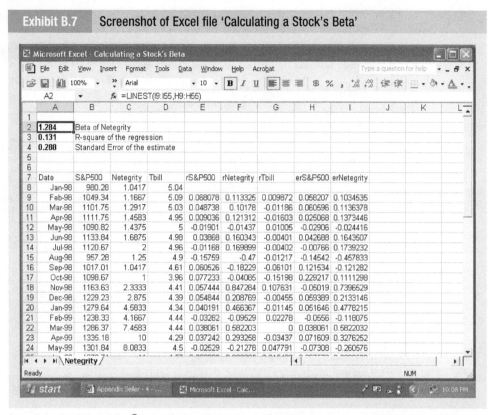

Source: Screenshot of Microsoft Excel® reprinted by permission from Microsoft Corporation. © 2003 Microsoft Corporation, One Microsoft Way, Redmond, Washington 98052-6399, USA. All rights reserved.

formula '=LINEST(I7:I53,H7:H53)'. The result is the beta of Netegrity of 1.28. As discussed in the body of the text, it is also important to report the R-squared value and standard error of the estimate. These values are reported in cells A3 and A4, respectively.

B.4   Performing event studies

As discussed in Chapter 12, an event study is a financial methodology used to determine whether a corporate event has a systematic effect on the company's stock price. There are many variations of an event study. While it is not our purpose here to explain fully how an event study works, we do want to take the opportunity to demonstrate how even a complex methodology like this one can be programmed in Excel. As with the other programs discussed in this appendix, users can download the complete event study model from the website referenced at the beginning of this appendix.

In the current example, we want to know whether new and relevant information is released in 'special stockholder meetings'. If new and relevant information is released in these meetings, then the stock price associated with the firm that held the meeting should adjust accordingly. To view the event study program, open the Excel file titled, 'Event Study – 2' (Exhibit B.8).

By taking a large sample of firms that have experienced the same corporate event, the researcher hopes to effectively remove, or wash out, all other influences that might have an impact of the stock price. For each firm in the sample, we need to gather stock returns for

Exhibit B.8 Screenshot of Excel file 'event study – 2' (I)

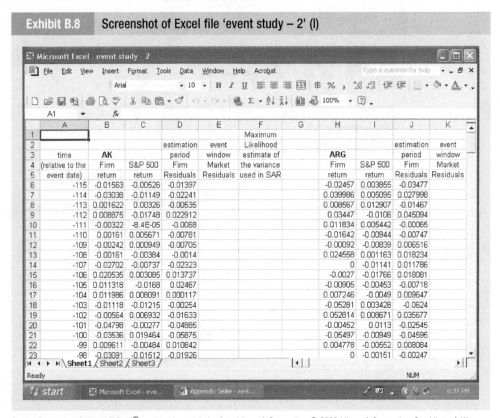

Source: Screenshot of Microsoft Excel® reprinted by permission from Microsoft Corporation. © 2003 Microsoft Corporation, One Microsoft Way, Redmond, Washington 98052-6399, USA. All rights reserved.

many days[5] before and after the event. The actual return realised over the event window minus what was expected is called an abnormal return. Ultimately, we need to compute a standardised abnormal return for each firm and for each day in the event window. This is accomplished through the following formulas.

$$SAR_{jt} = \frac{AR_{jt}}{\sqrt{s^2_{AR_{jt}}}}$$

where, SAR_{jt} = standardised abnormal return for firm j at time t, AR_{jt} = abnormal return for firm j at time t,

$$s^2_{AR_{jt}} = \left(\frac{\sum\limits_{t=-115}^{-16} (AR_{jt(est.period)} - \overline{AR}_{j(est.period)})^2}{D_j - 2} \right) \times \left(1 + \frac{1}{D_j} + \frac{(R_{mt(event.window)} - \bar{R}_{m(est.period)})^2}{\sum\limits_{t=-115}^{-16} (R_{mt(est.period)} - \bar{R}_{m(est.period)})^2} \right)$$

where: $s^2_{AR_{jt}}$ = variance of the abnormal return for firm j at time t, $AR_{jt(est.period)}$ = abnormal return for firm j at time t over the estimation period, $\overline{AR}_{j(est.period)}$ = mean abnormal return for

---

[5] We use 115 days before through 15 days after the event. However, there is no set number agreed upon in the field.

firm j over the estimation period, D_j = number of observed trading day returns for firm j over the estimation period, $R_{mt(event.window)}$ = return on the market (S&P500) at time t over the event window, $R_{mt(est.period)}$ = return on the market (S&P500) at time t over the estimation period, $\bar{R}_{m(est.period)}$ = mean return on the market (S&P500) over the estimation period.

In cells D140 through D143, we perform several intermediate estimation period statistics: alpha, beta and variance in the firm and market residuals. These will all be used to compute the maximum likelihood estimate of the variance used in the *SAR* equation. These calculations are shown in column F. The procedures described above must now be carried out for all firms in the sample. Since we have 40 firms in our sample, we will replicate this process through column IF.

Since the variance (denominator) in the *SAR* equation has been computed, all we have left to do is calculate the *AR* (numerator) and divide the two. To calculate AR, we use the following formula:

$$AR_{jt(event.window)} = R_{jt(event.window)} - \alpha_{j(est.period)} - \beta_{j(est.period)} \times R_{mt(event.window)}$$

where: $AR_{jt(event.window)}$ = abnormal return on stock j for each day in the event window, $R_{jt(event.window)}$ = return on stock j for each day in the event window, $\alpha_{j(est.period)}$ = intercept term for stock j measured over the estimation period, $\beta_{j(est.period)}$ = slope term for stock j measured over the estimation period, $R_{mt(event.window)}$ = return on the market for each day in the event window.

These values are reported for each firm over each day in the event window in cells B152 through AO182. After dividing these values by the variance, we arrive at the *SAR*. These values are reported in cells AQ152 through CD182. Summing across all firms yields the total standardised abnormal returns (TSARs). TSARs are calculated for each day in the event window. To determine whether these values are significant, we must calculate a corresponding Z-statistic based on the equation:

$$Z - statistic_t = \frac{TSAR_t}{\sqrt{\sum_{j=1}^{N} \frac{D_j - 2}{D_j - 4}}}$$

where: $Z - statistic_t$ = Z-statistic for each day in the event window, $TSAR_t$ = total standardised abnormal return for each day in the event window, D_j = number of observed trading day returns for firm j over the estimation period, N = number for firms in the sample.

To see these values, go to cells CF152 through CH182 (Exhibit B.9). *P*-values below 0.05 are statistically significant at 95%. *P*-values below 0.01 are statistically significant at 99%.

On day 0, the event day, the TSAR is statistically significant.[6] This means that we are 95% confident in concluding that new and relevant information is released in 'special stockholder meetings'. A graphical representation can be seen in Exhibit B.10.

It is of interest to some readers to examine the cumulative TSARs for each day in the event window. The formula can be written as:

$$CumulativeTSAR_{T_1,T_2} = \sum_{t=T_1}^{T_2} TSAR_t$$

where: $CumulativeTSAR_{T_1,T_2}$ = cumulative TSAR for each day in the event window, $TSAR_t$ = total standardised abnormal return for each day in the event window, T_1 = earliest date in the event window (-15), T_2 = later date in the event window (ranges from -15 through $+15$).

---

[6] The significance levels are based on the calculation of a Z-statistic where each TSAR is divided by the square root of the variance of the TSARs.

Exhibit B.9   Screenshot of Excel file 'event study – 2' (II)

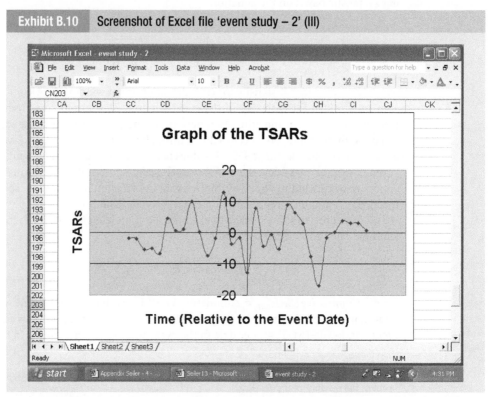

time (relative to the event date)	(Total SAR) TSAR	TSAR Z-statistic	TSAR p-value		Qjt: (intermediate calculations to get the Z-statistics AK	ARG	AGN	AHC	AMH
-15	-1.9387333	-0.3034	0.761588		1.020833333	1.020833	1.020833	1.020833	1.02083
-14	-2.1099081	-0.33018	0.741261		2.041666667	2.041667	2.041667	2.041667	2.04166
-13	-5.4310309	-0.84991	0.395373		3.0625	3.0625	3.0625	3.0625	3.062
-12	-5.0241229	-0.78624	0.431729		4.083333333	4.083333	4.083333	4.083333	4.0833
-11	-6.6488246	-1.04049	0.298113		5.104166667	5.104167	5.104167	5.104167	5.10416
-10	4.353193	0.681241	0.495719		6.125	6.125	6.125	6.125	6.12
-9	0.4948358	0.077438	0.938275		7.145833333	7.145833	7.145833	7.145833	7.14583
-8	0.9769076	0.152878	0.878494		8.166666667	8.166667	8.166667	8.166667	8.16666
-7	9.9688583	1.560048	0.118749		9.1875	9.1875	9.1875	9.1875	9.187
-6	0.0546589	0.008554	0.993175		10.20833333	10.20833	10.20833	10.20833	10.2083
-5	-7.4396264	-1.16424	0.244326		11.22916667	11.22917	11.22917	11.22917	11.2291
-4	-1.816525	-0.28427	0.776202		12.25	12.25	12.25	12.25	12.2
-3	12.797925	2.002775	0.045201		13.27083333	13.27083	13.27083	13.27083	13.2708
-2	-3.6178245	-0.56616	0.571284		14.29166667	14.29167	14.29167	14.29167	14.2916
-1	-1.6711423	-0.26152	0.793691		15.3125	15.3125	15.3125	15.3125	15.312
0	-12.869768	-2.01402	0.044008		16.33333333	16.33333	16.33333	16.33333	16.3333
1	7.8251076	1.224568	0.220738		17.35416667	17.35417	17.35417	17.35417	17.3541
2	-4.3755339	-0.68474	0.49351		18.375	18.375	18.375	18.375	18.37

Exhibit B.10   Screenshot of Excel file 'event study – 2' (III)

Exhibit B.11 Screenshot of Excel file 'event study – 2' (IV)

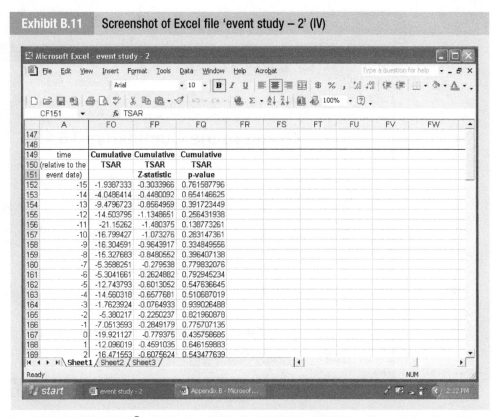

The statistical significance level is based on the formula:

$$Z_t = \left(\frac{1}{\sqrt{N}}\right)\left(\frac{\left(\displaystyle\sum_{T_1}^{T_2} SAR_{jt}\right)}{\sqrt{(T_2 - T_1 + 1)\left(\dfrac{D_j - 2}{D_j - 4}\right)}}\right)$$

where: Z_t = the Cumulative TSAR Z-statistic for each day in the event window, N = number of firms in the sample (40), SAR_{jt} = standardised abnormal return for firm j for each day in the event window, T_1 = earliest date in the event window (−15), T_2 = later date in the event window (ranges from −15 through +15), D_j = number of observed trading day returns for firm j over the estimation period.

The cumulative TSARs, Z-statistics, and corresponding P-values are reported in cells FO152 through FQ182 (Exhibit B.11).

An examination of the P-values found in cells FQ152 through FQ182 reveals that none of the cumulative TSARs is statistically significant. This finding results in the conclusion that no 'leakage (the premature seeping out of new information that is relevant to the firm's stock price)' occurs before special stockholder meetings. Graphically, the results can be presented as in Exhibit B.12.

| Exhibit B.12 | Screenshot of Excel file 'event study – 2' (V) |

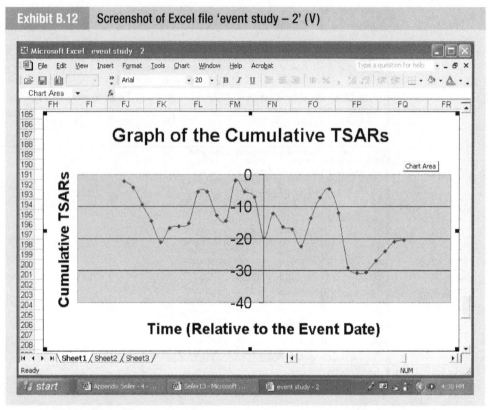

B.5 Bond analysis

There are four key calculations in bond analysis: valuation, yield to maturity (YTM), duration and convexity. Each of these concepts will be programmed in Excel below.[7]

Bond valuation

As discussed in Chapter 13, the intrinsic value of a bond is the present value of all future coupon payments as well as the par value of the bond when discounted at the YTM. Hence, for bond pricing, we need to know the par value, the coupon rate, the number of coupon payments remaining, the frequency of coupon payments and the YTM. After selecting the Excel file titled 'Bond Calculations', your screen should look like that in Exhibit B.13.

In cells A1 through A5, values must be entered for the YTM, par value, coupon rate, number of remaining coupon payments and the number of coupon payments per year (one for an annual bond, two for a semiannual bond). If we assume a YTM of 13%, a par value of $1000,

---

[7] All calculations shown in this section represent time periods that coincide exactly with coupon payments. Adjustments would have to be made in each formula to account for the time that passes between each coupon payment.

Exhibit B.13	Screenshot of Excel file 'Bond Calculations' (I)

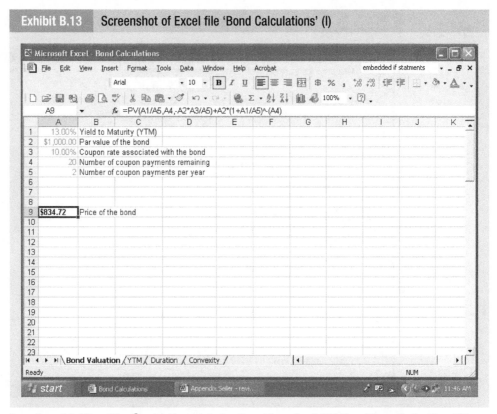

a coupon rate of 10%, and that there are 20 remaining coupon payments, the price of the bond with semiannual coupon payments will be $834.72. This value (and the corresponding formula) is shown in cell A9.

Yield to maturity

Instead of solving for the left-hand side of the equation for pricing bonds, we can solve for the denominator in the right-hand side of the equation. That is, if we know the price of the bond, we can solve for the YTM associated with the bond. To find the YTM, click on the tab marked YTM (Exhibit B.14).

In this case, cells A2 through A6 contain the values of the par value, coupon rate, number of remaining coupon payments, number of coupon payments per year and price of the bond. Assuming a current price of $834.72, a par value of $1000, a 10% coupon rate, and a bond that pays interest semiannually and has 20 remaining coupon payments, the YTM on the bond is equal to 13.00%. These numbers were chosen specifically to show the connection between the bond's price and its YTM. To find the YTM, we use the internal rate of return function in Excel. This function involves providing Excel with the range over which a stream of payments are given as well as our best guess as to the YTM. This best guess gives Excel a place to start. From there, Excel performs a series of trial-and-error substitutions until a value for YTM equations the two sides of the equation.

Exhibit B.14	Screenshot of Excel file 'Bond Calculations' (II)

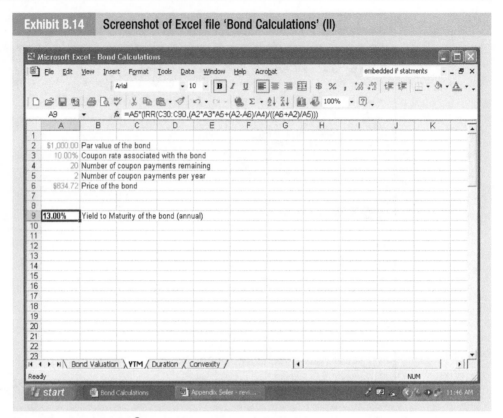

Source: Screenshot of Microsoft Excel® reprinted by permission from Microsoft Corporation. © 2003 Microsoft Corporation, One Microsoft Way, Redmond, Washington 98052-6399, USA. All rights reserved.

Duration

In Appendix 14A of Chapter 14, we learned that duration is the weighted average time it takes to receive the cash flows associated with a bond. For zero-coupon bonds, time to maturity is equal to duration. For all other bonds, duration is a smaller number. Duration is a fundamentally important concept in bond management because duration measures how sensitive a bond's price is to a change in interest rates. As demonstrated in Chapter 14, duration can be calculated within a single cell. Click on the tab marked Duration (Exhibit B.15).

The duration of a bond with a YTM of 12%, a par value of $1000, a coupon rate of 10%, ten remaining semiannual payments and no time elapsed since the last coupon payment is equal to four years.

Convexity

In order to capture the curvature of the price–yield relationship, it is necessary to calculate the convexity of a bond. Convexity measures how duration changes when the YTM changes. Begin by clicking on the tab titled Convexity (Exhibit B.16).

To match the example provided in Section 14.3, we consider a bond with a coupon rate and YTM of 10.68%, a par value of $1000 and ten remaining semiannual coupon payments. The annual convexity of this bond is equal to 18.29. Notice that the formula automatically converts the calculation to state the value for convexity in annual terms.

Exhibit B.15　Screenshot of Excel file 'Bond Calculations' (III)

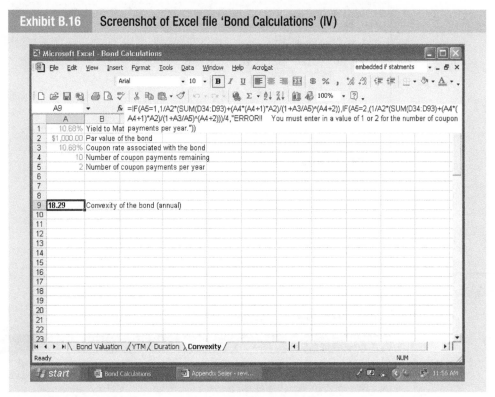

Source: Screenshot of Microsoft Excel® reprinted by permission from Microsoft Corporation. © 2003 Microsoft Corporation, One Microsoft Way, Redmond, Washington 98052-6399, USA. All rights reserved.

Exhibit B.16　Screenshot of Excel file 'Bond Calculations' (IV)

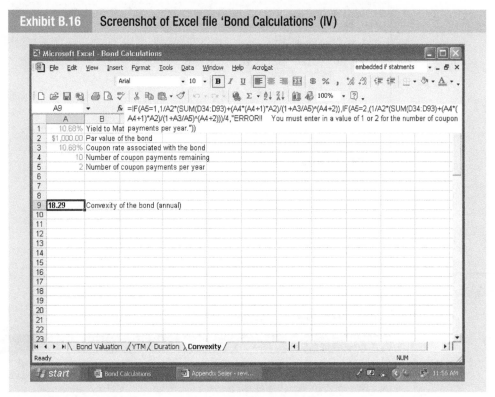

Source: Screenshot of Microsoft Excel® reprinted by permission from Microsoft Corporation. © 2003 Microsoft Corporation, One Microsoft Way, Redmond, Washington 98052-6399, USA. All rights reserved.

B.6 Calculating the price of a stock

As discussed in Chapter 15, the price of an asset is the present value of all expected future dividends, discounted at the appropriate, risk-adjusted discount rate. Since common stock has no maturity, these dividends can conceivably go on forever. Instead of creating formulas that contain an infinite number of terms, we can make a few simplifying assumptions about this future stream of dividends that will allow the infinitely long formula to reduce down to a manageable size. The two models below reflect such assumptions concerning the future growth rate in the dividends.

Constant growth case

The Gordon growth model assumes that dividends will grow at some fixed rate forever (with no growth, the growth rate is zero). Although this is very likely an oversimplification of reality, it allows the discounted dividend formula to reduce from an infinite number of terms down to the simple formula given in Equation 15.7 of Chapter 15. To perform the calculation in Excel, open the file named 'Common Stock Valuation Models'. Your screen should show the worksheet in Exhibit B.17.

In cells A1, A2 and A3, enter the most recently paid dividend, the required rate of return and the growth rate, respectively. The resulting stock price is shown in cell A10. In our case, we assumed that the most recently paid dividend is $2.00, the required rate of return is 16%, and the growth rate is 4%. Accordingly, the resulting stock price is $17.33.

Exhibit B.17	Screenshot of Excel file 'Common Stock Valuation Models' (I)

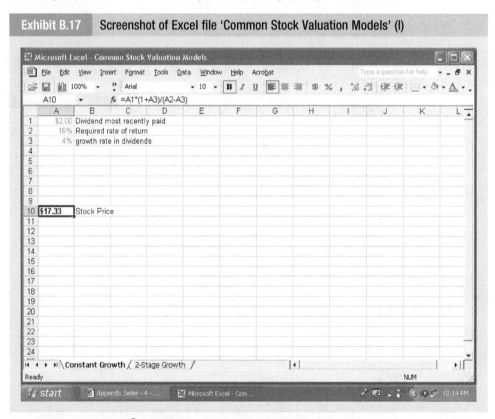

Two-stage growth case

Although convenient, it is not always appropriate to assume that dividends will grow at a constant rate forever. It might be a better assumption that a company will experience a higher growth rate for the next few years followed by a tapering off of that growth rate. If we assume there are not one but two constant growth rates in the future, we can use the two-stage growth model. In the same file, click on the tab marked 2-Stage Growth (Exhibit B.18).

Cell A8 includes the present value of the dividends over the first growth stage, and cell A9 includes the present value of the dividends over the second growth stage. The stock price in cell A10 is the sum of the two present value terms.

To keep our examples consistent, we will assume the same starting inputs for this model. The additional assumption we must make concerns the growth rate over the first growth period. We will assume that dividends grow at a higher rate of 10% for the first 12 years. Then, they will grow at 4% forever, as we assumed previously. Since the resulting dividend stream will be higher than in our previous example, we should anticipate that the resulting stock price will also be higher. If this is not the case, then there must be an error in the formula. Based on the results in cell A10, we confirm that this is exactly the case.[8]

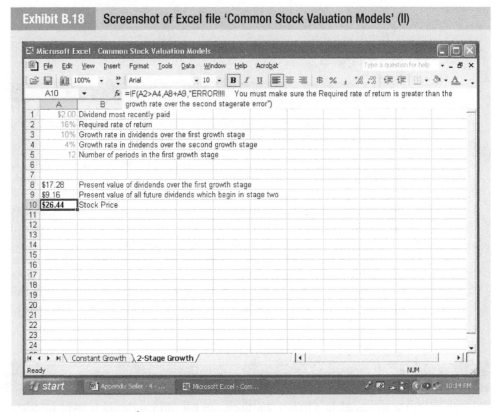

Exhibit B.18 Screenshot of Excel file 'Common Stock Valuation Models' (II)

---

[8] The intermediate calculations shown in cells A8 and A9 are for the user's reference, as these are commonly used as check figures.

Exhibit B.19	Screenshot of Excel file 'Common Stock Valuation Models' (III)

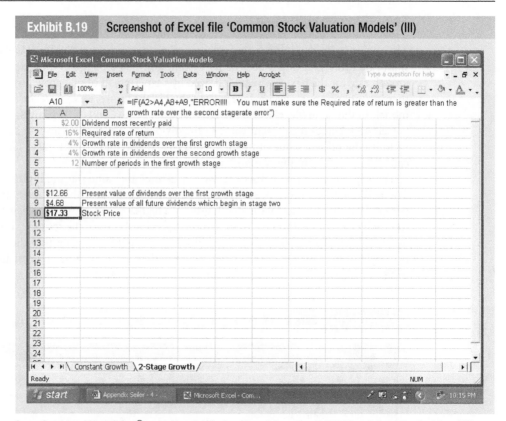

Source: Screenshot of Microsoft Excel® reprinted by permission from Microsoft Corporation. © 2003 Microsoft Corporation, One Microsoft Way, Redmond, Washington 98052-6399, USA. All rights reserved.

To show the connection between the constant growth model and the two-stage growth model, let's see what would happen if we assume the growth rates over both the first and the second period equal 4%. In this example, we should see that the stock price is $17.33. In this sense, the two-stage growth model has collapsed to become a one-stage, or constant, growth model, as presented in the previous section. The same results would occur if we changed the number of periods in the first growth stage to zero (Exhibit B.19).

Of course, the two-stage growth model can be extended to show three or four or even an infinite number of different growth periods. In fact, if we assume an infinite-stage growth model, then we revert back to our original formula for the price of a stock. This generic formula will have an infinite number of terms. In other words, we will have come full circle in our assumption process.

B.7 Option valuation

As discussed in Chapter 20, there are two primary models used to calculate the price of an option: the Black and Scholes (BS) model and the binominal model. The BS model is a continuous-time option-pricing model, whereas the binominal model is a discrete-time pricing model. Both can be used to price call and put options. The BS model is especially useful for valuing European options (which can be exercised only at maturity). The binominal model is also useful for valuing American options (which may also be exercised before maturity).

Exhibit B.20	Screenshot of Excel file 'Option Pricing Models' (I)

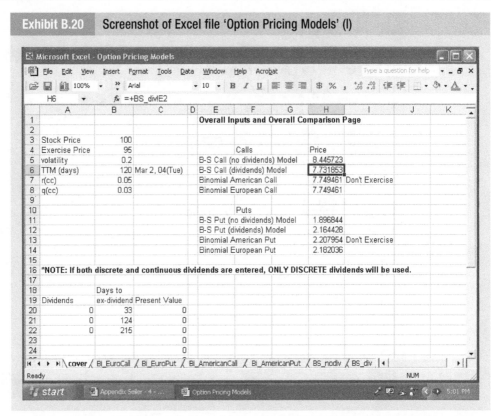

Source: Screenshot of Microsoft Excel® reprinted by permission from Microsoft Corporation. © 2003 Microsoft Corporation, One Microsoft Way, Redmond, Washington 98052-6399, USA. All rights reserved.

These various applications are all included in the spreadsheet file 'Option Pricing Models'. After opening the file, you should see the screen shown in Exhibit B.20.

There are six variables that affect the price of an option: stock price, exercise price, volatility, time to maturity ('TTM'), the risk-free rate of return ('rcc'), and the dividend yield (qcc). These inputs are to be entered by the user in cells B3 through B8, respectively.[9] Entering the dividend yield in B8 is appropriate when we can assume that the dividends are spread out evenly over the life of the option. This is a valid assumption for index options where all the firms within the index pay dividends at different times. However, if you are pricing an option on an individual stock, it is better to enter the discrete dividends directly into cells A20 through A37.[10] In sum, no cells in the file, except B3 through B8, and possibly A20 through A37, should be altered.

The option prices for calls are provided in cells H5 through H8. Prices for put options are given in cells H11 through H14. Exact formulas and calculations for all the models can be seen by clicking on the various tabs at the bottom of the file.

Let's focus on just two of the models for the purpose of illustration. Begin by selecting the tab marked BS_div to examine the BS value for a European call option for stocks that pay dividends (Exhibit B.21).

---

[9] The date in cell C6 is for the user's benefit only. Options mature on the third Saturday of the particular month. Since the user will not necessarily know the number of days from the present that represents, he or she can plug in various guesses into cell B6 until the correct expiration date appears.

[10] Both dividend amounts and days until the ex-dividend date must be entered in cells A20 through B37. Dividends should only entered over the life of the option. Once dividend values are entered, cells C20 through C37 will incorporate them into the various option prices.

Exhibit B.21 Screenshot of Excel file 'Option Pricing Models' (II)

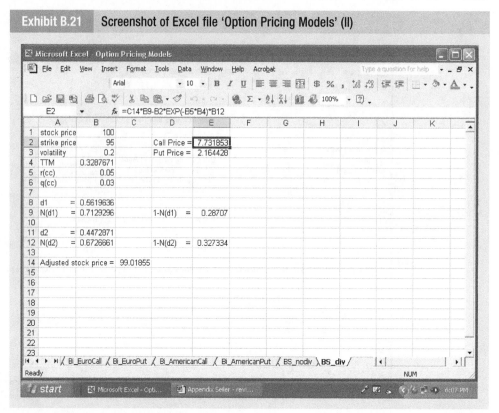

Source: Screenshot of Microsoft Excel® reprinted by permission from Microsoft Corporation. © 2003 Microsoft Corporation, One Microsoft Way, Redmond, Washington 98052-6399, USA. All rights reserved.

The formula for the BS model does not require a lengthy series of computations. In fact, you can see the calculation represented in the formula bar right above the spreadsheet. Since the stock pays a dividend in our example, we needed to make a simple adjustment to the stock price before using it in the formula. The adjustment involves simply subtracting the present value of all future dividends from the current price. This calculation is performed in cell C14. Based on the inputs from the cover sheet, we see that the value of the option with an underlying stock price of $100, a strike price of $95, a volatility of 20%, time to maturity of 0.3288 years, a risk-free rate of 5% and a continuously compounded dividend of 3% is equal to $7.73.

Now let's consider the binominal model for an American put option. To highlight the decision as to whether to exercise early, let's make the option deep in the money (so the time value of the option will be small). Since we are considering a put option, this means we should use an example where the stock price is far below the exercise price. Click on the tab titled Bi_AmericanPut (Exhibit B.22).

The binominal model is named for its assumption that stock prices can go up (B54) and down (B55) by a certain percentage. To determine the stock prices at each node, or period, multiply this number by cells B54 and B55. Doing so once gives the stock prices at node 2. This procedure is carried out for as many nodes as you have in the model. The black numbers in the binominal tree represent stock prices. Red numbers represent the corresponding option values. Now it is time to work backwards and fill in the option prices. Beginning in cell BA4, write the formula for the value of the option. Then, in the previous column, in addition to the basic formula we need to include our possible decision to exercise early. The formula can be expressed as shown in Exhibit B.23.

Exhibit B.22 Screenshot of Excel file 'Option Pricing Models' (III)

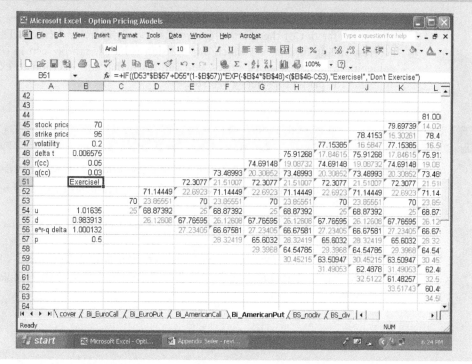

Exhibit B.23 Screenshot of Excel file 'Option Pricing Models' (IV)

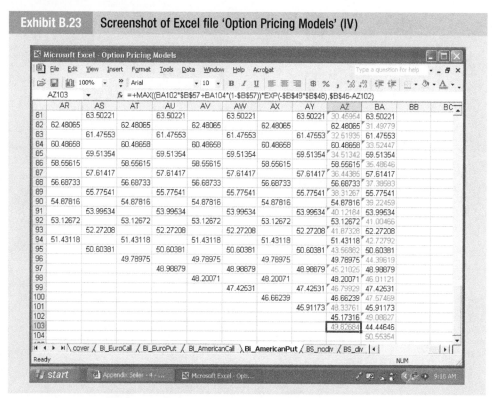

Copy this formula back throughout the entire binominal tree. In our example, we priced the stock far out of the money to invoke the early-exercise decision. This result, and the corresponding formula on which our decision is based, can be seen in cell B51. If you try plugging in different stock prices, you can learn that this decision to exercise early kicks in when the price drops below $78.58.

Selected references

Benninga, S., 2000, *Financial Modeling*, 2nd edn, Cambridge, MA: MIT Press.

Jackson, M. and M. Staunton, 2001, *Advanced Modelling in Finance Using Excel and VBA*, Chichester: John Wiley & Sons.

Seiler, M. J., 2004, *Performing Financial Studies: A Methodological Cookbook*, 1st edn, Upper Saddle River, NJ: Prentice Hall.

Walkenbach, J.; 2001a, *Excel 2002 Power Programming with VBA*, Hoboken, NJ: John Wiley & Sons.

Walkenbach, J., 2001b, *Microsoft Excel 2002 Formulas (With CD-ROM)*, Hoboken, NJ: John Wiley & Sons.

Chapter One

1   Corporate finance involves the interaction between firms and financial markets; the field of Investments addresses the interaction between investors and financial markets. There are also important differences regarding the relevant research methods of both fields: corporate finance problems often do not allow for quantitative research methods, and have to rely more on qualitative methods such as surveys and case studies.

2   The five basic components of the investment process are: investor characteristics; investment vehicles; strategy development; strategy implementation; and strategy monitoring.

3   The first component of the investment process is investor characteristics. Since each investor has unique investor characteristics (preferences, constraints, expectations), different investors have different optimal investment strategies.

4   The investment process is dynamic and never-ending. For example, financial markets, tax laws and security regulations change, the personal circumstances of investors change as they go through different stages of their lifecycle, and economic outlooks change as the economy moves through different stages of the business cycle.

5   The six most important developments in the capital market in recent years have been:

   a. Institutionalization: that is, the growing importance of institutional investors in capital markets.
   b. Advances in computer and telecommunication technology: these are changing security markets to virtual marketplaces.
   c. The introduction of new investment vehicles and strategies: examples include exchange traded funds (ETFs) and electronic communication networks (ECNs).
   d. Market globalisation: the globalisation of capital markets has increased the possibility of diversifying one's portfolio.
   e. Advances in academic knowledge: the field of finance has witnessed important academic developments that have also been adapted for practical applications.
   f. Increased focus on security regulation and investment ethics: a series of financial scandals have damaged the public's confidence in the financial system and led to increased regulation of the industry.

Chapter Two

1. a. Financial assets are easily divisible, while most physical assets (such as factories) are not.
   b. Financial assets are typically more marketable than physical assets. In other words, financial assets (such as stocks) are generally much more liquid than physical assets (such as stamps).
   c. Investors who purchase physical assets usually intend to hold them for a long time; in contrast, investors who buy financial assets face relatively low transactions costs and can therefore afford shorter holding periods.
   d. Information is usually more widely available for financial assets than for physical assets, and therefore often less costly to investors.

2. Treasury notes: Capital market
   Municipal bonds: Capital market
   Federal funds: Money market
   Eurodollars: Money market
   Repurchase agreements: Money market
   Commercial paper: Money market
   Mortgages: Capital market
   Treasury bills: Money market
   Corporate bonds: Capital market
   Negotiable CDs: Money market

3. This statement refers to the fact that common shareholders receive what is left over after all other claims on the firm have been settled.

4. a. The conversion ratio is the number of shares obtainable per bond: in this case 40.
   b. The conversion price is the par value divided by the conversion ratio: which in this case is $1000/40 = $25.
   c. The conversion value is the intrinsic value of a bond if converted immediately: which in this case is 40 × ($26) = $1040.

5. a. *Interest-rate risk*: the exposure to adverse changes in interest rates.
   b. *Equity risk*: the exposure to adverse changes in the stock market as a whole.
   c. *Commodity risk*: the exposure resulting from holding securities with an underlying sensitivity to commodity prices, for example, oil and precious metals.
   d. *Default risk*: the exposure to the possibility that one's counterparty won't be able to pay his or her financial obligation in a timely manner.
   e. *Credit migration risk*: the exposure arising from the possible adverse effect to the value of an investor's investment if the creditworthiness of his or her counterparty decreases unexpectedly.

Chapter Three

1. The most widely accepted model explaining IPO underpricing is Rock's (1986) winner's curse model. This model is based on the assumption of the existence of two types of investors in the marketplace: perfectly informed investors and relatively uninformed investors. The perfectly informed investors will apply only for underpriced issues leaving the uninformed investors to face a winner's curse in overpriced issues.

2   From Equation 3.2 we have:

$$P' = \frac{B}{N(1 - MM)}$$

However, Equation 3.1 is:

$$IM = \frac{N \times P - B}{N \times P}$$

And calculating the loan balance we get:

$$B = N \times P - IM \times (N \times P) = N \times P \times (1 - IM)$$

Substituting for B our result above, we get:

$$P' = \frac{N \times P(1 - IM)}{N(1 - MM)}$$

Dividing all terms by N, we get:

$$P' = \frac{P(1 - IM)}{(1 - MM)}$$

3   **a.** From Equation 3.2 we know that $P' = \dfrac{B}{N(1 - MM)}$. Assuming that Heloise borrowed as much as possible to open the account, $B = (400)(\$33)(0.45) = \$5940$. The price that will trigger a margin call is:

$$P' = \frac{5940}{400(1 - 0.25)} = \$19.80$$

   b. The actual margin will be 55% if the value of Heloise's claim on the account's assets, expressed as a percentage of the account's assets, is equal to 0.55. The assets in the account are the 400 shares of ABC stock plus Heloise's new deposit. Let X be $X = \$6000 + X$.

   The value of Heloise's claim on the assets is equal to the value of the assets minus the loan balance, or $(\$6000 + X) - \$5940 = \$60 + X$. The actual margin will be 55% if $0.55 = (60 + X)/(6000 + X)$. Solving, $X = \$7200$.

4   Example 1 is shallow and broad.
    Example 2 is deep and broad.
    Example 3 is shallow and thin.
    Example 4 is deep and thin.

5   The specialist is a market-maker who maintains a fair and orderly market for one or more securities. In addition, the specialists buy and sell for their own accounts (if there are no outstanding orders in the specialist's limit order book for the same security at the same price) to counteract any temporary imbalance in supply and demand for the stock.

Chapter Four

1   The retirement benefits of a defined-contribution plan are entirely dependent on the investment performance of the contributed funds; there's no predetermined benefit promised by the plan sponsor.

2 Life insurers invest more in long-term financial assets than property-casualty insurers; this is because typical property-casualty insurance usually has a much shorter term than typical life insurance. Also, property-casualty insurers' risks are 'insurance risks' that benefit less from the 'law of large numbers', which makes them less predictable and thus requiring more liquidity.

3 Open-end funds must be ready to repurchase shares from the public at all times. To be able to do this, these funds must keep some cash on hand. If they did not, they would be forced to sell assets every time investors redeemed their shares and would incur significant transaction costs while doing so.

   Closed-end funds do not have to be concerned with the above day-to-day liquidity issues because they do not allow investors to redeem shares.

4 $\text{NAV} = [1000(\$35) + 2000(\$45) + 3000(\$55) - \$87\,000]/10\,000$

   $= [\$35\,000 + \$90\,000 + \$165\,000 - \$87\,000]/10\,000 = \$203\,000/10\,000 = \$20.30$

5 Recall that the load is a one-time fee of 2%, whereas the management fee is an annual fee of 1.5%. Thus, your preferences will depend on your holding period. The value of investing \$100 in the S&P 500 after n years would be:

$$Value_{SP} = \$100(1 + 0.12)^n$$

and the value of the mutual fund would be:

$$Value_{MF} = \$100(1 - 0.02)(1 + 0.15 - 0.015)^n$$

For a one-year holding period, we have:

$$Value_{SP} = \$100(1 + 0.12) = \$112$$

$$Value_{MF} = \$100(1 - 0.02)(1 + 0.15 - 0.015) = \$111.23$$

and the S&P 500 is a better investment.

   However, if the holding period is 10 years, we have:

$$Value_{SP} = \$100(1 + 0.12)^{10} = \$310.58$$

$$Value_{MF} = \$100(1 - 0.02)(1 + 0.15 - 0.015)^{10} = \$347.68$$

and the mutual fund is the better investment. We can solve for the number of years such that both investments yield the same rate of return. Specifically:

$$Value_{SP} = Value_{MF}$$

$$100(1 + 0.12)^n = \$100(1 - 0.02)(1 + 0.15 - 0.015)^n$$

$$1.12^n = 0.98(1.135)^n$$

Taking the natural log of both sides, we have:

$$n \ln(1.12) = \ln(0.98) + n \ln(1.135)$$

Solving for n, we have:

$$n[\ln(1.12) - \ln(1.135)] = \ln(0.98)$$

$$n = \frac{\ln(0.98)}{\ln(1.12) - \ln(1.135)}$$

$$n = \frac{-0.0202}{0.1133 - 0.1266}$$

$$n = \frac{-0.0202}{0.0133} = 1.519 \text{ years}$$

Investors will prefer the S&P 500 for any holding period less than 1.519 years. For any holding period greater than 1.519 years, investors will prefer the mutual fund.

Chapter Five

1 Regulation is needed to eliminate unnecessary barriers to entry, stimulating efficiency and innovation and, eventually, lower prices and higher service quality for investors.

2 ▪ Securities Act of 1933
 ▪ Glass–Steagall Banking Act of 1933
 ▪ Securities Exchange Act of 1934
 ▪ Public Utilities Holding Company Act of 1935
 ▪ The Maloney Act of 1938

3 Yes, this investment decision is based on material non-public information and is therefore illegal.

4 Ethics embodies the ideals one should strive for and how one should behave; regulations are rules established by governments for the purpose of identifying unacceptable behaviour, but it's obvious that legislators cannot possibly impose regulations on every possible unethical action. It can therefore be the case that behaviour that is unacceptable from an ethical stand-point can be acceptable under existing regulations.

5 The two primary issues are:

 ▪ *Late trading*: Illegal practice of allowing certain investors to purchase fund shares at the day's closing price, even several hours after the markets close – when they should technically be buying the fund at the following day's opening price.
 ▪ *Market timing*: The technique of timing is designed to exploit market inefficiencies when the NAV price of the mutual fund shares does not reflect the current market value of the stocks held by the mutual fund.

Chapter Six

1 **a.** Using the linking method:

Date	Price	Dividend	Rate of return	Time-weighted rate of return
Purchase date	$100.00	–	–	–
Six months later	$108.00	$4.00	12%	12%
One year later	$116.64	$4.32	12%	25.44%

After 6 months, the price of the stock is $100(1.08) = $108. Every 6 months, dividends provide a 4% return on investment. The dividend received at 6 months will satisfy 4% = Dividend/$100. Solving, the dividend is $4.00. Using Equation 6.1 to calculate the return after 6 months we get: $(108 - 100 + 4)/100 = 12\%$.

After 1 year, the price of the stock is $108(1.08) = $116.64. The dividend received at one year will satisfy 4% = Dividend/$108. Solving, the dividend is $4.32. The return during the last 6 months of the year is $(116.64 - 108 + 4.32)/108 = 12\%$. The time-weighted return for the full year is $(1.12)(1.12) - 1 = 25.44\%$.

b. Using the index method:

Date	Price	Dividend	Additional shares purchased	Number of shares owned
Purchase date	$100.00	–	–	1
Six months later	$108.00	$4.00	0.037037	1.037037
One year later	$116.64	$4.32	0.038409	1.075446

At each dividend payment date, the number of additional shares purchased is:

$$AS_{6\,months} = (1)(\$4)/\$108 = 0.037037 \text{ share, and}$$

$$AS_{1\,year} = (1.037037)(\$4.32)/\$116.64 = 0.038409 \text{ share.}$$

Using Equation 6.3 to calculate the rate of return using the index method we get:

$$R = [(116.64)(1.075446)/(100)(1)] - 1 = 25.44\%.$$

2 Use Equation 6.5. Note that $EMV_i = BMV_i$ since the price of the preferred stock remains constant. The equation reduces to $R_i = I_i(1 - T)/BMV_i$.

a. R_i is 6% since investors require a 6% after-tax return. Because corporations pay tax on only 30% of dividends received, we must compute the effect of the corporate tax rate on dividend income. The after-tax cash flow is equal to:

$$I_i - \text{tax paid} = I_i - (0.3)I_i(0.34) = I_i - 0.102I_i$$

therefore, the effective corporate tax rate on dividend income is 10.2%. Corporate investors will pay a price that will provide a 6% return:

$$0.06 = \$4(1 - 0.102)/BMV_i$$

Solving:

$$BMV_i = \$59.87$$

b. Individual investors face a higher tax rate on dividend income than corporate investors (28% vs 10.2%). Therefore, individuals receive less after-tax cash flow from the preferred stock and will not pay as much as corporate investors. Use Equation 6.5 to determine the initial market value that will provide individuals a 6% after-tax return:

$$0.06 = \$4(1 - 0.28)/BMV_i$$

Solving:

$$BMV_i = \$48$$

c. If individuals pay $59.87 for the preferred stock, their after-tax return would be $R_i = \$4(1 - 0.28)/\$59.87 = 4.81\%$. At a price of $59.87, individuals would not earn their required after-tax return. Since corporations purchase most preferred stock, it is priced to provide a fair return to corporations instead of to individuals.

3 ■ Nominal ending wealth is $10 747(1.12)^{40} = \$1\,000\,019$.
   ■ Equation 6.8 gives the real annual return: $R_{real} = 1.12/1.03 - 1 = 8.738\%$.
   ■ Real ending wealth is only $10 747(1.08738)^{40} = \$306\,578$.

If Joaquin's goal was to collect real wealth of $1 000 000, inflation of only 3% caused him to fall short of his goal by $693 422.

4 Using Equation 6.13, first calculate the return on each stock for Tuesday and Wednesday:

		Return	
Stock	Monday	Tuesday	Wednesday
A	NA	10%	8%
B	NA	0%	2%

The average return is 5% on both Tuesday and Wednesday. The value of the index on Tuesday is $100(1.05) = 105$, and the value on Wednesday is $105(1.05) = 110.25$.

5 a. The rates of return are based on Equation 6.1 and are given in the following table:

End of year	NYSE composite	Rate of return
1988	156.26	–
1989	195.01	0.2480
1990	180.49	−0.0746
1991	229.44	0.271
1992	240.21	0.047
1993	259.08	0.078
1994	250.94	−0.0314
1995	329.51	0.31
1996	392.30	0.1905
1997	511.19	0.303
1998	595.81	0.166
1999	650.30	0.091
2000	656.87	0.010
2001	589.80	−0.102
2002	472.87	−0.198
2003	646.40	0.367

b. The arithmetic average of these 15 rates of return is (see Equation 6.15):

$$\bar{R}_A = (1/15) \times (0.2480 - 0.0746 + 0.271 + 0.047 + 0.078 - 0.0314 + 0.31 + 0.1905$$
$$+ 0.303 + 0.166 + 0.091 + 0.010 - 0.102 - 0.198 + 0.367)$$
$$= (1/15) \times 1.6755 = 0.1117 \text{ or } 11.17\%$$

c. The geometric average of these 15 rates of return is based on Equation 6.16:

$$\bar{R}_G = \left(\frac{646.40}{156.26} \right)^{1/15} - 1 = 9.93\%$$

d. The differences between Parts b and c is due to the variability of the rates of return over the years. When there is no variability, the averages are identical.

Chapter Seven

1 **a.** ■ Utility is represented by an increasing function; in other words, marginal utility (the utility derived from an additional unit of return) is always positive.

   ■ The added value from an additional unit of return falls as the return level increases and the investor becomes wealthier. In mathematical terms this is described by a concave utility function and, consequently, diminishing marginal utility.

   ■ Different investors have different utility functions, depending on, among other things, their wealth, income, education and age. Moreover, the shape of the utility function of a given investor changes through time. Thus, we cannot directly compare the level of utility and marginal utility of different utility functions associated with different investors or different points in time.

   b. Probability distributions are used to describe an investor's subjective expectations about future returns.

   c. Generally speaking, expansion of investment possibilities makes an investor better off, while imposing investment restrictions reduces the investment possibilities and makes investors worse off by limiting their choices. Restrictions and possibilities can be formulated in the form of limits on the amount invested in risky assets (such as stocks, junk bonds and derivatives), in social and environmental screens (socially responsible investments), or in the prohibition of short-selling. Restrictions are imposed on investors by, for example, regulators, investment mandates and industry codes of ethical conduct. Of course, society as a whole may benefit from restrictions that prevent investors from pursuing illegal or unethical investment strategies.

2 ■ Expected return and variance on the portfolio consisting of all three stocks, equally weighted (1/3; 1/3; 1/3):

$$E(R_P) = \frac{1}{3} \times 0.08 + \frac{1}{3} \times 0.08 + \frac{1}{3} \times 0.08 = 0.08$$

$$\sigma_{R_P}^2 = w_1^2 \times \sigma_1^2 + w_2^2 \times \sigma_2^2 + w_3^2 \times \sigma_3^2 + 2 \times w_1 \times w_2 \times \sigma_{12} + 2 \times w_1 \times w_3 \times \sigma_{13}$$
$$+ 2 \times w_2 \times w_3 \times \sigma_{23}$$

$$\sigma_{R_P}^2 = \left(\frac{1}{3}\right)^2 \times 0.0026 + \left(\frac{1}{3}\right)^2 \times 0.0007 + \left(\frac{1}{3}\right)^2 \times 0.0001 + 2 \times \frac{1}{3} \times \frac{1}{3} \times (-0.0005)$$

$$+ 2 \times \frac{1}{3} \times \frac{1}{3} \times 0.0003 + 2 \times \frac{1}{3} \times \frac{1}{3} \times (-0.0002) \approx 0.0003$$

   ■ Expected return and variance on the portfolio consisting of all three stocks in proportion (0; 1/4; 3/4):

$$E(R_P) = 0 \times 0.08 + \frac{1}{4} \times 0.08 + \frac{3}{4} \times 0.08 = 0.08$$

$$\sigma_{R_P}^2 = w_1^2 \times \sigma_1^2 + w_2^2 \times \sigma_2^2 + w_3^2 \times \sigma_3^2 + 2 \times w_1 \times w_2 \times \sigma_{12} + 2 \times w_1 \times w_3 \times \sigma_{13}$$
$$+ 2 \times w_2 \times w_3 \times \sigma_{23}$$

$$\sigma_{R_P}^2 = \left(\frac{1}{4}\right)^2 \times 0.0007 + \left(\frac{3}{4}\right)^2 \times 0.0001 + 2 \times \frac{1}{4} \times \frac{3}{4} \times (-0.0002) \approx 0.00003$$

Both portfolios have the same return, but the risk of the second portfolio where stock 1 is eliminated and stocks 2 and 3 are not equally weighted is ten times lower.

The utility of each portfolio equals:

$$u(R) = E(R_p)^{0.5} = 0.08^{0.05} = 0.28$$

The shape of the function indicates diminishing marginal utility, meaning that the investor is risk-averse. If presented with two portfolios with the same average return, but with different levels of risk, then the investor will choose the least risky one. Thus, the second portfolio will be preferred to the first one.

3 **a.** The expected utility of the investor in case he or she does not invest at all equals:

$$u(R_p) = \exp^0 = 1$$

since the return will be zero.

If the investment yields 10% return with a probability of 25%, or a loss of 5% with a probability of 75%, the expected utility equals:

$$E(u(R_p)) = 0.25 \times \exp^{0.1} + 0.75 \times \exp^{-0.05} = 0.9897$$

which means that the investor won't undertake the investment opportunity.

b. The investor will be eager to undertake the investment given the possible returns of 10% and −5%, if the expected utility of holding such a portfolio exceeds:

$$u(R_p) = \exp^0 = 1$$

As can be calculated:

$$p \times \exp^{0.1} + (1 - p) \times \exp^{-0.05} > 1$$

when $p > 0.3168$.

4 ■ The current asset pricing models do not, possibly, properly account for the risk perception and the risk attitude of investors.

■ Historical average rates of return have been overstated. For example, the computations typically assume that dividend payments to stocks are reinvested and that no taxes are paid.

■ Historically observed average rates of return are not representative of the returns that investors actually expected in the past (for example, due to a few unexpected catastrophic events such as world wars). They are also not representative of the returns that investors currently expect for the future (for example, because investment vehicles such as index funds and ETFs make low-cost, low-risk equity portfolios available even to small individual investors).

5 The expected utility criterion shows the theoretically correct link between investor objectives, expectations and constraints. Also, many operational investment tools, such as the mean–variance analysis (discussed in Chapter 8), rely on the principles of the expected utility framework.

Chapter Eight

1 **a.** The mean-variance efficiency criterion postulates that 'an asset or portfolio of assets is mean-variance efficient if there exists no other asset or portfolio that yields a higher mean and a lower variance'. This means that the investor will choose a portfolio with the least variance for a given level of return, or the portfolio of the highest return at a given level of risk.

b. Using this criterion, one can identify the efficient mean–variance frontier. Every mean–variance investor, irrespective of the shape of his or her indifference curves, will select a portfolio from this efficient frontier. Depending on his or her own preferences and possibilities, an investor will choose the portfolio that will belong to the highest possible indifference curve, tangent to the efficient frontier.

2 **a.** Expected return on a portfolio is the sum of the weights invested in an asset times the expected return on that asset, where we sum across all assets. The variance of a portfolio is a function of the proportions invested in each asset, the variance of each asset, and the covariances between assets.

b. The variance of the returns on the asset is the measure of risk of that asset when an investor holds only one asset. However, when the investor holds more than one risky asset, the risk of an individual asset is a function not only of its own variance but also of its degree of dependency on the other assets in the portfolio.

c. The covariance measures the degree of dependency of the rates of return of the two assets. If the rates of return of two assets tend to go up and down together, they will have a positive covariance. When one asset's return is relatively high and the other asset's return is relatively low, the covariance will be negative.

d. Correlation is a measure of the dependency of two variables, which is useful for comparing the benefits of diversifying a portfolio. When everything else is held constant, the lower the asset's correlation is, the lower a portfolio's variance will be. This is an attractive feature for risk-averse investors.

3 The two methods are the direct and the indirect method. The direct method is the simplest, but requires information about the returns of all individual assets in the different countries around the world. If one knows all the probability distributions of returns for the portfolio's assets, it is usually easier to use the direct method. However, it is rare that one knows all the probability distributions. Instead, one will typically know only summary statistics, such as the means, variances and covariances of the portfolio's assets. If so, it is easier to use the indirect method. The indirect method requires the means, variances and covariances of the individual assets. The increased computational burden of the indirect method is compensated by the lower data requirements.

4 The direct method requires computing the portfolio's return in each country. In each case, the return is the weighted average of the returns of Stock H and Stock I (see Equation 7.1). The proportion of wealth invested in Stock H is $5000/20\,000 = 25\%$, with the rest (75%) invested in Stock I.

State of economy	Probability	Stock H	Stock I	Portfolio return
Terrifying	0.2	−30%	−12%	$0.25(-30\%) + 0.75(-12\%) = -16.5\%$
Bothersome	0.3	−10%	0%	$0.25(-10\%) + 0.75(0\%) = -2.5\%$
Pleasant	0.5	6%	20%	$0.25(6\%) + 0.75(20\%) = 16.5\%$

The direct method uses Equation 7.4 to calculate expected return and Equation 7.5 to calculate variance:

$$E(R_p) = 0.2(-16.5\%) + 0.3(-2.5\%) + 0.5(16.5\%) = 4.2\%$$

$$\sigma_p^2 = 0.2(-0.165 - 0.042)^2 + 0.3(-0.025 - 0.042)^2 + 0.5(0.165 - 0.042)^2 = 0.017481, \text{ and}$$

$$\sigma_p = 13.22\%$$

The indirect method requires the variances of Stock H and Stock I and their covariance. To compute variance (Equation 7.5) and covariance (Equation 7.6), it is necessary to compute expected returns for Stock H and Stock I using Equation 7.4:

$$E(R_H) = 0.2(-30\%) + 0.3(-10\%) + 0.5(6\%) = -6\%$$

$$E(R_I) = 0.2(-12\%) + 0.3(0\%) + 0.5(20\%) = 7.6\%$$

$$\sigma_H^2 = 0.2[-0.30 - (-0.06)]^2 + 0.3[-0.10 - (-0.06)]^2 + 0.5[0.06 - (-0.06)]^2 = 0.0192$$

$$\sigma_I^2 = 0.2(-0.12 - 0.076)^2 + 0.3(0 - 0.076)^2 + 0.5(0.20 - 0.076)^2 = 0.017104$$

$$\sigma_{H,I} = 0.2[-0.30 - (-0.06)](-0.12 - 0.076) + 0.3[-0.10 - (-0.06)](0 - 0.076)$$
$$+ 0.5[0.06 - (-0.06)](0.20 - 0.076) = 0.01776.$$

Use Equation 8.6 to complete the computation:

$$\sigma_p^2 = 0.25^2(0.0192) + 0.75^2(0.017104) + 2(0.25)(0.75)(0.01776) = 0.017481, \text{ and}$$
$$\sigma = 13.22\%, \text{ as with the direct method.}$$

5 ■ The first two events imply the expansion of the portfolio possibility set and a favourable shift (a shift in the 'northwestern' direction) of the efficient frontier, making higher means (given the standard deviation) and lower standard deviations (given the mean) available.

   ■ The increased correlation of individual assets reduces the diversification benefits and implies a contraction of the portfolio possibility set and an unfavourable shift (a shift in the 'southeastern' direction) of the efficient frontier, making lower means (given the standard deviation) and higher standard deviations (given the mean) available.

Chapter Nine

1 a. The basic argument for international diversification is that international assets raise the mean–variance efficient frontier above that for portfolios with only domestic assets.
   b. Higher integration of capital markets has increased the systematic risk of the broad capital market as a whole, diminishing the amount of non-systematic, country-specific risk that can be diversified away. This increased correlation is especially typical for the markets of the developed countries, and significantly reduces the efficacy of international diversification.
   c. One can diversify a portfolio either across sectors and industries, or across asset classes, or between regions and countries. There is no superior strategy, and one can best diversify across countries, industries and asset classes. Some studies indicate that international diversification is quite effective, especially if combined with investment in international small caps and emerging markets.

2 From the standpoint of reducing risk, in general, the more stocks there are in a portfolio, the better off the investor is. Thus the larger the number of stocks in a portfolio, the smaller the portfolio's variance. However, as the number of stocks increases, the incremental contribution to the reduction in the portfolio's variance becomes smaller and smaller. Also, one should bear in mind that diversification does not only depend on how many stocks an investor holds, but especially on the correlations between those stocks. An investor who holds stocks of 15 different computer manufacturers is probably less diversified than an investor who holds stocks of companies from six different industries.

3 Investing in foreign securities results in two additional risks compared to investing in domestic securities:

   a. Foreign exchange risk: the rates of return on international investments are influenced by movements in foreign exchange prices.
   b. Political risk: the rates of return on international investments can be influenced by actions taken by foreign governments.

4 Most mutual funds are focused on a single type of asset category, such as domestic stocks. Diversifying across mutual funds that invest in different asset types can reduce risk. However, if you buy two mutual funds specialising in the same type of asset – for example, stocks – the gain from such diversification is very small indeed.

5 These viewpoints can both be correct. For the individual investor the added benefit of moving from seven securities to 100 securities might not be sufficient to compensate the transaction and information costs associated with portfolio diversification. However, the money manager has $10 000 000 to invest and for such a large portfolio the transaction and information cost per dollar would remain small; so, for the money manager, the benefit might very well be greater than the cost.

Chapter Ten

1 a. The separation theorem states that investment decisions are separated from financing decisions. At Stage 1, all investors select the market portfolio, which is the best portfolio of risky assets. At Stage 2, investors choose the optimal mix of the market portfolio and the risk-free asset to maximise their utility.
   b. Beta measures the relative contribution of an asset to the risk (variance) of the market portfolios. If the beta of a stock exceeds unity, then increasing the portfolio weight of the stock relative to its market capitalisation will make the portfolio riskier than the market portfolio.
   c. Alpha is the excess return above and beyond the risk premium. Investors try to find stocks with a large alpha because these stocks are underpriced and are located above the security market line.
   d. In equilibrium, all stocks and portfolios lie on a straight line called the SML. According to the CAPM, the higher the beta of a stock, the higher the expected rate of return. Any deviation from the SML implies that the market is not in CAPM equilibrium.
   e. An investor can mix any risky asset with a risk-free asset, creating a large set of investment opportunities all lying on the opportunity line. All investors, regardless of their indifference curves, will choose a portfolio from the opportunity line with the highest slope. This line is the CML. All portfolios lying on the CML are efficient, and are composed of various mixes of the market portfolio and the risk-free asset.

2 a.

Year	R_A	R_m	$R_A \times R_m$	R_m^2	R_A^2
1	0.05	0.08	0.004	0.0064	0.0025
2	0.03	−0.02	−0.0006	0.0004	0.0009
3	0.20	0.30	0.06	0.09	0.04
Sum	0.2800	0.3600	0.0634	0.0968	0.0434
Average	0.0933	0.1200	0.0211	0.0323	0.0145

Using Equation (10.6) we get:

$$\beta_i = \sigma_{i,m}/\sigma_m^2 = \frac{E(R_i \times R_m) - E(R_i) \times E(R_m)}{E(R_m^2) - E(R_m)^2}$$

$$\beta_a = [0.0211 - (0.0933) \times (0.12)]/[0.0323 - 0.12^2] = 0.556$$

b. The variance of the stock σ_A^2 is:

$$E(R_A^2) - E(R_A)^2 = 0.0145 - 0.0933^2 = 0.005765$$

c. To calculate the systematic and the unsystematic risk component, we first need to calculate the variance of the market portfolio:

The variance of the market σ_M^2 is:

$$E(R_M^2) - E(R_M)^2 = 0.0323 - 0.12^2 = 0.017787$$

The systematic risk component is:

$$\beta_A^2 \times \sigma_m^2 = 0.556^2 \times 0.017787 = 0.0055$$

The unsystematic risk component is:

$$\sigma_{eA}^2 = \sigma_A^2 - (\beta_A^2 \times \sigma_m^2) = 0.005765 - 0.0055 = 0.000266$$

The proportion of systematic risk is:

$$(\beta_A^2 \times \sigma_m^2)/\sigma_A^2 = 0.0055/0.005765 = 0.954 \text{ or } 95.4\%$$

The proportion of unsystematic risk:

$$\sigma_{eA}^2/\sigma_A^2 = 0.000266/0.005765 = 0.046 \text{ or } 4.6\%$$

So the stock's risk is almost completely determined by the systematic component (95.4%), which means that the stock is close to efficient.

3 **a.** Recall from Equation 10.2 that the expected rate of return of an efficient portfolio can be expressed as:

$$E(R_i) = w_r r + (1 - w_r)E(R_m)$$

Using $E(R_m) = 10\%$, and $E(R_i) = 15\%$:

$$15 = w_r r + (1 - w_r)10$$

Before we can determine the amount of borrowing or lending, we must first determine the risk-free rate.

Recall from Equation 10.5:

$$E(R_p) = r + [E(R_m) - r](\sigma_p/\sigma_m)$$

$$15 = r + (10 - r)(20/10)$$

$$15 = -r + 20$$

$$r = 5\%$$

Substituting this result in equation 10.2, we have:

$$15 = 5w_r + (1 - w_r)10$$

$$15 = -5w_r + 10$$

$$5 = -5w_r$$

$w_r = -1$, which indicates a -100% investment in the risk-free asset (thus borrowing) and a 200% investment in the market portfolio.

b. The risk-free rate has been calculated above; $r = 5\%$.

4 CAPM is used for:

- *Portfolio selection*: the beta is a popular measure of market timing.
- *Performance evaluation*: the alpha and beta allow an investor to assess whether or not a fund manager is earning his or her pay.
- *Risk management*: beta measures the dependency of an asset on the other available assets by a single number. It can be used in the Value-at-Risk framework.
- *Capital budgeting*: financial managers can calculate the cost of equity using CAPM.

5 The following well-documented stock market anomalies exist:

- *The size effect*: firms with a low market capitalisation seem to earn positive abnormal average returns; while firms with high market capitalisation earn negative abnormal returns.
- *The value effect*: stocks with a low market value relative to firm fundamentals (low price-to-earnings ratio, and high dividend-to-price ratio, as well as a high book-to-market ratio) seem to earn positive abnormal average returns; while growth stocks (high price-to-earnings ratio, and low dividend-to-price ratio, as well as a low book-to-market ratio) earn negative abnormal average returns.
- *The momentum effect*: in the short run (periods up to a year) one seems to be able to predict abnormal returns based on abnormal returns from the past. That is, the losers from the past continue to lose while the winners continue to win.

Chapter Eleven

1 The SIM assumes that returns are generated by a single factor (say, I) and firm-specific factors; specifically, the SIM assumes that:

$$E(R_i) = \alpha_i + \beta_i E(I) + e_i$$

where $Cov(I, e_i) = 0$, and that for any two stocks, $Cov(e_i e_j) = 0$. With these assumptions the SIM drastically reduces the inputs needed in solving for the optimum portfolios on the efficient frontier, because the covariances can be calculated as follows:

$$Cov(R_i, R_j) = \beta_i \beta_j \sigma_I^2$$

Thus, the investor only needs to estimate the betas for each stock rather than all possible covariances.

2 The SIM states that $R_i = \alpha_i + \beta_i \times I + e_i$ (see Equation 11.1). Taking the expectations of both sides, the SIM requires that:

$$E(R_i) = \alpha_i + \beta_i \times E(I)$$

Therefore, to calculate $E(R_F)$, we must first calculate α_F and β_F. We know the beta is formally calculated as $\beta_i = \sigma_{i,I}/\sigma_I^2$. We also know that:

$$E(R_F) = (10\% + 22\% + 18\% - 5\% + 12\%)/5 = 11.4\%$$

$$E(I) = (3\% + 2\% - 1\% - 2\% + 5\%)/5 = 1.4\%$$

$$\sigma_{F,I} = [(0.10 - 0.114)(0.03 - 0.014) + (0.22 - 0.114)(0.02 - 0.014)$$
$$+ (0.18 - 0.114)(-0.01 - 0.014) + (-0.05 - 0.114)(-0.02 - 0.014)$$
$$+ (0.12 - 0.114)(0.05 - 0.014)]/5 = 0.000924$$

$$\sigma_I^2 = [(0.03 - 0.014)^2 + (0.02 - 0.014)^2 + (-0.01 - 0.014)^2 + (-0.02 - 0.014)^2$$
$$+ (0.05 - 0.014)^2]/5 = 0.000664$$

Thus:

$$\beta_F = 0.000924/0.000664 = 1.391566$$

Then:

$$\alpha_F = 0.114 - 1.391566(0.014) = 0.094518$$

Finally:

$$E(R_F) = 0.094518 + 1.391566(0.04) = 15.018\%$$

3 **a.** The APT is an equilibrium model developed by Professor Stephen Ross. The primary assumption of the APT is that security returns are generated by a linear factor model. The APT is based on the no-arbitrage condition. That is, an investor should not be able to build a zero-risk, zero-investment portfolio that has positive returns. In general, the expected return on a security under the APT with multiple factors is:

$$E(R_i) = a_0 + a_1\beta_1 + a_2\beta_2 + \ldots + a_K\beta_K$$

where a_0 is the risk-free interest rate, β_i is the security's sensitivity to each factor, and a_i is the market price per unit of sensitivity.

The assumptions of the APT are:

i.   The capital market is characterised by perfect competition and individual investors cannot influence the prices.
ii. All investors have the same expectations regarding the future in terms of mean, variance and covariance terms. Rates of return depend on some common factors and some noise, which is firm-specific.
iii. A very large number of assets exist in the economy.
iv. Short sales are allowed, and the proceeds are available to the short sellers.
v.   Investors prefer more wealth to less.

b. In contrast to the CAPM, the APT does not assume that investors make decisions according to the mean–variance rule, and investors do not have to be risk-averse.

4 The APT line can be written as:

$$E(R_i) = E(R_Z) + (E(R_I) - E(R_Z))\beta_i$$

The slope of the line is given by the rate of change between any two of the assets:

$$(E(R_I) - E(R_Z)) = \frac{8\% - 4\%}{2 - 1} = \frac{12\% - 8\%}{3 - 2} = \frac{12\% - 4\%}{3 - 1} = 4\%, \text{ or } 0.04$$

Then, the intercept is given by:

$$E(R_Z) = E(R_i) - (E(R_I) - E(R_Z))\beta_i = E(R_i) - 0.04\beta_i$$

If we take Portfolio A, we get:

$$E(R_Z) = 0.04 - (0.04 \times 1) = 0.0$$

If we take Portfolio B, we get:

$$E(R_Z) = 0.08 - (0.04 \times 2) = 0.0$$

If we take Portfolio C, we get:

$$E(R_Z) = 0.12 - (0.04 \times 3) = 0.0$$

Thus, the APT line with these figures is given by:

$$E(R_i) = 0 + 0.04\beta_I$$

5 Since similar choices often have to be made for testing the CAPM, as well as the APT, empirical tests of the APT suffer many of the same problems as tests of the CAPM. These include: time variation of the return distribution; choice of appropriate statistical methods; and problems with the data, such as data mining, data snooping and sample selection bias.

Empirical testing of the APT suffers from an additional problem, since one also has to identify the relevant set of common risk factors. The CAPM predicts that the market portfolio is the only priced risk factor. By contrast, the APT gives no clues regarding the appropriate number of factors and the identity of the factors. In this respect, any test of the APT is a joint test of the hypothesis that the APT is a correct equilibrium model and the hypothesis that the set of risk factors is correct.

Chapter Twelve

1 a. An efficient market is a market in which prices reflect all relevant information. If a financial market is efficient, then the best estimate of the true value of a security is given by its current market price. The efficient market theory implies that technical analysis and fundamental analysis are worthless because all information that can be obtained with these techniques is already reflected in the market prices.

   b. *Weak form*: this form of the EMH holds that the prices of securities fully reflect all stock market information, such as price trends, volume information and the put–call ratio. If the weak form of the hypothesis is true, trading on the basis of this type of information will not produce returns that exceed those available from a buy-and-hold strategy, after accounting for transactions costs.

   Semi-strong form: this form of the EMH holds that the prices of securities fully reflect all publicly available information, such as price trends, volume information and public announcements issued by the management of companies with traded securities. If the semi-strong form of the hypothesis is true, trading on the basis of public information will not produce returns that exceed those available from a buy-and-hold strategy, after accounting for transactions costs.

   Strong form: this form of the EMH holds that the prices of securities fully reflect all information, whether public or private. If the strong form of the hypothesis is true, trading on the basis of any information, including inside information, will not produce returns that exceed those available from a buy-and-hold strategy, after accounting for transactions costs.

2 The empirical evidence suggests the following:

   a. The weak form of the EMT cannot be completely backed up, due to anomalous results, such as the 'January effect'.
   b. The semi-strong form of the EMT cannot be completely backed up, due to significant anomalous results, such trading based on the 'size-effect' and the 'market-to-book-value ratio'.
   c. The strong form of the EMT cannot be backed up in most cases.

3 It is difficult to make a profit based on the volume of trading activity. Although volume may increase before a takeover, volume also increases for other reasons, making it difficult to discern exactly what is causing the volume to increase. Also, even if volume increases because of an expected takeover that does not mean that one can systematically earn abnormal returns.

4 A market anomaly is any event that can be exploited to produce abnormal profits. There are four categories of anomalies: seasonal, event, firm and accounting anomalies. Firm anomalies are anomalies that result from firm-specific characteristics, such as the 'size effect'. Seasonal anomalies are anomalies that depend solely on time, such as the 'January effect'. Event anomalies are price changes that occur after some easily identified event, such as a listing announcement. Accounting anomalies are changes in stock prices that occur after the release of accounting information, such as an earnings announcement.

5 **a.** Errors of judgement and errors of preference are specific to the BF theory.

   b. Errors of preference are not really mistakes. If it is explained to people that they have committed errors of preference, then they typically will continue to make these errors.

   c. In this instance the error of judgement committed is availability bias. That is, the investor places undue weight on easily available information, as everyone who uses the Internet can get this information for free.

   d. In this instance the error of preference committed is that of risk-seeking for losses. That is, the investor is willing to take chances in an attempt to escape from a losing position.

Chapter Thirteen

1 This statement is not true for any bond with annual coupons larger than zero ($C > 0$). To illustrate this, suppose we have a bond with one year to maturity, a par value of $1000 and an annual coupon of $C = \$100$. If $y = 0$ then, with Equation (13.2), we get:

$$P = \frac{\$100}{1.0} = \frac{\$1000}{1.0} = \$1100$$

which is greater than $Par = \$1000$. This statement is true only if the annual coupon is zero because then the sum of the future coupons is zero, and the price will equal the par value (because there is no discounting).

2 Yield to call will exceed yield to maturity because the amount paid, if called, exceeds the par value of the bond. If yield curve is flat, bonds with similar characteristics – except maturity – will also trade at par. Thus, the yield must be higher for yield to call.

3 The local expectations hypothesis (LEH) states that all bonds with similar characteristics – except maturity – regardless of maturity, will have the same expected holding period rate of return. That is, a one-month bond and a 30-year bond should, on average, provide the same rate of return if one buys a one-month bond and holds it to maturity or buys a 30-year bond and sells it after one month.

   The unbiased expectations hypothesis (UEH) states that the current implied forward rates are unbiased estimators of future expected spot rates. Therefore, if the yield curve is upward sloping, UEH states that the market expectation is that rates will rise.

   The liquidity preference hypothesis (LPH) states that the yield curve should normally be upward-sloping, reflecting investors' preferences for the liquidity and lower risk of shorter-term securities. In its purest form, LPH is invalidated by casual observation of the historical behaviour of term structure. That is, there have been numerous occasions when the yield curve has been inverted.

The market segmentation hypothesis (MSH) states that for each type of maturity there exists an entirely separate market. For example, banks tend to participate exclusively in the short-term maturity, whereas insurance companies tend to participate exclusively in the long-term maturity as they have long-term obligations. Thus, the supply-and-demand considerations of participants within each sub-market will be the sole factors determining the equilibrium interest rate without any regard to the equilibrium point of neighbouring maturities.

4 Intelo's bond price will probably fall as a result of the downgrade. Conversely, the yield on maturity will rise in order to compensate for the reduction in price, as the bond carries more risk than before and the company must offer higher returns to entice investors.

5 **a.** The conversion ratio is 5, which means that for every bond converted the firm will issue 5 shares of common stock:

$$Conversion\ value = Conversion\ Ratio \times Current\ stock\ price$$
$$= 5 \times \$25 = \$125$$
$$Conversion\ Price = Par/Conversion\ Ratio$$
$$= \$100/5 = \$20$$

b. You should convert now as at the current stage the price exceeds the conversion price.

c. The value of the zero-coupon bond without the warrant should be equal to its future discounted cash flow; that is the repayment of the principal:

$$\frac{100}{1.1^{10}} = \$38.55$$

Hence, the value of the convertible option is equal to:

$$52 - 38.55 = \$13.45$$

d. The value of the convertible bond will increase. Just like any other option, the value of the option feature within the convertible depends positively on the risk of the underlying asset, that is the share.

Chapter Fourteen

1 The bond's par value is $1000. Assuming that before the inflation the two bonds sell at par, we obtain the following prices for the two bonds *after* the onset of inflation:

For the junk bond:

$$P_{junk} = \frac{\$91.30}{(1.092)} + \frac{\$91.30}{(1.092)^2} + \ldots + \frac{\$91.30}{(1.092)^{29}} + \frac{\$1091.30}{(1.092)^{30}} = \$992.93$$

and for the five-year bond:

$$P_{5-year} = \frac{\$59}{(1.079)} + \frac{\$59}{(1.079)^2} + \frac{\$59}{(1.079)^3} + \frac{\$59}{(1.079)^4} + \frac{\$1059}{(1.079)^5} = \$919.93$$

The capital loss on the junk bond is $7.07 (= $992.93 − $1000) and on the five-year bond the loss is $80.07 (= $919.93 − $1000). Thus, in the case of inflation, holders of the short-term bond suffer greater losses: the yield of the short-term bond rises due to inflation, but the yield of the junk bond behaves differently. The relatively high yield of junk bonds stems from the high probability of bankruptcy and, therefore, when the economy expands, as is generally the case in inflation, the probability of bankruptcy goes down, taking the yield on junk bonds down with it. This is why the yield on junk bonds is less sensitive to inflation. If there is a depression and the economy contracts, interest rates go down and the probability of bankruptcy goes up; hence, the yield to maturity on junk bonds will go down less than the yield to maturity on other short-term bonds. In such a case, a higher capital gain is obtained on the other short-term bonds.

2   Recall from Equation 14.5 that:

$$D = \sum_{i=1}^{n} w_i D_i$$

where:

$w_i = MV_i/MV$
MV_i is the market value of the portfolio holding of Bond i
MV is the market value of the total bond portfolio
D_i is the duration of Bond i
n is the number of bonds in the portfolio

Using Equation 14.5 to express D in this case, we get:

$$D = w_A D_A + w_B = w_A D_A + (1 - w_A)D_B$$

Setting $D = 12$ and solving for w_A, we get:

$$12 = w(8) + (1 - w_A)15$$

$$15w_A - 8W_A = 3$$

$$w_A = 3/7$$

and hence:

$$W_B = 0/7$$

In this case, $MV_i = Q_i P_i$ (where Q_i denotes quantity); thus we know:

$$w_A = \frac{Q_A P_A}{Q_A P_A + Q_B P_B} = \frac{Q_A(\$900)}{\$500\,000}$$

Solving for Q_A we get:

$$\frac{3}{7} = Q_A \frac{\$900}{\$500\,000}$$

$$Q_A = \frac{3}{7} = \frac{\$500\,000}{\$900} = 238.10$$

and solving for Q_B, we get:

$$\frac{4}{7} = Q_B \frac{\$1100}{\$500\,000}$$

$$Q_B = \frac{4}{7} \frac{\$500\,000}{\$1100} = 259.74$$

Thus, to minimise interest rate risk, you should buy 238.1 A bonds and 259.74 B bonds.

3 Recall from Equation 14.6 that convexity can be calculated as follows:

$$C = \sum_{t=1}^{n} t \times (t+1) \times \frac{CF_t/(1+y)^{t+2}}{P}$$

When applied to Bond M:

$$C = \sum_{t=1}^{6} \frac{t(t+1)}{(1.048)^2} \left[\frac{CF_t \Big/ \left(1 + \dfrac{0.096}{2}\right)^t}{\$1000} \right] = \left[\frac{1}{\$1000} \sum_{t=1}^{6} \frac{t \times (t+1) \times C}{(1.048)^{t+2}} + \frac{1}{\$1000} \times \frac{6 \times 7 \times Par}{1.048^8} \right]$$

$$= 0.001 \left[\frac{1 \times 2 \times 48}{(1.048)^3} + \frac{2 \times 3 \times 48}{(1.048)^4} + \frac{3 \times 4 \times 48}{(1.048)^5} + \frac{4 \times 5 \times 48}{(1.048)^6} + \frac{5 \times 6 \times 48}{(1.048)^7} + \frac{6 \times 7 \times 48}{(1.048)^8} \right.$$

$$\left. + \frac{6 \times 7 \times \$1000}{1.048^8} \right]$$

$$\cong 0.001(\$3925.005 + \$28\,864.167) = \$32\,789$$

To convert the calculated semiannual convexity to the annual convexity:

$$\$32\,789/4 = \$8197.25$$

Duration is a measure of the slope of the price–yield relationship. This can be a very imprecise measure for interest-rate risk in case of large yield changes. Convexity is a measure of the *curvature* of the price–yield relationship; it measures the degree by which the duration changes as the yield to maturity changes.

4 There are three income immunisation strategies discussed in this chapter: cash matching, duration matching and horizon matching. The least flexible is cash matching, which requires each year's cash flow to be matched exactly. The most flexible is duration matching, where the duration of the assets is matched with the duration of the liabilities. In between these two strategies is horizon matching, which requires cash matching for the first several years and duration matching thereafter.

5 a. Active management is implemented when the market is assumed to be inefficient, and hence, one can benefit from forecasting future interest rates and identifying overpriced and underpriced bonds.
   b. To avoid excessive risk-taking the manager can use a contingent immunisation strategy, which combines active management and passive management. By doing so, he or she can profit from pursuing timing strategies or duration mismatches, and at the same time limit the risk arising from adverse movements of interest rates.

Chapter Fifteen

1 Recall that the reciprocal of the P/E ratio (that is, E/P) is related directly to the expected rate of return for normal growth firms (Equation 15.20). Thus:

$$k = \frac{E(EPS_1)}{P_0} = \frac{1}{10} = 0.1 \text{ or } 10\%$$

Substituting this information in the CDGM (Equation 15.7), we get:

$$\$20 = \frac{E(DPS_1)}{k-g} = \frac{\$10}{0.1-g}$$

and solving for g, we get:

$$\$20(0.1-g) = \$10$$
$$0.1-g = 0.5$$

or:

$$g = 0.1 - 0.5 = -0.4 \text{ or } -40\%$$

Thus, the firm has a negative growth rate.

2 **a.** The 12% required rate of return is:

$$E(DPS_1) = 5 \times (1+0.06)^1 = 5.3$$

$$P_0 = \frac{5.3}{0.12-0.06} = \$88.33$$

b. The 14% required rate of return is:

$$P_0 = \frac{5.3}{0.14-0.06} = \$66.25$$

c. The 6% required rate of return is:

$$P_0 = \frac{5.3}{0.06-0.06} = \text{Undefined}$$

d. The 4% required rate of return is:

$$P_0 = \frac{5.3}{0.04-0.06} = -\$265.00$$

The model does not work in Parts c and d because $k < g$ violates the assumption of the constant dividend growth model. If Part d were correct, the Sugar Corporation would give an investor $265 and a share of stock!

3 With the revised estimate of the growth rate, the new price by the dividend discount model is:

$$P_0 = \frac{E(DPS_1)}{k-g} = \frac{\$6}{0.12-0.04} = \$75$$

Hence, the decline in the growth rate caused a $25 decrease in the market value of IBM.

4 To answer this question, we must first rearrange the CDGM. First, we define d_t as the company's dividend payout ratio, so that (see Equation 15.3):

$$DPS_t = d_t \times EPS_t$$

Then we rearrange Equation 15.7 to express the P/E ratio:

$$P_0 = \frac{E(DPS_1)}{k-g} = \frac{DPS_0(1+g)}{k-g} = \frac{d_0(EPS_0)(1+g)}{k-g} \Rightarrow \frac{P_0}{EPS_0} = d_0 \left[\frac{1+g}{k-g} \right]$$

a. Consider the last term in the equation above. Holding everything else constant, increasing g increases the numerator and decreases the denominator. Both indicate that increasing g increases the P/E ratio. Remember, however, that the growth rate for a normal-growth firm depends on the firm's payout (or, equivalently, retention) ratio; so that g increases only if d_t decreases. The effects exactly offset one another for a normal-growth firm. For a super-growth firm, increased growth comes from investment in positive-NPV projects and occurs without changing the payout ratio.

b. Increasing risk increases the required return (k), which causes the P/E ratio to decrease.

c. Increasing the payout ratio increases the P/E ratio for super-growth firms. For normal-growth firms, increases in the payout ratio are exactly offset by decreases in growth.

5 This statement is only sometimes true and reflects the reality that investors must be very careful when interpreting the results of any analysis based on a DDM. If the DDM indicates that the stock is undervalued, it does not guarantee that it will soon be correctly valued. In fact, the stock could become more undervalued before turning around, creating losses for investors unwilling or unable to wait for the mispricing to be corrected. Also, investors must be confident of the information on which the conclusion that the stock is mispriced is based. It is possible that the market price of the stock is correct and that the analyst's estimate of true value is incorrect.

Chapter Sixteen

1 The cash flow is:

$$190 + 100 - 10 - 15 = \$265 \text{ million}$$

The cash flow is:

$$265 - 25 + 5 = \$245 \text{ million}$$

2 Reporting revenues when a product is shipped to a company's own warehouse will result in higher reported earnings but will not impact the statement of cash flows, because this is not a cash transaction.

3 a. The ending inventory according to the FIFO method would be:

$$(55 \times \$850) + (5 \times \$780) = \$50\,650$$

Recall that FIFO assumes that goods inventoried first are sold first. Thus, with 60 elements in stock, their values would be based on the costs of the last elements purchased.
   The ending inventory according to the LIFO method would be:

$$(30 \times \$750) + (30 \times \$780) = \$45\,900$$

Recall that LIFO assumes goods inventoried last are sold first. Thus, with 60 elements in stock, their values would be based on the cost of the first elements purchased.
   The ending inventory according to the average cost method would be based on the average cost of all purchases and beginning inventories. That is:

$$\text{Total Cost} = (30 \times \$750) + (85 \times \$780) + (55 \times \$850) = \$135\,550$$

$$\text{Number of elements} = 30 + 85 + 55 = 170$$

And the average cost is:

$$\$135\,550/170 = \$797.35$$

Thus, the ending inventory would be valued at:

$$(60 \times \$797.35) = \$47\,841$$

b. Recall that cost of goods sold (COGS) is calculated as:

$$COGS = Beginning\ Inventory + Purchases - Ending\ Inventory$$

$$COGS = (30 \times \$750) + (85 \times \$780) + (55 \times \$850) - Ending\ Inventory$$

$$COGS = \$135\,550 - Ending\ Inventory$$

Based on results above, one finds:

$$FIFO: COGS = \$135\,550 - \$50\,650 = \$84\,900$$

$$LIFO: COGS = \$135\,550 - \$45\,900 = \$89\,650$$

Average costs:

$$COGS = \$135\,550 - \$47\,841 = \$87\,709$$

c. Recall our net income is sales less cost of goods sold less taxes. We use the following table for the solutions:

Income statement	FIFO	LIFO	Average cost
Sales	$99 000	$99 000	$99 000
COGS	$84 900	$89 650	$87 709
EBIT	$14 100	$9 350	$11 291
Taxes	$3 807	$2 524.50	$3 048.57
Net Income	$10 293	$6 825.50	$8 242.43

4 R&D is one of the most difficult expense items to assess. The main reason for this is that R&D expenditure does not necessarily add value to the firm, making actual R&D costs as a measure of R&D effectiveness inadequate. However, investors view R&D expenses differently to accountants: typically, accountants treat R&D as a non-asset-generating expense and they do not add it to the balance sheet; while investors often regard R&D as an asset-generating expense.

5 Based on the consolidated balance sheet given above, the following liquidity ratios can be constructed:

Quick ratio:

$$(Current\ Assets - Inventory - Other\ Current\ Assets)/Current\ Liabilities$$

$$(9702 - 2384 - 954)/8460 \approx 0.752$$

Current ratio:

$$Current\ Assets/Current\ Liabilities$$

$$9702/8460 \approx 1.147$$

Cash ratio:

$$(Cash + Marketable\ Securities)/Current\ Liabilities$$

$$(1725 + 731)/8460 \approx 0.29$$

Chapter Seventeen

1 Consider Equation 17.1:

$$GDP = C + I + G + (X - M)$$

where consumption (C), when increased by \$10 billion, has a positive impact on GDP. However, imports (M), also increased by \$10 billion, have a negative impact on GDP. The net impact on GDP will, therefore, be zero.

2 This statement is false because predicting the business cycle is different to predicting stock prices. Also, predicting stock prices does not yield abnormal returns if the predicted prices reflect only a change in risk or risk premiums.

3 Both fiscal and monetary policy aim to promote real GDP growth, relatively full employment and stable prices. However, while fiscal policy refers to the taxation and spending policy of a government and its effects on the business environment, monetary policy refers to the actions of a central bank taken to control the supply of money and interest rates which directly influence the financial markets.

4 Open market operations affect interest rates through their influence on the level of bank reserves. Every bank must deposit a minimum level of funds into a Federal Reserve Bank; the amount deposited must be a certain percentage of the bank's deposits. Therefore, reserves are liabilities to the Fed and assets to the banks.

   If the Fed buys Treasury securities in the open market from banks, the Fed pays for the securities by increasing the banks' reserves. Now that banks have more reserves on deposit than required, the excess reserves can be withdrawn and used to make new loans. Since credit is more readily available, interest rates decrease.

   A sale of Treasury securities by the Fed has exactly the opposite effect. Banks that buy the securities pay for them by having the balances of their reserve accounts at the Fed reduced. The banks must attract new deposits or borrow money to make up the shortfalls in their reserve accounts. Because the demand for credit has increased, interest rates increase.

5 a. Using Purchasing Power Parity (see Equation 17.7), with $E(h_{FC}) = 2.5\%$, $E(h_{DC}) = 3\%$ and $fx_0(FC/DC) = 1.2$, we find:

$$E[fx_1(FC/DC)] \approx [E(h_{FC} - h_{DC}) + 1] \times [fx_0(FC/DC)] \approx \$1.194/€$$

   b. Using the International Fisher Relationship (see Equation 17.8), with $E(h_{FC}) = 2.5\%$, $E(h_{DC}) = 3\%$ and $R_{n,FC} = 1\%$, $R_{n,DC} = 2.5\%$, we find:

$$R_{n,FC} - R_{n,DC} = -1.5 \neq E(h_{FC} - h_{DC}) = -0.5$$

   The International Fisher Relationship does not hold; the data is not consistent with that of Part (a). According to equation:

$$\frac{1 + R_{n,DC}}{1 + R_{n,FC}} = \frac{1 + R_{r,DC}}{1 + R_{r,FC}} \times \frac{1 + h_{DC}}{1 + h_{FC}}$$

   an arbitrage opportunity must exist, due to the real interest rates not being the same across the two countries, and money should flow to Europe due to a higher real rate.

c. Using the Interest Rate Parity (see Equation 17.10), we find:

$$F[fx_1(FC/DC)] \approx [(R_{n,FC} - R_{n,DC}) + 1] \times [fx_0 \, (FC/DC)] = [0.985 \times 1.2] = \$1.182/€$$

d. With the forward rate at \$1.15/€, Interest Rate Parity would state that the dollar is too highly priced; this means that a US investor could invest his money in Europe, earn an interest rate of 2.5% and then convert his money back into dollars and make a profit.

Chapter Eighteen

1 Fundamental analysis is based on fundamental values such as the firm's earnings, its dividends and the strength of its balance sheet. Technical analysis, on the other hand, is based on historical market data: for example, the past market prices, the amounts of short-selling, and the volume of trading. Technical analysis can thus only be beneficial if the market is not weak-form efficient.

2 Technical analysis assumes that asset prices can be predicted by observing and identifying a repetitive pattern of primary, intermediate and short-term waves. This idea originates from Charles Dow, who first identified these trends.

3 Technical analysts plot market data on charts, such as bar charts, point-and-figure charts, and candlestick charts. The charts display historical information that enables technical analysts to extrapolate trends into the future.

The candlestick chart was developed in Japan and only became popular in the United States recently. Each observation on a candlestick chart is based on a day's opening, high, low and closing prices. For each day, the chart contains a candlestick line, which has two parts. The real body is the broad part consisting of the difference between the opening and closing prices, and the shadows are the vertical thin line above and below the real body. If the opening price is above the closing price, then the real body is shaded dark. If the opening price is below the closing price, then the real body is not shaded.

4 The following point-and-figure chart could be constructed:

65			
64			
63			
62			
61			X
60			X
59			X
58			X
57			X
56			X
55			X
54		X	X
53		X	O	X
52		X	O	
51	O	X		
50	O			
49				

The closing prices first show a decline from 51.38 to 49.75. Hence, two Os are placed in the first column. Over the next three days the price increases to a peak of 54.13. Thus, we place 4 Xs in the second column from 51 to 54 (55 was never hit). Next the price fell to 52.25 and Os are placed in the third column for 53 and 52. Finally, the run-up in price for the last series of days is recorded in the fourth column.

5 This statement is false. Researchers have discovered patterns in security prices. For example, Lehmann (1990) found evidence of trends that do not always occur, but that have occurred with sufficient frequency to create many profit opportunities. Jegadeesh (1990) also found predictable patterns in stock prices for monthly returns over a long time period (1934–1987). Specifically, Jegadeesh found strong evidence that stocks which experience large losses in one month are likely to experience a significant reversal in the next month, and that stocks with large gains in one month are likely to experience a significant loss in the next month. These findings suggest that technical analysis may be useful.

Chapter Nineteen

1 a. First, it takes many transactions to mimic the payoff structure of an option over time. Derivatives contribute to the investment possibilities by making these payoff patterns available to a wider group of investors at a lower cost.

   Second, derivatives can be used to reduce risk. This risk reduction can be a gain to an investor.

   Third, and very much related to the above, investors may be willing to pay a premium for bonds and stocks if derivatives are available to manage the risk of these securities. Put differently, the availability of derivatives can lower funding costs.

   b. The four basic strategies investors use derivative contracts in are: hedging, speculating, arbitrage, and portfolio diversification.

   ■ In hedging strategies, derivative contracts are used to transfer price risk by offsetting an existing long or short position.
   ■ In speculative strategies, derivative contracts are used to expose oneself to more risk and are based on assumptions about future prices.
   ■ In arbitrage strategies, derivative contracts are used to re-create a particular asset synthetically. The synthetic asset is then traded against the original asset, so as to exploit price differences between the two.
   ■ In diversification strategies, derivative contracts are combined in a portfolio of assets in order to gain further diversification.

2 a. In an interest-rate swap, one counterparty promises to make a fixed periodic payment, while the second counterparty promises to make a floating periodic payment. The reason for this type of swap is to eliminate one party's exposure to changing interest rates while increasing the other party's exposure.

   In a currency swap, two counterparties agree to exchange equivalent holdings (based on a locked in exchange rate) of different currencies. Besides this, the details are the same as the interest-rate swap above.

   b. The financial manager can engage in an interest-rate swap paying a fixed long-term rate and receiving a floating short-term rate. If the short-term rate does in fact rise more than the market expected this swap will rise in value.

3 The calculations of cash flows are represented in the table below:

Day	Futures price	Daily gain (loss)	Cumulative gain (loss)	Margin account balance	Margin call
0	1218			30.000	
1	1220	1.000	1.000	31.000	
2	1225	2.500	3.500	33.500	
3	1218	−3.500	0	30.000	
4	1215	−1.500	−1.500	28.500	
5	1219	2.000	500	30.500	
6	1222	1.500	2.000	32.000	
7	1217	−2.500	−500	29.500	
8	1210	−3.500	−4.000	26.000	4.000[c]
9	1215	2.500	−1.500	32.500	
10	1220	2.500	1.000	35.000	

[a] When the index rises the futures contract buyer benefits:

$$\$1000 = 500 \times (\$1220 - \$1218)$$

[b] Cumulative gain/loss is calculated as the sum of all the previous days' losses/profits:

$$\$3500 = \$1000 + \$2500$$

[c] The margin call is issued as soon as the margin account balance becomes lower than the required maintenance margin of $27 000.

4 a. The profit from the contract with the fast-food chain with respect to future cacao prices can be represented as a function of the future cacao price P_c:

$$\text{Profit} = 5\ 200\ 000 - (3\ 000\ 000 + 2000 \times P_c) = 2\ 200\ 000 - 2000 \times P_c$$

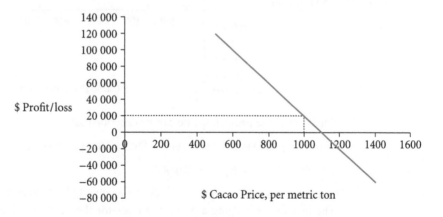

b. Purchasing one five-month cacao futures contract the chocolate producer locks in the cacao costs for 10 tons. This contract can be viewed as a loss if the market price of cacao in five months will be lower than $1000 per metric ton. The hedge is not perfect, because the producer locks in the costs for only 10 tons out of the 2000 needed for production. The profit and loss on the purchase of one futures contract is illustrated below:

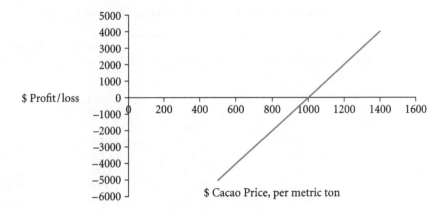

It is obvious, that if the market price is equal to $1000 per metric ton, the profit from the futures contract is zero.

c. To make a perfect hedge, the chocolate-producing company has to buy 200 futures contracts, because the production requires 2000 tons of cacao, and each futures contract is for 10 tons only.

In this case the profit/loss line will look as follows:

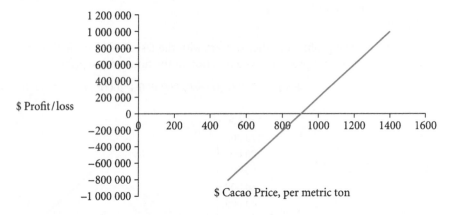

Analytically the profit/loss line can be described as:

Profit = $5 200 000 − $3 000 000 − (200 × 10 × $1000) + (200 × 10 × ($P_c$ − $1000))

Profit = ($2000 × P_c) − $1 800 000

Given the cacao price is equal to $1000 the profit will be $200 000, as initially planned.

The benefits of hedging are that the costs for the cacao are fixed. There is no chance of any changes in prices being passed on to the fast-food chain if they suddenly increase. On the other hand, if the prices decrease, the chocolate producer will still be obliged to purchase cacao at $1000, as fixed by the futures contract. If its competitors do not hedge, they will make more profit. It is important to note that hedging mainly refers to insurance against downside risk, and not to a strategy for deriving profit.

d. If one expects stable prices in the future, one is unlikely to profit from speculating on futures. The payoff from speculation will be about zero. One can, however, speculate on futures due to the price *changes*.

Option contracts and their combinations are more suitable for this purpose. There are a number of different strategies to benefit:

■ *Long Butterfly*: a Long Butterfly consists of buying two call options, one with a strike price of X_L, lower than $1000, and one with a strike price of X_H, higher than $1000. Then one writes two calls with an intermediate strike price of $1000. This results in a payoff pattern as shown below:

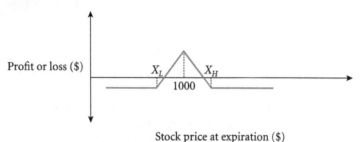

■ *Short Straddle*: this is a combination of a short put and a short call, with the same strike price:

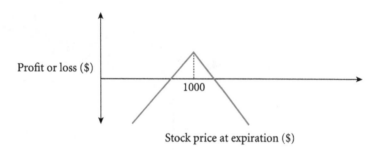

■ *Short Strangle*: a Short Strangle is similar to a Short Straddle, but the strike price of the short call (X_H) should be higher than that of the short put (X_L), with the forecasted price of $1000 being in between:

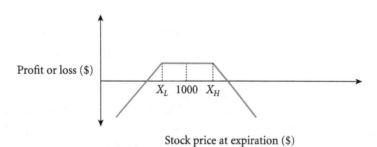

5 Recall that call options are in the money when the strike price is above the exercise price; and that calls are out of the money when the strike price is under the exercise price.

a. Writing a call option:
When the stock price rises to $110 the holder of the call will exercise the option. The option writer will lose $5 ($110 − $105), exactly offsetting the amount he has gained

before as option premium. The option writer's payoff is thus exactly zero (see payoff diagram below).

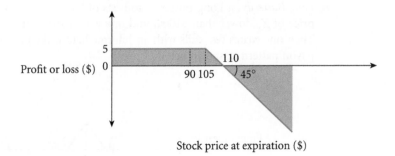

Stock price at expiration ($)

When the stock price goes down to $90 the holder of the call option won't exercise it. The option writer will thus retain the $5 option premium.

b. Writing a covered call option; that is, writing a call and buying the stock:

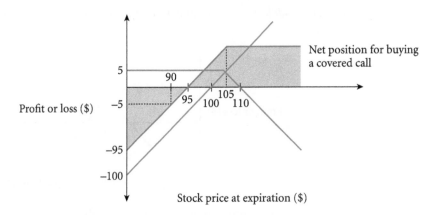

Stock price at expiration ($)

The combination of long call and short position on stock creates the payoff diagram similar to a short position in a put (see payoff diagram above).

Period t_0:
At the moment when an investor writes a call and buys the stock his or her cash flow is:

$$-\$100 + \$5 = -\$95$$

Period t_1:
When the stock price rises to $110 the option writer's counterparty exercises the call at the strike price of $105. The writer's payoff on the option is zero (as described above). However the writer also holds the stock, bought for $100, which is now worth $110. Therefore, the writer's total payoff can be calculated as:

$$-\$95 - \$5 + \$110 = \$10$$

When the stock prices goes down to $90 the option is not exercised, but the writer suffers a loss from the decrease of the price of the stocks he or she holds. His or her total payoff can therefore be calculated as:

$$-\$95 + \$90 = -\$5$$

Chapter Twenty

1 a. $B_{1/4} = 340 - 344.28$
$B_{1/4} = -4.28$

$B_{1/2} = 340 - 348.61$
$B_{1/2} = -\$8.61$

$B_{3/4} = 340 - 353.00$
$B_{3/4} = -13.00$

$B_1 = 340 - 357.43$
$B_1 = -17.43$

b. $344.28 = 340(1 + 0.03 - d)^{1/4}$

$(1 + 0.03 - d)^{1/4} = \dfrac{344.28}{340} = 1.0126$

$d = -0.0213, d = -2.13\%$

$353 = 340(1 + 0.03 - d)^{3/4}$

$(1 + 0.03 - d)^{3/4} = \dfrac{353.00}{340} = 1.0382$

$d = -0.0213, d = -2.13\%$

$348.61 = 340(1 + 0.03 - d)^{1/2}$

$(1 + 0.03 - d)^{1/2} = \dfrac{348.61}{340} = 1.0253$

$d = -0.0213, d = -2.13\%$

$357.43 = 340(1 + 0.03 - d)$

$(1 + 0.03 - d) = \dfrac{357.43}{340} = 1.0513$

$d = -0.0213, d = -2.13\%$

2

Trading strategy	Today (0)	At expiration $S_{t \geq X}$	At expiration $S_{t < X}$
Short one put	$+P_0$	$-S_t + X$	0
Borrow $X/(1 + r)^t$	$+X/(1 + r)^t$	$-X$	$-X$
Net cash flow	$+C_0 + X/(1 + r)^t$ (positive)	$-S_t$	$-X$

One could earn a positive payoff today if P_0 exceeded the strike price. Even in extremes, where X and S_t are zero, a profit can be made today by selling the overpriced call. It therefore follows that $C_0 \leq S_0$, and that $P_0 \leq X/(1 + r)^t$.

3

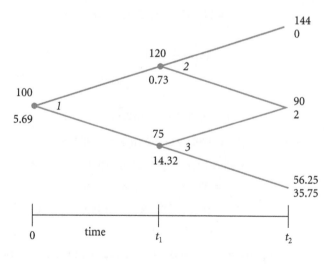

Put price at node *2*:

$$\text{Hedge ratio} = \frac{(0 - 2)}{120(1.2 - 0.75)} = -0.03704$$

$$\text{Put price} = -0.03704 \times 120 + \frac{2 - (-0.03704 \times 60)}{1.03} = 0.73$$

Put price at node *3*:

$$\text{Hedge ratio} = \frac{2 - 35.75}{120(1.2 - 0.75)} = -1$$

$$\text{Put price} \quad = -1 \times 75 + \frac{35.75 - (-1 \times 56.25)}{1.03} = 14.32$$

Put price at node *1*:

$$\text{Hedge ratio} = \frac{0.73 - 14.32}{100(1.2 - 0.75)} = -0.302$$

$$\text{Put price} \quad = -0.302 \times 100 + \frac{14.32 - (-0.302 \times 75)}{1.03} = 5.69$$

4

$$d_1 = \frac{\ln\left(\dfrac{100}{100}\right) + \left[0.02 + \left(\dfrac{0.3^2}{2}\right)\right] \times 0.5}{0.3\sqrt{0.5}} = \frac{0.0325}{0.21213} = 0.1532$$

$$d_2 = 0.1532 - (0.3\sqrt{0.5}) \qquad\qquad = -0.0589$$

so that $N(d_1) = 0.56089$ and $N(d_2) = 0.47652$

$$\text{Call} = 100e^{-(0.03\times0.5)} \times 0.56089 - 100e^{-(0.05\times0.5)} \times 0.47652$$

$$= 55.2539 - 46.4755 = 8.78$$

$$\text{Put} = 100e^{-(0.05\times0.5)} \times [1 - 0.47652] - 100e^{-(0.03\times0.5)} \times [1 - 0.56089]$$

$$= 51.0555 - 43.2573 = 7.80$$

5 a.

$$d_1 = \frac{\ln\left(\dfrac{101}{101}\right) + \left[0.02 + \left(\dfrac{0.3^2}{2}\right)\right] \times 0.5}{0.3\sqrt{0.5}} = \frac{0.04245}{0.21213} = 0.2001$$

$$d_2 = 0.2001 - (0.3\sqrt{0.5}) = -0.012$$

so that $N(d_1) = 0.579299$ and $N(d_2) = 0.495213$

$$\text{Call} = 101e^{-(0.03\times0.5)} \times 0.579299 - 100e^{-(0.05\times0.5)} \times 0.495213$$

$$= 57.6381 - 48.2986 = 9.34$$

$$\text{Put} = 100e^{-(0.05\times0.5)} \times [1 - 0.495213] - 101e^{-(0.03\times0.5)} \times [1 - 0.579299]$$

$$= 49.2324 - 41.8582 = 7.37$$

In comparison to Question 4, an increase of the stock price of 1% causes the call price to increase with 6.4%. The effect on the put is a 5.5% decrease of the price.

b.

$$\Delta \text{ Call} = e^{-(0.03\times0.5)} \times 0.579299 = 0.57067$$

$$\text{Call} = 8.78 + 0.57067 \times (101 - 100) = 9.35$$

$$\Delta \text{ Put} = e^{-(0.03\times0.5)} \times [0.579299 - 1] = -0.41444$$

$$\text{Put} = 7.80 + (-0.41444) \times (101 - 100) = 7.39$$

Using the formula for delta to estimate the effect of a 1% increase of the stock price, the call price is overestimated with 0.01 and the put price is overestimated with 0.02 in comparison to the Black–Scholes approach.

c. $$\Gamma = \frac{e^{-0.015-0.5(0.2001)^2}}{101 \times 0.3 \times \sqrt{2\pi 0.5}} = \frac{1.00503}{53.7054} = 0.01871$$

$$\text{Call} = 8.78 + 0.57067 \times (101 - 100) + 0.5 \times 0.01871 \times (101 - 100)^2 = 9.36$$

$$\text{Put} = 7.80 + (-0.41444) \times (101 - 100) + 0.5 \times 0.01871 \times (101 - 100)^2 = 7.40$$

Using both delta and gamma to estimate the effect of a 1% increase of the stock price, the call price is overestimated with 0.02 and the put price is overestimated with 0.03 in comparison to the Black–Scholes approach.

d. Repeating Part a:

$$d_1 = \frac{\ln\left(\frac{110}{100}\right) + \left[0.02 + \left(\frac{0.3^2}{2}\right)\right] \times 0.5}{0.3\sqrt{0.5}} = \frac{0.12781}{0.21213} = 0.6025$$

$$d_2 = 0.6025 - (0.3\sqrt{0.5}) \qquad\qquad = 0.3904$$

so that $N(d_1) = 0.72657$ and $N(d_2) = 0.65187$

$$\text{Call} = 110e^{-(0.03\times0.5)} \times 0.72657 - 100e^{-(0.05\times0.5)} \times 0.65187$$

$$= 78.7328 - 63.5775 = 15.16$$

$$\text{Put} = 100e^{-(0.05\times0.5)} \times [1 - 0.65187] - 110e^{-(0.03\times0.5)} \times [1 - 0.72657]$$

$$= 33.9535 - 29.6295 = 4.32$$

In comparison to Question 4, an increase of the stock price of 10% causes the call price to increase with 72.7%. The effect on the put is a 44.6% decrease of the price.

Repeating Part b:

$$\Delta \text{ Call} = e^{-(0.03\times0.5)} \times 0.72657 = 0.715753$$

$$\text{Call} = 8.78 + 0.715753 \times (110 - 100) = 15.94$$

$$\Delta \text{ Put} = e^{-(0.03\times0.5)} \times [0.72657 - 1] = -0.266679$$

$$\text{Put} = 7.80 + -0.266679 \times (110 - 100) = 5.13$$

Using the formula for delta to estimate the effect of a 10% increase of the stock price, the call price is overestimated with 0.78 and the put price is overestimated with 0.81 in comparison to the Black–Scholes approach.

Repeating Part c:

$$\Gamma = \frac{e^{-(0.015-[0.5\times0.6025^2])}}{101 \times 0.3 \times \sqrt{2\pi 0.5}} = \frac{1.18117}{58.491} = 0.020194$$

$$\text{Call} = 8.78 + 0.715753 \times (110 - 100) + 0.5 \times 0.020194 \times (110 - 100)^2 = 16.95$$

$$\text{Put} = 7.80 + (-0.266679) \times (110 - 100) + 0.5 \times 0.020194 \times (110 - 100)^2 = 6.14$$

Using both delta and gamma to estimate the effect of a 10% increase of the stock price, the call price is overestimated with 1.79 and the put price is overestimated with 1.82 in comparison to the Black–Scholes approach.

Chapter Twenty-one

1 Individual investors have a strong incentive to manage the risk of their portfolio, because investment losses reduce their possibilities for future expenses. Institutional retail investors should also have strong incentives to manage risk, because they invest the money of their clients who are generally risk-averse. Further, pension funds or insurance companies which have to cater for fixed liabilities will generally restrict the flexibility of the external money managers that invest their funds. Finally, regulatory bodies may force institutional investors to adopt particular risk management policies so as to mitigate systemic risk.

2 a. First, the standard deviation of the portfolio can be calculated as follows (see Equation 8.6):

$$\sigma_p = \sqrt{w_A^2 \sigma_A^2 + w_B^2 \sigma_B^2 + 2 w_A w_B \sigma_{A,B}}$$

$$\sigma_p = \sqrt{(^2/_7)^2 \times 1.6^2 + (^5/_7)^2 \times 1.2^2 + 2 \times ^2/_7 \times ^5/_7 \times 1.6 \times 1.2 \times 0.3}$$

$$\sigma_p = \sqrt{1.788}$$

$$\sigma_p \cong 1.086$$

The VaR should be calculated as followed (see Equation 21.1):

$$VaR(\gamma, T) = z^{-1}(\gamma) \times \sigma_p \times \sqrt{T} \times P$$

$$VaR(95.1) = 1.645 \times 0.01086 \times \sqrt{1 \times 700\,000} = 12\,505.29$$

b. (See Equation 21.1):

$$VaR(\gamma, T) = z^{-1}(\gamma) \times \sigma_p \times \sqrt{T \times P}$$

$$VaR(99.5) = 2.326 \times 0.01086 \times \sqrt{5 \times 700\,000} = 39\,528.71$$

c. Increasing the investment horizon also increases VaR.

3 a. An asset correlation of 20%, as in the table above (p. 759), has a joint probability of a default of 0.003%, which can be read from the right-hand bottom corner of the table.

b. If the asset correlation is 0%, the joint probability of a default is equal to the product of the individual default probabilities. The probability of default for the BB obligor is 1.07% (right-hand column). The probability of default for the A obligor is 0.06% (bottom row). Hence the joint probability of default is 0.06% × 1.07% (= 0.0006%). Clearly, lowering the correlation also lowers the joint default probability.

4 A disadvantage of the Monte Carlo method is that some statistical distribution for the factor returns has to be specified in advance, and hence specification error may arise. Further, although MCS does not use historical data, it is still exposed to sampling error: specifically, there is a risk of running too few simulations to adequately capture the return distribution and this could result in unreliable results. This is true especially if many risk factors are included in the model.

5 As head of the front office and the back office, Leeson was perfectly placed to relay false information back to London. Also, the senior management of the organisation should not

have taken for granted the enormous profits reported by Leeson, as arbitrage strategies are associated with low risk and low profit. Another problem was the lack of an independent risk management unit to provide an additional layer of checks and balances. Finally, there was an enormous lack of clearly defined rules within the organisation's structure; too many people did not know what their responsibilities were and to whom they had to report.

Chapter Twenty-two

1 a. *Sharpe's index*:

Fund A $(14\% - 6.5\%)/5.7 = 2.34$
Fund B $(16\% - 6.5\%)/7.1 = 1.34$

Although Firm B achieved higher returns, it failed to outperform Fund A on a risk-adjusted basis.

Treynor's index:

Fund A $(14\% - 6.5\%)/1.20 = 6.25\%$
Fund B $(16\% - 6.5\%)/0.91 = 10.44\%$

Fund B outperformed Fund A according to Treynor's index.

b. Fund A:

$$14\% - [6.5\% + (13.5\% - 6.5\%)(1.20)] = -0.9\%$$

Fund B:

$$16\% - [6.5\% + (13.5\% - 6.5\%)(0.91)] = 3.13\%$$

Fund B performed better than Fund A, because $PI_{J,Fund\ B} > PI_{J,Fund\ A}$. Fund B also outperformed the market (which has $PI_{J,Market} = 0$).

c. *The APT performance index*:

$$13.7\% - 12\% = 1.7\%$$

The fund outperformed by 1.7%.

2 Which index is better depends on each investor's situation. Sharpe's ratio uses standard deviation as a measure of risk, while Treynor's ratio uses beta to measure risk. Recall that standard deviation measures the total risk of an asset and beta measures the systematic risk. Therefore, Sharpe's index is more relevant for investors who do not hold any other portfolios, whereas Treynor's index is more relevant for investors who hold many other assets apart from the mutual fund.

3 ■ The portfolio manager decides what percentage of the portfolio will be stocks, bonds and cash. This decision is known as *asset allocation*.
   ■ The *sector allocation* decision concerns how much of an asset should be placed in a specific sector.
   ■ The *industry allocation* is the allotment of investment dollars given to a sector's industry components.
   ■ *Security selection*: for example, of the allocation given to the water industry, what portion should be invested in American Water Works (AWW)?

4   **a.** The HBSA determines investment style by examining the characteristics of the individual securities in the portfolio; it then maps these characteristics into the style of the portfolio. The RBSA does not use information on the individual securities but rather determines investment style by regressing the historical returns of the entire portfolio on a set of style indices.

  b. Mutual funds publish portfolio values on a daily basis, which means that the rate of return for each day is available publicly.

     Investors need not examine every individual security in the portfolio, and therefore the RBSA is less costly and time-consuming. The RBSA is especially useful, or even preferable, in situations where current portfolio information is not readily available. The focus is on the style of the entire portfolio.

  c. The RBSA is a 'black box' because the regression cannot explain why a particular blend of style indexes gives the best fit.

     The RBSA is very sensitive to style rotation or changes in asset allocation over time.

     A common problem for the RBSA is the selection of the appropriate set of styles and style indices.

  d. Managers of mutual funds are required to disclose the exact composition of their portfolios only on a quarterly basis.

     Investors need to keep track of, and examine, the portfolio composition and the properties of every stock in the portfolio, which – when done properly – will require a costly and time-consuming effort.

     The HBSA requires the investor to evaluate all individual securities in the portfolio.

5   The empirical evidence consistently finds that, on average, mutual fund managers lag behind the market when figures are corrected for risk and costs. There seems to be little evidence for stock-picking and market-timing ability on the part of mutual fund managers. Furthermore, turnover, expenses and management fees seem to have a negative impact on the performance of mutual funds. Finally, there appears to be little (if any) consistency in the performance of funds over time, which greatly reduces the effectiveness of performance evaluation for selecting funds.

Glossary

abnormal rate of return Return above what one would expect to earn, given the level of risk taken.

accounting anomaly Trading strategies that generate abnormal returns based on observed accounting numbers.

accounting scandals Scandals surrounding the misstatement of corporations' books. Examples include ENRON, WorldCom and Ahold.

active bond management Bond management style aimed at earning long-run returns by predicting future interest movements or selecting mispriced bonds.

active investment strategy Investment strategy in which the portfolio manager actively manages investments by altering the proportions of assets in the portfolio to time the market or to pick winners.

actual margin Percentage of total current market value that an investor posted as a guarantee in a transaction.

adjusted rate of return Simple rate of return adjusted for the effects of dividends.

advance–decline line Measure that compares the number of stocks that rose with the number of stocks that fell.

advanced estimate First estimate of gross domestic product (GDP) released about one month after the measurement period.

advance-funded pension plan Pensions paid from the proceeds of pensioners' prior investments.

after-tax rate of return Rate of return based on investment revenues after payment of all relevant taxes.

aggressive asset Asset with a beta greater than one.

alpha Intercept of a regression line.

alternative trading system (ATS) Electronic trading mechanism developed independently from the established marketplaces.

American depository receipt (ADR) Certificate issued by a US depository bank, representing foreign shares held by a bank, usually by a branch or correspondent in the country of issue.

American-style option Option that can be exercised early.

appraisal ratio Jensen's index divided by the residual standard deviation.

APT performance index Performance index based on the APT.

arbitrage Strategy aimed to yield returns with zero investment and zero risk.

arbitrage opportunity Opportunity to construct an arbitrage portfolio.

arbitrage portfolio Zero-investment portfolio that yields positive future returns.

arbitrage pricing theory (APT) A linear relationship between expected return and risk exposure coefficients derived by assuming that there is no arbitrage profit in the market.

arbitrage profit Positive return from exploiting an arbitrage opportunity.

arithmetic average Figure obtained by adding up the returns of n observations and dividing this sum by n.

arithmetic method Adds the rates of return and divides by the number of observations.

asked price Price at which investors can sell a security.

asset Something owned by a business, institution, partnership or individual that has monetary value.

asset allocation Proportioning of an investment portfolio among asset classes.

asset pricing theory Theory addressing the questions as to why certain capital assets have higher expected returns than others and why the expected returns are different at different points in time.

asset-liability management (ALM) Matching of investment assets with insurance or pension liabilities.

asset-specific events Events not related to the economy or industry sector as a whole, such as a fire.

asset-specific risk Risk that can be diversified away, being risk related to asset-specific factors.

at the money Describes an option that would generate no cash flow if exercised now and liquidated.

auction system Market system without designated dealers; investors trade directly with each other or with the intervention of a broker acting only as an intermediary.

back office In trading operations, the back office records, confirms and settles trades transacted by the front office.

back-testing Technique to test for abnormal profits by observing how historical prices behaved in response to some event.

backwardation Situation in which a futures contract has a positive basis.

balance sheet Overview of a firm's assets and liabilities at a given moment in time.

bank discount rate Interest rate charged to banks when they borrow directly from the Federal Reserve.

bank reserves Percentage of deposits that banks must hold in non-interest-bearing assets.

bankers' acceptance Money-market security that facilitates international trade.

bar chart Graph showing price movements over time with high, low and closing prices.

Barings Bank UK's oldest merchant bank, bankrupted by rogue trading in 1995.

basis Difference between the current spot price and the futures price.

bears Investors who believe that market prices will fall.

behavioural finance Field of finance that assumes that the psychology of decision-making under uncertainty may lead to market inefficiency and market anomalies.

benchmark error Use of an inappropriate benchmark proxy for the true market portfolio.

benchmark revision Revisions to gross domestic product (GDP) made in July for estimates covering the past three years.

best efforts Underwriting agreement in which the underwriter does not take ownership of the unsold securities.

best linear unbiased estimators (BLUE) Regression estimates with the lowest possible variance among all unbiased linear estimators.

beta Measure of the (systematic) risk of an asset relative to that of the market portfolio.

bid–ask spread Difference between the bid price and the ask price of a security.

bid price Price at which investors can buy a security.

bid yield Yield at which investors can buy a security.

binominal model Discrete derivatives-valuation model that assumes that prices can change only at predetermined moments, and stay constant in between.

binominal tree Graphical representation of the binominal model.

Black–Scholes option valuation model (BS model) Continuous option-valuation model based on the creation of a dynamic hedge portfolio.

blue-chip stock Stock of a large, financially sound corporation.

bond indenture Document detailing the terms of a bond issue.

bond index Index of a broad segment of the bond market.

bookbuilding Initial public offering (IPO) selling mechanism in which investors submit orders based on a price range published in a preliminary prospectus.

bookrunner Investment bank that maintains the order book during an equity subscription period and that plays a decisive role with regard to final pricing and allocation.

breadth Availability of a large volume of orders at prices above and below the current price.

breadth indicator Measure of overall market strength or weakness.

broker loan rate See *Call loan rate*.

budget deficit Government spending in a given period of more than its tax revenues.

bullet bond Bond that cannot be redeemed before maturity.

bulls Investors who believe that market prices will rise.

bull spread Option strategy designed to allow investors to profit if prices rise, but limit their losses if prices fall.

business cycle Period of expansion and contraction of aggregate economic activity as measured by real gross domestic product (GDP).

butterfly Option construction that involves buying and selling options on the same asset and with the same expiration date, but with different strike prices.

buyback of shares Repurchasing by a corporation of previously issued shares.

calendar anomaly Anomalous phenomenon that trading strategies based on calendar events generate systematic abnormal returns.

callable bond Bond that can be repurchased by the issuing corporation at a stated price.

call loan rate Interest rate charged by a broker on the borrowed funds in case of margin trading.

call market Market where trading and prices are determined at prespecified times and no trading occurs outside the specified times.

call option Contract giving the right to buy a specified amount of an underlying asset during some period in the future at a predetermined price; gives an investor the right to buy a specified stock at a specified price on or before a specified date.

candlestick chart Bar chart that includes the opening price as well as the high, low and closing prices.

candlestick line Graphical representation of the open, high, low and closing prices.

capital asset pricing model (CAPM) Equilibrium asset-pricing model that predicts a linear relationship between expected return and beta.

capital gains Profits earned when assets are sold at a higher price than purchased.

capital loss Losses incurred when assets are sold at a lower price than purchased.

capital market line (CML) Highest-sloped line achievable in the expected return, standard deviation space.

capital market securities Long-term bonds and stocks.

cash-matching strategy Income-immunisation strategy that assures future cash needs are supplied.

cash settlement Exchange of cash rather than the physical asset in a futures contract.

certificates of deposit Debt instruments issued by banks with maturity ranges from a few weeks to several years; usually interest-bearing.

chained (1996) dollar estimates Measure of real gross domestic product (GDP) that accounts for changes in the relative prices of goods and services in addition to changes in the overall level of prices (1996 is often taken as base year).

channel Pattern formed when two parallel lines are drawn on a bar chart, showing the up and down prices.

characteristic line Linear relationship between an asset and the market portfolio.

churning Excessive trading for the purpose of generating commissions.

civilian unemployment rate Number of unemployed people as a percentage of civilians working or actively seeking work.

clearing Verification of information between the two brokers in a securities transaction and the subsequent settlement.

closed-end fund Mutual fund that cannot issue more shares.

closing transaction Transaction that offsets an asset already held.

coefficient of determination (R-squared) Ratio of explained variance to total variance in regression analysis.

cognitive biases Mental biases linked to information identification and gathering, as well as understanding the meaning and consequences of information.

coincident indicator Economic statistics that are supposed to move with the business cycle.

cold IPO Initial public offering (IPO) with negative initial returns.

commercial paper Unsecured notes of corporations, usually issued at a discount.

commodity risk Risk that arises from holding securities with an exposure to a particular commodity, such as gold or oil.

commodity swap Contract to exchange payments based on a specific commodity price.

common risk factor Risk factor that affects the prices of securities, such as the inflation rate, gross domestic product (GDP) or the S&P 500 index.

common size statement See *Percentage financial statement*.

common stock Securities that represent part ownership in a firm.

comparison universe Group of investors with a similar investment style, used to assess the relative performance of an individual investor.

conduit Firm that sells pooled mortgages.

conduit theory Capital gains and ordinary income should not be double-taxed with investment companies.

confidence interval Area in which the estimates will probably lie.

confidence level Complement of the significance level.

consolidated limit order book (CLOB) Trading system in which all limit orders for a given security are submitted anonymously to a centralised book.

consolidation Process of connecting the various marketplaces.

constant dividend growth model (CDGM) Stock-valuation model that assumes that dividends grow at a constant rate.

consumption capital asset-pricing model (CCAPM) Generalisation of the capital asset-pricing model (CAPM) that treats investing as a means to fund future consumption.

consumption-to-wealth ratio Ratio of aggregate consumption to aggregate wealth, used to capture the effect of the business cycle.

contango Situation in which a futures contract has a negative basis.

contingent claim See *Derivative security*.

contingent immunisation Investment strategy designed to accommodate both the desire of bond managers to actively trade and the desire of investors to minimise interest-rate risk.

continuous distribution Probability distribution involving an infinite number of states of the world.

continuous market system System in which trades in each security occur at any time the stock exchange is open.

contraction Phase of the business cycle after a peak and before a trough.

convergence Process of the basis converging to zero when a futures contract reaches maturity.

conversion premium Value of the option to convert in a bond.

conversion price Par value divided by the conversion ratio.

conversion ratio Number of stocks per bond issued when the bond is converted.

conversion value Intrinsic value of a bond if converted immediately.

convertible bond Bond containing an option to convert it into some stock.

convexity Measure of the curvature of the bond's price–yield relationship used in price-immunisation strategies.

corporate bonds Debt securities issued by corporations to finance investment in new plant and equipment.

corporate finance Field of finance covering issues such as project analysis, capital structure, capital budgeting and working capital management.

corporate governance Distribution of rights and responsibilities among the board, managers, shareholders and other stakeholders in a business corporation.

correlation matrix Matrix used to display the correlation coefficients between more than two assets, with each element in the matrix containing the covariance between a pair of assets.

cost-of-carry model Futures-pricing model based on the implied cost of owning the underlying asset.

coupon payment Fixed periodic interest payment on a bond.

coupon yield Interest rate stated on a bond, note or other fixed-income security, expressed as a percentage of the principal (face value).

coupon-bearing bond Bond that pays period interest payments.

covered call Option strategy composed of buying a stock and writing a call option. The profit/loss from this strategy corresponds to that of writing a put option.

covered position Using options when the underlying asset is already owned.

credit migration risk Risk that the credit quality of a bond falls due to, for instance, unexpectedly poor corporate earnings or the issuance of new debt.

credit quality Measure of the likelihood of default; letters are assigned such as AAA, AA, and so forth.

credit risk Risk that the bond issue's interest or principal will not be paid.

credit spread See *Spread over Treasuries.*

credit swap Agreement to exchange default risk by reimbursing any losses on the loans covered by the swap due to default, in exchange for a similar reimbursement for defaults on other loans owned by the counterparty or a set of fixed payments.

credit value at risk (C-VaR) Maximum dollar loss that a portfolio may be expected to suffer due to credit risk over a given holding period, at a given level of confidence.

critical values Threshold with which the value of a test statistic is compared to determine whether the null hypothesis is rejected at a given level of significance.

cross-border bond Bond that a firm issues in the international market.

crossing network Alternative trading system that crosses multiple orders at a single price at prespecified times and that does not allow orders to be crossed or executed outside of the specified times.

cross-section data Refers to observations on different objects during the same time period.

cumulative abnormal rate of return (CAR) Sum of all abnormal rates of return during a given period.

cumulative distribution function Function that gives the probability that a random variable takes a value that is smaller than or equal to a specified value.

cumulative preferred stocks Preferred stock on which dividends accrue in the event that the issuer does not make timely dividend payments. Most preferred stock is cumulative preferred.

currency swap Contract to exchange different currencies on specified dates.

current ratio Ratio of current assets to current liabilities.

current yield Stated annual coupon payment divided by the current bond price.

cyclical stock Stock that moves with the business cycle.

date of record Date on which ownership is assessed for dividends.

day order Order expiring at the end of the trading day.

day trader Trader who conducts many buy and sell transactions on a single day and who closes his or her positions before leaving the trading room.

dealer system System in which dealers are the counterparties to every transaction.

debenture Unsecured bonds.

declaration date Date on which dividend is announced.

default mode (DM) model Portfolio credit risk model that focuses solely on the risk of default and doesn't consider migration risk.

default risk Risk of a bond issuer failing to pay either the coupon payments or the face value in a timely manner.

defensive asset Asset with a beta of less than one.

defensive stock Stock with a beta of less than one; moves in the opposite way to the business cycle.

defined-benefit pension plan Pension plan that promises employees a specific benefit when they retire; the sponsor has to make sufficient contributions to fund these benefits.

defined-contribution pension plan Pension plan that specifies only what will be contributed into a pension fund; the benefit depends on the investment return.

delta Linear approximation of the sensitivity of the option price to the price of the underlying stock.

delta-gamma method Method that relies on a quadratic relationship between asset returns and the risk factors instead of relying on a linear relationship.

deep market A market where a sufficient number of (limit) orders exists at prices above and below the price at which shares are currently trading.

derivative security Asset that derives its value from another asset.

descriptive statistics Statistics summarising the data set that was used to generate the regression output.

diagnostic test Test that determines whether the maintained assumptions of the ordinary least squares (OLS) regression technique hold.

direct approach Method of reporting the statement of cash flow that gives the cash receipts and payments.

discount Closed-end fund trading below net asset value (NAV), as a percent of NAV.

discount broker Broker who solely executes trades and doesn't offer additional services.

discount rate Method of quoting Treasury bill interest rates; the required rate of return, given the riskiness of the stock.

discrete distribution Probability distribution involving a finite number of states of the world.

diversifiable risk Risk that can be diversified away, being risk related to asset-specific factors.

diversification Spreading a portfolio over many investments to avoid excessive exposure to a few sources of risk.

dividend Taxable payment declared by a company's board of directors and given to its shareholders out of the company's current or retained earnings, usually quarterly.

dividend discount model (DDM) Valuation model based on the present value of cash dividends.

dividend yield Amount of dividends paid per share over the course of a year and dividing by the stock's price.

divisible Describes assets that you are able to buy small portions of.

divisor Number used in price-weighted indices that is adjusted for security changes such as stock splits.

dollar-weighted average rate of return Method of calculating an average rate of return that takes into account the amount invested in each time period.

dot.com bubble Rise in value of many Internet-related stocks in the late 1990s.

Dow diamonds Exchange-traded fund based on the Dow Jones Industrial Average.

Dow theory Technical analysis that is based on primary, intermediate- and short-term trends.

duration Holding period that balances the price effect against the reinvestment effect.

duration drift Change in duration due to the passage of time.

duration-matching strategy Income-immunisation strategy that matches asset duration with the duration of the liabilities.

Dutch auction Initial public offering (IPO)-selling mechanism that sets the introduction price at the highest price that allows for selling all shares.

dynamic hedge Hedge strategy in which a portfolio is rebalanced after each movement in price in order to remains riskless.

earnings per share Ratio of net income to outstanding shares.

EBITDA Earnings before interest, taxation, depreciation and amortisation.

efficient frontier Set of all investment strategies with the highest mean for a given variance.

efficient market Market in which prices reflect all relevant information about the stock.

efficient market theory (EMT) Theory that all assets are priced correctly and that there are no 'bargains' in the market.

electronic communication network (ECN) Computer-based trading system that allows investors to clear trades via an electronic limit order book.

electronic limit order book (ELOB) Electronic auction market system in which investors submit limit orders to a centralised order book and market orders are executed at the most favourable limit prices.

Elliott wave theory Outgrowth of the original technical analysis of Dow theory based on Fibonacci numbers.

equally weighted index Index that assigns each individual security an equal weight.

equilibrium rate of return Rate of return if the capital market is in equilibrium, or if demand equals supply for all capital assets.

equity premium Difference in the expected rate of return between stocks and Treasury bills.

equity risk Exposure to the stock market as a whole.

error of judgement Systematic over- or underestimation of the true probability of chance events.

errors of preference 'Mistakes' made in assigning values to future outcomes or from improper combinations of probabilities and values.

estimated beta See *Beta*.

estimation risk Risk of wrongly estimating the input parameters to a model.

ethics Principles on which the correctness of specific actions are determined.

eurodollars Deposit denominated in US dollars held in a bank outside of the USA.

European-style option Option that cannot be exercised early.

event anomaly Trading strategy that generates abnormal returns based on specific events.

ex-ante rate of return Forecasted rate of return used in estimating statistics.

excess return Deviation from the return predicted by the capital asset-pricing model (CAPM).

exchange-rate-adjusted rate of return Rate of return that has been adjusted to take into account the rate of inflation.

exchange-rate risk Exposure to adverse changes in exchange rates.

exchange-traded fund Closed-end fund that tracks a specific basket of securities and trads continuously on the major exchanges like an ordinary stock.

ex-dividend date First day on which stockholders no longer receive dividends if stock is purchased.

exercise price See *Strike price*.

exercising Buying or selling assets through an option contract.

expansion Phase of the business cycle after a trough and before a peak.

expected return Measure of the central tendency of the return distribution.

expected utility criterion Criterion that seeks the portfolio that maximises the expected utility of the investor.

expected utility theory (EUT) Theory in which decision-makers choose to maximise their expected utility given their expectations, utility and restrictions.

expiration date Date on which the option contract expires.

exponentially weighted moving average (EWMA) Moving average that uses weights that decrease exponentially as observations lie further in the past.

ex-post rate of return Historical rate of return used in estimating statistics.

extreme value theory (EVT) Branch of statistics that describes the tail behaviour of return distributions.

face value See *Par value*.

factor loading Measures the sensitivity of an asset's return to changes in a common risk factor.

factor portfolio Well-diversified portfolio with zero non-systematic risk, a unity beta for the risk factor under consideration and a zero beta for all other risk factors.

factor risk models Models that explain security returns based on their exposure to a set of common risk factors.

failure prediction Modelling of the probability of an issuer not being able to meet its obligations.

fallen angel Investment-grade bond that has subsequently been downgraded to a speculative grade.

family of funds Several different mutual funds offered by the same investment company.

federal agency bonds Bonds issued by government agencies such as the Federal National Mortgage Association (FNMA).

federal funds Money-market securities facilitating interbank borrowing.

federal funds rate Interest rate charged to banks when they borrow other banks' excess reserves.

financial assets Intangible assets, such as stocks and bonds.

financial engineering Design, development and implementation of innovative financial instruments and processes, and the formulation of creative solutions in finance.

financial ratio analysis Methods used to compare financial statements across different firms and, for a given firm, across different periods and points in time.

Financial Services Action Plan (FSAP) European agreement aiming to create a single market for financial services by the end of 2005.

financial statement Report that contains basic accounting data that helps investors understand the firm's financial history.

firm anomaly Trading strategies that generate abnormal returns based on firm-specific characteristics.

firm commitment Underwriting agreement in which the underwriter agrees to purchase all unsold shares for his or her own account at a predetermined price.

first notice day Earliest day on which traders with a short position can signal they are going to deliver.

fiscal policy Taxation and spending policies by a government designed to achieve gross domestic product (GDP) growth, relatively full employment and stable prices.

fixed-charge coverage Profits before income taxes and interest payments, divided by long-term interest, for a given period of time.

fixed price Offering that commences with a complete prospectus, including both offer size and price.

fixed-rate bond Bond with contractually fixed coupon payments, normally defined as a percentage of the par value.

floating-rate bond Bond with variable coupon payments, with the coupon rate tied to market interest rates.

floor broker A person who handles buying and selling futures contracts for others; broker who is willing to work for other member firms to assist in the trading process.

foreign exchange expectations Relationship between the current forward foreign exchange rate and the expected future spot exchange rate.

forward contract Contract to do something in the future, for example borrow or lend money.

forward foreign exchange contract Contract that obligates an investor to deliver a specified quantity of one currency in return for a specified amount of another currency.

forward foreign exchange rate Exchange rate available today to exchange currency at some specified date in the future.

forward rate Yield covering a period of time starting in the future.

frictionless market Market where trading is costless to conduct.

front office In trading operations, the front office performs the actual trading.

front running The illegal delaying of transactions by fund managers to trade privately in anticipation of the expected result of the pending transaction.

full-service broker Broker who provides a wide range of services to clients.

fundamental analysis Analysis that assesses the intrinsic value of a firm; trading strategies are based on the asset's publicly available information.

funding risk Potential for unanticipated costs or losses due to a mismatch between asset yields and liability funding costs.

futures commission merchants (FCMs) People qualified to trade futures contracts.

futures contract Agreement to make or take delivery of an asset at a later date at a given price; the trading price of a futures contract.

gamma Quadratic measure of the sensitivity of an option's price to the price of the underlying asset.

general capital asset-pricing model (GCAPM) Generalisation of the captial asset-pricing model (CAPM) that allows investors to hold a small number of assets in portfolio.

general obligation bond Municipal bond secured by the taxing and borrowing power of the municipality issuing it.

geometric average Figure obtained by the product of n observations and years (1 + rates of return), taking the $1/n$ root and subtracting 1.

geometric method Compound rate of return that mimics an investor's actual performance.

gilts Treasury securities (bills and bonds) issued by the British government.

global coordinator Leading investment bank in international (often large) equity offerings involving multiple investment banks.

going public Whole process of preparing and executing an initial public offering (IPO).

good-till-cancelled (GTC) order Order that remains in effect until it is executed or cancelled.

Green Shoe option Possibility for an underwriter to buy additional shares at the offering price.

gross domestic product (GDP) Total of goods and services produced in an economy.

growth rate Year-over-year change in value, expressed as a percentage.

growth stocks Stocks of firms having expected sales and earnings growth in excess of the industry average.

hedge fund Unregistered, privately offered, managed pool of capital for wealthy, financially sophisticated investors.

hedge ratio Number of stocks to buy or sell with options such that the future portfolio value is risk-free.

hedging Use of a technique used to limit loss potential.

high-grade bonds Bonds with credit quality of AAA or AA.

historical simulation Simulation method using a sample of historical observations for the risk factors.

holding period Time between the trade date of the purchase and the trade date of the sale of an asset.

holding period rate of return Rate of return earned on a bond by holding it for the next period.

holdings-based style analysis (HBSA) Method used to determine an investor's investment style based on the characteristics of the individual securities in his or her portfolio.

home bias Investors holding a substantially larger proportion of their wealth portfolios in domestic assets than standard portfolio theory would suggest.

horizon-matching strategy Income-immunisation strategy that cash matches over the next few years and duration matches the rest.

hot IPO Initial public offering (IPO) with positive initial returns.

human capital Skills and knowledge that people acquire through their investments in education and experience.

hybrid market system Market system that combines elements of the dealer system and the auction system.

hypothesis test Test statistic that indicates the degree to which the estimation results violate the null hypothesis.

immunisation strategy Strategy that seeks to neutralise the adverse effects of changes in yield to maturity.

implied distribution Market's opinion about the future distribution of returns, derived from market data.

income-immunisation strategy Strategy that ensures adequate future cash flow.

income statement Accounting statement showing the flow of sales, expenses and earnings during a specified period.

income stock (value stock) High-dividend-paying stock.

independent investment advice Investment advice that is not biased by a conflict of interest of the advisor.

independent regulator Regulator that is not biased by a conflict of interest.

index fund Passively managed fund that tries to mimic a specified index.

indexing Constructing a replicating portfolio designed to mirror the performance of a benchmark index.

index method Method for calculating rates of return that is based on initial and terminal values.

indirect approach Method of reporting the statement of cash flow that takes net income and through a series of adjustments reconciles it to cash from operations.

industry allocation Decision as to what proportion to invest in each industry.

inefficient frontier Set of all investment strategies with the lowest variance (below the minimum variance portfolio).

inflation-indexed bonds Bonds with coupon and pay payments linked to a cost of living index.

information-acquisition costs Costs of acquiring information on investment opportunities.

information asymmetry Differences in information available to different participants.

information availability Degree to which financial information is available, for example on past transactions, current quotes and the limit order book.

information costs See *Information-acquisition costs*.

information ratio See *Appraisal ratio*.

initial margin (IM) Percentage of the dollar amount originally required by the lender to be put up by the borrower when trading on margin.

initial public offering (IPO) Company changing from a privately held firm into a publicly held firm.

initial return Return on the first day after going public.

insider information Material information about a company that has not yet been made public.

institutional investors Specialised financial intermediaries that manage saving collectively on behalf of individuals and sometimes non-financial companies.

insurance Promise of compensation for specific potential future losses in exchange for a periodic payment.

insurance company Company that is in the business of assuming the risk of adverse events in exchange for a flow of insurance premiums.

intercept Measures the expected value of the regressand y if the regressors equal zero.

interest-rate parity Relationship between the forward foreign exchange rate and nominal interest rates.

interest-rate risk Risk faced by bond investors when market interest rates change.

interest-rate swap Contract to exchange payments based on interest rates.

intermarket spread swap Speculation on the spread between two different bond markets, such as Eurodollar bonds and domestic bonds.

intermediate trend Trend lasting from three weeks to six months in price data.

international Fisher relationship Relationship between nominal interest rates and inflation rates in different countries.

intertemporal capital asset-pricing model (ICAPM) Generalisation of the capital asset-pricing model (CAPM) that accounts for investors re-allocating their portfolios when the economic situation changes before the end of the investment period.

in the money Describes an option that would generate positive cash flow if exercised now and liquidated.

intrinsic value Value of the option if exercised immediately or zero, whichever is greater.

investment bank Bank handling the issuance of securities in the primary market. Most investment banks also offer broker/dealer operations, offer investment advice and facilitate mergers, private placements and corporate restructuring.

investment company Organisation that pools investors money by issuing shares and invests it in securities.

investment-grade bond Bond rated BBB (or Baa) or above.

investments Financial discipline that studies securities, security markets and investor behaviour.

investment trust Closed-end fund.

investment vehicles Asset classes that one can invest in.

investor characteristics Distinct characteristics that an investor exhibits.

investor education Independently acting equity research analyst affiliated to the underwriter visiting institutional clients and informing them about the forthcoming initial public offering (IPO).

Jensen's performance index Performance measure based on the security market line (SML).

jump Sudden increase or decrease of market prices after important new information reaches the market.

junior bond Bond that is either unsecured or has a lower priority than that of another debt claim on the same asset or property.

junk bond Bond with a low credit quality.

laddering Underwriter requiring investors to purchase additional shares in the aftermarket in return for being assigned substantial quantities of initial public offering (IPO) shares.

lagging indicator Economic statistics that are supposed to move behind the business cycle.

late trading Illegally allowing investors to buy fund shares after market's close at that day's closing price while they should only be allowed to buy these funds at the next day's opening price.

law of one price Law based on no arbitrage, stating that two items that are essentially the same cannot sell at different prices.

leading indicator Economic statistics that are supposed to move ahead of the business cycle.

lead manager Investment bank that manages an equity offering (often smaller equity offerings, orientated towards local investors) on its own.

legal risk Risk of loss incurred by contracts that cannot be enforced because of legal issues.

levered portfolio Portfolio financed partially by borrowing.

life insurance company Company that is in the business of assuming the risk of early death in exchange for a flow of insurance premiums.

limit order Order to buy or sell a specified quantity of a security at a specified price or better.

limit order book Current set of active limit orders that is sent to, and maintained by, a security exchange or a security dealer.

linking method Method for calculating rates of return that multiplies one plus the interim rate of return.

liquidity Ability to convert an asset into cash quickly, without significantly affecting its price.

liquidity preference hypothesis (LPH) Hypothesis stating that longer-term bonds should have a higher yield due to investors' preferences for liquidity.

liquidity premium Difference between the yield based on the unbiased expectations hypothesis and the actual yield.

load Fee paid as a sales commission to vendors of mutual funds.

load mutual funds Mutual funds sold in an over-the-counter (OTC) market by dealers who receive an up-front sales commission.

local expectations hypothesis (LEH) Hypothesis stating that all similar bonds, except maturity, will have the same holding period rate of return.

local Persons who trades for his or her own account in a futures pit.

log-normal distribution Statistical distribution that is skewed positively, in contrast to a normal distribution, which has no skewness.

long position Agreement to take delivery of a security.

Long Term Capital Management (LTCM) Hedge fund that nearly collapsed in 1998 after the Russian default.

maintenance margin Percentage of the dollar amount of the securities market value that must always be set aside as a margin when engaging in margin trading.

margin call Request from a broker to post additional margin when engaging in margin trading.

margin trading Investor borrowing a portion of the funds needed to buy securities from its broker.

marginal utility Additional satisfaction derived from a unit of additional return.

margin Percentage of the dollar amount of the securities market value that is set aside when engaging in margin trading.

marked to market Taking profits and losses daily on futures contracts.

market beta See *Beta*.

market capitalisation Market value of all shares outstanding.

market fragmentation Splintering of order flow and liquidity provision that occurs when several market-places are available to execute an order.

market globalisation International integration of financial markets.

market liquidity risk Risk that an investor cannot dispose of his or her securities at a fair value because no-one who wishes to buy the securities.

market makers Traders who stand ready to buy or sell securities from other traders at their own account, for example National Association of Securities Dealers Automated Quotations (NASDAQ) dealers and New York Stock Exchange (NYSE) specialists.

market microstructure Actual mechanisms in a security market that facilitate trading.

market order Order to buy or sell a certain quantity of a security at the best price currently available.

marketplace Place where the actual buy and sell orders of securities are executed.

market portfolio Optimum portfolio with riskless borrowing and lending.

market risk Non-diversifiable part of an asset's variance attributable to the overall market fluctuation.

market segmentation hypothesis (MSH) Hypothesis stating that different maturity bonds trade in separate segmented markets.

market timing Active investment strategy exploiting market inefficiency by moving into underpriced asset classes and out of overpriced asset classes.

marketability See *Liquidity*.

mark-to-market (MTM) model Portfolio credit risk model that focuses on both the risk of default and migration risk.

maturity Date on which a debt becomes due for payment.

maturity date See *Maturity*.

mean Measure of the central tendency of the return distribution.

mean reversion Variable showing reversion to a fixed average, or mean, in the long run.

mean–variance analysis Evaluation of investment strategies based on the expected value and variance of future returns.

mean–variance-efficiency criterion Prefers a higher mean and/or a lower variance.

mean–variance-efficient All investment strategies on the mean–variance frontier with the highest mean for a given variance and the lowest.

mean–variance frontier Set of investment strategies with the lowest variance for all possible means.

mean–variance indifference curve Curve representing the mean–variance combinations that provide the same utility level to an investor.

mean–variance possibilities set Set of all feasible mean–variance combinations, including all possible portfolios.

Merton model Generalised version of the Black and Scholes option-valuation model that accounts for dividend payments.

minimum variance portfolio (MVP) Portfolio with the smallest variance of all portfolios in the mean–variance set.

mixed market system See *Hybrid market system*.

momentum effect Continuation of security-price movements in a given direction; winners continue to win, losers continue to lose.

monetary policy Actions by a central bank to control the supply of money and interest rates that influence the financial markets directly.

money-market securities Short-term bonds, usually of less than one year.

moneyness Ratio of an option's strike price to the value of the underlying asset.

monte carlo simulation (MCS) Simulation method using a large number of random draws that are generated from a prespecified return distribution.

mortgage Collateralised bond, usually real estate.

mortgage-backed security Security whose value depends on a set of mortgages.

moving average Method of averaging the most recent past price data.

M-squared Measure of the return that an investor would have earned if the portfolio had been altered by risk-free lending or borrowing so as to match the standard deviation of the market portfolio.

multicollinearity Problem of strong individual inter-correlations among the independent variables and the dependent variable, compromising the least square estimates.

Multiple index model (MIM) Factor risk model that includes multiple common risk factors.

multiple regression Regressing a single independent variable, accounting for possible correlation between the regressors.

multistage growth model Valuation model assuming that a firm experiences multiple growth stages with different growth rates.

multivariate probability distribution Probability distribution function for the movements of several random variables.

municipal bonds State and local government securities.

mutual fund Managed pool of money invested in securities.

naked position Using options without holding to any underlying security.

Nasdaq 100 share Exchange-traded fund based on the National Association of Securities Dealers Antomated Quotations (NASDAQ) 100 stock index.

National Association of Securities Dealers (NASD) US self-regulatory non-governmental agency that regulates the sales of securities and oversees licences for brokers and brokerage firms.

net asset value (NAV) Current market value of securities in fund, less liabilities on a per share basis.

neutral asset Asset with a beta of one.

no arbitrage Rule stating that in equilibrium no arbitrage profit can be made.

no-load mutual fund Mutual fund that does not have any sales commissions.

nominal rate of return Rate of return denoted in nominal terms, ignoring inflation effects.

nominal yield See *Coupon yield*.

non-constant volatility When an option has a long time left to expiration, it is unlikely that volatility will remain constant over that period.

non-diversifiable risk See *Systematic risk*.

non-market risk See *Diversifiable risk*.

non-systematic risk See *Diversifiable risk*.

normal distribution Statistical distribution characterised by a symmetrical bell shape.

normal portfolio Passive benchmark portfolio consistent with the long-term investment policy.

normal-growth firm Firm whose earnings grow at a constant rate.

not-held (NH) order Order in which the broker is not held liable if he or she is unable to trade.

notional principal Basis on which swap interest payments are based, similar to the par value of bonds.

objective probability True unobservable underlying probability.

odd-lot trading Trading in orders not in sizes of 100s.

one-on-one Discrete meeting between management/bankers and representatives of institutional investors.

online broker Brokerage firm that allows investors to execute trades electronically using the Internet.

open-end fund Mutual fund that can issue more shares.

opening transaction Transaction when the initial position is taken.

open interest Number of futures contracts outstanding at a point in time.

open market operations US Treasury transactions by the Federal Reserve used to influence bank reserves.

operational risk Umbrella term for various investment risks other than market risk and credit risk.

opportunity line Represents portfolios that are achieved by combining different levels of borrowing and lending with a single risky portfolio.

optimisation Maximising an objective function in a situation characterised by restrictions.

option Legal contract that gives its holder the right to buy or sell a specified amount of an underlying asset at a fixed price.

option buyer Owner of the option contract.

option class All options of the same type (puts or calls) with the same underlying asset.

option premium Initial purchase or sales price of an option.

option series Part of an option class that has the same expiration date and strike price.

option value boundaries Boundaries to option prices that follow from no-arbitrage rules.

option writer Person from whom the option buyer purchases the option contract.

option-implied volatility Estimate for the volatility of the underlying asset derived from the market value of an option.

Options Clearing Corporation (OCC) Clearing corporation in the USA facilitating the validation, delivery and settlement of security transactions and, most importantly, guaranteeing that obligations are met.

ordinary least squares (OLS) method Regression method that selects estimates to minimise the sum of squared errors.

out of the money Describes an option that would generate negative cash flow if exercised now and liquidated.

overallotment option See *Green Shoe option*.

panel data Data set on different objects and different time periods.

par value Lump sum paid at maturity.

participating preferred stocks Dividends tied to earnings.

passive bond management See *Passive investment strategy*.

passive investment strategy Investment strategy in which the portfolio manager does not actively manage investments.

pay-as-you-go (PAYG) pension plan Pension system that pays pensions from the yearly proceeds of taxes that are paid by the actively working people in the system.

payment date Date on which dividend cheque is mailed.

payoff diagram Graph illustrating the value line or the profit and loss line.

peak Top of the business cycle.

pension fund Asset pool that accumulates over an employee's working years and pays retirement benefits during the employee's non-working years.

pension plan Agreement about the amounts and timing of the contribution to a pension fund and distributions from the pension fund.

p/e ratio Ratio of the current stock price to the current year's annual earnings per share (EPS).

percentage financial statement Balance sheet and income statements converted to percentages.

performance attribution Means to assess the sources of portfolio performance.

physical assets Tangible assets, such as precious metals and real estate.

pink herring Preliminary version of the preliminary prospectus.

pit Place where all buying and selling of futures contracts takes place.

plain vanilla swap Swap in which counterparties exchange fixed-rate interest payments for floating-rate interest payments.

point-and-figure chart Graph with *X*s and *O*s used to plot price reversals without consideration of time.

political risk Possibility that a country will take over a firm.

population correlation coefficient Coefficient of correlation function in a sample of historical returns.

population covariance Covariance between the returns of two assets as found in a sample of historical returns.

population mean Mean relative to the true (ex ante) return distribution.

population standard deviation Square root of the population variance.

population statistics Ex-ante statistics for summarising the statistical distribution of before-the-fact returns.

population variance Variance relative to the true (ex ante) return distribution.

portfolio diversification See *Diversification*.

portfolio mean Weighted average of the means of the individual assets making up a portfolio.

portfolio possibilities set Collection of all portfolios that satisfy the investment restrictions faced by an investor.

portfolio variance Complex weighted average of the individual assets' variances and covariances (or correlations).

portfolio weights Relative proportions of assets kept in a portfolio expressed as a percentage of the total wealth invested.

preference shares Preferred shares that have first claim to preferred dividends.

preferred habitat hypothesis Hypothesis that states that suppliers and demanders of funds have a preferred region of the yield curve but can be induced to move.

preliminary estimate Second estimate of gross domestic product (GDP) released about two months after the measurement period.

premarketing Informal contact between investment banks and institutional investors to assess demand and inform about a forthcoming initial public offering (IPO).

premium Closed-end fund trading above net asset value (NAV), as a percent of NAV.

price discovery Process that leads to market prices reflecting all available information.

price effect Impact on bond prices when interest rates change.

price immunisation Immunisation strategy that focuses on the current market value of assets and liabilities.

price risk Risk that bond prices will fall when interest rates rise.

price-weighted index Index that weighs individual securities according to their market price.

pricing error See *Abnormal rate of return*.

primary market Mechanism through which firms raise additional capital by selling stocks, bonds and other securities, and through which suppliers of capital (mainly shareholders) can sell their privately held stake.

primary shares Newly created shares rather than existing shares that are offered in an initial public offering (IPO). The proceeds go to the issuing firm.

primary tide Trend of successive higher highs and higher lows (a bull market), or successive lower highs and lower lows (a bear market).

primary trend Long-term trends lasting 4–4.5 years in price data.

prime rate Interest rate that banks charge their most creditworthy customers.

principal value See *Par value*.

private pension plan Non-public pension plan.

probability density Relative probability that a continuous random variable takes a given value.

probability distribution Function describing probabilities of future returns.

probability of exceedance (P-value) Gives the probability that the test statistic takes a value that is equal to or greater than the observed value if the null hypothesis was true.

programme trading Simultaneous purchase or sale of an entire basket of securities in a coordinated programme.

property holdings Wealth invested in real estate.

prospectus Legal document containing a business plan and other information for investors regarding an initial public offering (IPO).

protective put Strategy of holding a stock and buying an out-of-the-money option on this stock.

purchasing power parity Relationship between two countries' inflation rates and their foreign exchange rates.

pure yield pickup swap Moving to bonds with a higher yield.

put–call parity (PCP) Establishes the pricing relationship between the underlying security, the risk-free interest rate, call options and put options.

put–call ratio Measure based on the volume of put and call option trading.

put option Contract giving the right to sell a specified amount of an underlying asset during some period in the future at a predetermined price.

PVGO Present value of growth opportunities of a company.

quadratic utility Approximation of an investor's utility function based on a second-order Taylor' series.

quality of earnings Analyst's confidence in the quality of reported earnings of a firm.

quick ratio Ratio of current assets minus inventory and other non-marketable assets to current liabilities, a ratio often used in financial ratio analysis.

random walk Statistical concept in which future price changes are unpredictable, not based on prior outcomes.

rate-anticipation swap Positioning a bond portfolio based on the perceived direction of future interest-rate moves.

rating agency Firm that assesses the credit risk of a bond.

rating transition matrix Matrix that gives the estimated probability that a bond with a given grade will migrate to another grade.

real body On a candlestick line, the broad part consisting of the difference between opening and closing prices.

real GDP Inflation-adjusted measure of gross domestic product (GDP).

realised yield Holding period return actually generated from an investment in a bond.

real rate of return Inflation-adjusted rate of return.

recession Typically defined as two consecutive quarters of negative real gross domestic product (GDP) growth.

recombinant Property of a binominal tree that the outcome of an upward move followed by a downward move is equal to the outcome of a downward move followed by an upward move.

recovery rate Percentage of the face value that can be expected to be recovered in case of default.

red herring Preliminary version of the prospectus (so-called because the cover contains a disclaimer printed in red ink).

regressand Dependent variable.

regression coefficients Intercept and slope coefficients.

regression equation Stochastic relationship between regressand and regressor.

regression residual Distance of an observation from the estimated regression line.

regressor Independent variable.

regulated investment company Investment company that satisfies Regulation M of the Internal Revenue Service (IRS) and avoids taxes on security transactions.

regulation Rules established by governments for the purpose of identifying unacceptable behaviour.

reinvestment effect Impact on the reinvestment rate when interest rates change.

reinvestment risk Risk that future cash flows will be invested at a lower rate.

relative strength Measure of the price performance of one index against another.

repurchase agreement Sale of a money-market security with an agreement to buy it back at a higher price at a specified time.

resiliency Speed of new orders when prices change.

resistance Upper bound on prices due to many investors willing to sell at that price.

retained ownership percentage Remaining fraction of post-initial public offering (IPO) outstanding share capital in hands of the orignal (private) owners.

return on equity Ratio of net income to shareholders' equity, a ratio often used in financial ratio analysis.

returns-based style analysis (RBSA) Method for determining the style of an investment portfolio based on the past correlation with style indices.

revenue bond Bond backed by a specific project's income.

reverse repo Opposite side of a repurchase agreement, where one buys securities with an agreement to sell them at a later day at a specified price.

revised estimate Third estimate of gross domestic product (GDP) released about three months after the measurement period.

rho Measure for the sensitivity of option prices to the interest rate.

ripples Short-term movements of security prices that typically last from one day to three weeks.

risk Situation in which more than one future outcome is possible and the probability of each outcome is known to investors.

risk-averter A person who dislikes risk, everything else the same.

risk management Process of recognition, measurement and control of risks that an investor faces.

risk-neutral Describes a person who is indifferent about risk.

risk premium Higher return required to take higher risk.

risk-seeker A person who likes to take risk and is even willing to pay for it.

risk-adjusted performance measure Performance measurement that corrects for risk, such as Sharpe's performance index.

risk-free asset Asset whose return is known with certainty (with probability 1).

road show Directors of a company presenting themselves and their company to the community of institutional investors.

round lots Orders in sizes of 100s.

sample correlation coefficient Coefficient of correlation in a sample of historical return observations.

sample covariance Measure for the covariability of the returns of two securities in a sample of historical returns.

sample mean Measure of central tendency of security returns in a historical sample of returns.

sample standard deviation Square root of the sample variance.

sample statistics Ex-post statistics for summarising the statistical distribution of past rates of return.

sample variance Measure for the variability of the returns of a security in a historical sample.

seasoned equity offering Sale of shares through the primary market.

secondary market Previously issued securities being traded between investors.

secondary reactions Intermediate, corrective reactions to a primary tide retracing the primary swing in price, generally lasting two weeks to three months.

secondary shares Existing shares rather than newly created shares that are offered in an initial public offering (IPO). The proceeds go to the selling shareholders.

sector allocation Decision as to what proportion to invest in each sector.

secured bonds Bonds backed with collateral.

Securities Act of 1933 US act designed to require issuers to disclose all important financial information to investors.

Securities Exchange Act of 1934 Act that regulates the secondary market in the USA, that established the Securities and Exchange Commission (SEC), that gives the federal government authority to establish a margin, and that forbids insider trading.

Securities and Exchange commission (SEC) Independent, quasi-judiciary regulatory agency responsible for enforcing securities legislation in the USA.

security Instrument that signifies an ownership position in a stock or a bond, or the right to ownership by an option.

security broker Person who acts as an intermediary between buyers and sellers of securities in exchange for brokerage commission.

security exchange Facility for exchange members to trade securities.

security market line (SML) Linear relationship between expected return and beta.

security selection Decision as to what proportion to invest in each security; the process of determining the securities within each asset class that are most suitable.

self-regulatory organisation (SRO) Organisation required to perform a high degree of internal regulation of its members.

selling group Group linked to the syndicate, whose sole task is to distribute shares.

semi-strong form of the efficient market theory (EMT) Prices reflect all relevant publicly available information.

senior bonds Bonds having priority over junior bonds in case of default.

seniority Priority that a claimholder has relative to other claimholders in the event of default.

sensitivity analysis Analysis of the sensitivity of the value at risk (VaR) for different modelling and estimation choices.

sentiment indicator Indicator of traders' opinions about the market.

separation principle Decision of the optimal portfolio of risky assets (denoted m) is separate from the actual portfolio of the riskless asset and m.

settlement Delivery of certificates in exchange for payment after a securities trade.

settle price Average of the trading prices that occur during the last few minutes of the day.

shadow Thin lines above and below the real body on a candlestick line.

shallow market Market in which an insufficient number of (limit) orders exists at prices above and below the price at which shares are currently trading.

Sharpe's performance index Performance measure based on the capital market line (CML).

short position Agreement to deliver a security at a future moment.

short-selling See *Short position.*

short-term trend Trend that lasts less than three weeks and that is very erratic.

significance level Maximum acceptable frequency of type I error.

simple rate of return Dollar capital gain or loss and dollar income from the investment during a period as a percentage of the dollar amount invested.

simple regression Regression analysis involving only one independent variable or regressor.

simulation method Method for computing value at risk (VaR) using random computer-generated scenarios.

single index model (SIM) Factor risk model allowing for one factor to influence security returns.

sinking fund Money set aside to repay a bond principal in the future.

size effect Describes the phenomenon in which firms with a low market capitalisation ('small caps') seem to earn positive abnormal average returns, while large caps earn negative abnormal returns.

slope coefficient Measures the expected increase in the regressand from a unit increment in the regressors.

socially responsible investment (SRI) Integration of socially responsibility and environmental sustainability in investment strategies.

sounding out investors Investment bankers directly (without an intervening analyst) gauging interest from institutional investors.

specialist Appointed market maker on the New York Stock Exchange (NYSE).

speculating Taking uncovered positions based on a belief about future prices.

speculative stocks Very risky stocks.

spinning Allocation of attractive initial public offering (IPO) shares to the personal brokerage accounts of individuals with investment banking business to offer.

spot rate Yield to maturity of a zero-coupon bond with some stated maturity.

spread Option strategy in which the investor holds long and short positions on the same type of option, but the contracts have different expiration dates and exercise prices.

spread over Treasuries Difference in yield between a corporate bond and a Treasury bond with similar characteristics.

squared sum of residuals (SSR) Measures the sum of squared deviations from the estimated regression line.

standard deviation Measure of risk; square root of the variance.

standard error of regression Unbiased estimator of the standard deviation of the regression coefficient.

standard normal distribution Normal distribution with mean zero and standard deviation one.

state pension fund Tax-funded pension plan ensuring a minimum income for elderly people.

Standard & Poor's depository receipts Exchange-traded fund based on the S&P 500 index.

statement of cash flows Accounting statement showing the flow of cash through the firm.

statement of stockholders' equity Financial statement that reports the amounts and sources of changes in equity from capital transactions with owners.

static hedge Arbitrage trade in which a portfolio is used that remains riskless by construction after the initial purchase.

stock dividend Special form of dividend in which a corporation pays dividend in the form of stocks.

stock index Index measuring the performance of a certain basket of stocks.

stock split Issuing by a company of more new shares in return for existing shares.

stop order Order to trade if adverse price movement occurs.

straddle Option strategy in which the investor buys or sells both puts and calls on the same underlying item with the same exercise price and expiration date.

strangle Option strategy similar to that of a straddle, but in this case the call has a higher exercise price than the put, creating an interval where the movement of the stock price doesn't change the profit or loss.

strategy development Optimising the objectives and constraints (characteristics) of an investor.

strategy implementation Implementation of an investment strategy.

strategy monitoring Periodic re-evaluation of the investment strategy employed.

stratified sampling Approach that replicates the general characteristics of a market index, without the burden of having to replicate the exact composition of the index.

stress test Test used to examine a portfolio under a specific set of market events (scenarios) that are considered plausible, without developing a statistical model for such event.

strike price Predetermined price to buy or sell within the option contract.

strong form of the efficient market theory (EMT) Prices reflect all relevant publicly and privately available information.

style analysis Umbrella term for a set of techniques to determine the investment style of portfolios and to determine the relevant style benchmark portfolio.

style benchmark portfolio Benchmark portfolio that is designed to match the investment style of a fund.

style box Box in which the style of each investment in portfolio is classified according to a set of rules.

style index Index used in constructing style benchmark portfolios.

subjective probability One's beliefs regarding the actual underlying probabilities.

subordinated bonds Bonds that stand behind other bonds in the credit line.

substitution swap Selling overpriced bonds and buying underpriced bonds.

super-growth firm Firm whose earnings grow at a high rate for a period of time.

support Lower bound on prices due to the quantity of willing buyers at that price level.

survivorship bias Data sets overstating true performance due to the fact that when a security is liquidated (ceases to exist), its past performance is also deleted from the database.

swap Contract to exchange payments of some sort at a future date.

syndicate Group of investment bankers who participate in an initial public offering (IPO), taking some of the risk.

systematic risk Non-diversifiable part of an asset's variance attributable to overall market fluctuations.

systemic risk Risk that the unscrupulous actions of a few market participants could undermine public confidence in the entire financial system.

tangency portfolio Portfolio with the highest possible value for Sharpe's performance index.

T-bills See *Treasury bill*.

technical analysis Process of identifying trends in historical price data and extrapolating them to the future.

tender Attempt to buy large portions of a publicly held firm.

term repo Repo with a term of more than one day.

term structure of interest rates See *Yield curve*.

thin market Market with a small volume of orders at prices above and below the current price.

three-factor model Factor risk model allowing for a market factor, a size factor and a book-to-market ratio factor.

three-moment capital asset-pricing model (3M CAPM) Generalisation of the capital asset-pricing model (CAPM) in which stock portfolio selection is based on mean, variance and skewness.

three-stage growth model Valuation model assuming that a firm first experiences super growth and then,

through a transition stage in which the super-growth rate falls, enters a period of normal growth.

time decay Phenomenon in which an option loses part of its value as time passes if the underlying asset value does not increase.

time-series data Observations on a single object at different points in time or for different time periods.

time-series estimation method Estimation method that provides more accurate estimates for risk parameters by allowing recent observations to have greater influence on volatility estimates than stale observations.

time-weighted rate of return Calculating returns that measure how invested wealth would grow.

Tobin's q Ratio of the market value of a company to the replacement cost (the cost of replicating the firm's assets and liabilities).

top-down approach Security selection approach that starts with asset allocation and works systematically through sector and industry allocation to individual security selection.

tracking error Difference in the return of a benchmark index and a portfolio tracking that benchmark index.

transaction costs Costs associated with an investment transaction, including brokerage commission and bid–ask spread.

transparency Amount of prices and trading information that is disseminated to investors.

Treasury bill Negotiable debt obligation issued by the US government and backed by its full faith and credit, issued with a maturity of one year or less.

Treasury bond Negotiable, coupon-bearing debt obligation issued by the US government and backed by its full faith and credit, issued with a maturity of more than seven years.

Treasury inflation-protected securities (TIPS) Treasury bonds with coupons and the principal linked to a cost of living index.

Treasury note Negotiable debt obligation issued by the US government and backed by its full faith and credit, issued with a maturity of between one and seven years.

trendline Line drawn on a bar chart to identify current trends.

trough Bottom of the business cycle.

trust company Value of securities purchased (or sold, whichever is less) divided by average net asset value (NAV), a measure of transaction cost.

T-statistic Measure of the deviation of the estimated regression coefficient from the hypothesised value b, standardised by the standard error of the regression coefficient.

turnover Number of times per year that an average dollar of assets is reinvested.

two-stage growth models Valuation model assuming that a firm first experiences super growth and then enters a period of normal growth.

type I error Wrongly rejected if the null hypothesis is true.

type II error Wrongly not rejected if the null hypothesis is false.

unbiased Having no systematic error.

unbiased expectations hypothesis (UEH) Hypothesis stating that the current implied forward rate is an unbiased predictor of future spot rates.

uncertainty Situation that more than one future outcome is possible and the probability of each outcome is unknown to investors.

underpricing New issues on average being significantly underpriced compared with their aftermarket value.

underwriter Person that acts as an intermediary between the firm and the investors.

underwriting commission Syndicate members' compensation for risk and efforts.

unit trust Investment company that buys and holds a fixed portfolio of stocks, bonds or other securities.

univariate probability distribution Probability distribution function that considers the possible outcomes of an individual random variable.

unseasoned equity offerings See *Initial public offering (IPO)*.

unsecured bond Bond that is not backed by the guarantee of collateral.

unsystematic risk Risk that can be diversified away, being risk related to asset-specific factors.

utility function Measure of an investor's level of 'satisfaction' or preference.

valuation multiples Ratio of the market price of a share or the total market value of a firm's equity to a value driver.

value at risk (VaR) Maximum dollar loss that a portfolio may be expected to suffer due to market risk over a given holding period, at a given level of confidence.

value effect The phenomenon in which value stocks seem to earn positive abnormal average returns, while growth stocks earn negative abnormal returns.

value of assets in place Firm's value if its super-growth possibilities are ignored.

value-weighted index Index in which the individual securities are weighted according to their market capitalisation.

variance Measure of risk or the dispersion around the mean.

variance–covariance matrix Matrix used to display the covariability between more than two assets, with each element in the matrix containing the covariance between a pair of assets.

vega Sensitivity of an option price to the volatility of the underlying asset.

volatility peak Peak in the variance of a security.

volatility smile Graph that plots the empirical volatility against the strike price of options with the same underlying asset and the same maturity.

warehousing swaps Swaps in which a bank acts temporarily as the counterparty and tries to find a final counterparty later on.

warrant Similar to a regular option, but written by the firm that issued the underlying stocks.

weak form of the (EMT) States that efficient market theory prices reflect information revealed by historical market-based data.

winner's curse Paying more for an item than its value. The winner finds out that the other bidders valued the item less than him- or herself, hence discovering that he or she has erred in his or her valuation.

world equity benchmark shares (WEBS) Exchange-traded funds based on the Morgan Stanley Capital International (MSCI) stock market indices of a single foreign country.

yield Expected rate of return.

yield to call Yield to maturity of a callable bond in the case that the bond is called at the earliest possible date.

yield curve Relationship between yield to maturity and maturity for similar bonds.

yield to maturity Internal rate of return on a bond when held to maturity.

zero beta rate Asset with zero beta has a zero correlation with the market portfolio. The expected return on such an asset in equilibrium equals the risk-free interest rate.

zero-beta capital asset-pricing model Version of capital asset-pricing model (CAPM) in which investors cannot borrow at the riskless rate.

zero-coupon bond Bond that pays no interest and trades at a discount.

zero-investment portfolio Portfolio requiring zero initial investment, usually constructed by combining long and short positions.

Subject index